FREE WITH NEW COPIES OF THIS TEXTBOOK*

Scratch here for access code

Scratch here for access code

azeAPTaTeyDwKyct

Start using *my*BusinessCourse Today: **www.mybusinesscourse.com**

*my*BusinessCourse is a web-based learning and assessment program intended to complement your textbook and faculty instruction.

Student Benefits

- **eLectures**: These videos review the key concepts of each Learning Objective in each chapter.
- **Guided examples**: These videos provide step-by-step solutions for select problems in each chapter.
- **Auto-graded assignments**: Provide students with immediate feedback on select assignments. (**with Instructor-Led course ONLY**).
- **Quiz and Exam preparation**: myBusinessCourse provides students with additional practice and exam preparation materials to help students achieve better grades and content mastery.

You can access *my*BusinessCourse 24/7 from any web-enabled device, including iPads, smartphones, laptops, and tablets.

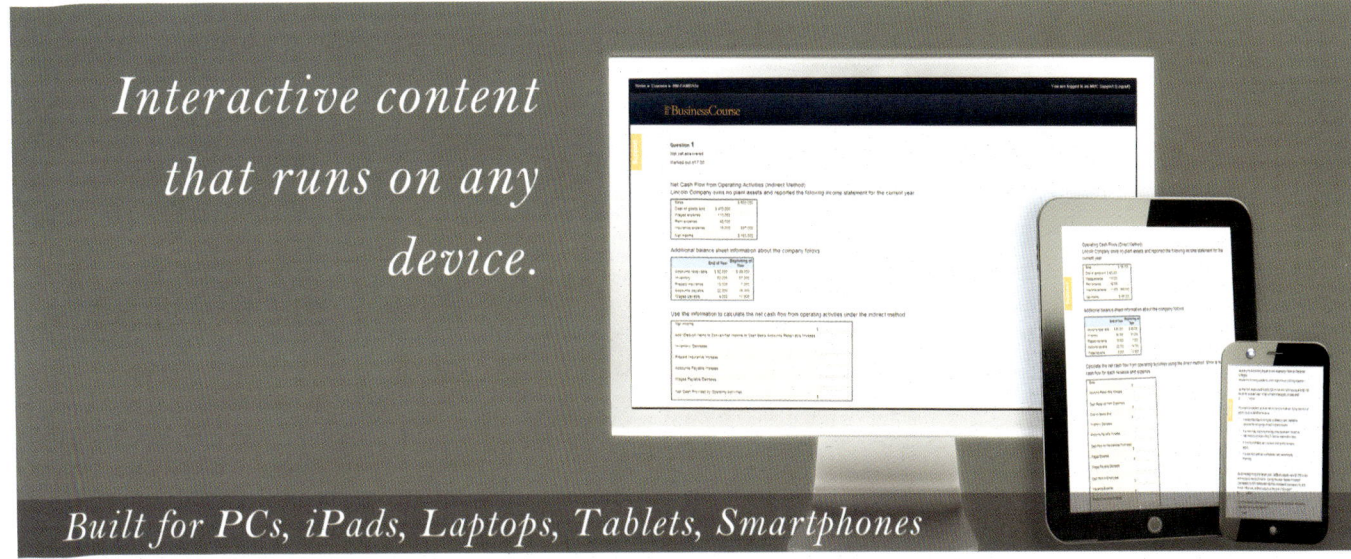

Interactive content that runs on any device.

Built for PCs, iPads, Laptops, Tablets, Smartphones

*Each access code is good for one use only. If the textbook is used for more than one course or term, students will have to purchase additional *my*BusinessCourse access codes. In addition, students who repeat a course for any reason will have to purchase a new access code. If you purchased a used book and the protective coating that covers the access code has been removed, your code may be invalid.

Access to *my*BusinessCourse is free ONLY with the purchase of a new textbook.

Cost Accounting
with Data Analytics

Eleventh Edition

MICHAEL R. KINNEY
TEXAS A&M UNIVERSITY

CECILY A. RAIBORN
TEXAS STATE UNIVERSITY

AMIE L. DRAGOO
FORMERLY EDGEWOOD COLLEGE

Photo Credits
Chapter 1: iStock
Chapter 2: iStock
Chapter 3: Shutterstock
Chapter 4: Shutterstock
Chapter 5: Shutterstock
Chapter 6: Shutterstock
Chapter 7: iStock
Chapter 8: Shutterstock
Chapter 9: Shutterstock
Chapter 10: iStock
Chapter 11: Shutterstock
Chapter 12: iStock
Chapter 13: iStock
Chapter 14: iStock
Chapter 15: Shutterstock
Chapter 16: iStock
Chapter 17: iStock
Chapter 18: Shutterstock
Chapter 19: iStock

Materials from the Certified Management Accountant Examinations, Copyright © 2022 by the Institute of Certified Management Accountants are reprinted and/or adapted with permission.

Cambridge Business Publishers

Cost Accounting with Data Analytics, Eleventh Edition, by Michael R. Kinney, Cecily A. Raiborn, and Amie L. Dragoo.

COPYRIGHT © 2025 by Cambridge Business Publishers, LLC. Published by Cambridge Business Publishers, LLC. Exclusive rights by Cambridge Business Publishers, LLC for manufacture and export. Previous editions of this work were published by Cengage Learning, Inc.

ALL RIGHTS RESERVED. No part of this publication may be reproduced, distributed, or stored in a database or retrieval system in any form or by any means, without prior written consent of Cambridge Business Publishers, LLC, including, but not limited to, in any network or other electronic storage or transmission, or broadcast for distance learning.

Student Edition ISBN 978-1-61853-614-3

Bookstores & Faculty: to order this book, call **800-619-6473** or email customerservice@cambridgepub.com.

Students: to order this book, please visit the book's website and order directly online.

Printed in Canada.
10 9 8 7 6 5 4 3 2 1

Preface

Welcome to *Cost Accounting with Data Analytics*. As the title suggests, our new edition is enhanced with an expanded and well-integrated coverage of Data Analytics. This update is in line with the rapid technological advances that we are experiencing in our academic settings and in the global business environment. We believe that the integration of data analytics provides a more meaningful and effective learning platform and better prepares students for their next steps in a career in business. The visual display of data provides students a new way to more deeply grasp accounting concepts that may simply get lost in a paragraph of text. We are also excited about the increased opportunities for critical thinking that the analysis provides for students.

Our market research indicates that students' preferred approach to learning has shifted from reading dense text to a more learn-by-doing approach. In response, we have enhanced our pedagogy this edition by making chapter demonstrations more focused: we now pose specific questions and show step-by-step solutions in demonstration problems for each chapter's learning objectives to facilitate active learning. What has not changed, however, is our unmatched, straightforward, and readable approach.

Cost accounting has been and remains a dynamic discipline that must respond to the evolving needs of managers. Along these lines, we have updated the organization and content of the text. We have rearranged some topics to provide a better progression of material, to highlight more relevant topics, and to provide a more logical grouping of related topics. We have also enhanced the content of the text through additional topics or the expansion of existing topics. Our redesign process resulted in the inclusion of two new chapters: Chapter 3 on cost behavior and estimation and Chapter 14 on pricing, sales variances, and customer profitability. We are excited to share these new changes with our current and future customers.

NEW TO THIS EDITION

Greater Emphasis on Data Analytics

Guided by skills required of new graduates and those outlined in the Evolution Model Curriculum presented by the AICPA and NASBA, we have expanded our focus on data analytics. New data visualizations are included within the text and new assignments are available in the end-of-chapter assignments.

- **In-Text Descriptive Data Visualizations:** In each chapter, we present data in spreadsheets and visualizations that provide students a new perspective and a deeper understanding of the results.

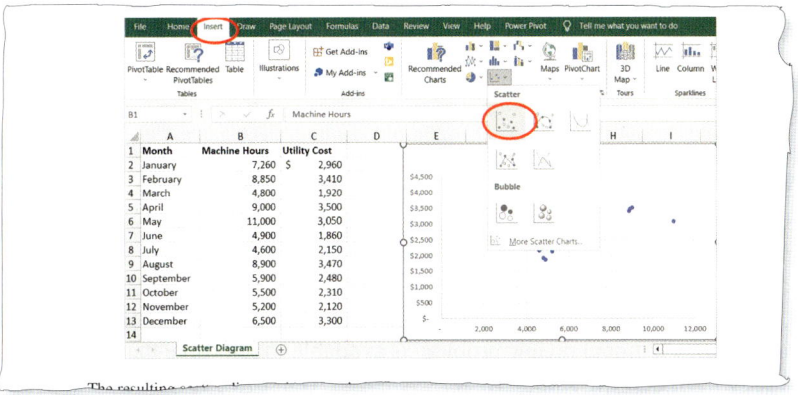

See examples on pages 4-7, 5-10, 6-20, and 10-10

iv   Preface

See examples on pages **3-7, 10-4, 15-18, and 17-5.**

- **In-Text Data Visualization with Analysis Questions:** A new question-and-answer section has been added to each chapter. The answers appear at the end of the chapter (following the answers to the Review questions). This allows students to engage in chapter concepts with visual tools, allowing for a deeper analysis and improved comprehension of the concepts.

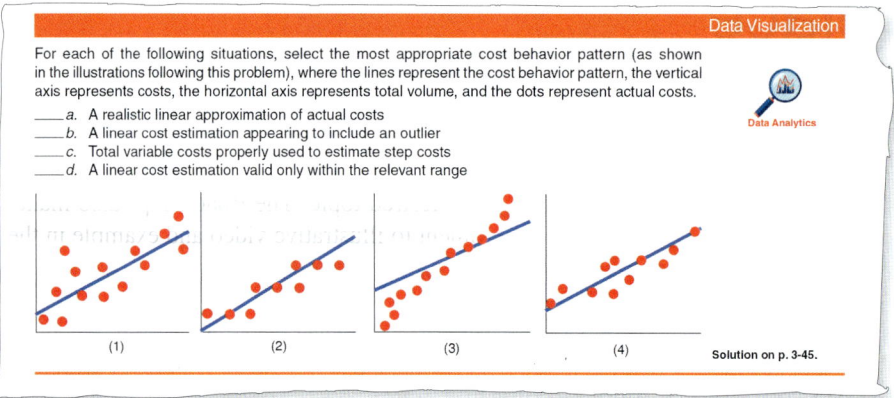

- **Data Analytic and Data Visualization Assignments:** New Data Analytics problems have been added to the assignment section in each chapter, requiring students to create and analyze visualizations in Excel and Tableau. Reference to a set of Data Visualization problems can also be found at the end of each chapter. The problems require analysis of (but not creation of) charts. This coverage is added to address requirements in the CPA and CMA exam and to improve the career readiness of students.

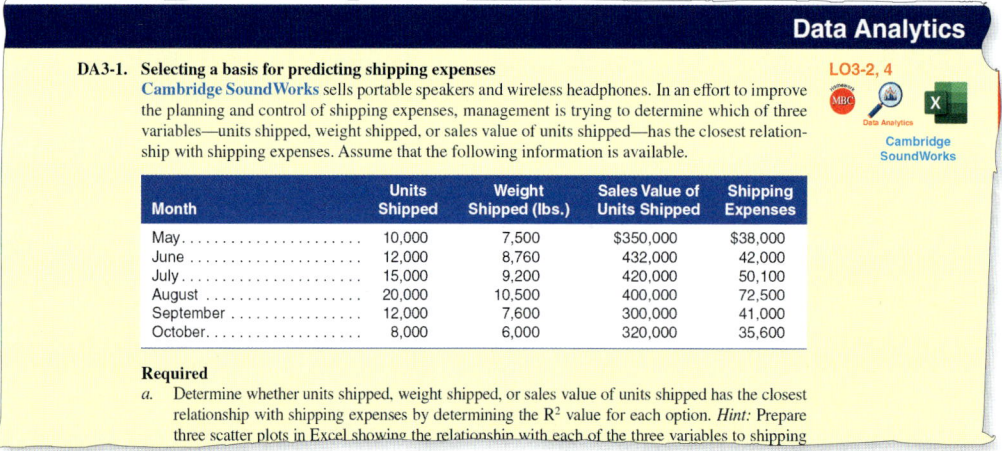

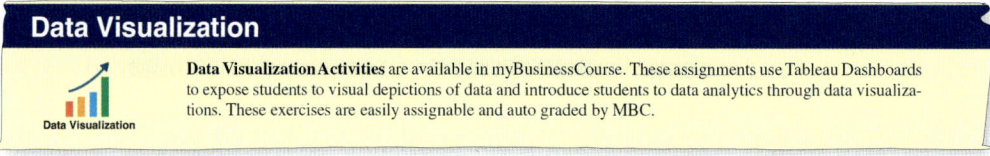

Active Learning

In this edition, we have pedagogically enhanced our active-learning approach by incorporating at least one demonstration problem for each learning objective. Our research has shown that today's students want to see how concepts are applied. They would prefer to see an application rather than read about a concept in the abstract. Each demonstration problem is supported by an **author-prepared video**. As in the prior edition, an additional review problem is available to reinforce the concepts presented in each learning objective. In this way, students see the application of concepts through a step-by-step illustration and then have the opportunity to immediately practice similar review problems. This **concept**

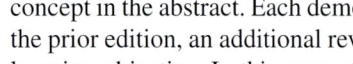

Preface

overview/illustration/practice approach keeps students engaged and ensures they have mastered one learning objective before proceeding to the next.

- **Road Maps:** The Road Maps highlight the user-friendly organization of each chapter and act as a guide for an active approach to student learning. Each chapter's **Road Map** identifies each learning objective for the chapter, the related page numbers, the guided lecture videos, the demonstration videos, the review problems, and the corresponding assignments. New to this edition, the Road Map has been enhanced with a list of key terms for each learning objective. This raises students' awareness of key terms and allows faculty to quickly see what key concepts are covered in each learning objective. In addition, the new demonstrations displayed in each chapter are listed on the Road Map. This table allows students and faculty to quickly grasp at a glance the chapter contents and to efficiently navigate to the desired topic. The Road Maps also make it easier for students to work backwards from assignment to illustrative video and example in the text.

Road Maps summarize each chapter's resources and categorize them by learning objective.

Demos are accompanied by videos that show how to solve the application problems for each learning objective.

Assignments reinforce learning and can be completed by hand or within MBC.

Road Map

LO	Learning Objective	Topics	Page	eLecture	Demo	Review	Assignments
3-1	**How is a linear total cost estimating equation used to estimate costs?** Cost Behavior Patterns :: Variable Costs :: Fixed Costs :: Mixed Costs :: Step Costs :: Total Cost Estimating Equation :: Factors Affecting Cost Behavior	3-2	e3–1	D3-1	Rev 3-1	MC3-11, MC3-12, E3-22, E3-23, E3-24, E3-25, E3-26, E3-27, E3-28, E3-29, E3-33, P3-47
3-2	**How is a scatter diagram used to analyze cost behavior?** Scatter Diagram :: Scatter Plot :: Outliers :: Representative Observations	3-5	e3–2	D3-2	Rev 3-2	MC3-13, E3-24, E3-25, E3-30, E3-31, E3-34, P3-47, **DA3-1, DA3-3, DA3-5**
3-3	**How is the high-low method used in analyzing mixed costs?** High-Low Method of Cost Estimation :: Two Representative Data Points :: Cost Prediction	3-8	e3–3	D3-3A D3-3B	Rev 3-3	MC3-14, E3-30, E3-31, E3-32, E3-33, E3-35, E3-36, E3-37, E3-38, P3-47, P3-49, **DA3-3, DA3-5**

Learning Objectives identify the key learning goals of the chapter.

Key Terms are listed for each learning objective.

eLectures are videos available in MBC that provide 3-5 minute reviews of each learning objective.

Reviews are accompanied by videos that demonstrate how to solve various types of problems and are available in MBC.

- **eLecture Videos:** Created by the authors, the eLecture videos are the concept overviews and provide the foundation for students to complete the demonstration problems that follow.

- **New Demonstrations and Accompanying Videos:** We include at least one demonstration problem for each learning objective. A key aspect to each demonstration is the positioning of a key question (signaled with a red diamond) that is solved in a step-by-step approach. Our aim with this approach is to actively engage students in the content of the learning objective. Students will better understand (1) the goal of the learning objective and (2) how to solve a related problem. Instead of skimming a section and moving on to the next, we hope to engage students in the topic, before they move on to the assignments.

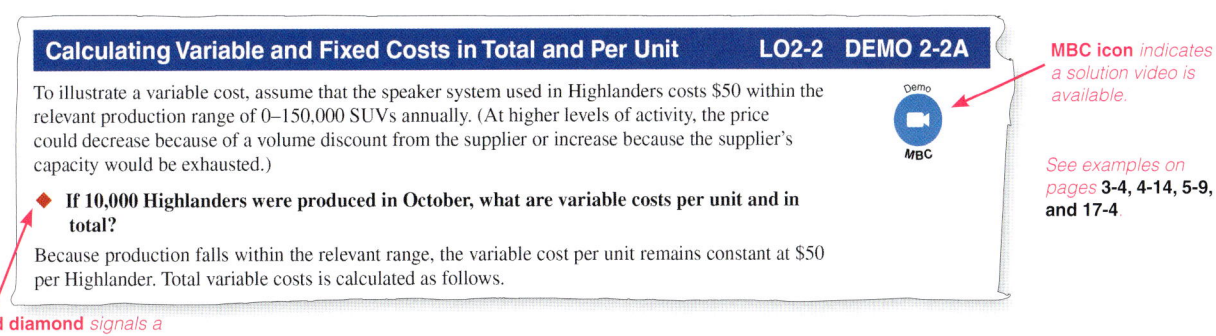

Calculating Variable and Fixed Costs in Total and Per Unit — LO2-2 DEMO 2-2A

To illustrate a variable cost, assume that the speaker system used in Highlanders costs $50 within the relevant production range of 0–150,000 SUVs annually. (At higher levels of activity, the price could decrease because of a volume discount from the supplier or increase because the supplier's capacity would be exhausted.)

♦ If 10,000 Highlanders were produced in October, what are variable costs per unit and in total?

Because production falls within the relevant range, the variable cost per unit remains constant at $50 per Highlander. Total variable costs is calculated as follows.

MBC icon indicates a solution video is available.

See examples on pages **3-4, 4-14, 5-9, and 17-4**

Red diamond signals a demonstration question.

- **In-Chapter Review Problems:** The emphasis in our approach is to provide students with a demonstration problem and review problem for each deliberately selected, key learning objective. In this way, students see the application of concepts through a step-by-step illustration and then

© Cambridge Business Publishers

Preface

have the opportunity to **immediately practice** similar review problems. At the conclusion of each learning objective, a review problem is provided with answers included at the end of the chapter. These review problems are presented to reinforce concepts presented in the section and ensure student comprehension. By not providing the review solutions on the same page as the review, we are encouraging students to "learn by doing." In addition, each review problem is **accompanied by a short video** (typically 3 minutes or less) that walks students through the solution to the review.

See examples on pages **2-22, 5-5, 6-21, and 18-22**.

MBC icon *indicates a solution video is available.*

Critical Thinking Question *is included as the last question of each review.*

Assignments *similar to the Reviews have been identified for students interested in additional practice.*

Solutions *to the reviews are presented at the end of the chapter.*

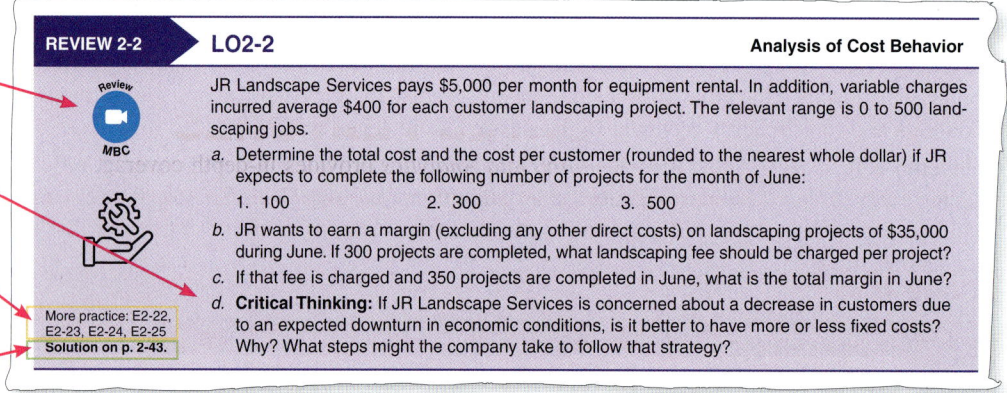

Increased Focus on Critical Thinking, ESG Implications, and Nonmanufacturing Examples

As part of our deep dive into the content and organization of the new edition, we thought it was particularly important to highlight, and supplement where needed, the following three areas.

- **Critical thinking:** Students often fall into the trap of thinking that there is only one correct answer to a problem. To emphasize the reality of open-ended questions in the accounting profession, we started with a brief explanation of how critical thinking skills are used in problem solving in Chapter 1. Also new to this edition, we added a question to each Review of every learning objective that requires students to apply higher-order, critical thinking skills. In addition, end-of-chapter assignments that rise to the level of critical thinking are marked with a new critical thinking icon.

- **Environmental, Social, and Governance (ESG):** The demand for companies to understand and address the risks and strategies related to ESG considerations is growing. To that end, we have identified and in some cases, supplemented the examples used in text explanations or assignments that touch on ESG issues. To make these connections more transparent to both faculty and students, we have identified these references with a special ESG icon that is used to mark in-text and end-of-chapter assignment examples.

See examples on pages **1-9, 3-16, 9-27, and 14-13**.

Changes in Technology or Prices

Changes in technology and prices make cost estimation and prediction difficult. For example, **FedEx** is committing to a fleet of zero-emission electric vehicles by 2040.[4] The replacement of gas-powered vehicles with electric vehicles is an ongoing process. This means that care must be taken to make sure that historical data used in developing future transportation cost estimates takes into account the mix of costs. Professional judgment may be required to make appropriate adjustments to the data. Only data reflecting a single price level should be used in cost estimation and prediction. If prices

- **Nonmanufacturing Examples:** Our text is carefully worded to include the application of cost accounting concepts to industries other than manufacturing. To make these expanded discussions and end-of-chapter problems more visible, we have adopted a new icon to mark the nonmanufacturing examples—**primarily that of the service industry**.

© Cambridge Business Publishers

Preface **Nonmanufacturing icon** *indicates the discussion or assignment pertains to a nonmanufacturing industry.* vii

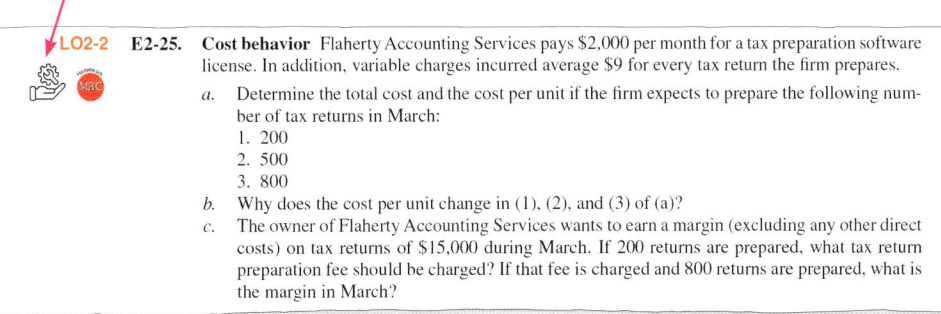

LO2-2 **E2-25. Cost behavior** Flaherty Accounting Services pays $2,000 per month for a tax preparation software license. In addition, variable charges incurred average $9 for every tax return the firm prepares.
  a. Determine the total cost and the cost per unit if the firm expects to prepare the following number of tax returns in March:
     1. 200
     2. 500
     3. 800
  b. Why does the cost per unit change in (1), (2), and (3) of (a)?
  c. The owner of Flaherty Accounting Services wants to earn a margin (excluding any other direct costs) on tax returns of $15,000 during March. If 200 returns are prepared, what tax return preparation fee should be charged? If that fee is charged and 800 returns are prepared, what is the margin in March?

See examples on pages **2-17, 5-11, 6-18, and 9-29**.

RETAINED AND UPDATED FEATURES

The eleventh edition of *Cost Accounting with Data Analytics* provides in-depth coverage of current cost management concepts and procedures in a straightforward and reader-friendly framework. The clean, concise presentation of materials and the updated illustrations reinforce and clarify the topics that readers traditionally struggle with most. The following features have been retained and updated in this edition.

■ **Real examples and ethical considerations**: As with previous editions, real examples and ethical coverage are woven into the text so readers immediately see the relevance of the cost accountant's role in managerial decisions and learn to go beyond the numbers to think critically. Related illustrations and real-world examples appeal to today's students and clearly exemplify the chapters' concepts. These examples connect today's business world with the classroom experience immediately.

Potential Ethical Issues

1. When using the high-low method, management could select particular data points to fit a predetermined cost structure.
2. When using the high-low method for budget estimates, management could select an outlier point to estimate budgeted costs in order to inflate the cost budget in order to justify higher costs.
3. Management could manipulate data or omit certain data used in a simple regression analysis in order to support a desired cost estimating equation.
4. Management uses an aggressive learning curve in pricing out a contract that puts unrealistic pressures

■ **High-quality end-of-chapter assignments:** Students practice accounting skills with a wide array of assignment types, including Internet research exercises, group activities, writing assignments, ethical problems, and Excel® template activities. Questions test basic chapter comprehension, exercises offer quick concept checks, and problems delve deeper into the concepts, testing students' application of critical topics and procedures.

Many new updates to the end-of-chapter assignments resulted in over 400 new or updated problems over the prior edition. New to this edition is a multiple-choice section, CMA questions from Gleim, and Data Analytic and Data Visualization assignments. In addition, all chapters have a varying number of new exercises or problems to supplement the current coverage that are quantitative and autogradable in mBC.

A new multiple-choice *section is now offered in the end-of-chapter assignments.*

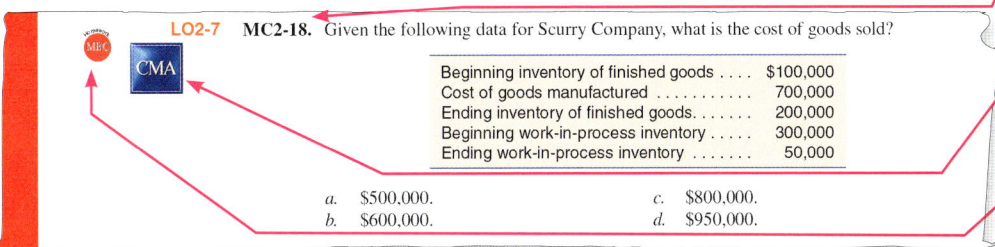

LO2-7 **MC2-18.** Given the following data for Scurry Company, what is the cost of goods sold?

Beginning inventory of finished goods	$100,000
Cost of goods manufactured	700,000
Ending inventory of finished goods	200,000
Beginning work-in-process inventory	300,000
Ending work-in-process inventory	50,000

  a. $500,000.   c. $800,000.
  b. $600,000.   d. $950,000.

CMA adapted *questions are included in the end-of-chapter assignments.*

MBC Icon *indicates assignment is available in MBC.*

■ **Gleim CMA Review Questions:** Cambridge Business Publishers has partnered with Gleim to provide students with CMA prep materials within MBC that will give them a competitive advantage as they transition from the accounting classroom to taking the CMA Exam.

CMA REVIEW

© Cambridge Business Publishers

- **Streamlined, student-friendly approach:** Recognized for its unmatched readability, the book's thought-provoking writing keeps concepts intriguing and easy to comprehend. This edition's solid blend of concepts and practices will help students clearly understand how to solve actual business problems.

- **Developing ethical business leaders:** The need for students to analyze business situations and make informed, ethical decisions is essential in today's business world. *Cost Accounting with Data Analytics* weaves ethical considerations throughout the chapter so that students learn to think consistently of the ethical implications of their actions. Potential Ethical Issues at the end of the chapter emphasize dilemmas students may encounter in business, and exercises and problems involving ethical considerations are marked with an ethics icon.

> **LO10-2**  **E10-33. Ethics; writing** Most hospitals are reimbursed according to diagnostic-related groups (DRGs). Each DRG has a specified standard "length of stay." If a patient leaves the hospital early, the hospital is financially impacted favorably, but a patient staying longer than the specified time costs the hospital money.
>
> a. From the hospital administrator's point of view, would you want favorable length-of-stay variances? How might you try to obtain such variances?
> b. From a patient's point of view, would you want favorable length-of-stay variances? Answer this question from the point of view of (1) a patient who has had minor surgery and (2) a patient who has had major surgery.
> c. Would favorable length-of-stay variances necessarily equate to high-quality care?

- **Comprehensive Chapter Review:** Comprehensive Chapter Reviews conclude each chapter to ensure your students' mastery of concepts through a list of key chapter terms, succinct chapter summaries, potential ethical issues, solution strategies highlighting key equations and concepts, and demonstration problems that students can use as a framework for solving similar examples in homework assignments or exams. These comprehensive reviews reinforce the critical concepts from the chapter and show how to apply them. For an example, refer to pages 2-23 to 2-25.

- **Solution Strategies:** Each chapter includes a section with an overview of key strategies for the more complex learning objectives. The strategies reinforce the content of the LO through a key formula, schedule, or an outline of steps. These are just another tool beyond the reviews and videos to assist students in working through the assignments.

Chapter Specific Changes

Chapter 1—Introduction to Cost Accounting
- New content added (some from former Chapter 19) on data analytics, block chain, artificial intelligence, and critical thinking
- Discussion on balance scorecard moved to Chapter 15
- Added sample organization chart, reference to the AICPA and CIMA code of ethics, and a section on career opportunities in managerial/cost accounting

Chapter 2—Cost Terminology and Classification
- Added service company illustrative examples
- Added illustration using real company financial statements
- Moved journal entry presentation to Chapter 6

Chapter 3—Cost Behavior and Analysis
- **New chapter**, incorporating new topics such as learning curves and some topics from the former Chapter 3 that are enhanced including an Excel application of least squares regression

Chapter 4—Cost-Volume-Profit Analysis
- Formerly Chapter 9
- Broke out incremental analysis into a separate learning objective
- Made contribution statement a focal point
- Simplified the algebraic formula presentations

Chapter 5—Relevant Information for Decision Making
- Formerly Chapter 10
- Updated chapter exhibits

Preface

- Added or emphasized sections on qualitative decision factors

Chapter 6—Job Order Costing
- Formerly Chapter 5
- Merged in discussion on overhead application formerly in Chapter 3
- Added a discussion section on plant-wide versus departmental overhead rates
- Added learning objective on job order in the service industry
- Added section on materiality
- Changed the main job order illustration to include multiple jobs, individual job cost sheets, and added T-accounts
- Streamlined discussion of documents used in job order costing
- Specified the accounting for rework in LO6-7
- Moved appendix to Chapter 10

Chapter 7—Process Costing
- Formerly Chapter 6
- Incorporated Appendix 3 into the main chapter content
- Improved the presentation of the production report

Chapter 8—Activity-Based Management and Activity-Based Costing
- Formerly Chapter 4
- Added new learning objective on time-driven activity-based costing
- Incorporated a process map
- Improved presentation of allocation schedules

Chapter 9—The Master Budget
- Formerly Chapter 8
- Added a section on general approaches to budgeting
- Added an application related to generative AI and the budget process
- Created new learning objective highlighting a service company example
- Added section on ESG impacts on the master budget
- Supplemented LO9-7 with new examples

Chapter 10—Flexible Budget, Standard Costing, and Variance Analysis
- Formerly Chapter 7 and a subtopic of former Chapter 3
- Incorporated new learning objective on flexible budgeting and tied it to the standard cost example
- Updated main company example to improve topical coverage throughout the chapter
- Adjusted the content across learning objectives, including the appendix coverage
- Added appendix formerly in Chapter 6

Chapter 11—Absorption/Variable Costing and Capacity Analysis
- Formerly subtopics of Chapter 3
- Expanded discussion and examples of absorption/variable costing including the connection to volume variance
- Expanded discussion on capacity to encompass volume variance and profit discussions
- Added topic of downward demand spiral

Chapter 12—Allocation of Joint Costs and Accounting for By-Product/Scrap
- Formerly Chapter 11
- Changed main company example to make more student-friendly
- Updated demonstrations and graphics throughout the chapter

Chapter 13—Responsibility Accounting, Support Department Cost Allocations, and Transfer Pricing
- Added content from former Chapter 12 as LO13-1
- Revamped some sections and updated examples to show a better flow
- Streamlined the presentation of transfer pricing

Chapter 14—Pricing, Sales Variances, and Customer Profitability
- **New chapter** and new content
- Utilized some content from former Chapter 18

Preface

Chapter 15—Performance Measurement, Balanced Scorecards, and Performance Rewards
- Formerly Chapter 14 and merged in some content from former Chapters 1 and 12
- Included new content on segment reporting
- Added content on pay versus performance
- Added scope-level discussion on greenhouse gas emissions
- Supplemented the quantitative assignment offerings

Chapter 16—Approaches to Cost Control and Managing Uncertainty
- Added some content from the former Chapter 12 and Chapter 19
- Added quantitative example on the topic of inflation
- Added new real company examples
- Added new ratio examples and other quantitative examples in the chapter and in the assignments

Chapter 17—Implementing Quality Concepts
- Reorganized chapter content
- Expanded the application of statistical process control charts
- Added new company examples

Chapter 18—Inventory and Production Management
- Reorganized and streamlined chapter content, including that of the appendix
- Added new ratio calculations and discussion
- Expanded economic order quantity discussion
- Added calculations for the opportunity cost of inventory

Chapter 19—Capital Budgeting
- Formerly Chapter 15
- Rearranged some content across learning objectives

TECHNOLOGY THAT IMPROVES LEARNING AND COMPLEMENTS FACULTY INSTRUCTION

myBusinessCourse is an online learning and assessment program intended to complement your textbook and faculty instruction. Access to **myBusinessCourse** is FREE ONLY with the purchase of a new textbook, but can be purchased separately.

MBC is ideal for faculty seeking opportunities to augment their course with an online component. MBC is also a turnkey solution for online courses. The following are some of the features of MBC.

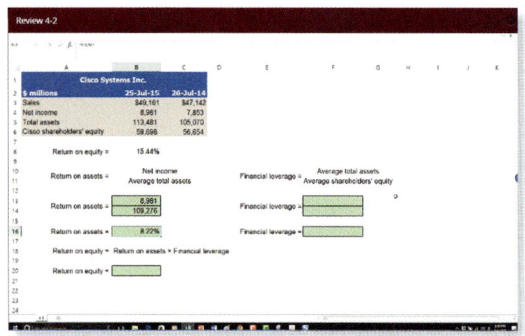

Increase Student Readiness
- **eLectures** explain each chapter's learning objectives and, in many cases, provide demonstrations. Consistent with the text and created by the authors, these videos are ideal for remediation and online instruction. However, our experiences have shown that students in traditional learning environments utilize these learning tools to master the topics.
- **Guided Examples** are narrated video demonstrations created by the authors that show students how to solve the Demonstration and Review problems from the textbook.
- Immediate feedback with **auto-graded homework**.
- **Test Bank** questions that can be incorporated into your assignments.
- Instructor **gradebook** with immediate grade results.

Make Instruction Needs-Based
- Identify where your students are struggling and customize your instruction to address their needs.
- Gauge how your entire class or individual students are performing by viewing the easy-to-use gradebook.

© Cambridge Business Publishers

Preface

- Ensure your students are getting the additional reinforcement and direction they need between class meetings.

Provide Instruction and Practice 24/7

- Assign homework from your Cambridge Business Publishers' textbook and have MBC grade it for you automatically.
- With our videos, your students can revisit accounting topics as often as they like or until they master the topic.
- Make homework due before class to ensure students enter your classroom prepared.
- For an additional fee, upgrade MBC to include the eBook and you have all the tools needed for an online course.

95.5% of students who used MBC, responded that MBC helped them learn accounting.*

88.3% of students said they would encourage their professor to continue using MBC in future terms.*

Integrate with LMS

myBusinessCourse integrates with many learning management systems, including **Canvas**, **Blackboard**, **Moodle**, **D2L**, **Schoology**, and **Sakai**. Your gradebooks sync automatically.

SUPPLEMENT PACKAGE
For Instructors

myBusinessCourse: A web-based learning and assessment program intended to complement your textbook and classroom instruction. Access to myBusinessCourse is FREE with the purchase of a new textbook and can also be purchased separately. This easy-to-use program grades homework automatically and provides students with additional help. Assignments with the logo in the margin are available in myBusinessCourse.

Solutions Manual: Created by the authors, the Excel-based *Solutions Manual* contains complete solutions to all the assignment material in the text.

PowerPoint: The PowerPoint slides outline key elements of each chapter.

Instructor's Manual: The Instructor's Manual includes explanations of key topics for each chapter along with a set of questions that can be used for student practice during classroom instruction.

Test Bank: The Test Bank includes true/false, multiple choice, exercises, and problems.

Excel Templates: We provide Excel spreadsheets for select assignments. These spreadsheets will save time in data entry and allow students to dedicate additional time to learning the material. The assignments accompanied by Excel spreadsheets are identified by the Excel icon.

Website: All instructor materials are accessible via the book's website (password protected) along with other useful links and marketing information: www.cambridgepub.com

For Students

myBusinessCourse: A web-based learning and assessment program intended to complement your textbook and faculty instruction. This easy-to-use program grades homework automatically and provides you with additional help when your instructor is not available. Assignments with the logo in the margin are available in myBusinessCourse. Access is free with new copies of this textbook (look for page containing the access code towards the front of the book). If you buy a used copy of the book, you can purchase access at www.mybusinesscourse.com.

Excel Templates: We provide Excel spreadsheets for select assignments. These spreadsheets will save time in data entry and allow students to dedicate additional time to learning the material. The assignments accompanied by Excel spreadsheets are identified by the Excel icon.

Website: Updates and other useful links are available to students free of charge on the book's website.

---

* These statistics are based on the results of five surveys in which 4,195 students participated.

© Cambridge Business Publishers

ACKNOWLEDGMENTS

This text benefited greatly from the valuable feedback of focus group attendees, reviewers, students, and colleagues. We are extremely grateful to them for their help in making this project a success.

Heba Abdel-Rahim	Dennis George	Lois Mahoney	G. Stevenson Smith
Daniel Acheampong	Mary Beth Goodrich	Roger Mayer	Neal Smith
John Alpers	Jamie Grandstaff	Gwen Meador	Jan Smolarski
Yunita Anwar	Sanjay Gupta	David Medved	Liang Song
Rowland Atiase	Heidi Hansel	Robin Meehan	Mohsen Souissi
Thomas Badley	Lizhong Hao	Lindsay Meermans	George Starbuck
Charles Bailey	Gregory Haselden	Mary Michel	Randall Stone
Sarah Bailey	Jacques Hendieh	Brian Miller	Jeffrey Strawser
Laura Bearden	Mike Hoppe	Christopher Mills	Ron Stunda
Eileen Beiter	Qianyun Huang	Donald Minyard	Kanaiya Sugandh
Cassie Bennett	Ronald J Jastrzebski	Cheryl Moore	Todd Thornock
Gary Bridges	Keting Jiang	Philip Morris	Greg Treadwell
Jake Brock	Wei Jiang	Barbara Muller	Mark Ulrich
Marilyn Brooks-Lewis	Cynthia Johnson	Martin Mulyadi	Timothy Swenson
Holly Caldwell	El-Sayed Kandiel	Alice Muncy	Ara Volkan
Magan Calhoun	Kaimee Kellis	Pamela Neely	Inna Voytsekivska
Alan Campbell	Daniel Kerch	Cynthia L. Nye	David Waizmann
Sandra Cereola	Hyunpyo Kim	Felicia Olagbemi	Edward Walker
Charles Chambers	Rebecca Kiser	Gary Page	Scott Wang
Kathryn Chang	Polly Knutson	Shanshan Pan	Cammy Wayne
Bih Horng Chiang	Mehmet Kocakulah	Grace Peng	Christine Wayne
Wen-Wen Chien	John Koeplin	Lincoln Pinto	Stephen Weiss
Thomas Clausen	Yauheni Koraneu	Micki Pitcher	Cassie Weitzenkamp
Cheryl Corke	Leslie Kren	Ronald Premuroso	Lynn White
Michael Coyne	Anthony Kurek	Debra Prendergast	Donna Whitten
Tim Creel	Scott Lail	Robert Rambo	Alisa Williams
Alan Czyzewski	John Lauck	Robert Rankin	Gayle Williams
Sebahattin Demirkan	David Laurel	William Rhodes	Alex Wu
Beatrix DeMott	Howard Lawrence	Iyad Rock	Di Wu
Amanda Dore	Marina Layvand	Jonathan Ross	Patricia Wynn
Augustine Duru	Deborah Leitsch	Stephanie Anne Rowe	Li Xu
Gertrude Eguae-Obazee	Bruce Leung	Norman Rush	Dimitri Yatsenko
James Emig	Marc Lewis	Audrey Scarlata	Josh Zender
Farima Fakoor	Lingxiang Li	Paul Schloemer	Kenny Zheng
Jeffrey Fisher	Haijin Lin	Haeyoung Shin	Aner Zhou
Mark Gale	Hu Liu	Manny Sicre	Katheryn Zielinski
Jace Garrett	Christopher Lynch	Larry Simpson	
Xin Geng	Nace R. Magner	Philip Slater	

We extend a special thanks to Brian Miller and Gayle Williams for their thorough job accuracy checking the chapter content and solutions. In addition, we are grateful to George Werthman, Lorraine Gleeson, Jocelyn Mousel, Debbie McQuade, Terry McQuade, and the entire team at Cambridge Business Publishers for their encouragement, enthusiasm, and guidance.

Michael   Cecily   Amie

March 2024

Brief Contents

Chapter	1	Introduction to Cost Accounting	1-1
Chapter	2	Cost Terminology and Classification	2-1
Chapter	3	Cost Behavior and Estimation	3-1
Chapter	4	Cost-Volume-Profit Analysis	4-1
Chapter	5	Relevant Information for Decision Making	5-1
Chapter	6	Job Order Costing	6-1
Chapter	7	Process Costing	7-1
Chapter	8	Activity-Based Management and Activity-Based Costing	8-1
Chapter	9	The Master Budget	9-1
Chapter	10	Flexible Budget, Standard Costing, and Variance Analysis	10-1
Chapter	11	Absorption/Variable Costing and Capacity Analysis	11-1
Chapter	12	Allocation of Joint Costs and Accounting for By-Product/Scrap	12-1
Chapter	13	Responsibility Accounting, Support Department Cost Allocations, and Transfer Pricing	13-1
Chapter	14	Pricing, Sales Variances, and Customer Profitability	14-1
Chapter	15	Performance Measurement, Balanced Scorecards, and Performance Rewards	15-1
Chapter	16	Approaches to Cost Control and Managing Uncertainty	16-1
Chapter	17	Implementing Quality Concepts	17-1
Chapter	18	Inventory and Production Management	18-1
Chapter	19	Capital Budgeting	19-1
Appendix	A	Compound Interest Tables	A-1
		Index	I-1

Contents

Preface iii

Chapter 1
Introduction to Cost Accounting 1-1

Introduction 1-2
Financial, Management, and Cost Accounting 1-2
   Financial Accounting 1-2
   Management Accounting 1-2
   Cost Accounting 1-4
Review 1-1 Financial and Cost Accounting 1-5
Organizational Strategy 1-6
   Core Competencies 1-6
   Organizational Structure 1-8
   Management Style and Organizational Structure 1-9
   Organizational Constraints 1-9
   Environmental Constraints 1-9
Review 1-2 Identification of Organizational Strategy 1-10
Value Chain 1-10
Review 1-3 Value Chain Activities 1-11
   Data Analytics 1-12
   Artificial Intelligence 1-13
   Blockchain Technology 1-16
   Applying Critical Thinking Skills in Problem-Solving 1-17
Review 1-4 Data Analytics, Artificial Intelligence, and Blockchain 1-19
Professional Ethics 1-19
   Unethical Practices 1-19
   Ethical Standards in Accounting 1-19
   Ethics in Multinational Corporations 1-22
Review 1-5 IMA's Statements of Ethical Professional Practice 1-22
Comprehensive Chapter Review 1-23
   Key Terms 23
   Chapter Summary 23
   Data Analytics 1-25
   Data Visualization 1-25
   Potential Ethical Issues 1-26
   Questions 1-26
   Multiple Choice 1-26
   Exercises 1-27
Review Solutions 1-34
   Data Visualization Solutions 1-35

Chapter 2
Cost Terminology and Classification 2-1

Introduction 2-2
Associating Costs with a Cost Object 2-2
   Direct vs. Indirect Costs 2-3
Review 2-1 Association with Cost Object 2-3
Costs Reacting to Changes in Activity 2-4
   Variable Cost 2-4
   Fixed Cost 2-4
   Mixed Cost 2-6
   Step Cost 2-7
   Relation Between a Cost and a Cost Driver 2-7
Review 2-2 Analysis of Cost Behavior 2-8
Classifying Costs for Different Purposes 2-9
   Classification of Costs for Financial Reporting 2-9
   Classification of Costs for Managerial Purposes 2-11
   Direct Material 2-11
Review 2-3 Financial Statement Classification of Costs 2-11
Components of Product Cost 2-11
   Direct Material 2-11
   Direct Labor 2-12
   Overhead 2-13
Review 2-4 Classifying Product Costs 2-13
The Conversion Process 2-14
   Retailers versus Manufacturers and Service Companies 2-15
   Manufacturers versus Service Companies 2-17
Review 2-5 Degree of Conversion 2-18
Product Cost Flow in a Cost System 2-18
Review 2-6 Determining Manufacturing Cost Flow 2-21
Cost of Goods Manufactured and Sold 2-21
Review 2-7 Preparing a Schedule of Goods Manufactured Statement Cost of Goods Sold 2-22
Comprehensive Review Module 2-23
   Key Terms 2-23
   Chapter Summary 2-23
   Solution Strategies 2-24
   Chapter Demonstration Problem 2-25
   Data Analytics 2-26
   Data Visualization 2-26
   Potential Ethical Issues 2-27
   Questions 2-27
   Multiple Choice 2-27
   Exercises 2-28
   Problems 2-36
Review Solutions 2-43
   Data Visualization Solutions 2-45

Chapter 3
Cost Behavior and Estimation 3-1

Introduction 3-2
Cost Behavior Analysis 3-2
   Linear Total Cost Estimating Equation 3-3
   Factors Affecting Cost Behavior Patterns 3-4

Contents

Review 3-1 Estimating Costs Using a Linear Total Cost Estimating Equation **3-5**
Cost Estimation **3-5**
    Scatter Diagrams **3-5**
Review 3-2 Preparing a Scatter Diagram **3-7**
    High-Low Cost Estimation **3-8**
Review 3-3 High-low Method **3-9**
    Least Squares Regression **3-9**
Review 3-4 Applying Regression Analysis **3-14**
Using Learning Curves to Estimate Costs **3-14**
Review 3-5 Using Learning Curves to Estimate Costs **3-16**
Additional Issues in Cost Estimation **3-16**
    Changes in Technology or Prices **3-16**
    Matching Activity and Costs **3-17**
    Identifying Relevant Cost Drivers **3-17**
    Ensuring the Reliability of Data **3-17**
Review 3-6 Identifying Problems in Cost Estimation **3-18**
Alternative Cost Driver Classifications **3-19**
    Manufacturing Cost Hierarchy **3-19**
    Customer Cost Hierarchy **3-20**
Review 3-7 Classifying Costs Using a Customer Cost Hierarchy **3-21**
Comprehensive Chapter Review **3-21**
    Key Terms **3-21**
    Chapter Summary **3-22**
    Solution Strategies **3-22**
    Chapter Demonstration Problem **3-23**
    Data Analytics **3-25**
    Data Visualization **3-28**
    Potential Ethical Issues **3-28**
    Questions **3-28**
    Multiple Choice **3-29**
    Exercises **3-31**
    Problems **3-39**
Review Solutions **3-43**
    Data Visualization Solutions **3-45**

Chapter 4
Cost-Volume-Profit Analysis **4-1**

Introduction **4-2**
Contribution Margin **4-2**
Review 4-1 Contribution Income Statement **4-4**
Break-Even Point **4-4**
    Identifying the Break-Even Point **4-5**
    Contribution Income Statement Proof **4-8**
Review 4-2 Break-Even Point **4-9**
Sales at a Fixed Level of Profit **4-9**
    Fixed Amount of Profit **4-10**
    Specific Amount of Profit per Unit **4-11**
Review 4-3 Cost Volume Profit Analysis **4-14**
Incremental Analysis for Short-Run Changes **4-14**
Review 4-4 Incremental Analysis **4-16**
CVP Analysis in a Multiproduct Environment **4-16**
    Break-Even in a Multiple Product Mix **4-17**
    Analysis Considering a Shift in Sales Mix **4-18**
Review 4-5 Cost Volume Profit Analysis—Multiproduct **4-19**
Managing Risks of CVP Relationships **4-19**
    Margin of Safety **4-19**
    Operating Leverage **4-20**
Review 4-6 Operating Leverage and Margin of Safety **4-22**
Underlying Assumptions of CVP Analysis **4-22**
Review 4-7 Assumptions of CVP Analysis **4-23**
Comprehensive Chapter Review **4-24**
    Key Terms **4-24**
    Chapter Summary **4-24**
    Solution Strategies **4-25**
    Chapter Demonstration Problem **4-26**
    Data Analytics **4-27**
    Data Visualization **4-29**
    Potential Ethical Issues **4-29**
    Questions **4-30**
    Multiple Choice **4-30**
    Exercises **4-31**
    Problems **4-37**
Review Solutions **4-43**
    Data Visualization Solutions **4-46**

Chapter 5
Relevant Information for Decision Making **5-1**

Introduction **5-2**
The Concept of Relevance **5-2**
    Association with Decision **5-2**
    Importance to Decision Maker **5-3**
    Bearing on the Future **5-3**
Review 5-1 Identifying Relevant Costs, Sunk Costs, and Opportunity Costs **5-5**
Relevant Costs for Specific Decisions **5-5**
    Outsourcing Decisions **5-6**
Review 5-2 Outsourcing Decisions **5-11**
    Scarce Resource Decisions **5-11**
Review 5-3 Scarce Resource Decision **5-14**
    Sales Mix Decisions **5-14**
Review 5-4 Sales Mix **5-19**
    Special Order Decisions **5-19**
Review 5-5 Special Order **5-21**
    Product Line and Segment Decisions **5-22**
Review 5-6 Decision to Keep or Drop a Division **5-24**
Comprehensive Chapter Review **5-24**
    Key Terms **5-24**
    Chapter Summary **5-25**
    Solution Strategies **5-26**
    Chapter Demonstration Problem **5-26**
    Data Analytics **5-27**
    Data Visualization **5-28**
    Potential Ethical Issues **5-28**
    Questions **5-29**
    Multiple Choice **5-29**
    Exercises **5-31**
    Problems **5-37**
Review Solutions **5-48**
    Data Visualization Solutions **5-50**

Chapter 6
Job Order Costing   6-1

Introduction   6-2
Systems and Methods of Product Costing   6-2
   Cost Accumulation Systems   6-2
   Valuation Methods   6-4
Review 6-1   Cost Accumulation System Choice   6-5
Applying Overhead in a Normal Costing System   6-6
   Calculating Predetermined OH Rate   6-6
   Applying Overhead to Production   6-6
Review 6-2   Plantwide vs. Department OH Rates   6-9
Underapplied or Overapplied Overhead   6-10
   Causes of Underapplied or Overapplied Overhead   6-10
   Disposition of Underapplied and Overapplied Overhead   6-10
Review 6-3   Underapplied or Overapplied Overhead   6-12
Job Order Costing System   6-12
Review 6-4   Journal Entries; Cost Accumulation   6-18
Job Costing in Service Organizations   6-18
Review 6-5   Illustrating Job Order Costing with a Service Provider   6-21
Job Order Costing to Assist Managers   6-22
   Managing Profitability Across Jobs   6-22
Review 6-6   Management Decision Making   6-23
Product and Material Losses in Job Order Costing   6-24
   Normal Loss Accounted for in Predetermined OH Rate   6-24
   Normal Loss Applied to a Specific Job   6-25
   Abnormal Loss Expensed as Incurred   6-25
Review 6-7   Job Order Costing; Rework   6-26
Comprehensive Chapter Review   6-27
   Key Terms   6-27
   Chapter Summary   6-27
   Solution Strategies   6-28
   Chapter Demonstration Problem   6-29
   Data Analytics   6-31
   Data Visualization   6-31
   Potential Ethical Issues   6-31
   Questions   6-32
   Multiple Choice   6-32
   Exercises   6-33
   Problems   6-44
Review Solutions   6-56
   Data Visualization Solutions   6-59

Chapter 7
Process Costing   7-1

Introduction   7-2
Unit Cost Calculation in Process Costing   7-2
   Production Costs: The Numerator   7-3
   Equivalent Units of Production: The Denominator   7-4
Review 7-1   Computing Equivalent Units   7-6
Weighted Average Costing Method   7-6
Review 7-2   Weighted Average Method of Process Costing   7-13
FIFO Method   7-13
Review 7-3   FIFO Method of Process Costing   7-17
Process Costing in a Multidepartment Setting   7-18
Review 7-4   Accounting for Second Department   7-19
Hybrid Costing Systems   7-20
Review 7-5   Hybrid Costing   7-21
Spoilage   7-21
Review 7-6   FIFO; Normal and Abnormal Loss   7-24
Appendix 7-1: Alternative Calculations of Weighted Average and FIFO Methods   7-24
Review 7-7   Alternative EUP Calculation Methods   7-25
Appendix 7-2: Process Costing With Standard Costs   7-26
Review 7-8   Standard Process Costing   7-28
Comprehensive Chapter Review   7-29
   Key Terms   7-29
   Chapter Summary   7-29
   Solution Strategies   7-30
   Chapter Demonstration Problem   7-31
   Data Analytics   7-34
   Data Visualization   7-34
   Potential Ethical Issues   7-35
   Questions   7-35
   Multiple Choice   7-35
   Exercises   7-37
   Problems   7-46
Review Solutions   7-56
   Data Visualization Solutions   7-59

Chapter 8
Activity-Based Management and Activity-Based Costing   8-1

Introduction   8-2
Activity-Based Management   8-2
   Activity Analysis   8-3
   Minimizing NVA Activities   8-5
Review 8-1   Activity Analysis   8-6
   Manufacturing Cycle Efficiency   8-6
   Service Cycle Efficiency   8-7
   Improving Manufacturing (Service) Cycle Efficiency   8-7
Review 8-2   Manufacturing Cycle Efficiency   LO8-2   8-7
Cost Driver Analysis   8-8
   Levels at Which Costs Are Incurred   8-9
   Product Profitability Analysis   8-11
Review 8-3   Cost Drivers   8-13
Activity-Based Costing   8-14
   Two-Stage Allocation Method   8-14
Review 8-4   OH Allocation Using Cost Drivers   8-18
Determining Whether ABC is Useful   8-18
   Large Product or Service Variety   8-19
   High Product/Process Complexity   8-19
   Lack of Commonality in Overhead Costs   8-20
   Irrationality of Current Cost Allocations   8-21
   Changes in Business Environment   8-21
Criticisms of Activity-Based Costing   8-22
Review 8-5   ABC; Product Profitability   8-23
Time-Driven Activity-Based Costing   8-23
Review 8-6   Applying Time-Driven Activity-Based Costing   8-25
Comprehensive Chapter Review   8-25
   Key Terms   8-25

Contents

   Chapter Summary 8-25
   Solution Strategies 8-27
   Chapter Demonstration Problem 8-28
   Data Analytics 8-29
   Data Visualization 8-30
   Potential Ethical Issues 8-30
   Questions 8-31
   Multiple Choice 8-31
   Exercises 8-32
   Problems 8-41
Review Solutions 8-55
   Data Visualization Solutions 8-57

Chapter 9
The Master Budget 9-1

Introduction 9-2
The Budgeting Process 9-2
   Long-Term Strategic Planning 9-2
   Short-Term Tactical Planning 9-3
   General Approaches to Budgeting 9-5
Review 9-1 Planning and Budgeting 9-7
The Master Budget 9-7
   Sales Budget 9-9
Review 9-2 Sales Budget 9-11
   Production Budget 9-12
   Purchases Budget 9-13
   Direct Labor Budget 9-14
   Overhead Budget 9-14
   Selling and Administrative Expense Budget 9-15
Review 9-3 Sales, Production, and Operating Cost Budgets 9-16
   Capital Budget 9-17
   Cash Budget 9-17
Review 9-4 Cash Budget 9-23
   Budgeted Financial Statements 9-23
Impact of Environmental Considerations on the Budgeting Process 9-27
Review 9-5 Operating Income Budget 9-28
Master Budget for a Service Provider 9-29
Review 9-6 Preparing a Budgeted Income Statement for a Service Provider 9-31
Quality of the Master Budget 9-31
Review 9-7 Understanding the Budgeting Process 9-35
Comprehensive Chapter Review 9-36
   Key Terms 9-36
   Chapter Summary 9-36
   Solution Strategies 9-37
   Chapter Demonstration Problem 9-39
   Data Analytics 9-40
   Data Visualization 9-41
   Potential Ethical Issues 9-42
   Questions 9-42
   Multiple Choice 9-43
   Exercises 9-44
   Problems 9-54
Review Solutions 9-67
   Data Visualization Solutions 9-70

Chapter 10
Flexible Budget, Standard Costing, and Variance Analysis 10-1

Introduction 10-2
Flexible Budgets 10-2
   Flexible Budgets for Planning 10-2
   Flexible Budgets for Performance Measurement 10-3
Review 10-1 Flexible Budget 10-4
Developing a Standard Cost System 10-5
   Benefits of a Standard Cost System 10-5
   Considerations in Establishing Standards 10-7
   Establishing Standards 10-8
Review 10-2 Setting Standard Costs 10-10
Material and Labor Variances 10-10
   General Variance Analysis Model 10-11
   Material Variances: Point-of-Usage Model 10-11
   Material Variances: Point-of-Purchase Model 10-14
   Labor Variances 10-14
Review 10-3 Calculating Material and Labor Variances 10-16
Overhead Variances 10-16
   Variable Overhead (Four-Variance Approach) 10-17
   Fixed Overhead (Four-Variance Approach) 10-18
   Alternative Overhead Variance Approaches 10-21
Review 10-4 Calculating Overhead Variances 10-23
Disposition of Standard Cost Variances 10-24
Adjusting Standards 10-25
Review 10-5 Disposing of Standards 10-26
Mix and Yield Variances 10-27
   Material Price, Mix, and Yield Variances 10-27
   Labor Rate, Mix, and Yield Variances 10-29
Review 10-6 Mix and Yield Variances 10-30
Appendix 10A: Job Order Costing Using Standard Costs 10-31
Review 10-7 Standard Costing 10-33
Appendix 10B: Conversion Cost as an Element in Standard Costing 10-33
Review 10-8 Variances and Conversion Cost Category 10-35
Comprehensive Chapter Review 10-35
   Key Terms 10-35
   Chapter Summary 10-36
   Solution Strategies 10-37
   Chapter Demonstration Problem 10-39
   Data Analytics 10-41
   Data Visualization 10-43
   Potential Ethical Issues 10-43
   Questions 10-43
   Multiple Choice 10-44
   Exercises 10-45
   Problems 10-56
Review Solutions 10-67
   Data Visualization Solutions 10-72

Chapter 11
Absorption/Variable Costing and Capacity Analysis 11-1

Introduction 11-2
Overview of Absorption and Variable Costing 11-2
   Absorption Costing 11-2
   Variable Costing 11-3
Review 11-1 Calculating Costs Under Absorption vs. Variable Costing 11-5
Income Under Absorption and Variable Costing 11-5
Review 11-2 Net Income; Absorption vs. Variable Costing 11-11
Income Statement Impact of a Volume Variance 11-11
   Reconciliation of Variable and Absorption Costing Before-Tax Profit 11-13
Review 11-3 Absorption and Variable Costing Income Statement with Volume Variance 11-14
Implications of Capacity Measurements 11-14
   Alternative Capacity Measures 11-15
   Capacity Measurement Effect on Absorption Income 11-16
Review 11-4 Predetermined OH Rates; Capacity Measures 11-18
Comprehensive Chapter Review 11-18
   Key Terms 11-18
   Chapter Summary 11-18
   Solution Strategies 11-19
   Chapter Demonstration Problem 11-19
   Data Analytics 11-21
   Data Visualization 11-21
   Potential Ethical Issues 11-22
   Questions 11-22
   Multiple Choice 11-22
   Exercises 11-24
   Problems 11-29
Review Solutions 11-36
   Data Visualization Solutions 11-38

Chapter 12
Allocation of Joint Costs and Accounting for By-Product/Scrap 12-1

Introduction 12-2
The Joint Process 12-2
   Decisions in the Joint Process 12-4
   The Decision to Sell or Process Further 12-5
Review 12-1 Deciding Whether to Sell or Process Further 12-7
Outputs of a Joint Process 12-7
Review 12-2 Classification of Output from a Joint Process 12-8
Allocation of Joint Cost 12-9
   Physical Measure Allocation 12-10
   Monetary Measure Allocation 12-11
   Comparison of Four Methods of Joint Cost Allocation 12-15
Review 12-3 Allocation of Joint Costs and Decision on Processing Further 12-16
Accounting for By-Product and Scrap 12-16
   Net Realizable Value Approach 12-16
   Realized Value Approach 12-19
   By-Product and Scrap in Job Order Costing 12-20
Review 12-4 Accounting for By-Products 12-21
Joint Costs in Non-Manufacturing Businesses and Not-for-Profit Organizations 12-22
Review 12-5 Retail Organization Joint Cost 12-23
Comprehensive Chapter Review 12-23
   Key Terms 12-23
   Chapter Summary 12-23
   Solution Strategies 12-25
   Chapter Demonstration Problem 12-25
   Data Analytics 12-27
   Data Visualization 12-28
   Potential Ethical Issues 12-28
   Questions 12-28
   Multiple Choice 12-28
   Exercises 12-30
   Problems 12-37
Review Solutions 12-45
   Data Visualization Solutions 12-47

Chapter 13
Responsibility Accounting, Support Department Cost Allocations, and Transfer Pricing 13-1

Introduction 13-2
Management Information and Control Systems 13-2
   Components of a Management Control System 13-3
   Defining a Cost Management System 13-4
Review 13-1 Cost Management System Roles in an Organization 13-6
Decentralization 13-7
   Shared Services 13-8
Review 13-2 Centralization vs. Decentralization 13-9
Responsibility Accounting Systems 13-10
   Control Activities in a Responsibility Accounting System 13-10
   Responsibility Reports 13-10
Review 13-3 Responsibility Report 13-13
Types of Responsibility Centers 13-13
   Cost Center 13-13
   Revenue Center 13-14
   Profit Center 13-14
   Investment Center 13-14
Review 13-4 Responsibility Centers 13-15
Support Department Cost Allocation 13-15
   Allocation Bases 13-16
   Methods of Allocating Support Department Costs 13-17
   Determining Overhead Application Rates 13-24
Review 13-5 Comprehensive Support Department Allocations 13-25
Transfer Pricing 13-26
   Types of Transfer Prices 13-28
   Selecting a Transfer Pricing System 13-30
   Transfer Prices in Multinational Settings 13-30
Review 13-6 Transfer Pricing 13-31
Comprehensive Chapter Review 13-32
   Key Terms 13-32

Contents

Chapter Summary 13-32
Solution Strategies 13-34
Chapter Demonstration Problem 13-34
Data Analytics 13-36
Data Visualization 13-36
Potential Ethical Issues 13-37
Questions 13-37
Multiple Choice 13-38
Exercises 13-39
Problems 13-46
Review Solutions 13-58
Data Visualization Solutions 13-62

Chapter 14
Pricing, Sales Variances, and Customer Profitability 14-1

Introduction 14-2
Cost-Based Approaches to Pricing 14-2
Comparing Economic Pricing to Cost-Based Pricing 14-2
Cost-Based Pricing Approaches 14-2
Review 14-1 Applying Cost-Based Approaches to Pricing 14-7
Life Cycle and Target Costing 14-8
Product Life Cycles 14-8
Target Costing 14-9
Advantages of Target Costing 14-11
Disadvantages of Target Costing 14-12
Review 14-2 Target Costing 14-13
Continuous Improvement Costing 14-13
Review 14-3 Analyzing the Impact of Continuous Improvement Initiatives 14-15
Revenue Variance 14-15
Review 14-4 Decomposing the Revenue Variance 14-17
Contribution Margin Variance 14-17
Contribution Margin Volume Variance 14-19
Sales Quantity Variance 14-21
Review 14-5 Decomposing the CM Volume Variances and the Sales Quantity Variances 14-22
Customer Profitability Analysis 14-23
Review 14-6 Analyzing Customer Profitability 14-26
Comprehensive Chapter Review 14-27
Key Terms 14-27
Chapter Summary 14-27
Solution Strategies 14-28
Chapter Demonstration Problem 14-29
Data Analytics 14-30
Data Visualization 14-31
Potential Ethical Issues 14-31
Questions 14-31
Multiple Choice 14-32
Exercises 14-33
Problems 14-39
Review Solutions 14-47
Data Visualization Solutions 14-50

Chapter 15
Performance Measurement, Balanced Scorecards, and Performance Rewards 15-1

Introduction 15-2
Designing Performance Measurement Systems 15-2
Organization Mission Statements 15-2
Critical Elements for Performance Measurement 15-3
Performance Measurement System Criteria 15-5
Review 15-1 Classifying Performance Measures 15-7
Financial Performance Measures 15-7
Segment Margin 15-7
Statement of Cash Flows 15-11
Review 15-2 Calculating Segment Margin and Ratios 15-11
Return on Investment 15-12
Residual Income 15-15
Economic Value Added 15-15
Limitations of Return on Investment, Residual Income, and Economic Value Added 15-16
Multi-Year Financial Performance Measures 15-17
Review 15-3 Calculating ROI, RI, and EVA 15-18
Nonfinancial, Quantitative Performance Measures 15-18
Selection of Nonfinancial Quantitative Measures 15-19
Types of Nonfinancial Performance Measures 15-20
Establishment of Comparison Bases 15-23
Review 15-4 Calculating Throughput 15-24
Using a Balanced Scorecard for Measuring Performance 15-24
Leading and Lagging Indicators 15-24
Need for Multiple Performance Measures 15-25
Balanced Scorecard Approach 15-26
Performance Evaluation in Multinational Settings 15-30
Review 15-5 Balanced Scorecard 15-31
Compensation Strategy 15-32
Pay-for-Performance Plans 15-32
Pay Versus Performance 15-35
Links Between Performance Measures and Rewards 15-36
Tax Implications of Compensation Elements 15-38
Global Compensation 15-38
Ethical Considerations of Compensation 15-39
Review 15-6 Compensation and Goal Congruence 15-39
Comprehensive Chapter Review 15-39
Comprehensive Chapter Review 15-39
Key Terms 15-39
Chapter Summary 15-40
Solution Strategies 15-41
Chapter Demonstration Problem 1 15-43
Chapter Demonstration Problem 2 15-44
Data Analytics 15-45
Data Visualization 15-46
Potential Ethical Issues 15-47
Questions 15-47
Multiple Choice 15-48
Exercises 15-49
Problems 15-55
Review Solutions 15-65
Data Visualization Solutions 15-67

Chapter 16
Approaches to Cost Control and Managing Uncertainty 16-1

Introduction 16-2
Functions of a Cost Control System 16-2
   Cost Control Implications in the Planning Phase 16-3
Review 16-1 Identifying Functions in a Cost Control System 16-5
Cost Consciousness Attitude 16-5
   Understanding Cost Changes 16-6
Review 16-2 Factors Causing Cost Changes 16-9
   Cost Containment 16-9
   Cost Avoidance and Cost Reduction 16-10
Review 16-3 Approaches to Cost Control 16-13
Classifying Fixed Costs 16-13
   Committed Fixed Costs 16-13
   Discretionary Fixed Costs 16-14
Review 16-4 Identifying Committed and Discretionary Fixed Costs 16-14
Planning and Controlling Discretionary Fixed Costs 16-15
   Planning for Discretionary Costs 16-15
   Controlling Discretionary Activities 16-16
Review 16-5 Controlling Discretionary Costs 16-22
Cash Management 16-23
   What Variables Influence the Optimal Level of Cash? 16-23
   What Are the Sources of Cash? 16-24
   What Variables Influence the Cost of Carrying Cash? 16-27
Review 16-6 Cash Conversion Cycle 16-28
Coping with Uncertainty 16-29
   The Nature and Causes of Uncertainty 16-29
   Four Strategies for Dealing with Uncertainty 16-30
Review 16-7 Uncertainty in Estimating Costs 16-33
Comprehensive Chapter Review 16-34
   Key Terms 16-34
   Chapter Summary 16-34
   Solution Strategies 16-35
   Chapter Demonstration Problem 16-36
   Data Analytics 16-37
   Data Visualization 16-37
   Potential Ethical Issues 16-37
   Questions 16-38
   Multiple Choice 16-38
   Exercises 16-39
   Problems 16-47
Review Solutions 16-54
   Data Visualization Solutions 16-55

Chapter 17
Implementing Quality Concepts 17-1

Introduction 17-2
What is Quality? 17-2
   Production View of Quality 17-2
   Consumer View of Quality 17-5
Review 17-1 Statistical Process Control Chart 17-7
Benchmarking 17-8
   Types of Benchmarking 17-8
   Benchmarking Steps 17-11
Review 17-2 Benchmarking 17-11
Total Quality Management 17-12
   Tenets of TQM 17-12
   Quality as an Organizational Culture 17-15
Review 17-3 Total Quality Management 17-16
Types of Quality Costs 17-16
Review 17-4 Identifying Quality Costs 17-19
Measuring the Cost of Quality 17-19
   Identifying and Tracking Quality Costs 17-19
   Preparing a Cost of Quality Report 17-20
   Determining the Causes of Variances 17-21
   Calculating the Total Cost of Quality 17-22
   Incorporating Quality into a Balanced Scorecard 17-24
Review 17-5 Measuring Cost of Quality 17-26
Comprehensive Chapter Review 17-27
   Key Terms 17-27
   Chapter Summary 17-27
   Solution Strategies 17-29
   Chapter Demonstration Problem 17-29
   Data Analytics 17-30
   Data Visualization 17-31
   Potential Ethical Issues 17-31
   Questions 17-32
   Multiple Choice 17-32
   Exercises 17-34
   Problems 17-42
Review Solutions 17-47
   Data Visualization Solutions 17-48

Chapter 18
Inventory and Production Management 18-1

Introduction 18-2
Buying/Producing and Carrying Inventory 18-2
   Financial Statement Presentation of Inventory Costs 18-2
   Primary Inventory Costs 18-3
Review 18-1 Calculating Inventory Costs 18-4
Economic Order Quantity in a Push System 18-4
   Push System Versus a Pull System 18-4
   Economic Order Quantity 18-5
   Economic Production Run 18-7
   Order Point and Safety Stock 18-8
   Pareto Inventory Analysis 18-9
Review 18-2 Economic Order Quantity and Economic Production Run 18-10
Just-In-Time in a Pull System 18-10
   Changes Needed to Implement JIT Manufacturing 18-11
   Performance Measures Under JIT 18-13
   Flexible and Lean Manufacturing Systems 18-15
Review 18-3 JIT Variances 18-16
Backflush Costing used in Just-in-time Systems 18-17
Review 18-4 Backflush Costing 18-20
Theory of Constraints 18-20
Review 18-5 Theory of Constraints 18-22
Comprehensive Chapter Review 18-22
   Key Terms 18-22

Contents

Chapter Summary **18-23**
Solution Strategies **18-24**
Chapter Demonstration Problem **18-25**
Data Analytics **18-26**
Data Visualization **18-27**
Potential Ethical Issues **18-27**
Questions **18-27**
Multiple Choice **18-28**
Exercises **18-29**
Problems **18-35**
Review Solutions **18-39**
Data Visualization Solutions **18-40**

Chapter **19**
Capital Budgeting **19-1**

Introduction **19-2**
Payback Period **19-2**
Identifying Cash Flows **19-2**
Calculating the Payback Period **19-4**
Review 19-1 Payback Period **19-5**
Discounted Cash Flow Methods **19-5**
Net Present Value Method **19-6**
Profitability Index **19-8**
Internal Rate of Return **19-9**
Review 19-2 Net Present Value, Profitability Index, Internal Rate of Return **19-12**
Relevant After-Tax Cash Flows **19-12**
After-Tax Net Present Value LO19-3 Review 19-3 **19-15**
Evaluating and Ranking Projects Using Different Methods **19-15**
Investment Decision **19-15**
Ranking Multiple Capital Projects **19-19**
Review 19-4 Ranking Capital Projects **19-20**

Compensating for Risk in Capital Project Evaluation **19-20**
Judgmental Method **19-20**
Risk-Adjusted Discount Rate Method **19-21**
Sensitivity Analysis **19-22**
Review 19-5 Sensitivity Analysis **19-24**
Postinvestment Audit **19-24**
Review 19-6 Postinvestment Audit **19-26**
Appendix 19A: Time Value of Money **19-26**
Review 19-7 Present Value Computations **19-28**
Appendix 19B: Accounting Rate of Return **19-28**
Review 19-8 Accounting Rate of Return **19-29**
Comprehensive Chapter Review **19-30**
Key Terms **19-30**
Chapter Summary **19-30**
Solution Strategies **19-32**
Chapter Demonstration Problem **19-33**
Data Analytics **19-34**
Data Visualization **19-35**
Potential Ethical Issues **19-35**
Questions **19-35**
Multiple Choice **19-36**
Exercises **19-37**
Problems **19-43**
Review Solutions **19-49**
Data Visualization Solutions **19-53**

Appendix **A**
Compound Interest Tables

Index **I-1**

Chapter 1
Introduction to Cost Accounting

Road Map

Road Maps summarize each chapter's resources and categorize them by learning objective.

Demos are illustrative examples accompanied by videos that are available in MBC.

Assignments reinforce learning and can be completed by hand or within MBC.

LO	Learning Objective | Topics	Page	eLecture	Demo	Review	Assignments
1-1	**What are the relationships among financial, management, and cost accounting?** Financial Accounting :: Management Accounting :: Cost-Benefit Analysis :: Cost Accounting :: Upstream Costs :: Downstream Costs :: Institute of Management Accountants (IMA) :: Cost Accounting Standards Board (CASB)	1-2	e1-1	D1-1	Rev 1-1	MC1-15, MC1-16, E1-24, E1-25, E1-26, E1-27, E1-28
1-2	**What is a mission statement, and why is it important to organizational strategy?** Mission Statement :: Strategy :: Core Competencies :: Cost Leadership :: Differentiation :: Organization Chart :: Line Personnel :: Staff Personnel :: CEO :: CFO :: Treasurer :: Controller :: Environmental, Social, and Governance (ESG)	1-6	e1-2	D1-2	Rev 1-2	MC1-17, MC1-18, E1-29, E1-30, E1-31, E1-32, E1-33, E1-34, E1-35, E1-36, E1-37, E1-38, E1-39, E1-40, **DA1-1**
1-3	**What is a value chain, and what are the major value chain functions?** Value Chain :: Research and Development :: Design :: Supply :: Production :: Marketing :: Distribution :: Customer Service	1-10	e1-3	D1-3	Rev 1-3	MC1-19, E1-41, E1-42, E1-43
1-4	**What are current trends that impact the role of cost accountants?** Data Analytics :: Descriptive :: Diagnostic :: Predictive :: Prescriptive :: Artificial Intelligence :: Machine Learning :: Blockchain :: Critical Thinking Skills	1-12	e1-4	D1-4A D1-4B	Rev 1-4	MC1-20, MC1-21, E1-44, E1-45, E1-46, E1-47, E1-48, E1-49, E1-50, E1-51, E1-52, E1-53, E1-54, E1-55, E1-56, **DA1-2**
1-5	**Why is ethical behavior so important in organizations?** IMA Statement of Ethical Professional Practice :: Competence :: Confidentiality :: Integrity :: Credibility :: Whistle-Blower :: Ethics in Multinational Corporations	1-19	e1-5	D1-5	Rev 1-5	MC1-22, MC1-23, E1-33, E1-57, E1-58, E1-59, E1-60, E1-61, E1-62, E1-63, E1-64, E1-65

Learning Objectives identify the key learning goals of the chapter.

eLectures are videos available in MBC that provide 3–5 minute reviews of each learning objective.

Reviews are accompanied by videos that demonstrate how to solve various types of problems and are available in MBC.

© Cambridge Business Publishers

INTRODUCTION

Your ultimate career goal may be to become the chief financial officer of **Starbucks**, a partner in the public accounting firm **KPMG**, a controller for the **Mayo Clinic** hospital, or a business analyst for a technology start-up company. Possible career positions for management or cost accountants span across every industry and field, providing many possibilities for you to apply your skills. This text presents techniques that will help management and cost accountants *think critically* in order to *solve problems* and *make decisions* necessary to achieve company goals. Such knowledge is important to anyone who wants to become technically proficient but also wants to use the skills to become a business advisor and problem solver. Cost accounting is foundational to the testing required to become a Certified Public Accountant (CPA), a Certified Management Accountant (CMA), or a Chartered Global Management Accountant (CGMA). The first part of this text presents the traditional tools of management and cost accounting, which are the building blocks for generating information used to satisfy internal and external user needs. The second part of the text presents innovative management and cost accounting topics and methods used in many organizations.

FINANCIAL, MANAGEMENT, AND COST ACCOUNTING

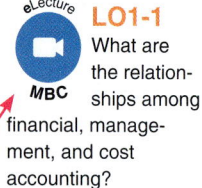

LO1-1 What are the relationships among financial, management, and cost accounting?

eLecture icons identify topics for which there are instructional videos in myBusinessCourse (MBC). See the Preface for more information on MBC.

Key Terms *are highlighted in bold, red font.*

Accounting is often called the *language of business* because it is the means by which information about a company is communicated. This language of business has different forms.

- **Financial accounting** is concentrated on the preparation and provision of financial statements: the balance sheet, statement of comprehensive income, statement of cash flows, and statement of changes in stockholders' equity. Financial accounting information is typically historical, quantitative, monetary, and verifiable. Such information usually reflects activities of the whole organization.

The second form of accounting is that of management and cost accounting.[1]

- **Management accounting** (also called **managerial accounting**) is concerned with providing information to parties inside an organization so that they can plan, control operations, make decisions, and evaluate performance.

- **Cost accounting** is directly concerned with the determination and use of product or service costs. While cost information is prepared for financial reporting, the most significant impact that a cost accountant can have on a company is the cost analysis that is provided for decision making.

Financial Accounting

The objective of financial accounting is to provide useful information to external parties, primarily investors and creditors. Financial accounting requires compliance with generally accepted accounting principles (GAAP), which are issued by the **Financial Accounting Standards Board (FASB)**. Most large, and many small, businesses are required to use GAAP to prepare their financial statements, which may be audited by an independent public accounting firm. Oversight of auditing standards for public companies is the responsibility of the **Public Company Accounting Oversight Board (PCAOB)**, created by the Sarbanes-Oxley Act of 2002.

Management Accounting

While financial accounting serves an important function in providing periodic information to external investors and creditors, management within a company has a need for decision-oriented information on a real-time basis. Business managers of for-profit organizations need an accounting system that can help implement and monitor organizational goals in a globally competitive, multiple-product/service, or multi-service environment. Not-for-profit organization (NFP) managers need an accounting system that focuses on the manner in which resources are used and measures the benefits provided by such use. Access to data and to methods to analyze data creates enormous opportunities for management accountants to capture and communicate more useful information to improve business success. However, managerial accounting information is subject to a **cost-benefit analysis** and should be developed only if the perceived benefits exceed the costs of development and use.

---

[1] Other forms of accounting, such as tax and auditing, are beyond the scope of this text.

Chapter 1 Introduction to Cost Accounting

Management accounting is used to gather the financial and nonfinancial information needed by internal users. In a production environment, managers are concerned with fulfilling organizational goals, communicating and implementing strategy, and coordinating product design, manufacturing, and marketing while simultaneously operating distinct business segments. Except for manufacturing issues, similar concerns exist in a business service environment. In a not-for-profit organization, the focus is still on strategy and goal fulfillment, but managers are also extremely concerned with budgeting, controlling costs, and determining the cost of providing distinct organizational services. Management accounting information commonly addresses individual or divisional concerns rather than those of the organization as a whole. Management accounting is not required to adhere to GAAP but provides both historical and forward-looking information for managers.

To prepare plans, evaluate performance, and make more complex decisions, management needs forward-looking information rather than only the historical data provided by financial accounting. The **upstream costs** (research, development, product design, and supply chain) and **downstream costs** (marketing, distribution, and customer service) incurred are a growing percentage of total enterprise costs. To make more effective pricing decisions, managers need to add these upstream and downstream internal costs to the GAAP-determined product cost.

SERVICE PROVIDER

Upstream costs
↓
GAAP-determined product costs
↓
Downstream costs

Distinguishing between Financial and Managerial Accounting   LO1-1   DEMO 1-1

♦ What are the differences between financial and management accounting as they relate to (1) primary users, (2) primary organizational focus, (3) information characteristics, (4) overriding criteria, and (5) reporting?

The primary differences between financial and management accounting are as follows.

Financial and Management Accounting Differences		
	Financial Accounting	**Management Accounting**
1. Primary users	External	Internal
2. Primary organizational focus	Whole (aggregated)	Parts (segmented)
3. Information characteristics	Must be • Historical • Quantitative • Monetary • Verifiable	May be • Current or forecasted • Quantitative or qualitative • Monetary or nonmonetary • Timely and, at a minimum, reasonably estimated
4. Overriding criteria	Generally accepted accounting principles Relevance Faithful representation	Situational relevance (usefulness) Decision-driven Benefits in excess of costs Flexibility
5. Reporting	Formal Longer reporting periods	Combination of formal and informal Reporting periods depend on need

Career Opportunities in Management Accounting

Management accountants are needed in positions of decision, support, planning, and control across all areas of businesses. Currently, there are over 1.4 million accountants and auditors in the U.S.[2] The Institute of Management Accountants (IMA) estimates that nearly 75 percent of accountants are management accountants.[3] Looking ahead, employment of accountants and auditors is expected to grow by 6 percent from 2021 to 2031.[4]

---

[2] U.S. Bureau of Labor Statistics, *Occupational Outlook Handbook, Accountants and Auditors*. Accessed August 2, 2023, https://www.bls.gov/ooh/business-and-financial/accountants-and-auditors.htm#tab-6%20%0D.

[3] Institute of Management Accountants, "Who Are Management Accountants?" Accessed August 2, 2023, https://www.imanet.org/membership/students/management-accounting-careers#:~:text=IMA%20estimates%20that%20nearly%2075,chief%20financial%20officers%2C%20and%20more.

[4] U.S. Bureau of Labor Statistics, *Occupational Outlook Handbook, Accountants and Auditors*. Accessed August 2, 2023, https://www.bls.gov/ooh/business-and-financial/accountants-and-auditors.htm#tab-6.

Even with increased efficiencies in accounting tasks due to rapid advancements in technology, the demand for accountants is expected to grow. This means that as more and more routine tasks are automated, the demand for management accountants' strategic and problem-solving skills will increase. This trend is evident in the small sample of job duties found in recent job postings included in **Exhibit 1.1**. Reviewing, analyzing, reporting, and partnering are an essential part of a management accountant's typical work day.

Exhibit 1.1	Sample Job Duties of Management Accountants
Chief financial officer	Work closely with the chief executive officer Perform strategic analysis Analyze market segments for expansion
Controller	Analyze changes in product design for effects on production costs Support programs for productivity improvements Partner with business lines and advise on relevant accounting Responsible for the accuracy of standard costs
Budget analysis	Track, monitor, and report information Prepare ad hoc reporting as needed Analyze budgeting trends and make recommendations
Senior cost accountant	Analyze costs and recommend cost savings initiatives Estimate costs for new or proposed products Create new tools to help drive operational success
Cost accountant	Review and investigate cost variances Coordinate inventory cycle counts Provide analytical support for capital projects

Cost Accounting

Cost accounting can be viewed as the intersection between financial and management accounting (see **Exhibit 1.2**). Cost accounting addresses the informational demands of both financial and management accounting by providing product or service cost information to

- external parties (stockholders, creditors, regulatory bodies, and donors) for investment and credit decisions and for reporting purposes, and
- internal managers for planning, controlling, decision making, and evaluating organizational performance.

Exhibit 1.2 Relationship of Financial, Management, and Cost Accounting

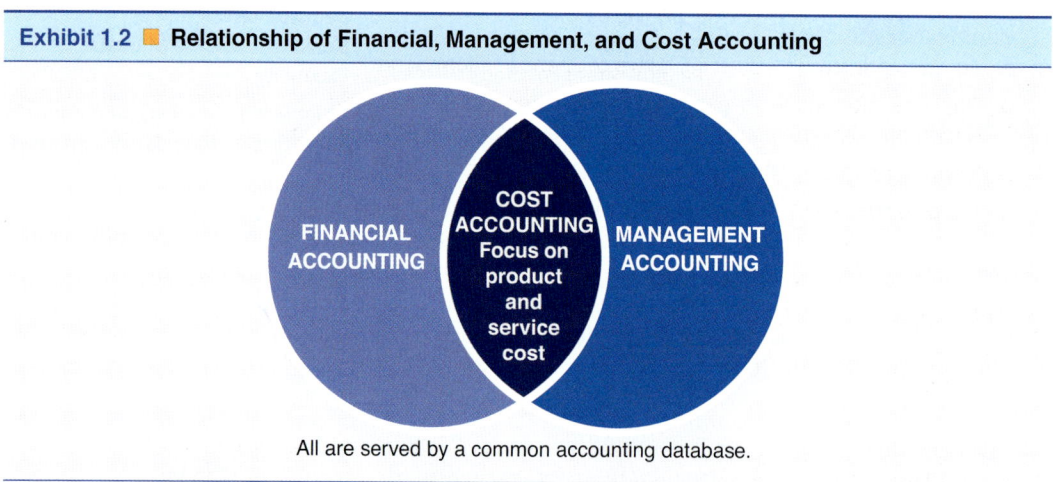

All are served by a common accounting database.

For a manufacturing company, **product cost** consists of the sum of all manufacturing costs (materials, labor, and manufacturing overhead) incurred to make one unit of product and is developed in

Chapter 1 Introduction to Cost Accounting

compliance with GAAP for financial reporting purposes. In nonmanufacturing companies or NFPs, a **service cost** is more likely to be computed. But product/service cost information can also be developed outside of the constraints of GAAP to assist management in its needs for planning and controlling operations.

Cost Accounting Guidelines

Although internal accounting reports need not comply with GAAP, two bodies, Institute of Management Accountants and Cost Accounting Standards Board, issue cost accounting guidelines.

The **Institute of Management Accountants** (IMA) is a voluntary membership organization of accountants, finance specialists, academics, and others focused exclusively on advancing the management accounting profession. The IMA issues directives on the practice of management and cost accounting called Statements on Management Accounting (SMAs). SMAs are not legally binding, but their rigorous developmental and exposure process helps ensure their wide support. The **Cost Accounting Standards Board (CASB)** is part of the U.S. Office of Federal Procurement Policy. The CASB's purpose is to issue cost accounting standards for defense contractors and federal agencies to help ensure uniformity and consistency in government contracting. Compliance with CASB standards is required for companies bidding on or pricing cost-related contracts of the federal government.

Although the IMA and CASB have been influential in standards development, most management accounting procedures have been developed within the industry and influenced by economic and finance theory. Thus, no "official" agency publishes generic management accounting standards for all companies, but there is wide acceptance of (and, therefore, authority for) the methods presented in this text.

Because accounting and other types of information are used to measure an organization's performance, managers may be tempted to manipulate the information to alter others' perceptions about an organization's performance. A strong organizational commitment to ethical behavior can curb deceptive uses of information.

Cost accounting information is needed by both financial and management accountants. Although financial accounting must be prepared in compliance with GAAP, management accounting must be prepared in accordance with management needs. Managers need information to develop mission statements, implement strategy, create efficiencies in the value chain, make sense of big data, and navigate trends attributed to technology advancements.

Financial and Cost Accounting **LO1-1** **REVIEW 1-1**

1. Indicate which type of accounting (financial or cost) best applies to each statement. More than one type of accounting may apply to a statement.

Statement	Financial Accounting	Cost Accounting
a. Focus is primarily on external users of financial information		
b. Provides information for purposes of management planning and decision making and for purposes of investment and credit decisions		
c. Reports product or service cost information		
d. Reports information primarily at the end of a period such as a month, quarter, or year		
e. May include non-GAAP costs in determining product costs		
f. Provides forecasted information		
g. Primarily focused on compliance with authoritative standards issued by the FASB		

2. **Critical Thinking:** What are additional costs beyond the GAAP-determined product costs for the following manufactured goods: (1) downstream costs of a shirt sold by **Gap Inc.**, and (2) upstream costs of a smart phone sold by **U.S. Cellular**?

More practice: MC1-16, E1-24
Solution on p. 1-34.

© Cambridge Business Publishers

ORGANIZATIONAL STRATEGY

LO1-2 What is a mission statement, and why is it important to organizational strategy?

Each organization (whether for-profit or not-for-profit) should have a **mission statement** that expresses the purposes for which the organization exists, what the organization wants to accomplish, and how its products and services can uniquely meet its targeted customers' needs. These statements are used to develop the organization's **strategy** or plan for how the firm will fulfill its goals and objectives by deploying its resources to create value for customers and shareholders. Mission statements are modified over time to adapt to the everchanging organizational environment. Each organization is unique; therefore, even organizations engaged in selling similar products or providing similar services have unique missions and strategies.

Organizational strategy should be designed to help the firm achieve an advantage over its competitors. For instance, **Amazon** has expanded its presence across a number of markets by following its mission statement. Amazon's customer-based mission statement is: "to be earth's most customer-centric company, earth's best employer, and earth's safest place to work."[5] An example of Amazon taking advantage of an opportunity to serve customers in new ways is its strategy of offering free, 2-hour delivery of grocery items from **Whole Foods** (an Amazon subsidiary).

Small organizations frequently develop only a single strategy, whereas large organizations often design an overall entity strategy as well as individual strategies for each organizational unit (such as a division or a location). Unit strategies flow from the organization's overall strategy to ensure effective and efficient resource allocations that are compatible with corporate goals. To be *effective*, the desired result must be achieved successfully. To be *efficient,* however, success is achieved with minimum waste.

In **Exhibit 1.3** is a model of the major factors that influence an organization's strategy. These factors include core competencies, organizational structure, management style and organizational culture, organizational constraints, and environmental constraints.

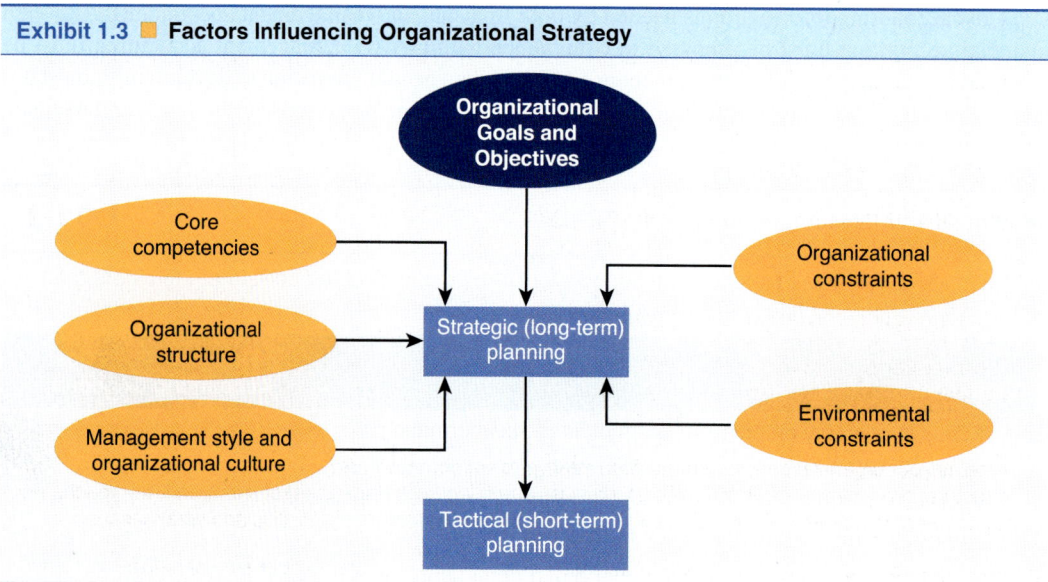

Exhibit 1.3 ■ Factors Influencing Organizational Strategy

Core Competencies

Strategy decisions should reflect the organization's core competencies. A **core competency** is any critical function or activity in which an organization seeks a higher proficiency than its competitors, making that function or activity the root of competitiveness and competitive advantage. Technological innovation, engineering, product development, and after-sales service are examples of core competencies. Other examples include product/service quality, speed to market, environmental policies, marketing skills, and organizational culture and ethics.

---

[5] "Who We Are." *Amazon.com*, Accessed August 3, 2023, www.aboutamazon.com/about-us.

Chapter 1 Introduction to Cost Accounting

- **Microsoft** believes its core competencies are collaboration, drive for results, customer focus, influencing for impact, judgment, and adaptability.[6]
- **Disney** asserts its core expertise in leadership, engagement, and service.[7]
- **MD Anderson Cancer Center** in Houston, Texas, believes its core competency is cancer patient care, research, education, and prevention.[8]

Cost Leadership and Product (Service) Differentiation Regardless of the type of organization, managers are concerned with formulating strategy, and cost accountants are charged with providing management with the information necessary for making choices about, and assessing progress toward, strategic achievement. For example, Who are our customers? Which customers are the most profitable? Least profitable? What is the lowest price that we can charge to not be worse off? What are past trends and forecasts for costs? Most companies employ either a cost leadership or a product (or service) differentiation strategy. **Cost leadership** refers to a company's ability to maintain its competitive edge by undercutting competitor prices. Successful cost leaders sustain a large market share by focusing almost exclusively on manufacturing products or providing services at a low cost. **Product** or **service differentiation** refers to a company's ability to offer superior quality products or more unique services than competitors. Such products and services are generally sold at premium prices.

Distinguishing between Cost Leadership and Differentiation Strategies   LO1-2   DEMO 1-2

◆ **Do the following companies follow a cost leadership or a product (service) differentiation strategy: Walmart, Lululemon, Volkswagen, BMW, Rent a Wreck, Beverly Hills Rent-a-Car?**

Walmart, **Volkswagen**, and **Rent-a-Wreck** primarily compete in their markets based on price under a cost leadership strategy. **Lululemon**, **BMW**, and **Beverly Hills Rent-a-Car** compete on quality and features under a product (service) differentiation strategy.

Real Companies and Institutions are highlighted in bold, blue font.

Exhibit 1.4 provides a checklist of questions that help indicate whether an organization has a comprehensive strategy in place.

Exhibit 1.4 ■ Strategy Checklist

1. What are the most important factors in your organization's operating environment? These factors could include the economy, population demographics, competitors, suppliers, resource availability, innovation, and the environment.

2. What are your organization's core competencies?

3. Have your organization's core competencies become competitive advantages? If yes, can these competitive advantages be maintained? How? If not, why has the organization failed to capitalize on those core competencies?

4. What is your organization's current position relative to your competitors? Factors to consider include cost structure, product/service lines, ability to innovate and adapt to change, market share, market "reach," customer perceptions of quality and service, and profitability. Analyze similarities and weaknesses.

5. What are your customers' purchase or selection criteria? Are your products or services designed to fit these criteria as well as or better than your competitors' products or services?

6. What is the organizational vision identified by your management, shareholders, and other internal and external stakeholders? Is the vision supported by identifiable goals and objectives? Is the vision amenable to change with a changing environment?

7. Does your organization have the appropriate resources (financial, personnel, and technological) to fulfill its vision? If not, what else is needed, and how can it be obtained?

continued

---

[6] "Know Our Competencies." *Microsoft*, Accessed August 3, 2023, https://careers.microsoft.com/v2/global/en/hiring-tips#.

[7] "About Disney Institute." *Disney Institute*. Accessed August 3, 2023, https://www.disneyinstitute.com/about/.

[8] "About MD Anderson." *MD Anderson Cancer Center*. Accessed August 3, 2023, https://www.mdanderson.org/about-md-anderson.html.

continued from previous page

8. Have appropriate performance measurements been established to determine if progress is being made toward your organization's mission and vision?

9. Are operating conditions continuously monitored to detect changes so that your organization can adapt with flexibility and sensitivity, especially to new trends in technology?

Organizational Structure

An organization is composed of people, resources other than people, and commitments that are acquired and arranged to achieve organizational strategies and goals. The organization evolves from its mission, strategies, goals, and managerial personalities. **Organizational structure** reflects the way in which authority and responsibility for making decisions are distributed among personnel. Organizational structure is often depicted graphically in an **organization chart**, as shown in **Exhibit 1.5**. **Authority** refers to the right of an individual or team (usually by virtue of position or rank) to use resources to accomplish a task or achieve an objective. **Responsibility** is the obligation of an individual (or team) to accomplish a task or achieve an objective.

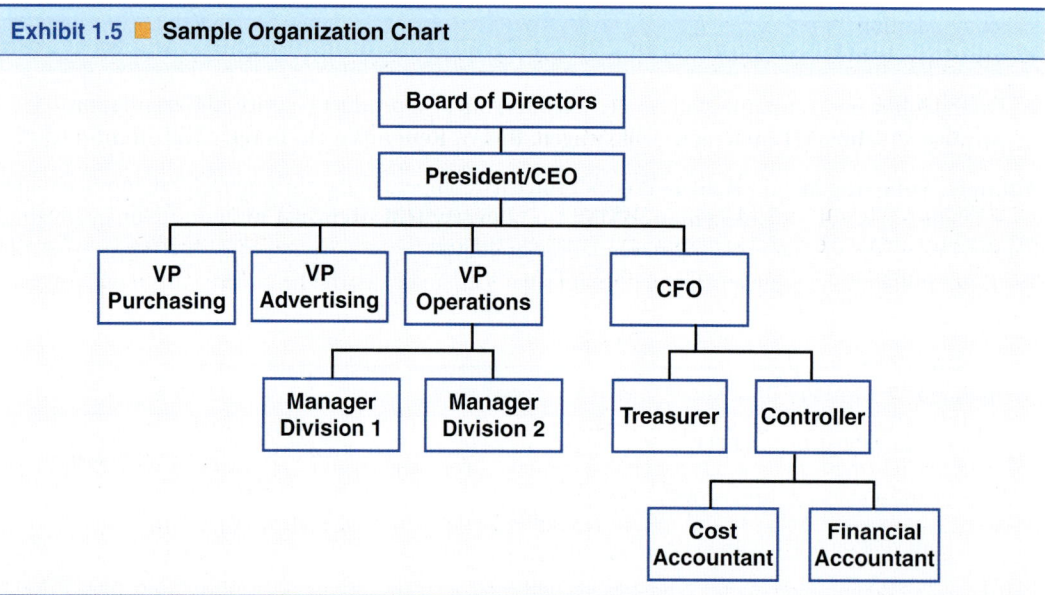

Exhibit 1.5 ■ Sample Organization Chart

The **board of directors** is elected by the shareholders as the overall governing body of the company. The top staff position as the leader of the company's executive group or leadership team is the president of the company. A company may also have a separate position above the president called a **chief executive officer (CEO)**. The role of the CEO is to manage the operations of the company but is also the key liaison between the company and the board of directors. However, the roles of the CEO and president could be filled by one individual. The vice presidents and the **chief financial officer (CFO)** would typically report to the president of the company. The CFO oversees all financial activities of the company. The treasurer and controller would typically report to the CFO. **Treasurers** are generally responsible for achieving short- and long-term financing, investing, and cash management goals, while **controllers** are responsible for both the financial and management (cost) accounting functions.

Positions within an organization are viewed as line or staff positions. **Line personnel** work directly toward attaining organizational goals. Persons in these positions are held responsible for achieving performance targets or budgeted income for their departments, divisions, or geographic regions. **Staff personnel** give assistance and advice to line personnel. For example, in **Exhibit 1.5**, the division managers would be considered line personnel because they would be responsible for the performance of the divisions, while the cost accountants would be considered staff personnel because they support the division managers.

Management Style and Organizational Structure

Going global, expanding core competencies, and investing in new technology require organizational change, and an organization's ability to change depends heavily on its management style and organizational culture. Different managers exhibit different preferences for interacting with the entity's stakeholders, especially employees. Management style is exhibited in decision-making processes, risk-taking, willingness to encourage change, and employee development, among other issues. Typically, management style is also reflected in an organization's culture: the basic manner in which the organization interacts with its business environment, the manner in which employees interact with each other and with management, and the underlying beliefs and attitudes held by employees about the organization. Culture plays a significant role in determining whether the communication system tends to be formal or informal, whether authority is likely to be concentrated in management or distributed throughout the organization, and whether organizational members are experiencing feelings of well-being or stress.

Organizational Constraints

A variety of organizational constraints may affect a firm's strategy options. Most constraints exist only in the short term because they can be overcome by existing business opportunities. Four common organizational constraints are monetary capital, intellectual capital, technology, and the environment. Although additional monetary capital can almost always be acquired through debt (short- or long-term borrowings) or equity (common or preferred stock) sales, management should decide

- whether the capital can be obtained at a reasonable cost and/or
- whether a reallocation of current capital would be more effective and efficient.

Intellectual capital encompasses all of an organization's intangible assets: knowledge, skills, and information. Companies rely on their intellectual capital to create ideas for products or services, to train and develop employees, and to attract and retain customers. As for technology, companies must adopt emerging technologies to stay at the top of their industry and achieve an advantage over competitors.

Environmental Constraints

Environmental constraints also impact organizational strategy. An **environmental constraint** is any limitation caused by external cultural, fiscal (such as taxation structures), legal/regulatory, or political situations and by competitive market structures. One cultural constraint that is becoming more prevalent in its effects on organizational strategy is **sustainability**. More organizations are aware of the need to integrate economic longevity with sustainability concerns, often referred to as **environmental, social, and governance (ESG)**. Some of the pressure for sustainability considerations comes from legal requirements, while other pressure has been exerted by internal and external organizational stakeholders. Because environmental constraints cannot be directly controlled by an organization's management, they tend to be long- rather than short-run influences.

In some cases ESG concerns are evident in a company's overall mission statement. For example, **Allbirds** is on a mission to "prove that comfort, good design and sustainability don't have to be mutually exclusive."[9] Other times, ESG concerns influence the company's overall mission statement but consist of a separate set of strategies. These strategies are often documented in a separate sustainability report. While these statements have thus far been voluntary, at the time of the writing of this text, the SEC is expected to announce new sustainability standards that will affect publicly traded companies. The following are a sample of environmental goals that could be found in ESG reports.

- Decrease carbon emissions
- Increase usage of renewable energy
- Decrease water usage in production
- Reduce rate material usage
- Increase use of recycled materials
- Increase the expected product life

Both financial and managerial accountants are well-positioned in companies to measure, assess, and report sustainability performance. This process is similar to what accountants have always done in providing relevant information necessary for decision making and the assessment of progress toward strategic goals.

---

[9] Allbirds, *Careers*, https://www.allbirds.com/pages/careers (Accessed December 20, 2023).

| REVIEW 1-2 | LO1-2 | Identification of Organizational Strategy |

1. For each of the following excerpts from company strategy, mission, purpose, value, or related statements (obtained from the company's website), indicate whether the company has a more dominant (1) cost leadership strategy or a (2) product or service differentiation strategy. (Note: Company names and sources are provided with the solutions.)
   a. "To win, [we] will lead on price, invest to differentiate on access, be competitive on assortment and deliver a great experience."
   b. "Our collections of timeless, updated classics and authentic reproductions provide a unique point of view and an unmatched combination of inspired design and unparalleled quality."
   c. "Excellence is our way of life. It has always been integral to our business. We expect our products, people, practices and leadership to exemplify it."
   d. "Connect People to what's important in their lives through friendly, reliable, and low-cost air travel."
   e. "Through quality products, superior customer service and unique opportunities we aim to be the hub of the cycling community."
2. **Critical Thinking:** Assume that you have been hired as a management accountant by a small manufacturing company that locally produces its products. The company follows a product differentiation strategy but would like to further support their strategy with environmental goals. How could you support this process?

More practice: MC1-18
E1-29
Solution on p. 1-34.

VALUE CHAIN

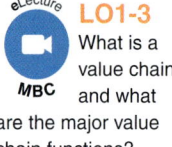

LO1-3
What is a value chain, and what are the major value chain functions?

Strategic management's foundation is the value chain, which is used to identify the upstream and downstream organizational processes that lead to cost leadership or product differentiation. The **value chain** is a set of value-adding functions or processes that convert inputs into products and services for customers.

| DEMO 1-3 | LO1-3 | Identifying Activities in the Value Chain Functions |

The generic value chain includes the functions of research and development, design, supply, production, marketing, distribution, and customer service. **Exhibit 1.6** defines each of these functions within the value chain.

◆ Using the function definitions, what is a specific activity at **General Motors (GM)** within each of the functions? Refer to **Exhibit 1.6** for the illustrative examples.

Company managers communicate organizational strategy to all members in the value chain so that the strategy can be effectively implemented. The communication network needed for coordination among internal functions is designed in part with input from cost accountants who integrate information needs of managers of each value chain function.

Exhibit 1.6 ■ Value Chain Functions, Definitions, and Examples

Function	Definition	Activity within the Function at GM
Research and Development	Experimenting to reduce costs or improve quality.	GM experiments with various paint formulas to produce the most lasting exterior paint finish.

continued

Chapter 1 Introduction to Cost Accounting

continued from previous page

Exhibit 1.6 — Value Chain Functions, Definitions, and Examples (concluded)

Function	Definition	Activity within the Function at GM
Design	Developing alternative product, service, or process designs.	In 2022, GM announced that it would offer the first-ever 2024 Sierra electric vehicle with 654 horsepower and a 400-mile range on a full charge.*
Supply	Managing raw materials received from vendors. Companies often develop long-term alliances with suppliers to reduce costs and improve quality.	GM annually honors its top suppliers for contributions toward innovation, quality, and performance.
Production	Acquiring and assembling resources to manufacture a product or render a service.	For GM, production reflects the acquisition of tires, metal, paint, fabric, glass, electronics, brakes, and other inputs and the assembly of those items into an automobile.
Marketing	Promoting a product or service to current and prospective customers.	GM launches social media advertising campaigns, places automobiles on a showroom floors, and designs billboard advertisements.
Distribution	Delivering a product or service to a customer.	GM uses trains and trucks to deliver automobiles to dealerships.
Customer Service	Supporting customers after the sale of a product or service.	GM provides an 800 number for its customers to call if they have questions or need roadside service.

* General Motors, "GMC Continues the Electric Truck Revolution: Introducing the First-Ever 2024 Sierra EV," Press Release (October 20, 2022); https://news.gm.com/newsroom.detail.html/Pages/news/us/en/2022/oct/1020-sierra-ev.html.

Value Chain Activities — REVIEW 1-3 (LO1-3)

1. Match each of the seven activities listed with one of the components of the value chain, *a* through *g*.

Value Chain Components	Activities
a. Research and development b. Design c. Supply d. Production e. Marketing f. Distribution g. Customer service	1. ___ Negotiating a price with a supplier for direct material 2. ___ Running a product ad on Instagram 3. ___ Adding a label and packaging materials to manufactured product 4. ___ Cost of testing a prototype for a new product 5. ___ Providing a replacement part in satisfaction of a warranty claim 6. ___ Generating a new product idea by conducting focus group studies 7. ___ Cost of storing finished product in a warehouse before delivery

2. **Critical Thinking:** Relate the value chain to a service industry by providing an example of an activity for each component of the value chain for a cellular phone repair service company. Use the value chain components of supply, operations, marketing, and customer service.

More practice: E1-41
Solution on p. 1-35.

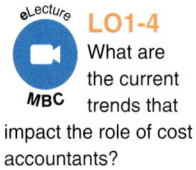

LO1-4
What are the current trends that impact the role of cost accountants?

Data Analytics

This section discusses the impact of innovation on accounting. The "age of change" is an apt description for the current environment in which managers and financial professionals must function. The most recent changes have been driven by the rapid evolution of technology, as can be seen with data analytics, artificial intelligence, and block chain initiatives. Management accountants are challenged to maximize the value that the company delivers to its customers, given the range of new options that new technology provides. To do so, management accountants will need to apply problem-solving and critical thinking skills.

Advances in technology have enabled companies to use data more effectively and efficiently to make key business decisions. **Data analytics** can broadly be defined as the process of examining sets of data with the goal of discovering useful information from patterns found in the data. Increasingly, data analysis is performed using programs ranging from basic spreadsheet software, such as **Microsoft Excel** and **Google Sheets**, to specialized software, such as **Tableau** and **Microsoft Power BI**. Using technology to analyze large amounts of data can reveal trends and insights that would otherwise be difficult to observe. Consider that a large company may be producing millions of data items every hour of the day.

Types of Data Analytics

Data analytics can be categorized into four mains types, ranging in sophistication from relatively straightforward to very complex.

Descriptive Analytics The first category is descriptive analytics, which describes what has happened over a given period of time. Simple examples include determining cost trends over a period of time or the relative effectiveness on sales of various social media promotions based on click-through rates. Microsoft Excel and other spreadsheet programs include built-in functions that greatly simplify performing descriptive analytics.

The summarized results from descriptive analytics can be presented with visualization tools included in specialized software packages. These displays enhance the message and help to communicate key findings to the intended audience. For example, results may be presented in a formal presentation for a review of monthly financial results. In another example, a manager may personalize a dashboard (which is a computer screen of critical information) of key financial measures updated continually that can be referred to during multiple points in a day.

Diagnostic Analytics The second category, diagnostic analytics, focuses more on why something occurred. This data analytics technique is used to monitor changes in data and often includes a certain amount of hypothesizing: Which social marketing campaigns generated the greatest sales impact? Did changing the beverage items affect food choices? Did the opening of competing restaurants negatively impact sales growth? Diagnostic analytics is useful because past performance is often a reliable predictor of future outcomes and can greatly aid in planning and forecasting. In addition, when diagnostic analytics are performed in real time, companies can quickly adjust business decisions to achieve desired outcomes.

Predictive Analytics Whereas descriptive and diagnostic analytics use data to try to understand what happened and why, predictive analytics uses data to try to determine what will happen. Predictive analysis relies on statistical modeling and forecasting methods. Banks use predictive analytics to identify and prevent fraudulent transactions by monitoring customer credit card transactions and red flagging those that deviate from a customer behavior profile that was developed from previous transaction and geographic data. Predictive analysis may benefit from the use of artificial intelligence discussed in the next section.

Prescriptive Analytics Finally, prescriptive analytics moves beyond predicting what is going to happen to suggesting a course of action for what *should* happen to optimize outcomes. Forecasts created using predictive analytics can be used to make recommendations for future courses of action. For example, if we own a sports bar and determine there is a high likelihood of our local sports team winning the championship this year, we should expand the bar area and add more big-screen televisions to maximize revenues.

Illustrating the Four Types of Data Analytics — LO1-4 DEMO 1-4A

◆ **What is an example of each type of data analytics?**

An example of each type of data analytics is provided in the table that follows.

Type of Data Analytics	Purpose	Example
Descriptive	To explain what happened	Continually updated sales data by product line
Diagnostic	To understand why it happened	Did the new advertising campaign cause sales to increase last quarter?
Predictive	To predict what will happen	Predicting fraudulent charges based on past behaviors
Prescriptive	To determine what should happen	Expand t-shirt production to optimize sales based on predicted team champion

Accountants Applying Data Analytics

Most accountants are likely already performing *descriptive analytics* in their regular work. This includes, for example, determining sum totals, averages, and period-to-period changes in such measures as sales, product costs, and gross margin by product. Other examples include average collection periods and day's sales in inventory by product type. A key source for such information is the data embedded in a company's **enterprise resource planning (ERP) system**, the company's customized business software system.

Through *diagnostic analytics*, accountants use data to try to explain why a change took place. Did an increase in sales relate to a change in new customers or new purchases from existing customers? Was a decrease in sales caused by less web traffic or a lower conversion of web visits to sales? Understanding the cause of the change can prompt discussion and action by management.

Accountants can provide even more value by employing *predictive* and *prescriptive analytics*. Accountants obtain data from a variety of sources in order to obtain insights into future outcomes and to provide guidance for future actions. The area of credit granting provides an example. Predictive analytics can help compute credit scores to predict the likelihood of future payments. As a result, prescriptive analytics can aid in suggesting terms for granting credit.

Using a variety of sources for data analytics provides additional points of view and helps to balance biases that may be internalized by the company. Using external data can increase a company's response time to a changing business environment. For example, the web movements of individuals using their personal computers and mobile devices are noted and captured by a plethora of network servers. This voluminous body of data reveals information about individual preferences, personal habits, shopping tendencies, social interactions, and so forth that can be exploited for a variety of purposes. These data could be used to identify social clusters, potential criminal activity, risk exposures, or emotional reactions to news and events and to product introductions.

The amount and sources of data are vast and can add insights to improve decision-making abilities. In fact, the term **big data** refers to extremely large data sets that can be analyzed. However, value can only be derived from data that is of high quality and is accurate. Decisions made on data will only be as good as the quality of the data used. Because data changes quickly, it is important that systems used to evaluate data quality provide feedback on a timely basis.

Artificial Intelligence

Some say artificial intelligence is the most important technological innovation of the coming decades, if not century. **Artificial intelligence (AI)** are machines or computer systems that simulate human intelligence in that they are programmed to sense, recognize speech, learn, problem solve, and act or react. An example of AI at work is a chatbot on a website that processes and responds to a customer's written questions in a customer help text box. An **artificial intelligence system** includes the staff, data, processes, hardware, and software required to develop the machine or computer system. Advancements in algorithms for analyzing data, improved computing power, and accessibility to large data sets provided the groundwork for the recent surge in AI initiatives.

The use of AI is causing and is expected to continue to cause vast changes in all industries. In fact, a report by PWC suggests that AI could contribute up to $15.7 trillion to the global economy in 2030. This economic impact is expected to be gained through additional productivity from automating business processes and using AI technologies with the current labor force, as well as increased consumer demand from high-quality, personalized products or services.[10]

Artificial intelligence initiatives can take on different forms. Will the human make the ultimate decision or the machine? Will the human and machine collaborate in decision making? **Augmented intelligence** assists humans in making better decisions as seen with a vehicle that assists the driver with steering. **Autonomous intelligence** allows for automated decision making without human involvement exhibited in a self-driving car.

Examples of new technologies that are the basis of some AI initiatives include machine learning and natural language processing. **Machine learning** is where computers use algorithms to learn from experience and improve performance over time. As new data is presented, new patterns are recognized, and learning results. Have you noticed that if you order something online the website recommends additional items that you may be interested in? This is a simple case where machine learning is processing web clicks in order to provide new recommendations. **Natural language processing (NLP)** software can understand and react to statements made in human language in speech or in text. The NLP software makes it possible for the virtual assistants and chatbots to respond to a customer's written or oral questions. In another example, NLP is used to identify obligations in legal contracts where the process could take seconds instead of hours of detailed reading by an attorney. In some cases, the outcomes of using NLP are faster and more accurate than work done by humans.

DEMO 1-4B LO1-4 Applying Artificial Intelligence to the Value Chain

◆ **How can AI initiatives improve processes in the different functions of the value chain?**

Exhibit 1.7 provides examples of artificial intelligence applied to each step of the value chain.

Exhibit 1.7 ■ AI Initiatives in the Value Chain

Component of the Value Chain	Application of Artificial Intelligence
Research and development	Continuous processing of real-time data on customer preferences as input into the development of new products.
Design	Creation of a digital prototype based upon a history of user preferences and data on current product feedback.
Supply	Automatic ordering of parts from a supplier based upon sales patterns and an analysis of lead times.
Production	Automation of assembly lines.
Marketing	Promotional material for personalized products/services is shared with potential customers based upon a history of prior purchases, personal demographics, web clicks, etc.
Distribution	Autonomous delivery vehicles.
Customer service	Use of a chatbot to troubleshoot issues from a customer calling a helpline.

The adoption of AI technology is or will be required for companies to remain competitive. A recent survey of executives indicated that 63 percent of respondents thought that AI adoptions were driven by the need to catch up with or narrow the lead of competitors.[11] The transformative changes brought on by AI are affecting not only the customer experience, but the nature of how work is done. The speed in which new AI technologies are being developed and deployed is unprecedented. The adoption of artificial intelligence and robotics technologies has the following potential benefits:

---

[10] PwC, "Sizing the Prize: What's the Real Value of AI for Your Business and How Can You Capitalise?" p. 3, accessed December 20, 2023, https://www.pwc.com.au/training/rolanda/artificial-intelligence-study.html.

[11] Deloitte, "State of AI in the Enterprise, 2nd Edition," p. 5, accessed August 4, 2023, https://www2.deloitte.com/content/dam/insights/us/articles/4780_State-of-AI-in-the-enterprise/DI_State-of-AI-in-the-enterprise-2nd-ed.pdf.

Chapter 1 Introduction to Cost Accounting   1-15

- Automating routine, repetitive and historically labor-intensive tasks and processes
- Reducing operating costs and increasing efficiency
- Providing 24/7 operational service
- Developing innovative new products and services
- Ensuring that products and services meet customer needs
- Scaling up operations with fewer and cheaper resources, and
- Extracting more value from existing investments in technology[12]

Artificial intelligence systems can be developed internally (or codeveloped with partners) or purchased. There are increasing levels of AI capabilities embedded in systems that are purchased. For example, some AI capabilities that can be purchased work directly with the company's enterprise software. While a physically on-site AI system could be pursued, the current trend is for companies to purchase cloud-based services. Cloud-based services are available on demand through an Internet connection from the AI service provider's server. This limits the company's initial investment and doesn't require the expertise of on-site staff to manage the system. The cloud-based service may reduce the risk incurred by companies interested in piloting an AI system.

Ethical Considerations with Artificial Intelligence

Because the use of algorithms in artificial intelligence can impact society in a variety of ways, it is important that developers and adopters of AI capabilities consider ethical impacts. AI systems should follow laws and values and protect the safety and privacy of humans. The following guiding ethical principles of AI have been presented by Google and Microsoft. Across these two set of principles, you can see significant overlap of the core concepts of safety, privacy, accountability, quality, and fairness.

Google Objectives for AI Applications
AI should
1. Be socially beneficial
2. Avoid creating or reinforcing unfair bias
3. Be built and tested for safety
4. Be accountable to people
5. Incorporate privacy design principles
6. Uphold high standards of scientific excellence
7. Be made available for uses that accord with these principles

Microsoft AI Principles
1. Fairness
2. Inclusiveness
3. Reliability and safety
4. Transparency
5. Privacy and security
6. Accountability

Sources: https://ai.google/principles/ (last accessed 1/9/20) and https://www.microsoft.com/en-us/ai/our-approach-to-ai (last accessed 1/9/20).

Data Visualization

Generative AI is a learning model, such as ChatGPT, that can produce new content, based on the data that it is trained on. Results from a March 2023 survey performed by KPMG of 300 business leaders, summarized in the report, *Generative AI: From Buzz to Business Value*, is included in the following data visualization.

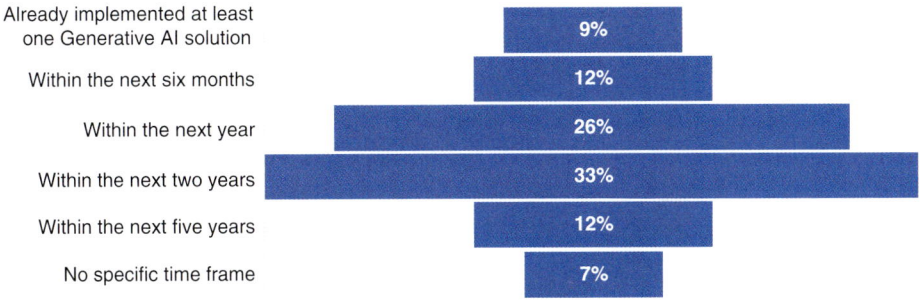

Time Frame for Implementation of Generative AI Solutions

Time Frame	Percentage
Already implemented at least one Generative AI solution	9%
Within the next six months	12%
Within the next year	26%
Within the next two years	33%
Within the next five years	12%
No specific time frame	7%

Note: Data does not total to 100 percent due to rounding.

continued

---

[12] Institute of Management Accountants and Association of Chartered Certified Accountants, "Digital Darwinism: Thriving in the Face of Technology Change," p. 25; accessed on August 4, 2023, https://www.imanet.org/research-publications/c-suite-reports/digital-darwinism-thriving-in-the-face-of-technology-change#:~:text="Digital%20Darwinism%3A%20thriving%20in%20the,continue%20to%20drive%20economic%20growth.

continued from previous page

Based on the data visualization, answer the following questions.
a. What percentage of the survey respondents already have or expect to implement Generative AI solutions within the next two years?
b. What percentage of the survey respondents expect to implement Generative AI within the next two years?
c. What does this data indicate about the survey respondents' interest in the implementation of Generative AI in their companies?

Solution on p. 1-35.

*Loh, T., et al., Generative AI: From buzz to business value, May 2023, https://kpmg.com/kpmg-us/content/dam/kpmg/pdf/2023/generative-ai-survey.pdf.

Blockchain Technology

Blockchain technology differs from the traditional accounting ledger in a fundamental way that has significant implications for the accounting profession. A traditional ledger system is a closed system controlled at a centralized location with individuals at the centralized location responsible for the maintenance and integrity of the ledger. In contrast, a **blockchain** is an open, decentralized ledger, where the ledger is distributed across multiple computers called **nodes**. The blockchain ledger is managed autonomously by the distributed nodes such that data is authenticated by mass collaboration rather than by a central authority. Each node on the blockchain maintains a complete copy of all past transactions that have been added to the ledger. Thus, by comparing to the other nodes' copies, the ledger is continuously synchronized. Unlike traditional accounting ledgers, none of the nodes has any special rights that differ from those of the other nodes.

Blockchains get their name because new ledger data are periodically bundled into **blocks**, which are then added to previous blocks to form a chain. Each block can contain a cryptocurrency exchange, as is the case with Bitcoin, but other possibilities include sales transactions, equity trades, loan payments, election votes—pretty much any contract transaction. In addition, the block contains a timestamp and a hash #, which together form a cryptographic signature associated with the previous blocks. This timestamp and hash make the blockchain essentially tamper-proof because the blocks cannot be changed without the change being apparent to all other nodes. While the chain propagates in only a single chronological order, it can be audited in both directions. **Exhibit 1.8** is a visual depiction of the blockchain process.

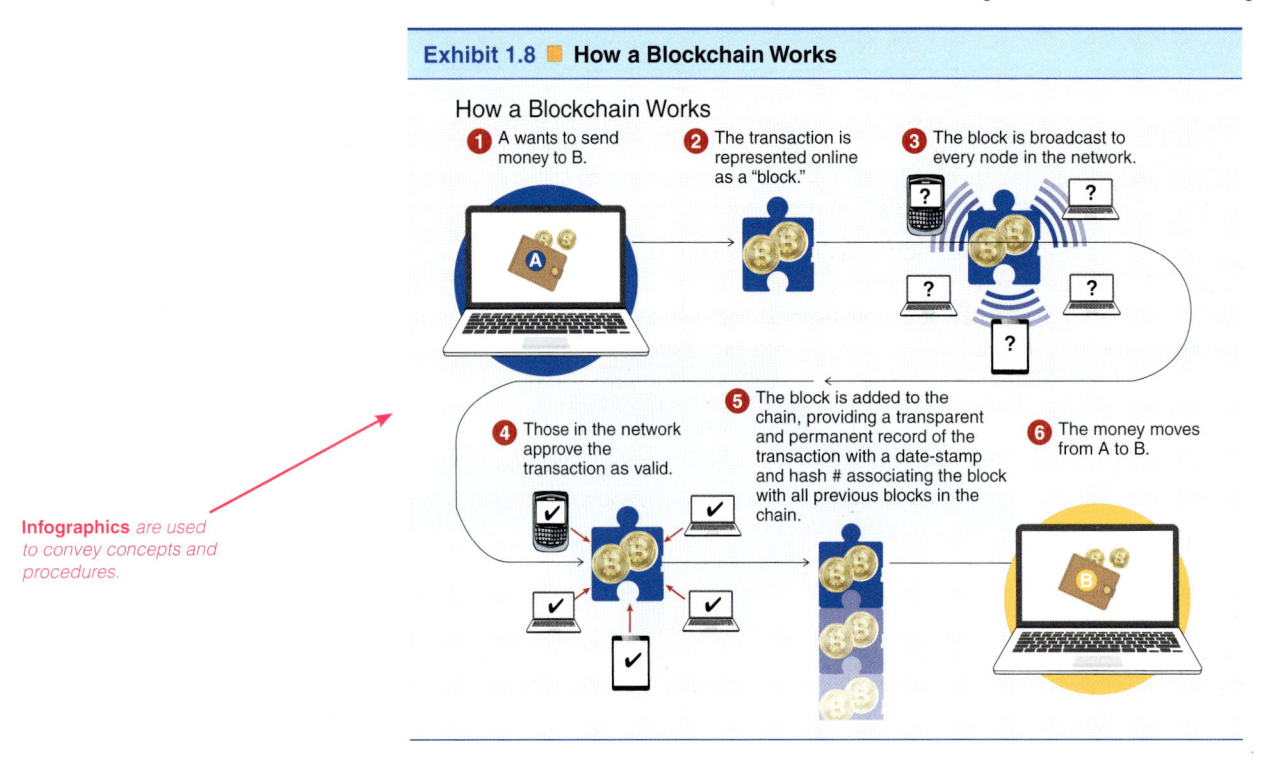

Exhibit 1.8 ■ How a Blockchain Works

How a Blockchain Works

1. A wants to send money to B.
2. The transaction is represented online as a "block."
3. The block is broadcast to every node in the network.
4. Those in the network approve the transaction as valid.
5. The block is added to the chain, providing a transparent and permanent record of the transaction with a date-stamp and hash # associating the block with all previous blocks in the chain.
6. The money moves from A to B.

Infographics *are used to convey concepts and procedures.*

The accounting profession has seen changes arising from a vast array of technological innovations, from computer spreadsheets to general ledger software to ERP systems. Blockchain technology represents another innovation in the way accounting is and will be performed. The invention of double-entry accounting, the bedrock of financial accounting, allowed managers to trust their own financial recordkeeping. Unfortunately, the same level of trust does not exist with outsiders, which is why companies rely on independent auditors for an opinion on the integrity of an entity's financial statements. These audits are often very time consuming and costly.

Accountants working in the traditional centralized-ledger environment are likely to spend a large amount of time reconciling accounts and amounts. This involves comparing balances at their company with external documents from outside entities, including banks, brokerages, and business partners, among others. In addition to the time-consuming process of acquiring all the needed sources of information and performing the comparisons, additional time and effort are often needed to reconcile any differences. In a blockchain's distributed ledger system, all node participants can continually confirm all transactions, greatly reducing the effort involved in periodic reconciliations. This allows for efficiencies in many aspects affecting the accounting function.

Continuous Financial Reporting Accountants working in the traditional environment are expected to produce internal, ad hoc reports. This often requires considerable effort reconciling internal documents, perhaps from multiple departments or divisions. In a blockchain environment, accountants spend far less time verifying transactional data, freeing up time for more valuable advisory activities. Consider, for example, the traditional closing of the books at the end of each period. Instead of needing to acquire the necessary data, verify its accuracy, and make all the necessary adjustments, one could envision a far more automated process with the use of blockchain technology. Financial statements could be updated continuously from data provided by the blockchain, making the period-ending closing process much less time-consuming. For example, having immediate access to financial information will improve decision-making capabilities for management accountants when determining the cost of products (Chapters 6–8), managing sales mix (Chapter 14), or managing cash levels (Chapter 16).

Connection of ERP Systems with External Sources The potential impact of blockchain technologies reaches far beyond internal financial accounting. ERP systems consolidate internal company data. However, the current ERP systems are not equipped to automate external transactions, such as an approval of a vendor purchase where both parties have a digital timestamp with a permanent record. The potential for combining blockchain with ERP systems to automate external transactions economically is a tremendous opportunity. Envision a scenario where a supplier, manufacturer, and customer each have their own ERP system but are joined together by one blockchain network. The flow of product from supplier to customer would be visible by each party, and each transaction between parties would be automatically and permanently recorded.

Efficiencies with Transfer Pricing Blockchain could simplify the process involved with transfer pricing (Chapter 13). A transfer price is an internal charge for services (or goods) transferred between organizational units. In a case where multinational subsidiaries use different ERP systems, a blockchain system could streamline transactions between subsidiaries and eliminate the need for reconciling items.

Applying Critical Thinking Skills in Problem-Solving

While there is no universal definition of critical thinking, the Foundation for Critical Thinking defines it as the "art of analyzing and evaluating thinking with a view to improving it" and further describes a critical thinker as someone who

- Identifies and clearly articulates questions and problems
- Identifies and analyzes relevant information
- Tests solutions and reaches conclusions
- Recognizes and assesses assumptions, implications, and consequences with an open mind

- Communicates effectively with others in problem-solving[13]

Let's consider some tasks performed by accountants.

- Preparing a trial balance based on monthly journal entries.
- Calculating straight-line depreciation expense for a 3-month period
- Determining the unit cost of a job in job order costing
- Determining sales dollars to break even given cost information.

Would any of these rise to the level of requiring critical thinking skills? Given a specified data set, these accounting tasks would rely more on remembering and understanding how to perform the calculation and applying that knowledge to a data set. While understanding and applying calculations is a foundational building block, moving beyond these skill sets to a level of critical thinking is now, more than ever, expected of accounting graduates. As mentioned in this section, with changes in technology, routine accounting tasks will continue to be replaced with more strategic and problem-solving tasks.

Recognizing that data sets are not always provided and that solutions are not always "black and white" is a step toward the use of critical thinking skills. An open-ended problem does not have one correct answer; in fact, it often has multiple viable solutions in which experts may disagree as to the best solution. Thus, even a well-supported answer still leaves room for uncertainty and incompleteness.[14]

Earlier in Review 1-2, we identified whether the following statement from Southwest's annual report was an indication of a more dominant cost leadership strategy or a service differentiation strategy: "Connect People to what's important in their lives through friendly, reliable, and low-cost air travel." Based on this specified information, it is clear that the company follows a cost leadership strategy, competing primarily on cost rather than on differentiation.

Continuing with the Southwest example, let's assume that the marketing department of Southwest proposes a sales promotion where a customer buys one flight and receives a companion ticket at 50 percent off. The question is whether or not to offer the promotion in support of the company's low-cost strategy. Related to this decision, the management accountant's task is to determine company profit implications of this promotion. First, the management accountant would want to identify relevant information such as

- How many new flights are forecasted based on this promotion?
- What are ticket prices on eligible promotion dates to destinations that fall under the promotion?
- What are the incremental costs of flying the additional passengers under the promotion?
- What are incremental costs of advertising the promotion?
- How many flights that would have been sold at full price will now be sold at half price?

In order to compete based upon a cost leadership strategy, it is important to offer a low-cost option of acceptable quality but still remain profitable. The answer to the question on profit implications is not clear cut. The accuracy of the answer will not be known until months after the promotion has ended. The goal now is to gather relevant information and generate a supportable conclusion that will contribute to the decision as to whether or not to offer the promotion. The management accountant will gather relevant data, assess the data, and perform data analytics to make sense of the data. Understanding the implications of a promotion and estimating the hidden costs are important in fulfilling the company's strategy while still maximizing profits. (Special order decisions will be discussed further in Chapter 5.)

Given the need to analyze relevant data and to incorporate new technology such as artificial intelligence and blockchain into accounting tasks, the demand for critical thinking skills will only increase. To this end, answering the last question of each chapter review and certain end-of-chapter assignments require higher-level critical thinking skills. Practicing these skills sets is an important step toward competence in the accounting profession, which is an ethical standard discussed in the next section.

---

[13] "Why Critical Thinking?" The Foundation for Critical Thinking. Accessed on August 2, 2023, https://www.criticalthinking.org/template.php?pages_id=796.

[14] Wolcott, S. "How to Help Your Students Become Better Critical Thinkers." *AICPA*. Accessed on August 4, 2023, https://www.thiswaytocpa.com/collectedmedia/files/critical-thinking-faculty-guide.pdf.

Data Analytics, Artificial Intelligence, and Blockchain — LO1-4 — REVIEW 1-4

a. Match each of the terms, 1 through 8, with the most appropriate definition, choosing from items *a* through *h*.

Term	Definitions
1. Artificial intelligence	a. ____ Bundled ledger data that form a chain
2. Blockchain	b. ____ Computer technology that results in learning and problem-solving
3. Blocks	c. ____ Decentralized ledger distributed across multiple computers
4. Descriptive analytics	d. ____ Determines the cause of trends in historical data
5. Diagnostic analytics	e. ____ Use computers to analyze trends to improve future performance
6. Machine learning	f. ____ Uses data to forecast future trends
7. Predictive analytics	g. ____ Uses data to suggest a future course of action
8. Prescriptive analytics	h. ____ Visually describes what took place in the past

b. **Critical Thinking:** Assume that a new artificial intelligence application was recently implemented in your company. It analyzes historical and current cost information of your company and other publicly available information in order to estimate costs for a proposed product. Because this process is far more sophisticated and uses significantly more data than was used under past procedures, is the management accountant's role now irrelevant in this process?

More practice: MC1-20, MC1-21, E1-44, E1-45, E1-48
Solution on p. 1-35.

PROFESSIONAL ETHICS

Most businesses participate in the global economy, which encompasses the international trade of goods and services, movement of labor, and flows of capital and information. The world has essentially become smaller through technology advances, improved communication capabilities, and trade agreements that promote international movement of goods and services among countries. Multinational corporation managers must achieve their organization's strategy within a global structure and under international regulations while exercising ethical behavior.

Unethical Practices

In business, managers need to attain their financial targets by concentrating on acquiring a targeted market share and achieving desired levels of customer satisfaction. However, executives at many companies have exhibited unethical behavior in trying to "make their numbers." **Earnings management** is any accounting method or practice used by managers or accountants to deliberately "adjust" a company's profit to meet a predetermined internal or external target. Earnings management allows a company to meet earnings estimates, preserve a specific earnings trend, convert a loss to a profit, increase management compensation (tied to stock performance), or hide illegal transactions. When the boundaries of reason are exceeded in applying accounting principles, companies are said to be engaging in "aggressive" accounting. Such aggression may range from simply stretching the limits of legitimacy all the way to outright fraud.

WorldCom, Enron, Tyco, and HealthSouth are but a few of the many companies whose managers faced criminal penalties from acting unethically within the parameters of their jobs. Some of the aggressive accounting practices that have been exposed involved the manipulation of cost accounting information. As a result of many large financial frauds, the U.S. Congress passed the Sarbanes-Oxley Act of 2002 (SOX). This act holds chief executive officers (CEOs) and chief financial officers (CFOs) personally accountable for their organizations' financial reporting.

Ethical Standards in Accounting

The accounting profession promotes high ethical standards for accountants through several of its professional organizations. The IMA administers the CMA exam, which is focused on the professional expertise required by accounting and financial management professionals. The CMA credential demonstrates expertise in financial planning, analysis, control, decision support, and professional

LO1-5 Why is ethical behavior so important in organizations?

ethics.[15] CMAs are required to adhere to the **IMA's Statement of Ethical Professional Practice**. This set of standards (shown in **Exhibit 1.9**) focuses on competence, confidentiality, integrity, and credibility. Adherence to these standards helps management accountants attain a high level of professionalism, thereby facilitating the development of trust from people inside and outside the organization.

Exhibit 1.9 ■ IMA Statement of Ethical Professional Practice

Members of IMA shall behave ethically. A commitment to ethical professional practice includes overarching principles that express our values and standards that guide member conduct.

Principles
IMA's overarching ethical principles include: Honesty, Fairness, Objectivity, and Responsibility. Members shall act in accordance with these principles and shall encourage others within their organizations to adhere to them.

Standards
IMA members have a responsibility to comply with and uphold the standards of Competence, Confidentiality, Integrity, and Credibility. Failure to comply may result in disciplinary action.

I. COMPETENCE
1. Maintain an appropriate level of professional leadership and expertise by enhancing knowledge and skills.
2. Perform professional duties in accordance with relevant laws, regulations, and technical standards.
3. Provide decision support information and recommendations that are accurate, clear, concise, and timely. Recognize and help manage risk.

II. CONFIDENTIALITY
1. Keep information confidential except when disclosure is authorized or legally required.
2. Inform all relevant parties regarding appropriate use of confidential information. Monitor to ensure compliance.
3. Refrain from using confidential information for unethical or illegal advantage.

III. INTEGRITY
1. Mitigate actual conflicts of interest. Regularly communicate with business associates to avoid apparent conflicts of interest. Advise all parties of any potential conflicts of interest.
2. Refrain from engaging in any conduct that would prejudice carrying out duties ethically.
3. Abstain from engaging in or supporting any activity that might discredit the profession.
4. Contribute to a positive ethical culture and place integrity of the profession above personal interests.

IV. CREDIBILITY
1. Communicate information fairly and objectively.
2. Provide all relevant information that could reasonably be expected to influence an intended user's understanding of the reports, analyses, or recommendations.
3. Report any delays or deficiencies in information, timeliness, processing, or internal controls in conformance with organization policy and/or applicable law.
4. Communicate professional limitations or other constraints that would preclude responsible judgment or successful performance of an activity.

Resolving Ethical Issues
In applying the Standards of Ethical Professional Practice, the member may encounter unethical issues or behavior. In these situations, the member should not ignore them, but rather should actively seek resolution of the issue. In determining which steps to follow, the member should consider all risks involved and whether protections exist against retaliation. When faced with unethical issues, the member should follow the established policies of his or her organization, including use of an anonymous reporting system if available. If the organization does not have established policies, the member should consider the following courses of action:
- The resolution process could include a discussion with the member's immediate supervisor. If the supervisor appears to be involved, the issue could be presented to the next level of management.
- IMA offers an anonymous helpline that the member may call to request how key elements of the *IMA Statement of Ethical Professional Practice* could be applied to the ethical issue.
- The member should consider consulting his or her own attorney to learn of any legal obligations, rights, and risks concerning the issue.

If resolution efforts are not successful, the member may wish to consider disassociating from the organization.

Source: Institute of Management Accountants, IMA Statement of Ethical Professional Practice (July 2017). Copyright by Institute of Management Accountants, Montvale, NJ; https://www.imanet.org/-/media/b6fbeeb74d964e6c9fe654c48456e61f.ashx.

The organization **AICPA & CIMA** (American Institute of CPAs and the Chartered Institute of Management Accountants) has also issued a code of ethics. The code of ethics is composed of five

---

[15] The CMA Exam is composed of two parts: Part 1 covers financial planning, performance, and analytics; Part 2 covers strategic financial management. Additional information about the CMA can be found at https://www.imanet.org/cma-certification?ssopc=1.

fundamental principles of integrity, objectivity, professional competence and due care, confidentiality, and professional behavior. Members are expected to abide by the standards and to uphold the integrity and reputation of the accounting profession.

Applying Standards in the IMA Statement of Ethical Practice — LO1-5 DEMO 1-5

◆ **What are illustrative examples of how cost accountants follow the four standards of competence, confidentiality, integrity, and credibility in the IMA Statement of Ethical Professional Practice?**

- **Competence** means that individuals will develop and maintain the skills needed to practice their profession.

  Example: *Cost accountants involved in government contracts must be familiar with both GAAP and CASB standards.*

- **Confidentiality** means that individuals will refrain from disclosing company information to inappropriate parties.

  Example: *Cost accountants should not share proprietary company information during casual discussions at a trade show with company competitors.*

- **Integrity** means that individuals will not participate in organizationally or professionally discreditable actions.

  Example: *Cost accountants should not accept gifts from suppliers because they could bias accountants' ability to fairly evaluate the suppliers and their products.*

- **Credibility** means that individuals will provide full, fair, and timely disclosure of all relevant information.

  Example: *Cost accountants should not intentionally miscalculate product cost data to misstate financial statements.*

Resolving Ethical Issues Cost and management accountants may find that others within the organization have acted illegally or immorally. Such actions could include financial fraud, theft, environmental violations, or employee discrimination. As indicated in **Exhibit 1.9**, the IMA's code of ethical conduct provides guidance on what to do when confronted with ethical issues. Accountants should document what (if any) regulations have been violated, obtain evidence of violation of such actions, and research and record the appropriate actions that should have been taken. This information should be kept confidential but be reported and discussed with a superior who is not involved in the situation—meaning that it could be necessary to communicate up the corporate ladder, even as far as the audit committee. If accountants cannot resolve the matter, their only recourse could be to resign and consult a legal advisor before reporting the matter to regulatory authorities.

Management accountants must focus on competence, confidentiality, integrity, and credibility in order to attain a high level of professionalism and trust.

Punishment for Fraudulent Acts and Rewards for Whistle-Blowers Managers and accountants who knowingly provide false information in public financial reports can be severely punished. For example, a CEO or CFO who knowingly certifies false financial reports may be punished with a maximum penalty of a $5 million fine, 20 years in prison, or both under SOX. Accountants who believe that a fraudulent situation exists should evaluate that situation and, if appropriate, "blow the whistle" on the activities by disclosing them to appropriate persons or agencies. Federal laws, including SOX, provide for some legal protection of whistle-blowers. The False Claims Act (FCA) allows whistle-blowers to receive 15 to 30 percent of any settlement proceeds resulting from the identification of such activities related to fraud against the U.S. government. In 2010, the Dodd-Frank Wall Street Reform and Consumer Protection Act (Dodd-Frank) was passed with several provisions to encourage whistle-blowing by persons who provide original information to the SEC. Awards can range from 10 to 30 percent of the amount recouped.

All accountants, regardless of organizational or geographical placement, should recognize their obligations to their profession and to professional ethics. Ethics is one aspect of business that should be practiced consistently worldwide.

Ethics in Multinational Corporations

Accountants and other individuals should be aware of not only their company's and profession's codes of ethical conduct but also the laws and ethical parameters within any countries in which their company operates. After some American companies were found to have given substantial bribes in connection with business activities, the United States passed the **Foreign Corrupt Practices Act (FCPA)**, which prohibits U.S. corporations (and certain other foreign issuers of securities that are sold in the United States) from offering or giving bribes (directly or indirectly) to foreign officials to influence those individuals (or cause them to use their influence) to help companies obtain or retain business. In 1998, the FCPA was amended to apply to foreign entities that make bribes or corrupt payments within the United States. The FCPA is directed at payments that cause officials to perform in a way specified by the firm rather than in a way prescribed by their official duties.

The SEC recently filed suit against **Panasonic Corp.**'s U.S. subsidiary, **Panasonic Avionics Corp.** (provider of in-flight entertainment and communication systems) for offering a lucrative consulting position to a government official at a state-owned airline to induce the official to help the company obtain business from the airline. Panasonic agreed to pay more than $280 million to U.S. authorities to resolve the charges of Foreign Corrupt Practices Act along with other accounting fraud violations.[16]

In another FCPA case, the SEC filed suit against **Goldman Sachs** for paying more than $1 billion in bribes to 12 government officials in the United Arab Emirates and Malaysia in order to obtain business for Goldman Sachs. Goldman Sachs agreed to pay more than $1 billion to the SEC to settle the charges.[17]

Anti-Bribery Convention Globally, the Organisation of Economic Co-operation and Development (OECD) issued an Anti-Bribery Convention in February 1999 to combat bribery. This document criminalizes any offer, promise, or giving of a bribe to a foreign public official so as to obtain or retain international business deals. By signing the OECD convention, a country acknowledges that bribery should not be considered an appropriate means of doing business. Countries that are parties to the Anti-Bribery Convention put in new measures to reinforce efforts to combat bribery through recommendations released by the OECD. For instance, parties to the convention participate in peer review examinations by member countries. Participating countries are listed in **Exhibit 1.10**.

Exhibit 1.10 Implementing the OECD Anti-Bribery Convention

Argentina	Colombia	Germany	Korea	Peru	Spain
Australia	Costa Rica	Greece	Latvia	Poland	Sweden
Austria	Croatia	Hungary	Lithuania	Portugal	Switzerland
Belgium	Czechia	Iceland	Luxembourg	Romania	Turkey
Brazil	Denmark	Ireland	Mexico	Russia	United Kingdom
Bulgaria	Estonia	Israel	Netherlands	Slovak Republic	United States
Canada	Finland	Italy	New Zealand	Slovenia	
Chile	France	Japan	Norway	South Africa	

Source: OECD (Organisation for Economic Co-operation and Development) Country reports on the implementation of the OECD Anti-Bribery Convention, https://www.oecd.org/daf/anti-bribery/countryreportsontheimplementationoftheoecdanti-briberyconvention.htm (Accessed December 20, 2023)

REVIEW 1-5   **LO1-5**   IMA's Statements of Ethical Professional Practice

1. For each scenario, assume that you are an accounting staff member working for a large, publicly traded manufacturer in the cost accounting department. Indicate whether each of the following scenarios, listed *a* through *e*, may be in conflict with the IMA's Statements of Ethical Professional Practice related to (1) competence, (2) confidentiality, (3) integrity, or (4) credibility.
   a. You casually mention to a friend that your company will report earnings above the financial analyst forecasts. You have full confidence that your friend will not pass along this information.

continued

---

[16] U.S. Securities and Exchange Commission, *Press Release* 2018-73 (April 30, 2018) https://www.sec.gov/news/press-release/2018-73 and United States Department of Justice, *Press Release* 18-551 (April 30, 2018) https://www.justice.gov/opa/pr/panasonic-avionics-corporation-agrees-pay-137-million-resolve-foreign-corrupt-practices-act.

[17] U.S. Securities and Exchange Commission, Litigation Release 2020-265 (October 22, 2020), https://www.sec.gov/news/press-release/2020-265.

b. In your role in supervising the physical inventory count for the first time, you didn't notice that a large lot of inventory was not tagged. It was later discovered that inventory was understated due to inadequate controls over the physical inventory count.

c. As a token of appreciation for the business, the members of the software purchasing committee (of which you are a member) all receive restaurant gift cards from the software vendor.

d. You notice that an internal control procedure is deliberately being circumvented by your colleague. Because the company's report on internal controls has already been issued for this year, and that in your estimation, this doesn't seem to be a big deal, you decide that it is best to wait until next year to communicate the deficiency.

e. In order to meet the current year's financial forecasts, your manager has asked you to contact three suppliers to see if they will delay December billings until January of the following year.

2. **Critical Thinking:** Continuing with the example, assume that you are a staff member working for a large, publicly traded manufacturer as a cost accountant. You are working on a multi-disciplinary team that is evaluating a segment that has been showing unprofitable trends for the last few years. In the process of gathering detailed cost information on the segment, you notice some unusual trends in the data. As a follow-up, you discuss your findings with the segment manager, who indicates that the accounts in question are not significant to the operations and would not make a difference in overall operations. While it is true that the account is not material to total expenses, are there ethical standards that apply, or does materiality override the need for further investigation?

More practice: MC1-23, E1-47
Solution on p. 1-35.

Comprehensive Chapter Review

Key Terms

AICPA & CIMA, p. 1-20
artificial intelligence (AI), p. 1-13
artificial intelligence system, p. 1-13
augmented intelligence, p. 1-14
authority, p. 1-8
autonomous intelligence, p. 1-14
big data, p. 1-13
blockchain, p. 1-16
blocks, p. 1-16
board of directors, p. 1-8
chief executive officer (CEO), p. 1-8
chief financial officer (CFO), p. 1-8
competence, p. 1-21
confidentiality, p. 1-21
controllers, p. 1-8
core competency, p. 1-6
cost accounting, p. 1-2
Cost Accounting Standards Board (CASB), p. 1-5

cost-benefit analysis, p. 1-2
cost leadership, p. 1-7
credibility, p. 1-21
data analytics, p. 1-12
downstream costs, p. 1-3
earnings management, p. 1-19
enterprise resource planning (ERP) system, p. 1-13
environmental constraint, p. 1-9
environmental, social, and governance (ESG), p. 1-9
financial accounting, p. 1-2
Foreign Corrupt Practices Act (FCPA), p. 1-22
IMA's Statement of Ethical Professional Practice, p. 1-20
Institute of Management Accountants (IMA), p. 1-5
integrity, p. 1-21
intellectual capital, p. 1-9
line personnel, p. 1-8

machine learning, p. 1-14
management accounting, p. 1-2
managerial accounting, p. 1-2
mission statement, p. 1-6
natural language processing (NLP), p. 1-14
nodes, p. 1-16
organizational structure, p. 1-8
organization chart, p. 1-8
product, p. 1-7
product cost, p. 1-4
responsibility, p. 1-8
service cost, p. 1-5
service differentiation, p. 1-7
staff personnel, p. 1-8
strategy, p. 1-6
sustainability, p. 1-9
treasurers, p. 1-8
upstream costs, p. 1-3
value chain, p. 1-10

Chapter Summary

Accounting Information, Types (Page 1-2)   LO1-1
- Accounting
  - provides information to external parties (stockholders, creditors, and various regulatory bodies) for investment and credit decisions.

- helps an organization estimate the cost of its products and services.
- provides information useful to internal managers who are responsible for planning, controlling, decision making, and evaluating performance.

■ The purposes of financial, management, and cost accounting are as follows:
- financial accounting is designed to meet external information needs and to comply with generally accepted accounting principles;
- management accounting is designed to satisfy internal users' information needs; and
- cost accounting overlaps financial accounting and management accounting by providing product costing information for financial statements and quantitative, disaggregated, cost-based information that managers need to perform their responsibilities.

■ Generally accepted cost accounting standards
- do not exist for companies that are not engaged in contracts with the federal government; however, the Statements on Management Accounting are well-researched suggestions related to high-quality management accounting practices.
- are prepared by the Cost Accounting Standards Board for companies engaged in federal government cost/bidding contracts.

LO1-2 Mission Statements, Organizational Strategy (Page 1-6)

■ The organizational mission and strategy are important to cost accountants because such statements help to
- indicate appropriate measures of accomplishment.
- define the development, implementation, and monitoring processes for the organizational information systems.

■ Two common corporate strategies are
- cost leadership, which refers to maintaining a competitive edge by undercutting competitor prices, and
- product/service differentiation, which refers to offering (generally at a premium price) superior quality products, more unique services, or a greater number of features than competitors.

■ Organizational strategy may be constrained by
- monetary capital, intellectual capital, and/or technology.
- environmental factors, such as external cultural, fiscal, legal/regulatory, or political situations (including sustainability concepts).
- competitive market structures.

■ The organizational structure
- is composed of people, resources other than people, and commitments that are acquired and arranged relative to authority and responsibility to achieve the organizational mission, strategy, and goals.
- is used by cost accountants to understand how information is communicated between managers and departments as well as the level of each manager's authority and responsibility.
- has line personnel who seek to achieve the organizational mission and strategy.
- has staff personnel, such as cost accountants, who advise and assist line personnel.
- is influenced by management style and organizational culture.

LO1-3 Value Chain (Page 1-10)

■ The value chain is a set of value-adding functions or processes that convert inputs into products and services for company customers.

■ Value chain functions include
- research and development,
- product design,
- supply,
- production,
- marketing,
- distribution, and
- customer service.

LO1-4 Current Trends (Page 1-12)

■ Data Analytics
- The purpose of descriptive analytics is to explain what happened.
- The purpose of diagnostic analytics is to understand why it happened.
- The purpose of predictive analytics is to predict what will happen.
- The purpose of prescriptive analytics is to determine what should happen.

■ Artificial Intelligence
- Initiatives range from augmented intelligence where machines assist humans to autonomous intelligence where decisions are automated.
- AI initiatives apply to all components of the value chain.

Chapter 1 Introduction to Cost Accounting

- Blockchain
  - Blockchain is a transparent system where data is distributed across nodes.
  - Blockchain allows for cryptographic signatures to be associated with blocks of data.
  - Blockchain greatly reduces the need for reconciliations across parties in the blockchain.
- Management accountants must use critical thinking skills to problem-solve as routine tasks are replaced with more strategic and analytic tasks, often using large data sets and new technology.

Ethical Standards and Behavior (Page 1-19)   LO1-5

- Ethical behavior in organizations is addressed in part in the following items:
  - IMA's *Statement of Ethical Professional Practice*, which refers to issues of competence, confidentiality, integrity, and credibility.
  - Sarbanes-Oxley Act, which requires corporate CEOs and CFOs to sign off on the accuracy of financial reports.
  - False Claims Act, which provides for whistle-blowing protection related to frauds against the U.S. government.
- Accountants need to be aware of ethical conduct and laws globally, not just in the United States.
- Ethical behavior has been addressed internationally:
  - The Foreign Corrupt Practices Act and the OECD's Anti-Bribery Convention prohibit companies from offering or giving bribes to foreign officials to influence those individuals to help obtain or retain business.
  - The OECD's Anti-Bribery Convention has been adopted by 44 countries worldwide.

Assignments with the MBC logo in the margin are available in myBusinessCourse.
Resources include demonstration videos, guided examples, and auto-graded homework.
See details in the Preface, and ask your professor how you can access the system.

Data Analytics

DA1-1. Analyzing trends in consumer behavior   LO1-2

Access the **IBM** Research Insights Report: Consumers Want it All: Hybrid Shopping, Sustainability, and Purpose-Driven Brands at https://www.ibm.com/thought-leadership/institute-business-value/en-us/report/2022-consumer-study and answer the following questions.

a. Referring to the data visualization in Figure 6, what type of consumer represented the largest segment of the population in 2020? In 2022? What implications does this have for companies regarding performance metrics in the area of sustainability?

b. If purpose-driven consumers are likely to pay a premium for products that align with their priorities, what does this imply for companies competing as cost leaders?

c. Why is it important for managerial accountants to understand how product costing is affected by sustainability initiatives?

IBM Institute for Business Values

DA1-2. Analyzing trends in AI technology   LO1-4

Access the **PwC** 2022 AI Business Survey found at https://www.pwc.com/us/en/tech-effect/ai-analytics/ai-business-survey.html and answer the following questions by analyzing the data visualizations included in the report.

a. What percentage of leaders in companies have been trying to achieve improved decision making through artificial intelligence (AI) initiatives?

b. What do business leaders project are the top two and bottom two areas of a business to be supported by AI initiatives?

c. What are AI simulations? What are the top five ways that leaders project that companies will use AI simulations? Which of these top five areas would managerial accountants likely partner in decision making?

d. What top three steps do leaders expect to take to develop and deploy responsible AI systems?

e. What percentage of company leaders surveyed have already implemented plans to accelerate AI initiatives in order to reduce general hiring needs?

PwC

Data Visualization

Data Visualization Activities are available in myBusinessCourse. These assignments use Tableau Dashboards to expose students to visual depictions of data and introduce students to data analytics through data visualizations. These exercises are easily assignable and auto graded by MBC.

Potential Ethical Issues

1. Using earnings management techniques to generate materially misleading financial statements
2. Achieving the "low-cost producer" strategy at any sacrifice
3. Retaliating against whistle-blowers within an organization
4. Developing a strategic alliance with another organization that would restrict fair trade (such as by fixing prices)
5. Not disclosing the categories of data collected, disclosed, or sold before or at the point of collection
6. Relying on biased information, obtained through artificial intelligence, for decision making
7. Engaging in bribery or other forms of corruption to obtain or retain business
8. Using accounting practices that hide illegal or improper managerial acts

Questions

Q1-1. Flexibility is said to be the hallmark of management accounting, whereas standardization and consistency describe financial accounting. Explain why the focus of these two accounting systems differs.

Q1-2. Why are legally binding cost accounting standards more critical for defense contractors than for other entities?

Q1-3. Why is a mission statement important to an organization?

Q1-4. What is organizational strategy? Why would each organization have a unique strategy or set of strategies?

Q1-5. What is a core competency, and how do core competencies impact the feasible set of alternative organizational strategies?

Q1-6. Why should a business be concerned with "being green" when polluting might be substantially less expensive—thereby helping in the pursuit of a "low-cost producer" strategy and making that organization's products less expensive for consumers?

Q1-7. Differentiate between authority and responsibility. Can a manager have one without the other? Explain.

Q1-8. "If an organization can borrow money or sell stock, it does not have a capital constraint." Is this statement true or false? Discuss the rationale for your answer.

Q1-9. How does workplace diversity affect organizational culture? Include in your answer a discussion of both the potential benefits and the potential difficulties of hiring workers with diverse backgrounds.

Q1-10. How can a change in governmental laws or regulations create a strategic opportunity for an organization? Give an example.

Q1-11. What is an organization's value chain, and how does it interface with strategy?

Q1-12. What are three current trends that impact the role of managerial accountants?

Q1-13. Why would operating in a global (rather than a strictly domestic) marketplace create a need for additional information for managers? Discuss some of the additional information managers would need and why such information would be valuable.

Q1-14. What ethical issues might affect a U.S. company considering opening a business in Venezuela?

Multiple Choice

LO1-1 MC1-15. Research and development costs are considered
- a. upstream costs.
- b. production process costs.
- c. downstream costs.
- d. manufacturing costs.

LO1-1 MC1-16. Which of the following is *not* a characteristic of management accounting?
- a. Information is aggregated
- b. Reports primarily on past decisions
- c. No external standards
- d. Provides information for internal users

LO1-2 MC1-17. A company is in the process of developing its mission statement. Which one of the following is least appropriate for a company's mission statement?
- a. Defining the purpose of the company.
- b. Identifying what product or service the company is providing.

Chapter 1 Introduction to Cost Accounting

      c. Promoting a common shared goal on the part of employees.
      d. Explaining the tactics for increasing market share in a specific region.

MC1-18. A company sells a product that is aimed at the broad mass market but is perceived as unique throughout its industry. The company is earning above average returns on the product. Which one of the following is the most appropriate term for the competitive strategy followed by the company?
      a. Market focus.
      b. Financial leadership.
      c. Cost leadership.
      d. Differentiation.

MC1-19. Which one of the following lists of functions is in proper value chain order?
      a. Research and development, marketing, and customer services.
      b. Production, marketing, and production design.
      c. Production design, distribution, and marketing.
      d. Research and development, customer service, and distribution.

MC1-20. To improve efficiency, a company is considering utilizing a tool developed by a third party that reviews sales contracts and identifies elements and clauses relevant to revenue recognition. The company is most likely using a tool that is employing
      a. business intelligence.
      b. artificial intelligence.
      c. blockchain.
      d. control monitoring.

MC1-21. The type of data analytics that is most likely to yield the most impact for an organization but is also the most complex is called
      a. diagnostic.
      b. predictive.
      c. descriptive.
      d. prescriptive.

MC1-22. Andrew Babbitt is a management accountant at Ace Mining Corporation (AMC), a processor of ores and minerals. He learned that AMC had been disposing hazardous waste materials in a nearby residential landfill. Babbitt knew that the waste materials could pose a danger to the residents in the area and that there could be legal ramifications for disposing hazardous waste in a residential landfill. When Babbitt discussed the issue with his supervisor the next morning, he was told to ignore it. Due to the significance of the matter, Babbitt decided to discuss the matter with his attorney. In accordance with IMA's Statement of Ethical Professional Practice, which one of the following is the correct evaluation of Babbitt's decision to contact his attorney?
      a. Babbitt's actions were appropriate as an immediate action.
      b. Babbitt's actions were inappropriate because they violated the confidentiality standard.
      c. Babbitt's actions were inappropriate because he should have immediately resigned from the organization.
      d. Babbitt's actions were inappropriate because they involved insubordination.

MC1-23. Which one of the following is an example of an overarching ethical principle from IMA's Statement of Ethical Professional Practice?
      a. Competence.
      b. Confidentiality.
      c. Fairness.
      d. Integrity.

Exercises

E1-24. Distinguishing between management and financial accounting Indicate whether each phrase is more descriptive of management accounting or financial accounting.
      a. Decision-making tool
      b. Emphasizes situational relevance
      c. Conforms to external standards
      d. Highly aggregated reports
      e. Has a greater emphasis on cost-benefit analysis
      f. Typically prepared on a quarterly or annual basis
      g. Longer reporting periods
      h. Income statement, balance sheet, and statement of cash flows
      i. Informal and formal reporting
      j. Future oriented

LO1-1 E1-25. Identifying upstream costs, product costs, and downstream costs Identify each of the following costs as upstream costs, GAAP-determined products costs, or downstream costs.

    a. Direct labor (manufacturing cost)
    b. Cost of promotional materials
    c. Direct materials (manufacturing cost)
    d. Research and development costs
    e. Costs to maintain customer service chatbot
    f. Engineering design costs
    g. Costs to ship finished products
    h. Website marketing costs
    i. Manufacturing overhead (manufacturing cost)
    j. Legal costs to obtain a design patent

LO1-1 E1-26. Accounting information; writing You are a partner in a local accounting firm that does financial planning and prepares tax returns, payroll, and financial reports for medium-size companies. Your monthly financial statements show that your organization is consistently profitable. Cash flow is becoming a small problem, however, and you need to borrow from your bank. You have also been receiving some customer complaints about time delays and price increases.

    a. What accounting information do you think is most important to take with you to discuss a possible loan with your banker?
    b. What accounting information do you think is most important to address the issues of time delays and price increases in your business? What nonaccounting information is important?
    c. Can the information in parts (a) and (b) be gathered from the organization's internal records directly? Indirectly? If the information cannot be obtained from internal records, where would you obtain such information?

LO1-1 E1-27. Organizational accountants; research; writing Use library or Internet resources to find how the jobs of management accountants have changed in the past 10 years.

    a. Prepare a "then-versus-now" comparison.
    b. What five skills do you believe are the most important for management accountants to possess? Discuss the rationale for your choices. Do you think these skills have changed over the past 10 years? Why or why not?

LO1-1 E1-28. Interview; research Call a local company and set up an interview with the firm's cost or management accountant. The following questions can be used as starting points for the interview:

- What is your educational background?
- What was your career path to attain this position?
- What are your most frequently recurring tasks?
- What aspects of your job do you find to be the most fun? The most challenging?
- What college courses would be the most helpful in preparing a person for your job? Why did you select these courses?

    a. Compare and contrast your interview answers with those of other students in the class.
    b. Which one or two items from the interview were of the most benefit to you? Why?

LO1-2 E1-29. Identifying cost leadership and differentiation strategies For each of the following statements, indicate whether the company is more oriented toward a (1) cost leadership strategy or a (2) product or service differentiation strategy.

    a. Leverage technology to improve guest experiences.
    b. Maximize profitability through the use of standardized processes that are designed for maximum efficiency.
    c. To produce luxury clothing products that are customized according to customer preference.
    d. Deliver affordable products to our guests.
    e. Offer customers national and private brand products at everyday low prices.
    f. Benefit people, the planet, and our business while offering a unique shopping experience.

LO1-2 E1-30. Strategic information; research; writing Select a multinational manufacturing company and access its three most recent annual financial reports. Assume that you have just been offered a position as this company's CFO. Use the information in the annual report (or Form 10-K) to develop answers to each of the following questions.

    a. What is the company's mission?

Chapter 1 Introduction to Cost Accounting

    b. What is the company's strategy? Does it differ from the strategy of two years ago?
    c. What are the company's goals as they relate to ESG?
    d. What are the company's core competencies?
    e. What are the value chain processes for this company?
    f. What products (services) does the company manufacture (offer)?
    g. What is the company's organizational structure? Prepare an organizational chart.
    h. What would be your top priorities for this company in the coming year?
    i. Based on your findings, would you accept employment? Why or why not?

E1-31. Mission statement; research; writing Obtain a copy of the mission statement of your college or university. Draft a mission statement for this cost accounting class that supports the school's mission statement. **LO1-2**
    a. How does your mission statement reflect the goals and objectives of the college mission statement?
    b. How can the successful accomplishment of your college's objectives be measured?

E1-32. Mission statement; writing You have managed Indiana's Best Appliances franchises for 15 years and have 100 employees. Business has been profitable, but you are concerned that the Indianapolis locations could soon experience a downturn in growth. You have decided to prepare for such an event by engaging in a higher level of strategic planning, beginning with a company mission statement. **LO1-2**
    a. How does a mission statement add strength to the strategic planning process?
    b. Who should be involved in developing a mission statement and why?
    c. What factors should be considered in the development of a mission statement? Why are these factors important?
    d. Prepare a mission statement for Best Appliances and discuss how your mission statement will provide benefits to strategic planning.

E1-33. Mission statement; writing Mission statements are intended to indicate what an organization does and why it exists. Some of them, however, are simply empty words with little or no substance used by few people to guide their activities. **LO1-2, 5**
    a. Does an organization really need a mission statement? Explain the rationale for your answer.
    b. How could a mission statement help an organization in its pursuit of evoking ethical behavior from employees?
    c. How could a mission statement help an organization in its pursuit of making high-quality products and providing high levels of customer service?

E1-34. Strategy; writing You are the manager of a large home improvement store. What are the five factors that you believe are most critical to your store's success? How would these factors influence your store's strategy? **LO1-2**

E1-35. Strategy; writing You are the manager of a small restaurant in your hometown. **LO1-2**
    a. What information would you obtain for making the decision of whether to add quiche and rack of lamb to your menu?
    b. Why would each of the information items in (a) be significant?

E1-36. Strategy; research; writing Choose a company that might use each of the following strategies relative to its competitors and discuss the benefits that might be realized from that strategy. Indicate the industry in which the company does business, the company's primary competitors, and whether a code of conduct or corporate governance appears on its Web site. **LO1-2**
    a. Differentiation
    b. Cost leadership

E1-37. Organizational constraints; writing Three common organizational constraints are monetary capital, intellectual capital, and technology. Additionally, the environment in which the organization operates may present one or more types of constraints: cultural, fiscal, legal/regulatory, or political. **LO1-2**
    a. Discuss whether each of these constraints would be influential in the following types of organizations:
        (1) city hall of a major metropolitan city
        (2) a franchised quick-copy business
        (3) a new firm of attorneys, all of whom recently graduated from law school
        (4) an international oil exploration and production company

b. For each of the previously listed organizations, discuss your perceptions about which of the constraints would be most critical and why.

LO1-2 E1-38. Strategy; research; writing Select a major manufacturing company. Use library, Internet, or other resources to answer as completely as possible the questions in **Exhibit 1.5** about the manufacturer you have chosen.

LO1-2 E1-39. Core competencies; group activity; research In a team of three or four students, list the core competencies of your local public school district and explain why these items are core competencies. Make an appointment with the principal of one of the high schools or the superintendent of the public school system and, without sharing your team's list, ask this individual what he or she believes the core competencies to be and why. Prepare a written or video presentation that summarizes, compares, and contrasts all of the competencies on your lists. Share copies of your presentation with the individuals whom you contacted.

LO1-2 E1-40. Organizational structure; writing Early this year, you started a financial planning services firm and now have 20 clients. Because of other obligations (including attending classes in pursuit of an advanced degree), you have hired three employees to help service the clients.
- *a.* What types of business activities would you empower these employees to handle and why?
- *b.* What types of business activities would you keep for yourself and why?

LO1-3 E1-41. Classifying activities using the value chain Within the value chain, classify each of the following activities of a furniture manufacturer as research and development, design, supply, production, marketing, distribution, or customer service.
- *a.* Web-based advertising
- *b.* Inspecting incoming red cedar planks
- *c.* Placing shipping labels on finished tables
- *d.* Shipping finished tables to customers
- *e.* Paying line employee salaries
- *f.* Replacing a table that was returned as defective
- *g.* Sanding tables
- *h.* Requisitioning trim for tables for jobs

LO1-3 E1-42. Value chain; writing You are the management accountant for a small company that makes and distributes hot sauce. You have been asked to prepare a presentation that will illustrate the company's value chain.
- *a.* What activities or types of companies would you include in the upstream (supplier) part of the value chain?
- *b.* What activities would you include in the internal value chain?
- *c.* What activities or types of companies would you include in the downstream (distribution and retailing) part of the value chain?

LO1-3 E1-43. Value chain; writing Strategic alliances represent an important value chain arrangement. In many organizations, suppliers are beginning to provide more and more input into customer activities.
- *a.* In the United States, would a strategic alliance ever be considered illegal? Explain.
- *b.* What do you perceive are the primary reasons for pursuing a strategic alliance?
- *c.* With whom might the manager of an online merchant selling flowers and plants want to establish strategic alliances? What issues might the manager want to consider prior to engaging in the alliance?

LO1-4 E1-44. Descriptive, diagnostic, predictive, and prescriptive data analyses Indicate which type of data analytics, 1 through 4, is described in each of the following statements, *a* through *h*.

Data Analytics
1. Descriptive analytics
2. Diagnostic analytics
3. Predictive analytics
4. Prescriptive analytics

Data Analytic Statement
- *a.* _____ Analytics focused on why something occurred.
- *b.* _____ Study of key trends and patterns with the purpose of predicting future outcomes.
- *c.* _____ Real-time data on customer orders by product item number allowing management to see any sudden changes in volume.
- *d.* _____ Based on a predicted outcome, three courses of actions are suggested along with potential implications of each course of action.
- *e.* _____ The CFO has a dashboard that updates automatically showing key financial indicators by department.
- *f.* _____ Exploring data in order to make correlations.
- *g.* _____ Use of analytics to forecast future demand for manufactured products.
- *h.* _____ Focusing on what should happen versus what could happen.

Chapter 1 Introduction to Cost Accounting   1-31

E1-45. Application of data analytics Indicate which type of data analytics, 1 through 4, is described in each of the following statements describing a data analytics application, *a* through *h*.

LO1-4

Data Analytics
1. Descriptive analytics
2. Diagnostic analytics
3. Predictive analytics
4. Prescriptive analytics

Data Analytic Statement
a. _____ Based upon the predicted supplies of inventory required for the next 12 months, the validation of a new supplier is recommended.
b. _____ A report summarizes average sales per customer per month for the past 5 years.
c. _____ Statistical analysis of purchases for a key supplier for the last 12 months is used to predict supplier purchases for the next 12 months.
d. _____ Determination of why a website had increased traffic was ascertained from the patterns discovered in external data sets.
e. _____ Data on equipment usage was statistically analyzed to predict the asset's useful life under three different scenarios.
f. _____ Inventory levels by product per day for the past week are summarized.
g. _____ A university summarized data on how often each room on campus was utilized during the day for a one-month period.
h. _____ Because of a university's predicted classroom usage based upon forecasted enrollment rates and historical usage, an option to lease excess capacity was suggested.

E1-46. Artificial intelligence Match each item in the value chain, 1 through 7, with an example of an artificial intelligence initiative, choosing from items *a* through *g*.

LO1-4

Value Chain
1. Research and development
2. Design
3. Supply
4. Production
5. Marketing
6. Distribution
7. Customer service

Artificial Intelligence Initiative
a. _____ System to optimize delivery traffic
b. _____ Tool that creates a variety of labels based upon some designated parameters
c. _____ System generation of a next-buy recommendation for individual customers
d. _____ Tool to continually discover trends, innovations, and price changes in vendor markets
e. _____ AI assistant that suggests answers to customer questions that a human can use to improve response time
f. _____ Self-learning robotic arm that can be utilized as a third arm by an employee on a manufacturing line
g. _____ Tool to analyze existing patents in order to assist in a company's strategic decisions

E1-47. Artificial intelligence Match each item in the value chain, 1 through 7, with an impact of an artificial intelligence initiative, choosing from items *a* through *g*.

LO1-4

Value Chain
1. Research and development
2. Design
3. Supply
4. Production
5. Marketing
6. Distribution
7. Customer service

Impact of Artificial Intelligence Initiative
a. _____ Increased customer sales through AI that writes personalized messages to customers and posts personalized social media ads.
b. _____ Avoidance of inventory shortages by equipping vendors with sensors that identify potential delays early on, allowing time for any necessary adjustments.
c. _____ Timely and predictable delivery of goods through the use of predictive analytics that identify possible delivery problems and make adjustments to optimize routing.
d. _____ Identification of defective product during the manufacturing process based on a sensor that identifies potential issues based on the sound of the equipment running and reacts accordingly.
e. _____ Generation of product ideas based on an analysis of social media data, sales data, customer review data, and customer preference data.
f. _____ Improved customer experience by providing an app that will give the customer step-by-step directions to a specific product in a particular store.
g. _____ Quicker time to market results because an electronic prototype is efficiently adapted to international markets through language translation and other adjustments.

LO1-4 **E1-48. Blockchain** Match each of the blockchain terms, 1 through 7, with the most appropriate definition, choosing from items *a* through *g*.

Blockchain Term	Definitions
1. Block	a. ____ Allows for automation of external transactions
2. Blockchain ledger	b. ____ Controlled centrally
3. Chain	c. ____ Decentralized system distributed across nodes
4. Cryptographic signature	d. ____ Made up of a series of blocks
5. ERP combined with block chain	e. ____ Maintains a copy of all past transactions
6. Node	f. ____ Timestamp and hash #
7. Traditional ledger system	g. ____ Transaction data sent to nodes in a system

LO1-4 **E1-49. Benefits of data analytics** Access the Institute of Management Accountant's report titled "The Data Analytics Implementation Journey in Business and Finance," (https://www.imanet.org/insights-and-trends/the-future-of-management-accounting/the-data-analytics-implementation-journey-in-business-and-finance?ssopc=1).

 a. Based upon the results of the survey, indicate which areas of an organization respondents identified as benefiting from leading-edge analytic techniques.
 b. What are examples of topics in this text that relate to your answer in part *a*?

LO1-4 **E1-50. Data analytics; artificial intelligence; blockchain** Go to PWC.com, KPMG.com, Deloitte.com, or EY.com. Search for a topic on data analytics, artificial intelligence, or blockchain and write about how the firm is using data analytics, artificial intelligence or blockchain to help its clients.

LO1-4 **E1-51. Artificial intelligence** Select five job descriptions for job openings with artificial intelligence in the description at linkedin.com or monster.com. Review the responsibilities and qualifications for each position.

 a. What similarities and differences do you see across the positions?
 b. Do the qualifications fall within one field or across multiple fields? Comment on your findings.
 c. What skills will accountants need to possess in order to work jointly on projects with colleagues in artificial intelligence fields?

LO1-4 **E1-52. Blockchain technology** Watch Bettina Warburg's **TED Talk** titled "How the Blockchain Will Radically Transform the Economy," dated June 2016, at https://www.ted.com/talks/bettina_warburg_how_the_blockchain_will_radically_transform_the_economy (last accessed December 21, 2023).

 a. Explain how blockchain can be used for personal identity.
 b. Explain how blockchain can be used to reduce uncertainties when value is exchanged across parties.

LO1-4 **E1-53. Trust in data analytics** KPMG described four anchors of trusted analytics in a report titled "Building Trust in Analytics: Breaking the Cycle of Mistrust in D&A," accessed at https://assets.kpmg.com/content/dam/kpmg/xx/pdf/2016/10/building-trust-in-analytics.pdf (last accessed December 21, 2023). Review the article and answer the following questions.

 a. Describe a data set that is maintained by a large retailer of consumer goods that sells both in physical stores and online. For each anchor of trusted analytics, develop a set of five questions that help determine whether the data is considered trusted.
 b. Why is it important for users to trust data sources?

LO1-4 **E1-54. Sources of data analytics** Companies can use a variety of sources for data analytics, both internal and external to the company.

 a. Based on an Internet search, what is the estimated number of companies using external sources of data for analytic purposes?
 b. What are the advantages and disadvantages of applying data analytics to data external to the company?

LO1-4 **E1-55. Ethical considerations of AI** Microsoft considers six principles important to the ethical development and deployment of AI: fairness, reliability and safety, privacy and security, inclusiveness, transparency, and accountability. Access Microsoft's, "The Future Computed: AI and Manufacturing" at https://news.microsoft.com/futurecomputed/?cid=CS_CS_G_AIM_G (last accessed 4 August 2023) to review the application of these principles and answer the following questions.

 a. Describe the six principles as they relate to the manufacturing industry.
 b. Describe a violation of each AI ethical principle in a manufacturing setting with a specified AI initiative.

Chapter 1 Introduction to Cost Accounting   1-33

   c. Describe specific aspects of an artificial intelligence initiative(s) that can be implemented in a manufacturing setting and that support each of the six principles.

E1-56. **ERP and blockchain** Blockchain provides an opportunity for companies to interact with other companies in a secure, transparent way. Using sources from the Internet, determine how a company would maximize its use of a blockchain if it currently uses an ERP system.

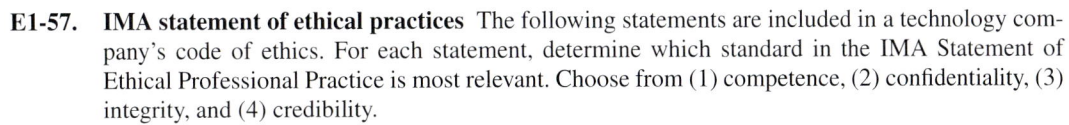

E1-57. **IMA statement of ethical practices** The following statements are included in a technology company's code of ethics. For each statement, determine which standard in the IMA Statement of Ethical Professional Practice is most relevant. Choose from (1) competence, (2) confidentiality, (3) integrity, and (4) credibility.
   a. Never disclose operational, financial, or trade-secret information without your manager's approval.
   b. Business gifts received in value of $30 or more should be declined or returned and reported to management.
   c. Do not misstate or omit critical information or change reports or other records with the intention of misleading the user of the information.
   d. Ascertain that all policies relating to the accurate reporting of meals and entertainment reimbursable expenses are in compliance with all relevant regulations.
   e. Do not use your company position to obtain preferential treatment or other resources while participating in an activity outside of the company.
   f. Employees in the purchasing department will rotate the suppliers that they work with every four years.
   g. Maintain credentials essential to your job position, including compliance with continuing education requirements.

E1-58. **Ethics; writing** In pursuing organizational strategy, cost and management accountants want to instill trust between and among themselves and their constituents, including other organizational members and the independent auditing firm. The IMA has a code of conduct for management accountants.
   a. List and explain each of the major guidelines of the IMA's code.
   b. What steps should a cost or management accountant who detects unethical behavior by his or her supervisor take before deciding to resign?

E1-59. **Ethics; writing** Intellectual capital is extremely important to an organization's longevity. There are, however, "intellectual capital pirates" who make their living from stealing.
   a. Assume you have made several popular music recordings that are being pirated overseas. Discuss your feelings about these intellectual capital pirates and what (if anything) should be done to them.
   b. Sharing passwords for apps or streaming services is also intellectual capital piracy. Do you perceive any difference between this type of copying and the copying of music recordings? Discuss the rationale for your answer.

E1-60. **Ethics; writing** You have recently been elected president of the United States. One of your most popular positions is that you want to reduce the costs of doing business in the United States. When asked how you intend to accomplish this, you reply, "By seeking to repeal all laws that create unnecessary costs. Repealing such laws will be good not only for business but also for the consumer since product costs, and therefore selling prices, will be reduced." Congress heard the message loud and clear and has decided to repeal all environmental protection laws.
   a. Discuss the short- and long-term implications of such a policy.
   b. How would such a policy affect the global competitiveness of U.S. companies?
   c. What reactions would you expect to such a policy from (1) other industrialized nations and (2) developing countries?

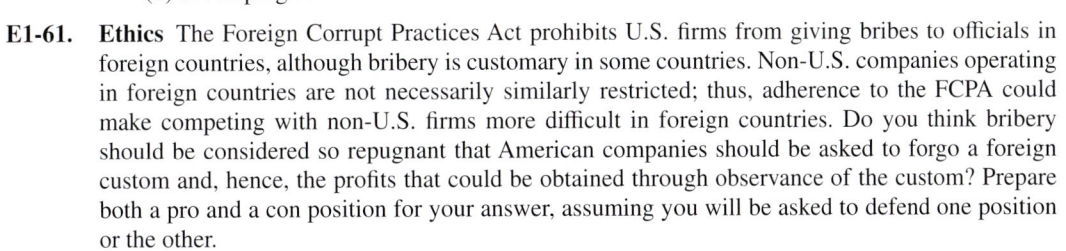

E1-61. **Ethics** The Foreign Corrupt Practices Act prohibits U.S. firms from giving bribes to officials in foreign countries, although bribery is customary in some countries. Non-U.S. companies operating in foreign countries are not necessarily similarly restricted; thus, adherence to the FCPA could make competing with non-U.S. firms more difficult in foreign countries. Do you think bribery should be considered so repugnant that American companies should be asked to forgo a foreign custom and, hence, the profits that could be obtained through observance of the custom? Prepare both a pro and a con position for your answer, assuming you will be asked to defend one position or the other.

© Cambridge Business Publishers

LO1-5 **E1-62. Ethics; writing** Accounting has a long history of being an ethical profession. In recent years, however, some companies have asked their accountants to help "manage earnings."

    a. Who is more likely to be involved in managing earnings: the financial or the management accountant? Why?

    b. Do you believe that "managing earnings" is ethical? Discuss the rationale for your answer.

LO1-5 **E1-63. Ethics; writing** You are a senior manager at Giganto Inc. All senior managers and the board of directors are scheduled to meet next week to discuss some questionable manipulations of earnings that were found by the outside independent auditors. The CEO has asked you to be prepared to start the discussion by developing questions that should be addressed before responding to the auditors.

    a. Why would the CEO be concerned about earnings management? After all, it is the auditor who attests to the fair presentation of financial reporting.

    b. If the earnings management were deemed to be "abusive" and you decided to resign and blow the whistle, would you have any protection? Explain.

LO1-5 **E1-64. Ethics; writing** "Few trends could so thoroughly undermine the very foundation of our free society," wrote Milton Friedman in *Capitalism and Freedom* (Chicago: University of Chicago Press, 1962), "as the acceptance by corporate officials of a social responsibility other than to make as much money for their shareholders as possible."

    a. Discuss your reactions to this quote from a legal standpoint.
    b. Discuss your reactions to this quote from an ethical standpoint.
    c. How would you resolve any conflicts that exist between your two answers?

LO1-5 **E1-65. Ethics; research; writing** Use library or Internet resources to find the major international stock exchanges on which **Volkswagen AG** is listed. Write a short paper on the complexities relative to ethics of listing on stock exchanges across multiple countries.

Review Solutions

Review 1-1

1. *a.* Financial   *c.* Financial, Cost   *e.* Cost   *g.* Financial
    b. Cost   *d.* Financial   *f.* Cost

2. Downstream costs of a shirt sold by **Gap Inc.** include the cost of advertising campaigns including internet ads, website maintenance costs, shipping costs, cost to maintain customer service phone lines and virtual help boxes, and costs of returns. Upstream costs of the latest smart phone sold by **U.S. Cellular** include the cost of market research to identify features that customers desire, research and development costs of the new version of the smart phone, design costs to create and test the prototype, costs to test the prototype before manufacturing begins, and legal costs to defend any new patents.

Review 1-2

1. *a.* **Cost leadership:** "To win, [we] will lead on price, invest to differentiate on access, be competitive on assortment and deliver a great experience." Walmart (https://stock.walmart.com/investors/our-strategy/ (accessed on 11/22/19)).

    b. **Product/Service Differentiation:** "Our collections of timeless, updated classics and authentic reproductions provide a unique point of view and an unmatched combination of inspired design and unparalleled quality." Restoration Hardware (https://www.restorationhardware.com/company-info/index.jsp (accessed 11/22/19)).

    c. **Product/Service Differentiation:** "Excellence is our way of life. It has always been integral to our business. We expect our products, people, practices and leadership to exemplify it." Bose (https://www.bose.com/en_us/about_bose/our_values.html (accessed 11/22/19)).

    d. **Cost leadership:** "Connect People to what's important in their lives through friendly, reliable, and low-cost air travel." Southwest (http://www.southwestairlinesinvestorrelations.com/our-company/purpose-vision-values-and-mission (accessed 11/22/19)).

    e. **Product/Service Differentiation:** "Through quality products, superior customer service and unique opportunities we aim to be the hub of the cycling community." Trek (https://www.trekbikesflorida.com/about/our-mission-values-pg437.htm (accessed 11/22/19)).

Chapter 1 Introduction to Cost Accounting

2. Management accountants can provide relevant information in the development of the goals, assist in developing performance measures, and assess progress toward these goals. For example, gathering information on types of environmental measures, current levels (if available), and publicly available information on measures in similar companies in a similar industry would be helpful in setting the company's goals. After the goals are determined, accountants can measure the goals periodically and report progress toward the goals.

Review 1-3

1. 1. *c.* Supply   3. *d.* Production   5. *g.* Customer Service   7. *f.* Distribution
    2. *e.* Marketing   4. *b.* Design   6. *a.* Research and
                                                  Development

2. *a.* Supply: The company establishes a supplier agreement with Apple for certified parts.
   b. Operations: The company offers same-day repair service of cellular phone screen replacements.
   c. Marketing: The company advertises on social media for same-day screen replacement.
   d. Customer service: The company offers a 6-month warranty on the cellular phone screen replacement.

Review 1-4

a. 1. *b*   3. *a*   5. *d*   7. *f*
     2. *c*   4. *h*   6. *e*   8. *g*

b. No, the management accountant's role is not irrelevant. It will be important for the management accountant to understand what data is used, the quality of the data, and how the cost recommendation was made based on the data. As has always been the case before AI, incorrect or irrelevant data used in a decision process will not result in a well-informed decision. In the end, the management accountant, not AI, is responsible for the data results. The management accountant needs to be able to justify the decisions and the quality of the inputs used to make the decisions.

Review 1-5

1. *a.* confidentiality   *c.* integrity   *e.* integrity
   b. competence   *d.* credibility

2. The degree of materiality should not override ethical considerations. Ethical issues that start out small can easily snowball into larger issues. Defending an action because it is simply not important or not material is a form of rationalization. While the irregularities may not be material, if they are at least reviewed and discussed, a conclusion can be made on the potential for related issues.

Data Visualization Solutions

(See page 1-15.)

a. 9% + 12% + 26% + 33% = 80%
b. 12% + 26% + 33% = 71%
c. The survey clearly indicates plans for increased adoption of Generative AI solutions over the next two years. It also indicates that as of March 2023, a large portion of the survey respondents had yet to see the impact of Generative AI solutions.

Chapter 2
Cost Terminology and Classification

Road Map

LO	Learning Objective | Topics	Page	eLecture	Demo	Review	Assignments
2-1	**Why are costs associated with a cost object?**	2-2	e2-1	D2-1	Rev 2-1	MC2-10, E2-19, E2-20, E2-21, P2-49
	Product Cost :: Service Cost :: Cost Object :: Direct Cost :: Indirect Cost					
2-2	**What assumptions do accountants make about cost behavior, and why are these assumptions necessary?**	2-4	e2-2	D2-2A D2-2B	Rev 2-2	MC2-11, MC2-12, MC2-13, E2-22, E2-23, E2-24, E2-25, E2-26, E2-27, E2-28, E2-29, E2-48, P2-49, P2-50, P2-51, P2-52, P2-53, P2-54, P2-55
	Time Frame :: Relevant Range :: Variable Cost :: Fixed Cost :: Total Cost :: Unit Cost :: Mixed Cost :: Step Cost :: Step Variable Cost :: Step Fixed Cost :: Cost Driver :: Cause-and-Effect Relationship					
2-3	**How does cost classification in the financial statements differ from cost classification for managerial purposes?**	2-9	e2-3	D2-3	Rev 2-3	MC2-14, E2-28, E2-30, E2-31, P2-49, P2-65, DA2-2
	Financial Reporting Purposes :: Product Costs :: Prime Cost :: Direct Material (DM) :: Conversion Cost :: Direct Labor (DL) :: Overhead (OH) :: Period Cost :: Managerial Purposes					
2-4	**What are the product cost categories for financial statement purposes, and what items comprise those categories?**	2-11	e2-4	D2-4	Rev 2-4	MC2-15, E2-29, E2-34, E2-35, E2-36, E2-37, E2-38, P2-56, P2-57, P2-58, P2-59, P2-60, P2-61, P2-65, P2-66
	Direct Materials :: Indirect Materials :: Direct Labor :: Indirect Labor :: Variable Overhead :: Fixed Overhead					
2-5	**How does the conversion process occur in manufacturing, retail, and service companies?**	2-14	e2-5	D2-5	Rev 2-5	MC2-16, E2-32, E2-33, E2-39, P2-61, P2-65, DA2-1, DA2-2
	Inputs :: Outputs :: Degree of Conversion :: Manufacturer :: Raw Materials (RM) :: Work in Process (WIP) :: Finished Goods (FG) :: Merchandiser or Retailer :: Service Company					
2-6	**How do product costs flow through a cost system?**	2-18	e2-6	D2-6A D2-6B	Rev 2-6	MC2-17, E2-40, E2-41, P2-56, P2-59, P2-60, P2-61, P2-62, P2-65, P2-66
	Cost Tracing :: Cost Allocation :: Cost Flow :: Cost of Goods Manufactured (CGM) :: Cost of Goods Sold (CGS)					
2-7	**How is cost of goods manufactured calculated and used in preparing an income statement?**	2-21	e2-7	D2-7	Rev 2-7	MC2-18, E2-42, E2-43, E2-44, E2-45, E2-46, E2-47, P2-59, P2-60, P2-61, P2-63, P2-64, P2-65, P2-66
	Schedule of Cost of Goods Manufactured :: Schedule of Cost of Goods Sold					

INTRODUCTION

No product can be produced without the incurrence of costs for material, labor, and overhead. At a minimum, no service can be produced without the incurrence of costs for labor and overhead; a cost for material may or may not be involved. **Cost** reflects the monetary measure of resources consumed to attain an objective such as making a good or performing a service. A **cost management system** is a set of formal methods developed for planning and controlling an organization's cost-generating activities relative to its strategy, goals, and objectives. This system is designed to communicate all value chain functions about product costs, product profitability, cost management, strategy implementation, and management performance. To effectively communicate information, accountants must clearly understand the differences among various types of costs, how those costs are computed, and how those costs are used. Cost concepts and terms have been developed to facilitate this communication process. Some important types of cost classification categories are summarized in **Exhibit 2.1**.

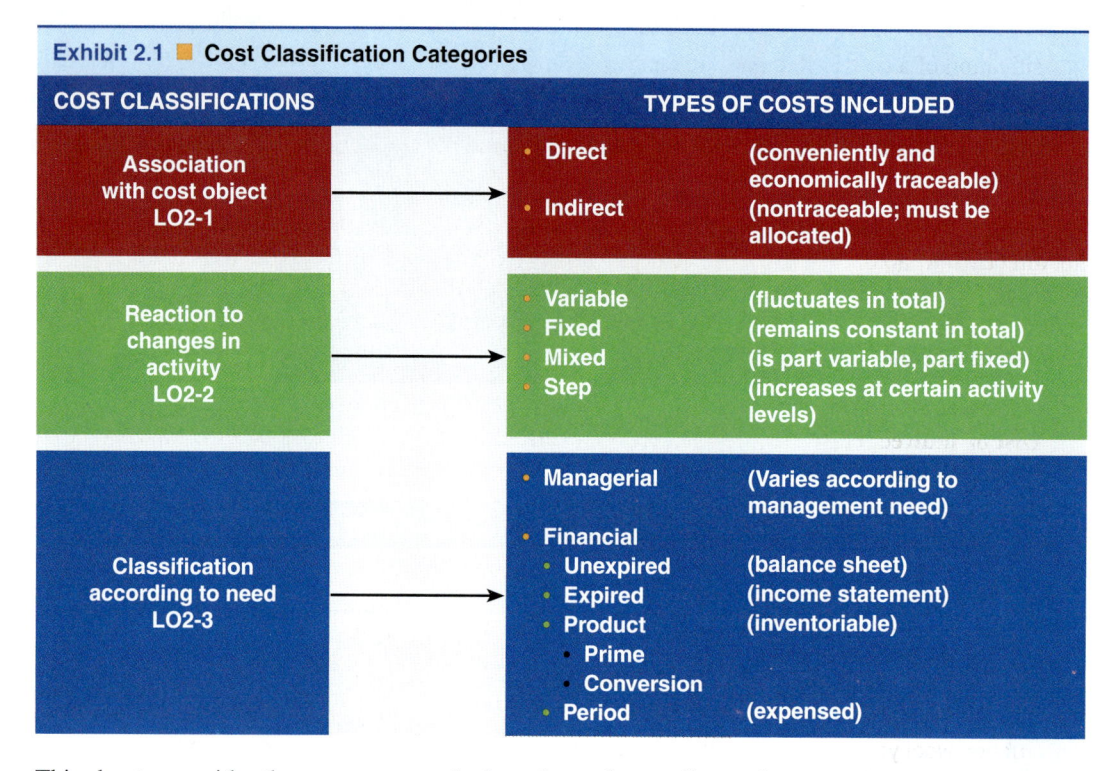

Exhibit 2.1 ■ Cost Classification Categories

COST CLASSIFICATIONS	TYPES OF COSTS INCLUDED
Association with cost object LO2-1	• Direct (conveniently and economically traceable) • Indirect (nontraceable; must be allocated)
Reaction to changes in activity LO2-2	• Variable (fluctuates in total) • Fixed (remains constant in total) • Mixed (is part variable, part fixed) • Step (increases at certain activity levels)

Classification according to need LO2-3	• Managerial (Varies according to management need)
	• Financial
	  • Unexpired (balance sheet)
	  • Expired (income statement)
	  • Product (inventoriable)
	    • Prime
	    • Conversion
	  • Period (expensed)

This chapter provides the necessary terminology for understanding and communicating cost and management accounting information. Additionally, cost flows and the process of cost accumulation in a production environment are presented.

ASSOCIATING COSTS WITH A COST OBJECT

LO2-1 Why are costs associated with a cost object?

A **cost object** is anything for which management wants to collect or accumulate costs. Production operations and service lines are common cost objects. For example, **Toyota**'s Princeton, Indiana, plant makes the Sienna minivans and the Highlander and Highlander Hybrid SUVs. Company managers could define the plant as the cost object and request information about production costs for a specific period. Alternatively, managers could define a specific Sienna minivan with its own unique vehicle identification number as the cost object and request information about production costs during the same period. In the first situation, production costs of all types of vehicles would be included in the information report, whereas in the second situation, production costs for one Sienna minvian would be included on the report. Collecting costs in different ways can help management make decisions regarding the efficiency of operations at the Princeton plant or the cost management effectiveness in producing one vehicle.

Chapter 2 Cost Terminology and Classification

Direct vs. Indirect Costs

Costs of making a product or performing a service are appropriately labeled *product* or *service* costs. The costs associated with any cost object can be classified according to their relation to the cost object. **Direct costs** are conveniently and economically traceable to the cost object. If management requested cost data about a Highlander, direct costs would include tires, sheet metal, speakers, leather, paint, and production line labor.

Indirect costs cannot be economically traced to the cost object but instead are allocated to the cost object. For example, Toyota uses glue in manufacturing each Highlander, but tracing that material would not be cost effective because the cost amount is insignificant. The clerical and information-processing costs of tracing the glue cost to a product would exceed any informational benefits that management might obtain from the information. Thus, glue cost for each SUV would be classified as an indirect cost.

Classifying Costs Associated with a Cost Object as Direct or Indirect — LO2-1 — DEMO 2-1

Classification of a cost as direct or indirect depends on the cost object specification.

◆ **Is plant depreciation for the Toyota Princeton plant a direct cost or indirect cost if the cost object is considered the (1) Toyota Princeton plant or (2) a specific Highlander Hybrid?**

If the Princeton plant is specified as the cost object, then the plant's depreciation is directly traceable. However, if the cost object is specified as a Highlander Hybrid, then the plant's depreciation cost is not directly traceable, in which case the depreciation is classified as indirect and must be allocated to the cost object.

Toyota Financial Services offers financing and leasing plans for Toyota customers and Toyota dealers. Assume that customer loans and dealer loans are serviced in different divisions of the company.

◆ **Is the salary of a credit analyst working in the retail division on customer loans a direct cost or indirect cost if the cost object is considered the (1) retail division or (2) a loan for a retail customer?**

If the cost object is the retail division, salary of the credit analyst is directly traceable to the retail division. However, if the cost object is an individual loan, then the salary of the credit analyst is indirect and must be allocated to an individual loan.

Association with Cost Object — LO2-1 — REVIEW 2-1

1. Following is a list of raw materials that might be used in the production of a baseball: cork, glue, rubber, wool yarn used for layering, thread for stitching, leather, miscellaneous supplies for equipment maintenance, and ink for logo. The baseballs are produced in the same production facility using the same equipment that produces bats. Classify each raw material as direct or indirect when the cost object is (a) the baseball and (b) the production facility.

	Cost Object	
Raw Material	**Baseball**	**Production Facility**
Cork		
Glue		
Rubber		
Layering yarn		
Thread		
Leather		
Maintenance supplies		
Ink for logo		

2. **Critical Thinking:** What are examples of management questions that would require the cost object to be a baseball? Production facility?

More practice: MC2-10, E2-19, E2-20, E2-21
Solution on p. 2-43.

COSTS REACTING TO CHANGES IN ACTIVITY

LO2-2 What assumptions do accountants make about cost behavior, and why are these assumptions necessary?

To manage costs, accountants must understand how total (rather than unit) cost behaves relative to a change in a related activity measure. Common activity measures include production volume, service and sales volumes, hours of machine or service time consumed, pounds of material moved, and number of purchase orders processed.

Every organizational cost will change if sufficient time passes or if an extreme shift in activity level occurs. Thus, to properly identify, analyze, and use cost behavior information, *a time frame is specified to indicate how far into the future a cost should be examined and a particular range of activity is assumed.* For example, the cost of a set of Highlander tires might be expected to increase by $25 next year but by $80 in three years. When Toyota estimates production costs for next year, the $25 increase would be relevant, but the $80 increase would be irrelevant. The assumed range of activity that reflects the company's normal operating range is referred to as the **relevant range**. Within the relevant range, the two primary cost behaviors are variable and fixed.

Variable Cost

A cost that varies in total proportionately with activity is a **variable cost**. Accordingly, a variable cost is a constant amount per unit. Variable costs are extremely important to a company's total profitability because each time a product is produced or sold, or a service is rendered, a specific amount of variable cost is incurred. Relative to volume of product or number of customers serviced, examples of variable costs include the costs of

- material,
- hourly wages, and
- sales commissions.

Although accountants view variable costs as linear relative to activity volume, economists view these costs as curvilinear, as shown in **Exhibit 2.2**. The cost line slopes upward at a given rate until a volume is reached, at which point the unit cost becomes fairly constant. Within this relevant range, the firm experiences stable effects on costs such as material price discounts and worker skill and productivity. Beyond the relevant range, the slope becomes quite steep as the firm enters a range of activity in which operations become inefficient and production capacity is overutilized. In this range, the firm finds that costs rise rapidly because of worker crowding, equipment shortages, and other operating inefficiencies. Although the curvilinear graph is more correct, it is awkward to use in planning or controlling costs. Accordingly, accountants choose the range in which these variable costs are assumed to behave as they are defined, and as such, the assumed cost behavior is an approximation of reality.

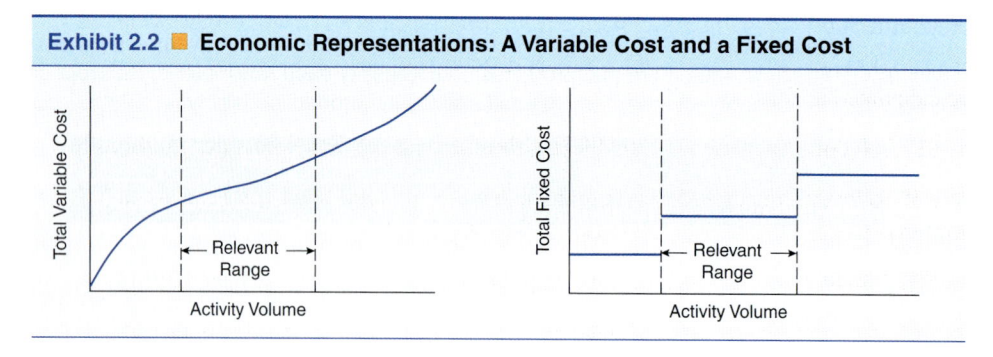

Exhibit 2.2 ■ Economic Representations: A Variable Cost and a Fixed Cost

Fixed Cost

In contrast, a cost that remains constant in total within the relevant range of activity is considered a **fixed cost**, as shown in **Exhibit 2.2**. On a per-unit basis, a fixed cost varies inversely with changes in the level of activity: the per-unit fixed cost decreases with increases in the activity level and increases with decreases in the activity level. Many fixed costs are incurred to provide a firm's production capacity.

Chapter 2 Cost Terminology and Classification

Fixed costs include

- salaries (as opposed to hourly wages),
- depreciation (computed using the straight-line method), and
- insurance.

Straight-Line Method:
$$\frac{(\text{Cost} - \text{Salvage value})}{\text{Useful Life}}$$

The respective total cost and unit cost definitions for variable and fixed cost behaviors are presented in **Exhibit 2.3**.

Exhibit 2.3 ■ Comparative Total and Unit Cost Behavior Definitions

	Total Cost	Unit Cost
Variable Cost	Varies in direct proportion to changes in activity	Is constant throughout the relevant range
Fixed Cost	Remains constant throughout the relevant range	Varies inversely with changes in activity throughout the relevant range

Calculating Variable and Fixed Costs in Total and Per Unit LO2-2 DEMO 2-2A

To illustrate a variable cost, assume that the speaker system used in Highlanders costs $50 within the relevant production range of 0–150,000 SUVs annually. (At higher levels of activity, the price could decrease because of a volume discount from the supplier or increase because the supplier's capacity would be exhausted.)

◆ **If 10,000 Highlanders were produced in October, what are variable costs per unit and in total?**

Because production falls within the relevant range, the variable cost per unit remains constant at $50 per Highlander. Total variable costs is calculated as follows.

$$10{,}000 \text{ Highlander} \times \$50 \text{ Variable cost per unit} = \$500{,}000 \text{ total variable costs}$$

To illustrate how to determine the total and unit amounts of a fixed cost, suppose that Toyota rents some Highlander manufacturing equipment for $12 million per year. The equipment has a maximum annual output capacity of 150,000 Highlanders.

◆ **If 120,000 Highlanders were produced in the year, what are fixed costs per unit and in total? How would your answer change if 125,000 Highlanders were produced in the year?**

Because 120,000 falls within the relevant range, fixed costs in total are $12 million and fixed costs per unit are calculated as follows.

$$\$12{,}000{,}000 \text{ Fixed cost} \div 120{,}000 \text{ Highlanders} = \$100 \text{ Fixed cost per Highlander}$$

However, if Toyota produces 125,000 Highlanders in a year, total fixed costs remain at $12,000,000, but rental expense per Highlander decreases to $96, as shown here.

$$\$12{,}000{,}000 \text{ Fixed cost} \div 125{,}000 \text{ Highlanders} = \$96 \text{ Fixed cost per Highlander}$$

From period to period, fixed costs may change. Business volume can increase or decrease sufficiently causing production capacity to be added or sold. Alternatively, management could decide to "trade" fixed and variable costs for one another. For example, a company installing new automated production equipment would incur a substantial additional fixed cost for depreciation but would eliminate (or reduce) the variable cost for hourly production workers' wages. In contrast, a company outsourcing its data processing function would eliminate the fixed costs of data processing equipment depreciation and personnel salaries but incur a variable cost based on transaction volume. Whether variable costs are traded for fixed costs or vice versa, a shift from one type of cost behavior to another type *changes a company's basic cost structure and can have a significant impact on profits.*

© Cambridge Business Publishers

Mixed Cost

Other costs exist that are not strictly variable or fixed. A **mixed cost** has both a variable and a fixed component. On a per-unit basis, a mixed cost does not fluctuate proportionately with changes in activity, nor does it remain constant with changes in activity. An electric bill that is computed as a flat charge for basic service (the fixed component) plus a stated rate for each kilowatt hour of usage (the variable component) is an example of a mixed cost.

DEMO 2-2B LO2-2 Calculating Total Mixed Costs

Exhibit 2.4 graphs a firm's electric bill, assuming a cost of $5,000 per month plus $0.018 per kilowatt hour (kWh) consumed.

◆ What is the total cost of electricity for a month if the company uses (1) 80,000 kWhs and (2) 90,000 kWhs of electricity?

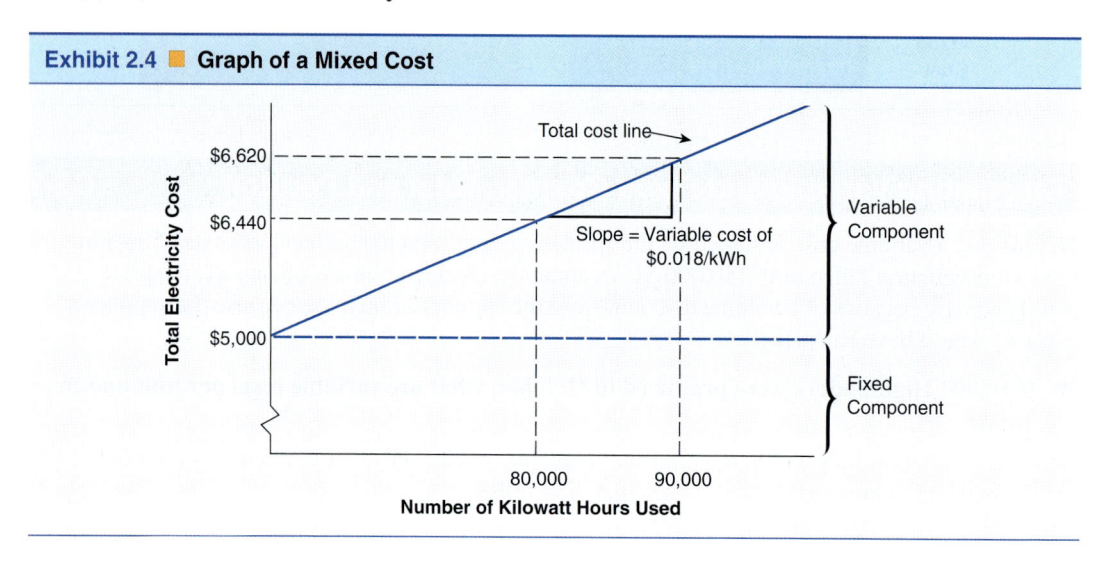

Exhibit 2.4 ■ Graph of a Mixed Cost

The total electricity bill is calculated as follows at the two consumption levels.

Total fixed costs + Total variable costs = Total cost of electricity

$5,000 + ($0.018 × 80,000 kWh) = $6,440 at 80,00kWhs

$5,000 + ($0.018 × 90,000 kWh) = $6,620 at 90,00kWhs

Complexities of Using an Average Cost per Unit In the last example, the total fixed cost of electricity would remain constant within the relevant range of production, but the fixed per unit declines with an increase in activity. This means that the mixed cost per kilowatt hour is different at different levels of energy consumption.

$6,440 ÷ 80,000 kWhs = $0.0805 per kWh

$6,620 ÷ 90,000 kWhs = $0.0736 per kWh (rounded)

Is the average cost per kilowatt hour $0.0805 or $0.0736? There is not one correct answer because it depends on the number of kilowatt hours used. Accountants need to use caution when applying an average cost per unit because it is always necessary to understand at what level of activity the per unit cost was calculated. At a different level of activity, the per-unit cost is not relevant. For example, at 95,000 kilowatt hours, using an average cost of $0.736 to estimate total costs would result in an estimate that is too high.

Understanding the types of behavior exhibited by costs is necessary to make valid estimates of total costs at various activity levels. Variable, fixed, and mixed costs are the typical types of cost behavior encountered in business. Within a specific time period and range, costs are separated into their variable and fixed components so that the behavior of these costs is more readily apparent. (Separation of mixed costs is discussed in Chapter 3.)

Assuming a variable cost is constant per unit and a fixed cost is constant in total within the relevant range can be justified for two reasons. First, if a company operates only in the relevant range of activity, the assumed conditions approximate reality. Second, selection of a constant per-unit variable cost and a constant total fixed cost provides a convenient, stable function for use in planning, controlling, and decision-making activities.

Step Cost

A **step cost** shifts upward or downward when activity changes by a certain interval or "step." A step cost can be variable or fixed. **Step variable costs** have small steps; step fixed costs have large steps. For instance, a water bill that changes in cost per gallon with usage is a step variable cost, as shown below.

Water Usage	Variable Cost per Gallon
0–1,000 gallons . . .	$0.002 per gallon
1001–2,000 gallons . . .	$0.003 per gallon
2001–3,000 gallons . . .	$0.005 per gallon

In contrast, the salary cost for airline reservations agents is a **step fixed cost**. Assume that each agent is paid $3,200 per month and can serve a maximum of 1,000 customers per month. Each additional 1,000 customers will result in an additional step fixed cost of $3,200. For step variable or step fixed costs, accountants must choose a specific relevant range of activity to use for analysis so that the step variable costs can be treated as variable and step fixed costs can be treated as fixed. Costs for 1 to 4 agents follow.

	Number of Agents	Monthly Salary Cost
0–1,000 customers	1	$ 3,200
1,001–2,000 customers	2	$ 6,400
2,001–3,000 customers	3	$ 9,600
3,001–4,000 customers	4	$12,800

If airline monthly volume increases from 2,500 customers to 3,800 customers, the airline will need four reservations agents rather than three.

Relation Between a Cost and a Cost Driver

Accountants use activities as predictors of cost changes. A **predictor** is an activity that, when changed, is accompanied by a consistent, observable change in a cost item. However, simply because two items change together does not prove that the predictor causes the change in cost. For instance, assume that every time you see a Highlander commercial during a sports event, the home team wins the game. If this is consistent, observable behavior, you can use a Highlander commercial to predict the winning team—but viewing the commercial does not cause the team to win!

In contrast, a predictor that has an absolute cause-and-effect relationship to a cost is called a **cost driver**. For example, production volume has a direct effect on the total cost of raw material used and can be said to "drive" that cost. **Exhibit 2.5** plots production volume on the X-axis and raw material cost on the Y-axis to show the linear cause-and-effect relationship between production volume and total raw material cost. This exhibit also illustrates the variable cost characteristic of raw material cost: the same amount of raw material cost is incurred for each unit produced. If the raw material is assumed to be engines and the units produced are assumed to be Highlanders, this illustration shows that as total Highlander production rises, total engine cost also rises proportionally. Graphically, the line slopes upward as it moves to the right. Thus, planned Highlander production volume could be used to predict total engine cost.

Exhibit 2.5 ■ Total Raw Material Cost Relative to Production Volume

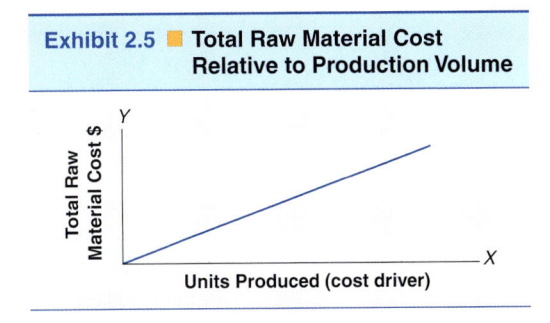

In most situations, the cause-and-effect relationship between a cost and a driver is less clear than as illustrated by engine cost and Highlander production because multiple factors commonly cause cost incurrence. For example, in addition to production volume, factors such as material quality, worker skill levels, and level of automation affect product spoilage cost. Although determining which factor actually caused a specific change in spoilage cost can be difficult, any of these factors could be chosen to predict that cost if confidence exists about the factor's relationship with cost changes. To be used as a predictor, the factor and the cost need only change together in a *reliable* manner.

Types of Cost Drivers The most basic cost driver is customer demand. Without customer demand for products or services, the organization cannot exist. Because the performance of activities consumes resources and resources cost money, the performance of activities also drives costs. The following is a list of potential cost drivers for a manufacturer.

- Number of purchase orders placed for raw materials
- Pounds of incoming raw materials inspected
- Number of items moved between workstations
- Hours of machine setup time
- Number of new employees hired and trained
- Number of orders packed for shipment
- Number of sales orders processed
- Cost of shipping product

A good decision requires an understanding of the linkages among the types of cost drivers and the costs of different activities.

Data Visualization

For each of the following situations, select the most appropriate cost behavior pattern, where the lines represent the cost behavior, the *Y*-axis represents costs, and the *X*-axis represents volume.
____ a. Total overtime premium paid to production employees
____ b. Total cost of interior designer salaries where each designer can handle a maximum of 10 projects
____ c. Average fixed cost per unit
____ d. Total selling & administrative costs
____ e. Labor cost per hour

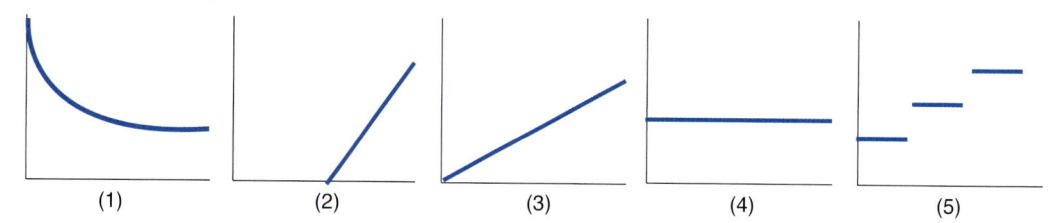

Solution on p. 2-45.

(1) (2) (3) (4) (5)

REVIEW 2-2 — LO2-2 — Analysis of Cost Behavior

JR Landscape Services pays $5,000 per month for equipment rental. In addition, variable charges incurred average $400 for each customer landscaping project. The relevant range is 0 to 500 landscaping jobs.

a. Determine the total cost and the cost per customer (rounded to the nearest whole dollar) if JR expects to complete the following number of projects for the month of June:
   1. 100
   2. 300
   3. 500

b. JR wants to earn a margin (excluding any other direct costs) on landscaping projects of $35,000 during June. If 300 projects are completed, what landscaping fee should be charged per project?

c. If that fee is charged and 350 projects are completed in June, what is the total margin in June?

d. **Critical Thinking:** If JR Landscape Services is concerned about a decrease in customers due to an expected downturn in economic conditions, is it better to have more or less fixed costs? Why? What steps might the company take to follow that strategy?

More practice: E2-22, E2-23, E2-24, E2-25
Solution on p. 2-43.

CLASSIFYING COSTS FOR DIFFERENT PURPOSES

Costs can be classified for different purposes. For example, inventory costs are classified in a certain way for financial reporting in order to ensure consistency across reporting entities. However, cost classifications made to complete a detailed inventory analysis by product type used for internal decision making do not need to follow financial reporting requirements. In this case, the objective is for the accountant to provide relevant information useful in decision making.

Classification of Costs for Financial Reporting

The balance sheet and income statement are two basic financial statements. The balance sheet is a statement of unexpired costs (assets), liabilities, and stockholders' equity; the income statement is a statement of revenues and expired costs (expenses and losses). An unexpired cost (asset) becomes an expired cost (an expense) when the asset is used or consumed. Thus, when *supplies* are purchased, they represent an asset, an unexpired cost. As supplies are consumed, the cost is recorded in *supplies expense*, an expired cost.

Identifying Unexpired and Expired Costs — LO2-3 DEMO 2-3

Exhibit 2.6 includes the balance sheet and income statement for General Motors Company.

◆ Considering inventories as an unexpired cost, what is the related expired cost, and where is it shown in the financial statements?

Inventories on the balance sheet is an example of an unexpired cost and represents goods held either for use in the manufacture of products or as products awaiting sale. *Cost of sales* (another word for cost of goods sold) on the income statement is an example of an expired cost and represents inventory cost for products sold.

Exhibit 2.6 — Financial Statements for General Motors Company

GENERAL MOTORS COMPANY AND SUBSIDIARIES
CONSOLIDATED BALANCE SHEETS (IN MILLIONS)* — Dec. 31, 2022

ASSETS	
Current assets	
Cash and cash equivalents	$ 19,153
Accounts and notes receivable, net of allowance	13,333
GM Financial receivables, net of allowance	33,623
Inventories	15,366
Other current assets	18,975
Total current assets	$100,451
Non-current assets	
Property, net	45,248
Other non-current assets	118,338
Total assets	$264,037
LIABILITIES AND EQUITY	
Current liabilities	
Accounts payable (principally trade)	27,486
Short-term debt and current portion of long-term debt	38,778
Accrued liabilities	24,910
Total current liabilities	91,174
Non-current liabilities	100,579
Total liabilities	$191,753
Commitments and contingencies	
Noncontrolling interest	357
Equity	$ 71,927
Total liabilities and equity	$264,037

GENERAL MOTORS COMPANY AND SUBSIDIARIES
CONSOLIDATED INCOME STATEMENTS (IN MILLIONS)*
Year ended — Dec. 31, 2022

Net sales and revenue	
Automotive	$143,975
GM Financial	12,760
Total net sales and revenue	156,735
Costs and expenses	
Automotive and other cost of sales	126,892
GM Financial interest, operating, and other expenses	8,862
Automotive and other selling, general, and administrative expense	10,667
Total costs and expenses	146,421
Operating income (loss)	10,315
Other income (loss)	1,282
Income (loss) before income taxes	11,597
Income tax expense	1,888
Net income (loss)	$ 9,708

*Presentation adjusted by authors for simplicity, including the combining of certain amounts into subtotals.
Per the General Motors 10-K, certain totals in the statements above may not add due to rounding.

Expenses and losses differ because expenses are intentionally incurred in the process of generating revenues, but losses are unintentionally incurred in the context of business operations. Cost of goods sold, advertising, and estimated product warranty costs are examples of expenses. Costs incurred for fire damage or abnormal production waste are examples of losses, as is selling a machine for less than book value.

When a product is the cost object, all costs can be classified as either product or period. **Product costs** are related to making or acquiring the products or providing the services that directly generate the revenues of an entity. **Period costs** are related to business functions other than production, such as selling and administration.

Cost Classifications of a Manufacturer

Product and period costs of a manufacturer as they relate to the financial statements are illustrated in **Exhibit 2.7**. A **manufacturer**, is a company that produces the goods that it sells.

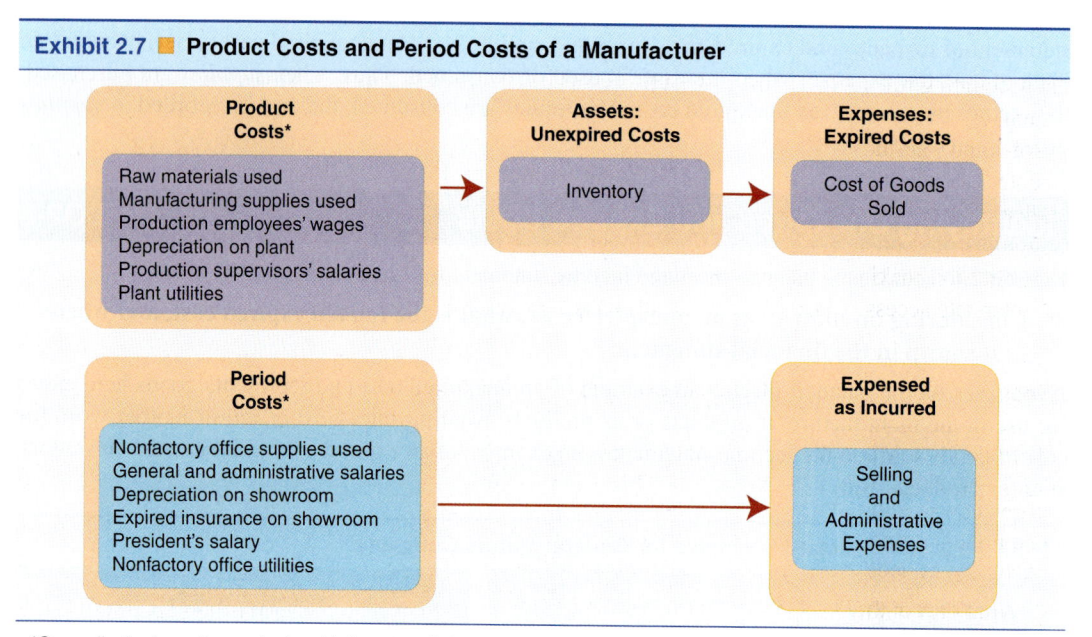

Exhibit 2.7 ■ Product Costs and Period Costs of a Manufacturer

Product Costs*:
- Raw materials used
- Manufacturing supplies used
- Production employees' wages
- Depreciation on plant
- Production supervisors' salaries
- Plant utilities

→ Assets: Unexpired Costs (Inventory) → Expenses: Expired Costs (Cost of Goods Sold)

Period Costs*:
- Nonfactory office supplies used
- General and administrative salaries
- Depreciation on showroom
- Expired insurance on showroom
- President's salary
- Nonfactory office utilities

→ Expensed as Incurred (Selling and Administrative Expenses)

*Generally, the largest unexpired cost is inventory. Other costs that may also be initially recorded as an asset (unexpired cost) before expensed include supplies and prepaid insurance.

Product costs are also called **inventoriable costs** and include direct costs (direct material and direct labor) and indirect costs (overhead). Precise classification of some costs into one of these categories can be difficult and requires judgment. However, the following categories and definitions (with General Motors Company examples) are useful.

- **Direct material (DM)** is any material that can be easily and economically traced to a product. Direct material includes raw material (sheet metal), purchased components from contract manufacturers (batteries), and manufactured subassemblies (engines and transmissions).
- **Direct labor (DL)** refers to the time spent by individuals who work specifically on manufacturing a product. The people bolting the chassis to the frame are considered direct labor, and their associated wages are direct labor costs.
- **Overhead (OH)** is any production cost that is indirect to the product. This cost element includes GM factory supervisors' salaries as well as depreciation, insurance, and utility costs on production machinery, equipment, and facilities.

Product costs are described further in the next section. The sum of direct labor and overhead costs is referred to as **conversion cost**—those costs that are incurred to convert materials into products. The sum of direct material and direct labor cost is referred to as **prime cost**.

Period costs are associated with a particular time period rather than with making a product. Period costs that have future benefit are classified as assets, whereas those having no future benefit are expenses (or losses). Prepaid insurance for an administration building represents an unexpired cost. When the insured period ends, the insurance becomes an expired or period cost (insurance expense). Salaries paid to the salesforce and depreciation on their laptop computers are also expired period costs.

Chapter 2 Cost Terminology and Classification

Classification of Costs for Managerial Purposes

Classification for financial accounting purposes is based on rules formulated in GAAP. However, as mentioned in Chapter 1, managerial accountants can summarize relevant information for decision making, without regard to GAAP. Thus, for internal managerial purposes, accountants and managers often use the term product costing to embrace all costs incurred in connection with a product or service throughout the value chain. This means that for internal analysis, the limitations on how product and period costs are defined and used do not apply. Costs accountants are integral in determining the costs required for GAAP financial statements, but they also have flexibility to change how costs are presented for decision making. Importantly, cost accountants must determine what information is relevant for the decision at hand.

One type of period cost that is often treated differently for managerial purposes is distribution costs. A **distribution cost** is any cost incurred to warehouse, transport, or deliver a product or service. Financial accounting rules require that distribution costs be expensed as incurred. However, managers should remember that these costs relate directly to products and services and should not adopt an "out-of-sight, out-of-mind" attitude about these costs simply because of the way they are handled under generally accepted accounting principles (GAAP). Distribution costs must be considered in relation to product/service volume, and these costs must be managed well for profitability to result from sales. Thus, even though distribution costs are not technically product costs, they can have a major impact on management decision making. For example, Teevin Bros. Land and Timber Company views its rail, water, and interstate access as providing a cost advantage for its timber and rock products over its competitors.

REVIEW 2-3

Financial Statement Classification of Costs — **LO2-3**

Moore Company purchased an $800,000 welding machine to use in production of commercial tooling. The welding machine was expected to have a life of 10 years and a salvage value at time of disposition of $50,000. The company uses straight-line depreciation. In addition, the company prepaid annual property taxes on its factory building of $85,000. During the first quarter of the year, the machine produced 800 product units, of which 560 were sold.

a. What part of the $885,000 in costs (welding machine and property taxes) expired in the first quarter of the year?

b. Where would each of the amounts related to this machine and the property tax appear on the financial statements at the end of the first quarter?

c. **Critical Thinking:** Assume that a certain line of the company's commercial tooling is expensive to ship due to size and weight. How might the company treat shipping costs for managerial costing purposes? What types of decisions could a company make using this cost information?

More practice: MC2-14, E2-30, E2-31
Solution on p. 2-43.

COMPONENTS OF PRODUCT COST

For a manufacturer, product costs are related to items that generate revenues and can be separated into three components.

LO2-4 What are the product cost categories for financial statement purposes, and what items comprise those categories?

Product Costs (GAAP Purposes)		
Direct Material	Direct Labor	Overhead

Direct Material

Any readily identifiable part of a product is a direct material. Theoretically, direct material cost should include the cost of all materials used to manufacture a product. However, some material costs are not conveniently or economically traceable to the final product. Such costs are treated and classified as **indirect material cost**, which is included as part of overhead. For instance, the cost of nails used by a furniture manufacturer is very small relative to a table's overall value. Accordingly, even though the nails can easily be traced to the final product (the table), nail cost is so insignificant that tracking it as a direct material is not justified.

Direct Labor

Direct labor refers to the effort of individuals who manufacture a product. Direct labor could also be considered effort that directly adds value to the final product. Direct labor cost is the total wages or salaries paid to direct labor personnel. Direct labor cost should include basic compensation, production efficiency bonuses, and the employer's share of Social Security and Medicare taxes. In addition, if a company's operations are relatively stable, direct labor cost should include all employer-paid insurance costs, holiday and vacation pay, and pension and other retirement benefits.[1]

As with materials, some labor costs that theoretically are direct costs are treated as indirect. **Indirect labor costs** are labor costs that are not directly related to the production of goods are considered overhead. One reason for classifying labor costs as indirect is that specifically tracing certain labor costs to production is inefficient. For instance, fringe benefit costs should be treated as direct labor cost, but the time, effort, and clerical expense of tracing this cost might not justify the additional accuracy such tracing would provide. Thus, the treatment of employee fringe benefits as indirect costs is often based on cost efficiencies.

A second reason for not treating certain labor costs as direct is that doing so could result in erroneous information about product costs.

DEMO 2-4 LO2-4 Classifying Labor as Direct and Indirect

Assume that Langley Corporation employs 20 assembly department workers who are paid $16 per hour; overtime wages are $24 (or time and a half) per hour. One week, the employees worked a total of 1,000 hours (including 200 hours of overtime) to complete all production orders.

♦ **What amount should be classified as direct labor and as indirect labor for the week?**

The full number of hours worked at the regular labor rate is classified as direct labor. The overtime premium of $8 ($24 − $16) for 200 overtime hours is classified as indirect labor, as shown in the following calculation.

Hours	Rate	Amount	Classification
1,000 ×	$16 =	$16,000	Direct labor
200 ×	$ 8 =	1,600	Indirect labor
		$17,600	Total

If the overtime cost were assigned to products made during the overtime hours, those products would have a labor cost 50 percent higher than items made during regular working hours. Because products are assigned to regular or overtime shifts randomly, items completed during overtime hours should not be forced to bear overtime charges. Thus, overtime or shift premiums are usually considered overhead rather than direct labor cost and are allocated *among all units*.

On some occasions, however, overtime or shift premiums should be considered direct labor cost. For example, if a customer is in a rush and requests a job to be scheduled during overtime or a night shift, overtime or shift premiums should be considered direct labor cost and attached to the customer's job that created the costs. Assume that on a Friday in July, Rosa Company asked Langley Corporation to deliver 100 units of product the following Monday.

♦ **If the overtime premium related to this rush job was $1,600, would the amount be classified as direct labor or indirect labor?**

Because the order's completion requires employees to work overtime, Langley Corporation should charge Rosa Company a higher selling price for each unit, and the overtime costs should be included as part of the direct labor cost of the Rosa Company order.

There are occasions when labor costs are being incurred but no work is being performed. For example, workers may be idle while they are waiting for machines to be maintained or for materials to arrive on the production floor. This cost of idle time should be assigned to overhead.

---

[1] Institute of Management Accountants, *Statements on Management Accounting Number 4C: Definition and Measurement of Direct Labor Cost* (Montvale, N.J.: NAA, June 13, 1985), p. 4.

Because people historically performed the majority of conversion activity, direct labor once represented a large portion of total manufacturing cost. In highly automated work environments, direct labor often represents only 10–15 percent of total manufacturing cost.

Overhead

Overhead is any factory or production cost that is indirect to manufacturing a product. Accordingly, overhead excludes direct material and direct labor costs but includes indirect material, indirect labor costs, and all other production costs. Overhead costs can be variable or fixed based on how they behave in response to changes in production volume or other activity measure.

Variable Overhead Included in **variable overhead** are the costs of indirect material, indirect labor paid on an hourly basis (such as wages for forklift operators, material handlers, and other workers who support the production process), lubricants used for machine maintenance, and the variable portion of factory utility charges. Depreciation calculated using either the units-of-production or service-life method is also a variable overhead cost. These depreciation methods reflect a decline in machine utility based on usage rather than time passage and are appropriate in an automated plant.

Fixed Overhead Included in **fixed overhead** are costs such as straight-line depreciation on factory assets, factory license fees, and factory insurance and property taxes. Fixed indirect labor costs include salaries for production supervisors, shift superintendents, and plant managers. The fixed portion of factory mixed costs (such as maintenance and utilities) is also part of fixed overhead.

Nonmanufacturers Unlike a manufacturer, a **merchandiser** (also called a **retailer**) purchases goods in finished or almost finished condition and resells those goods. Product costs for a merchandiser include the inventoriable cost to acquire and prepare the goods for sale. Because no manufacturing is involved, separate accounting for materials, labor, and overhead is not applicable. A **service provider** is in business to provide a service. For a *service provider*, costs of services (materials/supplies, labor, and overhead) can be accumulated by job or customer. However, costs of services are not inventoriable and are therefore expensed as incurred in the financial statements. Similar to a manufacturer, period costs are reported separately and include costs other than that of buying goods or providing a service. The conversion of inputs for manufacturers, merchandisers, and service providers is discussed in the next section.

REVIEW 2-4

Classifying Product Costs — LO2-4

The following factory costs were incurred by Diaz Inc. for the manufacture of tennis shoes for the month of July.

a. Classify each cost as one of the following: (a) direct material, (b) direct labor, or (c) overhead.

		Direct Material, Direct Labor, or Overhead
Material Costs:		
Leather	$1,000,000	
Thread	50,000	
Nylon	300,000	
Ink for logo	1,000	
Foam	200,000	
Rubber	400,000	
Glue	5,000	
Labor Costs:		
Sewing machine operators	$375,000	
Quality control supervisor	55,000	
Factory maintenance worker	10,000	
Assembly workers	80,000	

continued

continued from previous page

> b. Diaz Inc. is researching the purchase of an artificial intelligence system with machine vision technology that can identify defective product on the assembly line. The technology sends an alert so adjustments can be made to avoid additional defective product. The system would incur costs to (1) research the system options, (2) purchase the system, (3) adapt the system and setup processes by the engineers, (4) oversee the operations of the machine and coordinate any actions based on defects found, and (5) maintain the system.
> 1. How would the costs be classified for financial statement purposes?
> 2. **Critical Thinking:** What are nonmonetary considerations of this purchase?

More practice: MC2-15, E2-29
Solution on p. 2-44.

THE CONVERSION PROCESS

LO2-5 How does the conversion process occur in manufacturing, retail, and service companies?

To some extent, all organizations convert or change inputs into outputs. *Inputs* typically consist of material, labor, and overhead. In general, product (service) costs are incurred in the production (or conversion) area and period costs are incurred in all nonproduction (or nonconversion) areas. One exception is that a merchandiser typically requires little to no conversion of products in a production (or conversion) area. Conversion process *outputs* are usually either products or services. The level of input required to produce the output is expressed as a company's **degree of conversion**. See **Exhibit 2.8** for a comparison of the conversion activities of different types of organizations. Note that many service companies engage in a high degree of conversion. Firms of professionals (such as accountants, architects, or attorneys) convert labor and other resource inputs (material and overhead) into completed services (audit reports, building plans, or contracts).

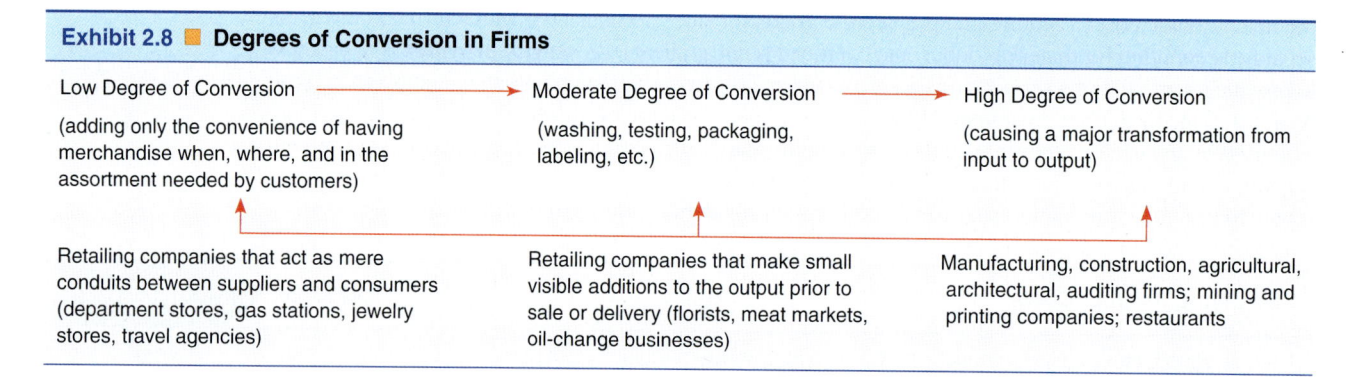

Exhibit 2.8 ■ Degrees of Conversion in Firms

Low Degree of Conversion	Moderate Degree of Conversion	High Degree of Conversion
(adding only the convenience of having merchandise when, where, and in the assortment needed by customers)	(washing, testing, packaging, labeling, etc.)	(causing a major transformation from input to output)
Retailing companies that act as mere conduits between suppliers and consumers (department stores, gas stations, jewelry stores, travel agencies)	Retailing companies that make small visible additions to the output prior to sale or delivery (florists, meat markets, oil-change businesses)	Manufacturing, construction, agricultural, architectural, auditing firms; mining and printing companies; restaurants

DEMO 2-5 LO2-5 Identifying How Degree of Conversion Affects Cost Assignment

◆ **Which type of company places a higher value on assigning costs to products or services: firms with a low degree of conversion or firms with a high degree of conversion? Why?**

Low Degree of Conversion Firms that engage in only a low degree of conversion can conveniently expense insignificant conversion costs of labor and overhead as period costs. The clerical cost savings from expensing outweigh the value of any slightly improved information that might result from assigning such costs to products or services. For example, when retail employees open shipping containers, hang clothing on racks, and tag merchandise with sales tickets, a labor cost for conversion is incurred. However, clothing stores do not attach the stock workers' wages to inventory; such labor costs are treated as period costs and expensed when incurred. The major distinction of retail firms relative to service and manufacturing firms is that retailers have much *lower* degrees of conversion than the other two types of firms.

High Degree of Conversion In contrast, in high-conversion firms, the informational benefits gained from accumulating the material, labor, and overhead costs incurred to produce output significantly exceed clerical accumulation costs. For instance, when constructing a house, certain types of costs are quite

© Cambridge Business Publishers

significant (see **Exhibit 2.9**). Direct labor cost of $50,000 is accumulated as a separate component of product cost because the amount is material and requires management's cost-control attention. Furthermore, direct labor cost is inventoried as part of the cost of the construction job until the house is complete.

Exhibit 2.9 ■ Building Construction Costs

	Manufacturing Cost	
Direct material	$ 80,000	40%
Direct labor	50,000	25%
Manufacturing overhead	70,000	35%
Total cost	$200,000	100%

- A manufacturer is engaged in a high degree of conversion of raw material input into a tangible output. Manufacturers typically use people and machines to convert raw material to output that has substance and can, if desired, be physically inspected.
- A **service company** is a firm that uses a significant amount of labor to engage in a high or moderate degree of conversion. A service company's output can be tangible (an architectural drawing) or intangible (insurance protection). Service firms can be either for-profit businesses or not-for-profit organizations.
- A **retailer** requires little if any conversion before the goods are sold to customers.

Retailers versus Manufacturers and Service Companies

Because little conversion of inventory is required by retailers, costs associated with such inventory are usually easy to determine, as are the valuations for financial statement presentation. Retail stores that engage in only low or moderate degrees of conversion ordinarily have only one inventory account (Merchandise Inventory).

In comparison, manufacturers and service companies engage in activities that involve the physical transformation of inputs into finished products or services. The materials or supplies and conversion costs of manufacturers and service companies must be assigned to output to determine the cost of both inventory produced and goods sold or services rendered. Cost accounting provides the structure and process for assigning material and conversion costs to products and services.

The production or conversion process for a manufacturer occurs in three stages:

1. work not started (**raw material** or **RM**),
2. work started but not completed (**work in process** or **WIP**), and
3. work completed (**finished goods** or **FG**).

Thus, manufacturers normally use three types of inventory accounts to accumulate costs as goods flow through the manufacturing process:

1. Raw Material Inventory (may include direct and indirect materials, for example, supplies),
2. Work in Process Inventory (for partially converted goods), and
3. Finished Goods Inventory.

Exhibit 2.10 compares the input–output relationships of a retail company with those of a manufacturing or service company. This exhibit illustrates that the primary difference between retail companies and manufacturing or service companies is the absence or presence of the area labeled "The Production Center." In a production center, input factors (raw material, supplies, and parts) enter, are transformed, and are stored until the goods or services are completed. If the output is a product, it can be warehoused or displayed until sold. Service outputs are directly provided to the client commissioning the work. Retail companies normally incur very limited conversion time, effort, and cost compared to manufacturing or service companies. Thus, although a retailer could have a department (such as one that adds store name labels to goods) that might be viewed as a "mini" production center, most often retailers have no designated "production center."

Exhibit 2.10 ■ Business Input–Output Relationships

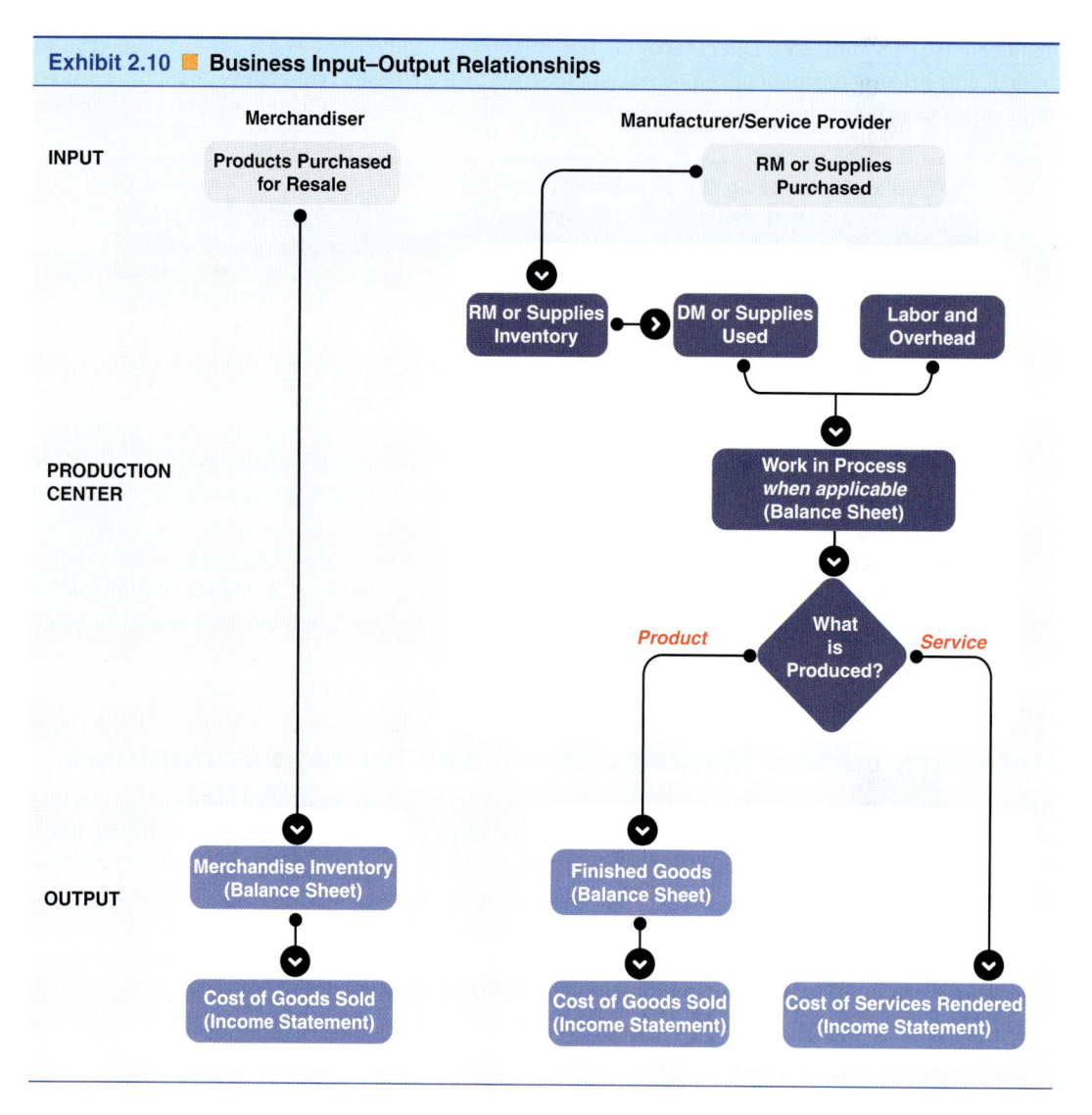

INPUT

Merchandiser: Products Purchased for Resale

Manufacturer/Service Provider: RM or Supplies Purchased
→ RM or Supplies Inventory → DM or Supplies Used → Labor and Overhead

PRODUCTION CENTER

Work in Process *when applicable* (Balance Sheet)

What is Produced?
- *Product*
- *Service*

OUTPUT

- Merchandise Inventory (Balance Sheet) → Cost of Goods Sold (Income Statement)
- Finished Goods (Balance Sheet) → Cost of Goods Sold (Income Statement)
- Cost of Services Rendered (Income Statement)

Costs are associated with each processing stage. The stages of production in a manufacturing firm and some of the costs associated with each stage are illustrated in **Exhibit 2.11**.

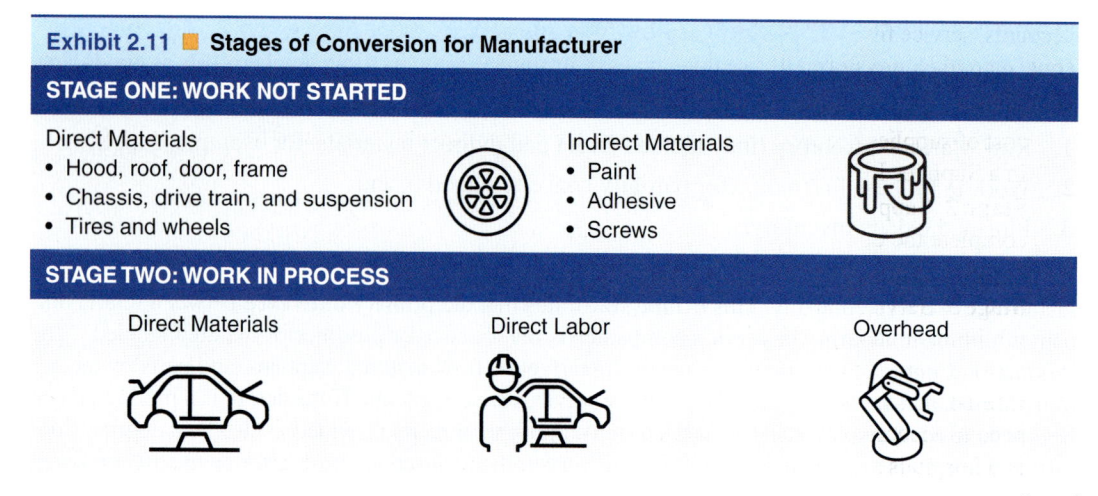

Exhibit 2.11 ■ Stages of Conversion for Manufacturer

STAGE ONE: WORK NOT STARTED

Direct Materials
- Hood, roof, door, frame
- Chassis, drive train, and suspension
- Tires and wheels

Indirect Materials
- Paint
- Adhesive
- Screws

STAGE TWO: WORK IN PROCESS

Direct Materials

Direct Labor

Overhead

continued

Chapter 2 Cost Terminology and Classification

continued from previous page.

Exhibit 2.11 ■ Stages of Conversion for Manufacturer (continued)

STAGE THREE: FINISHED WORK

Warehouse — Sold to Dealerships — Cost of Goods Sold

- **Stage 1** In the first stage of processing, the costs incurred reflect the prices paid for raw materials and/or supplies and quantities purchased.
- **Stage 2** As work progresses through the second stage, accrual-based accounting requires that labor and overhead costs related to the conversion of raw materials or supplies be accumulated and attached to the goods. Accumulating costs in appropriate inventory accounts for a manufacturer allows businesses to match the costs of buying or manufacturing a product with the revenues generated when the goods are sold.
- **Stage 3** For a merchandiser and a manufacturer, inventory costs will remain on the balance sheet until the inventory is sold. At the point of sale, costs will flow to cost of goods sold on the income statement. For a service provider, costs incurred during the period will be shown as cost of services rendered on the income statement. Simplified income statements for a manufacturer, merchandiser, and service provider follow.

Income Statement		
Manufacturer	**Merchandiser**	**Service Provider**
Sales	Sales	Sales
Costs of goods sold	Cost of goods sold	Cost of services rendered
Gross margin	Gross margin	Gross margin
Operating expenses	Operating expenses	Operating expenses
Other income/loss	Other income/loss	Other income/loss
Profit	Profit	Profit

Manufacturers versus Service Companies

Several differences in accounting for conversion activities exist between a manufacturer and a service company. Whereas manufacturers normally use three inventory accounts, service firms accumulate costs by job or customer. The three stages for a service provider are shown as follows.

- **Stage 1** The "work not started" stage of processing normally consists of the cost of supplies needed to perform the services; these costs are accounted for in a Supplies Inventory account.
- **Stage 2** Supplies are issued for a job, and labor and overhead are added to complete the conversion process. All of these costs may be accumulated by job or customer.
- **Stage 3** Service firms do not normally have Inventory accounts for a service job because most services cannot be warehoused. Determining the cost of services provided by job is extremely important in both profit-oriented service businesses and not-for-profit entities. For instance, architectural firms need to accumulate the costs incurred for designs and models of each project, and hospitals need to accumulate the costs of x-rays, MRIs, or other medical treatments for each patient. While costs can be accumulated by job, cost incurred on service jobs are typically treated as period costs and expensed as incurred on the income statement.

STAGE ONE: WORK NOT STARTED

Supplies

STAGE TWO: COST ACCUMULATION

Supplies
Labor
Overhead

STAGE THREE: COST OF SERVICES

Service completed and cost per job identified. Costs are reported as incurred in the income statement.

© Cambridge Business Publishers

Despite the accounting differences among retailers, manufacturers, and service firms, each type of organization can use management and cost accounting concepts and techniques, although to a different degree. Managers in all firms engage in planning, controlling, performance evaluation, and decision-making. Thus, management accounting is appropriate for all firms. Cost accounting techniques are essential to all firms engaged in significant conversion activities. In most companies, a main focus of managers is finding ways to reduce costs without sacrificing quality or productivity; both management and cost accounting techniques are used extensively in this pursuit.

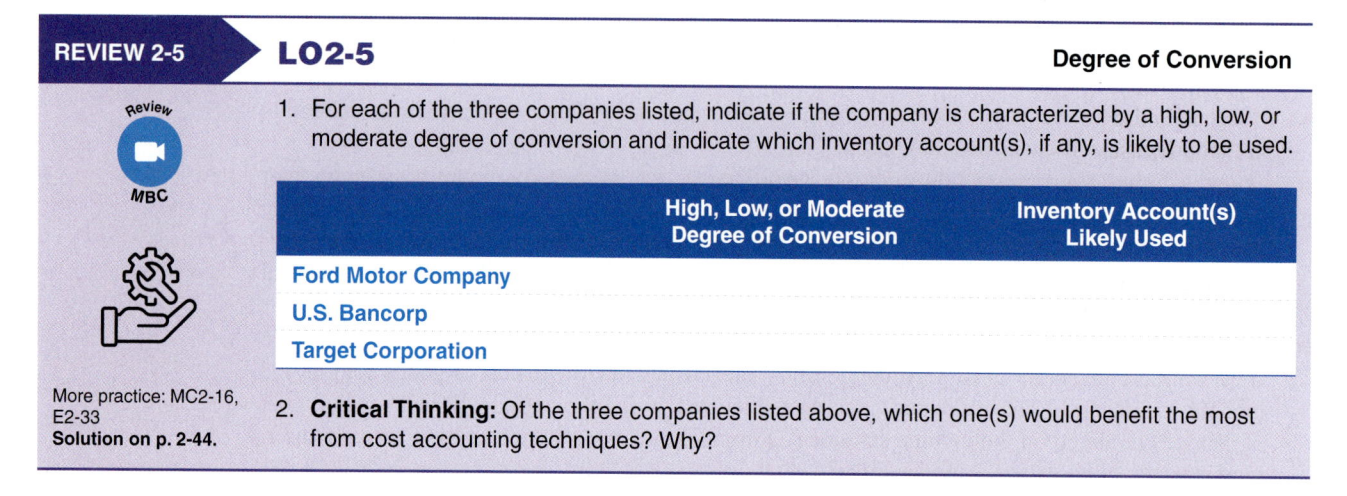

REVIEW 2-5 — **LO2-5** — **Degree of Conversion**

1. For each of the three companies listed, indicate if the company is characterized by a high, low, or moderate degree of conversion and indicate which inventory account(s), if any, is likely to be used.

	High, Low, or Moderate Degree of Conversion	Inventory Account(s) Likely Used
Ford Motor Company		
U.S. Bancorp		
Target Corporation		

More practice: MC2-16, E2-33
Solution on p. 2-44.

2. **Critical Thinking:** Of the three companies listed above, which one(s) would benefit the most from cost accounting techniques? Why?

PRODUCT COST FLOW IN A COST SYSTEM

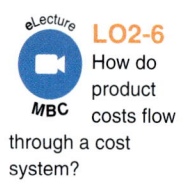

LO2-6 How do product costs flow through a cost system?

One goal of a cost system is to capture the cost of a product or service. With a high degree of conversion, a number of cost types must be attached to an individual product or service. Costs generally are traced to a product or allocated to a product. For a manufacturer, direct material and direct labor are clearly and easily traced to a product.

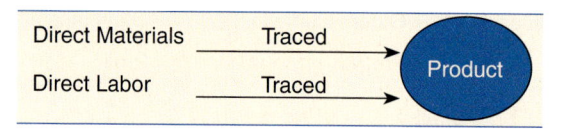

Direct Materials — Traced → Product
Direct Labor — Traced → Product

Overhead, on the other hand, must be accumulated throughout a period and allocated to the products manufactured or services rendered during that period. **Cost allocation** refers to the assignment of an indirect cost to one or more cost objects using some reasonable allocation base or driver. For a manufacturer, overhead is allocated to a product.

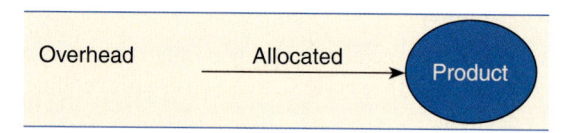

Overhead — Allocated → Product

Cost allocations can be made across time periods or within a single time period. For example, in financial accounting, a building's cost is allocated through depreciation charges over its useful or service life. The useful life is the period that revenue (that the asset helped produce) is recognized. In cost accounting, production overhead costs are allocated within a period through the use of allocation bases or cost drivers to products or services. This process reflects application of the measurement principle, which requires that all production or acquisition costs attach to the units produced, services rendered, or units purchased.

Reasons for Allocating Overhead

Overhead costs are allocated to cost objects for three reasons:

1. to determine the full cost of the cost object;
2. to motivate the manager in charge of the cost object to manage it efficiently; and

Chapter 2 Cost Terminology and Classification

3. to compare alternative courses of action for management planning, controlling, and decision-making.[2]

The first reason relates to financial statement valuations. Under GAAP, the "full cost" of a cost object of a manufacturer must include allocated production overhead. In contrast, the assignment of nonmanufacturing overhead costs to products is not normally allowed under GAAP.[3] The other two reasons for overhead allocations are related to internal purposes, and thus no specific rules apply to the allocation process.

Regardless of the reason overhead is allocated, the method and basis of allocation should be rational and systematic so that the resulting information is useful for product costing and managerial purposes. Traditionally, the information generated for satisfying the "full cost" objective was also used for the second and third objectives. However, because the first purpose is externally focused and the others are internally focused, different methods can be used to provide different costs for different purposes.

Allocating Overhead Costs — LO2-6 DEMO 2-6A

Let's consider a simple example of overhead allocation of a manufacturer. Assume that a company had two products with the following costs that are easily and clearly traceable to the products.

	Direct Materials	Direct Labor
Product 1	$50	$75
Product 2	$50	$25

In addition, the company incurred overhead (indirect) costs of $100 for costs shared between the two products. The company needs to allocate the $100 cost to the two products in order to estimate the costs of each product.

◆ **How could the company allocate the costs of $100 to the products since the cost is not clearly and easily traceable to the products?**

There are numerous ways that the cost could be allocated to the two products. One way is to allocate the overhead cost equally to each product: $50 to Product 1 and $50 to Product 2. However, a cost accountant's role is to report relevant information. Do the two products share equally the resources provided by the $100 cost? From the information presented, it appears that Product 1 uses 75% of total labor ($75 ÷ $100), so it might make sense to allocate $75 of the overhead costs to Product 1 and $25 to Product 2. Determining how to allocate overhead to products is not an exact science but an estimation process using relevant information. Allocation of overhead is discussed further in Chapter 6.

Cost Flow in a Perpetual Inventory System of a Manufacturer

The product costs of direct materials, direct labor, and overhead flow into the Work in Process (WIP) Inventory account. In a perpetual inventory system, all product costs flow from Work in Process (WIP) Inventory to Finished Goods (FG) Inventory and, ultimately, to Cost of Goods Sold (CGS); this cost flow is diagrammed below. The perpetual inventory system continuously provides current information for financial statement preparation and for inventory and cost control. All companies discussed in this text use a perpetual system.

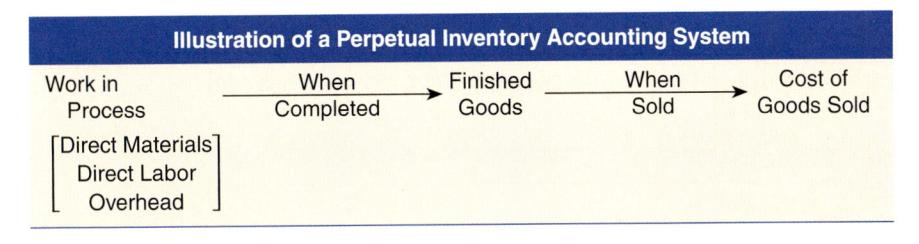

Illustration of a Perpetual Inventory Accounting System

Work in Process [Direct Materials, Direct Labor, Overhead] → When Completed → Finished Goods → When Sold → Cost of Goods Sold

---

[2] Institute of Management Accountants, *Statements on Management Accounting Number 4B: Allocation of Service and Administrative Costs* (Montvale, N.J.: NAA, June 13, 1985), pp. 9–10.

[3] Although potentially unacceptable for GAAP, certain nonmanufacturing overhead costs must be assigned to products for tax purposes.

© Cambridge Business Publishers

DEMO 2-6B LO2-6 Demonstrating the Flow of Production Costs Using T-Accounts

The Langley Corporation is used to illustrate the flow of products costs in a manufacturing company's actual cost system. April 1 and April 30 inventory account balances for the company follow.

	April 1	April 30
Raw Material (RM) Inventory (all direct)	$ 73,000	$ 69,000
Work in Process (WIP) Inventory	145,000	20,880
Finished Goods (FG) Inventory	87,400	91,600

Langley purchased $280,000 of raw materials during the month and incurred the following production costs: direct materials $284,000, direct labor $436,000, and overhead $214,080.

◆ How do the cost amounts flow through the cost system using T-accounts for the following accounts: Raw Materials Inventory, Work in Process Inventory, Finished Goods Inventory, and Cost of Goods Sold?

The presentation is shown in T-accounts in **Exhibit 2.12**. First, the beginning and ending balances are entered into the applicable T-accounts. Considering the amount of purchases for the month and the adjustment for inventory balances, direct materials used is calculated using the Raw Materials Inventory T-account as follows.

$73,000 Beg. bal. + $280,000 Purchases − $69,000 End. bal. = $284,000 Direct materials used

Considering the product costs added for the month and the adjustment for inventory balances, the cost of good manufactured can be determined through the Work in Process T-account. **Cost of goods manufactured (CGM)** is the total production cost of the goods that were completed and transferred to FG Inventory during the period and is calculated as follows.

$145,000 Beg. bal. + $284,000 DM + $436,000 DL + $214,080 OH − $20,880 End. bal. = $1,058,200 CGM

Considering CGM and the adjustment for inventory balances, cost of goods sold can be determined through the Finished Goods T-account. **Cost of goods sold (CGS)** is the total production cost of the goods that were transferred out of FG Inventory and sold during the period and is calculated as follows.

$87,400 Beg. bal. + $1,058,200 CGM − $91,600 End. bal. = $1,054,000 CGS

Exhibit 2.12 ■ Selected T-Accounts for Langley Corporation's April Production and Sales

Raw Material Inventory (all direct)			
Beg. bal.	73,000	(2)	284,000
(1)	280,000		
End. bal.	69,000		

Finished Goods Inventory			
Beg. bal.	87,400	(13)	1,054,000
(11) CGM	1,058,200		
End. bal.	91,600		

Work in Process Inventory			
Beg. bal.	145,000	(11)	1,058,200
(2) DM	284,000		
(3) DL	436,000		
(10) OH	214,080		
End. bal.	20,880		

Cost of Goods Sold	
(13) CGS	1,054,000

Chapter 2 Cost Terminology and Classification 2-21

REVIEW 2-6 — Determining Manufacturing Cost Flow — LO2-6

Lazer Corp. makes one product line. During the month of January, the company transferred costs of $302,000 to finished goods. January 1 and January 31 Work in Process balances were $44,000 and $91,000, respectively. The company credited materials inventory for $98,000 in January. Actual direct labor costs were $1.60 per unit. Lazer produced 75,000 units of product in the month of January.

a. What amount of overhead was allocated to production costs for the month of January?
b. Prepare a Work in Process T-account for the month of January.
c. What was the per-unit cost of goods manufactured in January? Round answer to two decimal places.
d. If finished goods inventory decreased by $28,000 from January 1 to January 31, what was the cost of goods sold for the month of January?
e. **Critical Thinking:** Now assume that prices are expected to remain constant and that the company forecasts production of 80,000 units in February. Could the per-unit cost calculated in part b be used to estimate cost of production in February? Why or why not?

More practice: MC2-17, E2-40
Solution on p. 2-44.

COST OF GOODS MANUFACTURED AND SOLD

The T-accounts in **Exhibit 2.12** provide detailed information about the cost of material used, goods transferred from work in process, and goods sold. This information is needed to prepare financial statements. A schedule of cost of goods manufactured is prepared as a preliminary step to the determination of cost of goods sold. This amount is similar to the cost of net purchases in the cost of goods sold schedule for a retailer. Thus, a retailer only prepares a schedule of cost of goods sold. A service business prepares a schedule of cost of services rendered.

LO2-7 How is cost of goods manufactured calculated and used in preparing an income statement?

DEMO 2-7 — Preparing a Schedule of Cost of Goods Manufactured and Cost of Goods Sold — LO2-7

◆ How are the amounts shown in Exhibit 2.12 displayed in a Schedule of Cost of Goods Manufactured and a Schedule of Cost of Goods Sold?

Formal schedules of cost of goods manufactured and cost of goods sold are presented in **Exhibit 2.13** using the amounts from **Exhibit 2.12**. The schedule of cost of goods manufactured starts with the beginning balance of WIP Inventory and details all product cost components. The cost of material used in production during the period is equal to the beginning balance of RM Inventory plus raw material purchased minus the ending balance of RM Inventory. (If RM Inventory includes both direct and indirect materials, the cost of direct material used is assigned to WIP Inventory, and the cost of indirect material used is included in overhead.) Because direct labor cannot be warehoused, all charges for direct labor during the period are part of WIP Inventory. Overhead costs are added to direct material and direct labor costs to determine total manufacturing costs.

Beg RM + Purch − DM used = End RM

Beginning WIP Inventory cost is added to total current manufacturing costs to obtain a subtotal amount referred to as **total cost to account for**. After the value of ending WIP Inventory is calculated (through techniques discussed in later chapters), it is subtracted from the subtotal to provide the CGM for the period. *The schedule of cost of goods manufactured is an internal schedule and is not provided to external parties.*

Beg WIP + DM used + DL + OH − CGM = End WIP

In the schedule of cost of goods sold, the CGM is added to the beginning balance of FG Inventory to find the cost of goods available for sale during the period. Ending FG Inventory is calculated by multiplying a physical unit count by a unit cost. If a perpetual inventory system is used, the actual amount of ending FG Inventory can be compared to the amount shown in the accounting records; any differences can be attributed to losses that could have arisen from theft, breakage, evaporation, or accounting errors. Ending FG Inventory is subtracted from the cost of goods available for sale to determine the CGS.

Beg FG + CGM − CGS = End FG

Exhibit 2.13 — Cost of Goods Manufactured and Cost of Goods Sold Schedules

LANGLEY CORPORATION
Schedule of Cost of Goods Manufactured
For the Month Ended April 30

Beginning balance of work in process inventory, April 1		$ 145,000
Manufacturing costs for the period		
Raw material inventory (assumed all direct)		
Beginning balance	$ 73,000	
Purchases of material	280,000	
Raw material available	$353,000	
Ending balance	(69,000)	
Total raw material used	$284,000	
Direct labor	436,000	
Overhead	214,080	
Total current period manufacturing costs		934,080
Total costs to account for		$1,079,080
Ending balance of work in process inventory, April 30		(20,880)
Cost of goods manufactured		$1,058,200

LANGLEY CORPORATION
Schedule of Cost of Goods Sold
For the Month Ended April 30

Beginning balance of finished goods inventory, April 1	$ 87,400
Cost of goods manufactured	1,058,200
Cost of goods available for sale	$1,145,600
Ending balance of finished goods inventory, April 30	(91,600)
Cost of goods sold	$1,054,000

REVIEW 2-7 — LO2-7: Preparing a Schedule of Goods Manufactured and Cost of Goods Sold

Crafters Inc. produces custom cabinetry. The company's Raw Material Inventory account includes the costs of both direct and indirect materials. Account balances for the company at the beginning and end of September follow:

	September 1	September 30
Raw Material Inventory	$102,000	$ 88,000
Work in Process Inventory	220,000	296,000
Finished Goods Inventory	388,000	425,000

During the month, the company purchased $814,000 of raw material and direct material used during the period amounted to $568,000. Factory payroll costs for September were $765,000, of which 65 percent was related to direct labor. Overhead charges for depreciation, insurance, utilities, and maintenance totaled $900,000 for September.

a. Prepare a schedule of cost of goods manufactured.
b. Prepare a schedule of cost of goods sold.
c. **Critical Thinking:** Crafters Inc. is considering a purchase of equipment that reduces material scrap and uses less energy. How would this purchase generally affect amounts in a schedule of cost of goods manufactured?

More practice: MC2-18, E2-42, E2-43, E2-44
Solution on p. 2-45.

Chapter 2 Cost Terminology and Classification

Comprehensive Review Module

Key Terms

conversion cost, p. 2-10
cost, p. 2-2
cost allocation, p. 2-18
cost driver, p. 2-7
cost management system, p. 2-2
cost object, p. 2-2
cost of goods manufactured (CGM), p. 2-20
cost of goods sold (CGS), p. 2-20
degree of conversion, p. 2-14
direct costs, p. 2-3
direct labor (DL), p. 2-10
direct material (DM), p. 2-10
distribution cost, p. 2-11

finished goods (FG), p. 2-15
fixed cost, p. 2-4
fixed overhead, p. 2-13
indirect costs, p. 2-3
indirect labor costs, p. 2-12
indirect material cost, p. 2-11
inventoriable costs, p. 2-10
manufacturer, p. 2-10
merchandiser, p. 2-13
mixed cost, p. 2-6
overhead (OH), p. 2-10
period costs, p. 2-10
predictor, p. 2-7
prime cost, p. 2-10

product costs, p. 2-10
raw material (RM), p. 2-15
relevant range, p. 2-4
retailer, p. 2-13, 2-15
service company, p. 2-15
service provider, p. 2-13
step cost, p. 2-7
step fixed cost, p. 2-7
step variable costs, p. 2-7
total cost to account for, p. 2-21
variable cost, p. 2-4
variable overhead, p. 2-13
work in process (WIP), p. 2-15

Chapter Summary

Cost Association (Page 2-2) — LO2-1
- Costs associated with a cost object are classified according to their relation to the cost object.
- Direct costs are traceable to the cost object.
- Indirect costs are allocated to the cost object.

Assumptions Used to Estimate Product Cost within Relevant Range of Activity (Page 2-4) — LO2-2
- Variable, fixed, or mixed depending on the cost's reaction to a change in a related activity level.
- Variable costs are constant per unit and will change in total in direct proportion to changes in activity.
- Fixed costs are constant in total and will vary inversely on a per-unit basis with changes in activity.
- Mixed costs fluctuate in total with changes in activity and can be separated into their variable and fixed components.
- Step costs are either variable or fixed, depending on the size of the changes (width of the steps) in cost that occur with changes in activity.

Cost Classification (Page 2-9) — LO2-3
- For financial reporting purposes, product (inventoriable) or period (selling, administrative, and financing) cost classification depends on the cost's association with the revenue-generating items sold by the company.
- Unexpired (assets) or expired (expenses or losses) depending on whether the cost has a future value to the company.
- Cost classification for managerial purposes depends on relevancy, without regard to GAAP rules.

Product Cost Categories (Page 2-11) — LO2-4
- Direct material, which is the cost of any item that is physically and conveniently traceable to the product or service.
- Direct labor, which is the wages or salaries of the people whose work is physically and conveniently traceable to the product or service.
- Overhead, which is any cost incurred in the conversion (or production) area that is not direct material or direct labor; overhead includes indirect material and indirect labor costs.

Conversion Process Differences (Page 2-14) — LO2-5
- Manufacturers require extensive activity to convert raw material into finished goods; the primary costs in these companies are direct material, direct labor, and overhead; manufacturers use three inventory accounts (Raw Material, Work in Process, and Finished Goods).

© Cambridge Business Publishers

- Service companies often require extensive activity to perform a service; the primary costs in these companies are direct labor and overhead; service companies may use Supplies Inventory and Work in Process Inventory accounts but typically have no Finished Goods Inventory.
- Retailers require little, if any, activity to make purchased goods ready for sale; the primary costs in these companies are prices paid for goods and labor wages; retailers use a Merchandise Inventory account.

LO2-6 Product Cost Flow (Page 2-18)
- For accounting purposes, all product costs attach to the units produced, services rendered, or units purchased.
- Direct material and direct labor are traced to a product or service.
- Overhead is allocated to a product or service using a reasonable allocation base or driver.
- Product costs flow through a cost system from the occurrence of product costs, to the assignment and allocation of costs to work in process, finished goods, and cost of goods sold.

LO2-7 Cost of Goods Manufactured (Page 2-21)
- CGM equals the costs that were in the conversion area at the beginning of the period plus production costs (direct material, direct labor, and overhead) incurred during the period minus the cost of incomplete goods that remain in the conversion area at the end of the period.
- CGM is shown on an internal management report called the schedule of cost of goods manufactured; it is equivalent to the cost of goods purchased in a retail company.
- CGM is added to beginning Finished Goods Inventory to determine the cost of goods available (CGA) for sale for the period; CGA is reduced by ending Finished Goods Inventory to determine cost of goods sold on the income statement.

Solution Strategies

LO2-7 Schedule of Cost of Goods Manufactured

Beginning balance of work in process inventory		$ XXX
Manufacturing costs for the period:		
Raw material (all direct):		
Beginning balance	$ XXX	
Purchases of material	XXX	
Raw material available for use	$ XXX	
Ending balance	(XXX)	
Direct material used	$XXX	
Direct labor	XXX	
Variable overhead	XXX	
Fixed overhead	XXX	
Total current period manufacturing costs		XXX
Total cost to account for		$ XXX
Ending balance of work in process inventory		(XXX)
Cost of goods manufactured		$ XXX

LO2-7 Cost of Goods Sold

Beginning balance of finished goods inventory	$ XXX
Cost of goods manufactured	XXX
Cost of goods available for sale	$ XXX
Ending balance of finished goods inventory	(XXX)
Cost of goods sold	$ XXX

Chapter Demonstration Problem

Latourneau Company had the following account balances as of August 1 and August 31.

LO2-6, 7

	August 1	August 31
Raw Material (direct only) Inventory	$20,300	$4,300
Work in Process Inventory	7,000	8,000
Finished Goods Inventory	18,000	5,600

During August, the company recorded sales of $700,000 and incurred the following costs.

1. Purchased $118,000 of raw material on account.
2. Accrued $62,000 in factory payroll costs for direct labor.
3. Applied actual overhead of $122,600 to Work in Process Inventory.
4. Incurred selling and administrative costs of $280,000.

Required:
a. Post transactions to T-accounts for Raw Material Inventory, Work in Process Inventory, Finished Goods Inventory, and Cost of Goods Sold.
b. Prepare a schedule of cost of goods manufactured for August using actual costing.
c. Prepare an income statement, including a detailed schedule of cost of goods sold.

Solution to Demonstration Problem

a.

Raw Material Inventory

BB	20,300	(2)	134,000
(1)	118,000		
EB	4,300		

Work in Process Inventory

BB	7,000	(9)	320,000
(2)	134,000		
(3)	62,000		
(8)	122,600		
EB	5,600		

Finished Goods Inventory

BB	18,000	(11)	330,000
(9)	320,000		
EB	8,000		

Cost of Goods Sold

(11)	330,000		

where BB = beginning balance
       EB = ending balance

b.

LATOURNEAU COMPANY
Schedule of Cost of Goods Manufactured
For the Month Ended August 31

Balance of work in process inventory, August 1		$ 7,000
Manufacturing costs for the period		
Raw material		
Beginning balance	$ 20,300	
Purchases of material	118,000	
Raw material available	$138,300	
Ending balance	(4,300)	
Total direct material used	$134,000	
Direct labor	62,000	
Overhead	122,600	
Total current period manufacturing costs		318,600
Total cost to account for		$325,600
Balance of work in process inventory, August 31		(5,600)
Cost of goods manufactured*		$320,000

*Note the similarity between the schedule of CGM and the WIP Inventory T-account.

c.

LATOURNEAU COMPANY
Income Statement
For the Month Ended August 31

Sales.		$700,000
Cost of goods sold		
Finished goods, August 1	$ 18,000	
Cost of goods manufactured.	320,000	
Cost of goods available.	$338,000	
Finished goods, August 31	(8,000)	
Cost of goods sold		(330,000)
Gross margin		$370,000
Selling and administrative expenses		(280,000)
Income from operations		$ 90,000

Assignments with the MBC logo in the margin are available in *myBusinessCourse*.
Resources include demonstration videos, guided examples, and auto-graded homework.
See details in the Preface, and ask your professor how you can access the system.

Data Analytics

LO2-5

U.S. Census Bureau

DA2-1. Analyzing trends in manufacturing

Access the file included in MBC from the **U.S. Census Bureau** that details manufacturing construction spending in the U.S. over time and complete the following requirements.

Required

a. Prepare a clustered column chart in Excel for total spending for the years 2002 to 2022. Hint: You will need to subtotal amounts for each year before preparing your chart. First, In a new column, use the RIGHT function to extract the year from the data in the Period column. Next, use the SUMIF function to total the values by year.
b. Describe the general trend over time and the recent trend in 2022.
c. Reference the article "America Is Back in the Factory Business" in the *Wall Street Journal*, dated April 3, 2023, or another article that explains the recent trends depicted for 2022. What are the main reasons for the recent trend?

LO2-3, 5

Cleveland Clinic
Ford Motor Company
General Motors
Mayo Clinic
Target
Walmart

DA2-2. Differentiating financial reporting for manufacturers, retailers, and service providers

Access the file included in MBC that includes amounts from recent, publicly available financial statements for **Cleveland Clinic**, **Ford Motor Company**, **General Motors**, **Mayo Clinic**, **Target**, and **Walmart**.

Required

a. Classify each of the companies as a manufacturer, retailer, or service provider.
b. Grouping the companies by the classification in part a, calculate the percentage of inventory over total assets for each of the years presented.
c. Prepare a stacked bar chart showing the percentage calculated in part b for each company for the years in which the data is provided.
d. Describe the trends that you observe within the company types and outside of the company types.
e. Discuss possible reasons for the trends that you observed in part d.
f. Do the percentages shown in part c correlate with the degree of conversion for each company (i.e. higher percentage, higher degree of conversion and lower percentage, lower degree of conversion)? Why or why not?

Data Visualization

Data Visualization Activities are available in myBusinessCourse. These assignments use Tableau Dashboards to expose students to visual depictions of data and introduce students to data analytics through data visualizations. These exercises are easily assignable and auto graded by MBC.

Potential Ethical Issues

1. Leaving expired costs on the balance sheet as assets, thereby not recognizing expenses or losses that would reduce net income
2. Treating period costs as product costs to inflate inventory assets and increase net income
3. Treating product costs as period costs to reduce the cost of goods manufactured and increase gross profit on the income statement, thereby making the conversion area appear more profitable than it actually was
4. Attaching the "random" costs of direct labor (such as overtime) to specific production units to inflate the cost of those units—especially if the buyer is required to pay for production cost plus a specified profit percentage
5. Overstating the cost of ending inventory accounts to reduce the cost of goods manufactured, reduce the cost of goods sold, and increase net income
6. Moving manufacturing operations to countries with weak environmental protection to reduce operating costs

Questions

Q2-1. Why must the word *cost* be accompanied by an adjective to be meaningful?

Q2-2. Why is it necessary to specify a cost object before being able to distinguish between a direct cost and an indirect cost?

Q2-3. Why is it necessary for a company to specify a relevant range of activity when making assumptions about cost behavior?

Q2-4. How do cost drivers and cost predictors differ, and why is the distinction important?

Q2-5. How do a product cost and a period cost differ?

Q2-6. What are conversion costs? Why are they called this?

Q2-7. What is the difference between tracing and allocating costs?

Q2-8. What are the types of companies that have a low degree of conversion and a high degree of conversion?

Q2-9. What is meant by the term *cost of goods manufactured*? Why does this item appear on an income statement?

Multiple Choice

MC2-10. Considering an accounting firm with an audit and tax department, which of the following costs would be classified indirect when the cost object is the tax department?
 a. Tax accountant salaries plus bonuses
 b. Annual fee for software used to complete tax returns
 c. Depreciation on laptop computers used by the tax accountants
 d. Depreciation on building shared by the two departments

MC2-11. Which one of the following refers to a cost that remains the same as the volume of activity decreases within the relevant range?
 a. Average cost per unit.   c. Unit fixed cost.
 b. Variable cost per unit.   d. Total variable cost.

MC2-12. Within the relevant range, fixed cost per unit will
 a. increase as the activity level increases.
 b. decrease as the activity level decreases.
 c. remain the same as the activity level decreases.
 d. decrease as the activity level increases.

MC2-13. Cell Company has discovered that the cost of processing customer invoices is strictly variable within the relevant range. Which one of the following statements concerning the cost of processing customer invoices is incorrect?

a. The total cost of processing customer invoices will increase as the volume of customer invoices increases.
b. The cost per unit for processing customer invoices will decline as the volume of customer invoices increases.
c. The cost of processing the 100th customer invoice will be the same as the cost of processing the first customer invoice.
d. The average cost per unit for processing a customer invoice will equal the incremental cost of processing one more customer invoice.

LO2-3 MC2-14. A review of Plunkett Corporation's accounting records for last year disclosed the following selected information.

Variable costs		Fixed costs	
Direct materials used	$ 56,000	Manufacturing overhead	$267,000
Direct labor	179,100	Selling costs	121,000
Manufacturing overhead	154,000	Administrative costs	235,900
Selling costs	108,400		

What were Plunkett's product costs and period costs for last year?

	Product	Period
a.	$235,100	$886,300
b.	$497,500	$623,900
c.	$656,100	$465,300
d.	$389,100	$465,300

LO2-4 MC2-15. In practice, items such as wood screws and glue used in the production of school desks and chairs would most likely be classified as
a. direct labor.
b. factory overhead.
c. direct materials.
d. period costs.

LO2-5 MC2-16. A company with a high degree of conversion
a. rarely benefits from the cost of assigning overhead to inventory or products.
b. Is most likely a merchandiser.
c. Is never a service provider.
d. Physically transform inputs into finished products or services.

LO2-6 MC2-17. A company incurred $200,000 of manufacturing cost during the month, with a beginning finished goods inventory of $20,000 and an ending finished goods inventory of $15,000. Assuming no work-in-process inventories, the company's cost of goods sold was
a. $220,000.
b. $205,000.
c. $200,000.
d. $105,000.

LO2-7 MC2-18. Given the following data for Scurry Company, what is the cost of goods sold?

Beginning inventory of finished goods	$100,000
Cost of goods manufactured	700,000
Ending inventory of finished goods	200,000
Beginning work-in-process inventory	300,000
Ending work-in-process inventory	50,000

a. $500,000.
b. $600,000.
c. $800,000.
d. $950,000.

Exercises

LO2-1 E2-19. Association with cost object Chase University's College of Business has five departments: Accounting, Economics, Finance, Management, and Marketing. Each department chairperson is responsible for the department's budget preparation.

Indicate whether each of the following costs incurred in the Accounting Department is direct or indirect to the department:

a. Accounting faculty salaries

Chapter 2 Cost Terminology and Classification

    b. Accounting chairperson's salary
    c. Cost of computer time of university server used by members of the department
    d. Cost of office assistant salaries (office assistants are shared by the entire college)
    e. Cost of travel by department faculty paid from externally generated funds contributed directly to the department
    f. Cost of equipment purchased by the department from allocated state funds
    g. Depreciation allocation of the college building cost for the number of offices used by department faculty
    h. Cost of digital subscriptions purchased by the department
    i. Cost of software on faculty computers

E2-20. Association with cost object Following is a list of raw materials that might be used in the production of a laptop computer: touch pad and buttons, glue, network connector, battery, paper towels used by line employees, keyboard, random access memory, motherboard, screws, and oil for production machinery. The laptops are produced in the same building using the same equipment that produces desktop computers and servers. Classify each raw material as direct or indirect when the cost object is the

    a. laptop.
    b. computer production plant.

E2-21. Association with cost object Morris & Assoc., owned by Cindy Morris, provides accounting services to clients. The firm has two accountants (Jo Perkins, who performs basic accounting services, and Steve Tompkin, who performs tax services) and one office assistant. The assistant is paid on an hourly basis for the actual hours worked. One client the firm served during April was Vic Kennedy. During April the following labor time was incurred. Classify the labor time as direct, indirect, or unrelated based on whether the cost object is (1) Kennedy's services, (2) tax services provided, or (3) the accounting firm.

    a. Four hours of Perkins's time in preparing Kennedy's financial statements
    b. Six hours of the assistant's time in copying Kennedy's tax materials
    c. Three hours of Morris's time playing golf with Kennedy
    d. Eight hours of continuing education paid for by the firm for Tompkin to attend a tax update seminar
    e. One hour of the assistant's time spent at lunch on the day that Kennedy's tax return was prepared
    f. Two hours of Perkins's time spent with Kennedy and his banker discussing Kennedy's financial statements
    g. One-half hour of Tompkin's time spent talking to an IRS agent about a deduction taken on Kennedy's tax return
    h. Forty hours of janitorial wages
    i. Seven hours of Tompkin's time preparing Kennedy's tax return

E2-22. Cost behavior Spirit Company produces baseball caps. The company incurred the following costs to produce 12,000 caps last month:

Cardboard for the brims	$ 4,800
Cloth	12,000
Plastic for headbands	6,000
Straight-line depreciation	7,200
Supervisors' salaries	19,200
Utilities	3,600
Total	$52,800

    a. What did each cap component cost on a per-unit basis?
    b. What is the probable type of behavior that each of the costs exhibits?
    c. The company expects to produce 10,000 caps this month. Would you expect each type of per-unit cost to increase or decrease? Why? Can the total cost of 10,000 caps be determined? Explain.

E2-23. Cost behavior Merry Olde Games produces croquet sets. The company makes fixed monthly payments to the local utility based on the previous year's electrical usage. Any difference between actual and expected usage is paid in January of the year following usage. In February, Merry Olde Games made 2,000 croquet sets and incurred the following costs:

© Cambridge Business Publishers

Cardboard boxes (1 per set)	$ 1,000
Mallets (2 per set)	12,000
Croquet balls (6 per set)	9,000
Wire hoops (12 per set, including extras)	3,600
Total hourly wages for production workers	8,400
Supervisor's salary	2,600
Building and equipment rental	2,800
Utilities	1,300
Total	$40,700

    a. What was the per-unit cost of each component of a croquet set?
    b. What was the total cost of each croquet set?
    c. Production for March is expected to be 2,500 croquet sets. Last November, when 2,500 sets were made, utility cost was $1,400. There have been no rate changes at the local utility companies since that time. What is the estimated cost per set for March?

LO2-2 E2-24. Cost behavior A local band will perform at your fraternity's charity event for free at your school's basketball arena (25,000-person capacity) on January 28. The school is charging your fraternity $37,500 for the facilities and $10 for each ticket sold. The fraternity asks you, their only numbers-astute member, to determine how much to charge for each ticket. The group wants to make a profit of $8 per ticket sold. You assume that 15,000 tickets will be sold.

    a. What is the total cost incurred by the fraternity if 15,000 tickets are sold?
    b. What price per ticket must be charged for the fraternity to earn its desired profit margin?
    c. Suppose that on the morning of January 28, a major snowstorm hits your area, bringing in 36 inches of snow and ice. Only 5,000 tickets are sold because most students were going to buy their tickets at the door. What is the total profit or loss to the fraternity?
    d. What assumptions did you make about your calculations that should have been conveyed to the fraternity?
    e. Suppose instead that fair weather prevails and, by show time, 20,000 concert tickets are sold. What is the total profit or loss to the fraternity?

LO2-2 E2-25. Cost behavior Flaherty Accounting Services pays $2,000 per month for a tax preparation software license. In addition, variable charges incurred average $9 for every tax return the firm prepares.

    a. Determine the total cost and the cost per unit if the firm expects to prepare the following number of tax returns in March:
        1. 200
        2. 500
        3. 800
    b. Why does the cost per unit change in (1), (2), and (3) of (a)?
    c. The owner of Flaherty Accounting Services wants to earn a margin (excluding any other direct costs) on tax returns of $15,000 during March. If 200 returns are prepared, what tax return preparation fee should be charged? If that fee is charged and 800 returns are prepared, what is the margin in March?

LO2-2 E2-26. Predictors and cost drivers; team activity Lawrence & Sluyter CPAs often use factors that change in a consistent pattern with costs to explain or predict cost behavior.

    a. As a team of three or four, select factors to predict or explain the behavior of the following costs:
        1. Staff accountant's travel expenses
        2. Office supplies inventory
        3. Laptop computers used in audit engagements
        4. Maintenance costs for the firm's lawn & grounds service
    b. Prepare a presentation of your chosen factors that also addresses whether the factors could be used as cost drivers in addition to cost predictors.

LO2-2 E2-27. Cost drivers Assume that Dover Hospital performs the following activities in providing outpatient service:

    a. Verifying patient's insurance coverage
    b. Scheduling patient's arrival date and time
    c. Scheduling staff to prepare patient's surgery room
    d. Scheduling doctors and nurses to perform surgery

Chapter 2 Cost Terminology and Classification

    e. Ordering patient's tests
    f. Moving patient to laboratory to administer lab tests
    g. Administering laboratory tests
    h. Moving patient to the operating room
    i. Administering anesthetic
    j. Performing surgery
    k. Administering postsurgical medications
    l. Moving patient to recovery room
    m. Discharging patient
    n. Billing patient's insurance company

Assume that the patient is the cost object and determine the appropriate cost driver or drivers for each activity.

E2-28. Cost behavior and classification Indicate whether each of the following items is a variable (V), fixed (F), or mixed (M) cost and whether it is a product/service (PT) or period (PD) cost. If some items have alternative answers, indicate the alternatives and the reasons for them.   LO2-2, 3

    a. Wages of factory maintenance workers
    b. Wages of forklift operators who move finished goods from a central warehouse to the outbound loading dock
    c. Insurance premiums paid to insure the headquarters of a manufacturing company
    d. Cost of labels attached to shirts made by a company
    e. Property taxes on a manufacturing plant
    f. Paper towels used in factory restrooms
    g. Salaries of office assistants in a law firm
    h. Freight costs of acquiring raw material from suppliers
    i. Computer paper used in an accounting firm
    j. Cost of wax to make candles
    k. Freight-in on a truckload of furniture purchased for resale

E2-29. Cost behavior and classification Classify each of the following costs incurred in manufacturing bicycles as variable (V), fixed (F), or mixed (M) cost (using number of units produced as the activity measure). Also indicate whether the cost is direct material (DM), direct labor (DL), or overhead (OH).   LO2-2, 4

    a. Factory supervision
    b. Aluminum tubing
    c. Rims
    d. Emblem
    e. Gearbox
    f. Straight-line depreciation on painting machine
    g. Fenders
    h. Raw material inventory clerk's wages
    i. Quality control inspector's salary
    j. Handlebars
    k. Metal worker's wages
    l. Roller chain
    m. Spokes (assuming cost is considered significant)
    n. Paint (assuming cost is considered significant)

E2-30. Financial statement classification Wayside Machine Tool Company purchased a $600,000 welding machine to use in production of large machine tools and robots. The welding machine was expected to have a life of 10 years and a salvage value at time of disposition of $60,000. The company uses straight-line depreciation. During its first operating year, the machine produced 600 product units, of which 480 were sold.   LO2-3

    a. What part of the $600,000 machine cost expired?
    b. Where would each of the amounts related to this machine appear on the financial statements at the end of the first year of operations?

E2-31. Financial statement classification Babineaux Company incurred the following costs in May: LO2-3

- Paid a six-month (May through October) premium for insurance of company headquarters, $18,600.
- Paid $1,000 fee for a salesperson to attend a seminar in July.

- Paid three months (May through July) of property taxes on its factory building, $15,000.
- Paid a $10,000 bonus to the company president for his performance during May.
- Accrued $20,000 of utility costs, of which 40 percent was for the headquarters and the remainder was for the factory.

    a. What expired period costs are associated with the May information?
    b. What unexpired period costs are associated with the May information?
    c. What product costs are associated with the May information?
    d. Discuss why the product cost cannot be described specifically as expired or unexpired in this situation.

LO2-5 E2-32. Company type Indicate whether each of the following terms is associated with a manufacturing (Mfg.), a retailing or merchandising (Mer.), or a service (Ser.) company. There can be more than one correct answer for each term.

    a. Depreciation—factory equipment   *f.* Finished goods inventory
    b. Prepaid rent   *g.* Cost of services rendered
    c. Auditing fees expense   *h.* Cost of goods sold
    d. Merchandise inventory   *i.* Direct labor wages
    e. Sales salaries expense

LO2-5 E2-33. Degrees of conversion Indicate whether each of the following types of organizations is characterized by a high, low, or moderate degree of conversion.

    a. Textbook publisher   *f.* Bakery in a grocery store
    b. Convenience store   *g.* Greek restaurant
    c. Sporting goods retailer   *h.* Jelly manufacturer
    d. Christmas tree farm   *i.* Auto manufacturer
    e. Custom print shop   *j.* Concert ticket seller

LO2-4 E2-34. Product cost classifications Barbieri Co. makes aluminum canoes. The company's June costs for material and labor were as follows:

Material costs	
Janitorial supplies	$ 1,800
Chrome rivets to assemble canoes	12,510
Sealant	1,230
Aluminum	1,683,000
Labor costs	
Janitorial wages	$ 9,300
Aluminum cutters	56,160
Salespeople's salaries	43,050
Welders	156,000
Factory supervisors' salaries	101,250

    a. What is the direct material cost for June?
    b. What is the direct labor cost for June?

LO2-4 E2-35. Product cost classifications Forham Inc. manufactures stainless steel knives. Following are factory costs incurred during the year:

Material costs	
Stainless steel	$800,000
Equipment oil and grease	6,000
Plastic for handles	5,600
Wood blocks for knife storage	24,800
Labor costs	
Equipment operators	$500,000
Equipment mechanics	82,000
Factory supervisors	272,000

    a. What is the direct material cost for the year?
    b. What is the direct labor cost for the year?
    c. What is the total indirect material cost and the indirect labor cost for the year?

E2-36. Product cost classifications
In June, Carolyn Gardens incurred the following costs. One of several projects in process during the month was a landscaped terrace for Pam Beattie. Relative to the Beattie landscaping job, classify each of the costs as direct material, direct labor, or overhead. The terrace required two days to design and one five-day work week to complete. Some costs may not fit entirely into a single classification; in such cases, and if possible, provide a systematic and rational method to allocate such costs.

Mulch purchased for Beattie's landscaping	$ 320
June salary of Z. Trumble, the landscape designer, who worked 20 days in June	3,000
Construction permit for Beattie's landscaping	95
Gardeners' wages; all worked on Beattie's landscaping; gardeners work eight hours per day, five days per week; there were 20 working days in June	3,840
June depreciation on the company loader, driven by a gardener and used on Beattie's landscaping one day	200
Landscaping rock purchased for Beattie's landscaping	1,580
June rent on Carolyn Gardens offices, where Z. Trumble has an office that occupies 150 square feet of 3,000 total square feet	2,400
June utility bills for Carolyn Gardens	1,800
Plants and pots purchased for Beattie's landscaping	1,950

E2-37. Labor cost classification
Woodlands Restaurant Supply operates in two shifts, paying a late-shift premium of 10 percent and an overtime premium of 75 percent. The May payroll follows:

Total wages for 6,000 hours	$54,000
Normal hourly employee wage	$ 9
Total regular hours worked, split evenly between the shifts	5,000

All overtime was worked by the early shift during May. Shift and overtime premiums are considered part of overhead rather than direct labor.

a. How many overtime hours were worked in May?
b. How much of the total labor cost should be charged to direct labor? To overhead?
c. What amount of overhead was for second-shift premiums? For overtime premiums?

E2-38. Labor cost classification
Tidy House produces a variety of household products. The firm operates 24 hours per day with three daily work shifts. The first-shift workers receive "regular pay." The second shift receives an 8 percent pay premium, and the third shift receives a 12 percent pay premium. In addition, when production is scheduled on weekends, the firm pays an overtime premium of 50 percent (based on the pay rate for first-shift employees). Labor premiums are included in overhead. The October factory payroll is as follows:

Total wages for October for 32,000 hours	$435,600
Normal hourly wage for first-shift employees	$ 12
Total regular hours worked, split evenly among the three shifts	27,000

a. How many overtime hours were worked in October?
b. How much of the total labor cost should be charged to direct labor? To overhead?
c. What amount of overhead was for second- and third-shift premiums? For overtime premiums?

E2-39. Classifying inventory costs
Below is a list of accounts that a company may maintain in its accounting records.

1. Cost of Goods Sold
2. Costs of Services Rendered
3. Finished Goods Inventory
4. Merchandise Inventory
5. Raw Materials Inventory
6. Supplies Inventory
7. Work in Process Inventory

For each of the accounts, answer the following questions:

a. Determine which type of company is most likely to maintain the account in its records: manufacturer, merchandiser, or a service provider. More than one type of company may apply.
b. Identify whether the account represents an expired cost or an unexpired cost.
c. Indicate on which financial statement the amount would be recognized.

	Company Type	Expired/Unexpired	Financial Statement
Cost of Goods Sold			
Costs of Services Rendered			
Finished Goods Inventory			
Merchandise Inventory			
Raw Materials Inventory			
Supplies Inventory			
Work in Process Inventory			

LO2-6 E2-40. Analyzing activity in inventory accounts Goodman Manufacturing, a manufacturer in Dallas, Texas, makes air conditioning products. Assume the following represents data related to its manufacturing operations for one month.

Manufacturing costs incurred during the year:	
Direct materials used (all direct)	180,000
Direct labor	360,000
Overhead	480,000
Selling and administrative expenses	336,000

	June 1	June 30
Raw Materials Inventory	$132,000	$126,000
Work in Process Inventory	90,000	110,000
Finished Goods Inventory	150,000	162,000

Determine each of the following amounts.

a. Cost of raw materials purchased
b. Cost of goods manufactured
c. Cost of goods sold

LO2-6 E2-41. Analyzing product costs Tamra Corp. makes one product line. In February, Tamra paid $530,000 in factory overhead costs. Of that amount, $124,000 was for January's factory utilities and $48,000 was for property taxes on the factory for the year. February's factory utility bill arrived on March 12, and was only $81,000 because the weather was significantly milder than in January. Tamra Corp. produced 50,000 units of product in both January and February.

a. What were Tamra's actual factory overhead costs for February?
b. Actual per-unit direct material and direct labor costs for February were $24.30 and $10.95. What was actual total product cost per unit for February?
c. Assume that, other than factory utilities, all direct material, direct labor, and overhead costs for Tamra Corp. were the same for January and February. Will product cost for the two months differ? How can such differences be avoided?

LO2-7 E2-42. Cost of goods manufactured The Work in Process Inventory account of Phelan Corporation increased $23,000 during November. Costs incurred during November included $24,000 for direct material, $126,000 for direct labor, and $42,000 for overhead. What was the cost of goods manufactured during November?

LO2-7 E2-43. CGM; CGS Wasik Company had the following inventory balances at the beginning and end of August:

	August 1	August 31
Raw Material Inventory	$ 58,000	$ 84,000
Work in Process Inventory	372,000	436,000
Finished Goods Inventory	224,000	196,000

All raw material is direct to the production process. The following information is also available about August manufacturing costs:

Cost of raw material used	$612,000
Direct labor cost	748,000
Manufacturing overhead	564,000

Chapter 2 Cost Terminology and Classification

a. Calculate the cost of goods manufactured for August.
b. Determine the cost of goods sold for August.

E2-44. **CGM; CGS** Irresistible Art produces collectible pieces of art. The company's Raw Material Inventory account includes the costs of both direct and indirect materials. Account balances for the company at the beginning and end of July follow:

	July 1	July 31
Raw Material Inventory	$ 93,200	$ 69,600
Work in Process Inventory	146,400	120,000
Finished Goods Inventory	72,000	104,800

During the month, the company purchased $656,000 of raw material; direct material used during the period amounted to $504,000. Factory payroll costs for July were $788,000, of which 75 percent was related to direct labor. Overhead charges for depreciation, insurance, utilities, and maintenance totaled $600,000 for July.

a. Prepare a schedule of cost of goods manufactured.
b. Prepare a schedule of cost of goods sold.

E2-45. **CGM; CGS** The cost of goods sold in March for Targé Co. was $2,644,100. The March 31 Work in Process Inventory was 25 percent of the March 1 Work in Process Inventory. Overhead was 225 percent of direct labor cost. During March, $1,182,000 of direct material was purchased. Other March information follows:

Inventories	March 1	March 31
Direct Material	$ 30,000	$42,000
Work in Process	90,000	?
Finished Goods	125,000	18,400

a. Prepare a cost of goods sold schedule for March.
b. Prepare the March cost of goods manufactured schedule.
c. What was the amount of prime cost incurred in March?
d. What was the amount of conversion cost incurred in March?

E2-46. **Service industry; CSR** Kalogrides & McMillan CPAs incurred the following costs in performing audits during September. The firm uses a Work in Process Inventory account for audit engagement costs and records overhead in fixed and variable overhead accounts. The following transactions took place during the month.

- Used $5,000 of previously purchased supplies on audit engagements.
- Paid $8,000 of partner travel expenses to an accounting conference.
- Recorded $6,500 of depreciation on laptops used in audits.
- Recorded $1,800,000 of annual depreciation on the Kalogrides & McMillan Building, located in downtown New York; 65 percent of the space is used to house audit personnel.
- Accrued audit partner salaries, $200,000.
- Accrued remaining audit staff salaries, $257,900.
- Paid credit card charges for travel costs for client engagements, $19,400.
- One month's prepaid insurance and property taxes expired on the downtown building, $17,300.
- Accrued $3,400 of office assistant wages; the office assistant works only for the audit partners and staff.
- Paid all accrued salaries and wages for the month.

Determine the cost of audit services rendered for September.

E2-47. **Cost of services rendered** The following information is related to North Zulch Veterinary Clinic for April, the firm's first month of operation:

Veterinarian salaries for April	$8,100
Assistants' salaries for April	3,140
Medical supplies purchased in April	2,400
Utilities for month (90% related to animal treatment)	2,000
Office salaries for April (20% related to animal treatment)	1,900
Medical supplies on hand at April 30	1,200
Depreciation on medical equipment for April	3,700
Building rental (80% related to animal treatment)	3,100

Compute the cost of services rendered.

LO2-2   E2-48.   Activities and cost drivers For each of the following activities, select the most appropriate cost driver. Each cost driver may be used only once.

Activity		Cost Driver
1. Pay vendors	a.	Number of different raw material items
2. Receive material deliveries	b.	Number of classes offered
3. Inspect raw materials	c.	Number of machine hours
4. Plan for purchases of raw materials	d.	Number of employees
5. Packaging	e.	Number of maintenance hours
6. Supervision	f.	Number of units of raw materials received
7. Employee training	g.	Number of new customers
8. Operating machines	h.	Number of deliveries
9. Machine maintenance	i.	Number of electronic fund transfers
10. Opening accounts at a bank	j.	Number of customer orders

Problems

LO2-1, 2, 3   P2-49.   Cost classifications Joe Reynolds painted four houses during April. For these jobs, he spent $2,400 on paint, $160 on mineral spirits, and $300 on brushes. He also bought two pairs of coveralls for $100 each; he wears coveralls only while he works. During the first week of April, Reynolds placed a $200 virtual ad for his business. He hired an assistant for one of the painting jobs; the assistant was paid $25 per hour and worked 50 hours.

Being a very methodical person, Reynolds kept detailed records of his mileage to and from each painting job. The average operating cost per mile for his van is $0.70. He found a $30 receipt in his van for a metropolitan map that he purchased in April. He uses the map as part of a contact file for referral work and for bids that he has made on potential jobs. He also had $30 in receipts for bridge tolls ($2 per trip) for a painting job he completed across the river.

Using the following headings, indicate how to classify each of the April costs incurred by Reynolds. Assume that the cost object is a house-painting job.

Type of Cost	Variable	Fixed	Direct	Indirect	Period	Product

LO2-2   P2-50.   Cost behavior PlumView Printers makes wedding invitation sets of 100 percent rag content edged in 24 karat gold. In an average month, the firm produces 80,000 boxes of invitations; each box contains 100 pages of stationery and 80 envelopes. Production costs are incurred for paper, ink, glue, and boxes. The company manufactures this product in batches of 500 boxes of a specific design. The following data have been extracted from the company's accounting records for June:

Cost of paper for each batch	$10,000
Cost of ink and glue for each batch	1,000
Cost of 1,000 gold boxes for each batch	32,000
Direct labor for producing each batch	16,000
Cost of designing each batch	20,000

Overhead charges total $408,000 per month and are considered fully fixed for purposes of cost estimation.

Chapter 2 Cost Terminology and Classification

  a. What is the cost per box of invitations based on average production volume?
  b. If sales volume increases to 120,000 boxes per month, what will be the cost per box (assuming that cost behavior patterns remain the same as in June)?
  c. If sales volume increases to 120,000 boxes per month but the firm does not want the cost per box to exceed its current level [based on (a)], what amount can the company pay for design costs, assuming all other costs are the same as June levels?
  d. Assume that PlumView Printers is now able to sell, on average, each box of invitations at a price of $195. If the company is able to increase its volume to 120,000 boxes per month, what sales price per box will generate the same per-unit gross margin that the firm is now achieving on 80,000 boxes per month?
  e. Would it be possible to lower total costs by producing more boxes per batch, even if the total volume of 80,000 is maintained? Explain.

P2-51. Cost behavior Creative Catering prepares meals for several airlines, and sales average 150,000 meals per month at a selling price of $25.32 per meal. The significant costs of each meal prepared are for the meat, vegetables, and plastic trays and utensils; no desserts are provided because the airlines are concerned about cost control. The company prepares meals in batches of 2,000. The following data are shown in the company's accounting records for June:

Cost of meat for 2,000 meals	$3,600
Cost of vegetables for 2,000 meals	1,440
Cost of plastic trays and utensils for 2,000 meals	480
Direct labor cost for 2,000 meals	3,800

Monthly overhead charges amount to $1,200,000 and are fully fixed. Company management has asked you to answer the following items.

  a. What is the cost per meal based on average sales and June costs?
  b. If sales increase to 300,000 meals per month, what will be the cost per meal (assuming that the cost behavior patterns remain the same as in June)?
  c. Assume that sales increase to 300,000 meals per month. Creative Catering wants to provide a larger meat portion per meal and has decided that, since the airlines are willing to incur the cost determined in (a), the company will simply increase its per-unit spending for meat. If all costs other than meat remain constant, how much can Creative Catering increase its cost per meal for meat?
  d. The company's major competitor has bid a price of $21.92 per meal to the airlines. The profit margin in the industry is 100 percent of total cost. If Creative Catering is to retain the airlines' business, how many meals must the company produce and sell each month to reach the bid price of the competitor and maintain the 100 percent profit margin? Assume that June cost patterns will not change and meals must be produced in batches of 2,000.
  e. Consider your answer to (d). Under what circumstances might the manager for Creative Catering retain the airlines' business but cause the company to be less profitable than it currently is? Show calculations.

P2-52. Cost behavior Toni Rankin has been elected to handle the local Little Theater summer play. The theater has a maximum capacity of 1,000 patrons. Rankin is trying to determine the price to charge Little Theater members for attendance at this year's performance of *The Producers*. She has developed the following cost estimates associated with the play:

- Cost of printing invitations will be $360 for 100–500; cost to print between 501 and 1,000 will be $450.
- Cost of readying and operating the theater for three evenings will be $900 if attendance is 500 or less; this cost rises to $1,200 if attendance is above 500.
- Postage to mail the invitations will be $0.60 each.
- Cost of building stage sets will be $1,800.
- Cost of printing up to 1,000 programs will be $350.
- Cost of security will be $110 per night plus $30 per hour; five hours will be needed each night.
- Cost to obtain script usage, $2,000.
- Costumes will be donated by several local businesses.

The Little Theater has 300 members, and each member is allowed two guests. Ordinarily only 60 percent of the members attend the summer offering. Of those attending, half bring one guest and the other half bring two guests. The play will be presented from 8 to 11 P.M. each evening.

Invitations are mailed to those members calling to say they plan to attend and also to each of the guests they specify. Rankin has asked you to help her by answering the following items.

a. Indicate the type of cost behavior exhibited by each of the items Rankin needs to consider.
b. If the ordinary attendance occurs, what will be the total cost of the summer production?
c. If the ordinary attendance occurs, what will be the cost per person attending?
d. If 90 percent of the members attend and each invites two guests, what will be the total cost of the play? The cost per person? What primarily causes the difference in the cost per person?

LO2-2 P2-53. Cost behavior Mason Company's cost structure contains a number of different cost behavior patterns. Following are descriptions of several different costs; match these to the appropriate graphs. On each graph, the vertical axis represents cost, and the horizontal axis represents level of activity or volume.

Identify, by letter, the graph that illustrates each of the following cost behavior patterns. Each graph can be used more than once.

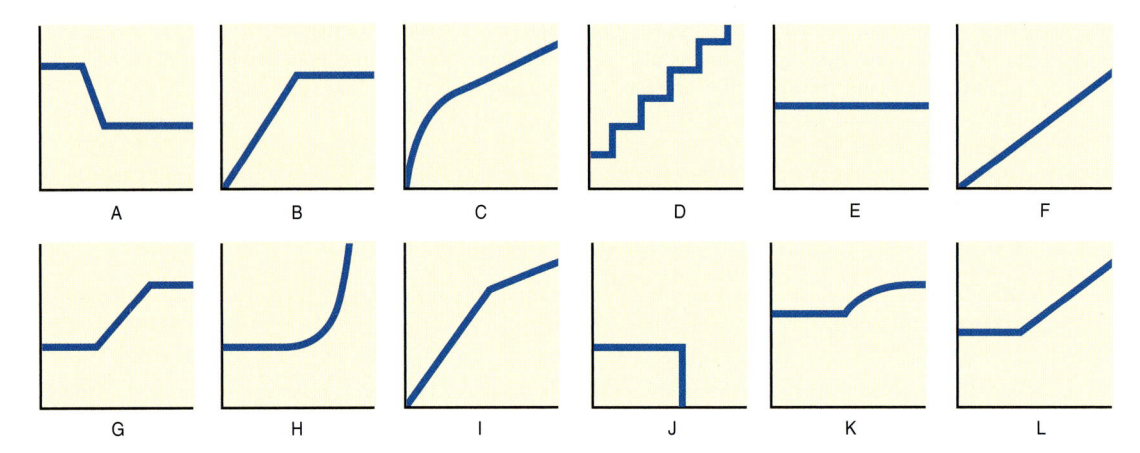

1. Cost of raw material, where the cost decreases by $0.06 per unit for each of the first 150 units purchased, after which it remains constant at $2.75 per unit.
2. City water bill, which is computed as follows: first 750,000 gallons or less, $1,000 flat fee; next 15,000 gallons, $0.002 per gallon used; next 15,000 gallons, $0.005 per gallon used; next 15,000 gallons, $0.008 per gallon used; and so on.
3. Salaries of maintenance workers, assuming one maintenance worker is needed for every 1,000 hours or less of machine time.
4. Electricity rate structure—a flat fixed charge of $250 plus a variable cost after 150,000 kilowatt hours are used.
5. Depreciation of equipment using the straight-line method.
6. Rent on a machine that is billed at $1,000 for up to 500 hours of machine time. After 500 hours of machine time, an additional charge of $1 per hour is paid up to a maximum charge of $2,500 per period.
7. Rent on a factory building donated by the county; the agreement provides for a monthly rental of $100,000 less $1 for each labor hour worked in excess of 200,000 hours. However, a minimum rental payment of $20,000 must be made each month.
8. Cost of raw material used.
9. Rent on a factory building donated by the city with an agreement providing for a fixed-fee payment unless 250,000 labor hours are worked, in which case no rent needs to be paid.

AICPA ADAPTED

LO2-2 P2-54. Cost drivers and predictors Customers demand a wide variety of "personalized" products and want those products delivered quickly. With an increase in automation to accommodate these demands, once products are designed, it is difficult to change the method of production or product components.

a. Why is determining the cost to manufacture a product quite a different activity from determining how to control such costs?
b. Why has the advancement of technology made costs more difficult to control?
c. For many production costs, why should "number of units produced" not be considered a cost driver even though it is certainly a valid cost predictor?

Chapter 2 Cost Terminology and Classification

P2-55. Cost behavior; cost management; ethics An extremely important and expensive variable cost per employee is employer-provided health care. This cost is expected to rise each year as more and more expensive technology is used on patients and as the costs of that technology are passed along through the insurance company to the employer. One simple way to reduce these variable costs is to reduce employee insurance coverage.

a. Discuss the ethical implications of reducing employee health-care coverage to reduce the variable costs incurred by the employer.

b. Assume that you are an employer with 600 employees. You are forced to reduce some insurance benefits. Your coverage currently includes the following items: mental health coverage, long-term disability, convalescent facility care, nonemergency but medically necessary procedures, dependent coverage, and life insurance. Select the two you would eliminate or dramatically reduce and provide reasons for your selections.

c. Prepare a plan that might allow you to "trade" some variable employee health-care costs for a fixed or mixed cost.

P2-56. Analyzing CGM The following transactions were incurred by Dimasi Industries during January:
1. Issued $800,000 of direct material to production.
2. Paid 28,800 hours of direct labor at $25 per hour.
3. Completed goods costing $1,749,300 and transferred them to finished goods.
4. Accrued 5,485 hours of indirect labor cost at $20 per hour.
5. Recorded $102,100 of depreciation on factory assets.
6. Accrued $32,800 of supervisors' salaries.
7. Issued indirect material to production (originally recorded in Supplies Inventory account).

a. If Work in Process Inventory had a beginning balance of $18,900 and an ending balance of $59,600, what total amount of manufacturing overhead was included in Work in Process Inventory during January? Consider parts 1, 2, and 3.

b. What amount of indirect materials was included in the total amount of manufacturing overhead?

P2-57. Direct labor; writing A portion of the costs incurred by business organizations is designated as direct labor cost. As used in practice, the term *direct labor cost* has a wide variety of meanings. Unless the meaning intended in a given context is clear, misunderstanding and confusion are likely to ensue. If a user does not understand the elements included in direct labor cost, erroneous interpretations of the numbers may occur and can result in poor management decisions. In addition to understanding the conceptual definition of direct labor cost, management accountants must understand how direct labor cost should be measured. Discuss the following issues:

a. Distinguish between direct labor and indirect labor.

b. Discuss why some nonproductive labor time (such as coffee breaks and personal time) can be and often is treated as direct labor, whereas other nonproductive time (such as downtime and training) is treated as indirect labor.

c. Following are labor cost elements that a company has classified as direct labor, manufacturing overhead, or either category depending on the situation.
- *Direct labor*: Included in the company's direct labor are production efficiency bonuses and certain benefits for direct labor workers such as FICA (employer's portion), group life insurance, vacation pay, and workers' compensation insurance.
- *Manufacturing overhead*: Included in the company's overhead are costs for wage continuation plans in the event of illness, the company-sponsored cafeteria, the personnel department, and recreational facilities.
- *Direct labor or manufacturing overhead*: Included in this category are maintenance expenses, overtime premiums, and shift premiums.

Explain the rationale used by the company in classifying the cost elements in each of the three categories.

d. The two aspects of measuring direct labor costs are (1) the quantity of labor effort that is to be included, and (2) the unit price by which the labor quantity is multiplied to arrive at labor cost. Why are these considered separate and distinct aspects of measuring labor cost?

P2-58. Ethics You are the chief financial officer for a small manufacturing company that has applied for a bank loan. In speaking with the bank loan officer, you are told that two minimum criteria for granting loans are (1) a 40 percent gross margin and (2) operating income of at least 15 percent of sales. Looking at the last four months' income statements, you find that gross margin has been between

30 and 33 percent, and operating income ranged from 18 to 24 percent of sales. You discuss these relations with the company president, who suggests that some of the product costs included in Cost of Goods Sold should be moved to the selling and administrative categories so that the income statement will conform to the bank's criteria.

 a. Which types of product costs might be most easily reassigned to period cost classifications?
 b. Because the president is not suggesting that any expenses be excluded from the income statement, do you see any ethical problems with the request? Discuss the rationale for your answer.
 c. Write a short memo to convince the banker to loan funds to the company in spite of its non-compliance with the specified loan criteria.

LO2-4, 6, 7 P2-59. CGS, CGM, FG, Income statement DeeZees makes evening dresses. The following information was gathered from the company records for the year, the first year of company operations. Work in Process Inventory at the end of the year was $15,750.

Direct material purchased on account	$ 555,000
Direct material issued to production	447,000
Direct labor payroll accrued	322,500
Indirect labor payroll accrued	93,000
Prepaid factory insurance expired	3,000
Factory utilities paid	21,450
Depreciation on factory equipment recorded	32,550
Factory rent paid	126,000
Sales (all on account)	1,431,000

The company's gross profit rate for the year was 35 percent.

 a. Compute the cost of goods sold for the year.
 b. What was the total cost of goods manufactured for the year?
 c. What is Finished Goods Inventory at December 31?
 d. If net income was $125,000, what were total selling and administrative expenses for the year?
 e. Prepare t-accounts for Work in Process Inventory, Finished Goods Inventory, and Cost of Goods Sold.

LO2-4, 6, 7 P2-60. CGM Weatherguard manufactures mailboxes. The following data represent transactions and balances for December, the company's first month of operations.

Purchased direct material on account	$248,000
Issued direct material to production	186,000
Direct labor (December)	134,000
Paid factory rent	3,600
Factory utilities	16,200
Recorded factory equipment depreciation	15,800
Paid supervisor salary	6,400
Ending work in process inventory (6,000 units)	35,000
Ending finished goods inventory (3,000 units)	?
Sales on account ($24 per unit)	648,000

 a. How many units were sold in December? How many units were completed in December?
 b. What was the total cost of goods manufactured in December?
 c. What was the per-unit cost of goods manufactured in December?
 d. Prepare t-accounts for Work in Process Inventory, Finished Goods Inventory, and Cost of Goods Sold.
 e. Compute gross profit for December.

LO2-4, 5, 6, 7 P2-61. Cost flows; CGM; CGS For each of the following cases, compute the missing amounts.

Chapter 2 Cost Terminology and Classification

	Case 1	Case 2	Case 3
Sales	$9,300	$ (g)	$112,000
Direct material used	1,200	(h)	18,200
Direct labor	(a)	4,900	(m)
Prime cost	3,700	(i)	(n)
Conversion cost	4,800	8,200	49,300
Manufacturing overhead	(b)	(j)	17,200
Cost of goods manufactured	6,200	14,000	(o)
Beginning work in process inventory	500	900	5,600
Ending work in process inventory	(c)	1,200	4,200
Beginning finished goods inventory	(d)	1,900	7,600
Ending finished goods inventory	1,200	(k)	(p)
Cost of goods sold	(e)	12,200	72,200
Gross profit	3,500	(l)	(q)
Operating expenses	(f)	3,500	18,000
Net income	2,200	4,000	(r)

P2-62. OH allocation; writing In a manufacturing company, overhead allocations are made for three reasons: (1) to determine the full cost of a product, (2) to encourage efficient resource usage, and (3) to compare alternative courses of action for management purposes.   LO2-6

    a. Why must overhead be considered a product cost under generally accepted accounting principles?

    b. Ryan Company makes plastic dog carriers. The manufacturing process is highly automated, and the machine time needed to make any size carrier is approximately the same. Ryan's management decides to begin producing plastic lawn furniture. To do so, two additional pieces of automated equipment are acquired. Annual depreciation on the new pieces of equipment is $38,000. Should the new overhead cost be allocated over all products manufactured by Ryan? Explain.

    c. Assume that the company produces two different styles of plastic lawn furniture. Considering only the lawn furniture line, under what conditions would it be accurate to apply the cost of overhead (depreciation on the equipment) to the two lines of furniture based upon units produced?

P2-63. CGM; CGS August inventory and cost data for Petersham Company are as follows: LO2-7

Direct labor	$182,400
Direct material purchased	196,300
Direct material used	195,800
Selling and administrative expenses	171,200
Factory overhead	205,700

	August 1	August 31
Direct material	$12,300	$?
Work in process	25,900	33,300
Finished goods	62,700	55,500

    a. Compute the inventory value for direct materials at August 31.
    b. Compute total product costs for August.
    c. Prepare a schedule of cost of goods manufactured for August.
    d. Compute cost of goods sold for August.
    e. Prepare an income statement for August. Assume that Petersham's income tax rate is 40 percent. Sales for August were $985,000.

P2-64. CGM; CGS Flex-Em began business in July. The firm makes an exercise machine for home and gym use. Following are data taken from the firm's accounting records that pertain to its first month of operations.   LO2-7

Direct material purchased on account	$ 900,000
Direct material issued to production	377,000
Direct labor payroll accrued	126,800
Indirect labor payroll paid	40,600
Factory insurance expired	6,000
Factory utilities paid	17,800
Factory depreciation recorded	230,300
Ending work in process inventory	51,000
Ending finished goods inventory (30 units)	97,500
Sales on account ($5,200 per unit)	1,040,000

a. How many units did the company sell in July?
b. Prepare a schedule of cost of goods manufactured for July.
c. How many units were completed in July?
d. What was the per-unit cost of goods manufactured for the month?
e. What was the cost of goods sold in the first month of operations?
f. What was the gross margin for July?

LO2-3, 4, 5, 6, 7

P2-65. Product and period costs; CGM; CGS On August 1, Sietens Corporation had the following account balances:

Raw Material Inventory (both direct and indirect)	$ 72,000
Work in Process Inventory	108,000
Finished Goods Inventory	24,000

During August, the following transactions took place:
1. Raw material was purchased on account, $570,000.
2. Direct material ($121,200) and indirect material ($15,000) were issued to production.
3. Factory payroll consisted of $180,000 for direct labor employees and $42,000 for indirect labor employees.
4. Office salaries totaled $144,600 for the month.
5. Utilities of $40,200 were accrued; 70 percent of the utilities cost is for the factory.
6. Depreciation of $60,000 was recorded on plant assets; 80 percent of the depreciation is related to factory machinery and equipment.
7. Rent of $66,000 was paid on the building. The factory occupies 60 percent of the building.
8. At the end of August, the Work in Process Inventory balance was $49,800.
9. At the end of August, the balance in Finished Goods Inventory was $53,400.

Sietens Corporation uses an actual cost system and debits actual overhead costs incurred to Work in Process Inventory.

a. Determine the total amount of product cost (cost of goods manufactured) and period cost incurred during August.
b. Compute the cost of goods sold for August.

LO2-4, 6, 7

P2-66. Missing data Grand Rapids Industrial suffered major losses in a fire on June 18. In addition to destroying several buildings, the blaze destroyed the company's Work in Process Inventory for an entire product line. Fortunately, the company was insured; however, it needs to substantiate the amount of the claim. To this end, the company has gathered the following information that pertains to production and sales of the affected product line:

1. The company's sales for the first 18 days of June amounted to $230,000. Normally, this product line generates a gross profit equal to 40 percent of sales.
2. Finished Goods Inventory was $29,000 on June 1 and $42,500 on June 18.
3. On June 1, Work in Process Inventory was $48,000.
4. During the first 18 days of June, the company incurred the following costs:

Direct material used	$76,000
Direct labor	44,000
Manufacturing overhead	42,000

Chapter 2 Cost Terminology and Classification

a. Determine the value of Work in Process Inventory that was destroyed by the fire, assuming Grand Rapids Industrial uses an actual cost system.
b. What other information might the insurance company require? How would management determine or estimate this information?

Review Solutions

Review 2-1

1.

Raw Material	Cost Object — Baseball	Cost Object — Production Facility
Cork	Direct	Direct
Glue	Indirect	Direct
Rubber	Direct	Direct
Layering yarn	Direct	Direct
Thread	Indirect	Direct
Leather	Direct	Direct
Maintenance supplies	Indirect	Direct
Ink for logo	Indirect	Direct

2. If the cost object is the baseball, the company is making a decision that requires knowledge of its cost, such as the following. What are the component costs of the baseball? Have the costs changed from the prior period requiring management attention? How does the production cost compare to the cost to outsource production of a baseball? What price should we charge for the baseball?

    If the cost object is the production facility, the company is making a decision that requires knowledge of the facility cost such as the following. How do the costs of this facility compare to other facilities owned by the company? How have facility costs changed from the prior period? Is the facility profitable? What is the impact on the company if the facility were to close?

Review 2-2

a. 1. Total cost: $45,000 ($5,000 + (100 × $400)); Cost per project: $450 ($45,000 ÷ 100)
   2. Total cost: $125,000 ($5,000 + (300 × $400)); Cost per project: $417 ($125,000 ÷ 300)
   3. Total cost: $205,000 ($5,000 + (500 × $400)); Cost per project: $410 ($205,000 ÷ 500)

b. Total cost plus margin of $160,000 ($125,000 + $35,000) ÷ 300 projects = $533 fee per project

c. Total costs: $145,000 ($5,000 + (350 × $400))
   Total margin: ($533 × 350) − $145,000 = $41,550

d. The company would be better off having fewer fixed costs if they are worried about volatility in the number of customers and thus the number of jobs. A lower number of jobs means that there are less jobs to spread over the fixed costs. This is evident in part *a* in that the average cost per job is greater at lower volumes. With variable costs, the costs are not incurred unless the jobs materialize. Thus, costs are automatically cut back when volume is lower. The fixed cost item is the equipment rental. It may be possible to negotiate the contract so that the equipment is used for a partial month and rented per day. This means that jobs are scheduled around a reduced work period. Alternatively, perhaps less equipment is rented at a fixed rate per month. Extra equipment is rented on a case-by-case basis when there are capacity issues that can't be resolved through scheduling.

Review 2-3

a. Expired costs $28,000, equal to depreciation of $13,125 (($800,000 − $50,000)/10 × 25% × 560/800) plus property taxes of $14,875 ($85,000/4 × 560/800).

b. Cost of goods sold on the income statement of $28,000 and finished goods inventory on the balance sheet of $12,000 ((($800,000 − $50,000)/10 × 25%) + $85,000/4) − $28,000).
   Prepaid taxes of $63,750, Property Plant and Equipment of $800,000, and Accumulated depreciation of $18,750 on the balance sheet.

c. For internal managerial purposes, the shipping costs may be included as part of the total cost of the product, even though for financial accounting purposes, such costs are classified as period costs. This information about shipping costs would be important to the pricing of the product, if for example, the selling price was determined through a markup on cost. An analysis of product costs that includes

© Cambridge Business Publishers

distribution costs may prompt management to initiate a product design change with a goal of reducing distribution costs.

Review 2-4

a.

		Direct Material, Direct Labor, or Overhead
Material Costs:		
Leather	$1,000,000	Direct Material
Thread	50,000	Overhead
Nylon	300,000	Direct Material
Ink for logo	1,000	Overhead
Foam	200,000	Direct Material
Rubber	400,000	Direct Material
Glue	5,000	Overhead
Labor Costs:		
Sewing machine operators	375,000	Direct Labor
Quality control supervisor	55,000	Overhead
Factory maintenance worker	10,000	Overhead
Assembly workers	80,000	Direct Labor

b. 1. Salary cost incurred to research the system would be expensed as a period cost. The cost to purchase the system and make it ready for use would be capitalized and depreciated over the useful life of the system. Periodic depreciation would be considered overhead. The salary costs to oversee the artificial intelligence processes during production would be classified as overhead as well as maintenance costs of the system.

2. Nonmonetary considerations include the potential for higher quality output. Defects that may not have been spotted before or only after products were completed will be identified as the defects happen. Identifying issues as they happen reduces spoilage and rework costs because the issue is identified on the spot and can be remedied without affecting a multitude of products. In addition, producing a higher quality product increases the potential for satisfied customers and repeat sales.

Review 2-5

1.

	High, Low, or Moderate Degree of Conversion	Inventory Account(s) Likely Used
Ford Motor Company	High	Raw Materials, Work in Process, Finished Goods
U.S. Bancorp	High	n/a
Target Corporation	Low	Merchandise Inventory

2. Of the three firms, cost accountants could provide the most benefit to Ford Motor Company and U.S. Bankcorp because of the high level of conversion activities. For a manufacturer, processes must be in place to track costs (direct materials, labor, and overhead) through the production process. Unlike a merchandiser that purchases an item for resale and the price of the product is primarily derived from an invoice, the cost of a product of a manufacturer is a total of the materials and conversion costs. In a similar way, the cost of a service requires tracking of costs and an allocation of those costs to a particular service. Understanding costs by product or by service provides necessary information for managerial decision making.

Review 2-6

a. $131,000 [$91,000 + $302,000 − $44,000 − $98,000 − ($1.60 × 75,000)]

b.

Work in Process	
44,000	302,000
98,000	
120,000	
131,000	
91,000	

c. $302,000/75,000 = $4.03

d. $330,000 ($302,000 + $28,000)

e. The issue in using a per-unit cost to estimate future costs is that the per-unit cost is based on a different level of activity. The average cost per unit includes fixed costs, which were calculated based on 75,000 units of production. If the average cost for 75,000 units is applied to 80,000 units, the estimate will be too high.

Review 2-7

a.

Schedule of Cost of Goods Manufactured
For the Month Ended September 30

Beginning WIP inventory		$ 220,000
Beginning RM inventory	$102,000	
Raw material purchased	814,000	
Raw material available	$916,000	
Ending RM inventory	(88,000)	
Raw material used	828,000	
Indirect material used ($828,000 − $568,000)	(260,000)	
Direct material used		568,000
Direct labor ($765,000 × 0.65)		497,250
Overhead:		
Various	$900,000	
Indirect material (from above)	260,000	
Indirect labor ($765,000 × 0.35)	267,750	1,427,750
Total cost to account for		$2,713,000
Ending WIP inventory		(296,000)
Cost of goods manufactured		$2,417,000

b.

Schedule of Cost of Goods Sold
For the Month Ended September 30

Beginning FG inventory	$ 388,000
Cost of goods manufactured	2,417,000
Goods available for sale	$2,805,000
Ending FG inventory	(425,000)
Cost of goods sold	$2,380,000

c. In general, the purchase of new equipment will increase depreciation expense (allocated as overhead in products costs). However, the amount of direct materials (product cost) should decrease with the efficiencies gained, and a drop in utilities costs would decrease overhead (product cost). The cost accountant would be able to estimate the amount of the potential savings over the life of the equipment.

Data Visualization Solutions

(See page 2-8.)

a. 2   *b.* 5   *c.* 1   *d.* 3   *e.* 4

Chapter 3
Cost Behavior and Estimation

Road Map

LO	Learning Objective | Topics	Page	eLecture	Demo	Review	Assignments
3-1	**How is a linear total cost estimating equation used to estimate costs?** Cost Behavior Patterns :: Variable Costs :: Fixed Costs :: Mixed Costs :: Step Costs :: Total Cost Estimating Equation :: Factors Affecting Cost Behavior	3-2	e3–1	D3-1	Rev 3-1	MC3-11, MC3-12, E3-22, E3-23, E3-24, E3-25, E3-26, E3-27, E3-28, E3-29, E3-33, P3-47
3-2	**How is a scatter diagram used to analyze cost behavior?** Scatter Diagram :: Scatter Plot :: Outliers :: Representative Observations	3-5	e3–2	D3-2	Rev 3-2	MC3-13, E3-24, E3-25, E3-30, E3-31, E3-34, P3-47, DA3-1, DA3-3, DA3-5
3-3	**How is the high-low method used in analyzing mixed costs?** High-Low Method of Cost Estimation :: Two Representative Data Points :: Cost Prediction	3-8	e3–3	D3-3A D3-3B	Rev 3-3	MC3-14, E3-30, E3-31, E3-32, E3-33, E3-35, E3-36, E3-37, E3-38, P3-47, P3-49, DA3-3, DA3-5
3-4	**How is least squares regression used in analyzing mixed costs?** Least Squares Regression Analysis :: Simple Regression Line :: Coefficients :: Coefficient of Determination :: Multiple Regression	3-9	e3–4	D3-4A D3-4B D3-4C	Rev 3-4	MC3-15, MC3-16, E3-39, E3-40, P3-47, P3-48, P3-49, P3-50, DA3-1, DA3-2, DA3-3, DA3-4
3-5	**How is the learning curve used to estimate nonlinear costs?** Learning Curve :: Incremental Unit Time Learning Curve :: Cumulative Average Time Learning Curve	3-14	e3–5	D3-5A D3-5B	Rev 3-5	MC3-17, MC3-18, E3-41, E3-42, E3-43, P3-51, P3-52, DA3-6
3-6	**What are problems encountered in cost estimation?** Technology :: Price Changes :: Matching Activity and Cost :: Identifying Cost Drivers :: Data Integrity	3-16	e3–6	D3-6	Rev 3-6	MC3-19, E3-44, E3-45, P3-47, P3-53, P3-58
3-7	**What is an alternative classification for cost drivers?** Manufacturing Cost Hierarchy:: Unit-Level Activity :: Batch-Level Activity :: Product/Process-Level Activity :: Organizational/Facility-Level Activity :: Customer Cost Hierarchy	3-19	e3–7	D3-7	Rev 3-7	MC3-20, MC3-21, E3-46, P3-54, P3-55, P3-56, P3-57, P3-58

INTRODUCTION

This chapter expands on the concept of *cost behavior* introduced in Chapter 2, which refers to the relationship between a given cost item and the quantity of its related cost driver. Cost behavior, therefore, explains how the total amount for various costs responds to changes in activity volume. Understanding cost behavior is essential for *estimating* future costs. In this chapter we examine several typical cost behavior patterns and methods for developing cost equations that are useful for predicting future costs.

COST BEHAVIOR ANALYSIS

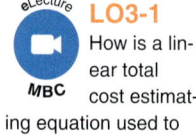

LO3-1 How is a linear total cost estimating equation used to estimate costs?

As discussed in Chapter 2, cost behavior can be classified into four categories: variable costs, fixed costs, mixed costs, and step costs. We expand our discussion of these cost behaviors by examining graphical presentations as shown in **Exhibit 3.1**. Observe that total cost is measured on the vertical axis, and total activity is measured on the horizontal axis. Consider pizza franchise **Domino's**. Domino's specializes in quick delivery and online order tracking. Customers can pick from signature pies like ExtravaganZZa, or they can create their own and choose the type of dough, sauce, and toppings. Domino's has been the global pizza chain leader in revenue since 2017. To manage its growth, the company must understand the behavior underlying its cost structure. In the discussion that follows, we assume that the activity that drives cost is sales volume.

Exhibit 3.1 — Cost Behavior Patterns

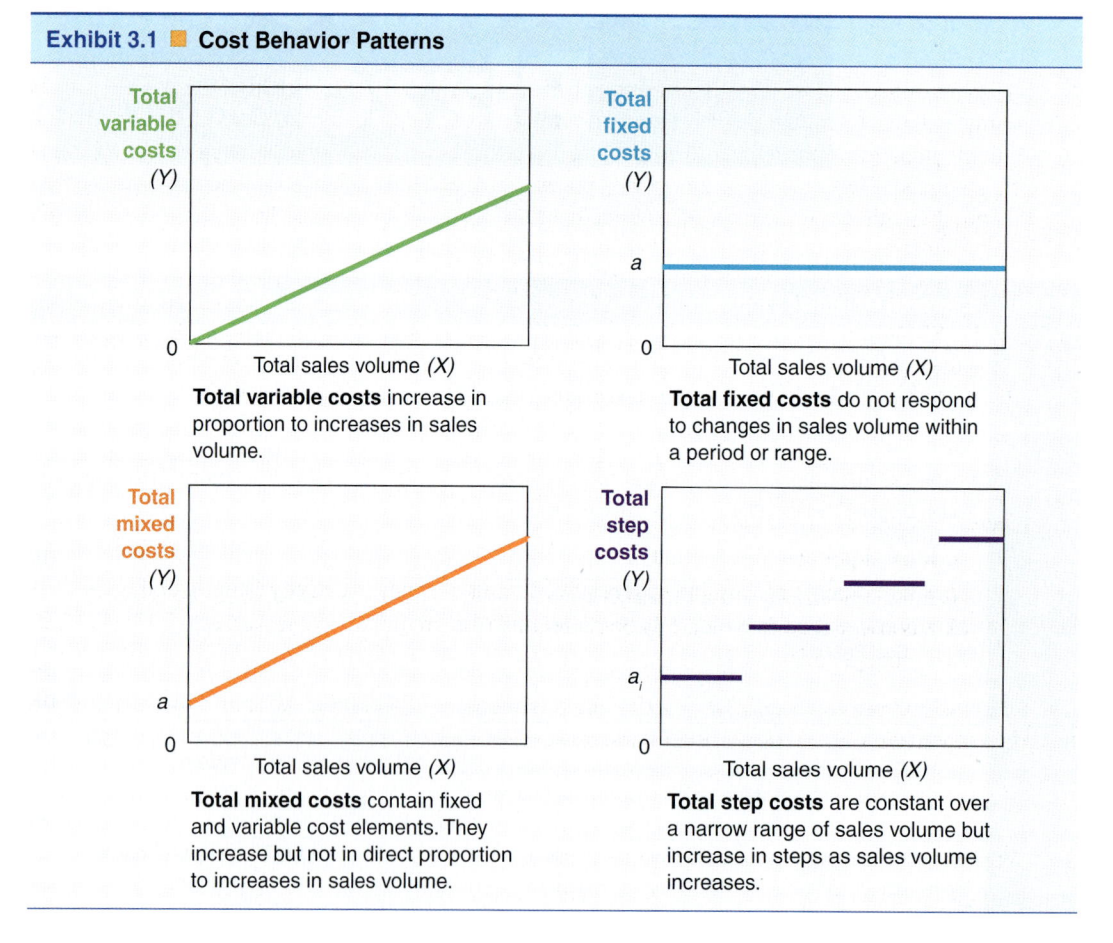

Total variable costs (Y) vs Total sales volume (X)
Total variable costs increase in proportion to increases in sales volume.

Total fixed costs (Y) vs Total sales volume (X)
Total fixed costs do not respond to changes in sales volume within a period or range.

Total mixed costs (Y) vs Total sales volume (X)
Total mixed costs contain fixed and variable cost elements. They increase but not in direct proportion to increases in sales volume.

Total step costs (Y) vs Total sales volume (X)
Total step costs are constant over a narrow range of sales volume but increase in steps as sales volume increases.

- *Variable costs* change in total in direct proportion to changes in the number of units sold. Total variable cost increases as sales volume increases, equaling zero dollars when sales volume is zero and increasing at a constant amount per unit of sales. Variable cost per unit can be determined by

Chapter 3 Cost Behavior and Estimation

dividing total costs by activity at two activity levels. The quotients of variable costs will be the same at both levels of activity. The higher the variable cost per unit, the steeper the slope (incline) of the line representing total cost. With the number of pizzas served as the cost driver for Domino's locations, the cost of cheese is an example of a variable cost.

- *Fixed costs*, in total, are easily identified. They are the same in total at each activity level within a relevant range. Hence, a line representing total fixed costs is flat with a slope of zero. Fixed costs per unit, however, change inversely with changes in activity. With the number of Domino's pizzas sold as the cost driver, annual depreciation, property taxes, and property insurance are examples of fixed costs. Fixed costs do not respond to short-run changes in cost drivers.
- *Mixed costs* (sometimes called *semivariable costs*) contain a fixed and a variable cost element. Total mixed costs are positive (like fixed costs) when sales volume is zero, and they increase in a linear fashion (like total variable costs) as sales volume increases. Mixed costs per unit will be lower at the higher activity level. This is because the fixed costs are spread over a larger number of units. With the number of pizzas sold as the cost driver for Domino's, the cost of electric power is an example of a mixed cost. Some electricity is required to provide basic lighting (fixed cost), while an increasing amount of electricity is required to prepare food as the number of pizzas served increases (variable cost).
- *Step costs* are constant within a narrow range of sales volume but shift to a higher level when sales volume exceeds the range. Total step costs increase in a steplike fashion as sales volume increases. With the number of pizzas served as the cost driver for Domino's, employee wages is an example of a step cost. Up to a certain number of pizzas, only a small staff needs to be on duty. Beyond that number, additional employees are needed for quality service and so forth.

Linear Total Cost Estimating Equation

To simplify estimation of costs, accountants typically assume that costs are linear rather than curvilinear. Because of this assumption, the general formula for a straight line can be used to describe any type of cost within a relevant range of activity. The straight-line formula is as follows.

$$Y = a + bX$$

where Y = total cost (dependent variable),
a = fixed portion of total cost,
b = unit change of variable cost relative to unit changes in activity (slope), and
X = activity base to which Y is being related (the predictor, cost driver, or independent variable).

The relationship between total cost (Y-axis) and total activity (X-axis) for the four cost behavior patterns is mathematically expressed as follows.

Variable cost	$Y = \$0.00 + bX$	If a cost is entirely variable, the *a* value in the formula is zero.
Fixed cost	$Y = a + \$0.00X$	If the cost is entirely fixed, the *b* value in the formula is zero
Mixed cost	$Y = a + bX$.	If the cost is mixed, the formula includes both the variable and fixed cost components: The resulting cost function is illustrated in **Exhibit 3.2**.
Step cost	$Y = a_i$	If the cost is step, the step cost within a specific range of activity is identified with the subscript *i*: $Y = a_i$

Exhibit 3.2 ■ Total Cost Behavior

Total costs (Y)

Total costs
$Y = a + bX$
where slope $b = \Delta Y/\Delta X$

Variable costs*

a

Fixed costs

0

Total activity (X)*

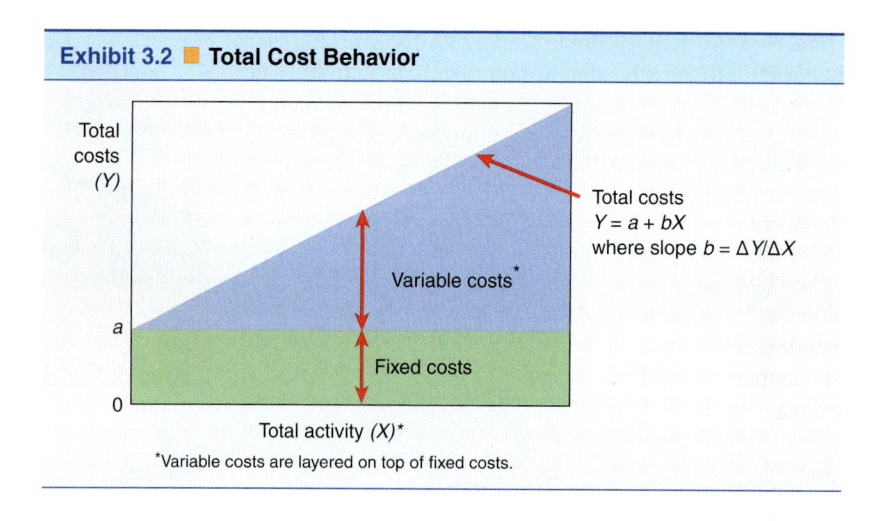

*Variable costs are layered on top of fixed costs.

DEMO 3-1 LO3-1 Predicting Costs Using the Cost Estimating Equation

In situations where the variable, fixed, and mixed costs and the related cost functions can be determined, a total cost equation can be useful in predicting future costs for various activity levels. For example, assume that **Domino's** fixed costs include rent and depreciation on equipment, totaling $3,000 per month. Also assume that the variable cost per pizza is $3.25.

◆ **What is the total cost estimating equation for Domino's?**

The total cost equation for Domino's is as follows.

$$Y = \$3,000 + \$3.25 \text{ (number of pizzas)}$$

◆ **What are total estimated costs for July if the store expects to sell 1,600 pizzas?**

The estimated cost for July is $8,200, calculated as follows.

$$Y = \$3,000 + \$3.25 \,(1,600) = \$8,200$$

Additional Cost Behavior Patterns Although we have considered the most frequently used cost behavior patterns, remember that there are numerous ways that costs can respond to changes in activity. It is important to think through each situation and then select a behavior pattern that seems logical and fits the known facts.

Factors Affecting Cost Behavior Patterns

The four cost behavior patterns presented are based on the fundamental assumption that a unit of final output is the primary cost driver. The implications of this assumption are examined later in this chapter.

Time Period Another important assumption is that the time period is too short to incorporate longer-term structural changes such as the scale of operations. Although this assumption is useful for short-range planning, for the purpose of developing plans for extended time periods, it is more appropriate to consider possible variations in the size and scope of operations. When this is done, many costs otherwise classified as fixed are better classified as variable.

Even the cost of depreciable assets can be viewed as variable if the time period is long enough. Assuming that the number of pizzas served is the cost driver, for a single month straight-line depreciation on all Domino's locations in the world is a fixed cost. Over several years, if sales are strong, a strategic decision will be made to open additional restaurants. If sales are weak, strategic decisions will likely be made to close some restaurants. Hence, over a multiple-year period, the number of restaurants varies with sales volume, making depreciation appear as a variable cost with sales revenue as the cost driver.

Cost Type Particular care needs to be taken with the vertical axis. So far, all graphs have placed *total costs* on the vertical axis. However, miscommunication is likely if one party is thinking in terms of total costs while the other is thinking in terms of variable or average costs. As mentioned in the previous chapter, applying an average cost from one period to another period with a different volume will result in inaccurate cost estimations.

> **Estimating Costs Using a Linear Total Cost Estimating Equation**   **LO3-1**   **REVIEW 3-1**
>
> The total monthly operating costs for a financial consulting firm is estimated to be $45,000 in fixed costs plus an additional $1,800 in variable costs per client. These estimates are valid as long as the number of clients does not exceed 50 clients per month.
> 1. Determine the linear total cost estimating equation for the consulting firm.
> 2. Determine the total monthly cost and the average cost per client if the firm is expecting the following number of clients for the month:
>   a. 25 clients   b. 30 clients   c. 36 clients
> 3. Determine the number of clients at which the average cost per client is $2,925.
> 4. **Critical Thinking:** Under what condition would the number of clients not be an accurate predictor of total costs for the consulting firm?
>
> More practice: MC3-12, E3-26, E3-29
> Solution on p. 3-43.

COST ESTIMATION

Cost estimation, the determination of the relationship between activity and cost, is an important part of cost management. In this section, we estimate the relationship between total activity and total costs.

To properly estimate the relationship between activity and cost, we must be familiar with basic cost behavior patterns and cost-estimating techniques. Costs known to have a variable or a fixed pattern are readily estimated by interviews or by analyzing available records. Sales commission per sales dollar, a variable cost, might be determined to be 15 percent of sales. In a similar manner, annual property taxes might be determined by consulting tax documents. Mixed (semivariable) costs, which contain fixed and variable cost elements, are more difficult to estimate. Three methods of estimating fixed and variable cost components include the following.

Scatter Diagrams LO3-2	High-Low Method LO3-3	Least Squares Regression LO3-4

Scatter Diagrams

One approach is to first graph historical activity and cost data in order to determine whether visually costs can be approximated by a straight line. A **scatter diagram** (also called a **scatter plot**) is a graph of past activity and cost data, with individual observations represented by dots. Plotting historical cost data on a scatter diagram is a useful approach to cost estimation, especially when used in conjunction with other cost-estimating techniques. A scatter diagram helps in selecting high and low activity levels representative of normal operating conditions. The periods of highest or lowest activity may not be *representative* because of the cost of overtime, the use of less efficient equipment, strikes, and so forth. If the goal is to develop an equation to predict costs under normal operating conditions, then the equation should be based on observations of normal operating conditions. Occasionally, operations occur at a level outside the relevant range (a special rush order could require excess labor or machine time), or cost distortions occur within the relevant range (a leak in a water pipe could go unnoticed for a period of time). Such nonrepresentative or abnormal observations are called **outliers** and should be disregarded when analyzing a mixed cost. A scatter diagram is also useful in determining whether costs can be reasonably approximated by a straight line.

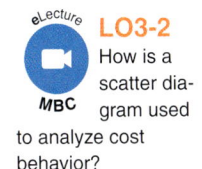

LO3-2 How is a scatter diagram used to analyze cost behavior?

> **Using a Scatter Diagram to Analyze Cost Behavior and Identify Outliers**   **LO3-2**   **DEMO 3-2**

Tri-State Industrial would like to calculate its predetermined overhead utility rate to use in the following calendar year. Tri-State Industrial gathered information for machine hours and utility costs for the past twelve months as shown in **Exhibit 3.3**. During the current year, the company's normal operating range of activity was between 4,000 and 10,000 machine hours per month.

Exhibit 3.3 ■ Machine Hours and Utility Cost Information for Tri-State Industrial

	A	B	C
1	Month	Machine Hours	Utility Cost
2	January	7,260	$2,960
3	February	8,850	3,410
4	March	4,800	1,920
5	April	9,000	3,500
6	May	11,000	3,050
7	June	4,900	1,860
8	July	4,600	2,180
9	August	8,900	3,470
10	September	5,900	2,480
11	October	5,500	2,310
12	November	5,200	2,120
13	December	6,500	3,300

◆ **How is a scatter diagram prepared and used to analyze cost data and identify outliers for Tri-State Industrial?**

By plotting the 12 months of data points in Excel, we can assess visually whether machine hours is a predictor of utility costs and whether any data points represent outliers. After entering the data in Excel, we can highlight the data and select Insert and the Scatter chart option.

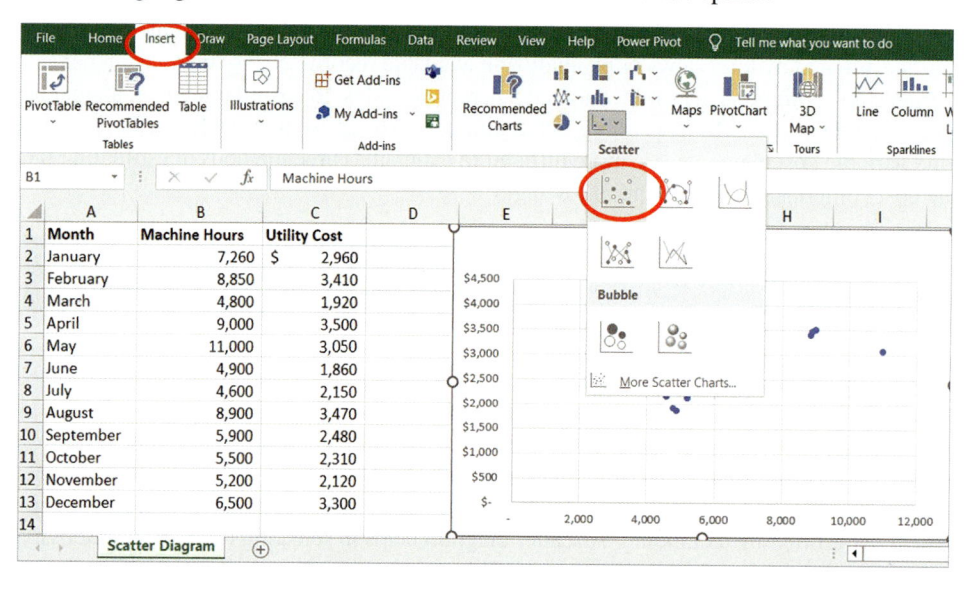

The resulting scatter diagram is shown below.

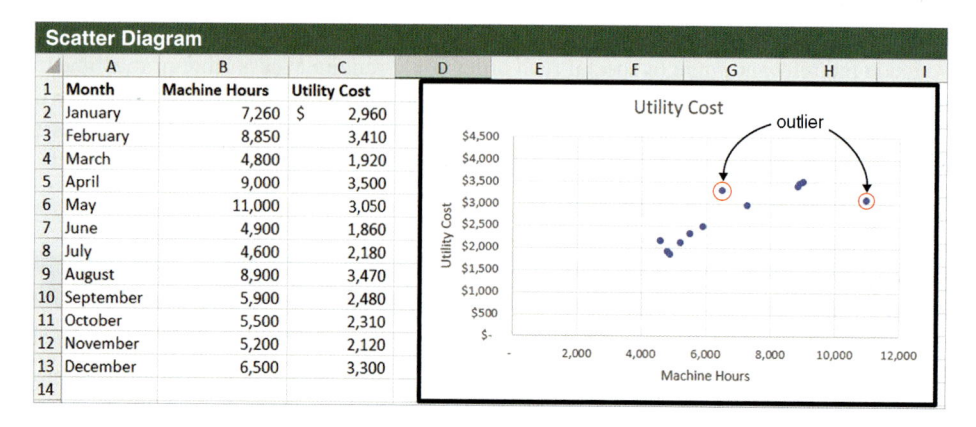

© Cambridge Business Publishers

Chapter 3 Cost Behavior and Estimation

May activity is viewed as an outlier and should *not* be used in the analysis of utility cost. This point does not appear to fit the pattern of the observations in the scatter plot. In addition, the amount of utility cost in December also appears to be an outlier and should *not* be used in the analysis of utility cost. Generally, machine hours appear to be a predictor of utility costs as the data points rise as machine hours increase indicated by data points that move up and to the right, approximating a straight-line.

Scatter diagrams are sometimes used alone as a basis of cost estimation. This requires the use of professional judgment to draw a representative straight line through the plot of historical data. Typically, the analyst tries to ensure that an equal number of observations are on either side of the line while minimizing the total vertical differences between the line and actual cost observations at each value of the independent variable. Once a line is drawn, cost estimates at any representative volume are made by studying the line. Where the line crosses the *Y*-axis represents total fixed costs. Variable cost per unit is calculated by solving the cost-estimating equation using total cost and activity from one of the points closest to the line. Alternatively, an equation for the line may be developed by applying the high-low method to any two points on the line as discussed in the next section.

Data Visualization

For each of the following situations, select the most appropriate cost behavior pattern (as shown in the illustrations following this problem), where the lines represent the cost behavior pattern, the vertical axis represents costs, the horizontal axis represents total volume, and the dots represent actual costs.

____ a. A realistic linear approximation of actual costs
____ b. A linear cost estimation appearing to include an outlier
____ c. Total variable costs properly used to estimate step costs
____ d. A linear cost estimation valid only within the relevant range

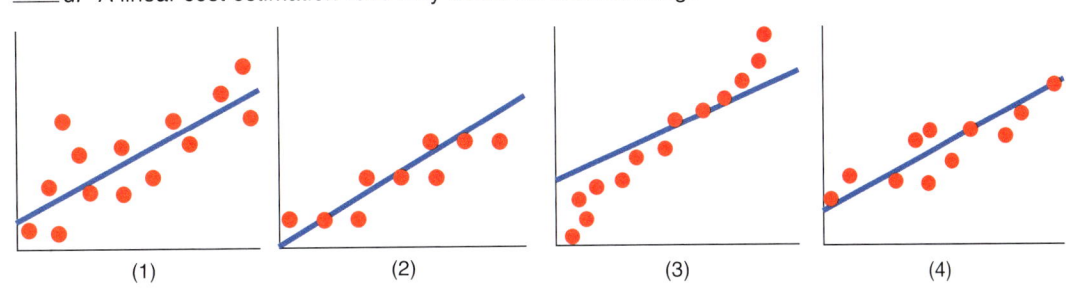

(1) (2) (3) (4)

Solution on p. 3-45.

REVIEW 3-2 — Preparing a Scatter Diagram — LO3-2

Appalachia Inc. has compiled the following data to analyze maintenance costs.

Appalachia Inc. Maintenance Costs

Month	Labor Hours	Maintenance Cost
January	730	$15,100
February	600	14,650
March	550	14,100
April	630	15,400
May	700	15,400
June	600	14,900
July	725	15,608
August	750	16,300
September	800	16,480
October	860	16,900

a. Prepare a scatter diagram to analyze the cost data and identify any outliers. The relevant range of activity is 500 to 1,000 labor hours.
b. **Critical Thinking:** Is the identification of outliers a clear-cut process? Why or why not?

More practice: MC3-13, E3-34
Solution on p. 3-43.

LO3-3 How is the high-low method used in analyzing mixed costs?

High-Low Cost Estimation

The most straightforward approach to determining the variable and fixed elements of mixed costs is to use the **high-low method of cost estimation**. This method utilizes data from two time periods, a *representative* high-activity period and a *representative* low-activity period, to estimate fixed and variable costs. This means that the outliers identified in a scatter diagram should be ignored in this analysis. Assuming identical fixed costs in both periods, any difference in total costs between these two periods is due entirely to variable costs.

After the outliers are excluded, changes in activity and cost are determined by subtracting low values from high values. These changes are used to calculate the b (variable unit cost) value in the $Y = a + bX$ formula as follows.

$$b = \frac{\text{Cost at High Activity Level} - \text{Cost at Low Activity Level}}{\text{High Activity Level} - \text{Low Activity Level}}$$

$$b = \frac{\text{Change in Total Cost}}{\text{Change in Activity Level}}$$

The b value is the unit variable cost per measure of activity. This value is multiplied by the activity level to determine the total variable cost contained in the total cost at either the high or the low level of activity. The fixed portion of a mixed cost is found by subtracting total variable cost from total cost.

$$\text{Fixed costs} = \text{Total costs} - \text{Total Variable costs}$$

As the activity level changes, the change in total mixed cost equals the change in activity multiplied by the unit variable cost. By definition, the fixed cost element does not fluctuate with changes in activity.

DEMO 3-3A   LO3-3   Estimating a Cost Equation Using the High-Low Method

◆ **Referring to the Tri-State Industrial data in Exhibit 3.3, what is an estimating cost equation for utility costs using the high-low method?**

The high-low method is illustrated in the following six steps.

STEP 1: Select the highest and lowest levels of activity within the relevant range (range of activity that reflects the company's normal operating range) and obtain the costs associated with those levels. These levels and costs are 9,000 and 4,600 hours, and $3,500 and $2,180, respectively. When choosing these points, the two outliers are ignored.

STEP 2: Calculate the change in cost compared to the change in activity.

	Machine Hours	Associated Total Cost
High activity........	9,000	$3,500
Low activity.........	4,600	2,180
Changes............	4,400	$1,320

STEP 3: Determine the relationship of cost change to activity change to find the variable cost element.

$$b = \$1{,}320 \div 4{,}400 \text{ MH} = \$0.30 \text{ per machine hour}$$

STEP 4: Compute total variable cost (TVC) at either level of activity.

High level of activity: TVC = $0.30(9,000) = $2,700

Low level of activity: TVC = $0.30(4,600) = $1,380

STEP 5: Subtract total variable cost from total cost at the associated level of activity to determine fixed cost.

High level of activity: a = $3,500 − $2,700 = $800

Low level of activity: a = $2,180 − $1,380 = $800

STEP 6: Substitute the fixed and variable cost values in the straight-line formula to get an equation that can be used to estimate total cost at any level of activity within the relevant range.

$$Y = \$800 + \$0.30X$$

where X = machine hours

Cost prediction, the forecasting of future costs, is a common purpose of cost estimation. Previously developed estimates of cost behavior are often the starting point in predicting future costs.

Using the High-Low Method to Predict Future Costs — LO3-3 — DEMO 3-3B

◆ Continuing the Tri-State Industrial example, what are predicted utility costs for January of the following year if machine hours are expected to be 8,000?

If machine hours are predicted to be 8,000 hours, utility costs are estimated as follows using the estimating equation developed through the high-low method.

$$Y = \$800 + \$0.30 \,(8{,}000 \text{ machine hours}) = \$3{,}200$$

Weaknesses of High-Low Method One potential weakness of the high-low method is that outliers can inadvertently be used in the calculation. Estimates of future costs calculated from a line drawn using such points will not indicate actual costs and probably are not good predictions. A second weakness of this method is that it considers only two data points. A more precise method of analyzing mixed costs is least squares regression analysis. This method is discussed in the next section.

High-low Method — LO3-3 — REVIEW 3-3

Use the data from Appalacia Inc. in Review 3-2 to answer the following questions.
a. Using the high-low method, develop the equation for predicting monthly maintenance costs using labor hours.
b. What is the predicted amount of maintenance costs for a month in which 650 labor hours are incurred?
c. **Critical Thinking:** If you are working as a management accountant and presented your findings in part *b* to management, what disclosure would you need to make regarding your analysis?

More practice: MC3-14, E3-32, E3-35, E3-36, E3-37, E3-38
Solution on p. 3-44.

Least Squares Regression

Least squares regression analysis uses a mathematical technique to fit a cost-estimating equation to observed data. **Simple regression** analysis uses one independent variable to predict the dependent variable based on the $Y = a + bX$ formula for a straight line. In **Exhibit 3.4**, actual observation values are designated as Y values. Numerous straight lines or trend lines can be drawn through the set of data observations, but most of these lines would provide a poor fit to the data. The simple regression method mathematically fits the best possible trend line, called a **regression line**, to observed data points. The method fits this regression line by minimizing the sum of the squares of the vertical deviations between the actual observation points and the regression line. Each of these differences is an estimating error. Values of *a* and *b* can be calculated manually using a set of equations developed by mathematicians[1] or by using programs such as **Microsoft** Excel.

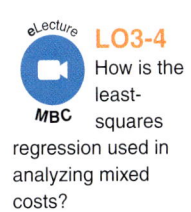

LO3-4 How is the least-squares regression used in analyzing mixed costs?

---

[1] The equations necessary to compute *b* and *a* values using the method of least squares are as follows. Note that The symbol Σ means "the summation of."

$$b = \frac{\Sigma xy - n(\bar{x})(\bar{y})}{\Sigma x^2 - n(\bar{x})^2}$$

where
$\bar{x}$ = mean of the independent variable
$\bar{y}$ = mean of the dependent variable
n = number of observations

$$a = \bar{y} - b\bar{x}$$

Exhibit 3.4 Illustration of Least Squares Regression Line

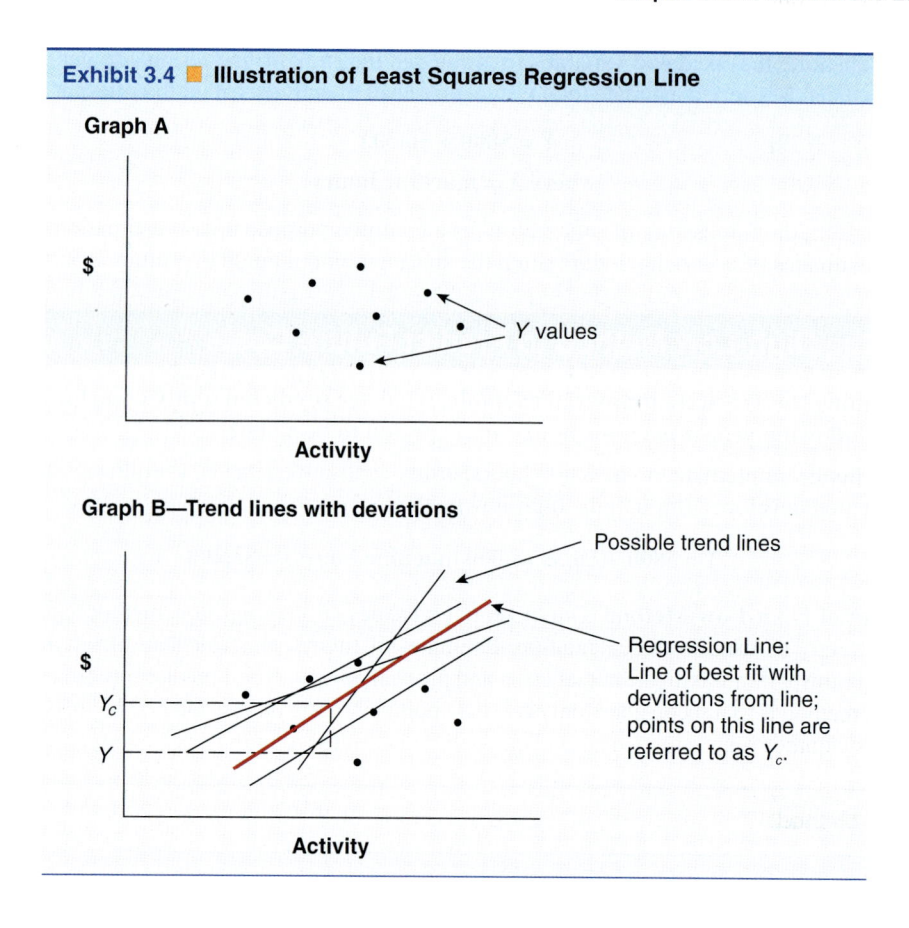

Graph A

(scatter plot of Y values vs. Activity)

Graph B—Trend lines with deviations

Possible trend lines

Regression Line: Line of best fit with deviations from line; points on this line are referred to as Y_c.

DEMO 3-4A   LO3-4   Using Regression to Estimate Cost Equation

◆ Continuing with the Tri-State Industrial example, what is the estimating cost equation using a regression analysis, excluding the outliers of May and December noted in Demo 3-2?

In Excel, we select the Data tab, Data Analysis, and Regression.

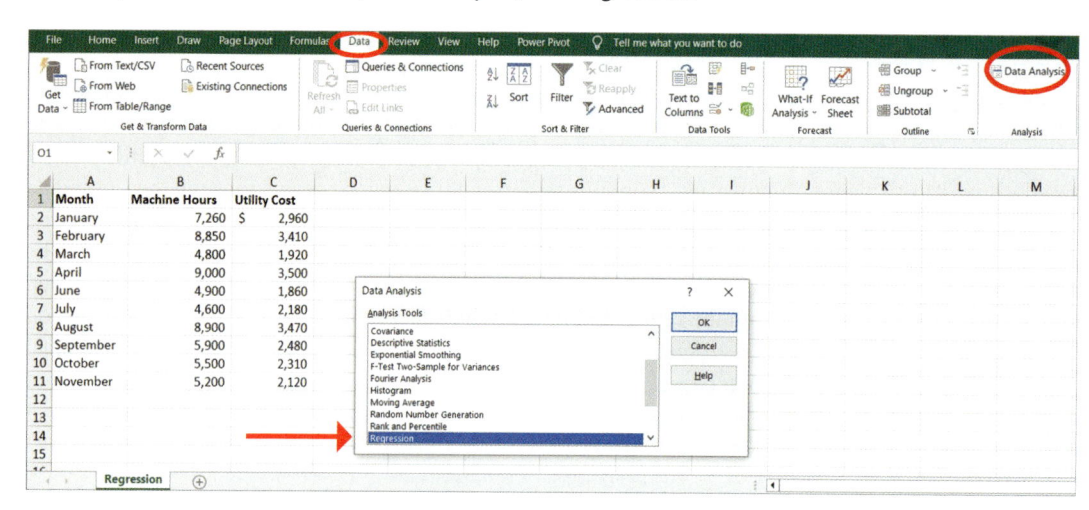

Note: Excel's regression tool can be found in the addin: Analysis Toolpak. To load the add-in, search for "regression" in the Excel Help box and click on the Analysis ToolPak add-in.

Month	Machine Hours	Utility Cost
January	7,260	$ 2,960
February	8,850	3,410
March	4,800	1,920
April	9,000	3,500
June	4,900	1,860
July	4,600	2,180
August	8,900	3,470
September	5,900	2,480
October	5,500	2,310
November	5,200	2,120

In the screen that opens, we enter the Y range (costs) and the X range (activity, which in this case, is machine hours). If you highlight the column headers, click on Labels, which will display the header names in the summary output. The default option that is checked will place the regression analysis in a new worksheet tab.

Chapter 3 Cost Behavior and Estimation

Regression Dialog Box

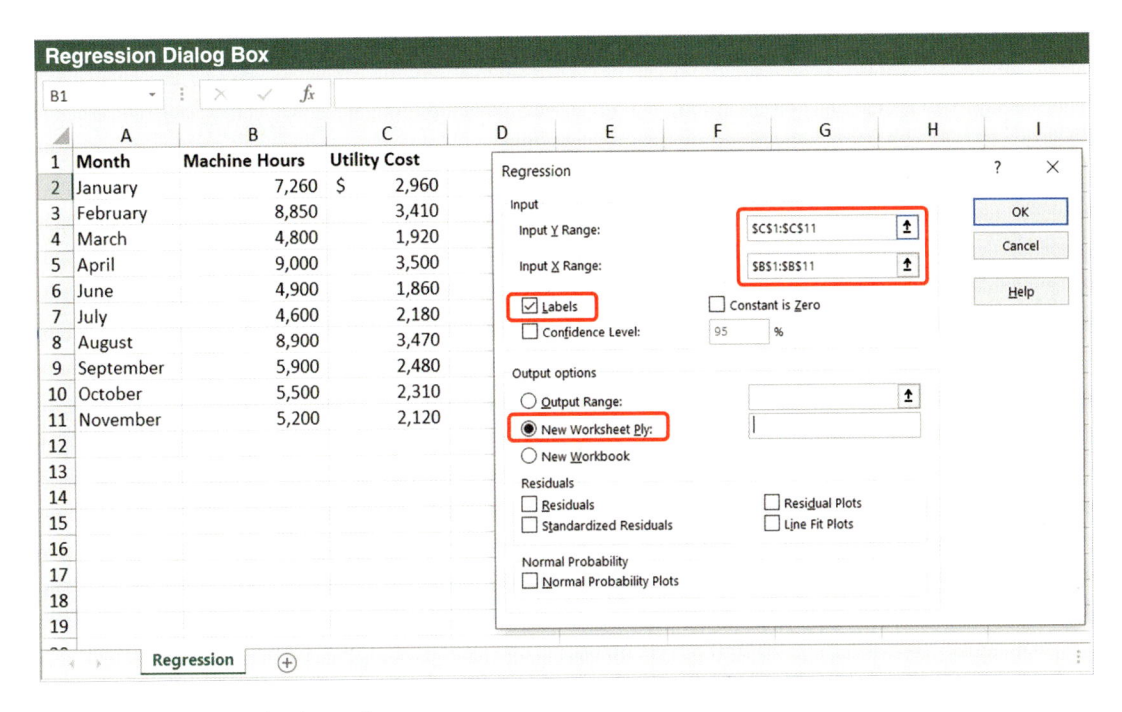

Month	Machine Hours	Utility Cost
January	7,260	$ 2,960
February	8,850	3,410
March	4,800	1,920
April	9,000	3,500
June	4,900	1,860
July	4,600	2,180
August	8,900	3,470
September	5,900	2,480
October	5,500	2,310
November	5,200	2,120

Regression dialog box settings: Input Y Range: $C$1:$C$11; Input X Range: $B$1:$B$11; Labels checked; Confidence Level: 95%; New Worksheet Ply selected.

The summary output is shown here.

Regression Summary Output

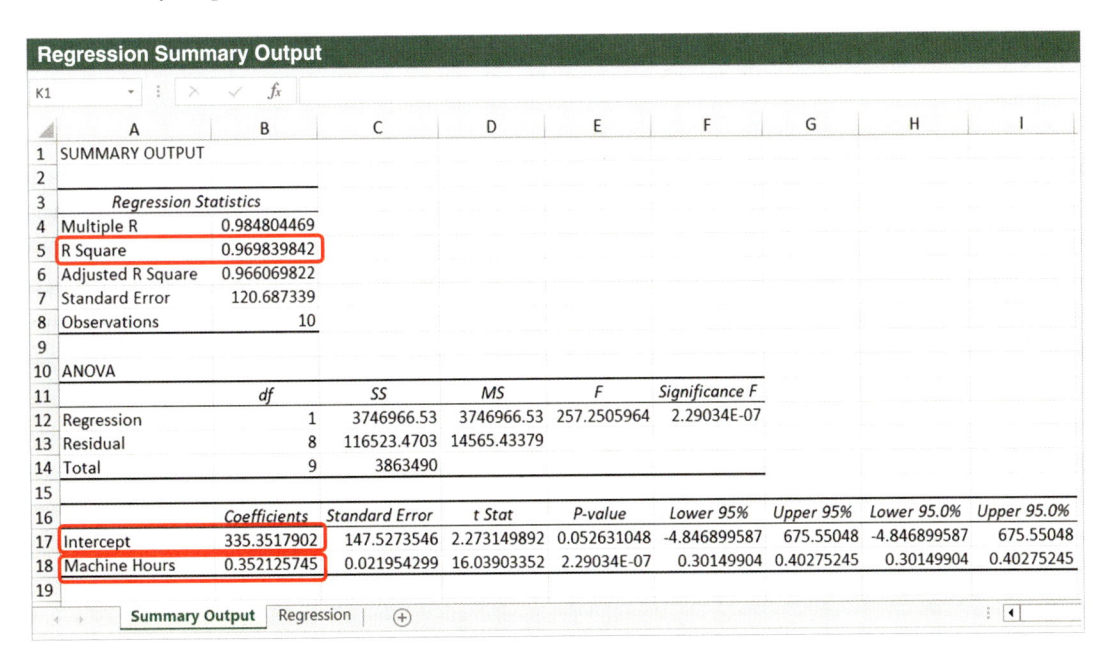

SUMMARY OUTPUT

Regression Statistics
Multiple R	0.984804469
R Square	0.969839842
Adjusted R Square	0.966069822
Standard Error	120.687339
Observations	10

ANOVA

	df	SS	MS	F	Significance F
Regression	1	3746966.53	3746966.53	257.2505964	2.29034E-07
Residual	8	116523.4703	14565.43379		
Total	9	3863490			

	Coefficients	Standard Error	t Stat	P-value	Lower 95%	Upper 95%	Lower 95.0%	Upper 95.0%
Intercept	335.3517902	147.5273546	2.273149892	0.052631048	-4.846899587	675.55048	-4.846899587	675.55048
Machine Hours	0.352125745	0.021954299	16.03903352	2.29034E-07	0.30149904	0.40275245	0.30149904	0.40275245

The least-squares equation for monthly utility costs is as follows.

$$Y = \$335.35 + 0.3521X$$

The *a* value (fixed cost labeled at intercept) and the *b* value (variable cost per machine hour) are listed as **coefficients** in the regression summary output.

Alternatively, the equation developed through simple regression can be added to the scatter chart along with the trend line. Right-click on any point in the chart, add Trendline, and then click on Display Equation on chart and Display R-squared on chart. The line drawn will be the line of best fit for the data. Because actual costs do not generally fall directly on the regression line and predicted costs naturally do, these two costs differ at their related activity levels. It is acceptable for the regression line not to pass through the majority (or even any) of the actual observation points because the line has been determined to mathematically "fit" the data.

© Cambridge Business Publishers

Formatting Trendline

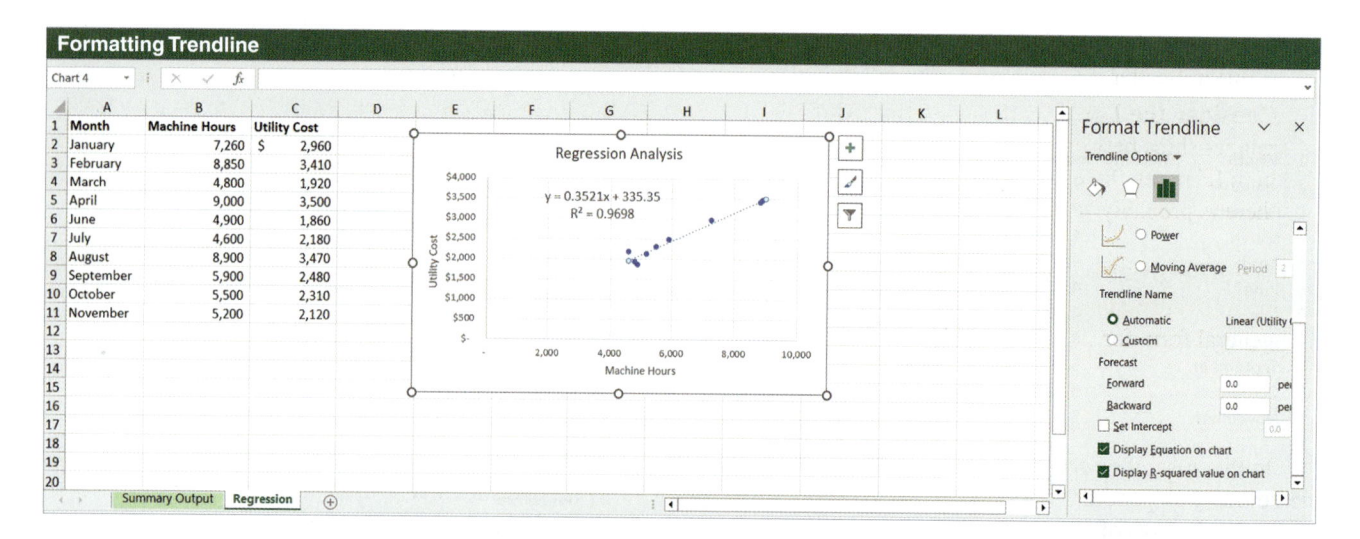

Month	Machine Hours	Utility Cost
January	7,260	$ 2,960
February	8,850	3,410
March	4,800	1,920
April	9,000	3,500
June	4,900	1,860
July	4,600	2,180
August	8,900	3,470
September	5,900	2,480
October	5,500	2,310
November	5,200	2,120

Regression Analysis: $y = 0.3521x + 335.35$, $R^2 = 0.9698$

DEMO 3-4B LO3-4 Using Regression to Predict Future Costs

- Using the estimating equation derived through the regression analysis, what are predicted utility costs for January of the following year if machine hours are expected to be 8,000?

$$Y = \$335.35 + 0.3521(8,000 \text{ machine hours}) = \$3,152.15$$

Recall that the high-low method predicted January costs of $3,200. Although this difference is small, we should consider which prediction is more reliable.

Advantage of Least-Squares Regression

Mathematicians regard least-squares regression analysis as superior to both the high-low and the scatter diagram methods. It uses all available data, rather than just two observations, and does not rely on subjective judgment in drawing a line.

In addition to the vertical axis intercept and the slope, least-squares regression calculates the coefficient of determination. The **coefficient of determination** is a measure of the percent of variation in the dependent variable (such as total utility costs) that is explained by variations in the independent variable (such as total machine hours). Statisticians often refer to the coefficient of determination as R-squared and represent it as R^2.

The coefficient of determination can have values between zero and one, with values close to zero suggesting that the equation is not very useful and values close to one indicating that the equation explains most of the variation in the dependent variable. The coefficient of determination for the Tri-State Industrial utility cost-estimating equation, determined using least-squares regression analysis, is 0.97. This is found both in the regression output summary and on the chart above. This means that approximately 97 percent of the variation in utility costs is explained by the number of shipments.

When multiple independent variables exist, least squares regression also helps to select the independent variable that is the best predictor of the dependent variable. When choosing between two cost-estimating equations, the *one with the higher coefficient of determination is generally preferred.* For instance, managers can use least squares to decide whether machine hours, direct labor hours, or pounds of material moved best explain and predict changes in a specific overhead cost. Creating scatter plots and determining the R^2 for each option allows companies a means of comparison.

Managers, Not Models, Are Responsible

Although computers make least-squares regression easy to use, the generated output should not automatically be accepted as correct. Statistics and other mathematical techniques are tools to help managers make decisions. Managers, not mathematical models, are responsible for decisions. Judgment should always be exercised when considering the validity of the least-squares approach, the solution, and the data.

- **Delete Outliers** If the objective is to predict future costs under normal operating conditions, observations reflecting abnormal operating conditions should be deleted.

Chapter 3 Cost Behavior and Estimation

- **Check for Linear Cost Pattern** Also examine the cost behavior pattern to determine whether it is linear. Scatter diagrams assist in both identifying outliers and cost behavior patterns.
- **Consider the Logic of the Cost Behavior** Finally, the results should make sense. When the relationships between total cost and several activity drivers are examined, it is possible to have a high R^2 purely by chance. Even though the relationship has a high R^2, if it "doesn't make sense" there is probably something wrong.

Multiple Regression

In **multiple regression**, two or more independent variables are used to predict the dependent variable. The general form for multiple regression analysis is as follows.

$$Y = a + \Sigma b_i X_i$$

In this case, the subscript i is a general representation of each independent variable. When there are several independent variables, i is set equal to 1 for the first, 2 for the second, and so forth. The total variable costs of each independent variable are computed as $b_i X_i$, with b_i representing the variable cost per unit of independent variable X_i. The Greek symbol sigma, Σ, indicates that the costs of all independent variables are summed in determining total variable costs.

Applying Multiple Regression Analysis — LO3-4 DEMO 3-4C

As an illustration, assume that **Tri-State Industrial**'s costs are expressed as a function of the unit sales of its two industrial products: standard and customized. Assume fixed costs are $18,000 per month and the variable costs are $250 per customized product and $120 per standard product. The mathematical representation of monthly costs with two variables is as follows.

$$Y = a + b_1 X_1 + b_2 X_2$$

where

a = $18,000
b_1 = $250 per customized product
b_2 = $120 per standard product

X_1 = unit sales of customized products
X_2 = unit sales of standard products

♦ During a month, if 105 customized products and 200 standard products are sold, what are Tri-State Industrial's estimated total costs?

$$Y = \$18{,}000 + \$250(105) + \$120(200)$$
$$= \$68{,}250$$

In addition to estimating costs, multiple regression analysis can be used to determine the effect of individual product features on the market value of a product or service. Multiple regression can be done in Excel in a similar way as explained for simple regression. With multiple regression, we instead identify more than one X column.

Assumptions in Regression Analysis

Like all mathematical models, regression analysis is based on certain assumptions that produce limitations on the model's use. Three of these assumptions follow; others are beyond the scope of the text.

- First, for regression analysis to be useful, the independent variable must be a valid predictor of the dependent variable; the relationship can be tested by determining the coefficient of correlation.
- Second, like the high-low method, regression analysis should be used only within a relevant range of activity.
- Third, the regression model is useful only as long as the circumstances existing at the time of its development remain constant; consequently, if significant additions are made to capacity or if there is a major change in technology usage, the regression line will no longer be valid.

REVIEW 3-4 — LO3-4 — Applying Regression Analysis

Using the data from Review 3-2, answer the following questions.

Required

a. Develop a cost-estimating equation using simple regression.

b. **Critical Thinking:** Why is it important to evaluate the data used in simple regression analysis? To support your answer, increase machine hours in June by 25 percent (without changing the maintenance cost) and determine the impact of the change on the R^2 value.

More practice: MC3-16, E3-39, E3-40
Solution on p. 3-44.

USING LEARNING CURVES TO ESTIMATE COSTS

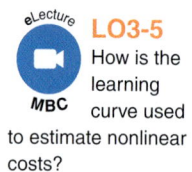

LO3-5 How is the learning curve used to estimate nonlinear costs?

The basis of a learning curve is simple: Typically, the more times that we work through a particular task, the more effective we are at the task. For example, the more times that you practice cost estimation techniques, the more you gain efficiencies, which reduces the time it takes for you to complete a similar type of assignment. Estimating the efficiencies gained through learning is *quantifiable* because people generally learn according to a predictable pattern. This concept of learning curves can be applied by managerial and cost accountants as they estimate costs of new products, services, projects, or processes or the upfront costs of training new employees. Consider the following examples:

- New manufacturing facilities are emerging to produce semiconductors based upon recent legislation such as a new factory in Arizona by Intel.
- Amazon.com revamped its distribution network from a national model to a model of eight, self-sufficient regions.
- Yum Brands which owns fast food restaurants such as Taco Bell, has a goal of 100 percent of its sales to be digitally placed.[2]

These examples highlight how understanding learning curves and their effect on cost predictions could be beneficial to companies. How will the cost to manufacture semiconductors in a new plant change over time? What labor efficiencies can be gained if a new distribution network is established? What is the training period for employees transitioning from order-taking to other responsibilities?

With each change, employees become more familiar with the process and efficiencies are gained. Because each additional activity is completed using less resources, the amount of resources used per output is not constant. This means that there is a nonlinear relationship between activity and output.

Engineers can study the time it takes to produce the same product again and again. Assuming a learning curve, the products will take less time to complete, the more the product is made. The origins of the study of learning curves is in the aerospace industry where an 80 percent learning curve was documented. We apply an 80 percent learning curve in the following examples, using an incremental unit time learning curve and a cumulative average time learning curve. The results of the two models vary because there are *different assumptions* built into the two models about how quickly learning takes place.

Incremental Unit Time Learning Curve Under the **incremental unit time learning curve model**, the time required to produce the *latest unit* is reduced by a constant rate as the cumulative quantity of units doubles. In the case of an 80 percent learning curve, the incremental time it takes to produce the last unit declines by 20 percent after the quantity doubles. An incremental unit time 80 percent learning curve is illustrated in the following demonstration.

DEMO 3-5A — LO3-5 — Applying the Incremental Unit Time Learning Curve

♦ If it takes 6.4 minutes to produce the 4th unit, how much time is estimated to produce the 8th unit, using the incremental unit time 80 percent learning curve?

If we double 4 units, we arrive at 8 units. The learner is estimated to take 5.12 minutes to produce the 8th unit, calculated as follows.

---
[2] Maurer, M., "Yum Brands CFO Has a Plan for 100% Digital Transactions," *Wall Street Journal*, August 16, 2023.

$$6.4 \text{ minutes} \times 80\% = 5.12 \text{ minutes}$$

The time it takes to produce each unit 5 through 7 decreases from 6.4 minutes until 5.12 minutes is reached at unit 8. To simplify this presentation, we focus only on the incremental time it takes to produce the unit at the point where the quantity doubles. Thus, we are not estimating the time it takes to complete units 5, 6, or 7.[3]

The *lower* the learning curve percentage, the *higher* the rate of learning. Thus, if instead a 70 percent learning curve was estimated, the 8th unit would be estimated to take only 4.48 minutes (6.4 minutes × 70 percent).

Cumulative Average Time Learning Curve
Under the **cumulative average time learning curve model**, the cumulative average time it takes to produce one unit is reduced by a constant rate as the cumulative quantity of units doubles. In the case of an 80 percent learning curve, the cumulative time it takes to produce one unit declines by 20 percent after the quantity doubles. The cumulative average time 80 percent learning curve is illustrated in the following demonstration.

Applying the Cumulative Average Time Learning Curve — LO3-5 — DEMO 3-5B

◆ Assume it takes 6.4 minutes to produce the 4th unit. If 8 units are produced, what is the cumulative average time estimate to produce one unit using the cumulative average time 80 percent learning curve?

The cumulative average time to produce one of the eight units is 5.12 minutes, calculated as follows.

$$6.4 \text{ minutes} \times 80\% = 5.12 \text{ minutes}$$

This means that the 8th unit took less time than 5.12 minutes in order for the cumulative average time to produce each unit to be 5.12 minutes. Compared to the incremental unit time method, learning is assumed to take place at a faster pace. The relationship between the cumulative average time per unit and cumulative number of units is graphed in **Exhibit 3.5**.

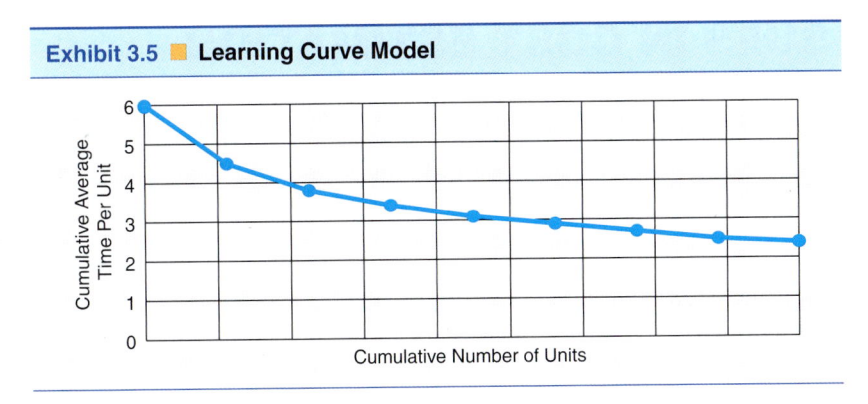

Exhibit 3.5 ■ Learning Curve Model

Uses of Learning Curves
Learning curves can used to inform estimates such as the following.

- Forecasting labor or service hours depending on the level of experience and expected turnover of employees.
- Measuring performance against standards that developed based on the experience of the employee.
- Scheduling a production line, taking into account the experience of workers.
- Negotiating a production contract knowing that initial products will take longer to produce than later products in a contract.

---

[3] The learning curve is represented by the equation $Y = aX^b$ where Y = Time to produce last single unit; X = Cumulative number of units produced; a = Time required to produce the first unit; b = Factor used to calculate incremental time equal to (ln) of the learning rate divided by the (ln) of 2 whereas (ln) means natural logarithm. For example, at the 4th unit, time is calculated as $y = 10(8^{-0.3219}) = 5.12$ minutes. Note: In Excel, b is calculated in an 80% learning curve as =LN(0.8)/LN(2) = −0.3219.

REVIEW 3-5 — LO3-5: Using Learning Curves to Estimate Costs

Part One: Applying the Incremental Unit Time Learning Curve

Aviators Inc. produces ultralight airplanes used for personal recreation. Aviators recently accepted an order for four airplanes from a dealer. The production of the first airplane required 12,000 direct labor hours. Based on historical data, Aviators anticipates an 80 percent incremental unit time learning curve.

a. What is the expected number of labor hours expected to be incurred to produce the second airplane?
b. What is the expected number of labor hours expected to be incurred to produce the fourth airplane?
c. Calculate the expected number of labor hours to produce the fourth airplane as a percentage of the expected number of labor hours to produce the first airplane.
d. How do your answers to parts *a* through *c* change with a 90 percent incremental unit time learning curve?

Part Two: Applying the Cumulative Average Time Learning Curve

Use the information from Part One, but now assume that Aviators anticipates an 80 percent cumulative average time learning curve.

a. What is the cumulative average number of expected labor hours expected to be incurred per airplane when only two planes are produced? What are the total hours to produce two planes?
b. What is the cumulative average number of expected labor hours expected to be incurred per airplane when all four planes are produced? What are the total hours to produce four planes?

Part Three: Analysis of Learning Curves

a. Why do the answers in Part One change when using a 90 percent vs. an 80 percent learning curve?
b. Which method, the incremental unit time or cumulative average time learning curve estimates a faster rate of learning?
c. **Critical Thinking:** How are learning curve assumptions useful for Aviators when negotiating the contract for the four airplanes?

More practice: MC3-18, E3-41, E3-42
Solution on p. 3-44.

ADDITIONAL ISSUES IN COST ESTIMATION

LO3-6 Identify and discuss problems encountered in cost estimation.

We have mentioned several items to be wary of when developing cost-estimating equations.

- Data that are not based on normal operating conditions
- Nonlinear relationships between total costs and activity
- Obtaining a high R^2 purely by chance

Additional items of concern include the following

- Changes in technology or prices
- Matching activity and cost within each observation
- Identifying activity cost drivers
- Ensuring the reliability of data

Changes in Technology or Prices

Changes in technology and prices make cost estimation and prediction difficult. For example, **FedEx** is committing to a fleet of zero-emission electric vehicles by 2040.[4] The replacement of gas-powered vehicles with electric vehicles is an ongoing process. This means that care must be taken to make sure that historical data used in developing future transportation cost estimates takes into account the mix of costs. Professional judgment may be required to make appropriate adjustments to the data.

Only data reflecting a single price level should be used in cost estimation and prediction. If prices have remained stable in the past but then uniformly increase by 20 percent cost-estimating equations based on data from previous periods will not accurately predict future costs. In this case, all that is required is a 20 percent increase in the prediction. Unfortunately, adjustments for price changes are seldom this simple. The prices of various cost elements are likely to change at different rates and at

---

[4] "FedEx Commits to Carbon-Neutral Operations by 2040." Fedex, March 3, 2021, https://newsroom.fedex.com/newsroom/asia-english/sustainability2021.

different times. Furthermore, there are probably several different price levels included in the past data used to develop cost-estimating equations. If data from different price levels are used, an attempt should be made to restate them to a single price level.

Matching Activity and Costs

The development of accurate cost-estimating equations requires the matching of the activity to related costs within each observation. This accuracy is often difficult to achieve because of the time lag between an activity and the recording of the cost of resources consumed by the activity. Current activities usually consume electricity, but the electric bill won't be received and recorded until next month. Driving an automobile requires routine maintenance for items such as lubrication and oil, but the auto can be driven several weeks or even months before the maintenance is required. Consequently, daily, weekly, and perhaps even monthly observations of miles driven and maintenance costs are unlikely to match the costs of oil and lubrication with the cost-driving activity, miles driven.

In general, the shorter the time period, the higher the probability of error in matching costs and activity. The cost analyst must carefully review the database to verify that activity and cost are matched within each observation. If matching problems are found, it may be possible to adjust the data (perhaps by moving the cost of electricity from one observation to another). Adjusting information to an accrual basis allows for matching of events with the corresponding time period. Under other circumstances, it may be necessary to use longer periods to match costs and activity.

Additionally, cost data should be examined to determine whether variable and fixed costs are classified accurately. Assuming that fixed costs for example, vary with a cost driver such as machine hours, will not result in accurate cost models.

Identifying Relevant Cost Drivers

Identifying the appropriate cost driver for a particular cost requires judgment and professional experience. In general, the cost driver should have a logical, causal relationship with costs. In many cases, the identity of the most appropriate cost driver, such as miles driven for the cost of automobile gasoline, is apparent. In other situations, where different cost drivers might be used, scatter diagrams and statistical measures, such as the coefficient of determination, are helpful in selecting the cost driver that best explains past variations in cost. When scatter diagrams are used, the analyst can study the dispersion of observations around the cost-estimating line. In general, a small dispersion is preferred. If regression analysis is used, the analyst considers the coefficient of determination. In general, a higher coefficient of determination is preferred. The relationship between the cost driver and the cost must seem logical, and the activity data must be available.

Ensuring the Reliability of Data

The quality of data analysis depends on the quality of the data used for the analysis. If cost predictions are inaccurate due to faulty data, management will lose trust in the process and in the reliability of the supporting data. A research report prepared by KPMG indicates that trust in data analytics is based on four anchors: quality, effectiveness, integrity, and resilience.[5]

- *Quality* refers to the level of accuracy, completeness, and timeliness of data. For example, what is the quality of the data sources? Still in the early stages of development, AI-powered language models such as **ChatGPT** and **Bard** are trained to provide detailed responses to human questions. But what is the source of the responses? Even when prompted for citations, books or articles cited by ChatGPT at times are not existent. Knowing the source of information is critical to assessing the quality of the information.

- *Effectiveness* refers to the accuracy of the outputs of data analytics and whether it benefits decision makers. How well did the predictions match actual events? Monitoring how effective the output is can inform how reliable future results will likely be. Importantly, understanding what went wrong can prompt changes to improve effectiveness in the future.

---

[5] "Building Trust in Analytics," KPMG, October 2016, https://assets.kpmg.com/content/dam/kpmg/xx/pdf/2016/10/building-trust-in-analytics.pdf.

- *Integrity* refers to whether data analytics is aligned with legal requirements and ethical standards. For example, is it transparent to a customer as to what data is being collected, how long it is held, and how it is used? Is maintaining the privacy of data a priority of the company? Some laws regulate transparency such as the *California Consumer Privacy Act*, which allows residents to limit the use and disclosure of collected personal information.
- *Resilience* refers to long term strategy of ensuring governance and security of data. Those in a position to oversee data security need to be skilled and able to adapt to a constantly changing landscape. Cyber security, which is the protection of a company from digital attacks is an application of resilience. Breaks downs, such as data breaches, have the potential of affecting the personal information of millions of customers.

DEMO 3-6 — LO3-6 — Identifying Potential Issues in Cost Estimation

The following is a list of items that could potentially cause issues in the cost estimation process.

◆ **Would the potential issue primarily relate to (a) a change in technology, (b) a change in price levels, (c) matching of activities to costs, (d) identifying relevant cost drivers, or (e) ensuring the integrity of data?**

1. Determining whether a cost estimating equation is a good predictor of future costs.

   The potential issue in cost estimation is in not identifying the most relevant *cost driver*. Selection of a cost driver requires a logical assessment of causation and an examination of statistical factors such as the level of R-squared.

2. Classifying maintenance costs on AI-powered manufacturing equipment as fixed or variable.

   A potential issue is the *matching of activity with a cost*, where a misclassification of a cost as either fixed or variable can affect cost estimation.

3. Estimating the future costs of batteries of electric vehicles.

   Changing technology is a potential issue because of the rapid pace of change in advancing technology for electric vehicle batteries making cost estimation difficult.

4. Limited supply of semiconductors during a pandemic.

   Limited supply can cause drastic and swift *increases in prices* of supplies, which can cause issues in the estimation of costs.

5. Using data that is collected from customer to increase future sales.

   Using customer data can cause potential issues in cost estimations if there is a lack of *data integrity*. Safeguards must be in place to protect the data and inform the customer of its usage in accordance with legal and ethical requirements.

REVIEW 3-6 — LO3-6 — Identifying Problems in Cost Estimation

a. In deciding which activity driver is the most appropriate for a particular manufacturing cost, would the following items make the driver more desirable or less desirable? Consider each scenario separately.
   1. A scatter plot reveals a small dispersion of points around the cost-estimating line.
   2. The coefficient of determination is 0.65 which is less than the coefficient of the other options.
   3. There is a logical relation between the activity and the cost but the activity data is not reliably available.
   4. Observations on a scatter plot do not reasonably approximate a straight-line.
   5. The cost changes with changes in the level of the activity driver.
   6. The coefficient of determination is 0.88, which is greater than the coefficient of the other options.

b. **Critical Thinking:** Identify potential activity drivers that would have logical and causal relations with costs in a manufacturing operation.

More practice: E3-44
Solution on p. 3-45.

ALTERNATIVE COST DRIVER CLASSIFICATIONS

So far we have examined cost behavior and cost estimation using only a unit-level approach, which assumes changes in costs are best explained by changes in the number of units of product or service provided customers. This approach may have worked for **Carnegie Steel Company**, but it is inappropriate for multidimensional organizations, such as **Square**. The unit-level approach becomes increasingly inaccurate for analyzing cost behavior when organizations experience the following types of changes:

- From face-to-face customer interactions to web-based interface,
- From stand-alone products to products with multiple layers of customer interface, such as Square's hardware versus the processing of payments executed by Square for its customers, and
- From internet-based operations to mobile platforms, thus engaging a more geographically diverse set of customers.

LO3-7 Describe and develop alternative classifications for cost drivers.

Manufacturing Cost Hierarchy

The most well-known framework, developed by Cooper[6] and Cooper and Kaplan[7] for manufacturing situations, classifies activities into the following four categories.

1. A **unit-level activity** is performed *for each unit* of product produced. **Christofle** is a French manufacturer of high-end silver flatware. In the production of forks, the stamping of each fork into the prescribed shape is an example of a unit-level cost driver.
2. A **batch-level activity** is performed *for each batch* of product produced. At Christofle, a batch is a number of identical units (such as a fork of a specific design) produced at the same time. Batch-level activities include setting up the machines to stamp each fork in an identical manner, moving the entire batch between workstations (i.e., molding, stamping, and finishing), and inspecting the first unit in the batch to verify that the machines are set up correctly.
3. A **product/process-level activity** is performed *to support* the production of *each different type of product/process*. At Christofle, product/process-level activities for a specific pattern of fork include initially designing the fork, producing and maintaining the mold for the fork, and determining manufacturing operations for the fork.
4. An **organizational/facility-level activity** is performed *to maintain* general manufacturing capabilities. At Christofle, organizational/facility-level activities include plant management, building maintenance, property taxes, and electricity required to sustain the building.

When using a cost hierarchy for analyzing and estimating costs, total costs are broken down into the different cost levels in the hierarchy, and a separate cost driver is determined for each level of cost. For example, using the above hierarchy, the costs that are related to the number of units produced (such as direct materials or direct labor) may have direct labor hours or machine hours as the cost driver; whereas batch costs may be driven by the number of setups of production machines or the number of times materials are moved from one machine to another. Other costs may be driven by the number of different products produced. Organizational/facility-level costs are generally regarded as fixed costs and do not vary unless capacity is increased or decreased.

Providing Examples of Activity Costs in the Manufacturing Setting — LO3-7 — DEMO 3-7

- Given the four cost categories in the manufacturing cost hierarchy, what are examples of activity costs for a manufacturer?

Several examples of the costs driven by activities at each level are presented in the following table.

---

[6] Robin Cooper, "Cost Classification in Unit-Based and Activity-Based Manufacturing Cost Systems," *Journal of Cost Management*, Fall 1990, pp. 4–14.

[7] Robin Cooper and Robert S. Kaplan, "Profit Priorities from Activity-Based Costing," *Harvard Business Review*, May-June 1991, pp. 130–135.

Hierarchy of Activity Costs

Activity Level	Reason for Activity	Examples of Activity Cost
1. Unit level	Performed for each unit of product produced or sold	• Cost of raw materials • Cost of inserting a component • Cost of direct labor • Some costs of packaging • Sales commissions
2. Batch level	Performed for each batch of product produced or sold	• Cost of processing sales order • Cost of issuing and tracking work order • Cost of equipment setup • Cost of moving batch between workstations • Cost of inspection (assuming same number of units inspected in each batch)
3. Product/Process level	Performed to support each different product that can be produced	• Cost of product development • Cost of product marketing such as advertising • Cost of specialized equipment • Cost of maintaining specialized equipment
4. Organizational/Facility level	Performed to maintain general manufacturing capabilities	• Cost of maintaining general facilities such as buildings and grounds • Cost of nonspecialized equipment • Cost of maintaining nonspecialized equipment • Cost of real property taxes • Cost of general advertising • Cost of general administration such as the plant manager's salary

Customer Cost Hierarchy

The manufacturing hierarchy presented is but one of many possible ways of classifying activities and their costs. Classification schemes should be designed to fit the organization and meet user needs.

Cost of individual products/services or individual customers A merchandising or service organization or the sales division of a manufacturing organization might use the following hierarchy.

1. **Unit-level activity:** performed for each unit sold.
2. **Order-level activity:** performed for each sales order.
3. **Customer-level activity:** performed to obtain or maintain each customer.
4. **Organizational/Facility-level activity:** performed to maintain the general sales or store function.

This classification scheme assists in answering questions concerning the cost of individual orders or individual customers.

Costs of market segments If an organization sells to distinct market segments (for profit, not for profit, and government), the cost hierarchy can be modified as follows:

1. Unit-level activity
2. Order-level activity
3. Customer-level activity
4. **Market-segment-level activity:** performed to obtain or maintain operations in a segment.
5. Organizational/Facility-level activity

The market-segment-level activities and their related costs differ with each market segment. This classification scheme assists in answering questions concerning the profitability of each segment.

Cost of unique projects Finally, an organization that completes unique projects for different market segments (such as buildings for **IBM** and the **U.S. Department of Defense**) can use the following hierarchy to determine the profitability of each segment:

Chapter 3 Cost Behavior and Estimation

1. **Project-level activity**: performed to support the completion of each project.
2. Market-segment-level activity
3. Organizational/Facility-level activity

The possibilities are endless. The important point is that both the cost hierarchy and the costs included in the hierarchy be tailored to meet the specific circumstances of an organization and the interests of management.

Classifying Costs Using a Customer Cost Hierarchy — LO3-7 — REVIEW 3-7

a. Consider the pizza chain **Blaze Pizza**. It custom builds and cooks each pizza to order. Items 1–6 represent cost activities associated with a particular store.
   1. Pepperoni on the pizza
   2. Wood to fuel the fire used to cook the pizzas
   3. Insurance on the building
   4. The labor costs of the employee building and cooking each pizza
   5. The cost of the sales calls made to local organizations to promote the pizzas for catering special events
   6. The costs associated with employees taking pizza orders

   Classify each cost activity above, in the most appropriate level of the proposed customer cost hierarchy. Each cost activity may be used more than once.

   _____ i. Unit-level—performed for each unit sold
   _____ ii. Order-level—performed for each sales order
   _____ iii. Customer-level—performed to obtain or maintain each customer
   _____ iv. Store (facility)-level—performed to maintain the general store functions

b. **Critical Thinking:** When will the incorporation of the hierarchy of activity costs into a cost estimating equation improve the accuracy of cost predictions?

More practice: E3-46
Solution on p. 3-45.

Comprehensive Chapter Review

Key Terms

batch-level activity, p. 3-19
coefficient of determination, p. 3-12
coefficients, p. 3-11
cost estimation, p. 3-5
cost prediction, p. 3-9
cumulative average time learning curve model, p. 3-15
customer-level activity, p. 3-20
high-low method of cost estimation, p. 3-8

incremental unit time learning curve model, p. 3-14
least squares regression analysis, p. 3-9
market-segment-level activity, p. 3-20
multiple regression, p. 3-13
order-level activity, p. 3-20
organizational/facility-level activity, p. 3-19, p. 3-20
outliers, p. 3-5

product/process-level activity, p. 3-19
project-level activity, p. 3-21
regression line, p. 3-9
scatter diagram, p. 3-5
scatter plot, p. 3-5
simple regression, p. 3-9
unit-level activity, p. 3-19, p. 3-20

Chapter Summary

LO3-1 **Linear Cost Estimating Equations Used to Estimate Costs (Page 3-2)**
- Costs behavior categories include variables costs, fixed costs, mixed costs, and step costs.
- The relationship between total cost (Y-axis) and total activity (X-axis) for the four cost behaviors can be mathematically expressed in a total cost estimating equation.
- A total cost equation can be used to predict costs.
- Factors affecting cost behavior patterns include the cost driver, the time period, and cost type.

LO3-2 **Scatter Diagram Used to Analyze Cost Behavior (Page 3-5)**
- Scatter plot is useful in determining whether costs can be reasonably approximated by a straight line.
- Any nonrepresentative observations identified are called outliers and should be ignored when analyzing a mixed cost.
- Scatter diagrams could be used alone as a basis of cost estimation but often are used in conjunction with other methods.

LO3-3 **Scatter Diagram Used to Analyze Cost Behavior (Page 3-8)**
- High-low method uses just two points (low and high activity) to estimate fixed and variable costs.
- Because fixed costs are the same at the low and high activity level, the difference in costs relates entirely to variable costs.

LO3-4 **Scatter Diagram Used to Analyze Cost Behavior (Page 3-9)**
- Least square regression analysis uses a mathematical technique to fit a cost estimating equation to observed data.
- Simple regression uses one independent variable to predict costs.
- Multiple regression uses more than one independent variable to predict costs.
- The coefficient of determination measures the percent of variation in the dependent variable explained by variations in the independent variable.

LO3-5 **Learning Curve Used to Estimate Nonlinear Costs (Page 3-14)**
- People generally learn according to predictable patterns that can be quantified.
- Learning curves estimate how efficiencies gained through learning impact cost predictions.
- The incremental unit time learning curve estimates the incremental time to produce the last unit.
- The cumulative average time learning curve measures the average-time of production for each unit.

LO3-6 **Learning Curve Used to Estimate Nonlinear Costs (Page 3-16)**
- Problems encountered in cost estimation are due to the following:
  - Changes in price levels
  - Changes in technology
  - Matching activity and cost within each observation
  - Identifying cost drivers
  - Maintaining data integrity

LO3-7 **Learning Curve Used to Estimate Nonlinear Costs (Page 3-19)**
- Using only unit-level cost drivers is not an accurate approach for multidimensional organizations.
- A manufacturing cost hierarchy can include unit-level activities, batch-level activities, product-level activities, and organizational/facility-level activities.
- A customer cost hierarchy can include unit-level activities, order-level activities, customer-level activities, and organizational/facility-level activities.

Solution Strategies

LO3-1 **Linear Cost Estimating Equations**

Variable costs: $Y = bX$

Where b = the variable cost per unit, sometimes referred to as the slope of the cost function.

Fixed costs: $Y = a$

Where a = total fixed costs. The slope of the fixed cost function is zero because fixed costs do not change with activity.

Mixed costs: $Y = a + bX$

Where a = total fixed cost element and b = variable cost element per unit of activity.

Step cost: $Y = a_i$

Where a_i = the step cost within a specific range of activity, identified by the subscript i.

Total costs: $Y = a + bX$

Where Y = total costs, a = vertical axis intercept (an approximation of fixed costs), b = slope (an approximation of variable costs per unit of X), and X = value of independent variable.

High-Low Method

LO3-3

$$\text{Variable costs per unit} = \frac{\text{Difference in total costs}}{\text{Difference in activity}}$$

Fixed costs = Total costs – Variable costs

Cost Estimating Equations Using Regression Analysis

LO3-4

General form for simple regression analysis: $Y = a + bX$

Where a = total fixed cost element and b = the variable cost per unit of independent variable X.

General form for multiple regression analysis is: $Y = a + \Sigma b_i X_i$

Where the subscript i is a general representation of each independent variable. When there are several independent variables, i is set equal to 1 for the first, 2 for the second, and so forth. The total variable costs of each independent variable are computed as $b_i X_i$, with b_i representing the variable cost per unit of independent variable X_i. The Greek symbol sigma, Σ, indicates that the costs of all independent variables are summed in determining total variable costs.

Chapter Demonstration Problem

Assume **Pottery Barn** wants to develop a monthly cost function for its packaging department and that the number of shipments is believed to be the primary cost driver. The following observations are available for the most recent twelve months.

LO3-2, 3, 4, 6

Shipping and Packaging Data

Month	Number of Shipments	Packaging Costs
January	6,000	$17,000
February	9,000	24,000
March	6,500	16,000
April	10,000	26,500
May	3,600	16,000
June	11,000	27,000
July	8,000	19,000
August	8,800	19,800
September	10,500	28,000
October	11,000	27,500
November	11,800	28,000
December	7,800	21,500

Required:

a. Plot the data on a scatter diagram using Excel. Identify any outlier(s).
b. Using the information from representative high- and low-volume months, use the high-low method to develop a cost-estimating equation for monthly packaging costs.
c. Use simple regression analysis to develop a cost-estimating equation for total packaging costs.
d. Use the cost estimating equation in parts b and c to estimate packaging costs for monthly shipments of 8,500.
e. Why do the results in part d differ? What advantages does simple regression analysis have in comparison with the high-low method of cost estimation?

Solution to Demonstration Problem

a.

Scatter Diagram

[Scatter diagram with Packaging Costs on y-axis ($0–$30,000) and Number of Shipments on x-axis (0–14,000). One point labeled "Outlier" at approximately (3,500, $16,000).]

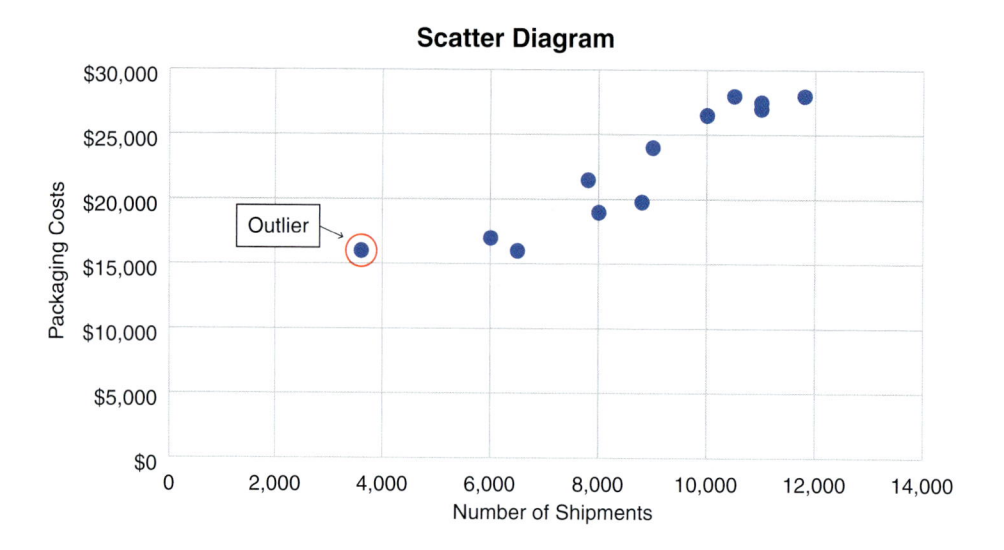

A review of the scatter diagram indicates the May unit volume is not representative.

b. $b = \dfrac{(\$28{,}000 - \$17{,}000)}{(11{,}800 - 6{,}000)} = \$1.90$ (rounded)

$a = \$28{,}000 - (\$1.90 \times 11{,}800) = \$5{,}580$

$Y = \$5{,}580 + \$1.90X$

c. $Y = \$5{,}580 + \$1.90\,(8{,}000) =$

Regression Summary Output

	A	B	C	D	E	F	G	H	I
1	SUMMARY OUTPUT								
2									
3	Regression Statistics								
4	Multiple R	0.948638306							
5	R Square	0.899914635							
6	Adjusted R Square	0.888794039							
7	Standard Error	1538.462623							
8	Observations	11							
9									
10	ANOVA								
11			df	SS	MS	F	Significance F		
12	Regression		1	191534558.4	191534558.4	80.92323682	8.57123E–06		
13	Residual		9	21301805.19	2366867.243				
14	Total		10	212836363.6					
15									
16		Coefficients	Standard Error	t Stat	P-value	Lower 95%	Upper 95%	Lower 95.0%	Upper 95.0%
17	Intercept	2250.409368	2365.664249	0.951280119	0.366308267	–3101.094958	7601.913695	–3101.094958	7601.913695
18	Number of Shipments	2.286309731	0.254154874	8.995734368	8.57123E–06	1.711371463	2.861247998	1.711371463	2.861247998

$Y = \$2{,}250 + \$2.29X$

d. $Y = \$5{,}580 + \$1.90\,(8{,}000) = \$20{,}780$

$Y = \$2{,}250 + \$2.29\,(8{,}000) = \$20{,}570$

e. The answers differ because the high-low method is based on two points whereas the results using simple regression takes into account all representative data points. The simple regression equation has two advantages over that developed in part *b*.
- It uses all observations (except May), rather than just two representative observations.
- It provides information on how well the cost-estimating equation explains the variation in the dependent variable. In this case, the cost-estimating equation explains approximately 90 percent of the variation in total packaging costs.

Data Analytics

DA3-1. Selecting a basis for predicting shipping expenses

Cambridge SoundWorks sells portable speakers and wireless headphones. In an effort to improve the planning and control of shipping expenses, management is trying to determine which of three variables—units shipped, weight shipped, or sales value of units shipped—has the closest relationship with shipping expenses. Assume that the following information is available.

Month	Units Shipped	Weight Shipped (lbs.)	Sales Value of Units Shipped	Shipping Expenses
May.	10,000	7,500	$350,000	$38,000
June	12,000	8,760	432,000	42,000
July.	15,000	9,200	420,000	50,100
August	20,000	10,500	400,000	72,500
September	12,000	7,600	300,000	41,000
October.	8,000	6,000	320,000	35,600

Required

a. Determine whether units shipped, weight shipped, or sales value of units shipped has the closest relationship with shipping expenses by determining the R^2 value for each option. *Hint:* Prepare three scatter plots in Excel showing the relationship with each of the three variables to shipping expenses. Highlight the data to be included in the chart. Open the insert tab and select the Scatter chart in the Charts group. *Hint:* Right-click a data point on the scatter chart, select Add trendline and check Display equation on chart and Display R^2 value on chart.

b. Using the independent variable that appears to have the closest relationship to shipping expenses, develop a cost-estimating equation for total monthly shipping expenses.

c. Use the equation developed in requirement (b) to predict total shipping expenses in a month when 14,000 units; weighing 9,380 lbs.; with a total sales value of $420,000 are shipped.

DA3-2. Multiple regression analysis for a special decision

For billing purposes, assume **Phoenix Family Medical Clinic** classifies its services into one of four major procedures, X1 through X4. Assume that a local business has proposed that Phoenix provide health services to its employees and their families at the following set rates per procedure.

X1.	$100	X3.	$ 60
X2.	200	X4.	300

Because these rates are significantly below the current rates charged for these services, management has asked for detailed cost information on each procedure. The following information is available for the most recent 12 months.

		Number of Procedures			
Month	Total Cost	X1	X2	X3	X4
1	$17,250	30	25	155	19
2	18,750	38	30	135	23
3	20,250	50	20	105	38
4	14,250	20	25	90	25
5	15,000	68	15	120	20
6	20,250	90	19	158	14
7	19,125	20	30	143	28
8	16,125	16	30	132	20
9	19,500	60	21	93	35
10	16,500	20	22	75	35
11	17,100	20	18	113	33
12	19,875	72	15	150	30

Required

a. Use multiple regression analysis to determine the unit cost of each procedure. How much variation in monthly cost is explained by your cost-estimating equation? *Hint:* Under the Data tab, click on Data analysis, Regression, and select the cells for the Y Range and X Range.

b. Evaluate the rates proposed by the local business. Assuming Phoenix has excess capacity and no employees of the local business currently patronize the clinic, what are your recommendations regarding the proposal?

c. Evaluate the rates proposed by the local business. Assuming Phoenix is operating at capacity and would have to turn current customers away if it agrees to provide health services to the local business, what are your recommendations regarding the proposal?

DA3-3. Cost estimation, interpretation, and analysis

Kendrick Anderson Furniture Maker, LLC creates custom tables in Atlanta. Assume that the following represents monthly information on production volume and manufacturing costs since the company started operations.

	Total Manufacturing Costs	Total Tables Produced	Living Room Tables Produced	Dining Room Tables Produced
Year 1: June	$71,000	110	25	85
July	57,500	90	45	45
August	79,724	130	15	115
September	64,250	95	36	59
October	57,300	76	24	52
November	60,900	92	48	44
December	62,700	105	24	81
Year 2, January	70,130	110	50	60
February	68,400	102	20	82
March	57,400	81	25	56
April	105,790	142	102	40
May	74,750	125	22	103
June	74,290	115	15	100
July	66,500	106	18	88
August	49,888	85	28	57
September	72,668	116	55	61
October	71,700	120	81	39
November	74,200	120	30	90
December	54,900	72	18	54

Required

a. Use the high-low method to develop a cost-estimating equation for total manufacturing costs driven by total tables produced.

b. In Excel, create a scatter graph of total manufacturing costs and total units produced. Use the graph to identify any unusual observations. *Hint:* Highlight the data to be included in the chart. Open the insert tab and select the Scatter chart in the Charts group.

c. Excluding any unusual observations, use the high-low method to develop a cost-estimating equation for total manufacturing costs. Comment on the results, comparing them with the results from requirement (*a*).

d. Use simple regression analysis in Excel to develop a cost-estimating equation for total manufacturing costs. How much variation in manufacturing costs is explained by your cost-estimating equation? What advantages does simple regression analysis have in comparison with the high-low method of cost estimation? Why must analysts carefully evaluate the data used in simple regression analysis? *Hint:* Exclude any outlier point(s). *Hint:* Under the Data tab, click on Data analysis, Regression, and select the cells for the Y Range and X Range.

e. A customer has offered to purchase 50 dining room tables for $452 per table. Management has asked your advice regarding the desirability of accepting the offer. What advice do you have for management? Complete a multiple regression analysis in Excel to support your answer.

DA3-4. Simple and multiple regression

Dan Mullen is employed by a mail-order distributor and reconditions used personal computers, routers, and printers. Dan is paid $12 per hour, plus an extra $6 per hour for work in excess of 40 hours per week. The distributor just announced plans to outsource all reconditioning work, so Dan will need to start looking for a new job. Because the distributor is pleased with the quality of Dan's work, he has been asked to enter into a long-term contract to recondition used computers at a rate of $50 per computer, plus all parts. The distributor also offered to rent all necessary equipment to Dan at a rate of $300 per month. Dan has been informed that he should plan on reconditioning as many computers as he can handle, up to a maximum of 20 per week.

Dan has room in his basement to set up a work area, but he is unsure of the economics of accepting the contract, as opposed to working for a local computer repair shop at $14 per hour. Data related to the time spent and the number of units of each type of electronic equipment Dan has reconditioned in recent weeks is as follows.

Week	Printers	Routers	Computers	Total Units	Total Hours
1	3	6	6	15	42
2	0	8	7	15	40
3	3	3	8	14	41
4	1	3	13	17	46
5	10	7	5	22	50
6	4	9	4	17	43
7	4	9	4	17	43
8	4	5	6	15	44
9	1	5	11	17	48
10	7	5	6	18	44
Total				167	441

Required

Assuming he wants to work an average of 40 hours per week, what should Dan do? Answer the question using (a) an analysis of average time to recondition electronic equipment, (b) simple regression, and (c) multiple regression.

a. Analysis of average time to recondition electronic equipment
   1. What is the average time to repair a piece of electronic equipment based upon the data? How many computers could Dan recondition in a week?
   2. Estimate net profit to recondition desktop computers for a month under the proposed contract.
   3. What is the net amount that Dan would receive for a month to work at the store?
   4. What should Dan do based on this analysis? Are there any flaws in the analysis?

b. Simple regression
   1. Complete a simple regression analysis (using total units and total hours). *Hint:* Under the Data tab, click on Data analysis, Regression, and select the cells for the *Y* Range and *X* Range. What is the estimating equation using total units and total hours and what percentage of the variation in total weekly hours is explained by the estimating equation?
   2. How many computers could Dan recondition in a week?
   3. Estimate net profit to recondition desktop computers for a month under the proposed contract.
   4. What should Dan do based on this analysis?

c. Multiple regression
   1. Complete a multiple regression analysis (using total units and total hours). What is the estimating equation using total units and total hours and what percentage of the variation in total weekly hours is explained by the estimating equation?
   2. How many computers could Dan recondition in a week based on this analysis?
   3. Estimate net profit to recondition desktop computers for a month under the proposed contract.
   4. What should Dan do based on this analysis?

DA3-5. Analyzing data visualizations: purchasing department costs

Assume you are the purchasing manager at **Block** for materials used in the chip reader. You have observed that as the company has increased its sales volume, the total cost to process purchase orders has increased as well, but not at a constant rate. You would like to estimate the cost to process purchase orders next month. You gather the following data for the last eight quarters.

Quarters	No. of Purchase Orders	Purchase Department Costs
1	8,000	246,686
2	8,160	238,521
3	8,405	247,881
4	8,573	253,340
5	8,763	247,031
6	8,938	260,066
7	9,161	261,603
8	9,344	259,959

Required

a. Prepare a scatter diagram in Excel that shows the relationship between the number of purchase orders and purchase department costs for the last eight quarters. Based upon the scatter diagram, are purchasing department costs fixed, variable or mixed?
b. Estimate the average purchasing cost per purchase order at the low and high point of purchase orders using data from the chart. Assume no outliers in your analysis.
c. Use the high-low method to develop a cost-estimating equation for total annual operating costs.
d. If purchases for next quarter are expected to be 9,600 units, what are expected purchasing department costs?
e. What are some reasons why the total cost to process purchase orders is not increasing at a constant rate? What trends do you expect in the average cost per unit in the purchasing department?

LO3-5 DA3-6. Determining the rate of the learning curve

Custom Accessories Inc. creates limited lines of furniture accessories for dealers and designers. The new lines are distinctive, and the process has a direct labor component. With each new line, the company estimates a learning curve in order to determine the pricing required for their desired profits. For each of the scenarios listed below, assume that the first unit uses 18.4 minutes of direct labor.

Required

Using the Goal Seek function in Excel, determine the rate of the learning curve for each of the four separate scenarios below. Each scenario assumes an incremental unit time learning curve with the following estimated minutes of direct labor for the 2,048th accessory item.

a. 0.77712 minutes
b. 2.07382 minutes
c. 3.50188 minutes
d. 5.77411 minutes

Hint: First, set up formulas to compute the labor minutes using an assumed learning curve rate (i.e., 60%). Link your formulas to a single cell with the assumed learning curve rate. Use Goal Seek (found under the Data tab, What-if Analysis) to calculate the cell for labor hours at the 2048th item by changing the learning curve rate cell.

Data Visualization

Data Visualization Activities are available in myBusinessCourse. These assignments use Tableau Dashboards to expose students to visual depictions of data and introduce students to data analytics through data visualizations. These exercises are easily assignable and auto graded by MBC.

Potential Ethical Issues

1. When using the high-low method, management could select particular data points to fit a predetermined cost structure.
2. When using the high-low method for budget estimates, management could select an outlier point to estimate budgeted costs in order to inflate the cost budget in order to justify higher costs.
3. Management could manipulate data or omit certain data used in a simple regression analysis in order to support a desired cost estimating equation.
4. Management uses an aggressive learning curve in pricing out a contract that puts unrealistic pressures on employees to increase productivity.
5. In order to achieve learning curve targets, new employees may be pressured to decrease quality or override safety measures.
6. A lack of data governance provided an opportunity for unauthorized changes to a data set.
7. A company collects personal information and sells it to a third party without the customer's consent.

Questions

Q3-1. Briefly describe variable, fixed, mixed, and step costs and indicate how the total cost function of each changes as activity increases within a time period.

Q3-2. Why is presenting all costs of an organization as a function of a single independent variable, although useful in obtaining a general understanding of cost behavior, often not accurate enough to make specific decisions concerning products, services, or activities?

Chapter 3 Cost Behavior and Estimation

Q3-3. Explain the term "relevant range" and why it is important in estimating total costs.

Q3-4. The high-low method of analyzing mixed costs uses only two observation points: the high and the low points of activity. Are these always the best points for prediction purposes? Why or why not?

Q3-5. Distinguish between cost estimation and cost prediction.

Q3-6. Why is a scatter diagram helpful when used in conjunction with other methods of cost estimation?

Q3-7. Why would regression analysis provide a more accurate cost formula than the high-low method for a mixed cost?

Q3-8. Why is it important to match activity and costs within each observation? When is this matching problem most likely to exist?

Q3-9. What are benefits of estimating costs using learning curves?

Q3-10. Distinguish between the unit-, batch-, product-, and organizational/facility-level activities of a manufacturing organization.

Multiple Choice

MC3-11. A graph of the total cost of ingredients used in **Papa Murphy's** pizzas most closely resembles this total cost behavior pattern:
- a. Variable cost
- b. Fixed cost
- c. Mixed cost
- d. Step cost

MC3-12. At a sales volume of 50 units, the average cost is $410 per unit and the variable cost is $10 per unit. Assuming a linear cost behavior pattern, if sales double to 100 units, the average cost will be
- a. $10
- b. $200
- c. $205
- d. $210

MC3-13. Plotting data points on a scatter chart
- a. can highlight whether a cost is a good predictor of activity.
- b. is the best way to develop a total cost estimating equation.
- c. helps determine whether costs approximate a straight-line.
- d. does not typically highlight outliers within a relevant range of activity.

MC3-14. Employees of Chelsea, a financial consulting firm, often travel to client sites for project meetings. The firm's business manager is attempting to better understand the costs associated with the employees' company cars. Below is data for the first four months of the year related to miles incurred and costs associated with the cars, including leases, insurance, maintenance, and gas. Use the high-low method to calculate the fixed costs associated with the company cars.

	Mileage	Costs
Jan.	450	$29,300
Feb.	325	$22,550
Mar.	418	$27,572
Apr.	380	$25,520

- a. $0.54
- b. $3,215
- c. $5,000
- d. $4,500

MC3-15. Which of the following situations would cause concern when an analyst is developing a cost-estimating equation?
- a. A relatively linear relationship exists between total costs and activity.
- b. The data is based on normal operating conditions.
- c. The industry incurs significant changes in technology.
- d. The cost driver has a logical, causal relationship with costs.

MC3-16. In order to analyze sales as a function of advertising expenses, the sales manager of Smith Company developed a simple regression model. The model included the following equation, which was based on 32 monthly observations of sales and advertising expenses with a related coefficient of determination of 0.90.

$$S = \$10{,}000 + 2.50A$$
$$S = \text{sales}$$
$$A = \text{advertising expenses}$$

If Smith Company's advertising expenses in one month amounted to $1,000, the related point estimate of sales would be

- a. $2,500
- b. $11,250
- c. $12,250
- d. $12,500

LO3-5 MC3-17. A manufacturing firm plans to bid on a special order of 80 units that will be manufactured in lots of 10 units each. The production manager estimates that the direct labor hours per unit will decline by a constant percentage each time the cumulative quantity of units produced doubles. The quantitative technique used to capture this phenomenon and estimate the direct labor hours required for the special order is

- a. cost-profit-volume analysis.
- b. the Markov process.
- c. linear programming analysis.
- d. learning curve analysis.

LO3-5 MC3-18. Aerosub Inc. has developed a new product for spacecraft that includes the manufacturing of a complex part. The manufacturing of this part requires a high degree of technical skill. Management believes there is a good opportunity for its technical force to learn and improve as they become accustomed to the production process. The production of the first unit requires 10,000 direct labor hours. If an 80% learning curve is used and eight units are produced, the cumulative average direct labor hours required per unit of the product will be

- a. 5,120 hours.
- b. 6,400 hours.
- c. 8,000 hours.
- d. 10,000 hours.

LO3-6 MC3-19. Increasing the length of the time period included in each observation of activity and cost will assist in overcoming this possible problem in cost estimation:

- a. Data not based on normal operations
- b. Nonlinear relationship between total costs and activity
- c. Changes in technology or prices
- d. Failure to match activity and costs within each observation

LO3-7 MC3-20. Arch manufactures a product with the following manufacturing cost hierarchy for its only current product:

	Cost
Unit	$20/unit
Batch	$500/batch
Product	$10,000/year
Facility	$50,000/year

Next year Arch plans to manufacture 50,000 units of product in batches of 500 units. Arch's predicted manufacturing costs for next year are

- a. $1,560,000
- b. $1,500,000
- c. $1,110,000
- d. $660,000

LO3-7 MC3-21. West sells specialized products produced by electronics companies to 100 engineering firms. West sells these products at a price based on West's purchase price. West's customer cost hierarchy is as follows:

	Cost
Unit	80% of selling price
Batch	$200 per sales order
Customer	$1,000 per customer per year
Facility	$120,000 per year

Next year West plans to sell $4,000,000 of product to the 100 engineering firms it serves. It anticipates that each firm will place an average of 4 orders. West's predicted customer costs for next year are

- a. $80,000
- b. $300,000
- c. $3,200,000
- d. $3,500,000

Exercises

E3-22. Classifying cost behavior   LO3-1

Classify the total costs of each of the following as variable, fixed, mixed, or step. Sales volume is the cost driver.
- a. Salary of the department manager
- b. Memory chips in a computer assembly plant
- c. Real estate taxes
- d. Salaries of quality inspectors when each inspector can evaluate a maximum of 1,000 units per day
- e. Wages paid to production employees for the time spent working on products
- f. Electric power in a factory
- g. Raw materials used in production
- h. Electric vehicle rented on the basis of a fixed charge per day plus an additional charge per mile driven
- i. Sales commissions
- j. Straight-line depreciation on office equipment

E3-23. Classifying cost behavior   LO3-1

Classify the total costs of each of the following as variable, fixed, mixed, or step.
- a. Straight-line depreciation on a building
- b. Maintenance costs at a hospital
- c. Rent on video conferencing equipment charged as a fixed amount per month plus an additional charge per call
- d. Cost of goods sold in a bookstore
- e. Salaries paid to temporary instructors in a college as the number of course sessions varies
- f. Lumber used by a house construction company
- g. The costs of operating a research department
- h. The cost of hiring a dance band for three hours
- i. Laser printer paper for a department printer
- j. Electric power in a restaurant

E3-24. Classifying cost behavior   LO3-1, 2

For each of the following situations, select the most appropriate cost behavior pattern (as shown in the illustrations following this problem) where the lines represent the cost behavior pattern, the vertical axis represents costs, the horizontal axis represents total volume, and the dots represent actual costs. Each pattern may be used more than once.
- a. Variable costs per unit
- b. Total fixed costs
- c. Total mixed costs
- d. Average fixed costs per unit
- e. Total current manufacturing costs
- f. Average variable costs
- g. Total costs when employees are paid $15 per hour for the first 40 hours worked each week and $20 for each additional hour
- h. Total costs when employees are paid $15 per hour and guaranteed a minimum weekly wage of $300
- i. Total costs per day when a consultant is paid $200 per hour with a maximum daily fee of $1,000
- j. Total variable costs
- k. Total costs for salaries of social workers where each social worker can handle a maximum of 25 cases
- l. A water bill where a flat fee of $800 is charged for the first 100,000 gallons and additional water costs $0.005 per gallon
- m. Total variable costs properly used to estimate step costs
- n. Total materials costs
- o. Rent on exhibit space at a convention

Graphs for Exercise E3-24

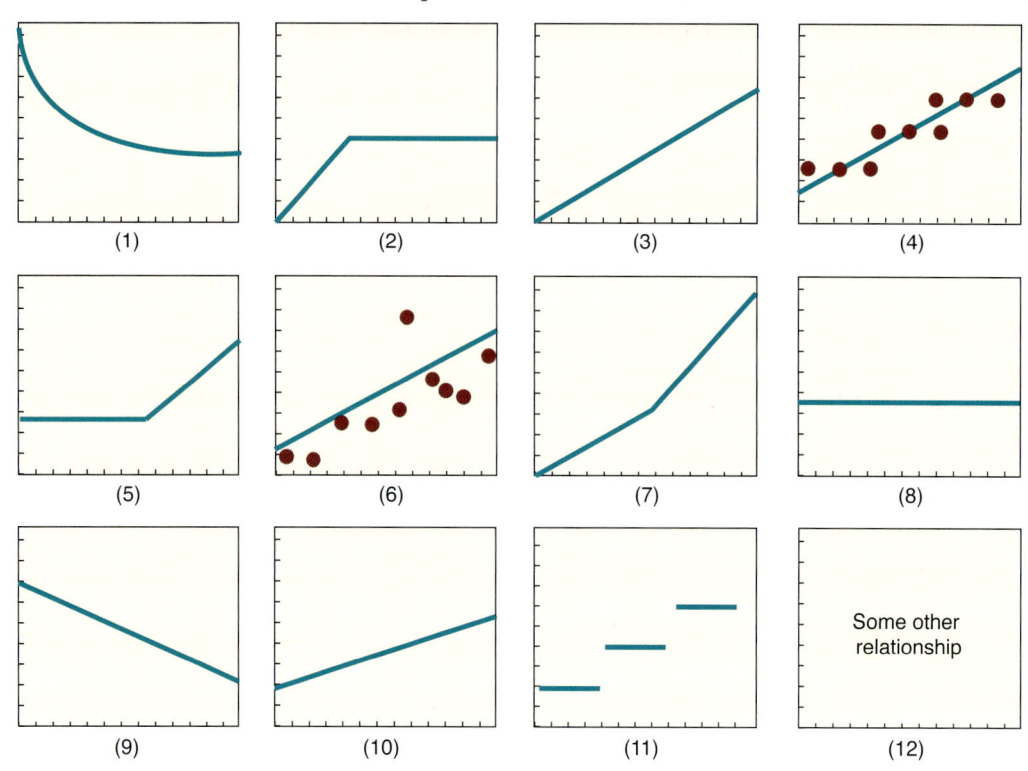

(1) (2) (3) (4)
(5) (6) (7) (8)
(9) (10) (11) (12) Some other relationship

LO3-1, 2 **E3-25. Classifying cost behavior**

For each of the graphs displayed following this problem, select the most appropriate cost behavior pattern where the lines represent the cost behavior pattern, the vertical axis represents total costs, the horizontal axis represents total volume, and the dots represent actual costs. Each pattern may be used more than once.

a. A cellular bill when a flat fee is charged for the first TB of data of use per month and additional data costs a set rate per GB.
b. Total selling and administrative costs
c. Total labor costs when employees are paid per unit produced
d. Total overtime premium paid production employees
e. Average total cost per unit
f. Salaries of supervisors when each one can supervise a maximum of 10 employees
g. Total idle time costs when employees are paid for a minimum 40-hour week
h. Materials costs per unit
i. Total sales commissions
j. Electric power consumption in a restaurant, assumed to have a variable and fixed component
k. Total costs when high volumes of production require the use of overtime and obsolete equipment
l. A good linear approximation of actual costs
m. A linear cost estimation valid only within the relevant range

Graphs for Exercise E3-25

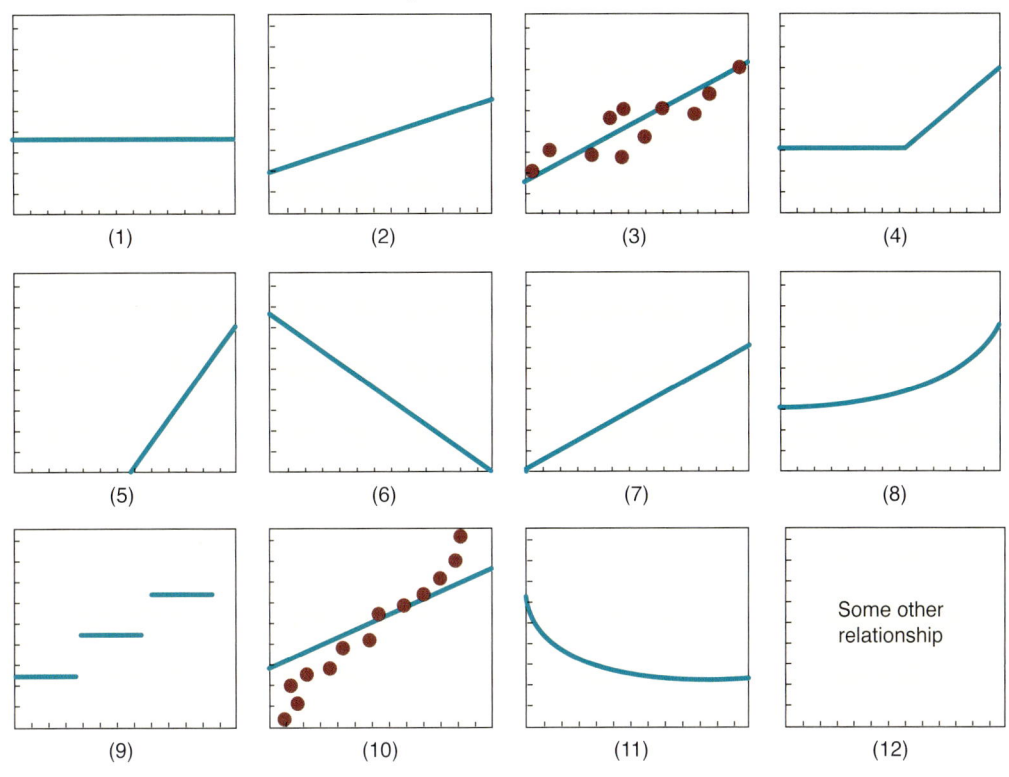

(1) (2) (3) (4)
(5) (6) (7) (8)
(9) (10) (11) (12) Some other relationship

E3-26. Computing average unit costs

Assume the total monthly operating costs of a **Panera's** restaurant are:

$$\$40,000 + \$0.75X$$

where

$$X = \text{Number of salad orders}$$

Required
a. Determine the average cost per salad at each of the following monthly volumes: 1,000; 10,000; 50,000; 100,000.
b. Determine the monthly volume at which the average cost per serving is $2.35.

E3-27. Automatic versus manual processing

Bartell's, a Seattle area drug store, operates an in-store printing service for photo printing. The current service, which requires employees to access photos uploaded by customers on their website, has monthly operating costs of $5,500 plus $0.15 per photo printed. Management is evaluating the desirability of acquiring a machine that will allow customers to download and make prints without employee assistance. If the machine is acquired, the monthly fixed costs will increase to $7,000 and the variable costs of printing a photo will decline to $0.05 per photo.

Required
a. Determine the total costs of printing 10,000 and 25,000 photos per month:
  1. With the current employee-assisted process.
  2. With the proposed customer self-service process.
b. Determine the monthly volume at which the proposed process becomes preferable to (costs less than) the current process.

E3-28. Automatic versus manual processing

Assume **Office Depot** processes 2,500,000 photocopies per month at its service center. Approximately 50% of the photocopies require collating. Collating is currently performed by high school and college students who are paid $10 per hour. Each student collates an average of 5,000 copies per hour. Management is contemplating the lease of an automatic collating machine that has a monthly capacity of 6,000,000 photocopies, with lease and operating costs totaling $3,000, plus $0.05 per 1,000 units collated.

Required
a. Determine the total costs of collating 1,000,000 and 2,000,000 per month:
   1. With student help.
   2. With the collating machine.
b. Determine the monthly volume at which the automatic process becomes preferable to (costs less than) the manual process.

LO3-1

E3-29. Developing an equation from average costs

Tucker Pup's Pet Resort offers dog boarding services in Chicago. Assume that in March, when dog-days occupancy was at an annual low of 150 days, the average cost per dog-day was $65. In July, when dog-days were at a capacity level of 600, the average cost per dog-day was $20.

Required
a. Develop an equation for monthly operating costs.
b. Determine the average boarding cost per dog-day at an annual volume of 4,500 dog-days.

LO3-2, 3

E3-30. Scatter diagrams and high-low cost estimation

Assume the local **Pearle Vision** has the following information on the number of sales orders received and order-processing costs.

Month	Sales Orders	Order-Processing Costs
1	3,300	$ 90,970
2	1,650	55,412
3	4,840	68,750
4	3,080	90,090
5	2,530	76,752
6	1,320	47,410
7	2,200	68,750

Required
a. Plot the data on a scatter diagram. Identify any outliers.
b. Use information from the high- and low-volume months to develop a cost-estimating equation for monthly order-processing costs using *representative points only*.

LO3-2, 3

E3-31. Scatter diagrams and high-low cost estimation

From April 1 through October 31, **Coles County Highway Department** hires temporary employees to mow and clean the right-of-way along county roads. The County Road Commissioner has asked you to help her in determining the variable labor cost of mowing and cleaning a mile of road. The following information is available regarding current-year operations:

Month	Miles Mowed and Cleaned	Labor Costs
April	240	$6,800
May	305	7,680
June	325	8,310
July	275	7,200
August	220	6,550
September	200	5,760
October	75	6,720

Required
a. Plot the data on a scatter diagram and identify any outliers.
b. Using the information from *representative* high- and low-volume months, use the high-low method to develop a cost-estimating equation for monthly labor costs.
c. Adjust the equation developed in requirement (b) to incorporate the effect of an anticipated 5% increase in wages.

LO3-3

E3-32. High-low cost estimation

Assume the local **YRC Worldwide** delivery service hub has the following information available about fleet miles and operating costs:

Year	Miles	Operating Costs
Year 1	695,000	$219,500
Year 2	855,000	267,500

Required
Use the high-low method to develop a cost-estimating equation for total annual operating costs.

E3-33. Cost behavior analysis in a restaurant: high-low cost estimation LO3-1, 3
Assume a **Potbelly's** restaurant has the following information available regarding costs at representative levels of monthly sales (meals served):

	Monthly Sales in Units		
	5,000	7,000	10,000
Cost of food sold	$ 7,500	$10,500	$15,000
Wages and fringe benefits	5,900	5,940	6,000
Fees paid delivery help	6,000	8,400	12,000
Rent on building	3,500	3,500	3,500
Depreciation on equipment	850	850	850
Utilities	600	640	700
Supplies (soap, floor wax, etc.)	400	480	600
Administrative costs	1,200	1,200	1,200
Total	$25,950	$31,510	$39,850

Required
a. Identify each cost as being variable, fixed, or mixed.
b. Use the high-low method to develop a schedule identifying the amount of each cost that is mixed or variable per unit. Total the amounts under each category to develop an equation for total monthly costs.
c. Predict total costs for a monthly sales volume of 8,500 units.

E3-34. Selecting an independent variable: scatter diagrams LO3-2
Brenthaven produces protective cases for mobile technology. The cases are sold internationally, online, and through retail partners. Presented is information on production costs and inventory changes for five recent months:

	January	February	March	April	May
Finished goods inventory in units:					
Beginning	20,000	30,000	20,000	5,000	35,000
Manufactured	35,000	45,000	40,000	50,000	60,000
Available	55,000	75,000	60,000	55,000	95,000
Sold	(25,000)	(55,000)	(55,000)	(20,000)	(65,000)
Ending	30,000	20,000	5,000	35,000	30,000
Manufacturing costs	$525,000	$615,000	$550,000	$745,000	$800,000

Required
a. With the aid of scatter diagrams, determine whether units sold or units manufactured is a better predictor of manufacturing costs.
b. Prepare an explanation for your answer to requirement (a).
c. Which independent variable, units sold or units manufactured, should be a better predictor of selling costs? Why?

E3-35. High-low method LO3-3
Information about Indiana Industrial's utility cost for the last six months of the current year follows. The high-low method will be used to develop a cost formula to predict next year's utility charges, and the number of machine hours has been found to be an appropriate cost driver. Data for the first half of the year are not being considered because the utility company imposed a significant rate change as of July 1.

Month	Machine Hours	Utility Cost
July	33,750	$13,000
August	34,000	12,200
September	33,150	11,040
October	32,000	11,960
November	31,250	11,500
December	31,000	11,720

    a. What is the cost formula for utility expense?
    b. What is the budgeted utility cost for September of the following year if 31,250 machine hours are projected?

LO3-3   **E3-36.**   **High-low method**

Wyoming Wholesale has gathered the following data on the number of shipments received and the cost of receiving reports for the first seven weeks of the year.

Number of Shipments Received	Weekly Cost of Receiving Reports
50	$175
44	162
40	154
35	142
53	185
58	200
60	202

    a. Using the high-low method, develop the equation for predicting weekly receiving report costs based on the number of shipments received.
    b. What is the predicted amount of receiving report costs for a week in which 72 shipments are received?
    c. What are the concerns you have regarding your prediction from (b)?

LO3-3   **E3-37.**   **High-low method**

La Mia's Casas builds replicas of residences of famous and infamous people. The company is highly automated, and the new accountant-owner has decided to use machine hours as the basis for predicting maintenance costs. The following data are available from the company's most recent eight months of operations:

Machine Hours	Maintenance Costs
4,000	$1,470
7,000	1,200
3,500	1,680
6,000	1,100
3,000	1,960
9,000	880
8,000	1,020
5,500	1,200

    a. Using the high-low method, determine the cost formula for maintenance costs with machine hours as the basis for estimation.
    b. What aspect of the estimated equation is bothersome? Provide an explanation for this situation.
    c. Within the relevant range, can the formula be reliably used to predict maintenance costs? Can the *a* and *b* values in the cost formula be interpreted as fixed and variable costs? Why or why not?

LO3-3   **E3-38.**   **High-low method**

Tijuana Tile has gathered the following information on its utility cost for the past six months.

Chapter 3 Cost Behavior and Estimation

Machine Hours	Utility Cost
1,300	$ 940
1,700	1,075
1,250	900
1,800	1,132
1,900	1,160
1,500	990

Using the high-low method, determine the cost formula for utility cost.

E3-39. Least squares regression
Wyoming Wholesale has gathered the following data on the number of shipments received and the cost of receiving reports for the first seven weeks of the year.

Number of Shipments Received	Weekly Cost of Receiving Reports
50	$175
44	162
40	154
35	142
53	185
58	200
60	202

a. Using regression tools in Excel, develop the equation for predicting weekly receiving report costs based on the number of shipments received.
b. What is the predicted amount of receiving report costs for a month (assume a month is exactly four weeks) in which 165 shipments are received?

E3-40. Least squares regression
UpTop Mining has compiled the following data to analyze utility costs:

Month	Machine Hours	Utility Cost
January	200	$300
February	325	440
March	400	480
April	410	490
May	525	620
June	680	790
July	820	840
August	900	900

Using regression tools in Excel, develop a formula for budgeting utility cost.

E3-41. Applying the incremental unit time learning curve
Large Vessels Inc. accepted an order for 4 ships. The production process is lengthy due to the customization required in the specification outlined in the contract. The production of the first ship required 48,000 direct labor hours. Based on past projects, the company anticipates an 80% *incremental* unit time learning curve.

a. What is the expected number of labor hours expected to be incurred to produce the second ship?
b. What is the expected number of labor hours expected to be incurred to produce the fourth ship?
c. Recalculate your answers to parts a & b using a 70% incremental unit time learning curve.
d. Recalculate your answers to parts a & b using a 90% incremental unit time learning curve.

E3-42. Applying the cumulative average time learning curve
In competing as a subcontractor on a military contract, Aerosub Inc. has developed a new product for spacecraft that includes the manufacturing of a complex part. Management believes there is a good opportunity for its technical force to learn and improve as they become accustomed to the production process. Accordingly, management estimates an 80% *cumulative* average time learning curve would apply to this unit. The overall contract will call for supplying eight units. Production of the first unit requires 10,000 direct labor hours.

What is the estimated total direct labor hours required to produce the seven additional units?

LO3-5 **E3-43. Applying the cumulative average time learning curve**

Propeller Inc. plans to manufacture a newly designed high-technology propeller for airplanes. Propeller forecasts that as workers gain experience, they will need less time to complete the job. Based on prior experience, Propeller estimates a 70% *cumulative* average time learning curve and has projected the following costs.

Cumulative Number of Units Produced	Manufacturing Projections Average Cost Per Unit	Total Costs
1	$20,000	$20,000
2	14,000	28,000

a. If Propeller manufactures four propellers, what would the total manufacturing costs be?
b. If Propeller manufactures eight propellers, what would the total manufacturing costs be?
c. Calculate the cumulative average cost of producing the eighth propeller as a percentage of the cost of producing the first propeller.

LO3-6 **E3-44. Identifying potential issues in cost estimation**

Determine whether each of the following is an indication of more or less reliable cost estimation effectiveness for data analysis in a manufacturing plant. Consider each scenario separately.

1. Data analysis of one potential driver of manufacturing defects shows a lower coefficient of determination compared to the analysis of other sources.
2. A scatter plot reveals a small dispersion of points around the cost-estimating line.
3. Data sets are pulled from verified sources and are checked for completeness.
4. Internal controls are in place to protect cost data from unauthorized access.
5. Direct material costs are expected to increase by an uncertain amount, due to a recent global supply shortage.
6. The relationship between the cost driver of machine hours and maintenance cost appears to be logical.
7. Potential for high inflation causes uncertainty in the prediction of supply costs.
8. The plant anticipates supplementing its manufacturing processes with AI technology in the upcoming year which could impact labor costs.

LO3-6 **E3-45. Identifying potential gaps in the effectiveness of data analytics**

Access KPMG's report, Building Trust in Analytics, at https://assets.kpmg.com/content/dam/kpmg/xx/pdf/2016/10/building-trust-in-analytics.pdf and answer the following questions.

a. What are four areas of concern for employees that rely on data for decision making?
b. What are potential gaps in each of these areas?
c. What are suggestions for closing these gaps in an organization?

LO3-7 **E3-46. Classifying costs using a manufacturing cost hierarchy**

One Degree Organic Foods, based in Canada, produces a line of organic cereal. The following represent activity costs for one of its manufacturing plants.

1. Leasing costs of its manufacturing facilities
2. Cost of sourcing organically grown oats
3. Cost of random quality inspection in every case of product
4. Cost to recalibrate machines after extended use
5. Cost of digital ads promoting its line of organic cereals
6. Cost of sustainable packaging materials for each box of cereal
7. Cost to research and develop a new flavor of cereal
8. Costs to prepare for and facilitate governmental compliance inspections
9. Mixing costs for an order of its brown rice crisp cereal.
10. Direct labor costs of employees working on the assembly line.

Required

Classify each cost activity above, in the most appropriate level of the manufacturing cost hierarchy. Choose from unit-level activity, batch-level activity, product-level activity, and facility-level activity. Each cost activity may be used more than once.

Problems

P3-47. High-low and scatter diagrams with implications for regression
Midnight Cookie Company produces and delivers gourmet cookies and ice cream until 1:30 a.m. from its three Seattle area locations. Presented is monthly cost and sales information for cookies at one of Midnight's locations.

LO3-1, 2, 3, 4, 6
Midnight Cookie Company

Month	Sales (Dozens)	Total Costs
January	6,800	$30,650
February	7,800	35,336
March	5,500	29,700
April	5,700	30,250
May	6,100	30,600
June	4,500	28,670

Required
a. Plot the data points and identify any outliers.
b. Using the high-low method, develop a cost-estimating equation for total monthly costs, using representative observations.
c. If you decided to develop a cost-estimating equation using least-squares regression analysis, should you include all the observations? Why or why not?
d. Using regression tools in Excel, develop a formula for budgeting total monthly costs.
e. Mention two reasons that the least-squares regression is superior to the high-low and scatter diagram methods of cost estimation.

P3-48. Estimating machine repair costs
In an attempt to determine the best basis for predicting machine repair costs, the production supervisor accumulated daily information on these costs and production over a one-month period. Applying simple regression analysis to the data, she obtained the following estimating equation:

LO3-4

$$Y = \$800 - \$2.60X$$

where

Y = total daily machine repair costs
X = daily production in units

Because of the negative relationship between repair costs and production, she was somewhat skeptical of the results, even though the R-squared was a respectable 0.765.

Required
a. What is the most likely explanation of the negative variable costs?
b. Suggest an alternative procedure for estimating machine repair costs that might prove more useful.

P3-49. High-low; least squares regression
Sympco Glass manufactures insulated windows. The firm's repair and maintenance (R&M) cost is mixed and varies most directly with machine hours worked. The following data have been gathered from recent operations:

LO3-3, 4

Month	MHs	R&M Cost
May	1,400	$ 9,000
June	1,900	10,719
July	2,000	10,900
August	2,500	13,000
September	2,200	11,578
October	2,700	13,160
November	1,700	9,525
December	2,300	11,670

a. Use the high-low method to estimate a cost formula for repairs and maintenance.
b. Using regression tools in Excel, develop a formula for budgeting R&M costs.
c. Does the answer to *a* or to *b* provide the better estimate of the relationship between repairs and maintenance costs and machine hours? Why?

LO3-4 **P3-50.** **Least squares regression**

Bon Voyage provides charter cruises in the eastern Caribbean. Tina Louise, the owner, wants to understand how her labor costs change per month. She recognizes that the cost is neither strictly fixed nor strictly variable. She has gathered the following information and has identified two potential predictive bases, number of charters and gross receipts.

Month	Labor Costs	Number of Charters	Gross Receipts ($000)
January.........	$ 8,000	10	$ 12
February........	9,200	14	18
March..........	12,000	22	26
April...........	14,200	28	36
May............	18,500	40	60
June...........	28,000	62	82
July............	34,000	100	120
August.........	30,000	90	100
September......	24,000	80	96

Using the least squares method, develop a labor cost formula using
1. Using regression tools in Excel, develop a formula for budgeting labor costs
   a. number of charters
   b. gross receipts
2. Which cost driver appears to have a strong relationship with labor costs?

LO3-5 **P3-51.** **Applying the cumulative average time learning curve**

Coe Company is a manufacturer of semi-custom motorcycles. The company used 500 labor hours to produce a prototype of a new motorcycle for one of its key customers. The customer then ordered three additional motorcycles to be produced over the next six months. Coe estimates that the manufacturing process for these additional motorcycles is subject to a 90% cumulative average time learning curve. Although the production manager was aware of the learning curve projections, he decided to ignore the learning curve when compiling his budget in order to provide a cushion to prevent exceeding the budgeted amount for labor.

a. By using the cumulative average-time learning curve, estimate the total number of labor hours that are required to manufacture the first four units of product.
b. Assume the 90% learning curve is realized. Calculate Coe's cost savings in producing the three additional units if the cost of direct labor is $25 per hour. Show your calculations.
c. Assume that Coe actually used 1,740 labor hours to produce the four units.
   1. If the company ignored the learning curve when creating the budget, how would the number of labor hours compare to the budgeted labor hours if the budget was based on the time to produce the first unit?
   2. If the learning curve had been considered when creating the budget, how would the number of labor hours compare to the budgeted labor hours?
d. Explain the effect on your answer to part c if the manufacturing process were instead subject to an 80% learning curve.
e. Identify and explain one limitation of learning curve analysis.

LO3-5 **P3-52.** **Applying the cumulative average time learning curve**

Rosewood Designs produces customized textiles, such as dresses, formal attire, and uniforms.
Rosewood is a small sole proprietorship owned and managed by Samuel Wood. Rosewood uses a job order costing system. During July, Rosewood completed Job 431, an order for 2,000 school uniforms. Rosewood incurred a total of 3,500 direct labor hours for the job. Based on the success of this large order, Wood is contemplating a drastic change in business strategy. Wood is considering mass producing school uniforms and gradually phasing out custom orders.

After completing Job 431, management analyzed the direct labor hours. Rosewood normally experiences an 80% *cumulative* average time learning curve, and management expects that the learning curve will level off after producing 8,000 uniforms.

Required

a. Define and explain the concept of the learning curve.

b. Compute the cumulative average hours per uniform for the following production levels: (1) 2,000 uniforms, (2) 4,000 uniforms, and (3) 8,000 uniforms?
c. Compute the cumulative total hours for the following production levels: (1) 2,000 uniforms, (2) 4,000 uniforms, and (3) 8,000 uniforms?
d. After completing 8,000 uniforms, what is the estimated direct labor cost per uniform? Assume an average labor rate of $12 per hour. How does this compare to a direct labor cost budget prepared after the initial 2,000 uniforms were produced?

P3-53. Ethical problem uncovered by cost estimation

Westfield owns and provides management services for several shopping centers. After five years with the company, James Heller was recently promoted to the position of manager of one of Westfield's smaller malls on the outskirts of a downtown area. When he accepted the assignment, James was told that he would hold the position for only a couple of years because that mall would likely be torn down to make way for a new sports stadium. James was also told that if he did well in this assignment, he would be in line for heading one of the company's new 200-store operations that were currently in the planning stage.

While reviewing the mall's financial records for the past few years, James observed that last year's oil consumption was up by 8%, even though the number of heating degree days was down by 4%. Somewhat curious, James uncovered the following information:

- The mall is heated by forced-air oil heat. The furnace is five years old and has been well maintained.
- Fuel oil is kept in four 5,000-gallon underground oil tanks. The oil tanks were installed 25 years ago.
- Replacing the tanks would cost $80,000. If pollution was found, cleanup costs could go as high as $2,000,000, depending on how much oil had leaked into the ground and how far it had spread.
- Replacing the tanks would add more congestion to the mall's parking situation.

Required
What should James do? Explain.

P3-54. Multiple cost drivers

Newman's Own manufactures a variety of specialty salad dressings. Production runs are both high-volume and low-volume activities, depending on customer orders. Assume the following represents general manufacturing costs (manufacturing overhead) and each cost's related cost driver for Newman's Own.

Level	Total Cost	Units of Cost Driver
Unit..................................	$600,000	20,000 machine hours
Batch...............................	40,000	400 customer orders
Product............................	84,000	15 products

The lime vinaigrette dressing required 1,000 machine hours to fill 60 customer orders for a total of 4,000 cases.

Required
a. Assuming all manufacturing overhead is estimated and predicted on the basis of machine hours, determine the predicted total overhead costs to produce the 4,000 cases of lime vinaigrette.
b. Assuming manufacturing overhead is estimated and predicted using separate rates for machine hours, customer orders, and products (a multiple-level cost hierarchy), determine the predicted total overhead costs to produce the 4,000 cases of lime vinaigrette.
c. Calculate the error in predicting manufacturing overhead using machine hours versus using multiple cost drivers. Indicate whether the use of only machine hours results in overpredicting or underpredicting the costs to produce 4,000 cases of lime vinaigrette.
d. Looking just at batch level costs, calculate the error in predicting those costs using machine hours versus using customer orders. Indicate whether the use of only machine hours results in overpredicting or underpredicting the batch-level costs to produce 4,000 cases of lime vinaigrette.
e. Looking just at product-level costs, calculate the error in predicting those costs using machine hours versus using number of products. Indicate whether the use of only machine hours results in overpredicting or underpredicting the product-level costs to produce 4,000 cases of lime vinaigrette.

LO3-7 P3-55. Unit- and batch-level cost drivers

Kentucky Fried Chicken (a reportable operating segment of **Yum Brands Inc.**), a fast-food restaurant, serves fried chicken. The managers are considering an "all you can eat" promotion and want to know the costs before setting a price. Each batch must be 50 pieces. The chicken is precut by the chain headquarters and sent to the stores in 10-piece bags. Each bag costs $5. Preparing a batch of 50 pieces of chicken with KFC's special coating takes one employee two hours. The current wage rate is $10 per hour. Another cost driver is the cost of putting fresh oil into the fryers. New oil, costing $9, is used for each batch.

Required
a. Determine the cost of preparing one batch of 50 pieces.
b. If management projects that it will sell 150 pieces of fried chicken, determine the total cost and the cost per piece.
c. If management estimates the sales to be 350 pieces, determine the total costs.
d. How much will the batch costs increase if the government raises the minimum wage to $12 per hour?
e. If management decided to increase the number of pieces in a batch to 100, determine the cost of preparing 350 pieces. Assume that the batch would take twice as long to prepare, pay rate stays at $10 per hour, and management wants to replace the oil after 100 pieces are cooked. Assume no change in expected sales volume. Note that only full batches can be prepared.

LO3-7 P3-56. Optimal batch size

This is a continuation of parts *c* and *e* of P3-55.

Required
Should management increase the batch size to 100? Why or why not?

LO3-7 P3-57. Cost drivers and cost estimation

Market Street Soup Company produces ten varieties of soup in large vats, several thousand gallons at a time. The soup is distributed to several categories of customers. Some soup is packaged in large containers and sold to college and university food services. Some is packaged in half-gallon or small containers and sold through wholesale distributors to grocery stores. Finally, some is packaged in a variety of individual servings and sold directly to the public from trucks owned and operated by Market Street Soup Company. Management has always assumed that costs fluctuated with the volume of soup, and cost-estimating equations have been based on the following cost function:

$$\text{Estimated costs} = \text{Fixed costs} + \text{Variable costs per gallon} \times \text{Production in gallons}$$

Lately, however, this equation has not been a very accurate predictor of total costs. At the same time, management has noticed that the volumes and varieties of soup sold through the three distinct distribution channels have fluctuated from month to month.

Required
a. What *relevant* major assumption is inherent in the cost-estimating equation currently used by Market Street Soup Company?
b. Why might Market Street Soup Company wish to develop a cost-estimating equation that recognizes the hierarchy of activity costs? Explain.
c. Develop the general form of a more accurate cost-estimating equation for Market Street Soup Company. Clearly label and explain all elements of the equation, and provide specific examples of costs for each element.

LO3-6, 7 P3-58. Verifying data sources

ChatGPT and **Bard** are examples of AI-powered, language driven sites that offer answers to user questions. These sites are currently offering free access to certain versions of the system.

Required
a. Using one of these sites (or a similar site), ask the following three questions, generating two responses for each. Save your search results.
   1. What is the manufacturing cost hierarchy developed by Cooper and Kaplan? Include citations.
   2. What is the customer hierarchy? Include citations.
   3. Give examples of unit level, batch level, product level, and facility level costs. Include citations.

Chapter 3 Cost Behavior and Estimation

b. Assess the quality of the source data. Do the citations link to valid sources? How do you validate the responses provided?
c. Using the two generated responses and information from the textbook in LO3-7, create an updated response to questions in part *a*. Are there any inconsistencies with the AI-generated response and the text book information?
d. Assess the effectiveness of the answer provided in part *a*. How is your updated response different from the AI-generated response?

Review Solutions

Review 3-1
1. Total costs = $45,000 + $1,800X
2. X = number of clients
   Total costs = $45,000 + $1,800X
   a. $45,000 + $1,800(25) = $90,000
      $90,000 ÷ 25 clients = $3,600 per client
   b. $45,000 + $1,800(30) = $99,000
      $99,000 ÷ 30 clients = $3,300 per client
   c. $45,000 + $1,800(36) = $109,800
      $109,800 ÷ 36 clients = $3,050 per client
3. $2,925 − $1,800 = $1,125 fixed costs per client
   $45,000 ÷ $1,125 = 40 clients
4. This scenario assumes that variable costs of $1,800 are incurred for each client. However, if the resources expended per client differ (ignoring fixed costs), then the number of clients would not be an accurate predictor of total variable costs for the firm.

Review 3-2

a.

Scatter Diagram

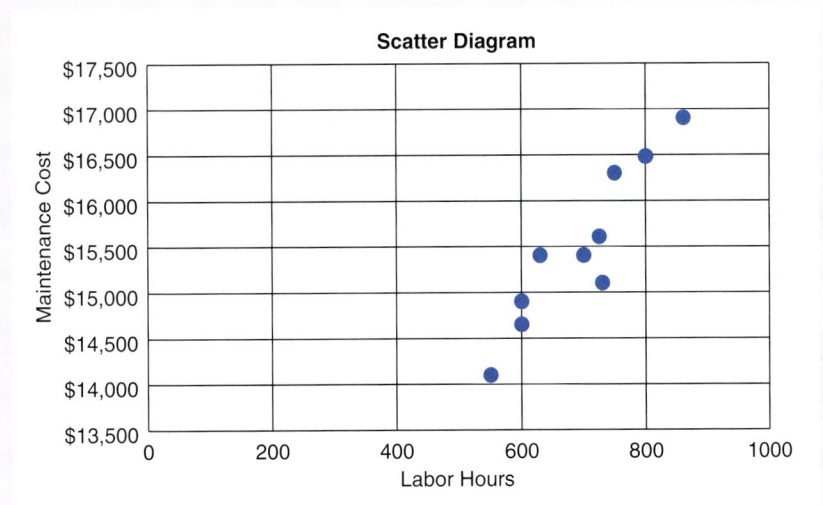

[Scatter diagram showing Maintenance Cost (y-axis, $13,500 to $17,500) vs Labor Hours (x-axis, 0 to 1000) with data points plotted.]

No observation points in the scatter diagram appear to be outliers.

b. The identification of outliers is not always a clear-cut process. Visually, a point may clearly be distanced from the other observation points to make it stand out as an outlier. Other times, it may not be as clear. In those cases, examining the details regarding the specific data point could help inform the management accountant as to whether there were unique circumstances that indicate that the point is not representative of activity for the period.

Review 3-3

a. $\dfrac{\text{Change in Costs}}{\text{Change in Activity}}$ $\dfrac{(\$16{,}900 - \$14{,}100)}{(860 - 550)} = \$9.03$ (rounded)

Fixed costs = $16,900 − ($9.03 × 860) = $9,134

$Y = \$9{,}134 + \$9.03X$

b. $Y = \$9{,}134 + \$9.03(650) = \$15{,}004$ (rounded)

c. If you were presenting your findings in part b, you would need to disclose that your analysis considered only two data points (high- and low-activity data points). If these two points are not representative of normal operations, the estimate will be inaccurate.

Review 3-4

a. **Regression Summary Output**

	A	B	C	D	E	F	G	H	I
1	SUMMARY OUTPUT								
3	Regression Statistics								
4	Multiple R	0.930077669							
5	R Square	0.865044471							
6	Adjusted R Square	0.84817503							
7	Standard Error	338.4911005							
8	Observations	10							
10	ANOVA								
11		df	SS	MS	F	Significance F			
12	Regression	1	5875329.799	5875329.799	51.2787866	9.60566E-05			
13	Residual	8	916609.8011	114576.2251					
14	Total	9	6791939.6						
16		Coefficients	Standard Error	t Stat	P-value	Lower 95%	Upper 95%	Lower 95.0%	Upper 95.0%
17	Intercept	9767.401712	805.421488	12.12706869	1.97842E-06	7910.09643	11624.70699	7910.09643	11624.70699
18	Labor Hours	8.230955058	1.14942691	7.160920793	9.60566E-05	5.580371851	10.88153826	5.580371851	10.88153826

$Y = \$9{,}767 + \$8.23X$

b. The analyst must evaluate the data used in regression analysis and exclude unusual observations. Otherwise, a single large squared deviation will have a disproportionate influence in the cost-estimating equation. If for example, we change machine hours in June to 750 hours (a 25% increase), the R^2 value changes from 0.865 to 0.734. It also results in a change in the cost estimating equation.

Review 3-5
PART ONE

a.&b.

Incremental Number of Units Produced	Manufacturing Projections: Average Hours per Unit
1	12,000
2	9,600
4	7,680

c. 7,680/12,000 = 64.0%

d.

Incremental Number of Units Produced	Manufacturing Projections: Average Hours per Unit
1	12,000
2	10,800
4	9,720

9,720/12,000 = 81.0%

Chapter 3 Cost Behavior and Estimation

PART TWO

a.&b.

Cumulative Number of Units Produced	Manufacturing Projections Average Hours per Unit	Total Hours
1	12,000	12,000
2	9,600	19,200
4	7,680	30,720

PART THREE

a. An 80% learning curve implies a higher rate of learning. Thus, the number of hours saved through efficiencies is much greater with an 80% learning curve.

b. In Part One, the fourth plane is estimated to take 7,680 hours. Each of the planes prior to the fourth plane will take more hours to produce than the final, fourth plane.

In Part Two, the average of the four planes is 7,680 hours. In fact, the third and fourth plane used significantly fewer hours than that: 30,720 – 19,200 = 11,520 hours for planes 3 and 4. On average, planes 3 and 4 took 5,760 hours each or 11,520/2. Thus, learning took place at a faster pace under the assumption of Part Two.

Incremental and Cumulative are simply two different methods applied. The important thing is for companies to use the method that best predicts future activity.

c. Knowing how labor hours will change will help the company determine the appropriate price to charge for the work. For example, if the company uses the estimate of labor hours of the first plane for all four planes, the bid would be too high and the company could lose the work to a competitor.

Review 3-6

a.
1. More desirable
2. Less desirable
3. Less desirable
4. Less desirable
5. More desirable
6. More desirable

b. Some common activity drivers for stating volume of activity in a manufacturing operation might include direct labor hours, machine hours, units of material produced, and units of finished product. The selection of the most appropriate basis requires judgment and professional experience. The relationship between the cost driver and the cost must seem logical and the activity data must be available.

Review 3-7

a.
1. Unit-level
2. Store-level
3. Store-level
4. Unit-level
5. Customer-level
6. Order-level

b. Incorporating the hierarchy of activity costs into the cost estimating equation recognizes the variability of each cost element. This will improve the accuracy of the predicting equation in cases where resources are not used evenly across products, products are customized, or where there are complex processes.

Data Visualization Solutions

(See page 3-7.)

a. 4   b. 1   c. 2   d. 3

Chapter 4

Cost-Volume-Profit Analysis

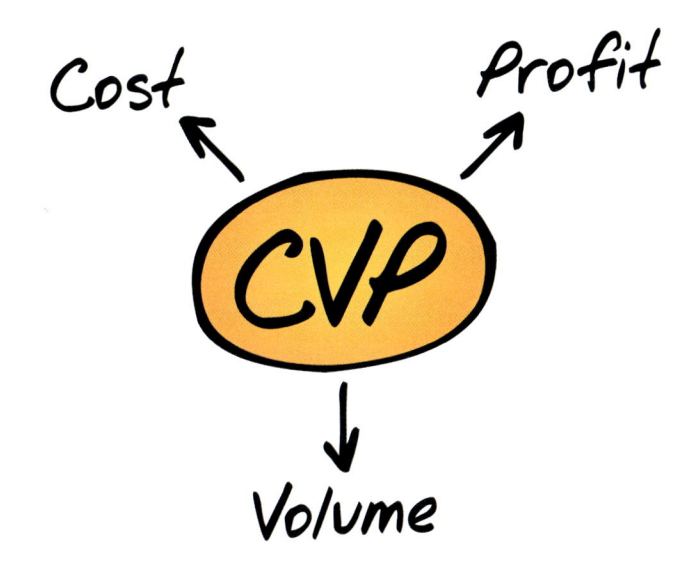

Cost *Profit*

CVP

Volume

Road Map

LO	Learning Objective | Topics	Page	eLecture	Demo	Review	Assignments
4-1	**What is contribution margin and why is it important?** Cost-Volume-Profit (CVP) :: Contribution Margin (CM) :: Contribution Income Statement :: Variable Costs :: Fixed Costs :: Contribution Margin Per Unit (CM per Unit) :: Contribution Margin Ratio (CM%)	4-2	e4-1	D4-1A D4-1B	Rev 4-1	MC4-8, E4-15, E4-16, E4-17, E4-23, E4-33, E4-35, E4-38, P4-41, P4-42, P4-44, P4-53, P4-55, DA4-1, DA4-2
4-2	**How is the break-even point (BEP) determined, and what methods are used to identify BEP?** Break-Even Point (BEP) :: Formula Approach :: Graphing Approach :: Traditional Break-Even Graph :: Profit-Volume Graph :: Contribution Income Statement Proof	4-4	e4-2	D4-2A D4-2B D4-2C D4-2D	Rev 4-2	MC4-9, E4-18, E4-19, E4-20, E4-22, E4-23, E4-28, E4-32, E4-33, E4-34, E4-35, E4-37, E4-40, P4-41, P4-42, P4-43, P4-45, P4-49, P4-50, P4-51, P4-52, P4-53, P4-55, P4-56
4-3	**How are sales estimated at a fixed level of profit, both before and after tax?** Fixed Before-Tax Profit :: Fixed After-Tax Profit :: Specified Before-Tax Profit Per Unit :: Specified After-Tax Profit Per Unit ::Contribution Income Statement Proof	4-9	e4-3	D4-3A D4-3B D4-3C D4-3D	Rev 4-3	MC4-10, E4-21, E4-22, E4-23, E4-24, E4-25, E4-27, E4-28, E4-33, E4-37, P4-41, P4-42, P4-43, P4-46, P4-47, P4-48, P4-49, P4-50, P4-51, P4-53, P4-55
4-4	**How is incremental analysis used for decision making in cost-volume-profit (CVP) situations?** Incremental Analysis :: CVP Situations	4-14	e4-4	D4-4	Rev 4-4	MC4-11, E4-26, E4-29, E4-33, P4-41, P4-42, P4-43, P4-44, P4-51, P4-52, P4-53, DA4-3
4-5	**How do break-even and CVP analysis differ for single-product and multiproduct firms?** Multiproduct Environment :: Break-Even Analysis :: CM Per "Bag" :: Weighted Average CM% Per "Bag" :: Shift in Sales Mix	4-16	e4-5	D4-5A D4-5B	Rev 4-5	MC4-12, E4-30, E4-31, P4-46, P4-47, P4-48, P4-49, P4-50, DA4-4
4-6	**How are margin of safety and operating leverage concepts used in business?** Margin of Safety (MS):: Operating Leverage ::Degree of Operating Leverage (DOL) :: Financial Risk	4-19	e4-6	D4-6A D4-6B	Rev 4-6	MC4-13, E4-32, E4-33, E4-34, E4-35, E4-37, P4-42, P4-48, P4-49, P4-52, P4-53, P4-55, P4-56
4-7	**What are the underlying assumptions of CVP analysis?** CVP Model :: Assumptions	4-22	e4-7	D4-7	Rev 4-7	MC4-14, E4-36, E4-39, E4-40, P4-54

© Cambridge Business Publishers

4-1

INTRODUCTION

To achieve company goals, managers must choose a specific course of action and then develop plans and controls to pursue that course. Because *planning* is future oriented, uncertainty exists, and information helps reduce that uncertainty. *Controlling* is making actual performance align with plans, and information is necessary in that process. Much of the information managers use to plan and control reflects relationships among product cost, selling price, and sales volume. Changing one of these essential components in the mix will cause changes in other components. For example, increasing advertising expenditures for a particular product would be justified by the increase in product sales volume and contribution margin that would be generated.

This chapter focuses on understanding how cost, volume, and profit interact. Examining shifts in cost and volume and the resulting effects on profits is called **cost-volume-profit (CVP) analysis**. Understanding these relationships helps in predicting future conditions (planning) as well as in explaining, evaluating, and acting on results (controlling). Before generating profit, a company must first reach its break-even point, which means that it must generate sufficient sales revenue to cover all cost. Then, by linking cost behavior and sales volume, managers can use the cost-volume-profit model to plan and control.

The chapter also presents the concepts of margin of safety and degree of operating leverage. Information provided by these models helps managers focus on the implications that volume changes would have on organizational profitability.

CONTRIBUTION MARGIN

LO4-1 What is contribution margin and why is it important?

A *traditional income statement* that is used for external reporting purposes classifies costs according to function, such as manufacturing, selling and administrative. This is the type of income statement typically included in corporate annual reports and official quarterly and annual filings of public companies with the Securities and Exchange Commission. (Refer to **Exhibit 4.1**.) The difficulty in using a traditional statement for internal purposes is that the relationship between sales volume, costs, and profits is not readily apparent. As a result, companies may choose to classify cost by behavior (variable vs. fixed) for internal reporting purposes. Consequently, we emphasize contribution income statements because they provide better information to *internal* decision makers.

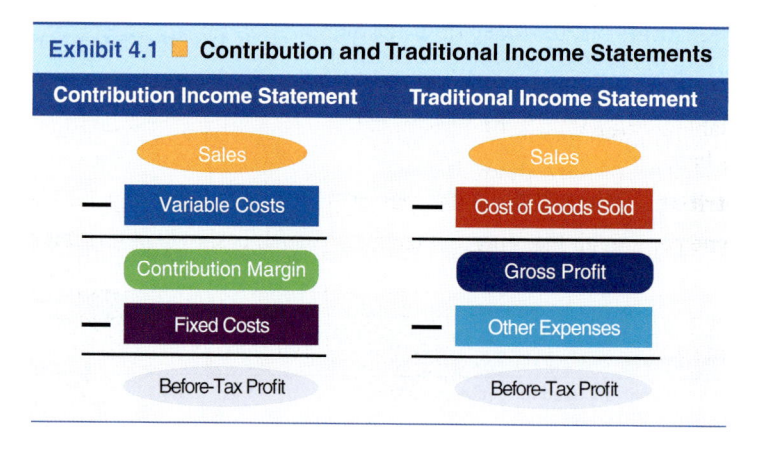

Exhibit 4.1 — Contribution and Traditional Income Statements

Contribution Income Statement	Traditional Income Statement
Sales	Sales
− Variable Costs	− Cost of Goods Sold
Contribution Margin	Gross Profit
− Fixed Costs	− Other Expenses
Before-Tax Profit	Before-Tax Profit

In a **contribution income statement**, costs are classified according to behavior as variable or fixed as illustrated in **Exhibit 4.1**. This format emphasizes **contribution margin (CM)**, which is the difference between total revenues and total variable costs. Contribution margin is the amount available to cover fixed costs and provide a profit. Contribution margin can be defined on either a per-unit or a total basis.

DEMO 4-1A   LO4-1   Preparing a Contribution Income Statement

Calispell Company manufactures a high-quality line of desk clocks. Product specifications have been established that will continue through production models for two more years. Annual sales are

Chapter 4 Cost-Volume-Profit Analysis

budgeted of 600,000 units. The following additional data is available for the company and is used in this demonstration and throughout this chapter.

Budgeted Information			
Sales price per unit.............	$40.00	Fixed production costs (in total)...............	$3,200,000
Variable production cost per unit...	25.00	Fixed selling and administrative costs (in total)...	1,200,000
Variable selling cost per unit.......	4.00		

◆ **How is a contribution income statement prepared for Calispell?**

The contribution income statement for Calispell is shown in **Exhibit 4.2**.

Exhibit 4.2 ■ Calispell Company Annual Budgeted Contribution Income Statement

		Total
Sales (600,000 × $40)...		$24,000,000
Variable cost		
Production (600,000 × $25)................................	$15,000,000	
Selling (600,000 × $4).......................................	2,400,000	
Total variable cost...		(17,400,000)
Contribution margin...		$ 6,600,000
Fixed cost		
Production...	$ 3,200,000	
Selling and administrative...................................	1,200,000	
Total fixed cost...		(4,400,000)
Before-tax profit...		$ 2,200,000

This statement shows a contribution margin of $6,600,000, which covers fixed costs of $4,400,000, with the remaining $2,200,000 making up before-tax profit.

Preparing a Presentation of Contribution Margin Per Unit and Percentage   LO4-1   DEMO 4-1B

While the contribution income statement (shown in **Exhibit 4.2**) presents information on total sales revenue, total variable costs, and so forth, it is sometimes useful to present information on a per-unit or portion of sales basis.

◆ **How is a contribution income presented per unit and as a percentage for Calispell?**

Contribution income per unit and as a percentage for Calispell is shown in **Exhibit 4.3**.

Exhibit 4.3 ■ Calispell Company Contribution Margin Per Unit and Percentage

	Per Unit	Percentage
Sales...	$40.00	100.0 ($40 ÷ $40)
Variable cost		
Production..	25.00	62.5 ($25 ÷ $40)
Selling...	4.00	10.0 ($ 4 ÷ $40)
Total variable cost......................................	(29.00)	(72.5) ($29 ÷ $40)
Contribution margin...	$11.00	27.5 ($11 ÷ $40)

The per-unit information assists in short-range planning. The **contribution margin per unit (CM per unit)** equals selling price per unit minus total variable cost per unit, which includes production, selling, and administrative costs. It is the amount, $11.00 in this case, that each unit contributes toward covering fixed costs and earning a profit. When expressed as a ratio to sales, the sales margin is identified as

© Cambridge Business Publishers

the **contribution margin ratio (CM%)**. This ratio indicates the proportion of revenue remaining after variable cost has been deducted from sales, or that portion of the revenue dollar that can be used to cover fixed cost and provide profit. *The CM% can be calculated using either per-unit or total revenue and variable cost information.* As a percentage of total sales, Calispell has a total variable production cost of 62.5 percent, a variable selling expense of 10.0 percent, and a contribution margin of 27.5 percent. These data are used throughout this chapter to illustrate break-even and cost-volume-profit computations.

REVIEW 4-1 | **LO4-1** | **Contribution Income Statement**

Leopold manufactures plastic component parts for refrigeration units. The following information is available for the company's first year of business when it produced 80,000 units. Revenue of $160,000 was generated by the sale of 80,000 units.

	Variable Cost	Fixed Cost
Production		
Direct material.	$0.40 per unit	
Direct labor	$0.20 per unit	
Overhead	$0.60 per unit	$30,000
Selling and administrative.	$0.20 per unit	10,000

a. What is the variable production cost per unit?
b. What is contribution margin per unit and the contribution margin ratio?
c. Prepare a contribution income statement.
d. If sales increased by 1,000 units, what is the increase in before-tax profit?
e. **Critical Thinking:** What are ways that this company could increase its contribution margin?

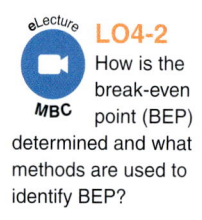

More practice: E4-15, E4-16
Solution on p. 4-43.

BREAK-EVEN POINT

LO4-2 How is the break-even point (BEP) determined and what methods are used to identify BEP?

The CVP model can be expressed mathematically or graphically. The CVP model considers all costs, regardless of whether they are product, period, variable, or fixed. CVP analysis originates in the profit equation. CVP analysis requires substitution of known amounts in the profit equation to solve for an unknown amount. The profit equation mirrors the income statement when known amounts are used for selling price per unit, variable cost per unit, volume of units, and fixed cost to find the amount of profit generated under given conditions. Our application of the CVP model will start with the concept of break-even. A company's **break-even point (BEP)** is that level of activity, in units or dollars, at which total revenue equals total cost. In **Exhibit 4.2**, the company reported income before income tax of $2.2 million. At break-even, the income before income tax would be $0. Thus, at BEP, the company generates neither a profit nor a loss on operating activities. Companies, however, do not wish merely to "break even" on operations. The BEP is calculated to establish a point of reference so that managers are better able to set sales goals that should result in operating profits rather than losses.

Finding the BEP first requires understanding company revenue and cost. A short summary of revenue and cost assumptions is presented at this point to provide a foundation for cost-volume-profit (CVP) analysis. These assumptions, and some challenges to them, are discussed in more detail at the end of the chapter.

CVP Assumptions

- **Relevant range:** The company is assumed to operate within the relevant range of activity specified in determining the revenue and cost information used in each of the following assumptions.[1]
- **Revenue:** Revenue per unit is assumed to remain constant; fluctuations in per-unit revenue for factors such as quantity discounts are ignored. Thus, total revenue fluctuates in direct proportion to level of activity or volume.

---

[1] As discussed in Chapter 2, the relevant range is the range of activity over which a variable cost will remain constant per unit and a fixed cost will remain constant in total.

Chapter 4 Cost-Volume-Profit Analysis

- **Variable cost:** On a per-unit basis, variable costs are assumed to remain constant. Therefore, total variable cost fluctuates in direct proportion to the level of activity or volume. Variable production costs include direct material, direct labor, and variable overhead; variable selling costs include charges for items such as commissions and shipping. Variable administrative costs can exist in areas such as purchasing; however, in the illustrations that follow, administrative costs are assumed to be fixed.
- **Fixed cost:** Total fixed cost is assumed to remain constant, and as such, per-unit fixed cost decreases as volume increases. (Per-unit fixed cost increases as volume decreases.) Fixed costs include both fixed manufacturing overhead and fixed selling and administrative expense.
- **Mixed cost:** Mixed cost is separated into variable and fixed elements for use in BEP or CVP analysis. Any method (such as regression analysis or the high–low method) that validly separates the mixed cost in relation to one or more predictors can be used.

Unit contribution margin is assumed to be constant because revenue and variable cost have been defined as being constant per unit in the assumptions described above. Total CM however, fluctuates in direct proportion to sales volume.

Identifying the Break-Even Point

Break-even calculations can be demonstrated using the formula or graph approach. A contribution income statement can be prepared to verify the results.

Formula Approach to Break-Even

The formula approach to break-even analysis uses an algebraic equation to calculate the BEP. In this analysis, sales volume, rather than production activity, is the focus of the relevant range. The equation represents the contribution income statement and shows the relationships among revenue, fixed cost, variable cost, volume, and profit as follows.

$$\text{SP per unit}(X) - \text{VC per unit}(X) - \text{Total FC} = \text{Profit}$$

where   SP = selling price   VC = variable cost
         X = volume (number of units)   FC = fixed cost

Solving for Break-Even in Sales Units Because the equation above simply represents an income statement, profit can be set equal to zero to solve for the break-even point. At the point where Profit = $0, total revenue equals total cost, and break-even point (BEP) in units can be found by solving the equation for X.

$$\text{SP per unit}(X) - \text{VC per unit}(X) - \text{Total FC} = \$0$$
$$(\text{SP per unit} - \text{VC per unit})(X) = \text{Total FC}$$
$$X = \text{Total FC} \div (\text{SP per unit} - \text{VC per unit})$$
$$X = \text{Total FC} \div \text{CM per unit}$$

We will illustrate examples in this chapter using the simplified formula for the break-even point.

> **Break-even in sales units = Fixed costs ÷ CM per unit**

Computing Break-Even in Sales Units   LO4-2   DEMO 4-2A

◆ Using the Calispell information given in Exhibit 4.2 ($40 selling price per clock, $29 variable cost per clock, and $4,400,000 of total fixed cost), what is the company's BEP in sales units?

The company's BEP in sales units is calculated as

> **Break-even in sales units = Fixed costs ÷ CM per unit**

$$= \$4,400,000 \div (\$40 - \$29)$$
$$= 400,000 \text{ clocks}$$

Solving for Break-Even in Sales Dollars BEP can be expressed in either units or dollars of revenue. One way to convert a unit BEP to dollars is to multiply the number of units by the selling price per unit. For Calispell, the BEP in sales dollars is $16,000,000.

$$400,000 \text{ BEP units} \times \$40 \text{ selling price per unit} = \$16,000,000$$

Another method of computing BEP in sales dollars uses the contribution margin ratio. Dividing total fixed cost by the CM% gives the BEP in sales dollars.[2] An advantage of this method is that it allows the BEP to be determined even if unit selling price and unit variable cost are not known.

DEMO 4-2B	LO4-2	Computing Break-Even in Sales Dollars

◆ Using the Calispell information, what is the company's BEP in sales dollars?

Calispell's CM% is 27.5% as calculated in **Exhibit 4.3**. The company's BEP in sales dollars is calculated as follows.

$$\text{Break-even in sales dollars} = \text{Fixed costs} \div \text{CM\%}$$

$$= \$4,400,000 \div 0.275$$
$$= \$16,000,000$$

BEP in units can be determined by dividing the BEP in sales dollars by the unit selling price, or as follows.

$$\text{BEP in units} = \$16,000,000 \div \$40$$
$$= 400,000 \text{ clocks}$$

The CM% allows the BEP to be determined even if unit selling price and unit variable cost are not known. Subtracting the contribution margin ratio from 100 percent gives the **variable cost ratio (VC%)**, which represents variable cost as a proportion of revenue.

Graphing Approach to Break-Even

Although solutions to BEP problems can be determined using equations, sometimes the information is more effectively conveyed to managers through a data visualization. A **break-even chart** can be prepared to graph the relationships among revenue, volume, and cost. The BEP on a break-even chart is located at the point where the total cost and total revenue lines intersect. Two approaches to graphing can be used to prepare break-even charts: the traditional approach and the profit-volume graph approach.

Traditional Break-Even Graph The traditional break-even graph shows the relationships among revenue, cost, and profit/loss, but does not show contribution margin.

DEMO 4-2C	LO4-2	Preparing a Traditional Break-Even Graph

◆ How is a traditional break-even graph prepared for Calispell?

A traditional break-even graph for Calispell Company is prepared by completing the following steps.

Step 1: As shown in **Exhibit 4.4**, label each axis and graph the total cost and fixed cost lines. The fixed cost line is drawn parallel to the *X*-axis (volume). The variable cost line begins where the fixed cost line intersects the *Y*-axis. The slope of the variable cost line is the per-unit

---

[2] Derivation of the contribution margin ratio formula is as follows:

$$\text{Sales} - [(\text{VC\%})(\text{Sales})] = \text{FC}$$
$$(1 - \text{VC\%})\text{Sales} = \text{FC}$$
$$\text{because } (1 - \text{VC\%}) = \text{CM\%}$$
$$\text{then Sales} = \text{FC} \div \text{CM\%}$$

where VC% = variable cost ratio or variable cost as a percentage of sales,
       CM% = contribution margin ratio or contribution margin as a percentage of sales

Thus, the VC% plus the CM% is equal to 100 percent.

© Cambridge Business Publishers

Chapter 4 Cost-Volume-Profit Analysis

variable cost ($29). The resulting line represents total cost. The distance between the fixed cost and the total cost lines represents total variable cost at each activity level.

Exhibit 4.4 ■ Calispell Company Graph of Total and Variable Cost

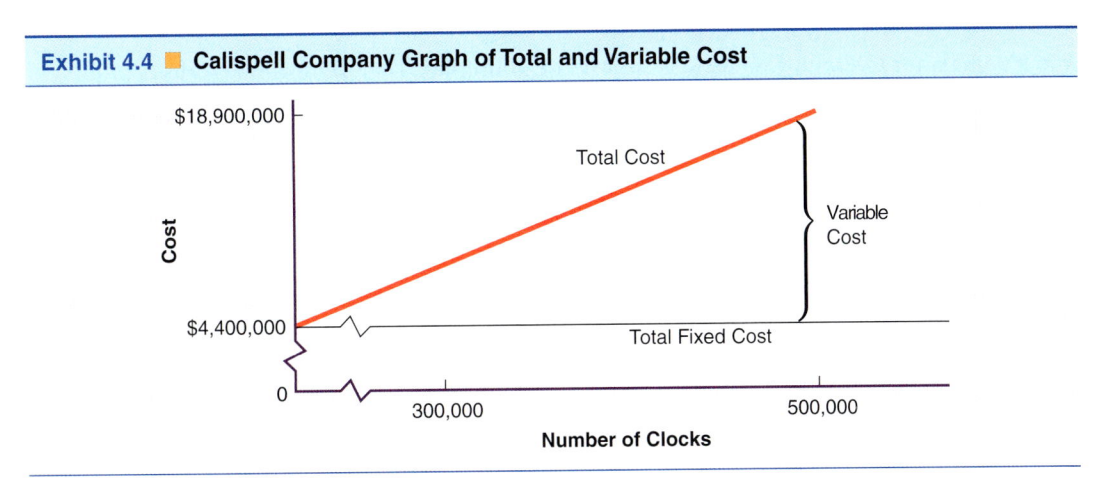

Step 2: Chart the revenue line, beginning at $0. The BEP is located at the intersection of the revenue line and the total cost line. The vertical distance to the right of the BEP and between the revenue and total cost lines represents profit. The distance between the revenue and total cost lines to the left of the BEP represents loss. If exact readings could be taken on the graph in **Exhibit 4.5**, Calispell's break-even point would be $16,000,000 of sales, or 400,000 clocks.

Exhibit 4.5 ■ Calispell Company Traditional Approach of Graphing

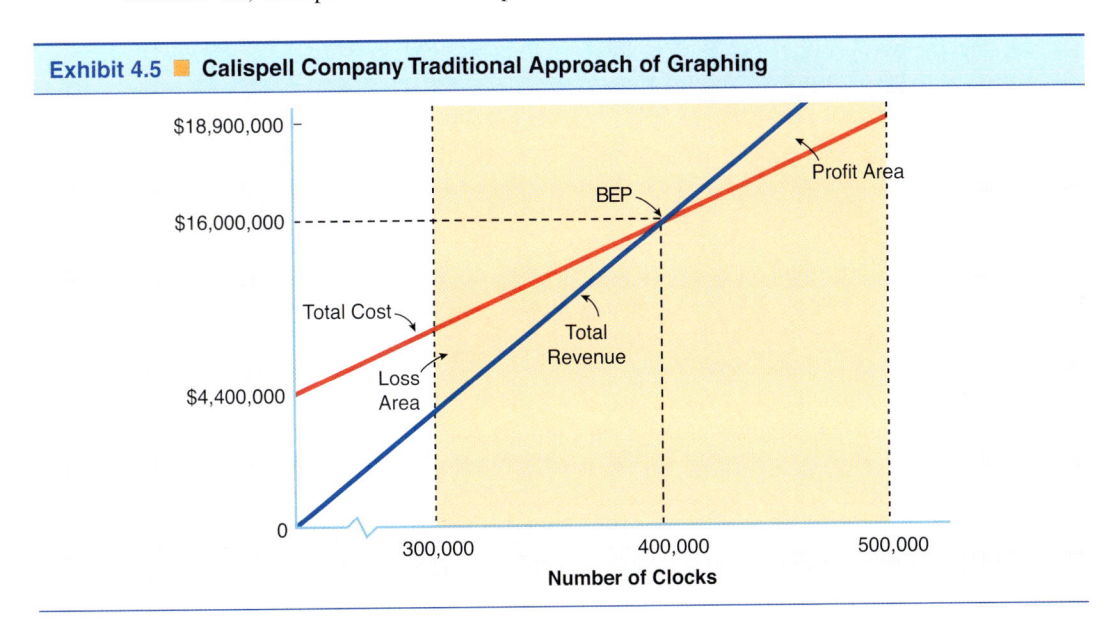

Profit-Volume Graph The **profit-volume (PV) graph** depicts the profit or loss associated with each sales level. The horizontal, or X, axis on the PV graph represents sales volume. The vertical, or Y, axis represents dollars of profit or loss. Amounts shown above the X-axis are positive and represent profits. Amounts shown below the X-axis are negative and represent losses.

Two points can be located on the graph: total fixed cost and break-even point. Total fixed cost is shown on the Y-axis below the sales volume line as a negative amount. If no products were sold, the fixed cost would still be incurred and a loss of that amount would result. Location of the BEP in units may be determined algebraically and is shown at the point where the profit line intersects the X-axis; at that point, there is no profit or loss. The amount of profit or loss for any sales volume can be read from the Y-axis. The slope of the profit (diagonal) line is determined by the unit contribution margin ($11), and the points on the line represent the contribution margin earned at each volume level. The line shows that no profit is earned until total contribution margin covers total fixed cost.

© Cambridge Business Publishers

DEMO 4-2D LO4-2 — Preparing a Profit-Volume Graph

◆ **How is a profit-volume graph prepared for Calispell?**

The PV graph for Calispell Company is shown in **Exhibit 4.6**. The diagonal line reflects profits (or losses) at any level of volume. For example, at the BEP of 400,000 clocks, the line crosses the horizontal line to indicate zero profit or loss. The original **Exhibit 4.2** income statement data indicating a profit of $2,200,000 at a sales volume of 600,000 clocks is also visible on this graph.

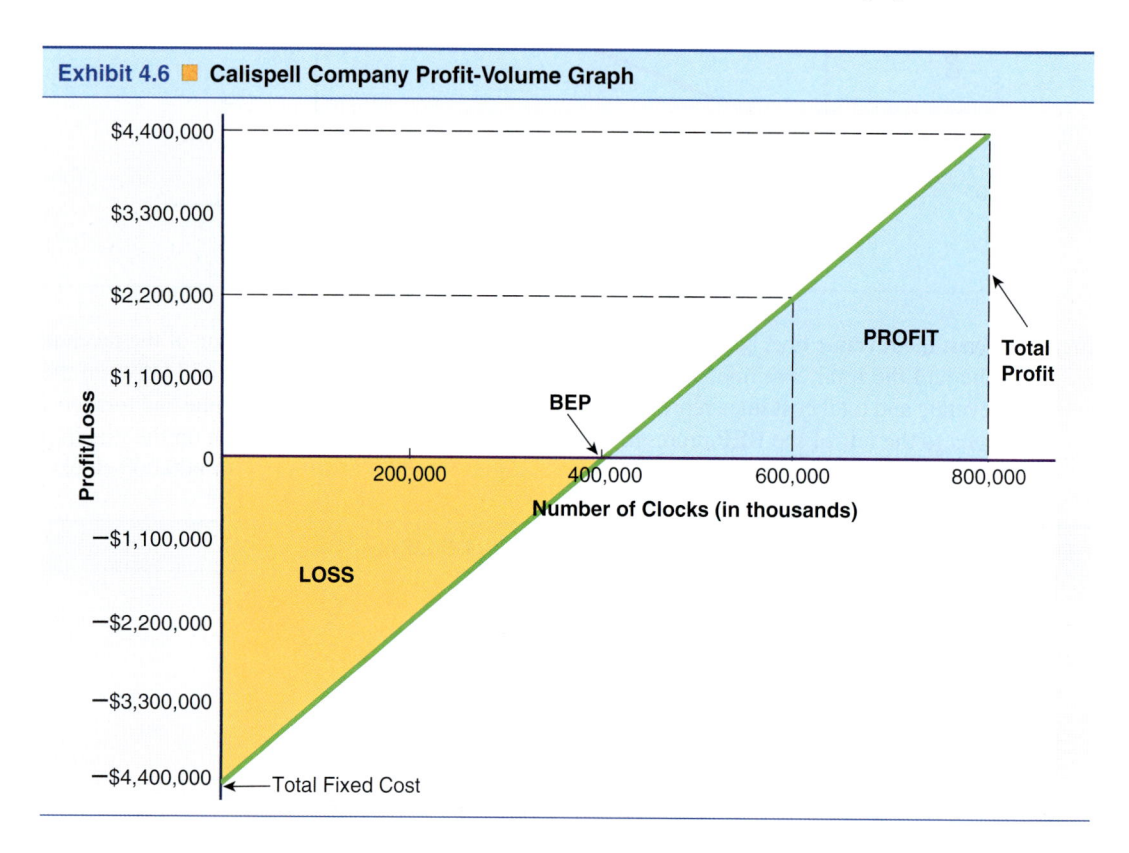

Exhibit 4.6 ■ Calispell Company Profit-Volume Graph

The graphing approach to breakeven provides a detailed visual display of the BEP. It does not, however, provide a precise solution because exact points cannot be determined on a graph. A definitive computation of the BEP can be found algebraically using the formula approach or a computer software application.

Contribution Income Statement Proof

Contribution income statements can be used to prove the accuracy of computations made using the BEP formulas or graphs. For example, the preparation of a contribution income statement using sales units at break-even, will result in a before-tax profit of zero.

The BEP provides a starting point for planning future operations. Managers want to earn operating profit rather than simply cover costs. Cost-volume-profit analysis considering target profit is illustrated in the next section.

Chapter 4 Cost-Volume-Profit Analysis

Data Visualization

A retailer's current sales volume is 4,000 units. For each of the items (a) through (e), indicate what the identified item represents and the amount. Note: For part (e), review LO4-6.

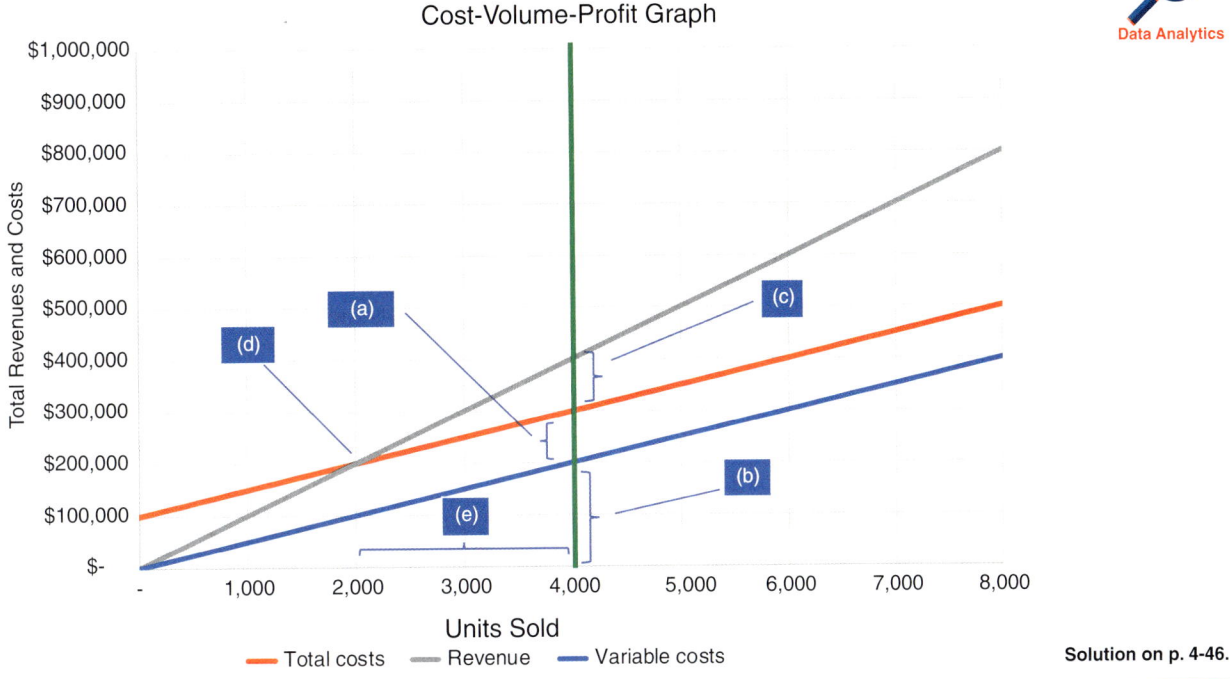

Cost-Volume-Profit Graph

— Total costs   — Revenue   — Variable costs

Solution on p. 4-46.

Break-Even Point — LO4-2 — REVIEW 4-2

Shalton Inc. makes and sells customized t-shirts. Operating information is as follows:

Selling price per unit....	$20	Annual fixed costs	
Variable cost per unit		Selling............	$15,000
Fabric............	4	Administrative.......	38,000
Sales commissions...	1	Manufacturing.......	60,000
Overhead..........	5		

a. What is Shalton's break-even point in units?
b. What is Shalton's break-even point in sales dollars?
c. What would Shalton's break-even point in units be if variable overhead increased to $6 per unit?
d. What would Shalton's break-even point in units be if fixed administrative expenses decreased by $2,000 (otherwise using the original data)?
e. **Critical Thinking:** How can Shalton use the knowledge of the break-even point in units to better manage its operations?

More practice: MC4-9, E4-18, E4-19
Solution on p. 4-44.

SALES AT A FIXED LEVEL OF PROFIT

Managers use CVP analysis to effectively plan and control by concentrating on the relationships among revenues, cost, volume changes, taxes, and profit. The analysis is usually performed on a companywide basis. The same basic CVP model and calculations can be applied to a single or multiproduct business. The following quote indicates the pervasive utility of the CVP model:

LO4-3 How are sales estimated at a fixed level of profit, both before and after tax?

© Cambridge Business Publishers

> Cost Volume Profit (CVP) analysis is one of the most hallowed, and yet one of the simplest, analytical tools in management accounting. [CVP] allows managers to examine the possible impacts of a wide range of strategic decisions [in] such crucial areas as pricing policies, product mixes, market expansions or contractions, outsourcing contracts, idle plant usage, discretionary expense planning, and a variety of other important considerations in the planning process. Given the broad range of contexts in which CVP can be used, the basic simplicity of CVP is quite remarkable. Armed with just three inputs of data—sales price, variable cost per unit, and fixed cost—a managerial analyst can evaluate the effects of decisions that potentially alter the basic nature of a firm.[3]

An important application of CVP analysis allows managers to set a desired target profit and focus on the relationships between it and other known income statement amounts to find an unknown. One common unknown in such applications is the sales volume that is needed to generate a particular profit amount. Because CVP analysis is concerned with relationships among the elements affecting continuing operations, in contrast with nonrecurring activities and events, *profits*—as used in this chapter—refer to operating profits before extraordinary and other nonoperating, nonrecurring items.

In many organizations, selling price is often market determined and not a management decision variable. Additionally, selling price and volume are often directly related, and fixed costs are assumed to be constant within a period. *Thus, variable cost is the amount in a CVP computation that can most likely be affected in the short-run.* Managers often use CVP analysis to determine how high variable cost can rise and still allow the company to generate a desired amount of profit. Variable cost can be affected by modifying product specifications or material quality as well as by being more efficient or effective in the production, service, and/or distribution processes.

A product's selling price is often market-related rather than being a management decision variable.

The following examples continue using the Calispell Company data with different amounts of target profit.

Fixed Amount of Profit

Because contribution margin represents the sales dollars remaining after variable cost is covered, each dollar of CM generated by product sales goes first to cover fixed cost and then to produce profits. After the BEP is reached, each dollar of CM is a dollar of before-tax profit.

Solving for Sales Units (Dollars) at a Fixed **Before-Tax** Profit

Profit can be treated in the break-even formula as an *additional cost* to be covered. Inclusion of a target or "fixed" profit changes the break-even formula as follows.

> Sales units for fixed before-tax profit = (Fixed costs + Before-tax profit) ÷ CM per unit
>
> Sales dollars for fixed before-tax profit = (Fixed costs + Before-tax profit) ÷ CM%

DEMO 4-3A LO4-3 Calculating Sales Given a Fixed Before-Tax Profit

◆ Referring to the information in Exhibit 4.2 for Calispell Company, what are sales in units and in dollars required for the company to achieve a desired profit of $3,300,000 *before* tax?

In sales units:

> Sales units for fixed before-tax profit = (Fixed costs + Before-tax profit) ÷ CM per unit
>
> = ($4,400,000 + $3,300,000) ÷ $11 = 700,000 units

---

[3] Flora Guidry, James O. Horrigan, and Cathy Craycraft, "CVP Analysis: A New Look," *Journal of Managerial Issues* (Spring 1998), pp. 74ff.

Chapter 4 Cost-Volume-Profit Analysis

In sales dollars:

> Sales dollars for fixed before-tax profit = (Fixed costs + Before-tax profit) ÷ CM%

$$= (\$4{,}400{,}000 + \$3{,}300{,}000) \div 0.275 = \$28{,}000{,}000$$

Solving for Sales Units (Dollars) at a Fixed After-Tax Profit

In choosing a target profit amount, managers must recognize that income tax represents a significant influence on business decision making. A company wanting a particular amount of profit after tax must first determine, given the applicable tax rate, the amount of profit that must be earned on a before-tax basis. This means that to apply the formulas used in the prior section, it is first necessary to convert the *desired after-tax profit* amount to a *before-tax profit* amount through the following formula.

Before-tax profit (1 − Tax rate) = After-tax profit

or

> Before-tax profit = After-tax profit ÷ (1 − Tax rate)

Calculating Sales Given a Fixed After-Tax Profit LO4-3 DEMO 4-3B

◆ Referring to the information in Exhibit 4.2 for Calispell Company, what are sales in units and in dollars required for the company to achieve a desired profit of $3,300,000 after tax? Assume a tax rate of 25 percent.

Convert after-tax profit to before-tax profit:

> Before-tax profit = After-tax profit ÷ (1 − Tax rate)

$$= \$3{,}300{,}000 \div (1 - 0.25) = \$4{,}400{,}000$$

In sales units:

> Sales units for fixed before-tax profit = (Fixed costs + Before-tax profit) ÷ CM per unit

$$= (\$4{,}400{,}000 + \$4{,}400{,}000) \div \$11 = 800{,}000 \text{ units}$$

In sales dollars:

> Sales dollars for fixed before-tax profit = (Fixed costs + Before-tax profit) ÷ CM%

$$= (\$4{,}400{,}000 + \$4{,}400{,}000) \div 0.275 = \$32{,}000{,}000$$

Converting the after-tax amount to a before-tax amount increased the desired profit from $3,300,000 to $4,400,000. The increase was necessary in order to account for the deduction required to pay taxes. As a result, the amount of sales units and sales dollars increased in order to achieve the after-tax profit target.

Specific Amount of Profit per Unit

Managers may desire to conduct an analysis of profit on a per-unit basis. As in the prior examples, profit can be stated on either a before-tax or an after-tax basis. For these alternatives, the CVP formula must be adjusted to recognize that profit is related to volume of activity.

Solving for Sales Units at a Specified Before-Tax Profit Per Unit

In this situation, the adjusted CVP formula for computing the necessary unit sales volume to earn a specified amount of profit per unit before tax is as follows.

$$\text{SP per unit}(X) - \text{VC per unit}(X) - \text{Total FC} = \text{Profit per unit}(X)$$

Solving for *X* (volume) gives the following:

SP per unit(*X*) − VC per unit(*X*) − Profit per unit(*X*) = Total FC

CM per unit − Profit per unit(*X*) = Total FC

X = Total FC ÷ (CM per unit − Profit per unit)

We will illustrate examples in this chapter using the simplified formula.

> **Sales units for fixed before-tax profit per unit = Fixed costs ÷ (CM per unit − Before-tax profit per unit)**

The per-unit profit is treated in the CVP formula as if it were an additional variable cost to be covered. This treatment effectively "adjusts" the original contribution margin and contribution margin ratio. When setting the desired profit as a percentage of selling price, the *profit percentage cannot exceed the contribution margin ratio*. If it does, an infeasible problem is created because the "adjusted" contribution margin is negative. In such a case, the variable cost ratio plus the desired profit percentage would exceed 100 percent of the selling price, and such a condition cannot exist.

Solving for Sales Units at a Specified After-Tax Profit Per Unit

In order to apply the formulas used in the prior section, it is first necessary to convert the desired after-tax profit amount to a *before-tax profit* amount through the following formula.

> **Before-tax profit per unit = After-tax profit per unit × (1 − Tax rate)**

DEMO 4-3C LO4-3 Calculating Sales Given Target Before-Tax Profit on Unit Sales

♦ Referring to the information in Exhibit 4.2 for Calispell Company, what are the sales in units and in dollars required for the company to achieve a 15 percent before-tax profit on unit sales?

With sales revenue of $40 per unit, the desired before-tax profit amount is equal to $6 ($40 × 0.15). Sales in units to achieve a profit of $6 per unit is calculated as follows.

In sales units:

> **Sales units for fixed before-tax profit per unit = Fixed costs ÷ (CM per unit − Before-tax profit per unit)**

= $4,400,000 ÷ ($11 − $6) = 880,000 units

In sales dollars:

First, compute the "adjusted" contribution margin % as follows.

	Per Unit*	Percentage
Selling price	$40	100.0
Variable cost	(29)	(72.5)
Set amount of profit before tax	(6)	(15.0)
"Adjusted" contribution margin ratio	$ 5	12.5

*It is not necessary to have per-unit data; all computations can be made with percentage information only.

> **Sales dollars for fixed before-tax profit per unit = Fixed costs ÷ "Adjusted" CM%**

= $4,400,000 ÷ 0.125
= $35,200,000

DEMO 4-3D LO4-3 Calculating Sales Given Target After-Tax Profit on Unit Sales

♦ Referring to the information in Exhibit 4.2 for Calispell Company, what are sales in units and in dollars required for the company to achieve a 11.25 percent after-tax profit on unit sales?

Chapter 4 Cost-Volume-Profit Analysis

Assume a tax rate of 25 percent.

With sales revenue of $40 per unit, the desired before-tax profit amount is equal to $4.50 ($40 × 0.1125). Sales in units to achieve a profit of $4.50 per unit is calculated as follows.

Convert after-tax profit per unit to a before-tax profit per unit:

$$\$4.50 \text{ Fixed after-tax profit per unit} \div (1 - 0.25) = \$6.00 \text{ Before-tax profit per unit}$$

In sales units:

Sales units for fixed before-tax profit per unit = Fixed costs ÷ (CM per unit − Before-tax profit per unit)

$$= \$4,400,000 \div (\$11.00 - \$6) = 880,000 \text{ units}$$

In sales dollars:
First, compute the "adjusted" contribution margin % (i.e., CM% − Profit % per unit).

	Per Unit	Percentage
Selling price	$40.00	100.00
Variable cost	(29.00)	(72.50)
Set amount of profit before tax	(6.00)	(15.00)
"Adjusted" contribution margin	$ 5.00	12.50

Sales dollars for fixed before-tax profit per unit = Fixed cost ÷ "Adjusted" CM ratio

$$= \$4,400,000 \div 0.125$$
$$= \$35,200,000$$

Contribution Income Statement Proof

Exhibit 4.7 proves the computations made in the earlier demonstrations. This means that the profit before tax calculated in each of the contribution income statements matches the desired profit in each of the demonstrations referenced.

The answers provided by CVP analysis are valid only in relation to specific selling price and cost relationships. Any change that occurs in the company's selling price or cost structure will cause a change in the BEP or in the sales needed to obtain a desired profit. However, the effects of revenue and cost changes on a company's BEP or sales volume can be determined through incremental analysis, as discussed in the next section.

Exhibit 4.7 ■ Calispell Company's Contribution Income Statements—Proof of Computations

Units Sold	Demo 4-2B 400,000	Demo 4-3A 700,000	Demo 4-3B 800,000	Demo 4-3C 880,000	Demo 4-3D 880,000
Sales ($40 per unit)	$16,000,000	$28,000,000	$32,000,000	$35,200,000	$35,200,000
Total variable cost ($29 per unit)	(11,600,000)	(20,300,000)	(23,200,000)	(25,520,000)	(25,520,000)
Contribution margin	$ 4,400,000	$ 7,700,000	$ 8,800,000	$ 9,680,000	$ 9,680,000
Total fixed cost	(4,400,000)	(4,400,000)	(4,400,000)	(4,400,000)	(4,400,000)
Profit before tax	$ 0	$ 3,300,000	$ 4,400,000	$ 5,280,000[a]	$ 5,280,000
Tax (25%)			(1,100,000)		(1,320,000)
Profit after tax (NI)			$ 3,300,000		$ 3,960,000[b]

[a] Desired profit before tax = 15% on revenue; 15% × $35,200,000 = $5,280,000; or $6 × 880,000 = $5,280,000.
[b] Desired profit after tax = 11.25% on revenue; 11.25% × $35,200,000 = $3,960,000.

REVIEW 4-3 — **LO4-3** — **Cost Volume Profit Analysis**

Atlanta Inc. sells a water filtration component part for $70 per unit. The company's variable cost per unit is $15 for direct material, $10 per unit for direct labor, and $8 per unit for overhead. Annual fixed production overhead is $15,000, and fixed selling and administrative overhead is $10,000. Atlanta's tax rate is 25 percent. Using this information, answer the following questions. Round all answers in units up to the nearest whole unit.

a. What is the contribution margin per unit?
b. What is the contribution margin ratio? Round answer to the nearest whole percentage point.
c. What is the break-even point in units?
d. Using the contribution margin ratio, what is the break-even point in sales dollars?
e. If Atlanta Inc. wants to earn a before-tax profit of $21,000, how many units must the company sell?
f. If Atlanta Inc. wants to earn an after-tax profit of $5,400, how many units must the company sell?
g. If Atlanta Inc. wants to earn an after-tax profit of $3.25 on each unit sold, how many units must the company sell?
h. **Critical Thinking:** Would the company need to sell more units for a before-tax profit of $21,000 or an after-tax profit of $21,000? How does an increase in the tax rate affect the number of units sold to achieve an after-tax profit of $21,000?

More practice: MC4-10, E4-21, E4-22, E4-23, E4-24, E4-25
Solution on p. 4-44.

INCREMENTAL ANALYSIS FOR SHORT-RUN CHANGES

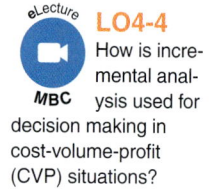

LO4-4 How is incremental analysis used for decision making in cost-volume-profit (CVP) situations?

Incremental analysis is a process that focuses on factors that change only from one course of action or decision to another. In CVP situations, incremental analysis is focused on revenue, cost, and/or volume changes. For example, the break-even point can increase or decrease, depending on revenue and cost changes.

- Other things being equal, the BEP will *increase* if there is an increase in the total fixed cost or a decrease in the unit (or percentage) contribution margin. A decrease in contribution margin could arise because of a reduction in selling price, an increase in variable cost per unit, or a combination of the two.
- The BEP will *decrease* if total fixed cost decreases or unit (or percentage) contribution margin increases.

A change in the BEP will also cause a shift in total profit or loss at any level of activity. The quantitative information derived from the incremental analysis can help inform decisions made by management related to pricing, advertising expenditures, cost structures, and more.

DEMO 4-4 — **LO4-4** — **Applying Incremental Analysis through the CVP Model**

Following are some examples of changes that could occur in a company and the incremental computations used to determine the effects of those changes on BEP or on profit. In most situations, incremental analysis is sufficient to determine the feasibility of contemplated changes, and a complete income statement need not be prepared. The basic facts presented for Calispell Company in **Exhibit 4.2** are continued. (All of the following examples use before-tax information to simplify the computations. After-tax analysis would require the application of the [1 − Tax rate] adjustment to all profit figures.)

◆ **Case 1** Calispell is estimating that sales units will increase by 1,000 clocks during the year. What is the net effect on profit?

The increase in profit is readily determined by multiplying the 1,000-unit increase in sales by the $11 unit contribution margin as follows.

1,000 Unit sales increase × $11 Contribution margin per unit = $11,000 Increase in before-tax profit

There is no increase in fixed costs, so the new profit level becomes $2,211,000 ($2,200,000 + $11,000) per year.

Chapter 4 Cost-Volume-Profit Analysis

◆ **Case 2** Calispell estimates that sales revenue will increase by $60,000 for the year. What is the net effect on before-tax profit?

$60,000 Sales increase × 27.5% Contribution margin ratio = $16,500 Increase in before-tax profit

The contribution margin ratio is especially useful in situations involving several products or when unit sales information is not available.

◆ **Case 3** Calispell wants to earn a before-tax profit of $2,750,000. How many clocks must the company sell to achieve that profit?

The incremental analysis relative to this question addresses the number of clocks above the BEP that must be sold. Because each dollar of contribution margin after BEP is a dollar of profit, the incremental analysis focuses only on the profit desired.

$2,750,000 ÷ $11 = 250,000 clocks above BEP

Because the BEP has already been computed as 400,000 clocks, the company must sell a total of 650,000 clocks.

◆ **Case 4** Calispell estimates that spending an additional $425,000 on digital advertising will result in an additional 50,000 clocks being sold. Should the company incur this extra fixed cost?

The contribution margin from the additional clock sales must first cover the additional fixed cost before additional profits can be generated.

Increase in contribution margin (50,000 clocks × $11 CM per clock)	$550,000
− Increase in fixed cost	(425,000)
= Net incremental benefit	$125,000

Because there is a net incremental profit of $125,000, the company should increase advertising spending.

An alternative computation is to divide the additional fixed cost of $425,000 by the $11 contribution margin. The result indicates that 38,636 clocks (rounded) would be required to cover the additional cost. Because the company expects to sell 50,000 clocks, the remaining 11,364 clocks would produce $11 of profit per clock, or $125,004.

◆ **Case 5** Calispell estimates that reducing a clock's selling price to $37.50 will result in an additional 90,000 clocks per year being sold. Should the company reduce the clock's selling price?

Budgeted sales volume, given in **Exhibit 4.2**, is 600,000 clocks. If the selling price is reduced, the contribution margin per unit will decrease to $8.50 per clock ($37.50 − $29.00). Sales volume will increase to 690,000 clocks (600,000 + 90,000).

Total new contribution margin (690,000 clocks × $8.50 CM per clock)	$ 5,865,000
− Total fixed cost (unchanged)	(4,400,000)
= New before-tax profit	$ 1,465,000
− Current budgeted profit before tax (from **Exhibit 4.2**)	(2,200,000)
= Net incremental loss	$ (735,000)

Because the sales price reduction will reduce profit by $735,000, Calispell Company should not lower the clock's selling price. The company, however, might want to investigate the possibility that a price reduction could, in the long run, increase demand to more than the additional 90,000 clocks per year and, thus, make the action profitable.

◆ **Case 6** Calispell has an opportunity to sell 100,000 clocks to a nonrecurring customer for $27 per clock. The clocks will be packaged and sold using the customer's own logo. Packaging cost will increase by $1 per clock, but the company will not incur any of the current variable selling cost for these 100,000 clocks. Acceptance of the job will require the company to pay a $30,000 commission to the salesperson calling on this customer.

We will assume that this sale will not interfere with budgeted sales and is within the company's relevant range of activity. Should Calispell make this sale?

The new variable cost per clock is $26 ($25 total budgeted variable production cost + $0 variable selling cost + $1 additional variable packaging cost). The $27 selling price minus the $26 new total variable cost provides a contribution margin of $1 per clock sold to the nonrecurring customer.

Total additional contribution margin (100,000 clocks × $1 CM per clock)	$100,000
− Additional fixed cost (commission) related to this sale	(30,000)
= Net incremental benefit	$ 70,000

The total CM generated by the sale more than covers the additional fixed cost. Thus, the sale produces incremental profit and, therefore, should be made.

However, as with all proposals, this one should be evaluated on the basis of its long-range potential. Is the commission a one-time payment? Will the customer possibly return in future years to buy additional clocks? Will such sales affect regular business in the future? Is the sales price to the new customer a legal one?[4] If all of these questions can be answered "yes," Calispell should seriously consider this opportunity. In addition, referral business from the new customer could also increase sales.

The incremental approach is often used to evaluate alternative pricing strategies in economic downturns. In such stressful times, companies must confront the reality that they might be unable to sell a normal volume of goods at normal prices. With this understanding, companies can choose to maintain normal prices and sell a lower volume of goods or reduce prices and attempt to maintain market share and normal volume.

REVIEW 4-4 — LO4-4 — Incremental Analysis

Leopold manufactures plastic component parts for refrigeration units. The following information is available for the company's first year of business when it produced 80,000 units. Revenue of $160,000 was generated by the sale of 80,000 units.

	Variable Cost	Fixed Cost
Direct material cost (per unit)	$0.40	
Direct labor cost (per unit)	0.20	
Overhead cost (per unit)	0.60	
Selling and administrative (per unit)		
Overhead (in total)		$30,000
Selling and administrative (in total)		$10,000

1. Compute the effects on profit of each of the following suggestions. Consider each suggestion separately.
   a. Changing to biodegradable materials would increase the per unit material cost by 50 percent, but would result in 20,000 units of additional sales.
   b. Increasing the advertising budget by $4,000 would increase sales by 15 percent.
   c. Lowering the price by 5 percent will increase demand in units by 15 percent.
2. **Critical Thinking:** What are some qualitative considerations for each of the three proposals?

More practice: E4-29
Solution on p. 4-44.

CVP ANALYSIS IN A MULTIPRODUCT ENVIRONMENT

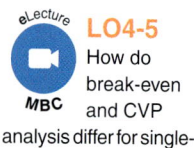

LO4-5 How do break-even and CVP analysis differ for single-product and multiproduct firms?

Companies typically produce and sell a variety of products, some of which may be related (such as bats and baseballs or sheets, towels, and comforters). To perform CVP analysis in a multiproduct company, one must assume either that the

---

[4] The Robinson-Patman Act addresses the legal ways in which companies can price their goods for sale to different purchasers.

Chapter 4 Cost-Volume-Profit Analysis

- product sales mix stays constant as total sales volume changes or
- average contribution margin ratio stays constant as total sales volume changes.

Break-Even in a Multiple Product Mix

The constant mix assumption can be referred to as the "bag" (or "basket") analogy. The analogy is that the sales mix represents a "bag" of products that are sold together. For example, when some product A is sold, set amounts of products B and C are also sold. Use of an assumed constant sales mix allows a weighted average contribution margin ratio to be computed for the "bag" of products being sold. Without the assumption of a constant sales mix, BEP cannot be calculated, nor can CVP analysis be used effectively. After the constant percentage contribution margin in a multiproduct firm has been determined, all situations regarding profit points can be treated in the same manner as they were earlier in the chapter. One must remember, however, that the answers reflect the "bag" assumption.

In a multiproduct company, the CM% is weighted by the quantities of each product included in the "bag." This weighting process means that the CM% of the product composing the largest proportion of the "bag" has the greatest impact on the average contribution margin of the product mix. The CM per "bag" can be used to determine break-even in total units and the weighted average CM% per "bag" can be used to determine break-even in total sales dollars. In either case, the estimated sales mix is used to determine the break out of sales by product.

Computing Break-Even for Multiple Products — LO4-5 DEMO 4-5A

Suppose that, because of the success of its desk clocks, Calispell management is considering the production of clock wall-mounting kits. The vice president of marketing estimates that the company will sell one clock wall-mounting kit for every three clocks sold. Therefore, the "bag" of products has a 3:1 product ratio. Calispell will incur an additional $514,000 in fixed plant asset costs (depreciation, insurance, and so forth) to support a higher relevant range of production. Other relevant information is shown in the following table.

	Clocks	Clock Wall-Mounting Kits
	Per unit	Per unit
Selling price	$40	$10
Total variable cost	(29)	(4)
Contribution margin	$11	$6

Total fixed cost (FC) = $4,400,000 previous + $514,000 additional = $4,914,000

◆ **What is the number of "bags" to break even and how many clocks and wall mounting kits are considered part of the "bags?"**

The following table shows the computation of the $39 CM per "bag" and the 30% weighted average CM% per "bag".

	Clocks	Clock Wall-Mounting Kits	Total	Percentage
Number of products per "bag"	3	1		
Total revenue per "bag"	$120	$10	$130	100
Total variable cost per "bag"	(87)	(4)	(91)	(70)
Contribution margin—"bag"	$33	$6	$39	30

BEP in "bags" is calculated as follows.

$$\text{BEP in "bags"} = \text{Fixed costs} \div \text{CM per "bag"}$$

$$= \$4,914,000 \div \$39$$

$$= 126,000 \text{ "bags"}$$

Note: Each "bag" consists of 3 clocks and 1 clock wall-mounting kit; therefore, it will take sales of 378,000 (=126,000 × 3) clocks and 126,000 (=126,000 × 1) clock wall-mounting kits to break even, assuming the constant 3:1 mix.

In sales dollars:

> **BEP in sales dollars = Fixed costs ÷ Weighted average CM% per "bag"**

$$= \$4,914,000 \div 0.30$$
$$= \$16,380,000^5$$

Proof of these computations through contribution income statements follow.

Units Sold	Clocks 378,000	Clock Wall-Mounting Kits 126,000	Total
Sales.	$ 15,120,000	$1,260,000	$ 16,380,000
Variable cost.	(10,962,000)	(504,000)	(11,466,000)
Contribution margin	$ 4,158,000	$ 756,000	$ 4,914,000
Fixed cost.			(4,914,000)
Income before tax.			$ 0

Analysis Considering a Shift in Sales Mix

Any shift in the product sales mix will change the weighted average CM% and BEP. If the sales mix shifts toward a product with a lower dollar contribution margin, the BEP will increase and profits will decrease unless there is a corresponding increase in total revenues. A shift toward higher dollar contribution margin products without a corresponding decrease in revenues will decrease the BEP and increase profits.

DEMO 4-5B   **LO4-5**   **Analysis of a Change in Sales Mix**

Now assume that instead of a 3:1 ratio, the sales mix for Calispell was 2.5 clocks to 1.5 clock wall-mounting kits.

◆ **What are the number of "bags" to break even assuming the shift in sales mix?**

The following table shows the computation of the $36.50 CM per "bag" and the 31.7% weighted average CM% per "bag".

	Clocks	Clock Wall-Mounting Kits	Total	Percentage
Number of products per "bag".	2.5	1.5		
Total revenue per "bag".	$100.00	$15	$115.00	100.0
Total variable cost per "bag"	(72.50)	(6)	(78.50)	(68.3)
Contribution margin—"bag".	$ 27.50	$ 9	$ 36.50	31.7

> **BEP in "bags" = Fixed costs ÷ CM per "bag"**

$$= \$4,914,000 \div \$36.50$$
$$= 134,631 \text{ "bags" (rounded up to nearest unit)}$$

More bags are required now to break even because the company sold a higher proportion of the clock wall-mounting kits, which have a lower unit contribution margin than the clocks.

---

[5] The break-even sales dollars also represent the assumed constant sales mix of $120 of clocks to $10 of clock wall-mounting kits to represent a 92.3% to 7.7% ratio (both percentages are rounded). Thus, the company must have $15,120,000 ($16,380,000 × 0.923) in sales of clocks and $1,260,000 in sales of clock wall-mounting kits to break even.

Chapter 4 Cost-Volume-Profit Analysis

◆ **What is the before-tax profit or loss if 126,000 "bags" were sold at the adjusted sales mix?**

With a sales mix ratio of 2.5 clocks to 1.5 clock wall-mounting kits, the company would have sold 315,000 (=126,000 × 2.5) clocks and 189,000 (=126,000 × 1.5) clock wall-mounting kits at a loss of $315,000 as shown below.

Units Sold	Clocks 315,000	Clock Wall-Mounting Kits 189,000	Total
Sales.	$12,600,000	$1,890,000	$14,490,000
Variable cost.	(9,135,000)	(756,000)	(9,891,000)
Contribution margin	$ 3,465,000	$1,134,000	$ 4,599,000
Fixed cost.			(4,914,000)
Before-tax loss			$ (315,000)

Cost Volume Profit Analysis—Multiproduct — LO4-5 — REVIEW 4-5

Applications Inc. makes three types of electronic kits. The company's total fixed cost is $424,800. Selling prices, variable cost, and sales percentages for each type of kit follow:

	Selling Price	Variable Cost	Percentage of Total Unit Sales
Basic.	$ 600	$300	50%
Intermediate	750	350	30%
Advanced	1,000	550	20%

a. What is the company's break-even point in units and sales dollars?
b. If the company has an after-tax income goal of $200,000 and the tax rate is 25 percent, how many units of each type of kit must be sold for the goal to be reached at the current sales mix?
c. Assume the sales mix shifts to 20 percent Basic, 50 percent Intermediate, and 30 percent Advanced. How does this change affect your answer to *a*?
d. **Critical Thinking:** Without performing the break-even calculations, how do you predict whether the number of break-even "bags" would be higher in part *a* or part *c*?

More practice: MC4-12, E4-30, E4-31
Solution on p. 4-45.

MANAGING RISKS OF CVP RELATIONSHIPS

CVP relationships can be formally analyzed using standard metrics to evaluate risk/reward relationships at existing sales levels or prospective sales levels. Two of these metrics are margin of safety and degree of operating leverage.

LO4-6 How are margin of safety and operating leverage concepts used in business?

Margin of Safety

When making decisions about business opportunities and changes in sales mix, managers often consider the **margin of safety (MS)**, which is the excess of budgeted or actual sales over break-even sales. The MS is the amount that sales can decline before reaching the BEP and, thus, provides a measure of the amount of "cushion" against losses.

The MS can be expressed in units, in dollars, or as a percentage (MS%). The following formulas are applicable.

> Margin of safety in units = Actual (or budgeted) sales in units − Break-even sales in units
> Margin of safety in $ = Actual (or budgeted) sales in $ − Break-even sales in $
> Margin of safety % = Margin of safety in units ÷ Actual (or budgeted) sales in units
> Margin of safety % = Margin of safety in $ ÷ Actual (or budgeted) sales in $

DEMO 4-6A   LO4-6   Computing Margin of Safety

The BEP for Calispell based on the **Exhibit 4.2** data is 400,000 units or $16,000,000 of sales. The company's budgeted income statement presented in **Exhibit 4.2** shows annual sales of $24,000,000 for 600,000 clocks.

◆ **What is Calispell's margin of safety in sales units, sales dollars, and as a percentage?**

In sales units: 600,000 budgeted units − 400,000 BEP units = 200,000 units
In sales $: $24,000,000 budgeted sales − $16,000,000 BEP sales = $8,000,000
As a percentage: 200,000 ÷ 600,000 = 33.33%
                       or
                       $8,000,000 ÷ $24,000,000 = 33.33%

Calispell's MS is quite high because the company is operating far above its BEP.

Risk Indicator The MS calculations allow management to determine how close to a "danger level" the company is operating and, as such, provide an indication of risk. The lower the MS, the more carefully management must watch revenue and control cost to avoid operating losses. At low margins of safety, managers are less likely to take advantage of opportunities that, if incorrectly analyzed or forecasted, could put the company in a loss position.

Operating Leverage

Another measure that is closely related to the MS and provides useful management information is the company's degree of operating leverage. The relationship between a company's variable and fixed costs is reflected in its **operating leverage**. Typically, highly labor-intensive organizations have high variable cost and low fixed cost; these organizations have low operating leverage.[6]

Conversely, organizations that are highly capital intensive or automated have cost structures that include low variable and high fixed cost, providing high operating leverage. Because variable cost is low relative to selling price, the contribution margin is high. However, high fixed cost means that the BEP also tends to be high. If the market determines selling prices, volume has the primary impact on profitability. Greater automation creates such a cost structure and companies become more dependent on volume increases to raise profits. *Thus, cost structure strongly influences the degree to which its profits respond to sales volume changes.*

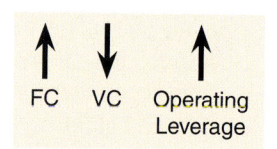

Companies with high operating leverage have high contribution margin ratios. Although such companies must establish fairly high sales volumes to initially cover fixed cost, once that cost is covered, each unit sold after breakeven adds significantly to profits. Thus, a small increase in sales can have a major impact on a company's profits.

The **degree of operating leverage (DOL)** measures how a percentage change in sales from the current level will affect company profits. DOL indicates how sensitive the company's profit is to sales volume increases and decreases. The computation for DOL follows.

$$\text{DOL} = \text{CM} \div \text{Before-tax profit}$$

This calculation assumes that fixed costs do not increase when sales increase.

DEMO 4-6B   LO4-6   Computing Degree of Operating Leverage

Assume that Calispell Company is currently selling 600,000 clocks.

◆ **How would a 20 percent increase in sales impact profits? How would a 20 percent decrease in sales impact profits?**

---

[6] An exception to this rule is a sports team, which is highly labor intensive, but its labor cost is fixed rather than variable.

First, Calispell's degree of operating leverage is calculated as follows.

$$\text{DOL} = \text{CM} \div \text{Before-tax profit}$$
$$= \$6,600,000 \div \$2,200,000$$
$$= 3$$

The impact of a 20 percent change to sales can be estimated using the DOL as follows.

$$\text{Predicted percentage change in profits} = \text{DOL} \times \text{Percentage change in sales}$$
$$= 3 \text{ DOL} \times 20\% \text{ Increase in sales}$$
$$= 60\% \text{ Increase in profits}$$

$$\text{Predicted percentage change in profits} = \text{DOL} \times \text{Percentage change in sales}$$
$$= 3 \text{ DOL} \times 20\% \text{ Decrease in sales}$$
$$= 60\% \text{ Decrease in profits}$$

These amounts are confirmed below.

Units Sold	Current 600,000	20 Percent Increase 720,000	20 Percent Decrease 480,000
Sales ($40 per clock)	$ 24,000,000	$ 28,800,000	$ 19,200,000
Variable cost ($29 per clock)	(17,400,000)	(20,880,000)	(13,920,000)
Contribution margin	$ 6,600,000	$ 7,920,000	$ 5,280,000
Fixed cost	(4,400,000)	(4,400,000)	(4,400,000)
Profit before tax	$ 2,200,000	$ 3,520,000[a]	$ 880,000[b]

[a] Profit increase = $3,520,000 − $2,200,000 = $1,320,000 (or 60% of the original profit).
[b] Profit decrease = $880,000 − $2,200,000 = ($1,320,000) (or −60% of the original profit).

Relationship Between MS Percentage and DOL

The DOL decreases as sales move upward from the BEP. Thus, when the margin of safety is low, the degree of operating leverage is high. In fact, at the BEP, the DOL is infinite because any increase from zero is an infinite percentage change. If a company is operating close to BEP, each percentage increase in sales can make a dramatic impact on net income. As the amount of sales increases from the BEP, margin of safety increases, but the degree of operating leverage declines. The relationship between the MS percentage (MS%) and DOL is as follows.

$$\text{MS\%} = 1 \div \text{DOL}$$
$$\text{DOL} = 1 \div \text{MS\%}$$

This relationship is proved below using the 600,000-clock sales level information for Calispell. Therefore, if one of the two measures is known, the other can be easily calculated.

$$\text{MS\%} = 1 \div \text{DOL}$$
$$= 1 \div 3 = 33\% \text{ (rounded)}$$

$$\text{DOL} = 1 \div \text{MS\%}$$
$$= 1 \div 33\% = 3 \text{ (rounded)}$$

REVIEW 4-6 — LO4-6 — Operating Leverage and Margin of Safety

Ring Co. makes office products. The selling price per package is $20, and variable cost of production is $14. Total fixed cost per year is $1,000,000. The company is currently selling 190,000 packages per year.

a. What is break-even in packages?
b. What is the margin of safety in dollars and in packages?
c. What is the degree of operating leverage?
d. If the company can increase sales in packages by 30 percent, what percentage increase will it experience in income? Prove your answer using a contribution income statement.
e. If the company increases advertising by $120,000, sales in packages will increase by 10 percent.
   (1) What will be the new break-even point in sales dollars?
   (2) The new degree of operating leverage?
f. **Critical Thinking:** Ring Co. is considering making a new line of kitchen products. In order to mitigate the financial risk of a new investment, should the company aim for a higher or lower degree of operating leverage?

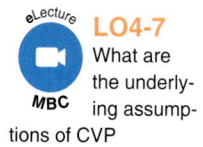

More practice: MC4-13, E4-34
Solution on p. 4-45.

UNDERLYING ASSUMPTIONS OF CVP ANALYSIS

LO4-7 What are the underlying assumptions of CVP analysis?

CVP analysis is a short-run model that focuses on relationships among selling price, variable cost, fixed cost, volume, and profit. This model is a useful planning tool that can provide information about the impact on profit when changes are made in the cost structure or in the sales level. Although limiting the accuracy of the results, several important but necessary assumptions are made in the CVP model. These assumptions follow.

1. All revenue and variable cost behavior patterns are constant per unit and linear within the relevant range.
2. Total contribution margin (Total revenue − Total variable cost) is linear within the relevant range and increases proportionally with output. This assumption follows directly from assumption 1.
3. Total fixed cost is constant within the relevant range. This assumption, in part, indicates that no capacity additions will be made during the period under consideration.
4. Mixed costs can be accurately separated into fixed and variable elements. Although accuracy of separation can be questioned, reliable estimates can be developed from the use of regression analysis or the high–low method (as discussed in Chapter 3).
5. Sales and production are equal; thus, there is no material fluctuation in inventory levels. This assumption is necessary because fixed cost can be allocated to inventory at a different rate each year.
6. In a multiproduct firm, the sales mix remains constant. This assumption is necessary so that a weighted average contribution margin and CM% can be computed.
7. Labor productivity, production technology, and market conditions will not change. If any of these changes were to occur, cost would change correspondingly, and selling prices might change. Such changes would invalidate assumptions 1 through 3.

DEMO 4-7 — LO4-7 — Analyzing CVP Assumptions

◆ **Which of the following scenarios would violate one or more of the CVP assumptions?**

1. Sales volume extends outside of the company's relevant range.
   Yes, this would violate CVP assumptions because the assumptions only apply within a company's relevant range of activity.
2. A CVP analysis extends over a two-year period.

Yes, *this would violate CVP assumptions because the results are generally valid in the short-run only, defined as one year or less. However, if the cost structure is not predicted to change, the assumptions could be revisited after a year to see if any adjustments need to be made in order to continue relying on the analysis.*

3. Variable costs in total increase with sales volume, while variable cost per unit remains constant within the relevant range.

   No, *this would not violate CVP assumptions because it indicates a linear cost pattern.*

4. The selling price per unit has changed due to a recent sales promotion.

   Yes, *this would violate CVP assumptions which would require new computations for CVP analyses with a change in selling price per unit.*

5. Estimates of variable and fixed costs obtained through regression are reliable but are not 100 percent accurate.

   No, *this would not violate CVP assumptions because the estimates must be reliable, but need not be perfect.*

Fixed Costs as Long-Term Variable Costs

The preceding seven assumptions are the traditional ones associated with CVP analysis. An additional assumption must be noted with regard to the distinction between variable and fixed cost. Accountants have generally assumed that cost behavior, once classified, remains constant as long as operations remain within the relevant range. Thus, for example, once a cost was determined to be "fixed," it would be fixed next year, the year after, and 10 years from now.

It is more appropriate, however, to regard fixed cost as long-term variable cost. *Over the long run, through managerial decisions, companies can change fixed cost; thus, a fixed cost is not fixed forever.* Generating cost information in a manner that yields a longer-run perspective is presented in Chapter 6 on activity-based costing/management. Part of the traditional "misclassification" of fixed cost has been caused by improperly specifying drivers of cost. As production and sales volumes are less often viewed as cost drivers, companies will begin to recognize that a "fixed cost" exists only in a short-term perspective.

Such a reclassification of cost simply means that cost drivers for long-term variable cost must be specified in break-even and CVP analyses. The formula will need to be expanded to include these additional drivers, and more information and a longer time frame will be needed to make the calculations. No longer will sales volume necessarily be the overriding nonmonetary force in the computations.

These adjustments to the CVP formula will force managers to take a long-run, rather than a short-run, view of product opportunities. Such a perspective could produce better organizational decisions. As the time frame is extended, both the time value of money and life cycle costing become necessary considerations. Additionally, the traditional income statement becomes less useful for evaluating projects that will take several years to mature. A long-run perspective is important in a variety of circumstances, such as when variable or fixed costs arise only in the first year that a product or service is provided to customers.

REVIEW 4-7 — Assumptions of CVP Analysis — LO4-7

a. Based on the underlying assumptions of the CVP analysis, indicate whether the following items are assumed to (a) remain constant, (b) fluctuate with output, or (c) not addressed specifically in the CVP assumptions.

1. Degree of operating leverage
2. Inventory levels
3. Labor productivity
4. Market conditions
5. Production technology
6. Sale per unit
7. Sales mix
8. Total contribution margin
9. Total fixed costs
10. Variable cost per unit

b. **Critical Thinking:** How can a cost such as straight-line depreciation on equipment be considered a fixed cost in the short-term but a variable cost in the long-term?

More practice: MC4-14, E4-39
Solution on p. 4-46.

Comprehensive Chapter Review

Key Terms

break-even chart, p. 4-6
break-even point (BEP), p. 4-4
contribution income statement, p. 4-2
contribution margin (CM), p. 4-2
contribution margin per unit (CM per unit), p. 4-3
contribution margin ratio (CM%), p. 4-4
cost-volume-profit (CVP) analysis, p. 4-2
degree of operating leverage (DOL), p. 4-20
incremental analysis, p. 4-14
margin of safety (MS), p. 4-19
operating leverage, p. 4-20
profit-volume (PV) graph, p. 4-7
variable cost ratio (VC%), p. 4-6

Chapter Summary

LO4-1 Contribution margin (Page 4-2)
- Contribution margin is the difference between total revenues and variable costs.
- Contribution income statement classifies costs according to behavior vs. function.
- Contribution margin indicates the proportion of revenue that contributes toward covering fixed costs and earning a profit

LO4-2 Determining the Break-Even Point (BEP) (Page 4-4)
- BEP identifies the volume level where total revenues equal total costs.
- BEP requires organizing costs by behavior.
- BEP requires assumptions, relative to volume, of linear revenue, and linear cost behavior.
- BEP relies on the existence of a relevant range of activity.
- BEP can be determined using
  - the following formulas where X = BEP:
    - X = Fixed cost ÷ Contribution margin per unit, where X = BEP in units
    - X = Fixed cost ÷ Contribution margin ratio, where X = BEP in sales dollars
  - graphing approach
    - by reading the Y-axis at the point where the total revenue and total cost lines intersect using the traditional CVP graph.
    - by reading where the profit line intersects the X-axis using the profit-volume graph.
- Contribution income statement is often used to prove the solutions found with other approaches.

LO4-3 Sales Computed for Desired Level of Profit (Page 4-9)
- CVP analysis can be used by a company to
  - study the interrelationships of
    - price,
    - volume,
    - fixed and variable cost, and
    - contribution margin.
  - calculate the level of sales volume necessary to achieve specific before- or after-tax target profit objectives.
  - enhance a manager's ability to positively influence current operations and to predict future operations, thereby reducing the risk of uncertainty.

LO4-4 Incremental Analysis for Short-Run Changes (Page 4-14)
- Incremental analysis focuses on factors that change only from one decision (course of action) to another.
- Quantitative analysis derived from incremental analysis is useful in management decision making.
- Quantitative results should be combined with qualitative factors in the decision process.

LO4-5 BEP and CVP Analysis for Single-Product and Multi-Product Firms (Page 4-16)
- In a multiproduct environment, break-even and CVP analysis
  - require that a constant product sales mix or "bag" assumption be used for the various products.
  - require that a weighted average contribution margin or CM ratio be calculated for each "bag" of product sold.

Chapter 4 Cost-Volume-Profit Analysis

- state solutions in terms of "bags" of product, which means the solutions must be converted (using the original product sales mix) to actual units (or sales dollars) of individual products.

MS and DOL (Page 4-19)   LO4-6
- Companies use the margin of safety (MS) and degree of operating leverage (DOL) concepts as follows:
  - the MS indicates how far (in units, in sales dollars, or as a percentage) a company is operating from its BEP; the MS% is equal to (1 ÷ DOL).
  - the DOL shows the percentage change that would occur in profit given a specified percentage change in sales from the current level; the DOL is equal to (1 ÷ MS%).

Underlying Assumptions of CVP Analysis (Page 4-22)   LO4-7
- The break-even and CVP models are based on several assumptions that limit their ability to reflect reality. Underlying assumptions are that
  - revenue and variable cost per unit are constant and linear within the relevant range.
  - contribution margin is linear within the relevant range.
  - total fixed cost is constant within the relevant range.
  - mixed cost can be accurately separated into its variable and fixed components.
  - sales and production levels are equal.
  - sales mix is constant in a multiproduct setting.
  - labor productivity, production technology, and market conditions will not change during the period under consideration.

Solution Strategies

Total Contribution Margin = Sales – Variable Costs   LO4-1

Contribution margin per unit = Selling price per unit – Variable cost per unit
Contribution margin ratio = Contribution margin/Sales or Contribution per unit/Selling price per unit
Contribution income statement:

Sales
 Less variable costs
Contribution margin
 Less fixed costs
Before-tax profit

Cost-Volume-Profit (CVP)   LO4-2, 3, 4, 5

The fundamental equation for break-even and CVP problems is

$$\text{Total revenue} - \text{Total cost} = \text{Profit}$$

CVP problems can also be solved by using a numerator/denominator approach. All numerators and denominators and the types of problems that each relates to follow. The formulas relate to both single- and multiproduct firms, but results for multiproduct firms are per bag and should be converted to units of individual products.

Problem Situation	Numerator	Denominator
BEP in sales units.	FC	CM per unit
BEP in sales dollars	FC	CM%
Sales Units for Fixed Before-Tax Profit.	FC + P	CM per unit
Sales Dollars for Fixed Before-Tax Profit	FC + P	CM%
Sales Units for Fixed Before-Tax Profit Per Unit.	FC	CM per unit – P_u
Sales Dollars for Fixed Before-Tax Profit Per Unit	FC	CM% – P_u%

where FC = fixed cost
       CM = contribution margin
       CM% = contribution margin ratio
       P = total profit (on a before-tax basis)
       P_u = profit per unit (on a before-tax basis)
       P_u% = profit percentage per unit (on a before-tax basis)

To convert after-tax profit to before-tax profit, divide after-tax profit by (1 – tax rate).

LO4-6 Margin of Safety (MS)

Margin of safety in units = Actual sales in units − Break-even sales in units
Margin of safety in dollars = Actual sales $ − Break-even sales $
Margin of safety % = (Margin of safety in units or $) ÷ (Actual sales in units or $)

Degree of Operating Leverage (DOL)

Degree of operating leverage = Contribution margin ÷ Before-tax profit
Predicted percentage change in profits = DOL × Percentage change in sales

Chapter Demonstration Problem

LO4-1, 2, 3, 4, 6 SunnyVale makes small plant stands that sell for $25 each. The company's annual level of production and sales is 120,000 units. In addition to $430,500 of fixed manufacturing overhead and $159,050 of fixed administrative expenses, the following per-unit costs have been determined for each plant stand:

Direct material	$ 6.00
Direct labor	3.00
Variable manufacturing overhead	0.80
Variable selling expense	2.20
Total variable cost	$12.00

Required:

a. Prepare a contribution income statement at the current level of production and sales.
b. Calculate the unit contribution margin in dollars and the contribution margin ratio for a plant stand.
c. Determine the break-even point in number of plant stands.
d. Calculate the dollar break-even point using the contribution margin ratio.
e. Determine SunnyVale's margin of safety in units, in sales dollars, and as a percentage.
f. Compute the company's degree of operating leverage. If sales increase by 25 percent, by what percentage will before-tax income increase?
g. How many plant stands must the company sell to earn $996,450 in before-tax income?
h. If the company wants to earn $657,800 after tax and is subject to a 20 percent tax rate, how many units must be sold?
i. How many plant stands must be sold to break even if SunnyVale's fixed manufacturing cost increases by $7,865? (Use the original data.)
j. The company has received an offer from a Brazilian company to buy 4,000 plant stands at $20 per unit. The per-unit variable selling cost of the additional units will be $2.80 (rather than $2.20), and $18,000 of additional fixed administrative cost will be incurred. This sale would not affect domestic sales or their costs. Based on quantitative factors alone, should SunnyVale accept this offer?

Solution to Demonstration Problem

a.

SunnyVale
Contribution Income Statement

Sales (120,000 × $25.00)		$ 3,000,000
Variable production cost		
Direct material (120,000 × $6.00)	$720,000	
Direct labor (120,000 × $3.00)	360,000	
Overhead (120,000 × $0.80)	96,000	
Variable selling expenses (120,000 × $2.20)	264,000	(1,440,000)
Contribution margin		$ 1,560,000
Fixed cost		
Manufacturing overhead	$430,500	
Administrative	159,050	(589,550)
Income before income tax		$ 970,450

© Cambridge Business Publishers

Chapter 4 Cost-Volume-Profit Analysis

b. CM   = SP – VC = $25 – $12 = $13 per unit
   CM% = CM ÷ SP = $13 ÷ $25 = 52 percent
c. BEP = FC ÷ CM per unit = $589,550 ÷ $13 = 45,350 plant stands
d. BEP = FC ÷ CM% = $589,550 ÷ 0.52 = $1,133,750 in sales
e. MS_u = Current unit sales – BEP unit sales = 120,000 – 45,350 = 74,650 plant stands
   MS$ = Current sales in dollars – BEP sales in dollars = $3,000,000 – $1,133,750 = $1,866,250
   MS% = MS in units ÷ Current unit sales = 74,650 ÷ 120,000 = 62 percent (rounded)
f. DOL = Current CM ÷ Current Before-tax profit = $1,560,000 ÷ $970,450 = 1.61 (rounded)
   Increase in Income = DOL × % Increase in Sales = 1.61 × 0.25 = 40.25 percent
   Proof:
     New sales   = 120,000 × 1.25 = 150,000
     New CM   = 150,000 × $13.00 = $1,950,000
     New before-tax profit = New CM – FC = $1,950,000 – $589,550 = $1,360,450
     Increase   = New before-tax profit – Old before-tax profit = $1,360,450 – $970,450 = $390,000
     Increase in % terms   = $390,000 ÷ $970,450 = 40.19 percent (rounded)
g. Sales units at a fixed profit = (FC + Before-tax profit) ÷ CM per unit
                                 = ($589,550 + $996,450) ÷ $13
                                 = 122,000 plant stands
h.   Before-tax profit = After-tax profit ÷ (1 – Tax rate) = $657,800 ÷ (1 – 0.20)
                                             = $657,800 ÷ 0.80 = $822,250
   Sales units at a fixed profit = (FC + Before-tax profit) ÷ CM per unit
                                 = ($589,550 + $822,250) ÷ $13
                                 = 108,600 plant stands
i.   X = Increase in FC ÷ CM
     X = $7,865 ÷ $13
     X = 605 units over BEP
   BEP = 45,350 + 605 = 45,955 plant stands
j. CM for each additional unit = $20.00 – $12.60 = $7.40
   CM = $7.40 × 4,000 = $29,600
   Increase in Before-tax profit = Increase in CM – Increase in FC = $29,600 – $18,000 = $11,600
   Yes, the company should accept the offer.

Assignments with the MBC logo in the margin are available in *myBusinessCourse*.
Resources include demonstration videos, guided examples, and auto-graded homework.
See details in the Preface, and ask your professor how you can access the system.

Data Analytics

DA4-1. Determining fixed vs. variable cost components using Excel   LO4-1

Genessee Industries introduced a new product last year (6582-D). Although it was very popular, it wasn't very profitable. Management has asked you to provide them with information to help them set a sales price that will provide them with a monthly gross profit of $7,500. (Last year's sales price was $75 per unit.)

You know that the direct costs per unit are $25 for direct materials and $5 for direct labor. You are given information about last year's monthly production levels and manufacturing overhead costs (indirect materials, indirect labor, and other). The Excel file is available on the textbook's website.

Required
a. Determine the cost formula for 6582-D. Use Excel's regression analysis tool to develop a cost-estimating equation for total fixed and variable manufacturing costs. Use the regression tool three times (once for indirect materials, once for indirect labor, and once for other overhead). Use the information from each analysis, along with the direct cost information to estimate the cost equation. *Hint:* Click on the 95% confidence level box *and* check the box to add a Line fit plot for each indirect cost element to show the relationship in chart form. *Hint:* You may need to change the minimum bound on the horizontal axis to 700 to see the line clearly on each chart.
b. Use the prior year data to create a graph of the various overhead costs by month. Create a Combo chart as follows. *Hint:* Under the Insert tab, click on Create custom combo chart.

1. The primary vertical axis is in dollars, and the secondary vertical axis is units of production. *Hint:* Click the Secondary axis box for units produced.
2. The horizontal axis is Months.
3. Units produced should be a Clustered column type; the overhead cost elements should be Line type.
4. Describe the trend in the overhead components based on a review of your chart.

c. Use Excel's Goal Seek tool to determine the sales price required to meet the $7,500 gross profit goal. Management believes monthly sales in units will average 1,500 next year. Assume the company will not maintain any inventory of finished goods. *Hint:* In a schedule in Excel, enter number of units, variable manufacturing cost per unit, total fixed costs, and a formula for gross profit. Use the Goal Seek tool to find the sales price. Goal Seek is found under the Data tab and under What-If Analysis.

d. Discuss how Goal Seek (or any other Excel tool) might help management with CVP analysis.

DA4-2. Determining fixed vs. variable cost components using Tableau
Available in MBC, this problem uses Tableau to determine fixed and variable cost components using Tableau.

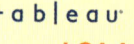

DA4-3. Segment reporting including CVP analysis
Fashion at Home sells three models of sewing machines (Traditional, Computerized, and Computerized with Quilting). Net operating income for the prior year was $232,500. The company president has asked the sales, production, and accounting managers for ideas for increasing profitability. Information about prior year operations is included in MBC.

Four proposals are presented to the president.

a. Raise prices by 10% on the Traditional model and 5% on the Computerized model. (No increase in the price of the Computerized with Quilting model is proposed.) The higher sales price is expected to reduce demand for those two products by 5%. *Note*: Round new selling price to the nearest whole dollar.

b. Add a new feature to the Computerized model. The feature will cost $20 in materials cost per unit. Labor costs will not change. Demand is expected to increase by 400 units per year if $20,000 is spent on advertising the new feature.

c. Lower the price of the Computerized with Quilting model to $695. The lower sales price is expected to result in an additional 400 Computerized with Quilting units being sold.

d. Eliminate the Traditional product. $15,000 of the fixed costs directly related to the product would be eliminated. The balance of the $25,000 in fixed costs would be shared (equally) by the remaining two products. In addition, some of the administrative employees would move into the space now used for manufacturing the Traditional product. This would eliminate $4,000 in monthly corporate rental expenses.

Required

a. Create a contribution format statement for Fashion At Home based on last year's operating results. The statement should reference amounts in your data table.

b. Use the prior year data to create four scenarios in Excel. In each scenario, assume only one of the four changes could be made. No other changes in quantities or costs are expected. *Hint*: Scenario Manager is located under the Data tab, under What-if Analysis. *Hint*: In Scenario Manager, highlight the data in the file profiled as the amounts to change; highlight the Net Operating Income from your contribution statement as the Result cell. For each new scenario, simply change the data amounts affected by the new scenario.
1. What was the prior year's contribution margin?
2. What were the prior year's segment margins for:
   i. Traditional?
   ii. Computerized?
   iii. Computerized with Quilting?
3. What are the expected profits under:
   i. Scenario A
   ii. Scenario B
   iii. Scenario C
   iv. Scenario D
4. The sales manager is concerned that the expected increase in the number of Computerized with Quilting models sold in Scenario C will result in a 10% decrease in unit sales of the Computerized models. Run another scenario that includes that reduction. How does this Scenario E that impact profitability?

Chapter 4 Cost-Volume-Profit Analysis

5. What should the president consider (other than the financial impacts described) before deciding whether to eliminate a product line (Scenario D)?

DA4-4. Analyzing changes in product mix over time

The **Fastenal Company** engages in the wholesale distribution of industrial and construction supplies. The following percentages of sales by product line was included in the 2021 10-K disclosures for Fastenal Company.

Type	Twelve-month Period Ended Dec. 31		
	2021	2020	2019
Other.	3.7%	3.3%	2.9%
Welding supplies	3.8%	3.5%	4.2%
Electrical supplies.	4.3%	4.1%	4.7%
Cutting tools	5.0%	4.7%	5.7%
Material handling	5.6%	5.1%	5.9%
Hydraulics & pneumatics	6.4%	5.9%	6.8%
Janitorial supplies.	8.2%	9.8%	7.8%
Tools.	8.5%	8.2%	9.9%
Safety supplies.	21.2%	25.5%	17.9%
Fasteners	33.3%	29.9%	34.2%
	100.0%	100.0%	100.0%

Required

a. Prepare a bar chart showing the trend in each product line over the three-year period. *Hint:* Each product line should have three bar graphs, one for each year. Based on your bar chart, answer the following questions.
   1. Visually from the bar chart, which product lines are the largest of the ten product lines?
   2. Of the three years 2019, 2020, and 2021, which year visually shows the most change in product mix?
   3. What product lines do you think were most affected by the COVID-19 pandemic in 2020? Why?

b. The company indicated in its 10-K disclosures that the portion of sales attributable to Fasteners has been decreasing for approximately 25 years. The company also indicated that non-fastener products generally carry lower gross profit margins than its Fastener products. Comment on the impact of these trends on the company's profitability.

Data Visualization

Data Visualization Activities are available in myBusinessCourse. These assignments use Tableau Dashboards to expose students to visual depictions of data and introduce students to data analytics through data visualizations. These exercises are easily assignable and auto graded by MBC.

Potential Ethical Issues

1. Ignoring the relevant range when setting assumptions about cost behavior to disregard the implications of cost changes on the calculation of BEP or CVP analysis
2. Treating some or all fixed costs as per-unit costs in calculating BEP or performing CVP analysis
3. Using untested or inaccurate assumptions about the relationship between variables such as advertising and sales volume or sales price and sales volume to ensure a particular decision outcome
4. Assuming a constant sales mix ratio while ignoring expected changes in demand for individual products when conducting CVP analysis for multiproduct firms
5. Using CVP analyses to support long-term cost management strategies
6. Visually distorting BEP graphs to project improper conclusions
7. Including irrelevant information in incremental analysis to manipulate calculation results

Questions

Q4-1. What information provided by a contribution income statement is used in computing the break-even point? Is this information on a traditional income statement? Explain your answer.

Q4-2. How is "break-even point" defined? What are the differences among the formula and the graph approaches for computing breakeven? How is a contribution income statement used to verify the results?

Q4-3. What is the contribution margin ratio? How is it used to calculate the break-even point?

Q4-4. Why is CVP analysis generally used as a short-run tool? Would CVP ever be appropriate as a long-run model?

Q4-5. How is the "bag" assumption used in CVP analysis for a multiproduct firm? What additional assumption must be made in multiproduct CVP analysis that does not pertain to a single-product CVP situation?

Q4-6. A multiproduct company has a sales mix of nine widgees to three squigees. Widgees have a contribution margin ratio of 45 percent, and squigees have a contribution margin ratio of 80 percent. If the sales mix changes to six widgees to six squigees, will the company have a higher or lower weighted average contribution margin ratio and a higher or lower break-even point (in sales dollars)? Explain the rationale for your answer.

Q4-7. Define and explain the relationship between margin of safety and degree of operating leverage.

Multiple Choice

MC4-8. (LO4-1) Manchester Airlines is in the process of preparing a contribution income statement that will allow a detailed look at its variable costs and profitability of operations. Which one of the following cost combinations should be used to evaluate the variable cost per flight of the company's Boston-Las Vegas flights?

a. Flight crew salary, fuel crew salary, and engine maintenance.
b. Fuel, food service, and airport landing fees.
c. Airplane depreciation, baggage handling, and airline marketing.
d. Communication system operation, food service, and ramp personnel.

MC4-9. (LO4-2) Phillips & Company produces educational software. Its unit cost structure, based upon an anticipated production volume of 150,000 units, is as follows.

Sales price	$160
Variable costs	60
Fixed costs	55

The marketing department has estimated sales for the coming year at 175,000 units, which is within the relevant range of Phillip's cost structure. Phillip's break-even volume (in units) and anticipated operating income for the coming year would amount to

a. 82,500 units and $7,875.000 of operating income.
b. 82,500 units and $9,250,000 of operating income.
c. 96,250 units and $3,543,750 of operating income.
d. 96,250 units and $7,875,000 of operating income.

MC4-10. (LO4-3) A detergent company sells large containers of industrial cleaner at a selling price of $12 per container. Each container of cleaner requires $4.50 of direct materials, $2.50 direct labor, and $1.00 of variable overhead. The company has total fixed costs of $2,000,000 and an income tax rate of 40%. Management has set a goal to achieve a targeted after-tax net income of $2,400,000. What amount of dollar sales must the company achieve in order to meet its goal?

a. $14,400,000.
b. $18,000,000.
c. $22,000,000.
d. $24,000,000.

MC4-11. (LO4-4) Bolger and Co. manufactures large gaskets for the turbine industry. Bolger's per unit sales price and variable costs for the current year are as follows.

Sales price per unit	$300
Variable costs per unit	210

Bolger's total fixed costs aggregate $360,000. As Bolger's labor agreement is expiring at the end of the year, management is concerned about the effect a new agreement will have on its unit breakeven point. The controller performed a sensitivity analysis to ascertain the estimated effect of a $10 per unit direct labor increase and a $10,000 reduction in fixed costs. Based on these data, it was determined that the breakeven point would

a. decrease by 1,000 units.
b. decrease by 125 units.
c. increase by 375 units.
d. increase by 500 units.

MC4-12. Specialty Cakes Inc. produces two types of cakes, a 2 lbs. round cake and a 3 lbs. heart-shaped cake. Total fixed costs for the firm are $94,000. Variable costs and sales data for the two types of cakes are presented below.

	2 lbs. Round Cake	3 lbs. Heart-shaped Cake
Selling price per unit.	$12	$20
Variable cost per unit	$ 8	$15
Current sales (units).	10,000	15,000

If the product sales mix were to change to three heart-shaped cakes for each round cake, the breakeven volume for each of these products would be

a. 8,174 round cakes, 12,261 heart-shaped cakes.
b. 12,261 round cakes, 8,174 heart-shaped cakes.
c. 4,947 round cakes, 14,842 heart-shaped cakes.
d. 15,326 round cakes, 8,109 heart-shaped cakes.

MC4-13. Projected sales for a tent manufacturer are $510,000. Each tent sells for $850 and requires $350 of variable costs to produce. The tent manufacturer's total fixed costs are $145,000. The tent manufacturer's margin of safety is

a. 310 units.
b. 710 units.
c. 730 units.
d. 1,310 units.

MC4-14. All of the following are assumptions of cost-volume-profit analysis except
a. total fixed costs do not change with a change in volume.
b. revenues change proportionately with volume.
c. variable costs per unit change proportionately with volume.
d. sales mix for multi-product situations do not vary with volume changes.

Exercises

E4-15. **Contribution income statement** Sports Drinks, Inc. began business in the current year selling bottles of a thirst-quenching drink. Production for the first year was 104,000 bottles, and sales were 104,000 bottles. The selling price per bottle was $3.10. Costs incurred during the year were as follows:

Ingredients used.	$ 56,000
Direct labor.	26,000
Variable overhead.	48,000
Fixed overhead.	5,200
Variable selling expenses.	10,000
Fixed selling and administrative expenses	28,000
Total actual cost	$173,200

For the year:
a. What was variable cost of goods sold?
b. What was the contribution margin per bottle?
c. What was the contribution margin ratio?

E4-16. **Contribution income statement** Top Disc manufactures flying disks. The following information is available for the year, the company's first year in business when it produced 325,000 units. Revenue of $812,500 was generated by the sale of 325,000 flying disks.

	Variable Cost	Fixed Cost
Production		
Direct material..............	$150,000	
Direct labor.................	100,000	
Overhead...................	75,000	$112,500
Selling and administrative.........	90,000	100,000

    a. What is the total contribution margin per unit?
    b. What is the contribution margin ratio?
    c. Prepare a contribution income statement.

LO4-1   **E4-17. Cost and revenue behavior** The following financial data have been determined from analyzing the records of Joe's Ceramics (a one-product firm):

Contribution margin per unit.....................	$25
Variable cost per unit	$21
Annual fixed cost	$90,000

How does each of the following measures change when product volume goes up by one unit at Joe's Ceramics?

    a. Total revenue   *b.* Total cost   *c.* Before-tax profit

LO4-2   **E4-18. Break-even point** Llano Lamps has the following revenue and cost functions:

$$\text{Revenue} = \$70 \text{ per unit}$$
$$\text{Cost} = \$90,000 + \$40 \text{ per unit}$$

    a. What is the break-even point in units?
    b. What is the break-even point in dollars?

LO4-2   **E4-19. Break-even point** Diamond Jim's makes and sells class rings for local schools. Operating information is as follows:

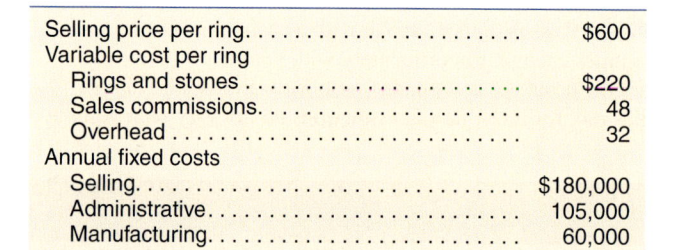

Selling price per ring........................	$600
Variable cost per ring	
Rings and stones.........................	$220
Sales commissions.......................	48
Overhead................................	32
Annual fixed costs	
Selling..................................	$180,000
Administrative...........................	105,000
Manufacturing...........................	60,000

    a. What is Diamond Jim's break-even point in rings?
    b. What is Diamond Jim's break-even point in sales dollars?
    c. What would Diamond Jim's break-even point be in rings if sales commissions increased to $54 per ring?
    d. What would Diamond Jim's break-even point be in rings if fixed selling expenses decreased by $6,000?

LO4-2   **E4-20. Formula; graph; contribution income statement** Pittsburg Tar Co. had the following income statement for the year:

Sales (30,000 gallons × $8)...............		$ 240,000
Variable cost		
Production (40,000 gallons × $3)........	$120,000	
Selling (30,000 gallons × $0.50).........	15,000	(135,000)
Contribution margin		$ 105,000
Fixed cost		
Production	$ 46,000	
Selling and administrative	6,200	(52,200)
Income before tax......................		$ 52,800
Income tax (40%)......................		(21,120)
Net income		$ 31,680

Chapter 4 Cost-Volume-Profit Analysis

a. Compute the break-even point using the equation approach.
b. Prepare a CVP graph to reflect the relationships among cost, revenue, profit, and volume.
c. Prepare a profit-volume graph.
d. Prepare a short explanation for company management about each of the graphs.
e. Prepare a contribution income statement at break-even point. Use the break-even gallons for both production and selling costs.

E4-21. Sales with fixed before-tax profit Salina Sports Wear has designed a new athletic suit. The company plans to produce and sell 30,000 units of the new product in the coming year. Annual fixed costs are $600,000, and variable costs are 70 percent of selling price. If the company wants a before-tax profit of $300,000, at what minimum price must it sell its product? *LO4-3*

E4-22. BEP, sales with fixed before-tax profit Hamlet House makes portable garden sheds that sell for $1,800 each. Costs are as follows: *LO4-2, 3*

	Per Unit	Total
Direct material	$800	
Direct labor	90	
Variable production overhead	60	
Variable selling and administrative cost	50	
Fixed production overhead		$200,000
Fixed selling and administrative		60,000

a. How many garden sheds must the company sell to break even?
b. If Hamlet House's management wants to earn a before-tax profit of $200,000, how many garden sheds must be sold?
c. If Hamlet House's management wants to earn a before-tax profit of $280,000, how many garden sheds must be sold?

E4-23. CM, BEP, sales with fixed before-tax profit Austin Automotive sells an auto accessory for $180 per unit. The company's variable cost per unit is $30 for direct material, $25 per unit for direct labor, and $17 per unit for overhead. Annual fixed production overhead is $37,400, and fixed selling and administrative overhead is $25,240. *LO4-1, 2, 3*

a. What is the contribution margin per unit?
b. What is the contribution margin ratio?
c. What is the break-even point in units?
d. Using the contribution margin ratio, what is the break-even point in sales dollars?
e. If Austin Automotive wants to earn a before-tax profit of $51,840, how many units must the company sell?

E4-24. Sales with fixed after-tax profit Use the information for Hamlet House in Exercise E4-22 and assume a tax rate for the company of 35 percent. *LO4-3*

a. If Hamlet House wants to earn an after-tax profit of $182,000, how many garden sheds must be sold?
b. How much revenue is needed to yield an after-tax profit of 8 percent of revenue? How many garden sheds does this revenue amount represent?

E4-25. Sales with fixed after-tax profit Use the information for Austin Automotive in Exercise E4-23 and assume a tax rate for the company of 30 percent. *LO4-3*

a. If Austin Automotive wants to earn an after-tax profit of $135,800, how many units must the company sell?
b. If Austin Automotive wants to earn an after-tax profit of $7.20 on each unit sold, how many units must the company sell?

E4-26. Incremental sales Pantene Paints has annual sales of $2,250,000 with variable expenses of 60 percent of sales and fixed expenses per month of $25,000. By how much must annual sales increase for Pantene Paints to have before-tax profit equal to 30 percent of sales? *LO4-4*

E4-27. Sales with fixed after-tax profit Golf Glider makes gasoline-powered golf carts. The selling price is $5,000 each, and costs are as follows: *LO4-3*

Cost	Per Unit	Total
Direct material	$2,000	
Direct labor	625	
Variable overhead	325	
Variable selling	50	
Annual fixed production overhead		$250,000
Annual fixed selling and administrative		120,000

Golf Glider's income is taxed at a 40 percent rate.

a. How many golf carts must Golf Glider sell to earn $600,000 after tax?
b. What level of revenue is needed to yield an after-tax income equal to 20 percent of sales?

LO4-2, 3 **E4-28. Volume and pricing** Dim Witt is the county commissioner of Clueless County. He decided to institute tolls for local ferry boat passengers. After the tolls had been in effect for four months, Astra Astute, county accountant, noticed that collecting $1,450 in tolls incurred a daily cost of $2,000. The toll is $0.50 per passenger.

a. How many people are using the ferry boats each day?
b. If the $2,000 cost is entirely fixed, how much must each passenger be charged for the toll process to break even? How much must each passenger be charged for the toll process to make a profit of $250 per day?
c. Assume that only 80 percent of the $2,000 is fixed and the remainder varies by passenger. If the toll is raised to $0.60 per person, passenger volume is expected to fall by 10 percent. If the toll is raised and volume falls, will the county be better or worse off than it is currently and by what amount?
d. Assume that only 80 percent of the $2,000 is fixed and the remainder varies by passenger. If passenger volume will decline by 5 percent for every $0.20 increase from the current $0.50 rate, at what level of use and toll amount would the county first make a profit?
e. Discuss the saying "We may be showing a loss, but we can make it up in volume."

LO4-4 **E4-29. Incremental analysis** Following are abbreviated income statements for two companies, Ainsley and Bard:

	Ainsley	Bard
Sales	$2,000,000	$2,000,000
Variable cost	(1,400,000)	0
Contribution margin	$ 600,000	$2,000,000
Fixed cost	0	(1,400,000)
Operating income	$ 600,000	$ 600,000

Ainsley and Bard produce an identical product and both sell that product at $40. Both companies are searching for ways to increase operating income. Managers of both companies are considering three identical strategies. Consider each of the following strategies, and discuss which company is best situated to adopt that strategy.

a. Decrease sales price 30 percent to increase sales volume 60 percent.
b. Increase sales price per unit 30 percent, which will cause sales volume to decline by 15 percent.
c. Increase advertising by $200,000 to increase sales volume by 15,000 units.

LO4-5 **E4-30. CVP; multiproduct** Mel's Accessories sells wallets and money clips. Historically, the firm's sales have averaged three wallets for every money clip. Each wallet has an $8 contribution margin, and each money clip has a $6 contribution margin. Mel's incurs fixed cost in the amount of $180,000. The selling prices of wallets and money clips, respectively, are $30 and $15. The corporate-wide tax rate is 40 percent.

a. How much revenue is needed to break even? How many wallets and money clips does this represent?
b. How much revenue is needed to earn a before-tax profit of $150,000?
c. How much revenue is needed to earn an after-tax profit of $150,000?
d. If Mel's earns the revenue determined in (b) but does so by selling five wallets for every two money clips, what would be the before-tax profit (or loss)? Why is this amount not $150,000?

Chapter 4 Cost-Volume-Profit Analysis

E4-31. Multiproduct Green Rider makes three types of electric scooters. The company's total fixed cost is $1,080,000,000. Selling prices, variable cost, and sales percentages for each type of scooter follow:

LO4-5

	Selling Price	Variable Cost	Percent of Total Unit Sales
Mod.	$2,200	$1,900	30
Rad.	3,700	3,000	50
X-treme.	6,000	5,000	20

a. What is Green Rider's break-even point in units and sales dollars?
b. If the company has an after-tax income goal of $1 billion and the tax rate is 50 percent, how many units of each type of scooter must be sold for the goal to be reached at the current sales mix?
c. Assume the sales mix shifts to 50 percent Mod, 40 percent Rad, and 10 percent X-treme. How does this change affect your answer to (a)?
d. If Green Rider sold more X-treme scooters and fewer Mod scooters, how would your answers to (a) and (b) change? No calculations are needed.

E4-32. Break-even; margin of safety Farmer Ned wants to cash in on the increased demand for ethanol. Accordingly, he purchased a corn farm in Iowa. Ned believes his corn crop can be sold to an ethanol plant for $9.60 per bushel. Variable cost associated with growing and selling a bushel of corn is $7.60. Ned's annual fixed cost is $264,000.

LO4-2, 6

a. What is the break-even point in sales dollars and bushels of corn? If Ned's farm is 1,200 acres, how many bushels must he produce per acre to break even?
b. If Ned actually produces 174,000 bushels, what is the margin of safety in bushels, in dollars, and as a percentage?

E4-33. Break-even; operating leverage; contribution income statement Racine Tire Co. manufactures tires for all-terrain vehicles. The tires sell for $60, and variable cost per tire is $30; monthly fixed cost is $450,000.

LO4-1, 2, 3, 4, 6

a. What is the break-even point in units and sales dollars?
b. If Ronnie Rice, the company's CEO, wants the business to earn a before-tax profit of 25 percent of revenues, how many tires must be sold each month?
c. If the company is currently selling 20,000 tires monthly, what is the degree of operating leverage?
d. If the company can increase sales volume by 15 percent above the current level, what will be the increase in net income? What will be the new net income? Prove your calculations with a contribution income statement.

E4-34. Operating leverage; margin of safety; break-even Titan Foods makes a high-energy frozen meal. The selling price per package is $7.20, and variable cost of production is $4.32. Total fixed cost per year is $316,600. The company is currently selling 125,000 packages per year.

LO4-2, 6

a. What is the margin of safety in packages?
b. What is the degree of operating leverage?
c. If the company can increase sales in packages by 30 percent, what percentage increase will it experience in income? Prove your answer with a contribution income statement.
d. If the company increases advertising by $41,200, sales in packages will increase by 15 percent. What will be the new break-even point in sales dollars? The new degree of operating leverage?

E4-35. Leverage factors; writing A group of prospective investors has asked for your help in understanding the comparative advantages and disadvantages of starting a company that is either labor intensive or, in contrast, one that uses significant cutting-edge technology and is, therefore, capital intensive. Prepare a report addressing the issues. Include discussions regarding cost structure, BEP, CVP, MS, DOL, risk, customer satisfaction, and the relationships among these concepts.

LO4-1, 2, 6

E4-36. Product cost; writing A friend of yours, attending another university, states she learned that CVP is a short-run-oriented model and is, therefore, of limited usefulness. Your professor, however, has often discussed CVP in presentations about long-run planning to your cost accounting class. You decide to investigate your friend's allegation by preparing a report addressing your friend's contention. Your professor is also asking you to prepare a separate report for internal management's use that addresses how the CVP model could be adapted to become more useful for making long-run decisions. Prepare these two reports, one for your friend's understanding and one for your professor.

LO4-7

LO4-2, 3, 6 E4-37. Comprehensive Compute the answers to each of the following independent situations.

a. Orlando Ray sells liquid and spray mouthwash in a sales mix of 1:2, respectively. The liquid mouthwash has a contribution margin of $10 per unit; the spray's CM is $5 per unit. Annual fixed cost for the company is $100,000. How many units of spray mouthwash would Orlando Ray sell at the break-even point?

b. Piniella Company has a break-even point of 4,000 units. At BEP, variable cost is $6,400 and fixed cost is $1,600. If one unit over breakeven is sold, what will be the company's before-tax profit?

c. Montreal Company's product sells for $10 per bottle. Annual fixed costs are $216,000 and variable cost is 40 percent of selling price. How many units would Montreal Company need to sell to earn a 25 percent before-tax profit on sales?

d. York Company has a BEP of 2,800 units. The company currently sells 3,200 units at $65 each. What is the company's margin of safety in units, in sales dollars, and as a percentage?

LO4-1 E4-38. Ethics; writing Niobrara Pesticide Company's new president has learned that, for the past four years, the company has been dumping its industrial waste into the local river and falsifying reports to authorities about the levels of suspected carcinogens in that waste. The plant manager says that there is no proof that the waste causes cancer and that only a few fishing villages are within 100 miles downriver. If the company must treat the substance to neutralize its potentially injurious effects and then transport it to a legal disposal site, the company's variable and fixed costs would rise to a level that might make the firm uncompetitive. If the company loses its competitive advantage, 10,000 local employees could become unemployed and the town's economy could collapse.

a. What specific variable and fixed costs can you identify that would increase (or decrease) if the waste were treated rather than dumped? How would these costs affect product contribution margin?

b. What ethical conflicts does the president face?

c. What rationalizations can you detect that plant employees have devised?

d. What options and suggestions can you offer the president?

LO4-7 E4-39. CVP assumptions Identify which of the CVP assumptions is violated in each of the circumstances described below.

a. Price per unit declines as the volume of sales and production increase.
b. Labor productivity increases as the volume of production declines.
c. The sales mix in a multiproduct firm varies as the volume of total sales changes.
d. Mixed cost cannot be separated into variable and fixed components.
e. Costs behave according to a curvilinear function.
f. Sales and production volume differ.
g. Fixed cost and capacity can be adjusted within the period.

LO4-2, 7 E4-40. CVP assumptions; break-even; writing A local businesswoman, Jane Aire, has hired you and a colleague, Joanna, from your cost accounting class to advise her regarding her small manufacturing business that makes leather valises. The business was organized just two years ago and has failed to become profitable, which is why the business owner has hired you and Joanna. After analyzing the client's books, Joanna prepared the following simple income statement for the current year.

Sales....................	$ 200,000
Variable cost...............	(120,000)
Contribution margin	$ 80,000
Fixed cost.................	(140,000)
Operating loss	$ (60,000)

After studying the income statement, Joanna worked out the break-even point for the firm and advised the client, "Ms. Aire, you will need to achieve sales of $350,000 before this business is producing enough revenues to cover all cost."

Ms. Aire replied, "That's a 75 percent increase over existing sales; I don't see any way this business will reach that level of sales."

"Then," said Joanna, "you should shut the business down today to cut your losses." After considering Joanna's income statement and the conversation between Joanna and Aire, discuss whether you agree with Joanna's recommendation.

Problems

P4-41. CM, BEP, sales with fixed before-tax profit and after-tax profit Casper Karts manufactures a three-wheeled shopping cart that sells for $60. Variable manufacturing and variable selling cost are, respectively, $35 and $10 per unit. Annual fixed cost is $975,000.

 a. What is the contribution margin per unit and the contribution margin ratio?
 b. What is the break-even point in units?
 c. How many units must the company sell to earn a before-tax profit of $900,000?
 d. If the company's tax rate is 40 percent, how many units must be sold to earn an after-tax profit of $750,000?
 e. If labor costs are 60 percent of the variable manufacturing cost and 40 percent of the fixed cost, how would a 10 percent decrease in both variable and fixed labor costs affect the break-even point?
 f. Assume that the total market for three-wheeled shopping carts is 600,000 units per year and that Casper Karts currently has 18 percent of the market. The company wants to obtain a 25 percent market share and also wants to earn a before-tax profit of $1,350,000. By how much must variable cost be reduced? Provide some suggestions for variable cost reductions.

LO4-1, 2, 3, 4

P4-42. CVP single product; comprehensive Beantown Baseball Company makes baseballs that sell for $13 per two-pack. Current annual production and sales are 960,000 baseballs. Costs for each baseball are as follows:

Direct material	$2.00
Direct labor	1.25
Variable overhead	0.50
Variable selling expenses	0.25
Total variable cost	$4.00
Total fixed overhead	$1,250,000

 a. Calculate the unit contribution margin in dollars and the contribution margin ratio for the company.
 b. Determine the break-even point in number of baseballs.
 c. Calculate the dollar break-even point using the contribution margin ratio.
 d. Determine the company's margin of safety in number of baseballs, in sales dollars, and as a percentage.
 e. Compute the company's degree of operating leverage. If sales increase by 30 percent, by what percentage would before-tax profit increase?
 f. How many baseballs must the company sell if it desires to earn $1,096,000 in before-tax profit?
 g. If the company wants to earn $750,000 after tax and is subject to a 40 percent tax rate, how many baseballs must be sold?
 h. How many baseballs would the company need to sell to break even if its fixed cost increased by $50,000? (Use original data.)
 i. Beantown Baseball Company has received an offer to provide a one-time sale of 20,000 baseballs at $8.80 per two-pack to the Lowell Spinners. This sale would not affect other sales, nor would the cost of those sales change. However, the variable cost of the additional units would increase by $0.20 for shipping, and fixed cost would increase by $6,000. Based solely on financial information, should the company accept this offer? Show your calculations. What other factors should the company consider in accepting or rejecting this offer?

LO4-1, 2, 3, 4, 6

P4-43. CVP Aqua Gear, in business for 20 years, makes swimwear for professional athletes. Analysis of the firm's financial records for the current year reveals the following:

Average swimsuit selling price	$70
Variable swimsuit expenses	
Direct material	$28
Direct labor	12
Variable overhead	8
Annual fixed cost	
Selling	$10,000
Administrative	24,000

LO4-2, 3, 4

The company's tax rate is 40 percent. Samantha Waters, company president, has asked you to help her answer the following questions. (Round CM% to the nearest tenth of a percent and BE in units to the nearest whole unit.)

a. What is the break-even point in number of swimsuits and in dollars?
b. How much revenue must be generated to produce $40,000 of before-tax profits? How many swimsuits would this level of revenue represent?
c. How much revenue must be generated to produce $40,000 of after-tax earnings? How many swimsuits would this represent?
d. What amount of revenue would be necessary to yield an after-tax profit equal to 20 percent of revenue?
e. Aqua Gear is considering purchasing a faster sewing machine that will save $6 per swimsuit in cost but will raise annual fixed cost by $40,000. If the equipment is purchased, the company expects to make and sell an additional 5,000 swimsuits. Should the company make this investment?
f. A marketing consultant told Aqua Gear managers that they could increase the number of swimsuits sold by 30 percent if the selling price was reduced by 10 percent and the company spent $10,000 on advertising. The company has been selling 3,000 swimsuits. Should the company make the changes advised by the consultant?

LO4-1, 4 P4-44. CVP decision alternatives Mitch Weatherby owns a sports brokerage agency and sells tickets to major league baseball, football, and basketball games. He also sells sports travel packages that include game tickets, airline tickets, and hotel accommodations. Revenues are commissions based as follows:

Game ticket sales.........	8% commission
Airline ticket sales.........	10% commission
Hotel bookings sales	20% commission

Monthly fixed costs include advertising ($2,200), rent ($1,800), utilities ($500), and other costs ($4,400). There are no variable costs. A typical month generates the following sales amounts that are subject to the stated commission structure:

Game tickets..................	$60,000
Airline tickets	9,000
Hotel bookings	14,000
Total.......................	$83,000

a. What is Weatherby's normal monthly profit or loss?
b. Weatherby estimates that airline bookings can be increased by 40 percent if he increases advertising by $1,200. Should he increase advertising?
c. Weatherby's friend Rusty has asked him for a job in the travel agency. Rusty has proposed that he be paid 50 percent of any additional commissions he can bring to the agency plus a salary of $400 per month. Weatherby has estimated that Rusty can generate the following additional bookings per month:

Game tickets..................	$ 8,000
Airline tickets	1,500
Hotel bookings	6,000
Total.......................	$15,500

Hiring Rusty would also increase fixed cost by $600 per month inclusive of salary. Should Weatherby hire Rusty?
d. Weatherby hired Rusty and in the first month, Rusty generated an additional $13,000 of bookings for the agency. The bookings, however, were all airline tickets. Was the decision to hire Rusty a good one? Why or why not?

LO4-2 P4-45. Graph The Real Deal is a social organization that performs charitable work in its local community. The club has the following monthly cost and fee information: monthly membership fee per member, $60; monthly variable cost of service per member, $25; and monthly fixed service cost, $3,500. Costs are extremely low because volunteers provide almost all services and supplies. Excess of fees over service cost are used to support charitable activities.

a. Prepare a break-even chart for The Real Deal.
b. Prepare a profit-volume graph for The Real Deal.

Chapter 4 Cost-Volume-Profit Analysis

    c. At this time, The Real Deal has only 120 members. Which of the preceding items (break-even chart or profit-volume graph) would you use in a speech to the membership about the benefits of recruiting additional members? Why?

P4-46. Multiproduct firm Yard Bird manufactures commercial and residential riding lawnmowers. The company sells one commercial mower per three residential mowers sold. Selling prices for the commercial and residential mowers are, respectively, $5,600 and $1,800, and variable selling and production cost are, respectively, $3,800 and $1,000. The company's annual fixed cost is $8,400,000. Compute the sales volume of each mower type needed to
    a. break even.
    b. earn $1,260,000 of income before tax.
    c. earn $1,008,000 of income after tax, assuming a 40 percent tax rate.
    d. earn 12 percent on sales revenue in before-tax income.
    e. earn 8 percent on sales revenue in after-tax income, assuming a 40 percent tax rate. (Round percentages and units to the nearest whole number.)

LO4-3, 5

P4-47. Multiproduct firm The Glass Menagerie makes small, pressed-resin ducks and ducklings. For every duck sold, the company sells five ducklings. The following information is available about the company's selling prices and cost:

LO4-3, 5

	Ducks	Ducklings
Selling price	$24	$12
Variable cost.	12	8
Annual fixed cost	$288,000	

    a. What is the average contribution margin ratio?
    b. Calculate the monthly unit break-even point if fixed cost is incurred evenly throughout the year. At the BEP, indicate how many units of each product will be sold monthly.
    c. If the company wants to earn $96,000 before-tax profit monthly, how many units of each product must it sell?
    d. Company management has specified $31,680 as monthly net income, and the company is in a 40 percent tax bracket. However, marketing information has indicated that the sales mix has changed to one duck to nine ducklings. How much total revenue and what number of products must be sold to achieve the company's profit objective?
    e. Refer to the original information. If the company can reduce variable cost per duckling to $4 by raising monthly fixed cost by $8,500, how will the break-even point change? Should the company make these changes? Explain your answer.

P4-48. Multiproduct firm The Pink Flamingo, Inc., manufactures plastic lawn ornaments. Currently the firm manufactures three items: reindeer, snowmen, and flamingos. For each reindeer, two snowmen and four flamingos are sold.

LO4-3, 5, 6

	Reindeer	Snowmen	Flamingos
Variable product cost	$12.00	$15.00	$25.00
Variable selling expenses.	6.00	4.50	8.00
Variable administrative expenses	3.00	5.50	6.00
Selling price	40.00	35.00	60.00
Annual fixed factory overhead	$420,000		
Annual fixed selling expenses	150,000		
Annual fixed administrative expenses.	80,178		

The firm is in a 40 percent tax bracket.
    a. What is the annual break-even point in revenues?
    b. How many reindeer, snowmen, and flamingos are expected to be sold at the breakeven point?
    c. If the firm desires before-tax profit of $250,428, how much total revenue is required, and how many units of each product must be sold?
    d. If the firm desires after-tax income of $155,718, how much total revenue is required, and how many units of each product must be sold?
    e. If the firm achieves the revenue determined in (d), what is its margin of safety in dollars and as a percentage? (Round to the nearest tenth of a percent.)

LO4-2, 3, 5, 6 P4-49. Comprehensive; multiproduct Nature's Own makes three types of wood flooring: Oak, Hickory, and Cherry. The company's tax rate is 40 percent. The following costs are expected for the year:

	Oak	Hickory	Cherry
Variable cost (on a per-square-yard basis)			
Direct material	$10.40	$6.50	$17.60
Direct labor	3.60	0.80	12.80
Production overhead	2.00	0.30	3.50
Selling expense	1.00	0.50	4.00
Administrative expense	0.40	0.20	0.60
Fixed overhead	$760,000		
Fixed selling expense	240,000		
Fixed administrative expense	200,000		

Per-square-yard expected selling prices are as follows: Oak, $32.80; Hickory, $16.00; and Cherry, $50.00. The expected sales mix is as follows:

	Oak	Hickory	Cherry
Square yards	9,000	72,000	6,000

a. Calculate the break-even point for the year. (Round to the next highest whole unit.)
b. How many square yards of each product are expected to be sold at the break-even point? (Round CM% to the nearest tenth of a percent.)
c. If the company wants to earn before-tax profit of $800,000, how many square yards of each type of flooring would it need to sell? How much total revenue would be required? (Round to the next highest whole unit.)
d. If the company wants to earn an after-tax profit of $680,000, determine the revenue needed using the contribution margin ratio approach. (Round CM% to the nearest tenth of a percent and amounts to the nearest whole dollar.)
e. If the company achieves the revenue determined in (d), what is the margin of safety (1) in dollars and (2) as a percentage? (Round to the nearest tenth of a percent.)

LO4-2, 3, 5 P4-50. CVP analysis; multiproduct Ted Tyner owns Sixth Man Hotel, a luxury hotel with 60 two-bedroom suites for coaches and their players. Capacity is 10 coaches and 50 players. Each suite is equipped with extra-long king-sized beds, super-tall and extended shower heads, extra-tall bathroom vanities, a laptop, and a printer. Each suite has a Pacific Ocean view. Hotel services include airport limousine pickup and drop-off, a daily fruit basket, champagne on the day of arrival, and a Hummer for transportation. Coaches and players are interviewed about their dietary restrictions and room service requirements before arrival. The hotel's original cost was $1,920,000, and depreciation is $160,000 per year. Other hotel operating costs include:

Labor	$320,000 per year plus $5 per suite per day
Utilities	$158,000 per year plus $1 per suite per day
Miscellaneous	$100,000 per year plus $6 per suite per day

In addition to these costs, costs are also incurred on food and beverage for each guest. These costs are strictly variable and (on average) are $40 per day for coaches and $15 per day for players.

a. Assuming that the hotel is able to maintain an average annual occupancy of 80 percent in both coach and player suites (based on a 360-day year), determine the minimum daily charge that must be assessed per suite per day to generate $240,000 of income before tax.
b. Assume that the per-day price Tyner charges is $240 for coaches and $200 for players. If the sales mix is 12:48 (12 coach days of occupancy for every 48 player days of occupancy), compute the following (rounding BEP to the nearest whole bag):
  1. The break-even point in total occupancy days.
  2. Total occupancy days required to generate $400,000 of income before tax.
  3. Total occupancy days to generate $400,000 of after-tax income. Tyner's personal tax rate is 35 percent.
c. Tyner is considering adding a massage service for guests to complement current hotel services. He has estimated that the cost of providing such a service would largely be fixed because all necessary facilities already exist. He would, however, need to hire five certified masseurs at

a cost of $500,000 per year. If Tyner decides to add this service, how much would he need to increase his daily charges (assume equal dollar increases to coach and player room fees) to maintain the break-even point computed in (b)?

P4-51. CVP analysis; advanced Fairbanks Express is a luxury passenger carrier in Alaska. All seats are first class, and the following data are available:

Number of seats per passenger train car..............	60
Average load factor (percentage of seats filled)...........	75%
Average full passenger fare........................	$140
Average variable cost per passenger..................	$60
Fixed operating cost per month.....................	$2,400,000

LO4-2, 3, 4

a. What is the break-even point in passengers and revenues per month? (Round CM% to the nearest tenth of a percent and BEP to the nearest dollar.)
b. What is the break-even point in number of passenger train cars per month? (Round to the nearest whole unit.)
c. If Fairbanks Express raises its average passenger fare to $170, it is estimated that the load factor will decrease to 60 percent. What will be the monthly break-even point in number of passenger cars? (Round to the nearest whole unit.)
d. (Refer to original data.) Fuel cost is a significant variable cost to any railway. If crude oil increases by $16 per barrel, it is estimated that variable cost per passenger will rise to $80. What would be the new break-even point in passengers and in number of passenger train cars? (Round to the nearest whole unit.)
e. Fairbanks Express has experienced an increase in variable cost per passenger to $70 and an increase in total fixed cost to $3,000,000. The company has decided to raise the average fare to $160. If the tax rate is 40 percent, how many passengers per month are needed to generate an after-tax profit of $800,000? (Round to the nearest whole dollar and unit.)
f. (Use original data.) Fairbanks Express is considering offering a discounted fare of $100, which the company believes would increase the load factor to 80 percent. Only the additional seats would be sold at the discounted fare. Additional monthly advertising cost would be $160,000. How much before-tax profit would the discounted fare provide Fairbanks Express if the company has 40 passenger train cars per day, 30 days per month?
g. Fairbanks Express has an opportunity to obtain a new route that would be traveled 15 times per month. The company believes it can sell seats at $150 on the route, but the load factor would be only 60 percent. Fixed cost would increase by $200,000 per month for additional crew, additional passenger train cars, maintenance, and so on. Variable cost per passenger would remain at $60.
   1. Should the company obtain the route?
   2. How many passenger train cars must Fairbanks Express operate to earn before-tax profit of $101,000 per month on this route? (Round to the nearest whole unit.)
   3. If the load factor could be increased to 75 percent, how many passenger train cars must be operated to earn before-tax profit of $101,000 per month on this route? (Round to the nearest whole unit.)
   4. What qualitative factors should be considered by Fairbanks Express in making its decision about acquiring this route?

P4-52. Incremental analysis Calypso Canvas makes canvas window awnings. You have been asked to predict the potential effects of some proposed company changes. The following information is available:

LO4-2, 4, 6

Variable cost per unit	
Direct material.....................	$18.40
Direct labor........................	13.00
Production overhead................	8.60
Selling expenses....................	4.60
Administrative expenses..............	3.00
Annual fixed cost	
Production overhead................	$1,200,000
Selling...........................	960,000
Administrative......................	480,000

The selling price is $94 per unit, and expected sales volume for the current year is 150,000 units. Following are some changes proposed by various members of the company.

1. Engineers suggest that adding color accents to each unit at a cost of $14.40 would increase product sales by 20 percent.
2. The sales manager suggests that a $520,000 increase in advertising will increase sales by 15 percent.
3. The sales force believes that lowering the price by 5 percent will increase demand in units by 10 percent.
    a. Compute the current break-even point in units and dollars. (Round to the nearest unit.)
    b. Compute the current margin of safety in dollars, in units, and as a percentage. (Round to the nearest whole percentage.)
    c. Compute the independent effects on profit and dollar break-even point of each of the suggestions. For each proposal, advise company management about acceptability.

LO4-1, 2, 3, 4, 6 **P4-53.** **MS; DOL; PV graph** You are considering buying one of two local firms (Olson Corp. and Miami Inc.). Olson Corp. uses a substantial amount of direct labor in its manufacturing operations, and its salespeople work on commission. Miami Inc. uses the latest automated technology in manufacturing; its salespeople are salaried. The following financial information is available for the two companies:

	OLSON CORP.		MIAMI INC.	
	Year 1	Year 2	Year 1	Year 2
Sales	$600,000	$960,000	$600,000	$840,000
Expenses including taxes	(528,000)	(823,200)	(528,000)	(667,200)
Net income	$72,000	$136,800	$72,000	$172,800

After examining cost data, you find that the fixed cost for Olson Corp. is $60,000; the fixed cost for Miami Inc. is $300,000. The tax rate for both companies is 40 percent.

a. Recast the income statements into the contribution income statement format.
b. What are the break-even sales for each firm for each year? (Round to the next highest whole dollar.)
c. Assume that you could acquire either firm for $1,200,000, and you want an after-tax return of 12 percent on your investment. Determine what sales level for each firm would allow you to reach your goal.
d. What is the margin of safety for each firm for each year? What is the degree of operating leverage?
e. Assume that product demand for Year 3 is expected to rise by 15 percent from the Year 2 level. What will be the expected net income for each firm?
f. Assume that product demand for Year 3 is expected to fall by 20 percent from the Year 2 level. What will be the expected net income for each firm?
g. Prepare a profit-volume graph for each firm.

LO4-7 **P4-54.** **CVP assumptions; writing** You were talking to your roommate one day about CVP analysis and the approaches that are used to calculate the break-even point. You also described the assumptions that underlie this type of analysis.

Your roommate proclaimed, "Wow, you people in accounting are pretty simple. Do you realize how unrealistic it is to assume that, no matter how many units you sell, you will realize the same price per unit? And, I've never heard any serious person suggest that costs are linear. How can you possibly state that assumption with a straight face? In your world, profit maximization is simple … just produce the maximum amount possible."

Provide a written justification of the assumptions accountants make in conducting CVP analysis that will satisfy your critical economist roommate.

LO4-1, 2, 3, 6 **P4-55.** **CVP; DOL; decision making** Atlantic Fish Company is a wholesale distributor of cod. The company services restaurants in the Boston area. Small but steady growth in sales has been achieved by Atlantic Fish Company over the past few years, while cod prices have been increasing. The company is formulating its plans for the year and has gathered the following information:

Average selling price per pound	$9.00
Costs	
Cost of cod per pound	$5.60
Shipping expense per pound	0.40
Selling and administrative expense (rent and salaries)	$650,000
Sales commissions	10% of sales

Chapter 4 Cost-Volume-Profit Analysis

Expected annual sales volume: 400,000 pounds of cod
The company's estimated tax rate is 40 percent.

a. What is the expected net income for the coming year? Prepare a contribution income statement.
b. Compute the contribution margin per unit and the contribution margin ratio. (Round to the nearest tenth of a percent.)
c. What is the break-even point in pounds sold and revenues? (Round to the nearest whole unit and dollar.)
d. Compute the degree of operating leverage and margin of safety expected for the coming year. (Round to the nearest tenth of a percent.)
e. Refer to the original data. Using the degree of operating leverage you computed in (d), compute the expected profit if sales are 20% above the expected level.
f. Refer to the original data. How many pounds of cod must be sold to earn an after-tax net income of $900,000? (Round to the nearest dollar.)

P4-56. Break even; DOL; decision making Buckeye Grain, a corn and wheat processing company, has decided to introduce a new product that can be manufactured by either a capital-intensive method or a labor-intensive method. The method chosen will have no effect on the quality of the finished product. Estimated manufacturing costs for the two methods are as follows.

LO4-2, 6
CMA

	Capital-intensive	Labor-intensive
Direct raw materials per unit.	$10.00	$11.20
Direct labor ($24/hour) per unit.	12.00	14.40
Variable overhead ($12/hour) per unit	6.00	9.60
Total fixed costs	$4,880,000	$2,640,000

Buckeye Grain sells the new product at $60 per unit during its initial stage of product life cycle. The incremental selling expenses are estimated to be $1,000.000 annually plus $4 for each unit sold, regardless of the manufacturing method. Fixed costs are all directly traceable incremental costs. When deciding which manufacturing method to use, the company's management team take into account the operating leverage.

Required
a. Calculate the estimated breakeven point in annual unit sales of the new product if the company uses the capital-intensive manufacturing method and labor-intensive manufacturing method, respectively.
b. Calculate the annual unit sales volume at which the company would be indifferent between the two manufacturing methods.
c. Explain how the level of sales can affect the company's choice of manufacturing method.
d. Explain operating leverage and its relationship with business risk.

Review Solutions

Review 4-1
a. $1.20 = $0.40 + $0.20 + $0.60
b. $0.60 = ($160,000 ÷ 80,000) − ($1.20 + $0.20)
   30% = $0.60 ÷ $2.00

c.

Contribution Income Statement		
Sales revenue.		$160,000
Variable cost		
Cost of goods sold	$96,000	
Selling and administrative.	16,000	(112,000)
Contribution margin		48,000
Fixed cost		
Manufacturing overhead.	$30,000	
Selling and administrative.	10,000	(40,000)
Before-tax profit		$ 8,000

© Cambridge Business Publishers

d. 1,000 units × $0.60 contribution margin per unit = $600 (increase in before-tax profit)
e. The company could increase its contribution margin by increasing it sales units. If sales units do not increase, the company could increase contribution margin by increasing the selling price per unit and/or by decreasing the variable cost per unit (for example, negotiate a lower cost of direct materials purchased for the production of component parts).

Review 4-2

a. 11,300 units = (Fixed cost of $113,000 ÷ CM per unit of $10)
b. $226,000 = (Fixed cost of $113,000 ÷ CM percentage of 50%)
c. 12,556 units = (Fixed cost of $113,000 ÷ CM per unit of $9)
d. 11,100 units = (Fixed cost of $111,000 ÷ CM per unit of $10)
e. Knowledge of break-even unit sales gives Shalton the baseline number of units that it must sell to incur no loss, but achieve no profit. Knowing this baseline amount can help the company manage its operations more efficiently in a number of ways including:
   - Provides information on setting sales targets and budgets. Can the company meet the baseline? What is a realistic goal above the baseline amount?
   - Helps management assess risk levels. Is the base line level achievable? What is the risk of not exceeding the baseline amount and thus reporting a loss?
   - Allows for sensitivity analyses. If the company exceeds or does not meet its baseline sales, what is the impact on profits? Is the selling price per unit set or can it be adjusted and how would the adjustment impact break-even unit sales?

Review 4-3

a. $37 = $70 − $15 − $10 − $8
b. 53% (rounded) = $37 ÷ $70
c. 676 units = ($15,000 + $10,000) ÷ $37
d. $47,297 = ($15,000 + $10,000) ÷ 52.857%
e. 1,244 units (1,243.2 rounded up) = ($15,000 + $10,000 + $21,000) ÷ $37
f. 871 units (870.3 rounded up) = ($15,000 + $10,000 + [$5,400/(1 − 0.25)]) ÷ $37
g. 766 units (765.3 rounded up) = ($15,000 + $10,000) ÷ ($37 − [$3.25 /(1 − 0.25)])
h. The company would need to sell more units for an after-tax profit of $21,000 because that amount actually equates to $28,000 before-tax. In other words, the amount of profit needed has to be greater in order to have enough to pay the taxes on the profits. An increase in the tax rate also increases the amount of units that the company must sell because more profit is required to be paid in taxes.

Review 4-4

1. a.

Contribution margin on new units sold [20,000 × ($2.00 − $1.40)]	$12,000
Less contribution margin lost on existing sales (80,000 × $0.20)	(16,000)
Net incremental loss	$ (4,000)

b.

Increase in contribution margin [(15% × 80,000) × ($2 − $1.20)]	$ 9,600
Less increase in fixed costs	(4,000)
Net incremental benefit	$ 5,600

c.

Contribution margin on new units sold (80,000 × 0.15) × (($2.00 × 95%) − $1.20)	$ 8,400
Less contribution margin lost on existing sales (80,000 × ($2.00 × 0.05))	(8,000)
Net incremental benefit	$ 400

2. Qualitative considerations:
   a. Although the switch to biodegradable materials results in a loss, is the change in line with corporate sustainability initiatives? Are there cost savings to consider through lower disposal costs or other production process cost savings? Are there any tax incentives that would offset the cost increase?
   b. Will the increase in sales extend into future periods if customers repeat sales?
   c. The incremental benefit is small. In fact, if the increase in demand turns out to be 14%, the change would be a net incremental loss of $160. Is the risk worth the small potential monetary benefit? How reliable is the forecast of increased sales?

Chapter 4 Cost-Volume-Profit Analysis

Review 4-5

a. The percentage of sales of 50%, 30% and 20% of basic, intermediate, and advanced converts to 5, 3, and 2 units, respectively, in a "bag" of 10 units. Sales mix = 118 bags = $424,800 ÷ [(5 × ($600 − $300)) + (3 × ($750 − $350)) + (2 × ($1,000 − $550)]

Basic:	590 units = 118 × 5	Basic:	$354,000 = 590 × $600
Intermediate:	354 units = 118 × 3	Intermediate:	$265,500 = 354 × $750
Advanced:	236 units = 118 × 2	Advanced:	$236,000 = 236 × $1,000

b. Sales mix = 192 bags = ($424,800 + [$200,000/(1− 0.25)]) ÷ [(5 × ($600 − $300)) + (3 × ($750 − $350)) + (2 × ($1,000 − $550))]

Basic:	960 units = 192 × 5	Basic:	$576,000 = 960 × $600
Intermediate:	576 units = 192 × 3	Intermediate:	$432,000 = 576 × $750
Advanced:	384 units = 192 × 2	Advanced:	$384,000 = 384 × $1,000

c. Sales mix = 107.54 bags = $424,800 ÷ [(2 × ($600 − $300)) + (5 × ($750 − $350)) + (3 × ($1,000 − $550))]

Basic:	215 units (rounded) = 107.54 × 2	Basic:	$129,000 = 215 × $600
Intermediate:	538 units (rounded) = 107.54 × 5	Intermediate:	$403,500 = 538 × $750
Advanced:	323 units (rounded) = 107.54 × 3	Advanced:	$323,000 = 323 × $1,000

Note: Due to the rounding of the number of sales units (company is unable to sell partial units), at the break-even point in this scenario, a slight profit would be recognized of $250.

d.

	Selling Price	Variable Cost	CM	CM%
Basic	$ 600	$300	$300	50%
Intermediate	750	350	400	53%
Advanced	1,000	550	450	45%

Based on a review of the CM% per item, break-even in part c should require less "bags" because it is weighted more heavily toward Intermediate which has the highest CM%. In part a, the "bags" are weighted more heavily toward Basic, which has the second highest CM%.

Review 4-6

a. 166,667 packages (rounded) = $1,000,000 ÷ ($20 − $14)

b. Margin of safety in dollars: $466,660 = ($20 × 190,000) − ($20 × 166,667)

Margin of safety in units: $190,000 − 166,667 = 23,333 units

c.
Sales ($20 × 190,000)	$3,800,000
Variable cost ($14 × 190,000)	2,660,000
Contribution margin	1,140,000
Fixed cost	1,000,000
Income before income tax	$ 140,000

Degree of operating leverage = 8.143 = $1,140,000 ÷ $140,000

d. 244% = 8.143 × 30%

Sales ($20 × 190,000 × 1.3)	$4,940,000
Variable cost ($14 × 190,000 × 1.3)	3,458,000
Contribution margin	1,482,000
Fixed cost	1,000,000
Income before income tax	$ 482,000

Percentage increase = 244% = ($482,000 − $140,000) ÷ $140,000

© Cambridge Business Publishers

e. (1) $3,733,333 = ($1,000,000 + $120,000)/[($20 − $14)/$20]

(2)
Sales ($20 × 1.10 × 190,000)	$4,180,000
VC ($14 × 1.10 × 190,000)	2,926,000
CM	1,254,000
FC ($1,000,000 + $120,000)	1,120,000
Pretax operating income	$ 134,000

Degree of operating leverage = 9.36 = $1,254,000 ÷ $134,000

f. If Ring invests in a new line of products, initially aiming for a lower degree of operating leverage will mitigate some risks. The BEP with higher fixed costs will be higher. Thus, Ring will need to secure more sales to break-even on the new venture if it opts for a higher fixed cost structure. A lower degree of operating leverage allows more flexibility because costs will adjust to changes in sales volume (due to sales demand, market conditions, etc.) more readily when costs are more variable than fixed.

Review 4-7

a. 1. c   3. a   5. a   7. a   9. a
    2. a   4. a   6. a   8. b   10. a

b. Depreciation on equipment is an allocation of costs over the useful life of the equipment. Once the straight-line depreciation amount is determined, it is fixed over the asset's useful life. However, in the longer term, the equipment could be replaced with different equipment with a different allocated cost which would change the periodic depreciation amount. The equipment could be sold and subsequently leased which could affect the operating costs. In another example, volume could change which could impact the level of equipment needed in the longer term which would also impact the amount of periodic depreciation.

Data Visualization Solutions

(See page 4-9.)

a. Fixed costs, $100,000
b. Variable costs, $200,000
c. Profit, $100,000
d. Breakeven point, $200,000 (or 2,000 units)
e. Margin of safety in units, 2,000 units

Chapter 5

Relevant Information for Decision Making

Road Map

LO	Learning Objective | Topics	Page	eLecture	Demo	Review	Assignments
5-1	**What makes a cost relevant or irrelevant for purposes of decision making?** Relevant :: Incremental Revenue : Incremental Cost :: Incremental Profit :: Incremental Loss :: Opportunity Cost :: Sunk Cost:: Nonmonetary Benefits and Costs	5-2	e5-1	D5-1	Rev 5-1	MC5-10, E5-16, E5-17, E5-18, E5-19, E5-20, E5-21, E5-22, P5-35, P5-36, P5-37, P5-44, P5-45, P5-51, P5-52, P5-54
5-2	**What information is relevant in an outsourcing decision?** Outsourcing :: Make-or-Buy :: Opportunity Costs :: Throughput :: Quantitative Factors :: Qualitative Factors	5-6	e5-2	D5-2	Rev 5-2	MC5-11, E5-16, E5-23, E5-24, E5-25, P5-38, P5-39, P5-40, P5-42, P5-43, P5-53
5-3	**How can management achieve the highest return from use of a scarce resource?** Scarce Resources :: Contribution Margin per Scarce Resource :: Qualitative Factors	5-11	e5-3	D5-3	Rev 5-3	MC5-12, E5-26, E5-27, P5-41, P5-43, P5-47, **DA5-1**
5-4	**What variables do managers use to manipulate sales mix?** Sales Mix :: Sales Price Changes :: Sales Compensation Changes :: Advertising Budget Changes :: Qualitative Factors	5-14	e5-4	D5-4A D5-4B D5-4C	Rev 5-4	MC5-13, E5-28, E5-29, E5-30, P5-45, P5-46, P5-47
5-5	**How are special prices set, and when are they used?** Special Order Decisions :: Qualitative Factors	5-19	e5-5	D5-5	Rev 5-5	MC5-14, E5-31, E5-32, P5-44, P5-48, P5-53, **DA5-2**
5-6	**How do managers determine whether a product line should be retained or discontinued?** Direct Variable Expenses :: Avoidable Fixed Expenses :: Unavoidable Fixed Expenses :: Allocated Common Expenses :: Segment Margin :: Qualitative Factors	5-22	e5-6	D5-6	Rev 5-6	MC5-15, E5-33, E5-34, P5-41, P5-49, P5-50, P5-51, P5-52, P5-54

INTRODUCTION

Relevant costing focuses managerial attention on a decision's relevant (or pertinent) information. Relevant costing techniques are applied in virtually all business decisions in both short- and long-term contexts. This chapter examines the application of relevant costing techniques to recurring *short-term* business decisions, such as replacing an asset, outsourcing a product or part, allocating scarce resources, manipulating sales mix, and evaluating special pricing of orders. Discussion of analysis tools that are applied to longer-term decisions, generally decisions with implications greater than one year, is deferred to Chapter 19. Long-term decisions generally require consideration of costs and benefits that are mismatched in time; that is, the cost is incurred currently, but the benefit is derived in future periods.

Steps in the Decision Process The concepts of relevant costing are applied in the process of making decisions, using a step-wise approach to select the best decision choice. There are four steps in this decision process.

Step 1: The necessity of making a decision becomes evident. To illustrate, assume a machine crucial to the manufacture of skin care products by **Estee Lauder** suffers a major breakdown. This event triggers the need to make a decision to choose an action that will restore the machine's productive function.

Step 2: Decision choices or alternatives are identified. Continuing with the Estee Lauder example, two obvious choices would be to repair or replace the machine. However, less obvious choices might also be considered, such as outsourcing the work normally performed on the broken machine to a third-party vendor that possesses and operates this type of machine.

Step 3: The relevant costs and benefits associated with each decision alternative identified in step 2 are calculated. *This chapter is largely dedicated to this step in the decision process.*

Step 4: The decision alternative providing the largest net benefit to the organization is selected. This step naturally follows from the pursuit of profit maximization in business organizations and efficient cost management in governmental and not-for-profit entities.

THE CONCEPT OF RELEVANCE

LO5-1 What makes a cost relevant or irrelevant for purposes of decision making?

In decision making, managers should consider only relevant costs and revenues associated with each decision alternative. For information to be **relevant**, it must possess three characteristics:

- be associated with the decision under consideration;
- be important to the decision maker; and
- have a connection to, or bearing on, some future endeavor.

Association with Decision

Cost accountants assist managers in determining which costs and revenues are decision relevant. Costs or revenues are relevant when they are logically related to a decision and vary (incrementally or differentially) from one decision alternative to another. **Incremental revenue** (or **differential revenue**) is the amount of revenue that varies across decision choices. **Incremental cost** (or **differential cost**) is the amount of cost that varies across decision choices. For example, if the annual operating cost of an existing machine is $30,000 and that of a potential replacement machine is $22,000, the incremental annual cost to operate the existing machine is $8,000.

$30,000 − $22,000 = $8,000 Incremental annual operating cost of existing machine

Stated differently, $22,000 of operating cost is in common between the two machines, but $8,000 is incremental or differential. *Only the incremental cost is relevant to a decision.*

The process of relevant costing requires comparing the incremental revenues and incremental costs of alternative choices. Although incremental costs can be variable or fixed, a *general guideline is that most variable costs are relevant but most existing fixed costs are not*. The logic of this guideline is that, as an activity measure (such as sales or production volume) changes within the relevant range, total variable cost changes but total fixed cost remains constant. However, there are exceptions to this general rule, particularly in the long-run. There is a relationship between time and relevance. In the longer term, management action can influence virtually all costs, including fixed costs.

The difference between the incremental revenue and incremental cost of a particular alternative is the **incremental profit (incremental loss)** of that course of action. Management can compare incremental effects of alternatives in choosing the most profitable (or least costly) alternative. Although such a comparison sounds simple, for two reasons often it is not. First, the concept of relevance is an inherently individualistic determination; second, technological changes have increased the amount of available information to consider in making a decision. One challenge is to obtain and process the vast amount of data available, and to determine what reflects relevant costs and benefits.

Opportunity Cost

Some relevant factors, such as sales commissions or direct production costs, are easily identified and quantified because they are captured by the accounting system. Other factors are relevant and quantifiable but are not captured by the accounting system. Such factors cannot be ignored merely because they are difficult to obtain or require the use of estimates. For example, an **opportunity cost** represents the benefit forgone because one course of action is chosen over another. These costs are extremely important in decision making but are not directly obtainable from the accounting records.

To illustrate the concept of opportunity cost, assume that on August 1, Joey bought a ticket for $90 to attend a concert in December. In October, Joey's friend offers to buy the ticket for $120. Joey now must make a decision in which there are two mutually exclusive choices: attend the concert or sell the ticket. The $120 price offered by Joey's friend is an opportunity cost or the benefit that Joey will sacrifice if he chooses to attend the concert rather than sell the ticket.

Importance to Decision Maker

The need for specific information depends on how important that information is relative to achieving managerial objectives. Additionally, precise information is given more credence in the decision process over less precise information. However, if information is extremely important, but less precise, a manager must weigh importance against precision.

Bearing on the Future

Information may pertain to past or present events but is relevant only if it pertains to a future decision choice. All managerial decisions are made to affect future events, so the information on which decisions are based should reflect future effects. The future can be the short run (two hours from now, or next month) or the long run (three years from now). Costs that have no relevance to the future are sunk costs and are discussed next.

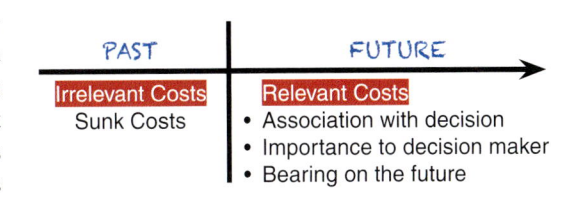

Sunk Costs

Only future costs and revenues can be influenced by current decisions and, as the time horizon lengthens, a larger set of future costs are differential, avoidable, and relevant. The challenge in relevant costing is to remove from consideration those costs that are not relevant, such as **sunk costs** that have been incurred in the past. One common misconception or error in decision making is treating a sunk cost, such as a previously purchased asset's acquisition cost or book value, as though it were relevant.

Sunk costs cannot be changed no matter what future course of action is taken because historical transactions cannot be reversed. For example, managers could find that a previously acquired asset is no longer adequate for its intended purpose, does not perform to expectations, is technologically obsolete, or is no longer marketable. Managers must then decide whether to keep the asset. This decision uses the current or future selling price that can be obtained for the asset, but that price is the result of current or future conditions and does not "recoup" the historical or sunk cost. The historical cost is irrelevant to the decision.

Although asset acquisition decisions are covered in depth in Chapter 19, they provide an excellent setting to introduce the concept of relevant information. The following illustration includes simplistic assumptions regarding asset acquisitions but demonstrates why sunk costs are not relevant costs.

DEMO 5-1 LO5-1 Identifying Relevant Costs in an Asset Replacement Decision

Landry Mechanical purchases a robotic warehouse management system for $12,000,000 on December 9. This "original" system is expected to have a useful life of five years, annual operating costs of $855,000, and no salvage value. Five days later, on December 14, Jill Landry, vice president of production, notices an advertisement for a similar system for $10,800,000. This "new" system also has an estimated life of five years and no salvage value, but it has features that enable it to perform better than the original system as well as save $355,000 per year in labor costs. On investigation, Landry discovers that the original system can be sold currently for $8,900,000. The following schedule provides data on the original and new robotic warehouse management systems.

Landry Decision Data	Original System Purchased Dec. 9	New System Available on Dec. 14
Cost	$12,000,000	$10,800,000
Life in years	5	5
Salvage value	$ 0	$ 0
Current resale value	$ 8,900,000	Not applicable
Annual operating cost	$ 855,000	$ 500,000

Landry Mechanical has two options:
- use the original system or
- sell the original system and buy the new system.

◆ **What are the relevant costs Landry should consider in making her decision?**

The following analysis indicates the relevant costs Landry should consider in making her decision.

Relevant Costs in Asset Replacement Decision	B	C
Alternative (1): Use original system		
Operating cost over life of original system ($855,000 × 5 years)		$ 4,275,000
Alternative (2): Sell original system and buy new		
Cost new system	$10,800,000	
Resale value of original system	(8,900,000)	
Effective net outlay for new system	$ 1,900,000	
Operating cost over life of new system ($500,000 × 5 years)	2,500,000	
Total cost of new system		(4,400,000)
Benefit of keeping the original system		$ 125,000
The alternative incremental calculation follows:		
Savings from operating the new system for five years		$ 1,775,000
Less effective incremental outlay for new system		(1,900,000)
Incremental advantage of keeping the original system		$ 125,000

Relevant costs to retain: $4,275,000
Relevant costs to replace: $4,400,000

- As the computations show, the original system's $12,000,000 purchase cost does not affect the decision outcome. This amount was sunk when the company bought the system. However, by selling the original system, the company would have net cash outlay for the new system of only $1,900,000.

© Cambridge Business Publishers

Chapter 5 Relevant Information for Decision Making

- Using either system, Landry Mechanical will incur operating costs over the next five years, but will spend $355,000 less each year using the new system (calculated as $855,000 − $500,000) for lifetime operating savings of $1,775,000.

Ignoring Sunk Costs A common analytical tendency is to include the $12,000,000 sunk cost of the old system in the analysis. However, this cost does not differ between the decision alternatives. If Landry keeps the original system, the company will deduct the $12,000,000 as depreciation expense over the system's life. Alternatively, if the system is sold, Landry will charge the $12,000,000 against the revenue realized from the system's sale. Thus, the $12,000,000 depreciation charge or its equivalent loss is the same in magnitude whether the company retains the original system or sells it and buys the new one. Because the amount is the same under both alternatives, it is not relevant to the decision process.

Landry must consider only the following relevant factors in deciding whether to purchase the new system:

- annual savings of the new system ($355,000) and the number of years (five) such savings would be enjoyed;[1]
- cost of the new system ($10,800,000); and
- current resale value of the original system ($8,900,000).

This example demonstrates the difference between relevant and irrelevant costs, including sunk costs. The next section discusses how the concepts of relevant costing, incremental revenues, and incremental costs are applied in making routine, recurring managerial decisions.

Identifying Relevant Costs, Sunk Costs, and Opportunity Costs — LO5-1 — REVIEW 5-1

Certain production equipment used by Lazer Inc. has become obsolete relative to current technology. The company is considering whether it should keep or replace its existing equipment. To aid in this decision, the company's controller gathered the following data:

	Old Equipment	New Equipment
Original cost	$90,000	$104,000
Remaining life	6	6
Accumulated depreciation	$15,000	n/a
Annual cash operating costs	$26,000	$10,000
Current salvage value	$18,000	n/a
Salvage value in five years	0	0

a. What three factors determine the relevance of information?
b. Identify any sunk costs in the data.
c. Identify any irrelevant (nondifferential) future costs.
d. Identify all relevant costs to the equipment replacement decision.
e. What are the opportunity costs associated with the alternative of keeping the old equipment?
f. What is the incremental cost to purchase the new equipment?
g. **Critical Thinking:** What nonmonetary factors could impact the decision to retain or replace the equipment?

More practice: MC5-10, E5-16, E5-19
Solution on p. 5-48.

RELEVANT COSTS FOR SPECIFIC DECISIONS

In evaluating courses of action, managers should select the alternative that provides the highest incremental benefit to the company. In doing so, managers must compare the net benefits of all courses of action against a baseline alternative. One course of action that is often used as the baseline alternative is the "change nothing" or "do nothing" option.

---

[1] In addition, two factors that were not discussed are important: the potential tax effects of the transactions and the time value of money. The authors have chosen to defer consideration of these factors to Chapter 19, which covers capital budgeting. Because of the time value of money, both systems were assumed to have zero salvage values at the end of their lives—a fairly unrealistic assumption.

Baseline Alternative Although certain incremental revenues and incremental costs are associated with other alternatives, the "change nothing" alternative has a zero incremental benefit because it reflects the status quo. Some situations involve specific government regulations or mandates in which a "change nothing" alternative does not exist. For example, assume a regulatory governmental agency issues an injunction against a company for polluting river water. Delays in the installation of pollution control devices could create fines that management should consider as incremental costs of the decision to delay. Not installing the devices would result in company closure, creating an opportunity cost equal to the lifetime income that would have been generated had sales continued.

Monetary and Nonmonetary Benefits and Costs Rational decision-making behavior includes a comprehensive evaluation of the monetary effects of all alternative courses of action. The chosen course should be one that provides the greatest benefit to the business relative to all other possible choices. In making decisions, managers must also find a way to include any inherently nonquantifiable considerations. Inclusion can be made by attempting to quantify those items or by simply making instinctive value judgments about nonmonetary benefits and costs.

Decisions outlined in the remainder of this chapter include the following.

Outsourcing Decisions	Scarce Resource Decisions	Sales Mix Decisions	Special Order Decisions	Product Line and Segment Decisions
LO5-2	LO5-3	LO5-4	LO5-5	LO5-6

Outsourcing Decisions

LO5-2 What information is relevant in an outsourcing decision?

Deciding how to source required inputs is an important decision for every business. In some cases, companies ensure the availability as well as the desired level of quality of parts and services by controlling all functions internally. In other cases, companies purchase more of the required materials, components, and services through an outsourcing process. **Outsourcing** refers to having work performed for one company by an off-site, nonaffiliated supplier. This process allows a company to buy a product (or service) from an outside supplier rather than making the product or performing the service in-house.

Benefits of Outsourcing An **outsourcing decision** (or **make-or-buy decision**) is made only after comparing internal production and opportunity costs to external purchase cost and then assessing the best use of facilities. Having an insourcing (make) option implies that the company has the capacity available for that purpose or has considered the cost of obtaining the necessary capacity. Relevant information for this type of decision includes both **quantitative factors** and **qualitative factors**. Exhibit 5.1 summarizes the primary motivations for companies to pursue outsourcing. Most outsourcing activities are less strategic and more routine such as the outsourcing of information processing.

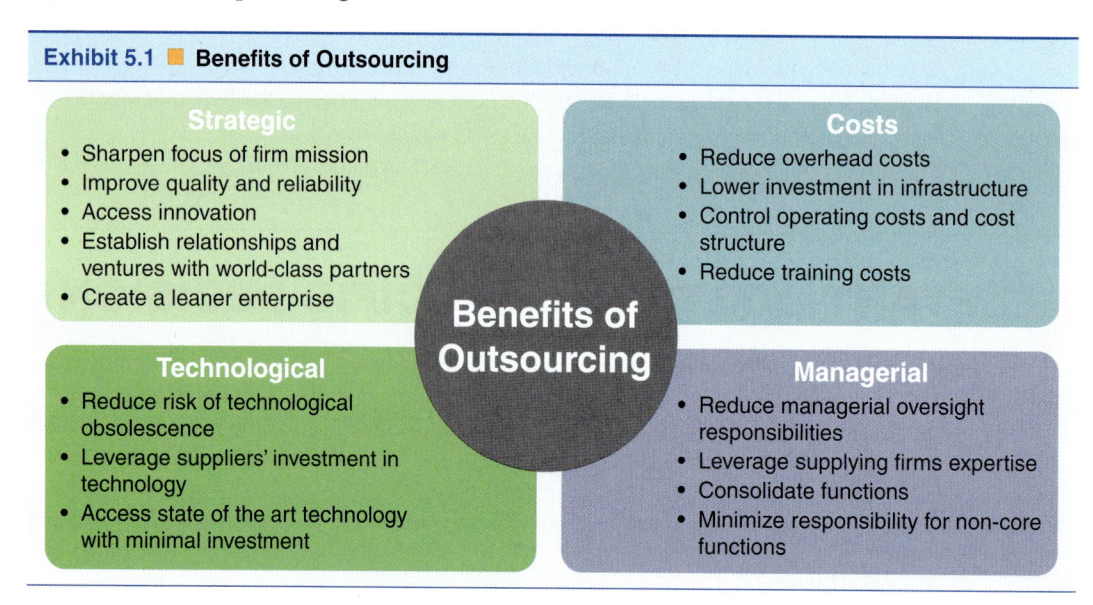

Exhibit 5.1 Benefits of Outsourcing

Strategic
- Sharpen focus of firm mission
- Improve quality and reliability
- Access innovation
- Establish relationships and ventures with world-class partners
- Create a leaner enterprise

Costs
- Reduce overhead costs
- Lower investment in infrastructure
- Control operating costs and cost structure
- Reduce training costs

Technological
- Reduce risk of technological obsolescence
- Leverage suppliers' investment in technology
- Access state of the art technology with minimal investment

Managerial
- Reduce managerial oversight responsibilities
- Leverage supplying firms expertise
- Consolidate functions
- Minimize responsibility for non-core functions

Chapter 5 Relevant Information for Decision Making

Outsourcing Decision Factors Numerous factors, such as those included in **Exhibit 5.2**, should be considered in the outsourcing decision. Several quantitative factors, such as incremental direct material and direct labor costs per unit, are known with a high degree of certainty. Other factors, such as variable overhead per unit and opportunity cost for production facilities, must be estimated. Qualitative factors should be evaluated by more than one individual so personal biases do not distort business judgment.

Exhibit 5.2 ■ Outsource Decision Considerations

Relevant Quantitative Factors
- Incremental production costs for each unit
- Unit cost of purchasing from outside supplier (price less any discounts available plus shipping, etc.)
- Number of available suppliers
- Availability of production capacity
- Opportunity costs of using facilities for production rather than for other purposes
- Amount of space available for storage
- Costs associated with carrying inventory
- Increase in throughput generated by buying components

Relevant Qualitative Factors
- Reliability of supply sources
- Ability to control quality of inputs purchased and company sustainability standards
- Nature of the work to be subcontracted
- Impact on customers and markets
- Future bargaining position with supplier(s)
- Perceptions regarding possible future price changes
- Perceptions about current product prices
- Protection of intellectual property

Assessing Outsourcing Risk Although companies can access better knowledge, experience, and process methodology through outsourcing, they also lose some control. Thus, company management should carefully evaluate the activities to be outsourced. The pyramid in **Exhibit 5.3** is one model for assessing outsourcing risk.

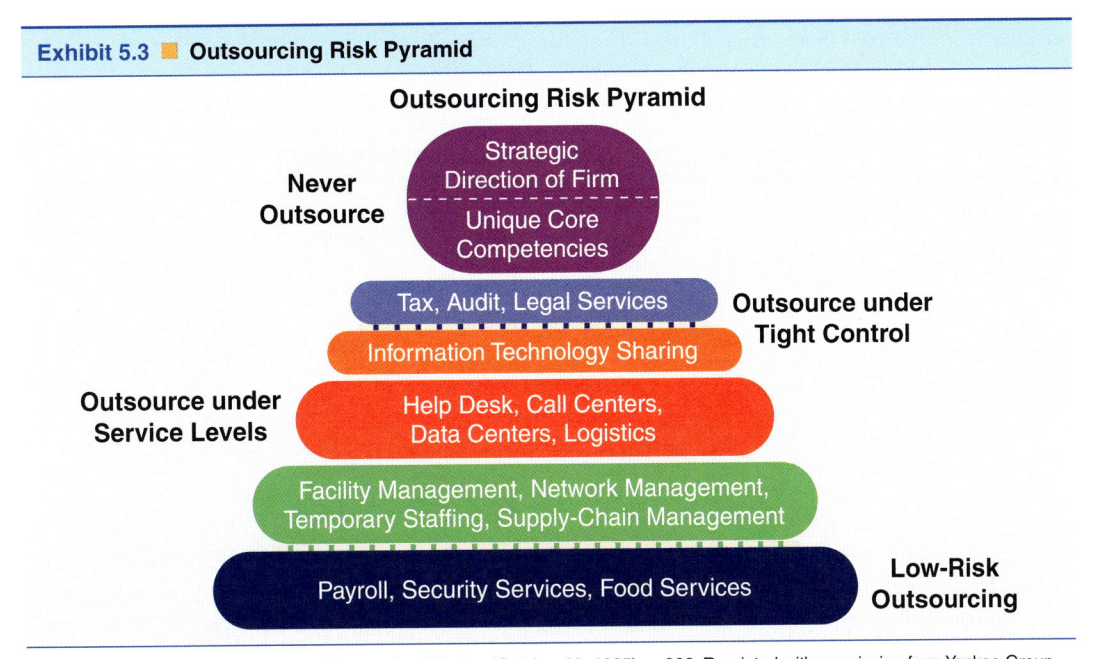

Exhibit 5.3 ■ Outsourcing Risk Pyramid

Outsourcing Risk Pyramid

- **Never Outsource**: Strategic Direction of Firm; Unique Core Competencies
- **Outsource under Tight Control**: Tax, Audit, Legal Services; Information Technology Sharing
- **Outsource under Service Levels**: Help Desk, Call Centers, Data Centers, Logistics; Facility Management, Network Management, Temporary Staffing, Supply-Chain Management
- **Low-Risk Outsourcing**: Payroll, Security Services, Food Services

Source: Yankee Group, "Innovators in Outsourcing," *Forbes* (October 23, 1995), p. 266. Reprinted with permission from Yankee Group.

Factors to consider include whether

- a function is considered critical to the organization's long-term viability (such as product research and development);
- the organization is pursuing a core competency relative to this function; and
- issues such as product/service quality, time of delivery, flexibility of use, sustainability considerations, or reliability of supply can be resolved to the company's satisfaction.

DEMO 5-2 — LO5-2 — Determining Whether to Outsource or Make Internally

Information about hinges for a door casing manufactured by Landry Mechanical (Landry) is shown below. The total cost to manufacture one hinge set is $7.90, or a set can be purchased externally for $7.00.

Landry Unit Cost Information

	A	B
1		Current Manufacturing Cost per Hinge Set
2	Direct material	$2.40
3	Direct labor	3.00
4	Variable overhead	0.80
5	Fixed overhead	1.70
6	Total unit cost	$7.90

Variable production cost of each set consists of $6.20 for material, labor, and variable overhead ($2.40 + $3.00 + $0.80). Of the $1.70 fixed overhead, only $0.50 is actually caused by hinge production and could be avoided if the firm chooses not to produce hinges. The remaining $1.20 of fixed overhead is an indirect (common) cost that would continue even if hinge production ceases.

◆ **Should Landry continue to make the hinges or purchase them from the outside supplier?**

The variable production cost of each set of $6.20 (=$2.40 + $3.00 + $0.80) is a relevant cost. In addition, $0.50 of the fixed overhead is considered a direct product cost because that amount can specifically be traced to hinge manufacturing. This $0.50 is an incremental cost because it *could be avoided* if Landry outsources the hinge sets. The remaining fixed overhead ($1.20) is not relevant to the outsourcing decision. This amount is a common cost incurred by general production activity that is unassociated with the cost object (hinge sets). Therefore, the $1.20 of fixed overhead cost is not relevant because it would continue under either alternative. The total relevant cost for the insource alternative is $6.70 or the cost that would be avoided if the hinge sets are purchased externally as shown below.

Relevant Unit Costs in Outsource Decision

	A	B	C
1		Insource	Outsource
2	**Per hinge set**		
3	Direct production costs		
4	Direct material	$2.40	
5	Direct labor	3.00	
6	Variable overhead	0.80	
7	Fixed overhead	0.50	
8	Purchase cost		$7.00
9	Cost per set	$6.70	$7.00

This $6.70 relevant cost for the insource alternative amount should be compared to the $7.00 price quoted by the supplier under the outsource alternative. The $6.70 and $7.00 are the incremental costs of making and buying, respectively. All else being equal, management should choose to make the hinge sets rather than purchase them because the company will save $0.30 on each hinge set. Relevant costs, regardless of whether they are variable or fixed, are avoidable because one decision alternative was chosen over another. In an outsourcing decision, variable production costs are relevant. Fixed production costs are relevant only if they can be avoided by discontinuing production.

Outsource Decision with Opportunity Cost

The opportunity cost of the facilities being used by production is also relevant in this decision. Choosing to outsource, rather than make, a product component allows the company to use its facilities for an alternative purpose. If a more profitable alternative is available, management should consider diverting the capacity to this use. Assume that Landry Mechanical can lease out the physical space now used to produce hinges for $360,000 per year.

◆ **If the company produces 500,000 hinge sets annually, should Landry continue to make the hinges or purchase them from the outside supplier, given the leasing option?**

Landry has an opportunity cost of $0.72 per set ($360,000 ÷ 500,000 hinge sets) for using, rather than leasing, the production space. The lease opportunity makes the outsource alternative more attractive to Landry because it would forgo this amount if the hinges are produced internally. Thus, the lease opportunity cost is essentially an "additional" production cost. Sacrificing potential revenue is as much a relevant cost as is the incurrence of expenses. The following comparison on a per-set cost basis indicates that there is a $0.42 advantage to outsourcing over insourcing for each hinge set.

Relevant Unit Costs in Outsource Decision with Opportunity Cost

	A	B	C
1		Insource	Outsource
2	**Per hinge set**		
3	Direct production costs	$6.70	
4	Opportunity cost (lease revenue)	0.72	
5	Purchase cost		$7.00
6	Cost per set	$7.42	$7.00

The net advantage of outsourcing in total is calculated as $7.42 − $7.00 = $0.42 × $500,000 = $210,000 or as follows.

Relevant Total Costs in Outsource Decision with Opportunity Cost

	A	B	C	D
1		Insource	Outsource	Difference in Favor of Outsourcing
2	**In total**			
3	Revenue from leasing capacity	$ 0	$ 360,000	$360,000
4	Cost for 500,000 hinge sets	(3,350,000)	(3,500,000)	(150,000)
5	Net cost	$(3,350,000)	$(3,140,000)	$210,000

Outsource Decision with Multiple Opportunity Costs

Another opportunity cost that can be associated with insourcing is manufacturing capacity used by a component's production. Assume that hinge production at Landry Mechanical uses a resource that has been determined to be a bottleneck in the manufacturing plant. This means that this resource would be more widely available for use in the production of Landry's other products if hinge sets were no longer produced internally. Management calculates that plant *throughput can be increased by one percent per year* on all other products if the company buys rather than makes the hinges. **Throughput** reflects the movement of inputs through a process to become outputs. Assume this increase in throughput would provide an estimated additional annual contribution margin of $180,000 with no incremental fixed costs.

◆ **If the company produces 500,000 hinge sets annually, should Landry continue to make the hinges or purchase them from the outside supplier, given the leasing option and potential for increased throughput?**

Dividing the amount of additional annual contribution margin of $180,000 by the 500,000 hinge sets currently being produced results in a $0.36 per-unit opportunity cost related to manufacturing. When added to the previously calculated relevant cost of $7.42, the relevant cost of manufacturing hinges becomes $7.78 as shown below.

	A	B	C
	Relevant Unit Costs in Outsource Decision with Multiple Opportunity Costs		
1		Insource	Outsource
2	**Per hinge set**		
3	Direct production costs	$6.70	
4	Opportunity cost (lease revenue)	0.72	
5	Opportunity cost (increased throughput)	0.36	
6	Purchase cost		$7.00
7	Cost per set	$7.78	$7.00

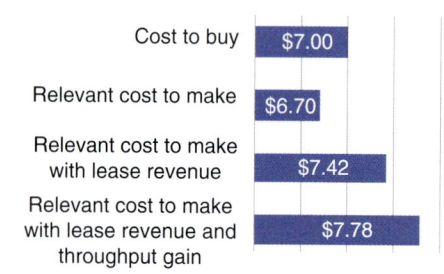

Cost to buy: $7.00
Relevant cost to make: $6.70
Relevant cost to make with lease revenue: $7.42
Relevant cost to make with lease revenue and throughput gain: $7.78

In summary, without considering opportunity costs, the decision to continue to make the hinge sets is supported by a lower cost per hinge set. However, given opportunity costs, the cost to outsource becomes the lower cost option. Thus, based on the *quantitative analysis* completed above which considered opportunity costs, Landry would conclude that it is more economical to purchase hinge sets for $7.00 than to manufacture them. This type of analysis—determining which alternative is preferred based on the *quantitative factors*—is the typical starting point of the decision process. Managers then use judgment to assess the decision's *qualitative aspects*.

Qualitative Decision Factors

Suppose Landry Mechanical's purchasing agent accessed a business blog that indicated the hinge supplier being considered is in poor financial condition and might file for bankruptcy. In this instance, management would decide to continue hinge production rather than outsource to this supplier. Although quantitative analysis supports purchase of the units, qualitative considerations suggest outsourcing would not be a wise action because the supplying source's stability as a going concern is questionable.

Other qualitative factors that might be considered include the following.

- Is the outside supplier interested in developing a long-term relationship or merely attempting to use some temporarily idle capacity? If so, what will happen at the end of the contract period?
- What impact would a decision to outsource have on the morale of a company's employees?
- Will the company be forced to rehire laid-off employees after the contract expires?
- Will the outside supplier meet delivery schedules?
- Will the supplier continually improve its manufacturing operations in order to remain competitive?
- Does the supplied part meet quality standards?
- Does the supplier meet acceptable environmental standards?

Short-Run Versus Long-Run Decision Making

In outsourcing decisions, a short-run decision can have many potentially long-run effects. Let's assume that after Landry stops hinge production and rents out its facilities, its supplier claims bankruptcy and ceases operations. Landry could face high start-up costs and delays if it tries to reestablish its hinge production process. At one point **Stonyfield Farm**, a New Hampshire-based yogurt company, faced such a situation: the firm subcontracted its yogurt production and one day found its supplier bankrupt, making Stonyfield unable to fill customer orders. It took Stonyfield two years to acquire the necessary production capacity and regain market strength.

This viewpoint suggests that the term *fixed cost* may actually be a misnomer. Although certain costs may not vary with volume in the short run, they will vary in the long run. *Thus, fixed costs are relevant for long-run decision making.* To illustrate this reasoning, assume that a company manufactures (rather than outsources) a particular part and expects demand for that part to increase in the future.

Chapter 5 Relevant Information for Decision Making

If the company expands capacity in the future, additional "fixed" capacity costs will be incurred. In turn, product costs would likely increase as a result of additional overhead allocated to production. To suggest that products made before capacity is increased would cost less than those made afterward is a short-run view. The long-run viewpoint should consider both the current and long-run variable costs over the product life cycle: capacity costs were "fixed" only until the relevant range of capacity changed. However, many firms actively engage in cooperative efforts with their suppliers to control costs and reduce prices. Strong supplier relationships are required for companies using the just-in-time (JIT) technologies discussed in Chapter 18.

Outsourcing in Service Organizations Outsourcing decisions are not confined solely to manufacturing entities. Many service organizations also make such decisions. For example, accounting and law firms must decide whether to prepare and present in-house continuing education programs or to outsource them. Consider also that some of the larger accounting firms have established a presence in India and other countries, where they prepare routine client tax reports or perform audit testing. In fact, U.S. based audit teams can submit overnight requests for testing to be done by their India counterparts which take place during India's work hours due to time zone differences. Many schools use independent contractors to bus their students. Doctors investigate the differences in cost, quality of results, and convenience to patients from having blood samples drawn and tested in the office or at an independent lab. Outsourcing can include product and process design activities, accounting and legal services, utilities, engineering services, and employee health services.

REVIEW 5-2

Outsourcing Decisions — LO5-2

Lopez Company manufactures various types of health food products. Management is evaluating an offer from Packaging Inc. to provide all packaging for a line of products at a cost of $2.80 each. Lopez's management has estimated the variable production costs of the packaging to be $2.10 per unit and that the company could avoid $31,000 per year in fixed costs if it purchased rather than produced the packaging. Unavoidable fixed costs total $40,000. The relevant range of production is 25,000 to 55,000 units.

a. If 28,000 units require packaging per year, should Lopez Company make them or buy them from the supplier?

b. If 50,000 units require packaging per year, should Lopez Company make them or buy them from the supplier?

c. **Critical Thinking:**
   1. What is causing the quantitative analysis in parts *a* and *b* to differ?
   2. How could qualitative factors affect the outsourcing decisions reached in parts *a* and *b*?

More practice: MC5-11, E5-23, E5-25
Solution on p. 5-48.

Scarce Resource Decisions

Managers frequently confront the short-run problem of making the best use of **scarce resources** that are essential to production activity or service provision but have limited availability. Scarce resources include the following.

- Machine time
- Skilled labor time
- Raw materials
- Production capacity
- Other inputs

LO5-3 How can management achieve the highest return from use of a scarce resource?

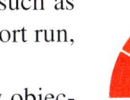

In the long run, company management could obtain a higher quantity of a scarce resource, such as by purchasing additional machines to increase the available machine time. However, in the short run, management must make the most efficient use of currently available scarce resources.

Determining the best use of a scarce resource requires management to identify company objectives. To maximize company profits, a scarce resource is best used to produce and sell the product generating the highest contribution margin (CM) per unit of the scarce resource. The quantity of the product produced however, should be limited to the customer demand for that product. Recall that contribution margin is equal to sales revenue minus variable costs.

Contribution margin per unit ÷ Scarce resource per unit = Contribution margin per scarce resource

This strategy assumes that the company must ration only one scarce resource. Notice that contribution margin, not gross margin (or gross profit) is used. You may recall that gross margin is unit selling price minus total production cost per unit. Total production cost includes allocated fixed manufacturing overhead. Because fixed costs do not change with production levels within the relevant range, they are typically not relevant in a short-run scarce resource decision.

DEMO 5-3 LO5-3 Determining the Best Use of Scarce Resources

The following schedule gives the unit contribution for two products that Landry Mechanical manufactures: drills and table saws. Fixed annual overhead related to these two product lines totals $9,220,000 and is allocated to products for purposes of inventory valuation. Because fixed overhead per unit is not relevant in the short run, unit CM rather than unit gross margin is the appropriate profitability measure of the two products. No variable selling or administrative costs are related to either product.

Landry Unit Contribution Margin Information

	A	B	C
1		Drill	Table Saw
2	Selling price per unit (a)	$80.00	$120.00
3	Variable production cost per unit:		
4	Direct material	45.00	60.00
5	Direct labor	12.50	15.00
6	Variable overhead	9.50	18.00
7	Total variable cost (b)	67.00	93.00
8	Unit contribution margin (c = a − b)	$13.00	$27.00

◆ **If Landry desires to achieve the highest level of profit possible and given no constraining resources, should Landry produce drills or table saws?**

The information indicates that table saws are more profitable than drills because the unit contribution margin of $27 is greater than that of drills of $13 per unit.

Now let's assume that a certain electrical switch is common to the production of both products. Each drill requires one electronic switch, and each table saw requires three electronic switches. Currently, because of a fire in a key supplier's facility, Landry has access to only 62,000 switches per month to make drills, table saws, or some combination of both. Because Landry's demand for switches exceeds the 62,000 per month that are available, the purchased switch is a scarce resource for the company.

◆ **If Landry desires to achieve the highest level of profit possible, should Landry produce drills or table saws, given the constrained resource?**

Dividing unit contribution margin by the required scarce resource quantity gives the CM per unit of scarce resource. The last line in the schedule below shows the $13 CM per switch for the drill compared to $9 for the table saw. Thus, it is more profitable for Landry Mechanical to produce drills than table saws.

Contribution Margin per Scarce Resource

	A	B	C
1		Drill	Table Saw
2	Unit contribution margin	$13.00	$27.00
3	Number of switches required per set	÷ 1	÷ 3
4	Contribution margin per switch	$13.00	$ 9.00

Because the table saw requires three times as many switches as a drill, drill production generates a higher CM per switch. If Landry Mechanical makes only these two types of products and wants to achieve the highest possible profit, it would dedicate all available switches to the production of drills. If Landry sells all units produced, this strategy would provide a total CM of $806,000 per month.

62,000 Switches × $13 Contribution margin per switch = $806,000 Total contribution margin

Multiple Scarce Resources If a company has only one scarce resource, managers will schedule production or other activity in a way that maximizes the scarce resource's use—which would be to produce and sell a single product. Most situations, however, involve several factors that limit a firm's ability to attain business objectives. Solving problems having several limiting factors requires the use of mathematical programming, which refers to a variety of techniques used to allocate limited resources among activities to achieve a specific goal or purpose. **Linear programming (LP)** is one method used to find the optimal allocation of scarce resources in a situation involving one objective and multiple limiting factors.[2]

Qualitative Decision Factors

In addition to considering the monetary effects related to scarce resource decisions, managers must remember that all factors cannot be readily quantified and that a situation's qualitative aspects must be evaluated in addition to the quantitative ones.

- *Are the products competitively related?* Before choosing to produce only drills, Landry Mechanical's managers should assess the potential damage to the firm's reputation and customer markets if the company were to limit its product line to a single item. Such a choice severely restricts a company's customer base and is especially important if the currently manufactured products are competitively related. For example, if Landry Mechanical stopped manufacturing table saws, customers wanting a drill and a table saw might decide to make their purchase from a company that could supply both products.

- *Are we focused on the most viable product?* Concentrating on a single product can also create market saturation or company stagnation. Some products, such as refrigerators and Rolex watches, are purchased infrequently. Other products, such as exercise equipment, may be purchased only in single units. Making products that are purchased infrequently or only in single units limits the company's opportunity for repeat business. If a company concentrates on the wrong single product, that exclusionary choice can be the beginning of the company's end.

- *Are the products considered part of a set?* In some cases, the revenues and expenses of a group of products must be considered as a set in allocating scarce resources. Multiple products could be complementary or part of a package in which one product cannot be used effectively without another product or is the key to revenue generation in future periods. To illustrate these possibilities, consider the following products: **Gillette**'s Atra razor and razor blades, **Hewlett Packard**'s ink jet printers and printer cartridges, and **Mattel**'s Barbie "family" of products. Would it be reasonable for Gillette to make only razors, HP to make only printers, or Mattel to make only Barbie dolls? In the case of Gillette, the company is known for giving away its razors—simply because of the future benefit of razor blade purchases. Mattel's management would probably choose to manufacture and sell Barbie dolls at zero contribution margin because of the profits that Barbie accessories generate.

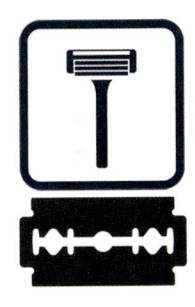

Thus, company management could decide that production and sale of some number of less profitable products is necessary to maintain either customer satisfaction or sales of other products. Discussed in the next section is the revenue side of production mix called sales mix.

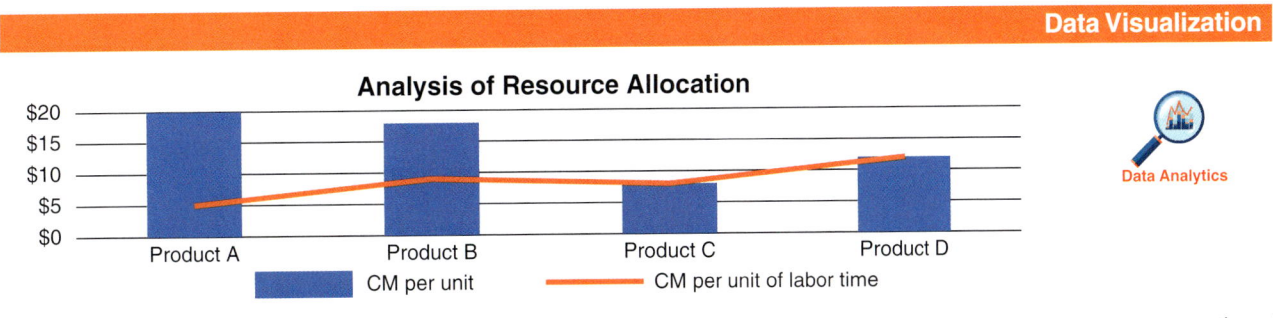

Data Visualization

Analysis of Resource Allocation

(Bar and line chart showing Product A, Product B, Product C, Product D with CM per unit as bars and CM per unit of labor time as line)

continued

---
[2] Finding the best allocation of resources when multiple goals exist is called goal programming. This topic is beyond the scope of this text.

continued from previous page

Rex Inc. manufactures four products: Product A, B, C, and D.
Based on the data visualization above, answer the following questions.

a. Which product has the highest and which product has the lowest contribution margin per unit?
b. Which product has the highest and which product has the lowest contribution margin per unit of labor time?
c. If the company has excess capacity and labor is not considered a scarce resource, which product would you recommend be produced?
d. If the company has excess capacity and labor is considered a scarce resource, which product would you recommend be produced?
e. As a cost accountant interested in cost control, what questions might you ask based on this data visualization?

Solution on p. 5-50.

REVIEW 5-3   **LO5-3**   **Scarce Resource Decision**

Madison Cycles manually manufactures three unique bicycle models: racing, touring, and basic. All of the skilled craftspeople employed at Madison Cycles can make each of the three models. Because it takes about a year to train each craftsperson, labor is a fixed production constraint over the short term. For the year, the company expects to have available 40,000 labor hours. The average hourly labor rate is $35. Fixed costs are $360,000 for factory costs and $90,000 for selling and administrative costs. Data regarding the current product line follow.

	Racing	Touring	Basic
Selling price	$3,240	$2,500	$805
Variable costs			
Direct material	792	576	216
Direct labor	1,365	945	280
Variable factory overhead	648	432	145
Variable selling	72	54	36

a. If a maximum of 1,200 items of any product is determined can be sold, how many of each product should the company make?
b. What before-tax profit will the company earn given your answer to part *a*?
c. **Critical Thinking:** If there is no limit to the number of items of any product that can be sold, does your answer to part *a* change? What other considerations might factor into the product mix decision?

More practice: E5-26, E5-27
Solution on p. 5-49.

Sales Mix Decisions

LO5-4
What variables do managers use to manipulate sales mix?

Managers continuously strive to achieve a variety of company objectives such as maximization of profit, maintenance of or increase in market share, and generation of customer goodwill and loyalty. Managers must be effective in selling products or performing services to accomplish these objectives. Regardless of whether the company is a retailer, manufacturer, or service organization, **sales mix** refers to the relative product quantities composing a company's total sales. Some important factors affecting a company's sales mix are

- product selling prices,
- sales force compensation, and
- advertising expenditures.

Because a change in one or all of these factors could cause sales mix to shift, managing these factors is fundamental to managing profit.

A company must continually monitor the sales prices of its products, with respect to both each other and competitors. Such monitoring can provide information that causes management to change one or more sales prices. Factors that might influence price changes include

Chapter 5 Relevant Information for Decision Making

- fluctuations in demand,
- changes in production/distribution cost,
- changes in economic conditions, and
- changes in competition.

Any shift in the selling price of one product in a multiproduct firm normally causes a change in sales mix of that firm because of the economic law of demand elasticity with respect to price. The law of demand elasticity indicates how closely price and demand are related. Product demand is highly elastic if a small price reduction generates a large demand increase. If demand is less elastic, large price reductions are needed to bring about moderate sales volume increases. In contrast, if demand is highly elastic, a small price increase results in a large drop in demand.

Sales Price Changes and Relative Profitability of Products — LO5-4 — DEMO 5-4A

Assume that Landry Mechanical has a line of meat slicers in addition to drills and table saws. The following schedule provides information on that line. This information is used to illustrate the effects of the three factors—selling prices, sales compensation, and advertising—on sales mix. The product line includes standard, home deluxe, and professional slicers. Each type of slicer has different features and is targeted at a different market segment. All slicers compete on the basis of high quality and are priced at the high end of their market niches. The current annual sales volume is 52,000 standard slicers, 39,000 home deluxe slicers, and 15,000 professional slicers. From the information below, the Professional slicers sell at the highest unit price while the Home Deluxe slicers show the highest contribution margin per unit.

Landry Unit Sales, Unit Variable Cost, and Total Fixed Cost Information

	A	B	C	D	E
1	Product Information		Standard	Home Deluxe	Professional
2	Unit selling price (SP)		$80	$450	$900
3	Variable costs				
4	Direct material		$33	$185	$425
5	Direct labor		12	75	245
6	Variable overhead		15	45	90
7	Total variable production cost		$60	$305	$760
8	Product contribution margin		$20	$145	$140
9	Variable selling expense (10% of SP)		(8)	(45)	(90)
10	Contribution margin per unit		$12	$100	$50
11	Total fixed costs:				
12	Production	$4,200,000			
13	Selling & administrative	1,100,000			
14	Total	$5,300,000			

For Landry Mechanical, profit maximization is the primary corporate objective. This strategy does not necessarily translate into maximizing unit sales of the product with the highest selling price and minimizing unit sales of the product with the lowest selling price. *The highest selling price per unit does not necessarily yield the highest contribution margin per unit or per dollar of sales.* In Landry Mechanical's case, the slicer with the highest sales price (the professional model) yields the second-highest unit CM of the three products but the lowest CM as a percent of sales. The company generates more profit by selling a dollar's worth of the home deluxe slicer than a dollar's worth of either the standard or the professional model, as shown in the following calculations (amounts rounded).

Home deluxe slicer	$100 Unit CM ÷ $450 Sales per unit = $0.22 CM per sales dollar
Standard slicer	$12 Unit CM ÷ $80 Sales per unit = $0.15 CM per sales dollar
Professional slicer	$50 Unit CM ÷ $900 Sales per unit = $0.06 CM per sales dollar

◆ **What is Landry's total annual income (loss) based on the current cost structure and sales mix?**

Total company CM is the sum of the contribution margins provided by the sale of all products. The following schedule shows product sales volumes and the respective total CMs from the three slicer types.

© Cambridge Business Publishers

Loss at Current Volume and Sales Mix

	A	B	C	D
1		Unit Contribution Margin	Current Sales Volume in Units	Income Statement Information
2	Standard slicers	$ 12	52,000	$ 624,000
3	Home deluxe slicers	100	39,000	3,900,000
4	Professional slicers	50	15,000	750,000
5	Total contribution margin of product sales mix			$ 5,274,000
6	Fixed expenses			(5,300,000)
7	Product line income (loss) at current volume and sales mix			$ (26,000)

If profit maximization is the goal, managers should consider each product's sales volume and unit contribution margin. A product's sales volume typically is related to its selling price. Generally, when a product's or service's price increases and demand is elastic with respect to price, demand for that product decreases.[3] Thus, if Landry Mechanical's management decides to raise the standard slicer price to $100, the company should experience some decline in demand for that product. Landry's marketing researchers have indicated that a $20 price increase would cause product demand to drop from 52,000 to 30,000 slicers per period.

◆ **What is Landry's total annual income (loss) based on the sales price change for the standard slicer, considering the expected impact on sales mix?**

The adjusted unit contribution margin for standard slicers is calculated as follows (all amounts are per unit).

$100 SP − $60 Variable production cost − $10 Variable selling expense (10% × $100) = $30

Based on the unit contribution margin of $30 for standard slicers at a new volume of 30,000 units, and assuming no adjustments to the amounts for the other products, the projected total product line income is $250,000 as shown the schedule below. This represents a $276,000 increase in profit over the current loss of $26,000.

Projected Profit with a Change in Sales Price and Volume

	A	B	C	D
1		Unit Contribution Margin	New Sales Volume in Units	Income Statement Information
2	Standard slicers	$ 30	30,000	$ 900,000
3	Home deluxe slicers	100	39,000	3,900,000
4	Professional slicers	50	15,000	750,000
5	Total contribution margin of product sales mix			$ 5,550,000
6	Fixed expenses			(5,300,000)
7	Product line income (loss) at new volume and sales mix			$ 250,000

Because CM per unit of the standard slicer increased, the total dollar contribution margin generated by sales of that product increased despite the decrease in unit sales. This example assumed that customers did not switch their purchases from the standard slicer to other Landry Mechanical products when the price of the standard slicer went up. When some product prices in a product line remain stable and others increase, customers might *substitute one product for another*. This example ignored switching between company products, but some customers might purchase a more expensive slicer after the standard slicer price increased. For example, customers might believe that the difference in functionality between the standard and home deluxe slicers is worth the price difference and make such a purchasing switch.

Quantitative Factors In making decisions to raise or lower prices, relevant quantitative factors include
- new contribution margin per unit of product,
- short-term and long-term changes in product demand and production volume because of the price change, and
- best use of the company's scarce resources.

---

[3] Such a decline in demand would generally not occur when the product in question has no close substitutes or is not a major expenditure in consumers' budgets.

© Cambridge Business Publishers

Chapter 5 Relevant Information for Decision Making

Qualitative Factors Some relevant qualitative factors involved in pricing decisions are

- impact of changes on customer goodwill toward the company,
- customer loyalty toward company products, and
- competitors' responses to the firm's new pricing structure.

Sales Compensation Changes — LO5-4 — DEMO 5-4B

Many companies compensate salespeople by paying a fixed rate of commission on gross sales dollars. This approach motivates salespeople to sell the highest-priced product rather than the product providing the highest contribution margin to the company. If the company has a profit maximization objective, such a compensation policy will be ineffective in achieving that objective.

Assume that Landry Mechanical has set a price structure for its slicers as follows: standard, $100; home deluxe, $450; and professional, $900. The company's current policy is to pay sales commissions equal to 10 percent of selling price. This commission structure encourages sales of professional slicers rather than home deluxe or standard slicers. Landry is considering a new compensation structure that should allow sales personnel to achieve the same or higher income as before the change given a similar level of effort. The new compensation structure provides base salaries for all salespeople totaling $2,000,000 per period. In addition, Landry would pay salespeople a commission equal to 15 percent of product contribution margin. The per-unit product CMs of the slicers are $40, $145, and $140, respectively, for standard, home deluxe, and professional slicers. (See Demo 5-4A, with the exception of the unit product CM for standard slicers which increased by $20 based upon the proposed increase in selling price.) The new compensation policy should motivate sales personnel to sell more of the slicers that produce the highest commission, which would correspondingly be the company's most profitable products.[4] As a result, Landry estimates sales volume under the new commission policy to be 40,000, 49,000, and 10,000 of standard, deluxe and professional slicers, respectively.

◆ How does Landry's total contribution margin for product sales change under the new commission policy?

The following schedule compares Landry Mechanical's total contribution margin using the current sales mix and commission structure with that of the new compensation structure focused on total CM.

Projected Profit with a Change in Sales Commission Structure

	A	B	C	D	E	F	G	H	I	J
1		Product CM	−	Commission	=	Product CM after Commission	×	Volume	=	Total CM
2	Old Policy—Commissions Equal 10% of Selling Price									
3	Standard	$ 40		(0.10 × $100) = $10.00		$ 30.00		30,000		$ 900,000
4	Home deluxe	145		(0.10 × $450) = $45.00		100.00		39,000		3,900,000
5	Professional	140		(0.10 × $900) = $90.00		50.00		15,000		750,000
6	Total contribution margin for product sales							84,000		**$5,550,000**
7	New Policy—Commissions Equal 15% of Product Contribution Margin per Unit and Incremental Base Salaries of $2,000,000									
8	Standard	$ 40		(0.15 × $ 40) = $ 6.00		$ 34.00		40,000		$1,360,000
9	Home deluxe	145		(0.15 × $145) = $21.75		123.25		49,000		6,039,250
10	Professional	140		(0.15 × $140) = $21.00		119.00		10,000		1,190,000
11	Total contribution margin for product sales							99,000		$8,589,250
12	Less sales force base salaries									(2,000,000)
13	Contribution margin adjusted for sales force base salaries									**$6,589,250**

The new structure increases profits by shifting sales from slicers with a lower CM ratio to those with a higher CM ratio. As a result, total contribution margin increases to $6,589,250. Salespeople also benefit from the new pay structure through higher total compensation, as shown in the following schedule.

---

[4] This statement relies on the assumption that the salespersons' efforts are more highly correlated with unit sales than dollar sales. If this assumption is accurate, the commission structure should encourage sales of products with higher CM ratios.

Current Sales Commissions Compared to New Sales Commissions

	A	B	C	D	E	F	G
1		Old Policy				New Policy	
2	Rate	Volume	Total		Rate	Volume	Total
3	$10.00	30,000	$ 300,000		$ 6.00	40,000	$ 240,000
4	$45.00	39,000	1,755,000		$21.75	49,000	1,065,750
5	$90.00	15,000	1,350,000		$21.00	10,000	210,000
6			$3,405,000				$1,515,750
7							2,000,000
8							$3,515,750
9	Net increase	$110,750					

Reflected in the sales mix change is the fact that standard slicers can be sold with substantially less salesperson effort per unit than that required for the other models. Fixed expenses would not be considered in setting compensation structures unless those expenses were incremental relative to the new policy or to changes in sales volumes. The new base salaries were an incremental cost of Landry Mechanical's proposed compensation plan.

DEMO 5-4C — LO5-4 — Advertising Budget Changes

Adjusting the advertising budgets of specific products or increasing the company's total advertising budget could lead to shifts in the sales mix. This section uses the data for Landry Mechanical to examine a proposed increase in the company's total advertising budget.

Landry Mechanical's advertising manager, Joe Malanga, has proposed increasing the advertising budget from $500,000 to $650,000 per year. He believes the increased advertising will result in the following additional slicer sales during the coming year: standard, 2,500; home deluxe, 1,500; and professional, 750. Assume per-unit CMs of the slicers are $30, $100, and $150, respectively, for standard, home deluxe, and professional slicers.

◆ **Will spending the additional $150,000 for advertising to generate the additional 4,750 units of sales produce higher profits than the slicer line is currently generating?**

The original fixed costs, as well as the CM generated by the *current* sales levels, are irrelevant to the decision. The relevant items are the increased sales revenue, increased variable costs, and increased fixed cost—the incremental effects of the advertising change. The difference between incremental revenues and incremental variable costs is the incremental contribution margin from which the incremental fixed cost is subtracted to obtain the incremental benefit (or loss) of the decision.[5]

See the following schedule for calculations of the expected increase in contribution margin if the company makes the increased advertising expenditure. Importantly, unlike the prior schedules which were based on a full analysis of sales and costs, this schedule only includes the amounts that differ under this new scenario.

Profit with a Change in Advertising Cost

	A	B	C	D	E
1		Standard	Home Deluxe	Professional	Total
2	Increase in volume	2,500	1,500	750	4,750
3	Contribution margin per unit	× $30	× $100	× $50	
4	Incremental contribution margin	$75,000	$150,000	$37,500	$ 262,500
5	Incremental fixed cost of advertising				(150,000)
6	Incremental benefit from increased advertising expenditure				$ 112,500

---

[5] This same type of incremental analysis is shown in Chapter 4 in relation to cost-volume-profit computations.

Because the $262,500 additional CM more than covers the $150,000 incremental cost for advertising, company management should increase advertising by $150,000. Increased advertising can cause changes in the sales mix or in the number of units sold by targeting advertising efforts at specific products. Sales can also be influenced by opportunities that allow companies to obtain business at a sales price that differs from the normal price.

REVIEW 5-4 — **LO5-4**

Sales Mix

Zen Salon Inc. provides two types of salon services: manicures and facials. All company personnel can perform each service equally well. To expand sales and market share, Zen Salon's manager relies heavily on local internet marketing advertising, but the annual advertising budget is expected to be very limited. Information on projected operations for the year follows.

	Manicures	Facials
Revenue per billable hour	$60	$84
Variable cost of labor	24	50
Material cost per billable hour	7	8
Allocated fixed cost per year	125,000	90,000
Projected billable hours for the year	15,000	8,000

a. What is Zen Salon's projected before-tax profit (or loss) for the year?

b. If $1 spent on advertising could increase manicure revenue by $20 or facial revenue by $20, on which service should the advertising dollar be spent?

c. If $1 spent on advertising could increase either manicure billable time or facial billable time by one hour, on which service should the advertising dollar be spent?

d. **Critical thinking:** In order to maximize profits, can management assume that advertising dollars should always be spent on the service that provides a higher contribution margin per service?

More practice: MC5-13, E5-28, E5-29
Solution on p. 5-49.

Special Order Decisions

In a **special order decision**, management computes sales prices for production or service jobs that are not part of the company's normal operations. Special order situations include jobs

- that require a bid,
- are accepted during slack periods, or
- are made to a particular buyer's specifications.

Typically, the sales price quoted on a special order job should be high enough to cover the job's variable and incremental fixed costs and generate a profit. In addition, company management should consider any effects that the additional job will have on normal company activities and whether this job will create additional, unforeseen costs. For example, if a company must give up a portion of regular sales, the associated contribution margin must be *subtracted* from the contribution margin gained from the special order. Specific instances of special orders are described as follows.

Introductory Low Bid Sometimes companies depart from their price-setting routine and deliberately offer a low selling price. This low price may cover only costs and produce no profit or even be below cost. The rationale of deliberately low introductory bids is to obtain the job and have the opportunity to introduce company products or services to a particular market segment. Special pricing of this nature could provide work for a period of time, but cannot be continued over the long run. To remain in business, a company must set selling prices to cover total costs and provide a reasonable profit margin.[6]

LO5-5 How are special prices set, and when are they used?

---

[6] An exception to this general rule can occur when a company produces related or complementary products. For instance, an electronics company can sell a video game at or below cost and allow the ancillary software program sales to be the primary source of profit.

Private-Label Products Special pricing also arises for private-label orders in which the buyer's (rather than the producer's) name is attached to the product. Companies may accept these jobs during slack periods to more effectively use available capacity. Fixed costs are typically not allocated to special order, private-label products. Some variable costs (such as sales commissions) can be reduced or eliminated by the very nature of the private-label process. Prices on this type of special order are typically set high enough to generate a positive contribution margin.

Unusual, Tailor-Made, or One-Time Jobs Special prices can also be justified when orders are of an unusual nature (because of the quantity, method of delivery, or packaging) or when products are tailor-made to customer instructions. Special pricing is also used when goods are produced for a one-time job, such as an overseas order that will not affect domestic sales.

DEMO 5-5   LO5-5   Determining Whether to Accept a Special Order

Assume that Landry Mechanical has the opportunity to bid on a special order for 60,000 private-label slicers for a major kitchen products retailer. Unit cost information related to the slicers is included in the schedule that follows.

	A	B
1	**Landry Unit Cost Information**	**Normal Costs**
2	Per-unit cost for slicers:	
3	Direct material and components	$ 90
4	Direct labor	25
5	Variable overhead	35
6	Variable selling expense (commission)	20
7	Total variable cost	$170
8	Fixed factory overhead (allocated)	30
9	Fixed selling & administrative expense	20
10	Total cost per slicer	$220

Company management is interested in the special order if the additional business will provide a satisfactory contribution to profit. Landry has unused production capacity available and can obtain the necessary components and raw material from suppliers. Landry will pay no sales commission on the sale and fixed costs are not expected to increase because of this sale. Also, Landry has no immediate opportunity for its currently unused capacity, so there is no opportunity cost associated with the unused capacity.

◆ **What is the minimum price that Landry could charge for the private-label slicers to be no worse off in profitability than its current position?**

Direct material and components, direct labor, and variable overhead costs are relevant to setting the bid price because these costs will be incurred for each slicer produced. Although all variable costs are normally relevant to a special pricing decision, variable selling expense is irrelevant in this instance because no sales commission will be paid on this sale. Because fixed expenses are not expected to increase due to this sale, these expenses are not relevant in the pricing decision.

Using the available cost information, the relevant cost for determining the bid price for each slicer is $150.

> **$90 Direct material and components + $25 Direct labor + $35 Variable overhead = $150**

This cost is the minimum price at which the company should sell one slicer. Any price higher than $150 will provide some incremental contribution margin and profit.

Now assume that the company does not have the capacity to complete the full order without giving up regular sales. In order to accept the special order, the company would have to forgo 10,000 units of sales to regular customers in order to supply the full special order of 60,000 units. Assume that slicers are sold at an average price of $200 to regular customers.

Chapter 5 Relevant Information for Decision Making

◆ **What would be the dollar effect on before-tax profit if this order was accepted for 60,000 units at a selling price of $155 per unit, given the capacity constraints?**

While the company would gain contribution margin from the special order, it would lose contribution margin on its regular sales as shown in the following calculation.

	Special Order with Capacity Constraints	
	A	B
1	Incremental revenue ($155 × 60,000 units)	$9,300,000
2	Incremental costs ($150 × 60,000 units)	(9,000,000)
3	Incremental contribution margin	$300,000
4	Lost contribution margin (($200 − $150) × 10,000 units)	(500,000)
5	Incremental loss from accepting the special order	$ (200,000)

Accepting the special order results in an incremental loss to the company because the loss on regular sales is larger than the gain on the special order.

Qualitative Factors When setting a special order price, management must consider qualitative as well as quantitative issues. For instance, management should answer questions such as the following:

- Will setting a low bid price establish a precedent for future prices?
- Will the contribution margin on a bid, set low enough to acquire the job, be sufficient to justify the additional burdens placed on management and employees by this activity?
- Will the additional production activity require the use of bottleneck resources and reduce company throughput?
- How will special order sales affect the company's normal sales?
- If production of the special order is scheduled during a period of low business activity (off-season or recession), is management willing to take the business at a lower contribution or profit margin simply to keep a trained workforce employed?

REVIEW 5-5 — Special Order — LO5-5

Wayflaire Inc. produces home products. The cost to manufacture a case (36 sets) of its most popular set of casual dinnerware is as follows.

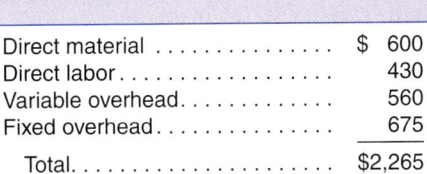

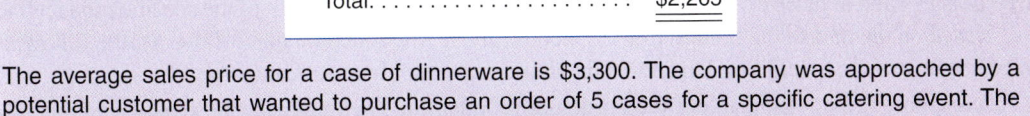

Direct material	$ 600
Direct labor	430
Variable overhead	560
Fixed overhead	675
Total	$2,265

The average sales price for a case of dinnerware is $3,300. The company was approached by a potential customer that wanted to purchase an order of 5 cases for a specific catering event. The potential customer suggested a price of $2,100 per case for this special order.

a. What costs are relevant to the decision to accept this special order?

b. What would be the dollar effect on before-tax profit if this order was accepted, assuming that the company had the capacity to manufacture the additional 5 cases?

c. What would be the dollar effect on before-tax profit if this order was accepted, assuming that the company did not have the capacity to manufacture the additional 5 cases? Assume that the company had to forego 5 cases of normal sales to supply the special order.

d. **Critical thinking:** Assuming that the company has the capacity to manufacture the additional 5 cases, is there the risk that the company's regular customers will demand a price cut? If the company is forced to drop prices by 5 percent to its regular customers, what is the net impact on profits assuming normal sales of 100 cases per month?

More practice: MC5-14, E5-31, E5-32
Solution on p. 5-50.

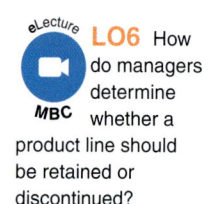

Product Line and Segment Decisions

LO6 How do managers determine whether a product line should be retained or discontinued?

Operating results of multiproduct environments are often disaggregated to show results by product lines. In reviewing these disaggregated statements, managers must distinguish relevant from irrelevant information regarding individual product lines. If all costs (variable and fixed) are allocated to product lines, a product line or segment could be perceived as operating at a loss when actually it is not. The commingling of relevant and irrelevant information on the statements could cause such perceptions.

DEMO 5-6 — LO5-6: Determining Whether to Keep or Drop a Segment

The following schedule provides basic earnings information for Landry Mechanical's Steel Door Division, which manufactures three product lines: Economy, Standard, and Deluxe. The data suggest that the Deluxe line is operating at a net loss of $165,000.

Product Line Income Statements (in $000s)

	A	B	C	D	E
1		Economy	Standard	Deluxe	Total
2	Sales	$ 8,000	$ 9,800	$ 3,000	$20,800
3	Total direct variable expenses	(5,400)	(5,700)	(2,200)	(13,300)
4	Total contribution margin	$ 2,600	$ 4,100	$ 800	$ 7,500
5	Total fixed expenses	(2,100)	(3,700)	(965)	(6,765)
6	Net income (loss)	$ 500	$ 400	$ (165)	$ 735
7	Details of fixed expenses				
8	(1) Avoidable fixed expenses	$ 1,200	$ 3,000	$ 450	$ 4,650
9	(2) Unavoidable fixed expenses	600	420	300	1,320
10	(3) Allocated common expenses	300	280	215	795
11	Total	$ 2,100	$ 3,700	$ 965	$ 6,765

◆ **In order to maximize company profits, should Landry drop the Deluxe product line?**

Managers reviewing the results might reason that the division would be $165,000 more profitable if the Deluxe line were dropped. Such a conclusion could be premature because relevant and irrelevant information are combined within the income statement. Specifically, all fixed expenses have been allocated to the individual product lines. Such allocations are traditionally based on one or more measures of "presumed" equity for each product line, such as the following:

- square footage occupied in the manufacturing plant,
- number of machine hours incurred for production, and
- number of direct labor employees.

In all cases, however, allocations could force fixed expenses into specific product line operating results even though some of those expenses were not actually incurred for the benefit of the specific product line.

Based on the data at the bottom of the schedule above, the schedule that follows on the following page segregates the Steel Door Division's fixed expenses into three subcategories:

- **Avoidable fixed:** Avoidable if the particular product line is eliminated (these expenses can also be referred to as *attributable expenses*).
- **Unavoidable fixed:** Directly associated with a particular product line but not avoidable.
- **Allocated common expense:** Incurred for the benefit of the company as a whole, but are allocated to individual product lines.

The latter two subcategories are irrelevant in deciding whether to eliminate a product line. If one product line is eliminated, an unavoidable expense merely shifts to another product line. Common expenses will be incurred regardless of which product lines are eliminated. An example of a common cost is the insurance premium on a manufacturing facility that houses all product lines.

Segment Margin Income Statements (in $000s)

	A	B	C	D	E
1		Economy	Standard	Deluxe	Total
2	Sales	$ 8,000	$ 9,800	$ 3,000	$ 20,800
3	Total direct variable expenses	(5,400)	(5,700)	(2,200)	(13,300)
4	Total contribution margin	$ 2,600	$ 4,100	$ 800	$ 7,500
5	(1) Avoidable fixed expenses	(1,200)	(3,000)	(450)	(4,650)
6	Segment margin	$ 1,400	$ 1,100	$ 350	$ 2,850
7	(2) Unavoidable fixed expenses	(600)	(420)	(300)	(1,320)
8	Product line result	$ 800	$ 680	$ 50	$ 1,530
9	(3) Allocated common expenses	(300)	(280)	(215)	(795)
10	Net income (loss)	$ 500	$ 400	$ (165)	$ 735

If the Steel Door Division eliminates the Deluxe line, total divisional profit will decline by the $350,000 segment margin of that line to $385,000. **Segment margin** represents the excess of revenues over direct variable expenses and avoidable fixed expenses. It is the amount remaining to cover unavoidable direct fixed expenses and common expenses and to provide profit.[7] The appropriate figure on which to base the continuation or elimination decision is segment margin because it measures the segment's contribution to the coverage of indirect and unavoidable expenses. The new net income of $385,000 that would result from having only two product lines (Economy and Standard) is in the following alternative computations.

Total Income After Dropping a Product Line (in $000s)

	A	B
1		Total
2	Current net income	$ 735
3	Decrease in income due to elimination of Deluxe (segment margin)	(350)
4	New net income	$ 385
5	Proof:	
6	Total contribution margin of Economy and Standard lines	$ 6,700
7	Less avoidable fixed expenses of the Economy and Standard lines	(4,200)
8	Segment margin of Economy and Standard lines	$ 2,500
9	Less all remaining unavoidable and allocated expenses ($1,320 + $795)	(2,115)
10	Remaining income with two product lines	$ 385

Based on this information, the Steel Door Division should not eliminate the Deluxe product line because it is generating a positive segment margin and covering its relevant expenses.

Classifying Costs as Avoidable or Unavoidable In classifying product line costs, managers should be aware that some costs can appear to be avoidable but are actually not. This determination must be made before costs can be appropriately classified in product line elimination decisions. Examples of the complexities that can arise in classifying costs follow.

- The salary of a supervisor working directly with a product line appears to be an avoidable fixed cost if the product line is eliminated. However, if such supervisors are transferred to other areas upon disposition of a product line, their salaries will continue and must be treated as unavoidable.
- Depreciation on factory equipment used to manufacture a specific product is an irrelevant cost in product line decisions. Even if the equipment will be kept in service and used to make other products, the depreciation expense is unavoidable and irrelevant to the decision.
- If the equipment can be sold, the selling price is relevant to the decision because the sale increases the benefit of discontinuing the product line.

---

[7] All common expenses are assumed to be fixed; this is not always the case. Some common costs could be variable, such as expenses of processing purchase orders or computer time-sharing expenses for payroll or other corporate functions.

Qualitative Factors Before deciding to discontinue a product line, management should carefully consider what resources would be required to make the product line profitable as well as the long-term ramifications of product line elimination. For example, product line elimination shrinks market assortment, which could cause some customers to seek other suppliers that maintain a broader market assortment. And, as in other relevant costing situations, decisions have qualitative as well as quantitative factors that must be analyzed. Individual customers also should be assessed (in the same manner as product lines) for profitability. When necessary, ways to improve the cost-benefit relationship should be determined.

Management's task is to effectively and efficiently allocate its finite stock of resources to accomplish its objectives. A cost accountant must always be diligent in providing information that is relevant to the decision at hand. Managers must have a reliable quantitative basis on which to analyze problems, compare viable solutions, and choose the best course of action. Because management is a social rather than a natural science, it has no fundamental "truths," and few related problems are susceptible to black-or-white solutions. Relevant costing is a process of making human approximations of the costs of alternative decision results.

REVIEW 5-6 — LO5-6 — Decision to Keep or Drop a Division

Celestial Inc. is organized into 3 distinct divisions. The company is currently contemplating the elimination of either Division 1 or Division 2 because they are showing a before-tax loss. An annual income statement follows.

(in $000s)	Division 1	Division 2	Division 3	Total
Sales	$5,300	$8,200	$30,240	$43,740
Cost of sales	3,920	7,000	18,144	29,064
Gross margin	$1,380	$1,200	$12,096	$14,676
Avoidable fixed costs*	1,484	600	5,836	7,920
Avoidable variable costs*	280	300	2,900	3,480
Allocated fixed costs	252	940	1,764	2,956
Operating profit	$ (636)	$ (640)	$ 1,596	$ 320

*Selling and administrative costs; there are no unavoidable fixed costs included in cost of sales.

a. How would the company's before-tax profit be affected if it dropped Division 1?
b. How would the company's before-tax profit be affected if it dropped Division 2?
d. **Critical thinking:** Does your analysis in parts *a* and *b* pertain to short-term and/or the long-term decision making?

More practice: MC5-15, E5-33, E5-34
Solution on p. 5-50.

Comprehensive Chapter Review

Key Terms

differential cost, p. 5-2
differential revenue, p. 5-2
incremental cost, p. 5-2
incremental profit (incremental loss), p. 5-3
incremental revenue, p. 5-2
linear programming (LP), p. 5-13

make-or-buy decision, p. 5-6
opportunity cost, p. 5-3
outsourcing, p. 5-6
outsourcing decision, p. 5-6
qualitative factors, p. 5-6
quantitative factors, p. 5-6
relevant, p. 5-2

sales mix, p. 5-14
scarce resources, p. 5-11
segment margin, p. 5-23
special order decision, p. 5-19
sunk costs, p. 5-3
throughput, p. 5-10

Chapter Summary

Decision Making (Page 5-2) — LO5-1
- Because of their association with the decision, importance to the decision maker, and bearing on the future, the following items are relevant in decision making:
  - costs that vary between decision choices (incremental or differential costs) and
  - benefits sacrificed by pursuing one decision choice rather than another (opportunity costs).
- Sunk costs are
  - incurred in the past to acquire assets or resources.
  - not relevant to decision making because they cannot be changed regardless of which decision choice is selected.
  - not recoverable regardless of current circumstances.

Outsourcing (Page 5-6) — LO5-2
- Relevant considerations in outsourcing (or offshoring) decisions include
  - quantitative factors such as
    - incremental/differential production costs,
    - opportunity costs,
    - external purchase costs, and
    - cash flow.
  - qualitative factors such as
    - capacity availability,
    - quality control,
    - technology availability,
    - organizational core competencies,
    - employee skill levels in-house and externally,
    - business risk, and
    - supplier availability and reliability.

Scarce Resources (Page 5-11) — LO5-3
- A scarce resource
  - is essential to production but is available only in limited quantity.
  - includes machine hours, skilled labor hours, raw materials or components, and production capacity.
  - requires management to base decisions on the contribution margin per unit of scarce resource available from alternative uses of the scarce resources; organizational profitability will be maximized by producing and selling the product or service that has the highest contribution margin per unit of scarce resource.

Sales Mix (Page 5-14) — LO5-4
- Sales mix is a key determinant of organizational profitability.
- Sales mix can be managed by manipulating
  - sales prices,
  - sales compensation methods, or
  - advertising budgets.

Special Prices (Page 5-19) — LO5-5
- Special prices for products or services
  - are generally set based on relevant variable production and selling costs and, if any, incremental fixed costs.
  - may or may not include a profit amount.
  - are used when companies bid on special order jobs, such as those that
    - require a bid,
    - are accepted during slack periods,
    - are made to a particular buyer's specifications, or
    - are of an unusual nature because of the order quantity, method of delivery, or packaging.

Product Line Decisions (Page 5-22) — LO5-6
- Segment margin
  - is the excess of revenues over direct variable expenses and avoidable fixed expenses for a specific product/service line.

- measures the segment's contribution to the coverage of indirect and unavoidable expenses and profit.
- is used to decide whether a product line should be retained or eliminated; a positive segment margin indicates retention and a negative segment margin indicates elimination.

Solution Strategies

General rule of decision making: Choose the alternative that yields the greatest incremental benefit.

> Incremental (additional) revenues
> − Incremental (additional) costs
> Incremental benefit (positive or negative)

LO5-1 Relevant Costs

- Direct material
- Direct labor
- Variable production overhead
- Variable selling expenses related to each alternative (can be greater or less than the "change nothing" alternative)
- Avoidable fixed production overhead
- Avoidable fixed selling/administrative costs (if any)
- Opportunity cost of choosing some other alternative (either increases the cost of one alternative or reduces the cost of another alternative)

Relevant Cost Analysis of Specific Decisions

LO5-3 Single Scarce Resource
1. Identify the scarce resource.
2. Determine the per-unit consumption of the scarce resource for each product.
3. Determine the contribution margin per unit of the scarce resource for each product.
4. Produce and sell the product with the highest contribution margin per unit of scarce resource to maximize profits, considering quantities that can reasonably be sold.

LO5-6 Product Line Analysis

> Sales
> − Direct variable expenses
> = Product line contribution margin
> − Avoidable fixed expenses
> = Segment (product line) margin*
> − Unavoidable fixed expenses
> = Product line operating results

*Make decision to retain or eliminate based on this line item.

Chapter Demonstration Problem

LO5-2 HD Sound Systems produces various equipment for home theatre and sound systems. One key component in all of the company's products is a module requiring two speakers configured in custom combinations. The firm currently incurs the following costs to make each speaker module:

Direct material	$24
Direct labor.	16
Variable overhead.	10
Fixed overhead.	20

Of the per-unit fixed overhead, the firm could avoid $8 if the modules were purchased from a company that has offered to sell an equivalent module for $56. HD produces 20,000 modules annually.

Chapter 5 Relevant Information for Decision Making

Required:
(Consider each requirement to be independent of the others.)
a. Should HD outsource the production of the module? Show calculations.
b. HD's vice president, Fred Flick, estimates that the company can rent out the facilities used to make the modules for $120,000 annually. What should the company do? Show calculations.
c. What are some qualitative factors that HD should consider in making the speaker module outsourcing decision?

Solution to Demonstration Problem

a. Relevant cost of making:

Direct material	$24
Direct labor	16
Variable overhead	10
Avoidable fixed overhead	8
Total	$58
Cost to outsource	$56

The cost to outsource is below the relevant cost to manufacture. Therefore, HD should outsource the speaker module.

b. $120,000 rental income ÷ 20,000 modules = $6 opportunity cost per module

Relevant cost to insource [from (a)]	$58
Opportunity cost	$ 6
Total	$64

The cost to insource is now even more inferior to outsourcing. Therefore, HD should outsource the item.

c. Some qualitative factors include the following:
- HD's future control of quality, supply, cost, and price of the speaker module;
- supplier's long-run going concern prospects;
- existence and number of qualified suppliers;
- impact on customers and markets;
- impact on employees; and
- reaction of financial and business press.

    a. $5,000.   c. $30,000.
    b. $10,000.   d. $40,000.

Assignments with the MBC logo in the margin are available in *BusinessCourse*.
Resources include demonstration videos, guided examples, and auto-graded homework.
See details in the Preface, and ask your professor how you can access the system.

Data Analytics

DA5-1. Utilization of constrained resources   LO5-3

Backyard Helpers, Inc. is a small manufacturing company with 18 different gardening tools in its product line. All of the products are fabricated using the same equipment.

Recently, sales demand has increased. Unfortunately, Backyard Helpers cannot produce enough products with existing equipment to meet that demand. Facilities can be expanded, and new equipment purchased, but it will be at least two years before that happens. The production manager needs to make production scheduling decisions now.

The Excel file available in MBC includes assumed information about demand, sales price, cost, and fabrication time on the shared equipment for each of Backyard Helpers' products.

Maximum machine time is 40,500 minutes per month. The demand for all products is spread equally throughout the month. Fixed costs (manufacturing, selling, and administrative) total $755,750 per month. Backyard Helpers maintains no inventory of finished goods: all units produced are sold during the month.

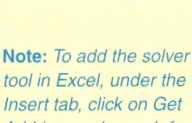

Note: To add the solver tool in Excel, under the Insert tab, click on Get Add-ins, and search for Solver. After it is added, the link will be available in the menu bar.

Required
a. Ignore machine time limits in answering the following:
   1. Which product has the highest contribution margin per unit? How many units of that product should be produced each month?
   2. If Backyard could meet demand, what would be the total net operating income per month?
b. If demand was unlimited for all products, which products should Backyard Helpers produce?
c. Given the maximum number of machine minutes per month and the expected demand per month, use Solver in Excel to answer the following questions. To prepare your worksheet to use the Solver tool, add columns with formulas for (1) contribution margin per unit, (2) total quantity in units, (3) total machine minutes, and (4) total contribution margin. In the Solver tool window, enter the cell that you would like to maximize (*Hint:* It is a single cell), identify the variables (*Hint:* Use quantity in units column) and enter the constraints (*Hint:* There are two constraints relating to demand and machine minutes).
   1. How many of the following products should be produced each month?
      i. R25
      ii. JK369
   2. Which products would be temporarily eliminated from Backyard Helpers product line under the Excel solution?
   3. What is the total net operating income per month given the machine time constraints and the quantities determined by Solver?
   4. What is the maximum amount Backyard Helpers should be willing to pay to rent fabrication time from another company? (Assume transportation and other costs would total $50,000.)
d. In Questions c2, you identified products that would be temporarily eliminated if Backyard followed the Excel solution. What reasons, if any, might management have for continuing to produce some of those products even if it means reducing the supply of some of the other products?

LO5-5 **DA5-2.** **Using data to analyze decisions on special order**

Kendrick Anderson Furniture Maker, LLC

Kendrick Anderson Furniture Maker, LLC creates custom tables in Atlanta. Assume that you are the product manager for the Living Room Table segment. Your company is planning to meet with a local not-for-profit company that is presenting a proposal for the production of tables for its senior center. Monthly manufacturing costs for the Living Room Table segment are included in the Excel file located in MBC. Assume that the data includes no outliers.

Required
a. What is the weighted average cost to manufacture a living room table based upon the historical data provided?
b. Using regression analysis, determine the cost-estimating equation to manufacture dining room tables. *Hint:* Under the Data tab, click on Data analysis, Regression, and select the cells for the *Y* Range and *X* Range.
c. What is the lowest price that your company would accept without making the company worse off?
d. What other information should you compile in advance of the meeting?

Data Visualization

Data Visualization Activities are available in myBusinessCourse. These assignments use Tableau Dashboards to expose students to visual depictions of data and introduce students to data analytics through data visualizations. These exercises are easily assignable and auto graded by MBC.

Potential Ethical Issues

1. Ignoring important qualitative factors in making relevant decisions, such as the impact on domestic employees, when companies choose to offshore operations
2. Choosing to move production offshore to a developing country to exploit lax environmental and labor regulations
3. Making decisions based on how they will impact reported financial earnings rather than by using relevant information
4. Using bait-and-switch advertising techniques to manage sales mix
5. Handling a scarce material circumstance by substituting materials that pose high risks to human health or the environment

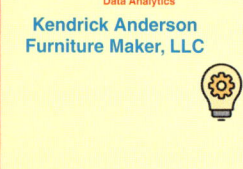

Questions

Q5-1. What does the term *relevance* mean in the context of making management decisions?
Q5-2. How does the passage of time affect the set of costs that is relevant to a decision?
Q5-3. What are opportunity costs, and why are they often the most difficult costs to analyze in decision making?
Q5-4. Describe sunk costs. Are there circumstances in which sunk costs are relevant to decisions? Discuss.
Q5-5. What is outsourcing?
Q5-6. What is a scarce resource? Why is an organization's most scarce resource likely to change from time to time?
Q5-7. What is the objective of managing the sales mix of products? What are the major factors that influence sales mix?
Q5-8. What is a special order decision? Under what circumstances would a company refuse to accept a special order?
Q5-9. What is segment margin? How is segment margin used in the quantitative analysis of a decision to drop or keep a product line?

Multiple Choice

MC5-10. Capital Company has decided to discontinue a product produced on a machine purchased four years ago at a cost of $70,000. The machine has a current book value of $30,000. Due to technologically improved machinery now available in the marketplace the existing machine has no current salvage value. The company is reviewing the various aspects involved in the production of a new product. The engineering staff advised that the existing machine can be used to produce the new product. Other costs involved in the production of the new product will be materials of $20,000 and labor priced at $5,000.

Ignoring income taxes, the costs relevant to the decision to produce or not to produce the new product would be

a. $25,000.
b. $30,000.
c. $55,000.
d. $95,000.

LO5-1

MC5-11. Synergy Inc. produces a component that is popular in many refrigeration systems. Data on three of the five different models of this component are as follows.

LO5-2

	Model A	Model B	Model C
Volume needed (units)	5,000	6,000	3,000
Manufacturing costs			
Variable direct costs	$10	$24	$20
Variable overhead	5	10	15
Fixed overhead	11	20	17
Total manufacturing costs	$26	$54	$52
Cost if purchased	$21	$42	$39

Synergy applies variable overhead on the basis of machine hours at the rate of $2.50 per hour. Fixed overhead costs are not avoidable.

Models A and B are manufactured in the Freezer Department, which has a capacity of 28,000 machine processing hours. Which one of the following options should be recommended to Synergy's management?

a. Purchase all three products in the quantities required.
b. Manufacture all three products in the quantities required.
c. The Freezer Department's manufacturing plan should include 5,000 units of Model A and 4,500 units of Model B.
d. The Freezer Department's manufacturing plan should include 2,000 units of Model A and 6,000 units of Model B.

LO5-3 MC5-12. Milton Manufacturing occasionally has capacity problems in its metal shaping division, where the chief cost driver is machine hours. In evaluating the attractiveness of its individual products for decision-making purposes, which measurement tool should the firm select?

	If machine hours do not constrain the number of units to be produced	If machine hours constrain the number of units to be produced
a.	Contribution margin	Contribution margin per machine hour.
b.	Gross profit	Contribution margin.
c.	Contribution margin	Contribution margin ratio.
d.	Contribution margin per machine hour	Contribution margin.

LO5-4 MC5-13. Raymund Inc., a bearings manufacturer, has the capacity to produce 7,000 bearings per month. The company is planning to replace a portion of its labor-intensive production process with a highly automated process, which would increase Raymund's fixed manufacturing costs by $30,000 per month and reduce its variable costs by $5 per unit.

Raymund's Income Statement for an average month is as follows.

Sales (5,000 units at $20 per unit)		$100,000
Variable manufacturing costs	$50,000	
Variable selling costs	15,000	65,000
Contribution margin		35,000
Fixed manufacturing costs	16,000	
Fixed selling costs	4,000	20,000
Operating income		$ 15,000

If Raymund installs the automated process, the company's monthly operating income would be

a. $5,000.
b. $10,000.
c. $30,000.
d. $40,000.

LO5-5 MC5-14. A company manufactures a product that has the following unit price and costs.

Selling price		$ 300
Costs		
Direct materials	$40	
Direct labor	30	
Variable manufacturing overhead	24	
Fixed manufacturing overhead	60	
Variable selling	6	
Fixed selling and administrative	20	
Total costs		(180)
Operating margin		$ 120

The company received a special order for 1,000 units of the product. The special order would still incur variable selling costs. The company currently has excess capacity but has an alternative use for this capacity that will result in a contribution margin of $20,000. What is the minimum price that the company should charge for this special order?

a. $120, because it covers the costs of manufacturing the product and allows the company to break even.
b. $140, because operating margin will increase by $20,000.
c. $180, because it covers the costs of manufacturing the product and allows the company to break even.
d. $200, because operating margin will increase by $20,000.

LO5-6 MC5-15. Current business segment operations for Whitman, a mass retailer, are presented below.

	Merchandise	Automotive	Restaurant	Total
Sales..................	$500,000	$400,000	$100,000	$1,000,000
Variable costs..............	300,000	200,000	70,000	570,000
Fixed costs...............	100,000	100,000	50,000	250,000
Operating income (loss)......	$100,000	$100,000	$ (20,000)	$ 180,000

Management is contemplating the discontinuance of the Restaurant segment since "it is losing money." If this segment is discontinued, $30,000 of its fixed costs will be eliminated. In addition, Merchandise and Automotive sales will decrease 5% from their current levels. What will Whitman's total contribution margin be if the Restaurant segment is discontinued?

a. $160,000.
b. $220,000.
c. $367,250.
d. $380,000.

Exercises

E5-16. Relevant costs; sunk costs Prior to the Super Bowl, a Boston-area retailer ordered 50,000 T-shirts that read: New England Patriots—Super Bowl Champs. The company paid $11.75 for each of the custom T-shirts. Following the loss of New England to the New York Giants, the retailer found itself with 15,000 unsold T-shirts after the Super Bowl. Before the Super Bowl, the retailer was able to sell 35,000 of the T-shirts at an average per-unit price of $25. The company is currently deciding how to dispose of the 15,000 remaining T-shirts. The retailer has learned from one of its suppliers that each shirt could be reworked at an average cost of $5.50 per shirt (which involves removing the Super Bowl reference from the shirts). Management of the retailer believes the reworked shirts could be sold at an average price of $10.25 during the coming football season. Alternatively, the company could sell the shirts at an average price of $2.60 as scrap material.

LO5-1, 2

a. Identify at least three alternative courses of action management could take with regard to the leftover T-shirts.
b. Which costs are sunk in this decision?
c. Identify the relevant costs of each alternative you listed in (a).
d. Based on your answer to (c), what is the best alternative and what is the relative financial advantage of the best alternative over the second-best alternative?

E5-17. Relevant costs; writing Because of a monumental error committed by its purchasing department, Corner Grocery ordered 5,000 heads of lettuce rather than the 1,000 that should have been ordered. The company paid $0.65 per head for the lettuce. Although management is confident that it can sell 2,000 units through regular sales, the market is not large enough to absorb the other 3,000 heads. Management has identified two ways to dispose of the excess heads of lettuce. First, a wholesaler has offered to purchase them for $0.25 each. Second, a restaurant chain has offered to purchase the lettuce if Corner Grocery will agree to convert it into packaged lettuce for salads. This option would require Corner Grocery to incur $2,500 for conversion, and the heads of lettuce could then be sold for the equivalent of $1.05 each.

LO5-1

a. Which costs are sunk in this decision?
b. Actually, Corner Grocery can consider three alternatives in this decision. Describe the alternative that is not mentioned in the problem.
c. What are the relevant costs of each decision alternative, and what should the company do?

E5-18. Relevant costs High Frequency manufactures and sells wireless headphones. Information on last year's operations (sales and production of last year's model) follows.

LO5-1

Sales price per unit...........................	$70
Costs per unit	
Direct material.............................	$16
Direct labor................................	14
Overhead (50% variable)....................	12
Selling costs (40% variable).................	20
Production in units............................	10,000
Sales in units.................................	9,500

In April of the current year, the new model is in production, and it renders last year's model obsolete. If the remaining 500 units of last year's model are to be sold through regular channels, what is the minimum price the company would accept for the headphones?

LO5-1 E5-19. Relevant costs Assume that you are about to graduate from your university and are deciding whether to apply for graduate school or enter the job market. To help make the decision, you have gathered the following data:

Costs incurred for the bachelor's degree	$163,000
Out-of-pocket costs for a master's degree	$94,000
Estimated starting salary with B.A.	$49,400
Estimated starting salary with M.A.	$66,800
Estimated time to complete master's degree	2 years
Estimated time from the present to retirement	40 years

a. Which of these factors is relevant to your decision?
b. What is the opportunity cost associated with earning the master's degree?
c. What is the out-of-pocket cost to obtain the master's degree?
d. What other factors should you consider before making a decision?

LO5-1 E5-20. Relevant vs. sunk costs; writing Your roommate, Jill Catanac, purchased a new laptop computer just before this school term for $300. Shortly after the semester began, her new computer was damaged when it was accidentally dropped. Returning the equipment to the retailer, Catanac was informed that the estimated cost of repairs was $200 (at a minimum) because the damage was not covered by the manufacturer's warranty.

Pondering the figures, Catanac was ready to decide to make repairs; after all, she had recently paid $300 for the computer. However, before making a decision, she asked for your advice.

a. Using concepts from this chapter, prepare a brief presentation outlining factors that Catanac should consider in making her decision.
b. Continue the presentation in (a) by discussing the options Catanac should consider in making her decision. Start by defining a base case against which alternatives can be compared.

LO5-1 E5-21. Asset replacement Certain production equipment used by Dayton Mechanical has become obsolete relative to current technology. The company is considering whether it should keep or replace its existing equipment. To aid in this decision, the company's controller gathered the following data:

	Old Equipment	New Equipment
Original cost	$350,000	$396,000
Remaining life	5 years	5 years
Accumulated depreciation	$158,000	$0
Annual cash operating costs	$64,000	$16,000
Current salvage value	$88,000	NA
Salvage value in five years	$0	$0

a. Identify any sunk costs in the data.
b. Identify any irrelevant (nondifferential) future costs.
c. Identify all relevant costs to the equipment replacement decision.
d. What are the opportunity costs associated with the alternative of keeping the old equipment?
e. What is the incremental cost to purchase the new equipment?
f. What qualitative considerations should be considered before making any decision?

LO5-1 E5-22. Asset replacement On April 1, Topeka Brake Mfg. purchased new production scheduling software for $480,000. On May 15, a representative of a computerized manufacturing technology company demonstrated new software that was clearly superior to that purchased by the firm in April. The price of this software is $840,000. Corporate managers estimate that the new software would save the company $32,000 annually in schedule-related costs compared to the recently installed software. Both software packages should last 10 years (the expected life of the computer hardware) and have no salvage value at that time. The company can sell its existing software for $356,000 if the new software is purchased. Should the company keep and use the software purchased earlier or buy the new software? Show computations to support your answer.

E5-23. Outsourcing Glass Tech manufactures fiberglass housings for portable generators. One part of the housing is a metal latch. Currently, the company produces the 120,000 metal latch units required annually. Company management is considering purchasing the latch from an external vendor. The following data are available for making the decision:

Cost per Unit to Manufacture	
Direct material	$1.40
Direct labor	1.36
Variable overhead	0.72
Fixed overhead—applied	1.12
Total cost	$4.60

Cost per Unit to Purchase	
Purchase price	$3.92
Freight charges	0.08
Total cost	$4.00

a. Assuming that all of Glass Tech's internal production costs are avoidable if the company purchases rather than makes the latch, what would be the net annual cost advantage to purchasing the latches?
b. Assume that some of Glass Tech's fixed overhead costs could not be avoided if it purchases rather than makes the latches. How much of the fixed overhead must be avoidable for the company to be indifferent as to making or buying the latches?

E5-24. Outsourcing Tuff Tach produces pickup truck bumpers that are sold on a wholesale basis to new car retailers. The average bumper sales price is $170. Normal annual sales volume is 300,000 units, which is the company's maximum production capacity. At this capacity, the company's per-unit costs are as follows:

Direct material	$ 53 (including mounting hardware @ $15 per unit)
Direct labor	17
Overhead (2/3 is fixed)	45
Total	$115

A key component in producing bumpers is the mounting hardware used to attach the bumpers to the vehicles. Birmingham Mechanical has offered to sell Tuff Tach as many mounting units as the company needs for $20 per unit. If Tuff Tach accepts the offer, the released facilities currently used to produce mounting hardware could be used to produce an additional 4,800 bumpers. What alternative is more desirable and by what amount? (Assume that the company is currently operating at its capacity of 300,000 units.)

E5-25. Outsourcing Pneu Shoe Company manufactures various types of athletic shoes. Several types require a gel insole. Presently, the company makes all gel insoles it requires. However, management is evaluating an offer from Ram Air Co. to provide gel insoles at a cost of $3.60 each. Pneu Shoe's management has estimated that the variable production costs of the insole total $2.70 per unit and that the company could avoid $27,000 per year in fixed costs if it purchased rather than produced the insoles.
a. If 25,000 insoles per year are required, should Pneu Shoe make them or buy them from Ram Air Co.?
b. If 60,000 insoles per year are required, should Pneu Shoe make them or buy them?
c. Assuming that all other factors are equal, at what level of production would the company be indifferent between making and buying the insoles?

E5-26. Allocation of scarce resources Sierra Sound Systems makes electronic products. Because the employees of one of the company's plants are on strike, the Chicago plant is operating at peak capacity. It makes two electronic products: wireless headphones and earbuds. Presently, the company can sell as many of each product as can be made, but making earbuds takes twice as long in production labor time as headphones. The company's production capacity is 100,000 labor hours per month. Data on each product are as follows:

	Headphones	Earbuds
Sales.	$72	$108
Variable costs.	(58)	(88)
Contribution margin	$14	$20
Labor hours required	1	2

Fixed costs are $240,000 per month.

a. How many of each product should the Chicago plant make? Explain your answer.
b. What qualitative factors would you consider in making this product mix decision?

LO5-3 E5-27. Allocation of scarce resources Since LaNora White graduated with an accounting degree, she has obtained significant experience in a variety of job settings. Her skills include auditing, income and estate taxation, and business consulting. White currently has her own practice, and her skills are in such demand that she limits her practice to taxation issues. Most of her engagements are one of three types: individual income taxation, estate taxation, or corporate taxation. Following are data pertaining to the revenues and costs of each tax area (per tax return):

	Individual	Estate	Corporate
Revenue.	$350	$1,200	$750
Variable cost.	$50	$200	$150
Hours per return of White's time.	2	8	5

Fixed costs of operating the office are $80,000 per year. White has such significant demand for her work that she must ration her time. She desires to work no more than 2,000 hours in the coming year. She can allocate her time so that she works only on one type of tax return or on any combination of the three types.

a. How should White allocate her time in the coming year to maximize her income?
b. Based on the optimal allocation, what is White's projected before-tax profit for the coming year?
c. What other factors should White consider in allocating her time?
d. What could White do to overcome the scarce resource constraint?

LO5-4 E5-28. Sales mix Pet Palace provides two types of services to dog owners: grooming and training. All company personnel can perform each service equally well. To expand sales and market share, Pet Palace's manager, Jim Jones, relies heavily on internet and billboard advertising, but next year's advertising budget is expected to be very limited. Information on projected operations for next year follows.

	Grooming	Training
Revenue per billable hour.	$50	$70
Variable cost of labor	$20	$41
Material cost per billable hour.	$6	$7
Allocated fixed cost per year.	$250,000	$260,000
Projected billable hours for the year	30,000	20,000

a. What is Pet Palace's projected before-tax profit (or loss) for next year?
b. If $1 spent on advertising could increase grooming revenue by $20 or training revenue by $20, on which service should the advertising dollar be spent?
c. If $1 spent on advertising could increase either grooming billable time or training billable time by one hour, on which service should the advertising dollar be spent?

LO5-4 E5-29. Sales mix One product produced and sold by Outfitters Inc. is a sleeping bag for which annual projections are as follows:

Projected volume in units	120,000
Sales price per unit.	$60
Variable production cost per unit	$25
Variable selling cost per unit.	$12
Fixed production cost	$805,000
Fixed selling and administration costs	$435,000

Chapter 5 Relevant Information for Decision Making

a. Compute the projected before-tax profit to be earned on the sleeping bags during the year.
b. Corporate management estimates that unit volume could be increased by 20 percent if sales price was decreased by 10 percent. How would such a change affect the profit level projected in (a)?
c. Rather than cutting the sales price, management is considering holding the sales price at the projected level and increasing advertising by $185,000. Such a change would increase volume by 20 percent. How would the level of profit under this alternative compare to the profit projected in (a)?

E5-30. Sales mix Trix Products Inc. manufactures smart watches and two accessories: ear buds and a charger. The ear buds and charger are compatible only with Trix smart watch. Sales prices and variable costs for each product are as follows:

LO5-4

	Smart Watch	Set of Ear Buds	Charger
Sales..................	$ 75	$ 20	$ 20
Variable production costs........	(60)	(4)	(5)
Variable selling costs...........	(4)	(1)	(2)
Contribution margin............	$ 11	$ 15	$ 13
Unit sales (next year's budget)....	1,400,000	400,000	200,000

The historical data of Trix Products Inc. suggest that, for each of the seven smart watches sold, two ear bud sets and one battery charger are sold. The company is currently exploring two options to increase overall corporate income for the upcoming year. The alternatives that follow would maintain the historical sales mix ratios:

1. Increase corporate advertising by $1,000,000. The company estimates doing so would increase total unit sales to 2,200,000.
2. Decrease the price of smart watches to $70. The company estimates doing so would increase smart watches sales to 3,150,000 units and have no effect on the unit selling price of the unit selling price of the other products.

a. Determine the effect of each proposal on budgeted profits for the coming year. Which alternative is preferred, and what is the relative financial benefit of that alternative?
b. How could the firm's management increase the ratio of ear buds and chargers to smart watches unit sales?

E5-31. Special order Wyoming Wire produces 12.5-gauge barbed wire that is retailed through farm supply companies. Presently, the company has the capacity to produce 100,000 tons of wire per year. It is operating at 80 percent of annual capacity, and at this level of operations, the cost per ton of wire is as follows:

LO5-5

Direct material	$560
Direct labor.........................	40
Variable overhead....................	50
Fixed overhead......................	190
Total	$840

The average sales price for the output produced by the firm is $900 per ton. The State of Texas has approached the firm to supply 200 tons of wire for the state's prisons for $670 per ton. No production modifications would be necessary to fulfill the order from the State of Texas.

a. What costs per ton are relevant to the decision to accept this special order?
b. What would be the dollar effect on before-tax profit if this order were accepted?

E5-32. Special order For The Ages Inc. produces solid-oak umbrella stands. Each stand is handmade and hand finished using the finest materials available. The firm has been operating at capacity (2,000 stands per year) for the past three years. Based on this capacity of operations, the firm's costs per stand are as follows:

LO5-5

Direct material	$ 50
Direct labor.........................	40
Variable overhead....................	10
Fixed overhead......................	30
Total	$130

© Cambridge Business Publishers

All selling and administrative expenses incurred by the firm are fixed. The average selling price of stands is $230. Recently, a large retailer approached Bill Wood, the president of For The Ages, about supplying three special stands to give as gifts to CEOs of key suppliers. Wood estimates that the following per-unit costs would be incurred to make the three stands:

Direct material	$250
Direct labor	350
Variable overhead	90
Total direct costs	$690

To accept the special order, the firm would have to sacrifice production of 20 regular units.

a. Identify all relevant costs that Wood should consider in deciding whether to accept the special order.
b. Assume the retailer offers to pay For The Ages a total of $3,800 for the three stands. How would accepting this offer affect For The Ages' before-tax profit?

LO5-6 E5-33. Product line Operations of Borderland Oil Drilling Services are separated into two geographical divisions: United States and Mexico. The operating results of each division for the year are as follows:

	United States	Mexico	Total
Sales	$ 7,200,000	$ 3,600,000	$10,800,000
Variable costs	(4,740,000)	(2,088,000)	(6,828,000)
Contribution margin	$ 2,460,000	$ 1,512,000	$ 3,972,000
Direct fixed costs	(800,000)	(490,000)	(1,290,000)
Segment margin	$ 1,660,000	$ 1,022,000	$ 2,682,000
Corporate fixed costs	(1,900,000)	(890,000)	(2,790,000)
Operating income (loss)	$ (240,000)	$ 132,000	$ (108,000)

Corporate fixed costs are allocated to the divisions based on relative sales. Assume that all of a division's direct fixed costs could be avoided by eliminating that division. Because the U.S. division is operating at a loss, Borderland's president is considering eliminating it.

a. If the U.S. division had been eliminated at the beginning of the year, what would have been Borderland's before-tax profit?
b. Recast the income statements into a more meaningful format than the one given. Why would total corporate operating results change from the $108,000 loss to the results determined in (a)?

LO5-6 E5-34. Product line Lakeland Financial Services provides outsourcing services for three areas: payroll, general ledger (GL), and tax compliance. The company is currently contemplating the elimination of the GL area because it is showing a before-tax loss. An annual income statement follows.

Lakeland Financial Services
Income Statement by Service Line
For the Year Ended July 31
(in thousands)

	Payroll	GL	Tax	Total
Sales	$ 4,400	$ 3,200	$ 3,600	$11,200
Cost of sales	(2,800)	(2,000)	(2,160)	(6,960)
Gross margin	$ 1,600	$ 1,200	$ 1,440	$ 4,240
Avoidable fixed and variable costs	$ 1,260	$ 1,470	$ 1,040	$ 3,770
Allocated fixed costs	180	140	210	530
Total fixed costs	$ 1,440	$ 1,610	$ 1,250	$ 4,300
Operating profit	$ 160	$ (410)	$ 190	$ (60)

a. Should corporate management drop the GL area? Support your answer with appropriate schedules.
b. If the GL area were dropped, how would the company's before-tax profit be affected?

Problems

P5-35. Relevant costs; writing Janet Cosgrove is the manager of Saratoga Sporting Goods, a division of Global Sports. Cosgrove's division sells a variety of sporting goods and supplies to wholesalers and retail chains throughout the Pacific Northwest and Latin America. Saratoga Sporting Goods has a single manufacturing facility located in Florida. As the manager of Saratoga Sporting Goods, Cosgrove is paid a salary and a bonus based on the profit she generates for the company. Recently, Cosgrove has been contemplating selling a warehouse owned by the division in Jacksonville. She has gathered the following information regarding the warehouse.

LO5-1

Age of warehouse.	17 years
Acquisition price	$17,500,000
Accumulated depreciation	$ 5,300,000
Current fair value	$ 7,000,000

Because the company has adopted JIT-based inventory management, the warehouse is no longer needed to store finished goods inventory. Furthermore, if the warehouse were sold, the $7,000,000 of current fair value would be realized on the sale. Cosgrove has consulted you, the CFO of the division, about the effect of the warehouse sale on divisional profits. You provided Cosgrove the following calculation:

Sales price	$ 7,000,000
Less net book value ($17,500,000 − $5,300,000)	(12,200,000)
Projected profit (loss) on sale.	$ (5,200,000)

    a. Discuss whether the loss that would be recognized on the sale is relevant to the decision to sell the warehouse.
    b. What would you recommend that Cosgrove do with respect to the warehouse?

P5-36. Asset replacement Arizona Mechanical recently created a new product, a computer-controlled, laser-precise lathe, and Ohio Ornamental Metals is considering purchasing one. Ohio's CFO received the following information from the accounting department regarding the company's existing lathe and the new Arizona Mechanical lathe. The savings in operating costs offered by the new lathe would mostly derive from reduced waste, reduced labor, and energy cost savings.

LO5-1

Old Machine	
Original cost	$875,000
Present book value.	$150,000
Annual cash operating costs	$450,000
Fair value now	$200,000
Fair value in five years	$0
Remaining useful life	5 years

New Machine	
Cost	$1,600,000
Annual cash operating costs	$155,000
Fair value in five years	$0
Useful life	5 years

    a. Based on financial considerations alone, should Ohio Ornamental Metals purchase the new lathe? Show computations to support your answer.
    b. What qualitative factors should Ohio Ornamental Metals consider before making a decision about purchasing the new lathe?

P5-37. Asset replacement Missouri River Energy Company provides electrical services to several rural counties in Nebraska and South Dakota. Its efficiency has been greatly affected by changes in technology. The company is currently considering the replacement of its main steam turbine, which was put in place approximately 30 years ago but is now technologically obsolete. The turbine's

LO5-1

operation is very reliable, but it is much less efficient than newer, computer-controlled turbines. The controller presented the following financial information to corporate management:

	Old Turbine	New Turbine
Original cost..........................	$4,000,000	$6,000,000
Fair value now	$400,000	$6,000,000
Remaining life........................	8 years	8 years
Quarterly operating costs.............	$210,000	$45,000
Salvage value in eight years..........	$0	$0
Accumulated depreciation	$800,000	N/A

a. Identify the costs that are relevant to the company's equipment replacement decision.
b. Determine whether it is more financially sound to keep the old turbine or replace it. Provide your own computations based on relevant costs only.
c. For this part only, assume that the acquisition cost of the new technology is unknown. What is the maximum amount that the company could pay for the new technology and be in the same financial condition as it is in currently?
d. What other considerations would come into play if, rather than a new turbine, the company were considering solar-powered technology to replace the old turbine system?

LO5-2 **P5-38. Outsourcing; ethics; writing** Tate Electronics manufactures computers and all required components. Its purchasing agent informed the company owner, Mervin Tate, that another company had offered to supply keyboards for Tate computers at prices below the variable costs at which Tate can make them. Incredulous, Tate hired an industrial consultant to explain how the supplier could offer the keyboards at less than Tate's variable costs.

The consultant suspects the supplier is using many undocumented laborers to work in its plant. The workers are poverty stricken and will take work at substandard wages. Tate's purchasing agent and the plant manager recommend to Mervin Tate that the company should outsource the keyboards because "no one can blame us for the supplier's hiring practices and if those practices come to light, no one will be able to show that we knew of those practices."

a. What are the ethical issues involved in this case?
b. What are the advantages and disadvantages of buying from this supplier?
c. What do you think Tate should do and why?

LO5-2 **P5-39. Outsourcing** Louisiana Luggage Components manufactures handles for suitcases and other luggage. Depending on the size of the luggage piece, attaching each handle to the luggage requires between two and six standard fasteners, which the company has historically produced. The costs to produce one fastener (based on capacity operation of 4,000,000 units per year) are as follows.

Direct material	$0.08
Direct labor......................	0.06
Variable factory overhead............	0.04
Fixed factory overhead..............	0.07
Total	$0.25

Fixed factory overhead includes $100,000 of depreciation on equipment for which there is no alternative use and no fair value. The balance of the fixed factory overhead pertains to the salary of the production supervisor, Jeff Wittier. Wittier has a lifetime employment contract and the skills that could be used to replace Brenda Gibbons, supervisor of floor maintenance. She draws a salary of $50,000 per year but is due to retire from the company.

Saratoga Suitcase Co. recently approached Louisiana Luggage Components with an offer to supply all required fasteners for $0.19 per unit. Anticipated sales demand for the coming year will require 4,000,000 fasteners.

a. Identify the costs that are relevant in this outsourcing decision.
b. What is the total annual advantage or disadvantage (in dollars) of outsourcing the fasteners rather than making them?
c. What qualitative factors should be taken into account in making this decision?

P5-40. Outsourcing Structural Steel Systems manufactures steel buildings for agricultural and home applications. Currently, managers are trying to decide between two alternatives regarding a major overhead door assembly for the company's buildings. The alternatives are as follows:

- Purchase new equipment with a five-year life and no salvage value at a cost of $10,000,000. The company uses straight-line depreciation and allocates that amount on a per-unit-of-production basis.
- Purchase the assemblies from an outside vendor who will sell them for $480 each under a five-year contract.

Following is Structural Steel Systems' present cost to produce one door assembly based on current and normal activity of 50,000 units per year.

Direct material	$278
Direct labor	132
Variable overhead	86
Fixed overhead*	72
Total	$568

*The fixed overhead includes $14 supervision cost, $18 depreciation, and $40 general company overhead.

The new equipment would be more efficient than the old equipment and would reduce direct labor costs and variable overhead costs by 25 percent. Supervisory costs of $700,000 would be unaffected. The new equipment would have a capacity of 75,000 assemblies per year. Structural Steel Systems could lease the space occupied by current assembly production to another firm for $228,000 per year if the company decides to buy from the outside vendor.

a. Show an analysis, including relevant unit and total costs, for each alternative of producing or buying the assemblies. Assume 50,000 assemblies are needed each year.
b. How would your answer differ if 60,000 assemblies were needed?
c. How would your answer differ if 75,000 assemblies were needed?
d. In addition to quantitative factors, what qualitative factors should be considered?

P5-41. Scarce resource; discontinued product lines; negative contribution margin The officers of Bardwell Company are reviewing the profitability of the company's four products and the potential effects of several proposals for varying the product mix. The following is an excerpt from the income statement and other data.

	Total	Product P	Product Q	Product R	Product S
Sales	$62,600	$10,000	$18,000	$12,600	$22,000
Cost of goods sold	(44,274)	(4,750)	(7,056)	(13,968)	(18,500)
Gross profit	$18,326	$5,250	$10,944	$(1,368)	$3,500
Operating expenses	(12,004)	(1,990)	(2,968)	(2,826)	(4,220)
Income before taxes	$6,322	$3,260	$7,976	$(4,194)	$(720)
Units sold		1,000	1,200	1,800	2,000
Sales price per unit		$10.00	$15.00	$7.00	$11.00
Variable cost of goods sold		2.50	3.00	6.50	6.00
Variable operating expenses		1.17	1.25	1.00	1.20

Each of the following proposals is to be considered independently of the other proposals. Consider only the product changes stated in each proposal; the activity of the other proposals remains stable.

a. What is the effect on income if Product P is discontinued?
b. What is the effect on income if Product R is discontinued?
c. What is the effect on income if Product R is discontinued and a consequent loss of customers causes a decrease in sales of 200 units of Product Q?
d. What is the effect on income if the sales price of product R is increased to $8.00 with a decrease in the number of units sold to 1,500?
e. Janet Poole, marketing manager at Bardwell Company, approaches Pamela Bardwell, the company's president. She proposes that Bardwell Company drop production of Product S to produce Product T, which is made on the same production equipment. Product T has a selling

price of $14.00, variable manufacturing costs of $9.00, and variable selling expenses of $2.46. Poole estimates that 2,100 units of Product T could be sold annually; she feels that this would be good for the company, as total sales revenue will increase by $7,400 and Product T would be replacing a product that is currently losing money for the company. Poole also believes that this would be good for the morale of the sales department, as total sales commissions will increase. Should Bardwell consider Poole's suggestion? Why or why not?

f. Explain why traditional cost accounting sometimes leads managers to make incorrect decisions.

P5-42. Outsourcing; opportunity cost Yoto Heavy Industrial uses ten units of Part No. T305 each month in the production of large diesel engines. The cost to manufacture one unit of T305 is presented below:

Direct material	$ 2,000
Material handling (20% of direct materials)	400
Direct labor	16,000
Manufacturing overhead (150% of direct labor)	24,000
Total manufacturing cost	$42,400

Material handling, which is not included in the manufacturing overhead, represents the direct variable costs of the receiving department that are applied to direct materials and purchased components on the basis of their cost. Yoto's annual manufacturing overhead budget is one-third variable and two-thirds fixed. Workman Hydraulic Company, one of Yoto's reliable vendors, has offered to supply T305 at a unit price of $30,000.

a. If Yoto Heavy Industrial purchases the ten T305 units from Workman Hydraulic Company, the capacity Yoto used to manufacture these parts would be idle. Compute the change in the out-of-pocket cost per unit to Yoto if it decided to purchase the parts from Workman Hydraulic Company.

b. Assume that Yoto Heavy Industrial is able to rent all idle capacity for $50,000 per month. If Yoto decides to purchase the ten units from Workman Hydraulic Company, what would be the change in the total monthly cost for T305?

P5-43. Outsourcing; scarce resources Callahan Manufacturing has assembled the data appearing below pertaining to two products. Past experience has shown that the unavoidable fixed factory overhead included in the cost per machine hour averages $10. Direct labor is paid $18 per hour. Callahan has a policy of filling all sales orders, even if it means purchasing units from outside suppliers at the same selling price per unit that Callahan currently charges.

	Blender	Electric Mixer
Direct material	$6	$11
Direct labor	$4	$9
Factory overhead at $16 per machine hour	$16	$32
Selling price per unit	$20	$38
Annual demand in units	20,000	28,000

a. Assume Callahan Manufacturing has 50,000 machine hours available. What would be the optimal production of each product to maximize Callahan's profits?

b. Refer to the original information. With all other things constant, if Callahan is able to reduce direct materials cost for the electric mixer by $6 per unit, what strategy should Callahan pursue?

c. Refer to the original information. Assume that an outbreak of the flu has left Callahan shorthanded on direct labor personnel. Approximately one-half of the workforce will be out of work for one month. During the month, what strategy should Callahan pursue?

P5-44. Relevant costs; special order pricing Kantrovitz Company is a manufacturer of industrial components. One of its products, AP110, is used as a subcomponent in appliance manufacturing. This product has the following information per unit:

Chapter 5 Relevant Information for Decision Making 5-41

Selling price	$150
Costs:	
Direct material	$ 20
Direct labor	15
Variable manufacturing overhead	12
Fixed manufacturing overhead	30
Shipping and handling	3
Fixed selling and administrative	10
Total per-unit cost	$ 90

   a. Kantrovitz has received a special, one-time order for 1,000 AP110 parts. Assuming Kantrovitz has excess capacity, what is the minimum price that is acceptable for beginning negotiations on this order?
   b. Kantrovitz has 5,000 units of AP110 in inventory that have some defects. The units cannot be sold through regular channels without a significant price reduction. What per-unit cost figure is relevant for setting a minimum selling price on these units?
   c. During the next year, sales of AP110 are expected to be 10,000 units. All costs will remain the same except that fixed manufacturing overhead will increase by 20 percent and direct material will increase by 10 percent. The selling price per unit for next year will be $160. Based on these data, calculate the total contribution margin generated by part AP110.
   d. Referring to (a), Kantrovitz has received a special, one-time order for 1,000 AP110 parts. Assume that Kantrovitz is operating at full capacity, and that the contribution of the output would be displaced by the one-time special order. Using the original data, compute the minimum acceptable selling price for this order.

P5-45. **Relevant costs; sales mix; writing** Microsoft announced it was extending the warranty on its video game player (introduced two years earlier) to three years for a certain type of malfunction indicated by three flashing red lights on the game console. The warranty extension would apply to previously sold units; however, the warranty for any other type of failure would not be extended beyond the original one-year warranty term. In making this announcement, Microsoft indicated it would take a charge of $1.05–1.15 billion for the costs of the warranty extension.   LO5-1, 4

   a. What relevant costs were likely considered by Microsoft management in reaching the decision to extend the warranty on the video game player and, in so doing, incur in excess of $1 billion of additional costs?
   b. Assume that one of the rationalizations for Microsoft to extend the warranty on the video game player was to manage sales mix. How could the extension of the video game player warranty affect the sales mix of Microsoft's entertainment and devices division?
   c. Comment on whether Microsoft was ethically obligated to extend the warranty on the video game player to three years.

   Source: Nick Wingfield, "Microsoft's Videogame Efforts Take a Costly Hit," *Wall Street Journal* (July 6, 2007), p. A3.

P5-46. **Sales mix** Leather Accessories produces leather belts and key fobs that sell for $40 and $10, respectively. The company currently sells 100,000 units of each type with the following operating results: LO5-4

Belts		
Sales (100,000 × $40)		$ 4,000,000
Variable costs		
Production (100,000 × $25)	$2,500,000	
Selling (100,000 × $6)	600,000	(3,100,000)
Contribution margin		$ 900,000
Fixed costs		
Production	$ 400,000	
Selling and administrative	180,000	(580,000)
Income		$ 320,000

continued

continued from previous page

Key Fobs		
Sales (100,000 × $10)		$ 1,000,000
Variable costs		
Production (100,000 × $6)	$ 600,000	
Selling (100,000 × $1)	100,000	(700,000)
Contribution margin		$ 300,000
Fixed costs		
Production	$ 100,000	
Selling and administrative	80,000	(180,000)
Income		$ 120,000

Corporate management has expressed its disappointment with the income being generated from the sales of these two products. Managers have asked for your help in analyzing three alternative plans to improve operating results.

1. Change the sales commission to 12 percent of sales price less variable production costs for each product from the current 5 percent of selling price. The marketing manager believes that the sales of the belts will decline by 5,000 units but those of key fobs will increase by 15,000 units.
2. Increase the advertising budget for belts by $75,000. The marketing manager believes this will increase the sales of belts by 19,000 units but will decrease the sales of key fobs by 9,000 units.
3. Raise the per-unit price of belts by $5 and of key fobs by $3. The marketing manager believes this will cause a decrease in the sales of belts by 6,000 units and of key fobs by 10,000 units. Variable costs per units will not change with the sales price increase.

a. Determine the effects on the income of each product line and the company in total if each alternative plan is put into effect.
b. What is your recommendation to the management of Leather Accessories?

LO5-3, 4   **P5-47.**   **Sales mix with scarce resources** San Fran Cycles manually manufactures three unique bicycle models: racing, touring, and basic. All of the skilled craftspeople employed at San Fran can make each of the three models. Because it takes about a year to train each craftsperson, labor is a fixed production constraint over the short term. For the year, the company expects to have available 34,000 labor hours. The average hourly labor rate is $30. Data regarding the current product line follow.

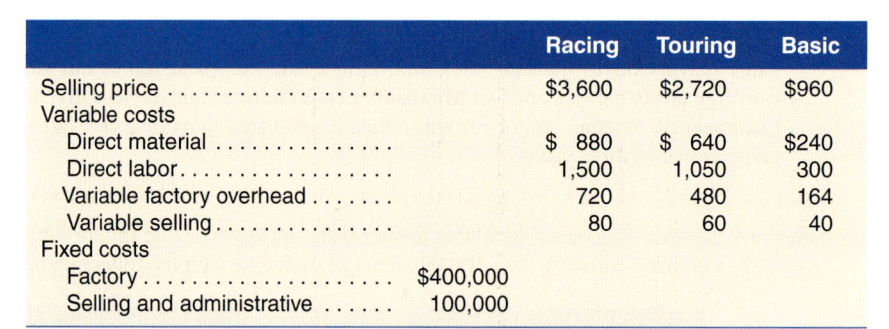

	Racing	Touring	Basic
Selling price	$3,600	$2,720	$960
Variable costs			
Direct material	$ 880	$ 640	$240
Direct labor.	1,500	1,050	300
Variable factory overhead	720	480	164
Variable selling	80	60	40
Fixed costs			
Factory	$400,000		
Selling and administrative	100,000		

The company pays taxes at the rate of 50 percent of operating income.

a. If an unlimited amount of any product can be sold, how many of each product should the company make? What before-tax profit will the company earn given your answer?
b. How many (rounded to the nearest whole unit) of each product must the company make if it has the policy to devote no more than 50 percent of its available skilled labor capacity to any one product but at least 20 percent to every product? What before-tax profit will the company earn given your answer?
c. Given the nature of the three products, is it reasonable to believe that there are market constraints on the mix of products that can be sold? Explain.
d. How does the company's tax rate enter into the calculation of the optimal labor allocation?

LO5-5   **P5-48.**   **Special order** Layton Ironworks manufactures a variety of industrial valves and pipe fittings sold primarily to customers in the United States. Currently, the company is operating at 70 percent of capacity and is earning a satisfactory return on investment.

Chapter 5 Relevant Information for Decision Making

Selling price	$150
Costs:	
Direct material	$ 20
Direct labor	15
Variable manufacturing overhead	12
Fixed manufacturing overhead	30
Shipping and handling	3
Fixed selling and administrative	10
Total per-unit cost	$ 90

a. Kantrovitz has received a special, one-time order for 1,000 AP110 parts. Assuming Kantrovitz has excess capacity, what is the minimum price that is acceptable for beginning negotiations on this order?

b. Kantrovitz has 5,000 units of AP110 in inventory that have some defects. The units cannot be sold through regular channels without a significant price reduction. What per-unit cost figure is relevant for setting a minimum selling price on these units?

c. During the next year, sales of AP110 are expected to be 10,000 units. All costs will remain the same except that fixed manufacturing overhead will increase by 20 percent and direct material will increase by 10 percent. The selling price per unit for next year will be $160. Based on these data, calculate the total contribution margin generated by part AP110.

d. Referring to (a), Kantrovitz has received a special, one-time order for 1,000 AP110 parts. Assume that Kantrovitz is operating at full capacity, and that the contribution of the output would be displaced by the one-time special order. Using the original data, compute the minimum acceptable selling price for this order.

P5-45. Relevant costs; sales mix; writing Microsoft announced it was extending the warranty on its video game player (introduced two years earlier) to three years for a certain type of malfunction indicated by three flashing red lights on the game console. The warranty extension would apply to previously sold units; however, the warranty for any other type of failure would not be extended beyond the original one-year warranty term. In making this announcement, Microsoft indicated it would take a charge of $1.05–1.15 billion for the costs of the warranty extension.

LO5-1, 4

a. What relevant costs were likely considered by Microsoft management in reaching the decision to extend the warranty on the video game player and, in so doing, incur in excess of $1 billion of additional costs?

b. Assume that one of the rationalizations for Microsoft to extend the warranty on the video game player was to manage sales mix. How could the extension of the video game player warranty affect the sales mix of Microsoft's entertainment and devices division?

c. Comment on whether Microsoft was ethically obligated to extend the warranty on the video game player to three years.

Source: Nick Wingfield, "Microsoft's Videogame Efforts Take a Costly Hit," *Wall Street Journal* (July 6, 2007), p. A3.

P5-46. Sales mix Leather Accessories produces leather belts and key fobs that sell for $40 and $10, respectively. The company currently sells 100,000 units of each type with the following operating results:

LO5-4

Belts		
Sales (100,000 × $40)		$ 4,000,000
Variable costs		
Production (100,000 × $25)	$2,500,000	
Selling (100,000 × $6)	600,000	(3,100,000)
Contribution margin		$ 900,000
Fixed costs		
Production	$ 400,000	
Selling and administrative	180,000	(580,000)
Income		$ 320,000

continued

continued from previous page

Key Fobs		
Sales (100,000 × $10)		$ 1,000,000
Variable costs		
Production (100,000 × $6)	$ 600,000	
Selling (100,000 × $1)	100,000	(700,000)
Contribution margin		$ 300,000
Fixed costs		
Production	$ 100,000	
Selling and administrative	80,000	(180,000)
Income		$ 120,000

Corporate management has expressed its disappointment with the income being generated from the sales of these two products. Managers have asked for your help in analyzing three alternative plans to improve operating results.

1. Change the sales commission to 12 percent of sales price less variable production costs for each product from the current 5 percent of selling price. The marketing manager believes that the sales of the belts will decline by 5,000 units but those of key fobs will increase by 15,000 units.
2. Increase the advertising budget for belts by $75,000. The marketing manager believes this will increase the sales of belts by 19,000 units but will decrease the sales of key fobs by 9,000 units.
3. Raise the per-unit price of belts by $5 and of key fobs by $3. The marketing manager believes this will cause a decrease in the sales of belts by 6,000 units and of key fobs by 10,000 units. Variable costs per units will not change with the sales price increase.

    a. Determine the effects on the income of each product line and the company in total if each alternative plan is put into effect.
    b. What is your recommendation to the management of Leather Accessories?

LO5-3, 4   **P5-47.**   **Sales mix with scarce resources** San Fran Cycles manually manufactures three unique bicycle models: racing, touring, and basic. All of the skilled craftspeople employed at San Fran can make each of the three models. Because it takes about a year to train each craftsperson, labor is a fixed production constraint over the short term. For the year, the company expects to have available 34,000 labor hours. The average hourly labor rate is $30. Data regarding the current product line follow.

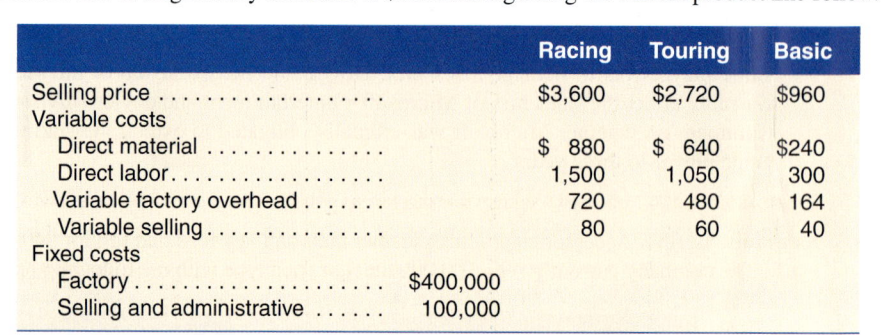

	Racing	Touring	Basic
Selling price	$3,600	$2,720	$960
Variable costs			
Direct material	$ 880	$ 640	$240
Direct labor	1,500	1,050	300
Variable factory overhead	720	480	164
Variable selling	80	60	40
Fixed costs			
Factory	$400,000		
Selling and administrative	100,000		

The company pays taxes at the rate of 50 percent of operating income.

    a. If an unlimited amount of any product can be sold, how many of each product should the company make? What before-tax profit will the company earn given your answer?
    b. How many (rounded to the nearest whole unit) of each product must the company make if it has the policy to devote no more than 50 percent of its available skilled labor capacity to any one product but at least 20 percent to every product? What before-tax profit will the company earn given your answer?
    c. Given the nature of the three products, is it reasonable to believe that there are market constraints on the mix of products that can be sold? Explain.
    d. How does the company's tax rate enter into the calculation of the optimal labor allocation?

LO5-5   **P5-48.**   **Special order** Layton Ironworks manufactures a variety of industrial valves and pipe fittings sold primarily to customers in the United States. Currently, the company is operating at 70 percent of capacity and is earning a satisfactory return on investment.

Chapter 5 Relevant Information for Decision Making

Prince Industries Ltd. of Scotland has approached Layton's management with an offer to buy 120,000 pressure valves. Prince manufactures an almost identical pressure valve, but a fire in Prince's valve plant has closed its manufacturing operations. Prince needs the 120,000 valves over the next four months to meet commitments to its regular customers; the company is prepared to pay $19 each for the valves.

Layton's product cost for the pressure valve based on current attainable standards is

Direct material	$ 5
Direct labor	6
Manufacturing overhead	9
Total cost	$20

Manufacturing overhead is applied to production at the rate of $18 per standard direct labor hour. This overhead rate is made up of the following components:

Variable factory overhead	$ 6
Fixed factory overhead—direct	8
Fixed factory overhead—allocated	4
Applied manufacturing overhead rate	$18

Additional costs incurred in connection with sales of the pressure valve include 5 percent sales commissions and $1 freight expense per unit. However, the company does not pay sales commissions on special orders that come directly to management.

In determining selling prices, Layton adds a 40 percent markup to product cost, which provides a $28 suggested selling price for the pressure valve. The marketing department, however, has set the current selling price at $27 to maintain market share.

Production management believes that it can handle Prince Industries' order without disrupting its scheduled production. The order would, however, require additional fixed factory overhead of $12,000 per month for supervision and clerical costs.

If management accepts the order, Layton will manufacture 30,000 pressure valves and ship them to Prince Industries each month for the next four months.

a. Determine how many additional direct labor hours would be required each month to fill the Prince Industries order.
b. Prepare an incremental analysis showing the impact of accepting the Prince Industries order.
c. Calculate the minimum unit price that Layton Ironworks' management could accept for the Prince Industries order without reducing net income.
d. Identify the factors, other than price, that Layton Ironworks should consider before accepting the Prince Industries order.

P5-49. Product line Gilfeather Food Service sells high-quality ice cream and steaks via overnight delivery. Income statements showing revenues and costs for the year for each product line are as follows. **LO5-6**

	Ice Cream	Steaks
Sales	$ 4,000,000	$ 2,000,000
Less: Cost of merchandise sold	(2,600,000)	(1,500,000)
Commissions to salespeople	(200,000)	(150,000)
Delivery costs	(600,000)	(120,000)
Depreciation on equipment	(200,000)	(100,000)
Salaries of division managers	(80,000)	(75,000)
Allocated corporate costs	(100,000)	(100,000)
Net income (loss)	$ 220,000	$ (45,000)

Management is concerned about profitability of steaks and is considering dropping the line. The equipment currently used to process steaks could be rented to a competitor for $8,500 annually. If the steaks line is dropped, allocated corporate costs would decrease from a total of $200,000 to $170,000, and all employees, including the product line manager, would be dismissed. Equipment depreciation would be unaffected by the decision, but $105,000 of the delivery costs charged to the steaks line could be eliminated if it is dropped.

a. Recast the preceding income statements in a format that provides more information in making this decision regarding the steaks product line.
b. What is the net advantage or disadvantage (change in total company before-tax profits) of continuing sales of steaks?
c. Should the company be concerned about losing ice cream sales if the steaks line is dropped? Explain.
d. How might the layoffs occurring from dropping the steaks line adversely affect the whole company?

LO5-6 **P5-50. Product line** You have been hired to assist the management of Great Bend Office Systems in resolving certain issues. The company has its home office in Montana and leases facilities in Montana, Idaho, and North Dakota, where it produces a high-quality bean bag chair designed for residential use. Great Bend management has provided you a projection of operations for next year, as follows:

	Total	Montana	Idaho	North Dakota
Sales...................	$ 17,600,000	$ 8,800,000	$ 5,600,000	$ 3,200,000
Fixed costs				
Factory..............	$ 4,400,000	$ 2,240,000	$ 1,120,000	$ 1,040,000
Administration........	1,400,000	840,000	440,000	120,000
Variable costs...........	5,800,000	2,660,000	1,700,000	1,440,000
Allocated home office costs	2,000,000	900,000	700,000	400,000
Total costs.............	$(13,600,000)	$(6,640,000)	$(3,960,000)	$(3,000,000)
Before-tax profit from operations ...	$ 4,000,000	$ 2,160,000	$ 1,640,000	$ 200,000

The sales price per unit is $100.

Due to the marginal results of operations in North Dakota, Great Bend has decided to cease operations there and sell that factory's machinery and equipment by the end of next year. Managers expect proceeds from the sale of these assets to exceed their book value by enough to cover termination costs.

Great Bend would like to continue serving its customers in that area if it is economically feasible. It is considering the following three alternatives:

1. Expand the operations of the Idaho factory by using space that is currently idle. This move would result in the following changes in that factory's operations:

Increase over Factory's Current Operations	
Sales............................	50%
Fixed costs	
Factory.......................	20%
Administration.................	10%

Under this proposal, variable costs would be $32 per unit sold.

2. Enter into a long-term contract with a competitor that will serve the area's customers and pay Great Bend a royalty of $16 per unit based on an estimate of 30,000 units being sold.
3. Close the North Dakota factory and not expand the Idaho factory's operations. Note: Total home office costs of $2,000,000 will remain the same under each situation.

To assist the company's management in determining which alternative is most economically feasible, prepare a schedule computing its estimated before-tax profit from total operations that would result from each of the following alternatives:

a. Expansion of the Idaho factory.
b. Negotiation of a long-term contract on a royalty basis.
c. Closure of the North Dakota operations with no expansion at other locations.

AICPA ADAPTED

LO5-1, 6 **P5-51. Comprehensive** Louisville Jar Co. has processing plants in Kentucky and Pennsylvania. Both plants use recycled glass to produce jars that a variety of food processors use in food canning. The jars sell for $10 per hundred units. Budgeted revenues and costs for the year ending December 31, in thousands of dollars, are:

Chapter 5 Relevant Information for Decision Making

	Kentucky	Pennsylvania	Total
Sales.	$1,100	$2,000	$3,100
Variable production costs			
Direct material	$ 275	$ 500	$ 775
Direct labor.	330	500	830
Factory overhead	220	350	570
Fixed factory overhead	350	450	800
Fixed regional promotion costs.	50	50	100
Allocated home office costs	55	100	155
Total costs	$1,280	$1,950	$3,230
Operating income (loss)	$ (180)	$ 50	$ (130)

Home office costs are fixed and are allocated to manufacturing plants on the basis of relative sales levels. Fixed regional promotional costs are discretionary advertising costs needed to obtain budgeted sales levels.

Because of the budgeted operating loss, Louisville Jar Co. is considering ceasing operations at its Kentucky plant. If it does so, proceeds from the sale of plant assets will exceed asset book values and exactly cover all termination costs; fixed factory overhead costs of $25,000 would not be eliminated. Louisville Jar Co. is considering the following three alternative plans:

PLAN A: Expand Kentucky's operations from its budgeted 11,000,000 units to a budgeted 17,000,000 units. It is believed that this can be accomplished by increasing Kentucky's fixed regional promotional expenditures by $120,000.

PLAN B: Close the Kentucky plant and expand the Pennsylvania operations from the current budgeted 20,000,000 to 31,000,000 units to fill Kentucky's budgeted production of 11,000,000 units. The Kentucky region would continue to incur promotional costs to sell the 11,000,000 units. All sales and costs would be budgeted by the Pennsylvania plant.

PLAN C: Close the Kentucky plant and enter into a long-term contract with a competitor to serve the Kentucky region's customers. This competitor would pay a royalty of $1.25 per 100 units sold to Louisville, which would continue to incur fixed regional promotional costs to maintain sales of 11,000,000 units in the Kentucky region.

    a. Without considering the effects of implementing Plans A, B, and C, compute the number of units that the Kentucky plant must produce and sell to cover its fixed factory overhead costs and fixed regional promotional costs.

    b. Prepare a schedule by plant and in total of Louisville's budgeted contribution margin and operating income resulting from the implementation of each of the following:

        1. Plan A.   2. Plan B.   3. Plan C.

AICPA ADAPTED
LO5-1, 6

P5-52. Sales and profit improvement Classic Clothes is a retail organization in the Northeast that sells upscale clothing. Each year, store managers (in consultation with their supervisors) establish financial goals; a monthly reporting system captures actual performance.

One of the firm's sales districts, District A, has three stores but has historically been a very poor performer. Consequently, the district supervisor has been searching for ways to improve the performance of her three stores. For May, she set performance goals with the managers of Stores 1 and 2. The managers will receive bonuses if the stores exceed certain performance measures. The manager of Store 3 decided not to participate in the bonus scheme. Because the district supervisor is unsure what type of bonus will encourage better performance, she offered the manager of Store 1 a bonus based on sales in excess of budgeted sales of $670,000; the manager of Store 2 was offered a bonus based on net income in excess of budgeted net income. The company's net income goal for each store is 12 percent of sales. Budgeted sales for Store 2 are $630,000.

    Other pertinent data for May follow.
- At Store 1, sales were 40 percent of total District A sales; sales at Store 2 were 35 percent of total District A sales. The cost of goods sold at both stores was 45 percent of sales.
- Variable selling expenses (sales commissions) were 8 percent of sales for all stores and districts.
- Variable administrative expenses were 3 percent of sales for all stores and districts.

- Maintenance cost including janitorial and repair services is a direct cost for each store. The store manager has complete control over this outlay; however, it should not be below 1 percent of sales.
- Advertising is considered a direct cost for each store and is completely under the store manager's control. Store 1 spent two-thirds of District A's total outlay for advertising, which was 10 times more than Store 2 spent on advertising.
- The rental expense at Store 1 is 40 percent of District A's total and at Store 2 is 30 percent of District A's total.

District A expenses are allocated to the stores based on sales.

a. Will Store 1 or Store 2 generate more profit under the new bonus scheme?
b. Will Store 1 or Store 2 generate more revenue under the new bonus scheme?
c. Why would Store 1 have an incentive to spend so much more on advertising than Store 2?
d. Which store manager has the most incentive to spend money on regular maintenance? Explain.
e. Which bonus scheme appears to offer the most incentive to improve the profit performance of the district in the short term? Long term?

LO5-2, 5 **P5-53.** **Analyzing one company's make or buy and special order proposals** OneCo is a retail organization in the Northeast that sells upscale clothing. Each year, store managers (in consultation with their supervisors) establish financial goals; a monthly reporting system captures actual performance.

OneCo Inc. produces a single product. Cost per unit, based on the manufacture and sale of 10,000 units per month at full capacity, is shown below.

Direct materials.	$ 4.00
Direct labor.	1.30
Variable overhead.	2.50
Fixed overhead.	3.40
Sales commission.	0.90
Total	$12.10

The $0.90 sales commission is paid for every unit sold through regular channels. Market demand is such that OneCo is operating at full capacity, and the firm has found it can sell all it can produce at the market price of $16.50.

Currently, OneCo is considering two separate proposals:
- Gatsby, Inc. has offered to buy 1,000 units at $14.35 each. Sales commission would be $0.35 on this special order.
- Zelda Productions, Inc. has offered to produce 1,000 units at a delivered cost to OneCo of $14.50 each.

Required

a. What would be the effect on OneCo's operating income if it accepts of the proposal from Gatsby, but rejects the proposal from Zelda?
b. What would be the effect on OneCo's operating income if it accepts of the proposal from Zelda, but rejects the proposal from Gatsby?
c. What would be the effect on OneCo's operating income if it accepts both proposals?
d. Assume Gatsby has offered a second proposal to purchase 2,000 units at the market price of $16.50, but has requested product modifications that would increase direct materials cost by $.30 per unit and increase direct labor and variable overhead by 15%. The sales commission would be $.35 per unit. Should OneCo accept this order? Explain your recommendation.
e. Under the situation described above, would your recommendation be different if the company had excess capacity? Explain your answer.

LO5-1, 6 **P5-54.** **Comprehensive; product line** Clean-N-Brite is a multiproduct company with several manufacturing plants. The Cincinnati plant manufactures and distributes two household cleaning and polishing compounds, regular and heavy-duty, under the HouseSafe label. The forecasted operating results for the first six months of the year, when 100,000 cases of each compound are expected to be manufactured and sold, are presented in the following statement:

Chapter 5 Relevant Information for Decision Making

HouseSafe Compounds—Cincinnati Plant
Forecasted Results of Operations
For the Six-Month Period Ending June 30

(In $000s)

	Regular	Heavy-Duty	Total
Sales.	$ 2,000	$ 3,000	$ 5,000
Cost of sales.	(1,600)	(1,900)	(3,500)
Gross profit.	$ 400	$ 1,100	$ 1,500
Selling and administrative expenses			
Variable	$ 400	$ 700	$ 1,100
Fixed*	240	360	600
Total selling and administrative expenses	$ (640)	$(1,060)	$(1,700)
Income (loss) before taxes	$ (240)	$ 40	$ (200)

*The fixed selling and administrative expenses are allocated between the two products on the basis of dollar sales volume on the internal reports.

The sales price per case for the regular compound will be $20 and for the heavy-duty will be $30 during the first six months of the year. The manufacturing costs by case of product follow.

	Cost per Case	
	Regular	Heavy-Duty
Raw material.	$ 7.00	$ 8.00
Direct labor.	4.00	4.00
Variable manufacturing overhead.	1.00	2.00
Fixed manufacturing overhead*	4.00	5.00
Total manufacturing cost.	$16.00	$19.00
Variable selling and administrative costs	$ 4.00	$ 7.00

*Depreciation charges are 50 percent of the fixed manufacturing overhead of each line.

Each product is manufactured on a separate production line. Annual normal manufacturing capacity is 200,000 cases of each product. However, the plant is capable of producing 250,000 cases of regular compound and 350,000 cases of heavy-duty compound annually.

The following schedule reflects top management consensus regarding the price/volume alternatives for the HouseSafe products for the last six months of the year, which are essentially the same as those during its first six months.

Regular Compound		Heavy-Duty Compound	
Alternative Prices (per case)	Sales Volume (in cases)	Alternative Prices (per case)	Sales Volume (in cases)
$18	120,000	$25	175,000
20	100,000	27	140,000
21	90,000	30	100,000
22	80,000	32	55,000
23	50,000	35	35,000

Top management believes the expected loss for the first six months reflects a tight profit margin caused by intense competition and that many competitors will be forced out of this market by next year, so the company's profits should improve.

a. What unit selling price should Clean-N-Brite select for each HouseSafe compound for the remaining six months of the year? Support your answer with appropriate calculations.

b. Without prejudice to your answer for (a), assume that the optimum price/volume alternatives for the last six months will be a selling price of $23 and volume level of 50,000 cases for the

regular compound and a selling price of $35 and volume of 35,000 cases for the heavy-duty compound.
1. Should Clean-N-Brite consider closing its Cincinnati operations until next year to minimize its losses? Support your answer with appropriate calculations.
2. Identify and discuss the qualitative factors that should be considered in deciding whether the Cincinnati plant should be closed during the last six months of the year.

Review Solutions

Review 5-1

a. The cost is associated with the decision under consideration, the cost is important to the decision maker, and the cost has a connection to some future endeavor.
b. Cost of old equipment, $90,000
c. Nondifferential operating costs, $10,000
d. Cost of new equipment, $104,000; salvage value of old equipment $18,000; differential operating costs, $16,000 (= $26,000 − $10,000)
e. Salvage value of old equipment $18,000; differential operating costs, $16,000 (= $26,000 − $10,000)
f. $86,000 = Cost of new equipment, $104,000 minus salvage value of old equipment $18,000
g. Nonmonetary factors could include environmental factors such as energy usage, amount of waste produced in the production process; equipment reliability which impacts unplanned downtime due to excessive maintenance and repair, and equipment safety risk levels to employees.

Review 5-2

a.
Costs to make ($31,000 + [$2.10 × 28,000])	$89,800
Costs to buy ($2.80 × 28,000)	(78,400)
Advantage of purchasing	$11,400

b.
Costs to make ($31,000 + [$2.10 × 50,000])	$136,000
Costs to buy ($2.80 × 50,000)	(140,000)
Disadvantage of purchasing	$ (4,000)

c. 1. In the short-run, the average cost to produce a unit decreases as volume increases when a company incurs fixed costs. Thus, the average cost per unit decreases from $3.21 in part *a* to $2.72 in part *b*.

   Average cost at 28,000 unit level: $89,800/28,000 = $3.21

   Average cost at 50,000 unit level: $136,000/50,000 = $2.72

   At a level of 50,000 units, it becomes less expensive to manufacture the product. At higher production levels, the company spreads its fixed costs over more units causing the per unit cost to decrease.

   2. There are many qualitative factors that could impact the quantitative conclusions reached in parts *a* and *b* such as the following.
   - Does the company expect the number of units packaged per year to be steady or vary? If the requirements are expected to be on the lower end, it may make sense for the company to outsource. However, if the packaging needs are expected to increase, perhaps the company would decide to package internally instead.
   - Is the supplier reliable and expected to meet quality standards as well as proposed delivery schedules?
   - Does the supplier meet the company's minimum environmental standards?

Chapter 5 Relevant Information for Decision Making

Review 5-3

a.

	Racing	Touring	Basic
Contribution margin (CM)	$363	$493	$128
Labor hours*	39	27	8
CM per scarce resource	$9.31	$18.26	$16.00

*Labor hours: Racing = 39 ($1,365 ÷ 35); Touring = 27 ($945 ÷ 35); Basic = 8 ($280 ÷ 35)

	Racing	Touring	Basic
Units to manufacture	0	1,200	950**
Labor hours allocated	0	32,400*	7,600

*1,200 × 27 hours = 32,400 hours
**40,000 labor hours − 32,400 hours = 7,600 hours ÷ 8 = 950 units

b.
CM for touring bikes	$591,600	($493 × 1,200)
CM for basic bikes	121,600	($128 × 950)
Fixed costs	(450,000)	($360,000 + $90,000)
Income for income tax	$263,200	

c. If there is no limit to the number of bikes that can be sold, the company would choose to make all touring bikes based on a quantitative assessment. However, there are qualitative items to consider in a product mix decision.

- Is the touring bike the product with the most potential for future sales? What are recent consumer trends and expected consumer trends?
- Do potential customers want to see all three types of bikes before making up their mind on the bike that they want to purchase? If so, customers may opt for stores with a wider selection.
- Does the company maintain a loyal group of customers who would be expecting to replace their bike with a racing or basic style in the upcoming year? Could not having an adequate selection hurt the company's reputation?

Review 5-4

a.

	Manicures	Facials	Total
Revenue	$900,000	$672,000	$1,572,000
Labor cost	360,000	400,000	760,000
Material cost	105,000	64,000	169,000
Contribution margin	435,000	208,000	643,000
Fixed cost	125,000	90,000	215,000
Income before taxes	$310,000	$118,000	$428,000

b.

$$\frac{\text{Contribution margin}}{\text{Sales}} \quad \frac{435,000}{900,000} \quad \frac{208,000}{672,000}$$

	Manicures	Facials
CM percentage	48%	31%

Advertising should be spent on manicures because it has a higher CM percentage.

c.

	Manicures	Facials
Revenue per hour	$60	$84
Variable cost per hour	(31)	(58)
CM per hour	$29	$26

Advertising should be spent on manicures because manicures provide a higher contribution margin per hour.

d. More advertising dollars should not always be spent on the service that provides a higher contribution margin per service. Is there sufficient demand for the service that is being advertised such that the number of services at a higher unit contribution margin will take place as planned? Is the labor force flexible and able to perform the required services or is training necessary? Are there any unforeseen additional costs or bottlenecks with a shift in sales mix?

Review 5-5

a. The relevant cost is $1,590 per case ($600 + $430 + $560).

b.
Incremental revenue (5 × $2,100)	$10,500
Incremental costs (5 × $1,590)	(7,950)
Incremental profit	$ 2,550

c.
Incremental revenue (5 × $2,100)	$10,500
Incremental costs (5 × $1,590)	(7,950)
Lost contribution margin (5 × [$3,300 − $600 − $430 − $560])	(8,550)
Net loss	$ (6,000)

d. It is a risk that regular customers will discover a price cut in the marketplace; however, if the one-time job is isolated and does not recur, the chances are slight. If however, discovery forces Wayflaire to drop prices to retain customers, the impact could be a costly one:

5% × $3,300 × 100 cases = $16,500 drop in profits for a month (without considering profit from special order).

The one time special order profits of $2,550 are more than offset by the loss in one month. If the price cut remains for a year, the estimated loss in profits from current customers is $198,000.

Review 5-6

a. If the company dropped Division 1, the company's pretax profit would increase because the negative segment margin of $384,000 would be eliminated, calculated as follows (in $000s):

Segment gross margin	$1,380
Avoidable costs	(1,764)
Segment margin	$ (384)

b. If the company dropped Division 2, the company's pretax profit would decrease because the positive segment margin of $300,000 would be eliminated, calculated as follows (in $000s):

Segment gross margin	$1,200
Avoidable costs	(900)
Segment margin	$ 300

c. The analysis in parts *a* and *b* pertain to the short-term. In the long-term, most costs are avoidable. Through down-sizing for example, facilities can be sold and employees can be terminated through restructuring. In another example, less costly options for services such as payroll can be obtained through outsourcing instead of maintaining internal payroll departments. In the long-term, these changes would reduce the amount of costs allocated to the divisions.

Data Visualization Solutions

(See page 5-13.)

a. Highest CM per unit: Product A
   Lowest CM per unit: Product C
b. Highest CM per unit of labor time: Product D
   Lowest CM per unit of labor time: Product A
c. Product A
d. Product D
e. Why does Product A take considerably more labor resources than the other products? Is there anything that can be learned from the production of Product D that could be utilized in the production of the other products?
   What factors are causing the CM per unit to vary so widely?

Chapter 6
Job Order Costing

Road Map

LO	Learning Objective | Topics	Page	eLecture	Demo	Review	Assignments
6-1	**How do job order and process costing systems, as well as their related valuation methods, differ?** Job Order Costing :: Process Costing :: Actual Cost System :: Normal Cost System :: Standard Cost System :: Predetermined OH Rate	6-2	e6-1	D6-1	Rev 6-1	MC6-10, E6-16, E6-17, E6-18, E6-19, E6-20, E6-21, P6-68
6-2	**How is overhead applied under a normal costing system?** Predetermined OH Rate :: Applied Overhead :: Manufacturing Overhead Control :: Fixed and Variable OH Rates :: Plantwide and Department OH Rates :: Cost Cross-Subsidization	6-6	e6-2	D6-2A D6-2B	Rev 6-2	MC6-11, E6-22, E6-23, E6-24, E6-25, E6-26, E6-33, E6-35, E6-37, E6-38, E6-39, E6-40, E6-43, E6-45, P6-53, P6-54, P6-55, P6-56, P6-57, P6-58, P6-60, P6-62, P6-63, P6-65, P6-68, P6-73, P6-74
6-3	**What causes underapplied or overapplied overhead, and how is it treated at the end of a period?** Underapplied Overhead :: Overapplied Overhead :: Disposition at Period-End :: Materiality	6-10	e6-3	D6-3A D6-3B	Rev 6-3	MC6-12, E6-22, E6-23, E6-25, E6-27, E6-28, E6-29, E6-32, E6-43, E6-45, P6-56, P6-59, P6-60, P6-63, P6-65, P6-68, P6-69
6-4	**How are costs accumulated in a job order costing system?** Material Requisition Document :: Payroll Summaries :: Applied Overhead :: Job Cost Sheet :: Work in Process :: Finished Goods :: Cost of Goods Sold :: Cost-Plus Contract :: Competitive Bidding	6-12	e6-4	D6-4	Rev 6-4	MC6-13, E6-30, E6-31, E6-32, E6-33, E6-34, E6-35, E6-36, E6-37, E6-38, E6-39, E6-40, E6-41, E6-42, E6-44, P6-57, P6-58, P6-59, P6-60, P6-61, P6-62, P6-63, P6-64, P6-65, P6-66, P6-67, P6-68, P6-69
6-5	**How is job order costing illustrated in the service industry?** Service Organization :: Cost of Services Provided	6-18	e6-5	D6-5	Rev 6-5	MC6-10, E6-42, E6-43, E6-44, E6-47, P6-66
6-6	**How does information from a job order costing system support management decision making?** Job Profitability :: Comparison Across Jobs :: Customized Job :: Decision Making	6-22	e6-6	D6-6	Rev 6-6	MC6-14, E6-45, E6-46, E6-47, E6-48, P6-70, P6-71, P6-72. DA6-1, DA6-2
6-7	**How are losses treated in a job order costing system?** Defects :: Spoilage Rework Costs :: Normal Loss :: Abnormal Loss :: Defective Units :: Rework	6-24	e6-7	D6-7A D6-7B D6-7C	Rev 6-7	MC6-15, E6-49, E6-50, E6-51, E6-52, P6-73, P6-74

INTRODUCTION

Cost accumulation systems are used to assign production or performance costs to *products or services* for internal and external financial reporting purposes. Such systems range from very simple to very complex. Systems with greater complexity are more expensive to operate and maintain because they require substantially more input data. When specifying the details of a costing system, the cost of generating the information must be less than the benefits of that information to management.

The two principal product costing systems are *job order* and *process*. Firms that produce distinct batches or custom outputs must track product costs to the product or customer level with a job order costing system. In contrast, firms that produce homogeneous output in continuous production processes use process costing to compute an "average" product cost. This average cost can satisfy most reporting needs and track costs by production process. Because they require the input of more cost and operating data, job order costing systems are more expensive and elaborate than process costing systems.

The chapter begins by distinguishing between job order and process costing and by addressing the three methods of valuation that can be used within these systems (actual, normal, and standard). After a discussion of overhead application, accounting under a job order costing systems follows. The chapter concludes by addressing how spoilage and losses are treated in a job order system. Chapter 10 discusses the use of predetermined input standards in job order systems.

SYSTEMS AND METHODS OF PRODUCT COSTING

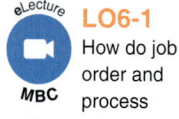

LO6-1 How do job order and process costing systems, as well as their related valuation methods, differ?

Before product costs can be computed, a determination must be made about the (1) cost accumulation system and (2) valuation method to be used. The cost accumulation system defines the cost object and method of assigning costs to production. The valuation method specifies how product costs are measured. Companies must have both a cost system and a valuation method; six possible combinations exist, as shown in **Exhibit 6.1**.[1]

Exhibit 6.1 ■ Costing Systems and Inventory Valuation

COST ACCUMULATION SYSTEMS	METHODS OF VALUATION		
	Actual	Normal	Standard
Job Order	Actual Direct Material Actual Direct Labor Actual Overhead (assigned to job at end of period)	Actual Direct Material Actual Direct Labor Overhead applied using predetermined rate(s) at completion of job or end of period	Standard Direct Material Standard Direct Labor Overhead applied using predetermined rate(s) when goods are completed or at end of period
Process	Actual Direct Material Actual Direct Labor Actual Overhead (assigned to job at end of period using FIFO or weighted average cost flow)	Actual Direct Material Actual Direct Labor Overhead applied using predetermined rate(s) (using FIFO or weighted average cost flow)	Standard Direct Material Standard Direct Labor Standard Overhead using predetermined rate(s) (will always be FIFO cost flow)

Cost Accumulation Systems

Regardless of the type of business, product costing is concerned with three things:

- cost identification,

---

[1] A third and fourth dimension (cost accumulation and cost presentation) are also necessary in this model. These dimensions relate to the use of absorption or variable costing and are covered in Chapter 11.

Chapter 6 Job Order Costing   6-3

- cost measurement, and
- product cost assignment.

Job order and process costing are the two primary cost accumulation systems.

Job Order Costing System	Process Costing System
Distinct batches of identical items or customized items	Large quantities of homogeneous items

Job Order Costing System

A **job order costing system** (covered in this chapter) is used by companies that make distinct batches of identical items or make products (perform unique services) that conform to specifications designated by the purchaser. Thus, job order costing is appropriate for

- a film and television producer
- a manufacturer producing custom shoes and boots,
- a screen printer making custom apparel,
- a publishing company producing educational textbooks,
- an accountant preparing tax returns,
- an architectural firm designing commercial buildings, and
- a research firm performing product development studies.

In these various settings, the word **job** is synonymous with client or customer, engagement, project, product, or contract.

Process Costing Systems

In contrast, **process costing systems** (covered in Chapter 7) are used by companies that make large quantities of homogeneous goods such as

- breakfast cereal,
- candy bars,
- detergent,
- gasoline, and
- bricks.

These products are produced in a continuous manufacturing environment, where production does not have a distinct start or finish. Given the mass manufacturing process, one unit of output cannot be readily identified with specific input costs within a given period—making the use of a cost-averaging approach necessary.

Identifying Cost Accumulation Systems   LO6-1   DEMO 6-1

♦ Which cost accumulation system, job order or process costing, would the following companies most likely follow?

1. **Stuller**, a fine jewelry manufacturer — Job order costing system
2. **Coca-Cola Company**, a beverage manufacturer — Process costing system
3. **Pfizer**, a bio-pharmaceutical company — Process costing system
4. **Paramount**, a film production company — Job order costing system
5. **A Perfect Event**, an event planning company — Job order costing system
6. **Nestlé**, manufacturer of yogurt and other food products — Process costing system

© Cambridge Business Publishers

Valuation Methods

As indicated in **Exhibit 6.1**, job order or process costing systems may be based on three alternative valuation methods: actual, normal, or standard.

Actual vs. Normal Cost Systems

In Chapter 2, we described how direct cost and indirect costs can be assigned to cost objects. The cost object relevant in job order and process costing systems is inventory. **Actual cost systems** assign the actual costs of direct material (DM), direct labor (DL), and overhead (OH) to Work in Process (WIP) Inventory. Service businesses that have few customers and/or low volume may use an actual cost system. However, many companies prefer to use a **normal cost system** that assigns actual direct material and direct labor to products but allocates overhead to products using a **predetermined OH rate**. The difference between the two systems relates to how overhead costs are assigned as noted in **Exhibit 6.1**. If the predetermined OH rate is substantially equivalent to what the actual OH rate would have been for an annual period, predetermined OH rates provide acceptable and useful costs.

The overhead allocation can occur in *real time* as products are manufactured or as services are delivered. Many accounting procedures are based on allocations. Cost allocations can be made across time periods or within a single time period. For example, in financial accounting, a building's cost is allocated through depreciation charges over its useful life. The useful life is the period that revenue (that the asset helped produce) is recognized. In cost accounting, manufacturing OH costs are allocated to products or services within a period using cost predictors or cost drivers. Such allocations reflect the cost principle requiring all production or acquisition costs to be attached to the units produced, services rendered, or units purchased.

Primary Reasons to Use a Normal Over an Actual Cost System

There are four primary reasons for using predetermined OH rates in product costing, which is the differentiating feature of a normal cost system.

- *Improves timeliness of information* First, predetermined OH rates facilitate overhead assignment during a period as goods are produced or sold and services are rendered. Thus, predetermined OH rates improve the timeliness of information. Managers do not want to wait until year end to determine which jobs are profitable and which ones are not.

- *Adjusts for cost variations unrelated to activity* Second, predetermined OH rates adjust for variations in actual overhead costs that are unrelated to fluctuations in activity. Overhead can vary monthly because of seasonal or calendar (days in a month) factors. For example, factory utility costs may be highest in summer because of the necessity to run air conditioning. If monthly production was constant at 3,000 units and actual overhead was assigned to production, the increase in utilities would cause product cost per unit to be higher in July than in March as illustrated in the following example.

	A	B	C
	Unit Cost Fluctuation Due to Seasonality		
1		March	July
2	Utility costs (assumed)	$ 1,200	$ 1,800
3	Divide by units produced	÷ 3,000	÷ 3,000
4	Utility cost per unit	$ 0.40	$ 0.60

- *Controls for cost fluctuations due to monthly changes in volume* Third, predetermined OH rates overcome the problem of fluctuations in activity levels that do not impact fixed overhead costs. Even if total manufacturing overhead costs were the same for each period, differences in activity levels between periods would cause a per-unit change in fixed overhead cost as illustrated in the schedule that follows. For this example, we assume 3,000 and 3,750 units produced in October and November, respectively.

Chapter 6 Job Order Costing

Unit Cost Fluctuation Due to Volume Differences

	A	B	C
1		October	November
2	Utility costs (assumed)	$ 600	$ 600
3	Divide by units	÷ 3,000	÷ 3,750
4	Utility cost per unit	$ 0.20	$ 0.16

Establishing a uniform annual predetermined OH rate for all units produced during the year overcomes the problems illustrated in this (and the prior) example.

- *Allows for product profitability analysis when combined with reasonable cost drivers* Finally, using predetermined OH rates—especially when the bases for those rates truly reflect overhead cost drivers—often allows managers to be more aware of individual product or product line profitability as well as the profitability of business with a particular customer or vendor. For instance, assume that a gift shop purchases a product from Vendor X for $20; the gift shop will sell that product to customers for $40. If the gift shop manager has determined that a reasonable OH rate per hour for vendor communication is $5 and that she often spends three hours on the phone with Vendor X because of customer complaints or shipping problems, the gift shop manager could decide that the $5 profit on the product [$40 selling price − ($20 product cost + $15 in overhead)] does not make it cost beneficial to continue working with Vendor X.

Standard Cost System

Companies using either job order or process costing may employ standards (or predetermined benchmarks) for costs to be incurred and/or quantities to be used. In a **standard cost system**, unit norms or standards are developed for direct material and direct labor quantities and/or costs. Overhead is applied to production using a predetermined rate that is considered the standard. These standards are used to plan for future activities and cost incurrence and to value inventories. Both actual and standard costs are recorded in the accounting records to provide an essential element of cost control—norms against which actual operating costs can be compared. A standard cost system allows companies to quickly recognize deviations or variances from expected production costs and to correct problems resulting from excess usage and/or costs. Actual cost systems do not provide this benefit, and normal cost systems cannot provide it in relation to material and labor. Although standards are most useful in environments characterized by repetitive manufacturing, standard costing can be used in some job order environments.

Because the use of predetermined OH rates is more common than the use of actual OH costs, this chapter addresses a job order, normal cost system and Chapter 10 describes job order using standard costs.[2]

REVIEW 6-1 — **LO6-1** — **Cost Accumulation System Choice**

1. For each of the following firm activities, determine whether the associated firm is more likely to use job order or process costing.
   - a. Provides tax services
   - b. Produces smart phones
   - c. Produces granola cereal
   - d. Produces commercial air jetliners
   - e. Manufactures custom inground pools
   - f. Manufactures bar soap
   - g. Is a hospital provider
   - h. Manufactures custom kitchen cabinetry
   - i. Manufactures dog food
   - j. Is a landscape contractor

2. **Critical Thinking:** Assume that the manufacturer of custom kitchen cabinetry is trying to decide between an actual and normal costing system. What factors would help the manufacturer make that determination?

More practice: MC6-10, E6-16, E6-17
Solution on p. 6-56.

---

[2] Although actual OH may be assigned to jobs, such an approach would be less customary because total overhead would not be known until the period ended, causing an unwarranted delay in overhead assignment. Activity-based costing (discussed in Chapter 8) can increase the validity of tracing OH costs to specific products or jobs.

APPLYING OVERHEAD IN A NORMAL COSTING SYSTEM

LO6-2 How is overhead applied under a normal costing system?

With one exception, normal cost system journal entries are identical to those made in an actual cost system. In both systems, overhead is debited during the period to a Manufacturing Overhead Control account and credited to the various accounts that "created" the overhead costs. In an actual cost system, the total amount of actual overhead cost is then transferred from the overhead account to Work in Process (WIP) Inventory. In contrast, a normal cost system assigns overhead cost to WIP Inventory using a predetermined OH rate.

Calculating Predetermined OH Rate

To calculate a predetermined OH rate, total budgeted overhead cost at a specific activity level is divided by the related budgeted activity level.

$$\text{Predetermined OH Rate} = \frac{\text{Total budgeted OH cost at a specified activity level}}{\text{Budgeted volume of specified activity level}}$$

Overhead cost and its related activity measure are typically budgeted for one year, although a longer or shorter period could be more appropriate in some organizations' production cycles. For example, a longer period is more appropriate in a company that constructs ships, bridges, or high-rise office buildings.

Companies should use an activity base that is logically related to actual overhead cost incurrence. Although production volume might be the first activity base considered, this base is reasonable only if the company manufactures one type of product or renders just one type of service. If a company makes multiple products or performs multiple services, production or service volumes cannot be summed to determine "activity volume" because the products and services are dissimilar.

A company that builds high-rise office buildings will likely budget overhead cost for a period longer than one year.

To effectively allocate overhead to heterogeneous products or services, a measure of activity that is common to all output must be selected. In Chapter 2, we described how a cost driver must have a cause-and-effect relationship to a cost for it to "drive" that cost. Direct labor hours and direct labor dollars are common activity measures; however, these bases could be inappropriate if a company is highly automated. Using any direct labor measure to allocate overhead costs in automated plants results in extremely high overhead rates because the costs are applied over a relatively small activity volume. In automated plants, machine hours could be a more appropriate base for allocating overhead. Other possible measures which we previously defined as *cost drivers* include the

- number of purchase orders,
- product-related physical characteristics such as tons or gallons,
- number of, or amount of time used performing, machine setups,
- number of parts,
- material handling time,
- product complexity, and
- number of product defects.

Applying Overhead to Production

Once calculated, the predetermined OH rate is used throughout the period to apply overhead to WIP Inventory. Applied overhead is calculated as the predetermined OH rate multiplied by the actual activity volume. Thus, **applied overhead** is the dollar amount of overhead assigned to WIP Inventory using the activity measure that was selected to develop the OH rate. Overhead can be applied when goods or services are transferred out of WIP Inventory or at the end of each month if financial statements are to be prepared. Or, under real-time systems, overhead can be applied continuously as production occurs.

$$\text{Applied overhead} = \text{Predetermined OH rate} \times \text{Actual activity volume}$$

Chapter 6 Job Order Costing

For convenience, both actual and applied overhead are recorded in a single general ledger account.[3] Debits to the account represent *actual* overhead costs, and credits represent *applied* overhead. Variable and fixed overhead may be recorded either in a single account or in separate accounts, although separate accounts provide better information to managers. **Exhibit 6.2** presents the alternative overhead recording possibilities.

Exhibit 6.2 ■ Cost Accounting System Possibilities for Manufacturing Overhead

Single overhead account for variable and fixed overhead:

Manufacturing Overhead Control

Total actual OH incurred	Total OH applied

Separate overhead accounts for variable and fixed overhead:

Manufacturing Variable Overhead (VOH) Control

Total actual VOH incurred	Total VOH applied

Manufacturing Fixed Overhead (FOH) Control

Total actual FOH incurred	Total FOH applied

Using Separate Variable and Fixed Predetermined OH Rates

If variable and fixed overhead are applied using separate rates, the general ledger will have separate variable and fixed OH accounts. Because overhead represents an ever-larger part of product cost in automated factories, the benefits of separating OH according to its variable or fixed behavior are generally thought to be greater than the time and effort needed to make that separation. (Separation of mixed costs into variable and fixed components was discussed in Chapter 3.)

Regardless of the number of predetermined OH rates used, actual overhead is debited to the general ledger overhead account and credited to the source of the overhead cost. Overhead is applied to WIP Inventory as production occurs, and as measured by the activity identified in the denominator in the predetermined OH rate formula. Applied overhead is debited to WIP Inventory and credited to the overhead general ledger account.

Applying Overhead Separately for Fixed and Variable Costs   LO6-2   DEMO 6-2A

Assume that Tri-State Industrial, a manufacturer of children's car seats, budgeted and then experienced the following amounts in the current year.

Tri-State Industrial—Budgeted and Actual Data

	A	B	C
1		Variable Overhead	Fixed Overhead
2	Budgeted annual overhead amount	$375,000	$630,000
3	Actual January overhead amount	$ 31,385	$ 55,970

The company budgeted 50,000 total machine hours for the year and incurred 4,300 actual machine hours in the month of January. Assume that both variable and fixed overhead costs are applied based on machine hours.

◆ **How does the company record entries for actual and applied overhead, recording variable and fixed costs separately?**

The journal entry to record actual overhead for this example follows.

---

[3] Some companies may use separate overhead accounts for actual and applied overhead. In such cases, the actual overhead account has a debit balance and the applied overhead account has a credit balance. The applied overhead account is closed at the end of the year against the actual overhead account to determine the amount of underapplied or overapplied overhead.

	Variable Manufacturing Overhead Control.................	31,385	
	Fixed Manufacturing Overhead Control...................	55,970	
	Various accounts...................................		87,355
	To record actual manufacturing overhead		

Applied overhead for January is calculated as follows.

	Tri-State Industrial—Applied Overhead		
	A	B	C
1		Variable Overhead	Fixed Overhead
2	Budgeted annual overhead amount	$375,000	$630,000
3	Budgeted annual machine hours	÷ 50,000	÷ 50,000
4	Predetermined overhead rate	$ 7.50	$ 12.60
5	Actual January machine hours	× 4,300	× 4,300
6	Applied January overhead	$ 32,250	$ 54,180

The journal entry to record applied overhead for this example follows.

	Work in Process Inventory...............................	86,430	
	Variable Manufacturing Overhead Control..............		32,250
	Fixed Manufacturing Overhead Control................		54,180
	To apply variable and fixed manufacturing overhead to WIP		

Using Plantwide or Departmental Predetermined OH Rates

A **plantwide overhead allocation method** is often used in situations where companies produce only one product in a plant, or where multiple products are very similar in regard to the cost of and use of resources, such as machine or labor hours, that drive most of the overhead costs.

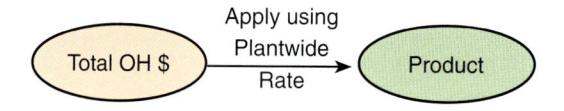

A **department overhead allocation method** will produce a more accurate allocation of overhead costs to the various products, if multiple products are produced that consume varying levels of activities in multiple production departments.

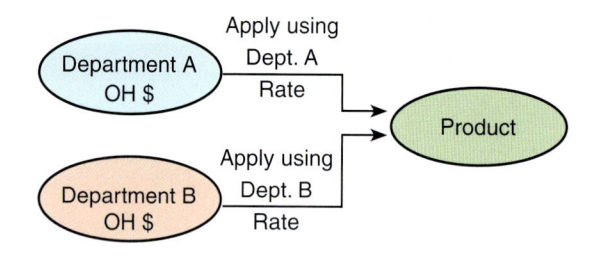

DEMO 6-2B LO6-2 Calculating Plantwide and Departmental Predetermined OH Rates

◆ If we assume that Tri-State Industrial has $1,005,000 in budgeted annual plantwide overhead and budgets 100,000 plantwide machine hours for the year, what is its plantwide predetermined overhead rate using machine hours as the cost driver?

The company's plantwide predetermined overhead rate is $10.05, calculated as follows.

Chapter 6 Job Order Costing

Plantwide Predetermined Overhead Rate

	A	B
1	Budgeted annual plantwide overhead	$1,005,000
2	Budgeted annual plantwide machine hours	÷ 100,000
3	Plantwide overhead rate per machine hour	$ 10.05

◆ **Continuing with the Tri-State example, how are department overhead rates calculated, assuming that the company has two departments?**

If we assume that Tri-State Industrial has two production departments, it is necessary first to assign the $1,005,000 of total overhead costs for the plant to the two production departments. Some of the plantwide costs will be directly assignable to the departments, while other costs must be allocated to the production departments. Assume that after these allocations, the total costs assigned to the departments were $255,000 for Department A and $750,000 for Department B for the year.

The next step in the product costing process is to assign the department costs to the products. For this example, assume that the manufacturing process in Department A is labor intensive, while the process in Department B is fully automated. Department overhead rates are calculated as follows assuming the department overhead costs and cost drivers provided.

Departmental Overhead Rates

	A	B	C
1		Department A	Department B
2	Budgeted annual department overhead cost	$255,000	$750,000
3	Budgeted annual direct labor hours	÷ 20,000	
4	Budgeted annual machine hours		÷ 75,000
5	Department predetermined overhead rates	$ 12.75	$ 10.00
6		Per direct labor hour	Per machine hour

In most multiproduct manufacturing environments, the department overhead allocation approach represents a cost system improvement over using a single, plantwide overhead rate. Department rates reduce the likelihood of **cost cross-subsidization**, which occurs when one product is assigned too much cost as a result of another being assigned too little cost.

In the next section, we discuss how to reconcile the difference between actual and applied overhead at period-end.

Plantwide vs. Department OH Rates   **LO6-2**   **REVIEW 6-2**

Blair Manufacturing Co. has gathered the following information to develop predetermined OH rates for the year. The company produces a wide variety of houseware products that are processed through two departments, Assembly (automated) and Finishing (labor intensive).

- Budgeted total overhead: $275,000 in Assembly and $458,000 in Finishing
- Budgeted total direct labor hours: 18,000 in Assembly and 30,000 in Finishing
- Budgeted total machine hours: 96,000 in Assembly and 9,000 in Finishing

Answer the following questions, rounding all answers to two decimal places.

a. Compute a plantwide predetermined OH rate using direct labor hours.
b. Compute a plantwide predetermined OH rate using machine hours.
c. Compute departmental predetermined OH rates using machine hours for Assembly and direct labor hours for Finishing.
d. Determine the amount of overhead that would be allocated to a product that required ten machine hours in Assembly and two direct labor hours in Finishing using the answers developed in (a), (b), and (c). Assume that the product required no labor hours in Assembly and no machine hours in Finishing.
e. **Critical Thinking:** How might some of the answers in part d, result in cost cross-subsidization?

More practice: MC6-11, E6-26
Solution on p. 6-56.

UNDERAPPLIED OR OVERAPPLIED OVERHEAD

LO6-3 What causes underapplied or overapplied overhead, and how is it treated at the end of a period?

At period-end, total actual overhead will differ from total applied overhead. The difference is called underapplied or overapplied overhead. **Underapplied overhead** occurs when the OH applied to WIP Inventory is less than the actual OH cost. **Overapplied overhead** occurs when the OH applied to WIP Inventory is more than actual OH cost. Underapplied or overapplied overhead must be closed at year-end because the overhead control account is temporary.

Causes of Underapplied or Overapplied Overhead

Under- or overapplication of overhead is caused by two factors that can work independently or jointly. These two factors are *cost differences* and *capacity utilization differences*. For example, if actual fixed overhead (FOH) cost differs from expected FOH cost, a fixed manufacturing overhead spending variance is created. If actual capacity utilization differs from expected utilization (i.e. actual activity level differs from budgeted activity level), a volume variance arises.[4] The independent effects of these differences (or for similar differences related to variable OH) are as follows.

Actual FOH Cost > Expected FOH Cost = Underapplied FOH
Actual FOH Cost < Expected FOH Cost = Overapplied FOH
Actual Utilization > Expected Utilization = Overapplied FOH
Actual Utilization < Expected Utilization = Underapplied FOH

In most cases, however, *both* cost and capacity utilization differ from estimates. When this occurs, no generalizations can be made as to whether overhead will be underapplied or overapplied.

Disposition of Underapplied and Overapplied Overhead

Overhead control accounts are temporary accounts and are closed at period-end. Closing the accounts requires disposition of the underapplied or overapplied OH. Disposition depends on the materiality of the amount involved. If the amount is immaterial, it is closed to Cost of Goods Sold (CGS). If the amount of applied OH differs materially from actual overhead costs, it should be prorated among the Inventory accounts and Cost of Goods Sold. Allocation in this case is more appropriate because OH costs are included in Inventory accounts and Cost of Goods Sold, so all accounts should reflect the adjustment.

Determining whether an amount is material requires *management judgment* because materiality level is specific to a company. There is no pre-established or universal threshold for **materiality**. Ultimately, an item is considered material if there is a substantial likelihood that a reasonable person would consider it material or important.

Immaterial Amount of Over/Under Applied Overhead

If the amount of underapplied or overapplied overhead is immaterial, the difference simply adjusts the Cost of Goods Sold balance. With underapplied (overapplied) overhead, not enough (too much) overhead was charged to jobs that eventually were sold, so we now need to make up the difference by charging (decreasing) the amount of underapplied (overapplied) overhead to (in) CGS. As shown in **Exhibit 6.3**, when overhead is underapplied (debit balance), an insufficient amount of OH was applied to production and the closing process causes Cost of Goods Sold to increase. Alternatively, overapplied overhead (credit balance) reflects the fact that too much OH was applied to production, so closing overapplied OH causes Cost of Goods Sold to decrease.

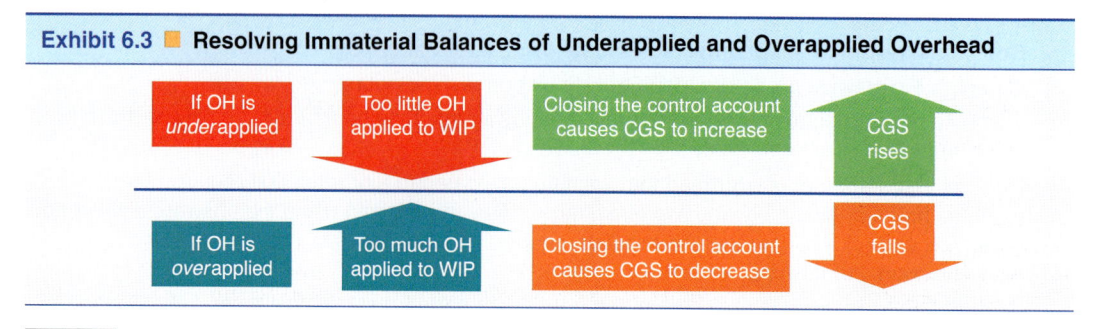

Exhibit 6.3 ■ Resolving Immaterial Balances of Underapplied and Overapplied Overhead

| If OH is *under*applied | Too little OH applied to WIP | Closing the control account causes CGS to increase | CGS rises |
| If OH is *over*applied | Too much OH applied to WIP | Closing the control account causes CGS to decrease | CGS falls |

---
[4] These variances are covered in depth in Chapter 10.

Chapter 6 Job Order Costing

Reconciling Immaterial Over/Under Applied OH at Period-End — LO6-3 DEMO 6-3A

To illustrate the closing process of overhead account balances, first assume that Tri-State Industrial determines separate variable and fixed overhead rates as follows.

	Variable Overhead	Fixed Overhead
Budgeted overhead amount	$375,000	$630,000
Budgeted machine hours	÷ 50,000	÷ 50,000
Predetermined overhead rate	$ 7.50	$ 12.60

Assume that Tri-State Industrial incurred and applied overhead as follows when 51,500 machine hours were incurred for the year.

	Variable Overhead	Fixed Overhead
Actual (given)	$383,000	$657,000
Applied		
Variable ($7.50 × 51,500)	386,250	
Fixed ($12.60 × 51,500)		648,900
Over- (under-) applied amount	$ 3,250	$ (8,100)

Variable OH Control: 383,000 | 386,250 ; 3,250
Fixed OH Control: 657,000 | 648,900 ; 8,100

◆ **What are the journal entries required to close out over- or underapplied variable and fixed overhead, assuming amounts are considered immaterial?**

The journal entries to close these amounts are as follows.

Variable Manufacturing Overhead Control	3,250	
Cost of Goods Sold		3,250
To close overapplied VOH		
Cost of Goods Sold	8,100	
Fixed Manufacturing Overhead Control		8,100
To close underapplied FOH		

Variable OH Control: 383,000 | 386,250 ; 3,250 ; 0
Cost of Goods Sold: | 3,250
Fixed OH Control: 657,000 | 648,900 ; 8,100 ; 0
Cost of Goods Sold: 8,100 | 3,250

Material Amount of Over/Under Applied Overhead

If the amount of overapplied or underapplied OH is material (significant), it should be prorated among the accounts in which applied OH resides: Work in Process Inventory, Finished Goods Inventory, and Cost of Goods Sold. Some of the overapplied overhead was charged to WIP and FG and still is part of its balance. (Or in the case of underapplied overhead, too little was charged.) Note that because overhead never gets charged to raw materials, no adjustment is made to raw materials. Proration of the underapplied or overapplied overhead makes the account balances conform more closely to actual cost as required by generally accepted accounting principles (GAAP) for external reporting.

Reconciling Material Over/Under Applied OH at Period-End — LO6-3 DEMO 6-3B

The following assumed data for Tri-State Industrial is used to illustrate proration of a material amount of overapplied fixed overhead based on year-end account balances for inventories and cost of goods sold.[5]

Fixed Manufacturing Overhead Control		Account Balances	
Actual FOH	$220,000	Work in Process Inventory	$ 45,640
Applied FOH	260,000	Finished Goods Inventory	78,240
Overapplied FOH	$ 40,000	Cost of Goods Sold	528,120

Fixed OH Control: 220,000 | 260,000 ; | 40,000
Work in Process: 45,640 |
Finished Goods: 78,240 |
Cost of Goods Sold: 528,120 |

---

[5] Theoretically, underapplied or overapplied OH should be allocated based on the amounts of applied OH contained in each account rather than on total account balances. Use of total account balances could cause distortion because they contain direct material and direct labor costs that are not related to actual or applied OH. In spite of this potential distortion, use of total balances is more common in practice for two reasons. First, the theoretical method is complex and requires detailed account analysis. Second, overhead tends to lose its identity after leaving Work in Process Inventory, thus making the determination of the amount of overhead in Finished Goods Inventory and Cost of Goods Sold account balances more difficult.

© Cambridge Business Publishers

◆ **What is the journal entry to close out overapplied fixed overhead assuming the amount is considered material?**

STEP 1: Add balances of accounts and determine proportional relationships.

Balance			Proportion		Percentage
Work in Process	$ 45,640		$45,640 ÷ $652,000		7
Finished Goods	78,240		$78,240 ÷ $652,000		12
Cost of Goods Sold*	528,120		$528,120 ÷ $652,000		81
Total	$652,000				100

*The account with the largest balance (CGS) will have the highest proportion, resulting in the largest adjustment.

STEP 2: Multiply percentages by the overapplied overhead amount to determine the adjustment amount.

Account	%	×	Overapplied FOH	=	Adjustment Amount
Work in Process	7	×	$40,000	=	$ 2,800
Finished Goods	12	×	$40,000	=	$ 4,800
Cost of Goods Sold	81	×	$40,000	=	$32,400

STEP 3: Prepare the journal entry to close manufacturing overhead account and assign adjustment amount to appropriate accounts.

Fixed OH Control		Work in Process	
220,000	260,000	45,640	2,800
40,000			
0		42,840	

Finished Goods		Cost of Goods Sold	
78,240	4,800	528,120	32,400
73,440		495,720	

Fixed Manufacturing Overhead Control	40,000	
Work in Process Inventory		2,800
Finished Goods Inventory		4,800
Cost of Goods Sold		32,400
To close overapplied fixed overhead		

After the journal entry above, Fixed OH Control has a zero balance and the Inventory and Cost of Goods Sold accounts are reduced because OH was overapplied. If instead, the OH had been *underapplied*, the accounts debited and credited in the journal entry would be reversed. This would result in an increase to the Inventory and Cost of Goods Sold accounts.

REVIEW 6-3 — LO6-3 — Underapplied or Overapplied Overhead

At the end of the year, Siri Company's accounts showed a $50,000 debit balance in Manufacturing Overhead Control. In addition, the company had the following account balances:

Work in Process Inventory	$ 200,000
Finished Goods Inventory	800,000
Cost of Goods Sold	3,000,000

a. Prepare the necessary journal entry to close the overhead account if the balance is considered immaterial.
b. Prepare the necessary journal entry to close the overhead account if the balance is considered material.
c. **Critical Thinking:** Is it possible for one company to consider an overapplied balance of $50,000 material while another company to consider that same balance to be immaterial? Why or why not?

More practice: MC6-12, E6-25, E6-27, E6-29
Solution on p. 6-57.

JOB ORDER COSTING SYSTEM

LO6-4 How are costs accumulated in a job order costing system?

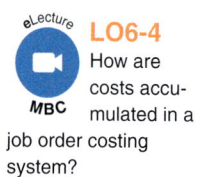

In a job order costing system, costs are accumulated by job, which is a single unit or multiple similar or dissimilar units that has or have been produced to distinct customer specifications.[6] If multiple outputs are produced, a per-unit cost can be computed only if the units are similar or if costs are accumulated

---
[6] To eliminate the need for repetition, the term units should be read to mean either products or services because job order costing is applicable to both manufacturing and service companies. For the same reason, the term produced can mean manufactured or performed.

Chapter 6 Job Order Costing

for each separate unit (such as through an identification number). Each job is treated as a unique cost entity or cost object. Because of the uniqueness of the jobs, costs of different jobs are maintained in separate subsidiary ledger accounts.

Let's assume that Motivating Building Solutions (MBS) builds portable buildings to clients' specifications. In its first month of operations (March), it obtained contracts on March 1 for three buildings: Job #1, Job #2, and Job #3.

- Job #1 to start March 1:   20- by 40-foot storage building
- Job #2 to start March 5:   35- by 35-foot commercial utility building
- Job #3 to start March 11: 30- by 40-foot portable classroom

Each distinct building represents a job. The company maintains three separate subsidiary ledger accounts which will accumulate the direct material, direct labor, and overhead costs for each job. The ending balance in the subsidiary accounts for all incomplete jobs will total the combined amount in the general ledger, in an account called Work in Process Inventory Control. During the month, assuming that all three jobs are in process, the total in the subsidiary ledgers for Jobs #1, #2, and #3 will equal the balance in Work in Process Inventory Control as illustrated below.

SUBSIDIARY LEDGERS			GENERAL LEDGER
Job #1	Job #2	Job #3	Work in Process Inventory Control
#	#	#	#

The source document that provides virtually all financial information about a particular job is the **job order cost sheet**. The set of job order cost sheets for all incomplete jobs composes the WIP Inventory subsidiary ledger. This means that Jobs #1, #2, and #3 *will each have an associated job order cost sheet that provides the details that support the subtotals in the subsidiary ledgers*. A job order cost sheet includes a job number, job description, customer identification, scheduling information, delivery instructions, and contract price as well as details regarding actual costs for direct material, direct labor, and applied overhead. After a job is completed, the job order cost sheet will contain the total and per-unit cost of the job. The per-unit cost can be helpful for planning and control purposes as well as for bidding on future contracts. If a job was exceptionally profitable, management might decide to pursue additional similar jobs. If a job was unprofitable, the job order cost sheet may indicate areas in which cost control was lax. Job order cost sheets provide information important to managing profitability and setting prices.

The job order cost sheet also might include *budgeted cost information*, especially if such information is used to estimate the job's selling price or to support a bid price. Custom manufacturers typically price their goods using two methods. A **cost-plus contract** allows producers to cover all direct costs and some indirect costs and to generate an acceptable profit margin. In other cases, producers may use a **competitive bidding** technique. In such instances, the company must accurately estimate the costs of making the unique products associated with each contract. Otherwise, the company can incur significant losses when actual costs exceed costs estimated during the bidding process. In bid pricing, budgeted and actual costs should be compared at the end of a job to determine any deviations from estimates. Budget-to-actual comparisons are also generally useful for planning and control purposes.

Illustrating a Job Order Cost System for a Manufacturer   LO6-4   DEMO 6-4

The logic of separating costs for individual jobs is illustrated as we continue with the example of MBS. This example will move through the three stages of production: contracted for but not yet started, in process, and completed. MBS has two departments: Parts Fabrication and Assembly.

- The Parts Fabrication Department designs and cuts the major components of the building and is highly automated.
- The Assembly Department assembles and installs the components and this department is highly labor intensive.

© Cambridge Business Publishers

The Assembly Department begins work on the buildings as soon as the floor components are available from the Parts Fabrication Department.

MBS bills its customers on a cost-plus basis, with profit set equal to 25 percent of costs. The firm uses a job order costing system based on normal costs.

♦ **For each of the following significant transactions that occurred in March, what is the journal entry required and T-account presentation?**

1. Purchase of Raw Materials

On March 1, direct material was purchased for $80,000 on account by the purchasing agent.

The Raw Material Inventory account may include the costs of both direct and indirect materials. The purchase entry is recorded as follows.

Raw Material Inventory	Accounts Payable
80,000	80,000

Raw Material Inventory............................ 80,000
    Accounts Payable............................ 80,000
    To record purchase of direct material

2. Requisition of Raw Materials

Direct material was issued to the Parts Fabrication Department and Assembly Department for use in the three jobs as follows.

Job	Parts Fabrication Department	Requisition No.	Assembly Department	Requisition No.
Job #1...	$ 8,000 on March 1	001-1	$ 500 on March 8	001-2
Job #2...	14,000 on March 5	002-1	1,200 on March 12	002-2
Job #3...	45,000 on March 11	003-1	6,600 on March 19	003-2

To begin a job, a **material requisition document** is initiated so material can be released from inventory, or purchased, and sent to the production area. This source document (likely in electronic form) indicates the types and quantities of material to be issued to production or used to perform a service job. This process makes it fairly easy to identify and associate direct materials with particular jobs. The material requisition document verifies material flow from the warehouse to the requisitioning department. Responsibility for material cost can be traced to users because the employees who authorize and issue or receive the materials are listed. Summary entries for March for the requisition of materials are as follows.

WIP Inventory—Parts Fabrication		Raw Material Inventory	
Job #1 8,000		80,000	67,000
Job #2 14,000			
Job #3 45,000			

WIP Inventory—Parts Fabrication (Job #1)............ 8,000
WIP Inventory—Parts Fabrication (Job #2)............ 14,000
WIP Inventory—Parts Fabrication (Job #3)............ 45,000
    Raw Material Inventory............................ 67,000
    To record requisition and issuance of direct material to Parts Fabrication Department

WIP Inventory—Assembly		Raw Material Inventory	
Job #1 500		80,000	67,000
Job #2 1,200			8,300
Job #3 6,600			

WIP Inventory—Assembly (Job #1)................. 500
WIP Inventory—Assembly (Job #2)................. 1,200
WIP Inventory—Assembly (Job #3)................. 6,600
    Raw Material Inventory............................ 8,300
    To record requisition and issuance of direct material to Assembly Department

When the first direct material associated with a job is issued to production, that job enters the second stage of its production cycle: *work in process*. At this point, cost information begins to be accumulated on the job order cost sheet. Direct labor is the second element of the production process.

3. Recording of Direct Labor

Payroll summaries indicated that the following direct labor costs were incurred in the month of March.

Chapter 6 Job Order Costing

Job	Parts Fabrication Department	Assembly Department
Job #1	$1,000	$2,400
Job #2	3,000	3,500
Job #3	5,000	9,500

Because factory employee hours are typically tracked by job number, labor costs can fairly easily be accumulated by job and department. For example, employees may swipe their employee ID cards and job cards through an electronic scanner when switching from one job to another. Summary entries for March for direct labor are as follows.

WIP Inventory—Parts Fabrication (Job #1)	1,000	
WIP Inventory—Parts Fabrication (Job #2)	3,000	
WIP Inventory—Parts Fabrication (Job #3)	5,000	
Wages Payable		9,000
To record direct labor cost for Parts Fabrication Department		

WIP Inventory—Parts Fabrication:
Job #1 8,000
Job #2 14,000
Job #3 45,000
Job #1 1,000
Job #2 3,000
Job #3 5,000

Wages Payable: 9,000

WIP Inventory—Assembly (Job #1)	2,400	
WIP Inventory—Assembly (Job #2)	3,500	
WIP Inventory—Assembly (Job #3)	9,500	
Wages Payable		15,400
To record direct labor cost for Assembly Department		

WIP Inventory—Assembly:
Job #1 500
Job #2 1,200
Job #3 6,600
Job #1 2,400
Job #2 3,500
Job #3 9,500

Wages Payable: 9,000; 15,400

4. Recording of Actual Overhead Costs

The following indirect costs were incurred in each department.

Job	Parts Fabrication Department	Assembly Department	Total
Materials	$ 800	$ 300	$ 1,100
Labor	4,200	4,500	8,700
Utilities/Fuel	5,900	2,300	8,200
Depreciation	9,500	3,300	12,800
Total	$20,400	$10,400	$30,800

Actual overhead incurred during production is debited to the Manufacturing Overhead control account. A summary entry for March for indirect costs is as follows.

Manufacturing Overhead Control—Parts Fabrication	20,400	
Manufacturing Overhead Control—Assembly	10,400	
Raw Material Inventory		1,100
Wages Payable		8,700
Utilities/Fuel Payable		8,200
Accumulated Depreciation		12,800
To record various overhead costs		

OH Control—Parts Fabrication: 20,400
OH Control—Assembly: 10,400

Raw Material Inventory: 80,000 | 67,000; 8,300; 1,100
Wages Payable: 9,000; 15,400; 8,700
Utilities/Fuel Payable: 8,200
Accumulated Depreciation: 12,800

5. Recording of Applied Overhead

Overhead is applied in Parts Fabrication at a predetermined rate of $100 per machine hour (MH). In the Assembly Department, overhead is applied at a predetermined rate of $10 per direct labor hour (DLH). The following information on actual machine and labor hours is provided for March.

	Parts Fabrication Department Machine Hours	Assembly Department Labor Hours
Job #1	20	40
Job #2	35	110
Job #3	145	800
	200	950

Overhead costs are usually not traceable to specific jobs as discussed earlier in this chapter. Instead, overhead costs must be applied to production using a predetermined OH rate multiplied by the actual measure of the activity that was recorded for each job during the period. If a job is completed within a period, OH is applied at completion of production so that a full product cost can be transferred to Finished Goods Inventory. If, however, a job is not complete at the end of a period, overhead must be applied at that time so that WIP Inventory on the period-end balance sheet contains costs for all three product elements (DM, DL, and OH). Applied overhead per job for MBS is calculated as follows.

Job	Parts Fabrication Department Applied OH	Assembly Department Applied OH
Job #1	20 MHs × $100 = $ 2,000	40 DLHs × $10 = $ 400
Job #2	35 MHs × $100 = $ 3,500	110 DLHs × $10 = $1,100
Job #3	145 MHs × $100 = $14,500	800 DLHs × $10 = $8,000

Summary entries for March for applied overhead are as follows.

WIP Inventory—Parts Fabrication (Job #1)	2,000	
WIP Inventory—Parts Fabrication (Job #2)	3,500	
WIP Inventory—Parts Fabrication (Job #3)	14,500	
Manufacturing Overhead Control—Parts Fabrication		20,000
To apply overhead in Parts Fabrication Department		
WIP Inventory—Assembly (Job #1)	400	
WIP Inventory—Assembly (Job #2)	1,100	
WIP Inventory—Assembly (Job #3)	8,000	
Manufacturing Overhead Control—Assembly		9,500
To apply overhead in Assembly Department		

6. Recording Job Completion

Job #1 was completed on March 31, while Jobs #2 and #3 were only partially complete.

When a job is completed, its total cost is removed from Work in Process Inventory and transferred to Finished Goods Inventory. Job order cost sheets for completed jobs are removed from the WIP Inventory subsidiary ledger and become the subsidiary ledger for the Finished Goods Inventory control account. The following entry is recorded for the completion of Job #1.

Finished Goods Inventory	14,300	
WIP Inventory—Parts Fabrication ($8,000 + 1,000 + 2,000)		11,000
WIP Inventory—Assembly ($500 + $2,400 + $400)		3,300
To record completion of Job #1		

7. Recording Sale of Job

Job #1 was sold for cash in the amount of the cost-plus contract, calculated as $14,300 × 1.25 = $17,875.

When a job is sold, its cost is transferred from Finished Goods Inventory to Cost of Goods Sold. The job cost sheet then becomes a subsidiary record for Cost of Goods Sold.

Cash	17,875	
Sales Revenue		17,875
To record sale of Job #1		

Cost of Goods Sold	14,300	
Finished Goods Inventory		14,300
To record CGS for Job #1		

Chapter 6 Job Order Costing

8. Reconciling Overhead Accounts

For MBS, any underapplied or overapplied overhead at month-end is considered immaterial and is assigned to Cost of Goods Sold.

The difference between actual and applied overhead is calculated as follows.

	Fabrication Department	Assembly Department
Actual OH	$20,400	$10,400
Applied OH	20,000	9,500
Over- (under-)applied amount	$ (400)	$ (900)

The amount of underapplied overhead of $1,300 ($400 + $900) is assigned to Cost of Goods Sold through the following entry.

Cost of Goods Sold	1,300	
Manufacturing Overhead Control—Parts Fabrication		400
Manufacturing Overhead Control—Assembly		900
To assign underapplied overhead to CGS		

```
         CGS
    14,300 |
     1,300 |

OH Control—Parts Fabrication     OH Control—Assembly
    20,400 | 20,000                 10,400 | 9,500
           |    400                        |   900
           |      0                        |     0
```

Presentation of Job Cost Sheets

◆ **What is the impact on the job cost sheets of the March transactions?**

Job cost sheets at the end of the period show costs of $14,300, $26,300, and $88,600 for Jobs #1, #2, and #3, respectively. The budgeted cost of each of the jobs is listed and can be compared to actual costs at the completion of the job for performance evaluation.

Job Order No.: 1
- Job Description: 20- by 40-foot storage building
- Contract Agreement Date: March 1
- Actual Start Date: March 1
- Actual Completion Date: March 31
- Contract Price: Cost + 25%

DIRECT MATERIALS

Date Received	Department	Requisition No.	Amount
March 01	Fabrication	001-1	$ 8,000
March 08	Assembly	001-2	500
			$ 8,500

DIRECT LABOR

Date	Department	Source	Amount
March #	Fabrication	Payroll	$ 1,000
March #	Assembly	Payroll	2,400
			$ 3,400

OVERHEAD

Date	Department	Source	Amount
March #	Fabrication	Machine meters	$ 2,000
March #	Assembly	Payroll	400
			$ 2,400

TOTAL COST IN FABRICATION	$11,000
TOTAL COST IN ASSEMBLY	3,300
TOTAL MANUFACTURING COST OF JOB	$14,300
TOTAL BUDGETED COST OF JOB	$14,000

Job Order No.: 2
- Job Description: 35- by 35-foot commercial utility building
- Contract Agreement Date: March 1
- Actual Start Date: March 5
- Actual Completion Date:
- Contract Price: Cost + 25%

DIRECT MATERIALS

Date Received	Department	Requisition No.	Amount
March 05	Fabrication	002-1	$14,000
March 12	Assembly	002-2	1,200
			$15,200

DIRECT LABOR

Date	Department	Source	Amount
March #	Fabrication	Payroll	$ 3,000
March #	Assembly	Payroll	3,500
			$ 6,500

OVERHEAD

Date	Department	Source	Amount
March #	Fabrication	Machine meters	$ 3,500
March #	Assembly	Payroll	1,100
			$ 4,600

TOTAL COST IN FABRICATION	$20,500
TOTAL COST IN ASSEMBLY	5,800
TOTAL MANUFACTURING COST OF JOB	$26,300
TOTAL BUDGETED COST OF JOB	$30,000

Job Order No.: 3
- Job Description: 40-foot portable classroom
- Contract Agreement Date: March 1
- Actual Start Date: March 11
- Actual Completion Date:
- Contract Price: Cost + 25%

DIRECT MATERIALS

Date Received	Department	Requisition No.	Amount
March 11	Fabrication	003-1	$ 45,000
March 19	Assembly	003-2	6,600
			$ 51,600

DIRECT LABOR

Date	Department	Source	Amount
March #	Fabrication	Payroll	$ 5,000
March #	Assembly	Payroll	9,500
			$ 14,500

OVERHEAD

Date	Department	Source	Amount
March #	Fabrication	Machine meters	$ 14,500
March #	Assembly	Payroll	8,000
			$ 22,500

TOTAL COST IN FABRICATION	$ 64,500
TOTAL COST IN ASSEMBLY	24,100
TOTAL MANUFACTURING COST OF JOB	$ 88,600
TOTAL BUDGETED COST OF JOB	$140,000

Job order costing documents and cost flows used in this illustration for MBS are depicted in **Exhibit 6.4**.

Exhibit 6.4 ■ Job Order Costing Documents and Cost Flows

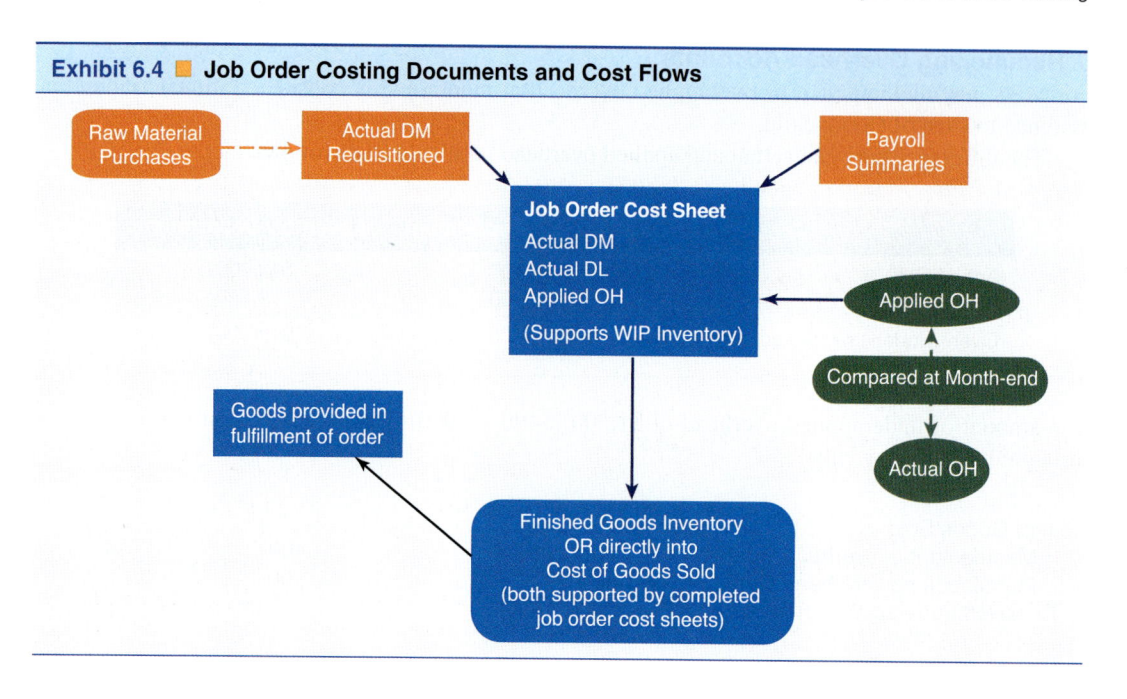

```
Raw Material Purchases --> Actual DM Requisitioned --> Job Order Cost Sheet
                                                       Actual DM
                                                       Actual DL
                          Payroll Summaries -------->  Applied OH
                                                       (Supports WIP Inventory)

                                                       <-- Applied OH
                                                            ↕ Compared at Month-end
                                                            Actual OH

Goods provided in fulfillment of order <-- Finished Goods Inventory
                                           OR directly into
                                           Cost of Goods Sold
                                           (both supported by completed
                                           job order cost sheets)
```

REVIEW 6-4 | LO6-4 — Journal Entries; Cost Accumulation

The following costs were incurred in April by Riders Corp., which produces customized bicycles.

Direct material purchased on account		$ 49,400
Direct material used for jobs:		
Job #301	$29,120	
Job #302	4,680	
Other jobs	34,840	$ 68,640
Direct labor costs for month:		
Job #301	$ 6,760	
Job #302	9,100	
Other jobs	12,740	$ 28,600
Actual overhead costs for April		$143,000

The balance in Work in Process Inventory on April 1 was $10,920, which consisted of $7,280 for Job #301 and $3,640 for Job #302. The April beginning balance in Direct Material Inventory was $28,990. Overhead is applied to jobs at a rate of $2.25 per dollar of direct labor cost. Job #301 was completed and transferred to Finished Goods Inventory during April. Job #301 was delivered to the customer at the agreed-upon price of cost plus 40 percent.

a. Prepare journal entries to record the preceding information.
b. Determine the April ending balance in WIP Inventory. How much of this balance relates to Job #302?
c. **Critical Thinking:** If overhead was underapplied for the month of April, and the company's policy is to reconcile overhead at year-end, was the job over or undercosted? Why?

More practice: E6-32, E6-34, E6-41
Solution on p. 6-57.

JOB COSTING IN SERVICE ORGANIZATIONS

LO6-5
How is job order costing illustrated in the service industry?

Service costing, the assignment of costs to services performed, uses job costing concepts to determine the cost of filling customer service orders in organizations such as automobile repair shops, charter airlines, CPA firms, hospitals, and law firms. Many of these organizations bill clients on the basis of resources consumed. Consequently, they maintain detailed records for billing purposes. On the invoice sent to the client, the organization itemizes any materials consumed on the job at a selling price per unit, the labor hours worked on the job at a billing rate per hour, and the time special facilities were

Chapter 6 Job Order Costing

used at a billing rate per unit of time. Employees with different capabilities and experience often have different billing rates. In a CPA firm, for example, a partner or a senior manager has a higher billing rate than a staff accountant.

The prices and rates must be high enough to cover costs not assigned to specific jobs and to provide for a profit. To evaluate the contribution to common costs and profit from a job, a comparison must be made between the price charged the customer and the actual cost of the job. This is easily done when the actual cost of resources itemized on the customer's invoice is presented on a job cost sheet. A CPA firm, for example, should accumulate the actual hardware and software costs incurred in an accounting system installation for a client, along with the actual wages earned by employees while working on the job and any related travel costs. Comparing the total of these costs with the price charged, the client indicates the total contribution of the job to common costs and profit.

Although service organizations may identify costs with individual jobs for management accounting purposes, there is considerable variation in the way job cost information is presented in financial statements. Some organizations report the cost of jobs completed in their income statements using an account such as **Cost of Services Provided**. They use procedures similar to those outlined in the prior section.

More often, however, service organizations do not formally establish detailed procedures to trace the flow of service costs. Instead, service job costs are left in their original cost categories such as materials expense, salaries and wages expense, travel expense, and so forth. Because all service costs are *typically regarded as expenses rather than product costs*, either procedure is acceptable for financial reporting. Regardless of the formal treatment of service costs in financial accounting records and statements, the managers of a well-run service organization need information regarding job cost and contribution.

All preceding examples of service costing involve situations in which the order is filled in response to a specific customer request. Job order costing can also be used to determine the cost of making services available even when the names of specific customers are not known in advance and the service is being provided on a speculative basis. A regularly scheduled airline flight, for example, could be regarded as a job. Management is interested in knowing the cost of the job in order to determine its profitability. This is but another example of the versatility of job order costing.

Illustrating Job Order Costing in Service Organization   LO6-5   DEMO 6-5

Cutwater, a consulting agency completes consulting projects for companies in the United States. To achieve cost control, assume Cutwater uses a job cost system similar to that found in a manufacturing organization. During the year, its northeast office tracked the cost of consulting jobs completed for three clients.

Cost of Consulting Projects

	A	B	C	D	E
1		Pinnacle Ltd.	Meridian Org.	Cascade Inc.	Total
2	Supplies	$27,720	$10,920	$17,040	$55,680
3	Staff cost	$39,750	$ 7,750	$21,600	$69,100
4	Number of projects	10	2	4	16

Supplies can be traced to each job because these costs are typically associated with specific consulting projects. Based on historical data, Cutwater has calculated an overhead charge of $40 per staff hour. The normal staff cost per hour is $50.

◆ **What is the total cost of each of the consulting projects for the year?**

The total number of staff hours per client is calculated as follows.

Cost of Consulting Projects

	A	B	C	D	E	F
1		Staff Cost		Staff Cost Per Hour		Total Staff Hours
2	Pinnacle Ltd.	$39,750	÷	$50	=	795
3	Meridian Org.	$ 7,750	÷	$50	=	155
4	Cascade Inc.	$21,600	÷	$50	=	432

The total staff hours calculated above are used to apply overhead to each client.

Applied Overhead by Client

	A	B	C	D	E	F
1		Total Staff Hours		Overhead Rate		Applied Overhead
2	Pinnacle Ltd.	795	×	$40	=	$31,800
3	Meridian Org.	155	×	$40	=	6,200
4	Cascade Inc.	432	×	$40	=	17,280
5	Total cost					$55,280

The total cost per client is calculated by adding the cost of supplies, staff, and overhead.

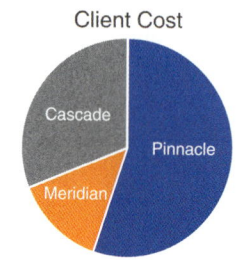

Total Cost by Client

	A	B	C	D	E
1		Pinnacle Ltd.	Meridian Org.	Cascade Inc.	Total
2	Supplies	$27,720	$10,920	$17,040	$ 55,680
3	Staff cost	39,750	7,750	21,600	69,100
4	Overhead	31,800	6,200	17,280	55,280
5	Total cost	$99,270	$24,870	$55,920	$180,060

◆ **What is the average cost per project per client for the year?**

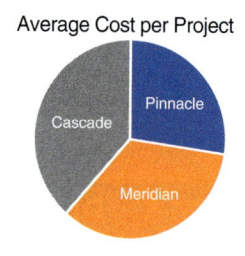

Average Cost by per Project per Client

	A	B	C	D	E	F
1		Total Cost		No. of Projects		Average Cost per Project
2	Pinnacle Ltd.	$99,270	÷	10	=	$ 9,927
3	Meridian Org.	24,870	÷	2	=	12,435
4	Cascade Inc.	55,920	÷	4	=	13,980

Based on this analysis, Pinnacle incurred the most client cost but at the lowest average cost per project. Cutwater charges $15,000 per consulting project and actual overhead for the year was $60,000.

◆ **How is the income statement prepared for the northeast office, adjusting for under- or overapplied overhead in the statement?**

Income Statement

	A	B	C
1			Total
2	Sales (16 × $15,000)		$240,000
3	Costs:		
4	Supplies	$55,680	
5	Staff cost	69,100	
6	Applied overhead	55,280	
7	Underapplied overhead ($60,000 − $55,280)	4,720	(184,780)
8	Before-tax profit		$ 55,220

Chapter 6 Job Order Costing

Data Visualization

The following data visualization provides information on a consultant's three jobs: Edgewood, Hilltop, and Sunset.

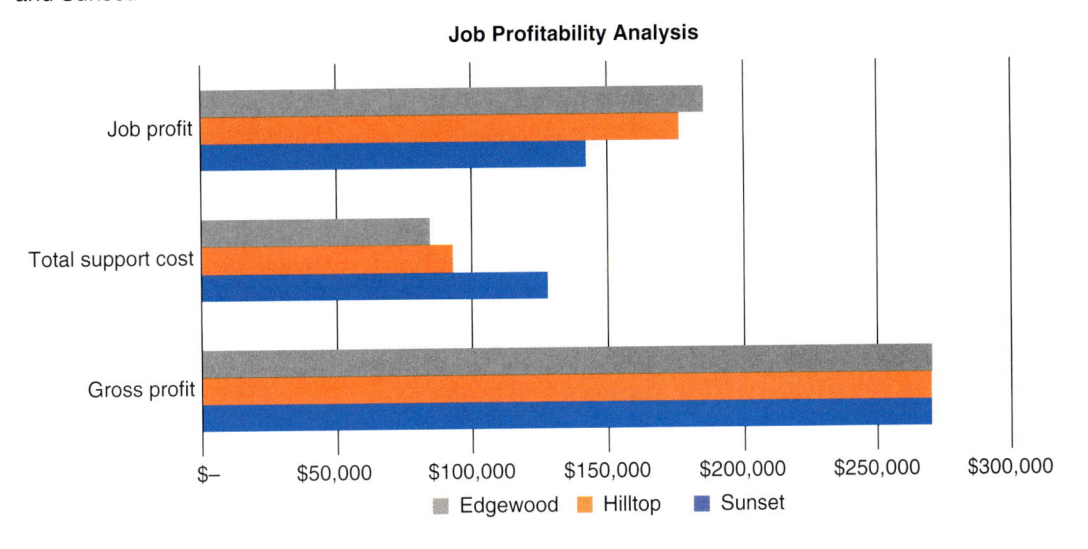

Job Profitability Analysis

(Horizontal bar chart showing Job profit, Total support cost, and Gross profit for Edgewood, Hilltop, and Sunset, with x-axis from $– to $300,000)

- Job profit: Edgewood ~$185,000; Hilltop ~$175,000; Sunset ~$140,000
- Total support cost: Edgewood ~$85,000; Hilltop ~$95,000; Sunset ~$130,000
- Gross profit: Edgewood ~$270,000; Hilltop ~$270,000; Sunset ~$270,000

Legend: Edgewood, Hilltop, Sunset

Based on the data visualization above, answer the following questions.
a. What does the data indicate about the gross profit per job vs. the profitability per job?
b. If support costs were not allocated to jobs, what information would management have for decision making regarding job profitability?
c. Which job appears to be an outlier?

Solution on p. 6-59.

REVIEW 6-5

Illustrating Job Order Costing with a Service Provider — LO6-5

Northridge Veterinary Clinic provides veterinarian (vet) appointments and technician appointments. Vet appointments are reserved for preventive and urgent care, while technician appointments are utilized for procedures not requiring a vet's exam. Approximately 40% of the technicians' time was spent on technician appointments and 60% was spent assisting during vet visits. All services performed during the month were completed. The following additional information relates to April (first month of operation).

1. Medical supplies purchased in April on account	4,320
2. Medical supplies used in April	?
3. Veterinarian salaries for April	14,580
4. Technician salaries for April	5,652
5. Utilities for month on account (90% related to animal treatment)	3,600
6. Office salaries for April (20% related to animal treatment)	3,420
7. Depreciation on medical equipment for April	6,640
8. Depreciation on building (80% related to animal treatment)	5,580

Also assume that medical supplies on hand at April 30 totaled $2,160.

Required

a. Determine the cost of services provided for animal treatment for the month of April for vet appointments and technician appointments. Medical supplies and technician salaries should be allocated 60% to vet appointments and 40% to technician appointments. Also, overhead costs related to animal treatment, should be allocated 60% to vet appointments and 40% to technician appointments.

b. **Critical Thinking:** What additional information could the company accumulate regarding the cost of services provided for animal treatment? How could this information be helpful to management for decision making?

More practice: E6-42, E6-43, E6-44
Solution on p. 6-58.

JOB ORDER COSTING TO ASSIST MANAGERS

LO6-6 How does information from a job order costing system support management decision making?

Managers are interested in controlling costs in each department as well as for each job. Actual direct material, direct labor, and factory overhead costs are accumulated in departmental accounts and are periodically compared to budgets so that managers can respond to significant deviations. Transactions must be recorded in a consistent, complete, and accurate manner to have information on actual costs available for periodic comparisons.

Managers in different types of job order organizations may stress different types of cost control. Companies such as **Harley-Davidson** are extremely concerned about labor hours and their related costs required to build custom motorcycles. Unlike most motorcycles that are built on a moving assembly line, each Harley-Davidson custom cycle takes up to 100 labor-hours to hand-make.[7] Other companies implement significant cost and physical controls for direct materials. For example, jewelers are concerned about the costs of platinum, gold, diamonds, and Australian black opals. Hospitals must be careful to control OH costs related to expensive but seldom-used equipment or to the processing of patient information.

Managing Profitability Across Jobs

One primary difference between job order costing for manufacturing and service organizations is that most service organizations use a fairly insignificant amount of material relative to the value of labor for each job. In such cases, only direct labor may be traced to each job and all material may be treated (for the sake of convenience) as part of OH. Overhead is then allocated to the various jobs, most commonly using a predetermined rate per direct labor hour or direct labor dollar. Other cost drivers that can effectively assign OH to jobs may also be identified.

Knowing the costs of individual jobs allows managers to better estimate future job costs and to establish realistic bids and selling prices. Using budgets in a job order costing system also provides information against which actual costs can be compared at regular time intervals for control purposes. These comparisons can also furnish some performance evaluation information. The following two examples demonstrate the usefulness of job order costing to managers.

DEMO 6-6   **LO6-6**   **Determining Job Profitability**

Lasting Landscaping specializes in commercial landscape projects. The firm has a diverse set of clients and job types. The company reported before-tax profits of $68,920 last year with a profit margin of 21 percent, calculated as follows.

$$\$68{,}920 \text{ Before-tax profits} \div \$336{,}000 \text{ Sales} = 21\%$$

However, its president, Joann Bradley, wants to know which of the firm's clients are the most profitable and which are the least profitable. To determine this information, she requested a breakdown of profit per job measured on both a percentage and an absolute dollar basis.

Bradley found that no client job cost records were kept. Costs had been accumulated only by type—cost of services provided, selling, and general & administrative. Stan Tobias, the sales manager, was certain that the largest profits came from the company's largest accounts. A careful job cost analysis produced the following results.

	Job 1	Job 2	Job 3	Job 4	Job 5	Job 6	Job 7	Job 8	Total
Sales........................	$80,000	$65,000	$45,000	$32,000	$34,000	$30,000	$28,000	$22,000	$336,000
Cost of services provided......	50,400	45,500	27,450	20,800	17,000	16,500	16,520	12,760	206,930
Selling expenses...............	8,000	2,600	1,350	320	340	750	560	330	14,250
General & administrative expenses...	16,000	9,750	6,750	3,520	4,080	2,400	2,520	880	45,900
Before-tax profits.............	$ 5,600	$ 7,150	$ 9,450	$ 7,360	$12,580	$10,350	$ 8,400	$ 8,030	$ 68,920
Profit Margin (Profit ÷ Sales).....	7%	11%	21%	23%	37%	35%	30%	37%	21%

---

[7] http://www.motorcyclenews.com/MCN/News/newsresults/Customs-modified-bikes/2011/April/apr2111-shaw-harley-davidson-custom-built-in-7-minutes/ (last accessed 12/26/23).

◆ Is the sales manager's assertion accurate that the largest profits came from the largest accounts?

The profitability analysis does not confirm the sales manager's assertions. In fact, the analysis shows that the largest accounts contributed most of the firm's revenue but the smallest percentage and absolute dollars of incremental profit. For instance, Job 1 with $80,000 in sales revenue had a profit margin of 7 percent, while Job 5 with $34,000 in sales revenue had a profit margin of 37 percent. Until Bradley requested this information, no one had totaled the costs associated with each client.

A company that has a large number of jobs that vary in size, time, or effort may not know which jobs are responsible for disproportionately large costs. Job order costing can assist in both determining which jobs are truly profitable and helping managers to better monitor costs. As a result of the cost analysis, Bradley can implement a formal system to track job costs. Bradley can also analyze why certain jobs are more profitable than other jobs. Cost cutting measures or more efficient strategies can be implemented to decrease costs. In some cases, unprofitable accounts could even be dropped. With job cost information, account managers will feel more responsibility to monitor and control costs related to their particular accounts.

Benefits of Cost Estimation in Job Costing

Paul Boudreaux and his employees custom manufacture small wooden boats to customer specifications. Before completing his MBA and learning about job order costing, Boudreaux had a vague notion of the costs associated with each boat's production. He would estimate selling prices by using vague information from past jobs and specifications for the new design and adding what he considered a reasonable profit margin. Often customers who indicated they thought the selling price was too high could convince Boudreaux to make price reductions.

Implementing the job order costing system provided Boudreaux with the following benefits:

- better cost control over the jobs that were in process;
- better inventory valuations for financial statements;
- better information with which to prevent part stockouts (not having parts in inventory) and production stoppages;
- a better ability to make certain that materials acquired for a particular custom boat were actually used for that job;
- more up-to-date information to judge whether to accept additional work and to determine when current work would be completed; and
- an informed means by which to understand how costs were incurred on jobs, estimate costs that would be incurred on future jobs, and justify price quotes on future jobs.

Whether an entity is a manufacturer or a service organization that tailors its output to customer specifications, company management will find that job order costing techniques help in performing managerial functions. This type of cost system is useful for determining the cost of goods produced or services rendered in companies that are able to attach costs to specific jobs. As product variety increases, the size of production lots for many items shrinks, and job order costing becomes more applicable.

Job order costing information can help managers trace costs associated with specific jobs, like custom boats, to estimate costs for future jobs.

REVIEW 6-6 — **LO6-6**

Management Decision Making in Job Order Costing

Specialized Products Inc. manufactures customized products for collegiate bookstores. Profits for the current months are $22,000 based on sales of $118,000, less total manufacturing costs of $96,000. Management has a target gross profit margin of 25 percent. In order to increase its margin, the company is interested in analyzing its costs using a job order costing system. Management obtained the following information on its five jobs.

continued

	Job 1	Job 2	Job 3	Job 4	Job 5
Sales.............	$50,000	$45,000	$15,000	$5,000	$3,000
Design hours	100	130	65	55	50
Machine hours	455	490	150	60	45

The Engineering and Design overhead cost pool (Overhead Pool #1) totals $18,000, and the cost driver is design hours. The Construction overhead cost pool (Overhead Pool #2) totals $78,000, and the cost driver is machine hours.

a. What is the current gross profit margin?
b. What is the gross profit margin per job?
c. **Critical Thinking:** What job(s) require further attention by management? Why?

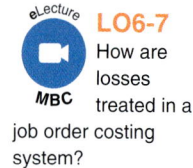

More practice: E6-45
Solution on p. 6-58.

PRODUCT AND MATERIAL LOSSES IN JOB ORDER COSTING

LO6-7 How are losses treated in a job order costing system?

Production processes may result in losses of direct material or partially completed products. Some losses, such as evaporation, leakage, or oxidation, are inherent in the manufacturing process; such reductions are called shrinkage. Modifying the production process to reduce or eliminate shrinkage may be difficult, impossible, or simply not cost beneficial. At other times, production process errors (either by humans or machines) cause a loss of units through rejection at inspection for failure to meet appropriate quality standards or designated product specifications. Such units are considered either **defects**, if they can be economically reworked and sold, or **spoilage**, if such rework cannot be performed.

Units not meeting quality specifications may be reworked to meet specifications or may be sold as irregulars. **Rework cost** is a product or period cost depending on whether the rework relates to defective production that is considered to be normal or abnormal. A **normal loss** of units falls within a tolerance level that is expected during production. For example, if a company sets its quality goal as 99 percent of goods produced, the company expects a normal loss of 1 percent. Any loss in excess of the set expectation level is considered an **abnormal loss**. Thus, the difference between normal and abnormal loss is merely one of degree and is determined by management.

In a job order situation, the accounting treatment for lost units depends on two issues:

- Is a loss generally incurred for most jobs or is it specifically identified with a particular job?
- Is the loss considered normal or abnormal?

Normal Loss Accounted for in Predetermined OH Rate

If a *normal loss is anticipated on all jobs,* the predetermined OH rate should include an amount for the net loss, which equals the cost of defective or spoiled work plus rework costs minus any estimated disposal value of that work. This approach assumes that losses are naturally inherent and unavoidable in the production of good units, and the estimated loss should be allocated to the good units produced.

DEMO 6-7A   **LO6-7**   **Recording Defective Work Inventory When a Normal Loss is Anticipated on all Jobs**

Assume that Kyndo Corp. produces special order cleaning compounds for use by manufacturers. Regardless of the job, some spoilage always occurs in the mixing process. In computing the predetermined OH rate related to the custom compounds, the following estimates are made.

Overhead costs other than spoilage...............................		$ 121,500
Estimated spoilage cost	$10,300	
Sales of improperly mixed compounds to foreign distributors	(4,300)	6,000
Total estimated overhead		$ 127,500
Estimated gallons of production during the year		÷ 150,000
Predetermined OH rate per gallon		$ 0.85

Chapter 6 Job Order Costing

During the year, Kyndo Corp. accepted a job (#38) from Husserl Co. to manufacture 100 gallons of cleaning compound. The compound is mixed in 20-gallon vats. In mixing the compound, one vat of ingredients was spoiled when a worker accidentally added a thickening agent meant for another job into a container of Job #38's cleaning compound. Actual cost of the defective mixture currently included in Work in Process Inventory is $57, but it can be sold at an outlet market for $22.

◆ **What is the adjusting entry to reclassify the cost of defective units in Work in Process?**

The following adjusting entry is made to account for the actual defect cost.

Defective Work Inventory	22	
Manufacturing Overhead Control	35	
Work in Process Inventory—Job #38		57
To record disposal value of defective work incurred on Job #38 for Husserl Co.		

The estimated cost of spoilage was originally included when calculating the predetermined OH rate. Therefore, as defects or spoilage occur, the disposal value of nonstandard work is (if salable) included in Inventory, and the net cost of the normal, nonstandard work is charged to the Manufacturing Overhead Control account, as is any other actual OH cost. Work in Process Inventory is reduced for the cost of spoilage (to offset the job cost previously recorded in Work in Process).

Rework Costs If Kyndo Corp. incurred any normal, incremental costs for rework, the rework costs would be debited to Manufacturing Overhead Control.

Normal Loss Applied to a Specific Job

If losses are not generally anticipated but are occasionally experienced on specific jobs because of job-related characteristics, the estimated cost should *not* be included in setting the predetermined OH rate. Because the defect/spoilage cost attaches to the job, disposal value of such goods reduces the cost of the job that created those goods. If no disposal value exists for the defective/spoiled goods or if rework costs are incurred, the cost of those lost units is assigned to the job that caused the defect or spoilage.

Recording Defective Work Inventory Identified with a Particular Job   LO6-7   DEMO 6-7B

Now assume that Kyndo Corp. did not typically experience spoilage in its production process. The company's predetermined OH rate would have been calculated as $0.81 per gallon ($121,500 ÷ 150,000). Assume that more ammonia than normal was added to one vat of the batch at Husserl Co.'s request. After inspecting those 20 gallons, Husserl Co. was unsatisfied and asked Kyndo Corp. to keep the original formula for the remaining gallons. The 20 gallons could be sold to another company for $22.

◆ **How is the $22 disposal value recorded by Kyndo Corp.?**

This amount would reduce the cost of the Husserl Co. job (which now includes the full value of the defective materials in the Work in Process account) as shown in the following entry.

Defective Work Inventory	22	
Work in Process Inventory—Job #38		22
To record disposal value of defective work incurred on Job #38 for Husserl Co.		

After this entry, the cost of the defective work (less the disposal value), remains in the Work in Process account as part of the job cost.

Rework Costs If Kyndo Corp. incurred any normal, incremental costs for rework, the rework costs would be debited to Work in Process Inventory for the specific job.

Abnormal Loss Expensed as Incurred

The cost of all *abnormal losses* (net of any disposal value) should be written off as a period cost. This treatment is justified because asset cost should include only those costs that are necessary to acquire or produce inventory. Unnecessary costs should be written off in the period in which they are incurred. Abnormal losses are not necessary to produce good units, and the cost is avoidable in the future. This cost should be separately identified and the cause investigated to determine how to prevent future similar occurrences.

DEMO 6-7C — LO6-7 — Recording an Abnormal Defect

Now assume Kyndo Corp. normally anticipates some losses on its custom orders and included the estimated cost of those losses in developing the predetermined OH rate. Job #135 produced defective units costing $198 (included in its Work in Process Inventory); however, a disposal value of $45 was associated with those units. Of the remaining $153 of cost, $120 was related to normal defects, and $33 was related to abnormal defects.

◆ What is the entry to reassign the cost of defective work on Job #135?

Defective Work Inventory	45	
Manufacturing Overhead Control	120	
Loss from Abnormal Spoilage	33	
Work in Process Inventory—Job #135		198

To record reassignment of cost of defective and spoiled work on Job #135

The first debit represents the defective inventory's disposal value; the debit to Manufacturing Overhead Control is for the net cost of normal spoilage. The debit to Loss from Abnormal Spoilage is for the portion of the net cost of spoilage that was unnecessary and unanticipated in setting the predetermined application rate. The credit to Work in Process eliminates the cost previously posted to Work in Process for the job. When the defective product is sold, Cash (or Accounts Receivable) is debited and Defective Work Inventory is credited.

Rework Costs If Kyndo Corp. incurred any abnormal, incremental costs for rework, the rework costs would be debited to Loss on Abnormal Rework.

REVIEW 6-7 — LO6-7 — Job Order Costing; Rework

Atlantae Corp. uses a job order costing system for client contracts related to custom-manufactured blinds. A customer recently ordered 15 blinds, and the job was assigned #380. Information for Job #380 revealed the following:

Direct material	$650
Direct labor	800
Overhead	700

Final inspection of the blinds revealed that one was defective. In correcting the defect, an additional $50 of cost was incurred ($20 for direct material and $30 for direct labor). After the defects were corrected, the blind was included with the other units and shipped to the customer. Assume no entry had been made for the $50 of rework costs.

a. Journalize the entry to record incurrence of the rework costs if Atlantae Corp.'s predetermined overhead rate includes normal rework costs.
b. Journalize the entry to record incurrence of the rework costs if rework is normal but specific to this job.
c. Journalize the entry to record incurrence of the rework costs, assuming that all rework is abnormal.
d. **Critical Thinking:** How is management judgment required in the steps leading up to the recording of the journal entries in parts *a* to *c*?

More practice: MC6-15, E6-49, E6-51
Solution on p. 6-59.

Chapter 6 Job Order Costing 6-27

Comprehensive Chapter Review

Key Terms

abnormal loss, p. 6-24
actual cost systems, p. 6-4
applied overhead, p. 6-6
competitive bidding, p. 6-13
cost cross-subsidization, p. 6-9
cost of services provided, p. 6-19
cost-plus contract, p. 6-13
defects, p. 6-24
department overhead allocation method, p. 6-8

job, p. 6-3
job order costing system, p. 6-3
job order cost sheet, p. 6-13
materiality, p. 6-10
material requisition document, p. 6-14
normal cost system, p. 6-4
normal loss, p. 6-24
overapplied overhead, p. 6-10

plantwide overhead allocation method, p. 6-8
predetermined OH rate, p. 6-4
process costing systems, p. 6-3
rework cost, p. 6-24
service costing, p. 6-18
spoilage, p. 6-24
standard cost system, p. 6-5
underapplied overhead, p. 6-10

Chapter Summary

Job Order vs. Process Costing; Valuation Systems (Page 6-2) LO6-1
- Job order costing is used in companies that make limited quantities of distinct products or perform customer-specific services. Process costing is used in companies that make mass quantities of homogeneous output on a continuous flow basis.
- Job order costing requires the use of a job order cost sheet to track the direct material, direct labor, and actual or applied overhead to each customer-specific job. Process costing accounts for direct material, direct labor, and actual or applied overhead by batch of goods per department.
- Job order costing does not allow for the computation of a cost per unit unless all units within the job are similar; process costing can and does create a cost per unit for each cost element.
- Job order costing may use an actual cost system, a normal cost system, or a standard cost system; process costing may use the same type of cost valuation systems but standard cost systems are significantly more prevalent in process costing than job order costing.
- There are three primary valuation systems.
  - An actual cost system combines actual direct material, direct labor, and overhead.
  - A normal cost system combines actual direct material and direct labor with applied overhead (which uses a predetermined OH rate).
  - A standard cost system combines budgeted norms (standards) for direct material, direct labor, and overhead.

Overhead Cost Allocation (Page 6-6) LO6-2
- Manufacturing overhead costs are allocated to products to
  - eliminate the problems caused by delays in obtaining actual cost data.
  - make the overhead allocation process more effective.
  - allocate a uniform amount of overhead to goods or services based on related production efforts.
  - allow managers to be more aware of individual product or product line profitability as well as the profitability of doing business with a particular customer or vendor.
- Cost allocations can be made using actual or normal costing; normal costing necessitates the computation of one or more predetermined overhead rates.
- A predetermined OH rate is calculated as total budgeted OH cost at a specified activity level divided by the volume at that specified activity level.
- Applied OH is the amount of overhead debited to Work in Process Inventory using the actual volume of the specified activity measure multiplied by the predetermined OH rate.

Underapplied and Overapplied Overhead (Page 6-10) LO6-3
- Underapplied (actual is more than applied) or overapplied (actual is less than applied) overhead is
  - caused by a difference between actual and budgeted OH costs and/or a difference between the actual and budgeted level of activity chosen to compute the predetermined OH rate.
  - closed at the end of each period (unless normal capacity is used for the denominator level of activity) to
    ➢ Cost of Goods Sold (CGS) if the amount of underapplied or overapplied overhead is immaterial (underapplied will cause CGS to increase, and overapplied will cause CGS to decrease) or

© Cambridge Business Publishers

➤ Work in Process Inventory, Finished Goods Inventory, and Cost of Goods Sold (based on their proportional balances), if the amount of underapplied or overapplied overhead is material.

LO6-4 Job Order Costing System Characteristics and Primary Documents (Page 6-12)
- Costs are accumulated by job, which is a single unit or multiple similar or dissimilar units that has or have been produced to distinct customer specifications.
- Costs of different jobs cannot logically be averaged; a unique cost must be determined for each job.
- Custom manufacturers typically price their goods using either a cost-plus contract or competitive bidding.
- The job order cost sheet contains all financial information about a particular job.
  - Cost sheets for incomplete jobs serve as the Work in Process Inventory subsidiary ledger.
  - Cost sheets for completed jobs not yet delivered to customers constitute the Finished Goods Inventory subsidiary ledger.
  - Cost sheets for completed and sold jobs comprise the Cost of Goods Sold subsidiary ledger.
- Material requisition forms trace the issuance of raw material to the specific jobs in WIP Inventory so that direct material can be included on the job order cost sheets.
- Payroll summaries provide the necessary information so that direct labor cost can be included on the job order cost sheets.
- Direct material and direct labor costs are included on the job order cost sheet.
- Indirect materials and indirect labor are included with other actual overhead costs in one or more Overhead Control accounts.
- Overhead is applied using predetermined overhead rates to jobs at completion or the end of the period, whichever is earlier.
- Jobs and their related costs are transferred between departments or, if completed, to Finished Goods Inventory.
- Goods are delivered to the requesting customers for cash or credit; the cost of those goods is removed from Finished Goods Inventory and expensed to Cost of Goods Sold.

LO6-5 Job Costing in Service Organizations (Page 6-18)
- Service costing uses job costing to determine the cost of a particular service job or customer service order.
- Generally, service organizations use the original cost categories when tracking cost flow.
- On the income statement, the cost of jobs can be recorded in an account called Cost of Services Provided.
- Job order costing for service providers can be used even when the names of specific customers are not known.
- Managers of a well-run service organization need information regarding job cost and contribution.

LO6-6 Job Order Costing and Management Decision Making (Page 6-22)
- Job order costing assists managers in planning, controlling, decision making, and evaluating performance.
- Job order costing allows managers to trace costs associated with specific current jobs to better estimate costs for future jobs.
- Job order costing provides a means by which managers can better control the costs associated with current production, especially if comparisons with budgets or standards are used.
- Job order costing allows costs to be gathered correctly for jobs that are contracted on a cost-plus basis.
- Job order costing highlights those jobs or types of jobs that are most profitable to the organization.

LO6-7 Losses in a Job Order Costing System (Page 6-24)
- Defective production can be economically reworked; spoilage cannot be economically reworked.
- Both normal and abnormal losses may occur in a job order system.
  - Normal losses that are generally anticipated on all jobs are estimated and included in the development of the predetermined OH rate.
  - Normal losses that are associated with a particular job are charged (net of any disposal value) to that job.
  - Abnormal losses are charged to a loss account in the period in which they are incurred.

Solution Strategies

LO6-2 Applied Overhead

$$\text{Applied Overhead} = \frac{\text{Total Budgeted OH Cost at a Specified Activity Level}}{\text{Budgeted Volume of Specified Activity Level}} \times \text{Actual Activity Volume}$$

Chapter 6 Job Order Costing

Underapplied and Overapplied Overhead

LO6-3

Manufacturing Overhead Control		Manufacturing Overhead Control	
Total actual OH incurred	Total OH applied	Total actual OH incurred	Total OH applied
Debit balance Underapplied OH			Credit balance Overapplied OH

A debit balance in Manufacturing Overhead at the end of the period is underapplied overhead; a credit balance is overapplied overhead. The debit or credit balance in the overhead account is closed at the end of the period to Cost of Goods Sold or is prorated to Work in Process Inventory, Finished Goods Inventory, and Cost of Goods Sold.

BASIC JOURNAL ENTRIES IN A JOB ORDER COSTING SYSTEM

LO6-4

Raw Material Inventory..	XXX	
Accounts Payable..		XXX
To record the purchase of raw material		
Work in Process Inventory—Dept. (Job #).................................	XXX	
Manufacturing Overhead Control..	XXX	
Raw Material Inventory...		XXX
To record the issuance of direct and indirect material requisitioned for a specific job		
Work in Process Inventory—Dept. (Job #).................................	XXX	
Manufacturing Overhead Control..	XXX	
Wages Payable...		XXX
To record direct and indirect labor payroll for production employees		
Manufacturing Overhead Control..	XXX	
Various accounts		XXX
To record the incurrence of actual overhead costs (Account titles to be credited must be specified in an actual journal entry.)		
Work in Process Inventory—Dept. (Job #).................................	XXX	
Manufacturing Overhead Control...................................		XXX
To apply overhead to a specific job (This may be actual OH or OH applied using a predetermined rate. Predetermined OH is applied at job completion or end of period, whichever is earlier.)		
Finished Goods Inventory (Job #)	XXX	
Work in Process Inventory..		XXX
To transfer completed goods to FG Inventory		
Accounts Receivable	XXX	
Sales..		XXX
To record the sale of goods on account		
Cost of Goods Sold	XXX	
Finished Goods Inventory...		XXX
To record CGS		

Chapter Demonstration Problem

LO6-2, 3, 4

Crown Fence Company is a firm that specializes in custom ornamental metal products. Work on several jobs was performed in the month of September. To help in establishing the price for the Willowdale Homeowners' Association, Crown's cost accountant provided the sales manager with budgeted cost information showing total budgeted costs of $17,200. The sales manager believed that a normal selling price was appropriate and, thus, set the sales price to yield a gross margin of roughly 20 percent [($21,500 - $17,200) ÷ $21,500]. The customer agreed to this sales price in a contract dated August 13. Crown's production manager scheduled the job to begin on September 1 and to be completed by November 15. The job is assigned the number PF108 for identification purposes.

    In the entries that follow, use separate WIP Inventory accounts for costs related either to Job #PF108 or to other jobs.

© Cambridge Business Publishers

1. During September, material requisition forms L40–L55 indicated that raw materials costing $5,420 were issued from the warehouse to production. The raw material requisitioned in September included $4,875 of DM used on Job #PF108 and $520 of DM used on other jobs. The remaining $25 of raw materials issued during September were indirect.
2. Total labor cost for September was $9,599. Job #PF108 required $6,902 of DL cost combining the two biweekly pay periods in September. The remaining jobs in process required $1,447 of DL cost, and indirect labor cost for the month totaled $1,250.
3. The company incurred overhead costs in addition to indirect material and indirect labor during September. Factory building and equipment depreciation of $2,500 was recorded. Insurance on the factory building was prepaid and one month ($200) of that insurance had expired. A $1,900 bill for factory utility costs was received and would be paid in October. Repair and maintenance costs of $500 were paid in cash. Additional miscellaneous OH costs of $800 were incurred. Credit the account "Various accounts" for this entry for simplification.
4. Overhead is applied using two predetermined OH rates: $12 per direct labor hour and $30 per machine hour. In September, Fabrication employees committed 260 hours of direct labor time to Job #PF108, and 65 machine hours were consumed on that job. Other jobs used 25 hours of direct labor time and 20 machine hours.
5. Job #PF108 is completed and costs are transferred to Finished Goods.
6. Job #PF108 is sold for cash for $35,250.
7. Any underapplied or overapplied overhead at month-end is considered immaterial and is assigned to Cost of Goods Sold.

Solution to Demonstration Problem

1. Work in Process Inventory—Job #PF108 4,875
   Work in Process Inventory—Other jobs 520
   Manufacturing Overhead Control—Indirect material 25
       Raw Material Inventory 5,420
   To record direct and indirect materials issued per September requisitions

2. Work in Process Inventory—Job #PF108 6,902
   Work in Process Inventory—Other jobs 1,447
   Manufacturing Overhead Control—Indirect labor 1,250
       Wages Payable 9,599
   To record direct and indirect labor wages for September

3. Manufacturing Overhead Control 5,900
       Accumulated Depreciation 2,500
       Prepaid Insurance 200
       Utilities Payable 1,900
       Cash 500
       Various accounts 800
   To record actual September OH costs exclusive of indirect material and indirect labor wages

4. OH applied to Job #PF108 = $5,070 [260 direct labor hours × $12] + [65 machine hours × $30]. The other jobs worked on during September received total applied OH of $900 [25 direct labor hours (assumed) × $12] + [20 machine hours (assumed) × $30].

   Work in Process Inventory—Job #PF108 5,070
   Work in Process Inventory—Other jobs 900
       Manufacturing Overhead Control 5,970
   To apply overhead for September using predetermined rates

5. Finished Goods Inventory—Job #PF108 16,847
       Work in Process Inventory—Job #PF108 16,847

6. Accounts Receivable—Willowdale Homeowners' Association .. 35,250
       Sales 35,250
   To record the sale of goods on account

   Cost of Goods Sold—Job #PF108 16,847
       Finished Goods Inventory—Job #PF108 16,847
   To record the CGS for the Willowdale sale

Chapter 6 Job Order Costing

7. Manufacturing overhead is overapplied by $70 ($5,970 − $5,900), thus, the following entry is required at period-end.

Manufacturing Overhead Control	70	
Cost of Goods Control		70

Assignments with the MBC logo in the margin are available in myBusinessCourse.
Resources include demonstration videos, guided examples, and auto-graded homework.
See details in the Preface, and ask your professor how you can access the system.

Data Analytics

DA6-1. Job profitability using Excel Harvard Products is a job shop (a company that manufactures custom products in small batches). Each batch is managed by one of Harvard's four project managers. Manufacturing facilities are located in Illinois, Wisconsin, Michigan, and Indiana.

Assume the President of Harvard Products has asked for information about costs and profits by job, location, customer, and project manager. A summary of costs (by job) is included in an Excel file available on the textbook's website. *Hint:* Add columns to the Data sheet to separate out account amounts (revenue, direct material, etc.). The IF function is useful here.

Required
Create PivotTables to answer the following questions.
  a. Which customer was the most profitable for Harvard? What was the job number for the most profitable job for that customer? What was the average revenue on jobs for that customer? What was the average revenue for all jobs?
  b. Which location was the least profitable (in dollars) for Harvard? What appears to have contributed more to the lower profits at that location – size of jobs (average revenue) or profit margin ratios? Which location had the highest average revenue per job?
  c. The President of Harvard Products has decided to give performance bonuses to project managers. Determine which project manager will receive the highest bonus if performance is based on:

   1. Average revenue per job?
   2. Number of jobs?
   3. Total profit?
   4. Profit margin ratios?

  d. Based solely on the information you have available, would you encourage management to close the facility with the lowest profit margin? Why or why not? Include in your answer the information you might need to have before making a final decision.

DA6-2. Job profitability using Tableau Available in MBC, this problem uses Tableau to analyze the profitability of manufacturing jobs and determine how bonus measurements are impacted by the metrics used for assessment.

Data Visualization

Data Visualization Activities are available in myBusinessCourse. These assignments use Tableau Dashboards to expose students to visual depictions of data and introduce students to data analytics through data visualizations. These exercises are easily assignable and auto graded by MBC.

Potential Ethical Issues

1. Inflating costs of cost-plus contracts so that the price of the contract increases as does the profit for the contract
2. Assigning costs from a fixed-fee contract to a cost-plus contract so that both contracts become more profitable
3. Substituting materials of a lower quality than specified in the contract to reduce costs and increase profits
4. Shifting costs from completed jobs (in Cost of Goods Sold) to incomplete jobs (in Work in Process Inventory) to both increase profits reported for financial accounting purposes and inflate assets on the balance sheet

© Cambridge Business Publishers

5. Using manufacturing methods or materials that violate the intellectual property rights of other firms (for example, patent rights of competitors)
6. Recording the disposal value from the sale of defective work in a cost-plus contract job as "Other Revenue" rather than reducing the inventory cost of the related job

Questions

Q6-1. In choosing a product costing system, what are the two choices available for a cost accumulation system? How do these systems differ?

Q6-2. In choosing a product costing system, what are the three valuation method alternatives? Explain how these methods differ.

Q6-3. Discuss the reasons a company would use a predetermined overhead rate rather than actual overhead to determine cost of products or services.

Q6-4. Why are departmental predetermined OH rates more useful for managerial decision making than plant-wide OH rates? Why do firms use separate variable and fixed rates rather than a total overhead rate?

Q6-5. How can information produced by a job order costing system assist managers in operating their firms more efficiently?

Q6-6. How does job order costing differ for a service provider as compared to a manufacturer?

Q6-7. How is the difference between actual and applied overhead reconciled at period-end?

Q6-8. If normal spoilage is generally anticipated to occur on all jobs, how should the cost of that spoilage be treated?

Q6-9. Why are normal and abnormal spoilage accounted for differently? Typically, how does one determine which spoilage is normal and which is abnormal?

Multiple Choice

LO6-1, 5

MC6-10. A company sells specialty advertising items that are designed and produced to meet each customer's specific needs. Prominently displaying the customer's company name, these items are used by the customer to give to its clients as a form of promotion. The most appropriate cost accumulation system for the company to use is
- *a.* actual costing.
- *b.* job order costing.
- *c.* life-cycle costing.
- *d.* process costing.

LO6-2

MC6-11. A manufacturer allocates overhead costs using labor hours under a normal costing system. The following information is available.

	Budget	Actual
Overhead costs	$500,000	$550,000
Labor hours	25,000	28,000

What is the amount of applied overhead for the period?
- *a.* $560,000
- *b.* $500,000
- *c.* $525,000
- *d.* $528,000

LO6-3

MC6-12. A company uses a normal costing system and a predetermined overhead rate to allocate its overhead costs. The manufacturing process requires the use of machining equipment, which is a primary driver of overhead. The actual factory overhead amount is $450 for Department A, Job 120 as of the end of the year. Production costs are shown below.

Estimated annual overhead for all departments	$220,000
Expected annual machine hours for all departments	20,000
Actual machine hours for Department A, Job 120	32
Actual labor hours for Department A, Job 120	21

The overhead cost for Department A, Job 120 is
- *a.* $98 overapplied.
- *b.* $98 underapplied.
- *c.* $219 overapplied.
- *d.* $219 underapplied.

Chapter 6 Job Order Costing

MC6-13. Baldwin Printing Company uses a job order costing system and applies overhead based on machine hours. A total of 150,000 machine hours have been budgeted for the year. During the year, an order for 1,000 units was completed and incurred the following.

Direct material costs.	$1,000
Direct labor costs	1,500
Actual overhead	1,980
Machine hours	450

The accountant calculated the inventory cost of this order to be $4.30 per unit. The annual budgeted overhead in dollars was

- a. $577,500.
- b. $600,000.
- c. $645,000.
- d. $660,000.

LO6-4

MC6-14. Benefits of determining the costs of individual jobs under job order costing include all of the following except for
- a. Provides average costs for cost control.
- b. Provides information for bidding on future jobs.
- c. Helps to establish selling prices.
- d. Provides a basis for estimating future job costs.

LO6-6

MC6-15. Assume that because a company anticipates some spoilage on jobs, its predetermined overhead rate includes an estimated amount related to these losses. If the company discovers $180 of defective inventory in WIP Inventory, and can dispose of the defective units for $30, how is the difference of $150 reflected in the required adjusting entry?
- a. $150 debit to Loss from Spoilage
- b. $150 debit to Defective Work Inventory
- c. $150 debit to Manufacturing Overhead Control
- d. $150 credit to Manufacturing Overhead Control

LO6-7

Exercises

E6-16. Costing system choice For each of the following firms, determine whether it is more likely to use job order or process costing. This firm
- a. provides legal services.
- b. is a health-care clinic.
- c. manufactures shampoo.
- d. makes custom jewelry.
- e. is an automobile repair shop.
- f. provides landscaping services for corporations.
- g. designs luxury yachts.
- h. manufactures paint.
- i. produces college textbooks.
- j. produces candles.
- k. provides property management services for real estate developers.
- l. manufactures baby food.
- m. manufactures canned vegetables.
- n. makes wedding cakes.
- o. designs custom software.
- p. is a film production company.
- q. manufactures air mattresses for swimming pool use.

LO6-1

E6-17. Job order costing and process costing applications For each of the following situations, indicate whether job order or process costing is more appropriate and why.
- a. Building contractor for residential condominiums.
- b. Manufacturer of wool yarn, sold to fabric-making textile companies.
- c. Battery manufacturer, that just received a special order for 100,000 batteries, tailored for a unique, new product.
- d. Manufacturer of carbonated water, that sells to chain grocery stores and member warehouses.
- e. Aerospace manufacturer, received an order for a commercial aircraft.

LO6-1

LO6-1 E6-18. Comparing actual and normal costing systems Holiday Décor Inc. produces seasonal products that are sold primarily in October through December. The company produces 100 units per month throughout the year incurring costs of $5,000 plus extra inventory storage costs. Inventory storage costs are $0 for January through March. Beginning in April, inventory storage costs are $200 per month and increase by $200 per month through September. Because inventory storage needs decrease later in the year, storage costs are $600, $400, and $200 for the months of October, November, and December, respectively.

   a. Using an actual costing system, where unit costs are computed monthly, what is the range of unit costs over the 12-month period?
   b. Using a normal costing system and considering unit costs on an annual basis, what is the cost per unit?
   c. Which option, a or b, provides a more accurate picture of the product's unit cost? Why?

LO6-1 E6-19. Comparing actual and normal costing systems Assume that **NordicTrack**, a manufacturer of personal training equipment, plans to hire an environmental consultant for one year to assist the company with its environmental initiatives. Assume that the cost of the consultant is $120,000 and the consultant will focus on one site location. Units produced at that location vary by quarter: 12,000, 15,000, 20,000, and 12,500 units, in quarters 1, 2, 3, and 4 respectively.

   a. Using an actual costing system, where indirect unit costs are computed quarterly, what is the range of indirect unit costs over the four quarters? Does the unit cost fluctuate per quarter? Why or why not?
   b. Using a normal costing system and considering costs on an annual basis, what is the indirect cost per unit?
   c. If the company is considering increasing the cost of its product in order to absorb the cost of the environmental consultant, what should be the increase in cost per unit per quarter?

LO6-1 E6-20. Costing system/valuation method Calista London, after spending 20 years working for a large engineering firm, has decided to start her own business. She has designed a product to remove jar lids with minimal physical effort. London believes this product will sell one million units per year. London has protected her design with appropriate patents, has acquired production space and required machinery, and is now training her newly hired employees to manufacture the product.

London has been your friend for many years and has asked your advice about what type of product cost and valuation system she should use. Based on the limited information given here, what recommendation would you make to London? Why?

LO6-1 E6-21. Costing system/valuation method; research; writing **Fraser** is a full service yacht brokerage company, specializing in yachts over 30 m. Access the company's Web site (https://www.fraseryachts.com) and locate one of the yachts that is currently available for sale ("Buy"). What features of this yacht indicate a critical need for the company to use job order costing?

LO6-2, 3 E6-22. Predetermined OH rates Lansing Mfg. prepared the following annual abbreviated budget for different levels of machine hours:

	40,000	44,000	48,000	52,000
Variable manufacturing overhead...	$ 80,000	$ 88,000	$ 96,000	$104,000
Fixed manufacturing overhead.....	325,000	325,000	325,000	325,000

Each product requires four hours of machine time, and the company expects to produce 10,000 units for the year. Production is expected to be evenly distributed throughout the year.

   a. Calculate separate predetermined variable and fixed OH rates using as the basis of application (1) units of production and (2) machine hours.
   b. Calculate the combined predetermined OH rate using (1) units of product and (2) machine hours.
   c. Assume that all actual overhead costs are equal to expected overhead costs for the year, but that Lansing Mfg. produced 11,000 units of product. If the separate rates based on units of product calculated in (a) were used to apply overhead, what amounts of underapplied or overapplied variable and fixed overhead exist at year-end?

LO6-2, 3 E6-23. OH application Use the information in Exercise E6-22 and assume that Lansing Mfg. has decided to use units of production to apply overhead to production. In April of the current year, the company produced 900 units and incurred $7,500 and $26,500 of variable and fixed overhead, respectively.

Chapter 6 Job Order Costing

    a. What amount of variable manufacturing overhead should be applied to production in April?
    b. What amount of fixed manufacturing overhead should be applied to production in April?
    c. Calculate the under- or overapplied variable and fixed overhead for April.

E6-24. Predetermined OH rate For the current year, Omaha Mechanical has a monthly overhead cost formula of $42,900 + $6 per direct labor hour. The firm's current year expected annual capacity is 78,000 direct labor hours, to be incurred evenly each month. Making one unit of the company's product requires 1.5 direct labor hours.   *LO6-2*

    a. Determine the total overhead to be applied per unit of product in the current year.
    b. Prepare journal entries to record the application of overhead to Work in Process Inventory and the incurrence of $128,550 of actual overhead in January, when 6,390 direct labor hours were worked.
    c. Given the actual direct labor hours in (b), how many units would you have expected to be produced in January?

E6-25. Predetermined OH rate Langston Automotive Accessories applies overhead using a combined rate for fixed and variable overhead. The rate is 250 percent of direct labor cost. During the first three months of the current year, actual costs incurred were as follows: *LO6-2, 3*

	Direct Labor Cost	Actual Overhead
January...............	$180,000	$440,000
February..............	165,000	420,400
March................	170,000	421,000

    a. What amount of overhead was applied to production in each of the three months?
    b. What was the underapplied or overapplied overhead for each of the three months and for the first quarter?

E6-26. Plantwide vs. departmental OH rates Roddickton Manufacturing Co. has gathered the following information to develop predetermined OH rates for the year. The company produces a wide variety of energy-saving products that are processed through two departments, Assembly (automated) and Finishing (labor intensive).   *LO6-2*

> Budgeted total overhead: $600,400 in Assembly and $199,600 in Finishing
> Budgeted total direct labor hours: 10,000 in Assembly and 40,000 in Finishing
> Budgeted total machine hours: 76,000 in Assembly and 4,000 in Finishing

    a. Compute a plantwide predetermined OH rate using direct labor hours.
    b. Compute a plantwide predetermined OH rate using machine hours.
    c. Compute departmental predetermined OH rates using machine hours for Assembly and direct labor hours for Finishing.
    d. Determine the amount of overhead that would be assigned to a product that required five machine hours in Assembly and one direct labor hour in Finishing using the answers developed in (a), (b), and (c).

E6-27. Underapplied or overapplied overhead At the end of the year, Jackson Tank Company's accounts showed a $66,000 credit balance in Manufacturing Overhead Control. In addition, the company had the following account balances: *LO6-3*

Work in Process Inventory...............	$384,000
Finished Goods Inventory................	96,000
Cost of Goods Sold	720,000

    a. Prepare the necessary journal entry to close the overhead account if the balance is considered immaterial.
    b. Prepare the necessary journal entry to close the overhead account if the balance is considered material.
    c. Which method do you believe is more appropriate for the company, and why?

LO6-3 **E6-28. Predetermined OH rates and underapplied/overapplied OH** Davidson's Dolls had the following information in its Work in Process Inventory account for June:

Work in Process Inventory

Beginning balance	10,000	Transferred out	335,000
Materials added	150,000		
Labor (5,000 DLHs)	90,000		
Applied overhead	120,000		
Ending balance	35,000		

All workers are paid the same rate per hour. Factory overhead is applied to Work in Process Inventory on the basis of direct labor hours. The only work left in process at the end of the month had a total of 2,860 direct labor hours accumulated to date.

a. What is the total predetermined OH rate per direct labor hour?
b. If actual total overhead for June is $121,500, what is the amount of underapplied or overapplied overhead?
c. Given your answer to (b), how would you recommend the over- or underapplied overhead be closed?

LO6-3 **E6-29. Underapplied or overapplied overhead** At year-end, Dub's Wind Generator Co. had a $40,000 debit balance in its Manufacturing Overhead Control account. Overhead is applied to products based on direct labor cost. Relevant account balance information at year-end follows:

	Work in Process Inventory	Finished Inventory	Cost of Goods Sold
Direct material	$20,000	$ 80,000	$120,000
Direct labor	10,000	40,000	50,000
Factory overhead	20,000	80,000	100,000
	$50,000	$200,000	$270,000

a. What predetermined OH rate was used during the year?
b. Provide arguments to be used for deciding whether to prorate the balance in the overhead account at year-end.
c. Prorate the overhead account balance based on the relative balances of the appropriate accounts.
d. Identify some possible reasons that the company had a debit balance in the overhead account at year-end.

LO6-4 **E6-30. Job order costing accounts** Following are specific types of information that can be located in a particular account. For each item listed, identify the account that would provide the relevant information. More than one item may apply. Choose from the following: Raw Materials Inventory, Manufacturing Overhead Control, Work in Process Inventory, Finished Goods Inventory, Cost of Goods Sold.

a. Total cost of goods manufactured during a period
b. Total cost of material issued to production for a period
c. Total manufacturing overhead cost incurred for a period
d. Total cost of material purchased during a period
e. Total cost of goods sold during a period
f. Total indirect labor cost incurred during a period
g. Total direct labor cost incurred during a period

LO6-4 **E6-31. Job costing documents; ethics; writing** Salem Corp. contracted for a specialized production machine from Quindo Industries, a tool company. The contract specified a price equal to "115 percent of production cost." A sales executive at Quindo told Salem's management that the machine's approximate price would be $1,725,000 based on the following estimates:

Chapter 6 Job Order Costing

Direct material cost.	$ 500,000
Direct labor cost	400,000
Manufacturing overhead (applied based on machine time)	600,000
Markup	225,000
Estimated price to Salem	$1,725,000

Two months later, Quindo Industries delivered the completed machinery, configured and manufactured as per the contract. However, the accompanying invoice caught Salem's executives by surprise. The invoice provided the following:

Direct material cost.	$ 658,000
Direct labor cost	625,000
Manufacturing overhead (applied based on machine time)	640,000
Markup	288,450
Estimated price to Salem	$2,211,450

Upon receiving the invoice, Salem executives requested an audit of the direct material charges because they were more than 30 percent higher than the original estimate. Quindo Industries granted the request and Salem hired your firm to conduct the audit.

a. Describe your strategy for validating the $658,000 charge for direct material and discuss specific documents you will request from Quindo Industries as part of the audit.
b. Describe your strategy for validating the $625,000 charge for direct labor and discuss specific documents you will request from Quindo Industries as part of the audit.
c. How might Quindo Industries have manipulated the predetermined overhead rate?
d. Even if all of the charges are validated, do you perceive the tool company's behavior in this case as ethical? Explain.

E6-32. Journal entries Nottaway Flooring produces custom-made floor tiles. The company's Raw Material Inventory account contains both direct and indirect materials. Until the end of April, the company worked solely on a large job (#4263) for a major client. Near the end of the month, Nottaway began Job #4264. The following information was obtained relating to April production operations.

1. Raw material purchased on account, $204,000.
2. Direct material issued to Job #4263 cost $163,800; indirect material issued for that job cost $12,460. Direct material costing $1,870 was issued to start production of Job #4264.
3. Direct labor hours worked on Job #4263 were 3,600. Direct labor hours for Job #4264 were 120. All direct labor employees were paid $15 per hour.
4. Actual factory overhead costs incurred for the month totaled $68,700. This overhead consisted of $18,000 of supervisory salaries, $21,500 of depreciation charges, $7,200 of insurance, $12,500 of indirect labor, and $9,500 of utilities. Salaries, insurance, and utilities were paid in cash, and indirect labor charges were accrued.
5. Overhead is applied to production at the rate of $18 per direct labor hour.

Beginning balances of Raw Material Inventory and Work in Process Inventory were, respectively, $4,300 and $11,400. Of the beginning WIP balance, $800 was related to Job #4263. Job #4263 was completed during April.

a. Prepare journal entries for Transactions 1–5.
b. Determine the balance in Raw Material Inventory at the end of the month.
c. Determine the balance in Work in Process Inventory at the end of the month.
d. Determine the cost of the goods manufactured during April. If completed goods consist of 10,000 similar units, what was the cost per unit?
e. What is the amount of underapplied or overapplied overhead at the end of April?

LO6-3, 4

E6-33. Cost accumulation Croftmark Co. began operations on May 1. Its Work in Process Inventory account on May 31 appeared as follows:

LO6-2, 4

Work in Process Inventory

Direct material	138,600	Cost of completed jobs	??
Direct labor	96,000		
Applied overhead	134,400		

The company applies overhead on the basis of direct labor cost. Only one job was still in process on May 31. That job had $37,725 in direct material and $18,100 in direct labor cost assigned to it.

a. What was the predetermined overhead application rate?
b. What was the balance in WIP Inventory at the end of May?
c. What was the total cost of jobs completed in May?

LO6-4 **E6-34.** **Journal entries; cost accumulation** The following costs were incurred in February by Container Corp., which produces customized steel storage bins:

Direct material purchased on account		$ 76,000
Direct material used for jobs:		
Job #217	$44,800	
Job #218	7,200	
Other jobs	53,600	105,600
Direct labor costs for month:		
Job #217	$10,400	
Job #218	14,000	
Other jobs	19,600	44,000
Actual overhead costs for February		220,000

The balance in Work in Process Inventory on February 1 was $16,800, which consisted of $11,200 for Job #217 and $5,600 for Job #218. The February beginning balance in Direct Material Inventory was $44,600. Actual overhead is applied to jobs at a rate of $4.95 per dollar of direct labor cost. Job #217 was completed and transferred to Finished Goods Inventory during February. Job #217 was delivered to the customer at the agreed-upon price of cost plus 35 percent.

a. Prepare journal entries to record the preceding information.
b. Determine the February ending balance in WIP Inventory. How much of this balance relates to Job #218?

LO6-2, 4 **E6-35.** **Cost accumulation** Blaine Corp. makes floats for Mardi Gras in New Orleans. The company's fiscal year ends on March 31. On January 1, the company's WIP Inventory account appeared as follows:

Work in Process Inventory

Beginning balance	916,650	Cost of completed jobs	??
Direct material	589,670		
Direct labor	159,600		
Applied overhead	127,680		

The direct labor cost contained in the beginning balance of WIP Inventory was for a total of 15,200 direct labor hours (DLHs). During January, 7,600 DLHs were recorded. Only one job was still in process on January 31. That job had $73,250 in direct material and 2,850 DLHs assigned to it.

a. If overhead is applied on the basis of DLHs, what predetermined OH rate was in effect during the company's previous fiscal year?
b. What was the average direct labor rate per hour?
c. What amount of direct material cost was in the beginning balance of WIP Inventory?
d. What was the balance in WIP Inventory at the end of January?
e. What was the total cost of jobs manufactured in January?

LO6-4 **E6-36.** **Cost accumulation** Barfield Mfg. Co. applies overhead to jobs at a rate of 140 percent of direct labor cost. The following account information is available.

Direct Material Inventory				Work in Process Inventory			
Beg. balance	24,600		?	Beg. balance	56,000		?
Purchases	?			Direct material	?		
				Direct labor	395,000		
				Overhead	?		
	4,100				27,640		

Finished Goods Inventory			Cost of Goods Sold	
Beg. balance 90,000	1,890,000		?	
Goods completed ?				
57,000				

Calculate the following items that are missing from Barfield's account information:
a. Cost of goods sold
b. Cost of goods manufactured
c. Amount of overhead applied to production
d. Cost of direct material used
e. Cost of direct material purchased

E6-37. Cost accumulation On September 25, a hurricane destroyed the work in process inventory of Biloxi Corporation. At that time, the company was in the process of manufacturing two custom jobs (B325 and Q428). Although all of Biloxi's on-site accounting records were destroyed, the following information is available from some backup off-site records:

- Biloxi Corp. applies overhead at the rate of 85 percent of direct labor cost.
- The cost of goods sold for the company averages 75 percent of selling price. Sales from January 1 to the date of the hurricane totaled $1,598,000.
- The company's wage rate for production employees is $12.90 per hour. A total of 25,760 direct labor hours were recorded from January 1 through September 25.
- As of September 25, $21,980 of direct material and 128 hours of direct labor had been recorded for Job B325. Also at that time, $14,700 of direct material and 240 hours of direct labor had been recorded for Job Q428.
- January 1 inventories (of the current year) were as follows: $19,500 of Raw Material and $68,900 of Finished Goods. Raw materials purchased during the year totaled $843,276.
- The amount of Work in Process Inventory at January (of the current year) was $14,600. Jobs B325 and Q428 were not in process on January 1.
- One job, R91, was completed and in the warehouse awaiting shipment on September 25. The total cost of this job was $165,600.

Determine the following amounts.
a. Cost of goods sold for the year
b. Cost of goods manufactured during the year
c. Amount of applied overhead for each job in WIP Inventory
d. Cost of WIP Inventory destroyed by the hurricane
e. Cost of RM Inventory destroyed by the hurricane

LO6-2, 4

E6-38. Cost accumulation; assigning costs to jobs Mystic Inc. uses a job order costing system and applies overhead to jobs at a predetermined rate of $4.25 per direct labor dollar. During April, the company spent $29,600 on direct material and $3,900 on direct labor for Job #344. Budgeted factory overhead for the company for the year was $1,275,000.

a. How did Mystic Inc. compute the predetermined overhead rate for the year?
b. Journalize the application of overhead to all jobs, assuming that April's total direct labor cost was $22,700.
c. How much overhead was assigned to Job #344 during April?
d. Job #344 had a balance of $18,350 on April 1. What was the April 30 balance?

LO6-2, 4

E6-39. Cost accumulation in two departments Rio Valde Co. uses a normal cost, job order costing system. In the Mixing Department, overhead is applied using machine hours; in Paving, overhead is applied using direct labor hours. In December of Year One, the company estimated the following data for its two departments for Year Two:

LO6-2, 4

	Mixing Department	Paving Department
Direct labor hours	12,000	28,000
Machine hours	60,000	12,000
Budgeted overhead cost	$480,000	$700,000

a. Compute the predetermined OH rate for each department of Rio Valde.
b. Job #220 was started and completed during March of Year Two. The job cost sheet shows the following information:

	Mixing Department	Paving Department
Direct material	$22,600	$3,400
Direct labor cost	$1,250	$4,050
Direct labor hours	24	340
Machine hours	290	44

Compute the overhead applied to Job #220 for each department and in total.

c. The president of Rio Valde suggested that, for simplicity, a single predetermined overhead rate be computed using machine hours. How much overhead would have been applied to Job #220 if that single rate had been used? Would such a rate have indicated the actual overhead cost of each job? Explain.

LO6-2, 4 **E6-40.** **Cost accumulation in two departments** Country Products manufactures quilt racks. Pine stock is introduced in Department 1, where the raw material is cut and assembled. In Department 2, completed racks are stained and packaged for shipment. Department 1 applies overhead on the basis of machine hours; Department 2 applies overhead on the basis of direct labor hours. The company's predetermined overhead rates were computed using the following information:

	Department 1	Department 2
Expected overhead	$465,000	$380,600
Expected DLHs	4,000	22,000
Expected MHs	30,000	2,500

Sue Power contacted Country Products to produce 500 quilt racks as a special order. Power wanted the racks made from teak and to be made larger than the company's normal racks. Country Products designated Power's order as Job #462.

During July, Country Products purchased $346,000 of raw material on account, of which $19,000 was teak. Requisitions were issued for $340,000 of raw material, including all the teak. There were 285 direct labor hours worked (at a rate of $11 per DLH) and 2,400 machine hours recorded in Department 1; of these hours, 25 DLHs and 320 MHs were on Job #462. Department 2 had 1,430 DLHs (at a rate of $18 per DLH) and 180 MHs; of these, 158 DLHs and 20 MHs were worked on Job #462. Assume that all wages are paid in cash.

Job #462 was completed on July 28 and shipped to Power. She was billed cost plus 20 percent.

a. What are the predetermined overhead rates for Departments 1 and 2?
b. Prepare journal entries for the July transactions.
c. What were the cost and selling price per unit of Job #462? What was the cost per unit of the raw material?
d. Assume that enough pine had been issued in July for 20,000 quilt racks. The raw material inventory manager is Power's friend, who conveniently "forgot" to trace the teak's cost specifically to Job #462. What would the effect of this "error" be on the raw material cost, total cost, and selling price for each unit in Job #462? (Round to the nearest cent.)

LO6-4 **E6-41.** **Actual costing system; journal entries** DeeZees makes evening dresses. The following information was gathered from the company records for the year, the first year of company operations. Work in Process Inventory at the end of the year was $15,750.

Direct material purchased on account	$ 555,000
Direct material issued to production	447,000
Direct labor payroll accrued	322,500
Indirect labor payroll accrued	93,000
Prepaid factory insurance expired	3,000
Factory utilities paid	21,450
Depreciation on factory equipment recorded	32,550
Factory rent paid	126,000
Sales (all on account)	1,431,000
Selling, general and administrative expenses	375,850

The company's gross profit rate for the year was 35 percent.

Prepare journal entries to record the flow of costs for the year, assuming the company uses a perpetual inventory system and a single Manufacturing Overhead Control account and that actual overhead is included in WIP Inventory.

E6-42. Cost accumulation; assigning costs to jobs The law firm of Taub & Lawson, LLP, currently has four cases in process. Following is information related to those cases as of the end of March:

	Case #1	Case #2	Case #3	Case #4
Direct material	$480	$8,800	$3,700	$850
Direct labor hours ($190 per hour)	40	90	70	15
Estimated court hours	12	65	120	40

Taub & Lawson allocates overhead to cases based on a predetermined rate of $150 per estimated court hour.

a. Determine the total cost assigned to each case as of March 31.
b. Case #3 was completed at the end of April. At that time, $10,100 of direct materials had been used and 174 direct labor hours had been incurred. Of the DLHs, 72 had been spent in court. Taub & Lawson's policy is to charge clients actual costs plus 45 percent. What amount will be billed to the client involved in Case #3?

E6-43. Cost accumulation; assigning costs to jobs Entrada, an interior decorating firm, uses a job order costing system and applies overhead to jobs using a predetermined rate of $17 per direct labor hour. On June 1, Job #918 was the only job in process. Its costs included direct material of $8,250 and direct labor of $500 (25 hours at $20 per hour). During June, the company began work on Jobs #919, #920, and #921. Direct material used for June totaled $21,650. June's direct labor cost totaled $6,300. Job #920 had not been completed at the end of June, and its direct material and direct labor charges were $2,850 and $800, respectively. All other jobs were completed in June.

a. What was the total cost of Job #920 as of the end of June?
b. What was the cost of goods manufactured for June?
c. If actual overhead for June was $5,054, was the overhead underapplied or overapplied for the month? By how much?

E6-44. Service industry; actual costing; journal entries Kalogrides & McMillan CPAs incurred the following costs in performing audit and tax services during September.

- Used $5,000 of previously purchased supplies: 40% for audit and 60% for tax engagements.
- Paid $8,000 of all partner travel expenses to an accounting conference, considered a common, unallocated expense.
- Recorded $6,500 of depreciation on laptops used in audits and $8,800 on laptops used in tax.
- Recorded $1,800,000 of annual depreciation on the Kalogrides & McMillan Building, located in downtown New York; 35 percent of the space is used to house audit personnel and 50 percent, tax personnel.
- Accrued audit partner salaries, $200,000; tax partner salaries, $225,000.
- Accrued remaining audit staff salaries, $257,900; tax audit staff salaries, $330,000.
- Paid credit card charges for travel costs for client engagements: audit, $19,400; tax, $2,600.
- One month's prepaid insurance and property taxes expired on the downtown building, $17,300.
- Accrued $3,400 of office assistant wages; the office assistant works 40% for the audit partners and staff and 60% for the tax partners and staff.

Determine the cost of audit and tax services rendered for September.

E6-45. Job profitability analysis The cost accountant for Party Planners Inc. summarized the following information for five jobs of the company.

	Jobs				
	A	B	C	D	E
Sales	$3,800	$4,500	$3,400	$5,600	$4,700
Cost of services provided	2,600	3,100	2,302	2,303	3,300
General & Administrative expenses	410	200	150	213	125

a. Prepare a profitability analysis by job, showing gross profit and before-tax profit.

b. Compute the gross profit % (gross profit ÷ sales) per job and the profit margin (before-tax profit ÷ sales) for each job.
c. Which job(s) seem to be overperforming and which job(s) seem to be underperforming relative to the other jobs? Support your conclusions.
d. What is the overall gross profit % and profit margin calculated on the total amounts of the five jobs? What information is not apparent from these average metrics as compared to the calculations in parts *a* to *c*?

LO6-6

E6-46. Job costing and decision making; writing Bonivo Inc. manufactures computers from commodity components to client specifications. The company has historically tracked only the cost of components to computers, and computer selling prices, or bids, have been based solely on the cost of components plus a markup sufficient to cover the other operating costs. In recent years, the company has encountered increasing price pressure from customers, and as a result, computers have often been sold at less than the full markup price—causing continually decreasing profits for the firm.

As you have provided other financial services to Bonivo Inc. in the past, company management has asked you for guidance regarding approaches that could be taken to better manage the firm's profits and prices. You decide that a job order costing system could be helpful to Bonivo.

a. Explain how a job order costing system could help Bonivo better control costs and profits.
b. Explain why Bonivo should not base computer prices only on component costs plus a markup.

LO6-5, 6

E6-47. Job costing and pricing Attorney Maria Conroe uses a job order costing system to collect costs of client engagements. Conroe is currently working on a case for Stacie Olivgra. During the first three months of the year, Conroe logged 95 hours on the Olivgra case.

In addition to direct hours spent by Conroe, her office assistant has worked 35 hours typing and copying 1,450 pages of documents related to the Olivgra case. Conroe's assistant works 160 hours per month and is paid a salary of $4,800 per month. The average cost per copy is $0.06 for paper, toner, and machine rental. Telephone and fax charges for long-distance calls on the case totaled $145. Last, Conroe has estimated that total office overhead for rent, utilities, parking, and so on amount to $9,600 per month and that, during a normal month, the office is open every hour that the assistant is at work. Overhead charges are allocated to clients based on the number of hours of assistant's time.

a. Conroe desires to set the billing rate so that she earns, at a minimum, $190 per hour, and covers all direct and allocated indirect costs related to a case. What minimum charge per hour (rounded to the nearest $10) should Conroe charge Olivgra? (Hint: Be sure to include office overhead.) What would be the total billing to Olivgra?
b. All the hours that Conroe spends at the office are not necessarily billable hours. In addition, Conroe did not consider certain other expenses such as license fees, country club dues, automobile costs, and other miscellaneous expenses when she determined the amount of overhead per month. Therefore, Conroe is considering billing clients for direct costs plus allocated indirect costs plus a 40 percent margin to cover nonbillable time as well as other costs. What will Conroe charge Olivgra in total for the time spent on her case?
c. Which billing method is more likely to be accepted by clients, and why?

LO6-6

E6-48. Cost control; writing Juneau Container makes steel storage canisters for various chemical products. The company uses a job order costing system and obtains jobs based on competitive bidding. For each project, a budget is developed.

One of the firm's products is a 55-gallon drum. In the past year, the company made this drum on four separate occasions for four different customers. Financial details for the four orders follow:

Date	Job No.	Quantity	Bid Price	Budgeted Cost	Actual Cost
Jan. 17	2118	60,000	$190,000	$120,000	$145,000
Mar. 13	2789	29,000	155,000	110,000	121,000
Oct. 20	4300	61,000	180,000	125,000	143,000
Dec. 3	4990	35,000	175,000	150,000	168,000

Assume that you are the company's controller. Write a memo to management describing any problems that you perceive in the data presented and the steps that should be taken to eliminate recurrence of these problems.

Chapter 6 Job Order Costing

E6-49. Job order costing; rework San Angelo Corp. uses a job order costing system for client contracts related to custom-manufactured pulley systems. Elmore Mechanical recently ordered 20,000 pulleys, and the job was assigned #BA468. Information for Job #BA468 revealed the following:

Direct material	$40,800
Direct labor	49,200
Overhead	36,800

LO6-7

Final inspection of the pulleys revealed that 230 were defective. In correcting the defects, an additional $1,150 of cost was incurred ($250 for direct material and $900 for direct labor). After the defects were corrected, the pulleys were included with the other good units and shipped to the customer. Assume no entry has been made for the $1,150 of rework costs.

a. Journalize the entry to record incurrence of the rework costs if San Angelo Corp.'s predetermined overhead rate includes normal rework costs.
b. Journalize the entry to record incurrence of the rework costs if rework is normal and rework costs are not included in the company's predetermined overhead rate. If San Angelo Corp. prices jobs on a cost-plus basis, should the rework costs be considered in determining the markup?
c. Journalize the entry to record incurrence of the rework costs, assuming that all rework is abnormal.

E6-50. Job order costing; rework and defective units Canyon City Co. uses a job order costing system that combines actual direct material and actual direct labor costs with a predetermined overhead charge based on machine hours. Expected overhead and machine hours of $1,421,000 and 145,000, respectively, were used in developing the predetermined rate for the year.

LO6-7

During the year, the company worked on Job #876 and incurred the following costs and machine hours:

Direct material	$47,500
Direct labor	21,800
Machine hours	325

a. What is the total cost of Job #876? What is the cost per unit if 1,500 units were made? (Round to the nearest cent.)
b. In completing Job #876, 30 units were defective and had to be reworked at a cost of $25 each. Assume that spoilage and rework costs were included in the original estimated overhead costs. Where does the $750 rework cost appear in the accounts of Canyon City Co.?
c. Now assume that rework costs were not included in the original estimated overhead costs. Upon completing Job #876, the quality control inspector determined that 30 units were spoiled and would be unacceptable to the customer. Thirty additional good units were made at a total cost of $1,390. The spoiled units were sold for $240 as "seconds" to an outlet store. What is the total cost of Job #876 assuming the spoilage was considered normal?

E6-51. Defective units and spoilage PaintCo produces commercial paint to customer specifications. For each separate situation, determine any required journal entries to properly reflect the defective units.

LO6-7

a. The company assumes that with each batch of paint produced, some spoilage naturally occurs. Therefore, the company includes rework costs in developing their overhead application rate. The company's cost accountant discovered that Work in Process Inventory for Job #108 includes costs of $100 for paint that did not meet specifications due to a *normal* cause. However, the paint can be sold to a dealer for $75.
b. The company assumes that with each batch of paint produced, some spoilage naturally occurs. Therefore, the company includes rework costs in developing their overhead application rate. The company's cost accountant discovered that Work in Process Inventory for Job #108 includes costs of $100 for paint that did not meet specifications due to an *abnormal* cause. However, the paint can be sold to a dealer for $75.
c. The company does not include rework costs in developing the overhead application rate because rework is related to specific jobs. The company's cost accountant discovered that Work in Process Inventory for Job #108 includes costs of $100 for paint that did not meet specifications due to a *normal* cause. However, the paint can be sold to a dealer for $75.

© Cambridge Business Publishers

LO6-7 **E6-52. Accounting for losses; writing** Describe how the following occurrences should be accounted for based on the fact pattern presented:

a. Certain amounts of spoilage and waste are normal in the production system and affect all jobs.
b. A certain amount of spoilage occurs that is unique to a particular job. There is no disposal value for the spoiled units.
c. Because of a nonroutine malfunction in a production machine, a number of products in Work in Process Inventory were ruined. The quantity of work lost is assumed to be abnormal. There is some salvage value for the spoiled units.

Problems

LO6-2 **P6-53. Overhead application** Last June, Lacy Dalton had just been appointed CFO of Garland & Wreath when she received some interesting reports about the profitability of the company's three most important product lines. One of the products, GW1, was produced in a very labor-intensive production process; another product, GW7, was produced in a very machine-intensive production process; and the third product, GW4, was produced in a manner that was equally labor and machine intensive. Dalton observed that all three products were produced in high volume and were priced to compete with similar products of other manufacturers. Prior to receiving the profit report, Dalton had expected the three products to be roughly equally profitable. However, according to the profit report, GW1 was actually losing a significant amount of money and GW7 was generating an impressively high profit. In the middle, GW4 was producing an average profit. After viewing the profit data, Dalton developed a theory that the "real" profitability of each product was substantially different from the reported profits. To test her theory, Dalton gathered cost data from the firm's accounting records. Dalton was quickly satisfied that the direct material and direct labor costs were charged to products properly; however, she surmised that the manufacturing overhead allocation was distorting product costs. To further investigate, she gathered the following information:

	GW1	GW4	GW7
Monthly direct labor hours	8,000	1,600	400
Monthly machine hours	800	2,400	12,800
Monthly allocated overhead cost	$80,000	$16,000	$4,000

Dalton noted that the current cost accounting system assigned all overhead to products based on direct labor hours using a predetermined overhead rate.

a. Using the data gathered by Dalton, calculate the predetermined OH rate based on direct labor hours.
b. Find the predetermined OH rate per machine hour that would allocate the current total overhead ($100,000) to the three product lines.
c. Dalton believes the current overhead allocation is distorting the profitability of the product lines. Determine the amount of overhead that would be allocated to each product line if machine hours were the basis of overhead allocation.
d. Why are the overhead allocations using direct labor hours and machine hours so different? Which is the better allocation?

LO6-2 **P6-54. Plant vs. departmental OH rates** Montana Metal Works has two departments: Fabrication and Finishing. Three workers oversee the 25 machines in Fabrication. Finishing uses 35 crafters to hand-polish output, which is then run through buffing machines. Product CG9832-09 uses the following amounts of direct labor and machine time in each department:

	Fabrication	Finishing
Machine hours	10.00	0.30
Direct labor hours	0.02	2.00

Following are the budgeted overhead costs and volumes for each department for the upcoming year:

	Fabrication	Finishing
Budgeted overhead	$635,340	$324,000
Budgeted machine hours	72,000	9,300
Budgeted direct labor hours	4,800	48,000

    a. What is the plantwide OH rate based on machine hours for the upcoming year? How much overhead will be assigned to each unit of Product CG9832-09 using this rate?

    b. The company's auditors inform management that departmental predetermined OH rates using machine hours in Fabrication and direct labor hours in Finishing would be more appropriate than a plantwide rate. Calculate departmental overhead rates for each department. How much overhead would have been assigned to each unit of Product CG9832-09 using departmental rates?

    c. Discuss why departmental rates are more appropriate than plantwide rates for Montana Metal Works.

P6-55. Plant vs. departmental OH rates Red River Farm Machine makes a wide variety of products, all of which must be processed in the Cutting and Assembly departments. For the year, Red River budgeted total overhead of $993,000, of which $385,500 will be incurred in Cutting and the remainder will be incurred in Assembly. Budgeted direct labor and machine hours are as follows: **LO6-2**

	Cutting	Assembly
Budgeted direct labor hours	27,000	3,000
Budgeted machine hours	2,100	65,800

Two products made by Red River are the RW22SKI and the SD45ROW. The following cost and production time information on these items has been gathered:

	RW22SKI	SD45ROW
Direct material	$34.85	$19.57
Direct labor rate in Cutting	$20.00	$20.00
Direct labor rate in Assembly	$ 8.00	$ 8.00
Direct labor hours in Cutting	6.00	4.80
Direct labor hours in Assembly	0.03	0.05
Machine hours in Cutting	0.06	0.15
Machine hours in Assembly	5.90	9.30

    a. What is the plantwide predetermined OH rate based on (1) direct labor hours and (2) machine hours for the upcoming year? Round all computations to two decimal places.

    b. What are the departmental predetermined OH rates in Cutting and Assembly using the most appropriate base in each department? Round all computations to two decimal places.

    c. What are the costs of products RW22SKI and SD45ROW using (1) a plantwide rate based on direct labor hours, (2) a plantwide rate based on machine hours, and (3) departmental rates calculated in (b)?

    d. A competitor manufactures a product that is extremely similar to RW22SKI and sells each unit for $310. Discuss how Red River's management might be influenced by the impact of the different product costs calculated in (c).

P6-56. Under/overapplied OH; OH disposition Grand Island Brake Co. budgeted the following variable and fixed overhead costs for the year: **LO6-2, 3**

Variable indirect labor	$100,000
Variable indirect material	20,000
Variable utilities	80,000
Variable portion of other mixed costs	120,000
Fixed machinery depreciation	62,000
Fixed machinery lease payments	13,000
Fixed machinery insurance	16,000
Fixed salaries	75,000
Fixed utilities	12,000

The company allocates overhead to production using machine hours. For the year, machine hours have been budgeted at 50,000.

    a. Determine the predetermined variable and fixed OH rates for Grand Island Brake Co. The company uses separate variable and fixed manufacturing overhead control accounts.

    b. During the year, the company used 53,000 machine hours during production and incurred a total of $273,600 of variable overhead costs and $185,680 of fixed overhead costs. Prepare journal entries to record the incurrence of the actual overhead costs and the application of overhead to production.

    c. What amounts of underapplied or overapplied overhead exist at year-end?

    d. The company's management believes that the fixed overhead amount calculated in (a) should be considered immaterial. Prepare the entry to close the Fixed Overhead Control account at the end of the year.

    e. Management believes that the variable overhead amount calculated in (c) should be considered material and should be prorated to the appropriate accounts. At year-end, balances were as follows for inventory and Cost of Goods Sold accounts:

Raw Material Inventory.............................	$ 25,000
Work in Process Inventory	234,000
Finished Goods Inventory...........................	390,000
Cost of Goods Sold	936,000

Prepare the entry to close the Variable Overhead Control account at the end of the year.

LO6-2, 4   **P6-57.**   **Journal entries** Summer Shade manufactures awnings on residential and commercial structures. The company had the following transactions for February:

- Purchased $790,000 of (raw) material on account.
- Issued $570,000 of (direct) material to jobs.
- Issued $120,000 of (indirect) material for use on jobs.
- Accrued wages payable of $874,000, of which $794,000 could be traced directly to particular jobs.
- Applied overhead to jobs on the basis of 55 percent of direct labor cost.
- Completed jobs costing $1,046,000. For these jobs, revenues of $1,342,000 were collected.

Journalize the above transactions.

LO6-2, 4   **P6-58.**   **Journal entries** Polaski Inc. uses an actual cost, job order system. The following transactions are for August. At the beginning of the month, Direct Material Inventory was $2,000, Work in Process Inventory was $10,500, and Finished Goods Inventory was $6,500.

- Direct material purchases on account totaled $90,000.
- Direct labor cost for the period totaled $75,600 for 8,000 DL hours; these costs were paid in cash.
- Actual overhead costs were $82,000 and are applied to production.
- The ending inventory of Direct Material Inventory was $3,500.
- The ending inventory of Work in Process Inventory was $7,750.
- Goods costing $243,700 were sold for $350,400 cash.

    a. What was the actual OH rate per direct labor hour?
    b. Journalize the preceding transactions.
    c. Determine the ending balance in Finished Goods Inventory.

LO6-3, 4   **P6-59.**   **Journal entries; assigning costs to jobs; cost accumulation** Ialani Corp. uses a job order costing system for the yachts it constructs. On September 1, the company had the following account balances:

Raw Material Inventory..............	$ 332,400
Work in Process Inventory	1,512,600
Cost of Goods Sold	4,864,000

On September 1, the three jobs in Work in Process Inventory had the following balances:

Chapter 6 Job Order Costing 6-47

Job #75............	$586,400
Job #78............	266,600
Job #82............	659,600

The following transactions occurred during September:

Sept.	1	Purchased $1,940,000 of raw material on account.
	4	Issued $1,900,000 of raw material as follows: Job #75, $289,600; Job #78, $252,600; Job #82, $992,200; Job #86, $312,400; and indirect material, $53,200.
	15	Prepared and paid the $757,000 factory payroll for September 1–15. Analysis of this payroll showed the following information:

Job #75.............	9,660 hours	$ 84,600
Job #78.............	26,320 hours	267,200
Job #82.............	20,300 hours	203,000
Job #86.............	10,280 hours	110,800
Indirect labor wages....		91,400

	15	On each payroll date, Ialani Corp. applies manufacturing overhead to jobs at a rate of $12.50 per direct labor hour.
	15	Job #75 was completed, accepted by the customer, and billed at a selling price of cost plus 30 percent. Selling prices are rounded to the nearest whole dollar.
	20	Paid the following monthly factory bills: utilities, $39,600; rent, $70,600; and accounts payable (accrued in August), $196,800.
	24	Purchased raw material on account, $624,000.
	25	Issued $716,400 of direct material as follows: Job #78, $154,800; Job #82, $212,600; Job #86, $349,000; indirect material issued was $55,800.
	30	Recorded additional factory overhead costs as follows: depreciation, $809,000; expired prepaid insurance, $165,400; and accrued taxes and licenses, $232,400.
	30	Recorded and paid the factory payroll for September 16–30 of $714,400. Analysis of the payroll follows:

Job #78.............	8,940 hours	$177,400
Job #82.............	13,650 hours	228,400
Job #86.............	9,980 hours	243,600
Indirect labor wages....		65,000

	30	Applied overhead for the second half of the month to jobs.

a. Journalize the September transactions.
b. Use T-accounts to post the information from the journal entries in (a) to the job cost subsidiary accounts and to general ledger accounts.
c. Reconcile the September 30 balances in the subsidiary ledger with the Work in Process Inventory account in the general ledger.
d. Determine the amount of underapplied or overapplied overhead for September.

P6-60. Journal entries; cost accumulation Stockman Co. began the year with three jobs in process.   LO6-2, 3, 4

	TYPE OF COST			
Job No.	Direct Material	Direct Labor	Overhead	Total
247.....................	$ 77,200	$ 91,400	$ 36,560	$ 205,160
251.....................	176,600	209,800	83,920	470,320
253.....................	145,400	169,600	67,840	382,840
Totals	$399,200	$470,800	$188,320	$1,058,320

© Cambridge Business Publishers

During the year, the following transactions occurred:
1. The firm purchased and paid for $542,000 of raw material.
2. Factory payroll records revealed the following:
   - Indirect labor incurred was $54,000.
   - Direct labor incurred was $602,800 and was associated with the jobs as follows:

Job No.	Direct Labor Cost
247	$ 17,400
251	8,800
253	21,000
254	136,600
255	145,000
256	94,600
257	179,400

3. Material requisition forms issued during the year revealed the following:
   - Indirect material issued totaled $76,000.
   - Direct material issued totaled $466,400 and was associated with jobs as follows:

Job No.	Direct Labor Cost
247	$ 12,400
251	6,200
253	16,800
254	105,200
255	119,800
256	72,800
257	133,200

4. Overhead is applied to jobs on the basis of direct labor cost. Management budgeted OH of $240,000 and total DL cost of $600,000 for the year. Actual total factory OH costs (including indirect labor and indirect material) for the year totaled $244,400.
5. Jobs #247 through #255 were completed and delivered to customers, who paid for the goods in cash. The revenue on these jobs was $2,264,774.

a. Journalize all preceding events.
b. Determine the ending balances for the jobs still in process.
c. Determine the cost of jobs sold, adjusted for underapplied or overapplied overhead.

LO6-4 **P6-61.** **Simple inventory calculation** Production data for the first week in November for Florida Fabricators were as follows:

WORK IN PROCESS INVENTORY					
Date	Job No.	DM	DL	Machine Time (Overhead)
Nov. 1	411	$1,900	36 hours	50 hours
1	412	1,240	10 hours	30 hours
5	417	620	8 hours	16 hours

Finished Goods Inventory, Nov. 1: $23,800

Finished Goods Inventory, Nov. 5: $0

MATERIAL RECORDS				
Type	Inv. Nov. 1	Purchases	Issuances	Inv. Nov. 5
Aluminum	$ 8,300	$98,300	$58,700	$?
Steel	12,800	26,500	34,200	?
Other	5,800	23,550	25,900	?

Direct labor hours worked in the first week of November were 680 at a cost of $15 per DL hour. Machine hours worked that week were 1,200. Overhead for the first week in November was as follows:

Depreciation	$ 9,000
Supervisor salaries	14,400
Indirect labor	8,350
Insurance	2,800
Utilities	2,250
Total	$36,800

Overhead is applied to production at a rate of $30 per machine hour. Underapplied or overapplied OH is treated as an adjustment to Cost of Goods Sold at year-end.

All company jobs are consecutively numbered, and all work not in ending Finished Goods Inventory has been completed and sold. The only job in progress on November 5 was #417.

Determine the following balances on November 5:

a. the three raw material inventory accounts
b. Work in Process Inventory
c. Cost of Goods Sold

P6-62. Job cost sheet analysis You have applied for a cost accounting position with Chelsea Containers. The company controller has asked all candidates to take a quiz to demonstrate their knowledge of job order costing. Chelsea's job order costing system is based on normal costs, and overhead is applied based on direct labor cost. The following information pertaining to May has been provided to you: **LO6-2, 4**

Job No.	DM	DL	Applied OH	Total Cost
67	$ 35,406	$13,840	$15,916	$ 65,162
69	109,872	14,480	16,652	141,004
70	2,436	4,000	4,600	11,036
71	308,430	57,000	?	?
72	57,690	4,400	5,060	67,150

You are informed that Job #68 had been completed in April. You are also told that Job #67 was the only job in process at the beginning of May. At that time, the job had been assigned $25,800 for DM and $7,200 for DL. At the end of May, Job #71 had not been completed; all others were complete. Answers to the following questions are required.

a. What is Chelsea Containers' predetermined OH rate?
b. What was the total cost of beginning Work in Process Inventory?
c. What were total direct manufacturing costs incurred for May?
d. What was cost of goods manufactured for May?

P6-63. Departmental rates All jobs at Frankfurt Inc., which uses a job order costing system, go through two departments (Fabrication and Assembly). Overhead is applied to jobs based on machine hours in Fabrication and on direct labor hours in Assembly. In December, corporate management estimated the following production data for the year in setting its predetermined OH rates: **LO6-2, 3, 4**

	Fabrication	Assembly
Machine hours	104,000	44,000
Direct labor hours	50,400	320,000
Departmental overhead	$1,560,000	$1,760,000

Two jobs completed during the year were #2296 and #2297. The job order cost sheets showed the following information about these jobs:

	Job #2296	Job #2297
Direct material cost	$118,500	$147,200
Direct labor hours—Fabrication	900	460
Machine hours—Fabrication	1,800	900
Direct labor hours—Assembly	850	400
Machine hours—Assembly	108	46

Direct labor workers are paid $12 per hour in the Fabrication Department and $10 per hour in the Assembly Department.

a. Compute the predetermined OH rates used in Fabrication and Assembly for the year.
b. Compute the direct labor cost associated with each job for both departments.
c. Compute the amount of overhead assigned to each job in each department.
d. Determine the total cost of Jobs #2296 and #2297.
e. Actual data for the year for each department are as follows:

	Fabricating	Assembly
Machine hours	103,200	43,200
Direct labor hours	47,800	324,000
Departmental overhead	$1,528,000	$1,790,000

What is the amount of underapplied or overapplied OH for each department for the year ended December 31?

LO6-4 P6-64. Comprehensive Birmingham Contractors uses a job order costing system. In May, the company made a $3,300,000 bid to build a pedestrian overpass over the beach highway at Gulf Shores, Alabama. Birmingham Contractors won the bid and assigned #515 to the project. Its completion date was set at December 15. The following costs were estimated for completion of the overpass: $1,240,000 for direct material, $670,000 for direct labor, and $402,000 for overhead.

During July, work began on job #515; DM cost assigned to Job #515 was $121,800, and DL cost associated with it was $175,040. The firm uses a predetermined OH rate of 60 percent of DL cost. Birmingham Contractors also worked on several other jobs during July and incurred the following costs:

Direct material (including Job #515) issued	$579,300
Direct labor (including Job #515) accrued	584,000
Indirect labor accrued	55,800
Administrative salaries and wages accrued	39,600
Depreciation on construction equipment	26,400
Depreciation on office equipment	7,800
Client entertainment (on accounts payable)	11,100
Advertising for firm (paid in cash)	6,600
Indirect material (from supplies inventory)	18,600
Miscellaneous expenses (design-related; to be paid in the following month)	10,200
Accrued utilities (for office, $1,800; for construction, $5,400)	7,200

During July, Birmingham Contractors completed several jobs that had been in process before the beginning of the month. These completed jobs sold for $1,224,000, and payment will be made to the company in August. The related job cost sheets showed costs associated with those jobs of $829,000. At the beginning of July, Birmingham Contractors had Work in Process Inventory of $871,800.

a. Prepare a job order cost sheet for Job #515, including all job details, and post the appropriate cost information for July.
b. Prepare journal entries for the preceding information.
c. Prepare a Cost of Goods Manufactured Schedule for July for Birmingham Contractors.
d. Assuming that the company pays income tax at a 40 percent rate, prepare an income statement for Birmingham Contractors.

LO6-2, 3, 4 P6-65. Comprehensive Edward Nabors owns Enclose, which designs and manufactures perimeter fencing for large retail and commercial buildings. Each job goes through three stages: design, production, and installation. Three jobs were started and completed during the first week of May. No jobs were in process at the end of April. Information for the three departments for the first week in May follows.

Job #2019	DEPARTMENT		
	Design	Production	Installation
Direct labor hours	800	NA	760
Machine hours	NA	720	NA
Direct labor cost	$81,600	$ 34,000	$10,080
Direct material	$ 9,600	$116,400	$10,400

continued

Chapter 6 Job Order Costing

continued from previous page

Job #2020	Design	Production	Installation
Direct labor hours	680	NA	640
Machine hours	NA	2,400	NA
Direct labor cost	$69,360	$ 59,600	$11,520
Direct material	$ 8,200	$268,800	$36,800

Job #2021	Design	Production	Installation
Direct labor hours	720	NA	3,280
Machine hours	NA	960	NA
Direct labor cost	$73,440	$ 21,600	$15,200
Direct material	$17,600	$232,000	$10,400

Overhead is applied using departmental rates. Design and Installation use direct labor cost as the base, with rates of 30 and 90 percent, respectively. Production uses machine hours as the base, with a rate of $15 per hour. Actual OH for the month was $105,600 in Design, $60,000 in Production, and $31,200 in Installation.

a. Determine the overhead to be applied to each job. By how much is the overhead underapplied or overapplied in each department? For the company?
b. Assume that no journal entries have been made to Work in Process Inventory. Journalize all necessary entries to both the subsidiary ledger and general ledger accounts. Accrue direct labor costs.
c. Calculate the total cost for each job.

P6-66. **Cost accumulation; assigning costs to jobs** Gigi LeBlanc is an advertising consultant who tracks costs for her jobs using a job order costing system. During September, LeBlanc and her staff worked on and completed jobs for the following companies: LO6-4, 5

	Reliant Company	Dumas Manufacturing	Omaha Inc.
Direct material cost	$7,800	$14,200	$19,800
Direct labor cost	$5,580	$18,000	$28,350
Number of promotions designed	3	10	8

Direct material can be traced to each job because these costs are typically associated with specific advertising campaigns. Based on historical data, LeBlanc has calculated an overhead charge of $58 per direct labor hour. The normal labor cost per hour is $45.

a. Determine the total cost for each of the advertising accounts for the month.
b. Determine the cost per promotion developed for each client. (Round to the nearest dollar.)
c. LeBlanc charges $8,600 per promotion. What was her net income for the month, assuming actual overhead for the month was $50,000? Adjust for under- or overapplied OH.
d. You suggest to LeBlanc that she bill ads on a cost-plus basis and suggest a markup of 30 percent on cost. How would her income have compared to her income computed in (c) if she had used this method? How would her clients feel about such a method?

P6-67. **Comprehensive; job cost sheet** Lincoln Construction Company builds bridges. In October and November, the firm worked exclusively on a bridge spanning the Calamus River in northern Nebraska. Lincoln Construction's Precast Department builds structural elements of the bridges in temporary plants located near the construction sites. The Construction Department operates at the bridge site and assembles the precast structural elements. Estimated costs for the Calamus River bridge for the Precast Department were $1,550,000 for direct material, $220,000 for direct labor, and $275,000 for overhead. For the Construction Department, estimated costs for the Calamus River bridge were $350,000 for DM, $130,000 for DL, and $214,500 for OH. Overhead is applied on the last day of each month. Overhead application rates for the Precast and Construction departments are $25 per machine hour and 165 percent of direct labor cost, respectively. LO6-4

Transactions for October

1	Purchased $1,150,000 of material (on account) for the Precast Department to begin building structural elements. All of the material was issued to production; of the issuances, $650,000 was considered direct.
5	Installed utilities at the bridge site at a total cost of $25,000. This amount will be paid at a later date.
8	Paid rent for the temporary construction site housing the Precast Department, $5,000.
15	Completed bridge support pillars by the Precast Department and transferred to the construction site.
20	Paid machine rental expense of $60,000 incurred by the Construction Department for clearing the bridge site and digging foundations for bridge supports.
24	Purchased additional material costing $1,485,000 on account.
31	Paid the following bills for the Precast Department: utilities, $7,000; direct labor, $45,000; insurance, $6,220; and supervision and other indirect labor costs, $7,900. Departmental depreciation was recorded, $15,200. The company also paid bills for the Construction Department: utilities, $2,300; direct labor, $16,300; indirect labor, $5,700; and insurance, $1,900. Departmental depreciation was recorded on equipment, $8,750.
31	Issued a check to pay for the material purchased on October 1 and October 24.
31	Applied overhead to production in each department; 6,000 machine hours were worked in the Precast Department in October.

Transactions for November

1	Transferred additional structural elements from the Precast Department to the construction site. The Construction Department incurred a cash cost of $5,000 to rent a crane.
4	Issued $1,000,000 of material to the Precast Department. Of this amount, $825,000 was considered direct.
8	Paid rent of $5,000 in cash for the temporary site occupied by the Precast Department.
15	Issued $425,000 of material to the Construction Department. Of this amount, $200,000 was considered direct.
18	Transferred additional structural elements from the Precast Department to the construction site.
24	Transferred the final batch of structural elements from the Precast Department to the construction site.
29	Completed the bridge.
30	Paid final bills for the month in the Precast Department: utilities, $15,000; direct labor, $115,000; insurance, $9,350; and supervision and other indirect labor costs, $14,500. Depreciation was recorded, $15,200. The company also paid bills for the Construction Department: utilities, $4,900; direct labor, $134,300; indirect labor, $15,200; and insurance, $5,400. Depreciation was recorded on equipment, $18,350.
30	Applied overhead in each department. The Precast Department recorded 3,950 machine hours in November.
30	Billed the state of Nebraska for the completed bridge at the contract price of $3,450,000.

a. Journalize the entries for the preceding transactions. For purposes of this problem, it is not necessary to transfer direct material and direct labor from one department to the other.

b. Post all entries to T-accounts.

Chapter 6 Job Order Costing

c. Prepare a job order cost sheet, which includes estimated costs, for the construction of the bridge.

d. Discuss Lincoln Construction Company's estimates relative to its actual costs.

P6-68. Comprehensive Pip Squeaks Inc. is a manufacturer of furnishings for infants and children. The company uses a job order costing system. Pip Squeaks' Work in Process Inventory on April 30, consisted of the following jobs:

LO6-1, 2, 3, 4
CMA

Job No.	Items	Units	Accumulated Cost
CBS102	Cribs	20,000	$ 900,000
PLP086	Playpens	15,000	420,000
DRS114	Dressers	25,000	1,570,000

The company's Finished Goods Inventory, carried on a FIFO (first-in, first-out) basis, consists of five items:

Item	Quantity and Unit Cost	Total Cost
Cribs	7,500 units × $64	$ 480,000
Strollers	13,000 units × $23	299,000
Carriages	11,200 units × $102	1,142,400
Dressers	21,000 units × $55	1,155,000
Playpens	19,400 units × $35	679,000
Total		$3,755,400

Pip Squeaks applies factory overhead on the basis of direct labor hours. The company's factory OH budget for the fiscal year ending May 31, totaled $4,500,000, and the company planned to work 600,000 DL hours during this year. Through the first 11 months of the year, a total of 555,000 DL hours were worked, and total factory OH amounted to $4,273,500.

At the end of April, the balance in Pip Squeaks' Raw Material Inventory account, which includes both raw material and purchased parts, was $668,000. Additions to and requisitions from the material inventory during May included the following:

	Raw Material	Parts Purchased
Additions	$242,000	$396,000
Requisitions:		
Job #CBS102	51,000	104,000
Job #PLP086	3,000	10,800
Job #DRS114	124,000	87,000
Job #STR077 (10,000 strollers)	62,000	81,000
Job #CRG098 (5,000 carriages)	65,000	187,000

During May, Pip Squeaks' factory payroll consisted of the following:

Job No.	Hours	Cost
CBS102	12,000	$122,400
PLP086	4,400	43,200
DRS114	19,500	200,500
STR077	3,500	30,000
CRG098	14,000	138,000
Indirect	3,000	29,400
Supervision		57,600
Total		$621,100

The jobs that were completed in May and the unit sales for May are as follows.

Job No.	Items	Quantity Completed
CBS102	Cribs	20,000
PLP086	Playpens	15,000
STR077	Strollers	10,000
CRG098	Carriages	5,000

Items	Quantity Shipped
Cribs	17,500
Playpens	21,000
Strollers	14,000
Dressers	18,000
Carriages	6,000

a. Describe when it is appropriate for a company to use a job order costing system.
b. Calculate the dollar balance in Pip Squeaks' Work in Process Inventory account as of May 31.
c. Calculate the dollar amount related to the playpens in Pip Squeaks' Finished Goods Inventory as of May 31.
d. Explain the treatment of underapplied or overapplied overhead when using a job order costing system.

LO6-3, 4 **P6-69.** **Missing amounts** Riveredge Manufacturing Company realized too late that it had made a mistake locating its controller's office and its electronic data processing system in the basement. Because of the spring thaw, the Mississippi River overflowed its banks on May 2 and flooded the company's basement. Electronic data storage was destroyed, and the company had not provided off-site storage of data. Some of the paper printouts were located but were badly faded and only partially legible. On May 3, when the flooding subsided, company accountants were able to assemble the following factory-related data from the debris and from discussions with various knowledgeable personnel. Data about the following accounts were found:

- Raw Material (includes indirect material) Inventory: Balance April 1 was $9,600.
- Work in Process Inventory: Balance April 1 was $15,400.
- Finished Goods Inventory: Balance April 30 was $13,200.
- Total company payroll cost for April was $58,400.
- Accounts payable balance April 30 was $36,000.
- Indirect material used in April cost $11,600.
- Other nonmaterial and nonlabor overhead items for April totaled $5,000.

Payroll records, kept at an across-town service center that processes the company's payroll, showed that April's direct labor amounted to $36,400 and represented 8,800 labor hours. Indirect factory labor amounted to $10,800 in April.

The president's office had a file copy of the production budget for the current year. It revealed that the predetermined OH rate is based on planned annual DL hours of 100,800 and expected factory OH of $302,400.

Discussion with the factory superintendent indicated that only two jobs remained unfinished on April 30. Fortunately, the superintendent also had copies of the job cost sheets that showed a combined total of $4,800 of DM and $9,000 of DL. The DL hours on these jobs totaled 2,144. Both of these jobs had been started during April.

A badly faded copy of April's Cost of Goods Manufactured and Sold Schedule showed cost of goods manufactured was $96,000, and the April 1 Finished Goods Inventory was $16,800.

The treasurer's office files copies of paid invoices chronologically. All invoices are for raw material purchased on account. Examination of these files revealed that unpaid invoices on April 1 amounted to $12,200; $56,000 of purchases had been made during April; and $36,000 of unpaid invoices existed on April 30.

a. Calculate the cost of direct material used in April.
b. Calculate the cost of raw material issued in April.
c. Calculate the April 30 balance of Raw Material Inventory.
d. Determine the amount of underapplied or overapplied overhead for April.
e. What is the Cost of Goods Sold for April?

Chapter 6 Job Order Costing

P6-70. Ethics; writing Two types of contracts are commonly used when private firms contract to provide services to governmental agencies: cost-plus and fixed-price contracts. The cost-plus contract allows the contracting firm to recover the costs associated with providing the product or service plus a reasonable profit. The fixed-price contract provides for a fixed payment to the contractor. When a fixed-price contract is used, the contractor's profits are based on its ability to control costs relative to the price received.

In recent years, a number of contractors have either been accused, or found guilty, of improper accounting or fraud in accounting for contracts with the government. One deceptive accounting technique that is sometimes the subject of audit investigations involves cases in which a contractor is suspected of shifting costs from fixed-priced contracts to cost-plus contracts. In shifting costs from the fixed-priced contract, the contractor not only influences costs assigned to that contract but also receives a reimbursement plus an additional amount on the costs shifted to the cost-plus contract.

a. Why would a company that conducts work under both cost-plus and fixed-price contracts have an incentive to shift costs from the fixed-price to the cost-plus contracts?
b. From an ethical perspective, do you believe such cost shifting is ever justified? Explain.

LO6-6

P6-71. Research; quality; writing Timbuk2 is a San Francisco company that makes a variety of messenger, cyclist, and laptop bags. The company's Web site (Timbuk2.com) allows customers to design their own size, color, and fabric bags with specific features and accessories; then the company sews the bags to the customers' specifications.

a. Visit the company's Web site and custom-design a bag. Compare the quoted price with a bag of similar quality and features at a local store. Explain whether you think the Timbuk2 bag is a good value.
b. Why would Timbuk2 be able to produce custom-made messenger bags for almost the same cost as mass-produced ones?
c. Would you expect the quality of the custom-produced messenger bags to be higher or lower than the mass-produced ones? Discuss the rationale for your answer.
d. Why would the custom-made messenger bags show a high profit margin?

LO6-6

Timbuk2

P6-72. Ethics; writing One of the main reasons for using a job order costing system is to achieve profitability by charging a price for each job that is proportionate to the related costs. The fundamental underlying concept is that the buyer of the product should be charged a price that exceeds all costs related to the job contract; thus, the price reflects the cost.

However, there are settings in which the price charged to the consumer does not reflect the costs incurred by the vendor to serve that customer. A case heard by the U.S. Supreme Court involved the University of Wisconsin, which charged all students a user fee and then redistributed the fees to student organizations.

The purpose of collecting the fee is to ensure that money is available to support diversity of thought and speech in student organizations. The user fee supports even unpopular causes so that the students hear a variety of voices. In total, the fee subsidized about 125 student groups. However, a group of students filed suit, claiming that students should not be required to fund causes that are inconsistent with their personal beliefs.

a. In your opinion, how would diversity of thought be affected if a student were allowed to select the organizations that would receive the student's user fee (e.g., as with dues)?
b. Is the University of Wisconsin treating its students ethically by charging them to support student organizations for causes that conflict with their personal beliefs?

LO6-6

P6-73. Defective units and spoilage Prudoe Compounds produces a variety of chemicals used by auto manufacturers in their painting processes. With each batch of chemicals produced, some spoilage naturally occurs. Prudoe Compounds includes normal spoilage cost in its predetermined OH rate. For the year, Prudoe Compounds estimated the following:

LO6-2, 7

Overhead costs, other than spoilage	$600,000
Estimated spoilage cost	50,000
Estimated sales value of spoiled materials	20,000
Estimated direct labor hours	40,000

a. Prudoe Compounds applies overhead based on direct labor hours. Calculate the predetermined OH rate for the year.
b. For a batch of chemicals mixed in May, the firm experienced normal spoilage on Job #788. The cost of the spoiled material amounted to $1,730 and the company estimated the salvage value of those materials to be $496. Journalize the entry for the spoilage.

© Cambridge Business Publishers

LO6-2, 7 **P6-74. Defective units and rework** PlastiCo produces plastic pipe to customer specifications. Losses of less than 5 percent are considered normal because they are inherent in the production process. The company applies overhead to products using machine hours. PlastiCo used the following information in setting its predetermined OH rate for the year:

Expected overhead other than rework	$850,000
Expected rework costs	75,000
Total expected overhead	$925,000
Expected machine hours for the year	100,000

During the year, the following production and cost data were accumulated:

Total good production completed	2,000,000 feet of pipe
Total defects	40,000 feet of pipe
Ending inventory	75,000 feet of pipe
Total cost of direct material for Job #B316	$687,100
Total cost of direct labor for Job #B316	$157,750
Total machine hours for Job #B316	3,080
Cost of reworking defects during the year	$ 75,500
Total actual overhead cost for the year	$862,000

a. Determine the overhead application rate for the year.
b. Determine the cost for Job #B316 in the year.
c. Assume that the rework is normal and those units can be sold for the regular selling price. How will PlastiCo account for the $75,500 of rework cost?
d. Assume that PlastiCo does not include rework costs in developing the overhead application rate because rework is related to specific jobs. Determine the cost of Job #B316 if rework was not associated specifically to this job.
e. Using the information from (d), assume that 20 percent of the rework cost was specifically related to 200 feet of pipe produced for Job #B316. The reworked pipe can be sold for $3.50 per foot. What is the total cost of Job #B316?

Review Solutions

Review 6-1

1. a. Job order
   b. Process costing
   c. Process costing
   d. Job order
   e. Job order
   f. Process costing
   g. Job order
   h. Job order
   i. Process costing
   j. Job order

2. The main difference between an actual and normal cost system is that actual overhead cost is assigned to products/services versus applied overhead that is assigned using a predetermined overhead rate.
   - If the manufacturer has a preference for timely data for decision making purposes, the normal system would be preferable as overhead costs can be allocated without having to wait for actual results.
   - If the manufacturer experiences seasonal fluctuations in utilities, maintenance, etc. due to extreme heat or cold, the normal system would be preferable as it smooths costs over an annual period.
   - If activity levels fluctuate within a relevant range, a normal costing system may be preferable as a fixed cost per unit is calculated on an annual basis and would not fluctuate month to month.
   - If the manufacturer has identified cost drivers with a causal relationship with costs, having timely information will allow for more effective profitability analysis.

Review 6-2

a. ($275,000 + $458,000) ÷ (18,000 + 30,000) = $15.27
b. ($275,000 + $458,000) ÷ (96,000 + 9,000) = $6.98

Chapter 6 Job Order Costing

c. Assembly: $275,000 ÷ 96,000 = $2.86
   Finishing: $458,000 ÷ 30,000 = $15.27

d. (a) $15.27 × 2 = $30.54
   (b) $6.98 × 10 = $69.80
   (c) ($2.86 × 10) + ($15.27 × 2) = $59.14

e. Using a plantwide rate with labor hours will result in the product being *undercosted*. Using only labor hours to apply overhead does not take into account the product's higher relative use of machine hours as compared to labor hours. On the other hand, using only machine hours will result in the product being *overcosted*. The emphasis is placed on the higher use of machine hours and doesn't take into account the lower relative use of labor hours in finishing. If one product is undercosted, this means that another product will carry too much cost (and vice versa). Thus cost cross-subsidization will more likely occur when a plantwide rate is used versus when department rates are used.

Review 6-3

a.
Cost of Goods Sold	50,000	
Manufacturing Overhead		50,000
To close underapplied overhead		

b.
Work in Process	2,500	
Finished Goods	10,000	
Cost of Goods Sold	37,500	
Manufacturing Overhead		50,000
To close underapplied overhead		

c. Determining materiality is entity specific. For example, in a company such as Ford Motor Company, $50,000 as a percentage of total assets is a negligible percentage. However, for a small manufacturer that supplies goods to Ford Motor, $50,000 may be 5% or more of total assets. Using a percentage threshold such as 5%, can provide a preliminary assessment of materiality. However, it must be combined with other analysis or review of all relevant considerations. Generally, a cost is considered material if there is a substantial likelihood that a reasonable person would consider it material (important) for that particular situation.

Review 6-4

a.
Raw Material Inventory	49,400	
Accounts Payable		49,400
WIP—Job #301	29,120	
WIP—Job #302	4,680	
WIP—Other jobs	34,840	
Direct Material Inventory		68,640
WIP—Job #301	6,760	
WIP—Job #302	9,100	
WIP—Other jobs	12,740	
Cash or Wages Payable		28,600
Manufacturing Overhead	143,000	
Various accounts		143,000
WIP—Job #301	15,210	
WIP—Job #302	20,475	
WIP—Other jobs	28,665	
Manufacturing Overhead		64,350
Finished Goods Inventory	58,370	
WIP—Job #301 ($7,280 + $29,120 + $6,760 + $15,210)		58,370
Cash	81,718	
Sales		81,718
Cost of Goods Sold	58,370	
Finished Goods Inventory		58,370

© Cambridge Business Publishers

b. Ending WIP $114,140 ($10,920 + $68,640 + $28,600 + $64,350 − $58,370).
$37,895 relates to Job #302 ($3,640 + $4,680 + $9,100 + $20,475).

c. If overhead was underapplied for April, that could mean that the total cost of Job #301 was understated because less overhead was applied to the job than actual costs. However, one month is only a fraction of the year. To date, is overhead over or underapplied? Is overhead expected to be underapplied at year-end? Also, is overhead underapplied by a material or immaterial amount? Without more information, it is impossible to know whether the job is over or undercosted.

Review 6-5

	Vet Appointments	Technician Appointments	Total
Supplies used[1]	$ 1,296	$ 864	$ 2,160
Labor:			
Veterinarian salaries	14,580		14,580
Technician salaries[2]	3,391	2,261	5,652
Overhead:			
Utilities[3]	1,944	1,296	3,240
Office salaries[4]	410	274	684
Depreciation on medical equipment[5]	3,984	2,656	6,640
Depreciation on building[6]	2,678	1,786	4,464
Cost of services rendered	$28,283	$9,137	$37,420

[1] Supplies used:
$0 + $4,320 − $2,160 = $2,160
Vet appointments: $2,160 × 60% = $1,296
Technician appointments: $2,160 × 40% = $ 864

[2] Veterinarian assistant salaries:
Vet appointments: $5,652 × 60% = $3,391 (rounded)
Technician appointments: $5,652 × 40% = $2,261 (rounded)

[3] Utilities:
Vet appointments: 90% × $3,600 × 60% = $1,944
Technician appointments: 90% × $3,600 × 40% = $1,296

[4] Office salaries:
Vet appointments: 20% × $3,420 × 60% = $ 410 (rounded)
Technician appointments: 20% × $3,420 × 40% = $ 274 (rounded)

[5] Depreciation on medical equipment:
Vet appointments: $6,640 × 60% = $3,984
Technician appointments: $6,640 × 40% = $2,656

[6] Depreciation on building:
Vet appointments: 80% × $5,580 × 60% = $2,678 (rounded)
Technician appointments: 80% × $5,580 × 40% = $1,786 (rounded)

b. The total cost of services provided for April is $37,420. However, if amounts were tracked by patient, direct materials could be tracked by job.

Direct labor could also be directly applied to jobs by using the time allocated per appointment. Overhead costs of $15,028 could be allocated to jobs by using a predetermined overhead rate such as direct labor hours.

With this additional information, management could have a costing system that tracks costs by job. Using this information, management could set prices and determine the profitability by job, which could determine which jobs were more profitable than others.

Review 6-6

a. 19% = $22,000 ÷ $118,000

b. Allocation of overhead pool #1: $18,000 ÷ 400 (100 + 130 + 65 + 55 + 50) = $45

Customer A: $4,500 ($45 × 100); Customer B: $5,850 ($45 × 130); Customer C: $2,925 ($45 × 65); Customer D: $2,475 ($45 × 55); Customer E: $2,250 ($45 × 50).

Allocation of overhead pool #2: $78,000 ÷ 1,200 (455 + 490 + 150 + 60 + 45) = $65

Customer A: $29,575 ($65 × 455); Customer B: $31,850 ($65 × 490); Customer C: $9,750 ($65 × 150); Customer D: $3,900 ($65 × 60); Customer E: $2,925 ($65 × 45).

Chapter 6 Job Order Costing

	Total	Customer A	Customer B	Customer C	Customer D	Customer E
Sales.............	$118,000	$50,000	$45,000	$15,000	$ 5,000	$ 3,000
Overhead Pool #1....	18,000	4,500	5,850	2,925	2,475	2,250
Overhead Pool #2....	78,000	29,575	31,850	9,750	3,900	2,925
Gross profit.........	$ 22,000	$15,925	$ 7,300	$ 2,325	$(1,375)	$(2,175)
Gross profit margin...	19%	32%	16%	16%	–28%	–73%

c. The jobs that require further investigation by management are Customers D and E. The company is unprofitable on jobs with sales of $5,000 or less.

Review 6-7

a.
Manufacturing Overhead Control.............	50	
Raw Material Inventory..................		20
Wages Payable.......................		30

b.
WIP—Job #380	50	
Raw Material Inventory..................		20
Wages Payable.......................		30

c.
Loss on Abnormal Rework..................	50	
Raw Material Inventory..................		20
Wages Payable.......................		30

d. Management judgment is required upfront in order to determine whether normal losses typically apply to all jobs or specific jobs. If it is determined that losses apply to all jobs, management must estimate the rework costs used in the predetermined overhead rate. If a loss is incurred, management judgment is required in determining whether the loss is normal or abnormal. If the defective units have a disposal value, management must estimate its value which also requires judgment.

Data Visualization Solutions
(See page 6-21.)

a. Each of the three jobs has the same gross profit; however, after allocating support costs to each job, the profitability varies by job. Edgewood is the most profitable followed by Hilltop, and then Sunset.

b. Without allocating support costs to each job, the company might assume that each job is equally profitable because each job has the same gross profit. Support costs might be reviewed in total, but not on a job basis. Management may assume incorrectly, that support costs are used equally by job.

c. The Sunset job appears to be an outlier. Information may be gained from reviewing what is working well on the other jobs to see if that could be applied to the Sunset job.

Chapter 7
Process Costing

Road Map

LO	Learning Objective | Topics	Page	eLecture	Demo	Review	Assignments
7-1	**Why are equivalent units of production used in calculating a unit cost in process costing?** Unit Cost :: Production Costs :: Equivalent Units of Production (EUP) :: Two-Period Production Sequence	7-2	e7-1	D7-1A D7-1B	Rev 7-1	M7-14, M7-15, E7-23, E7-24, E7-25, E7-26, E7-27, E7-28, E7-29, E7-30, E7-31, E7-32, E7-33, E7-37, E7-38, E7-39, E7-40, E7-44, E7-46, E7-47, E7-48, P7-58, P7-59, P7-62, P7-77
7-2	**How are equivalent units of production, unit costs, and inventory values determined using the weighted average (WA) method of process costing?** Weighted Average (WA) Process Costing Method :: Physical Units :: Equivalent Units :: WA Unit Cost :: Cost of Production Report	7-6	e7-2	D7-2	Rev 7-2	M7-14, M7-16, E7-25, E7-26, E7-27, E7-31, E7-32, E7-33, E7-34, E7-36, E7-37, E7-38, E7-41, E7-44, E7-45, E7-46, E7-48, E7-53, P7-58, P7-59, P7-60, P7-61, P7-65, P7-66, P7-67, P7-69, P7-70, P7-74, P7-75, P7-76, P7-77
7-3	**How are equivalent units of production, unit costs, and inventory values determined using the first-in, first-out (FIFO) method of process costing?** FIFO Process Costing Method :: Physical Units :: Equivalent Units :: FIFO Unit Cost :: Cost of Production Report	7-13	e7-3	D7-3	Rev 7-3	M7-15, M7-17, E7-28, E7-29, E7-30, E7-31, E7-32, E7-33, E7-35, E7-36, E7-39, E7-40, E7-42, E7-43, E7-44, E7-47, E7-48, E7-51, E7-52, E7-54, P7-62, P7-63, P7-64, P7-65, P7-66, P7-68, P7-71, P7-78, DA 7-1
7-4	**How are transferred-in costs and units accounted for in a multidepartment production setting?** Multidepartment Setting :: Transferred-In Cost	7-18	e7-4	D7-4	Rev 7-4	M7-18, E7-45, E7-46, E7-47, E7-48, P7-67, P7-68, P7-69, P7-70, P7-71, P7-74, P7-75, P7-76
7-5	**Why would a company use a hybrid costing system?** Hybrid Costing System :: Characteristics of Job Order and Process Costing	7-20	e7-5	D7-5	Rev 7-5	M7-19, E7-49, E7-50, P7-72, P7-73
7-6	**How are normal and abnormal spoilage losses treated in an equivalent units of production schedule?** Spoilage :: Continuous Loss :: Discrete Loss :: Normal Loss :: Abnormal Loss :: Method of Neglect :: Product Cost :: Period Cost	7-21	e7-6	D7-6	Rev 7-6	M7-20, E7-51, E7-52, E7-53, E7-54, P7-75, P7-77, P7-78
7-7	*(Appendix 7A)* **What alternative methods can be used to calculate equivalent units of production?** WA EUP Starting with Units Transferred Out :: WA EUP Starting with Total Units :: Reconciliation Between WA EUP and FIFO EUP	7-24	e7-7	D7-7	Rev 7-7	MC7-21, E7-31, E7-32, E7-33, E7-55
7-8	*(Appendix 7B)* **How are equivalent units of production, unit costs, and inventory values determined using the standard costing method of process costing?** Standard Costs :: FIFO Process Costing Method :: Variance Analysis	7-26	e7-8	D7-8	Rev 7-8	M7-22, E7-56, E7-57, P7-74, P7-76, P7-79, P7-80

INTRODUCTION

Companies choose product costing systems based, in part, on the types of products manufactured and services offered. As discussed in Chapter 6, companies that manufacture products or perform services conforming to distinct customer specifications and made in limited quantities use job order costing. However, some companies manufacture homogenous products in a continuous flow process or in batches of output containing units that are identical. Manufacturers of food products, bricks, gasoline, candles, and paper, among many other types of firms, commonly use the process costing method. For example, **Kellogg's** produces Rice Krispies in batches, and all "rice puffs" in each batch are the same. For Kellogg's Pop-Tarts, the external pastry is the same for all batches, but the flavoring inside may differ or some external pastries may be frosted while others are not. Kellogg's uses a process costing rather than a job order costing system to accumulate and assign costs to units of production.

Both job order and process costing systems accumulate costs by cost component (direct material, direct labor, and overhead) in each production department. However, the two systems assign costs to departmental output differently. In a job order system, costs are assigned to specific jobs and, if possible, to the units contained within each job. Process costing uses an averaging technique to assign costs to all units produced during the period. In both systems, unit costs are transferred between departments as goods flow from one department to the next so that a total production cost can be accumulated.

This chapter first illustrates the weighted average (WA) and first-in, first-out (FIFO) methods of calculating unit cost in a process costing system. These two methods differ only in the treatment of beginning Work in Process (WIP) Inventory units and costs. After unit cost has been determined, a total cost is assigned to (1) units transferred out of a department and (2) that department's ending WIP Inventory.

The chapter also describes the use of process costing in multidepartment organizations and hybrid systems. Hybrid systems are used in some companies that customize products that would commonly be accounted for using a process costing system. Next, the issue of accounting for spoilage in a process costing system is discussed. Appendix 7A provides alternative computations for equivalent unit of product calculations. Appendix 7B describes how standard costing systems are used as a simplification of the FIFO process costing system.

UNIT COST CALCULATION IN PROCESS COSTING

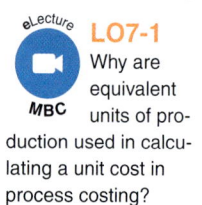

LO7-1 Why are equivalent units of production used in calculating a unit cost in process costing?

The cost accumulation process in a process costing system differs from that in a job order costing system due to the cost object to which the costs are assigned, which affects the unit cost calculation.

Production System	Cost Object	Unit Cost
Job Order	Specific customer's job	Cost per unit in a job
Process	Production run by department	Cost per unit in a process

The Candle Shop, which manufactures scented candles for two different customer groups, is used to illustrate the differences. In addition to its daily operations of making votive, 7-inch, and 12-inch taper candles, the company periodically contracts to make custom candles for client promotional activities.

Process Costing For its basic product lines, The Candle Shop uses a process costing system to accumulate periodic costs for each department and each product type. Because the company manufactures several types of candles each period, the costs assignable to each product type must be individually designated and attached to the specific production runs. *Production run costs for each department are then assigned to the units processed during the period.*

Job Order Costing In contrast, for specialty candle production, The Candle Shop uses job order costing to accumulate direct material and direct labor costs associated with each distinctive order and assigns those costs directly to the individual customer's job. Overhead is allocated using a predetermined overhead rate. After each job is completed, *the total material, labor, and allocated overhead costs are known and the cost for each unit in the job can be determined.*

The focus of this chapter is process costing. Assigning costs to product units requires the use of an *averaging process*. In a process costing system, a product's actual unit cost is found by dividing a period's departmental production costs by that period's departmental production quantity as expressed by the following formula.

$$\text{Unit cost} = \frac{\text{Production costs}}{\text{Equivalent Units of Production}}$$

Production Costs: The Numerator

The formula numerator is obtained by accumulating departmental costs incurred in a single period. **Exhibit 7.1** presents the sources of the initial cost assignments to production departments during a period. Costs are reassigned at the end of the period (usually each month) from the departments to the units produced. As goods are transferred from one department to the next, related departmental production costs are also transferred. When products are complete, their costs are transferred from WIP Inventory to Finished Goods (FG) Inventory.

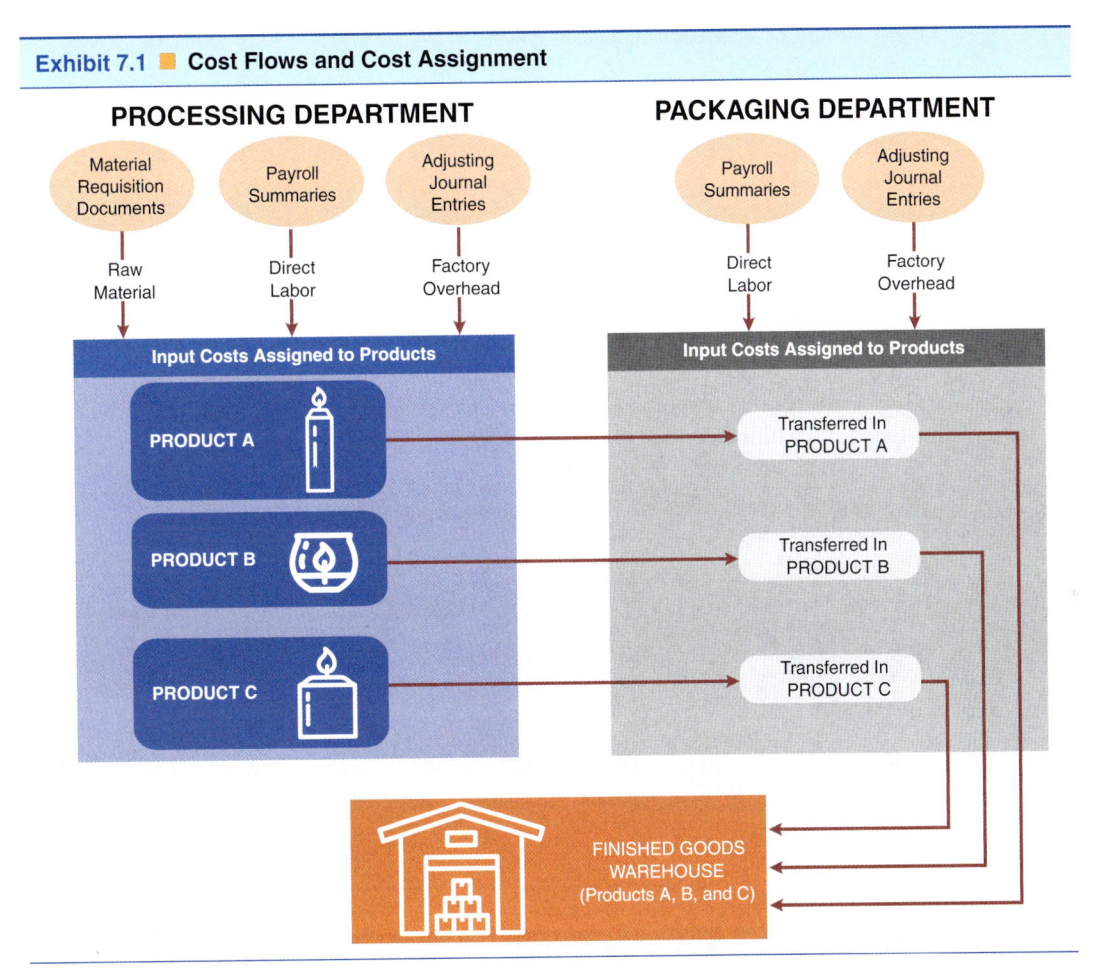

Exhibit 7.1 ■ Cost Flows and Cost Assignment

As in job order costing, direct material and direct labor costs present relatively few problems for cost accumulation and assignment in a process costing system. Direct material cost can be measured from material requisition documents; direct labor cost can be determined from payroll summaries. Overhead, however, must be allocated to output. If total overhead costs are relatively constant and production volume is relatively steady between periods, actual overhead costs may be used for product costing. Otherwise, as discussed in the last chapter, using actual overhead for product costing would result in fluctuating unit costs, and therefore, usage of predetermined application rates is more appropriate. As costs and production activities change, the base on which overhead is assigned to production may shift. For example, as a production plant becomes less labor intensive and more automated, management should change from a labor-based to a machine-based overhead allocation.

Equivalent Units of Production: The Denominator

The denominator in the unit cost formula represents total departmental production of a given product for the period. If all units started during a period were 100 percent complete at the end of the period, units could simply be counted to obtain the denominator. In most production processes, however, partially completed units comprise WIP Inventory at the end of one period and the beginning WIP Inventory of the next period. Process costing assigns costs to both fully and partially completed units by mathematically converting partially completed units to equivalent whole units. **Equivalent units of production (EUP)** are approximations of the number of whole units of output that could have been produced during a period from the actual resources expended during that period. For example, if two units were each 50 percent complete, EUP is one unit.

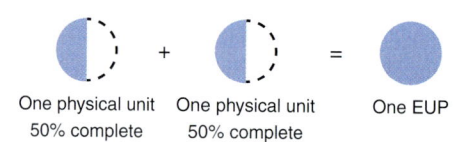

One physical unit 50% complete + One physical unit 50% complete = One EUP

Units in beginning WIP Inventory were started last period but will be completed during the current period. This *two-period production sequence* means that some costs for the units in beginning inventory were incurred last period and additional costs for those units will be incurred in the current period. For example, let's assume production of candles started in period one. Period one ending inventory becomes beginning inventory for period two. If beginning inventory for period two was 25 percent complete for direct labor and overhead, the remaining 75 percent would need to be completed in period two.

Additionally, the partially completed units in ending WIP Inventory were started in the current period but will not be completed until next period. Therefore, some of the current period costs should attach to the units in ending WIP Inventory, and additional costs will be incurred and attached to those units next period. For example, if ending inventory for period two was 40 percent complete as to direct labor and overhead, another 60 percent would need to be added in period three. This production sequence is illustrated in **Exhibit 7.2**.

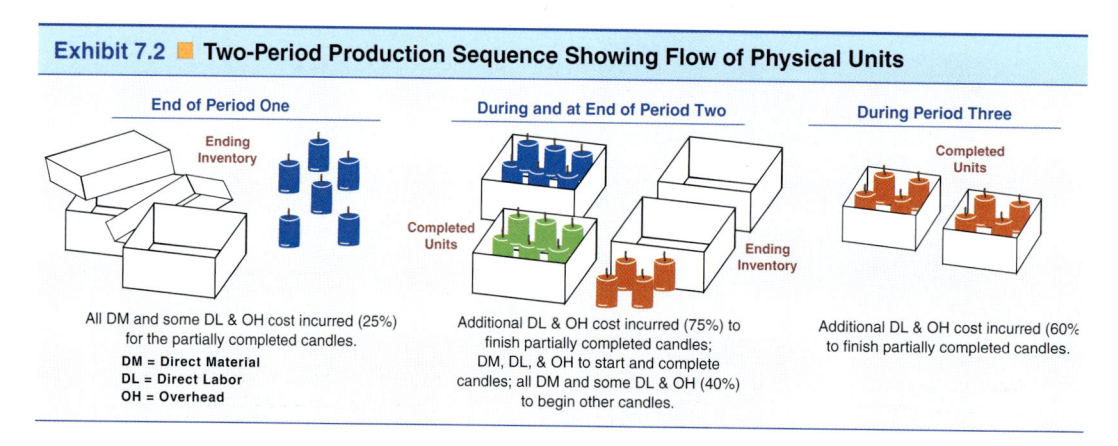

Exhibit 7.2 ■ Two-Period Production Sequence Showing Flow of Physical Units

End of Period One
All DM and some DL & OH cost incurred (25%) for the partially completed candles.
DM = Direct Material
DL = Direct Labor
OH = Overhead

During and at End of Period Two
Additional DL & OH cost incurred (75%) to finish partially completed candles; DM, DL, & OH to start and complete candles; all DM and some DL & OH (40%) to begin other candles.

During Period Three
Additional DL & OH cost incurred (60% to finish partially completed candles.

DEMO 7-1A LO7-1 Computing Equivalent Units for the Period

The following simple example indicates how EUP are calculated. Assume The Candle Shop had no WIP Inventory on November 1. During November, the company worked on 220,000 units: 200,000 units were fully completed and 20,000 units were 40 percent complete at the end of the period.

◆ **What are EUP for the period?**

The EUP for the period are as follows.

$$\text{EUP} = \text{BI (beginning inventory) units completed} + \text{Units started and completed} + \text{EI (ending inventory) units partially complete}$$

$$\text{EUP} = 0 + (200{,}000 \times 100\%) + (20{,}000 \times 40\%)$$

$$\text{EUP} = 208{,}000$$

Some quantity of direct material must be introduced at the start of production to begin the conversion process. For example, to make its various products, assume The Candle Shop's production process begins with candle wax. Any material added at the start of production is 100 percent complete at the outset of the process, regardless of the percentage of completion of labor and overhead.

When overhead is applied on a direct labor basis, or when direct labor and overhead are added to the product at the same rate, a *single percentage of completion* can be used for both **conversion cost (CC)** components, labor and overhead.

Calculating EUP for Multiple Direct Materials

Most production processes require multiple direct materials. Additional materials may be added at any point or even continuously during processing. A direct material, such as a box, may even be added at the end of processing. Until the end of the production process, the product would be zero percent complete as to the box but may be totally complete with regard to other materials. The Candle Shop's production process occurs as follows.

- Wicks and wax are added at the beginning of the process. Thus, these materials are 100 percent complete at any point in the process after the start of production; no additional quantities of these materials are added later in production.
- When enough conversion costs have been added to reach the 20 percent completion point, additional materials (color and scent) are added. Prior to 20 percent completion, these materials were 0 percent complete; after the 20 percent point, these materials are 100 percent complete.
- Almost at the end of the process, the candles are boxed and, after this step, the product is 100 percent complete. Thus, boxes are 0 percent complete until the candles are packaged; after packaging, the product is complete and transferred to the finished goods warehouse or directly to customers.

The production flow for candles is shown in **Exhibit 7.3** and visually illustrates the need for separate EUP computations for each cost component.

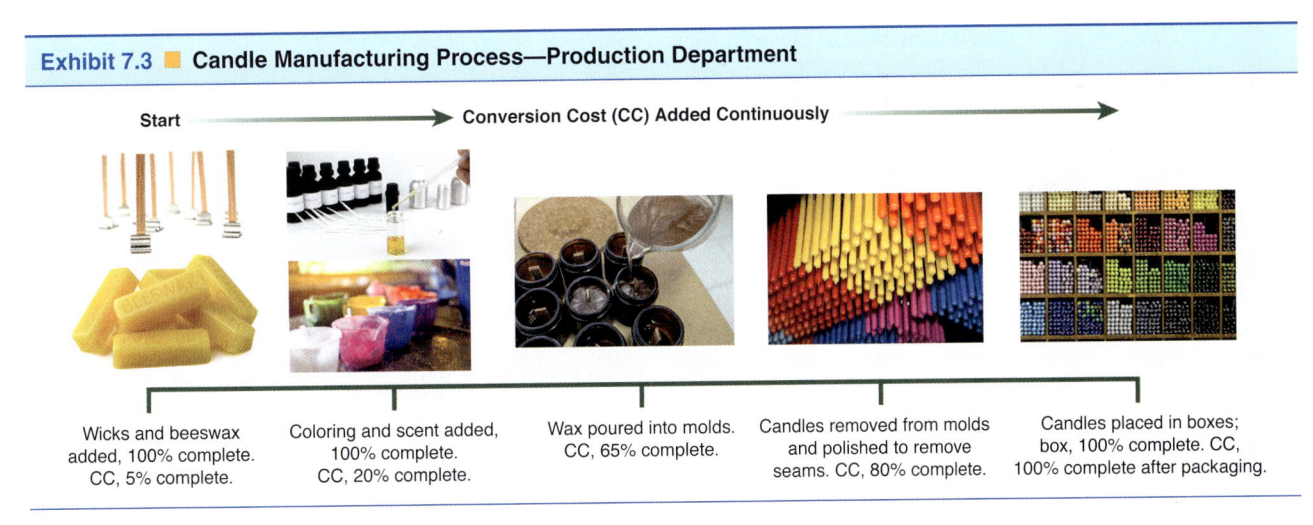

Exhibit 7.3 ■ Candle Manufacturing Process—Production Department

Start → Conversion Cost (CC) Added Continuously →

| Wicks and beeswax added, 100% complete. CC, 5% complete. | Coloring and scent added, 100% complete. CC, 20% complete. | Wax poured into molds. CC, 65% complete. | Candles removed from molds and polished to remove seams. CC, 80% complete. | Candles placed in boxes; box, 100% complete. CC, 100% complete after packaging. |

Computing Equivalent Units for DM and CC   LO7-1   DEMO 7-1B

Assume that The Candle Shop had no beginning inventory, but had enough wicks and wax to start to make 8,000 candles. At the end of the period, the process is 75 percent complete as to labor and overhead. The candles are 100 percent complete as to wicks, wax, color, and scent, but 0 percent complete as to boxes.

- ◆ **What are EUP for (1) wicks, wax, color, and scent, (2) boxes, and (3) conversion cost for the period?**

- The materials EUP calculations indicate that there are 8,000 EUP for wicks, wax, color, and scent.
- Because candles are not boxed until completed, there are 0 EUP for boxes.

© Cambridge Business Publishers

- The labor and overhead (conversion) cost components have an equivalency of 6,000 candles because the candles are 75 percent complete and labor and overhead are added continuously during the process.[1]

$$8,000 \text{ candles} \times 75\% = 6,000 \text{ EUP for conversion costs}$$

REVIEW 7-1 · LO7-1 · Computing Equivalent Units

a. Compute equivalent units of production for the period for each of the following separate scenarios. In your calculations, simply calculate work done during the period, ignoring the application of any particular costing method.

Scenario	EUP for Materials	EUP for Conversion Costs
1. The company worked on 135,000 units, 80,000 which are fully completed and 55,000 which are 45 percent complete at the end of the period for materials and conversion costs.		
2. The company worked on 54,000 units which are now in ending inventory. The units are 100 percent complete at the end of the period for materials and the process is 75 percent complete as to labor and overhead.		
3. The company finished work on the 12,000 units that were in its beginning inventory of the period. These units had 40 percent of materials added and were 20 percent complete as to labor and overhead at the start of the production period.		
4. The company started and completed 10,000 units and completed 4,000 units of its beginning inventory that had all of its materials but were only 25 percent complete as to labor and overhead at the start of the production period.		

More practice: E7-23
Solution on p. 7-56.

b. **Critical Thinking:** In what ways could a company estimate a percent complete as to labor and overhead? How can the accuracy of this estimate impact decision making?

WEIGHTED AVERAGE COSTING METHOD

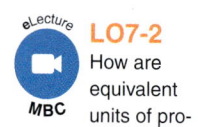

LO7-2 How are equivalent units of production, unit costs, and inventory values determined using the weighted average (WA) method of process costing?

The two methods of accounting for cost flows in process costing include the following.

| Weighted Average (WA) | First-in, First-out (FIFO) |

These methods reflect the way in which cost flows are assumed to occur in the production process.

Differentiating WA Method from FIFO Method

The **weighted average method** computes a single average cost per unit of the combined beginning WIP Inventory and current period production. The **first-in, first-out method** separates beginning WIP Inventory and current period production as well as their costs so that a *current period* cost per unit can be calculated. The denominator in the EUP cost formula differs, depending on which of the two methods is used.[2]

---

[1] Although the same number of equivalent units results for wicks, wax, color, and scent and for labor and overhead, separate calculations of unit cost may be desirable for each cost component. These separate calculations would give managers more information for planning and control purposes. Managers must weigh the costs of making separate calculations against the benefits of having the additional information. For illustrative purposes, however, single computations will be made when cost components are at equal percentages of completion.

[2] Note that the term *denominator* is used here rather than equivalent units of production. Based on its definition, EUP are related to current period production activity. Thus, for any given set of production facts, there is only one true measure of equivalent units produced—regardless of the cost flow assumption used—and that measure is FIFO EUP. However, this fact has been obscured over time due to the continued references to the "EUP" computation for weighted average. Thus, the term *EUP* has taken on a generic use to mean "the denominator used to compute the unit cost of production for a period in a process costing system." EUP is used in this generic manner throughout the process costing discussion.

Costing Method	Units and Costs	Cost per Unit
Weighted average	BI + Current period production and costs	Average cost for all EUP worked on during the period
First-in, first-out	BI separated from current period production and costs	Separate costs for BI units and units started during the period

Calculation of a unit product cost is essential for determining the journal entry amount to be transferred as goods move between departments as well as for preparing the financial statements (containing WIP Inventory, FG Inventory, and Cost of Goods Sold). The WA method provides a reasonable approximation of unit costs if inventory quantities are fairly constant and costs remain fairly steady over time. In such circumstances, the difference between the WA and FIFO inventory costs will be immaterial and management may choose the WA method because of its ease of calculation. *If, however, inventory quantities and costs have a high level of variability, the FIFO method will provide better information about periodic changes on unit costs.*

Steps in the Process Costing System

Exhibit 7.4 outlines the steps necessary in a process costing system for determining the costs assignable to the units completed and to those still in WIP inventory at the end of a period.

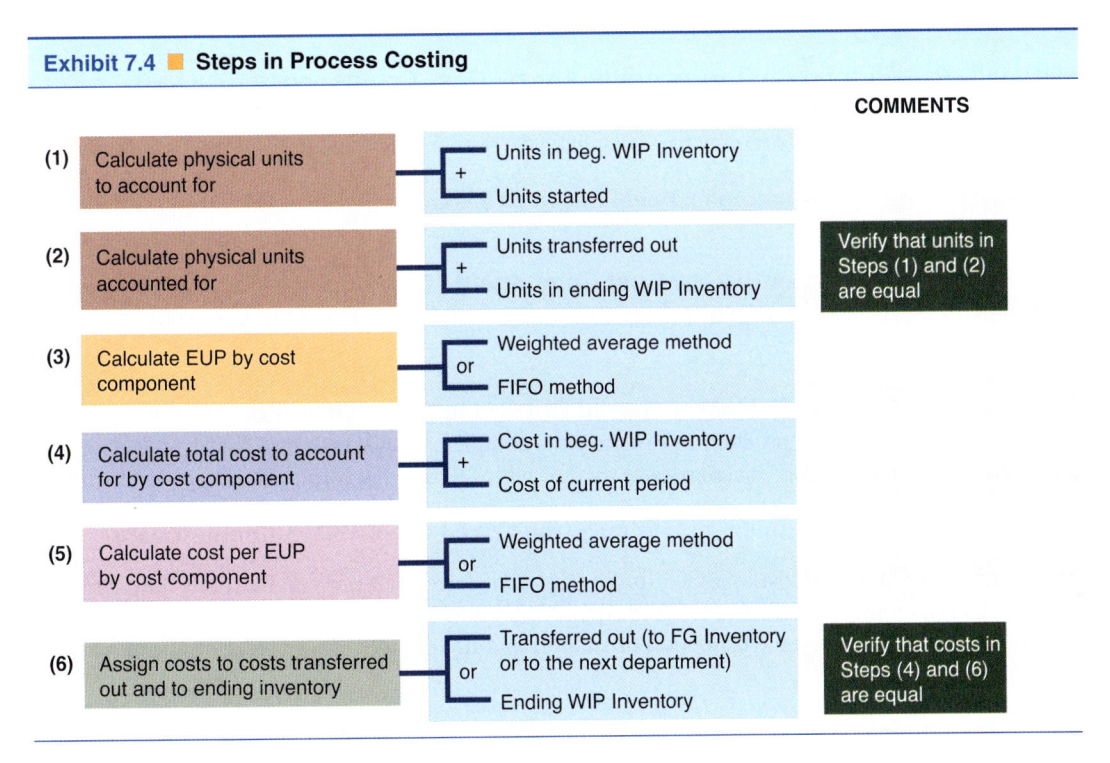

Exhibit 7.4 ■ Steps in Process Costing

Step	Action	Components	Comments
(1)	Calculate physical units to account for	Units in beg. WIP Inventory + Units started	
(2)	Calculate physical units accounted for	Units transferred out + Units in ending WIP Inventory	Verify that units in Steps (1) and (2) are equal
(3)	Calculate EUP by cost component	Weighted average method or FIFO method	
(4)	Calculate total cost to account for by cost component	Cost in beg. WIP Inventory + Cost of current period	
(5)	Calculate cost per EUP by cost component	Weighted average method or FIFO method	
(6)	Assign costs to costs transferred out and to ending inventory	Transferred out (to FG Inventory or to the next department) or Ending WIP Inventory	Verify that costs in Steps (4) and (6) are equal

Step 1: Calculate Physical Units to Account For Determine the total actual physical (whole) units for which the department is responsible. This amount is the sum of fully and partially completed units processed in the department during the current period.

Total units = Beginning WIP Inventory units + Units started this period

Step 2: Calculate Physical Units Accounted For Calculate the total physical units accounted for, which requires determining what happened to the units during the period. At period-end, the total physical units will be either (1) completed and transferred out or (2) partially completed and remaining in ending WIP Inventory.[3]

---

[3] A third category (spoilage/breakage) does exist. It is assumed at this point that no production losses occur. A later section in this chapter provides a discussion of spoilage in process costing situations.

> **Total units = Completed units + Ending WIP Inventory Units**

The number of completed units is equal to (a) beginning WIP units (assumed completed in the current period) plus (b) started and completed units (units produced *entirely* in the current period).

> **Completed units = Beginning WIP Inventory units + Started and completed units**

Verify that the total physical units for which the department is responsible is equal to the total physical units accounted for. If these amounts are not equal, any additional computations will be incorrect.

Step 3: Calculate EUP by Cost Component At this point, because of the lack of similarity in the work performed on completed and partially completed units, physical units are converted (using either the WA or FIFO method) to equivalent units of production using the percentage of completion for each cost component. If all direct material is added at the same stage of completion, a single computation for direct material can be made. If multiple materials are used but placed into production at different points in the production process, multiple direct material EUP calculations are necessary. If overhead is based on direct labor or if these two factors are always at the same degree of completion, a single EUP can be computed for conversion. If neither condition exists, separate EUP schedules must be prepared for labor and overhead.[4]

Step 4: Calculate Total Cost to Account For by Cost Component Find the **total cost to account for**, which is the beginning balance in WIP Inventory plus all current costs for direct material, direct labor, and overhead. Determine the costs that have been incurred in total and by cost component.

> **Total cost to account for = Beginning WIP $ + Current $ for DM, DL, and OH**

Step 5: Calculate Cost per EUP by Cost Component Using either the WA or the FIFO equivalent units of production calculated in step 3, calculate the cost per equivalent unit for each cost component.

Step 6: Assign Costs to Costs Transferred Out and to Ending Inventory Use the unit costs computed in step 5 to assign production costs to units completed and transferred out of WIP Inventory and to units remaining in WIP Inventory, the total of which equals the **total cost accounted for**.

> **Total cost accounted for = Total $ transferred out of WIP + Ending WIP $**

Verify that the total of the cost assigned to the units transferred out of WIP Inventory plus the cost of the units remaining in WIP Inventory is equal to the total cost to account for in step 4. If these amounts are not equal (with the exception of small rounding differences), an error has been made in the computations.

DEMO 7-2   LO7-2   Demonstrating Process Costing Using the WA Method

The Candle Shop makes a 7-inch unscented pillar candle that is popular with restaurants and hotels because it minimizes customer allergy concerns. The company manufactures this product in one department with a single direct material: wax. Costs of wicks and coloring are insignificant and are considered indirect materials and part of overhead. Candles are shipped in reusable containers to a central warehouse. From there, candles are distributed to wholesalers and retailers who supply their own containers. Wax is added at the start of processing, so all units in process are 100 percent complete as to this material. Labor and overhead are assumed to be at the same degree of completion throughout the production process. Overhead costs for The Candle Shop are exceptionally stable, so actual

---

[4] As discussed in the last chapter, overhead can be applied to products using a variety of traditional (e.g., direct labor hours or machine hours) or activity driven (e.g., number of machine setups, pounds of material moved, or number of material requisitions) bases. The number of equivalent unit computations required depends on the number of different cost pools and overhead allocation bases established in the organization.

Chapter 7 Process Costing

overhead is assigned to production at the end of each period. **Exhibit 7.5** presents April information regarding The Candle Shop's inventories and costs.

Exhibit 7.5 ■ Production and Cost Information for The Candle Shop for April

Candles in beginning WIP Inventory (40% complete as to conversion)			10,000
Candles started during current period			401,400
Candles completed and transferred to FG Inventory			406,000
Candles in ending WIP Inventory (80% complete as to conversion)			5,400
Costs of beginning WIP Inventory			
Direct material	$ 11,886		
Direct labor	5,658		
Overhead	19,858	$ 37,402	
Current period costs			
Direct material	$642,240		
Direct labor	122,638		
Overhead	385,262	1,150,140	
Total cost to account for		$1,187,542	

Solving for Physical Quantities Although the exhibit provides information on both the quantity of candles transferred out and the quantity in the ending WIP Inventory, both quantities do not have to be explicitly stated. The number of candles remaining in the ending WIP Inventory can be calculated as total candles to account for minus the candles that were completed and transferred to FG Inventory during the period. Alternatively, the number of candles transferred to FG Inventory can be calculated as the total candles to account for minus the candles in ending WIP Inventory.

◆ How is the Candle Shop Information included in Exhibit 7.5 used to illustrated each step in process costing under the WA method outlined in Exhibit 7.4?

Step 1: Calculate Physical Units to Account For The **total physical units to account for** is the sum of the physical units in the beginning inventory plus the physical units started during the current period.

Candles in beginning WIP Inventory	10,000
Candles started during current period	401,400
Candles to account for	411,400

Step 2: Calculate Physical Units Accounted For The items detailed in this step indicate the physical units transferred out and in ending inventory. While cost assignment in Step 6 will be based on equivalent units, this step is based on actual physical units. The **total physical units accounted for** in step 2 equals the total physical units to account for in step 1 as shown in **Exhibit 7.6**.

Candles completed and transferred to FG Inventory	406,000
Candles in ending WIP Inventory	5,400
Candles accounted for	411,400

Exhibit 7.6 ■ Unit Concepts

Total units to account for	=	Total units accounted for
Beginning WIP Inventory units + Units started		Units completed + Ending WIP Inventory units

Step 3: Calculate EUP by Cost Component The WA EUP computation focuses on two items: (1) the number of candles in the beginning WIP inventory and (2) the number of candles started

and completed during the period. Of the total units transferred out of WIP Inventory, some units had been part of beginning inventory while others were started and completed within the current period. Thus, the **units started and completed** during a period equal the units completed during the period minus units in the beginning inventory. Units started and completed can also be computed as units started during the period minus the units in the ending inventory.

For The Candle Shop, 396,000 candles were started and completed in April, calculated as follows.

> **Units started and completed = Completed units – Beginning WIP Inventory units**
>
> 396,000 units = 406,000 units – 10,000 units

OR

> **Units started and completed = Units started this period – Ending WIP Inventory units**
>
> 396,000 units = 401,400 units – 5,400 units

The ending WIP Inventory is 100 percent complete as to material because wax is added at the start of production. The ending WIP Inventory is 80 percent complete as to labor and overhead. One EUP computation of 4,320 units can be made for labor and overhead costs because these cost elements are assumed to be added at the same rate throughout the production process.

5,400 Physical units × 80% complete at period end = 4,320 EUP for conversion in ending WIP

The WA computation for equivalent units of production is as follows.[5]

	DM	Conversion
Candles in beginning WIP Inventory (physical units)	10,000	10,000
Candles started and completed (physical units)	396,000	396,000
Ending WIP Inventory (5,400 × % complete)	5,400	4,320
Equivalent units of production	411,400	410,320

Step 4: Calculate Total Cost to Account For by Cost Component The total cost to account for equals beginning WIP Inventory cost plus current period costs. **Exhibit 7.5** provides the cost for each component of production: direct material, direct labor, and overhead. Production costs can be determined from transfers of direct material from the warehouse, incurrence of direct labor, and either actual or applied overhead amounts. The sum of direct labor and overhead costs is the total conversion cost. For The Candle Shop, the total cost to account for is ($37,402 + $1,150,140) or $1,187,542.

	Total	DM	DL	OH
Beginning WIP Inventory costs	$ 37,402	$ 11,886	$ 5,658	$ 19,858
Current period costs	1,150,140	642,240	122,638	385,262
Total cost to account for	$1,187,542	$654,126	$128,296	$405,120

The total cost to account for must be assigned to two categories of goods: those transferred to FG Inventory (or, if appropriate, to the next department) and those in ending WIP Inventory. Assignments are made based on the whole or equivalent whole units contained in each inventory category.

Step 5: Calculate Cost per EUP by Cost Component A cost per EUP must be computed for each component for which a separate calculation of EUP is made. Under the WA method, the costs of beginning WIP Inventory and of the current period are summed for each cost component and divided by that component's weighted average EUP to obtain the per-unit cost as follows.

---

[5] Different approaches exist to compute equivalent units of production and unit costs under weighted average and FIFO. In addition to the computations shown within this chapter, other valid and commonly used approaches for computing and reconciling WA and FIFO EUP are shown in Appendix 7A to this chapter.

$$\text{WA unit cost for each component} = \frac{\text{(Beginning WIP Inventory cost + Current period cost)}}{\text{Total WA equivalent units of production}}$$

This computation divides total cost by total units to produce an average component cost per unit. Because labor and overhead are at the same degree of completion, their costs can be combined and shown as a single conversion cost (CC) per equivalent unit. The Candle Shop's WA cost per EUP calculations for material and conversion follow.

	Total	DM	CC
Beginning WIP Inventory costs (**Exhibit 7.5**)	$ 37,402	$ 11,886	$ 25,516
Current period costs (**Exhibit 7.5**)	1,150,140	642,240	507,900
Total cost to account for	$1,187,542	$654,126	$533,416
Divided by EUP (step 3)		÷ 411,400	÷ 410,320
Cost per EUP	$ 2.89	$ 1.59	$ 1.30

The material and conversion cost amounts are summed to find the total production cost of $2.89 for equivalent whole candles completed during April by The Candle Shop. Note that the total cost of $1,187,542 *cannot* be divided by a quantity because each of the two cost components has a different number of equivalent units of production.

Step 6: Assign Costs to Costs Transferred Out and to Ending Inventory
This step assigns total production costs to units of product by determining the cost of (1) goods completed and transferred out during the period and (2) units in the ending WIP Inventory.

Using the WA method, the cost of goods completed and transferred out is found by multiplying the total number of units transferred by the total cost per EUP.

Total cost transferred = 406,000 units × $2.89 = $1,173,340

Because the WA method is based on an averaging technique that combines both prior and current period work, the period in which the transferred units were started does not matter. All units and all costs, respectively, are commingled.

Ending WIP Inventory cost is calculated by multiplying the EUP for each cost component by the component cost per EUP computed in step 5. Cost of the ending WIP Inventory using the WA method is as follows.

Ending WIP Inventory	
Direct material (5,400 × $1.59)	$ 8,586
Conversion (4,320 × $1.30)	5,616
Total cost of ending WIP Inventory	$14,202

The total cost assigned to units transferred out and to units in the ending WIP Inventory must equal the total cost to account for. For The Candle Shop, total cost to account for (step 4) was determined as $1,187,542, which equals transferred-out cost ($1,173,340) plus the cost of the ending WIP Inventory ($14,202).

The steps just discussed can be combined into a **cost of production report**, which details all manufacturing quantities and costs, shows the computation of cost per EUP, and indicates the cost assigned to goods produced during the period. **Exhibit 7.7** shows The Candle Shop's cost of production report using the WA method.

Exhibit 7.7 ■ The Candle Shop's Cost of Production Report for the Month Ended April 30

Cost of Production Report

	A	B	C	D
1	**Weighted Average Method**		**Equivalent Units of Production**	
2	**Production Data**	**Physical Units**	**Direct Material**	**Conversion**
3	Beginning WIP Inventory	10,000		
4	Candles started	401,400		
5	Candles to account for	411,400		
6	Beginning WIP Inventory*	10,000	10,000	10,000
7	Started and completed	396,000	396,000	396,000
8	Candles completed	406,000		
9	Ending WIP Inventory**	5,400	5,400	4,320
10	Candles accounted for	411,400	411,400	410,320
11	**Cost Data**	**Total Costs**	**Direct Material**	**Conversion**
12	Costs in beginning WIP Inventory	$ 37,402	$ 11,886	$ 25,516
13	Current period costs	1,150,140	642,240	507,900
14	Total cost to account for	**$1,187,542**	$ 654,126	$533,416
15	Divided by EUP		÷ 411,400	÷ 410,320
16	Cost per EUP	$ 2.89	$ 1.59	$ 1.30
17	**Cost Assignment**			
18	Transferred out (406,000 × $2.89)		$1,173,340	
19	Ending WIP Inventory			
20	Direct material (5,400 × 100% × $1.59)	$8,586		
21	Conversion (5,400 × 80% × $1.30)	5,616	14,202	
22	Total cost accounted for		**$1,187,542**	
23	* 100% complete as to material; 40% complete as to conversion.			
24	** 100% complete as to material; 80% complete as to conversion.			

Information contained on the cost of production report indicates the actual flow of goods and dollar amounts through the general ledger accounting system. **Exhibit 7.8** provides summary journal entries and related T-accounts that show how the information in **Exhibit 7.7** is recorded in the WIP and FG Inventory accounts. Note that the total cost to account for must either be transferred out of WIP Inventory or remain as the ending balance of that account.

Exhibit 7.8 ■ The Candle Shop's Journal Entries (WA Method)

Work in Process Inventory	642,240	
Raw Material Inventory		642,240
To record issuance of material to production (Exhibit 7.5)		
Work in Process Inventory	122,638	
Wages Payable		122,638
To accrue wages for direct labor (Exhibit 7.5)		
Manufacturing Overhead	385,262	
Various accounts		385,262
To record actual overhead costs (Exhibit 7.5)		
Work in Process Inventory	385,262	
Manufacturing Overhead		385,262
To apply actual overhead to production		
Finished Goods Inventory	1,173,340	
Work in Process Inventory		1,173,340

continued

Chapter 7 Process Costing

continued from previous page

Exhibit 7.8 ■ The Candle Shop's Journal Entries (WA Method) (concluded)

To transfer cost of completed candles to finished goods (Exhibit 7.7)

Work in Process Inventory				Finished Goods Inventory			
Beginning balance	37,402			Beginning balance	XXX	Cost of goods sold	XXX
Direct material	642,240	Cost of goods manufactured	1,173,340 →	Cost of goods manufactured	1,173,340		
Direct labor	122,638						
Overhead	385,262						
Total cost to account for	1,187,542						
Ending balance	14,202			Ending balance	XXX		

REVIEW 7-2 — Weighted Average Method of Process Costing — LO7-2

Lathrop Inc. mass produces filters for drinking water. The following cost information is available for October:

Beginning inventory direct material cost	$ 5,800
Beginning inventory conversion cost	2,200
Direct material issued during October	88,000
Direct labor incurred during October	18,000
Overhead applied during October	15,000

On October 1, the company had 1,200 units in process, which were 80 percent complete as to materials and 20 percent complete as to conversion. Lathrop started 12,000 units into process during October and had 800 units still in process on October 31. The ending WIP units were 40 percent complete as to materials and 30 percent complete as to conversion.

a. Compute the unit costs for October for direct material and for conversion under the weighted average method.
b. Determine the cost transferred out for October using the weighted average method. Round your final answers to the nearest whole dollar.
c. Determine the cost of October 31 ending inventory using the weighted average method. Round your final answers to the nearest whole dollar.
d. **Critical Thinking:** For what reasons might Lathrop use the WA process costing method over the FIFO process costing method?

More practice: E7-34, E7-37, E7-38, E7-41
Solution on p. 7-56.

FIFO METHOD

As described in the last section, separating beginning WIP inventory from current period production under the *FIFO method* allows a cost for the current period to be calculated. (This is unlike the WA method where an average unit cost is calculated for all units worked on during the period.) The general steps in process costing shown in **Exhibit 7.4** apply to the FIFO method when the EUP calculations follow the first-in, first-out cost flow.

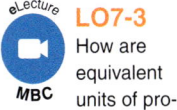

LO7-3 How are equivalent units of production, unit costs, and inventory values determined using the first-in, first-out (FIFO) method of process costing?

DEMO 7-3 — Demonstrating Process Costing Using the FIFO Method — LO7-3

◆ **How is The Candle Shop Information included in Exhibit 7.5 used to illustrated each step in process costing under the FIFO method outlined in Exhibit 7.4?**

Steps 1 and 2 are not repeated here because they use physical units and, as such, are the same in both the FIFO and WA methods.

Step 3: Calculate EUP by Cost Component Using the FIFO method, the work performed last period is not commingled with work performed in the current period. Only work completed on the beginning WIP Inventory during the current period is shown in the EUP schedule. This work equals the physical units in the beginning WIP Inventory times (1 − percentage of work done in the prior period). No additional material is needed in April to complete the 10,000 candles in the beginning WIP Inventory. Because the beginning WIP Inventory was 40 percent complete as to labor and overhead, the company will do 60 percent of the conversion work on those goods in the current period or the equivalent of 6,000 candles.

10,000 Physical units × 60% incomplete at beg. of period = 6,000 EUP for conversion in beg. WIP

The computation for units started and completed and ending WIP Inventory is the same for both the FIFO and WA methods.

The EUP schedule for the FIFO method is as follows.

	DM	Conversion
Candles in beginning WIP Inventory completed in the current period	0	6,000
Candles started and completed	396,000	396,000
Ending WIP Inventory (5,400 × % complete)	5,400	4,320
Equivalent units of production	401,400	406,320

Except for the different treatment of units in the beginning WIP Inventory, the remaining amounts in the FIFO EUP schedule are the same as those for the WA method. Thus, the only difference between the EUPs of the two methods is that the FIFO method *does not* include the equivalent units of work performed on the beginning inventory in the EUP schedule while the WA method *does* include those equivalent units in the EUP schedule.

	DM	Conversion
FIFO EUP	401,400	406,320
+ BI WIP (DM: 10,000 units × 100%; CC: 10,000 × 40%)	10,000	4,000
WA EUP	411,400	410,320

Step 4: Calculate Total Cost to Account For by Cost Component This step is the same as it was for the WA method. The total cost to account for is $1,187,542.

Step 5: Calculate Cost per EUP by Cost Component Because the FIFO EUP calculation ignores the work performed in the prior period on beginning WIP Inventory, the FIFO cost per EUP computation also ignores prior period costs in the current period computation. The calculation for each cost component at the end of the period is as follows.

$$\text{FIFO unit cost} = \frac{\text{Current period cost}}{\text{Total FIFO equivalent units of production}}$$

Given that the EUP computations and the costs used to compute cost per EUP both differ between the FIFO and weighted average methods, different cost per EUP results will be obtained for the WA and FIFO methods. The FIFO cost per EUP calculations are as follows.

	Total	DM	CC
Current period costs	$1,150,140	$642,240	$507,900
Divided by EUP (Step 3)		÷ 401,400	÷ 406,320
Cost per EUP	$ 2.85	$ 1.60	$ 1.25

It is useful to understand the underlying difference between the WA and FIFO total cost computations. The WA total unit cost of $2.89 reflects production costs for April and also production costs from the prior month due to the inclusion of beginning inventory costs. The FIFO total unit cost of $2.85 is the average cost of production *in the month of April only*. The $0.04 difference is caused solely by the difference in treatment of beginning WIP Inventory costs.

Step 6: Assign Costs to Costs Transferred Out and to Ending Inventory The FIFO method assumes that the units in beginning WIP Inventory are the first units completed during the current period and, therefore, are the first units transferred out. The remaining units transferred out during the period were both started and completed in the current period. As shown in the cost of production report in **Exhibit 7.9**, the two-step computation needed to determine the cost of goods transferred out distinctly presents this FIFO logic.

The first part of the cost assignment for units transferred out relates to beginning WIP Inventory units. Before April 1, these units had absorbed all material cost and some conversion cost in WIP Inventory. None of these prior period costs were included in the EUP cost calculations in step 5. These beginning inventory units were finished during the current period, so the cost of completion reflects only current period costs. Again, the BI units were complete as to material but needed an additional 60 percent of labor and overhead to be complete. Total cost of producing the units contained in the beginning WIP Inventory is equal to the beginning WIP Inventory costs plus the current period completion costs or $44,902. Next, the cost of units started and completed in the current period is computed using only current period costs. The total cost for all units completed and transferred to FG Inventory for April is $1,173,502.[6] This cost assignment process for The Candle Shop is as follows.

Transferred out		
(1) Beginning inventory (prior period costs)........................		$ 37,402
Completion of beginning inventory		
Direct material (10,000 × 0% × $1.60).....................		0
Conversion (10,000 × 60% × $1.25).......................		7,500
Total cost of beginning inventory transferred		$ 44,902
(2) Candles started and completed (396,000 × $2.85)............		1,128,600
Total cost transferred		$1,173,502

The process of calculating the FIFO cost of the ending WIP Inventory is the same as under the WA method. Ending WIP cost using FIFO is as follows.

Ending WIP Inventory	
Direct material (5,400 × $1.60)...	$ 8,640
Conversion (5,400 × 80% × $1.25)	5,400
Total cost of ending WIP Inventory...	$14,040

The total cost of the candles transferred out ($1,173,502) plus the cost of the candles in the ending WIP Inventory ($14,040) equals the total cost to be accounted for ($1,187,542).

---

[6] Whether to distinguish a per unit cost for beginning units transferred out separately from a per unit cost for started and completed units depends on whether a strict or modified FIFO method is used. Under a strict FIFO method, we consider the 10,000 candles in beginning inventory as transferred out at a cost of $4.49 ($44,902 ÷ 10,000) and started and completed units transferred out at a cost of $2.85. Under modified FIFO, $2.89 ($1,173,502 ÷ 406,000) is considered an average cost for all candles transferred out in April. If the unit costs are not significantly different, a company may use one unit cost for all candles transferred out in April to the next department or to Finished Goods Inventory for simplification.

Exhibit 7.9 ■ The Candle Shop's Cost of Production Report for the Month Ended April 30

Cost of Production Report

	A	B	C	D
1	**FIFO Method**		**Equivalent Units of Production**	
2	**Production Data**	Physical Units	Direct Material	Conversion
3	Beginning WIP Inventory	10,000		
4	Candles started	401,400		
5	Candles to account for	411,400		
6	Beginning WIP Inventory*	10,000	0	6,000
7	Started and completed	396,000	396,000	396,000
8	Candles completed	406,000		
9	Ending WIP Inventory**	5,400	5,400	4,320
10	Candles accounted for	411,400	401,400	406,320
11	**Cost Data**	Total Costs	Direct Material	Conversion
12	Costs in beginning WIP Inventory	$ 37,402		
13	Current period costs	1,150,140	$ 642,240	$507,900
14	Total cost to account for	**$1,187,542**		
15	Divided by EUP		÷ 401,400	÷ 406,320
16	Cost per EUP	$ 2.85	$ 1.60	$ 1.25
17	**Cost Assignment**			
18	Transferred out			
19	Beginning WIP Inventory costs	$ 37,402		
20	Cost to complete			
21	Conversion (10,000 × 60% × $1.25)	7,500	$ 44,902	
22	Started & completed (396,000 × $2.85)		1,128,600	
23	Total cost transferred		$1,173,502	
24	Ending WIP Inventory			
25	Direct material (5,400 × 100% × $1.60)	$ 8,640		
26	Conversion (5,400 × 80% × $1.25)	5,400	14,040	
27	Total cost accounted for		**$1,187,542**	
28	* 100% complete as to material; 40% complete as to conversion.			
29	** 100% complete as to material; 80% complete as to conversion.			

The journal entries provided for the issuance of direct material, accrual of direct labor wages, and recognition and application of actual overhead are the same as those shown in **Exhibit 7.8** for the WA method. If FIFO were used, when completed goods are transferred from WIP Inventory to FG Inventory for April, the amount transferred would be $1,173,502 rather than the $1,173,340 shown in **Exhibit 7.8**. It is assumed that the company began April with no FG Inventory, 400,000 candles were sold on account for $9 each, and a perpetual FIFO inventory system is used. **Exhibit 7.10** provides the sale and cost of goods sold journal entries; inventory T-accounts are given for the FIFO information. Under the FIFO assumption, the first 10,000 units sold relate to beginning inventory (cost of $44,902) and the remaining 390,000 units had a unit cost of $2.85.

Exhibit 7.10 ■ The Candle Shop's Sale Journal Entries (FIFO Method)

Accounts Receivable	3,600,000	
Sales..		3,600,000
To record sales on account (400,000 candles $9.00)		
Cost of Goods Sold*.............................	1,156,402	
Finished Goods Inventory......................		1,156,402
To transfer cost of goods sold, using strict FIFO:		

    First 10,000 units .... $ 44,902
    Remaining 390,000 units at $2.85 1,111,500
                                          $1,156,402

*Note: Using the information from **Exhibit 7.7**, this entry would be for $1,156,000 if weighted average were used: 400,000 × $2.89.

Work in Process Inventory

Beginning balance	37,402			
Direct material	642,240	Cost of goods		
Direct labor	122,638	manufactured	1,173,502	→
Overhead	385,262			
Total cost to account for	1,187,542			
Ending balance	14,040			

Finished Goods Inventory

Beginning balance	0	Cost of goods sold	1,156,402
Cost of goods manufactured	1,173,502		
Ending balance (6,000 × $2.85)	17,100		

Data Visualization

The data visualization shows per unit, budgeted, and actual materials cost for a manufacturer under the FIFO and WA costing methods for January. Assume that (1) beginning EUP (2) and total EUP for materials are the same between actual and budget.

Analyzing WA vs. FIFO Costing Methods for Materials

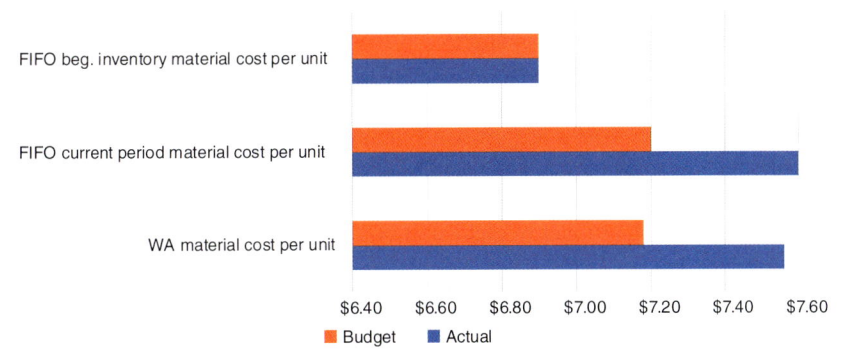

- FIFO beg. inventory material cost per unit: Budget ~$6.90, Actual ~$6.85
- FIFO current period material cost per unit: Budget ~$7.20, Actual ~$7.55
- WA material cost per unit: Budget ~$7.15, Actual ~$7.50

(scale: $6.40 $6.60 $6.80 $7.00 $7.20 $7.40 $7.60)
■ Budget ■ Actual

Based on the data visualization above, answer the following questions.
a. What could have caused the per unit changes in actual amounts compared to budget?
b. What does this indicate about the differences between the two methods?

Solution on p. 7-59.

REVIEW 7-3 — FIFO Method of Process Costing — LO7-3

Use the information from Review 7-2 to answer the following questions.
a. Compute the unit costs for October for direct material and for conversion under the FIFO method.
b. Determine the cost transferred out for October using the FIFO method. Round your final answers to the nearest whole dollar.

continued

continued from previous page

> c. Determine the cost of October 31 ending inventory using the FIFO method. Round your final answers to the nearest whole dollar.
>
> d. **Critical Thinking:** Compare the total cost per EUP in Review 7-2 under the WA method, to the total cost per EUP in Review 7-3 under the FIFO method. Based on this relationship, is the beginning inventory cost per EUP higher or lower than the EUP for current period costs? Does this indicate prices are rising or falling?

More practice: E7-39, E7-40, E7-42, E7-43
Solution on p. 7-57.

PROCESS COSTING IN A MULTIDEPARTMENT SETTING

LO7-4 How are transferred-in costs and units accounted for in a multidepartment production setting?

Most companies have multiple, rather than single, department processing facilities. In a multidepartment production environment, goods are transferred from a predecessor (upstream) department to a successor (downstream) department. Manufacturing costs always follow the physical flow of goods. Thus, when goods are transferred from one department to another, costs are also transferred. Thus, if The Candle Shop decided to place candles (rather than send them to a central warehouse in reusable containers) in eight-unit boxes, production activities could be divided into two departments: Processing and Packaging. A new material (a box) would be added at the end of the Packaging Department.

Costs of the completed units of predecessor departments are treated as input costs in successor departments. Such a sequential treatment requires the use of an additional cost component called **transferred-in cost** or prior department cost. This cost component is always 100 percent complete because the goods would not have been transferred out of the predecessor department if processing there were not complete. The transferred-in cost component is treated the same as any other cost component in the calculations of EUP and cost per EUP.

A successor department might add additional raw material to the units transferred in or might simply provide additional labor with a corresponding incurrence of overhead. In some situations, addition or expansion of materials may cause the number of units accounted for to be higher than those to be accounted for originally or in a previous department. Anything added in the successor department requires its own cost component column for calculating EUP and cost per EUP (unless the additional components have the same degree of completion, in which case they can be combined).

Occasionally, successor departments change the unit of measure used in predecessor departments. For example, at The Candle Shop, production in the Processing Department might be measured as the number of candles but the production measure in the Packaging Department might be number of eight-unit boxes.

In multidepartment production, goods are transferred from one department to another before they are complete.

DEMO 7-4   LO7-4   Demonstrating Process Costing in a Multidepartment Setting

We now assume that after units are completed in the Processing Department of the Candle Shop, the units move to the Packaging Department. For this example, we use the weighted average information from **Exhibit 7.7**. In Packaging, employees wrap each candle in transparent wrap and then place eight candles in a box. The wrap is considered an indirect material; the box is a direct material that is added at the end of the process. The following information for the Packaging Department is available.

Candles in beginning WIP inventory—Packaging Department (100% complete as to transferred in; 0% complete as to box; 45% complete as to conversion)	1,000
Candles transferred in from Processing	406,000
Candles in ending WIP Inventory—Packaging Department (100% complete as to transferred in; 0% complete as to box; 80% complete as to conversion)	2,800
Eight-pack boxes of candles sent to Finished Goods Inventory	50,525

	Transferred-In	DM	Conversion
Beginning WIP	$ 855	$ 0	$ 95
Current period	1,173,340*	20,210	10,066

*From **Exhibit 7.7**

Chapter 7 Process Costing

◆ **How is the cost of production report prepared for the Packaging Department? Exhibit 7.11** illustrates this report.

Exhibit 7.11 ■ The Candle Shop's Cost of Production Report for Packaging Department (Packaging)

Cost of Production Report

	A	B	C	D	E
1	**Weighted Average Method**		\multicolumn{3}{l|}{**Equivalent Units of Production**}		
2	Production Data	Physical Units	Trans. In	DM	Conversion
3	Beginning WIP Inventory	1,000			
4	Candles started	406,000			
5	Candles to account for	407,000			
6	Beginning WIP Inventory*	1,000	1,000	1,000	1,000
7	Started and completed	403,200	403,200	403,200	403,200
8	Candles completed (50,525 × 8)	404,200			
9	Ending WIP Inventory**	2,800	2,800	0	2,240
10	Candles accounted for	407,000	407,000	404,200	406,440
11	Divided by candles per box		÷ 8	÷ 8	÷ 8
12	EUP in boxes		50,875	50,525	50,805
13			\multicolumn{3}{l|}{**Equivalent Units of Production**}		
14	**Cost Data**	Total Costs	Trans. In	DM	Conversion
15	Costs in beginning WIP Inventory	$ 950	$ 855	$ 0	$ 95
16	Current period costs	1,203,616	1,173,340	20,210	10,066
17	Total costs to account for	$1,204,566	$1,174,195	$ 20,210	$ 10,161
18	Divided by EUP		÷ 50,875	÷ 50,525	÷ 50,805
19	Cost per box EUP	$ 23.68	$ 23.08	$ 0.40	$ 0.20
20	**Cost Assignment**				
21	Transferred out (50,525 × $23.68)		$1,196,432		
22	Ending WIP Inventory (2,800 candles = 350 boxes)				
23	Transferred in (350 × 100% × $23.08)	$ 8,078			
24	Direct material (350 × 0% × $0.40)	0			
25	Conversion (350 × 80% × $0.20)	56	8,134		
26	Total cost accounted for		$1,204,566		

* 100% complete as to transferred-in; 0 percent complete as to box; 45% complete as to conversion
**100% complete as to transferred-in; 0 percent complete as to box; 80% complete as to conversion

---

Accounting for Second Department

LO7-4

REVIEW 7-4

Holley Inc. produces shelving in a two-process, two-department operation. In the Manufacturing Department, shelving components are made. In the Assembly Department, the material received from Manufacturing is assembled into individual shelving units. Each department maintains its own Work in Process Inventory, and costs are assigned using weighted average process costing. In Assembly, conversion costs are incurred evenly throughout the process; direct material is added at the end of the process. For September, the following production and cost information is available for the Assembly Department:

- Beginning WIP Inventory: 1,150 units (20 percent complete as to conversion); transferred in cost, $17,400; conversion cost, $2,300
- Transferred in during September: 18,400 units

continued

continued from previous page

- Current period costs: transferred in, $188,000; direct material, $23,000; conversion, $33,000
- Ending WIP Inventory: 1,380 units (70 percent complete as to conversion)

For the Assembly Department, compute the following:

a. Cost per EUP for each cost component
b. Cost transferred to Finished Goods Inventory
c. Cost of ending WIP Inventory
d. **Critical Thinking:** Under what scenario would transferred-in costs have a percent complete of less than 100 percent?

More practice: MC7-18, E7-45, E7-46, E7-47
Solution on p. 7-57.

HYBRID COSTING SYSTEMS

LO7-5 Why would a company use a hybrid costing system?

Many companies now customize what were previously mass-produced items. In such circumstances, neither a job order nor process costing technique is perfectly suited to attach costs to output. Thus, companies may design a hybrid costing system that is appropriate for their particular processing situation. A **hybrid costing system** combines characteristics of both job order and process costing systems. Such a system would be used, for example, in a manufacturing environment in which various product lines have different direct materials but similar processing techniques.

DEMO 7-5 LO7-5 Demonstrating a Hybrid Cost System

To illustrate the need for hybrid systems, assume that you order an automobile with the following options: heated leather seats, an upgraded stereo system, security camera, and pearlized paint. Costs of these options must be traced specifically to your car, but the assembly processes of the upgrades for all cars produced by the plant are similar. Assume that the direct material costs per unit for the leather seats, upgraded stereo system, security camera, and pearlized paint are $600, $500, $300, and $200, respectively. All materials have been added at month end. Also assume that the related conversion costs for the upgrades are $1,000 per EUP and the process is 40 percent complete as to conversion at month end.

◆ What is the cost of the WIP of the customized car accessories for this particular car at month end using a hybrid approach?

	Unit Cost
Direct materials ($600 + $500 + $300 + $200).............	$1,600
Conversion cost (1 unit × 40% × $1,000).................	400
Cost of Ending WIP of car accessories..................	$2,000

The manufacturing process of a customized vehicle has aspects of both job order and process costing systems.

A hybrid system allows the job order costing feature of tracing direct material to specific jobs to be combined with the process costing feature of averaging labor and overhead costs over all homogeneous production to derive the total cost of your automobile. It would not be feasible to use a job order costing system to trace labor or overhead cost to your car individually, and it would be improper to average the costs of your options over all the cars produced during the period.

A hybrid costing system may be appropriate for companies producing items such as furniture, clothing, and special-order computers. In each instance, numerous kinds of raw materials could be used to create similar output. A table may be made from oak, teak, or mahogany; a blouse may be made from silk, cotton, or polyester; and computers may have different hard drives and other internal components. The material cost for a batch run would be traced separately, but the production process of the batch is repetitive.

Hybrid costing systems provide a more accurate accounting picture of the actual manufacturing activities in certain companies. Job order costing and process costing are two ends of a continuum and, as is typically the case for any continuum, neither end is necessarily the norm. As the use of flexible manufacturing processes increases, so will the use of hybrid costing systems.

Chapter 7 Process Costing   7-21

Hybrid Costing   LO7-5   REVIEW 7-5

M5 Inc. makes customized equipment components from aluminum, steel, or some combination of the two. The parts generally take the same amount of time and effort to assemble. M5 Inc. developed the following standard costs for each type of component.

	Aluminum	Steel	Combination
Direct material	$ 80	$ 60	$ 70
Direct labor (2 hours)	40	40	40
Overhead (based on 2 hours)	75	75	75
Total	$195	$175	$185

M5 Inc. began the year with no beginning WIP Inventory. During January, 500 components were started: 200 were made from aluminum, 175 were made from steel, and 125 were made from a combination of aluminum and steel. At the end of January, 80 components were not yet complete: 15 made from aluminum, 30 made from steel, and 35 made from a combination of aluminum and steel. The stage of completion for each cost component for the 80 unfinished components was as follows.

Material	100% complete
Conversion	40% complete

a. Calculate the cost of components completed during January.
b. Calculate the cost of components in ending WIP Inventory.
c. **Critical Thinking:** What about the manufacturing process in this example makes it a good candidate for a hybrid costing model?

More practice: E7-50
Solution on p. 7-57.

SPOILAGE

To this point, the examples assumed that all units to be accounted for have been transferred out or are in ending WIP Inventory. However, almost every process produces some units that do not meet production specifications. This section addresses two simple examples of spoilage in a process costing system.

Losses in a production process may occur continuously or at a specific point. For example, the weight loss in roasting coffee beans would be considered a **continuous loss** because it occurs fairly uniformly through the process. In contrast, a **discrete loss** is assumed to occur at a specific point and is detectable only when a quality check is performed. Control points can be either mechanically included in the production process or performed by inspectors.

Several methods can be used to account for units lost during production. Selection of the most appropriate method depends on whether the loss is considered normal or abnormal and whether the loss occurred continuously in the process or at a discrete point.[7] **Exhibit 7.12** summarizes the accounting for the cost of lost units.

LO7-6 How are normal and abnormal spoilage losses treated in an equivalent units of production schedule?

Normal Continuous Loss The costs of normal shrinkage and normal continuous losses in a process costing environment are accounted for using the **method of neglect**, which excludes the spoiled units in the equivalent units of production schedule. Ignoring the spoilage results in a smaller number of EUP and *dividing production costs by a smaller EUP raises the cost per equivalent unit*. Thus, the cost of lost units is spread proportionately over the good units transferred out and those remaining in WIP Inventory.

Discrete Continuous Loss Alternatively, the cost of normal discrete losses should be *assigned only to units that have passed the inspection point*. Such units should be good units (relative to the inspected characteristic), whereas the units prior to this point may be good or they may be defective or spoiled. Assigning loss costs to units that may be found to be defective or spoiled in the next period would not be reasonable.

---

[7] Normal and abnormal losses are defined in Chapter 6.

© Cambridge Business Publishers

Exhibit 7.12 ■ Continuous versus Discrete Losses

Loss Type	Assumed to Occur	May Be	Cost Handled How?	Cost Assigned To?
Continuous	Uniformly throughout process	Normal	Absorbed by all units in ending inventory and transferred out on an EUP basis	Product
		Abnormal	Written off as a loss on an EUP basis	Period
Discrete	At inspection point or at end of process	Normal	Absorbed by all units past inspection point in ending inventory and transferred out on an EUP basis	Product
		Abnormal	Written off as a loss on an EUP basis	Period

Abnormal Continuous and Discrete Losses The cost of all abnormal losses should be accumulated and *treated as a loss in the period in which those losses occurred.* Abnormal loss cost is always accounted for on an equivalent unit basis. Abnormal losses are extended in the EUP schedule at the percentage of completion at the end of production for continuous losses (100 percent complete for all cost elements) or at the point of inspection for discrete losses. For example, assume that a process added all direct material at the beginning of production and the inspection point for determining spoilage was at the 75 percent completion stage as to labor and overhead. If 100 units were found to be spoiled at the inspection point, the extension to the EUP schedule would be 100 EUP for DM and 75 EUP for conversion. The spoiled units would be removed at that point and no additional labor and overhead would be added to them.

DEMO 7-6 LO7-6 Accounting for Spoilage

Hanks Inc. will be used to illustrate the method of neglect for a normal loss and an abnormal loss. Hanks produces glass jars in a single department; the jars are then sold to candle manufacturers. All materials are added at the start of the process, and conversion costs are applied uniformly throughout the production process. Breakage commonly occurs at the end of the production process when a machine pushes air into the jars to form their openings. Hanks expects a maximum of 5 percent of the units started into production to be "lost" during processing. For convenience, quantities will be discussed in terms of jars rather than raw material inputs. Recyclable shipping containers are provided by buyers and, therefore, are not a cost to Hanks Inc. The company uses the WA method of calculating equivalent units. **Exhibit 7.13** provides the basic information for June.

Exhibit 7.13 ■ Production and Cost Data for Hanks Inc. for June

Jars

Beginning WIP Inventory (CC: 60% complete)	12,000
Started during month	90,000
Jars completed and transferred	79,200
Ending WIP Inventory (CC: 75% complete)	15,000
Spoiled jars	7,800

Costs

Beginning WIP Inventory		
Material	$ 16,230	
Conversion	3,459	$19,689
Current period		
Material	$101,745	
Conversion	19,041	120,786
Total cost to be accounted for		$140,475

In June, Hanks had 12,000 jars in the beginning WIP Inventory and started 90,000 jars into production. At the end of June, the company accounted for 94,200 jars (79,200 completed and 15,000 in ending WIP Inventory).

Total jars to be accounted for (12,000 + 90,000)	102,000
Total jars accounted for (79,200 + 15,000)	(94,200)
Jars spoiled during processing	7,800
Normal spoilage (0.05 × 90,000)	(4,500)
Abnormal spoilage	3,300

◆ **Using WA process costing, how is the cost of production report reflecting spoilage prepared for Hank Inc. for the month of June?**

Under the method of neglect, the normal spoilage is not included in the computation of EUP and, thus, simply "disappears" from the EUP schedule. Therefore, the cost per equivalent "good" jar made during the period is higher for each cost component.[8]

Exhibit 7.14 presents the cost of production report for Hanks Inc. for June. Use of the FIFO process costing method by Hanks Inc. would have created differences in the number of equivalent units of production, cost per equivalent unit, and cost assignment schedule.[9]

Exhibit 7.14 ■ Hanks Inc.'s Cost of Production Report for the Month Ended June 30

Cost of Production Report

	A	B	C	D
1	**Weighted Average Method**	**Equivalent Units of Production**		
2	Production Data	Physical Units	Direct Material	Conversion
3	Beginning WIP Inventory	12,000		
4	Jars started	90,000		
5	Jars to account for	102,000		
6	Beginning WIP Inventory*	12,000	12,000	12,000
7	Jars started and completed	67,200	67,200	67,200
8	Total jars completed	79,200		
9	Ending Inventory**	15,000	15,000	11,250
10	Normal spoilage (not extended)	4,500		
11	Abnormal spoilage	3,300	3,300	3,300
12	Jars accounted for	102,000	97,500	93,750
13	**Cost Data**	Total Costs	Direct Material	Conversion
14	Costs in beginning WIP Inventory	$ 19,689	$ 16,230	$ 3,459
15	Current period costs	120,786	101,745	19,041
16	Total cost to account for	**$140,475**	$117,975	$ 22,500
17	Divided by EUP		÷ 97,500	÷ 93,750
18	Cost per EUP	$ 1.45	$ 1.21	$ 0.24
19	**Cost Assignment**			
20	Transferred out (79,200 × $1.45)		$114,840	
21	Ending WIP inventory			
22	Direct material (15,000 × $1.21)	$ 18,150		
23	Conversion (11,250 × $0.24)	2,700	20,850	
24	Abnormal loss (3,300 × $1.45)		4,785	
25	Total costs accounted for		**$140,475**	
26	* 100% complete as to material; 60% complete as to conversion.			
27	** 100% complete as to material; 75% complete as to conversion.			

---

[8] There is a theoretical problem with the use of the method of neglect when a company uses weighted average process costing. Units in the ending WIP inventory have spoiled unit cost assigned to them in the current period and will have lost unit cost assigned to them again in the next period. But even with this flaw, this method provides a reasonable measure of unit cost if the rate of spoilage is consistent from period to period.

[9] For FIFO costing, the EUP would be 85,500 and 86,550, respectively, for DM and Conversion. Cost per EUP would be $1.19 and $0.22, respectively, for DM and Conversion. Total cost transferred out would be $115,497; total cost of ending WIP Inventory would be $20,325; and cost of abnormal loss would be $4,653.

REVIEW 7-6 — LO7-6 — FIFO; Normal and Abnormal Loss

Best Foods manufactures cereal in a continuous, mass production process. Cereal mix is added at the beginning of the process. Normal losses are minimal and abnormal losses infrequently occur when foreign materials are found in the cereal mix. Routine inspection occurs at the 95 percent completion point as to conversion.

During September, a machine malfunctioned and contaminated 5,000 pounds of cereal mix. This abnormal loss occurred when conversion was 75 percent complete on those pounds of product. The error was immediately noticed, and those pounds of cereal mix were pulled from the production process. Two thousand additional pounds of cereal mix were detected as unsuitable at the routine inspection point; this amount was considered within normal limits. Production data for the month follow.

Beg. WIP Inventory (65% complete)	125,000 pounds
Started during the month	675,000 pounds
Ending WIP Inventory (40% complete)	80,000 pounds

a. Determine the number of equivalent units of production for direct material and for conversion, assuming a FIFO cost flow.
b. If the costs per equivalent unit of production are $1.10 and $0.50 for direct material and conversion, respectively, what is the cost of the ending WIP Inventory?
c. What is the cost of abnormal loss? How is this cost treated in September?
d. **Critical Thinking:** Do normal and abnormal losses impact the income statement in the same period?

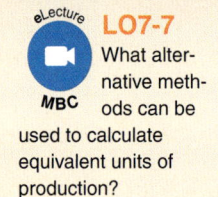

More practice: E7-51, E7-52 E7-53, E7-54
Solution on p. 7-58.

Appendix 7A: Alternative Calculations of Weighted Average and FIFO Methods

LO7-7 What alternative methods can be used to calculate equivalent units of production?

Various methods can be used to compute equivalent units of production under the WA and FIFO methods.

WA EUP Calculation Starting with Units Transferred Out

One common variation of the weighted average EUP calculation presented in the chapter is the following.

	Units transferred out (whole units)
+	Ending WIP Inventory (equivalent units)
=	WA EUP

WA EUP Calculation Starting with Total Units

Another method to compute equivalent units of production under the WA method begins with the total number of units to account for in the period. From this amount, the EUP to be completed next period are subtracted to give the WA EUP.

	Total units to account for
−	EUP to be completed next period
=	WA EUP

Reconciling Between WA EUP and FIFO EUP

The FIFO EUP can be quickly derived by subtracting the equivalent units in the beginning WIP Inventory that had been produced in the previous period from the WA EUP:

	WA EUP
−	Beginning WIP Inventory in equivalent units
=	FIFO EUP

This computation is appropriate because the WA method differentiates only between units completed and units not completed during the period. Since the WA method does not exclude the equivalent units in the

Chapter 7 Process Costing

beginning WIP Inventory, converting from WA to FIFO requires removal of the equivalent units produced in the previous period from beginning WIP Inventory.

Purpose of Alternative Calculations These alternative calculations can be used either as a confirmation of answers found by using beginning WIP Inventory units, units started and completed, and ending WIP Inventory units or as a shortcut to initially compute EUP.

Using Alternative Methods to Calculate EUP — LO7-7 — DEMO 7-7

The April production data for The Candle Shop are repeated here to illustrate these alternative calculations for the weighted average and FIFO methods.

Candles in beginning WIP Inventory (100% complete as to material; 40% complete as to conversion costs)	10,000
Candles started during the month	401,400
Candles completed during the month	406,000
Candles in ending WIP Inventory (100% complete as to material; 80% complete as to conversion costs)	5,400

◆ Using the data above, how do you calculate WA EUP beginning with units transferred out? How is WA EUP converted to FIFO EUP?

The EUP are computed as follows.

		DM	Conversion
	Candles transferred out	406,000	406,000
+	EI WIP (5,400 units × % work performed: 100% DM; 80% conversion)	5,400	4,320
=	**WA EUP**	411,400	410,320
−	BI WIP (10,000 units × % work in prior period: 100% DM; 40% conversion)	(10,000)	(4,000)
=	**FIFO EUP**	401,400	406,320

◆ Using the data above, how do you calculate WA EUP beginning with total units to account for? How is WA EUP converted to FIFO EUP?

Using The Candle Shop's data, these computations are as follows.

		DM	Conversion
	Total units to account for	411,400	411,400
−	EUP to be completed next period (5,400 EI units × % work not performed: 0% DM; 20% conversion)	0	(1,080)
=	**WA EUP**	411,400	410,320
−	BI EUP (10,000 units × % work completed in prior period: 100% DM; 40% conversion)	(10,000)	(4,000)
=	**FIFO EUP**	401,400	406,320

Alternative EUP Calculation Methods — LO7-7 — REVIEW 7-7

In manufacturing its products, Fritz Corp. adds all direct material at the beginning of the production process. The company's direct labor and overhead are considered to be continuously at the same degree of completion. May production information is as follows:

Beginning WIP Inventory	24,000 units
Started during September	600,000 units
Completed during September	608,000 units

continued

continued from previous page

> As of May 1, the beginning WIP Inventory was 45 percent complete as to labor and overhead. On May 31, the ending WIP Inventory was 65 percent complete as to conversion.
>
> a. Compute equivalent units of production using the weighted average method of process costing, starting with (1) total units transferred out and then (2) starting with total units to account for.
>
> b. **Critical Thinking:** Reconcile your answer in part *a* to the FIFO inventory method of process costing. Explain the logic of this calculation.

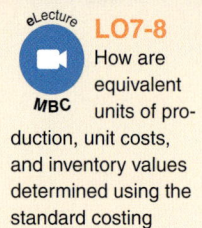

More practice: E7-55
Solution on p. 7-58.

Appendix 7B: Process Costing With Standard Costs

LO7-8 How are equivalent units of production, unit costs, and inventory values determined using the standard costing method of process costing?

Companies may prefer to use standard rather than actual costs for inventory valuation purposes. Actual costing requires that a new production cost be computed each period. However, once a production process is established, the "new" costs are often not materially different from the "old" costs, so standards for each cost component can be developed and used as benchmarks to simplify the costing process and eliminate periodic cost recomputations. Standards should be reviewed, and possibly revised, at least once per year to keep quantities and costs current.

EUP calculations for standard process costing are *identical to those of FIFO process costing*. Unlike the WA method, the emphasis of both standard costing and FIFO are on the measurement and control of current production activities and current period costs. The WA method commingles prior and current period units and costs, which reduces the emphasis on current effort that standard costing is intended to represent and measure.

DEMO 7-8 LO7-8 Demonstrating Process Costing with Standard Costs

To illustrate the differences between using actual and standard process costing, The Candle Shop example is continued. When a standard cost system is used, inventories are stated at standard rather than actual costs. Therefore, although the EUP and current period costs remain the same as shown in **Exhibit 7.8**, the beginning inventory cost data must be restated to reflect standard costs and to demonstrate the effect of consistent use of standard costs over successive periods. Thus, the adjusted beginning WIP Inventory is a follows.

	Standard Cost per Unit	# of Units	% Completion	Cost
Direct material	$1.58	10,000	100%	$15,800
Direct labor	0.24	10,000	40%	960
Overhead	1.00	10,000	40%	4,000
Total standard cost	$2.82			$20,760

Although direct labor and overhead are at the same degree of completion, these amounts are not combined into a conversion cost category under standard costing. To do so would eliminate the benefit of observing cost variances by category.

♦ **Using FIFO process costing and standard costs, how are the cost of production report for The Candle Shop for the month of April and its related summary journal entries prepared?**

Exhibit 7.15 presents the cost of production report using The Candle Shop's standard cost information.[10]

---

[10] Total material, labor, and overhead variances are shown for The Candle Shop. Variances from actual costs must be closed at the end of a period. If the variances are immaterial, they can be closed to Cost of Goods Sold; otherwise, they should be allocated among the appropriate inventory accounts and Cost of Goods Sold.

Chapter 7 Process Costing

Exhibit 7.15 ■ The Candle Shop's Cost of Production Report for the Month Ended April 30

Cost of Production Report

	A	B	C	D	E
1	**Standard Costing: FIFO Method**		\multicolumn{3}{c}{**Equivalent Units of Production**}		
2	Production Data	Physical Units	Direct Material	Direct Labor	Overhead
3	Beginning WIP Inventory	10,000			
4	Candles started	401,400			
5	Candles to account for	411,400			
6	Beginning WIP Inventory	10,000	0	6,000	6,000
7	Started and completed	396,000	396,000	396,000	396,000
8	Candles completed	406,000			
9	Ending WIP Inventory	5,400	5,400	4,320	4,320
10	Candles accounted for	411,400	401,400	406,320	406,320
11	**Cost Data**	Total Costs	Direct Material	Direct Labor	Overhead
12	Beginning inventory (at standard)	$ 20,760	$ 15,800	$ 960	$ 4,000
13	Current period costs (actual; see **Exhibit 7.8**)	1,150,140	642,240	122,638	385,262
14	(1) Total cost to account for	**$1,170,900**	$658,040	$123,598	$389,262
15	**Cost Assignment**				
16	Costs in beginning WIP Inventory	$ 20,760	$ 15,800	$ 960	$ 4,000
17	Beginning WIP Inventory costs				
18	Cost to complete				
19	Direct labor (6,000 × $0.24)			1,440	
20	Overhead (6,000 × $1.00)				6,000
21	Total cost to complete	7,440			
22	Started and completed:				
23	Direct materials (396,000 × $1.58)		625,680		
24	Direct labor (396,000 × $0.24)			95,040	
25	Overhead (396,000 × $1.00)				396,000
26	Total cost transferred	1,116,720			
27	Ending inventory				
28	Direct materials (5,400 × $1.58)		8,532		
29	Direct labor (4,320 × $0.24)*			1,037	
30	Overhead (4,320 × $1.00)				4,320
31	Total EI costs	13,889			
32	(2) Total	$1,158,809	$650,012	$ 98,477	$410,320
33	Variances from actual (1 − 2)	12,091	8,028	25,121	(21,058)
34	Total costs accounted for	**$1,170,900**	$658,040	$123,598	$389,262
35	* Rounded to the nearest dollar.				
36	NOTE: Favorable variances are shown in parentheses because they represent a cost reduction.				

Summary journal entries for The Candle Shop's April production, assuming a standard cost FIFO process costing system and amounts from **Exhibit 7.12**, are as follows.

1. WIP Inventory is debited for $634,212: the standard cost ($625,680) of material used to complete 396,000 units started in April plus the standard cost ($8,532) for the material used to produce the units in ending WIP Inventory. Raw Material Inventory is credited for the actual cost of the material withdrawn during April ($642,240).

```
Work in Process Inventory . . . . . . . . . . . . . . . . . . . . . . . . . .   634,212
Direct Material Variance . . . . . . . . . . . . . . . . . . . . . . . . . .     8,028
    Raw Material Inventory. . . . . . . . . . . . . . . . . . . . . . . .              642,240
    To record issuance of material at standard and
    unfavorable direct material variance
```

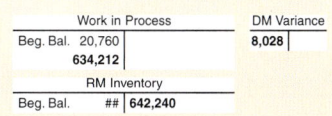

Work in Process		DM Variance	
Beg. Bal. 20,760		8,028	
634,212			

RM Inventory	
Beg. Bal. ##	642,240

2. WIP Inventory is debited for the standard cost of labor allowed based on the equivalent units produced in April. The EUP for the month reflect the production necessary to complete the beginning WIP Inventory candles (6,000), the candles started and completed (396,000), and the work performed on the ending inventory candles (4,320), or a total of 406,320 EUP. Multiplying this equivalent production by the standard labor cost per candle of $0.24 gives a total of $97,517 (rounded).

Work in Process Inventory	97,517	
Direct Labor Variance	25,121	
Wages Payable		122,638
To accrue direct labor cost; assign labor cost to WIP Inventory at standard; record unfavorable direct labor variance		

3. Actual factory overhead incurred in April is $385,262.

Manufacturing Overhead	385,262	
Various accounts		385,262
To record actual overhead cost for April		

4. WIP Inventory is debited for the standard cost of overhead based on the EUP produced in April. Multiplying the 406,320 EUP by the standard overhead rate of $1.00 per candle gives $406,320.

Work in Process Inventory	406,320	
Manufacturing Overhead		385,262
Overhead Variance		21,058
To apply overhead to WIP Inventory and record the favorable overhead variance		

5. Finished Goods Inventory is debited for the total standard cost ($1,144,920) of the 406,000 candles completed during the month (406,000 × $2.82).

Finished Goods Inventory	1,144,920	
Work in Process Inventory		1,144,920
To transfer standard cost of completed candles to FG Inventory		

Advantages of Standard Costing

Simplification of recordkeeping A standard costing system eliminates the need to differentiate between the per-unit cost of the beginning WIP Inventory units that were completed and the per-unit cost of the units started and completed in the current period. All units transferred out of a department are at the standard production cost for each cost component. Thus, recordkeeping is simplified, and variations from the norm are highlighted in the period of incurrence. Standard cost systems are discussed in depth in Chapter 10.

Useful in Cost Control Standard costing not only simplifies the cost flows in a process costing system but also provides a useful tool to control costs. By developing standards, managers have a benchmark against which actual costs can be compared. Managers may also use these standards as targets for performance measurements. For example, meeting standard costs 98 percent of the time may be set as a goal for the company.

Allows Variance Analysis Use of standard quantities and costs allows material, labor, and overhead variances to be computed during the period. Variances serve to identify differences between the benchmark (standard) cost and the actual cost. By striving to control variances, managers control costs. Managers should also benchmark, to the extent possible, their firm's costs against costs incurred by other firms. Such information may help indicate the organization's cost strengths and weaknesses.

REVIEW 7-8   **LO7-8**   **Standard Process Costing**

Randall Co. uses a standard costing system to account for its production of kitchenware. Plastic is added at the start of production; labor and overhead are incurred at equal rates throughout the process. The standard cost of one unit is as follows:

continued

Chapter 7 Process Costing   **7-29**

continued from previous page

Direct material	$ 4.25
Direct labor	4.50
Overhead	6.50
Total cost	$15.25

The following production and cost data are applicable for October:

Beg. WIP Inventory (CC: 45% complete)	25,000 units
Units started in October	120,000 units
Ending WIP Inventory (CC: 65% complete)	18,000 units
Current cost of direct material	$490,000
Current cost of direct labor	580,000
Current cost of overhead	820,000

a. What amount is carried as the October beginning balance of WIP Inventory?
b. What amount is carried as the October ending balance of WIP Inventory?
c. What amount is transferred to Finished Goods Inventory for October?
d. What are the total direct material, direct labor, and overhead variances for October?
e. Record the journal entries to recognize the direct material, direct labor, and overhead variances.
f. **Critical Thinking:** While it is the company's policy to update standards annually, what is an indication that standards may need to be updated more often than annually?

More practice: E7-56, E7-57
Solution on p. 7-59.

Comprehensive Chapter Review

Key Terms

continuous loss, p. 7-21
conversion cost, p. 7-5
cost of production report, p. 7-11
discrete loss, p. 7-21
Equivalent units of production (EUP), p. 7-4
first-in, first-out method, p. 7-6

hybrid costing system, p. 7-20
method of neglect, p. 7-21
total cost accounted for, p. 7-8
total cost to account for, p. 7-8
total physical units accounted for, p. 7-9

total physical units to account for, p. 7-9
transferred-in cost, p. 7-18
units started and completed, p. 7-10
weighted average method, p. 7-6

Chapter Summary

Equivalent Units of Production (EUP) (Page 7-2)   LO7-1
- EUP approximate the number of whole units of output that could have been produced during a period from the actual effort expended during that period.
- EUP assign production costs for direct material, direct labor, and overhead to complete and incomplete output of the period; a separate EUP calculation is required for each cost component that is at a different percentage of completion in the production process.
- Unit cost = production cost divided EUP

Weighted Average (WA) Method (Page 7-6)   LO7-2
- WA combines the beginning WIP Inventory and current period production activity and costs.
- WA determines
  - EUP (by cost component) by adding the physical units in beginning WIP Inventory, physical units started and completed during the period, and equivalent units in the ending WIP Inventory.

© Cambridge Business Publishers

- average unit cost (per cost component) by dividing total cost (equal to beginning-of-the-period costs plus current period costs) by EUP.
- transferred-out value by multiplying total units transferred out by total average cost per EUP.
- ending WIP Inventory value by multiplying the EUP for each cost component by the related cost per EUP.

LO7-3 First-In, First-Out (FIFO) Method (Page 7-13)
- FIFO does not commingle beginning WIP Inventory and current period production activity or costs.
- FIFO determines
  - EUP (by cost component) by the equivalent units in beginning WIP Inventory that were completed during the current period, physical units started and completed during the period, and equivalent units in ending WIP Inventory.
  - average unit cost (per cost component) by dividing current period cost by EUP.
  - transferred-out value by adding the cost of beginning WIP Inventory, current period cost needed to complete beginning WIP Inventory, and cost of units started and completed in the current period.
  - ending WIP Inventory value by multiplying the EUP for each cost component by the related cost per EUP.

LO7-4 Multidepartment Production Setting (Page 7-18)
- Costs transferred from a predecessor department to a successor department are called Transferred In or Prior Department costs and these are always 100 percent complete.
- Successor departments may change the unit of measurement from the predecessor department; such changes will need to be reflected in the EUP schedule.

LO7-5 Hybrid Costing (Page 7-20)
- Hybrid costing combines the characteristics of both job order and process costing systems.
- Hybrid costing traces direct material and/or direct labor that is related to a particular batch of goods to those specific goods using job order costing.
- Hybrid costing uses process costing techniques to account for cost components that are common to numerous batches of output.

LO7-6 Spoilage (Page 7-21)
- Normal continuous losses are accounted for using the method of neglect.
- Discrete continuous losses are assigned to units that have passed the inspection point.
- Abnormal continuous and discrete losses are expensed as a loss in the period incurred.

Solution Strategies

LO7-2, 3 Steps in Process Costing Computations

1. Calculate the physical units to account for:

       Beginning WIP Inventory in physical units
   + Units started (or transferred in) during the period

2. Calculate the physical units accounted for. This step involves identifying the groups to which costs are to be assigned (transferred out or remaining in ending WIP Inventory).

       Units completed and transferred
   + Units in ending WIP Inventory

3. Calculate the EUP per cost component. Cost components include transferred-in (if multidepartment), direct material, direct labor, and overhead. If multiple materials are used and have different degrees of completion, each material is considered a separate cost component. If overhead is applied on a direct labor basis or is incurred at the same rate as direct labor, the two cost elements can be combined as one cost component and referred to as conversion.

   a. WA

       Beginning WIP Inventory in physical units
   + Units started and completed*
   + (Ending WIP Inventory × % complete)

Chapter 7 Process Costing

    b. FIFO

        (Beginning WIP Inventory × % not complete at start of period)
    + Units started and completed*
    + (Ending WIP Inventory × % complete)

*Units started and completed = (Units transferred out − Units in beginning WIP Inventory)

4. Calculate total cost to account for by cost component:

        Cost in beginning WIP Inventory
    + Costs of the current period

5. Calculate cost per equivalent unit for each cost component:
    a. WA

        Cost of component in beginning WIP Inventory
    + Cost of component for current period
    = Total cost of component
    ÷ EUP for component
    = Cost per equivalent unit

    b. FIFO

        Cost of component for current period
    ÷ EUP for component
    = Cost per equivalent unit of component

6. Assign the costs to inventory accounts using the WA or FIFO method. The total cost assigned to units transferred out plus the units in the ending WIP Inventory must equal the total cost to account for.
    a. WA
      1. Transferred out:

        Units transferred out × Total cost per EUP for all components

      2. Ending WIP Inventory:

        The sum of EUP for each component × Cost per EUP for each component

    b. FIFO
      1. Transferred out:

        Beginning WIP Inventory cost
    + (Beginning WIP Inventory × % not complete at beginning of period
        for each component × Cost per EUP for each component)

      2. Ending WIP Inventory:

        The sum of EUP for each component × Cost per EUP for each component

Chapter Demonstration Problem

Plaid-Clad manufactures golf bags in a two-department process: Assembly and Finishing. The Assembly Department uses weighted average costing; the percentage of completion of overhead in this department is unrelated to direct labor. The Finishing Department adds hardware to the assembled bags and uses FIFO costing; overhead is applied in this department on a direct labor basis. For June, the following production data and costs were gathered:

LO7-1, 2, 3, 4

Assembly Department: Units
Beginning WIP Inventory (100% complete for DM;
    40% complete for DL; 30% complete for OH) 250
Units started 8,800
Ending WIP Inventory (100% complete for DM;
    70% complete for DL; 90% complete for OH) 400

Assembly Department: Costs	DM	DL	OH	Total
Beginning WIP Inventory	$ 3,755	$ 690	$ 250	$ 4,695
Current period	100,320	63,606	27,681	191,607
Total costs	$104,075	$64,296	$27,931	$196,302

Finishing Department: Units
Beginning WIP Inventory (100% complete for transferred in;
  15% complete for DM; 40% complete for conversion) 100
Units transferred in 8,650
Ending WIP Inventory (100% complete for transferred in;
  30% complete for DM; 65% complete for conversion) 200

Finishing Department: Costs	Transferred In	DM	Conversion	Total
Beginning inventory	$ 2,176	$ 30	$ 95	$ 2,301
Current period	188,570	15,471	21,600	225,641
Total costs	$190,746	$15,501	$21,695	$227,942

Required:
a. Prepare a cost of production report for the Assembly Department.
b. Prepare a cost of production report for the Finishing Department.
c. Prepare T-accounts to show the flow of costs through the Assembly and Finishing Departments.
d. Prepare the journal entries for the Assembly and the Finishing Department for June.

Solution to Demonstration Problem

a.

Assembly Department WA Method	Physical Units	DM (EUP)	DL (EUP)	OH (EUP)
Beginning WIP Inventory	250			
Units started	8,800			
Units to account for	9,050			
Beginning WIP Inventory	250	250	250	250
Started and completed	8,400	8,400	8,400	8,400
Units completed	8,650			
Ending WIP Inventory	400	400	280	360
Units accounted for	9,050	9,050	8,930	9,010

Cost Data	Total	DM	DL	OH
Beginning WIP Inventory	$ 4,695	$ 3,755	$ 690	$ 250
Current period	191,607	100,320	63,606	27,681
Total cost to account for	$196,302	$104,075	$64,296	$27,931
Divided by EUP		÷ 9,050	÷ 8,930	÷ 9,010
Cost per EUP	$ 21.80	$ 11.50	$ 7.20	$ 3.10

Cost Assignment		
Transferred out (8,650 × $21.80)		$188,570
Ending WIP Inventory		
DM (400 × $11.50)	$ 4,600	
DL (280 × $7.20)	2,016	
OH (360 × $3.10)	1,116	7,732
Total cost accounted for		$196,302

b.

Finishing Department FIFO Method	Physical Units	Equivalent Units of Production		
		Transferred In	DM	Conversion
Beginning WIP Inventory	100			
Units started	8,650			
Units to account for	8,750			
Beginning WIP Inventory	100	0	85	60
Started and completed	8,450	8,450	8,450	8,450
Units completed	8,550			
Ending WIP Inventory	200	200	60	130
Units accounted for	8,750	8,650	8,595	8,640

Cost Data	Total	Transferred In	DM	Conversion
Beginning WIP Inventory	$ 2,301			
Current period	225,641	$188,570	$15,471	$21,600
Total cost to account for	$227,942			
Divided by EUP		÷ 8,650	÷ 8,595	÷ 8,640
Cost per EUP	$ 26.10	$ 21.80	$ 1.80	$ 2.50

Cost Assignment

Transferred out		
Beginning inventory cost	$ 2,301	
Cost to complete		
TI (0 × $21.80)	0	
DM (85 × $1.80)	153	
Conversion (60 × $2.50)	150	$ 2,604
Started and completed (8,450 × $26.10)		220,545
Ending inventory		
TI (200 × $21.80)	$ 4,360	
DM (60 × $1.80)	108	
Conversion (130 × $2.50)	325	4,793
Total cost accounted for		$227,942

c.

WIP Inventory—Assembly Dept.			
Beg. bal:		Transferred Out to Finishing Dep.	188,570
Direct material	3,755		
Direct labor	690		
Overhead	250		
Current costs:			
Direct material	100,320		
Direct labor	63,606		
Overhead	27,681		
Total cost to account for	196,302		
Ending balance*	7,732		

*DM $4,600 + DL $2,016 + OH $1,116 = $7,732

WIP Inventory—Finishing Dept.			
Beg. bal:		CGM	223,149
Transferred in	2,176		
Direct material	30		
Conversion	95		
Current costs:			
Transferred in	188,570		
Direct material	15,471		
Conversion	21,600		
Total cost to account for	227,942		
Ending balance*	4,793		

*TI $4,360 + DM $108 + CC $325 = $4,793

FG Inventory			
Beg. bal.	XXX	CGS	XXX
CGM	223,149		
End. bal.	XXX		

d. **Assembly Dept.**

Work in Process Inventory—Assembly..........................	100,320	
Raw Material Inventory.................................		100,320
To transfer in direct material		
Work in Process Inventory—Assembly..........................	63,606	
Wages Payable.......................................		63,606
To record direct labor costs		
Work in Process Inventory—Assembly..........................	27,681	
Overhead—Assembly.................................		27,681
To apply overhead costs to WIP		
Work in Process Inventory—Finishing..........................	188,570	
Work in Process Inventory—Assembly.....................		188,570
To transfer completed goods to next department		

Finishing Dept.

Work in Process Inventory—Finishing..........................	15,471	
Raw Material Inventory.................................		15,471
To transfer in direct material		
Work in Process Inventory—Finishing..........................	21,600	
Conversion Cost—Finishing..............................		21,600
To apply direct labor and overhead costs to WIP		
Finished Goods Inventory....................................	223,149	
Work in Process Inventory—Finishing.....................		223,149
To transfer completed goods to FG		

Assignments with the MBC logo in the margin are available in *myBusinessCourse*. Resources include demonstration videos, guided examples, and auto-graded homework. See details in the Preface, and ask your professor how you can access the system.

Data Analytics

LO7-3

DA7-1. Analyzing trends in manufacturing costs

A machine parts manufacturer gathered data for its Cutting Department for the last three years. The data includes actual costs and equivalent units for direct materials and conversion costs. The data also includes budget information based on budgeted volume levels. The Excel file is available on the textbook's website. The volume of units in the Cutting Department is relatively consistent from month-to-month. Likewise, costs have remained steady and fairly consistent from year to year. However, a three-year analysis reveals some data points that would be considered outliers.

Required

Assuming that the company uses the FIFO method of process costing to track its manufacturing costs, answer the following questions.

a. Prepare a stacked column chart of actual total direct materials and actual total conversion costs showing each month over the three-year period. Indicate any months where data points appear to be outliers.

b. Prepare two clustered column charts, one comparing actual to budgeted direct materials and another comparing actual to budgeted conversion costs. Based on the review of the charts, which outlier(s) appear to be related to a change in volume? What is a possible cause for the change in volume?

c. Which outlier(s) appear to be due to a change in costs not related to volume? *Hint:* Prepare a chart comparing direct materials and conversion costs per unit to the related budgeted costs per unit. What is a possible cause for the change in costs?

Data Visualization

Data Visualization Activities are available in myBusinessCourse. These assignments use Tableau Dashboards to expose students to visual depictions of data and introduce students to data analytics through data visualizations. These exercises are easily assignable and auto graded by MBC.

Potential Ethical Issues

1. Estimating too high (or too low) a completion percentage for ending WIP Inventory to decrease (or increase) the cost per EUP and thereby distorting ending WIP and ending FG inventories on the balance sheet and Cost of Goods Sold on the income statement
2. Not updating standard costs to reflect new quantities or costs and thereby distorting ending WIP and ending FG inventories on the balance sheet and Cost of Goods Sold on the income statement and creating potentially significant variances that could be written off without management review
3. Ignoring the necessity to trace significant, direct costs to specific jobs in hybrid manufacturing situations and thereby understating the cost of products containing high-cost components or materials and overstating the cost of products containing low-cost components or materials
4. Treating abnormal spoilage as normal spoilage and thereby inflating the cost of "good" units and not reporting the abnormal spoilage as a current period loss on the income statement

Questions

Q7-1. What are the characteristics of a company that would be more likely to use process costing than job order costing?

Q7-2. How do the weighted average and first-in, first-out methods of process costing differ in their treatment of beginning Work in Process Inventory units?

Q7-3. What is an "equivalent unit of production," and why is it a necessary concept to employ in a process costing system?

Q7-4. Is one equivalent unit computation sufficient for all cost components? Explain your answer.

Q7-5. What is meant by the phrase *units started and completed*? Why is this phrase more closely associated with the first-in, first-out method of process costing than with the weighted average method?

Q7-6. What is meant by the phrase *transferred out cost*? Why does the transferred out cost under the WA method include only one computation, but the FIFO method includes multiple computations?

Q7-7. How is the cost of ending inventory calculated in a process costing system?

Q7-8. Which cost component can be found in a downstream department of a multidepartment production process that will not be present in the first upstream department? Discuss.

Q7-9. A company has two sequential processing departments. On the cost of production reports for the departments, will the cost per unit transferred out of the first department always be equal to the cost per unit transferred in to the second department? Explain.

Q7-10. What is a hybrid costing system? In what circumstances are hybrid costing systems typically employed?

Q7-11. In accounting for spoilage, what is meant by the "method of neglect"? How does the use of this method affect cost of good production?

Q7-12. In a process costing system, how are normal and abnormal spoilage typically treated? Why are normal and abnormal spoilage treated differently?

Q7-13. (Appendix 7-2) How is a standard costing system used to measure variances?

Multiple Choice

MC7-14. Colt Company uses a weighted-average process cost system to account for the cost of producing a chemical compound. As part of production, Material B is added when the goods are 80% complete. The company started 70,000 additional units during the month; and had the following work in process inventories at the beginning and end of the month.

Beginning	20,000 units, 90% complete
Ending	25,000 units, 60% complete

How many equivalent units would Material B costs have been assigned to at the end of the month?

a. 65,000.   c. 85,000.
b. 70,000.   d. 90,000.

LO7-1, 3 **MC7-15.** Jones Corporation uses a first-in, first-out (FIFO) process costing system. Jones has the following unit information for the month of August.

	Units
Beginning work-in-process inventory, 100% complete for materials, 75% complete for conversion cost	10,000
Units completed and transferred out.	90,000
Ending work-in-process inventory, 100% complete for materials, 60% complete for conversion cost	8,000

The number of equivalent units of production for conversion costs for the month of August is
- a. 87,300.
- b. 88,000.
- c. 92,300.
- d. 92,700.

LO7-2 **MC7-16.** Mack Inc. uses a weighted-average process costing system. Direct materials and conversion costs are incurred evenly during the production process. During the month of October, the following costs were incurred.

Direct materials	$39,700
Conversion costs	70,000

The work-in-process inventory as of October 1 consisted of 5,000 units, valued at $4,300, that were 20% complete. During October, 27,000 units were transferred out. Inventory as of October 31 consisted of 3,000 units that were 50% complete. The weighted-average inventory cost per unit completed in October was
- a. $3.51.
- b. $3.88.
- c. $3.99.
- d. $4.00.

LO7-3 **MC7-17.** Mack Inc. uses a first-in, first-out process costing system. Direct materials and conversion costs are incurred evenly during the production process. During the month of October, the following costs were incurred.

Direct materials	$39,700
Conversion costs	70,000

The work-in-process inventory as of October 1 consisted of 5,000 units, valued at $4,300, that were 20% complete. During October, 27,000 units were transferred out. Inventory as of October 31 consisted of 3,000 units that were 50% complete. The FIFO inventory cost per unit completed in October was
- a. $3.51.
- b. $3.88.
- c. $3.99.
- d. $4.00.

LO7-4 **MC7-18.** During December, Krause Chemical Company had the following selected data concerning the manufacture of Xyzine, an industrial cleaner.

Production Flow	Physical Units
Completed and transferred to the next department	100
Add: Ending work-in-process inventory	10 (40% complete as to conversion)
Total units to account for	110
Less: Beginning work-in-process inventory	20 (60% complete as to conversion)
Units started during December	90

All material is added at the beginning of processing in this department, and conversion costs are added uniformly during the process. The beginning work-in-process inventory had $120 of raw material and $180 of conversion costs incurred. Material added during December was $540 and conversion costs of $1,484 were incurred. Krause uses the weighted-average process-costing method. The total raw material costs in the ending work-in-process inventory for December is
- a. $120.
- b. $72.
- c. $60.
- d. $36.

Chapter 7 Process Costing

MC7-19. The following statements describe a hybrid costing system except for **LO7-5**
    a. Combines characteristics of job order and process costing.
    b. Can be used in a system with different materials but similar processing procedures.
    c. Can be useful for a manufacturer of customized products.
    d. Requires the same accounting treatment for material and conversion costs.

MC7-20. A company produces disk brakes for mountain bikes. During the current reporting period, the company has normal spoilage of 700 units. At the beginning of the current reporting period, the company had 3,400 units in inventory and started and completed 5,600 units. 4,900 units were transferred out, and ending inventory had 3,100 units. In this reporting period, the abnormal spoilage for the company disk brakes production was **LO7-6**
    a. 300 units.   *c.* 1,000 units.
    b. 400 units.   *d.* 5,200 units.

MC7-21. Appendix; Which of the following statements are incorrect? **LO7-7**
    a. WA EUP – Equivalent units of beginning inventory = FIFO EUP
    b. Beginning inventory completed during the period + Whole units transferred out + Equivalent units of ending inventory = FIFO EUP
    c. Whole units transferred out + Equivalent units of ending inventory = WA EUP
    d. Equivalent units of beginning inventory + Whole started and completed units + Equivalent units of ending inventory = WA EUP

MC7-22. Appendix; The following are advantages of standard costing in a process costing system except for **LO7-8**
    a. Relevant to both WA and FIFO process costing approaches.
    b. Provides benchmarks for performance measurement.
    c. Allows for variance computations.
    d. Streamlines the process of recording journal entries.

Exercises

E7-23. **Computing equivalent units** Compute equivalent units of production for the period for each of the following separate scenarios. In your calculations, simply calculate work done during the period, ignoring the application of any particular costing method. **LO7-1**

Scenario	Materials	Conversion
1. The company had 40,000 units in ending inventory that had 40% of materials added and were 30% complete as to conversion costs.		
2. The company worked on 325,000 units, 250,000 of which are fully completed and 75,000 which are 80 percent complete at the end of the period for materials and conversion costs.		
3. The company worked on 88,000 units which are now in ending inventory. Materials are added at the end of the process and the process is 60 percent complete as to labor and overhead.		
4. The company finished work on the 38,500 units that were in its beginning inventory of the period. These units had 70 percent of materials added and were 35 percent complete as to labor and overhead at the start of the production period.		
5. The company started and completed 25,000 units and completed 5,000 units of its beginning inventory that had all of its materials but were only 15 percent complete as to labor and overhead at the start of the production period.		

E7-24. **Research** In a team of three or four people, choose a company whose mass production process you would like to study. Use the library, the Internet, and (if possible) personal resources to gather information. Prepare a visual representation (similar to **Exhibit 7.3**) of that production process. In this illustration, indicate the approximate percentage of completion points at which various materials are added and where/how labor and overhead flow into and through the process. **LO7-1**

© Cambridge Business Publishers

Assume that 1,000 units of product are flowing through your production process and are now at the 60 percent completion point as to labor. Prepare a written explanation about the quantity of direct material equivalent units that are included in the 1,000 units. Also explain how much overhead activity and cost have occurred and why the overhead percentage is the same as or different from the percentage of completion for labor.

LO7-1, 2 **E7-25. WA EUP** In manufacturing its products, Trevano Corp. adds all direct material at the beginning of the production process. The company's direct labor and overhead are considered to be continuously at the same degree of completion. September production information is as follows:

Beginning WIP Inventory	10,000 pounds
Started during September	25,000 pounds
Completed during September.	32,000 pounds

As of September 1, the beginning WIP Inventory was 30 percent complete as to labor and overhead. On September 30, the ending WIP Inventory was 80 percent complete as to conversion.

a. Determine the total number of pounds to account for if Trevano uses the weighted average process costing method.
b. Determine the equivalent units of production for direct material.
c. Determine the equivalent units of production for direct labor and overhead.
d. How does the accuracy of the percent complete impact your answers to parts *b* and *c*?

LO7-1, 2 **E7-26. WA EUP** O'Malley Corp. uses a weighted average process costing system. Material is added at the beginning of the production process and overhead is applied on the basis of direct labor. O'Malley's records indicate that 70,000 units were in process at the beginning of May; these units were 30 percent complete as to conversion. In May, the company started 445,300 and completed 427,500 units. May's ending inventory was 35 percent complete as to conversion.

a. What are the equivalent units of production for direct material?
b. What are the equivalent units of production for conversion?

LO7-1, 2 **E7-27. WA EUP** For each of the following situations, use the weighted average method to determine the equivalent units of production for labor and overhead, assuming that they are continuously at the same percentage of completion:

a.
Beginning WIP Inventory (40% complete)	10,000
Units started in production	350,000
Units transferred out.	344,000
Ending WIP Inventory (70% complete).	16,000

b.
Beginning WIP Inventory (30% complete)	40,000
Units started in production	480,000
Units transferred out.	?
Ending WIP Inventory (80% complete).	26,000

c.
Beginning WIP Inventory (55% complete)	15,000
Units started in production	405,000
Units transferred out.	415,800
Ending WIP Inventory (90% complete).	?

d.
Beginning WIP Inventory (35% complete)	10,800
Units started in production	?
Units transferred out.	351,600
Ending WIP Inventory (45% complete).	18,300

LO7-1, 3 **E7-28. FIFO EUP** Assume that Trevano Corp. in Exercise E7-25 uses the FIFO method of process costing.

a. What proportion of work needs to be performed on the beginning inventory units to complete them?
b. What are the equivalent units of production for direct material?

c. What are the equivalent units of production for conversion?

E7-29. FIFO EUP Assume that O'Malley Corp. in Exercise E7-26 uses the FIFO method of process costing.
   a. What are the equivalent units of production for direct material?
   b. What are the equivalent units of production for conversion?

E7-30. FIFO EUP Using the information in Exercise E7-27 and assuming a FIFO method of process costing, determine the equivalent units of production for labor and overhead.

E7-31. WA & FIFO EUP Lazer Inc. makes small toys in a one-department production process. Plastic is added at the beginning of the process; all other materials are considered indirect. The following information is available relative to September production activities:

> Beginning WIP Inventory: 15,000 toys (60 percent complete as to labor; 75 percent complete as to overhead)
>
> Started into production: plastic for 620,000 toys
>
> Ending WIP Inventory: 25,400 toys (35 percent complete as to labor; 60 percent complete as to overhead)

   a. Compute the EUP for direct material, direct labor, and overhead using weighted average process costing.
   b. Compute the EUP for direct material, direct labor, and overhead using FIFO process costing.
   c. Reconcile the calculations in parts (a) and (b).

E7-32. WA & FIFO EUP Ramos Corp. uses a process costing system to assign costs to its steel production. During March, Ramos had beginning Work in Process Inventory of 180,000 tons of steel (100 percent complete as to material and 65 percent complete as to conversion). During the month, the raw material needed to produce 3,400,000 tons of steel was started in process. At month-end, 165,000 tons remained in WIP Inventory (100 percent complete as to material and 40 percent complete as to conversion).
   a. Compute the total units to account for.
   b. Determine how many units were started and completed.
   c. Determine the equivalent units of production using the weighted average method.
   d. Determine the equivalent units of production using the FIFO method.
   e. Reconcile your answers to parts (c) and (d).

E7-33. WA & FIFO EUP On April 30, Leander Co. had 21,600 units in process that were 85 percent complete as to material, 60 percent complete as to direct labor, and 45 percent complete as to overhead. During May, 561,000 units were started. The 13,700 units in ending inventory were 75 percent complete as to material, 25 percent complete as to direct labor, and 10 percent complete as to overhead.
   a. Calculate the physical units to account for in May.
   b. How many units were started and completed during May?
   c. Determine May's EUP for each category using the weighted average method.
   d. Determine May's EUP for each category using the FIFO method.
   e. Reconcile your answers to parts (c) and (d).

E7-34. Cost per WA EUP In October, Pedraza Corp.'s production was 53,600 equivalent units for direct material, 48,800 equivalent units for direct labor, and 42,000 equivalent units for overhead. During October, direct material, conversion, and overhead costs incurred were as follows:

Direct material	$158,688
Conversion	189,648
Overhead	85,200

Beginning WIP Inventory costs for October were $26,232 for direct material, $19,504 for direct labor, and $20,640 for overhead.
   a. How much did Pedraza Corp. spend on direct labor in October?
   b. What was the October weighted average cost per equivalent unit for direct material, direct labor, and overhead?

LO7-3 **E7-35. Cost per FIFO EUP** Assume that Pedraza Corp. in Exercise E7-34 had 7,200 EUP for direct material in October's beginning WIP Inventory, 8,000 EUP for direct labor, and 7,920 EUP for overhead.

a. What was the October FIFO cost per EUP for direct material, direct labor, and overhead?
b. Now assume that the EUP calculations for direct labor and overhead were overestimated by 20%. How does this affect your answer to part a and to decisions made using the information in part *a*?

LO7-2, 3 **E7-36. Cost per WA & FIFO EUP** Pylonic Mfg. produces concrete garden border sections. All material is added at the beginning of processing. Production and cost information for May are as follows:

WA EUP	
Direct material	160,000 sections
Direct labor	152,000 sections
Overhead	150,000 sections
FIFO EUP	
Direct material	120,000 sections
Direct labor	124,000 sections
Overhead	132,000 sections
Beginning WIP Inventory costs	
Direct material	$19,600
Direct labor	6,320
Overhead	10,020
Current period costs	
Direct material	$54,000
Direct labor	34,720
Overhead	84,480

a. What is the total cost to account for?
b. Using weighted average process costing, what is the cost per equivalent unit for each cost component?
c. Using FIFO process costing, what is the cost per equivalent unit for each cost component?
d. How many units were in beginning inventory and at what percentage of completion was each cost component?

LO7-1, 2 **E7-37. WA EUP; cost per WA EUP** BeGone manufactures spray cans of insect repellent. On August 1, the company had 9,800 units in the beginning WIP Inventory that were 100 percent complete as to canisters, 60 percent complete as to other materials, 40 percent complete as to direct labor, and 20 percent complete as to overhead. During August, BeGone started 81,500 units in the manufacturing process. Ending WIP Inventory included 4,600 units that were 100 percent complete as to canisters, 40 percent complete as to other materials, 20 percent complete as to direct labor, and 10 percent complete as to overhead. Cost information for the month is as follows:

Beginning WIP Inventory	
Canisters	$ 6,535
Other direct materials	6,174
Direct labor	5,594
Overhead	1,070
August costs	
Canisters	61,940
Other direct materials	86,793
Direct labor	82,026
Overhead	160,176

Prepare a schedule showing the BeGone August computation of weighted average equivalent units of production and cost per equivalent unit.

LO7-1, 2 **E7-38. WA EUP; cost per WA EUP** Kahil Mfg. makes skateboards and uses a weighted average process costing system. On May 1, the company had 400 boards in process that were 70 percent complete as to material and 85 percent complete as to conversion. During the month, 3,800 additional boards were started, and 300 boards were still in process (40 percent complete as to material and 60 percent complete as to conversion) at the end of May. Cost information for May is as follows:

Chapter 7 Process Costing

Beginning WIP Inventory costs	
Direct material	$ 4,349
Conversion	4,658
Current period costs	
Direct material	60,775
Conversion	46,750

    a. Calculate EUP for each cost component using the weighted average method.
    b. Calculate cost per EUP for each cost component.

E7-39. FIFO EUP; cost per FIFO EUP Use the information in Exercise E7-37 except assume that BeGone uses FIFO process costing. Prepare a schedule showing the BeGone August computation of FIFO equivalent units of production and cost per equivalent unit.   LO7-1, 3

E7-40. FIFO EUP; cost per FIFO EUP Use the information in Exercise E7-38 except assume that Kahil Mfg. uses FIFO costing. Prepare a schedule showing the August computation of FIFO equivalent units of production and cost per equivalent unit.   LO7-1, 3

E7-41. WA cost assignment Louvre Corp. applies the weighted average method for process costing. The following production and cost per EUP data are available for Louvre Corp. for February: LO7-2

Units completed during February	390,000
Units in ending inventory (100% complete as to direct material; 30% complete as to direct labor; 25% complete as to overhead)	55,500
Direct material cost per EUP	$7.50
Direct labor cost per EUP	$9.00
Overhead cost per EUP	$10.20

    a. What is the cost of the goods completed during February?
    b. What is the cost of ending inventory at February 28?
    c. What is the total cost to account for during February?

E7-42. FIFO cost assignment In October, Manchaca Company, who uses the FIFO method for process costing, had the following production and cost data: LO7-3

Beginning inventory units (80% complete as to DM; 45% complete as to DL; 30% complete as to OH)	42,600
October completed production	1,570,000
Units in ending inventory (35% complete as to DM; 15% complete as to DL; 25% complete as to OH)	28,400
Beginning inventory cost	$458,482
October direct material cost per EUP	$10.74
October direct labor cost per EUP	$13.88
October overhead cost per EUP	$24.80

    a. What is the cost of the beginning inventory transferred out in October?
    b. What is the total cost transferred out in October?
    c. What is the cost of ending inventory at the end of October?
    d. What is the total cost to account for during October?

E7-43. FIFO cost assignment In November, Lamb Co. computed its equivalent unit costs under FIFO process costing as follows: LO7-3

Direct material	$29.50
Packaging	3.00
Direct labor	10.84
Overhead	7.68

Direct material and packaging are added at the start and end of processing, respectively.
    Beginning inventory cost was $1,026,810 and consisted of

- $789,040 direct material cost for 54,000 EUP.
- $91,862 direct labor cost for 16,200 EUP.

- $145,908 overhead cost for 18,900 EUP.

Lamb Co. transferred a total of 370,000 units to finished goods during November and had 12,000 units in ending WIP Inventory. The ending inventory units were 30 percent complete as to direct labor and 55 percent complete as to overhead.

a. What percentage complete were the beginning inventory units as to direct material? Packaging? Direct labor? Overhead?
b. What was the total cost of the completed beginning inventory units?
c. What was the cost of the units started and completed in November?
d. What was the cost of November's ending inventory?

LO7-1, 2, 3 **E7-44. EUP; cost per EUP; cost assignment; WA & FIFO** Found Sound mass-produces miniature speakers for personal sound systems. The following cost information is available for June:

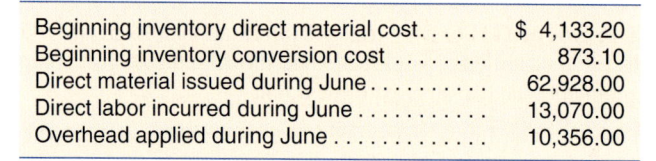

Beginning inventory direct material cost......	$ 4,133.20
Beginning inventory conversion cost	873.10
Direct material issued during June...........	62,928.00
Direct labor incurred during June............	13,070.00
Overhead applied during June...............	10,356.00

On June 1, the company had 1,000 units in process, which were 60 percent complete as to material and 30 percent complete as to conversion. Found Sound started 8,400 units into process during June and had 300 units still in process on June 30. The ending WIP units were 80 percent complete as to material and 70 percent complete as to conversion.

a. Compute the unit costs for June under the weighted average method for direct material and for conversion.
b. Determine the cost transferred out for June using the weighted average method.
c. Determine the cost of June 30 ending inventory using the weighted average method.
d. Compute the unit costs for June under the FIFO method for direct material and for conversion.
e. Determine the total costs transferred to Finished Goods Inventory during June using the FIFO method.
f. Determine the cost of June 30 ending inventory using the FIFO method.
g. Prepare the entries for the direct material, direct labor, and overhead cost assigned to production during June as well as the transfer of the completed goods during June using the weighted average method.

LO7-2, 4 **E7-45. Second department** During August, Tibbetts's Casing Department equivalent unit product costs, computed under the weighted average method, were as follows:

Transferred in	$10
Material.................	2
Conversion	6

All material is introduced at the end of the process in the Casing Department. August's ending Work in Process Inventory contained 4,000 units that were 80 percent complete as to conversion. Twenty-five thousand units were transferred out during August to Finished Goods Inventory.

a. Compute the total costs that should be assigned to the August 31, Work in Process.
b. Compute the total cost of units transferred to finished goods.
c. Prepare the journal entry that Tibbetts's accountant should make at the end of August related to the units transferred out.

LO7-1, 2, 4 **E7-46. WA EUP; second department** Angerstein Inc. produces calendars in a two-process, two-department operation. In the Printing Department, calendars are printed and cut. In the Assembly Department, the material received from Printing is assembled into individual calendars and bound. Each department maintains its own Work in Process Inventory, and costs are assigned using weighted average process costing. In Assembly, conversion costs are incurred evenly throughout the process; direct material is added at the end of the process. For September, the following production and cost information is available for the Assembly Department:

> Beginning WIP Inventory: 5,000 calendars (30 percent complete as to conversion); transferred in cost, $7,550; conversion cost, $1,093
>
> Transferred in during September: 80,000 calendars
>
> Current period costs: transferred in, $80,000; direct material, $10,270; conversion, $13,991
>
> Ending WIP Inventory: 6,000 calendars (80 percent complete as to conversion)

For the Assembly Department, compute the following:
a. equivalent units of production for each cost component
b. cost per EUP for each cost component
c. cost transferred to Finished Goods Inventory
d. cost of ending WIP Inventory

E7-47. FIFO EUP; second department Use the information in Exercise E7-46 and assume that Angerstein Inc. uses the FIFO method of process costing. For the Assembly Department, compute the following:

a. equivalent units of production for each cost component
b. cost per EUP for each cost component
c. cost transferred to Finished Goods Inventory
d. cost of ending WIP Inventory

E7-48. WA & FIFO EUP; two departments Baum Co. has two processing departments: Fabrication and Assembly. In the Fabrication Department, metal is cut and formed into various components, which are then transferred to Assembly. The components are welded, polished, and coated with sealant in the Assembly Department. April production data for these two departments follow.

Fabrication

Beginning WIP Inventory (100% complete as to material; 25% complete as to conversion)	5,000
Units started during month	40,000
Ending WIP Inventory (100% complete as to material; 60% complete as to conversion)	6,800

Assembly

Beginning WIP Inventory (0% complete as to sealant; 35% complete as to conversion)	2,000
Units started during month	?
Ending WIP Inventory (0% complete as to sealant; 15% complete as to conversion)	6,100

a. Determine the equivalent units of production for each cost component for each department under the WA method.
b. Determine the equivalent units of production for each cost component for each department under the FIFO method.

E7-49. Hybrid costing WrapAround makes one-size-fits-most capes. Each cape goes through the same conversion process, but three types of fabric (Dacron, denim, and cotton) are available. The company uses a standard costing system, and standard costs for each type of cape follow.

	Dacron	Denim	Cotton
Material (2 yards)	$10	$ 8	$12
Direct labor (1 hour)	9	9	9
Overhead (based on 1.5 machine hours)	6	6	6
Total	$25	$23	$27

Material is added at the start of production. In March, there was no beginning WIP Inventory and 2,500 capes were started into production. Of these, 300 were Dacron, 500 were denim, and 1,700 were cotton. At the end of March, 100 capes (50 Dacron, 20 denim, and 30 cotton) were not yet complete. The stage of completion for each cost component for the 100 unfinished capes is as follows:

Material	100% complete
Direct labor	25% complete
Overhead	35% complete

a. Determine the total cost of the capes completed and transferred to Finished Goods Inventory.
b. Determine the total cost of the capes in the ending WIP Inventory.

LO7-5   E7-50.   Hybrid costing Pat Koontz makes necklaces from glass beads, metal beads, and natural beads. After reading about hybrid costing, she realized that the different types of necklaces did not cost the same amount of money to make, even though they took the same amount of time and effort to assemble. Koontz developed the following standard costs for each type of necklace:

	Glass	Metal	Natural
Beads..	$24	$15	$ 7
Direct labor (1.5 hours).........................	15	15	15
Overhead (based on 1.5 hours)	8	8	8
Total	$47	$38	$30

Koontz began the year with no beginning WIP Inventory after she experienced an extreme holiday rush. During January, 130 necklaces were started: 70 were glass, 25 were metal, and 35 were natural. At the end of January, 25 necklaces were not yet complete: 5 glass, 13 metal, and 7 natural. The stage of completion for each cost component for the 25 unfinished necklaces was as follows:

Material...........................	100% complete
Conversion	60% complete

a. Calculate the cost of necklaces completed during January.
b. Calculate the cost of necklaces in ending WIP Inventory.

LO7-3, 6   E7-51.   FIFO EUP computations; normal loss Oehkle Inc. produces paint in a process in which spoilage occurs continually. Spoilage of 2 percent or fewer of the gallons of raw material placed into production is considered normal. The following operating statistics are available for June:

Beginning WIP Inventory (60% complete as to material; 70% complete as to conversion)...	16,000 gallons
Started during June	360,000 gallons
Ending WIP Inventory (40% complete as to material; 20% complete as to conversion)...	8,000 gallons
Spoiled..	2,800 gallons

a. How many gallons were transferred out?
b. What are the FIFO equivalent units of production for material? For conversion?

LO7-3, 6   E7-52.   FIFO; normal loss Lilliputian Inc. produces dog food. All direct material is entered at the beginning of the process. Some shrinkage occurs during the production process, but management considers any shrinkage of less than 8 percent to be normal. October data are as follows:

Beginning WIP Inventory (45% complete as to conversion).................	36,000 pounds
Started during the month	120,000 pounds
Transferred to FG Inventory	126,000 pounds
Ending WIP Inventory (15% complete as to conversion)	21,600 pounds
Loss	? pounds

The following costs are associated with October production:

Beginning WIP Inventory:		
Material	$14,000	
Conversion..................	10,800	$24,800
Current period:		
Material	$39,060	
Conversion..................	33,912	72,972
Total cost to account for		$97,772

Prepare an October cost of production report for Lilliputian Inc. using FIFO process costing.

LO7-2, 6   E7-53.   WA; normal vs. abnormal spoilage Hebert Industries uses a weighted average process costing system. Management has specified that the normal loss from shrinkage cannot exceed 3 percent

Chapter 7 Process Costing

of the units started in a period. All raw material is added at the start of the production process. Spoilage is determined upon inspection at the end of the production process. March processing information follows.

Beginning WIP Inventory (30% complete as to conversion)	20,000 units
Started during March	120,000 units
Completed during March	116,400 units
Ending WIP Inventory (20% complete as to conversion)	16,000 units

a. How many total units are there to account for?
b. How many units were spoiled during processing? Of the spoiled units, how many should be treated as a normal loss? As an abnormal loss?
c. What are the equivalent units of production for direct material? For conversion?
d. How are costs associated with the company's normal spoilage handled?
e. How are costs associated with the company's abnormal spoilage handled?

E7-54. **FIFO; normal and abnormal loss** Omaha Foods manufactures corn meal in a continuous, mass production process. Corn is added at the beginning of the process. Normal losses are minimal and abnormal losses infrequently occur when foreign materials are found in the corn meal. Routine inspection occurs at the 95 percent completion point as to conversion.

During May, a machine malfunctioned and dumped salt into 8,000 pounds of corn meal. This abnormal loss occurred when conversion was 70 percent complete on those pounds of product. The error was immediately noticed, and those pounds of corn meal were pulled from the production process. Two thousand additional pounds of meal were detected as unsuitable at the routine inspection point; this amount was considered within normal limits. Production data for the month follow.

LO7-3, 6

Beginning WIP Inventory (85% complete)	40,000 pounds
Started during the month	425,000 pounds
Ending WIP Inventory (25% complete)	10,000 pounds

a. Determine the number of EUP for direct material and for conversion, assuming a FIFO cost flow.
b. If the costs per EUP are $0.08 and $0.15 for direct material and conversion, respectively, what is the cost of the ending WIP Inventory?
c. What is the cost of abnormal loss? How is this cost treated in May?

E7-55. **Appendix; Alternative EUP calculation methods** In manufacturing its products, Russell Corp. adds all direct material at the beginning of the production process. The company's direct labor and overhead are considered to be continuously at the same degree of completion. September production information is as follows:

LO7-7

Beginning WIP Inventory	10,000 units
Started during September	25,000 units
Completed during September	32,000 units

As of June 1, the beginning WIP Inventory was 30 percent complete as to labor and overhead. On June 30, the ending WIP Inventory was 80 percent complete as to conversion.

a. Compute equivalent units of production using the weighted average method of process costing showing two alternative calculations.
b. Compute equivalent units of production using the FIFO method of process costing showing two alternative calculations.

E7-56. **Appendix; Standard process costing** Cherbock Company uses a standard costing system to account for its pita bread manufacturing process. The bread is sold in packages of one dozen pieces. The company has set the following cost standards for each package:

LO7-8

Direct material—ingredients	$0.25
Direct material—packaging	0.05
Direct labor	0.07
Overhead	0.30
Total cost	$0.67

© Cambridge Business Publishers

On June 1, the company had 12,000 pitas in process; these were 100 percent complete as to ingredients, 0 percent complete as to packaging, and 70 percent complete as to labor and overhead. During June, 310,000 pitas were started, and 314,000 were finished. Ending inventory was 100 percent complete as to ingredients, 0 percent complete as to the packaging, and 60 percent complete as to labor and overhead.

a. What were the equivalent units of production for June for each cost component?
b. What was the cost of the packages transferred to Finished Goods Inventory during June?
c. What was the cost of the ending WIP Inventory for June?

LO7-8 E7-57. Appendix; Standard process costing; variances Reischman Co. uses a standard costing system to account for its production of toys. Plastic is added at the start of production; labor and overhead are incurred at equal rates throughout the process. The standard cost of one toy is as follows:

Direct material	$0.10
Direct labor	0.02
Overhead	0.09
Total cost	$0.21

The following production and cost data are applicable to April:

Beginning WIP Inventory (45% complete)	180,000 units
Units started in April	1,300,000 units
Ending WIP Inventory (65% complete)	144,000 units
Current cost of direct material	$184,000
Current cost of direct labor	27,126
Current cost of overhead	118,500

a. What amount is carried as the April beginning balance of WIP Inventory?
b. What amount is carried as the April ending balance of WIP Inventory?
c. What amount is transferred to Finished Goods Inventory for April?
d. What are the total direct material, direct labor, and overhead variances for April?
e. Record the journal entries to recognize the direct material, direct labor, and overhead variances.

Problems

LO7-1, 2 P7-58. WA EUP & cost assignment GitAlong Inc. manufactures belt buckles in a single-step production process. The following information is available for June:

	Physical Units	Cost of Material	Cost of Labor
Beginning work in process	200,000	$1,200,000	$ 671,875
Units started during period	1,000,000	7,800,000	3,976,250
Units in ending inventory	300,000		

All material is added at the start of the production process. Beginning and ending inventory units were, respectively 80 percent and 70 percent complete as to conversion. Overhead cost is applied to production at the rate of 60 percent of direct labor cost.

a. Prepare a schedule to compute equivalent units of production by cost component assuming the weighted average method.
b. Determine the unit production costs for material and conversion.
c. Calculate the costs assigned to completed units and ending inventory for August.

LO7-1, 2 P7-59. WA EUP; cost assignment Spangenberg Products manufactures computer cases. All material is added at the start of production and overhead is assumed to be incurred at the same rate as labor. Overhead is applied to each product at the rate of 70 percent of direct labor cost. At the beginning of July, there were no units in the Finished Goods Inventory. The firm's inventory cost records provide the following information:

Chapter 7 Process Costing

	Units	DM Cost	DL Cost
Work in Process Inventory, 7/1 (70% complete as to labor)	100,000	$ 750,000	$ 215,000
Units started in production	1,500,000		
Costs for July		5,650,000	4,105,000
Work in Process Inventory, 7/31 (60% complete as to labor)	400,000		

At the end of July, the cost of the Finished Goods Inventory was determined to be $124,000.

a. Compute the following:
   1. Equivalent units of production using the weighted average method.
   2. Unit production costs for material, labor, and overhead.
   3. Cost of goods sold.
b. Prepare the journal entries to record the July transfer of completed goods and the July cost of goods sold.

P7-60. WA cost assignment Fresh Seasons is a contract manufacturer for Delectable Dressing Company. Fresh Seasons uses a weighted average process costing system to account for its salad dressing production. All ingredients are added at the start of the process. Delectable provides reusable vats to Fresh Seasons for the completed product to be shipped to Delectable for bottling, so Fresh Seasons incurs no packaging costs. Production and cost information for Fresh Seasons during April follow.

LO7-2

Gallons of dressing in beginning WIP Inventory	36,000
Gallons completed during April	242,000
Gallons of dressing in ending WIP Inventory	23,500
Costs of beginning WIP Inventory	
Direct material	$ 183,510
Direct labor	98,526
Overhead	78,273
Costs incurred in April	
Direct material	$1,136,025
Direct labor	451,450
Overhead	723,195

April beginning and ending WIP inventories had the following percentages of completion for labor and overhead:

	April 1	April 30
Direct labor	55%	15%
Overhead	70%	10%

a. How many gallons of dressing ingredients were started in April?
b. What is the total cost of the goods transferred out during April?
c. What is the cost of April's ending WIP Inventory?

P7-61. WA cost of production report; journal entries Delacroix Co. had 800 units of inventory at the beginning of March. Other information about that beginning Work in Process Inventory is as follows:

LO7-2

Quantity: 800 units	Percent Complete	Costs Incurred
Direct material	45	$ 6,748
Direct labor	65	8,680
Overhead	40	5,710
Total beginning inventory		$21,138

Direct labor costs were extremely high during February, because the company had a labor strike and paid a high premium to get production workers that month.

During March, Delacroix Co. started production of 11,400 units of product and incurred $259,012 for material, $58,200 for direct labor, and $188,210 for overhead. At the end of March, the company had 400 units in process (70 percent complete as to material, 90 percent complete as to direct labor, and 80 percent complete as to overhead).

    a. Prepare a cost of production report for March using the weighted average method.
    b. Journalize the March transactions.
    c. Prepare T-accounts to represent the flow of costs for Delacroix Co. for March. Use XXX where amounts are unknown and identify what each unknown amount represents.

LO7-1, 3   **P7-62.**   **FIFO cost per EUP**   Itzgood makes a variety of healthy snack foods. The following information for January relates to a trail mix. Materials are added at the beginning of processing; overhead is applied based on direct labor. The mix is transferred to a second department for packaging. Itzgood uses a FIFO process costing system.

Beginning WIP Inventory (40% complete as to conversion)	20,000 pounds
Mix started in January	321,600 pounds
Ending WIP Inventory (80% complete as to conversion)	16,000 pounds
Material cost incurred in January	$778,272
Conversion cost incurred in January	$277,536

Beginning inventory cost totaled $53,580. For January, compute the following:

    a. Equivalent units of production for material and conversion.
    b. Cost per equivalent unit by cost component.
    c. Cost of mix transferred to the packaging department in January.
    d. Cost of January's ending inventory.

LO7-3   **P7-63.**   **FIFO cost assignment**   Use the Fresh Seasons information from Problem E7-60, except assume that the company uses a FIFO process costing system.

    a. How many gallons of dressing ingredients were started in April?
    b. What is the total cost of the completed beginning inventory?
    c. What is the total cost of goods completed during April?
    d. What is the average cost per gallon of all goods completed during April? (Round to the nearest cent.)
    e. What is the cost of April's ending WIP Inventory?

LO7-3   **P7-64.**   **FIFO cost of production report**   Use the information from Problem E7-61 for Delacroix Co.

    a. Prepare a cost of production report for March using the FIFO method.
    b. In general, what differences exist between the WA and FIFO methods of process costing and why do these differences exist?

LO7-2, 3   **P7-65.**   **WA & FIFO; cost of production report**   In a single-process production system, Phunky Phingers produces wool gloves. For November, the company's accounting records reflected the following:

Beginning WIP Inventory (100% complete as to material; 30% complete as to direct labor; 60% complete as to overhead)	12,000 units
Units started during the month	90,000 units
Ending WIP Inventory (100% complete as to material; 40% complete as to direct labor; 80% complete as to overhead)	20,000 units

Cost Component	November 1	During November
Direct material	$13,020	$90,000
Direct labor	1,908	45,792
Overhead	4,636	70,824

    a. For November, prepare a cost of production report, assuming that the company uses the weighted average method.
    b. For November, prepare a cost of production report, assuming that the company uses the FIFO method.
    c. Compare the total cost per EUP in part *a* under the WA method to the total cost per EUP in part *b* under the FIFO method. Based on this comparison, is the beginning inventory cost per EUP higher or lower than the EUP for current period costs? Does this indicate prices are rising or falling?

Chapter 7 Process Costing 7-49

P7-66. **WA and FIFO; cost of production report** Springtime Paints makes quality paint in one production department. Production begins with the blending of various chemicals, which are added at the beginning of the process, and ends with the canning of the paint. Canning occurs when the mixture reaches the 90 percent stage of completion. The gallon cans are then transferred to the Shipping Department for crating and shipment. Labor and overhead are added continuously throughout the process. Factory overhead is applied at the rate of $3 per direct labor hour.

LO7-2, 3

Prior to May, when a change in the process was implemented, work in process inventories were insignificant. The change in process enables more production but results in large amounts of work in process. The company has always used the weighted average method to determine equivalent production and unit costs. Now production management is considering changing from the weighted average method to the first-in, first-out method.

The following data relate to actual production during May:

Work in process inventory, May 1	
Direct material—chemicals	$ 45,100
Direct labor ($10 per hour)	5,250
Factory overhead	1,550
Costs for May	
Direct material—chemicals	$228,900
Direct material—cans	7,000
Direct labor ($10 per hour)	35,000
Factory overhead	11,000
Units for May (Gallons)	
Work in process inventory, May 1 (25% complete)	4,000
Sent to Shipping Department	20,000
Started in May	21,000
Work in process inventory, May 31 (80% complete)	5,000

a. Prepare a cost of production report for May using the WA method.
b. Prepare a cost of production report for May using the FIFO method.
c. Discuss the advantages and disadvantages of using the WA method versus the FIFO method, and explain under what circumstances each method should be used.

P7-67. **WA; second department** Octavia Corp.'s products are manufactured in three separate departments: Molding, Curing, and Finishing. Materials are introduced in Molding; additional material is added in Curing. The following information is available for the Curing Department for May:

LO7-2, 4

Beginning WIP Inventory (degree of completion: transferred in, 100%; direct material, 80%; direct labor, 40%; overhead, 30%)	8,000 units
Transferred in from Molding	40,000 units
Ending WIP Inventory (degree of completion: transferred in, 100%; direct material, 70%; direct labor, 50%; overhead, 40%)	4,000 units
Transferred to Finishing	? units

Cost Component	BI Cost	Current Period Cost
Transferred in	$200,160	$1,620,000
Direct material	42,504	333,300
Direct labor	31,360	517,880
Overhead	4,848	267,840

Prepare, in good form, a weighted average cost of production report for the Curing Department for May.

CPA ADAPTED

P7-68. **FIFO; second department** Use the information for Octavia Corp. in Problem P7-67, except assume that the company uses FIFO costing. Prepare, in good form, a FIFO cost of production report for the Curing Department for May.

LO7-3, 4

CPA ADAPTED

P7-69. **Two departments; WA** Always Christmas makes artificial Christmas trees in two departments: Cutting and Boxing. In the Cutting Department, wire wrapped with green "needles" is placed into production at the beginning of the process and is cut to various lengths. The "branches" are then transferred to the Boxing Department, where the lengths are separated into the necessary groups to make a tree. The "limbs" are then placed in boxes and immediately sent to Finished Goods.

LO7-2, 4

© Cambridge Business Publishers

The following data are available related to the October production in each of the two departments:

	Units	Percent of Completion Transferred In	Percent of Completion Material	Percent of Completion Conversion
Cutting Department				
Beginning WIP Inventory	8,000	N/A	100	40
Started in process	36,000			
Ending inventory	3,600	N/A	100	70
Boxing Department				
Beginning WIP Inventory	2,500	100	0	65
Transferred in	?			
Ending inventory	1,200	100	0	70

	Costs Transferred In	Costs Material	Costs Conversion
Cutting Department			
Beginning WIP Inventory	N/A	$ 293,000	$ 80,000
Current period	N/A	1,379,000	1,293,440
Boxing Department			
Beginning WIP Inventory	$166,420	$ 0	$ 6,993
Current period	?	383,640	246,120

a. Prepare a cost of production report for the Cutting Department assuming a weighted average method.

b. Using the data developed from (a), prepare a cost of production report for the Boxing Department assuming a weighted average method.

LO7-2, 4 **P7-70. Cost flows; multiple departments** Elijah Inc. produces accent stripes for automobiles in 50-inch rolls. Each roll passes through three departments (Striping, Adhesion, and Packaging) before it is ready for shipment to customers. Product costs are tracked by department and assigned using a process costing system. Overhead is applied to production in each department at a rate of 80 percent of the department's direct labor cost.

The following T-account information pertains to departmental operations for June:

Work in Process—Striping

Beginning	20,000	
DM	90,000	?
DL	80,000	
Overhead	?	
Ending	17,000	

Work in Process—Adhesion

Beginning	70,000	
Transferred in	?	
DM	22,600	480,000
DL	?	
Overhead	?	
Ending	20,600	

Work in Process—Packaging

Beginning	150,000	
Transferred in	?	CGM ?
DM	?	
DL	?	
Overhead	90,000	
Ending	40,000	

Finished Goods

Beginning	185,000	
TI	880,000	720,000
Ending	?	

a. What was the cost of goods transferred from the Striping Department to the Adhesion Department for the month?

b. How much direct labor cost was incurred in the Adhesion Department? How much overhead was assigned to production in the Adhesion Department for the month?

c. How much direct material cost was charged to products in the Packaging Department?

d. Prepare the journal entries for all interdepartmental transfers of products and the cost of the units sold during June.

Chapter 7 Process Costing

P7-71. Comprehensive; FIFO; two departments KeepIn makes fencing in a two-stage production system. In the Cutting Department, wood is cut and assembled into 6-foot fence sections. In the Coating Department, the sections are pressure-treated to resist the effects of weather and then coated with a preservative. The following production and cost data are available for March (units are 6-foot fence sections):

Units	Cutting Dept.	Coating Dept.
Beginning WIP Inventory (March 1)	1,300	900
Complete as to material	80%	0%
Complete as to conversion	75%	60%
Units started in March	4,800	?
Units completed in March	?	4,500
Ending WIP Inventory (March 31)	1,100	?
Complete as to material	40%	0%
Complete as to conversion	20%	40%

Costs	Cutting Dept.	Coating Dept.
Beginning WIP Inventory		
Transferred in	N/A	$11,840
Material	$ 8,345	0
Conversion	7,720	1,674
Current		
Transferred in	N/A	?
Material	35,200	4,950
Conversion	21,225	11,300

a. Prepare EUP schedules for both the Cutting and Coating Departments.
b. Determine the cost per EUP for the Cutting Department.
c. Assign costs to goods transferred out of and in ending WIP Inventory in the Cutting Department.
d. Determine the cost per EUP in the Coating Department. Use the modified FIFO basis and round to the nearest cent. (See footnote 6, Page 7-15.)
e. Assign costs to goods transferred out of and in ending WIP Inventory in the Coating Department.

P7-72. Multiproduct; hybrid costing Be-at-Ease Industries manufactures a series of three models of molded plastic chairs: standard (without arms), deluxe (with arms), and executive (with arms and padding). All are variations of the same design. The company uses batch manufacturing and has a hybrid costing system.

Be-at-Ease has an extrusion operation and subsequent operations to form, trim, and finish the chairs. Plastic sheets are produced by the extrusion operation, some of which are sold directly to other manufacturers. During the forming operation, the remaining plastic sheets are molded into chair seats, and the legs are added; the standard model is sold after this operation. During the trim operation, the arms are added to the deluxe and executive models, and the chair edges are smoothed. Only the executive model enters the finish operation where the padding is added. All units produced complete the same steps within each operation.

The July production run had a total manufacturing cost of $898,000. The units of production and direct material costs incurred were as follows:

	Units Produced	Extrusion Materials	Form Materials	Trim Materials	Finish Materials
Plastic sheets	5,000	$ 60,000			
Standard model	6,000	72,000	$24,000		
Deluxe model	3,000	36,000	12,000	$ 9,000	
Executive model	2,000	24,000	8,000	6,000	$12,000
Totals	16,000	$192,000	$44,000	$15,000	$12,000

Manufacturing costs applied during July were as follows:

	Extrusion Operation	Form Operation	Trim Operation	Finish Operation
Direct labor	$152,000	$60,000	$30,000	$18,000
Factory overhead	240,000	72,000	39,000	24,000

a. For each product produced by Be-at-Ease during July, determine the
   1. Unit cost.
   2. Total cost.

   Account for all costs incurred during the month, and support your answer with appropriate calculations.

b. Without prejudice to your answer in (a), assume that only 1,000 units of the deluxe model remained in the Work in Process Inventory at the end of the month. These units were 100 percent complete as to material and 60 percent complete as to conversion in the trim operation. Determine the value of the 1,000 units of the deluxe model in Be-at-Ease's Work in Process Inventory at the end of July.

LO7-5 **P7-73.** **Multiproduct; hybrid costing** Randazzo Ltd. produces sports fan towels and uses the weighted average process costing method. All towels are cut to be the same size and from the same fabric but can be customized by adding one or more options: (1) embossed team logo, (2) streamers, and (3) a wooden handle. The following information is available for September:

Towels	
BI (70% complete as to conversion)	15,000
Started	520,000
EI (95% complete as to conversion)	9,000
Cost data	
Beginning inventory DM	$ 13,250
Beginning inventory logos	4,035
Beginning inventory conversion	5,703
Current period DM	468,250
Current period embossed logos	298,735
Current period streamers	119,977
Current period wooden handles	1,312
Current period conversion	282,954

At the beginning of September, 40 percent of the towels had been embossed. At the end of September, 70 percent of the towels in work in process were plain, 25 percent had been embossed, and 5 percent had streamers. Conversion is applied to all items equally.

Randazzo's production and sales for the month were as follows:

	Production	Sales
Plain towels	60,000	58,000
Towels with logos and streamers	418,000	417,500
Towels with logos, streamers, and handles	25,000	24,800
Towels with streamers	15,200	15,175
Towels with streamers and handles	2,800	2,730
Towels with handles	5,000	4,350
Total production for September	526,000	522,555

a. Determine the cost of Randazzo's ending WIP Inventory of towels.
b. Determine the cost of Randazzo's ending FG Inventory of towels.
c. Determine the cost of goods sold for September.
d. Should the conversion cost for all towels be the same amount?

LO7-2, 4, 8 **P7-74.** **WA; normal and abnormal loss** Turkburg produces frozen turkey patties. In the Forming Department, ground turkey is formed into patties and cooked; an acceptable shrinkage loss for this department is 1 percent of the pounds started. The patties are then transferred to the Finishing Department where they are placed on buns, boxed, and frozen.

Turkburg uses a weighted average process costing system and has the following production and cost data for the Forming Department for May:

Beginning WIP Inventory (80% complete as to conversion)	2,000 pounds
Started	250,000 pounds
Transferred to Finishing (357,300 patties)	238,200 pounds
Ending inventory (30% complete as to conversion)	6,000 pounds
Beginning inventory cost of turkey	$ 1,807
May cost of turkey	$240,208
Beginning inventory conversion cost	$ 150
May conversion cost	$ 24,380

    a. What is the total shrinkage (in pounds)?
    b. How much of the shrinkage is classified as normal? How is it treated for accounting purposes?
    c. How much of the shrinkage is classified as abnormal? How is it treated for accounting purposes?
    d. What are the May equivalent units of production in the Forming Department for direct materials and conversion?
    e. What is the total cost of the patties transferred to the Finishing Department? Cost of ending inventory? Cost of abnormal spoilage?
    f. How might Turkburg reduce its shrinkage loss? How, if at all, would your solution(s) affect costs and selling prices?
    g. What might have been the cause of the abnormally high spoilage in May? Use calculations to support your answer.

P7-75. WA; normal and abnormal discrete spoilage Gary's Tools manufactures one of its products in a two-department process. A separate Work in Process Inventory account is maintained for each department, and the company uses a weighted average process costing system. The first department is Molding; the second is Grinding. At the end of production in Grinding, a quality inspection is made and then packaging is added. Overhead is applied in the Grinding Department on a machine-hour basis. Production and cost data for the Grinding Department for August follow:

LO7-2, 4, 6

Production Data

Beginning WIP Inventory (percent complete: material, 0; labor, 30; overhead, 40)	1,000 units
Transferred in from Molding	50,800 units
Normal spoilage (found at the end of processing during quality control)	650 units
Abnormal spoilage (found at end of processing during quality control)	350 units
Ending WIP Inventory (percent complete: material, 0; labor, 40; overhead, 65)	1,800 units
Transferred to finished goods	? units

Cost Data

Beginning WIP Inventory		
Transferred in	$6,050	
Material (label and package)	0	
Direct labor	325	
Overhead	980	$ 7,355
Current period		
Transferred in	$149,350	
Material (label and package)	12,250	
Direct labor	23,767	
Overhead	50,190	235,557
Total cost to account for		$242,912

    a. Prepare the August cost of production report for the Grinding Department. Gary's Tools assigns the cost of normal spoilage only to the products that are transferred out. As such, the company extends both the normal and abnormal spoilage units in the EUP schedule to all cost components except packaging (as packaging is not added to spoiled units). The cost of normal spoilage is attached to the units transferred to Finished Goods Inventory; the cost of abnormal spoilage is considered a period loss.
    b. Prepare the journal entry to dispose of the cost of abnormal spoilage.

LO7-2, 4, 8

P7-76. WA; normal and abnormal discrete spoilage Strongarm manufactures various lines of bicycles. Because of the high volume of each type of product, the company employs a process cost system using the weighted average method to determine unit costs. Bicycle parts are manufactured in the Molding Department and transferred to the Assembly Department where they are partially assembled. After assembly, the bicycle is sent to the Packing Department. Annual cost and production figures for the Assembly Department follow:

Production Data

Beginning WIP Inventory (100% complete as to transferred in; 100% complete as to material; 80% complete as to conversion)	3,000 units
Transferred in during the year (100% complete as to transferred in)	45,000 units
Transferred to Packing	40,000 units
Ending WIP Inventory (100% complete as to transferred in; 50% complete as to material; 20% complete as to conversion)	4,000 units

COST DATA

	Transferred In	Direct Material	Conversion
Beginning WIP Inventory	$ 82,200	$ 6,660	$ 13,930
Current period	1,237,800	96,840	241,430
Totals	$1,320,000	$103,500	$255,360

Damaged bicycles are identified on inspection when the assembly process is complete. The normal rejection rate for damaged bicycles is 5 percent of those reaching the inspection point. Any damaged bicycles above the 5 percent quota are considered to be abnormal. Damaged bikes are removed from the production process, and when possible, parts are reused on other bikes. However, such salvage is ignored for the purposes of this problem.

Strongarm does not want to assign normal spoilage cost either to the units in ending inventory (because they have not yet been inspected) or to the bikes that are considered "abnormal spoilage." Thus, the company includes both normal and abnormal spoilage in the equivalent units schedule (at the appropriate percentage of completion). The cost of the normal spoilage is then added to the bikes transferred to the Packing Department. Abnormal spoilage is treated as a period loss.

a. Compute the number of damaged bikes that are considered to be
   1. Normal spoilage.
   2. Abnormal spoilage.
b. Compute the weighted average equivalent units of production for the year for
   1. Bicycles transferred in from the Molding Department.
   2. Bicycles produced with regard to Assembly material.
   3. Bicycles produced with regard to Assembly conversion.
c. Compute the cost per equivalent unit for the fully assembled bicycle.
d. Compute the amount of total production cost that will be associated with the following items:
   1. Normal damaged units.
   2. Abnormal damaged units.
   3. Good units completed in the Assembly Department.
   4. Ending Work in Process Inventory in the Assembly Department.
e. What amount will be transferred to the Packing Department?
f. Discuss some potential reasons for spoilage to occur in this company. Which of these reasons would you consider important enough to correct and why? How might you attempt to correct these problems?

LO7-1, 2, 6

P7-77. WA; normal and abnormal discrete spoilage LaToya Company produces door pulls, which are inspected at the end of production. Spoilage may occur because the door pull is improperly stamped or molded. Any spoilage in excess of 3 percent of the completed good units is considered abnormal. Direct material is added at the start of production. Labor and overhead are incurred evenly throughout production.

The company's May production and cost data follow:

Beginning WIP Inventory (50% complete)	5,600
Units started	74,400
Good units completed	70,000
Ending WIP Inventory (1/3 complete)	7,500

	DM	Conversion	Total
Beginning inventory	$ 6,400	$ 1,232	$ 7,632
Current period	74,400	31,768	106,168
Total	$80,800	$33,000	$113,800

Calculate the equivalent units schedule, prepare a weighted average cost of production report, and assign all costs. LaToya extends both the normal and abnormal spoilage units in the EUP schedule to all cost components that have been incurred to the point of detection (100 percent completion). The cost of normal spoilage is attached to the units transferred to Finished Goods Inventory; the cost of abnormal spoilage is considered a period loss.

P7-78. FIFO; normal and abnormal discrete spoilage Use the LaToya Company data given in Problem E7-70. However, assume that the spoiled goods were detected when conversion was 30 percent complete. Prepare a May cost of production report using the FIFO method. The cost of normal spoilage is attached to the units transferred to Finished Goods Inventory; the cost of abnormal spoilage is considered a period loss. Round all cost calculations to the nearest penny. **LO7-3, 6**

P7-79. Appendix; standard process costing Donbrowski Co. manufactures reflective lenses and uses a standard process costing system. For May, the following data are available: **LO7-8**

Standard Cost of One Unit	
Direct material	$ 5.50
Conversion	12.50
Total manufacturing cost	$18.00
Beginning WIP Inventory	10,000 units (100% DM; 70% conversion)
Started in May	180,000 units
Completed in May	150,000 units
Ending WIP Inventory	? units (100% DM; 60% conversion)
Actual costs for May:	
Direct material	$1,001,000
Conversion	2,136,000
Total actual cost	$3,137,000

a. Prepare an equivalent units of production schedule.
b. Prepare a cost of production report and assign costs to goods transferred and to ending work in process inventory.
c. Calculate and label the variances and close them to Cost of Goods Sold.

P7-80. Appendix; standard process costing MHR Inc. uses a standard process costing system. All material is added at the beginning of the production process. Per unit standard costs for one of the company's products are as follows: **LO7-8**

Direct material	$ 8.25
Direct labor	1.60
Overhead	4.90
Total standard cost	$14.75

October production and cost information for MHR follow:

Units in beginning inventory (40% complete as to DL, 70% complete as to OH)...	14,800
Units started..................................	385,000
Units in ending inventory (60% complete as to DL, 85% complete as to OH).....	4,300
Current period costs:	
Direct material	$3,201,032
Direct labor...................................	625,510
Overhead.....................................	1,904,390

    a.   Prepare an equivalent units of production schedule.
    b.   Determine the cost of the beginning inventory (in total and by cost component).
    c.   Assign costs to goods transferred and to ending WIP inventory.
    d.   Calculate and label (F or U) the variances.

Review Solutions

Review 7-1

a.

Scenario	EUP for Materials	EUP for Conversion Costs
1...........	104,750	104,750
2...........	54,000	40,500
3...........	7,200	9,600
4...........	10,000	13,000

b. The percent complete as to conversion could be estimated through a number of ways. The company could physically examine production and estimate completion, or physically weigh or measure units as a way to estimate completion. Alternatively, the company could estimate completion based on the number of actual direct labor or machine hours incurred compared to total budgeted labor or machine hours. A company could use past data or experience to determine the extent of progression of the units in the production process. Artificial intelligence with visual inspection capabilities could also be utilized to measure the percentage of completion.

    The number of equivalent units calculated depends upon the percent complete. The number of equivalent units directly impacts unit costs. Thus, if the percent complete is overestimated, unit cost would be underestimated for the period (and vice versa). Any decision based upon unit cost (such as setting a selling price or initiating cost control measures) would be impacted by an inaccurate unit cost.

Review 7-2

a.

Cost Data Total	Total Costs	Direct Material	Conversion
Costs in beginning WIP Inventory....	$ 8,000	$ 5,800	$ 2,200
Current period costs..............	121,000	88,000	33,000
Total cost to account for	$129,000	$93,800	$35,200
Divided by EUP		12,720[1]	12,640[2]
Cost per EUP....................	$10.1590	$7.3742	$2.7848

[1] 12,720 = 1,200 + 11,200 + (800 × 0.40)
[2] 12,640 = 1,200 + 11,200 + (800 × 0.30)

b. $125,972 = 12,400* × $10.1590
   *12,400 = 1,200 + 12,000 − 800

c. $3,028 [(320 × $7.3742) + (240 × $2.7848)]

d. Lathrop might choose the WA method over the FIFO method if material and conversion price levels were stable and inventory levels were stable. Changing either the cost per unit or the relative mix between units of ending inventory relative to transferred out inventory will cause the unit costs per period to vary. These changes by period would be buried in the averaging inherent in the WA method. Understanding the month-to-month fluctuations, if significant, would be important to management decision making, especially concerning pricing and cost control.

Chapter 7 Process Costing

Review 7-3

a.

Cost Data	Total Costs	Direct Material	Conversion
Costs in beginning WIP Inventory....	$ 8,000		
Current period costs...............	121,000	$88,000	$33,000
Total cost to account for	$129,000		
Divided by EUP		11,760	12,400
Cost per EUP	$10.1443	$7.4830	$2.6613

b. $125,967 = [$8,000 + ($10.1443 × 11,200) + ($7.4830 × 240) + ($2.6613 × 960)]

c. $3,033 = [($7.4830 × 320) + ($2.6613 × 240)]

d. The total cost per EUP under the WA method of $10.1590 is greater than the total cost per EUP under the FIFO method of $10.1443. This means that the beginning cost per EUP is greater than the current cost per EUP. Under the weighted average method, beginning inventory costs (relating to the prior period) are averaged in with current costs. Thus, to have an increase to the WA method means that beginning costs per unit were higher indicating prices went down in the current period. (Beginning cost per EUP = [$5,800/(1,200 × 80%)] + [$2,200/(1,200 × 20%)] = $15.21 which is greater than current cost per EUP of $10.14.)

Review 7-4

a.

Cost Data	Total Costs	Transferred-In	Direct Material	Conversion
Costs in beginning WIP Inventory....	$ 19,700	$ 17,400	$ —	$ 2,300
Current period costs...............	244,000	188,000	23,000	33,000
Total cost to account for	$263,700	$205,400	$23,000	$35,300
Divided by EUP		19,550[1]	18,170[2]	19,136[3]
Cost per EUP	$13.6169	$10.5064	$1.2658	$1.8447

[1] 19,550 = 1,150 + 17,020 + 1,380
[2] 18,170 = 1,150 + 17,020
[3] 19,136 = 1,150 + 17,020 + (1,380 × 0.70)

b. $247,419 ($13.6169 × 18,170)

c. $16,281 [($10.5064 × 1,380) + ($1.8447 × 966)]

d. Transferred-in costs would have a 100% completion rate by definition because they would not be transferred from the prior department unless complete. Thus, a percent less than 100% would likely indicate an error in recording.

Review 7-5

a.

Cost of goods manufactured:	
DM: Aluminum	$14,800 ($80 × (200 – 15))
DM: Steel	8,700 ($60 × (175 – 30))
DM: Combination ...	6,300 ($70 × (125 – 35))
Conversion	48,300 ($40 + $75) × (500 – 80)
Total	$78,100

b.

Ending inventory:	
DM: Aluminum	$1,200 ($80 × 15)
DM: Steel	1,800 ($60 × 30)
DM: Combination ...	2,450 ($70 × 35)
Conversion	3,680 ($40 + $75) × 80 × 40%
Total	$9,130

c. In this example, materials were customized by component and could easily be traced by component. This is similar to how costs are tracked under job order costing. However, labor and overhead were added at a similar rate and are tracked based upon percentage complete. This is conducive to process costing. Thus, a hybrid costing system is more relevant than choosing either job order or process costing.

Review 7-6

a.

FIFO Method	Materials	Conversion
Beginning WIP Inventory	—	43,750
Started and completed	588,000	588,000
Ending WIP Inventory	80,000	32,000
Normal spoilage	—	—
Abnormal spoilage	5,000	3,750
EUP (FIFO)	673,000	667,500

b. $104,000 [(80,000 × $1.10) + (32,000 × $0.50)]

c. $7,375 [(5,000 × $1.10) + (3,750 × $0.50)]
The cost of abnormal spoilage would be expensed (treated as a period cost).

d. Abnormal losses are recognized immediately. With the method of neglect, normal losses may be deferred to the next period. Any ending WIP would be allocated some of the normal spoilage costs. Thus, the allocated spoilage costs would not become expense until the subsequent period when the inventory was sold.

Review 7-7

	Physical Units
Beginning WIP Inventory	24,000
Started and completed	584,000
Units completed	608,000
Ending WIP Inventory	16,000
Units accounted for	624,000

a. 1.

EUP: Weighted Average Method	Materials	Conversion
Units completed	608,000	608,000
Ending WIP Inventory	16,000	10,400
EUP (WA)	624,000	618,400

2.

EUP: Weighted Average Method	Materials	Conversion
Total units to account for	624,000	624,000
EU to be completed next period	0	(5,600)
EUP (WA)	624,000	618,400

b.

EUP Reconciliation	Materials	Conversion
Weighted average EUP	624,000	618,400
Beg WIP in EUP	(24,000)	(10,800)
EUP (FIFO)	600,000	607,600

The only difference between the WA and FIFO methods in computing EUP is that the units of beginning inventory are considered in the WA method calculation, but not in the FIFO method calculation. Thus, the number of units of BI EUP calculated using the percentage completed in the prior period, is the reconciling item between the two methods. Excluding this amount in the FIFO calculation means that EUP relate only to the *current* period.

Chapter 7 Process Costing

Review 7-8

a. $230,000 [(25,000 × $4.25) + (25,000 × 45% × ($4.50 + $6.50))]
b. $205,200 [(18,000 × $4.25) + (18,000 × 65% × ($4.50 + $6.50))]
c. $1,936,750 [(25,000 + 120,000 − 18,000) × $15.25]

d.

FIFO Method	Materials	Labor	Overhead
Beginning WIP Inventory	0	13,750	13,750
Started and completed	102,000	102,000	102,000
Ending WIP Inventory	18,000	11,700	11,700
Equivalent units	120,000	127,450	127,450
Multiply by unit cost	$ 4.25	$ 4.50	$ 6.50
Standard cost of period	$510,000	$573,525	$828,425
Actual cost of period	(490,000)	(580,000)	(820,000)
Favorable (Unfavorable) Variance	$ 20,000	$ (6,475)	$ 8,425

e.
```
Work in Process Inventory .................................... 510,000
    Material Variance .........................................              20,000
    Raw Material Inventory ...................................             490,000

Work in Process Inventory .................................... 573,525
Labor Variance ..............................................   6,475
    Wages Payable (or Cash) ..................................             580,000

Work in Process Inventory .................................... 828,425
    Overapplied Overhead .....................................               8,425
    Manufacturing Overhead ...................................             820,000
```

f. Standard costing assumes a stable operating environment. When market conditions or production processes change significantly, the static nature of standard costs may lead to inaccuracies in costing. For example, changing market conditions could cause prices to increase or decrease such that the standard costs derived vary significantly from actual. In another example, a change in processing could impact the cost of conversion (such as the automation of additional processes) which may require a standard adjustment.

Data Visualization Solutions

(See page 7-17.)

a. If beginning EU did not change, that means beginning cost per unit did not change between the budget and actual. However, the costs per unit in the current period increased, causing the FIFO current cost per unit to increase. This caused the WA cost per unit to also increase.

b. While the WA cost per unit increased, it did not increase at the same rate as under the FIFO method. This is because the WA method averages in the cost of beginning inventory. Thus, the current period increase in cost is not fully transparent under the WA method, which averages costs across current costs and beginning inventory.

Chapter 8

Activity-Based Management and Activity-Based Costing

Road Map

LO	Learning Objective | Topics	Page	eLecture	Demo	Review	Assignments
8-1	**In an activity-based management system, what are value-added and non-value-added activities?** Activity-based management (ABM) :: Value-Added Activity (VA) :: Non-Value-Added Activity (NVA) :: Business-Value-Added Activities (BNA) :: Process Map :: Processing (Service) Time :: Inspection Time :: Transfer Time :: Idle Time :: Total Cycle Time :: Value Chart	8-2	e8-1	D8-1	Rev 8-1	MC8-13, E8-19, E8-20, E8-21, E8-22, E8-23, E8-24, E8-25, E8-26, E8-27, E8-28, E8-29, P8-61, P8-62
8-2	**How do value-added and non-value-added activities affect manufacturing cycle efficiency?** Manufacturing Cycle Efficiency :: Just-In-Time :: Service Cycle Efficiency :: Systemic Factors :: Physical Factors :: Human Factors	8-6	e8-2	D8-2	Rev 8-2	MC8-14, E8-24, E8-25, E8-26, E8-27, E8-28, E8-29, E8-30, E8-31
8-3	**Why must cost drivers be designated in an activity-based costing system?** Activity-Based Costing (ABC) :: Unit-Level Costs :: Batch-Level Costs :: Engineering Change Order (ECO) :: Product/Process Level Costs :: Organizational/Facility-Level Costs :: Product Profitability Analysis	8-8	e8-3	D8-3A D8-3B D8-3C	Rev 8-3	MC8-15, E8-32, E8-33, E8-34, E8-35, E8-36, E8-37, E8-38, P8-50, P8-51, P8-61, P8-62, P8-63, P8-69, P8-70, DA8-1
8-4	**How are product and service costs computed using an activity-based costing system?** Two-Step Allocation :: OH :: Cost Driver :: Activity Center :: Activity Driver :: Cost Objects :: Product Variety :: Product Complexity :: Process Complexity :: Cost Cross-Subsidization	8-14	e8-4	D8-4	Rev 8-4	MC8-16, E8-39, E8-40, E8-41, E8-42, P8-51, P8-52, P8-53, P8-54, P8-55, P8-56, P8-57, P8-58, P8-59, P8-60, P8-61, P8-62, P8-64, P8-65, DA8-1, DA8-2
8-5	**Under what conditions is activity-based costing useful in an organization, and what information do activity-based costing systems provide to management?** Mass Customization :: Pareto Principle :: Product/Process Complexity :: Barriers :: Non-GAAP Method	8-18	e8-5	D8-5	Rev 8-5	MC8-17, E8-42, E8-43, E8-44, E8-45, E8-46, P8-51, P8-52, P8-56, P8-57, P8-58, P8-59, P8-60, P8-61, P8-62, P8-63, P8-64, P8-65, P8-66, P8-67, P8-68, DA8-3
8-6	**How are product and service costs computed using a time-driven activity-based costing system?** Time-Driven Activity-Based Costing (TDABC) :: Cost of Activity :: Amount of Time Spent on Activity :: Capacity :: Unused Capacity	8-23	e8-6	D8-6	Rev 8-6	MC8-18, E8-47, E8-48, E8-49, P8-69, P8-70

INTRODUCTION

To succeed in today's global marketplace, companies must generate high-quality products or services and have competitive cost structures. Actions taken to create cost efficiencies require an understanding of the drivers, or underlying causes, of costs and not merely recognition of cost predictors. Chapter 6 discusses computation of predetermined overhead (OH) rates using traditional activity bases: direct labor costs, direct labor hours, and machine hours. However, many alternative activity bases are available to assign overhead to products and services. Using such "nontraditional" bases can improve management information about the cost of production or provision and enhance an organization's competitive advantage.

This chapter discusses activity-based management (ABM) and activity-based costing (ABC). These two concepts allow a more direct focus on organizational actions and the overhead costs created by those actions. Used together, ABM and ABC can help managers make better decisions about the design, production or performance, profitability, and pricing of products and services.

ACTIVITY-BASED MANAGEMENT

LO8-1 In an activity-based management system, what are value-added and non-value-added activities?

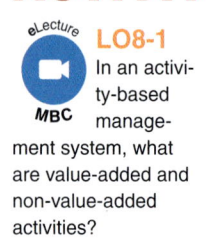

Although specifically designated as an accounting function, determination of product or service cost is a major concern for all managers. Pricing, profitability, and organizational investments to support production or service provision are issues that extend beyond accounting into the areas of corporate strategy, marketing, and finance. In theory, production or performance cost would not matter if a sufficient number of customers were willing to buy a product or service at a price that was high enough to cover that cost and provide a reasonable profit margin. However, in reality, customers purchase a product or service only if they perceive that it provides an acceptable value for the price. Given that reality, management must be concerned about an equitable relationship between selling price and value.

As shown in **Exhibit 8.1**, **activity-based management (ABM)** is a business process model focusing on the control of production or performance activities in order to improve customer value and enhance profitability.

Exhibit 8.1 ■ Components of Activity-Based Management

External Benefits
Improved Customer Value
Enhanced Profitability

Internal Benefits
More Efficient Production
More Accurate Cost Determination
More Effective Performance Evaluation

Activity Analysis | Cost Driver Analysis | Activity-Based Costing | Continuous Improvement | Operational Control | Quality Management | Business Process Improvement | Performance Measurement

CONCEPTS UNDERLYING ACTIVITY-BASED MANAGEMENT

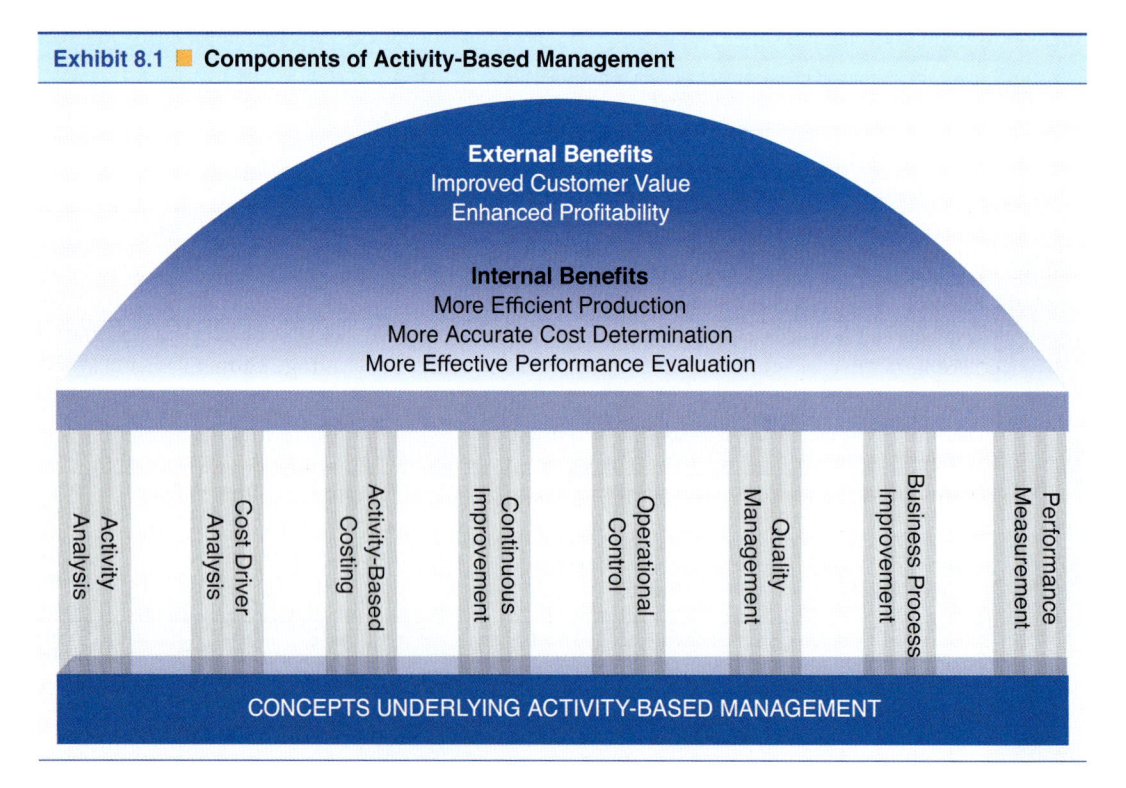

ABM includes a variety of concepts that help companies to produce or process more efficiently, determine product or service costs more accurately, and control and evaluate performance more effectively.

Activity Analysis

In a business context, an **activity** is any repetitive action that is performed in fulfillment of a business function. A primary component of activity-based management is **activity analysis**, which is the process of studying activities to (1) classify them as either value-added or non-value-added activities and (2) devise ways of minimizing or eliminating activities that increase costs but provide little or no customer value.

Activities can be labeled as either value-added or non-value-added. A **value-added (VA) activity** increases the worth of a product or service to a customer and is one for which the customer is willing to pay. Alternatively, a **non-value-added (NVA) activity** increases the time spent on a product or service but does not increase its worth and, thus, is viewed as unnecessary from the customer's perspective. *NVA activities can be reduced, redesigned, or eliminated without affecting the product's or service's market value or quality.*

Businesses can also engage in some activities that are essential (or appear to be essential) to business operations but for which customers would not *willingly* choose to pay. These activities are known as **business-value-added (BVA) activities**. For example, companies must prepare invoices for documenting sales and collections. Customers realize invoice preparation creates costs, and that such costs must be covered by product selling prices. However, because invoice preparation adds no direct value to products or services, customers would prefer not to pay for this activity through a higher selling price.

Asking "Why" Questions Often an easy way to determine the value provided by an activity is to ask "why" five times: if the answers represent valid business reasons, the activity generally adds value; otherwise, the activity adds no value. Consider the following "conversation" about storing a large quantity of flour at a pizza restaurant.

- Why are we storing flour? Because it was acquired before it was actually needed.
- Why was the flour acquired prior to its need? Because it was acquired in a bulk purchase.
- Why was the flour bought in bulk? Because it is less expensive that way.
- Why is buying in bulk less expensive if doing so creates costs for storing and moving the flour as well as possible costs of spillage or spoilage? Because those costs never occurred to me . . . maybe there's a better way. (In this case, only four "why" questions were needed!)

Identifying Processes To begin activity analysis, managers should first identify the organization's production or performance processes. A **process** is a series of activities that, when performed together, satisfy a specific objective. Companies engage in processes for production, distribution, selling, administration, and other company functions. Processes should be defined before a company tries to determine relationships among activities. Most processes occur horizontally across organizational functions and, thus, overlap multiple functional areas. For example, a production process also affects engineering, purchasing, receiving, warehousing, accounting, human resources, and marketing.

Identifying Activities within Processes For each distinct process, a **process map** (or detailed flowchart) should be prepared to indicate *every* step in *every* area that goes into making or doing something. Some steps on the process map are necessary and, therefore, must be performed for the process to be completed. Other steps reflect those activities for which a valid business answer to the "why" question cannot be found and, as such, are unnecessary. An example of a process map is shown in **Exhibit 8.2**. Activities that can be summarized from this process map include receiving goods, inspecting goods, corresponding with suppliers, performing quality checks, transporting goods, and storing goods.

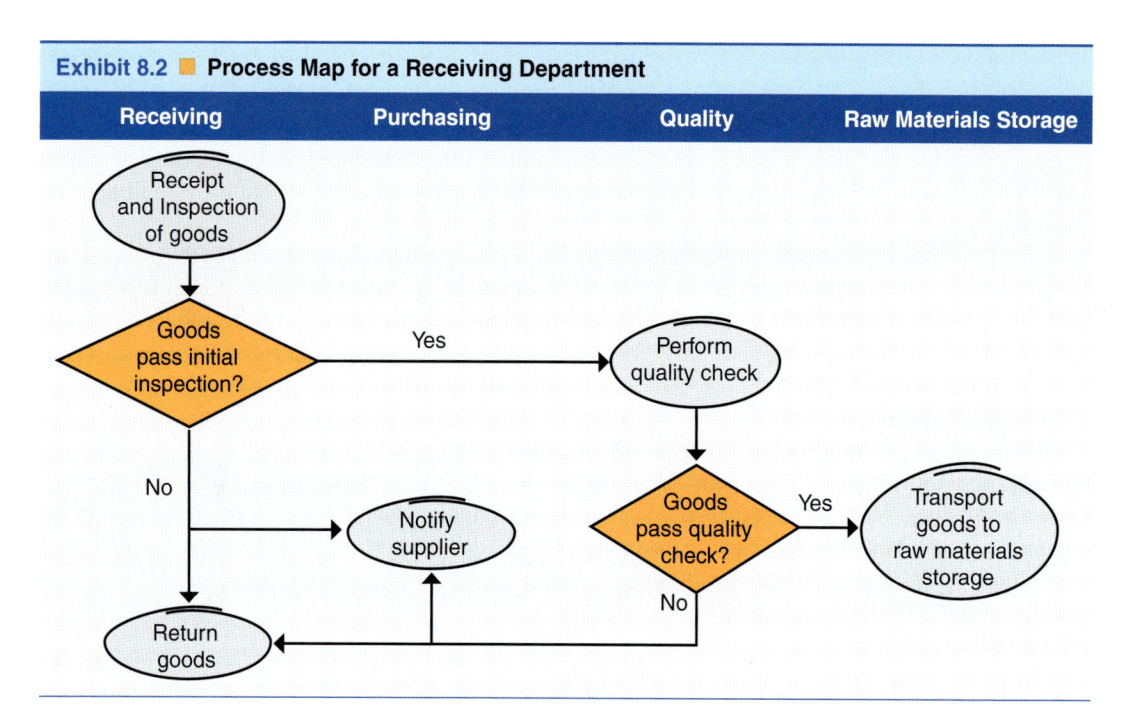

Exhibit 8.2 ■ Process Map for a Receiving Department

Receiving	Purchasing	Quality	Raw Materials Storage

- Receipt and Inspection of goods
- Goods pass initial inspection? — Yes → Perform quality check
- No → Return goods
- Notify supplier
- Goods pass quality check? — Yes → Transport goods to raw materials storage
- No → Notify supplier

Classifying Activities After a process map has been developed, the time needed to perform the activities should be noted and classified in one of four ways.

- **Processing (service) time**: the actual time spent performing all *necessary* functions to manufacture the product or to perform the service; this time is VA.
- **Inspection time**: the time required to perform quality control other than what is internal to the process. This time is usually considered NVA unless the consumer would actually be willing to pay for it (such as in the pharmaceutical or food industries).
- **Transfer time**: the time consumed moving products or components from one place to another; this time is NVA.
- **Idle time**: the time goods spend in storage or waiting at a production operation for processing; this time is NVA.

The time from the receipt to the completion of a product or service order is equal to value-added time plus non-value-added time or **cycle (lead) time**.

Total Cycle (or Lead) Time = Value-Added Time + Non-Value-Added Time

DEMO 8-1 LO8-1 Classifying Activities as VA or NVA

Assume that Prough Corporation, a chemical producer, identified the following seven activities.

◆ **Is each activity classified as VA or NVA and as processing, inspection, transfer, or idle time?**

1. Receiving	....	NVA	Transfer Time
2. Move to production	....	NVA	Transfer Time
3. Assembly	....	VA	Processing Time
4. Setup of Machinery	....	NVA	Idle Time
5. Inspection	....	NVA	Inspection Time
6. Packaging	....	VA	Processing Time
7. Storage	....	NVA	Idle Time

Packaging may be a VA activity for some companies and a NVA activity for others. Some products, such as liquids, require packaging; other products need little or no packaging. Because packaging takes up about a third of the U.S. landfills and creates a substantial amount of disposal cost, companies and consumers are focused on reducing or eliminating packaging. For instance, **Walmart** provides a resource called *Walmart Sustainable Packaging Position Statement and Playbook* to help its suppliers set recycled content goals for packaging.[1]

Creating a Value Chart Combining the process map and the time assessments produces a **value chart** that traces a process from beginning to end. **Exhibit 8.3** provides a value chart for a liquid chemical produced by Prough Corporation. Value is added to a product only when processing actually occurs. Note the excessive time consumed by storing and moving materials. Out of a total maximum 64 days of cycle time, the VA time for the production of this chemical is four days.

Exhibit 8.3 ■ Value Chart for Prough Corporation

Assembling Operations	Receiving	Quality control	Storage	Move to production	Waiting for use	Setup of machinery	Assembly	Move to inspection	Move to finishing
Average time (days)	1	0.5	5–30	0.25	0.5	0.25	2	0.25	0.25

Finishing Operations	Receiving	Move to production	Waiting for use	Setup	Finishing	Inspection	Packaging	Move to loading dock	Storage	Ship
Average time (days)	0.25	0.25	5–10	0.25	1	1	1	0.25	3–7	2–8

Non-value-added activities
Value-added activities

Total time in Assembling:	10–35 days
Total time in Finishing:	14–29 days
Total processing time:	24–64 days
Total value-added time:	**4 days**
Total non-value-added time:	**20–60 days***

*Next in this process, the company would determine the cost of the non-value-added time. Monetizing the amount of non-value-added time highlights its impact on company profitability.

Estimating the Cost of NVA Activities Constructing a value chart for every product or service would be extremely time-consuming, but a few such charts can quickly indicate where a company is losing time and money through NVA activities. The cost of such activities can be approximated by using estimates for storage facility depreciation, property taxes and insurance charges, wages for employees who handle warehousing, and the capital cost of funds tied up in stored inventory. Multiplying these cost estimates by times shown in the value chart will indicate the amount by which costs could be reduced by eliminating NVA activities.

Minimizing NVA Activities

Many product and service prices are set by the marketplace rather than by an individual organization attempting to cover its incurred costs. However, if the selling price of a product or service is insufficient to cover the cost of production or performance and produce a reasonable profit margin, management generally needs to find a way to reduce cost or, failing that, may need to exit the market for that product or service.[2] *The easiest way to reduce cost is to minimize or eliminate the NVA activities that are incurred during the production or performance process.* Such reductions will allow the company to obtain a larger profit margin when selling at market price than those companies with higher costs. Or cost reductions may allow the company to sell below the market price and thereby increase market share. Consider that the communications industry is heavily affected by customer turnover, so

---

[1] Source: https://www.walmartsustainabilityhub.com/project-gigaton/packaging

[2] Occasionally, product or service prices may be set at a level that is insufficient to cover costs. Such a pricing structure usually is imposed to meet market competition, to establish a "presence" in a particular market segment, or to encourage the purchase of related products or services.

companies try to contain costs without negatively affecting customer sales and service. For instance, artificial intelligence has led to customer service needs being met through a chatbot that can electronically return a response based on a question posed by a customer. If companies can reduce operational support costs and maintain quality, profit margins can be increased even if prices are not raised.

While a company's goal is to reduce NVA activities, few companies can completely eliminate, for example, all quality control functions and all transfer time. Understanding the NVA nature of these functions, however, should help managers strive to minimize such activities to the extent possible. Thus, companies should view VA and NVA activities as occurring on a continuum and strive to eliminate or minimize those activities that add the most time and cost and provide the least value.

REVIEW 8-1 — LO8-1 — Activity Analysis

MyBattery Inc. makes alkaline batteries and performs the following activities in the manufacturing process to produce a tray of 1,000 batteries.

Activity	Time (hours)
Receive raw materials	2.00
Store raw materials	48.00
Mix raw materials	0.50
Form can	0.10
Insert materials and close battery	0.10
Test batteries and insert into storage trays	0.10
Age batteries for 1 day before second battery test	24.00
Add label to batteries	0.10
Retest batteries	0.25
Move batteries to packaging department	6.00
Store batteries	24.00
Package batteries	1.00

a. Identify each of the tasks listed above as a value-added activity or a non-value-added activity. (Note: Assume customer views packaging as essential to the delivery of the product.)

b. **Critical Thinking:** How could a value chart be used by MyBattery Inc. to emphasize the cost of non-value-added activities? What information does this provide for management decision making?

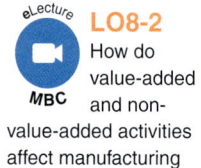

More practice: MC8-13, E8-22, E8-23
Solution on p. 8-55.

Manufacturing Cycle Efficiency

Dividing total value-added processing time by total cycle time results in a measurement referred to as **manufacturing cycle efficiency (MCE)**.

> **Manufacturing Cycle Efficiency = Total Value-Added Time ÷ Total Cycle Time**

MCE measures the proportion of value-added time to total cycle time. As non-value-added time decreases, the MCE measure increases.

DEMO 8-2 — LO8-2 — Calculating Manufacturing Cycle Efficiency

◆ **Using the information from Exhibit 8.3, what is Prough Corporation's manufacturing cycle efficiency?**

Prough Corporation's MCE has a range of 6 percent to 17 percent depending on the estimate used for total cycle time (which was calculated as a range of days in **Exhibit 8.3**).

> MCE: Lowest estimated NVA time   4 days ÷ 24 days = 17%
> MCE: Highest estimated NVA time   4 days ÷ 64 days = 6%

Although 100 percent efficiency can never be achieved, *most production processes add value to products only approximately 10 percent of the time* from raw material receipt until shipment to customers.

In other words, about 90 percent of manufacturing cycle time is wasted or NVA time. But products act like magnets in regard to costs: the longer the cycle time, the more opportunity the product has to "pull" costs to it.

A **just-in-time (JIT)** manufacturing process (discussed in detail in Chapter 18) seeks to achieve substantially higher efficiency by producing components and goods at the precise time they are needed by either the next production station or the consumer. JIT also often relies on the use of automated, robotic technologies that minimize downtime and maximize quality. Thus, JIT eliminates a significant amount of idle time (especially in storage) and reduces transfer time; both of these types of NVA activities substantially decrease MCE.

Service Cycle Efficiency

In a retail environment, cycle time relates to time between ordering and selling an item. NVA activities in retail include shipping time from the supplier, delays spent counting merchandise in a receiving department, and any storage time between receipt and sale. In a service company, cycle time refers to the time between service order and service completion. All time spent on activities that are not actual service performance or are "non-activities" (such as delays in beginning a job) are considered NVA activities for that job. A service company computes **service cycle efficiency (SCE)** by dividing total actual service time by total cycle time.

> Service Cycle Efficiency = Total Actual Service Time ÷ Total Cycle Time

Improving Manufacturing (Service) Cycle Efficiency

In order to improve manufacturing (service) cycle efficiency, a company must reduce non-value-added activities. Non-value-added activities are attributable to three types of factors:

Factor	Example	Change
Systemic	• The need to manufacture products in large batches to minimize setup cost • The need to respond to service jobs in order of urgency	• Invest in new equipment that has shorter setup times or can be adapted to the production of multiple products • Redesign products to reduce or eliminate the need for new setups • Reduce situations that create urgency
Physical	• The need to move goods because of inefficient plant or machine layout, especially when receiving and shipping are on different floors than storage and production	• Redesign plant and/or reconfigure machinery to improve product flow and alleviate machine bottlenecks
Human	• The need to rework products because of errors made by employees who have improper skills or received inadequate training • Delays caused by people who waste time by socializing at work	• Hire employees with the right skill set or train them in the right skills • Have employees accept responsibility for their work and strive for total quality control • Emphasize the proper performance measures related to production times

Attempts to reduce NVA activities should be directed at all of these factors, but management must concentrate on *reducing or eliminating the NVA activities that create the highest costs.* Doing so should cause product/service quality to increase with a simultaneous decrease in cycle time and cost.

REVIEW 8-2

Manufacturing Cycle Efficiency — **LO8-2**

Using the information from Review 8-1, answer the following questions.
a. Calculate the total cycle time of this manufacturing process.
b. Calculate the manufacturing cycle efficiency of this process.
c. **Critical Thinking:** How can management use the information derived in part *b* to make process improvements?

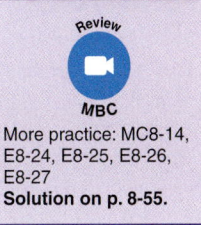

More practice: MC8-14, E8-24, E8-25, E8-26, E8-27
Solution on p. 8-55.

COST DRIVER ANALYSIS

LO8-3 Why must cost drivers be designated in an activity-based costing system?

Companies engage in many activities that consume resources and cause costs to be incurred. All activities have cost drivers, which are the factors that have direct cause-and-effect relationships to a cost. Cost drivers are classified as either *volume-related* (such as labor or machine hours) or *non-volume-related* (such as setups, work orders, or distance traveled), which generally reflect the incurrence of specific transactions. Many cost drivers can be identified for an individual business unit. For example, primary cost drivers for factory insurance are total value of plant assets, number of accidents or claims occurring in a period, quantity of workers, and inventory size.

Generally, more cost drivers can be identified for a given activity than should be used in activity-based costing. **Activity-based costing (ABC)** is a cost accounting system that

- focuses on an organization's activities,
- collects costs on the basis of the underlying nature and extent of those activities,
- uses the gathered information to determine product/service cost accumulation, and
- assesses the appropriateness of activity elimination.

For these purposes, a cost driver should be easy to understand, directly related to the activity being performed, and appropriate for performance measurement. Only a limited number of cost drivers should be selected and the cost of measuring a driver should not exceed the benefit of using it. For example, **Exhibit 8.4** shows six possible cost drivers for shipping cost, but the one that is the easiest to track and measure is trip distance.

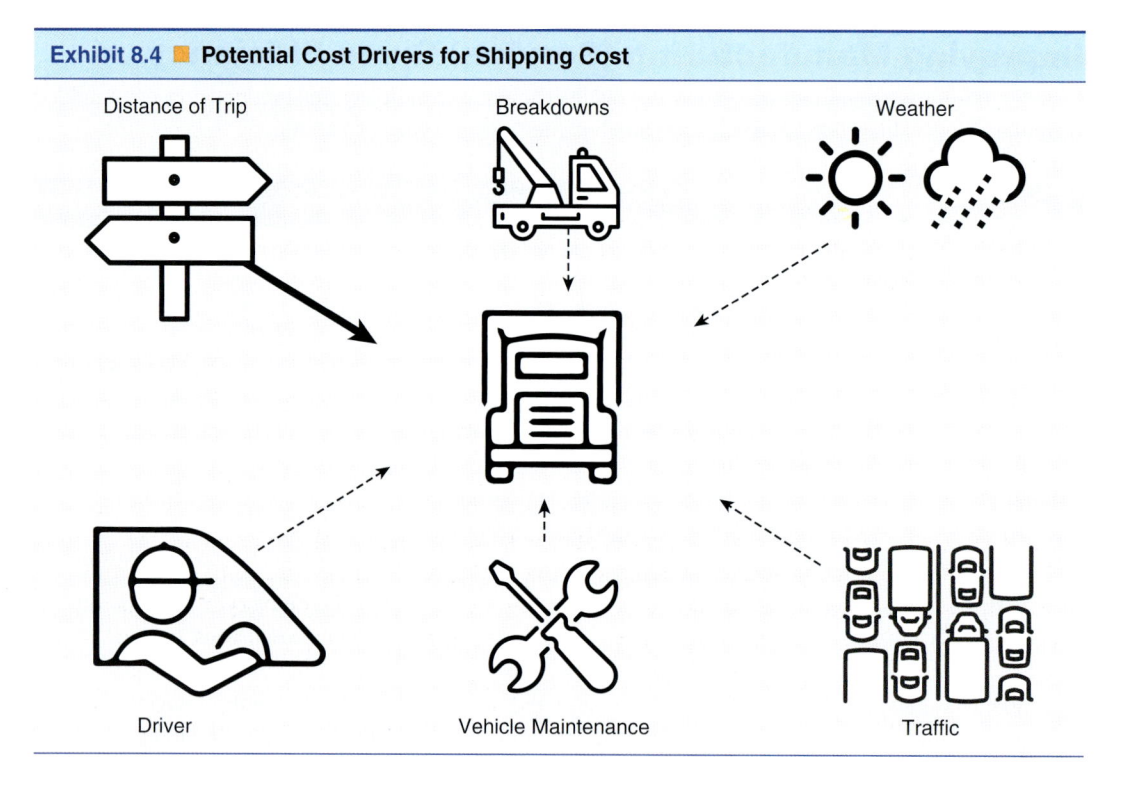

Exhibit 8.4 ■ Potential Cost Drivers for Shipping Cost

Distance of Trip · Breakdowns · Weather · Driver · Vehicle Maintenance · Traffic

Product and service costs are commonly identified as direct material, direct labor, and overhead. Accountants have had little difficulty in tracing direct material or direct labor to products and services. The primary impediment to a fair determination of product or service cost has always been the assignment of overhead. As discussed in Chapter 6, OH has traditionally been accumulated as a single total overhead—often using only one driver, such as direct labor hours or machine hours.

Such an allocation procedure causes few, if any, problems for financial statement preparation. However, the use of a minimal number of cost pools or cost drivers can produce illogical product or service costs for *internal managerial use* in complex production or service environments. However, organizations must limit the number of cost pools and cost drivers used so that the system will not become overly complicated and expensive. Thus, overhead should be divided into subgroups of costs that can be viewed as being primarily caused by one common or highly correlated cause.

Analyzing cost drivers in conjunction with activity analysis can highlight activities that do not add value and, as such, can be targeted for elimination to reduce costs and increase profitability. This information provides the basis for management's decisions for improving the process, benchmarking against competitors, and increasing profitability.

Levels at Which Costs Are Incurred

To reflect more complex environments, the accounting system must first recognize that costs are created and incurred because their drivers occur at different levels.[3] This realization necessitates using **cost driver analysis**, which investigates, quantifies, and explains the relationship of drivers to their related costs. The levels of cost classification illustrated in **Exhibit 8.5** include unit-level costs, batch-level costs, product/process level costs, and organizational/facility-level costs.

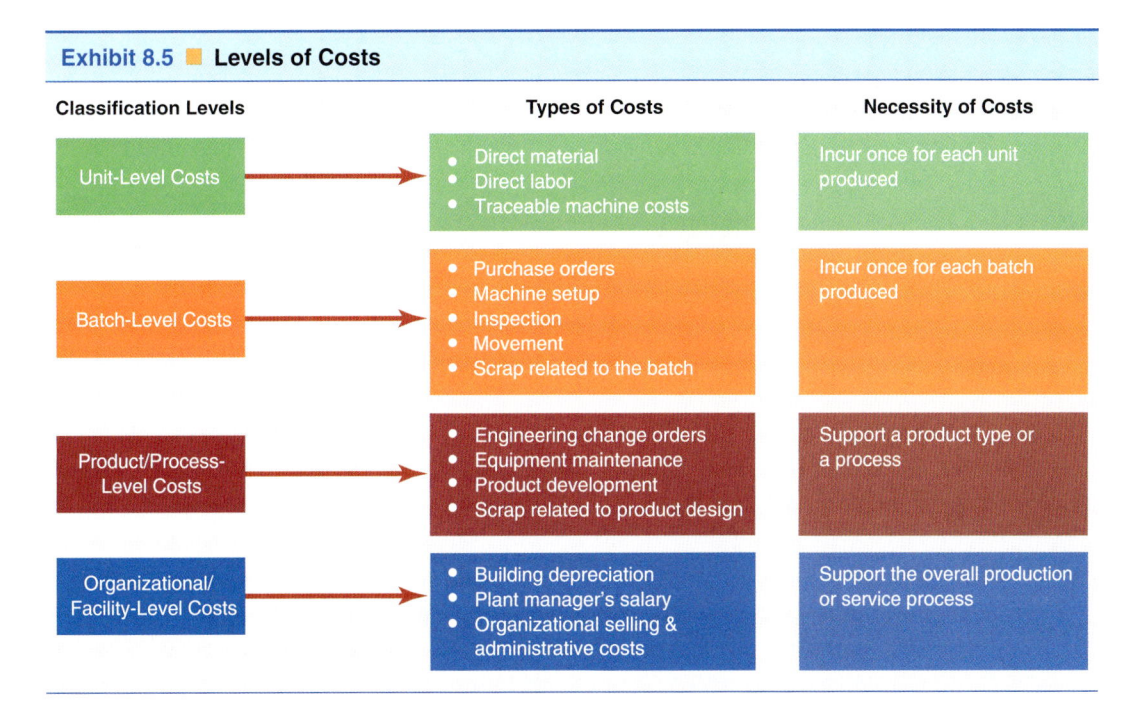

Exhibit 8.5 ■ Levels of Costs

Classification Levels	Types of Costs	Necessity of Costs
Unit-Level Costs	• Direct material • Direct labor • Traceable machine costs	Incur once for each unit produced
Batch-Level Costs	• Purchase orders • Machine setup • Inspection • Movement • Scrap related to the batch	Incur once for each batch produced
Product/Process-Level Costs	• Engineering change orders • Equipment maintenance • Product development • Scrap related to product design	Support a product type or a process
Organizational/Facility-Level Costs	• Building depreciation • Plant manager's salary • Organizational selling & administrative costs	Support the overall production or service process

Unit-Level Costs

Traditionally, cost drivers were viewed as existing only at the unit level: for example, the quantity of labor or machine time expended to make a product or render a service. Such **unit-level costs** are caused by the production or acquisition of a single unit of product or the delivery of a single unit of service. Direct material and direct labor are good examples of unit-level costs: each product uses a specific amount of raw material and requires a specific quantity of labor time to manufacture.

However, most overhead is not incurred on a per unit basis. There is no way to determine the exact amount of electricity or machine depreciation used to make one unit of product or perform one unit of service. Thus, overhead costs typically are incurred for broader-based categories of activity and, therefore, have cost drivers other than units, labor time, or machine hours. These broader-based activity levels have been categorized as batch, product/process level, and organizational/facility level, as previously introduced in Chapter 3.

Batch-Level Costs

Costs that are caused by a group of things being made, handled, or processed at a single time are referred to as **batch-level costs**. One overhead example of a batch-level cost is machine setup.

---

[3] This hierarchy of costs was introduced by Robin Cooper in "Cost Classification in Unit-Based and Activity-Based Manufacturing Cost Systems," *Journal of Cost Management* (Fall 1990), p. 6.

DEMO 8-3A LO8-3 Unit-Level Vs. Batch-Level Cost Assignment

Assume that the cost to prepare a machine to cast product parts is $900. Two different part types are to be manufactured during the day, so two setups will be needed at a total cost of $1,800. The first setup will generate 3,000 Type A parts. The machine will then be reset to generate 600 Type B parts. These specific quantities of parts are needed because the company uses a JIT production system.

◆ **Using this information, how are setup costs allocated to Type A and Type B parts using the number of parts as a cost driver compared to the number of batches as a cost driver?**

The following calculations show that the setup cost per unit depends on whether setup is considered unit-level or batch-level.

Allocation of Set Up Costs								
	A	B	C	D	E	F	G	H	I	J
1		Unit-Level Cost Assignment				Batch-Level Cost Assignment			
2/3		Number of Parts	Cost per Part*	Cost Assignment			Cost per Batch	Number of Parts in Batch	Cost per Part**	Cost Assignment
4	Type A	3,000	$0.50	$1,500		Type A	$ 900	3,000	$0.30	$ 900
5	Type B	600	0.50	300		Type B	900	600	1.50	900
6		3,600		$1,800			$1,800			$1,800

* $1,800 ÷ 3,600 parts = $0.50

**$900 ÷ 3,000 parts in batch = $0.30
$900 ÷ 600 parts in batch = $1.50

The unit-level method assigns the majority of setup cost to Type A parts. However, because setup cost is created by the incurrence of a batch being processed, the batch-level cost assignments are more appropriate. The batch-level perspective shows the commonality of the cost to the parts within the batch and is more indicative of the relationship between the activity (setup) and the cost driver (different parts production runs).

Product/Process-Level Costs

A cost caused by the development, production, or acquisition of different items is called a **product-level (process-level) cost**.

DEMO 8-3B LO8-3 Unit-Level Vs. Product-Level Cost Assignment

To illustrate the product cost level, assume that a manufacturer's engineering department issued five **engineering change orders (ECOs)** during May. In this case, the ECOs specify changes to an existing product, rather than specifying plans for a new product. Of these ECOs, four relate to Product R, one relates to Product S, and none relates to Product T. Each ECO costs $6,000 to issue, including charges for items such as labor review and redesign time, approval time, determination of new specifications, notification, and implementation. During May, the company made 7,500 products: 1,000 units of Product R, 1,500 units of Product S, and 5,000 units of Product T.

◆ **Using this information, how are ECO costs allocated to Products R, S, and T using the number of units of product versus the number of ECOs?**

If ECO costs are treated as unit-level costs, a unit cost of $4.00 would be allocated to all units.

5 ECOs × $6,000 per ECO = $30,000 total ECO cost ÷ 7,500 units = $4.00 per unit

Allocation of ECO Costs									
	A	B	C	D	E	F	G	H	I
1		Unit-Level Cost Assignment				Product-Level Cost Assignment			
2		Number of Units	Cost per Unit	Cost Assignment			Number of ECOs	Cost per ECO	Cost Assignment
4	Product R	1,000	$4.00	$ 4,000		Product R	4	$6,000	$24,000
5	Product S	1,500	4.00	6,000		Product S	1	6,000	6,000
6	Product T	5,000	4.00	20,000		Product T	0		0
7		7,500		$30,000			5		$30,000

Note that the unit-level method inappropriately assigns $20,000 of ECO cost to Product T, which had no ECOs!

This example indicates that using a product- or process-level driver (number of ECOs) for ECO costs would assign $24,000 of costs to Product R and $6,000 to Product S. However, the ECO costs should not attach solely to the current month's production. The ECO cost should be allocated to all units of Products R and S that have been and will be manufactured while these ECOs are in effect because the changed design will benefit all that production. Since future production of Products R and S is unknown at the end of May, no per-unit cost is shown in the product-level cost assignment table. If product-level cost assignments are required, reasonable estimates can be made about future production levels so that no significant product cost distortions should arise for either internal or external reporting.

Organizational/Facility-Level Costs

Organizational-level (facility-level) costs are incurred for the sole purpose of supporting facility operations. Such costs are common to many different products and services and *should theoretically not be assigned to products and services at all because any such assignment would only be arbitrary*. Many organizations, though, attach organizational-level costs to goods produced or services rendered because the amounts are insignificant relative to all other costs.

Accountants have traditionally (and incorrectly) assumed that when costs did not vary with changes in production at the unit level, those costs were fixed rather than variable. In reality, batch-, product/process-, and organizational-level costs are all variable, but they vary for reasons other than changes in production volume. Therefore, to determine a valid estimate of product or service cost, costs should be accumulated by cost level. Because unit-, batch-, and product/process-level costs are all associated with units of products or services (merely at different levels), these costs can be summed at the product/service level to match with the revenues generated by product sales. Organizational-level costs are not product or service related, so they should (again, in theory) be subtracted only in total from net product revenues.

Product Profitability Analysis

Exhibit 8.6 shows how costs collected at the unit, batch, and product/process levels can be aggregated to estimate a total product cost. Each product or service cost is multiplied by the number of units sold, and that amount (cost of goods sold or cost of services rendered) is subtracted from total sales revenues to obtain a product or service line profit or loss amount. These computations would be performed for each product or service line and summed to determine net product or service income (or loss) from which the unassigned organizational-level costs would be subtracted to find company profit or loss for internal management use. In this model, the traditional distinction between product and period costs (discussed in Chapter 2) can be and is ignored. The emphasis is on modifying product or service profitability analysis to focus on *internal* management purposes rather than on external reporting. The approach in **Exhibit 8.6** ignores the product/period cost distinction required by generally accepted accounting principles (GAAP) and, therefore, is *not* currently acceptable for external reporting.

General administration, rent, and building security costs are examples of organizational-level costs, which are incurred to support the facility operations in general.

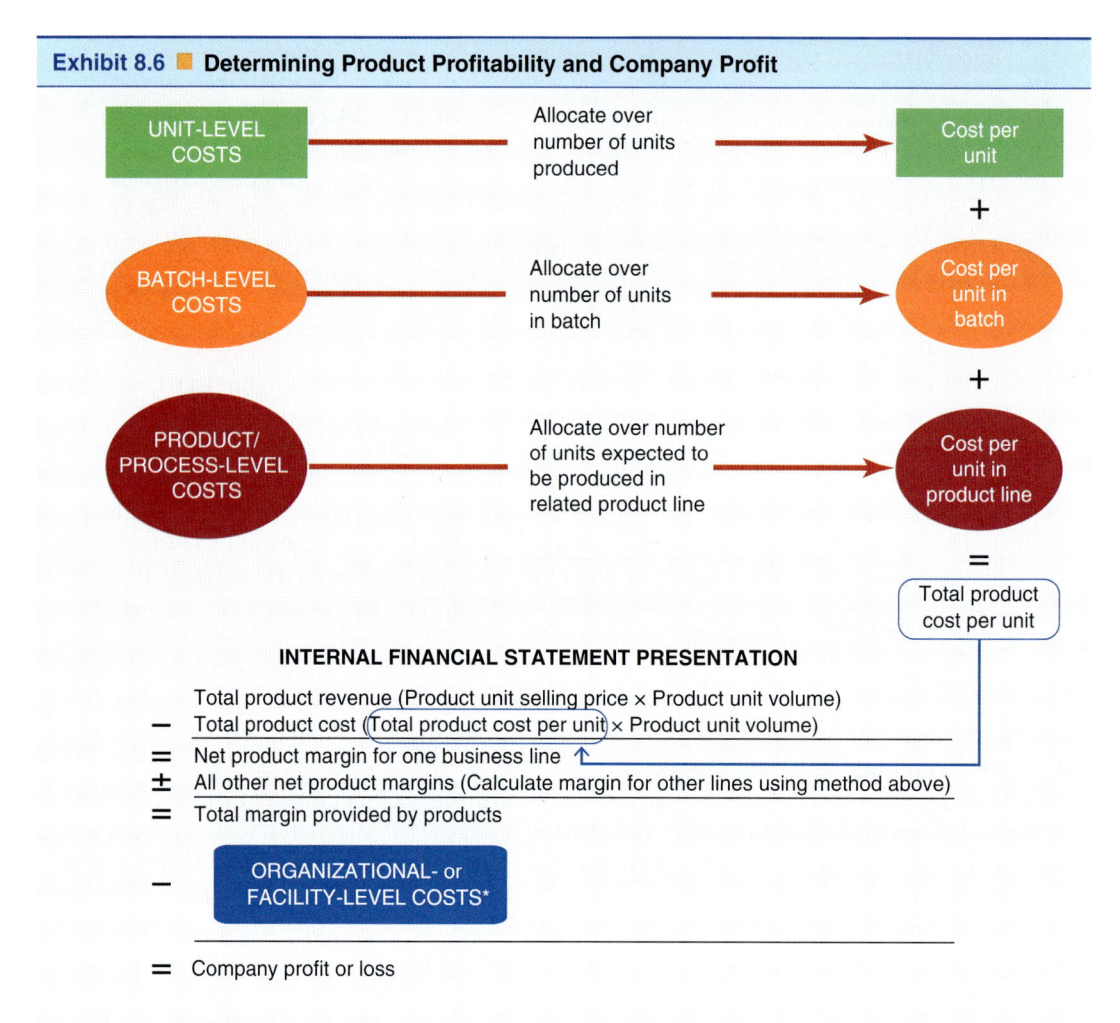

Exhibit 8.6 ■ Determining Product Profitability and Company Profit

UNIT-LEVEL COSTS → Allocate over number of units produced → Cost per unit

+

BATCH-LEVEL COSTS → Allocate over number of units in batch → Cost per unit in batch

+

PRODUCT/ PROCESS-LEVEL COSTS → Allocate over number of units expected to be produced in related product line → Cost per unit in product line

= Total product cost per unit

INTERNAL FINANCIAL STATEMENT PRESENTATION

Total product revenue (Product unit selling price × Product unit volume)
− Total product cost (Total product cost per unit × Product unit volume)
= Net product margin for one business line
± All other net product margins (Calculate margin for other lines using method above)
= Total margin provided by products
− ORGANIZATIONAL- or FACILITY-LEVEL COSTS*
= Company profit or loss

*Some of these costs could be assignable to specific products or services and would be included in determining product cost per unit.

A **product profitability analysis** shows a product line income(loss) for each product, which is equal to revenue minus direct costs and overhead for that product. Overhead in a product profitability analysis can be determined using traditional costing (unit-level analysis) or using ABC costing, where unit-, batch-, and product-level costs are all associated with the product.

DEMO 8-3C LO8-3 Product Profitability Analysis under Traditional versus ABC Costing

The following schedule for Bexar Manufacturing shows a product profitability analysis under traditional costing and under activity-based costing for the company's three products. While individual calculations are not detailed, the following information is provided.

- Under the traditional costing model, overhead costs are allocated based upon machine hours.
- Under the ABC costing model, costs were captured at the different levels and assigned to products based on appropriate cost drivers.
- The company's only three products, Product C, Product D, and Product E, had volumes of 5,000, 1,500, and 105,000 units, respectively, for the period.
- Product D is a low-volume, special order line.

◆ **How does the information shown in the product profitability analysis differ in the traditional costing presentation versus the activity-based costing presentation?**

Product Profitability Analysis

	A	B	C	D	E
1	**Traditional Costing**	Product C	Product D	Product E	Total
2	Product revenue	$250,000	$ 67,500	$4,200,000	$4,517,500
3	Product costs:				
4	Direct	$100,000	$ 30,000	$ 945,000	1,075,000
5	Overhead	67,500	20,250	1,417,500	1,505,250
6	Net income	$ 82,500	$ 17,250	$1,837,500	$1,937,250
7	**Activity-Based Costing**	Product C	Product D	Product E	Total
8	Product revenue	$250,000	$ 67,500	$4,200,000	$4,517,500
9	Product costs:				
10	Direct	$100,000	$ 30,000	$ 945,000	1,075,000
11	Overhead				
12	Unit level	31,000	9,300	651,000	691,300
13	Batch level	45,000	28,500	315,000	388,500
14	Product level	15,000	22,500	210,000	247,500
15	Product line income or (loss)	$ 59,000	$(22,800)	$2,079,000	$2,115,200
16	Organizational-level costs				177,950
17	Net income				$1,937,250

The cost information in the traditional costing section indicates that all three products are profitable for Bexar to produce and sell. However, the more refined approach under ABC costing shows that Product D is actually unprofitable for the company to produce. This example illustrates that a lack of consideration for underlying causes of costs can result in flawed cost data. Traditional cost allocations tend to subsidize low-volume specialty products by misallocating overhead to high-volume, standard products. This problem occurs because costs of the extra activities needed to make specialty products are assigned using the one or very few drivers of traditional costing—and usually these drivers are volume based. This is the case for Product D which incurred significant batch-level and product-level costs for its relatively low volume level which resulted in a product line loss. This concept called *cost-cross subsidization* is discussed further in the next section. Because all of the company's products are represented in the analysis, notice that the total company profit is the same under each costing system—it is the profit allocation by product that differs.

Cost Drivers

LO8-3 **REVIEW 8-3**

a. For each of the following costs that are commonly incurred in a manufacturing company, identify which cost driver would likely be the more appropriate choice. Support your answer.

Type of Cost	Cost Driver
1. Warehouse storage cost	Number of units *or* Square footage of occupied space
2. Freight cost for materials received	Pounds of materials received *or* Number of product types received
3. Equipment repair and maintenance cost	Machine hours *or* Direct labor hours
4. Product inspection costs	Annual plant operating hours *or* Number of quality inspections
5. Engineering costs to change products	Number of engineers *or* Number of engineering change orders
6. Information technology support cost	Number of service tickets *or* Number of products shipped
7. Digital marketing cost	Number of customer web clicks *or* Number of design changes

continued

More practice: MC8-15, E8-32, E8-33, E8-34, E8-35
Solution on p. 8-55.

b. **Critical Thinking:** Assume instead that all of the costs in part *a* were allocated to products using the number of units produced. What do you see as a potential result of using this approach?

ACTIVITY-BASED COSTING

LO8-4 How are product and service costs computed using an activity-based costing system?

ABC focuses on attaching costs to products and services based on the activities conducted to produce, perform, distribute, and support those products and services. The three fundamental components of activity-based costing are

- recognizing that costs are incurred at different organizational levels,
- accumulating related costs into individual cost pools, and
- using multiple cost drivers to assign costs to products and services.

Two-Stage Allocation Method

After being recorded in the general ledger and sub-ledger accounts, costs in an ABC system are accumulated in activity center cost pools.

Stage One: Cost Accumulation An **activity center** is any part of the production or service process for which management wants a separate reporting of costs. In defining these centers, management should consider the following issues:

- geographical proximity of equipment,
- defined centers of managerial responsibility,
- magnitude of product costs, and
- the need to keep the number of activity centers manageable.

Costs having the same driver are accumulated in pools reflecting the appropriate level of cost incurrence (unit, batch, or product/process). The fact that a relationship exists between a cost pool and a cost driver indicates that if the cost driver can be reduced or eliminated, the related cost should also be reduced or eliminated.

Gathering costs in pools having the same cost drivers allows managers to view an organization's activities cross-functionally. Companies not using ABC often accumulate overhead in departmental, rather than plantwide, cost pools. This type of accumulation reflects a vertical-function approach to cost accumulation; however, production and service activities are horizontal by nature. A product or service flows through an organization, affecting numerous departments as it goes. In Stage One, a cost driver approach is used to develop cost pools. This allows managers to more clearly focus on the cost effects created in making a product or performing a service than was traditionally possible.

Even in highly complex manufacturing environments, ABC systems usually have no more than 10 to 20 cost pools. Many ABC experts in practice have observed that creating a large number of activity cost pools for a given costing application normally does not significantly improve cost accuracy above that of a smaller number of cost pools. As with any information system design, the costs of developing and maintaining the system must not exceed its benefits; hence, although adding more activity cost pools may result in some small amount of increased accuracy, it may be so small as not to be cost effective.

Stage Two: Cost Allocation After accumulation, costs are allocated out of the activity center cost pools and assigned to products and services by use of a second type of driver. An **activity driver** measures the demands placed on activities and, thus, the resources consumed by products and services. An activity driver often indicates an activity's output. The process of cost assignment is the same as the overhead application process illustrated in Chapter 6. **Exhibit 8.7** illustrates the allocation process of tracing costs to products and services in an ABC system.

The *cost drivers* for the cost accumulation stage can differ from the *activity drivers* used for the allocation stage because some activity center costs are not traceable to lower levels of activity. Costs at the lowest (unit) level of activity should be allocated to products by use of volume- or unit-based drivers. Costs incurred at higher (batch and product/process) levels can also be allocated to products by use of volume-related drivers, but the volume measure should include only those units associated with the batch or the product/process. **Exhibit 8.8** provides some common drivers for various activity centers.

Exhibit 8.7 ■ Tracing Costs in an Activity-Based Costing System

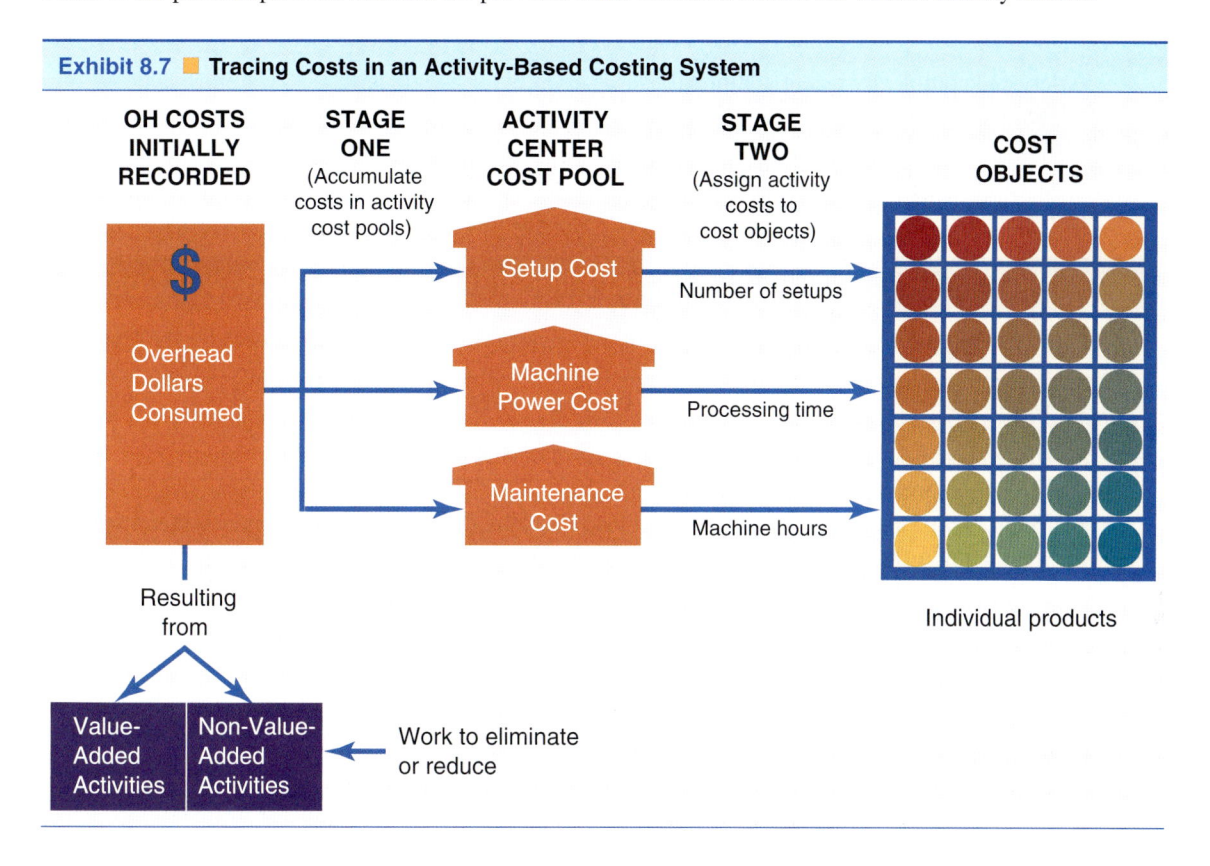

OH COSTS INITIALLY RECORDED → **STAGE ONE** (Accumulate costs in activity cost pools) → **ACTIVITY CENTER COST POOL** → **STAGE TWO** (Assign activity costs to cost objects) → **COST OBJECTS**

Overhead Dollars Consumed flows to:
- Setup Cost → Number of setups → Individual products
- Machine Power Cost → Processing time → Individual products
- Maintenance Cost → Machine hours → Individual products

Overhead Dollars Consumed resulting from:
- Value-Added Activities
- Non-Value-Added Activities ← Work to eliminate or reduce

Exhibit 8.8 ■ Activity Drivers

Activity Center	Activity Drivers
Accounting	Reports requested; dollars expended
Human resources	Job change actions; hiring actions; training hours; counseling hours
Data processing	Reports requested; transactions processed; programming hours; program change requests
Production engineering	Hours spent in each shop; job specification changes requested; product change notices processed
Quality control	Hours spent in each shop; defects discovered; samples analyzed
Plant services	Preventive maintenance cycles; hours spent in each shop; repair and maintenance actions
Material services	Dollar value of requisitions; number of transactions processed; number of personnel in direct support
Utilities	Direct usage (metered to shop); space occupied
Production shops	Fixed per-job charge; setups made; direct labor; machine hours; number of moves; material applied

Source: Michael D. Woods, "Completing the Picture: Economic Choices with ABC," *Management Accounting* (December 1992), p. 54. Reprinted from *Management Accounting.* Copyright by Institute of Management Accountants, Montvale, NJ.

Three significant cost drivers that have traditionally been disregarded are related to variety and complexity.

- **Product variety** refers to the number of different types of products made.
- **Product complexity** refers to the number of components included in a product.
- **Process complexity** refers to the number of processes through which a product flows.

Variety and complexity create additional overhead costs for activities such as warehousing, purchasing, setups, and inspections—all of which can be seen as "long-term variable costs" because they will increase as the number and types of products increase. Therefore, accountants should consider using items such as number of product types, number of components, and number of necessary processes as the cost drivers for applying ABC.

DEMO 8-4 LO8-4 Illustrating Traditional Cost Allocation and Activity-Based Costing

The following information is summarized for the Factory Maintenance Department for the year.

# of employees	9	Expected DLHs for the year	200,000
Cost per employee	$50,000	# of units of Z4395 produced this year	10,000
Total departmental cost for the year. . .	$450,000	# of DLHs used to produce Z4395 this year. . .	3,000

◆ **What is the cost allocation to a unit of Z4395 of the department's factory maintenance cost using a traditional cost allocation base of direct labor hours (DLHs)?**

Under traditional costing, overhead is considered to be part of one large cost pool. Overhead is allocated to products based on a rate of $2.25 per direct labor hour, calculated by dividing total OH costs by total budgeted direct labor hours.

$$\$450{,}000 \div 200{,}000 = \$2.25 \text{ per DLH}$$

Overhead applied to product Z4395 is calculated by multiplying the predetermined OH rate by the actual number of labor hours used to produce product Z4395.

$$\$2.25 \times 3{,}000 \text{ hours} = \$6{,}750 \text{ OH applied to Z4395}$$

Since 10,000 units of Z4395 were produced during the year, the cost per unit of Z4395 is calculated as follows.

$$\$6{,}750 \div 10{,}000 \text{ units} = \boxed{\$0.675 \text{ OH cost per unit of Z4395}}$$

◆ **What is the cost allocation to a unit of Z4395 of the department's factory maintenance cost using ABC costing?**

Stage One Assume in Stage One, total OH costs of $450,000 are assigned to the following three activity cost pools according to the number of employees.

Regular maintenance	Preventive maintenance	Repairs	Total
5 employees	2 employees	2 employees	9 employees

The Stage One cost allocation rate is calculated by dividing total budgeted OH by the total number of employees.

$$\$450{,}000 \div 9 \text{ employees} = \$50{,}000 \text{ per employee}$$

OH is assigned to each of the three activity cost pools as follows.

Cost Pool	Allocated Overhead
Regular maintenance	5 employees × $50,000 = $250,000
Preventive maintenance . . .	2 employees × $50,000 = $100,000
Repairs	2 employees × $50,000 = $100,000

Stage Two Now assume in Stage Two, costs are allocated to products using 500,000 machine hours (MHs) for Regular maintenance, 5,000 setups for Preventive maintenance, and 100,000 machine starts for Repairs. Stage Two allocation rates are calculated by dividing the budgeted OH in each activity pool by the activity pool's budgeted activity driver amount.

Cost Pool	Allocated Rate
Regular maintenance	$250,000 ÷ 500,000 MHS = $0.50 per MH
Preventive maintenance	$100,000 ÷ 5,000 setups = $20 per setup
Repairs	$100,000 ÷ 100,000 machine startups = $1 per machine startup

- Reg. Maint. $250,000 — $0.50 per MH
- Prevent. Maint. $100,000 — $20 per setup
- Repairs $100,000 — $1 per machine start

Next, assign OH costs to products by multiplying the allocation rates calculated above by the quantity of second-stage cost drivers consumed in making these products. Assume that 10,000 units of Z4395 incurred the following: 30,000 MHs; 30 setups; and 40 machine starts.

(30,000 MHs × $0.50) + (30 setups × $20) + (40 machine starts × $1) = $15,640 OH applied to Z4395

Since 10,000 units of Z4395 were produced during the year, the cost per unit of Z4395 is calculated as follows.

$$\$15{,}640 \div 10{,}000 \text{ units} = \boxed{\$1.564 \text{ OH cost per unit of Z4395}}$$

Note that the cost allocated to Z4395 with the ABC system is 132 percent higher than the cost allocated with the traditional allocation system ($1.564 versus $0.675)! This is due primarily to the complexity of the part which increased its use of resources.

Cost Cross-Subsidization

Discrepancies in cost assignments between traditional and activity-based costing methods are not uncommon. As illustrated in Demo 8-3C, ABC systems can reveal that significant resources are consumed by low-volume products or services and complex production operations. Some reasons for this conclusion are shown in **Exhibit 8.9**. Studies have shown that, after an ABC implementation, the costs of high-volume standard products are often from 10 to 30 percent lower than the costs determined by traditional cost systems for the same products. Costs assigned to low-volume, complex specialty products tend to increase from 100 to 500 percent after implementing ABC. *Thus, ABC typically shifts a substantial amount of overhead cost from standard high-volume products to premium special-order, low-volume products.* This means that **cost cross-subsidization** often exists under traditional costing methods, where one product is assigned too much cost as a result of another being assigned too little cost. The ABC costs of moderately complex products and services (those that are neither extremely simple nor complex nor produced in extremely low or high volumes) tend to remain approximately the same as costs calculated using traditional costing methods.

Exhibit 8.9 ■ Why Low Volume, Specialty Products/Services Cost More

Organizational Area	High Volume Items	Low Volume Items
Sales	• Customers order from stock products.	• Salespeople take extra time to help customers "create" specialty products that generate additional work for other areas.
Engineering	• Design is known and kept current. • Process has been kept current and adapted for new technology.	• Design must be developed or reviewed for necessary changes. • Process must be developed or reviewed to conform to new technology.
Purchasing	• Suppliers are known. • Raw material prices are standardized. • Components are in stock.	• New suppliers may have to be obtained. • Price quotes may need to be evaluated or negotiated. • Nonstandard raw materials may need to be found, ordered, and placed in stock.

continued

Exhibit 8.9	Why Low Volume, Specialty Products/Services Cost More (concluded)		
Organizational Area	**High Volume Items**	**Low Volume Items**
Production or Performance	• Setups are familiar and easily handled. • Labor is familiar with the process, thereby reducing labor time. • Changeovers from one process to another are scheduled in advance.	• Setups are unfamiliar and take more time. • Labor is unfamiliar with the process and must learn or relearn. • Process changeovers may need to be expedited or randomly scheduled, creating delays, additional work orders, and confusion.
Quality Control	• Potential problems are known and easily checked.	• Problems are unknown and more inspection must be performed.

Managers in many companies are concerned about the product and service cost information provided by traditional cost accounting systems. Although reasonable for use in preparing financial statements, such costs often have limited value for managerial decision making and cost control—the latter being a high priority concern, especially in difficult economic times, for managers in all types of organizations.

Activity-based costing is applicable to all organizational areas, including selling and administrative departments. Many companies use an ABC system to allocate corporate overhead costs to their revenue-producing units based on the number of reports, documents, customers, or other reasonable activity measures.

REVIEW 8-4 — LO8-4: Traditional and Activity-Based OH Cost Allocation

Manufacturing Inc. is concerned about the profitability of orders for athletic apparel. Orders consist of standard items and custom items. Custom orders allow the customer to add a logo or request a non-standard color. The company is currently assigning the $1,200,000 of overhead costs to its products based on machine hours. Of the overhead, $480,000 is utilities related and the remainder is primarily related to quality control costs. The following information about the products is also available.

	Standard Items	Custom Items
Number produced.	1,250,000	840,000
Machine hours	102,000	18,000
Inspection hours	6,000	30,000
Revenues	$3,840,000	$3,360,000
Direct costs	$3,000,000	$2,640,000

a. Determine the total overhead cost assigned to standard items and custom items using the current allocation system.
b. Determine the total overhead cost assigned to standard items and custom items if more appropriate cost drivers were used.
c. **Critical Thinking:** Is there evidence of cost cross-subsidization under traditional costing? How does cost-cross subsidization affect management decision making?

More practice: E8-41, P8-53, P8-54
Solution on p. 8-56.

DETERMINING WHETHER ABC IS USEFUL

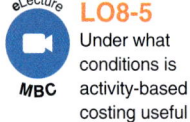

LO8-5 Under what conditions is activity-based costing useful in an organization, and what information do activity-based costing systems provide to management?

Although not every accounting system using direct labor or machine hours to assign overhead costs produces inaccurate cost information, a great deal of information can be lost in the accounting systems of companies that ignore activity and cost relationships. Some general indicators can alert managers to the need to review the relevance of the cost information their system is providing. Several of these indicators are more relevant to manufacturing entities, whereas others are equally applicable to both manufacturing and service businesses. Factors to consider include the

- number and diversity of products or services produced,
- diversity and differential degree of support services used for different products,

- extent to which common processes are used,
- effectiveness of current cost allocation methods, and
- rate of growth of period costs.[4]

Additionally, if ABC is implemented, the new information will change management decisions *only* if management is able to set product/service prices, there are no strategic constraints in the company, and the company has developed a culture of cost reduction. The following circumstances could indicate the need to consider using ABC.

Large Product or Service Variety

Product and service variety are commonly associated with the need to consider ABC. Whether items are variations of the same product line (such as **Hallmark**'s different types of greeting cards) or products are in numerous product families (such as **Procter & Gamble**'s detergents, diapers, fabric softeners, and shampoos), adding products causes numerous overhead costs to increase. Consider, for example, that **Walmart** has over 80 million products on its website, while a **Sally Beauty Salon** store carries between 5,000–10,000 SKUs of products.[5]

In the quest for product variety, many companies are striving for **mass customization** of products. Such personalized production can often be conducted at a relatively low cost. For example, **Mymüesli** lets customers create their own muesli from various ingredients and "566 quadrillion" possible combinations of base, grains, fruits, nuts, seeds, and extras. **MOD Pizza** allows customers to create their own pizzas choosing from over 30 toppings for one price. Although such customization can please some customers, it has some drawbacks.

- There can be too many choices, creating confusion for customers.
- Mass customization creates a tremendous opportunity for errors.
- Most companies have found that customers, given a wide variety of choices, typically make selections based on the 20:80 **Pareto principle**. This principle suggests that, in many situations, it is common to observe that approximately 20 percent of "inputs" (choices) are responsible for 80 percent of "outputs" (selections).[6]

Most traditional cost systems do not provide information such as the number of different parts that are used in a product, so management cannot identify products made with low-volume or unique components. ABC systems are flexible and can gather such details so that persons involved in reengineering efforts have information about relationships among activities and cost drivers. With these data, reengineering efforts can be focused both on the primary causes of process complexity and on the causes that create the highest levels of waste.

High Product/Process Complexity

Companies with complex products, services, or processes should investigate ways to reduce that complexity. Management could review the design of the company's products and processes to standardize them and reduce the number of different components, tools, and activities. Products should be designed to consider the Pareto principle and take advantage of *commonality of parts*. For instance, if a company finds that 20 percent of its parts are used in 80 percent of its products, the company should ask where the remaining parts are being used.

- If the remaining parts are being used in key products, could equal quality be achieved by using the more common parts? If so, customers would likely be satisfied if more common parts were used and product prices were reduced.

---

[4] T. L. Estrin, Jeffrey Kantor, and David Albers, "Is ABC Suitable for Your Company?" *Management Accounting* (April 1994), p. 40. Copyright Institute of Management Accountants, Montvale, NJ.

[5] Sources: "Walmart Sponsored Products Program Overview," (November 15, 2019), https://sellerhelp.walmart.com/s/guide?article=000008208 and "Operating Segments," (November 15, 2019), www.sallybeautyholdings.com/investor-relations/investor-overview/at-a-glance.

[6] The Italian economist Vilfredo Pareto found that about 85 percent of Milan's wealth was held by about 15 percent of the people. The term *Pareto principle* was coined by Joseph Juran in relationship to quality problems. Juran found that a high proportion of such problems were caused by a small number of process characteristics (the vital few) whereas the majority of process characteristics (the trivial many) accounted for only a small proportion of quality problems.

- If the remaining parts are not being used in key products, will the customers purchasing the low-volume products be willing to pay a premium price to cover the additional costs of using low-volume parts? If so, the benefits from the complexity would be worth the cost. Complexity is acceptable *only* if it adds value from the customer's point of view.

Process complexity can develop over time, or it can exist because of a lack of sufficient planning in product development. Processes are complex when they create difficulties for the people performing the operations (such as physical straining, awkwardness of motions, and wasted motions) or using the machinery (such as multiple and/or detailed setups, lengthy transfer time between machine processes, and numerous instrument recalibrations). Process complexity is indicative of abundant non-value-added activities that cause time delays and cost increases.

Data Visualization

A manufacturer of different types of pool cleaning kits recently adopted ABC costing. As part of the adoption process, the company prepared an analysis of its part usage by preparing a Pareto chart.

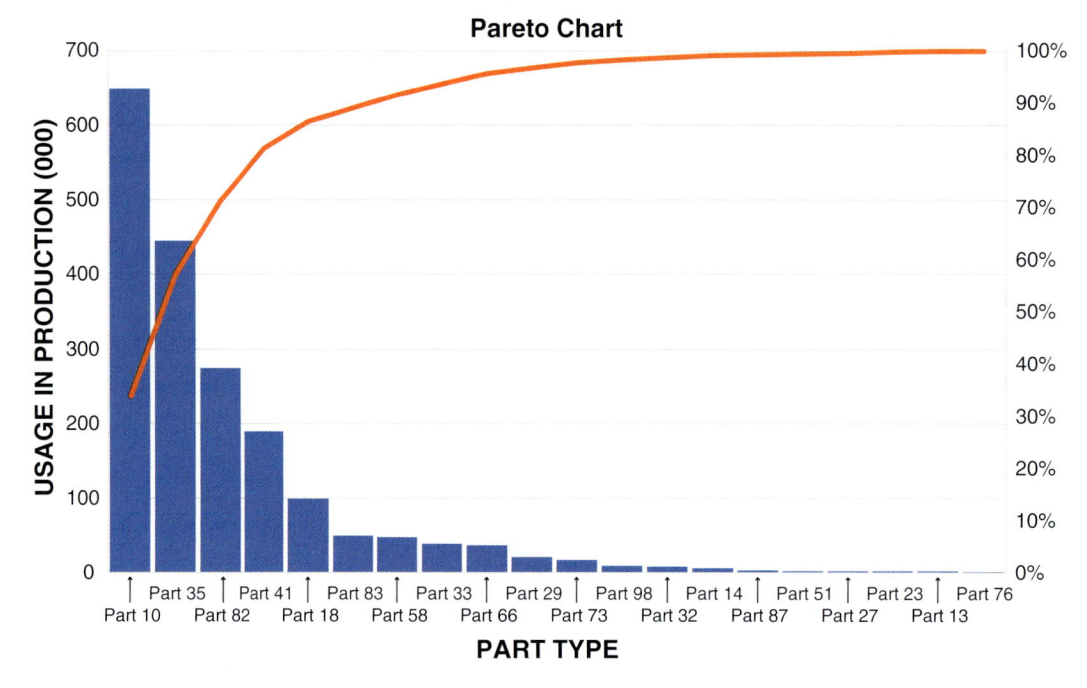

Pareto Chart

Based on the data visualization above, answer the following questions.
a. In what way are the different types of parts organized on the *X*-axis?
b. What is the minimum number of parts that comprise 80 percent of part usage?
c. How can this analysis help management to increase production efficiencies and enhance cost controlling efforts?

Lack of Commonality in Overhead Costs

Certain products and services create substantially more overhead costs than others do. Although some of these additional overhead costs are caused by product variety or product/process complexity, others are related to support services. For instance, some products require high levels of advertising; some use expensive distribution channels; and some require the use of high-technology machinery. If only one or two overhead pools are used, overhead costs related to specific products will be spread over all products. The result will be higher costs for products that are not responsible for the increased overhead.

Similarly, some customers cost more to serve than others. Customers who buy in small quantities create additional processing and shipping costs. Customers who do not pay bills on time create additional accounts receivable costs. Customers who need too much personalized attention create additional sales or travel and entertainment costs. Determination of a "cost to serve" using ABC will help organizations identify the customers who are the most profitable and will also allow consideration of ways to generate additional revenue from the higher cost-to-serve customers. Customer profitability is discussed further in Chapter 14. In general, cost to serve would include investigation of order size and frequency, sensitivity to price, level of repeat business, service requirements (especially in terms of time), return rates, and payment patterns. Referral business from a customer should be considered a "negative cost" or an additional revenue from that client.

Irrationality of Current Cost Allocations

Companies that have undergone a significant change in their products or processes (such as increasing product variety or reengineering business processes) often recognize that existing cost systems no longer provide a reasonable estimate of product or service cost. For example, after automating production processes, many companies have experienced large reductions in labor cost with equal or greater increases in overhead. Continuing to use direct labor as an OH allocation base produces extraordinarily high application rates: some highly automated companies have predetermined OH rates ranging from 500 to 2,000 percent of direct labor cost. In such instances, products made using automated equipment tend to be charged an insufficient amount of overhead, whereas products made using high proportions of direct labor tend to be overcharged.

Traditional overhead cost allocations also reflect the financial accounting perspective of expensing period costs as they are incurred. ABC recognizes that some period costs (such as R&D and logistics) are distinctly and reasonably associated with specific products; ABC traces and allocates such costs to the appropriate products or services. Such a perspective modifies the traditional delineation between period and product cost.

Changes in Business Environment

A change in a company's competitive environment could also indicate a need for better cost information. Increased competition can occur because

- other companies have recognized the profit potential of a particular product or service,
- other companies now find the product (service) has become cost feasible to make or perform, or
- an industry or market has been deregulated.

If additional companies are competing for the same "old" quantity of business, the best estimate of product or service cost must be available to management so that reasonable profit margins can be maintained or obtained. For instance, if the U.S. jewelry and watch market's compound annual growth rate is expected to be 1.5 percent, such companies would need to strictly control costs to achieve a profit margin level that allows them to remain in business.

Changes in management strategy can also signal the need for a new cost system. For example, if management wants to start a new production operation, the cost system must be capable of providing information on how costs will change. Showing costs as conforming only to the traditional unit-level variable and fixed classifications might not allow usable information to be developed. Viewing costs as batch-level, product/process-level, or organizational/facility-level focuses on cost drivers and on the changes the planned operations will have on activities and costs.

Eliminating NVA activities to reduce cycle time, making products (or performing services) with zero defects, reducing product costs on an ongoing basis, and simplifying products and processes reflect the concepts of continuous improvement. ABC, by promoting an understanding of cost drivers, allows the NVA activities to be identified and their causes eliminated or reduced.

Determining the Usefulness of ABC Costing LO8-5 DEMO 8-5

◆ **Referring to Demo 8-4, what factors indicate that ABC costing could provide useful cost information to managers? What additional information would have been helpful to make this assessment?**

Product Z4395 appears to be a complex product, using a fair amount of resources including 30,000 machine hours, 30 setups, and 40 machine starts. This is an indication that applying OH using a simple unit cost driver would *not* provide the information that an ABC system could provide. Additional information is required to answer the following questions.

- Do the company's products vary widely in type or design?
- Do the company's products use resources in different ways? For example, do products vary in the number of machines hours, setups, and machine starts required?
- Has the company experienced any recent changes in products or processes?
- Has there been a change in the company's competitive environment?

Answering "yes" to any of these additional questions would further support a change to ABC costing.

CRITICISMS OF ACTIVITY-BASED COSTING

Realistically assessing new models and accounting approaches to determine what they can help managers accomplish is always important. However, no accounting technique or system provides management *exact cost information* for every product or the information needed to make consistently perfect decisions. For certain types of companies, ABC typically provides better information than that generated from a traditional overhead allocation process, but ABC is not a cure-all for all managerial concerns. Following are some short-comings of ABC.

Barriers to Implementation First, ABC requires a significant amount of time and cost to implement. If implementation is to be successful, substantial support is needed throughout the firm. Management must create an environment for change that overcomes a variety of individual, organizational, and environmental barriers, such as the following:

Individual Barriers	Organizational Barriers	Environmental Barriers
• Fear of change	• Territorial issues	• Employee (often union) groups
• Shift in status	• Hierarchical issues	• Regulatory agencies
• Learning new skills	• Corporate culture issues	• Financial accounting mandates

To overcome these barriers, a firm must first recognize that these barriers exist, investigate their causes, and communicate information about the "what," "why," and "how" of ABC to all concerned parties. Top management must be involved with, and support, the implementation process. A shortfall in this area will make any progress toward the new system slow and difficult. Additionally, everyone in the company must be educated in new terminology, concepts, and performance measurements. Even if both of these conditions (support and education) are met, substantial time is needed to properly analyze the activities occurring in the activity centers, trace costs to those activities, and determine the cost drivers. One alternative to traditional ABC summarized in the next section is time-driven ABC, which focuses only on the cost of supplying resources to activities and the time it takes to perform activities using the concept of available capacity.[7]

Inconsistencies with GAAP Accounting Another problem with ABC is that it does not conform specifically to GAAP. ABC suggests that some nonproduct costs (such as those for R&D) *should* be allocated to products, whereas certain other traditionally designated product costs (such as factory building depreciation) *should not* be allocated to products. Therefore, most companies have used ABC for internal reporting but continue to prepare their external financial statements with a more traditional system—requiring even more costs to be incurred. As ABC systems become more accepted, more companies could choose to refine how ABC and GAAP determine product cost to make those definitions more compatible and, thereby, eliminate the need for two costing systems.

Companies attempting to implement ABC as a cure-all for product failures, sales volume declines, or financial losses will quickly find that the system is ineffective for these purposes. However, companies can implement ABC and its related management techniques in support of and in conjunction with total quality management, just-in-time production, or any of the other world-class methodologies. Companies doing so will provide the customer with the best variety, price, quality, service, and lead time of which they are capable—and, possibly, enjoy large increases in market share.

---

[7] Robert S. Kaplan and Steven R. Anderson, "Time-Driven Activity-Based Costing," *Harvard Business Review* (November 2004).

ABC and ABM are effective in supporting continuous improvement, short lead times, and flexible manufacturing by helping managers to

- identify and monitor significant technology costs;
- trace many technology costs directly to products;
- increase market share;
- identify the cost drivers that create or influence cost;
- identify activities that do not contribute to perceived customer value (i.e., non-value-added activities or waste);
- understand the impact of new technologies on all elements of performance;
- translate company goals into activity goals;
- analyze the performance of activities across business functions;
- analyze performance problems; and
- promote standards of excellence.

In summary, ABC assigns overhead costs to products and services differently from a traditional overhead allocation system. Implementation of ABC does not cause a company's overhead cost to be reduced; that outcome results from the implementation of ABM through its focus on identifying and reducing or eliminating non-value-added activities. Together, ABM and ABC assist managers by providing information that can help them produce products and perform services most efficiently and effectively and, thus, be highly competitive in the global business environment.

ABC; Product Profitability — **LO8-5** — **REVIEW 8-5**

Using the information from Review 8-4, answer the following questions.
a. Determine the total profit for standard items and custom items using the current allocation system.
b. Determine the total profit for standard items and custom items if more appropriate cost drivers were used.
c. What is the profit margin (Net income ÷ Revenues) for standard items and for custom items under the assumptions in part *a*?
d. What is the profit margin for standard items and for custom items under the assumptions in part *b*?
e. What is the difference between the overall profit calculated in part *a* and in part *b*?
f. **Critical Thinking:** As a sales manager, which product would you choose to prioritize for marketing expenditures given the profitability information in part *a*? Part *b*? What are the implications of these decisions?

More practice: E8-43
Solution on p. 8-56.

TIME-DRIVEN ACTIVITY-BASED COSTING

ABC's complexity is both a strength and a weakness. To successfully implement ABC, an organization must be able to model and measure its production process in great detail. In industries such as health care, this is all but impossible. Kaplan and his colleagues introduced a refinement to ABC called **time-driven activity-based costing (TDABC)** and tested its application to health care with the help of several hospitals.[8] Rather than defining complex sets of activities and their rates, TDABC uses historical data to estimate the relationship between the cost of an activity and the amount of time spent on the activity.

LO8-6 How are product and service costs computed using a time-driven activity-based costing system?

> **Predetermined rate per minute/hour = Budgeted activity cost ÷ Total available minutes/hours**

The total available minutes/hours is referred to as a company's available **capacity**. Any time not used for activities is considered **unused capacity**. Capacity can be measured in different ways as explained later in Chapter 11. For this section, we simply consider capacity as time available under normal operating circumstances.

Next, the predetermined rate is applied to the time for a particular transaction.

---

[8] Robert Kaplan and Michael Porter, "The Big Idea: How to Solve the Cost Crisis in Health Care," *Harvard Business Review*, September 2011

> Cost per transaction = Predetermined rate per minute/hour × Minutes/hours for a transaction
> Total activity cost = Cost per transaction × No. of Transactions

DEMO 8-6 LO8-6   Applying Time-Driven Activity-Based Costing

The total annual cost of $2,997,000 for a radiology department of a health clinic includes the cost of three full-time technicians, equipment, technology, and supplies. The total number of available technician hours is 5,400 for the year.

The department manager estimated times for each of the following activities.

Intake/Preparation	10 minutes
Imaging	15 minutes
Consultation/Exit	10 minutes

During the year, the radiology department treated 8,700 patients. Assume all patients participate in the three activities.

◆ **What is the cost per patient visit, estimated using TDABC?**

The cost per patient of $323.75 is calculated as follows.

Predetermined rate per minute = $2,997,000 ÷ (5,400 × 60 minutes)

= $2,997,000 ÷ 324,000 minutes = $9.25 per minute

Cost per patient visit = $9.25 × (10 minutes + 15 minutes + 10 minutes)

= $9.25 × 35 minutes = $323.75

◆ **What is the total estimated cost of the 8,700 patients and what is the cost of the unused capacity?**

Total estimated cost = 8,700 patients × $323.75 = $2,816,625

The cost of unused capacity is equal to the total cost of the department less the estimated cost of the actual patients treated.

$2,997,000 − $2,816,625 = $180,375 or approximately 6% ($180,375 ÷ $2,997,000)

The cost per activity and of unused capacity is summarized in the following table.

Activity	Quantity	Unit Time	Total Time	Rate per Minute	Total Cost
Intake/Preparation	8,700	10 minutes	87,000 minutes	$9.25	$ 804,750
Imaging	8,700	15 minutes	130,500 minutes	9.25	1,207,125
Consultation/Exit	8,700	10 minutes	87,000 minutes	9.25	804,750
Unused capacity					180,375
Total costs					$2,997,000

The estimated relationship between cost and time allows organizations to implement ABC without completely characterizing their activities. It also allows organizations to determine which resources are particularly costly and focus on those resources for cost control. Thus, the benefits of ABC can be realized without the implementation issues discussed in this chapter. TDABC integrates easily with existing resource planning processes and without the costs of a full ABC implementation.

The reports that are generated through a TDABC system are intuitive and useful to management. For example, in the summary report of Demo 8-6, the total time for each activity is summarized along with the cost of each activity. Management can focus on cost control by focusing efforts on reducing time per activity. Extra emphasis can be placed on reducing non-valued added activities as well as a reduction in unused capacity.

Chapter 8 Activity-Based Management and Activity-Based Costing

The **Mayo Clinic** is a successful example of the benefits of TDABC implementation. It treats the TDABC process like it would any other improvement in medical care—as a scientific inquiry. It assembles a project team from every level of the organization and the group uses Kaplan's principles to estimate time/resource cost relationships. These relationships lead to experiments for improvement where they test the changes suggested in the TDABC process. Their findings are then shared with the whole organization.[9]

Applying Time-Driven Activity-Based Costing — **LO8-6** — **REVIEW 8-6**

A drive-through, quick service automobile service center provides three services: oil change, air filter replacement, and wiper blade replacement. The following summary is provided for the year based on a TDABC analysis.

Activity	No. of Services	Total Minutes	Total TDABC Cost
Oil change	13,000	130,000	$481,000
Air filter replacement	5,000	30,000	111,000
Wiper blade replacement	2,000	6,000	22,200

a. What is the budgeted cost per minute for the auto services?
b. If total estimated technician hours of capacity for the year are 2,915, what is the total cost for the year?
c. What is the unit time in minutes for an oil change, air filter replacement, and wiper blade replacement?
d. What is the cost of unused capacity?
e. **Critical Thinking:** How would management decide on whether or not a new auto technician should be hired?

More practice: E8-47, E8-48, E8-49
Solution on p. 8-57.

Comprehensive Chapter Review

Key Terms

activity, p. 8-3
activity analysis, p. 8-3
activity-based costing (ABC), p. 8-8
activity-based management (ABM), p. 8-2
activity center, p. 8-14
activity driver, p. 8-14
batch-level costs, p. 8-9
business-value-added (BVA) activities, p. 8-3
capacity, p. 8-23
cost cross-subsidization, p. 8-17
cost driver analysis, p. 8-9
cycle (lead) time, p. 8-4

engineering change orders (ECOs), p. 8-10
idle time, p. 8-4
inspection time, p. 8-4
just-in-time (JIT), p. 8-7
manufacturing cycle efficiency (MCE), p. 8-6
mass customization, p. 8-19
non-value-added (NVA) activity, p. 8-3
organizational-level (facility-level) costs, p. 8-11
Pareto principle, p. 8-19
process, p. 8-3
process complexity, p. 8-16
processing (service) time, p. 8-4

process map, p. 8-3
product complexity, p. 8-16
product-level (process-level) cost, p. 8-10
product profitability analysis, p. 8-12
product variety, p. 8-16
service cycle efficiency (SCE), p. 8-7
time-driven activity-based costing (TDABC), p. 8-23
transfer time, p. 8-4
unit-level costs, p. 8-9
unused capacity, p. 8-23
value-added (VA) activity, p. 8-3
value chart, p. 8-5

Chapter Summary

Activity-Based Management; Value-Added and Non-Value-Added Activities (Page 8-2) — **LO8-1**
- Activity-based management (ABM)
  - analyzes activities and identifies their cost drivers.

---

[9] 2Derek Haas, Richard Helmers, March Rucci, Meredith Brady, and Robert Kaplan, "The Mayo Clinic Model for Running a Value-Improvement Program," *Harvard Business Review*, October 22, 2015

© Cambridge Business Publishers

- classifies activities relative to customer value and strives to eliminate or minimize those activities for which customers would choose not to pay.
- helps assure that customers perceive an equitable relationship between product selling price and value.
- improves processes and operational controls.
- analyzes performance problems.
- translates company goals into organizational activities.

■ A value-added (VA) activity
- increases the worth of a product or service.
- is one for which the customer is willing to pay.
- is an actual production or service task.

■ A non-value-added (NVA) activity
- lengthens the production or performance time.
- increases the cost of product or services without adding product or service value.
- is one for which the customer would not be willing to pay.
- is created by
  ➢ inspecting (except in certain industries such as food and pharmaceutical),
  ➢ moving,
  ➢ waiting,
  ➢ packaging (unless essential to the convenient or proper delivery of a product), or
  ➢ engaging in a task that is (or appears to be) essential to business operations but for which customers would not willingly choose to pay.

LO8-2 Manufacturing Cycle Efficiency (Page 8-6)
■ Manufacturing cycle efficiency (MCE) is computed as total value-added time divided by total cycle time.
■ MCE measures how well a company uses its time resources.
■ VA activities increase MCE, while NVA activities decrease MCE.
■ In a service company, cycle efficiency is computed as total actual service time divided by total cycle time (from original service order to service completion).

LO8-3 Importance of Cost Drivers (Page 8-8)
■ Cost drivers identify what causes a cost to be incurred so that it can be controlled.
■ Cost drivers should indicate at what level a cost occurs.
- Unit costs are caused by the production or acquisition of a single unit of product or the delivery of a single unit of service.
- Batch costs are caused by a group of things being made, handled, or processed at a single time.
- Product/process costs are caused by the development, production, or acquisition of different items.
- Organizational (facility) costs are caused by facility operations and the management of the organizational infrastructure.

■ Cost drivers allow costs to be pooled together such that they have a common activity base that can be used to allocate those costs to products or services.
■ Cost drivers promote the effective and efficient management of costs.
■ Cost drivers help identify costs related to product variety and product/process complexity.

LO8-4 Computation of Costs in Activity-Based Costing (Page 8-14)
■ Activity-based costing (ABC) is a cost accounting system that focuses on an organization's activities and collects costs on the basis of the underlying nature and extent of those activities.
■ ABC is a process of overhead allocation.
■ ABC differs from a traditional cost accounting system in that ABC
- identifies several levels of costs rather than the traditional concepts of variable (at the unit level) or fixed.
- collects costs in cost pools based on the underlying nature and extent of activities.
- assigns costs within the multiple cost pools to products or services using multiple drivers (both volume- and non-volume-related) that best reflect the factor causing the costs to be incurred.
- considers some costs that are considered product costs for external reporting as period costs.
- considers some costs that are considered period costs for external reporting as product costs.
- may, under certain conditions, provide a more realistic picture of actual production cost than has traditionally been available.

Chapter 8 Activity-Based Management and Activity-Based Costing

Conditions for Effective Use of ABC (Page 8-18) LO8-5
- ABC is appropriate in an organization that
  - produces and sells a wide variety of products or services.
  - customizes products to customer specifications.
  - uses a wide range of techniques to manufacture products or to provide services.
  - has a lack of commonality in overhead costs of products or services.
  - has experienced problems with its current overhead allocation system.
  - has experienced significant changes in its business environment, including widespread adoption of new technologies.
- Installation of an ABM or ABC system allows management to
  - see the cost impact of an organization's cross-functional activities.
  - understand that fixed costs are, in fact, long-run variable costs that change based on an identifiable driver.
  - realize the value of preparing process maps and value charts.
  - determine that the traditional bases (direct labor and machine hours) might not produce the most logical costs for products or services.
  - recognize that standard products/services often financially support premium products/services.
  - set prices that reflect the activities needed to produce special or premium products.
  - decide whether premium or low-volume products are actually profitable for the company.
  - calculate MCE and measure organizational performance.
  - be aware that the most effective way to control costs is to minimize or eliminate NVA activities.
  - accept that customers who are not profitable should not necessarily be retained.
- Criticisms of ABC
  - ABC requires substantial time and cost to implement.
  - ABC does not specifically conform to generally accepted accounting principles.
  - ABC cannot "cure" product failures, sales volume declines, or financial losses.
  - ABC does not reduce overhead costs.

Time-Driven Activity-Based Costing (Page 8-23) LO8-6
- Time-driven activity-based costing (TDABC) is a refinement to activity-based costing which
  - measures the relationship between the cost of an activity and the amount of time spent on the activity.
  - reduces complexity by reducing the number of cost pools and activity rates normally required under activity-based costing.
  - aids in cost control efforts by identifying which resources are more costly.

Solution Strategies

Manufacturing Cycle Efficiency LO8-2

Total Cycle Time = Value-Added Processing Time + Inspection Time + Transfer Time + Idle Time

MCE = Value-Added Processing Time ÷ Total Cycle Time

Note: Depending on the organization, packaging time may be part of value-added processing time or a type of non-value-added time. In either case, packaging time will add to total cycle time. Business-value-added time may need to be included as NVA time for certain types of functions.

Activity-Based Costing LO8-4

1. Determine the organization's costs.
2. Stage One Determine the drivers creating the costs and aggregate the costs into "pools" based on levels of costs.
3. Determine the organization's activity centers and allocate costs to those centers using cost drivers.
4. Stage Two Determine the activity drivers needed to assign costs to products and services.

Predetermined activity-based rate = Budgeted OH in activity center cost pool ÷ Budgeted activity driver amount

Allocated OH = Predetermined activity-based rate × Actual activity driver amount

5. Do not allocate organizational level costs to products (services) unless those costs are immaterial in amount.

LO8-6 Time-Driven Activity-Based Costing

Predetermined rate per minute/hour = Budgeted activity cost ÷ Total available minutes/hours

Cost per transaction = Predetermined rate per minute/hour × Minutes/hours for a transaction

Total activity cost = Cost per transaction × No. of Transactions

Chapter Demonstration Problem

LO8-4, 5 Potter Inc. manufactures wizard figurines. All figurines are approximately the same size, but some are plain ceramic whereas others are "fancy," with purple leather capes and a prism-headed wand. Management is considering producing only the fancy figurines because they appear to be substantially more profitable than the plain figurines. The company's total production overhead is $5,017,500. Some additional data follow.

	Plain	Fancy
Revenues	$15,000,000	$16,800,000
Direct costs	$ 8,050,000	$ 8,950,000
Production (units)	1,500,000	350,000
Machine hours	200,000	50,000
Direct labor hours	30,500	157,625
Number of inspections	600	6,900

Required:

a. Potter Inc. has consistently used machine hours to allocate overhead. Determine the profitability of each line of figurines, and decide whether the company should stop producing the plain figurines.
b. The cost accountant has determined that production overhead costs can be assigned to separate cost pools. Pool #1 contains $1,260,000 of overhead costs for which the most appropriate cost driver is machine hours; Pool #2 contains $2,257,500 of overhead costs for which the most appropriate cost driver is direct labor hours; and Pool #3 contains $1,500,000 of overhead costs for which the most appropriate cost driver is number of inspections. Compute the overhead cost that should be allocated to each type of figurine using this methodology.
c. Discuss whether the company should continue to manufacture both types of figurines.

Solution to Demonstration Problem

a. Overhead rate per MH = $5,017,500 ÷ 250,000 = $20.07 per MH
Overhead for plain figurines: 200,000 × $20.07 = $4,014,000
Overhead for fancy figurines: 50,000 × $20.07 = $1,003,500

	Plain		Fancy	
Revenue		$15,000,000		$16,800,000
Direct costs	$8,050,000		$8,950,000	
Overhead	4,014,000		1,003,500	
Total costs		(12,064,000)		(9,953,500)
Gross profit		$ 2,936,000		$ 6,846,500
Gross profit margin (rounded)		19.6%		40.8%

Total OH $5,017,500

$20.07 per MH

Gross profit margin:

$$\frac{\text{Gross profit}}{\text{Revenue}}$$

Chapter 8 Activity-Based Management and Activity-Based Costing

b.

	Plain	Fancy	Total
Machine hours	200,000	50,000	250,000
Rate per MH ($1,260,000 ÷ 250,000)	× $5.04	× $5.04	× $5.04
Pool #1 OH cost allocations	$1,008,000	$ 252,000	$1,260,000
Direct labor hours	30,500	157,625	188,125
Rate per DLH ($2,257,500 ÷ 188,125)	× $12	× $12	× $12
Pool #2 OH cost allocations	$ 366,000	$1,891,500	$2,257,500
Number of inspections	600	6,900	7,500
Rate per inspection ($1,500,000 ÷ 7,500)	× $200	× $200	× $200
Pool #3 OH cost allocations	$ 120,000	$1,380,000	$1,500,000
Total allocated overhead costs	$1,494,000	$3,523,500	$5,017,500

Pool #1 $1,260,000
$5.04 per MH

Pool #2 $2,257,500
$12 per DLH

Pool #3 $1,500,000
$200 per inspection

		Plain		Fancy
Revenue		$15,000,000		$16,800,000
Direct costs	$8,050,000		$8,950,000	
Overhead	1,494,000		3,523,500	
Total costs		(9,544,000)		(12,473,500)
Gross profit		$ 5,456,000		$ 4,326,500
Gross profit margin		36.4%		25.8%

c. Given the new allocations, management should continue to produce both types of figurines because both appear to be profitable. However, the cost accountant could consider developing additional overhead pools because of the large number of costs charged to Pool #2.

Assignments with the MBC logo in the margin are available in *myBusinessCourse*.
Resources include demonstration videos, guided examples, and auto-graded homework.
See details in the Preface, and ask your professor how you can access the system.

Data Analytics

DA8-1. Activity-based costing using Excel   LO8-3, 4

Assume Kirkland Industries (a contract assembly manufacturer) has decided to adopt activity-based costing techniques to determine its manufacturing overhead rates. The production manager has identified three activities (materials movement, assembly, and packaging/shipping) and a number of possible activity measures (# of jobs, direct labor hours, machine hours, # of boxes shipped, and # of components used). Working together, the production and accounting managers have used historical data from 2014 to 2021 to determine total activity costs by month. Those results are included in a data file on the textbook's website. The workbook also includes totals for the various activity measures from the same 2014–2021 period.

Budgeted overhead dollars and activities for the year are as follows.

Budgeted Overhead		Budgeted Measures	
Materials movement	$1,080,000	No. of jobs	480
Assembly	$1,950,000	Direct labor hours	16,000
Packaging/Shipping	$1,584,000	Machine hours	7,800
		No. of boxes shipped	48,000
		No. of components used	4,000,000

Note: *If the Analyze section does not appear, you will need to load the Analysis ToolPak. Click the File tab, click Options, and click Add-Ins. Make sure Excel Add-ins appears in the Manage field. Check the Analysis ToolPak option and click OK.*

Required

a. Use the correlation tool in Excel to determine which measure should be used for each activity.
Hint: The correlation tool can be found on the *Data Analysis* menu in the *Analyze* section of the Data tab in Excel. *Hint:* Open the Correlation Tool and highlight the data. If the first row is

highlighted, check the box for Labels in first row. From your results, determine which variable has the highest correlation value for each of the three overhead categories.
  b. Using the measures identified in part *a*, determine the activity rates for allocating manufacturing overhead to jobs.
  c. What would the predetermined rate be if direct labor hours were used to allocate all manufacturing overhead costs?
  d. Assume Kirkland had a job that required 36 direct labor hours, 16 machine hours, 1,875 components, and 68 boxes. How much manufacturing overhead would be applied to that job under ABC? How does that compare to the amount applied if direct labor hours were used to allocate overhead? What might account for the difference?

LO8-4 **DA8-2. Analyzing product costs using different overhead application methods**
The Windsor Company calculated overhead rates for its Job No. 845 using activity-based costing, departmental overhead allocation, and plantwide overhead allocation. A summary of product costs and components of applied OH for Job No. 845 under the three different costing methods is included in an Excel file available on the textbook's website.

Required
  a. Create three pie charts of the product costs of Job No. 845, one for each of the three costing methods. In each pie chart, include direct material, direct labor, and overhead costs. Display proportions in percentages. *Hint*: Right-click inside the pie and select Format Data Labels. Select Percentages under Label Options in the sidebar. Deselect Value, if necessary.
  b. Describe the differences in the charts in part *a*. How might the charts impact a manager's assessment of product costs under the different methods.
  c. Create three pie charts (one for each of the three costing methods) showing the components of overhead of Job No. 845.
  d. Which chart in part *c* provides a better management tool for decision making? Why?
  e. Create one bar chart comparing applied overhead in *total* calculated under each of the three costing methods.
  f. How do the differences shown in the bar chart in part *e* affect the costing of other jobs of the company?

LO8-5 **DA8-3. Analyzing travel costs using a Pareto Chart**
A consulting firm based in Chicago would like to implement cost controls on travel expenses to its on-going client base. A summary of travel costs by destination is included in an Excel file available on the textbook's website. Using this information, create and analyze a Pareto chart of the firm's travel costs.

Required
  a. Sort the cost data by destination, from the highest to the lowest cost. *Hint*: Under the Data tab, use the Sort function.
  b. Create a new column showing the cumulative cost.
  c. Create a new column showing the cumulative cost percentage. *Hint*: Each amount in the cumulative cost column should be divided by total travel costs.
  d. Create a Pareto chart. *Hint*: While highlighting the destination, cost, and cumulative percentage column, select the Pareto chart option in the histogram group of the All charts menu.
  e. Which cities comprise at least 77 percent of the travel costs?
  f. Which cities comprise 20 percent of the travel costs?
  g. How could this analysis be useful for managing travel expenses?

Data Visualization

Data Visualization Activities are available in myBusinessCourse. These assignments use Tableau Dashboards to expose students to visual depictions of data and introduce students to data analytics through data visualizations. These exercises are easily assignable and auto graded by MBC.

Potential Ethical Issues

1. Ignoring non-value-added activities and times in the development of a value chart to improve cycle efficiency as a performance metric

Chapter 8 Activity-Based Management and Activity-Based Costing

2. Using an unsubstantiated designation of "non-value-added" for specific activities merely to justify the elimination of the jobs of the individuals performing those activities
3. Misclassifying batch- or product/process-level activities as unit-level to spread the costs of those activities to higher-volume products/services and, thereby, reduce the cost of lower-volume products so as to justify a reduced selling price on the lower-volume products/services
4. Selecting an inappropriate cost driver to allocate costs to products or services in a way that intentionally distorts realistic cost calculations
5. Using activity-based costing to unethically justify no longer purchasing from a particular vendor or selling to a particular customer
6. Using activity-based costing to justify not allocating corporate funds to social or environmental causes
7. Using distorted activity-based costing allocations to transfer costs from fixed-price contracts to cost-plus contracts

Questions

Q8-1. What is activity-based management (ABM), and what specific management tools are used in ABM?

Q8-2. What is activity analysis, and how is it used with cost driver analysis to manage costs and increase profits?

Q8-3. Why are value-added activities defined from a customer viewpoint?

Q8-4. According to a *Wall Street Journal* article, a three-hour televised football game boils down to 10 minutes and 43 seconds of actual playing time.[10] What other activities take place during a televised football game? Of all the activities, which are value-added and which are non-value-added? Discuss whether everyone would agree with your choices. What is the cycle efficiency of the football game?

Q8-5. If five people from the same organization calculated manufacturing cycle efficiency for a specific process, would each compute the same MCE? Why or why not?

Q8-6. Why is service cycle efficiency generally a higher percentage than manufacturing cycle efficiency?

Q8-7. Do cost drivers exist in a traditional accounting system? Are they designated as such? How, if at all, does the use of cost drivers in a traditional accounting system differ from those in an activity-based costing system?

Q8-8. Why do more traditional methods of overhead assignment "overload" standard high-volume products or services with overhead costs? How does ABC improve overhead assignments?

Q8-9. Once an activity-based costing system has been developed and implemented in a company, will that system be appropriate for the long term? Why or why not?

Q8-10. Are all companies likely to benefit to an equal extent from adopting ABC? Discuss.

Q8-11. The Chrysler Fiat 500X offers customers a variety of combinations of model types, exterior colors, seat colors, and wheel styles (source: https://www.fiatusa.com/). Discuss the additional costs that Chrysler might incur from having options for the Fiat 500X. Do you think that customers will be willing to pay significantly different prices for option variations? Why or why not?

Q8-12. Significant hurdles, including a large time commitment, are often encountered in adopting ABC. What specific activities associated with ABC adoption require large investments of time?

Multiple Choice

MC8-13. Consider the following manufacturing-related activities.
  I. Conducting the final assembly of wooden furniture.
  II. Moving completed production to the finished goods warehouse.
  III. Painting newly-manufactured automobiles.
  IV. Setting up a machine related to a new production run.
  V. Reworking defective goods to bring them up to quality standards.

The activities that would be classified as value-added activities are
  a. II, III, IV, and V only.
  b. I, IV, and V only.
  c. I, III, and V only.
  d. I and III only.

LO8-1

---
[10] D. Biderman, "11 Minutes of Action," *WSJ* (January 15, 2010), W1

© Cambridge Business Publishers

LO8-2 **MC8-14.** Assume that **Stickley**, a furniture manufacturer with operations in New York and North Carolina, performed a time study on its operations for its dining tables.

Actual processing time on the machines for one batch of tables.......	3.75 hours
Time spent moving a batch of tables from one station to the next......	2.00 hours
Time spent on quality control testing, per batch.....................	45 minutes
Time spent setting up equipment, for batch processing..............	30 minutes

What is the company's manufacturing cycle efficiency?
- a. 100%
- b. 46%
- c. 7%
- d. 54%

LO8-3 **MC8-15.** When using activity-based costing techniques, which one of the following departmental activities would be expected to use machine hours as a cost driver to allocate overhead costs to production?
- a. Plant cafeteria.
- b. Machine setups.
- c. Material handling.
- d. Robotics painting.

LO8-4 **MC8-16.** A company is implementing an activity-based budgeting system. Set-up overhead is allocated based on set-up hours and manufacturing overhead is allocated based on direct manufacturing labor hours. Budget information is listed in the table below.

Cost Driver Information	Product A	Product B
Number of units per batch...................	50	25
Set-up time per batch......................	1.75 hours	1.25 hours
Direct manufacturing labor time per batch......	1.00 hours	0.75 hours

The company plans to produce 1,000 units of Product A and 750 units of Product B. The activity rates are $100 per set-up hour and $150 per direct manufacturing labor hour. What is the total budgeted overhead?
- a. $10,063.
- b. $13,625.
- c. $15,125.
- d. $22,188.

LO8-5 **MC8-17.** A company's operations include a high level of fixed costs and produce a variety of products. What type of costing system should be recommended?
- a. Job-order costing.
- b. Process costing.
- c. Process value analysis.
- d. Activity-based costing.

LO8-6 **MC8-18.** What is the primary advantage for a manufacturer that has adopted time-driven activity-based costing?
- a. It provides more accurate costing of products by using both unit-level and batch-level activity drivers.
- b. It provides a detailed analysis by showing actual time and costs for each activity.
- c. It minimizes cost pools and activity rates which reduces the complexity of cost allocation.
- d. Eliminates all barriers typical of traditional ABC costing.

Exercises

LO8-1 **E8-19.** **Activity analysis; writing** Choose an activity related to this class, such as attending lectures or doing homework. Write down the answers to the question "why" five times to determine whether your activity is value-added or non-value-added.

LO8-1 **E8-20.** **Activity analysis** Your boss wants to know whether quality inspections at your company add value. Use the "why" methodology to help your boss make this determination if you work at (a) a clothing manufacturer that sells to a discount chain and (b) a pharmaceutical manufacturer.

LO8-1 **E8-21.** **Activity analysis; research** Go to a local department or grocery store.
- a. List five packaged items for which it is readily apparent that packaging is essential and, therefore, would be considered value-added.
- b. List five packaged items for which it is readily apparent that packaging is nonessential and therefore adds no value.
- c. For each item listed in (b), indicate why you think the item was packaged rather than left unpackaged.

Chapter 8 Activity-Based Management and Activity-Based Costing

E8-22. Activity analysis The following activities are common at Pisana's Department Store. Goods are received with barcodes attached that can be read by scanners but not by customers. **LO8-1**

1. Attending trade shows to view new products
2. Reviewing supplier catalogs
3. Ordering merchandise
4. Waiting for shipments to be received
5. Inspecting goods for damage
6. Matching receiving reports and purchase orders
7. Placing customer-readable price tags on merchandise
8. Moving goods to retail area
9. Stocking shelves
10. Training salespersons in store merchandise
11. Checking out customer purchases
12. Handing customer receipts
13. Wrapping gift items when requested
14. Helping customers with returns or exchanges

  a. Indicate which activities are value-added (VA), business-value-added (BVA), and non-value-added (NVA).
  b. How might some of the business-value-added activities be reduced or eliminated?

E8-23. Activity analysis The Raleigh plant manager of Allentown Corp. has noticed the plant frequently changes the schedule on its production line. He has gathered the following information on the activities, estimated times, and average costs required for a single schedule change. **LO8-1**

Activity	Est. Time	Average Cost
Review impact of change on orders	30 min.– 2 hrs.	$ 300
Reschedule production orders	15 min.–24 hrs.	875
Stop production and change over to new process	10 min.– 3 hrs.	150
Locate inventory produced under old process	20 min.– 6 hrs.	1,500
Remanufacture old inventory to conform to new process	3 hrs.–20 hrs.	6,000
Generate new production paperwork	15 min.– 4 hrs.	500
Change purchasing schedule	10 min.– 8 hrs.	2,100
Collect paperwork from the floor	5 min.–15 min.	75
Review new line schedule	15 min.–30 min.	100
Pay overtime premiums	3 hrs.– 5 hrs.	1,000
Total costs required for a single schedule change		$6,600

  a. Which, if any, of these activities are value-added?
  b. What is the cost driver in this situation?
  c. How can the cost driver be controlled and the NVA activities eliminated?

E8-24. Activity analysis; MCE Elaydo Inc. makes flavored water and performs the following tasks in the beverage manufacturing process: **LO8-1, 2**

	Hours
Receive and transfer ingredients to storage	9.0
Store ingredients	264.0
Transfer ingredients from storage to production area	3.5
Mix and cook ingredients	6.5
Bottle water	3.0
Transfer bottles to finished goods warehouse	5.0

  a. Calculate the total cycle time of this manufacturing process.
  b. Calculate the manufacturing cycle efficiency of this process.

E8-25. Activity analysis Farrah Westin plans to build a concrete walkway for her home during her vacation. The following schedule shows how project time will be allocated: **LO8-1, 2**

Activity	Hours
Purchase materials.	5
Obtain rental equipment.	2
Remove sod and level site.	20
Build forms for concrete.	10
Mix and pour concrete into forms.	5
Level concrete and smooth.	6
Let dry.	24
Remove forms from concrete.	2
Return rental tools.	1
Clean up.	4

    a.   Identify the value-added activities. How much of the total time is value-added time?
    b.   Identify the non-value-added activities. How much total time is spent performing non-value-added activities?
    c.   Calculate the manufacturing cycle efficiency.

LO8-1, 2   **E8-26.**   **Activity analysis; MCE** Log Cabins Unlimited constructs vacation houses in the North Carolina mountains. The company has developed the following value chart:

Operations	Average Number of Days
Receiving materials.	2
Storing materials.	10
Measuring and cutting materials.	9
Handling materials.	7
Setting up and moving scaffolding.	6
Assembling materials.	3
Building fireplace.	12
Pegging logs.	8
Cutting and framing doors and windows.	5
Sealing joints.	4
Waiting for county inspectors.	6
Inspecting property (county inspectors).	1

    a.   What are the value-added activities and their total time?
    b.   What are the non-value-added activities and their total time?
    c.   Calculate the manufacturing cycle efficiency of the process.
    d.   Explain the difference between value-added and non-value-added activities.

LO8-1, 2   **E8-27.**   **Activity analysis; MCE** Spice-a-licious produces creole seasoning using the following process for each batch:

Function	Time (Minutes)
Receiving ingredients.	60
Moving ingredients to stockroom.	80
Storing ingredients in stockroom.	8,200
Moving ingredients from stockroom.	8
Measuring ingredients.	30
Mixing ingredients.	60
Packaging ingredients.	50
Moving packaged seasoning to warehouse.	100
Storing packaged seasoning in warehouse.	20,000
Moving packaged seasoning from warehouse to trucks.	120

    a.   Calculate the total cycle time of this manufacturing process.
    b.   Which of the functions add value?
    c.   Calculate the manufacturing cycle efficiency of this process.
    d.   What could Spice-a-licious do to improve its MCE?

Chapter 8 Activity-Based Management and Activity-Based Costing

E8-28. Activity analysis; SCE The following activities take place at Lohman CPAs during a recurring external audit of Reliance Corp. Classify the activities as value-added or non-value-added from the perspective of Reliance Corp. and compute the service cycle efficiency.

LO8-1, 2

Activity	Time (Hours)
Drafting engagement letter	4
Audit planning and discussion of audit risk	20
Internal control review	32
Preparing audit program	24
Fieldwork, transaction testing, completing work papers	125
Client discussions and rework	16
Drafting and issuing audit report; discussion with board of directors	23
Audit follow-up discussions	20

E8-29. Activity analysis; SCE Following are the activities that occur during a patient visit to a physician's office.

LO8-1, 2

Step	Time Spent
Patient arrives at doctor's office and checks in with receptionist	2 min.
Patient is asked to review previously provided information for changes; there are none	3 min.
Patient returns forms to receptionist	1 min.
Receptionist verifies patient insurance and collects co-pay	5 min.
Patient waits in waiting room	15 min.
Nurse escorts patient to exam room and takes vital signs	3 min.
Patient waits in exam room	7 min.
Physician examines and treats patient	8 min.
Patient checks out with receptionist, if needed	3 min.

    a. Classify each of the above activities as value-added or non-value-added.
    b. Determine the service cycle efficiency.

E8-30. SCE When problems occur with products that are purchased, buyers contact the manufacturer's call center. After being notified of a problem and requesting assistance from the appropriate parties, a call center agent can create a solution document for the problem in 30 minutes. A supervisor then takes 15 minutes to review the document and verify the solution. The document is then routed to Marketing for review (30 minutes) and on to Legal (two hours) to make certain that the document is ready for publication. However, because of time lags between each step, the total cycle time takes 15 days from creation to publication.[11]

LO8-2

    a. Which of the activities in the correction process are value-added?
    b. If the problem could not have been foreseen, how would you calculate the cycle efficiency for the correction process?
    c. Assume again that the problem could not have been foreseen. After being notified of a problem and requesting assistance from the appropriate parties, a call center agent can create a solution document for the problem in 30 minutes. Call center agents are "licensed" to publish a solution document after placing it in a queue for four hours after development to allow Marketing and Legal the option of review. After four hours, the solution document is automatically posted on the company's Web site to assist customers. What is the new cycle efficiency?
    d. Assume that the manufacturer sold 30,000 of the problem products just before Christmas. The first customer complaint call was received at 10 A.M. on December 25. The call center agent devised the solution document by 10:30 A.M. If a call will be received every ten minutes until the support document is posted and each call costs the company $15, what is the call center cost related to this problem if the process is handled as originally discussed? As discussed in (*c*)?

E8-31. Value chart McAllen Co. manufactures special-order office cubicle systems. Production time is two days, but the average cycle time for any order is three weeks. The company president has asked you, as the new controller, to discuss missed delivery dates. Prepare an oral presentation for the executive officers in which you address the following:

LO8-2

---

[11] Based on information accessed on September 12, 2023 at https://www.streetdirectory.com/travel_guide/16701/corporate_matters/increase_call_center_efficiency_with_knowledge_centered_support.html.

LO8-3 E8-32. **Cost drivers** For each of the following cost pools in a temporary employment agency, identify a cost driver and explain why it is appropriate.
  a. Advertising cost
  b. Accounts receivable department
  c. Property taxes and insurance on office building
  d. Information technology
  e. Payroll department
  f. Utilities

LO8-3 E8-33. **Cost drivers** For each of the following costs commonly incurred in a manufacturing company, identify a cost driver and explain why it is an appropriate choice.
  a. Factory depreciation
  b. Freight costs for materials
  c. Machine setup cost
  d. Computer operations
  e. Material storage
  f. Material handling
  g. Engineering changes
  h. Advertising expense
  i. Building utilities
  j. Quality control
  k. Equipment maintenance

LO8-3 E8-34. **Levels of costs** The following costs are incurred in a fast-food restaurant that relies on computer-controlled equipment to prepare customers' food. The majority of food is purchased daily for freshness. Classify each cost as unit level (U), batch level (B), product/process level (P), or organizational level (O).
  a. Maintenance of the restaurant building
  b. Store manager's salary
  c. Refrigeration of raw materials
  d. Oil for the deep-fat fryer (changed every four hours)
  e. Electricity expense for the pizza oven
  f. Ingredients for food orders
  g. Depreciation on equipment
  h. Cardboard boxes for food order
  i. Property taxes
  j. Frozen potatoes for french fries

LO8-3 E8-35. **Levels of costs** Carpenter Inc. designs industrial tooling parts and makes the molds for those parts. The following activities take place when the company creates a new mold. Classify each cost as unit level (U), batch level (B), product/process level (P), or organizational level (O).
  a. Consulting with equipment manufacturer on design specifications
  b. Engineering design of mold
  c. Creating mold
  d. Moving materials from warehouse for test quantity
  e. Using direct materials for test quantity to judge conformity to design specifications
  f. Inspecting test quantity
  g. Preparing design specification changes based on test molds
  h. Depreciating small kiln used solely for test quantities
  i. Depreciating manufacturing building

LO8-3 E8-36. **Levels of costs** Baldacci Inc. has a casting machine that is used for three of the company's products. Each machine setup costs $20,445, and the machine was set up in June for six different production runs. The following information shows the units of output from each of the setups.

Setup #	Product #453	Product #529	Product #663
1	22,800		
2			840
3		15,200	
4	27,900		
5			60
6	17,800		

Chapter 8 Activity-Based Management and Activity-Based Costing

a. If total machine setup cost is allocated to all units of product, what is the setup cost per unit and total setup cost for Products #453, 529, and 663 during June?

b. If machine setup cost is allocated to each type of product made, what is the setup cost per unit of Products #453, 529, and 663 and the total cost of those products during June? (Round to two decimal places.)

c. If Baldacci Inc. had manufactured all similar products in a single production run, how would unit and total costs have changed during June? (Round to two decimal places.)

E8-37. Levels of costs Three clients (A, B, and C) use Babineaux Call Service's call center. During October, Babineaux initiated four new equipment advancements. The following information indicates the cost and benefits of each service: **LO8-3**

Service Type	Cost	Benefits Client	Estimated Calls Benefited
Service #359	$ 5,810	A	7,000
Service #360	7,085	A and	2,200
		B	4,300
Service #361	3,198	C	1,300
Service #362	4,887	C	2,700
	$20,980		17,500

a. First assume that the total cost of new equipment is allocated to all units benefited.
  1. What is the cost per estimated call?
  2. What is the total cost allocated to each client?

b. Next, assume that the total cost of new equipment is allocated to clients benefited.
  1. What is the cost per call benefited for each service type?
  2. What is the total cost allocated to each client?

c. Assume that Babineaux Call Service charges the costs to the clients as indicated in (b). Client A estimates that a total of 30,000 calls will be processed by Babineaux over the life of the equipment advances. How should Client A allocate the new costs to its callers?

E8-38. Levels of costs Leopold & Olney LLP has five partners and 12 staff accountants. The partners each work 2,100 hours per year and earn $350,000 annually. The staff accountants each work 2,600 hours per year and earn $80,000 annually. The firm's total annual budget for professional support available to partners and staff accountants is $312,750. The firm also spends $125,100 for administrative support that is used only by the partners. **LO8-3**

a. Assume that total support cost is considered a unit-level cost based on number of work hours. What is the support rate per labor hour?

b. If one audit engagement requires 60 partner hours and 220 staff accountant hours, how much professional support cost would be charged to the engagement using the rate determined in (a)?

c. Assume that support costs are considered batch-level costs based on number of work hours. What are the professional and administrative support rates per labor hour? (Round to two decimal places.)

d. If an audit engagement requires 60 partner hours and 220 staff accountant hours, how much support cost would be charged to the engagement using the rates determined in (c)?

E8-39. OH allocation using cost drivers Wambaugh Corp. has decided to implement an activity-based costing system for its in-house legal department. The legal department's primary expense is professional salaries, which are estimated for associated activities as follows: **LO8-4**

Reviewing supplier or customer contracts (Contracts)	$270,000
Reviewing regulatory compliance issues (Regulation)	379,500
Court actions (Court)	862,500

Management has determined that the appropriate cost allocation base for Contracts is the number of pages in the contract reviewed, for Regulation is the number of reviews, and for Court is number of hours of court time. For the year, the legal department reviewed 500,000 pages of contracts, responded to 750 regulatory review requests, and logged 3,750 hours in court.

a. Determine the allocation rate for each activity in the legal department.

b. What amount would be charged to a department that had 21,000 pages of contracts reviewed, made 27 regulatory review requests, and consumed 315 professional hours in court services during the year?
c. How can the developed rates be used for evaluating output relative to cost incurred in the legal department? What alternative does the firm have to maintaining an internal legal department and how might this choice affect costs?

LO8-4 E8-40. OH allocation using cost drivers Regis Place is a health-care facility that has been allocating its overhead costs to patients based on number of patient days. The facility's overhead costs total $3,620,400 per year and the facility (which operates monthly at capacity) has a total of 60 beds available. (Assume a 360-day year.) The facility's accountant is considering a new overhead allocation method using the following information:

OH Cost		Cost Driver (Quantity)	
Rooms (depreciation, cleaning, etc.)	$ 504,000	# of rooms (25 double)	35
Laundry	151,200	# of beds	60
Nursing care	1,314,000	# of nurse-hours annually	43,800
Physical therapy	960,000	# of hours of rehab	8,000
General services	691,200	# of patient days	?

Rooms are cleaned daily; laundry for rooms is done, on average, every other day.

a. How many patient days are available at Regis Place?
b. What is the current overhead rate per patient day? (Round to the nearest dollar.)
c. Using the individual cost drivers, what is the overhead rate for each type of cost? (Round to the nearest dollar.)
d. Assume a patient stayed at Regis Place for six days. The patient was in a single room and required six hours of nursing care and 30 hours of physical therapy. What overhead cost would be assigned to this patient under the current method of overhead allocation? What overhead cost would be assigned to this patient under the ABC method of overhead allocation?
e. Assume a patient stayed at Regis Place for six days. The patient was in a double room and required six hours of nursing care but did not require any physical therapy. What overhead cost would be assigned to this patient under the current method of overhead allocation? What overhead cost would be assigned to this patient under the ABC method of overhead allocation?

LO8-4 E8-41. ABC Bernacke Corp. is instituting an activity-based costing project in its ten-person purchasing department. Annual departmental overhead costs are $731,250. Because finding the best supplier takes the majority of effort in the department, most of the costs are allocated to this activity area. Many purchase orders are received in a single shipment.

Activity	Allocation Measure	Quantity	Total Cost
Find best suppliers	Number of telephone calls	75,000	$375,000
Issue purchase orders	Number of purchase orders	46,875	187,500
Review receiving reports	Number of receiving reports	28,125	168,750

One special-order product manufactured by the company required the following purchasing department activities: 25 telephone calls, 50 purchase orders, and 35 receipts.

a. What amount of purchasing department cost should be assigned to this product?
b. If 100 units of the product are manufactured during the year, what is the purchasing department cost per unit?
c. If purchasing department costs had been allocated using telephone calls as the allocation base, how much cost would have been assigned to this product?

LO8-4, 5 E8-42. ABC; product profitability Outerwear Inc. is concerned about the profitability of its regular gloves. Company managers are considering producing only the top-quality, fleece lined, gloves. The company is currently assigning the $2,000,000 of overhead costs to both types of gloves based on machine hours. Of the overhead, $800,000 is utilities related and the remainder is primarily related to quality control inspectors' salaries. The following information about the products is also available:

	Regular	Fleece-Lined
Number produced	2,000,000	1,400,000
Machine hours	170,000	30,000
Inspection hours	10,000	50,000
Revenues	$6,400,000	$5,600,000
Direct costs	$5,000,000	$4,400,000

a. Determine the total overhead cost assigned to each type of gloves using the current allocation system.
b. Determine the total overhead cost assigned to each type of gloves if more appropriate cost drivers were used.
c. Should the company stop producing the regular gloves? Explain.

E8-43. Product profitability Sandford Inc. manufactures lawn mowers and garden tractors. Lawn mowers are relatively simple to produce and are made in large quantities. Garden tractors are customized to individual wholesale customer specifications. The company produces and sells 300,000 lawn mowers and 30,000 garden tractors annually. Revenues and costs incurred for each product are as follows:

	Lawn Mowers	Garden Tractors
Revenue	$19,500,000	$17,850,000
Direct material	4,000,000	2,700,000
Direct labor ($20 per hour)	2,800,000	6,000,000
Overhead	?	?

Manufacturing overhead totals $3,960,000.

a. Calculate the profit (loss) in total and per unit for each product if overhead is assigned to product using a per-unit basis.
b. Calculate the profit (loss) in total and per unit for each product if overhead is assigned to products using a direct labor hour basis.
c. Assume that manufacturing overhead can be divided into two cost pools as follows: $1,320,000, which has a cost driver of direct labor hours, and $2,640,000, which has a cost driver of machine hours (totaling 150,000). Lawn mower production uses 25,000 machine hours; garden tractor production uses 125,000 machine hours. Calculate the profit (loss) in total and per unit for each product if overhead is assigned to products using these two overhead bases.
d. Does your answer in (a), (b), or (c) provide the best representation of the profit contributed by each product? Explain.

E8-44. Controlling OH; writing SailAway has changed its product line from general paints to specialized marine coatings, which has caused overhead costs to double. Costs affected include customer service, production scheduling, inventory control, and laboratory work. The company has decided to analyze and update its cost information and pricing practices. Although some large orders are still received, most current business is generated from products designed and produced in small lot sizes to meet specifically detailed environmental and technical requirements. Management believes that large orders are being penalized and small orders are receiving favorable cost (and, thus, selling price) treatment.

a. Indicate why the shift in product lines would have caused such major increases in overhead.
b. Is it possible that management is correct in its belief about the costs of large and small orders? If so, why?
c. Write a memo to management suggesting how it might change the cost accounting system to reflect the changes in the business.

E8-45. Benefits of ABC; writing The cost systems at many companies selling multiple products have become less than adequate in today's global competition. Managers often make important product decisions based on distorted cost information because the cost systems have been primarily designed to focus on inventory measurement. Current literature suggests that many manufacturing companies should have at least three cost systems, one each for inventory measurement, operational control, and activity-based costing.

a. Identify the purpose and characteristics of each of the following cost systems:
  1. Inventory measurement

2. Activity-based costing
   b. Discuss why a cost system developed for inventory valuation could distort product cost information.
   c. Describe the benefits that management can obtain from using activity-based costing.
   d. List the steps that a company using a traditional cost system would take to implement activity-based costing.

LO8-5 E8-46. Decision making; ethics; writing Many manufacturers are deciding to service only customers that buy $10,000 or more of products from the manufacturers annually. Manufacturers defend such policies by stating that they can provide better service to customers that handle more volume and more diverse product lines.

   a. Relate the concepts in the chapter to the decision of manufacturers to drop small customers.
   b. Are there any ethical implications of eliminating groups of customers that could be less profitable than others?
   c. Does activity-based costing adequately account for all costs that are related to a decision to eliminate a particular customer base? (*Hint:* Consider opportunity costs such as those related to reputation.)

LO8-6 E8-47. Applying time-driven activity-based costing The Chocolate Baker specializes in chocolate baked goods. The firm has long assessed the profitability of a product line by comparing revenues to the cost of goods sold. However, Barry White, the firm's new accountant, wants to use an activity-based costing system that takes into consideration the cost of the delivery person. Listed below are activity and cost information relating to two of Chocolate Baker's major products.

	Muffins	Cheesecake
Revenue	$53,000	$46,000
Cost of goods sold	26,000	21,000
Delivery Activity		
Number of deliveries	150	85
Average length of delivery	10 Minutes	15 Minutes
Cost per hour for delivery	$20.00	$20.00

Required
   a. What is the cost of the muffin delivery?
   b. What is the cost of the cheesecake delivery?
   c. What is the actual profitability of muffins?
   d. What is the actual profitability of cheesecakes?

LO8-6 E8-48. Applying time-driven activity-based costing A small tax firm operating during busy season has four employees who each work a total of 562.50 hours over a four month period. Operating costs for the period total $249,750.

The estimated time for each of the following three types of tax returns that are prepared follow.

1040 without itemized deductions	60 minutes
Form 1040 with Schedule A	75 minutes
Form 1120S for S Corporation	240 minutes

During the tax year, the tax firm completed 1,150 Form 1040s without itemized deductions, 700 Form 1040s with Schedule A, and 50 Form 1120s for S Corporations.
   a. What is the cost per type of tax return estimated using TDABC?
   b. What is the total estimated cost of the prepared tax returns and what is the cost of the unused capacity?

LO8-6 E8-49. Applying time-driven activity-based costing An insurance agency manages a separate call center that only handles renter insurance policies. The two agents set up new polices, renew policies, or refer the potential customers to other services. The following summary is provided for the year based on a TDABC analysis.

Activity	Quantity	Total Minutes	Total Cost
New policy	2,200	132,000	145,200
Renewal	2,400	36,000	39,600
Referral of service	350	1,750	1,925

a. What is the budgeted cost per minute for the agency services?
b. If the cost to staff the agency for the year is $191,400, how many total hours were budgeted?
c. What is the unit time in minutes, estimated for an agent's time to set up a new policy, a renewal, and to refer services?
d. What is the cost and estimated hours of unused capacity?
e. Is an additional agent needed to handle the current volume?
f. If activity is expected to increase by 10% in the next year, is an additional agent needed?

Problems

P8-50. Activity analysis Management at Glover & Lamb Inc. is concerned about controlling factory labor-related costs. The following summary is the result of an analysis of the major categories of labor costs for the year:

Category	Amount
Base wages	$63,000,000
Health-care benefits	10,500,000
Payroll taxes	5,018,832
Overtime	8,697,600
Training	1,875,000
Retirement benefits	6,898,500
Workers' compensation	1,199,940

Following are some of the potential cost drivers identified by the company for labor-related costs, along with their current year volume levels:

Potential Activity Driver	Current Year Volume Level
Average number of factory employees	2,100
Number of new hires	300
Number of regular labor hours worked	3,150,000
Number of overtime hours worked	288,000
Total factory wages paid	$71,697,600
Volume of production in units	12,000,000
Number of production process changes	600
Number of production schedule changes	375

a. For each cost pool, determine the cost per unit of the activity driver using the activity driver that you believe has the closest relationship to the cost pool.
b. Based on your judgments and calculations in (a), which activity driver should receive the most attention from company managers in their efforts to control labor-related costs? How much of the total labor-related cost is attributable to this activity driver?
c. In the contemporary environment, many firms ask their employees to work record levels of overtime. What activity driver does this practice suggest is a major contributor to labor-related costs? Explain.

P8-51. Cost drivers; ABC; analysis Boerne Community Hospital has been under increasing pressure to be accountable for its patient charges. The hospital's current pricing system is ad hoc, based on pricing norms for the geographical area; only direct costs for surgery, medication, and other treatments are explicitly considered. The hospital's controller has suggested that the hospital improve pricing policies by seeking a tighter relationship between costs and pricing. This approach would make prices for services less arbitrary. As a first step, the controller has determined that most costs can be assigned to one of three cost pools. The three cost pools follow along with the estimated amounts and activity drivers.

Activity Center	Amount	Activity Driver	Quantity
Professional salaries	$13,125,000	Professional hours	75,000 hours
Building costs	6,187,500	Square feet used	56,250 sq. ft.
Risk management	850,000	Patients served	2,500 patients

The hospital provides service in three broad categories. The services follow with their volume measures for the activity centers.

Service	Professional Hours	Square Feet	Number of Patients
Surgery	3,750	12,500	500
Housing patients	70,000	27,500	1,250
Outpatient care	1,250	16,250	750

a. What bases might be used as cost drivers to allocate the service center costs among the patients served by the hospital? Defend your selections.
b. The hospital currently charges an "add-on" rate calculated using professional hours to patients' direct charges. What rate is Boerne Community Hospital charging per hour? (Round to the nearest dollar.)
c. Determine the allocation rates for each activity center cost pool.
d. Allocate the activity center costs to the three services provided by the hospital.
e. Boerne Community Hospital has decided to estimate costs by activity center using professional hours. What is the cost per professional hour of each service? What would cause the cost per hour difference for the three services? (Round to the nearest dollar.)

LO8-4, 5 P8-52. ABC; pricing; writing McNeil Office makes standard metal five-drawer desks. Occasionally, the company takes custom orders. McNeil's overhead costs for a month in which no custom desks are produced are as follows:

Purchasing Department for raw material and supplies (20 purchase orders)	$10,000
Setting up machines for production runs (4 times per month after maintenance checks)	2,480
Utilities (based on 6,400 machine hours)	320
Supervisor salaries	16,000
Machine and building depreciation (fixed)	11,000
Quality control and inspections performed on random selection of desks each day; one quality control worker	5,000
Total overhead costs	$44,800

Factory operations are highly automated, and overhead is allocated to products based on machine hours.

In July, six orders were filled for custom desks. Selling prices were based on charges for actual direct material, actual direct labor, and the overhead rate per machine hour. During July, the following costs were incurred for 6,400 hours of machine time:

Purchasing Department for raw material and supplies (44 purchase orders)	$12,400
Setting up machines for production runs (18 times)	3,280
Utilities (based on 6,400 machine hours)	320
Supervisor salaries	16,000
Machine and building depreciation (fixed)	11,000
Quality control and inspections performed on random selection of desks each day; one quality control worker	5,960
Engineering design and specification costs	6,000
Total overhead costs	$54,960

a. How much of the purchasing department cost is variable and how much is fixed? What types of purchasing costs would fit into each of these categories?

b. Why might the number of machine setups have increased from four to 18 when only six custom orders were received?
c. Why might the cost of quality control and inspections have increased?
d. Why were engineering design and specification costs included during July?
e. If McNeil Office were to adopt activity-based costing, what would you suggest as the cost drivers for each of the overhead cost items?
f. What is the current predetermined overhead rate based on machine hours? Do you think the custom orders should have been priced using this rate per machine hour? Explain the reasoning for your answer.

P8-53. ABC Odyssey Inc. has a total of $2,362,500 in production overhead costs. The company's products and related statistics follow.

LO8-4

	Product A	Product B
Direct material in pounds	139,500	190,500
Direct labor hours	30,000	37,500
Machine hours	52,500	22,500
Number of setups	430	860
Number of units produced	15,000	7,500

Additional data: The 330,000 pounds of material were purchased for $544,500. One direct labor hour costs $12.

a. Assume that Odyssey Inc. uses direct labor hours to apply overhead to products. Determine the total cost for each product and the cost per unit.
b. Assume that Odyssey Inc. uses machine hours to apply overhead to products. Determine the total cost for each product and the cost per unit.
c. Assume that Odyssey Inc. uses the following activity centers, cost drivers, and costs to apply overhead to products:

Cost Pool	Cost Driver	Cost
Utilities	# of machine hours	$750,000
Setup	# of setups	193,500
Material handling	# of pounds of material	1,419,000

Determine the total cost for each product and the cost per unit.

P8-54. ABC Outdoor Texas makes umbrellas, gazebos, and chaise lounges. The company uses a traditional overhead allocation scheme and assigns overhead to products at the rate of $30 per direct labor hour. The costs per unit for each product group in the current year were as follows:

LO8-4

	Umbrellas	Gazebo	Chaise Lounges
Direct material	$12	$120	$ 12
Direct labor	18	135	45
Overhead	24	180	60
Total	$54	$435	$117

Because profitability has been lagging and competition has been getting more intense, Outdoor Texas is considering implementing an activity-based costing system for the following year. In analyzing the current year data, management determined that its $12,030,000 of factory overhead could be assigned to four basic activities: quality control, setups, material handling, and equipment operation. Data for the current year costs associated with each of the four activities follow.

Quality Control	Setups	Material Handling	Equipment Operation	Total Costs
$630,000	$600,000	$1,800,000	$14,970,000	$18,000,000

Management determined that the following allocation bases and total current year volumes for each allocation base could have been used for ABC.

Activity	Base
Quality control	Number of units produced
Setups	Number of setups
Material handling	Pounds of material used
Equipment operation	Number of machine hours

Volume measures for the current year for each product and each allocation base were as follows:

	Umbrellas	Gazebos	Chaise Lounges
Number of units	300,000	30,000	90,000
Number of setups	600	1,300	1,100
Pounds of material	1,200,000	3,000,000	1,800,000
Number of machine hours	600,000	1,100,000	1,300,000

a. How much direct labor time is needed to produce an umbrella, a gazebo, and a chaise lounge?
b. For the year, determine the total overhead allocated to each product group using the traditional allocation based on direct labor hours.
c. For the year, determine the total overhead that would have been allocated to each product group if activity-based costing were used. Compute the cost per unit for each product group.
d. Outdoor Texas has a policy of setting sales prices based on product costs. How would the sales prices using activity-based costing differ from those obtained using the traditional overhead allocation?

LO8-4 P8-55. ABC Reschman Co. manufactures two products. Following is a production and cost analysis for each product for the current year:[12]

Cost Component	Product A	Product B	Both Products	Cost
Units produced	10,000	10,000	20,000	
Raw material used (units)				
X	50,000	50,000	100,000	$800,000
Y		100,000	100,000	$200,000
Labor hours used				
Department 1				$682,000
Direct labor	20,000	5,000	25,000	$375,000
Indirect labor				
Inspections	2,500	2,400	4,900	
Machine operations	5,000	10,000	15,000	
Setups	252	248	500	
Department 2				$462,000
Direct labor	5,000	5,000	10,000	$200,000
Indirect labor				
Inspection	2,680	5,000	7,680	
Machine operations	1,000	3,860	4,860	
Setups	250	310	560	
Machine hours used				
Department 1	5,000	10,000	15,000	$400,000
Department 2	5,000	20,000	25,000	$800,000
Power used (kW hours)				$400,000
Department 1			1,500,000	
Department 2			8,500,000	
Other activity data				
Building occupancy				$1,000,000
Purchasing				$100,000
Number of purchase orders				
Material X			200	
Material			300	
Square feet occupied				
Purchasing			10,000	
Power			40,000	
Department 1			200,000	
Department 2			250,000	

[12] Source: Adapted from Harold P. Roth and A. Faye Borthick, "Getting Closer to Real Product Costs," *Management Accounting* (May 1989), pp. 28–33. Reprinted from *Management Accounting*. Copyright by Institute of Management Accountants, Montvale, NJ.

Elysia Sanderson, the firm's cost accountant, has just returned from a seminar on activity-based costing. To apply the concepts she learned, she decides to analyze the costs incurred for Products A and B on an activity basis. In doing so, she specifies the following first and second allocation processes:

First Stage: Allocations to Departments

Cost Pool	Cost Object	Activity Allocation Base
Power	Departments	Kilowatt hours
Purchasing	Material	Number of purchase orders
Building occupancy	Departments	Square feet occupied

Second Stage: Allocations to Products

Cost Pool	Cost Object	Activity Allocation Base
Departments		
Indirect labor	Products	Hours worked
Power	Products	Machine hours
Machinery related	Products	Machine hours
Building occupancy	Products	Machine hours
Material purchasing	Products	Materials used

a. Determine the total overhead for Reschman Co.
b. Determine the plantwide overhead rate for the company, assuming the use of direct labor hours.
c. Determine the cost per unit of Product A and Product B, using the overhead rate found in (b).
d. Determine the cost allocations to departments (first-stage allocations). Allocate costs from the departments in the following order: building occupancy, purchasing, and power. Finish the cost allocations for one department to get an "adjusted" cost to allocate to the next department.
e. Using the allocations found in (d), determine the cost allocations to products (second-stage allocations).
f. Determine the cost per unit of Product A and Product B using the overhead allocations found in (e).

P8-56. ABC; pricing Chester Inc. has identified activity centers to which overhead costs are assigned. The cost pool amounts for these centers and their selected activity drivers for the year follow.

LO8-4, 5

Activity Centers	Costs	Activity Drivers
Utilities	$1,800,000	90,000 machine hours
Scheduling and setup	1,638,000	1,170 setups
Material handling	3,840,000	2,400,000 pounds of material

The company's products and other operating statistics follow.

	Products A	B	C
Direct costs	$120,000	$120,000	$135,000
Machine hours	45,000	15,000	30,000
Number of setups	195	570	405
Pounds of material	750,000	450,000	1,200,000
Number of units produced	60,000	30,000	90,000
Direct labor hours	48,000	27,000	75,000

a. Determine unit product cost using the appropriate cost drivers for each product.
b. Before it installed an ABC system, Chester used a traditional costing system that allocated factory overhead to products using direct labor hours. The firm operates in a competitive market and sets product prices at cost plus a 25 percent markup.
 1. Calculate unit costs based on traditional costing. (Round to two decimal places.)
 2. Determine selling prices based on unit costs for traditional costing and for ABC. (Round to two decimal places.)
c. Discuss the problems related to setting prices based on traditional costing and explain how ABC improves the information.

LO8-4, 5 P8-57. **ABC; pricing** Strickland Co. currently charges manufacturing overhead costs to products using machine hours. However, company management believes that the use of ABC would provide more realistic cost estimates and, in turn, give the company an edge in pricing over its competitors. Strickland's accountant and production manager have provided the following budgeted information for next year, given a budgeted capacity of 1,000,000 machine hours:[13]

Type of Manufacturing Cost	Cost Amount
Electric power	$ 500,000
Work cells	3,000,000
Material handling	1,000,000
Quality control inspections	1,000,000
Machine setups	350,000
Total budgeted overhead costs	$5,850,000

Type of Manufacturing Cost	Activity Driver
Electric power	200,000 kilowatt hours
Work cells	300,000 square feet
Material handling	200,000 material moves
Quality control inspections	50,000 inspections
Machine setups	25,000 setups

A national construction company approached Pete Lang, the VP of marketing, about a bid for 2,500 doors. Lang asked the cost accountant to prepare a cost estimate for producing the 2,500 doors; he received the following data:

Direct material cost	$ 50,000
Direct labor cost	$150,000
Machine hours	5,000
Direct labor hours	2,500
Electric power—kilowatt hours	500
Work cells—square feet	1,000
Number of material handling moves	20
Number of quality control inspections	15
Number of setups	6

   a. What is the predetermined overhead rate if the traditional measure of machine hours is used?
   b. What is the manufacturing cost per door as presently accounted for?
   c. What is the manufacturing cost per door under the proposed ABC method?
   d. If the two cost systems will result in different cost estimates, which cost accounting system is preferable as a pricing base, and why?
   e. If activity-based management were implemented prior to an ABC system, which of the manufacturing overhead costs might be reduced or eliminated? Why?

LO8-4, 5 P8-58. **ABC; decision making** Casito Corp. manufactures multiple types of products; however, most of the company's sales are from Product #347 and Product #658. Product #347 has been a standard in the industry for several years; the market for this product is competitive and price sensitive. Casito plans to sell 65,000 units of Product #347 next year at a price of $150 per unit. Product #658 is a recent addition to Casito's product line. This product incorporates the latest technology and can be sold at a premium price; the company expects to sell 40,000 units of this product next year for $300 per unit.

Casito's management group is meeting to discuss strategies, and the current topic of conversation is how to spend the sales and promotion budget. The sales manager believes that the market share for Product #347 could be expanded by concentrating Casito's promotional efforts in this area. However, the production manager wants to target a larger market share for Product #658. He says, "The cost sheets I get show that the contribution from Product #658 is more than twice that from Product #347. I know we get a premium price for this product; selling it should help overall profitability." Casito has the following costs for the two products:

---

[13] **Source:** Adapted from Nabil Hassa, Herbert E. Brown, and Paul M. Saunders, "Management Accounting Case Study: Beaver Window Inc.," *Management Accounting Campus Report* (Fall 1990). Copyright Institute of Management Accountants, Montvale, NJ.

Chapter 8 Activity-Based Management and Activity-Based Costing

	Product #347	Product #658
Direct material	$80	$140
Direct labor	1.5 hours	4.0 hours
Machine time	0.5 hours	1.5 hours

Variable manufacturing overhead is currently applied on the basis of direct labor hours. For next year, variable manufacturing overhead is budgeted at $1,120,000 for a total of 280,000 direct labor hours. The hourly rates for machine time and direct labor are $10 and $14, respectively. Casito applies a material handling charge at 10 percent of material cost; this material handling charge is not included in variable manufacturing overhead. Total expenditures for next year for materials are budgeted at $10,800,000.

Marc Alexander, Casito's controller, believes that before management decides to allocate marketing funds to individual products, it might be worthwhile to look at these products on the basis of the activities involved in their production. Alexander has prepared the following schedule to help the management group understand this concept:

	Budgeted Cost	Cost Driver	Annual Activity for Cost Driver
Material overhead			
Procurement	$ 400,000	Number of parts	4,000,000 parts
Production scheduling	220,000	Number of units	110,000 units
Packaging and shipping	440,000	Number of units	110,000 units
	$1,060,000		
Variable overhead			
Machine setup	$ 446,000	Number of setups	278,750 setups
Hazardous waste disposal	48,000	Pounds of waste	16,000 pounds
Quality control	560,000	Number of inspections	160,000 inspections
General supplies	66,000	Number of units	110,000 units
	$1,120,000		
Manufacturing			
Machine insertion	$1,200,000	Number of parts	3,000,000 parts
Manual insertion	4,000,000	Number of parts	1,000,000 parts
Wave soldering	132,000	Number of units	110,000 units
	$5,332,000		

Required per Unit		
	Product #347	Product #658
Parts	25	55
Machine insertions of parts	24	35
Manual insertions of parts	1	20
Machine setups	2	3
Hazardous waste	0.02 lb.	0.35 lb.
Inspections	1	2

Alexander wants to calculate a new cost, using appropriate cost drivers, for each product. The new cost drivers would replace the direct labor, machine time, and overhead costs in the current costing system.

a. Identify at least four general advantages associated with activity-based costing.
b. On the basis of current costs, calculate the total contribution expected for next year for
   1. Product #347.   2. Product #658.
c. On the basis of activity-based costs, calculate the total contribution expected for next year for
   1. Product #347.   2. Product #658.
d. Explain how the comparison of the results of the two costing methods could impact the decisions made by Casito's management group.

© Cambridge Business Publishers

LO8-4, 5 **P8-59. ABC; product profitability** Delgado Design provides a wide range of engineering and architectural consulting services through its three offices in Altamont, Ballard, and Circleville. The company allocates resources and bonuses to the three offices based on the net income reported for the period. Following are the performance results for the year:

	Altamont	Ballard	Circleville	Total
Sales	$1,500,000	$1,419,000	$1,067,000	$3,986,000
Less: Direct material	(281,000)	(421,000)	(185,000)	(887,000)
Direct labor	(382,000)	(317,000)	(325,000)	(1,024,000)
Overhead	(725,800)	(602,300)	(617,500)	(1,945,600)
Net income	$ 111,200	$ 78,700	$ (60,500)	$ 129,400

Overhead items are accumulated in one overhead pool and allocated to the offices based on direct labor dollars. For the year, this predetermined overhead rate was $1.90 for every direct labor dollar incurred. The overhead pool includes rent, depreciation, taxes, etc., regardless of which office incurred the expense. This method of accumulating costs forces the offices to absorb a portion of the overhead incurred by other offices.

Management is concerned with the results of the year's performance reports. During a review of overhead costs, it became apparent that many items of overhead are not correlated with direct labor dollars as previously assumed. Management decided that applying overhead based on activity-based costing and direct tracing, when possible, should provide a more accurate picture of the profitability of each office. An analysis of the overhead revealed that the following dollars for rent, utilities, depreciation, and taxes could be traced directly to the office that incurred the overhead:

	Altamont	Ballard	Circleville	Total
Office overhead	$195,000	$286,100	$203,500	$684,600

Activity pools and activity drivers were determined from the accounting records and staff surveys as follows:

Activity Pools		Activity Driver	Altamont	Ballard	Circleville
General administration	$ 409,000	Direct labor	$ 386,346	$ 305,010	$325,344
Project costing	48,000	# of timesheet entries	6,300	4,060	3,640
Accounts payable/receiving	139,000	# of vendor invoices	1,035	874	391
Accounts receivable	47,000	# of client invoices	572	429	99
Payroll/mail sort & delivery	30,000	# of employees	34	39	27
Personnel recruiting	38,000	# of new hires	8	4	8
Employee insur. processing	14,000	# of insur. claims filed	238	273	189
Proposals	139,000	# of proposals	195	245	60
Sales meetings, sales aids	202,000	Contracted sales	$1,821,600	$1,404,150	$569,250
Shipping	24,000	# of projects	100	125	25
Ordering	48,000	# of purchase orders	126	102	72
Duplicating costs	46,000	# of copies duplicated	160,734	145,782	67,284
Blueprinting	77,000	# of blueprints	38,790	31,032	16,378
	$1,261,000				

a. How much overhead cost should be assigned to each office based on activity-based costing concepts?
b. What is the contribution of each office before subtracting the results obtained in (a)?
c. What is the profitability of each office using activity-based costing?
d. Evaluate the concerns of management regarding the traditional costing technique currently used.

IMA ADAPTED

Chapter 8 Activity-Based Management and Activity-Based Costing

P8-60. ABC; pricing Craig Oldenettel owns and manages a commercial cold-storage warehouse that has 100,000 cubic feet of storage capacity. Historically, he has charged customers a flat rate of $0.16 per pound per month for goods stored.

LO8-4, 5

In the past two years, Oldenettel has become dissatisfied with the profitability of the warehouse operation. Despite the fact that the warehouse remains relatively full, revenues have not kept pace with operating costs. Recently, Oldenettel asked his accountant, Pamela Beattie, to improve his understanding of how activity-based costing could help him revise the pricing formula. Beattie has determined that most costs can be associated with one of four activities. Those activities and their related costs, volume measures, and volume levels for the year follow:[14]

Activity	Cost	Monthly Volume Measure	
Send/receive goods	$50,000	Weight in pounds	500,000
Store goods	16,000	Volume in cubic feet	80,000
Move goods	20,000	Volume in square feet	5,000
Identify goods	8,000	Number of packages	500

a. Based on the activity cost and volume data, determine the amount of cost assigned to the following customers, whose goods were all received on the first day of last month.

Customer	Weight of Order in Pounds	Cubic Feet	Square Feet	Number of Packages
Barfield	40,000	3,200	1,100	15
Glover	40,000	800	600	10
Dozier	40,000	1,400	1,900	50

b. Determine the price to be charged to each customer under the existing pricing plan.
c. Determine the price to be charged using ABC, assuming Oldenettel would base the price on the cost determined in (a) plus a markup of 40 percent.
d. How well does Oldenettel's existing pricing plan capture the costs for providing the warehouse services? Explain.

P8-61. Activity analysis, ABC; pricing; cost drivers Power Production manufactures two product models: Regular and Special. The following information was taken from the accounting records for the first quarter of the year.

LO8-1, 3, 4, 5

	Regular	Special	Total
Units produced	80,000	20,000	100,000
Material cost	$320,000	$180,000	$500,000
Labor cost	$480,000	$140,000	$620,000

Power currently uses a traditional cost accounting system where total overhead cost is assigned to products based on the total number of units produced. Company president Sue Power has approached the controller, Keisha Connaery, with concerns about sagging profit margins and her inability to explain competitors' pricing of similar products. Connaery suggests that the company explore the possibility of a costing system that is based less on volume and more on identifying the consumption of resources by products (given manufacturing process activities). Connaery identifies the following overhead costs related to the production process:

Wages and costs related to machine setups	$ 360,000
Material handling costs	480,000
Quality control costs	120,000
Other overhead costs related to units produced	240,000
Total	$1,200,000

---

[14] Source: Adapted from Harold P. Roth and Linda T. Sims, "Costing for Warehousing and Distribution," *Management Accounting* (August 1991), pp. 42–45. Reprinted from *Management Accounting*. Copyright by Institute of Management Accountants, Montvale, NJ.

During the quarter, there were 40 machine setups for production: 20 from Special to Regular and 20 from Regular to Special. Connaery believes that the number of setups is the most appropriate cost driver of machine setup costs and material cost is the primary indicator of material handling costs. The Special model uses more expensive and difficult-to-handle materials. Additionally, each Special unit is hand-inspected by quality control personnel because it is more complex and has more parts than a Regular unit. Quality control inspectors are paid $40 per hour; examination of payroll time sheets indicates that the inspectors spent 50 percent more hours inspecting Special units than Regular units. Finally, Connaery thinks the remaining 30 percent of overhead costs are related to the number of units produced.

a. Using a traditional, volume-based overhead rate, determine the overhead cost per unit of the Regular and Special units.
b. Using the information provided by Connaery, determine the overhead cost per unit of the Regular and Special Units using an activity-based costing system.
c. What is the total per-unit cost of the Regular and Special Units under each overhead costing system?
d. Compute the amount of product cross-subsidization per unit that was taking place under the traditional costing system.
e. Identify potential non-value-added activities in Power's current manufacturing system.
f. What suggestions would you have for Sue Power to improve the competitiveness of the company's products in the marketplace?

LO8-1, 3, 4, 5 **P8-62.** **Activity analysis, ABC; pricing; cost drivers; decision making** Jessica Corporation has identified the following overhead costs and cost drivers for the coming year:

Overhead Item	Cost Driver	Budgeted Cost	Budgeted Activity Level
Machine setup	Number of setups	$ 20,000	200
Inspection	Number of inspections	130,000	6,500
Material handling	Number of material moves	80,000	8,000
Engineering	Engineering hours	50,000	1,000
		$280,000	

The following information was collected on three jobs that were completed during the year:

	Job 101	Job 102	Job 103
Direct material	$5,000	$12,000	$8,000
Direct labor	$2,000	$ 2,000	$4,000
Units completed	100	50	200
Number of setups	1	2	4
Number of inspections	20	10	30
Number of material moves	30	10	50
Engineering hours	10	50	10

Budgeted direct labor cost was $100,000, and budgeted direct material cost was $280,000.

a. If Jessica Corp. uses activity-based costing, how much overhead cost should be assigned to Job 101?
b. If Jessica Corp. uses activity-based costing, compute the cost of each unit of Job 102.
c. Jessica Corp. prices its products at 140 percent of cost. If activity-based costing is used, what price should it set for each unit of Job 103?
d. If Jessica Corp. used a traditional accounting system and allocated overhead based on direct labor cost, by how much would each unit of Job 103 be over- or under-costed compared to activity-based costing? What would be the management implications of this difference?
e. Identify any non-value-added activities or activities that may be currently necessary but appear to be inefficient in Jessica Corp.'s production process. Explain what steps the company management could take to improve the production process and potentially lower manufacturing costs.
f. Jessica Corp. is considering outsourcing inspections to an outside company that would perform the inspections for $10 apiece. What are the potential total savings if Jessica outsources the inspections? What other factors should company management consider before making this decision?

P8-63. ABC; pricing; cost drivers Believing that its traditional cost system may be providing misleading information, Missoula Corporation is considering an activity-based costing (ABC) approach. Missoula Corporation employs a full-cost system and has been applying its manufacturing overhead on the basis of machine hours. The organization plans on using 50,000 direct labor hours and 30,000 machine hours in the following year. The following data show the manufacturing overhead that is budgeted:

LO8-3, 5

Activity	Cost Driver	Budgeted Cost Driver	Budgeted Activity Cost
Material handling	Number of parts handled	6,000,000	$ 720,000
Setup costs	Number of setups	750	315,000
Machining costs	Machine hours	30,000	540,000
Quality control	Number of batches	500	225,000
	Total manufacturing overhead cost		$1,800,000

Cost, sales, and production data for one of the company's products for the coming year are as follows:

Direct material cost per unit	$4.40
Direct labor cost per unit (0.05 DLH @ $15 per DLH)	0.75
Total	$5.15
Sales and production data:	
Expected sales	20,000 units
Batch size	5,000 units
Setups	2 per batch
Total parts per finished unit	5 parts
Machine hours required	80 MHs per batch

a. Compute the per-unit cost for this product if Missoula uses the traditional full-cost system.
b. Compute the per-unit cost for this product if Missoula employs an activity-based costing system.
c. Assume the company wishes to achieve a gross profit rate of 40 percent. Determine the selling price that would be required based on your answers to (a) and (b).

CIA ADAPTED

P8-64. ABC; pricing Classic Confections makes very elaborate wedding cakes to order. The company's owner, Sandra Tillson, has provided the following data concerning the activity rates in its activity-based costing system:

LO8-4, 5

Activity Cost Pools	Activity Rate
Guest related	$0.90 per guest
Tier related	$34.41 per tier
Order related	$150.00 per order

The measure of activity for the size-related activity cost pool is the number of planned guests at the wedding reception. The greater the number of guests, the larger the cake. The measure of complexity is the number of cake tiers. The activity measure for the order-related cost pool is the number of orders. (Each wedding involves one order.) The activity rates include the costs of raw ingredients such as flour, sugar, eggs, and shortening. The activity rates do not include the costs of purchased decorations such as miniature statues and wedding bells, which are accounted for separately. The average wedding has 125 guests and generally requires a three-tiered cake.

Data concerning two recent orders appear below:

	Sacks Wedding	Nussbaum Wedding
Number of reception guests	50	164
Number of tiers on the cake	1	5
Cost of purchased decorations for cake	$22.50	$58.86

a. What amount would the company have to charge for the Sacks wedding cake to break even on that cake?
b. Assuming that the company charges $650 for the Nussbaum wedding cake, what would be the overall gross margin on the order?
c. Karen O'Brien wants to order a special cake for her 25th wedding anniversary celebration. She wants the cake to be four tiers but, in addition, would like 20 special flowers added to the top of the cake, which requires very intricate detailing instead of purchased decorations. O'Brien expects that attendance at the anniversary party will be 200 people. If Tillson decides to charge $5 for each special flower, which price should she quote? What price should be charged if the company wants to make an overall gross margin of 35 percent on the O'Brien order?
d. Suppose that the company decides that the present activity-based costing system is too complex and that all costs (except for the costs of purchased decorations) should be allocated on the basis of the number of guests. In that event, what would you expect to happen to the costs of cakes for receptions with more than the average number of guests and for receptions with fewer than the average number of guests? Explain your answer.

CIA ADAPTED

LO8-4, 5 P8-65. ABC; pricing Treffle Molding Company manufactures two products: large jar covers and small bottle caps. Large jar covers require special handling. Each cover must be individually sanded on a special machine to remove excess material (referred to as "flash") from the units. Covers are sanded at the rate of 200 jar covers per hour. Jar covers also require special handling during the packaging process as they are hand-packed in special cartons with foam protection to avoid breakage during shipment. Special packaging materials are $5 per carton; each carton holds 250 jar covers.

Small bottle caps are processed in batches of 5,000 units and do not require use of the machine sander. One employee can process a load of small bottle caps in two hours.

The accounting department has established the following information related to overhead cost pools and cost drivers:

Overhead Cost Pool	Budgeted Annual Overhead Cost	Cost Driver	Budgeted Activity of Cost Driver
Engineering	$300,000	Engineering hours	3,000 hours
Machine setups	$ 50,000	Number of setups	100 setups
Material purchase and support	$200,000	Number of pounds of material	2,000,000 pounds
Machine sanding	$100,000	Machine hours	10,000 hours
Product certification	$270,000	Number of orders	6,000 orders

Treffle employs ten direct labor employees. Each employee averages 2,000 hours per year and is paid $25 per hour.

During August, Treffle received an order for 1,000 jar covers from Ravel Cosmetics and an order for 10,000 bottle caps from Nortell Skin Products. Additional information related to each order appears as follows:

	Ravel	Nortell
Machine setups	4	1
Raw material ($0.20 per pound)	$200	$500
Engineering hours	10	2
Direct labor hours	4	2

a. Compute the total overhead that should be charged to each order using activity-based costing.
b. Compute the total overhead that would be assigned to each order if Treffle uses a single, predetermined overhead rate based on direct labor hours.
c. Compute the full cost per unit under traditional costing and under activity-based costing. The company quotes all orders on a cost-per-1,000-units basis.
d. Analyze the difference in the cost per order between traditional and ABC. To what factors can the difference be attributed?
e. Based on the costs computed in (c), what selling price per unit would Treffle have to charge for each order to earn a gross profit of 40 percent on the order?
f. The president of Treffle Molding Company, James Mahoney, is upset that the buyer for Ravel Cosmetics insists on small deliveries of each order, resulting in frequent setups to complete each order. How can Mahoney improve this situation?

Chapter 8 Activity-Based Management and Activity-Based Costing   8-53

P8-66. Product complexity; writing Strategic Supply is a world leader in the production of electronic test and measurement instruments. The company had experienced almost uninterrupted growth, but recently, the low-priced end of its Portables Division's product line was challenged by the aggressive low-price strategy of several Japanese competitors. These Japanese companies set prices 25 percent below Strategic's prevailing prices. To compete, the division needed to reduce costs and increase customer value by increasing operational efficiency.

LO8-5

The division took steps to implement just-in-time delivery and scheduling techniques as well as a total quality control program and to involve people techniques that moved responsibility for problem solving down to the operating level of the division. The results of these changes were impressive: substantial reductions in cycle time, direct labor hours per unit, and inventory levels as well as increases in output dollars per person per day and in operating income. The cost accounting system was providing information, however, that did not seem to support the changes.

Total overhead cost for the division was $10,000,000; of this, 55 percent seemed to be related to materials and 45 percent to conversion. Material-related costs pertain to procurement, receiving, inspection, stockroom personnel, and so on. Conversion-related costs pertain to direct labor, supervision, and process-related engineering. All overhead was applied on the basis of direct labor.

The division decided to concentrate efforts on revamping the application system for material-related overhead. Managers believed the majority of material overhead (MOH) costs were related to the maintenance and handling of each different part number. Other types of MOH costs were driven by the value of parts, absolute number of parts, and each use of a different part number.

At this time, the division used 8,000 different parts, each in extremely different quantities. For example, annual usage of one part was 35,000 units; usage of another part was only 200 units. The division decided that MOH costs would decrease if a smaller number of different parts were used in the products.[15]

   a. Why would MOH have decreased if parts were standardized?
   b. Using the numbers given, develop a cost allocation method for MOH to quantify and communicate the strategy of parts standardization.
   c. Explain how the use of the method developed in (b) would support the strategy of parts standardization.
   d. Is any method that applies the entire MOH cost pool on the basis of one cost driver sufficiently accurate for complex products? Explain.
   e. Are MOH product costing rates developed for management reporting appropriate for inventory valuation for external reporting? Why or why not?

P8-67. Decision making; writing Companies that want to be more globally competitive can consider the implementation of activity-based management (ABM). Such companies often have used other initiatives that involve higher efficiency, effectiveness, or output quality. These same initiatives are typically consistent with and supportive of ABM.

LO8-5

   a. In what other types of "initiatives" might such global companies engage?
   b. How might ABM and activity-based costing (ABC) help a company in its quest to achieve world-class status?
   c. For any significant initiative, senior management commitment is generally required. Would it be equally important to have top management support if a company were instituting ABC rather than ABM? Justify your answer.
   d. Assume that you are a member of top management in a large organization. Do you think implementation of ABM or ABC would be more valuable? Explain the rationale for your answer.

P8-68. Decision making; ethics; writing As the chief executive officer of a large corporation, you have decided, after discussion with production and accounting personnel, to implement activity-based management concepts. Your goal is to reduce cycle time and, in turn, costs. A primary way to accomplish this goal is to install highly automated equipment in your plant, which would then displace approximately 60 percent of your workforce. Your company is the major employer in the area of the country where it is located.

LO8-5

   a. Discuss the pros and cons of installing the equipment from the perspective of your (1) stockholders, (2) employees, and (3) customers.
   b. How would you explain to a worker that his or her job is a non-value-added activity?
   c. What alternatives might you have that could accomplish the goal of reducing cycle time but not create economic havoc for the local area?

---

[15] **Source:** Adapted from Michael A. Robinson, ed., *Cases from Management Accounting Practice*, No. 5 (Montvale, NJ: National Association of Accountants, 1989), pp. 13–17. Copyright by Institute of Management Accountants (formerly National Association of Accountants), Montvale, NJ.

© Cambridge Business Publishers

LO8-3, 6 **P8-69. ABC costing for a service organization** **Molitor Financial Group** is a full-service residential mortgage company in the Chicago area that operates in a very competitive market. Assume management is concerned about operating costs associated with processing mortgage applications and has decided to install an ABC costing system to help them get a handle on costs. Although labor hours seem to be the primary driver of the cost of processing a new mortgage, the labor cost for the different activities involved in processing new loans varies widely. The Accounting Department has provided the following data for the company's five major cost pools for the current year.

Activity Cost Pools		Activity Drivers	
Taking customer applications	$ 306,000	Time—assistant managers	3,600 hours
Conducting credit investigations	378,000	Time—credit managers	5,400 hours
Underwriting	405,000	Time—Underwriting Department	5,400 hours
Preparing loan packages	594,000	Time—Processing Department	10,800 hours
Closing loans	396,000	Time—Legal Department	3,600 hours
	$2,079,000		28,800 hours

During the year, the company processed and issued 900 new mortgages, two of which are summarized here with regard to activities used to process the mortgages.

	Loan 7023	Loan 8955
Application processing hours	2.00	4.00
Credit investigating hours	3.00	5.00
Underwriting hours	6.00	6.00
Processing hours	9.00	18.00
Legal hours	4.00	6.00
Total hours	24.00	39.00

a. Determine the cost per unit of activity for each activity cost pool.
b. Determine the cost of processing loans 7023 and 8955.
c. Determine the cost of preparing loans 7023 and 8955 assuming that an average cost per hour for all activities is used.
d. Compare and discuss your answers to requirements (*b*) and (*c*).

LO8-3, 6 **P8-70. ABC—a service application** Grand Haven is a senior living community that offers a full range of services including independent living, assisted living, and skilled nursing care. The assisted living division provides residential space, meals, and medical services (MS) to its residents. The current costing system adds the cost of all of these services (space, meals, and MS) and divides by total resident days to get a cost per resident day. Recognizing that MS tends to vary significantly among the residents, Grand Haven's accountant recommended that an ABC system be designed to calculate more accurately the cost of MS provided to residents. She decided that residents should be classified into four categories (A, B, C, D) based on the level of services received, with group A representing the lowest level of service and D representing the highest level of service. Two cost drivers being considered for measuring MS costs are number of assistance calls and number of assistant contacts. A contact is registered each time an assistance professional provides medical services or aid to a resident. The accountant has gathered the following data for the most recent annual period.

Resident Classification	Annual Resident Days	Annual Assistance Hours	Number of Assistance Contacts
A	18,000	9,100	27,000
B	10,000	22,500	31,000
C	5,500	23,000	27,500
D	3,000	18,400	24,000
	36,500	73,000	109,500

Chapter 8 Activity-Based Management and Activity-Based Costing   8-55

> Other data
> Total cost of medical services for the period $4,927,500
> Total cost of meals and residential space $2,591,500

    a. Determine the total cost of a resident day using the current system.
    b. Determine the ABC cost of a resident day for each category of residents using assistance hours as the cost driver for medical services and resident days as the cost driver for meals and residential space.
    c. Determine the ABC cost of a resident day for each category of residents using assistance contacts as the cost driver for medical services and resident days as the cost driver for meals and residential space.
    d. Which cost driver do you think provides the more accurate measure of the cost per day for a Grand Haven resident?

Review Solutions

Review 8-1

a.

Activity	Time (hours)	Value-Added or Non-Value Added
Receive materials.	2.00	Non-value added
Store materials	48.00	Non-value added
Mix materials	0.50	Value added
Form can	0.10	Value added
Insert materials and close battery	0.10	Value added
Test batteries and insert into storage trays.	0.10	Non-value added
Age batteries for 1 day before second battery test.	24.00	Non-value added
Add label to batteries	0.10	Value added
Retest batteries	0.25	Non-value added
Move to packaging department	6.00	Non-value added
Store batteries	24.00	Non-value added
Package batteries.	1.00	Value added

    b. With the information from part *a* which differentiates value added from non-value added activities, the company could create a value chart. A value chart will monetize the time spent on non-value-added activities which emphasizes the cost of such activities. This allows the company to make decisions on possible cost controlling activities. Controlling costs increases the company's margins on sales, thus increasing overall profitability.

Review 8-2

    a. Cycle time: 2.00 + 48.00 + 0.50 + 0.10 + 0.10 + 0.10 + 24.00 + 0.10 + 0.25 + 6.00 + 24.00 + 1.00 = 106.15 hours
    b. MCE: 1.80 ÷ 106.15 = 1.7%
    c. Management can measure and track MCE as a way to control NVA activities. The lower the MCE, the greater proportion of NVA activities to total, overall activities. If 10% is a typical MCE level, at 1.7%, this company is well below that level. Management should determine which of the non-value-added activities are the most costly and first work to reduce those activities. By monitoring the MCE, management will be able to track its progress in reducing NVA.

Review 8-3

    a. 1. **Square footage of occupied space.** Because storage costs are typically driven by space, square footage occupied would likely be a better indicator of costs as compared to number of units. For example, the type of unit may be small and take up minimal storage space.
        2. **Pounds of materials received.** Freight charges are based upon weight and dimensions. Thus, pounds of material would be a better indicator than the number of product types received.
        3. **Machine hours.** Costs related to equipment would be driven by its related hours versus hours incurred by the laborers. In fact, in a highly automated environment, direct labor hours may be minimal.

© Cambridge Business Publishers

4. **Number of quality inspections.** Quality costs would likely be tied to the number of inspections versus a more general indicator such as an increase in hours of operation.
5. **Number of engineering change orders.** The number of change orders would be a better indicator of costs because this would indicate work being performed. Also, the number of engineers doesn't take into account actual hours worked or the amount of work performed.
6. **Number of service tickets.** If support is initiated with a service ticket, costs can be associated with the number of tickets. The number of products shipped doesn't indicate how much information technology support was needed.
7. **Number of design changes.** Costs would be driven by the number of design changes required. The number of clicks doesn't indicate what costs were required to establish the digital marketing asset(s).

b. Using a unit-level cost driver will result in less accurate cost allocation to the cost objects (products). Allocating indirect costs to products is an estimation process. However, if the cost driver used to allocate costs is not the cause of the cost, than the cost allocation is not an accurate measure of how costs were incurred across products. This means that with flawed cost allocations, some products will be undercosted and some products will be overcosted. If prices are based on cost estimates, some products will be priced too high and others too low.

Review 8-4

a. Overhead costs for standard items: ($1,200,000 ÷ 120,000) × 102,000 = $1,020,000
   Overhead costs for custom items: ($1,200,000 ÷ 120,000) × 18,000 = $180,000

b. Overhead costs for standard items: (($720,000 ÷ 36,000) × 6,000) + (($480,000 ÷ 120,000) × 102,000) = $528,000.
   Overhead costs for custom items: (($720,000 ÷ 36,000) × 30,000) + (($480,000 ÷ 120,000) × 18,000) = $672,000.

c. Yes, this example demonstrates cost-cross subsidization because standard units were overcosted while custom items were undercosted under the current (traditional) allocation system. In fact, standard item costs are almost two times higher under the current cost allocation system. This means that management is making decisions based on inaccurate information. For example, if management believes that custom items only cost $180,000 instead of $672,000, they could be drastically underpricing the custom products. If management thinks that custom products are profitable, they would not be prioritizing cost control efforts which results in lower overall profitability due to the custom product's excessive drain on resources.

Review 8-5

a. Total profit for standard items: $3,840,000 − $3,000,000 − $1,020,000 = $(180,000)
   Total profit for custom items: $3,360,000 − $2,640,000 − $180,000 = $540,000

b. Total profit for standard items: $3,840,000 − $3,000,000 − $528,000 = $312,000
   Total profit for custom items: $3,360,000 − $2,640,000 − $672,000 = $48,000

c. Profit margin for standard items: $(180,000)/$3,840,000 = −4.7%
   Profit margin for custom items: $540,000/$3,360,000 = 16.1%

d. Profit margin for standard items: $312,000/$3,840,000 = 8.1%
   Profit margin for custom items: $48,000/$3,360,000 = 1.4%

e. Total profit in part *a*: $(180,000) + $540,000 = $360,000
   Total profit in part *b*: $312,000 + $48,000 = $360,000

f. Using the information in part *a*, a sales manager would likely choose to promote the custom projects. However, using the information in part *b*, a sales manager would likely choose to promote standard products. Using the more refined costing system of activity-based costing, standard items have a much higher profit margin. Thus, if the sales manager promotes standard products and shifts the sales mix in that direction, overall profit margin will increase. However, if the sales mix shifts toward custom items with only a 1.4% profit margin, overall profit margin will decrease.

Review 8-6

a. $481,000 ÷ 130,000 = $3.70. (Same amount can be obtained from a similar calculation for the other two services).

b. X = $3.70 × (2,915 × 60)
   X = $647,130

c. Oil change: 130,000/13,000 = 10 minutes
   Air filter replacement: 30,000/5,000 = 6 minutes
   Wiper blade replacement: 6,000/2,000 = 3 minutes

d. $647,130 − $481,000 − $111,000 − $22,200 = $32,930

e. Currently, the company is operating with excess capacity of 8,900 minutes ($32,930/$3.70 = 8,900 minutes) or approximately 148 hours. If sales were expected to increase over 5.3% of current volume (8,900/166,000 minutes = 5.3%), than another technician would be required. However, based on current volume, another technician does not appear to be warranted.

Data Visualization Solutions

(See page 8-20.)

a. The parts are organized on the X-axis from the highest usage to the lowest usage.
b. Four parts (Part 10, Part 35, Part 82, and Part 41) comprise more than 80% of part usage.
c. This analysis shows that 20% of the parts (4/20 parts) provide 80% of the part usage. Cost savings can result by reducing complexity and narrowing the part types.

   The company could start by understanding how the less used parts are utilized and whether more common parts could be used instead. Also, in design of new products or redesign of current products, efforts can be made to use more common parts.

   Regarding purchasing of parts, the chart also indicates the key parts to be managed and where price fluctuations will have the most impact on the company's overall profits.

Chapter 9

The Master Budget

Road Map

LO	Learning Objective | Topics	Page	eLecture	Demo	Review	Assignments
9-1	**Why is strategy important to the budgeting process and what are some general approaches to budgeting?** Budgets :: Strategic Planning :: External Variables :: Internal Variables :: Tactical Planning :: Budgeting :: Budget Committee: Generative AI :: Output/Input Approach :: Activity-Based Approach :: Incremental Approach :: Minimum Level Approach :: Zero-Based Budgeting	9-2	e9-1	D9-1A D9-1B D9-1C D9-1D	Rev 9-1	MC9-14, E9-23, E9-24, E9-25, E9-26, E9-27, E9-28, E9-29, E9-30, DA9-1
9-2	**What are the various components of a master budget and why is the sales budget the starting point?** Master Budget :: Sales Budget :: Internal Factors :: External Factors :: Sales Forecast	9-7	e9-2	D9-2	Rev 9-2	MC9-15, MC9-16, E9-31, E9-32, P9-78, P9-79, DA9-2, DA9-3
9-3	**How are the production and operating cost budgets of the master budget prepared?** Operating Budgets :: Production Budget :: Purchases Budget :: Direct Labor Budget :: Overhead Budget :: Selling and Administrative Budget	9-12	e9-3	D9-3A D9-3B D9-3C D9-3D D9-3E	Rev 9-3	MC9-17, MC9-18, E9-33, E9-34, E9-35, E9-36, E9-37, E9-38, E9-39, E9-43, E9-47, E9-50, P9-62, P9-63, P9-64, P9-65, P9-66, P9-67, P9-68, P9-73, P9-76, P9-78, P9-79, P9-80, P9-81
9-4	**Why are the financial budgets important in the master budgeting process?** Capital Budget :: Cash Budget :: Cash Receipts :: Cash Disbursements :: Desired Minimum Cash Balance :: Financing	9-16	e9-4	D9-4A D9-4B D9-4C D9-4D	Rev 9-4	MC9-19, E9-39, E9-40, E9-41, E9-42, E9-43, E9-44, E9-45, E9-46, E9-47, E9-50, E9-53, E9-54, E9-55, P9-64, P9-66, P9-67, P9-69, P9-70, P9-71, P9-72, P9-73, P9-74, P9-76, P9-78, P9-79
9-5	**How are budgeted financial statements prepared and how do ESG initiatives impact the budgeting process?** Cost of Goods Manufactured Schedule :: Income Statement :: Balance Sheet :: Statement of Cash Flows :: Environmental Considerations :: Carbon Offsets :: Master Budget	9-23	e9-5	D9-5A D9-5B	Rev 9-5	MC9-20, E9-48, E9-49, E9-50, E9-51, E9-52, E9-56, P9-74, P9-75, P9-76, P9-77, P9-78, P9-79, P9-80, P9-81
9-6	**How does the budgeting process differ for a service provider?** Service Provider :: Master Budget	9-29	e9-6	D9-6	Rev 9-6	MC9-21, E9-24, E9-31, E9-53, E9-54, E9-55, E9-61, P9-71, P9-76, P9-80, P9-81
9-7	**What are factors that contribute to a well-prepared budget?** Forecasting :: Continuous (Rolling) Budget :: Budget Variances :: Participatory Budget :: Imposed Budget :: Budget Slack :: Ethics	9-31	e9-7	D9-7	Rev 9-7	MC9-22, E9-57, E9-58, E9-59, E9-60, P9-80, P9-81, P9-82

INTRODUCTION

In virtually any endeavor, organizing and coordinating behavior involves visualizing the future, specifying the desired outcomes, and determining the activities and resources needed to achieve those results. The last part of the behavioral process is essential because, as stated in *The Little Prince*, "a goal without a plan is just a wish."

Planning is the cornerstone of effective management, and in the complex business environment, successful planning requires that managers predict, with reasonable precision, the key variables that affect company performance. Such predictions provide managers with the foundation for effective problem solving, control, and resource allocation. Planning (especially in financial terms) is *important* even if future conditions are expected to approximate current ones; planning is *critical* when future conditions are expected to change.

This chapter covers the budgeting process and master budget preparation. Budgeting is important for organizations of all sizes, especially those with large quantities of monetary, human, and physical resources.

THE BUDGETING PROCESS

LO9-1 Why is strategy important to the budgeting process and what are some general approaches to budgeting?

Unlike a computer, human beings often have difficulty processing many facts and relationships simultaneously and also have a tendency to forget. Thus, as plans become more intricate, they should be documented in writing and include qualitative narratives of goals, objectives, and means of accomplishing the objectives. However, if plans consisted only of qualitative narratives, comparisons between expected and actual results would be vague generalizations that would not provide the ability to measure whether the organization succeeded. The process of formalizing plans and translating qualitative narratives into a documented, quantitative format is called **budgeting**. The end result of this process is a **budget**, which quantitatively expresses an organization's commitment to planned activities, resource acquisition, and resource usage. Although budgets are typically expressed in financial terms, the budgeting process must begin by considering *nonquantitative factors and all organizational resources,* such as raw material, inventory, supplies, personnel, and facilities.

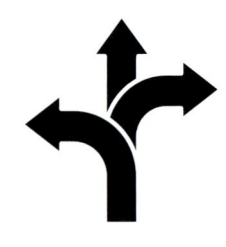

The budgeting process indicates a direction or path that management has chosen from many alternatives. Inclusion of quantifiable amounts provides specific criteria against which future performance (also recorded in accounting terms) can be compared. Thus, a budget is a type of standard that allows variances to be computed and feedback about those variances to be given to appropriate individuals. Budgets can be viewed from a long-term (strategic) or a short-term (tactical) perspective.

Long-Term Strategic Planning

Top-level managers, generally with the assistance of key staff members, who plan on a long-range basis (5–10 years) are engaged in **strategic planning**. The result is a statement of long-range organizational goals as well as the strategies and policies that will help achieve those goals. The strategic plan should identify key variables that will be the direct causes of the achievement (or nonachievement) of organizational goals and objectives. Key variables (shown in **Exhibit 9.1**) can be internal (under the control of management) or external (normally noncontrollable by management). *Effective strategic planning requires that managers build plans and budgets that integrate the key internal and external variables.* This information is used to adjust the previously gathered historical information for any changes in the key variables for the planning period.

During the strategic planning process, managers set organizational *goals* and *objectives* and agree on how to achieve them. Typically, goals are stated as desired abstract achievements (such as "to become a market leader for a particular product") and objectives are stated as desired quantifiable results for a specified time (such as "to manufacture 200,000 units of Product X with fewer than 1 percent defects next year"). Achieving goals and objectives requires organizing complex activities, managing diverse resources, and formalizing plans.

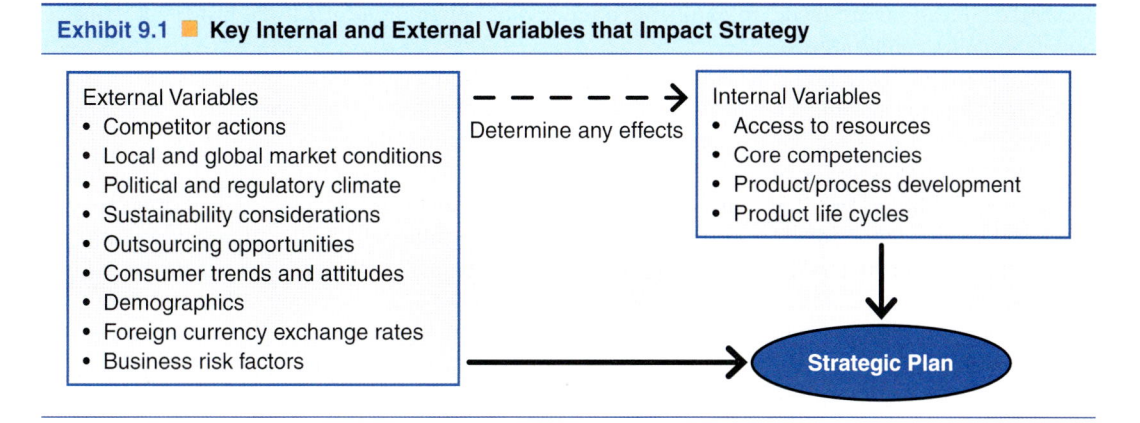

Exhibit 9.1 ■ Key Internal and External Variables that Impact Strategy

External Variables
- Competitor actions
- Local and global market conditions
- Political and regulatory climate
- Sustainability considerations
- Outsourcing opportunities
- Consumer trends and attitudes
- Demographics
- Foreign currency exchange rates
- Business risk factors

Determine any effects →

Internal Variables
- Access to resources
- Core competencies
- Product/process development
- Product life cycles

↓

Strategic Plan

Short-Term Tactical Planning

After identifying key variables, management should gather information useful for managing or reacting to changes in these variables. Often this information is historical and qualitative and provides a useful starting point for tactical planning activities. **Tactical planning** determines how the strategic plans will be achieved. Some tactical plans, such as corporate policy statements, exist for the long term and address repetitive situations. Most tactical plans, however, are short term (1–18 months). They are considered "single-use" plans and are developed to address a given set of circumstances or to cover a specific period of time.

The annual budget is an example of a single-use tactical plan. Shorter-term (quarterly and monthly) plans should also be included, so the budget contains the details necessary for the plan to work effectively. The monetary budget is the end product of the predictions and assumptions underlying organizational goals and objectives. Financial performance targets could include net income, earnings per share, or sales revenue. Nonfinancial performance targets could include a designated customer satisfaction level, defect reduction rates, and percentage of on-time deliveries. Quantifying potential difficulties in achieving organizational targets makes those difficulties visible. Thus, budgets help managers find ways to overcome problems before they are realized. **Exhibit 9.2** illustrates the relationships among strategic planning, tactical planning, and budgeting.

Exhibit 9.2 ■ Relationships among Planning Processes

Who?	What?	How?	Why?
Top management	Strategic planning	State organizational mission, goals, and strategies; long range (5–10 years)	Establish a long-range organizational vision and provide a sense of unity and commitment to specified purposes
Top management and mid-management	Tactical planning	State organizational plans; short range (1–18 months)	Provide direction for achievement of strategic plans; state strategic plans in terms for which managers can act; furnish a basis against which results can be measured
Top management, mid-management, and operational management	Budgeting	Prepare quantitative and monetary statements that coordinate company activities for a year or less	Allocate resources effectively and efficiently; indicate a commitment to objectives; provide a monetary control device

A well-prepared budget serves as a guide for company activities and is an effective tool for communicating objectives, constraints, and expectations to organizational personnel. Communication promotes understanding of

- what is to be accomplished,
- how those accomplishments are to be achieved, and
- the manner in which resources are to be allocated.

Resource allocations are made, in part, from a process of obtaining information, justifying requests, and negotiating compromises.

Employee participation is needed to effectively integrate information from various sources and to obtain individual managerial commitment to the resulting budget. Participation helps to produce a spirit of cooperation, motivate employees, and instill teamwork. However, the greater the employee participation in the budgeting process, the greater the time and cost involved. To say that a company uses a highly *participative budgeting process* implies that budgets are built from the bottom of the organization upward.

Managers review the budget prior to its approval to determine whether the forecasted results are acceptable. The budget could indicate that results expected from the planned activities do not achieve the desired objectives. In this case, planned activities are reconsidered and revised so that they more effectively achieve the desired outcomes expressed in the tactical planning stage.

After a budget is approved by upper management, or in some companies, by a formal **budget committee**, it is implemented and becomes a performance benchmark. A budget committee is a group of employees, designated to oversee the budgeting process. The budget sets the resource constraints under which managers must operate for the upcoming budget period. The control phase includes

- making actual-to-budget comparisons,
- determining variances,
- investigating variance causes,
- taking necessary corrective action, and
- providing feedback to operating managers.

Budgeting allows managers to effectively communicate organizational goals and objectives while producing a spirit of cooperation and participation in the planning process.

Feedback, both positive and negative, is essential to the control process and must be provided in a timely manner. This cyclical process is illustrated in **Exhibit 9.3**.

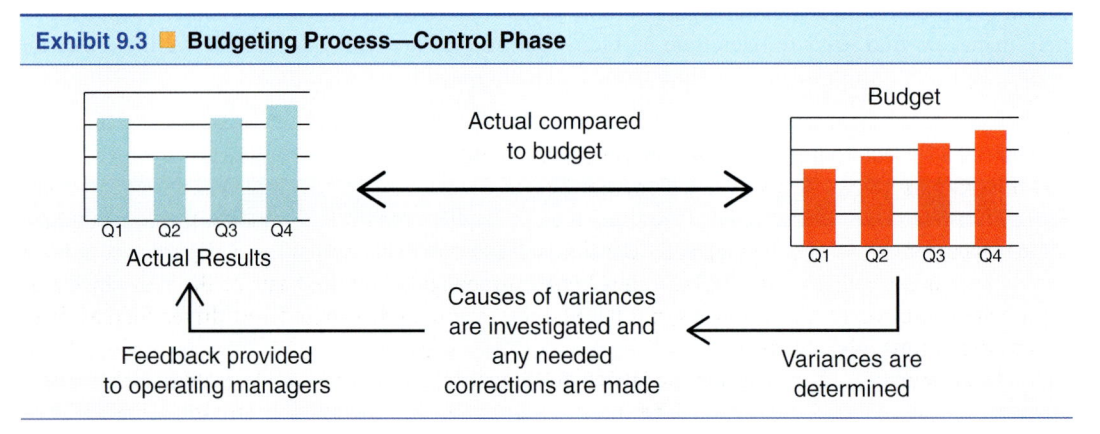

Exhibit 9.3 ■ Budgeting Process—Control Phase

Actual Results — Actual compared to budget — Budget

Variances are determined → Causes of variances are investigated and any needed corrections are made → Feedback provided to operating managers

The preceding discussion describes a budgeting process but, as with many other business practices, budgeting is unique to individual organizations. For example, some companies are taking advantage of the recent technological advances in **generative artificial intelligence (generative AI)** in the budgeting process. Generative AI is a learning model that can produce new content based on the data that it is trained on. This means that generative AI can be trained with company proprietary information along with other information relevant to that company. These models have the capability to analyze market data and produce reports on a variety of scenarios. In fact, generative AI trained with a company's information can even produce a draft of a master budget for a company. However, the draft, while saving time and providing valuable insights, will require critical review by cost accountants. The ideas in the draft need to be vetted. Does the budget follow the company's strategy? Which of the different scenarios is preferable? Are there other scenarios not considered? Are the calculations accurate and take into account all known data? Are there relationships in the schedules or data that are not logical? A budget can be

Chapter 9 The Master Budget

produced through various means, but ultimately, it must be accepted by the users for it to be functional. Thus, understanding the underlying aspects of budgeting may be more important than in the past because accountants will be more quickly immersed in analyzing the underlying data, the assumptions, and output of learning models. Regardless of how it is carried out, the budgeting process results in a **master budget**. This "budget" is actually a comprehensive set of budgets, budgetary schedules, and budgeted (also called pro forma) organizational financial statements.

General Approaches to Budgeting

Before an organization can develop its master budget, management must decide which approaches to budget planning will be used for the various revenue and expenditure activities and organizational units. Widely used planning approaches to budgeting include the output/input, activity-based, incremental, and minimum level approaches.

Output/Input Approach

The **output/input approach** budgets physical inputs and costs as a function of planned unit-level activities. This approach is often used for service, merchandising, manufacturing, and distribution activities that have defined relationships between effort and accomplishment.

Applying the Output/Input Approach — LO9-1 DEMO 9-1A

A manufacturer of equipment subcomponents produces a unit that requires 2 pounds of direct materials that cost $5 each.

◆ If planned production volume is 25 units, what is the budgeted input and cost for direct materials?

The budgeted input is 50 pounds and the budgeted cost is $250, calculated as follows.

25 units × 2 pounds per unit = 50 pounds × $5 per pound = $250 budgeted direct materials

The budgeted inputs are a function of the planned outputs. The output/input approach starts with the planned outputs and works backward to budget the inputs. It is difficult to use this approach for costs that do not respond to changes in unit-level cost drivers.

Activity-Based Approach

Managers could consider expanding their budgeting process to recognize the concepts of activities and cost drivers in a manner consistent with activity-based management. The **activity-based approach** is a type of output/input method, but it reduces the distortions in the transformation through emphasis on the expected cost of the planned activities that will be consumed for a process, department, service, product, or other budget objective. Overhead costs are budgeted on the basis of the cost objective's anticipated consumption of activities, not based only on some broad-based cost driver such as direct labor hours or machine hours.

The amount of each cost driver used by each budget objective (for example, product or service) is determined and multiplied by the cost per unit of the cost driver. The result is an estimate of the costs of each product or service based on cost drivers such as assembly-line setup or inspections, as well as the traditional volume-based drivers such as direct labor hours or units of direct materials consumed. Activity-based budgeting predicts costs of budget objectives by adding all costs of the cost drivers that each product or service is budgeted to consume.

Applying the Activity-Based Approach — LO9-1 DEMO 9-1B

A manufacturer of equipment subcomponents incurs inspection costs at an estimated cost of $40 per batch.

◆ If planned production volume is 30,000 units, and there are 300 units in a batch, what is the budgeted cost of inspections using the activity-based approach?

Budgeted inspection costs are $4,000, calculated as follows.

© Cambridge Business Publishers

$$30{,}000 \text{ units} \div 300 \text{ units in a batch} = 100 \text{ batches}$$

$$\$40 \times 100 \text{ batches} = \$4{,}000 \text{ budgeted inspection costs}$$

This type of budget can increase managerial awareness of non-value-added (NVA) activities and make managers question why such costs are being incurred. Based on this enhanced awareness, managers can plan to reduce or eliminate some of these NVA activities. In evaluating the proposed budget, management would focus their attention on identifying the *optimal* set of activities rather than just the output/input relationships.

Incremental Approach

The **incremental approach** budgets costs for a coming period as a dollar or percentage change from the amount budgeted for (or spent during) some previous period. This approach is often used when the relationships between inputs and outputs are weak or nonexistent. For example, it is often difficult to establish a clear relationship between sales volume and advertising expenditures. Consequently, the budgeted amount of advertising for a future period is often based on the budgeted or actual advertising expenditures in a prior period.

DEMO 9-1C   LO9-1   Applying the Incremental Approach

A merchandiser incurred advertising expenditures for the current year of $200,000.

◆ **If advertising expenditures for the upcoming year are estimated to increase by 5 percent over the current year, what are budgeted advertising costs for the upcoming year under the incremental approach?**

The current year advertising expenditures are increased by an increment of $10,000 to a level of $210,000, calculated as follows.

$$\$200{,}000 \times 5\% = \$10{,}000 \text{ incremental budget}$$

$$\$200{,}000 + \$10{,}000 = \$210{,}000 \text{ budgeted advertising costs}$$

In evaluating the proposed current year budget, management would accept the $200,000 base and focus attention on justifying the increment of $10,000.

The incremental approach is widely used in government and not-for-profit organizations. In seeking a budget appropriation, a manager using the incremental approach need only justify proposed expenditures in excess of the previous budget. The primary advantage of the incremental approach is that it simplifies the budget process by considering only the increments in the various budget items. A major disadvantage is that existing waste and inefficiencies could escalate year after year.

Minimum Level Approach

Using the **minimum level approach**, an organization establishes a base amount for budget items and requires explanation or justification for any budgeted amount above the minimum (base). This base is usually significantly less than the base used in the incremental approach. It likely is the minimum amount necessary to keep a program or organizational unit viable. For example, the corporate director of product development would need some basic amount to avoid canceling ongoing projects. Additional increments might also be included, first to support the current level of product development and second to undertake desirable new projects.

Some organizations, especially units of government, employ a variation of the minimum level approach, identified as zero-based budgeting. Under **zero-based budgeting** every dollar of expenditure must be justified.

DEMO 9-1D   LO9-1   Applying the Zero-Based Budgeting Approach

A merchandiser incurred advertising expenditures for the current year of $200,000.

◆ **If advertising expenditures for the upcoming year are estimated to be $205,000, how much of the budget of $205,000 must be justified?**

Chapter 9 The Master Budget

The entire amount of the proposed current year budget of $205,000 must be justified by the operating managers. For example, $5,000 will be used for digital ads in the first quarter . . . and this would continue until the $205,000 is fully accounted for.

The essence of zero-based budgeting is breaking an organizational unit's total budget into program packages with related costs. Management then ranks all program packages on the basis of the perceived benefits in relation to their costs. Program packages are then funded for the budget period using this ranking. High-ranking packages are most likely to be funded and low-ranking packages are least likely to be funded.

Planning and Budgeting — **LO9-1** — **REVIEW 9-1**

1. Match each of the following terms: budget, strategic plan, and tactical plan with the most appropriate description (*a* through *c*) and with the most relevant example (*d* through *f*).

   Description
   a. ___ Formalized plan expressed quantitatively to assist in resource allocation.
   b. ___ Long-term goals along with steps to achieving those goals.
   c. ___ Generally, a short-term plan developed to address a specific item.

   Example
   d. ___ The company will offer a 20 percent price reduction for all online sales next Monday as a way to attract new customers and reward current customers.
   e. ___ Marketing expenditures expected for the first quarter are $250,000, an increase of 10 percent over the prior quarter.
   f. ___ Over the next 5 years, the company will focus on increasing product awareness of its top products through social media campaigns in order to increase sales.

2. **Critical Thinking:** What internal or external variables might influence a company's decision to focus on increasing product awareness of its top products through social media campaigns?

More practice: E9-23
Solution on p. 9-67.

THE MASTER BUDGET

As described in the last section, the culmination of the budgeting process is the preparation of the master budget. The master budget is an organization-wide set of budgets that considers all interrelationships among organizational units. Because it explicitly considers organizational interrelationships, the master budget is more complex than budgets developed for products, services, organization units, or specific processes. The elements of the master budget depend on the nature of the business, its products or services, processes and organization, and management needs. After a brief overview of the various components of the master budget, we start at the top of the master budget with the sales budget. We continue with the remaining schedules in the master budget in later sections.

LO9-2 What are the various components of a master budget and why is the sales budget the starting point?

As shown in **Exhibit 9.4**, the master budget can be broken down into two components: operating and financial. An **operating budget** is a budget that is expressed in both units and dollars. It represents the activities of an organization that are performed in conducting its daily affairs. When an operating budget relates to revenues, the units are those expected to be sold, and the dollars reflect selling prices. In contrast, when an operating budget relates to costs, the input units are those expected to be either transformed into output units or consumed, and the dollars reflect costs.

Monetary details from the various operating budgets are combined to prepare **financial budgets**, which indicate the funds to be generated or consumed during the budget period. Financial budgets include cash and capital budgets as well as the budgeted financial statements that are the ultimate focal points for top management.

Exhibit 9.4 ■ Components of a Master Budget

MASTER BUDGET FOR A MANUFACTURER

Operating
Includes components of the various budgeted financial statements
- sales budget — LO9-2
- production budget
- purchases budget
- direct labor budget — LO9-3
- overhead budget
- selling and administrative budget

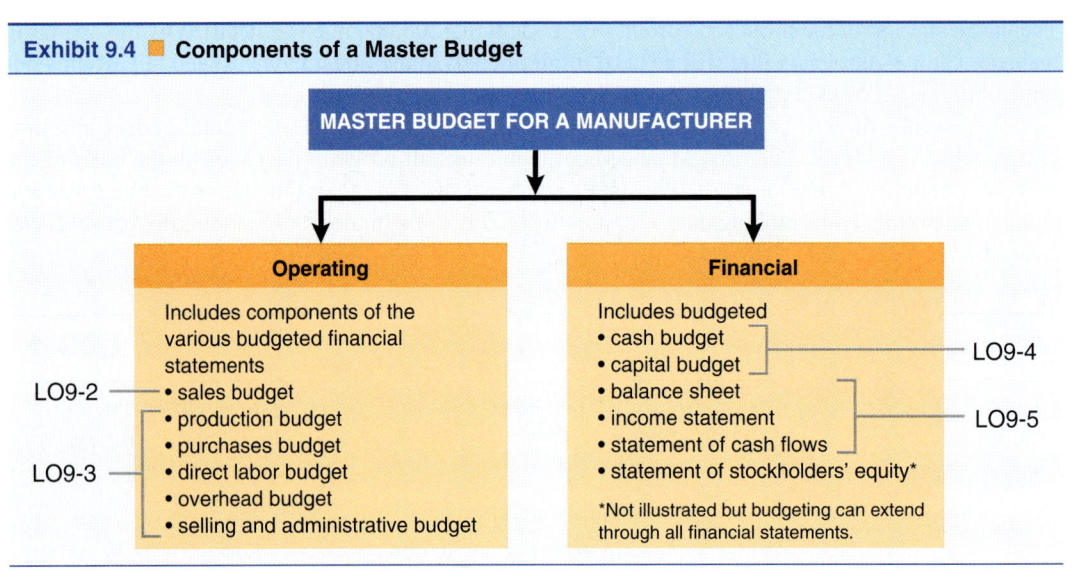

Financial
Includes budgeted
- cash budget — LO9-4
- capital budget
- balance sheet
- income statement — LO9-5
- statement of cash flows
- statement of stockholders' equity*

*Not illustrated but budgeting can extend through all financial statements.

Note: *Merchandiser:* Because the company is not manufacturing a product, a purchases budget is used for the purchase of merchandise inventory; *Service Provider:* Because the company's main focus is on service, a purchases budget will only be used for supplies or ancillary products that are sold in conjunction with services; *Nonmanufacturer:* If a company is not producing a product, a production budget is not used.

The master budget is prepared for a specific period and is static in the sense that it is based on a single level of output demand. The single level of output demand is the *amount of sales budgeted for the period*.[1] Developing the budget using a single demand level is necessary to identify the specific input quantities to be acquired. Arrangements must be made to assure that an adequate number of personnel are hired, needed production and/or storage space is available, and suppliers, prices, delivery schedules, and quality of resources are confirmed. This means that estimated sales impacts the level of resources required throughout the master budget.

Estimated sales is the organization's *source of inflows*. Primary sources of inflows vary by organization type.

- In manufacturing or retail companies, primary inflows come from the sale of products.
- In service providers, primary inflows are the result of providing services.
- In not-for-profits, the primary inflows would be contributions, interest on endowments, fees, and allocations from other entities.
- In governmental entities, the primary inflows are usually taxes and fees.

Regardless of the organizational source of inflows, all departmental budgets must interact in a coordinated manner because of the many budgetary relationships. A budget developed by one department is often an essential ingredient in developing another department's budget. **Exhibit 9.5** presents an overview of the budget preparation sequence, indicates departmental budget preparation responsibility, and illustrates how the budgets interrelate. Departments involved in the budgeting process both generate and use information. If top management encourages participation of lower-level managers in the budgeting process, each department either prepares its own budget or provides information for inclusion in a budget. The budget is typically prepared for a year and then subdivided into quarterly and monthly periods.

---

[1] Companies can engage in contingency planning, providing for multiple budgeting paths. For example, a company could construct three budgets, such as for a high level of activity, an expected level of activity, and a low level of activity. If actual activity turns out to be either higher or lower than expected, management has a budget ready.

Exhibit 9.5 ■ **The Master Budget: An Overview**

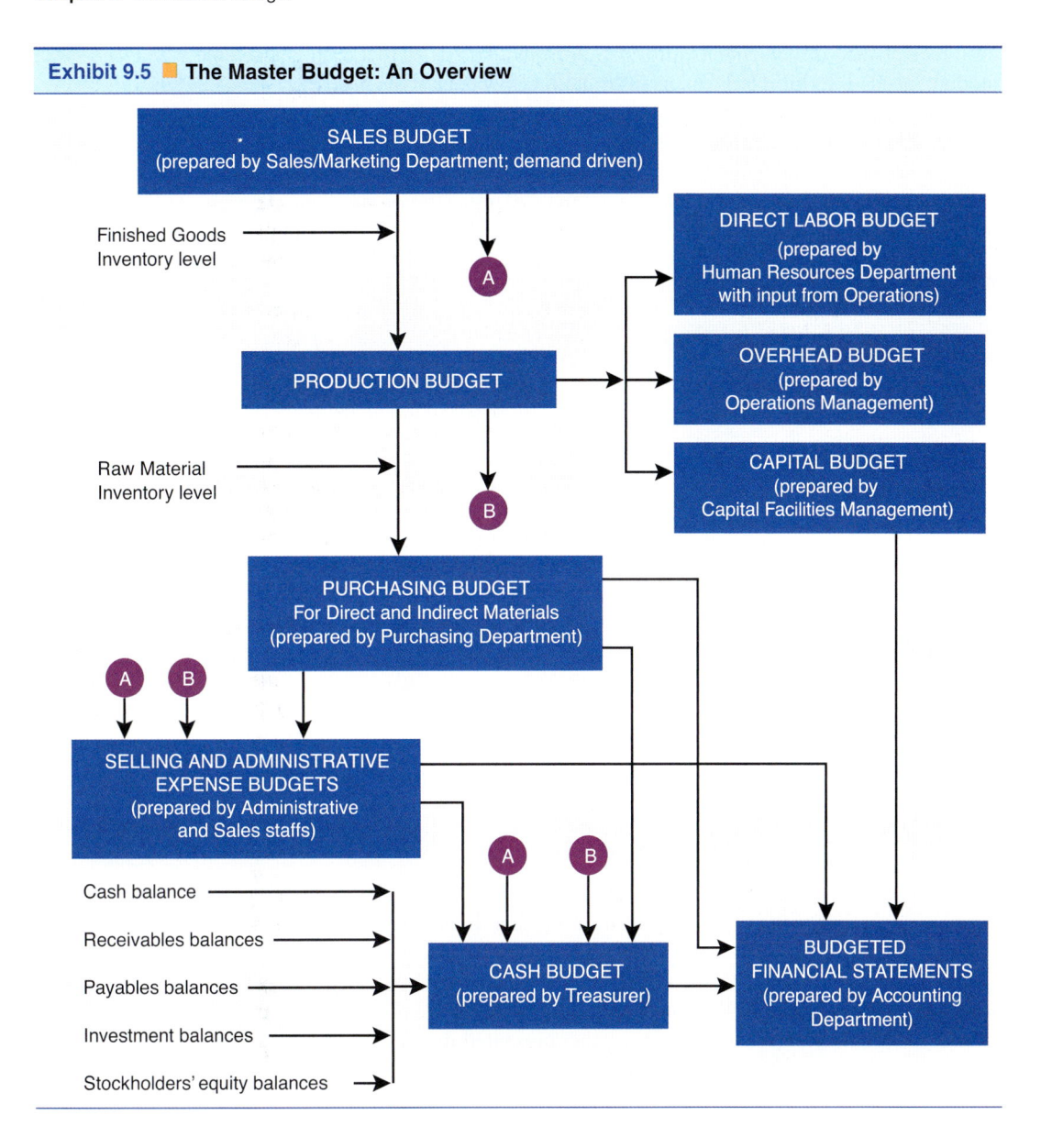

```
                    SALES BUDGET
          (prepared by Sales/Marketing Department; demand driven)
                          │
Finished Goods ──────────→│
Inventory level           │
                         (A)
                          │
                          ▼
                   PRODUCTION BUDGET ──────────→ DIRECT LABOR BUDGET
                          │                      (prepared by Human
                          │                       Resources Department
                          │                       with input from Operations)
                          │
                          ├────────────────────→ OVERHEAD BUDGET
Raw Material ────────────→│                      (prepared by
Inventory level           │                       Operations Management)
                         (B)
                          │                       CAPITAL BUDGET
                          ├────────────────────→ (prepared by
                          ▼                       Capital Facilities Management)
                   PURCHASING BUDGET
              For Direct and Indirect Materials
              (prepared by Purchasing Department)

  (A) (B)
   │  │
   ▼  ▼
SELLING AND ADMINISTRATIVE
   EXPENSE BUDGETS
 (prepared by Administrative
    and Sales staffs)
                         (A) (B)
Cash balance ──────────→  │   │
Receivables balances ──→  ▼   ▼
Payables balances ────→  CASH BUDGET ──────→ BUDGETED
Investment balances ──→  (prepared by        FINANCIAL STATEMENTS
Stockholders' equity ─→   Treasurer)         (prepared by Accounting
balances                                      Department)
```

Sales Budget

Estimating sales is a complex process that incorporates a wide variety of external and internal information. External information such as economic conditions and internal information such as production capabilities influence sales estimates. **Exhibit 9.6** highlights a number of factors that influence the final determination of a sales estimate. This estimate, often prepared by the sales or marketing department, includes the types, quantities, and timing of sales for the company's products or services. These estimates are used to prepare the **sales budget**, which is often presented with forecasted units multiplied by the selling price per unit as follows.

> **Sales budget = Forecasted sales in units × Expected selling price per unit**

A production manager combines sales estimates with information from Purchasing, Human Resources, Operations, and Capital Facilities to specify the types, quantities, and timing of products to be manufactured. Sales estimates, in conjunction with estimated cash collection patterns, are used to determine the amounts and timing of cash receipts. Resource consumption budgets are then integrated into budgeted financial statements. To properly manage the organization's funds, the treasurer needs

OPERATING BUDGET

Sales Budget

cash receipts and disbursements information from all areas so that cash is available when, and in the amount, needed. **Exhibit 9.5** depicts information flow but not the necessary details. Thus, this chapter discusses the specifics of preparing a master budget, starting first with the sales budget. Again, because the sales budget drives almost all other activities in the organization, it is prepared first. The in-depth example used to illustrate the master budget in this chapter, focuses on a manufacturing company. A shorter retail company example is provided in the demonstration problem at the end of the chapter. A budget example for a service provider is provided in LO9-6.

Exhibit 9.6 ■ Information for Sales Forecasting

Internal	External
• Seasonality of the product/service • Production capability and capacity • Advertising plans and media usage • Sales bonus plans • Capital availability • Distribution methods relied upon • Adjustments to product lines (new, modified, eliminations) • Utilization of technology • Operational efficiency • Changes in client base • Historical data (modified by known changes such as canceled contracts or pending new contracts) • Life cycle of products	• Local, domestic and global economic conditions (including employment rates, tax rates, interest rates, consumer purchasing power, age of population, and credit policy changes) • Competition and market share levels • Market demand for sustainable products/services • Political changes • Style or fashion trends • Selling price changes and add-on fees (such as those made by the airlines) • Industry growth

DEMO 9-2   LO9-2   Preparing the Sales Budget

Dresdill Corp. has been in business for several years. The company, which produces a single type of commercial stainless steel lock, is preparing its Year 4 annual budget and has estimated total annual sales at 350,000 locks. Although annual sales would be detailed on a monthly basis, Dresdill focuses on the budgets for only the first quarter of Year 4. The process of developing the master budget is the same regardless of whether the time frame is one year or one quarter.

The December 31, Year 3, balance sheet presented on the next page provides account balances needed to begin preparation of the master budget. The December 31, Year 3, balances are estimates rather than actual figures because the budget process for Year 4 must begin significantly before December 31, Year 3. The company's budgetary time schedule depends on many factors, including company size, degree of forecasting sophistication, and cyclical nature of the business. For example, in May and June, Dresdill Corp. begins analyzing historical November sales patterns to project the seasonal labor that will need to be hired before the holiday season over a half year away.[2] Assume that Dresdill Corp. begins its budgeting process in November, Year 3, when the Year 4 sales forecast is received by management or the budget committee.

---

[2] D. Amato-McCoy, "Holiday Preparations," Chain Store Age (August/September 2010), pp. 28, 30.

Chapter 9 The Master Budget

Balance Sheet, End of Year 3

	A	B	C	D	E	F
1			Dresdill Corp. Balance Sheet December 31, Year 3			
2	Assets			Liabilities & Stockholders' Equity		
3	Current assets			Current liabilities		
4	Cash		$ 10,000	Accounts payable		$ 42,504
5	Accounts receivable	$ 69,840		Dividends payable (payment scheduled for March 31)		45,000
6	Less allowance for uncollectibles	(1,248)	68,592			
7	Inventories			Total current liabilities		$87,504
8	Raw material (3,289 pounds)	$ 7,565*				
9	Finished goods (1,500 units)	4,800	12,365			
10	Total current assets		$90,957			
11	Plant assets			Stockholders' equity		
12	Property, plant, and equipment	$370,000		Common stock	$180,000	
13	Less accumulated depreciation	(90,000)	280,000	Retained earnings	103,453	283,453
14	Total assets		$370,957	Total liabilities and stockholders' equity		$370,957
15	*This amount is actually $7,564.70, or 3,289 pounds of steel multiplied by $2.30 per pound. It has been rounded for simplicity in this schedule. Retained Earnings has been similarly rounded.					

The selling price set for Year 4 is $5 per lock, regardless of sales territory or customer. Monthly demand for the first four months of Year 4 are shown below. April information is presented because some elements of the master budget for March require the subsequent month's information.

	January	February	March	April
Sales in units	30,000	28,000	33,000	32,000

◆ **How is the sales budget prepared for the first four months of Year 4?**

The sales budget is presented below in both units and sales dollars.

Sales Budget, First Quarter Year 4

	A	B	C	D	E	F
1		January	February	March	Total for Quarter	April*
2	Sales in units	30,000	28,000	33,000	91,000	32,000
3	Selling price per unit	× $5	× $5	× $5	× $5	× $5
4	Sales in dollars	$150,000	$140,000	$165,000	$455,000	$160,000
5	*Information for April is needed for subsequent computations.					

Sales Budget — LO9-2 — REVIEW 9-2

Madison Co.'s sales manager estimates that 200,000 units of product #486 and 7,000 units of product #890 will be sold next year. Quarterly sales estimates for product #486 are 25,000, 65,000, 50,000, and 60,000 units for Quarters 1, 2, 3, and 4, respectively. The selling price of product #486 is $10, but a 10 percent price increase is forecasted beginning in Quarter 3. Product #890 is a new product with more features. Sales are estimated to be 2,000 units in Quarter 3 and 5,000 units in Quarter 4. The selling price of Product #890 is expected to be $15.

a. Prepare a sales budget for the year for Madison Co.

b. **Critical Thinking:** If you are the cost accountant preparing the sales budget for the company, how might you account for the uncertainty of a possible economic downturn which could impact sales volume forecasts?

More practice: MC9-16, E9-31, E9-32
Solution on p. 9-67.

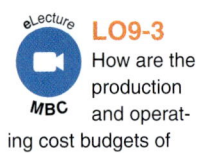

LO9-3 How are the production and operating cost budgets of the master budget prepared?

In this section, we illustrate the production and operating cost budgets which include the following budgets.

OPERATING BUDGETS
Production Budget	Purchases Budget	Direct Labor Budget	Overhead Budget	Selling & Administrative Expense Budget

Production Budget

For a manufacturing company, the **production budget** follows from the sales budget and is based on information about the type, quantity, and timing of units to be sold. (A retail or service company would not prepare a production budget.) Sales information is combined with beginning and ending Finished Goods (FG) Inventory information so that managers can schedule necessary production. The following formula provides the computation for units to be produced.

Number of units to be sold (from sales budget)	XXX
+ Number of units desired in ending FG Inventory	XXX
= Total units needed during period	XXX
− Number of units in beginning FG Inventory	(XXX)
= Units to be produced	XXX

Company management determines ending inventory policy. Desired ending FG Inventory balance is generally a function of the quantity and timing of demand in the upcoming period as related to the firm's capacity and speed to produce particular units. Frequently, management wants ending FG Inventory to equal a given percentage of the next period's projected sales. Other alternatives include

- a constant amount of inventory,
- a buildup of inventory for future high-demand periods, or
- near-zero inventory under a just-in-time system (discussed in depth in Chapter 18).

The decision about ending inventory levels often relates to whether a firm wants to have constant production with varying inventory levels or variable production with constant inventory levels. Managers should consider the high costs of stockpiling inventory before making a decision about how much inventory to keep on hand.

DEMO 9-3A LO9-3 Preparing a Production Budget

Assume that demand for Dresdill's products is relatively constant year-round. Because most sales are to recurring customers, Dresdill's policy is that ending FG Inventory should be 5 percent of the next month's unit sales.

Desired ending FG inventory = 5% × Next month's unit sales

◆ Considering this policy and using the sales information from Demo 9-2, how is the production budget prepared for the first quarter of Year 4?

Production Budget, First Quarter Year 4					
	A	B	C	D	E
1		January	February	March	Total
2	Sales in units (from **Demo 9-2**)	30,000	28,000	33,000	91,000
3	Desired ending inventory	1,400	1,650	1,600	1,600
4	Total needed	31,400	29,650	34,600	92,600
5	Beginning inventory	(1,500)	(1,400)	(1,650)	(1,500)
6	Units to be produced	29,900	28,250	32,950	91,100

Chapter 9 The Master Budget   9-13

January's beginning FG Inventory is the 1,500 units on hand at December 31, Year 3 as shown on page 9-11. (Alternatively, the 1,500 units can be computed as 5 percent of January's estimated sales of 30,000 units because the estimated ending inventory for December becomes the beginning inventory for January.) Desired February ending inventory is calculated as follows.

Desired February ending FG inventory = 5% × 33,000 units = 1,650 units

Desired March ending inventory is 5 percent of the April sales of 32,000 units.

Desired March ending FG inventory = 5% × 32,000 units = 1,600 units

Dresdill does not have any Work in Process Inventory because all units placed into production are assumed to be fully completed during each period.[3]

Purchases Budget

Direct material must be purchased each period in quantities sufficient to meet production needs and to conform to the company's desired ending inventory policies. Companies may have different policies for the raw material associated with different products or for different seasons of the year. For example, a company may maintain only a minimal ending inventory of a raw material that is consistently available in the quantity and quality desired. Alternatively, if a material is difficult to obtain at certain times of the year, a company may stockpile that material for use in future periods.

The **purchases budget** is first stated in whole units of finished products and then converted to direct material component requirements (quantity). Next, the desired ending inventory quantity of materials is added, and the beginning quantity of materials is subtracted, to arrive at the total quantity of materials required to purchase. Quantities are converted to dollars by multiplying by the price per unit of material. For a merchandiser, the purchases budget could be used to calculate the amount of merchandise inventory to purchase for the period.

Preparing a Purchases Budget   LO9-3   DEMO 9-3B

Dresdill Corp.'s management aligns its policy for ending Raw Material Inventory with its production needs for the following month. Because of occasional difficulty in obtaining the high quality of stainless steel needed, Dresdill's ending inventory for raw material is set at 10 percent of the quantity needed for the following month's production. Production of a Dresdill lock requires only one direct material: stainless steel. The cost of the appropriate grade of stainless steel has been estimated by the purchasing agent at $2.30 per pound, and it takes 1.1 pounds of steel to produce one lock.

♦ **How is the purchases budget prepared for the first quarter of Year 4?**

The schedule below shows Dresdill's purchase cost for each month of the first quarter of Year 4. Note that beginning and ending inventory quantities are expressed first in terms of locks and then are converted to the appropriate material quantity measure (pounds of steel). To complete the March budget, we assume that April production is 34,500 units, which would require 37,950 pounds of material. In addition, the beginning inventory of material for January is 3,289 pounds, found on the balance sheet on page 9-11.

---

[3] Most manufacturing entities do not produce only whole units during the period. Normally, partially completed beginning and ending Work in Process inventories will exist. These inventories create the need to use equivalent units of production (discussed in Chapter 7) when computing the production budget.

Purchases Budget, First Quarter Year 4

	A	B	C	D	E
1		January	February	March	Quarter
2	Units to be produced (from Demo 9-3A)	29,900	28,250	32,950	91,100
3	Pounds needed per unit	× 1.1	× 1.1	× 1.1	× 1.1
4	Total pounds needed	32,890	31,075	36,245	100,210
5	Desired EI (percentage of next month's needs)	3,108	3,625	3,795	3,795
6	Beginning inventory	(3,289)	(3,108)	(3,625)	(3,289)
7	Total pounds of steel to purchase	32,709	31,592	36,415	100,716
8	Price per pound	× $2.30	× $2.30	× $2.30	× $2.30
9	Total cost of steel purchases	$75,231	$72,662	$83,754	$231,647
10	**Note:** Cost of purchases is rounded. Total cost for steel for March was rounded down to balance to the quarter total.				

Direct Labor Budget

Given expected production, the Engineering and Human Resources Departments can work together to determine the necessary labor requirements for the factory, sales force, and office staff. Salaries (and associated costs) are included as appropriate in the overhead budget, the selling and administrative expense budget and in the direct labor budget. This section on the direct labor budget focuses on the costs of factory labor. Factory direct labor costs are based on standard hours of labor needed to produce the units in the production budget. The average wage rate includes the direct labor payroll rate, payroll taxes, and fringe benefits; these items usually add between 25 and 30 percent to the base labor cost. The **direct labor budget** is first stated in whole units of finished products and then converted to direct labor hours allowed based on standard direct labor hours allowed per unit. (*Standards* specify the expected costs and quantities needed to manufacture a single unit of product or perform a single service and are discussed further in the next chapter.) Next, total hours allowed are multiplied by the average wage rate.

DEMO 9-3C   LO9-3   Preparing a Direct Labor Budget

Assume that Dresdill's management has reviewed the staffing requirements and estimates 0.014 direct labor hour per finished unit and that the average wage rate is $25 per hour. All compensation will be paid in the month in which it is incurred.

◆ **How is the direct labor budget prepared for the first quarter of Year 4?**

The following schedule shows Dresdill's direct labor budget, which shows a total labor cost of $31,885 for the quarter.

Direct Labor Budget, First Quarter Year 4

	A	B	C	D	E
1		January	February	March	Total
2	Units to be produced (Demo 9-3A)	29,900	28,250	32,950	91,100
3	Standard hours allowed	× 0.014	× 0.014	× 0.014	× 0.014
4	Total hours allowed	418.60	395.50	461.30	1,275.40
5	Average wage rate (including fringe benefits)	× $25.00	× $25.00	× $25.00	× $25.00
6	Direct labor cost	$ 10,465	$ 9,888	$ 11,532	$ 31,885
7	**Note:** Direct labor cost for March was rounded down to balance to the quarter total.				

Overhead Budget

The third production cost of overhead is estimated in the **overhead budget**. The overhead amount used in the budget can be calculated using an applied overhead rate as discussed in prior chapters.

Preparing an Overhead Budget   LO9-3   DEMO 9-3D

Dresdill has determined that machine hours are the best predictor of overhead costs and determined ten units can be produced per machine hour.

Overhead is broken up into seven categories, with fixed costs and variable costs per machine hour estimated as follows.

Fixed and Variable Overhead

	A	B	C	D	E	F	G	H	I
1	Overhead Item	Depreciation	Indirect Material	Indirect Labor	Utilities	Property Tax	Insurance	Maintenance	Total
2	Fixed (in total)	$1,700	$ 0	$6,000	$ 500	$500	$450	$ 575	$9,725
3	Variable cost per machine hour	$ 0	$0.20	$ 1.50	$0.10	$ 0	$ 0	$0.30	$ 2.10

◆ **How is the overhead budget prepared for the first quarter of Year 4, showing both total cost and total cost net of depreciation?** (The net of depreciation cost is the amount expected to be paid in cash during the month and will be used in the cash budget in the next section.)

Overhead Budget, First Quarter, Year 4

	A	B	C	D	E
1		January	February	March	Total
2	Units to be produced (Demo 9-3A)	29,900	28,250	32,950	91,100
3	10 units per machine hour	÷ 10	÷ 10	÷ 10	÷ 10
4	Total machine hours	2,990	2,825	3,295	9,110
5	OH rate per machine hour	× $2.10	× $2.10	× $2.10	× $2.10
6	Variable OH costs	6,279	5,932	6,920	19,131
7	Fixed OH costs	9,725	9,725	9,725	29,175
8	Total OH costs	$16,004	$15,657	$16,645	$48,306
9	Less: depreciation fixed costs	(1,700)	(1,700)	(1,700)	(5,100)
10	Total OH costs net of depreciation	$14,304	$13,957	$14,945	$43,206
11	Note: variable overhead cost for February was rounded down to balance to the quarter total.				

Selling and Administrative Expense Budget

Selling expenses include costs in connection with sales and distribution such as sales commissions. Administrative expenses include costs in connection with the general administration of the organization, such as the cost of its accounting department. Selling and administrative (S&A) expenses can be predicted in the same manner as overhead costs in creating a **selling and administrative expense budget**. However, *sales levels*, rather than production levels, are used to measure activity in preparing this budget.

Preparing a Selling and Administrative Expense Budget   LO9-3   DEMO 9-3E

For Dresdill, assume that sales salaries are $2,000 per month plus a 2 percent commission on sales. Administrative salaries total $9,000 per month. The company has the following additional S&A expenses for the quarter: depreciation of $500 per month, miscellaneous costs of $100 per month, and variable costs of 3 percent of sales per month.

◆ **How is the selling and administrative expense budget prepared for the first quarter of Year 4 showing both total costs and total costs net of depreciation?** (The net of depreciation cost is the amount expected to be paid in cash during the month and will affect the cash budget in the next section.)

Total fixed selling and administrative costs are $2,000 + $9,000 + $500 + $100 = $11,600. Total variable selling and administrative costs are 5 percent (= 2% + 3%) of sales. The schedule below presents Dresdill's first quarter Year 4 S&A budget.

S&A Expense Budget, First Quarter Year 4					
	A	B	C	D	E
1		January	February	March	Total
2	Predicted sales (from Demo 9-2)	$150,000	$140,000	$165,000	$455,000
3	5% Variable S&A rate	× 5%	× 5%	× 5%	× 5%
4	Variable OH costs	7,500	7,000	8,250	22,750
5	Fixed OH costs	11,600	11,600	11,600	34,800
6	Total S&A costs	$19,100	$18,600	$19,850	$57,550
7	Less: depreciation fixed costs	(500)	(500)	(500)	(1,500)
8	Total cost net of depreciation	$ 18,600	$ 18,100	$ 19,350	$ 56,050

REVIEW 9-3 — LO9-3 — Sales, Production, and Operating Cost Budgets

Lakeside Inc. makes two boating products that use similar raw materials: #401 and #586. Estimated production needs for a unit of each product follow.

	#401	#586
Steel (in pounds)	4.0	3.0
Wood (in board feet)	0.6	0.3
Direct labor (in hours)	2.0	3.0
Machine hours	0.5	0.8

Estimated sales in units by product for the year are 96,000 of #401 and 36,000 of #586. Additionally, estimated beginning and desired ending inventory quantities for the year are as follows.

	Beginning	Ending
#401 (units)	960	768
#586 (units)	1,440	1,080
Steel (in pounds)	2,400	1,680
Wood (in board feet)	960	720

Overhead is applied to production at the rate of $20 per machine hour and the direct labor wage rate is $20.00 per hour.

1. Prepare the following for each of the products:
   a. Sales budget (in units)
   b. Production budget
   c. Purchases budget (steel and wood)
   d. Direct labor budget
   e. Overhead budget
2. What is the impact of a 20 percent decrease in the sales budget on the purchases budget, the direct labor budget, and the overhead?
3. **Critical Thinking:** If the drop in the sales budget of 20% is announced mid-year, does that automatically mean that the company can decrease operation costs by 20%?

More practice: E9-33, E9-34, E9-35
Solution on p. 9-67.

LO9-4 Why are the financial budgets important in the master budgeting process?

After the preceding budgets have been developed, the financial budgets can be constructed. In this section, we illustrate the capital budget and the cash budget.

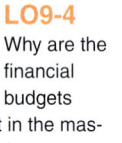

FINANCIAL BUDGETS

Capital Budget — Cash Budget

The cash budget, which incorporates the capital budget, might be the most important schedule prepared during the budgeting process because a company cannot survive without cash.

Capital Budget

The master budget focuses on the short-term or upcoming fiscal period. Managers, however, must also assess and budget for long-term needs such as plant and equipment purchases. Determining the current planned expenditures for long-term assets is referred to as capital budgeting.[4] A **capital budget** estimates costs over a period longer than a year, but the asset purchases included in the capital budget will impact cash outflows and periodic depreciation expense of the upcoming annual period. Thus, results of the capital budgeting process affect the cash and financial statement budgets.

Preparing a Capital Budget — LO9-4 DEMO 9-4A

Assume that Dresdill managers have decided to purchase a $28,000 machine in January and pay for the machine in February. The machine will be placed into service in April after installation, testing, and employee training. Depreciation on the new machine will not be included in the overhead calculation until installation is complete.

◆ How is the capital budget prepared for the first quarter of Year 4?

The schedule below shows Dresdill's capital budget.

	A	B	C	D	E
1	Capital Budget, First Quarter Year 4	January	February	March	Total
2	Acquisition—machinery	$28,000	$ 0	$ 0	$28,000
3	Cash payment for machinery	0	28,000	0	28,000

Cash Budget

The following model can be used to summarize cash receipts and disbursements in a way that assists managers in devising appropriate financing measures to meet company needs.

Cash Budget Model

Beginning cash balance	XXX
+ Cash receipts (collections)	XXX
= Cash available for disbursements exclusive of financing	XXX
− Cash needed for disbursements (purchases, direct labor, overhead, S&A, taxes, bonuses, etc.)	(XXX)
= Cash excess or deficiency (a)	XXX
− Minimum desired cash balance	(XXX)
= Cash needed or available for investment or loan repayment	XXX
Financing methods	
± Borrow (repay) XXX	
± Issue (reacquire) capital stock XXX	
± Sell (acquire) investments XXX	
± Sell (acquire) plant assets XXX	
± Receive (pay) interest or dividends XXX	
Total impact (+ or −) of planned financing (b)	XXX
= Ending cash balance (c), where [(c) = (a) ± (b)]	XXX

Cash Receipts and Accounts Receivable Because some sales are not made on a cash basis, managers must translate sales information into cash receipts through the use of an expected collection pattern. This process considers the collection patterns experienced in the recent past and management's judgment about changes that could disturb current collection patterns. For example, changes that could weaken current collection patterns include recessionary conditions, increases in interest rates, less strict credit-granting policies, and ineffective collection practices.

---

[4] Capital budgeting is discussed in depth in Chapter 19.

DEMO 9-4B   LO9-4   Preparing a Cash Receipts Schedule

Dresdill Corp. has two types of customers:

- cash customers who never receive a discount and
- credit customers.

Of the credit customers, manufacturers and wholesalers are allowed a 2 percent cash discount; retailers are not allowed the discount.

Dresdill has determined from historical data that the collection pattern diagrammed in **Exhibit 9.7** is applicable to its customers. Of each month's sales, 20 percent will be for cash and 80 percent will be on credit. The 40 percent of the credit customers who are allowed the discount pay in the month of the sale. Collections from the remaining credit customers are as follows: 20 percent in the month of sale, 50 percent in the month following the sale, and 29 percent in the second month following the sale. Uncollectible accounts amount to 1 percent of the credit sales that do not take a discount. Assume that November and December Year 3 sales were $125,000 and $135,000, respectively.

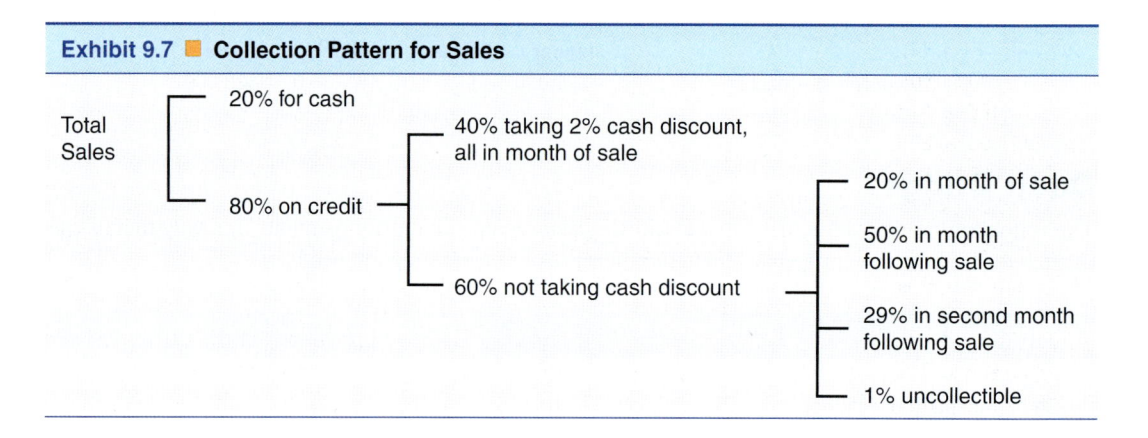

Exhibit 9.7 ■ Collection Pattern for Sales

Total Sales
- 20% for cash
- 80% on credit
  - 40% taking 2% cash discount, all in month of sale
  - 60% not taking cash discount
    - 20% in month of sale
    - 50% in month following sale
    - 29% in second month following sale
    - 1% uncollectible

◆ **Using the sales budget from Demo 9-2, information on November and December Year 3 sales, and the collection pattern described above, what are estimated cash receipts from sales during the first three months of Year 4?**

Using Dresdill's expected collection pattern, projected monthly collections in the first quarter of Year 4 are shown in the schedule that follows. Note that management will use November and December sales information because collections for credit sales extend over three months, meaning that collection of some of the previous year's sales occurs in the budget year.

Chapter 9 The Master Budget

	A	B	C	D	E	F	G	
	Cash Collections, First Quarter Year 4							
1	Sales From	January	February	March	Total	Discount	Uncollectible	
2	November Year 3 sales							AR Balance,
3	$125,000 × 80% × 60% × 29%	$ 17,400			$ 17,400			Dec. 31, Year 3:
4	$125,000 × 80% × 60% × 1%						$ 600	$17,400
5	December Year 3 sales							600
6	$135,000 × 80% × 60% × 50%	32,400			32,400			32,400
7	$135,000 × 80% × 60% × 29%		$ 18,792		18,792			18,792
8	$135,000 × 80% × 60% × 1%						648	648
9	January Year 4 sales							$69,840
10	$150,000 × 20%	30,000			30,000			
11	$150,000 × 80% × 40% × 98%*	47,040			47,040	$ 960		
12	$150,000 × 80% × 60% × 20%	14,400			14,400			
13	$150,000 × 80% × 60% × 50%		36,000		36,000			
14	$150,000 × 80% × 60% × 29%			$ 20,880	20,880			
15	$150,000 × 80% × 60% × 1%						720	
16	February Year 4 sales							
17	$140,000 × 20%		28,000		28,000			
18	$140,000 × 80% × 40% × 98%*		43,904		43,904	896		
19	$140,000 × 80% × 60% × 20%		13,440		13,440			
20	$140,000 × 80% × 60% × 50%			33,600	33,600			
21	March Year 4 sales							
22	$165,000 × 20%			33,000	33,000			
23	$165,000 × 80% × 40% × 98%*			51,744	51,744	1,056		
24	$165,000 × 80% × 60% × 20%			15,840	15,840			
25	Totals	$141,240	$140,136	$155,064	$436,440	$2,912	$1,968	
26	*Cash collected is equal to sales × 98% (= 100% − 2%). The discount amount is equal to sales × 2%.							

January Year 4 sales of $150,000 are used to illustrate the collection calculations in the cash collection schedule above. The first line for January represents cash sales equal to 20 percent of total sales, or $30,000. The next line represents the 80 percent of the customers who buy on credit and who take the discount.

Sales to credit customers (80% of $150,000)	$120,000
Sales to customers allowed discount (40% × $120,000)	$ 48,000
− Discount taken by customers (2% × $48,000)	(960)
= Net collections from customers allowed discount	$ 47,040

The third line for January in the cash collection schedule above reflects the 60 percent of credit customers who paid in the month of sale but were not allowed the discount. The remaining amounts for February and March are computed similarly.

♦ **What are the components of the Accounts Receivable balance as of December 31, Year 3?**

The amounts for November and December collections can be reconciled to the December 31, Year 3, balance sheet (Page 9-11), which indicates a balance of $69,840 in Accounts Receivable. This amount is also detailed below using amounts from the cash collection schedule above.

December 31, Year 3, Balance in Accounts Receivable	
January collections of November sales	$17,400
Estimated November bad debts	600
January collections of December sales	32,400
February collections of December sales	18,792
Estimated December bad debts	648
December 31, Year 3, Accounts Receivable balance	$69,840

© Cambridge Business Publishers

◆ **What are the balances in Accounts Receivable, Allowance for Uncollectible Accounts, and Sales Discounts as of March 31 of Year 4?**

After the cash collections schedule has been prepared, balances for Accounts Receivable, Allowance for Uncollectibles, and Sales Discounts can be projected. These T-accounts for Dresdill follow. Balances will be used to prepare budgeted, quarter-end Year 4 financial statements. For illustrative purposes only, all sales are initially recorded as Accounts Receivable. Immediate cash collections are then deducted from the Accounts Receivable balance.

Accounts Receivable (A/R)

Dec. 31, Year 3 Bal. (Page 9-11)	69,840	Decrease in accounts receivable based upon cash collections[1]	
January Year 4 sales (Demo 9-2)	150,000	January collections	142,200
February Year 4 sales (Demo 9-2)	140,000	February collections	141,032
March Year 4 sales (Demo 9-2)	165,000	March collections	156,120
March 31, Year 4 Bal.	85,488		

[1] Accounts receivable is credited for the full value of the receivable amount when the gross method is used. Thus, the decrease in accounts receivable due to the collection amounts are calculated as follows from information found in Demo 9-4B.

January: $141,240 cash collections + $960 cash discount = $142,200
February: $140,136 cash collections + $896 cash discount = $141,032
March: $155,064 cash collections + $1,056 cash discount = $156,120

Allowance for Uncollectible Accounts

	Dec. 31, Year 3 Bal. (Page 9-11)	1,248	
	January estimate (Demo 9-4B)	720	
	February estimate[1]	672	
	March estimate[2]	792	
	March 31, Year 4 Bal.	3,432	

Sales Discounts

January discounts (Demo 9-4B)	960		
February discounts (Demo 9-4B)	896		
March discounts (Demo 9-4B)	1,056		
March 31, Year 4 Bal.	2,912		

[1] [$140,000 × (80%) × (60%) × (1%)]
[2] [$165,000 × (80%) × (60%) × (1%)]

Uncollectible accounts Note that the estimated uncollectible accounts from November Year 3 through March Year 4 have not been written off as of the end of the first quarter of Year 4. Companies continue to make collection efforts for a substantial period before accounts are acknowledged as worthless. Thus, these receivables may remain on the books for six months or more from the original sales date. When accounts are written off, Accounts Receivable and the Allowance for Uncollectibles will both decrease; however, there will be no income statement impact relative to the write-off.

DEMO 9-4C LO9-4 Preparing a Cash Disbursements Schedule

Dresdill buys all raw material on account (which means, no cash purchases). Dresdill pays for 40 percent of each month's purchases in the month of purchase and is allowed a 2 percent discount for prompt payment. The remaining 60 percent is paid in the month following purchase, and no discounts are taken.

◆ **Using the purchases information from Demo 9-3B, what are estimated cash disbursements during the first three months of Year 4?**

The following schedule presents the first-quarter Year 4 cash disbursements information for purchases. The December 31, Year 3, Accounts Payable balance of $42,504 (Page 9-11) represents 60 percent of December purchases of $70,840. All amounts have been rounded to whole dollars.

Chapter 9 The Master Budget

	A	B	C	D	E	F
	Cash Disbursements for Accounts Payable, First Quarter Year 4					
1	Payment for Purchases of	January	February	March	Total	Discount
2	December Year 3	$42,504			$ 42,504	
3	January Year 4 (from Demo 9-3B)					
4	$75,231 × 40% × 98%*	29,491			29,491	$ 602
5	$75,231 × 60%		$45,139		45,139	
6	February Year 4 (from Demo 9-3B)					
7	$72,662 × 40% × 98%		28,484		28,484	581
8	$72,662 × 60%			$43,597	43,597	
9	March Year 4 (from Demo 9-3B)					
10	$83,754 × 40% × 98%			32,832	32,832	670
11		$71,995	$73,623	$76,429	$222,047	$1,853
12	*Cash paid is equal to cash purchases × 98% (= 100% − 2%). The discount amount is equal to cash purchases × 2%.					

◆ **What are the balances in Accounts Payable, and Purchase discounts as of March 31 of Year 4?**

Accounts payable activity is summarized in the following T-account. The March 31 balance of $50,251 represents 60 percent of March purchases of $83,754 that will be paid during April (slight difference due to rounding). Purchase discounts as of March 31, Year 4 total $1,853.

Accounts Payable

Decrease in accounts payable based upon cash payments[1]		Dec. 31, Year 3 Bal. (Page 9-11)	42,504
January payments	72,597	Jan. Year 4 purchases (Demo 9-3B)	75,231
February payments	74,204	Feb. Year 4 purchases (Demo 9-3B)	72,662
March payments	77,099	March Year 4 purchases (Demo 9-3B)	83,754
		March 31, Year 4 Bal.	50,251

Purchases Discounts

January discounts	602
February discounts	581
March discounts	670
March 31, Year 4 Bal.	1,853

[1] Accounts payable is debited for the full value of the payable amount when the gross method is used. Thus, the decrease in accounts payable due to the collection amounts are calculated as follows from the information found in the schedule above.
January: $71,995 cash payments + $602 cash discount = $72,597
February: $73,623 cash collections + $581 cash discount = $74,204
March: $76,429 cash collections + $670 cash discount = $77,099

Combining Cash Receipts and Cash Disbursements into a Cash Budget A cash budget shows the estimated cash balance after subtracting cash disbursements from cash receipts. Based on the estimated cash balance and the company's desired minimum cash balance, the company can determine how much cash is left for investments or how much is needed through financing.

There are two primary reasons for having a **desired minimum cash balance**: one is internal and the other is external.

- The first reason reflects the uncertainty associated with the budgeting process. Because managers cannot budget with absolute precision, they maintain a "cushion" to protect the company from potential errors in forecasting collections and payments.
- The second reason is that the company's bank may require a minimum cash balance in relation to an open line of credit.

Preparing a Cash Budget — LO9-4 DEMO 9-4D

Assume Dresdill has established $10,000 as its desired minimum cash balance. For simplicity, it is assumed that any investments or sales of investments are made in end-of-month $1,000 increments. Interest on company investments at 3 percent per year (or 0.25 percent per month) is added to the company's bank account at month's end. Dividends of $45,000 are estimated to be paid in March as indicated on page 9-11.

◆ **Given the cash receipt and disbursement information for Dresdill, how is the cash budget prepared for the first quarter of Year 4?**

The following schedule indicates that Dresdill expects $35,876 excess of cash available over disbursements in January. Such an excess, however, does not consider the need for the $10,000 minimum balance. Thus, the company has $25,876 available. It will use $25,000 of that amount to purchase temporary investments at the end of January.

Cash Budget, First Quarter Year 4

	A	B	C	D	E
1		January	February	March	Total
2	Beginning cash balance	$ 10,000	$ 10,876	$ 10,507	$ 10,000
3	Cash collections (Demo 9-4B)	141,240	140,136	155,064	436,440
4	Cash available exclusive of financing	$151,240	$151,012	$165,571	$446,440
5	**Disbursements**				
6	Accounts payable (for purchases, Demo 9-4C)	$ 71,995	$ 73,623	$ 76,429	$222,047
7	Direct labor (Demo 9-3C)	10,465	9,888	11,532	31,885
8	Overhead (Demo 9-3D)*	14,304	13,957	14,945	43,206
9	S&A expenses (Demo 9-3E)*	18,600	18,100	19,350	56,050
10	Total disbursements	$115,364	$115,568	$122,256	$353,188
11	Cash excess (deficiency) (a)	$ 35,876	$ 35,444	$ 43,315	$ 93,252
12	Minimum balance desired	(10,000)	(10,000)	(10,000)	(10,000)
13	Cash available (needed)	$ 25,876	$ 25,444	$ 33,315	$ 83,252
14	**Financing**				
15	Borrowings (repayments)	$ 0	$ 0	$ 0	$ 0
16	Issue (reacquire) stock	0	0	0	0
17	Sell (purchase) investments**	(25,000)	3,000	12,000	(10,000)
18	Sell (acquire) plant assets (Demo 9-4A)	0	(28,000)	0	(28,000)
19	Receive (pay) interest***	0	63	55	118
20	Receive (pay) dividends	0	0	(45,000)	(45,000)
21	Total impact of planned financing (b)	$ (25,000)	$ (24,937)	$ (32,945)	$ (82,882)
22	Ending cash balance (c); (c = a + b) (includes minimum cash balance)	$ 10,876	$ 10,507	$ 10,370	$ 10,370
23	* These amounts are net of depreciation. ** This is the net result of investments and disposals of investments. *** Interest is calculated assuming a 3 percent annual rate (0.25 percent per month); investments and disposals of investments are made at the end of the month in $1,000 increments. February interest: 0.0025 × $25,000 = $63 (rounded) March interest: 0.0025 × ($25,000 − $3,000) = $55				

In February, Dresdill will meet its desired minimum cash balance, but will have to sell $3,000 of its investments to pay for the machine. In March, Dresdill will have enough excess cash available, coupled with the liquidation of $12,000 of investments, to pay the $45,000 dividend declared in Year 3 (page 9-11).

Cash flow provides the short-run source of power in a business to negotiate and act. In addition to preparing and executing a sound cash budget, a business can take other measures. Examples of such measures include a rigorous review of the credit health of new customers, a customer cash discount program as an incentive for prompt payments, and timely follow-up procedures on overdue accounts.

Chapter 9 The Master Budget

Cash Budget — LO9-4 — REVIEW 9-4

Holley Ltd. is preparing its first-quarter monthly cash budget for the year. The following information is available about actual prior year sales and expected current year sales:

November Prior Year	December Prior Year	January Current Year	February Current Year	March Current Year
$125,000	$145,000	$109,000	$120,000	$122,000

Tracing collections from prior year monthly sales and discussions with the credit manager helped develop a profile of collection behavior patterns. Of a given month's sales, 45 percent is typically collected in the month of sale. Because the company terms are 2 percent (end of month) net 30, all collections within the month of sale are net of the 2 percent discount. Of a given month's sales, 30 percent is collected in the month following the sale. The remaining 25 percent is collected in the second month following the month of the sale. Bad debts are negligible and should be ignored.

a. Prepare a schedule of cash collections for Holley Ltd. for January, February, and March of the current year.
b. Calculate the Accounts Receivable balance at March 31, of the current year.
c. **Critical Thinking:** How can management use the cash budget in decision making?

More practice: E9-40, E9-41, E9-42
Solution on p. 9-68.

Budgeted Financial Statements

The final step in the budgeting process is development of budgeted financial statements that reflect the achieved results if the estimates and assumptions used for all previous budgets actually occur.

FINANCIAL BUDGETS

Budgeted Income Statement	Budgeted Balance Sheet	Budgeted Statement of Cash Flows

LO9-5 How are budgeted financial statements prepared and how do ESG initiatives impact the budgeting process?

Such statements allow management to determine whether the projected results are acceptable. If results are not acceptable, management has the opportunity to make adjustments before the beginning of the period for which the budget is being prepared.

When expected net income is unacceptably low, management can investigate the possibility of raising selling prices or finding ways to decrease costs. Any changes considered by management might have related effects that must be included in the revised projections. For example, raising selling prices could decrease volume. Alternatively, cost reductions from using lower-grade material could increase spoilage during production or cause a decline in demand. Changes in budget assumptions and their resultant effects can be simulated quickly and easily through scenario analysis.

Preparing Budgeted Financial Statements — LO9-5 — DEMO 9-5A

◆ **Using the prior budgets, how does Dresdill prepare the budgeted financial statements for the first quarter of Year 4?**

Cost of Goods Manufactured Schedule In a manufacturing environment, management must prepare a schedule of cost of goods manufactured before it can prepare an income statement. *This schedule is necessary to determine cost of goods sold.* Using information from previous budgets, Dresdill's budgeted cost of goods manufactured schedule is shown on the next page. Because it was assumed that no beginning or ending Work in Process Inventories exist, cost of goods manufactured equals the manufacturing costs of the period. Had a partially completed Work in Process Inventory existed, the computations would be more complex and would have involved the use of equivalent units of production (discussed in Chapter 7).

Income Statement Dresdill's budgeted income statement for the first quarter of Year 4 is presented on the next page. This statement uses much of the information previously developed in determining the revenues and expenses for the period.

© Cambridge Business Publishers

Budgeted Cost of Goods Manufactured Schedule

Dresdill Corp.
Budgeted Cost of Goods Manufactured Schedule
For Quarter Ending March 31, Year 4

	A	B	C
2	Beginning work in process inventory		$ 0
3	Cost of raw material used		
4	Beginning balance (Page 9-11)	$ 7,565	
5	Net purchases (Note A)	229,794	
6	Total raw material available	$237,359	
7	Ending balance of raw material (Note B)	(8,729)	
8	Cost of raw material used	$228,630	
9	Direct labor (Demo 9-3C)	31,885	
10	Overhead (Demo 9-3D)	48,306	
11	Total costs to be accounted for		308,821
12	Ending work in process inventory		0
13	Cost of goods manufactured		$308,821

14

Note A
Total purchases (Demo 9-3B)	$231,647	
Purchase discounts (p. 9-21)	(1,853)	
Net purchases	$229,794	

Note B
Ending balance (Demo 9-3B)	3,795	
Price per pound	× $2.30	
Ending balance of raw material	$8,729 (rounded)	

Budgeted Income Statement

Dresdill Corp.
Budgeted Income Statement
For Quarter Ending March 31, Year 4

	A	B	C
2	Sales (Demo 9-2)		$455,000
3	Less sales discounts (p. 9-20)		2,912
4	Net sales		$452,088
5	Cost of goods sold		
6	Finished goods—Dec. 31, Year 3 (Page 9-11)	$ 4,800	
7	Cost of goods manufactured	308,821	
8	Cost of goods available for sale	$313,621	
9	Finished goods—March 31, Year 4 (Note A)	(5,280)	(308,341)
10	Gross margin		$143,747
11	Expenses		
12	Uncollectible accounts expense (Note B)	$ 2,184	
13	S&A expenses (Demo 9-3E)	57,550	(59,734)
14	Income from operations		$ 84,013
15	Other revenue—interest earned (Demo 9-4D)		118
16	Income before income taxes		$ 84,131
17	Income taxes (assumed rate of 40%)		(33,652)
18	Net income		$ 50,479

19

Note A
Beginning finished goods units (p. 9-11)	1,500	
Production (Demo 9-3A)	91,100	
Units available for sale	92,600	
Sales (Demo 9-3A)	(91,000)	
Ending finished goods units	1,600	
Cost per unit:		
Material ($2.30 × 1.1)	$2.53	
Conversion (assumed)	0.77	× $3.30
Cost of ending inventory	$ 5,280	

Note B
Total sales	$455,000	
% credit sales	× 0.80	
Credit sales	$364,000	
% not taking discount	× 0.60	
Potential bad debts	$218,400	
% estimated uncollectible	× 0.01	
Estimated bad debts	$ 2,184	

Chapter 9 The Master Budget

Balance Sheet On completion of the income statement, a March 31, Year 4, balance sheet can be prepared.

Budgeted Balance Sheet

Dresdill Corp.
Budgeted Balance Sheet
March 31, Year 4

Assets			Liabilities and Stockholders' Equity		
Current Assets			**Current Liabilities**		
Cash (Demo 9-4D)		$ 10,370	Accounts Payable (p. 9-21)		$ 50,251
Accounts Receivable (p. 9-20)	$ 85,488		Income Tax Payable (Note C)		33,652
Less Allowance for Uncollectibles (p. 9-20)	(3,432)	82,056	Total Current Liabilities		$ 83,903
Inventories					
Raw Material (3,795 pounds) (p. 9-24)	$ 8,729				
Finished Goods (1,600 units) (p. 9-24)	5,280	14,009			
Investment (Demo 9-4D)		10,000			
Total Current Assets		116,435			
Plant Assets			**Stockholders' Equity**		
Property, Plant, and Equipment (Note A)	$398,000		Common Stock (p. 9-11)	$180,000	
Less Accumulated Depreciation (Note B)	(96,600)	301,400	Retained Earnings (Note D)	153,932	333,932
Total Assets		**$417,835**	**Total Liabilities and Stockholders' Equity**		**$417,835**

Note A
Beginning balance (Page 9-11) $370,000
Purchased new machine (Demo 9-4A) 28,000
Ending balance $398,000

Note B
Beginning balance (Page 9-11) . . . . $ 90,000
Factory depreciation (Demo 9-3D). 5,100
S&A depreciation (Demo 9-3E) 1,500
Ending balance . . . . $ 96,600

Note C
See income tax expense on the income statement on the prior page. Income tax is assumed to be paid in the second quarter.

Note D
Beginning balance (Page 9-11) $103,453
Net income (see prior page) 50,479
Ending balance $153,932

Statement of Cash Flows Information found on the income statement, balance sheet, and cash budget is also used to prepare a statement of cash flows (SCF). This statement can assist managers in performing the following functions:

- judging the company's ability to handle fixed cash outflow commitments,
- adapting to adverse changes in business conditions,
- undertaking new commitments, and
- assessing the quality of company earnings by indicating the relationship between net income and net cash flow from operations.

Whereas the cash budget is essential to current cash management, the budgeted SCF gives managers a more comprehensive view of cash flows by rearranging them into three distinct major activities (operating, investing, and financing). Such a rearrangement permits management to judge whether the specific anticipated flows are consistent with the company's strategic plans. In addition, the SCF would incorporate a schedule or narrative about significant noncash transactions if any have occurred, such as an exchange of stock for land.

The operating section (prepared on either a direct or an indirect basis) of the SCF is acceptable for external reporting. The direct basis uses pure cash flow information (cash receipts and cash disbursements) for operating activities. The operating section of an SCF prepared on an indirect basis begins with net income and makes reconciling adjustments to arrive at cash flow from operations. A statement of cash flows for Dresdill using the information from the cash budget in Demo 9-4D is shown on the next page.

Budgeted Statement of Cash Flows

	A	B	C	D
1	Dresdill Corp. Budgeted Statement of Cash Flows For Quarter Ending March 31, Year 4			
2	**Operating activities**			
3	Cash collections from sales (Demo 9-4D)		$436,440	
4	Interest collected (Demo 9-4D)		118	
5	Total		$436,558	
6	Cash payments			
7	For inventory:			
8	Raw material (Demo 9-4D)	$222,047		
9	Direct labor (Demo 9-4D)	31,885		
10	Overhead (Demo 9-4D)	43,206	(297,138)	
11	For S&A costs		(56,050)	
12	Net cash inflow from operating activities			$ 83,370
13	**Investing activities**			
14	Purchase of plant asset (Demo 9-4D)		$ (28,000)	
15	Purchase of short-term investments (Demo 9-4D)		(25,000)	
16	Sale of short-term investments (Demo 9-4D)		15,000	
17	Net cash outflow from investing activities			(38,000)
18	**Financing activities**			
19	Dividends paid		$ (45,000)	
20	Net cash outflow from financing activities			(45,000)
21	Net increase in cash			$ 370
22	Beginning balance of cash (January 1, Year 4)			10,000
23	Ending balance of cash (March 31, Year 4)			$ 10,370
24	Alternative (indirect) basis for operating activities			
25	Net income		$ 50,479	
26	+ Depreciation (Demo 9-3D and Demo 9-3E)	$ 6,600		
27	− Increase in net Accounts Receivable ($68,592 − $82,056)	(13,464)		
28	− Increase in total inventory ($12,365 − $14,009)	(1,644)		
29	+ Increase in Taxes Payable ($0 − $33,652)	33,652		
30	+ Increase in Accounts Payable ($42,504 − $50,251)	7,747	32,891	
31	= Net cash inflow from operating activities		$ 83,370	

The bottom of the statement shows the indirect method of presenting operating cash flows and uses information from the budgeted balance sheets on pages 9-11 and 9-25 and the budgeted income statement on page 9-24.

Dresdill's cash flow from operating activities ($83,370) is low compared to net sales revenue of $452,088, as is its net income per net sales dollar (11.2 percent). However, cash flow from operating activities does exceed net income of $50,479.

Dresdill may want to review the sales price for its locks and its production costs. Another issue that might be discussed is whether such a high proportion of retained earnings should be paid out as dividends.

Chapter 9 The Master Budget 9-27

Data Visualization

The following data visualization shows budgeted expenses for a casual dining restaurant for a month in which it estimated sales of $42,000.

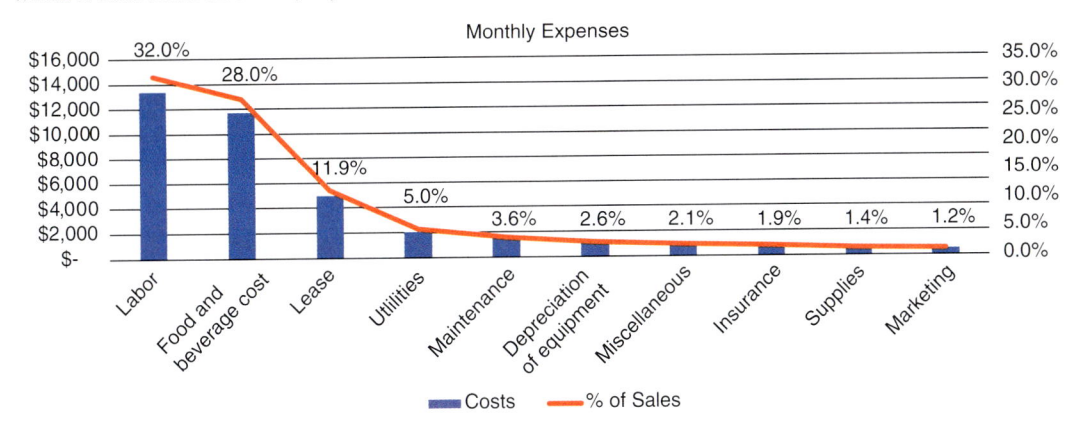

Monthly Expenses

Expense	Cost	% of Sales
Labor	~$13,440	32.0%
Food and beverage cost	~$11,760	28.0%
Lease	~$5,000	11.9%
Utilities	~$2,100	5.0%
Maintenance		3.6%
Depreciation of equipment		2.6%
Miscellaneous		2.1%
Insurance		1.9%
Supplies		1.4%
Marketing		1.2%

Based on the data visualization above, answer the following questions.
a. What is the company's current budgeted profit as a percentage of sales? For cost control purposes, which expenses should the manager focus on?
b. If both labor and food and beverage costs are projected to increase by 5% each, what is the adjusted percentage of sales for each expense?
c. What is profit as a percentage of sales after considering the increase in costs in part *b*?

Solution on p. 9-70.

IMPACT OF ENVIRONMENTAL CONSIDERATIONS ON THE BUDGETING PROCESS

The environmental impact of businesses is of increasing concern to governments, citizens, investors, and managers. Accountants are concerned with both measuring business performance in regard to environmental issues and managing environmental costs. Respondents of a 2019 survey of CEOs conducted by Deloitte considered the most important measures of success to be a company's impact on society, including income inequality, diversity, and the environment.[5] The importance of sustainability goals is further supported with the results of a 2023 survey of 753 business leaders by **Honeywell International, Inc.**, in collaboration with **Futurum Research**.[6] The results indicated that sustainability goals were the *top priority*, ahead of financial performance and market growth, over the coming six months. The study also indicated that 84 percent or more of respondents planned to *increase budgets* in the following sustainability categories: energy evolution and efficiency, emissions reduction, pollution prevention, and circularity and recycling.

The increase in planned spending is fueled by demand, but also by affordability as new technologies have driven costs down and in some cases, governmental subsidies have reduced company's investment costs. Management of environmental spending requires the consideration of environmental issues in every operational aspect. For example, environmental effects are related to the scrap and byproduct from manufacturing operations, cost of materials selected for product components, actions of suppliers providing necessary inputs, and product and packaging usage and disposition habits of customers. Planned green equipment purchases impact capital expenditures but can also make holding current equipment more costly. Does the useful live of the current equipment need to be reduced? Is there an estimated cost of disposal that needs to be capitalized immediately at fair value and expensed?[7] Some companies pur-

---

[5] Deloitte, "Leading the Social Enterprise: Reinvent with a Human Focus," https://www2.deloitte.com/content/dam/insights/us/articles/5136_HC Trends-2019/DI_HC-Trends-2019.pdf (accessed 1/9/20).

[6] Environmental Sustainability Index Q3 2023, Honeywell International, Inc. and Futurum Group, accessed September 18, 2023, https://www.honeywell.com/us/en/company/sustainability/environmental-sustainability-index.

[7] Disposal costs (AROs or asset retirement obligations) would be estimated at fair value, added to the carrying value of the asset while a corresponding liability would be recorded. Over time, the asset would be depreciated (at the higher amount) and accretion expense recorded for the liability until the asset is disposed of.

chase **carbon offsets**, or the direct support of projects that are proven to reduce carbon emissions. This action is intended to offset the company's unavoidable carbon emissions.

In short, environmental issues span the entire value chain. Thus, sustainability efforts will have an impact on various budgets within the master budget, especially as companies strive to achieve ESG goals, such as becoming carbon neutral by a specified date.

DEMO 9-5B   LO9-5   Identifying the Master Budget Impact of Sustainability Initiatives

◆ **What is the impact of each of the following new sustainability initiatives on the master budget for the upcoming year?** Consider each initiative separately.

Sustainability Initiative	Impact on Master Budget for Upcoming Year
1. Management approved a future purchase of more energy efficient equipment which will shorten the useful life of currently held equipment.	• With a decrease in estimate of useful asset life, depreciation will increase affecting the overhead and financial budgets. (In the future, the capital budget would be affected and operational cost savings, such as utilities cost, could decrease the overhead budget.)
2. Consumer trends indicate customers gravitating toward more "green" products in the company's portfolio of products.	• A sales shift in product types will have a ripple effect throughout the budgets starting with the sales budget and flowing through to the production, cost, and financial budgets. (The company will need to assess the impact on future budgets.)
3. The company applied for a governmental grant to purchase green technology which requires that certain metrics be met to qualify for the funding.	• Depending on the specific accounting for the grant, the amount could be recorded as revenue or as a reduction to the capital investment which would reduce depreciation (after metrics are met). Thus, it would impact the overhead and/or the financial budgets.
4. Management committed to increasing its spending on carbon offsets next year.	• Carbon offsets will impact overhead costs and financial budgets.
5. Management is committing to a research and development project to decrease packaging materials required per product.	• During the research stage, the costs would be expensed as research and development costs; thus, it would impact the selling & administrative expense and financial budgets.

REVIEW 9-5   LO9-5   Operating Income Budget

The operating results in summarized form for a computer and related supplies store for the prior year follow.

Revenue	
Computers	$ 6,240,000
Computer supplies	2,600,000
Maintenance contracts	1,560,000
Total revenue	$10,400,000
Costs and expenses	
Cost of computer	$ 4,368,000
Cost of computer supplies	520,000
Marketing expenses	780,000
Customer maintenance costs	832,000
Administrative expenses	1,456,000
Total costs and expenses	7,956,000
Operating income	$ 2,444,000

continued

Chapter 9 The Master Budget 9-27

Data Visualization

The following data visualization shows budgeted expenses for a casual dining restaurant for a month in which it estimated sales of $42,000.

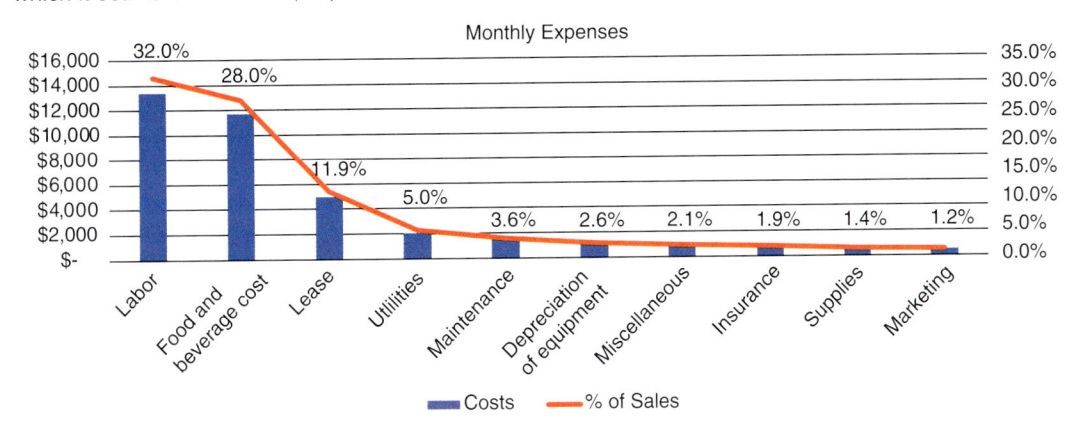

Monthly Expenses

Expense	Cost	% of Sales
Labor	~$13,440	32.0%
Food and beverage cost	~$11,760	28.0%
Lease	~$5,000	11.9%
Utilities	~$2,100	5.0%
Maintenance	~$1,512	3.6%
Depreciation of equipment	~$1,092	2.6%
Miscellaneous	~$882	2.1%
Insurance	~$798	1.9%
Supplies	~$588	1.4%
Marketing	~$504	1.2%

Based on the data visualization above, answer the following questions.
a. What is the company's current budgeted profit as a percentage of sales? For cost control purposes, which expenses should the manager focus on?
b. If both labor and food and beverage costs are projected to increase by 5% each, what is the adjusted percentage of sales for each expense?
c. What is profit as a percentage of sales after considering the increase in costs in part b?

Solution on p. 9-70.

IMPACT OF ENVIRONMENTAL CONSIDERATIONS ON THE BUDGETING PROCESS

The environmental impact of businesses is of increasing concern to governments, citizens, investors, and managers. Accountants are concerned with both measuring business performance in regard to environmental issues and managing environmental costs. Respondents of a 2019 survey of CEOs conducted by Deloitte considered the most important measures of success to be a company's impact on society, including income inequality, diversity, and the environment.[5] The importance of sustainability goals is further supported with the results of a 2023 survey of 753 business leaders by **Honeywell International, Inc.**, in collaboration with **Futurum Research**.[6] The results indicated that sustainability goals were the *top priority*, ahead of financial performance and market growth, over the coming six months. The study also indicated that 84 percent or more of respondents planned to *increase budgets* in the following sustainability categories: energy evolution and efficiency, emissions reduction, pollution prevention, and circularity and recycling.

The increase in planned spending is fueled by demand, but also by affordability as new technologies have driven costs down and in some cases, governmental subsidies have reduced company's investment costs. Management of environmental spending requires the consideration of environmental issues in every operational aspect. For example, environmental effects are related to the scrap and byproduct from manufacturing operations, cost of materials selected for product components, actions of suppliers providing necessary inputs, and product and packaging usage and disposition habits of customers. Planned green equipment purchases impact capital expenditures but can also make holding current equipment more costly. Does the useful live of the current equipment need to be reduced? Is there an estimated cost of disposal that needs to be capitalized immediately at fair value and expensed?[7] Some companies pur-

---

[5] Deloitte, "Leading the Social Enterprise: Reinvent with a Human Focus," https://www2.deloitte.com/content/dam/insights/us/articles/5136_HC Trends-2019/DI_HC-Trends-2019.pdf (accessed 1/9/20).

[6] Environmental Sustainability Index Q3 2023, Honeywell International, Inc. and Futurum Group, accessed September 18, 2023, https://www.honeywell.com/us/en/company/sustainability/environmental-sustainability-index.

[7] Disposal costs (AROs or asset retirement obligations) would be estimated at fair value, added to the carrying value of the asset while a corresponding liability would be recorded. Over time, the asset would be depreciated (at the higher amount) and accretion expense recorded for the liability until the asset is disposed of.

chase **carbon offsets**, or the direct support of projects that are proven to reduce carbon emissions. This action is intended to offset the company's unavoidable carbon emissions.

In short, environmental issues span the entire value chain. Thus, sustainability efforts will have an impact on various budgets within the master budget, especially as companies strive to achieve ESG goals, such as becoming carbon neutral by a specified date.

DEMO 9-5B LO9-5 Identifying the Master Budget Impact of Sustainability Initiatives

◆ **What is the impact of each of the following new sustainability initiatives on the master budget for the upcoming year?** Consider each initiative separately.

Sustainability Initiative	Impact on Master Budget for Upcoming Year
1. Management approved a future purchase of more energy efficient equipment which will shorten the useful life of currently held equipment.	• With a decrease in estimate of useful asset life, depreciation will increase affecting the overhead and financial budgets. (In the future, the capital budget would be affected and operational cost savings, such as utilities cost, could decrease the overhead budget.)
2. Consumer trends indicate customers gravitating toward more "green" products in the company's portfolio of products.	• A sales shift in product types will have a ripple effect throughout the budgets starting with the sales budget and flowing through to the production, cost, and financial budgets. (The company will need to assess the impact on future budgets.)
3. The company applied for a governmental grant to purchase green technology which requires that certain metrics be met to qualify for the funding.	• Depending on the specific accounting for the grant, the amount could be recorded as revenue or as a reduction to the capital investment which would reduce depreciation (after metrics are met). Thus, it would impact the overhead and/or the financial budgets.
4. Management committed to increasing its spending on carbon offsets next year.	• Carbon offsets will impact overhead costs and financial budgets.
5. Management is committing to a research and development project to decrease packaging materials required per product.	• During the research stage, the costs would be expensed as research and development costs; thus, it would impact the selling & administrative expense and financial budgets.

REVIEW 9-5 LO9-5   Operating Income Budget

The operating results in summarized form for a computer and related supplies store for the prior year follow.

Revenue	
Computers	$ 6,240,000
Computer supplies	2,600,000
Maintenance contracts	1,560,000
Total revenue	$10,400,000
Costs and expenses	
Cost of computer	$ 4,368,000
Cost of computer supplies	520,000
Marketing expenses	780,000
Customer maintenance costs	832,000
Administrative expenses	1,456,000
Total costs and expenses	7,956,000
Operating income	$ 2,444,000

continued

Chapter 9 The Master Budget

continued from previous page

The computer store is in the process of formulating its operating budget for the current year and has made the following assumptions.

- The selling prices of computers are expected to increase 8 percent but there will be no selling price increases for computer supplies and maintenance contracts.
- Computer unit sales are expected to increase 3 percent with a corresponding 6 percent growth in the number of maintenance contracts; growth in unit computer supplies is estimated at 5 percent.
- The cost of computers and computer supplies is expected to increase 5 percent.
- Marketing expenses will be increased 2 percent in the coming year.
- Three technicians will be added to the customer maintenance operations in the coming year, increasing the customer maintenance costs by $150,000.
- Administrative costs will be held at the same level.

a. Compute the computer store's budgeted operating income for the current year.
b. **Critical Thinking:** What contributed to the change in operating income between prior year results and the current year budget?

More practice: E9-48, E9-49, E9-51
Solution on p. 9-69.

MASTER BUDGET FOR A SERVICE PROVIDER

Preparing a master budget for a service provider is similar to that of a manufacturer. However, service organizations usually have a *low percentage* of their assets invested in inventory, typically consisting of the supplies needed to facilitate operations. The majority of a service organization's expenses however, will consist of salaries incurred to provide services. This reduces the number of budgets typically required, such as a production budget.

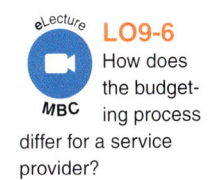

LO9-6 How does the budgeting process differ for a service provider?

Preparing Budgets for a Service Provider — LO9-6 DEMO 9-6

Shelby is the sole owner of a business that provides residential interior design services. She provides design consulting services and performs design projects. For design consulting services, her main cost is labor, but for design projects, she will provide consulting services, furnish spaces, and/or coordinate with contractors to complete design work. During peak times, she hires local students from a design program at a local university. Shelby has additional time in the upcoming year to devote to her business and would like to expand her project base by spending $5,000 in digital advertising.

Shelby summarized the following information based on her financial results from the prior year and her expected results of the current year.

- Shelby maintains a Materials and Furnishings Inventory balance for items that she has purchased for future projects. The December 31 balance is $12,000 and she anticipates the year-end balance to increase to $30,000.
- Prior year consulting revenue and project revenue were $50,000 and $160,000, respectively. Shelby estimates that consulting revenue and project revenue will increase in the current year by 10 percent and 15 percent respectively. At the beginning of the current year, the accounts receivable balance is zero. However, Shelby expects to have a $2,500 and $8,000 Accounts Receivable balances related to Consulting and Projects, respectively, at year end.
- To support the current year projects, Shelby expects to use $50,000 in materials and furnishings and to incur $60,000 in contractor fees.
- Shelby intends to hire two university students at $20 an hour for 300 hours each.
- Additional estimated costs for the upcoming year include $2,000 in rent and utilities for her home office, $1,500 in insurance costs, and $3,500 in miscellaneous costs. On June 30, Shelby anticipates joining a professional membership in a design organization at a cost of $1,500 for the year.
- The cash balance is $12,000 at the beginning of the current year and this represents the minimum required cash balance.

◆ **How does Shelby create a purchases budget for materials and furnishings?**

The amount of materials and furnishings estimated to be purchased in the current year is $68,000, calculated in the following purchases budget.

Purchases Budget	Annual
Materials and furnishings required for the period	$ 50,000
Projected ending balance	30,000
Total requirements	80,000
Less beginning inventory	(12,000)
Purchases	$ 68,000

◆ **Ignoring taxes, how does Shelby create a revenue and expense budget, before considering her salary?**

The revenue and expense budget shows a net profit of $104,250, before owner's salary.

Revenue and Expense Budget	Annual
Consulting revenue ($50,000 × 1.10)	$ 55,000
Project revenue ($160,000 × 1.15)	184,000
Total revenues	239,000
Expenses:	
Project materials and furnishings	$ 50,000
Project contractor fees	60,000
Salaries, part-time staff (2 employees × $20 × 300 hours)	12,000
Rent and utilities	2,000
Advertising	5,000
Insurance	1,500
Miscellaneous	3,500
Professional membership ($1,500 × 6 months/12 months)	750
Total expenses	(134,750)
Revenues less expenses	$104,250

◆ **Ignoring taxes, how does Shelby create a cash budget, considering her salary of $75,000?**

The cash budget shows $75,000 for owner salaries, while still maintaining the required ending cash balance of $12,000.

Cash Budget	Annual
Beginning cash	$ 12,000
Cash receipts:	
Consulting revenue ($55,000 − $2,500)	52,500
Consulting projects ($184,000 − $8,000)	176,000
Total cash receipts	228,500
Cash disbursements:	
Project materials and furnishings	68,000
Project contractor fees	60,000
Salaries, part-time staff	12,000
Rent and utilities	2,000
Advertising	5,000
Insurance	1,500
Miscellaneous	3,500
Professional membership	1,500
Total cash disbursements before owner salary	153,500
Net cash	87,000
Amount for owner salary	75,000
Ending cash	$ 12,000

Chapter 9 The Master Budget

Not-For-Profit Organizations Managers in not-for-profit organizations (NFPs) must recognize that their budgeting process is often more difficult than in for-profit entities. Because contribution or fee inflows are often tied closely to general economic conditions, estimates of these amounts may be less reliable than sales revenue estimates. Costs in NFPs may be less reasonably tied to inflows and more tied to the service activities of the NFPs. There is a strong emphasis in NFPs on stewardship responsibility so budget versus actual comparisons are critical as is cash management. Cash flows in NFPs often fluctuate greatly during the year even though expense items remain constant; thus, managers at NFPs must keep a close eye on whether sufficient cash is available to provide client services. "An increase in demand for a not-for-profit's services can lead to a management crisis" should insufficient funds exist.[8]

Preparing a Budgeted Income Statement for a Service Provider — LO9-6 — REVIEW 9-6

A small legal firm has two lines of business: full-service and virtual. Virtual services are streamlined services offered for more standardized transactions. The company summarized the following revenue and cost data using its historical information.

	Annual
Service revenue	
Virtual-service revenue	$ 280,000
Full-service revenue	1,250,000
Fixed expenses	
Salaries	800,000
Overhead	150,000
Variable expenses	
Overhead: 15% of Total revenue	
Client service: 5% of Full-service revenue	

For the first quarter of the following year, the firm expects the following changes.

- Virtual-service revenue will increase by 10 percent and Full-service revenue will decrease by 10 percent.
- Salaries expense will increase by 5 percent.
- Professional liability insurance expense will increase by $10,000 for the annual policy.
- Overhead as a percentage of total revenue is not expected to change, but Client service expense as a percentage of Full-service revenue is expected to increase to 8 percent.

a. Prepare a budgeted income statement for the first quarter.
b. **Critical Thinking:** How is the cost control focus different for a service provider compared to a manufacturer?

More practice: MC9-21, E9-53, P9-76
Solution on p. 9-69.

QUALITY OF THE MASTER BUDGET

A well-prepared master budget can act as a:

- guide to help managers align activities and resource allocations with organizational goals;
- vehicle to promote employee participation, cooperation, and departmental coordination;
- tool to enhance conduct of the managerial functions of planning, controlling, problem solving, and performance evaluating;
- basis on which to sharpen management's responsiveness to changes in both internal and external factors; and
- model that provides a rigorous view of future performance of a business in time to consider alternative measures.

Factors that contribute to a well-prepared budget include: the accuracy of sales forecasts, timing of budget preparation, the policy on budget revisions, level of employee participation, and ethical behavior.

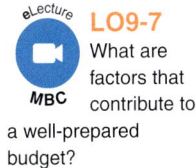

LO9-7 What are factors that contribute to a well-prepared budget?

---

[8] M. Pich., "Planning and Budgeting in Non-Profit Organizations," *CMA Magazine* (March 2009), pp. 22–27.

Accuracy of Sales Forecasts

Budget preparation requires the development of a variety of forecasts. The sales forecast is based on a variety of interrelated factors such as historical trends, product innovation, general economic conditions, industry conditions, and the organization's strategic position for competing on the basis of price, product differentiation, or market niche. Many organizations first determine the industry forecast for a given product or service and then extract from it their sales estimations.

Because of its fundamental role in the budgeting process, sales demand has a pervasive impact on the master budget. Projected sales must be predicted as accurately and with as many details as possible. Sales forecasts should indicate type and quantity of products to be sold, geographic locations of the sales, types of buyers, and timing of sales. Such detail is necessary because different products require different production and distribution facilities and channels; different customers have different credit terms and payment schedules; and different seasons or months can necessitate different shipping schedules or methods. Managers should use as much information as is available and can combine several estimation approaches. Combining prediction methods provides managers a way to confirm estimates and reduce uncertainty. Some ways of estimating future demand are

- canvassing sales personnel for a subjective consensus,
- making simple extrapolations of past trends,
- using market research, and
- employing statistical and other mathematical models.

Care should be taken to use realistic, rather than optimistic or pessimistic, forecasts of revenues and costs. Firms can develop computer models that allow repetitive simulations to be run after changes are made to one or more factors. These simulations permit managers to review results that would be obtained under various circumstances.

While the focus of this chapter is using budgets for internal decision making, it is interesting to note that many publicly traded companies share their forecasts of revenues, expenses, profits, losses, capital expenditures and/or other information for the upcoming months through earnings guidance. For example, **Kroger** released guidance in a company press release in the third quarter, that estimated full-year sales trends, and a range for its operating profits and capital expenditures, among other things.[9] The *earnings guidance* is voluntary information that is disclosed through press releases or other forms of investor communication. This practice puts even more pressure on companies to understand their current results and whether or not they will perform at or below budget in order to communicate relevant information before results are known.

Timing of Budget Preparation The master budget is normally prepared for a year and is detailed by quarters and months within those quarters. A survey conducted by the American Productivity & Quality Center found that high-performing organizations tend to complete their budgeting cycle in 25 days or less.[10] Some companies (such as **American Express**, **Group Health Cooperative**, and **Unilever**)[11] use a **continuous budget** (or **rolling budget**), which means that an ongoing 12-month budget is presented by successively adding a new budget month (12 months into the future) as each current month expires. Such a process allows management to work, at any time, within the present one-month component of a full 12-month annual budget. Continuous budgets make the planning process less sporadic. Rather than having managers "go into the budgeting period" at a specific time, they are continuously involved in planning and budgeting. Benefits of a continuous budget include

- eliminating a fiscal year mind-set by recognizing that business is an ongoing operation and should be managed accordingly;
- allowing management to take corrective steps as forecasted business conditions change;
- eliminating the unrealistic "gap" that occurs with the first iteration of each annual budget; and
- reducing or eliminating the budget planning process that occurs at the end of each fiscal year.[12]

---

[9] "Kroger Reports Second Quarter 2023 Results and Reaffirms Guidance," Kroger. Accessed September 18, 2023. https://ir.kroger.com/Corporate-Profile/press-releases/press-release/2023/Kroger-Reports-Second-Quarter-2023-Results-and-Reaffirms-Guidance/default.aspx.

[10] P. Wiggins, "Cycle Time to Complete the Annual Budget: Metric of the Month," CFO.com (November 1, 2021), https://www.cfo.com/news/cycle-time-to-complete-the-annual-budget-metric-of-the-month/655292/

[11] M. Lamoreaux, "Planning for Uncertainty," *Journal of Accountancy* (October 2011), pp. 32–36.

[12] S. Hunt and P. Klein, "Budgets Roll with the Times," *Optimize* (August 2003), p. 85.

A traditional year-long budget can become irrelevant very quickly in a crisis situation. During the pandemic, companies needed to rely on information that looked beyond the end of the year and that was updated for current conditions. For example, **Ascension**, a healthcare system based in St. Louis, accelerated its transition to a rolling 18- to 24-month budget, with quarterly spending plan reviews.[13]

Policy on Budget Revisions

If actual results differ from plans, managers should find the causes of the differences and then consider budget revisions. Arrangements usually cannot be made rapidly enough to revise the current month's budget. However, managers could revise future months' budgets under certain circumstances (such as if actual and expected performance deviated substantially). Certain budgetary times may be adjusted more frequently than others. For example, Southwest Airlines "updates its revenue forecast daily and its fuel forecast weekly. But other items may be forecast bimonthly, monthly or quarterly."[14]

If budget variance causes are beyond the organization's control and are cost related, management can decide to revise budget cost estimates upward or downward to be more realistic. If the causes are internal (such as the sales staff not selling the product), management can leave the budget in its original form so that the effects of operational control are visible in the comparisons. Regardless of whether the budget is revised, managers should commend those individuals responsible for positive performance and communicate the effects of such performance to other related departments. For example, if the sales force has sold significantly higher quantities of product than expected in the original budget, production and purchasing must be notified to increase the number of units manufactured and amount of raw material purchased.

Level of Employee Participation

A **participatory budget** is developed through joint decision making by top management and operating personnel. However, in **imposed budgets**, top management prepares with little or no input from operating personnel. After the budget has been developed, operating personnel are informed of the budget goals and constraints. The budgeting process can be represented by a continuum with participatory budgets on one end and imposed budgets on the other. Only rarely is a budget either purely participatory or purely imposed. The budget process in a company is usually defined by the degree to which the process is either participatory or imposed.

Budget Slack When budgets are used for performance evaluations, management often encounters the problem of **budget slack**, which is the intentional underestimation of revenues and/or overestimation of expenses. Slack can be incorporated into the budget during the development process in a participatory budget. Having budget slack allows subordinate managers to achieve their objectives with less effort than would be necessary without the slack. Slack also creates problems because of the significant interaction of the budget factors. For example, if sales volumes are understated or overstated, problems in the production, purchasing, and personnel areas can arise.

Budget Padding Another problem encountered in budgeting is **budget padding**. Managers may "pad" the budget by increasing budget amounts in areas that will likely be approved rather than in areas in which the funds are actually desired. "Diverting corporate funds for purposes not sanctioned by higher management can result in lower profit overall, less return for shareholders, difficulty meeting debt covenants, and fewer bonuses being paid."[15]

Top management can try to reduce slack or padding by tying actual performance to the budget through a bonus system. Operating managers are rewarded with large bonuses for budgeting relatively high performance levels and achieving those levels. If performance expectations are low, achievement of that performance is either not rewarded or only minimally rewarded. Top management must be aware that budget slack and padding have a tremendous negative impact on organizational effectiveness and efficiency.

---

[13] K. Broughton, "Corporate Spending Plans Tweaked as Recovery Pace Remains Uncertain," *The Wall Street Journal* (February 15, 2021), https://www.wsj.com/articles/corporate-spending-plans-tweaked-as-recovery-pace-remains-uncertain-11613399400.

[14] M. Lamoreaux, "Planning for Uncertainty," *Journal of Accountancy* (October 2011), pp. 32–36.

[15] T. Stephenson and J. Porter, "Part 6 of 6: Really Using an Excel-Based Budget You've Created," *Strategic Finance* (July 2010), pp. 38–43.

Ethical Behavior

Because most wrongful activities related to budgeting are unethical, rather than illegal, organizations often have difficulty dealing with them. However, when managers' actions cross the gray area between ethical and fraudulent behavior, organizations are not reluctant to dismiss employees or even pursue legal actions against them.

Although most managers have a natural inclination to be conservative in developing their budgets, at some level the blatant padding or building slack into the budget becomes unethical. In an extreme case, it might even be considered theft if an inordinate level of budgetary slack creates favorable performance variances that lead to significant bonuses or other financial gain for the manager. The deliberate falsification of budgets is unethical behavior and is grounds for dismissal in most organizations.

Ethical issues might also arise in the reporting of performance results, which usually compares actual data with budgeted data. Examples of unethical reporting of actual performance data include misclassification of expenses, overstating revenues or understating expenses, postponing or accelerating the recording of activities at the end of the accounting period, or creating fictitious activities.

DEMO 9-7 | **LO9-7** | **Classifying Actions in the Budget Process**

◆ **For each of the following descriptions of a budget action, what is the aspect of budgeting that is most relevant?**

Choose from forecasting, rolling budget, participatory budget, imposed budget, budget slack, and budget padding. Consider each scenario separately.

a. In estimating the budget category for wages, the top quartile of all wages was used as an estimate instead of an average amount.

   Budget slack: The budget will likely be higher than actual results. The amount of slack will depend on the known difference between the average and the top quartile average.

b. A production manager increased the repairs and maintenance budget but plans to use the extra funds for departmental computer upgrades instead.

   Budget padding: The manager desires to upgrade the computers by increasing a different budget that may be more easily approved.

c. As a result of the pandemic, budgets quickly became irrelevant, prompting upper management to make budget revisions without input from operation managers.

   Imposed budget: The crisis required a quick reaction which was directed by upper management and communicated to operation managers.

d. The first draft of a sales budget is prepared through generative AI, utilizing extensive statistical models based upon historical trends and a vast amount of market research.

   Forecasting: The sales forecast drives the numbers in the remaining budgets; thus, the accuracy in forecasting is essential to the validity of the master budget.

e. A new technology start-up company adopted a policy to produce ongoing 12-month budgets.

   Rolling budget: A startup faces uncertainty in the amounts of revenues and costs. A rolling budget would provide the flexibility to adjust the budget as the business grows.

f. In anticipation of the annual budgeting process, the purchasing department held a brainstorming session, focused on gathering ideas for cost-saving initiatives.

   Participatory budget: Obtaining input from operating personnel is a participatory budgeting practice.

Chapter 9 The Master Budget

REVIEW 9-7

Understanding the Budgeting Process — **LO9-7**

1. Match each of the following items 1 through 8 with the most appropriate description, *a* through *h*.

   Term
   1. Benefit of a master budget
   2. Budget padding
   3. Budget slack
   4. Continuous budget
   5. Imposed budget
   6. Method to estimate sales demand
   7. Participatory budget
   8. Sales projections

   Description
   a. ___ Essential to the budgeting process
   b. ___ Assists managers in the allocation of resources and in control and planning functions
   c. ___ Results in a full 12-month budget at any particular point in time
   d. ___ Intentional over (under) estimation of budgetary expenses (revenues)
   e. ___ Budget developed by management and operating staff
   f. ___ Budget developed by management without input from operating staff
   g. ___ Increasing the budget in one area with the intent to use the funds elsewhere
   h. ___ Use of statistical models

2. **Critical Thinking:** Under what circumstances would an imposed budget be preferable to a participatory budget?

More practice: E9-57
Solution on p. 9-70.

A Deeper Look into the Budgeting Process: A Budget Manual

To be useful, a budget requires a substantial amount of time and effort from the persons who prepare it. This process can be improved by the availability of an organizational **budget manual**, which is a detailed set of information and guidelines about the budgetary process. The manual should include:

- statements of the budgetary purpose;
- a listing of specific budgetary activities to be performed;
- a calendar of scheduled budgetary activities;
- sample budgetary forms; and
- original, revised, and approved budgets.

The statements of budgetary purpose and desired results communicate the reasons behind the process. These statements should flow from general to specific details. An example of a general statement of budgetary purpose might be as follows: "The cash budget provides a basis for planning, reviewing, and controlling cash flows from and to various activities; this budget is essential to the preparation of a pro forma statement of cash flows." Specific statements could include references to minimum desired cash balances and periods of intense cash needs.

Budgetary activities should be listed by position rather than by person because the responsibility for actions should be assigned to the individual holding the designated position at the time the budget is being prepared. The manual's activities section should indicate who has the final authority for revising and approving the budget. Budget approval can be delegated to a budget committee or reserved by one or several members of top management.

The budget calendar helps coordinate the budgetary process by providing a timetable for all budget activities. The larger the organization, the more time that will be needed to gather and coordinate information, identify weak points in the process or the budget itself, and take corrective action. The calendar should also indicate control points at which budget-to-actual comparisons are to be made.

Sample forms and templates are extremely useful because they provide for consistent presentations of budget information from all individuals, making summarization of information easier and quicker. Templates should be easy to understand and may include standardized worksheets or programmed spreadsheets that allow managers to update historical information to arrive at budgetary figures. This section of the budget manual may also provide standard cost tables for items on which the organization has specific guidelines or policies. For example, a company policy states that each salesperson's per diem meal allowance is $70, meal expenses would be budgeted as estimated travel days multiplied by $70.

The final section of the budget manual contains the budgets generated during the budgeting process. Numerous budgets may be proposed and rejected prior to actual budget acceptance and implementation. Understanding this revision process and why changes were made is helpful for future planning. The final approved master budget is included in the budget manual as a control document.[16]

---

[16] In the event of changes in economic conditions or strategic plans, the "final" budget can be revised during the budget period.

© Cambridge Business Publishers

Comprehensive Chapter Review

Key Terms

activity-based approach, p. 9-5
budget, p. 9-2
budget committee, p. 9-4
budgeting, p. 9-2
budget manual, p. 9-35
budget padding, p. 9-33
budget slack, p. 9-33
capital budget, p. 9-17
carbon offsets, p. 9-28
continuous budget, p. 9-32
desired minimum cash balance, p. 9-21
direct labor budget, p. 9-14
financial budgets, p. 9-7
generative artificial intelligence (generative AI), p. 9-4
imposed budgets, p. 9-33
incremental approach, p. 9-6
master budget, p. 9-5
minimum level approach, p. 9-6
operating budget, p. 9-7
output/input approach, p. 9-5
overhead budget, p. 9-14
participatory budget, p. 9-33
production budget, p. 9-12
purchases budget, p. 9-13
rolling budget, p. 9-32
sales budget, p. 9-9
selling and administrative expense budget, p. 9-15
strategic planning, p. 9-2
tactical planning, p. 9-3
zero-based budgeting, p. 9-6

Chapter Summary

LO9-1 Relationship of Strategic and Tactical Planning to Budgeting (Page 9-2)
- Strategic planning focuses on the long term (5–10 years).
- Tactical planning focuses on the short term (1–18 months).
- Both strategic and tactical planning need qualitative and quantitative information.
- Budgeting helps in the planning process by having management
  - visualize the future and move in a focused direction. agree on and communicate organizational goals and objectives.
  - translate strategic goals and objectives into quantifiable, monetary information.
  - tie the long-term and short-term (tactical) plans together.
  - harmonize external considerations and internal factors.
  - determine how to commit resources to desired activities.
  - establish financial performance indicators of success.
  - engage people to participate in the planning process.
  - produce a spirit of cooperation among employees and organizational departments or divisions.
  - control operations and resource usage.
- Budget approaches include
  - Output/Input approach
  - Activity-based approach
  - Incremental approach
  - Minimum level approach

LO9-2 Sales as the Starting Point of a Master Budget (Page 9-7)
- Determination of a sales projection requires current information regarding
  - the economy,
  - business environment,
  - technological developments,
  - and available resources.
- The sales projection provides a single level of output demand that is used as a base throughout the budget process.
- The use of a specific sales projection provides a static base to facilitate the numerous arrangements (employees, suppliers, prices, resource quality, capacity availability, etc.) that must be in place before operations begin.

LO9-3 Components and Preparation of a Master Budget (Page 9-12)
- The sales budget (prepared first) reflects unit sales volume and sales prices.
- The production budget adds unit sales to desired units in ending Finished Goods Inventory and subtracts units in beginning Finished Goods Inventory.
  - Retail and service companies do not have a production budget.
- The purchases budget adds production requirements to desired ending raw material or component inventories and subtracts beginning raw material or component inventories.

Chapter 9 The Master Budget

- Purchases quantities are multiplied by raw material or component costs.
- The direct labor budget multiplies units of production by standard hours allowed and then by average wage rate.
- The overhead budget indicates the type and amount of variable and fixed manufacturing overhead costs.
- The selling and administrative budget indicates the type and amount of variable and fixed nonmanufacturing costs.
- The capital budget contains fixed asset purchases and payment points for those assets.
- The cash budget reflects all cash received from and spent on items included in the other budgets.
- All of the individual budgets are combined to prepare budgeted financial statements.

Importance of the Cash Budget in Master Budgeting (Page 9-16)   LO9-4

- Cash is essential for an organization to survive.
- The cash budget
  - translates accrual-based information (such as sales revenues and purchases) into cash flows.
  - helps management assess the effectiveness of credit practices (i.e., whether customers are paying for purchases within the designated credit period).
  - indicates when cash borrowings might be necessary or when cash investments might be made (and for how long).
  - provides important information for preparing the budgeted statement of cash flows.

Reasons for Preparing Budgeted Financial Statements (Page 9-23)   LO9-5

- Such statements
  - indicate the results that will be achieved if the estimates and assumptions used actually occur.
  - allow management to determine if the budgeted results are acceptable.
  - provide management an opportunity, if necessary, to make adjustments to budget assumptions.
  - assess the effects of a change in one budget assumption on related budget assumptions or amounts.

Budgeting Process for a Service Provider (Page 9-29)   LO9-6

- Similar to the process required for a manufacturer, but with fewer types of budgets needed
- Service organizations typically have lower inventory levels
- Budgets can include purchases budget, revenue and expense budget, and cash budget

Budgeting Factors in a Well-Prepared Budget (Page 9-31)   LO9-7

- Accuracy of the sales budget has significant impact on the master budget.
- Rolling budgets can make planning less sporadic.
- Causes of variances should be considered and budget revisions should be made if appropriate.
- Management should try to reduce budget slack and budget padding due to the negative impact on the organization.
- Participatory budgets are developed jointly by top management and operating personnel while imposed budgets are prepared with little/no input from operating personnel.
- Blatant budget slack or padding can be considered unethical behavior.

Solution Strategies

Sales Budget

    Units of sales
× Selling price per unit
= Dollars of sales

Production Budget   LO9-2

    Units of sales
+ Units desired in ending inventory
− Units in beginning inventory
= Units to be produced

Purchases Budget

    Units to be produced*
+ Units desired in ending inventory
− Units in beginning inventory
= Units to be purchased

*Converted to direct material component requirements, if necessary

Direct Labor Budget

    Units to be produced
× Standard time allowed per unit
= Standard labor time allowed
× Per-hour direct labor cost
= Total direct labor cost

© Cambridge Business Publishers

Overhead Budget

    Predicted activity base
× Variable overhead rate per unit of activity

= Total variable overhead cost
+ Fixed overhead cost

= Total overhead cost

Selling and Administrative Budget

    Predicted sales dollars (or other variable measure)
× Variable S&A rate per dollar (or other variable measure)

= Total variable S&A cost
+ Fixed S&A cost

= Total S&A cost

LO9-4 Cash Budget

    Beginning cash balance
+ Cash receipts (collections)

= Cash available for disbursements
− Cash needed for disbursements:
    Cash payments for accounts payable for month
    Cost of compensation
    Total cost of overhead minus depreciation
    Total S&A cost minus depreciation

= Cash excess or deficiency
− Minimum desired cash balance

= Cash needed or available for investment or financing
± Various financing measures

= Ending cash balance

Schedule of Cash Receipts (Collections) from Sales

    Dollars of credit sales for month
× Percent collection for month of sale

= Credit to accounts receivable for month's sales
− Allowed and taken sales discounts

= Receipts for current month's credit sales
+ Receipts from cash sales
+ Current month's cash receipts for prior months' credit sales

= Cash receipts for current month

Schedule of Cash Payments for Purchases

    Units to be purchased
× Cost per unit

= Total cost of purchases
× Percent payment for current purchases

= Debit to accounts payable for month's purchases
− Purchase discounts taken

= Cash payments for current month's purchases
+ Cash purchases
+ Current month's payments for prior months' purchases

= Cash payments for accounts payable for current month

Chapter Demonstration Problem

LO9-2, 3, 4

The July 31, balance sheet for World Windows Inc. includes the following information:

Cash..	$ 40,000 debit
Accounts Receivable	270,000 debit
Merchandise Inventory of R#850 units................	8,750 debit
Merchandise Inventory of R#925 units................	7,200 debit

The firm's management has designated $35,000 as the firm's monthly minimum cash balance. Because a piece of equipment was sold at the end of July, the beginning cash balance was greater than the minimum desired amount. Other information about World Windows is as follows:

- Projected sales (all on account) for the following three months are

	August	September	October
R#850 units (unit selling price = $250).....	1,000	800	1,100
R#925 units (unit selling price = $480).....	500	700	1,300

- Cost of Goods Sold (CGS) for R#850 and R#925 units approximate 70 and 60 percent, respectively, of sales revenues.
- Management wants to end each month with 5 percent of the following month's sales in units. Unit costs are assumed to be stable.
- The collection pattern for accounts receivable is 55 percent in the month of sale, 44 percent in the month following the sale, and 1 percent uncollectible.
- All accounts payable for inventory are paid in the month of purchase.
- Other monthly expenses are $28,000, which includes $6,000 of depreciation but does not include uncollectible accounts expense.
- Investments of excess cash are made in $5,000 increments.

Required:
a. Prepare a sales budget for August, September, and October.
b. Prepare a purchases budget for August and September.
c. Forecast the August cash collections.
d. Prepare the cash budget for August including the effects of financing (borrowing or investing).

Solution to Demonstration Problem

a.

	August	September	October
R#850 units	1,000 × $250 = $250,000	800 × $250 = $200,000	1,100 × $250 = $275,000
R#925 units	500 × $480 = 240,000	700 × $480 = 336,000	1,300 × $480 = 624,000
	$490,000	$536,000	$899,000

b. R#850 units: Cost = 70% of sales revenue = 0.70 × $250 = $175 per unit
R#925 units: Cost = 60% of sales revenue = 0.60 × $480 = $288 per unit
R#850 units in beginning inventory = 5% of 1,000 = 50; 50 × $175 = $8,750 (as shown in beginning merchandise inventory)
R#925 units in beginning inventory = 5% of 500 = 25; 25 × $288 = $7,200 (as shown in beginning merchandise inventory)

R#850 units	August	September
Sales................................	1,000	800
Ending inventory.....................	40	55
Beginning inventory	(50)	(40)
Units to purchase	990	815
Cost per unit.........................	× $175	× $175
Purchases of R#850..................	$173,250	$142,625

R#925 units	August	September
Sales.	500	700
Ending inventory.	35	65
Beginning inventory	(25)	(35)
Units to purchase	510	730
Cost per unit.	× $288	× $288
Purchases of R#925.	$146,880	$210,240

Total purchases in August = $173,250 + $146,880 = $320,130
Total purchases in September = $142,625 + $210,240 = 352,865

c. A/R on July 31 = 0.45 July sales
$270,000 = 0.45X
X = $600,000 = total July sales

August Collections	
From July ($600,000 × 0.44)	$264,000
From August ($490,000 × 0.55)	269,500
Total	$533,500

d.

August Cash Budget		
Beginning cash balance		$ 40,000
August collections.		533,500
Total cash available for disbursements.		$573,500
Disbursements		
Purchase of merchandise	$320,130	
Other monthly expenses ($28,000 – $6,000)	22,000	(342,130)
Cash excess or deficiency (a)		$231,370
Less minimum cash balance desired		(35,000)
Cash available		$196,370
Financing:		
Acquire investment (b)		(195,000)
Ending cash balance (c); (c = a + b)		$ 36,370

Assignments with the [MBC] logo in the margin are available in *myBusinessCourse*.
Resources include demonstration videos, guided examples, and auto-graded homework.
See details in the Preface, and ask your professor how you can access the system.

Data Analytics

LO9-1 **DA9-1. Analyzing revenue budget data**

Access the data file from the **Connecticut Office of the State Comptroller** available on the textbook website and answer the following questions.

Required

a. Prepare a PivotChart showing the revenue actual totals by revenue category in a bar chart. *Hint:* With your cursor on a cell in the worksheet, click on Insert, PivotChart. Drag Revenue category into Axis (Rows) and Actual Amount into Values. Right click on chart to Select a new chart type and choose Bar chart.

b. Add two chart slicers: one for Fiscal Year and one for Fund type in order to capture data only for 2022 and for General fund. Add data labels to columns. *Hint:* Under the "PivotChart Analyze" label, select Insert slicer and select Fiscal year. Repeat steps but now select Fund type. To add data labels, with cursor on a bar (make sure all bars are highlighted), right click and select Add data labels.

Chapter 9 The Master Budget 9-41

    c. Sort bar chart from the largest expenditure to the smallest.
    d. Using your data visualization, answer the following questions.
        1. What are the top three revenue sources and dollar amounts for the General fund in 2022?
        2. What is the dollar amount of revenue for the category "Cigarettes and Tobacco"?
        3. Display the amounts as a percentage of the grand total. Starting from the category with the highest percentage, what categories make up 94.46 percent of the total? *Hint:* Open the dropdown menu next to the amount field in the Values section. Select Value Field Settings and open the Show values as tab. Select % of Grand Total.
    e. Create a revenue budget for 2023 using the incremental approach: increase each 2022 category by 2 percent as the basis for your 2023 revenue budget. Round the amounts to millions of dollar. *Hint:* Create an Excel worksheet using the data from your summary table. Arrange your budget from the largest to the smallest dollar amounts.
    f. What are some strengths and weaknesses of using the incremental approach to budgeting?

DA9-2. Forecasting using Excel
Melton Manufacturing opened in January 2023. Sales have increased significantly in the first two years of operations, and management is now looking to expand production capacity. To finance the purchase of a new factory, they would need to either raise capital or borrow funds. They have asked you to make some projections for the next year of operations. They intend to share these with potential investors and lenders. Information about unit sales, sales revenues, and net profits for the past two years is included in the file available on the textbook's website. A video demonstrating Excel tools used to answer the questions in this problem is also available on the website.

Required
1. Create three line graphs in Excel (one for units sold, one for sales revenue, and one for net operating income). Add trendlines to all graphs.
    a. Extend the trendline out for 12 months.
    b. Use the Polynomial (Order 2) trendline option for all charts
    c. To see how closely the trendline matches the data, check the Display R-squared value on chart box. The closer the R-square value is to 1, the better the match.
2. Create the same three graphs using the Forecast Sheet tool (line charts) in Excel. *Hint:* The Forecast Sheet tool is found under the Data tab. Highlight data to analyze, click on Forecast sheet, and click on Options to make the following adjustments.
    a. Set the Forecast End to 12/1/2025.
    b. Use an 85 percent Confidence Interval.
    c. Check the Include forecast statistics box.
    d. Leave remaining defaults as is.
3. Use the trendline graphs to determine: (*Hint:* To help identify the answers, display gridlines. Consider changing vertical axis bounds.)
    a. Expected unit sales in October 2025
    b. Expected sales revenue in June 2025
    c. Expected net profits in December 2025
4. Use the Forecast sheets to determine:
    a. Range of expected unit sales in October 2025 (Upper to lower Confidence bounds)
    b. Expected sales revenue in June 2025 (Upper to lower Confidence bounds)
    c. Range of expected net profits in December 2025 (Upper to lower Confidence bounds)
5. To evaluate the Forecast sheets, rerun the forecasts. This time change the Forecast Start date to 1/1/2024 to see what the model would have predicted for 2024. (Leave the confidence level at 85 percent.) Compare the forecasted results for 2024 to the actual results for 2024. Were the predictions higher or lower than the actual results? What could have caused the differences?

DA9-3. Forecasting using Tableau
Available in MBC, this problem uses Tableau to forecast sales and net profits.

Data Visualization

Data Visualization Activities are available in myBusinessCourse. These assignments use Tableau Dashboards to expose students to visual depictions of data and introduce students to data analytics through data visualizations. These exercises are easily assignable and auto graded by MBC.

© Cambridge Business Publishers

Potential Ethical Issues

1. Using a single budgeting system globally that may conflict with national cultures
2. Knowingly introducing, or allowing employees to introduce, budget slack into the process that will misallocate resources or generate inequitable performance rewards
3. Treating short-term conditions as long-term conditions (or vice versa) to intentionally distort the effects of those conditions on the budgeting process
4. Pressuring employees to meet or exceed budget goals through the use of fraudulent accounting techniques
5. Encouraging employee participation in the budgeting process only to disregard that input
6. Engaging in "backwards budgeting" that justifies management decisions that have been previously determined—especially relative to employee layoffs and plant closures
7. Disregarding contingencies during budget preparation because those conditions cannot be quantified with extreme accuracy
8. Ignoring external performance measures and benchmarks (such as comparisons with competitors or customer satisfaction levels) and concentrating only on meeting internally selected financial targets
9. Allowing lower-level managers to participate in the budgeting process but not communicating necessary "big picture" assumptions—causing participatory budgets to be unrealistic and managers to fail to achieve targets
10. Promoting a "spend-it-or-lose-it" attitude, whereby organizational units reducing expenditures are punished, and units that spend unnecessarily are rewarded, in future periods
11. Mandating a uniform "across-the-board" organizational budget cut without giving employees the opportunity to justify current expenditures or to suggest alternative methods of achieving the desired cost reduction

Questions

Q9-1. How does budgeting provide important information to managers and operating personnel?

Q9-2. How does the strategic plan influence preparation of the master budget?

Q9-3. Distinguish between a strategic plan and a tactical plan. How are these plans related?

Q9-4. After a master budget has been prepared, what is its role in managerial control?

Q9-5. Differentiate between the operating and financial budgets that are contained in a master budget. Why are both types needed?

Q9-6. Discuss the sequence in which the major components of the master budget are prepared. Why is it necessary to prepare the components in such a sequence?

Q9-7. Why is a firm's production budget influenced by the finished goods inventory policy?

Q9-8. Assume that in preparing the cash budget, the accountant discovers that a cash shortage will likely occur in a specific month. What actions might the accountant recommend to management to deal with the cash shortage?

Q9-9. The cash budget and the budgeted statement of cash flows both provide information about cash. What information about cash is common to these two sources, and what information is unique to the two sources?

Q9-10. Why is continuous (rolling) budgeting becoming more popular than it was in the past for organizational managers?

Q9-11. If the majority of companies find that their forecasts are inaccurate, why should managers engage in budgeting at all?

Q9-12. What is budgetary slack, and what might top managers do to rid their firms' budgets of slack?

Q9-13. Why is it helpful for a company to prepare a budget manual?

Chapter 9 The Master Budget

Multiple Choice

MC9-14. The management of a food-processing company is analyzing its internal strengths and weaknesses as part of its strategic planning process. Which one of the following is most likely considered a strategic internal variable for the company? *LO9-1*
   a. Changes in the legal code for food processors.
   b. The economic forces that regulate the local labor supply.
   c. Technological changes in food-processing methods.
   d. The culture at the company's food-processing plant.

MC9-15. Which one of following budgets is regarded as the foundation of the master budget? *LO9-2*
   a. Production.
   b. Sales.
   c. Operating.
   d. Cash.

MC9-16. Netco's sales budget for the coming year is as follows. *LO9-2*

Item	Volume in Units	Sales Price	Sales Revenue
1	200,000	$50	$10,000,000
2	150,000	10	1,500,000
3	300,000	30	9,000,000
Total sales revenue			$20,500,000

Items 1 and 3 are different models of the same product. Item 2 is a complement to Item 1. Past experience indicates that the sales volume of Item 2 relative to the sales volume of Item 1 is fairly constant. Netco is considering a 10 percent price increase for the coming year for Item 1, which will cause sales of Item 1 to decline by 20 percent while simultaneously causing sales of Item 3 to increase by 5 percent. If Netco institutes the price increase for Item 1, total sales revenue will decrease by
   a. $1,050,000.
   b. $850,000.
   c. $750,000.
   d. $550,000.

MC9-17. Data regarding Rombus Company's budget are shown below. *LO9-3*

Planned sales	4,000 units
Material cost	$2.50 per pound
Direct labor	3 hours per unit
Direct labor rate	$7 per hour
Finished goods beginning inventory	900 units
Finished goods ending inventory	600 units
Direct materials beginning inventory	4,300 units
Direct materials ending inventory	4,500 units
Materials used per unit	6 pounds

Rombus Company's production budget will show total units to be produced of
   a. 3,700.
   b. 4,000.
   c. 4,300.
   d. 4,600.

MC9-18. Stevens Company manufactures electronic components used in automobile manufacturing. Standard usage of the two materials required to produce one finished electronic component, as well as the current inventory, are shown below. *LO9-3*

Material	Standard Per Unit	Price	Current Inventory
Geo	2.0 pounds	$15/lb.	5,000 pounds
Clio	1.5 pounds	$10/lb.	7,500 pounds

Stevens forecasts sales of 20,000 components for each of the next two production periods, with a zero beginning finished goods inventory balance and a zero finished goods inventory balance forecasted at each period end. Company policy dictates that 25 percent of the raw materials needed to produce the next period's projected sales be maintained in ending direct materials inventory.

© Cambridge Business Publishers

Based on this information, what would the budgeted direct materials purchases for the coming period be?

	Geo	Clio
a.	$450,000	$450,000
b.	$675,000	$300,000
c.	$675,000	$400,000
d.	$825,000	$450,000

LO9-4 MC9-19. Brown Company estimates that monthly sales will be as follows.

January	$100,000
February	150,000
March	180,000

Historical trends indicate that 40 percent of sales are collected during the month of sale, 50 percent are collected in the month following the sale, and 10 percent are collected two months after the sale. Brown's accounts receivable balance as of December 31 totals $80,000 ($72,000 from December's sales and $8,000 from November's sales). The amount of cash Brown can expect to collect during the month of January is

a. $76,800.
b. $84,000.
c. $108,000.
d. $133,000.

LO9-5 MC9-20. Assume the following budgeted information.

Net sales	$447,000
Gross margin	135,800
Finished goods, ending balance	5,000
Finished goods, beginning balance	6,200
Income from operations	85,800

What are selling & administrative expenses and cost of goods manufactured?

a. $50,000, $310,000
b. $87,000, $322,400
c. $50,000, $322,400
d. $51,200, $312,400

LO9-6 MC9-21. A company operates 10 offices. In the prior year, the total cost of operating the offices was $1,000,000 of which $140,000 consisted of fixed costs. All else remaining equal, what will be the budgeted costs if the company were to operate 12 offices?

a. $1,028,000.
b. $1,032,000.
c. $1,172,000.
d. $1,200,000.

LO9-7 MC9-22. Which one of the following statements concerning approaches for the budget development process is correct?
a. The imposed approach to budgeting discourages strict adherence to strategic organizational goals.
b. To prevent ambiguity, once departmental budgeted goals have been developed, they should remain fixed even if the sales forecast upon which they are based proves to be wrong in the middle of the fiscal year.
c. With the information technology available, the role of budgets as an organizational communication device has declined.
d. Since department managers have the most detailed knowledge about organizational operations, they should use this information as the building blocks of the operating budget.

Exercises

LO9-1 E9-23. Strategy, tactics, budgets Match each of the following examples with one of the following terms: strategy, tactic, budget.
1. _____ Purchase solar panels for $750,000 in 6 months.
2. _____ Increase renewable energy sources.
3. _____ All of the company's production facilities will be carbon neutral by 2030.

Chapter 9 The Master Budget

E9-24. Output/input budget Lincoln Medical Clinic has the following resource input information available for a routine physical examination. *LO9-1, 6*
- Each exam normally requires 0.75 hour of examining room time, including
  - 30 minutes of nursing services,
- 15 minutes of physician services.
- Each exam also utilizes one package of examination supplies costing $50 each.
- Including benefits, physicians earn $100/hour and nurses earn $35/hour.
- Variable overhead is budgeted at $20 per examining room hour and fixed overhead is budgeted at $8,000 per month.

  a. Prepare an output/input budget for March when 600 routine examinations are planned.
  b. What are some of the likely benefits to Lincoln Medical Clinic of dedicating time to go through the budgeting process.

E9-25. Incremental budget Lima County uses an incremental approach to budgeting. The current year cash budget for the Lima County Department of Budling Inspections is presented as follows: *LO9-1*

	Current Year Budget
Supplies	$ 13,000
Temporary and seasonal wages	35,000
Wages of full-time employees	220,000
Supervisor salaries	66,000
Rent	54,000
Travel	16,000
Insurance	15,000
Utilities	11,000
Miscellaneous	12,000
Contingencies and equipment	28,000
Total	$470,000

Prepare an incremental cash budget for next year, assuming the planned total budget increase is 2.5 percent. Budget details include a budget increment for salaries and wages of 2 percent, no change in rent (lease terms), 4 percent increase for travel, and 2 percent increases in the budget for supplies and miscellaneous. Utility companies have received approvals for rate increases amounting to 2 percent and insurance companies have announced an increase in premiums of 4 percent. (Hint: The Contingencies and equipment budget is a plug.)

E9-26. Activity-based budget Highland Industries has the following budget information available for February: *LO9-1*

Units manufactured	25,000
Factory administration	$145,000
Assembly	¼ hour per unit × $20
Direct materials	3 pounds per unit × $6
Inspection	$40 per batch of 1,000 units
Manufacturing overhead	$8 per unit
Product development	$50,000
Setup cost	$100 per batch of 1,000 units

Use activity-based costing to prepare a manufacturing cost budget for February.

E9-27. Strategic planning; writing Before a budget can be prepared, company management considers "what if" changes that might occur during the forecast period. Prepare a list of five possible questions about changes that you might want to consider if you were a manager in a *LO9-1*
  a. global manufacturing company.
  b. local retailer.

E9-28. Strategic planning; research When engaging in strategic planning, company management often prepares a SWOT analysis. *LO9-1*
  a. Based on an internet search, explain a SWOT analysis, and its usefulness in the planning process.
  b. Choose an organization with which you are familiar and develop a SWOT analysis for that organization.

© Cambridge Business Publishers

LO9-1 **E9-29. Tactical planning; writing** People, as well as businesses, need to budget. Assume that you have recently moved to an apartment with significantly higher rent than your previous apartment, and you are now experiencing financial difficulties. Prepare a list of at least 10 recommendations on how to "do things differently" to help manage your finances.

LO9-1 **E9-30. Planning; writing** High-level executives have often indicated that competitors' actions are the top external factor affecting their businesses and their business plans.

    a. Why are competitors' actions so important to business planning?
    b. How would competitors' actions affect a business's internal planning?
    c. What other internal and external factors are key elements in a business's budgeting process?

LO9-2, 6 **E9-31. Revenue budget** In the prior year, Grand Falls Bank (GFB) had $4,000,000 in business loans at an average interest rate of 3.5 percent as well as $3,200,000 in consumer loans with an average rate of 8 percent. GFB also has $750,000 invested in government securities that pay interest at an average rate of 2.5 percent.

For the current year, GFB estimates that the volume of business loans will increase to $6,000,000, and the interest rate will rise to 5 percent. It projects that consumer loans will be $4,000,000 and have an average interest rate of 11 percent. The bank's government security investment will be $1,600,000 and will bear an average interest rate of 4.5 percent. What is GFB's projected revenue for the current year?

LO9-2 **E9-32. Sales budget** Pataky Co.'s sales manager estimates that 2,000,000 units of product RI#698 will be sold during the year. The product's selling price is expected to decline as the result of technology changes during the year and estimates of the sales price are as follows:

1st Quarter	2nd Quarter	3rd Quarter	4th Quarter
$17	$16	$14	$12

In talking with customers, the sales department discovered that sales quantities per quarter could vary substantially. Thus, the sales manager has prepared the following three sets of quarterly sales projections:

Unit Sales	1st Quarter	2nd Quarter	3rd Quarter	4th Quarter	Total
Scenario A....	600,000	300,000	640,000	460,000	2,000,000
Scenario B....	400,000	700,000	250,000	650,000	2,000,000
Scenario C....	530,000	480,000	800,000	190,000	2,000,000

If Pataky's sales department is able to influence customers, which of the potential sales scenarios would be most profitable for the company? Would that scenario possibly cause the company any difficulties?

LO9-3 **E9-33. Production budget** Seguin Inc. has the following projected unit sales for the first four months of the year:

Month	Unit Sales
January....................	102,400
February...................	96,000
March......................	128,000
April.......................	153,600

Company policy is to have an ending monthly inventory equal to 5 percent of next month's estimated sales; however, this criterion was not in effect at the end of the past year. Ending inventory at that time was 7,000 units. Determine the company's production requirements for each month of the first quarter of the year.

LO9-3 **E9-34. Production budget** Nafari Company's sales budget has the following unit sales projections for each quarter of Year 4:

Chapter 9 The Master Budget

Quarter	Unit Sales
January–March	1,080,000
April–June	1,360,000
July–September	980,000
October–December	1,100,000
Total	4,520,000

Sales for the first quarter of Year 5 are expected to be 1,200,000 units. Ending inventory of finished goods for each quarter is scheduled to equal 10 percent of the next quarter's budgeted sales. The company's ending inventory on December 31, Year 3, is estimated at 94,500 units. Develop a quarterly production budget for Year 4 and for Year 4 in total.

E9-35. Production, direct materials, and direct labor budgets Gerrad Manufacturing has projected sales of its product for the next six months as follows: LO9-3

January	300 units
February	700 units
March	1,000 units
April	900 units
May	400 units
June	300 units

The finished product requires 3 pounds of raw material and 10 hours of direct labor.

Gerrad tries to maintain a Finished Goods ending inventory equal to the next two months of sales and a Raw Material ending inventory equal to one-half of the current month's production needs. January's beginning inventories are expected to conform to company policy.

a. Prepare a production budget for February, March, and April.
b. Prepare a forecast of the units and cost of raw material that will be required for February, March, and April. The expected cost per pound of raw material is expected to be $2 in February, $2.30 in March, and $2.40 in April.
c. Prepare a direct labor budget (assuming a $12 per hour rate) for February, March, and April.

E9-36. Material purchases budget Gap'O has projected sales of 325,000 hospital gowns in October. Each gown requires 2.5 yards of fabric. The beginning inventory of fabric and gowns, respectively, are 5,000 yards and 21,000 gowns. Gap'O wants to have 4,550 yards of fabric and 15,800 gowns on hand at the end of October. The fabric comes in 15-yard bolts. If Gap'O has no beginning or ending Work in Process Inventory, how many bolts of fabric must the company purchase in October? LO9-3

E9-37. Material purchases budget Hard Core had budgeted sales of 190,000 feet of its concrete culvert products for June. Each foot of product requires 4 pounds of concrete ($0.10 per pound) and 7.5 pounds of gravel ($0.04 per pound). Actual beginning inventories and projected ending inventories follow. LO9-3

	June 1	June 30
Finished Goods Inventory (in feet)	12,250	10,000
Concrete (in pounds)	41,000	34,300
Gravel (in pounds)	32,650	46,250

a. How many pounds of concrete did Hard Core plan to purchase in June? What was the cost of those purchases?
b. How many pounds of gravel did Hard Core plan to purchase in June? What was the cost of those purchases?

E9-38. Production and related schedules Goldstein Inc. manufactures and sells plastic boxes and trays. Sales are projected to be evenly spread over the annual period. Estimated product sales and material needs for each unit of product follow. LO9-3

	Boxes	Trays
Annual sales	42,000	30,000
Material A	2.0 pounds	1.0 pound
Material B	1.5 pounds	0.8 pound
Direct labor	0.3 hour	0.2 hour

Overhead is applied at a rate of $1.60 per direct labor hour.

	Expected Beginning Inventories	Desired Ending Inventories
Material A......	1,780 pounds	1,500 pounds
Material B......	5,000 pounds	1,400 pounds
Boxes.........	1,200 units	1,800 units
Trays..........	800 units	650 units

Material A costs $0.05 per pound, and Material B costs $0.07 per pound. Prepare the following information:

a. Production schedule by product and in total.
b. Purchases budget in units by raw material, in total, and in dollars.
c. Direct labor budget in hours by product, in total, and in dollars. The average direct labor wage rate is $9.50 per hour.
d. Overhead to be charged to production by product and in total.

LO9-3, 4 E9-39. Budgeted purchases; budgeted cash payments Grenfell Company is preparing a cash budget for the year for purchases of Calvos. Budgeted data are as follows:

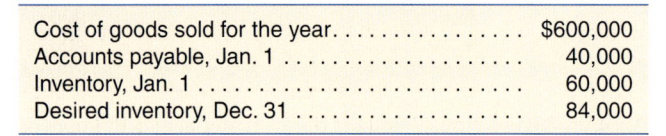

Cost of goods sold for the year...............	$600,000
Accounts payable, Jan. 1....................	40,000
Inventory, Jan. 1...........................	60,000
Desired inventory, Dec. 31	84,000

Purchases will be made in 12 equal monthly amounts and paid for in the following month. Compute the budgeted cash payment for purchases of Calvos for the year.

LO9-4 E9-40. Cash collections The treasurer of Homeyra Corp. needs to estimate cash collections from accounts receivable for September, October, and November. Forty percent of the company's customers pay in cash, and the rest are credit customers. The collection pattern for the credit customers is 20 percent in the month of sale and 80 percent in the following month. Because of Homeyra's established client base, the company experiences almost zero uncollectible accounts. Estimated total sales for August, September, October, and November follow.

Month	Sales
August	$78,000
September	80,000
October...............................	95,000
November.............................	91,000

Determine Homeyra Corp.'s cash collections for September, October, and November.

LO9-4 E9-41. Cash collections Ridenour Ltd. is preparing its first-quarter monthly cash budget for Year 4. The following information is available about actual Year 3 sales and expected Year 4 sales:

November	December	January	February	March
$83,000	$76,000	$79,000	$88,000	$59,000

Tracing collections from prior year monthly sales and discussions with the credit manager helped develop a profile of collection behavior patterns.

Of a given month's sales, 40 percent is typically collected in the month of sale. Because the company terms are 1 percent (end of month) net 30, all collections within the month of sale are net of the 1 percent discount. Of a given month's sales, 30 percent is collected in the month following the sale. The remaining 30 percent is collected in the second month following the month of the sale. Bad debts are negligible and should be ignored.

a. Prepare a schedule of cash collections for Ridenour Ltd. for January, February, and March of Year 4.
b. Calculate the Accounts Receivable balance at March 31, Year 4.

LO9-4 E9-42. Cash collections Miriam Irby is president of MI Corp. Irby has decided to take a month's vacation with her family to South Africa, Zimbabwe, and Angola. Irby has researched the trip and determined that the total cost of the trip for her family will be approximately $50,000. Her travel

Chapter 9 The Master Budget

agent says that a 10 percent discount can be obtained if Irby can write a check for the cost of the trip by the end of November. Irby says she sees no problem in doing that given that the company's expected billings for October, November, and December, respectively, are $100,000, $65,000, and $15,000 (Irby will leave on vacation in December).

As of September 30, MI Corp.'s accountant has estimated cash collections from billings to be 15 percent in the month of sale, 55 percent in the month following sale, and 30 percent in the second month following sale. The September 30 Accounts Receivable balance is $11,000; that amount is expected to be collected in October. Average monthly business costs are $22,500.

a. What are MI Corp.'s expected cash collections for October, November, and December?
b. Can Irby pay for her trip in November and obtain the 10 percent discount? Explain.
c. What would you suggest that Irby do?

E9-43. Direct material purchases and budgeted payments Campbell Manufacturing intends to start business on January 1. Production plans for the first four months of operations are as follows: **LO9-3, 4**

January............	20,000 units
February...........	50,000 units
March.............	70,000 units
April..............	70,000 units

Each unit requires two pounds of material. The firm would like to end each month with enough raw material to cover 25 percent of the following month's production needs. Raw material costs $7 per pound. Management pays for 40 percent of purchases in the month of purchase and receives a 10 percent discount for these payments. The remaining purchases are paid in the following month, with no discount available.

a. Prepare a purchases budget for the first quarter of the year in units, in total, and in dollars.
b. Determine the budgeted payments for purchases of raw material for each of the first three months of operations and for the quarter in total.
c. Where in the budgeted financial statements do the purchase discounts appear?

E9-44. Cash balance The following budgeted May cash information is available for Salado Corp.: **LO9-4**

Net after-tax income..........................	$336,000
Depreciation expense.........................	56,200
Accrued income tax expense..................	82,000
Increase in Accounts Receivable for month.....	8,000
Decrease in Accounts Payable for month.......	7,000
Estimated bad debts expense..................	4,100
Dividends declared in May....................	35,000
Dividends paid in May........................	47,000

If Salado's May 1 cash balance is $23,000, what is the company's budgeted May 31 cash balance?

E9-45. Cash disbursements The following budgeted information about Reeves Co. is available for September: **LO9-4**

Sales for September..........................	$2,700,000
Gross profit on sales..........................	40%
Decrease in Merchandise Inventory during September....	$ 43,750
Wages expense for September.................	$ 325,500
Increase in Wages Payable for September......	$ 42,000
Other cash expenses for September............	$ 245,000
Decrease in Accounts Payable during September........	$ 35,000

Reeves Co. only uses its Accounts Payable for inventory purchases.

a. How much does Reeves Co. expect to pay for inventory in September?
b. What are total budgeted cash disbursements for September?

E9-46. Cash budget The following cash budget is for the third quarter of this year. Solve for the missing numbers on the cash budget, assuming that the accountant has requested a minimum cash balance of $7,000 at the start of each month. All borrowings, repayments, and investments are made in even $1,000 amounts. No borrowings or investments exist at the beginning of July. **LO9-4**

© Cambridge Business Publishers

	July	August	September	Total
Beginning cash balance	$ 7,400	$?	$?	$?
Cash receipts	16,400	20,200	?	?
Total cash available	$?	$?	$41,000	$ 77,800
Cash disbursements				
Payments on account	$?	$ 7,800	$11,400	$?
Wages expense	10,000	?	12,400	34,600
Overhead costs	8,000	9,200	?	26,000
Total disbursements	$20,600	$?	$32,600	$?
Cash excess (deficiency)	$?	$?	$?	$?
Minimum cash balance	(7,000)	(7,000)	?	?
Cash available (needed)	$?	$ (8,800)	$?	$(11,600)
Financing				
Borrowings (repayments)	$ 4,000	$?	$ (1,000)	$?
Acquire (sell) investments	0	0	?	?
Receive (pay) interest	0	0	?	(20)
Ending cash balance	$ 7,200	$?	$?	$ 7,380

LO9-3, 4 **E9-47. Various budgets** Compute the required answer for each of the following independent situations.

a. For next year, Penny Suits projects $8,000,000 of sales and total fixed manufacturing costs of $2,000,000. Variable manufacturing costs are estimated at 65 percent of sales. Assuming no change in inventory, what is the company's projected cost of goods sold?

b. Tommy's Company has projected the following information for October:

Sales	$800,000
Gross profit (based on sales)	25%
Increase in Merchandise Inventory in October	$ 20,000
Decrease in Accounts Payable for October	$ 45,000

What are expected cash disbursements for inventory purchases for October?

c. Buda Corp. is attempting to budget its overhead costs for March of next year. Overhead is a mixed cost with the following flexible budget formula: $y = \$250,000 + \$17.50X$, where X represents machine hours. Fixed overhead includes $95,000 of depreciation. If Buda Corp. expects to utilize 7,500 machine hours in March, what is the company's budgeted March overhead cost? How much cash will the company pay for budgeted overhead in March?

d. Elizabeth Enterprises expects to begin next year with a cash balance of $15,000. Cash collections from sales and on account during the year are expected to be $470,500. The firm wants to maintain a minimum cash balance of $5,000. Budgeted cash disbursements for the year are as follows:

Payoff of note payable	$ 52,500
Interest on note payable	4,700
Purchase of computer system	17,900
Payments for operating costs and inventory purchases	193,500
Direct labor payments	110,000
Cash overhead payments	106,400
Cash selling and administrative payments	94,800

The company can, if necessary, borrow in $1,000 amounts. Prepare a cash budget for next year.

E9-48. Budgeted income statement Last year's income statement for Cooper Company is as follows: LO9-5

Sales (100,000 × $10)		$1,000,000
Cost of goods sold		
Direct material	$400,000	
Direct labor	200,000	
Overhead	100,000	(700,000)
Gross profit		$ 300,000
Expenses		
Selling	$104,000	
Administrative	120,000	(224,000)
Income before taxes		$ 76,000

This year, unit sales are expected to increase by 25 percent; material and labor costs are expected to increase by 10 percent per unit. Overhead is applied to production based on a percentage of direct labor costs. Fixed selling expenses total $24,000; the remainder varies with sales dollars. All administrative costs are fixed.

Management desires to earn 10 percent on sales this year and will adjust the unit selling price if necessary. Develop a budgeted income statement for the year for Cooper Company that incorporates the indicated changes.

E9-49. Budgeted income statement The operating results in summarized form for a retail computer store for this year are: LO9-5

Revenue:	
Hardware sales	$ 4,800,000
Software sales	2,000,000
Maintenance contracts	1,200,000
Total revenue	$ 8,000,000
Costs and expenses:	
Cost of hardware sales	$ 3,360,000
Cost of software sales	1,200,000
Marketing expenses	600,000
Customer maintenance costs	640,000
Administrative expenses	1,120,000
Total costs and expenses	$(6,920,000)
Operating income	$ 1,080,000

The computer store is in the process of formulating its operating budget for next year and has made the following assumptions:

- The selling prices of hardware are expected to increase 10 percent but there will be no selling price increases for software and maintenance contracts.
- Hardware unit sales are expected to increase 5 percent with a corresponding 5 percent growth in the number of maintenance contracts; growth in unit software sales is estimated at 8 percent.
- The cost of hardware and software is expected to increase 4 percent.
- Marketing expenses will be increased 5 percent in the coming year.
- Three technicians will be added to the customer maintenance operations in the coming year, increasing the customer maintenance costs by $120,000.
- Administrative costs will be held at the same level.

Compute the computer retail store's budgeted operating income for next year.

CIA ADAPTED

E9-50. Budgeted accounts receivable; cash; and income statement In preparing its budget for July, Wade Inc. has the following information available: LO9-3, 4, 5

Accounts Receivable at June 30	$750,000
Estimated credit sales for July	900,000
Estimated collections in July for credit sales in July and prior months	660,000
Estimated write-offs in July for uncollectible credit sales	27,000
Estimated provision for uncollectible accounts for credit sales in July	20,000

a. What is the projected balance of Accounts Receivable at July 31?
b. Which of these amounts (if any) will affect the cash budget?
c. Which of these amounts (if any) will affect the budgeted income statement for July?

LO9-5 E9-51. Budgeted income statement The following budget information is available for Sluyter Corp. for May:
- Sales are expected to be $400,000. All sales are on account, and a provision for bad debts is accrued monthly at 3 percent of sales.
- Inventory was $35,000 on April 30, and an increase of $10,000 is planned for May.
- All inventory is marked to sell at cost plus 60 percent.
- Estimated cash disbursements for selling and administrative expenses for the month are $55,000.
- Depreciation for May is projected at $8,000.

Prepare a budgeted income statement for Sluyter Corp. for May.

LO9-5 E9-52. Budgeted income statement Alyssa Co. is planning to purchase a new piece of production equipment. The equipment will increase fixed overhead by $700,000 per year in depreciation but reduce variable expenses per unit by 20 percent. Budgeted annual sales of the company's products are 240,000 units at an average selling price of $25. Variable expenses are currently 65 percent of sales, and fixed costs total $1,400,000 per year.
a. Prepare an income statement assuming that the new equipment is not purchased.
b. What is the current variable cost per unit? What will be the new variable cost per unit if the equipment is purchased?
c. Prepare an income statement assuming that the new equipment is purchased.
d. Should the equipment be acquired?

LO9-4, 6 E9-53. Cash collections, accounts receivable Total June sales for Roy's Catering are expected to be $450,000. Of each month's sales, 80 percent is expected to be on credit. The Accounts Receivable balance at May 31 is $119,600, of which $90,000 represents the remainder of May credit sales. There are no receivables from months prior to April. The collection pattern of Roy's Catering credit sales is 70 percent in the month of sale, 20 percent in the month following the sale, and 10 percent in the second month following the sale. Roy's Catering has no uncollectible accounts.
a. What were total sales for April?
b. What were credit sales for May?
c. What are projected cash collections for June?
d. What is the expected balance of Accounts Receivable at June 30?

LO9-4, 6 E9-54. Cash collections, accounts receivable The October 1, Accounts Receivable balance for Darin Landscaping is $632,500. Of that balance, $480,000 represents remaining accounts receivable from September billings. The normal collection pattern for the firm is 20 percent of billings in the month of service, 55 percent in the month after service, and 22 percent in the second month following service. The remaining billings are uncollectible. October billings are expected to be $750,000.
a. What were August billings for Darin Landscaping?
b. What amount of September billings is expected to be uncollectible?
c. What are the firm's projected cash collections in October?

LO9-4, 6 E9-55. Service company cash budget Presented are partial April, May, and June cash budgets for a consulting firm:

	Cash Budget			
	April	May	June	Total
Cash balance, beginning	$ 24,000	$?	$?	$?
Collections on service revenue	100,000	90,000	140,000	?
Cash available for operations	?	?	?	?
Disbursements for operating expenses	(115,000)	(110,000)	(115,000)	?
Cash excess (deficiency)	?	?	?	?
Minimum cash balance	?	?	?	?
Cash available (needed)	?	?	?	?
Financing				
Borrowings	?	?	?	?
Repayments	?	?	?	?
Interest	?	?	?	?
Cash balance, ending	$?	$?	$?	$?

Loans are obtained in increments of $1,000 at the start of each month to maintain a minimum end-of-month balance of $12,000. Interest is 1 percent simple interest (no compounding) per month, payable when a loan payment is made. Repayments are made as soon as possible, subject to the minimum end-of-month balance.

Complete the cash budget.

E9-56. **ESG considerations** For each of the following sustainability initiatives, determine the likely impact on the master budget.
1. A 10-year commitment to net zero carbon emissions decreases the useful lives of certain operational equipment.
2. Estimated environmental costs to dispose of equipment currently held has risen sharply.
3. The company has committed to switching to a new supplier with a lower environmental impact but at a higher material cost.
4. The company has committed to purchasing solar panels next year for its corporate office.
5. The company has committed to purchasing five electric vehicles to replace 5 fully depreciated vehicles to deliver finished goods.

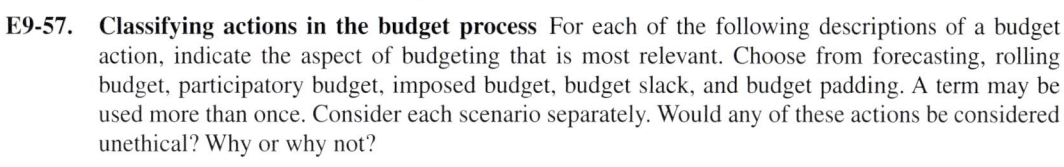

E9-57. **Classifying actions in the budget process** For each of the following descriptions of a budget action, indicate the aspect of budgeting that is most relevant. Choose from forecasting, rolling budget, participatory budget, imposed budget, budget slack, and budget padding. A term may be used more than once. Consider each scenario separately. Would any of these actions be considered unethical? Why or why not?
   a. A production manager intentionally overestimates the cost of materials to ensure that actual costs will be less than budget. The production manager's performance reviews take into account budget overruns.
   b. Computer models are used to generate alternate scenarios in order to estimate sales and expenses for the upcoming year.
   c. Due to the pandemic, the one-year master budget (created annually) quickly became outdated. To get needed information, the company quickly converted to an ongoing, 18-month budgetary planning process.
   d. A draft of the master budget is forward to each department for feedback.
   e. The budget for committed fixed costs is intentionally increased by management even though the amount is not expected to increase.
   f. A regulatory change to the minimum wage caused the annual budget for a fast-food restaurant to be irrelevant. Due to the complex strategic responses required to remain a going concern, upper management will manage the budgeting process for at least two-years.
   g. The prediction of sales of clothing takes into account seasonality.

E9-58. **Management control; writing** You are a managing partner for a 50-person CPA firm. What important detail items would you want to review in making a budget and year-end analysis in each of the following areas?
   a. Human resources
   b. Information technology
   c. Marketing/Business development
   d. Accounts receivable

E9-59. **Budgeting attitudes; writing** Many managers believe that if all amounts in their spending budgets are not spent during a period, they will lose allocations in future periods and that they will receive little or no recognition for the cost savings.

Prepare an essay that discusses the behavioral and ethical issues involved in a spend-it-or-lose-it attitude. Include in your discussion the issue of negotiating budget allocation requests prior to the beginning of the period.

E9-60. **Continuous budgeting; writing** You own a small boat manufacturing company. At a recent manufacturers' association meeting, you overheard one of the other company owners say that he liked using a continuous budgeting process. Discuss in a report to your top management group what you believe are the advantages and disadvantages of continuous budgeting for your company.

E9-61. **Research; writing** Find the Web page for a charitable organization that operates internationally as well as domestically.
   a. Prepare a list of activities in which this organization is currently involved.
   b. What would be the greatest challenges in budgeting for such an organization?
   c. Do you think not-for-profits should be as concerned as for-profit organizations with budgeting? Explain the rationale for your answer.

Problems

LO9-3 **P9-62. Production and purchases budgets** Caleb Corp. has prepared the following unit sales forecast for Year 2:

	January–June	July–December	Total Units
Sales.	1,160,000	1,440,000	2,600,000

Estimated ending Finished Goods Inventories are 50,000 units at December 31, Year 1; 72,000 units at June 30, Year 2; and 120,000 units at December 31, Year 2.

In manufacturing a unit of this product, Caleb Corp. uses 3 pounds of Material A and 0.75 gallons of Material B. Materials A and B cost, respectively, $2.50 per pound and $1.80 per gallon.

The company carries no Work in Process Inventory. Ending inventories of direct material are projected as follows:

	December 31, Year 1	June 30, Year 2	December 31, Year 2
Material A (in pounds)	240,000	270,000	284,000
Material B (in gallons).	90,000	70,000	76,000

Prepare a production and purchases budget for each semiannual period of Year 2.

LO9-3 **P9-63. Production and purchases budgets; writing** Narisho Supply is in the process of preparing the budget for the first quarter. The following projections for unit sales have been made:

	January	February	March	Total
Sales.	72,000	64,000	60,000	196,000

Each finished unit requires three direct materials: 4 pounds of Material M, 2.5 pounds of Material N, and 2 pounds of Material O. Based on company policies, the following estimates of finished units and pounds of direct material inventories are made:

	December	January	February	March
Finished, units	18,000	16,000	15,000	14,000
Direct material M, pounds.	13,500	12,000	11,250	10,500
Direct material N, pounds.	9,000	8,000	7,500	7,000
Direct material O, pounds.	7,300	9,400	8,200	8,500

a. Prepare a monthly production and purchases budget for the first quarter.
b. The production supervisor wants to purchase new production equipment for the year. Such equipment would largely replace the current labor-intensive production system. Write a memo to corporate management explaining why new production equipment could affect the production and purchases budget.
c. Who should be consulted to determine the new material requirements per unit if the new production equipment is installed?

LO9-3, 4 **P9-64. Production; purchases; cash disbursements** So Sweet! has budgeted sales of 600,000 cans of diet iced tea mix during June and 750,000 cans during July. Production of the mix requires 14.5 ounces of tea and 1.5 ounces of sugar substitute. June 1 inventories of tea and sugar substitute are as follows:

Iced tea mix	24,600 cans of finished product
Tea	750 pounds
Sugar substitute	200 pounds

So Sweet! generally carries a finished goods inventory equal to 5 percent of the following month's needs; raw material ending inventories should equal the production needs for 10 percent of ending Finished Goods Inventory. Assuming that the ending inventory policy is met, answer the following questions.

a. How many cans of iced tea mix will be produced in June?

b. How many pounds of tea will be purchased in June?
c. How many pounds of sugar substitute will be purchased in June?
d. Tea and sugar substitute cost $3.50 and $0.40 per pound, respectively. What dollar amount of raw material purchases is budgeted for June?
e. If the company normally pays for 40 percent of its budgeted purchases during the month of purchase and takes a 2 percent discount, what are budgeted cash disbursements in June for June purchases? How much will So Sweet! owe for June purchases in July?

P9-65. Production; purchases; direct labor & OH budgets Atkinson's Reliable Tools makes two products that use similar raw materials: #587Q and #253X. Estimated production needs for a unit of each product follow.

LO9-3

	#587Q	#253X
Steel (in pounds)	3	5
Wood (in board feet)	0.5	0.2
Direct labor (in hours)	2	3
Machine hours	0.5	0.7

Estimated sales in units by product for the year are 80,000 of #587Q and 30,000 of #253X. Additionally, estimated beginning and desired ending inventory quantities are as follows.

	Beginning	Ending
#587Q (units)	800	640
#253X (units)	1,200	900
Steel (in pounds)	2,000	1,400
Wood (in board feet)	800	600

Overhead is applied to production at the rate of $15 per machine hour and the direct labor wage rate is $10.50 per hour. Prepare (a) the production schedule by product, (b) the purchases budget in units by raw material, (c) direct labor in hours by product, in total, and in dollars, and (d) overhead budget by product and in total.

P9-66. Production; purchases; cash budgets Corner Brook Furniture Co. makes bookstands and expects sales and collections for the first three months of Year 2 to be as follows:

LO9-3, 4

	January	February	March	Total
Sales quantity (units)	6,400	5,200	7,400	19,000
Revenue	$128,000	$104,000	$148,000	$380,000
Collections	$116,200	$ 81,300	$101,500	$299,000

The December 31, Year 1, balance sheet revealed the following selected account balances: Cash, $18,320; Direct Material Inventory, $8,230; Finished Goods Inventory, $23,200; and Accounts Payable, $5,800. The Direct Material Inventory balance represents 1,580 pounds of scrap iron and 1,200 bookstand bases. The Finished Goods Inventory consists of 1,220 bookstands.

Each bookstand requires two pounds of scrap iron, which costs $3 per pound. Bookstand bases are purchased from a local lumber mill at a cost of $2.50 per unit. Company management decided that, beginning in Year 2, the ending balance of Direct Material Inventory should be 25 percent of the following month's production requirements and that the ending balance of Finished Goods Inventory should be 20 percent of the next month's sales. Sales for April and May are expected to be 8,000 bookstands per month.

The company normally pays for 75 percent of a month's purchases of direct material in the month of purchase (on which it takes a 1 percent cash discount). The remaining 25 percent is paid in full in the month following the month of purchase.

Direct labor is budgeted at $0.70 per bookstand produced and is paid in the month of production. Total cash manufacturing overhead is budgeted at $14,000 per month plus $1.30 per bookstand. Total cash selling and administrative costs equal $13,600 per month plus 10 percent of sales revenue. These costs are all paid in the month of incurrence. In addition, the company plans to pay executive bonuses of $35,000 in January Year 2 and make an estimated quarterly tax payment of $5,000 in March Year 2.

Management requires a minimum cash balance of $10,000 at the end of each month. If the company borrows funds, it will do so only in $1,000 multiples at the beginning of a month at a 12 percent annual interest rate. Loans are to be repaid at the end of a month in multiples of $1,000. Interest is paid only when a repayment is made. Investments are made in $1,000 multiples at the end of a month, and the return on investment is 8 percent per year.

a. Prepare a production budget by month and in total for the first quarter of Year 2.
b. Prepare a direct material purchases budget by month and in total for the first quarter of Year 2.
c. Prepare a schedule of cash payments for purchases by month and in total for the first quarter of Year 2.
d. Prepare a combined payments schedule for manufacturing overhead and selling and administrative cash costs for each month and in total for the first quarter of Year 2.
e. Prepare a cash budget for each month and in total for the first quarter of Year 2.

LO9-3, 4 **P9-67.** **Budgeted sales and S&A; other computations** Butler Inc. has projected Cost of Goods Sold (CGS) for June of $1,500,000. Of this amount, $80,000 represents fixed overhead costs. Total variable costs for the company each month average 70 percent of sales. The company's cost to retail (CGS to sales) percentage is 60 percent, and the company normally generates net income equal to 15 percent of sales. All purchases and expenses (except depreciation) are paid 65 percent in the month incurred and 35 percent in the following month. Depreciation is $45,000 per month.

a. What are Butler Inc.'s expected sales for June?
b. What are Butler Inc.'s expected variable selling and administrative costs for June?
c. What are Butler Inc.'s total fixed costs? How much of this is fixed selling and administrative cost?
d. Butler Inc. normally collects 55 percent of its sales in the month of sale and the rest in the next month. What are expected cash receipts and disbursements related only to June's transactions?

LO9-3 **P9-68.** **Budgeted cash collections; budgeted accounts receivable; bad debts** Cute and Cuddly Inc. sells teddy bears in walk-by kiosks in shopping malls. The company's balance sheet on March 31 showed the following balances related to Accounts Receivable and inventories:

Accounts Receivable	$346,000
Allowance for doubtful accounts.	35,000
Inventory.	208,000
Accounts payable to suppliers	455,000

The company's controller, Brad Jones, is making budget projections for the second quarter of the year and has made the following assumptions:

- Budgeted sales: April—60,000 units, May—140,000 units, June—46,000 units
- Selling price per bear—$12
- Cost per bear—$8

Expected cash collections from the March 31 balance of Accounts Receivable:

In April	$ 36,000
In May.	295,000
To be written off	15,000

Other information:

The Accounts Receivable balance at March 31 consists of $36,000 from February sales and $310,000 from March sales.

Eighty percent of sales are on credit. The remaining sales are cash sales. Twenty-five percent of credit sales are collected in the month of sale, with 55 percent in the month following and 18 percent in the second month following. The remaining 2 percent are uncollectible. The company expects to write off $15,000 of accounts receivable during the second quarter.

Thirty percent of purchases are paid for in the month of purchase with the remainder in the month following.

The company budgets ending inventory equal to 40 percent of the following month's sales in units. July's sales are budgeted at 30,000 units.

a. Prepare a sales budget for the quarter ended June 30.
b. Compute budgeted cash collections for the quarter ending June 30.

c. Compute budgeted Accounts Receivable at June 30.
d. Compute the estimated bad debt expense that will appear in the budgeted income statement for the quarter ending June 30.
e. How would the Accounts Receivable be presented on the budgeted balance sheet at June 30?
f. Compute budgeted purchases for the quarter ended June 30.
g. Compute budgeted cash payments for inventory for the quarter ended June 30.
h. Compute budgeted accounts payable at June 30.

P9-69. Cash budget Stabler Co.'s projected March 31 balance sheet follows.   LO9-4

Assets		Liabilities and Stockholders' Equity		
Cash	$ 24,000	Accounts Payable		$140,400
Accounts Receivable (net of Allowance for Uncollectibles of $2,880)	69,120			
Merchandise Inventory	104,800	Common Stock	$50,000	
Plant Assets (net of Accumulated Depreciation of $120,000)	72,000	Retained Earnings	79,520	129,520
Total Assets	$269,920	Total Liabilities and Stockholders' Equity		$269,920

Additional information about the company is as follows:

- Expected sales for April and May are $240,000 and $260,000, respectively. All sales are made on account.
- The monthly collection pattern from the month of sale forward is 50 percent, 48 percent, and 2 percent uncollectible. Accounts Receivable and the Allowance for Uncollectibles reflect only accounts for March.
- Cost of goods sold is 65 percent of sales.
- Purchases each month are 60 percent of the current month's sales and 30 percent of the next month's projected sales. All purchases are paid for in full in the month following purchase.
- Dividends of $20,000 will be declared and paid in April.
- Selling and administrative expenses each month are $43,000, of which $8,000 is depreciation.
- Investments and borrowings must be made in $1,000 amounts.

a. What were March budgeted sales?
b. What will be budgeted cash collections for April?
c. What will be the Merchandise Inventory balance at April 30?
d. What will be the projected balance in the Retained Earnings account at April 30?
e. If the company wishes to maintain a minimum cash balance of $16,000, how much will be available for investment, or be borrowed at the end of April?

P9-70. Cash budget Vassar Corp. has incurred substantial losses for several years and has decided to declare bankruptcy. The company petitioned the court for protection from creditors on March 31, Year 1, and submitted the following balance sheet: LO9-4

Vassar Corp.
Balance Sheet
March 31, Year 1

	Book Value	Liquidation Value
Assets		
Accounts Receivable	$100,000	$ 50,000
Inventories	90,000	40,000
Plant Assets (net)	150,000	160,000
Totals	$340,000	$250,000

Vassar's liabilities and stockholders' equity at this date are as follows:

Accounts Payable—General Creditors	$ 600,000
Common Stock	60,000
Retained Earnings Deficit	(320,000)
Totals	$ 340,000

Vassar's management informed the court that the company has developed a new product and that a prospective customer is willing to sign a contract for the purchase of 10,000 units during the year ending March 31, Year 2, and 12,000 units during the year ending March 31, Year 3, at a price of $90 per unit. Vassar expects to sell 15,000 units during the year ending March 31, Year 3. This product can be manufactured using Vassar's present facilities. Monthly production with immediate delivery is expected to be uniform within each year. Receivables are expected to be collected during the calendar month following sales. Unit production costs of the new product are estimated as follows:

Direct material	$20
Direct labor	30
Variable overhead	10

Fixed costs of $130,000 (excluding depreciation) are incurred per year. Purchases of direct material will be paid during the calendar month following purchase. Fixed costs, direct labor, and variable overhead will be paid as incurred. Inventory of direct material will equal 60 days' usage. After the first month of operations, 30 days' usage will be ordered each month.

The general creditors have agreed to reduce their total claims to 60 percent of their March 31, Year 1, balances under the following conditions:

- Existing accounts receivable and inventories are to be liquidated immediately, with the proceeds turned over to the general creditors.
- The reduced balance of accounts payable is to be paid as cash is generated from future operations but no later than March 31, Year 3. No interest will be paid on these obligations.

Under this proposed plan, the general creditors would receive $110,000 more than the current liquidation value of Vassar's assets. The court has engaged you to determine the feasibility of this plan.

Ignoring any need to borrow and repay short-term funds for working capital purposes, prepare a cash budget for the years ending March 31, Year 2 and Year 3, showing the cash expected to be available for paying the claims of the general creditors, the amount of payments to general creditors, and the cash remaining after payment of claims.

P9-71. Cash budget Collegiate Management Education (CME) Inc. is a nonprofit organization that sponsors a wide variety of management seminars throughout the Southwest. In addition, it is heavily involved in research into improved methods of teaching and motivating college administrators. Its seminar activity is largely supported by fees, and the research program is supported by membership dues.

CME operates on a calendar-year basis and is finalizing the budget for the year. The following information has been taken from approved plans, which are still tentative at this time:

Seminar Program

Revenue
The scheduled number of programs should produce $12,000,000 of revenue for the year. Each program is budgeted to produce the same amount of revenue. The revenue is collected during the month the program is offered. The programs are scheduled during the basic academic year and are not held during June, July, August, or December. Of the revenue, 12 percent is generated in each of the first five months of the year and the remainder is distributed evenly during September, October, and November.

Direct expenses
The seminar expenses are of three types:

- Instructors' fees are paid at the rate of 70 percent of seminar revenue in the month following the seminar. The instructors are considered independent contractors and are not eligible for CME employee benefits.

- Facilities fees total $5,600,000 for the year. They are the same for each program and are paid in the month the program is given.
- Annual promotional costs of $1,000,000 are spent equally in all months except June and July, when there is no promotional effort.

Research Program

Research grant

The research program has a large number of projects nearing completion. The main research activity this year includes feasibility studies for new projects to be started next year. As a result, the total grant expense of $3,000,000 for the year is expected to be incurred at the rate of $500,000 per month during the first six months of the year.

Salaries and Other CME Expenses

- Office lease—annual amount of $240,000 paid monthly at the beginning of each month.
- General administrative expenses—$1,500,000 annually, or $125,000 per month, paid in cash as incurred.
- Depreciation expense—$240,000 per year.
- General CME promotion—annual cost of $600,000, paid monthly.
- Salaries and benefits are as follows:

Number of Employees	Annual Cash Salary	Total Annual Salaries
1	$50,000	$ 50,000
3	40,000	120,000
4	30,000	120,000
15	25,000	375,000
5	15,000	75,000
22	10,000	220,000
50		$960,000

Employee benefits are $240,000, or 25 percent of annual salaries. Except for the pension contribution, the benefits are paid as salaries are paid. The annual pension payment of $24,000, based on 2.5 percent of total annual salaries, is due on April 15 of this year.

Other Information

- Membership income—CME has 100,000 members, each of whom pays a $100 annual fee. The fee for the calendar year is invoiced in late June.
- Collection schedule—July, 60 percent; August, 30 percent; September, 5 percent; and October, 5 percent.
- Capital expenditures—this program calls for a total of $510,000 in cash payments to be spread evenly over the first five months of this year.
- Cash and temporary investments at January 1 are estimated at $750,000.

a. Prepare a budget of the annual cash receipts and disbursements for the year.
b. Prepare a cash budget for CME for January of this year.
c. Using the information developed in (a) and (b), identify two important operating problems of CME.

CPA ADAPTED

P9-72. Cash budget Blackman Corp., a rapidly expanding crossbow distributor, is in the process of formulating plans for next year. Cara Jordan, director of marketing, has completed her annual forecast and is confident that sales estimates will be met or exceeded. The following forecasted sales figures show the growth expected and will provide the planning basis for other corporate departments.

LO9-4

	Sales		Sales
January	$3,600,000	July	$6,000,000
February	4,000,000	August	6,000,000
March	3,600,000	September	6,400,000
April	4,400,000	October	6,400,000
May	5,000,000	November	6,000,000
June	5,600,000	December	6,800,000

George Moore, assistant controller, has been given the responsibility for formulating the cash flow projection, a critical element during a period of rapid expansion. The following information will be used in preparing the cash analysis.

- Blackman has experienced an excellent record in accounts receivable collections and expects this trend to continue. The company collects 60 percent of its billings in the month after the sale and 40 percent in the second month after the sale. Uncollectible accounts are insignificant and should not be considered in the analysis.
- The purchase of crossbows is Blackman's largest expenditure; the cost of these items equals 50 percent of sales. The company receives 60 percent of the crossbows one month prior to sale and 40 percent during the month of sale.
- Prior experience shows that 80 percent of accounts payable is paid by Blackman one month after receipt of the purchased crossbows, and the remaining 20 percent is paid the second month after receipt.
- Hourly wages, including fringe benefits, are a function of sales volume and are equal to 20 percent of the current month's sales. These wages are paid in the month incurred.
- Administrative expenses are projected to be $5,280,000 for the year. All of these expenses are incurred uniformly throughout the year except the property taxes. Property taxes are paid in four equal installments in the last month of each quarter.

The composition of the expenses is:

Salaries	$ 960,000
Promotion	1,320,000
Property taxes	480,000
Insurance	720,000
Utilities	600,000
Depreciation	1,200,000
Total	$5,280,000

- Income tax payments are made by Blackman in the first month of each quarter based on income for the prior quarter. Blackman's income tax rate is 40 percent. Blackman's net income for the first quarter of the year is projected to be $1,224,000.
- Blackman has a corporate policy of maintaining an end-of-month cash balance of $200,000. Cash is invested or borrowed monthly, as necessary, to maintain this balance.

Blackman uses a calendar year reporting period.

a. Prepare a budgeted schedule of cash receipts and disbursements for Blackman Corp., by month, for the second quarter of the year. Ignore interest expense and/or interest income associated with the borrowing/investing activities.
b. Discuss why cash budgeting is particularly important for a rapidly expanding company such as Blackman Corp.
c. Do monthly cash budgets ignore the pattern of cash flows within the month? Explain.

CPA ADAPTED

LO9-3, 4 **P9-73.** **Comprehensive budgets** Shredder Manufacturing has the following projected unit sales (at $18 per unit) for four months of operations:

Month	Unit Sales
January	25,000
February	30,000
March	32,000
April	35,000

Twenty-five percent of the customers are expected to pay in the month of sale and take a 3 percent discount; 70 percent of the customers are expected to pay in the month following sale. The remaining 5 percent will never pay.

It takes two pounds of raw material (costing $0.75 per pound) to produce a unit of product. In January, no raw material is in beginning inventories, but management wants to end each month with enough material for 20 percent of the next month's production. (April's production is assumed to be 34,000 units.) Shredder Manufacturing pays for 60 percent of its material purchases in the month of purchase and 40 percent in the following month.

Chapter 9 The Master Budget   9-61

> Each unit of product requires 0.5 hours of labor time. Labor is paid $15 per hour and is paid in the same month as worked. Overhead is estimated to be $2 per unit plus $25,000 per month (including depreciation of $12,000). Overhead costs are paid as incurred.
>
> Shredder will begin January with no Work in Process or Finished Goods Inventory. Inventory policy for these two accounts is set at zero ending WIP and 25 percent of the following month's sales for FG.
>
> a. Prepare a sales budget for January, February, and March.
> b. Prepare a production budget for January, February, and March.
> c. Prepare a purchases budget for January, February, and March.
> d. Prepare a direct labor budget for January, February, and March.
> e. Prepare an overhead budget for January, February, and March.
> f. Prepare a cash receipts schedule for sales and a cash payments schedule for material purchased.

P9-74. Cash budget; budgeted income statement Davide's Arrangements purchases, wholesales, and retails fresh flowers. Company estimates reveal the following for the first three months of the company's fiscal year:

LO9-4, 5

	Purchases	Sales
June	$132,000	$204,000
July	116,000	184,000
August	160,000	232,000

Davide's pays 60 percent of any month's purchases in the month of purchase, receiving a 2 percent discount on those payments. The remaining amount is paid in the following month, with no discount given. Other monthly payments for expenses are $48,000 plus 12 percent of sales revenue. Depreciation is $8,000 per month. Davide's maintains a minimum cash balance of $28,000. Borrowings and repayments must be made in $1,000 amounts.

All sales transactions are on credit. Experience indicates the following expected collection pattern for credit sales: 25 percent in the month of sale, 60 percent in the month following the sale, and 15 percent in the second month following the sale. The company has no debt other than what is currently owed for purchases on account.

a. Calculate the July 31 balances for Accounts Receivable and Accounts Payable.
b. Calculate the expected total cash collections in August.
c. Calculate the expected total cash disbursements in August.
d. Prepare a cash budget for August, assuming that the beginning balance of cash was $28,470.
e. Prepare a budgeted income statement for August. Assume an average gross profit rate of 45 percent and ignore income taxes.
f. Explain how and why inventory management must be different for perishable commodities than for nonperishable commodities.

P9-75. Budgeted results GJO Corp. manufactures decorative, high-quality nutcrackers. Selling price of a nutcracker is full production cost plus 25 percent (rounded to the nearest dollar). Variable production cost is $55 per unit, and total fixed costs are $2,600,000. Fixed manufacturing costs are 80 percent of total fixed costs and are allocated to the product based on the number of units produced. Variable selling and administrative costs are 8 percent of sales. Variable and fixed costs are expected to increase by 15 and 7.5 percent, respectively, next year. Estimated production and sales are 400,000 units.

LO9-5

a. What is the expected full production cost per unit of GJO Corp.'s nutcrackers for next year?
b. What is the product's expected selling price?
c. What is budgeted income before tax using the selling price computed in (b)?
d. What is the required selling price (rounded to the nearest dollar) for the company to earn income before tax equal to 25 percent of sales?

P9-76. Service Company, purchases budget, income statement, cash budget Moore Medical Center is located in a summer resort community. During the summer months (June through August), the center operates an outpatient clinic for the treatment of minor injuries and illnesses.

LO9-3, 4, 5, 6

The clinic is administered as a separate department within the hospital. It has its own staff and maintains its own financial records. All patients requiring extensive or intensive care are referred to other hospital departments.

An analysis of past operating data for the outpatient clinic reveals the following:

- Staff: Seven full-time employees with total monthly salaries of $42,000. On a monthly basis, one additional staff member is hired for every 500 budgeted patient visits in excess of 3,000, at a cost of $7,000 per month.
- Facilities: Monthly facility costs, including depreciation of $2,500, total $15,000.
- Supplies: The supplies expense averages $20 per patient visit. The center maintains an end-of-month supplies inventory equal to 10 percent of the predicted needs of the following month, with a minimum ending inventory of $4,000, which is also the desired inventory at the end of August.
- Additional variable patient costs, such as medications, are charged directly to the patient by the hospital pharmacy.
- Payments: All staff and maintenance expenses are paid in the month the cost is incurred. Supplies are purchased at cost directly from the hospital with an immediate transfer of cash from the clinic cash account to the hospital cash account.
- Collections: The average bill for services rendered is $75. Of the total bills, 40 percent are paid in cash at the time the service is rendered, 10 percent are never paid, and the remaining 50 percent are covered by insurance. In the past, insurance companies have disallowed 30 percent of the claims filed and paid the balance two months after services are rendered.
- May 30 status: At the end of May, the clinic had $15,000 in cash and supplies costing $5,000.

Budgeted patient visits for next summer are as follows:

Month	Patient Visits
June	3,000
July	3,500
August	4,500

For the Moore Outpatient Clinic:

a. Prepare a supplies purchases budget for June, July, and August with a total column.
b. Prepare budgeted income statement for June, July, and August with a total column.
c. Prepare a cash budget for June, July, and August with a total column. Assume that the clinic has no source for financing.
d. Is the cash budget for the annual summer outpatient clinic feasible? If not, make appropriate recommendations for management's consideration.

LO9-5 P9-77. Budgeted income statement and balance sheet The projected October 31 balance sheet for Blanco Co. follows:

Assets	
Cash	$ 28,000,000
Accounts Receivable (net of Allowance for Uncollectibles of $3,000,000)	57,000,000
Inventory	52,500,000
Property, Plant, and Equipment (net of Accumulated Depreciation of $37,500,000)	112,500,000
Total Assets	$250,000,000
Liabilities and Stockholders' Equity	
Accounts Payable	$165,000,000
Common Stock	120,000,000
Retained Earnings (deficit)	(35,000,000)
Total Liabilities and Stockholders' Equity	$250,000,000

Additional information is as follows:

- Sales for November and December are budgeted at $330,000,000 and $360,000,000, respectively.
- Collections are expected to be 70 percent in the month of sale, 28 percent in the following month, and 2 percent uncollectible.
- The company's gross profit is projected at 30 percent of sales.
- Purchases each month are 70 percent of the following month's projected sales. Purchases are paid in full in the month following the purchase.
- Other monthly cash expenses are $46,500,000. Monthly depreciation is $15,000,000.

a. Prepare a budgeted income statement for November.
b. Prepare a budgeted balance sheet at November 30.
c. Describe any special problems this company may encounter because of its weak balance sheet. Recommend actions the firm might take to improve the balance sheet.

Chapter 9 The Master Budget

P9-78. Comprehensive Clarenville Kitchen Products produces and sells upscale mixers and breadmakers. In October Year 1, Clarenville's budget department gathered the following data to meet budget requirements for Year 2.

LO9-2, 3, 4, 5

Year 2 Projected Sales

Product	Units	Price
Mixers	60,000	$ 90
Breadmakers	40,000	140

Year 2 Inventories (Units)

Product	Expected Jan. 1, Year 2	Desired Dec. 31, Year 2
Mixers	15,000	20,000
Breadmakers	4,000	5,000

To produce one unit of each product, the following major internal components are used (in addition to the plastic housing for products, which is subcontracted in a subsequent operation):

Component	Mixer	Breadmaker
Motor	1	1
Beater	2	4
Fuse	2	3

Projected data for Year 2 with respect to components are as follows:

	Anticipated Purchase Price	Expected Inventory Jan. 1, Year 2	Desired Inventory Dec. 31, Year 2
Motor	$18.00	2,000	3,600 units
Beater	1.75	21,000	24,000 units
Fuse	2.40	6,000	7,500 units

Projected direct labor requirements for Year 2 and rates are as follows:

Product	Hours per Unit	Rate per Hour
Mixers	2	$ 8
Breadmakers	3	10

Overhead is applied at a rate of $7.50 per direct labor hour.

Based on these projections and budget requirements for Year 2 for mixers and breadmakers, prepare the following budgets for Year 2:

a. Sales budget (in dollars)
b. Production budget (in units)
c. Internal components purchases budget (in units and dollars)
d. Direct labor budget (in dollars)
e. The total production cost, excluding subsequent departments, per mixer and per breadmaker

CPA ADAPTED

P9-79. Master budget preparation Kalogridis Corp. manufactures industrial dye. The company is preparing its Year 2 master budget and has presented you with the following information:

LO9-2, 3, 4, 5

a. The projected December 31, Year 1, balance sheet for the company is as follows:

Assets			Liabilities		
Cash		$ 5,080	Notes Payable		$ 25,000
Accounts Receivable		26,500	Accounts Payable		2,148
Raw Material Inventory		800	Dividends Payable		10,000
Finished Goods Inventory		2,104	Total Liabilities		$ 37,148
Prepaid Insurance		1,200	Common Stock	$100,000	
Building	$300,000		Paid-in Capital	50,000	
Accum. Depreciation	(20,000)	280,000	Retained Earnings	128,536	278,536
Total Assets		$315,684	Total Liabilities and Stockholders' Equity		$315,684

© Cambridge Business Publishers

b. The Accounts Receivable balance at December 31, Year 1 represents the remaining balances of November and December credit sales. Sales were $70,000 and $65,000, respectively, in those two months.

c. Estimated sales in gallons of dye for January through May Year 2 are as follows:

January	8,000
February	10,000
March	15,000
April	12,000
May	11,000

Each gallon of dye sells for $12.

d. The collection pattern for accounts receivable is as follows: 70 percent in the month of sale, 20 percent in the first month after the sale, and 10 percent in the second month after the sale. Kalogridis Corp. expects no bad debts and gives no cash discounts.

e. Each gallon of dye has the following standard quantities and costs for direct material and direct labor:

1.2 gallons of direct material (some evaporation occurs during processing) × $0.80 per gallon	$0.96
0.5 hour of direct labor × $6 per hour	3.00

f. Variable overhead (VOH) is applied to the product on a machine-hour basis. Processing one gallon of dye takes five hours of machine time. The variable overhead rate is $0.06 per machine hour; VOH consists entirely of utility costs. Total annual fixed overhead is $120,000; it is applied at $1 per gallon based on an expected annual capacity of 120,000 gallons. Fixed overhead per year is composed of the following costs:

Salaries	$78,000
Utilities	12,000
Insurance—factory	2,400
Depreciation—factory	27,600

Fixed overhead is incurred evenly throughout the year.

g. There is no beginning Work in Process Inventory. All work in process is completed in the period in which it is started. Raw Material Inventory at the beginning of the year consists of 1,000 gallons of direct material at a standard cost of $0.80 per gallon. There are 400 gallons of dye in Finished Goods Inventory at the beginning of the year carried at a standard cost of $5.26 per gallon: direct material, $0.96; direct labor, $3.00; variable overhead, $0.30; and fixed overhead, $1.00.

h. Accounts Payable relates solely to raw material and is paid 60 percent in the month of purchase and 40 percent in the month after purchase. No discounts are received for prompt payment.

i. The dividend will be paid in January Year 2.

j. A new piece of equipment costing $9,000 will be purchased on March 1, Year 2. Payment of 80 percent will be made in March and 20 percent in April. The equipment has a useful life of three years, will have no salvage value, and will be placed into service on March 1.

k. The note payable has a 12 percent interest rate; interest is paid at the end of each month. The principal of the note is repaid as cash is available to do so.

l. Kalogridis Corp.'s management has set a minimum cash balance at $5,000. Investments and borrowings are made in even $100 amounts. Interest on any borrowings is expected to be 12 percent per year, and investments will earn 4 percent per year.

m. The ending Finished Goods Inventory should include 5 percent of the next month's sales. This situation will not be true at the beginning of Year 2 due to a miscalculation in sales for December. The ending inventory of raw materials also should be 5 percent of the next month's needs.

n. Selling and administrative costs per month are as follows: salaries, $25,000; rent, $7,000; and utilities, $800. These costs are paid in cash as they are incurred.

o. The company's tax rate is 35 percent. (Round to the nearest dollar.)

Prepare a master budget for each month of the first quarter of Year 2 and budgeted financial statements as of the end of the first quarter of Year 2.

Chapter 9 The Master Budget

P9-80. Preparing and analyzing a budget Norton Weymer & Collins, LLP, a local accounting firm, has a formal budgeting system. The firm has five partners, two managers, four seniors, two administrative assistants, and two bookkeepers. The budgeting process has a bottom-line focus; that is, the budget and planning process continues to iterate and evolve until an acceptable budgeted net income is obtained. The determination of an acceptable level of net income is based on two factors: (1) the amount of salary the partners could generate if they were employed elsewhere and (2) a reasonable return on the partners' investment in the firm's net assets.

For the year, after careful consideration of alternative employment opportunities, the partners agreed that the best alternative employment would generate the following salaries:

Partner 1	$150,000
Partner 2	225,000
Partner 3	110,000
Partner 4	90,000
Partner 5	125,000
Total	$700,000

LO9-3, 5, 6, 7

The second input to determining the desired net income level is more complex. This part of the desired net income is based on the value of the net assets owned by the accounting firm. The partners have identified two major categories of assets: tangible and intangible. The partners have agreed that the net tangible assets are worth $230,000. The intangible assets, consisting mostly of the accounting practice itself, are worth 1.1 times gross fees billed in the prior year, which totaled $1,615,000. The partners have also agreed that a reasonable rate of return on the net assets of the accounting firm is 12 percent. Thus, the partners' desired net income from return on investment is as follows:

Tangible assets	$ 230,000
Intangible assets ($1,615,000 × 110 percent)	1,776,500
Total investment	$2,006,500
Rate of return	× 0.12
Required dollar return	$ 240,780

The experience of the accounting firm indicates that other operating costs are incurred as follows:

Fixed expenses (per year)	
Salaries (other than partners)	$300,000
Overhead	125,000
Variable expenses	
Overhead	15 percent of gross billings
Client service	5 percent of gross billings

Source: Adapted from Jerry S. Huss, "Better Budgeting for CPA Firms," *Journal of Accountancy* (November 1977), pp. 65–72. Reprinted with permission from the *Journal of Accountancy*. Copyright© 2000 by American Institute of CPAs. Opinions of the authors are their own and do not necessarily reflect policies of the AICPA.

a. Determine the minimum level of gross billings that would allow the partners to realize their net income objective. Prepare a budget of costs and revenues at that level.
b. If the partners believe that the level of billings you have projected in (a) is not feasible given the time constraints at the partner, manager, and senior levels, what changes can they make to the budget to preserve the desired level of net income?

P9-81. Revising and analyzing an operating budget Attala Co., a division of Jackson Industries (JI), offers consulting services to clients for a fee. JI's corporate management is pleased with the performance of Attala Co. for the first nine months of the current year and has recommended that Attala Co.'s division manager, Jason Newport, submit a revised forecast for the remaining quarter because the division has exceeded the annual year-to-date plan by 20 percent of operating income. An unexpected increase in billed hour volume over the original plan is the main reason for this gain in income. The original operating budget for the first three quarters for Attala Co. is as follows:

LO9-3, 5, 6, 7

OPERATING BUDGET	1st Quarter	2nd Quarter	3rd Quarter	Total 9 Months
Consulting fees				
Management consulting	$ 315,000	$ 315,000	$ 315,000	$ 945,000
EDP consulting	421,875	421,875	421,875	1,265,625
Total	$ 736,875	$ 736,875	$ 736,875	$ 2,210,625
Other revenue	10,000	10,000	10,000	30,000
Total	$ 746,875	$ 746,875	$ 746,875	$ 2,240,625
Expenses				
Consultant salaries	$(386,750)	$(386,750)	$(386,750)	$(1,160,250)
Travel and entertainment	(45,625)	(45,625)	(45,625)	(136,875)
Administrative	(100,000)	(100,000)	(100,000)	(300,000)
Depreciation	(40,000)	(40,000)	(40,000)	(120,000)
Corporate allocation	(50,000)	(50,000)	(50,000)	(150,000)
Total	$(622,375)	$(622,375)	$(622,375)	$(1,867,125)
Operating income	$ 124,500	$ 124,500	$ 124,500	$ 373,500

When comparing the actuals for the first three quarters to the original plan, Newport analyzed the variances and will reflect the following information in his revised forecast for the fourth quarter.

The division currently has 25 consultants on staff, 10 for management consulting and 15 for EDP consulting, and has hired 3 additional management consultants to start work at the beginning of the fourth quarter to meet the increased client demand.

The hourly billing rates for consulting revenues will remain at $90 for each management consultant and $75 for each EDP consultant. However, due to the favorable increase in billing hour volume when compared to the plan, the hours for each consultant will be increased by 50 hours per quarter. New employees are equally as capable as current employees and their time will be billed at the same rates.

The annual budgeted salaries and actual salaries, paid monthly, are $50,000 for a management consultant and 8 percent less for an EDP consultant. Corporate management has approved a merit increase of 10 percent at the beginning of the fourth quarter for all 25 existing consultants, but the new consultants will be compensated at the planned rate.

The planned salary expense includes a provision for employee fringe benefits amounting to 30 percent of the annual salaries; however, the improvement of some corporate-wide employee programs will increase the fringe benefit allocation to 40 percent.

The original plan assumes a fixed hourly rate for travel and other related expenses for each billing hour of consulting. These expenses are not reimbursed by the client, and the previously determined hourly rate has proven to be adequate to cover these costs.

Other revenues are derived from temporary rentals and interest income and remain unchanged for the fourth quarter.

Administrative expenses are 7 percent below the plan; this 7 percent savings on fourth-quarter expenses will be reflected in the revised plan.

Depreciation for office equipment and computers will stay constant at the projected straight-line rate.

Due to the favorable experience for the first three quarters and the division's increased ability to absorb costs, JI corporate management has increased the corporate expense allocation by 50 percent.

a. Prepare a revised operating budget for the fourth quarter for Attala Co. that Jason Newport will present to Jackson Industries. Be sure to furnish supporting calculations for all revised revenue and expense amounts.
b. Discuss the reasons that an organization would prepare a revised forecast.
c. Discuss your feelings about the 50 percent increase in corporate expense allocations.

P9-82. Budgeting internationally; writing Preparing budgets for a multinational organization is significantly more complex than doing so for a solely domestic organization. What costs might managers find in budgets for international companies that might not commonly be included (or included at similar amounts) in budgets for domestic companies?

Review Solutions

Review 9-1

1. a. Budget
   b. Strategic plan
   c. Tactical plan
   d. Tactical plan
   e. Budget
   f. Strategic plan

2. External variables can impact the company's decision to focus on product awareness. (1) What is the level of competition for the products and how are the company's products viewed in comparison to competitor's products? (2) What are expected domestic and global economic conditions over the next several years? (3) Do the products meet the sustainability standards that customers expect? (4) Are there any expected customer trends that would either favorably or unfavorably impact customer preferences as they relate to the products? (5) Are there any current trends in technology that could impact the life cycle of the product?

   Internal variables can impact the company's decision to focus on product awareness. (1) Are there any potential sourcing issues of merchandise? (2) Are the products part of the company's core competencies? (3) Are there any corporate sustainability goals that will impact the production of the products? (4) Are any of the products reaching the end of their product life cycles?

Review 9-2

a.

Sales Budget	Quarter 1	Quarter 2	Quarter 3	Quarter 4	Total
Product #486					
Sales in units	25,000	65,000	50,000	60,000	200,000
Selling price per unit	$ 10.00	$ 10.00	$ 11.00	$ 11.00	
Sales in dollars	$250,000	$650,000	$550,000	$660,000	$2,110,000
Product #890					
Sales in units	0	0	2,000	5,000	7,000
Selling price per unit	$ 0	$ 0	$ 15.00	$ 15.00	
Sales in dollars	$ 0	$ 0	$ 30,000	$ 75,000	$ 105,000
Total sales in dollars	$250,000	$650,000	$580,000	$735,000	$2,215,000

b. A contingency budget could be prepared which is a second budget, modeling the possible decrease in sales volume. The contingency budget could be extended to the full master budget should the company need to pivot in the event of an economic downturn.

Review 9-3

1. a.

Annual Sales Budget	#401	#586
Product #401		
Sales in units	96,000	36,000

b.

Production Budget	#401	#586
Sales in units	96,000	36,000
Desired ending inventory	768	1,080
Total needed	96,768	37,080
Beginning inventory	(960)	(1,440)
Units to be produced	95,808	35,640

c.

Purchases Budget—Steel	#401	#586	Total
Units to be produced	95,808	35,640	
Pounds per unit.	× 4	× 3	
Total quantity needed	383,232	106,920	490,152
Desired ending inventory			1,680
Beginning inventory			(2,400)
Total pounds to purchase			489,432

Purchases Budget—Wood	#401	#586	Total
Units to be produced	95,808	35,640	
Pounds per unit.	× 0.60	× 0.30	
Total quantity needed	57,485	10,692	68,177
Desired ending inventory			720
Beginning inventory			(960)
Total pounds to purchase			67,937

d.

Direct Labor Budget	#401	#586	Total
Units to be produced	95,808	35,640	
Standard hours allowed	× 2.00	× 3.00	
Total hours allowed.	191,616	106,920	298,536
Average wage rate	× $20.00	× $20.00	× $20.00
Direct labor cost	$3,832,320	$2,138,400	$5,970,720

e.

Overhead Budget	#401	#586	Total
Units to be produced	95,808	35,640	
Machine hours	× 0.50	× 0.80	
Total machine hours	47,904	28,512	76,416
Overhead rate.	× $20.00	× $20.00	× $20.00
Overhead cost	$958,080	$570,240	$1,528,320

2. Because the budgets are all driven by the number of units produced, the pounds to purchase drops by 20 percent and the direct labor and overhead cost amounts drop by 20 percent.

3. While the sales budget dropped, it does not necessarily mean that operationally, the company can act quickly enough to drop costs. For example, does labor consist of full-time or temporary employees such that labor hours can contractually be reduced? Have materials already been purchased or have commitments been made to purchase the quantities per the budget? Are overhead costs fixed or variable? An unexpected adjustment to a sales budget has impacts throughout the organization that companies will need to react to in order to achieve desired profitability levels.

Review 9-4

a.

	January	February	March
Nov. sales	$31,250		
Dec. sales	43,500		
Dec. sales		$36,250	
Jan. sales	48,069		
Jan. sales		32,700	
Jan. sales			$27,250
Feb. sales		52,920	
Feb. sales			36,000
Mar. sales			53,802
Total collections	$122,819	$121,870	$117,052

Chapter 9 The Master Budget

b.
February sales to be collected in April	$30,000
March sales to be collected in April	36,600
March sales to be collected in May	30,500
Accounts receivable balance at March 31	$97,100

c. The cash budget is useful for making decisions on discretionary expenditures and provides an indication of whether financing will be necessary for an upcoming period. In addition, it allows management to evaluate its collection patterns and evaluate whether any changes should be made to credit terms offered.

Review 9-5

a.
Revenue
Computers ($6,240,000 × 1.08 × 1.03)	$ 6,941,376
Computer supplies ($2,600,000 × 1.05)	2,730,000
Maintenance contracts ($1,560,000 × 1.06)	1,653,600
Total revenue	$11,324,976

Costs and expenses
Cost of computers ($4,368,000 × 1.03 × 1.05)	$4,723,992
Cost of computer supplies ($520,000 × 1.05 × 1.05)	573,300
Marketing expenses ($780,000 × 1.02)	795,600
Customer maintenance costs ($832,000 + $150,000)	982,000
Administrative expenses	1,456,000
Total costs and expenses	8,530,892
Operating income	$2,794,084

b. Positive results: The increase in computer revenue was greater than the increase in computer costs. Because the sale of computers is 61 percent of overall sales, this had a significant impact on overall trends. Also, other costs such as marketing and administrative costs did not go up as much as the rate of sales.

Negative results: These positive trends were offset by the cost of supplies going up at a higher rate than the sale of supplies and the cost of contracts going up at a higher rate than revenue from contracts.

Overall, net income increased, per the budget, by over 14 percent over prior year results.

Review 9-6

a.

Revenue and Expense Budget	Quarter
Revenue:	
Virtual-service revenue ($280,000 × 1.10 ÷ 4)	$ 77,000
Full-service revenue ($1,250,000 × 0.90 ÷ 4)	281,250
Total revenues	358,250
Expenses:	
Salaries ($800,000 × 1.05 ÷ 4)	210,000
Overhead:	
Fixed [($150,000 + $10,000) ÷ 4]	40,000
Variable (15% × 358,250)*	53,738
Client service (8% × $281,250)	22,500
Total expenses	326,238
Net profit	$32,012

*Amount rounded.

b. The largest expense is labor making up over 64 percent of total expenses. The largest expense for a manufacturer is cost of goods sold which includes direct materials, direct labor, and overhead related to the products being manufactured. This means that the focus of cost control should differ between company types.

Review 9-7

1. a. 8   c. 4   e. 7   g. 2
   b. 1   d. 3   f. 5   h. 6

2. An imposed budget is dictated by top management without input from operating managers. In certain circumstances, this process is preferable such as in (1) start-up companies or companies going through high-growth periods, (2) down-sizing or liquidation scenarios, (3) crisis situations, such as the pandemic, (4) cases of extensive legal or regulatory changes; or (5) cases of new competitors or technology. In all of these cases, the situations have quickly disrupted budgets, making them less relevant or even irrelevant.

Data Visualization Solutions
(See page 9-27.)

a. 100% − 32.0% − 28.0% − 11.9% − 5.0% − 3.6% − 2.6% − 2.1% − 1.9% − 1.4% − 1.2% = 10.3%
Labor and food and beverage cost represent 60 percent of the cost of sales and should be the focus of cost control. (Lease expense represents 12 percent of sales but likely is a fixed cost.)

b. Labor: $42,000 × 32% = $13,440 × 5% = $672 increase
Adjusted % of sales = $13,440 + $672 = $14,112 ÷ $42,000 = 33.6%
Food and beverage cost: $42,000 × 28% = $11,760 × 5% = $588 increase
Adjusted % of sales = $11,760 + $588 = $12,348 ÷ $42,000 = 29.4%

c. 100% − 33.6% − 29.4% − 11.9% − 5.0% − 3.6% − 2.6% − 2.1% − 1.9% − 1.4% − 1.2% = 7.3%

Chapter 10
Flexible Budget, Standard Costing, and Variance Analysis

Road Map

LO	Learning Objective	Topics	Page	eLecture	Demo	Review	Assignments
10-1	**How is a flexible budget prepared and what is its purpose?** Static Budget :: Static Budget Variance :: Flexible Budget :: Flexible Budget Variance	10-2	e10-1	D10-1A D10-1B	Rev 10-1	MC10-15, E10-24, E10-25, E10-26, E10-27, E10-28, E10-29, P10-66, P10-67, P10-68, DA10-1
10-2	**How are material, labor, and overhead standards set in a standard costing system?** Material Standards :: Bill of Materials :: Labor Standards :: Overhead Standards :: Standard Quantity Allowed :: Standard Cost Card	10-5	e10-2	D10-2	Rev 10-2	MC10-16, E10-30, E10-31, E10-32, E10-33, E10-34, E10-35, E10-36, DA10-2
10-3	**How are material and labor variances calculated and recorded?** Material Price Variance (MPV) :: Material Quantity Variance (MQV) :: Total Material Variance (TMV) :: Point-of-Usage Model :: Point-of-Purchase Model :: Labor Rate Variance (LRV) :: Labor Efficiency Variance (LEV) :: Total Labor Variance (TLV)	10-10	e10-3	D10-3A D10-3B D10-3C D10-3D D10-3E	Rev 10-3	MC10-17, MC10-18, E10-37, E10-38, E10-39, E10-40, E10-41, E10-42, E10-43, E10-44, E10-45, E10-46, E10-47, E10-48, E10-49, P10-69, P10-70, P10-71, P10-72, P10-73, P10-74, P10-80, P10-81, P10-83, P10-84
10-4	**How are overhead variances calculated and recorded?** Four-Variance :: VOH Spending Variance :: VOH Efficiency Variance :: FOH Spending Variance :: Volume Variance :: Noncontrollable Variance :: Alternative Approaches :: One-Variance :: Two-Variance :: Three Variance	10-16	e10-4	D10-4A D10-4B D10-4C	Rev 10-4	MC10-19, E10-50, E10-51, E10-52, E10-53, E10-54, E10-55, E10-56, P10-75, P10-76, P10-77, P10-78, P10-79, P10-80, P10-81, P10-83
10-5	**How are variances reconciled at period end?** Disposition of Variances :: Insignificant Variances :: Significant Variances	10-24	e10-5	D10-5	Rev 10-5	MC10-20, E10-48, E10-51, E10-57, P10-76, P10-82
10-6	**How are variances affected by multiple material and labor categories?** Material Price Variance :: Material Mix Variance :: Material Yield Variance :: Labor Rate Variance :: Labor Mix Variance :: Labor Yield Variance	10-27	e10-6	D10-6A D10-6B	Rev 10-6	MC10-21, E10-58, E10-59, E10-60, P10-85, P10-86
10-7	**(Appendix 10A) How are standard costs used in a job order costing system?** Job Order Costing System :: Material Variances :: Labor Variances :: Hybrid of Actual and Standard Cost Systems	10-31	e10-7	D10-7A D10-7B	Rev 10-7	MC10-22, E10-61, E10-62, E10-63, P10-87, P10-88
10-8	**(Appendix 10B) How does the use of a single conversion element (rather than the traditional labor and overhead elements) affect standard costing?** Conversion Cost Variances :: Spending Variance :: Efficiency Variance :: Volume Variance	10-33	e10-8	D10-8	Rev 10-8	MC10-23, E10-64, E10-65, P10-89, P10-90

© Cambridge Business Publishers

INTRODUCTION

Organizations, even those not involved in production activities, develop and use standards for almost all tasks. For example, businesses set standards for employee sales expenses; pizza restaurants set standards to prepare and bake a pizza; and casinos set standards for revenue to be generated per square foot of playing space. The **MGM Grand** in Las Vegas has standards for housekeeping (30 minutes), room service (maximum of 30 minutes to deliver), maintenance calls (15 minutes to be handled), and car valet delivery (8 minutes).[1] A Big Mac at McDonald's should be assembled in 15 seconds; Taco Bell requires that Crunchwrap Supremes get grilled for 27 seconds; and Wendy's has an average of 134 seconds per vehicle in the drive-through lanes.[2]

Because of the variety of organizational activities and information objectives, no single standard costing system is appropriate for all situations. Some systems use standards for costs but not for quantities; other systems (especially those in service businesses) use standards for labor but not material. Standards act as target measures of performance and therefore may be met, exceeded, or failed to be met. Accountants help explain the financial consequences of exceeding or failing to achieve standards. Without a predetermined measure, managers have no way of knowing what performance level is expected or gauging actual performance. And without comparing the actual result to the predetermined measure, managers have no way of knowing whether the company met expectations or exercised reasonable operational control.

This chapter starts with a discussion of the variance between actual costs and the flexible budget. This variance can be examined in more detail through a standard cost system. The chapter discusses why standard cost systems are used, how standards are developed, how variances from standards are calculated, and what information can be gained from variance analysis. Journal entries used in a standard cost system are shown. The chapter also covers mix and yield variances that can arise from using multiple types of materials or groups of labor.

FLEXIBLE BUDGETS

LO10-1 How is a flexible budget prepared and what is its purpose?

A budget that is based on a single prediction of sales and production is called a **static budget**. The master budget discussed in the last section is a form of a static budget. **Flexible budgets** are budgets adjusted to a specific volume level(s). A flexible budget can be used as a

- planning document, presenting expected cost at different levels of activity, or as a
- performance measure, when adjusted to reflect actual volume.

Flexible Budgets for Planning

A flexible budget can be used as a planning document that presents *expected* variable and fixed costs at different activity levels. Activity levels shown on a flexible budget usually cover the contemplated range of activity for the current or future periods. If all activity levels are within the relevant range, costs at each successive level should equal the previous level plus an increment for each variable cost.

> **Increment = Variable cost per unit × Quantity of additional activity**

DEMO 10-1A LO10-1   Creating a Flexible Budget for Planning

Salinas Corporation (Salinas) produces one product, a high-quality, carbon fiber bike frame. Salinas developed an annual master budget based on monthly production of 1,000 bike frames. The monthly relevant range of activity is 800 to 1,200 bike frames. Assume for simplicity, that direct materials consist only of carbon fiber. Budgeted variable costs per bike frame for direct materials, direct labor, and variable overhead, are $260, $36, and $22.50, respectively. Budgeted annual fixed overhead cost is $381,600, expected to be incurred evenly at $31,800 per month.

◆ **How are flexible budgets prepared by Salinas for planning at monthly volumes of 800, 900, 1,000, 1,100, and 1,200 bike frames?**

---

[1] Andrea Petersen, "When 12,000 Guests Spend the Night," *Wall Street Journal* (September 22, 2011), p. D1.
[2] Karl Greenfeld, "Fast and Furious," *Bloomberg Businessweek* (May 9–May 15, 2011), pp. 64–69.

Chapter 10 Flexible Budget, Standard Costing, and Variance Analysis

	Flexible Budget	Flexible Budget	Flexible Budget	Flexible Budget	Flexible Budget
Volume (units)	800	900	1,000	1,100	1,200
Variable Costs					
Direct materials	$208,000	$234,000	$260,000	$286,000	$312,000
Direct labor	28,800	32,400	36,000	39,600	43,200
Variable overhead	18,000	20,250	22,500	24,750	27,000
Fixed overhead cost	31,800	31,800	31,800	31,800	31,800
Total	$286,600	$318,450	$350,300	$382,150	$414,000

Fixed cost is the same at each level of activity within the relevant range. The variable cost per unit is applied to each level of activity. For example, the direct material cost of $260 per unit is applied to each volume level, starting with 800 units.

The increment between flexible budgets of $31,850 (for example, $318,450 − $286,600) is due to variable costs, and is calculated as follows:

$$\text{Increment} = (\$260 + \$36 + \$22.50) \times 100 \text{ units} = \$31,850$$

Flexible Budgets for Performance Measurement

Rather than used for planning, a flexible budget can be set for a particular level of production *after* the fact. If actual production happened to equal budgeted production, the production department is evaluated by comparing the actual and budgeted costs. If production needs change, perhaps due to an unexpected increase or decrease in sales volume, the production department should attempt to make appropriate changes to the budget.

When the actual production volume is anything other than the originally budgeted amount, the production department's financial responsibility for costs should be based on the actual level of production. For the purpose of evaluating financial performance, a flexible budget is tailored, after the fact, to the actual level of activity.

Financial performance reports that include a comparison of actual and budgeted (or allowed) costs, identify the difference as a *flexible budget variance*. In performance reports, allowed costs are the flexible budget amounts for the actual level of activity. The variance is favorable if actual costs are less than budgeted (or allowed) costs and unfavorable if actual costs are more than budgeted (or allowed) costs. These comparisons are made in total and individually for each type of controllable cost assigned to the department.

Using a Flexible Budget to Measure Performance — LO10-1 DEMO 10-1B

Assume actual production for the month for Salinas totaled 1,200 bike frames rather than the 1,000 bike frames planned.

◆ Given the actual data provided below, what is the static budget variance, and the flexible budget variance for each of the manufacturing costs?

The performance report for manufacturing costs based on static and flexible budgets are presented as follows. Unfavorable variances are designated with a "U" and favorable variances are designated with an "F."

Production Department Performance Report

	Based on Static Budget			Based on Flexible Budget		
	Actual	Static Budget	Static Budget Variance	Actual	Flexible Budget	Flexible Budget Variance
Volume (units)	1,200	1,000		1,200	1,200	
Variable Costs						
Direct materials	$307,850	$260,000	$47,850 U	$307,850	$312,000	$ 4,150 F
Direct labor	43,475	36,000	7,475 U	43,475	43,200	275 U
Variable overhead	24,500	22,500	2,000 U	24,500	27,000	2,500 F
Fixed overhead cost	33,000	31,800	1,200 U	33,000	31,800	1,200 U
Total	$408,825	$350,300	$58,525 U	$408,825	$414,000	$ 5,175 F

© Cambridge Business Publishers

The static budget for one month is provided at a volume of 1,000 units. The flexible budget for the month is based on 1,200 units and is shown in the prior flexible budget used for planning. When the production department's financial performance is evaluated using the static budget, the actual cost of producing 1,200 bike frames is compared to the budgeted cost of producing 1,000 bike frames. The result is a series of unfavorable static budget variances totaling $58,525.

When the production department's financial performance is evaluated by comparing actual costs with costs allowed in a flexible budget drawn up for the actual production volume, the results are mixed. Direct materials have a $4,150 favorable variance. Direct labor has a $275 unfavorable variance. The variable overhead variance is $2,500 favorable. The fixed overhead variance remains $1,200 unfavorable since the static and flexible fixed budgets stay the same. The net flexible budget variance is $5,175 favorable, a substantial change from the static budget variance of $58,525 unfavorable.

Flexible budget variances are a better indicator of performance than static budget variances that do not reflect actual production levels. When production exceeds the planned level of activity, the static budget variances are usually unfavorable. Likewise, when actual production is substantially below the planned level of activity, the static variances are usually favorable.

Data Visualization

The flexible budget for Salinas is shown graphically for a month.

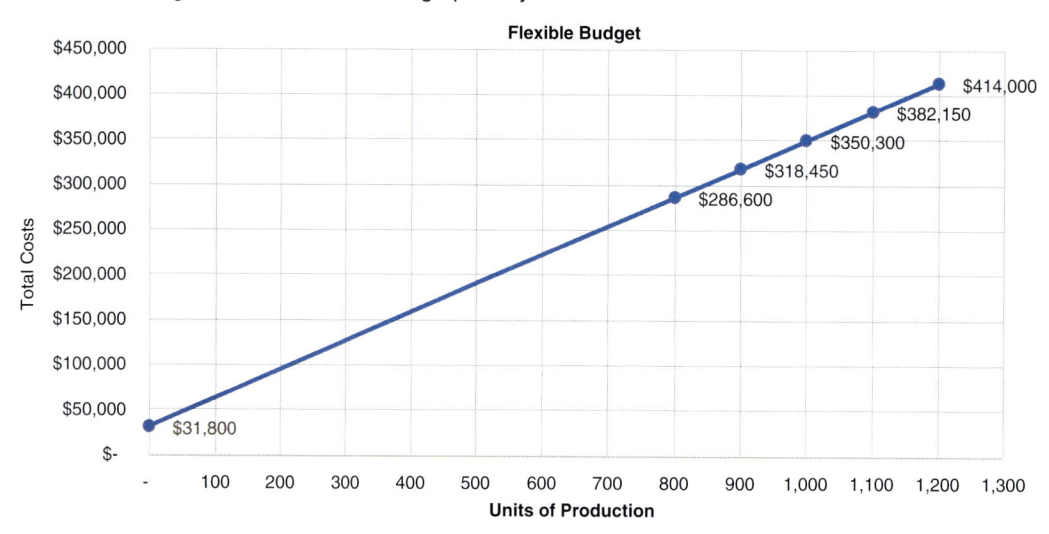

Flexible Budget

Units of Production	Total Costs
0	$31,800
800	$286,600
900	$318,450
1,000	$350,300
1,100	$382,150
1,200	$414,000

Based on this data visualization, answer the following questions.
a. What are total costs at the level of a master budget based on 1,000 units?
b. How do you determine which flexible budget total cost amount is appropriate to use for cost control?
c. If total actual cost is $302,100 when 800 units are produced, are the results over or under the master budget total cost amount? Over or under the relevant flexible budget total cost amount?
d. If total actual cost is $361,800 when 1,100 units are produced, are the results over or under the master budget total cost amount? Over or under the relevant flexible budget total cost amount?

Solution on p. 10-72.

REVIEW 10-1   **LO10-1**   *Flexible Budget*

Alterations Inc. provides a variety of clothing alterations. Analysis of monthly costs revealed the following cost formulas when direct labor hours are used as the basis of cost determination.
Supplies: = $0 + $5.00X
Production supervision and direct labor: y = 850 + $6.00X
Utilities: y = $575 + $4X
Rent: y = $600 + $0.00X
Advertising: y = $85 + $0.00X

continued

continued from previous page

> a. Prepare a flexible budget at 400, 450, 500, and 550 direct labor hours.
> b. Calculate a total cost per direct labor hour at each level of activity.
> c. **Critical Thinking:** How might management use a flexible budget for planning purposes and for control purposes?
>
> More practice: E10-24, E10-26
> Solution on p. 10-67.

DEVELOPING A STANDARD COST SYSTEM

A flexible budget provides a basis for control because it is based on actual volume. However, a more detailed system of control can be developed through a standard cost system, which provides information on input costs and quantities. A **standard cost system** tracks both standard and actual costs in the accounting records. This dual recording provides an essential element of cost control: having norms against which actual operations can be compared. Actual costs may differ each time materials are acquired. Labor rates may be adjusted during a period. Overhead costs fluctuate for a wide variety of reasons, some of which are not controllable within the organization. Additionally, material quantities, labor times, and machine hours may vary with production or service activities. In an actual cost system, each difference will have an impact on product cost. With an actual cost system, product or service unit costs would change continuously with changes in prices and usage of inputs.

In contrast to an actual cost system, a standard cost system uses **standards** that specify the *expected costs and quantities* needed to manufacture a single unit of product or perform a single service. By holding unit costs constant for some period of time, the use of standard costs provides the same benefits as the use of predetermined overhead rates. A standard cost system allows

- the allocation of costs in real time to products and services and
- the ability to adjust for cost or quantity fluctuations unrelated to activity differences. Standard cost systems are designed to provide an assessment measure of performance to managers for use in performing their various functions.

LO10-2 How are material, labor, and overhead standards set in a standard costing system?

Benefits of a Standard Cost System

Benefits of a standard cost system include the following.

Motivation	Planning	Controlling	Decision Making	Performance Evaluation

Motivation
Standards help communicate management's expectations to employees. When standards are achievable and rewards for attaining them are available, employees are likely to be motivated to strive to meet the targets that have been set. However, from a standpoint of organizational profitability and competitiveness, the standards must require a reasonable amount of effort on the employee's part. The use of tight standards can have undesirable behavioral effects if employees find that a second set of standards is used in the "real" budget or if they are constantly subject to unfavorable performance reports. These employees could come to distrust the entire budgeting and performance evaluation system, or they may quit trying to achieve any of the organization's standards.

Planning
Financial and operational planning requires estimates about future price and usage of inputs. Managers can use current standards to estimate future quantity needs and costs. These estimates help determine purchasing needs for material, staffing needs for labor, and capacity needs related to overhead and planning for company cash flows. Standards are also used to provide the cost basis needed to analyze relationships among the organization's costs, sales volume, and profits. But standards should not be considered long-term amounts and should be reviewed, and likely updated, at least annually, especially if an organization implements changes in production technology.

Controlling
The control process begins with the establishment of standards as a basis against which actual costs and quantities can be measured and variances calculated. **Variance analysis** is the process of categorizing

the nature (favorable or unfavorable) of the differences between actual and standard costs/quantities and seeking explanations for those differences. A well-designed variance analysis system computes variances as early as possible, subject to cost–benefit assessments. The system should help managers determine who or what was responsible for each variance and who is best able to explain it. An early measurement and reporting system allows managers to quickly monitor operations and take corrective action if necessary.

In analyzing variances, managers must recognize that they have a specific scarce resource: their time. They must distinguish between situations that can be ignored and those that need attention. To do this, managers establish upper and lower tolerance limits of acceptable deviations from the standard. If variances are small and within an acceptable range, no managerial action is required. If a variance differs significantly from standard, the manager responsible for the cost is expected to identify the variance cause(s) and then take actions to eliminate future unfavorable variances or, perhaps, to perpetuate favorable variances.

Setting upper and lower tolerance limits for deviations (as illustrated in **Exhibit 10.1**) allows managers to implement the **management-by-exception** concept. (The control limits can be established through a statistical process control chart discussed later in Chapter 17.) In the exhibit, the only significant deviation from standard occurred on Day 5, when the actual cost exceeded the upper limit of acceptable performance. An exception report describing the situation should be generated on this date so that the manager can investigate the underlying variance causes.

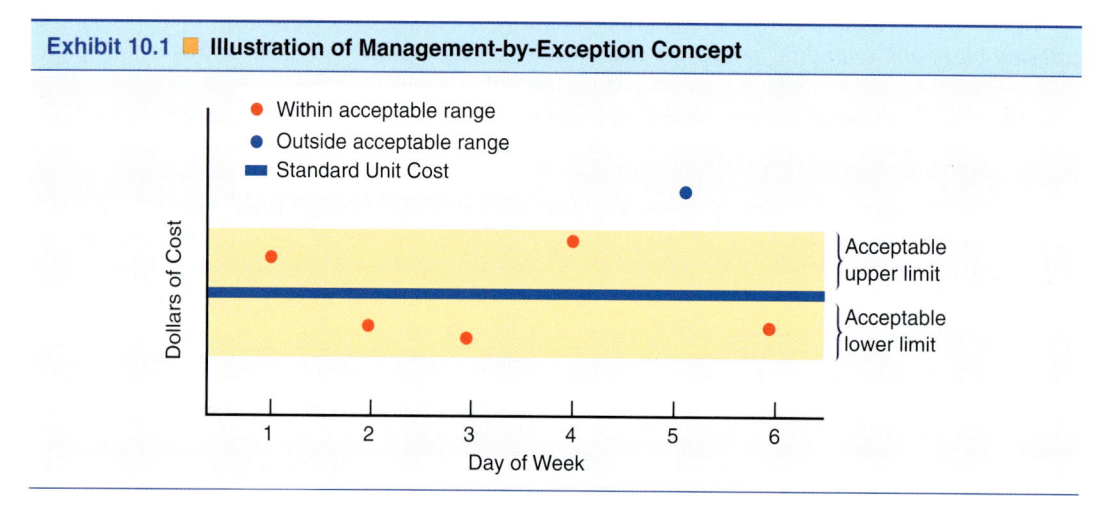

Exhibit 10.1 ■ Illustration of Management-by-Exception Concept

Variances large enough to fall outside the acceptability ranges often indicate problems. However, a mere computation of a variance does not reveal the variance's cause nor the person or group responsible for it. To determine variance causality, managers must investigate significant variances through observation, inspection, and inquiry. The investigation involves people at the operating level as well as accounting personnel. Operations personnel should spot variances as they occur and record the reasons for the variances to the extent that those reasons are discernible. For example, operating personnel could readily detect and report causes such as machine downtime or material spoilage.

One important point about variances must be made: a favorable variance is not necessarily a good variance. Although people often equate "favorable" with "good," an extremely favorable variance could mean that an error was made when the standard was set or that a related, offsetting unfavorable variance exists. For example, if low-grade material is purchased, a favorable price variance may result when the cost of the material is less than anticipated. However, use of the lower grade material may mean that more material than standard might have to be used to overcome defective production or that more labor time was required to complete a job as a result of using the inferior material—both results would create other unfavorable variances. Another common situation begins with labor rather than material. Using workers who are lower paid but less skilled than others will result in a favorable wage variance but can cause an excessive, unfavorable use of raw material and of labor time. Managers must be aware that such relationships exist and that *variances cannot be analyzed in isolation*.

Decision Making

Standard cost information facilitates decision making. For example, managers can compare a standard cost with a quoted price to determine whether an item should be manufactured in-house or purchased. Using actual cost information in such a decision could be inappropriate because the actual cost could fluctuate each period. Also, in deciding whether to offer a special price to customers, managers can use standard product cost to determine the lowest price limit. Similarly, a company bidding on contracts must have some idea of estimated product costs. Bidding too low and winning the contract could cause substantial operating income (and, possibly, cash flow) reduction; a bid that is too high could be noncompetitive and cause the contract to be awarded to another company.

Performance Evaluation

Variance reports should be analyzed for both positive and negative information as soon as they are received. Management needs to know which costs were and were not controlled and who is responsible. Such information allows management to provide feedback to employees, investigate areas of concern, and make performance evaluations and recommendations. For proper performance evaluations to be made, variance responsibility must be traced to specific managers.[3]

Considerations in Establishing Standards

When standards are established, the issues of appropriateness and attainability should be considered. Appropriateness, in relation to a standard, refers to the bases on which the standards are developed and how long they will be viable. Attainability refers to management's belief about the degree of difficulty or rigor that should be exerted in achieving the standard.

Appropriateness

Although developed from past and current information, standards must evolve to reflect relevant future technical and environmental factors. Consideration should be given to factors such as material quality, normal ordering quantities for material, expected employee wage rates, mix of employee skills, facility layout, and expected degree of plant automation. As mentioned earlier, standards will not remain useful forever. Current operating performance should not be compared to out-of-date standards because such comparisons will generate variances that are not logical bases for planning, controlling, decision making, or evaluating performance.

Attainability

Standards provide a target measure of performance and can be set at various levels of rigor that can affect employee motivation. Standards can be classified as expected, practical, and ideal. Depending on the rigor of the standard in effect, the acceptable ranges used to apply the management-by-exception principle will differ—especially on the unfavorable side.

Type of Standard	Ability to Achieve	Types of Variances
Expected	Almost always	Almost always favorable
Practical	60–70% of the time	Favorable and unfavorable
Ideal	Rarely, if ever	Almost always unfavorable

Expected Standards Expected standards reflect what is actually expected to occur. Such standards anticipate future waste and inefficiencies and allow for them. As such, expected standards are not of significant value for motivating, controlling, decision making, or evaluating performance. A company using expected standards should set a very small range of acceptable variation because actual costs should conform closely to standards. Expected standards tend to generate favorable variances.

Practical Standards Standards that can be reached or slightly exceeded approximately 60–70 percent of the time with reasonable effort are called practical standards. These standards allow for normal, unavoidable delays such as those caused by machine downtime and worker breaks. Practical standards

---

[3] Responsibility accounting, performance evaluation, and cost control relative to variances are discussed in greater depth in, respectively, Chapters 13 and 15.

represent an attainable challenge and traditionally have been thought to be the most effective in motivating workers and determining their performance levels. Both favorable and unfavorable variances result from the use of such moderately rigorous standards.

Ideal Standards Standards that provide for no inefficiency of any type are called **ideal** (or theoretical) **standards**. These standards are the most rigorous and do not allow for normal operating delays or human limitations such as fatigue, boredom, or misunderstanding. Unless a plant is entirely automated (and then the possibility of human error or power failure still exists), ideal standards are impossible to attain. Applying such standards has traditionally resulted in discouraged and resentful workers who ultimately ignored the standards. However, it can be argued that if a standard is set at a less-than-ideal level, managers are allowing and encouraging inefficient resource utilization.

Establishing Standards

A primary objective in manufacturing a product is to minimize unit cost while achieving certain quality and functionality specifications. Almost all products can be manufactured from a variety of alternative inputs that would generate similar output and output quality. *The input choices that are made affect the standards that are set.* Some possible input resource combinations are not necessarily practical or efficient. For instance, a labor team might consist only of skilled workers, but such a team might not be cost beneficial if the wage rates of skilled and unskilled workers differ significantly. Also, providing high-technology equipment to unskilled labor is possible, but doing so would not be an efficient use of resources. Developing a standard cost involves judgment and practicality in identifying the material and labor types, quantities, and prices as well as understanding the types of organizational overhead and how they behave.

After the desired output quality and the input resources needed to achieve that quality at a reasonable cost have been determined, price and quantity standards can be developed. Experts from cost accounting, industrial engineering, human resources, data processing, purchasing, and management contribute information and expertise toward developing standards. Inclusion of the various groups helps to ensure credibility of the standards and to motivate people to achieve the standards. The discussion of the standard-setting process begins with material.

Material Standards

The first step in developing material standards is to identify and list the specific direct material(s) needed to manufacture the product or provide the service.[4] This list is generally available on product specification documents prior to initial production. Four things must be known about material inputs:

- type of material needed,
- quality (grade) of material needed,
- quantity of material needed, and
- price per unit of material (must be based on level of quality specified).

For example, the direct material used in producing a baseball glove is cured and tanned leather; indirect materials include nylon thread and small plastic reinforcements at the base of the thumb and small finger. Because only about 30 percent of a cowhide can actually be used to make baseball gloves, each cowhide provides enough leather for only three or four gloves—but actual output depends on the glove size being produced (from gloves worn to play T-ball to those worn in the major leagues). Buffalo hide, kangaroo hide, pigskin, and human-made materials may be substituted for cowhide, but choice of material will affect production cost.

In making quality decisions, managers should remember that as the material grade rises, so generally does price. Decisions about material inputs usually seek to balance the relationships of price, quality, and projected selling prices with company objectives. Only after the quality level is selected for each component can estimates be made for the physical quantity of weight, size, volume, or other input measure(s). These estimates are based on the results of engineering tests, opinions of managers and

---

[4] For the remainder of the chapter, the text discussion will assume that a product is being manufactured. The discussion, however, is equally appropriate for service provision.

Chapter 10 Flexible Budget, Standard Costing, and Variance Analysis

workers using the material, past material requisitions, and review of the cost accounts. In addition, companies often make allowances for normal waste of components when determining quantities. The specifications for materials, including quality and quantity, are compiled on a product's **bill of materials**.

Next, component prices must be determined. Purchasing agents may be able to exercise substantial influence on input prices in the following ways:

- understanding the quantity and timing of company purchasing;
- knowing what alternative suppliers are available;
- recognizing the economic climate under which purchases are being made;
- performing "due diligence" as to the input costs incurred and profit margins desired by suppliers; and
- seeking single source suppliers or partnership alliances with suppliers, when appropriate.

When all quantity and price information is available, component quantities are multiplied by unit prices to obtain each component's total cost. These totals are summed to determine the total standard material cost of one unit of product.

Labor Standards

Developing labor standards requires the same basic procedures as those used for material. Each production operation performed by workers (such as bending, reaching, lifting, moving material, and packing) or by machinery (such as drilling, cooking, and assembling) should be identified. In specifying operations and movements, all necessary activities should be included when time standards are set, but all unnecessary movements of workers and material should be disregarded.[5]

To develop effective standards, a company obtains quantitative information for each production operation. Such information can be gathered from industrial engineering methods, in-house time-and-motion studies, or historical data. **Methods-time measurement (MTM)** is an industrial engineering process that analyzes work tasks to determine the time a trained worker needs to perform a given operation at a rate that can be sustained for an eight-hour workday. After all labor tasks have been analyzed, a company prepares an **operations flow document** that lists all tasks necessary to make one unit of product or perform a specific service.

Labor rate standards should reflect employee wages and related employer costs for fringe benefits, FICA (Social Security), and unemployment taxes. Once time and rate information are available, job task times are multiplied by wage rates to generate each operation's total cost. These totals are summed to provide the total standard labor cost of one unit (or batch) of product.

Overhead Standards

Overhead (OH) standards reflect the company's predetermined manufacturing overhead rate(s). As discussed in prior chapters, the most appropriate costing information will result when (1) overhead is assigned to separate cost pools based on cost drivers and (2) allocations are made using cost drivers directly related to the overhead costs being assigned.

Standard Cost Card

After the bill of materials, operations flow document, and predetermined OH rates per activity measure have been developed, a **standard cost card** is prepared that summarizes the standard quantities and costs needed to produce one unit. The **standard quantity allowed** is calculated by taking the number of units produced, multiplied by the standard quantity for one unit.

Preparing a Standard Cost Card — LO10-2 DEMO 10-2

For Salinas, assume the following standard input quantities and prices for one bike frame.

- Direct materials: Each bike frame requires four sheets of carbon fiber at a cost of $65 per sheet.
- Direct labor: Each bike frame requires 1.5 hours of labor at cost of $24 per hour.

---

[5] Similar to making "normal" allowances for wasted material in setting material standards, companies also include certain often unnecessary activities such as rework in determining labor standards. Problems related to assessing production efficiency also arise with such inclusions.

- Variable overhead (VOH): Budgeted annual VOH is $270,000 and is applied using direct labor hours at an applied rate of $15 per direct labor hour.
- Fixed overhead (FOH): Budgeted annual FOH is $381,600 and is applied using direct labor hours at an applied rate of $21.20 per direct labor hour.
- Planned output for the year: 12,000 bike frames.

◆ **How does Salinas prepare a standard cost sheet for one bike frame?**

Salinas Corporation's standard cost card is provided below, both in a table and visually through a chart. It is apparent that direct materials is a significant portion of the cost of one bike frame.

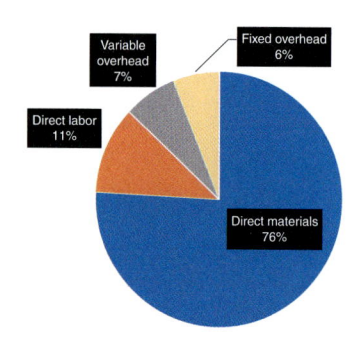

Standard Cost Card

Product Cost	Standard Quantity	Standard Price	Total Cost Per Unit
Direct material			
Carbon fiber	4 sheets	$65.00	$260.00
Direct labor	1.5 labor hours	24.00	36.00
Variable overhead	1.5 labor hours	15.00	22.50
Fixed overhead	1.5 labor hours	21.20	31.80
Total			$350.30

Pie chart: Direct materials 76%, Direct labor 11%, Variable overhead 7%, Fixed overhead 6%.

REVIEW 10-2 — LO10-2 — Setting Standard Costs

One of All-Natural Inc.'s bestselling products is its fruit smoothie, which is manufactured in 15-gallon batches. Each batch requires ten quarts of mixed berries. The mixed berries are sorted by hand before entering the production process, and because of imperfections, one quart of mixed berries is discarded for every five quarts of acceptable mixed berries. The standard direct labor sorting time to obtain one quart of acceptable mixed berries is four minutes. After sorting, mixed berries are blended with other ingredients; blending requires 15 minutes of direct labor time per batch. During the blending process, some product is lost because it adheres to the blending vats. After blending, the smoothie is packaged in 16-ounce containers. The following cost information is relevant:

- Mixed berries are purchased for $1.25 per quart.
- All other ingredients cost a total of $0.80 per gallon.
- Direct labor is paid $10.00 per hour.
- The total cost of material and labor required to package the smoothies is $0.25 per 16-ounce smoothie container.
- Overhead is applied at a rate of $20 per machine hour. One-half hour of machine hour is the standard for a 15-gallon batch of product.

a. Develop the standard cost for the cost components of a 15-gallon batch of fruit smoothies. The standard cost should identify standard quantity, standard price/rate, and standard cost per batch for each cost component.

b. If 10 batches of smoothies are produced, what is the *standard quantity allowed of* (1) quarts of mixed berries, (2) gallons of other ingredients, (3) hours of sorting and (4) hours of blending?

c. **Critical Thinking:** Should labor measurements used in the standard cost card be based on expected, practical, or ideal standards?

More practice: E10-35, E10-36
Solution on p. 10-68.

MATERIAL AND LABOR VARIANCES

LO10-3 How are material and labor variances calculated and recorded?

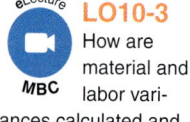

Before describing the material and labor variances, we start with a general variance analysis model to provide foundational concepts.

General Variance Analysis Model

The difference between total actual cost for production inputs and total standard cost applied to the production output is the total flexible budget variance. Total variances do not provide useful information for determining why standard and actual costs differed. For instance, was the variance caused by price factors, quantity factors, or both? To provide additional information, total variances are subdivided into *price* and *usage* components. The total flexible budget can be expanded to provide the following general model indicating the two subvariances, using a middle column that reflects a combination of standard price and actual quantity.

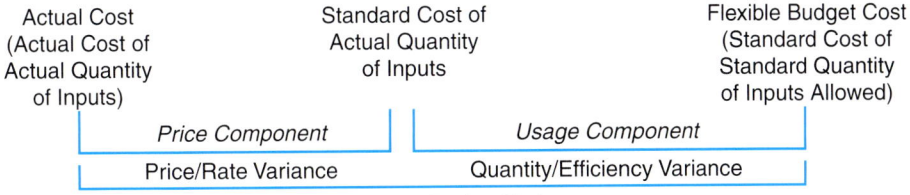

```
Actual Cost              Standard Cost of         Flexible Budget Cost
(Actual Cost of          Actual Quantity          (Standard Cost of
 Actual Quantity           of Inputs               Standard Quantity
 of Inputs)                                        of Inputs Allowed)
        |_____Price Component_____|_____Usage Component_____|
        |_____Price/Rate Variance_|_Quantity/Efficiency Variance_|
                       Total Flexible Budget Variance
```

Price Component The price component indicates the difference between the actual cost of the inputs and cost expected to be paid for inputs. The price (or rate) variance is calculated as the difference between the actual price (AP) and the standard price (SP) per unit of input multiplied by the actual input quantity (AQ).

$$\text{Price (or rate) variance} = (AP - SP)(AQ)$$

Usage Component The usage component of the total variance shows the efficiency of results or the relationship of input to output. The change from input to output reflects the fact that the actual ratio of inputs to outputs will not necessarily equal the standard ratio of inputs to outputs. The flexible budget amount shown in the right-hand column of the general variance analysis model is computed as the standard quantity allowed multiplied by the standard input price. The quantity/efficiency variance is calculated as the difference between the AQ and standard quantity of input allowed (SQ) multiplied by the standard price per unit of input.

$$\text{Quantity (or efficiency) variance} = (AQ - SQ)(SP)$$

If the actual price or quantity amounts are higher than the standard price or quantity amounts, the variance is unfavorable (U). If the actual amounts are lower than the standard amounts, the variance is favorable (F). The designation of unfavorable and favorable reflects the effect that the variances have on income as indicated in the following table.

Actual to Standard Relationship	Variance	Effect on Income
Actual Price > Standard Price	Unfavorable	Negative
Actual Price < Standard Price	Favorable	Positive
Actual Quantity > Standard Quantity	Unfavorable	Negative
Actual Quantity < Standard Quantity	Favorable	Positive

It is important to note that *unfavorable* is not necessarily equated with bad nor is *favorable* equated with good. Determination of "bad" or "good" must be made after identifying the variance's cause and its implications for other cost elements.

The following sections illustrate variance computations for each cost element.

Material Variances: Point-of-Usage Model

The general variance analysis model can be applied to materials to compute material price and material quantity variances. We first illustrate the **point-of-usage model** where the material quantity used to calculate the material price variance is the same material quantity used to calculate the material quantity variance.

DEMO 10-3A LO10-3 — Calculating Point-of-Usage Material Variances

During January, Salinas Corporation started and completed 1,200 bike frames. The following schedule shows the actual results for the period.

Actual Manufacturing Costs For Month of January	
Actual bike frames completed	1,200
Manufacturing costs	
Carbon fiber (4,700 sheets at $65.50 per sheet)	$307,850
Direct labor (1,850 hours at $23.50 per hour)	43,475
Variable overhead	24,500
Fixed overhead	33,000
Total	$408,825

This information is used to compute the January variances. We assume that the 4,700 sheets of carbon fiber used for the month equals the number of sheets purchased for the month. From the standard cost card, prepared in Demo 10-2, we know that the standard number of sheets for each bike frame is four. Therefore, the standard quantity allowed for 1,200 bike frames is 4,800 sheets.

Standard quantity allowed = 1,200 units × 4 sheets = 4,800 sheets

◆ How are the material price and quantity variances calculated for Salinas for January, when the quantity of materials purchased equals the quantity of materials used?

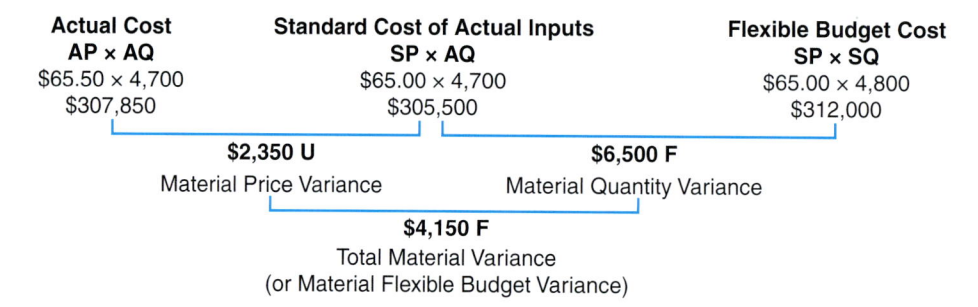

Actual Cost	Standard Cost of Actual Inputs	Flexible Budget Cost
AP × AQ	SP × AQ	SP × SQ
$65.50 × 4,700	$65.00 × 4,700	$65.00 × 4,800
$307,850	$305,500	$312,000

$2,350 U — Material Price Variance
$6,500 F — Material Quantity Variance
$4,150 F — Total Material Variance (or Material Flexible Budget Variance)

Material Price Variance The **material price variance (MPV)** indicates whether the amount paid for material was less or more than standard price. The material price variance is always based on the material quantity purchased. However, in this case, the quantity purchased is the same as the quantity used (i.e., all materials purchased were used). For carbon fiber, the price paid was $65.60 rather than the standard price of $65 per sheet, creating an unfavorable price variance. An unfavorable variance increases the cost of production, thus, a positive sign indicates a favorable variance. The MPV can also be calculated as follows.

MPV = (Actual price − Standard price) × Actual quantity

MPV = ($65.50 − $65) × 4,700 = $2,350 U

The purchasing manager should be able to explain why the price paid per sheet of carbon fiber was greater than standard.

Material Quantity Variance The **material quantity variance (MQV)** indicates whether the actual quantity purchased and used was less or more than the standard quantity allowed for the *actual* output. This difference is multiplied by the standard price per unit of material. Production used 100 less sheets of carbon fiber than the standard allowed, resulting in a $6,500 favorable (negative) material quantity variance. The MQV can also be calculated as follows.

MQV = Standard price × (Actual quantity − Standard quantity)

MQV = $65.00 × (4,700 − 4,800) = −$6,500 or $6,500 F

Chapter 10 Flexible Budget, Standard Costing, and Variance Analysis 10-13

The production manager should be able to explain why fewer carbon sheets were used than allowed for in January.

The **total material variance (TMV)** or the flexible material budget variance is the summation of the individual variances or can also be calculated by subtracting the total standard cost for carbon fiber from the total actual cost of carbon fiber.

$$\text{TMV} = \text{MPV} + \text{MQV}$$

$$= \$2{,}350 + -\$6{,}500 = -\$4{,}150 \text{ or } \$4{,}150 \text{ F}$$

or

$$\text{TMV} = \text{Total actual cost} - \text{Total standard cost}$$

$$= \$307{,}850 - \$312{,}000 = -\$4{,}150 \text{ or } \$4{,}150 \text{ F}$$

Importantly, the TMV ties back to Demo 10-1B where the flexible budget variance for materials was calculated as $4,150 F. Note how the MPV and MQV provide additional information that cannot be derived from the TMV by itself.

In a case where a company has multiple material components, price and quantity variance computations must be made for each direct material component, and these component variances are summed to obtain the total price and quantity variances. Such a summation, however, does not provide useful information for cost control.

Journal Entries for Material Variances

Although both actual and standard costs are recorded in a standard cost system, only standard costs are shown in the Raw (Direct) Material, Work in Process, and Finished Goods Inventory accounts. Note that all unfavorable variances have debit balances and favorable variances have credit balances. Unfavorable variances represent excess production costs; favorable variances represent savings in production costs. Standard production costs are shown in inventory accounts (which have debit balances); therefore, excess costs are also debits.

Recording Entries for Point-of-Usage Material Variances   LO10-3   DEMO 10-3B

◆ What journal entries would be recorded by Salinas in January for raw material inventory and the related variances?

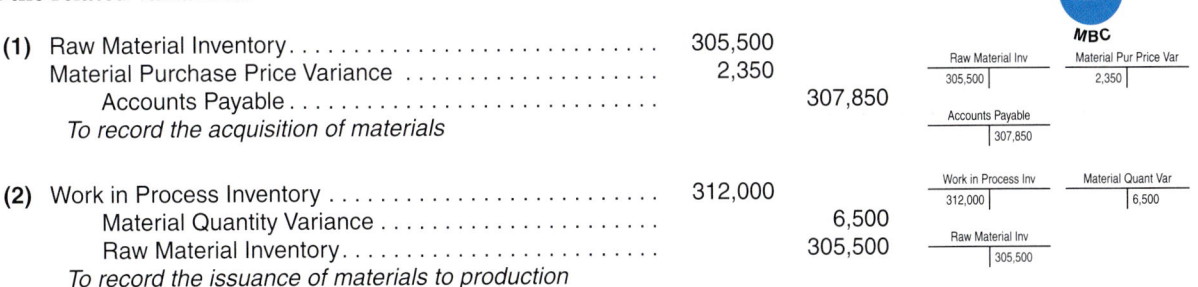

(1)	Raw Material Inventory.............................	305,500	
	Material Purchase Price Variance	2,350	
	Accounts Payable...............................		307,850
	To record the acquisition of materials		
(2)	Work in Process Inventory	312,000	
	Material Quantity Variance		6,500
	Raw Material Inventory..........................		305,500
	To record the issuance of materials to production		

(1) The debit to Raw Material Inventory is for the standard price of the actual quantity of carbon fiber purchased in January. The credit to Accounts Payable is for the actual price of the actual quantity of carbon fiber purchased. The variance debit reflects the unfavorable material price variance for carbon fiber.

(2) The debit to Work in Process Inventory is for the standard price of the standard quantity of carbon fiber used in January. The Raw Material Inventory credit is for the standard price of the actual quantity of carbon fiber used in production. The credit to the Material Quantity Variance account reflects the underuse (by 100 sheets) of carbon fiber valued at the standard price.

Material Variances: Point-of-Purchase Model

A total variance for a cost component generally equals the sum of the price and usage variances. An *exception* to this rule occurs when the actual quantity of material purchased is different from the actual quantity of material placed into production. Because the material price variance relates to the purchasing (rather than the production) function, the **point-of-purchase model** calculates the material price variance using the quantity of materials purchased (Q_p) rather than the quantity of materials used (Q_u). The general variance analysis model is altered slightly to isolate the variance as early as possible to provide more rapid information for management control purposes.

DEMO 10-3C LO10-3 Calculating Point-of-Purchase Material Variances

Assume that Salinas Corporation purchased 5,500 carbon fiber sheets at $65.50 per sheet during January, but only used 4,700 carbon fiber sheets for the 1,200 bike frames produced that month.

♦ **How are the material price and quantity variances calculated for Salinas for January, when the quantity of materials purchased does not equal the quantity of materials used?**

Using the point-of-purchase variance model, the computation for the material price variance is adjusted, but the computation for the material quantity variance remains the same as previously shown. The point-of-purchase material variance model is a "staggered" one as follows.

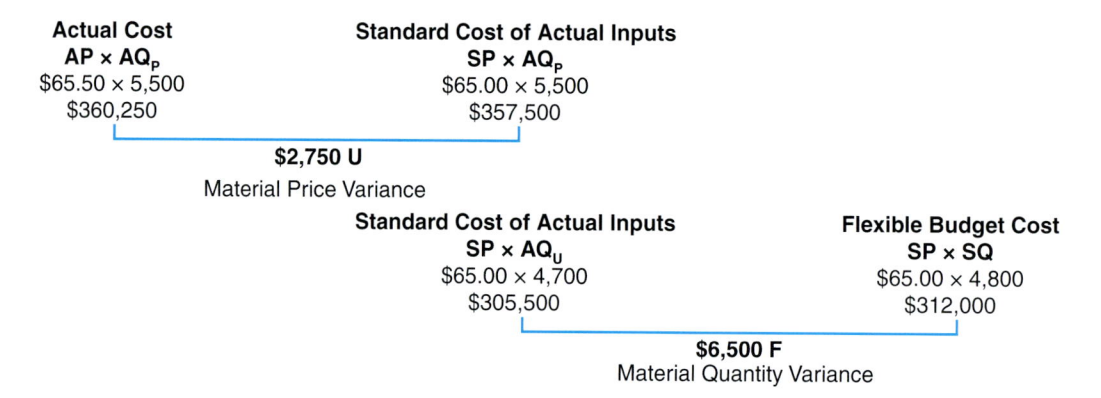

Actual Cost AP × AQ$_p$ $65.50 × 5,500 $360,250	Standard Cost of Actual Inputs SP × AQ$_p$ $65.00 × 5,500 $357,500	
	$2,750 U Material Price Variance	
	Standard Cost of Actual Inputs SP × AQ$_u$ $65.00 × 4,700 $305,500	Flexible Budget Cost SP × SQ $65.00 × 4,800 $312,000
	$6,500 F Material Quantity Variance	

The material quantity variance is still computed on the actual quantity used and, thus, remains at $6,500 F. However, because the price and quantity variances have been computed using different bases, they should not be summed. **Thus, the total material variance cannot be easily reconciled when the quantity of material purchased differs from the quantity of material used.**

Point-of-Purchase Variance Disadvantages

The material price variance computation generally occurs at the point-of-purchase, when amounts are entered into a company's ERP system. Although computing the material price variance at the purchase point allows managers to see the impact of buying decisions rapidly, such information might not be most relevant when the company aims for low inventory levels. Buying material that is not needed for current production requires that the material be stored and moved, both of which are non-value-added activities. The trade-off in price savings should be measured against the additional costs to determine the cost–benefit relationship of such a purchase.

Additionally, computing a material price variance on purchases rather than on usage can reduce the probability of recognizing a relationship between a favorable material price variance and an unfavorable material quantity variance. If a favorable price variance resulted from buying low-grade material, the potential negative effects of that purchase on material usage and labor efficiency will not be known until the material is actually used.

Labor Variances

Labor variances are calculated in a similar way to material variances.

Chapter 10 Flexible Budget, Standard Costing, and Variance Analysis 10-15

Calculating Labor Variances   LO10-3 DEMO 10-3D

Each bike frame at Salinas Corporation requires 1.5 direct labor hours at standard. Thus, the standard labor hours allowed for 1,200 bike frames is (1,200 x 1.5) or 1,800 direct labor hours.

◆ **How are the labor rate and efficiency variances calculated for Salinas for January?**

Calculations of the labor variances are as follows.

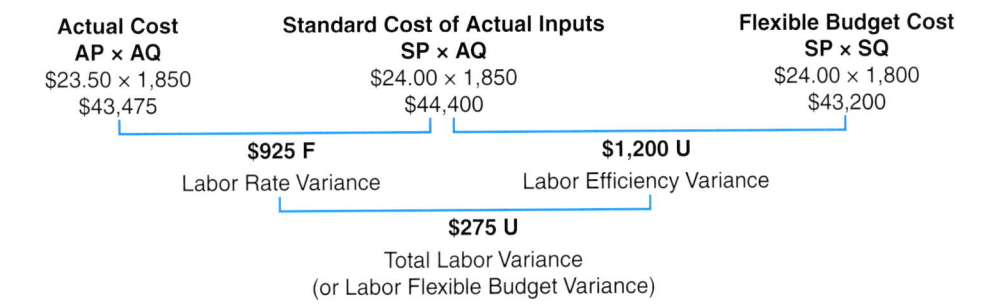

Actual Cost AP × AQ	Standard Cost of Actual Inputs SP × AQ	Flexible Budget Cost SP × SQ
$23.50 × 1,850 $43,475	$24.00 × 1,850 $44,400	$24.00 × 1,800 $43,200

$925 F — Labor Rate Variance

$1,200 U — Labor Efficiency Variance

$275 U — Total Labor Variance (or Labor Flexible Budget Variance)

Labor Rate Variance The **labor rate variance (LRV)** is the difference between the actual wages paid to labor for the period and the standard cost of actual hours worked. In January, the actual wage rate was $0.50 less than the standard wage rate per hour, giving a $925 favorable labor rate variance. An unfavorable variance might be created by a raise granted within the period to employees; a favorable variance would be generated if employees in a particular period opted to take a reduced hourly rate rather than having some of the workers laid off.

The LRV is computed as follows.

> **LRV = (Actual price − Standard price) × Actual quantity**
>
> LRV = ($23.50 − $24.00) × 1,850 hours = −$925 or $925 F

Labor Efficiency Variance The **labor efficiency variance (LEV)** indicates whether the amount of time worked was less or more than the standard quantity allowed for the actual output. This difference is multiplied by the standard rate per hour of labor time.

In January, 50 more hours were incurred than the standard allowed to produce 1,200 bike frames. The LEV is computed as follows.

> **LEV = Standard price × (Actual quantity − Standard quantity)**
>
> LEV = $24 × (1,850 − 1,800) = $1,200 U

The **total labor variance (TLV)** can be calculated as $275 U by either of the following formulas.

> **TLV = LRV + LEV**
>
> = −$925 + $1,200 = $275 U
>
> **TLV = Total actual cost − Total standard cost**
>
> = $43,475 − $43,200 = $275 U

As with the TMV, the TLV of $275 U ties back to the total labor flexible budget variance in Demo 10-1B.

Journal Entry for Labor Variance

The entry to record labor and variances in a standard costing system is illustrated in the following demonstration.

DEMO 10-3E LO10-3 — Recording Entry for Labor Variance

◆ What journal entry would be recorded by Salinas in January for direct labor and the related variances?

Work in Process Inventory	43,200	
Labor Efficiency Variance	1,200	
Labor Rate Variance		925
Wages Payable		43,475

To record incurrence of direct labor costs

T-accounts:
- Work in Process Inv: 43,200
- Labor Efficiency Var: 1,200
- Labor Rate Var: 925
- Wages Payable: 43,475

The debit to Work in Process Inventory is the flexible budget for producing 1,200 bike frames. The Wages Payable credit is for the actual amount of direct labor cost during the period. The Labor Rate Variance credit represents the difference between actual and standard rate, multiplied by actual labor hours. The Labor Efficiency Variance debit reflects the difference between actual and standard hours allowed multiplied by the standard wage rate. There is no point-of-purchase discrepancy for labor as labor cannot be inventoried or stored as is the case for materials.

REVIEW 10-3 LO10-3 — Calculating Material and Labor Variances

Central Manufacturing produces metal products with the following standard quantity and cost information.

Stainless steel	5 sheets at $6.40	$ 32.00
Copper	4 sheets at $8.50	34.00
Direct labor	7 hours at $20.00	140.00
Variable overhead	6 machine hours at $5.00	30.00
Fixed overhead	6 machine hours at $4.00	24.00

Overhead rates were based on normal monthly capacity of 7,800 machine hours. During March, the company produced 1,105 units. The following costs were incurred in March.

Direct Material
Stainless steel	5,000 sheets purchased at $6.20	5,500 sheets used
Copper	4,100 sheets purchased at $8.20	4,500 sheets used

Direct Labor
7,700 hours . . . . $19.00 per hour

Variable Overhead
$30,000 . . . . Based on 5,400 hours

Fixed Overhead
$27,000 . . . . Based on 5,400 hours

1. Compute the following variances.
   a. Total material price variance
   b. Total material quantity variance
   c. Labor rate variance
   d. Labor efficiency variance
2. Prepare the journal entries to record the standard costing information.
3. **Critical Thinking:** Analyze the variance results and indicate how the material price variance could be related to the material quantity variance.

More practice: E10-37, E10-39, E10-43, E10-46, E10-47
Solution on p. 10-68.

OVERHEAD VARIANCES

LO10-4 How are overhead variances calculated and recorded?

As discussed in Chapter 3, total variable cost changes in direct relationship with changes in activity and fixed cost per unit changes inversely with changes in activity. Thus, to develop a predetermined overhead (OH) rate, a specific capacity level must be selected to compute budgeted overhead costs.

To compute the variable and fixed predetermined OH rates, managers at Salinas Corporation used an annual capacity level of 12,000 bike frames, which corresponds to 18,000 direct labor hours

Chapter 10 Flexible Budget, Standard Costing, and Variance Analysis 10-17

(12,000 bike frames × 1.5 hours per bike frame). At that level of DLHs, budgeted annual variable and fixed overhead costs were calculated, respectively, as $270,000 and $381,600, as shown earlier in Demo 10-2. Company accountants decided to set both the variable overhead (VOH) rate and the fixed overhead (FOH) rate using number of direct labor hours as follows.

$$\text{VOH rate} = \frac{\text{Budgeted VOH}}{\text{Budgeted DLHs}} = \$270{,}000 \div 18{,}000 = \$15.00 \text{ per DLH}$$

$$\text{FOH rate} = \frac{\text{Budgeted FOH}}{\text{Budgeted DLHs}} = \$381{,}600 \div 18{,}000 = \$21.20 \text{ per DLH}$$

Because Salinas Corporation uses separate variable and fixed overhead application rates, separate price and usage components can be calculated for each type of overhead. This **four-variance approach** provides managers with the greatest detail and, thus, the greatest flexibility for control and performance evaluation.

Variable Overhead (Four-Variance Approach)

The computations for VOH variances are as follows.

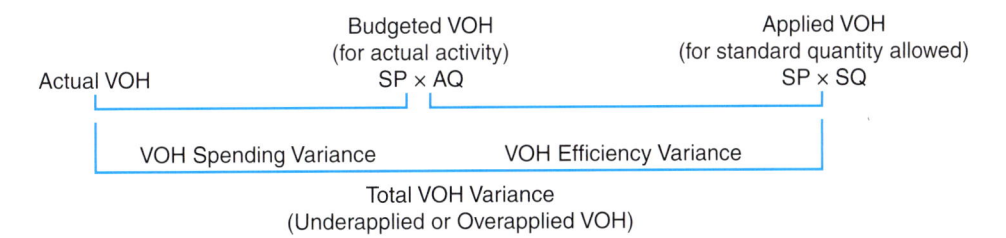

```
                    Budgeted VOH              Applied VOH
                    (for actual activity)     (for standard quantity allowed)
Actual VOH          SP × AQ                   SP × SQ
     └──────────────────┘└──────────────────────┘
       VOH Spending Variance    VOH Efficiency Variance
     └──────────────────────────────────────────┘
                    Total VOH Variance
                    (Underapplied or Overapplied VOH)
```

Because VOH increases with increases in activity, the budgeted amount of VOH will change with changes in actual production.

Calculating Variable Overhead Variances — LO10-4 DEMO 10-4A

Salinas Corp. worked a total of 1,850 DLHs. At a predetermined VOH rate of $15 per DLH, the company would have budgeted a total of $27,750 in VOH costs. The amount of $27,000 of applied VOH reflects the $15 standard predetermined VOH rate multiplied by the standard quantity allowed of time required for the period's actual output (1,200 bike frames × 1.5 direct labor hours per bike frame or 1,800 direct labor hours).

◆ **How are the VOH spending and efficiency variances calculated for Salinas for January?**

Using the actual January VOH cost information from Demo 10-3A, the VOH variances for bike frame production are calculated as follows.

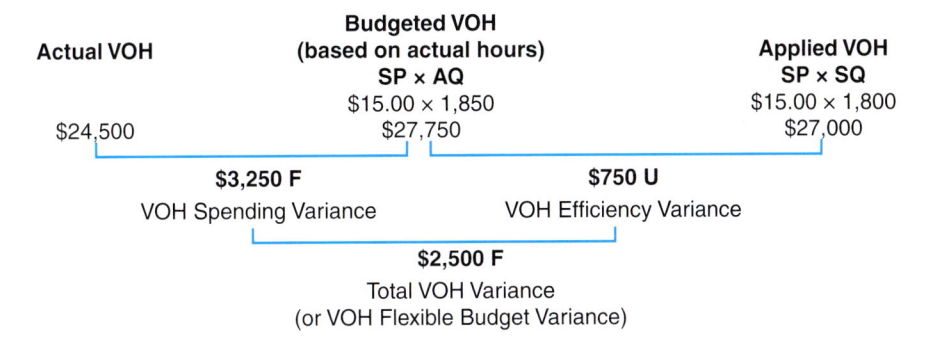

```
                    Budgeted VOH
                    (based on actual hours)    Applied VOH
   Actual VOH       SP × AQ                    SP × SQ
                    $15.00 × 1,850             $15.00 × 1,800
   $24,500          $27,750                    $27,000
        └─────────────┘   └────────────────────────┘
         $3,250 F              $750 U
      VOH Spending Variance    VOH Efficiency Variance
        └──────────────────────────────────────┘
                    $2,500 F
                 Total VOH Variance
             (or VOH Flexible Budget Variance)
```

Variable Overhead Spending Variance The difference between actual VOH and budgeted VOH based on actual hours is the **variable overhead spending variance**. VOH spending variances are caused by both component price and volume differences. For example, an unfavorable variable overhead spending variance could be caused by either paying a higher price or using more indirect material than the standard allows. Variable overhead spending variances associated with price differences can occur because, over time, changes in VOH prices have not been included in the standard rate. For example, average indirect labor wage rates or utility rates could have changed since the predetermined VOH rate was computed. Managers usually have little control over prices charged by external parties and should generally not be held accountable for variances arising because of such price changes. In these instances, the standard rates should be adjusted.

Variable overhead spending variances associated with quantity differences can be caused by waste or shrinkage of production inputs (such as indirect material). For instance, deterioration of material during storage or from lack of proper handling can be recognized only after the material is placed into production. Such occurrences usually have little relationship to the input activity basis used, but they do affect the VOH spending variance. If waste or spoilage is the cause of the VOH spending variance, managers should be held accountable and encouraged to implement more effective controls.

Nurseries have to be careful about the storage of seeds, which can rapidly deteriorate with high temperature or humidity. Spoiled seeds will create a higher variable overhead spending variance for future greenhouse operations.

Variable Overhead Efficiency Variance The difference between budgeted VOH for actual hours and applied VOH is the **variable overhead efficiency variance**. This variance quantifies the effect of using more or less of the activity or resource that is the base for VOH application. For example, Salinas Corporation applies VOH to bike frames using direct labor hours. If Salinas uses direct labor time inefficiently, higher variable overhead costs will occur. When actual input exceeds standard input allowed for the output achieved, production operations are considered to be inefficient. Excess input also indicates that an increased VOH budget is needed to support the additional activity base being used.

The total VOH variance for the period is equal to actual VOH minus applied VOH (also shown in Demo 10-1B). This total variance is the amount of underapplied or overapplied VOH for the period.

Fixed Overhead (Four-Variance Approach)

The total fixed overhead (FOH) variance is divided into price and volume components by inserting budgeted FOH in the middle column of the general variance analysis model as follows.

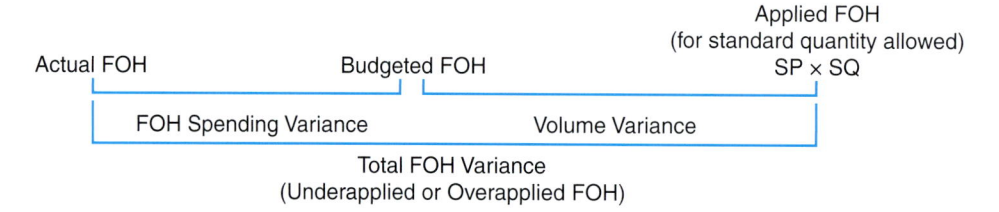

```
                                                    Applied FOH
                                             (for standard quantity allowed)
  Actual FOH         Budgeted FOH                    SP × SQ
       └──────────────────┬──────────────────┴──────────────────┐
          FOH Spending Variance         Volume Variance
                          Total FOH Variance
                   (Underapplied or Overapplied FOH)
```

The left column is the total actual fixed overhead incurred. Budgeted FOH is a constant amount throughout the relevant range of activity and was the amount used to develop the predetermined FOH rate. Thus, the middle column is a constant figure *regardless of the actual quantity of input or the standard quantity of input allowed*. Applied FOH reflects the standard predetermined FOH rate multiplied by the standard quantity of activity for the period's actual output. The total FOH variance at the end of the period equals the amount of underapplied or overapplied FOH.

DEMO 10-4B LO10-4   Calculating Fixed Overhead Variances

Total annual budgeted FOH for Salinas Corporation is given in Demo 10-2 as $381,600. Assuming that FOH is incurred steadily throughout the year, the monthly budgeted FOH is $31,800. As indicated in the computation for applied VOH, 1,800 DLHs is the standard quantity of time allowed for January's production of 1,200 bike frames. The amount of applied FOH reflects the $21.20 standard predetermined FOH rate (calculated on page 10-17) multiplied by the standard quantity allowed of 1,800 DLHs which equals $38,160.

◆ **How are the FOH spending and volume variances calculated for Salinas for January?**

Using the actual January FOH cost information from Demo 10-3A, the FOH variances for bike frame production are calculated as follows.

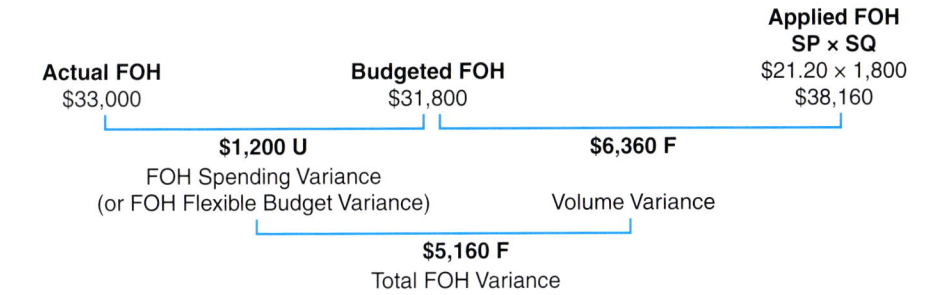

Actual FOH	Budgeted FOH	Applied FOH SP × SQ $21.20 × 1,800
$33,000	$31,800	$38,160

$1,200 U
FOH Spending Variance
(or FOH Flexible Budget Variance)

$6,360 F
Volume Variance

$5,160 F
Total FOH Variance

Fixed Overhead Spending Variance The difference between actual and budgeted FOH is the **fixed overhead spending variance**. This variance is also equal to the FOH flexible budget variance calculated in Demo 10-1B. This amount normally represents the spending differences for the numerous FOH components, although it can also reflect resource mismanagement. Individual FOH components would be shown in the company's flexible overhead budget, and individual spending variances should be calculated for each component.

Volume Variance As with variable overhead, applied FOH is related to the predetermined rate and the standard quantity for the actual production level achieved. Relative to FOH, the standard input allowed for the achieved production level measures capacity utilization for the period. The fixed overhead **volume variance** is the difference between budgeted and applied FOH. This variance is caused *solely* by producing at a level that differs from the level that was used to compute the predetermined FOH rate.

Assuming Actual Production = Planned Production In the case of Salinas Corporation, the $21.20 predetermined FOH rate was computed by dividing $381,600 of budgeted FOH cost by a capacity level of 18,000 DLHs for 12,000 bike frames. Had any other capacity level been chosen, the predetermined FOH rate would have been a different amount, even though the $381,600 budgeted fixed overhead would have remained the same. For example, if 14,400 bike frames (rather than 12,000) had been chosen as the expected capacity for the year, Salinas would have expected to produce 1,200 each month (the same as actual monthly production) and total expected capacity in direct labor hours would have been 21,600 DLHs (14,400 × 1.5 DLHs). At that level of expected capacity, the predetermined FOH would have been

$$\text{Predetermined FOH rate} = \frac{\$381,600}{21,600} = \$17.66667$$

Since the actual volume for January was 1,200 bike frames and the expected volume for January was 1,200 bike frames, there would be no volume variance as shown in the following calculation.

Applied FOH for January (1,200 bikes × 1.5 DLHs × $17.66667 per bike frame) . . .	$31,800
Budgeted FOH for January ($381,600 ÷ 12)	31,800
Volume variance.	$ 0

However, if actual capacity usage differs from the capacity used in determining the predetermined FOH rate, a volume variance will arise because, by using a predetermined rate per unit of activity, fixed overhead is treated as if it were a variable cost even though it is not.

Although capacity utilization is controllable to some degree, the volume variance is the variance over which production managers have the least influence and control, especially in the short run. Thus, a volume variance is also called a **noncontrollable variance**. Although managers cannot control the capacity level chosen to compute the predetermined FOH rate, they do have the ability to control capacity utilization. Capacity utilization should be viewed in relation to inventory level and sales demand. Underutilization of capacity is not always undesirable; it is more appropriate to properly regulate production than to produce inventory that ends up in stockpiles. Producing unneeded inventory generates substantial costs for material, labor, and overhead as well as storage and handling costs. The positive impact that such unneeded production will have on the volume variance is insignificant because this variance is of little or no value for managerial control purposes.

Management is usually aware, as production occurs, of capacity utilization even if a volume variance is not reported. The volume variance merely translates under- or overutilization into a dollar amount. An unfavorable volume variance indicates less-than-expected utilization of capacity. If available capacity is commonly being used at a level higher (or lower) than that which was anticipated or is available, managers should recognize that condition, investigate the reasons for it, and (if possible and desirable) initiate appropriate action. Managers can influence capacity utilization by

- modifying work schedules,
- taking measures to relieve any obstructions to or congestion of production activities,
- carefully monitoring the movement of resources through the production process, and
- acquiring needed, or disposing of unneeded, space and equipment.

Preferably, such actions should be taken before production starts rather than after it is completed. Efforts made after production is completed might improve next period's operations but will have no impact on past production.

Journal Entries for Overhead Variances

The entry to record overhead and variances in a standard costing system are illustrated in the following demonstration.

DEMO 10-4C LO10-4   Recording Entries for Overhead Variances

◆ **What journal entries would be recorded by Salinas in January for overhead and the related four-variances?**

(1) Variable Manufacturing Overhead Control 24,500
    Fixed Manufacturing Overhead Control 33,000
        Various accounts 57,500
    To record actual overhead costs

(2) Work in Process Inventory 65,160
        Variable Manufacturing Overhead Control ($15.00 × 1.5 × 1,200). . 27,000
        Fixed Manufacturing Overhead Control ($21.20 × 1.5 × 1,200) 38,160
    To apply overhead to the month's production

(3) Variable Manufacturing Overhead Control 2,500
    Variable Overhead Efficiency Variance 750
        Variable Overhead Spending Variance 3,250
    To close the VOH Control account and recognize VOH variances

(4) Fixed Overhead Spending Variance 1,200
    Fixed Manufacturing Overhead Control 5,160
        Volume Variance 6,360
    To close the FOH Control account and recognize FOH variances

VOH Control
| 24,500 | |
Various Accounts
| | 57,500 |

FOH Control
| 33,000 | |

VOH Control
| 24,500 | 27,000 |
Work in Process
| 65,160 | |

FOH Control
| 33,000 | 38,160 |

VOH Control
24,500	27,000
2,500	
0	
VOH Spending Var
| | 3,250 |
VOH Efficiency Var
| | 750 |

FOH Control
33,000	38,160
5,160	
0	
Volume Var
| | 6,360 |
FOH Spending Var
| 1,200 | |

(1) This entry reflects the incurrence of all company overhead for the month. During January, actual costs incurred for variable and fixed overhead are debited to the Manufacturing Overhead Control accounts. For convenience, credits to all actual overhead items are not shown; instead, "Various accounts" are indicated. In reality, credits would be provided to accounts representing the overhead items (such as indirect material inventory, wages payable, accumulated depreciation, and utility payables).

(2) Overhead is applied to production using the predetermined rates multiplied by the standard input allowed. Applied overhead is debited to Work in Process Inventory and credited to Manufacturing Overhead Control accounts. Overhead application is recorded at completion of production or at the end of the period, whichever occurs first. The difference between actual debits and applied credits in each overhead account represents the total variable and fixed overhead variances and is also the under- or overapplied overhead for the period. For January, variable overhead and fixed overhead are applied at the respective $15 per DLH and $21.20 per DLH predetermined rates.

(3) and (4) These entries assume an end-of-month closing of the Variable Manufacturing Overhead Control and Fixed Manufacturing Overhead Control accounts. These entries close the manufacturing overhead accounts and recognize the appropriate overhead variances. This entry is provided for illustration only. This process would typically not be performed at month-end but rather at year-end because an annual period was used to calculate the predetermined OH rates.

Variance Summary

The variances for Salinas Corporation are summarized in the following data visualization.

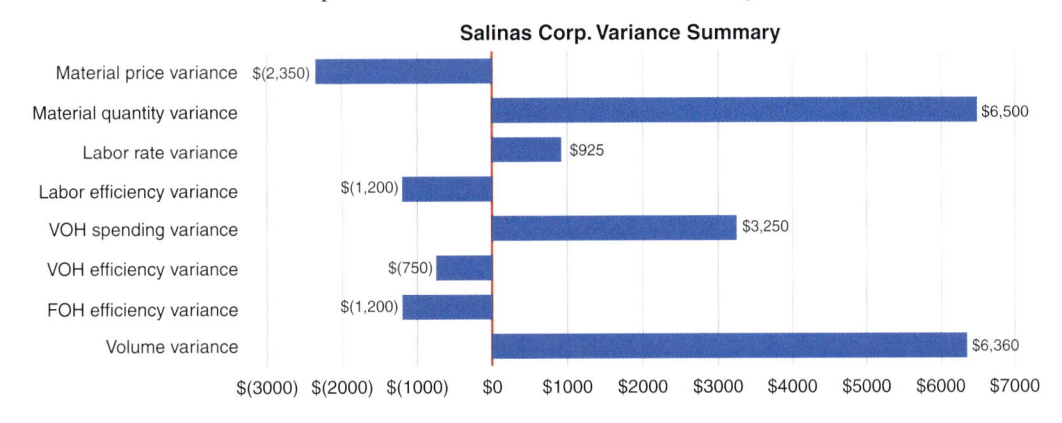

Salinas Corp. Variance Summary

Material price variance	$(2,350)
Material quantity variance	$6,500
Labor rate variance	$925
Labor efficiency variance	$(1,200)
VOH spending variance	$3,250
VOH efficiency variance	$(750)
FOH efficiency variance	$(1,200)
Volume variance	$6,360

The most significant variances are the material quantity variance and the volume variance. The favorable material quantity variance is due to the lower quantity of materials used as compared to the standard allowed. The favorable volume variance is due to the increase in bike frames produced over the budgeted quantity.

Alternative Overhead Variance Approaches

If the accounting system does not separate variable and fixed overhead costs, insufficient data will be available to compute four overhead variances. Use of a combined (variable and fixed) predetermined OH rate requires alternative overhead variance computations.

One-Variance Approach

One approach is to calculate only the **total overhead variance**, which is the difference between total actual overhead and total overhead applied to production. The amount of applied overhead is found by multiplying the combined rate by the standard quantity allowed for the actual production. The **one-variance approach** is as follows.

```
        Actual Overhead            Applied Overhead
     Variable OH + Fixed OH            SP × SQ
     └─────────────────────────────────────────┘
                Total Overhead Variance
```

Like other total variances, the total overhead variance provides limited information to managers. For Salinas Corporation, the total overhead application rate is $36.20 per DLH (or $15 per DLH for VOH + $21.20 per DLH for FOH). The total OH variance is calculated as follows.

Actual Overhead	Applied Overhead
VOH + FOH	SP × SQ
	$36.20 × 1,800
$57,500	$65,160

$7,660 F
Total Overhead Variance

Note that this amount is the same as the summation of the $2,500 F total VOH variance and the $5,160 F total FOH variance computed under the four-variance approach.

Two-Variance Approach

A **two-variance approach** is performed by inserting a middle column in the one-variance model:

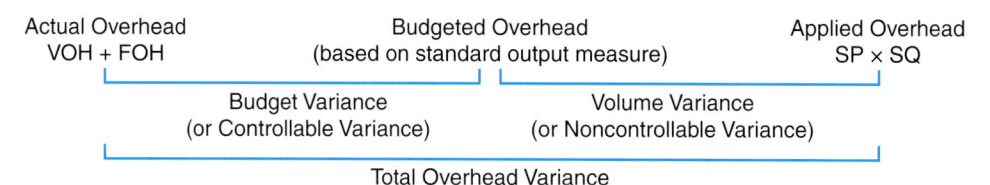

Actual Overhead	Budgeted Overhead	Applied Overhead
VOH + FOH	(based on standard output measure)	SP × SQ

Budget Variance   Volume Variance
(or Controllable Variance)   (or Noncontrollable Variance)

Total Overhead Variance

The middle column in the two-variance OH computation is the expected total overhead cost for the period's actual output. This amount represents total budgeted VOH at the standard quantity measure allowed plus the budgeted FOH, which is constant at all activity levels in the relevant range.

The **budget variance** equals total actual OH minus budgeted OH for the period's actual output. This variance is also referred to as the **controllable variance** because managers are able to exert some degree of influence on this amount during the short run. The difference between budgeted overhead for the period's actual output and total applied overhead is the volume (or noncontrollable) variance. This variance is the same as would be computed under the four-variance approach.

For Salinas Corporation, the two-variance OH computations are as follows.

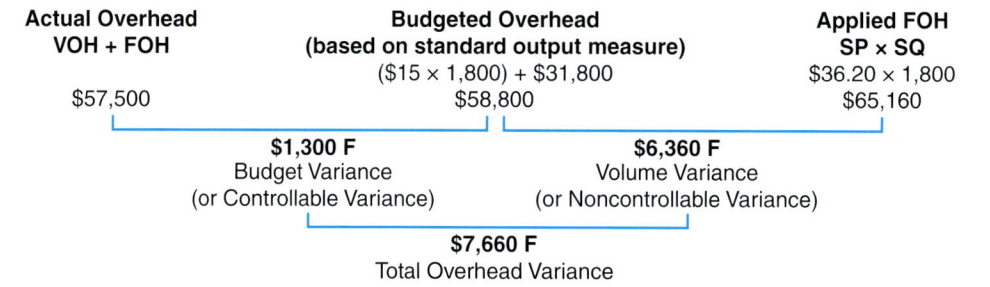

Actual Overhead	Budgeted Overhead	Applied FOH
VOH + FOH	(based on standard output measure)	SP × SQ
	($15 × 1,800) + $31,800	$36.20 × 1,800
$57,500	$58,800	$65,160

$1,300 F $6,360 F
Budget Variance   Volume Variance
(or Controllable Variance)   (or Noncontrollable Variance)

$7,660 F
Total Overhead Variance

Note that the favorable budget variance amount of $1,300 is the same as the summation of the $3,250 F VOH spending variance, the $750 U VOH efficiency variance, and the $1,200 U FOH spending variance computed under the four-variance approach. The $6,360 F volume variance is the same as the volume variance computed under the four-variance approach.

Three-Variance Approach

Inserting another column between the left and middle columns of the two-variance model provides a three-variance analysis by separating the budget variance into spending and efficiency variances. The new column represents the flexible budget based on the actual input measure(s).[6] The **three-variance approach** is as follows.

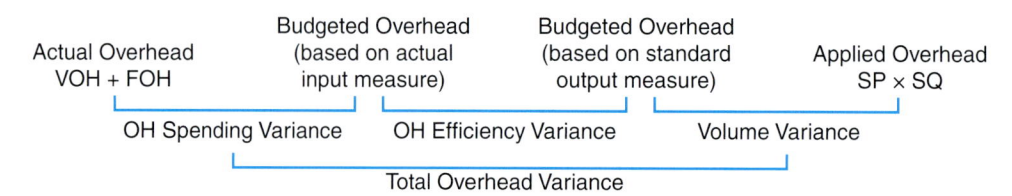

Actual Overhead	Budgeted Overhead	Budgeted Overhead	Applied Overhead
VOH + FOH	(based on actual input measure)	(based on standard output measure)	SP × SQ

OH Spending Variance   OH Efficiency Variance   Volume Variance

Total Overhead Variance

---

[6] Flexible budgets are discussed in Chapter 3.

The total **overhead spending variance** is computed as total actual overhead minus total budgeted overhead at the actual input activity level. Because FOH is the same at any level of activity, the **overhead efficiency variance** is related solely to variable overhead and is the difference between total budgeted overhead at the actual input activity level and total budgeted overhead at the standard activity level. This variance measures, at standard cost, the effect on VOH from using more or fewer inputs than standard for the actual production.

For Salinas Corporation, the three-variance computations are as follows.

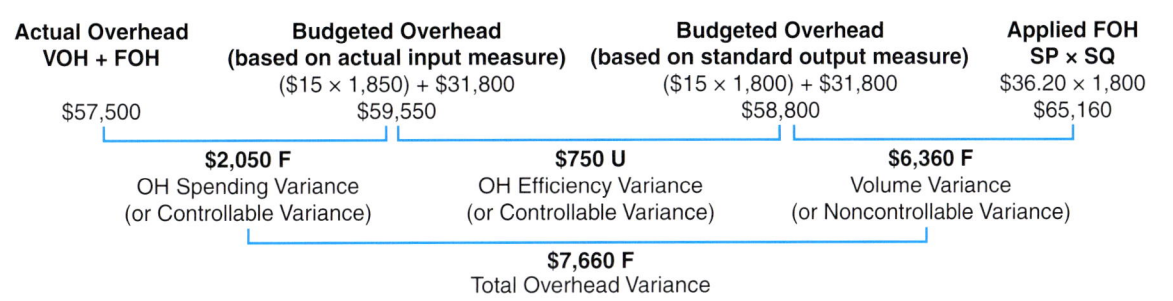

Actual Overhead VOH + FOH	Budgeted Overhead (based on actual input measure)	Budgeted Overhead (based on standard output measure)	Applied FOH SP × SQ
	($15 × 1,850) + $31,800	($15 × 1,800) + $31,800	$36.20 × 1,800
$57,500	$59,550	$58,800	$65,160

$2,050 F — OH Spending Variance (or Controllable Variance)
$750 U — OH Efficiency Variance (or Controllable Variance)
$6,360 F — Volume Variance (or Noncontrollable Variance)

$7,660 F — Total Overhead Variance

Note that the favorable OH spending variance amount of $2,050 is the same as the $3,250 F VOH spending variance plus the $1,200 U FOH spending variance computed under the four-variance approach. The $750 U OH efficiency variance is the same as the VOH efficiency variance computed under the four-variance approach. The sum of the overhead spending and overhead efficiency variances of the three-variance analysis equals the $1,300 F budget variance of the two-variance analysis. The $6,360 F volume (noncontrollable) variance is the same as was calculated using the two-variance or the four-variance approach.

If VOH and FOH are applied using a combined rate, the one-, two-, and three variance approaches will have the relationships shown in **Exhibit 10.2**. The amounts in the exhibit represent the data provided for Salinas Corporation. Managers should select the method that provides the most useful information and that conforms to the company's accounting system.

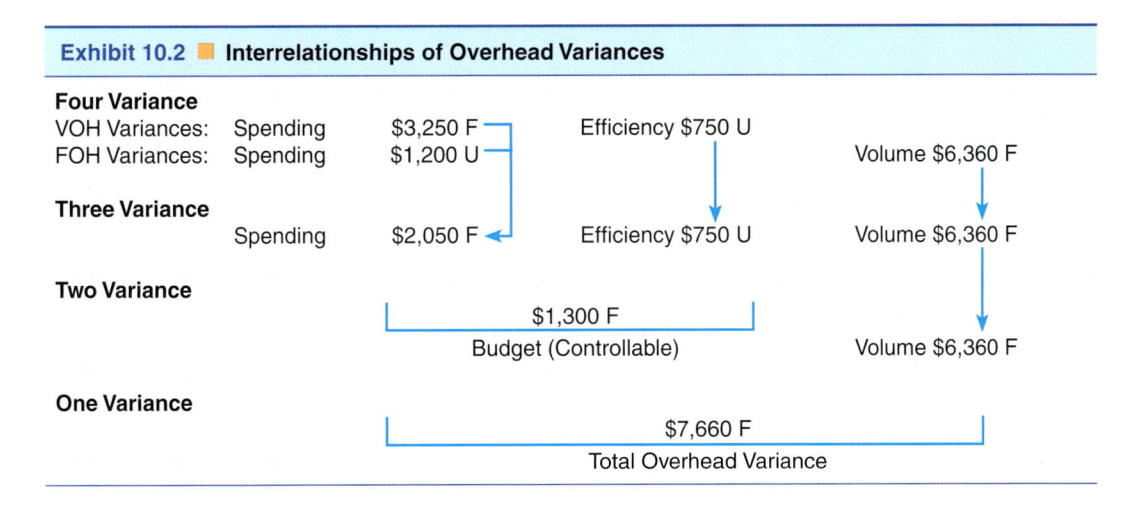

Exhibit 10.2 ■ Interrelationships of Overhead Variances

Four Variance
VOH Variances: Spending $3,250 F — Efficiency $750 U
FOH Variances: Spending $1,200 U — Volume $6,360 F

Three Variance
Spending $2,050 F — Efficiency $750 U — Volume $6,360 F

Two Variance
$1,300 F Budget (Controllable) — Volume $6,360 F

One Variance
$7,660 F Total Overhead Variance

Calculating Overhead Variances   **LO10-4**   **REVIEW 10-4**

Refer to the information provided in Review 10-3 to answer the following questions.
1. Compute the following variances under the overhead four-variance approach:
   a. Variable overhead spending variance
   b. Variable overhead efficiency variance
   c. Fixed overhead spending variance
   d. Volume variance
2. Prepare the journal entries to record the standard costing information.
3. **Critical Thinking:** Analyze the variance results.

More practice: E10-50, E10-53
Solution on p. 10-69.

DISPOSITION OF STANDARD COST VARIANCES

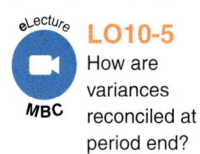

LO10-5
How are variances reconciled at period end?

Although standard costs are useful for internal reporting, they can be used in financial statements only if the amounts are substantially equivalent to those that would have resulted from using an actual cost system. If standards are achievable and current, this equivalency should exist. Standard costs in financial statements should provide fairly conservative inventory valuations because the effects of excess price and/or inefficient operations are eliminated.

Insignificant Variances At year-end, adjusting entries are made to eliminate standard cost variances. The entries depend on whether the variances are, in total, insignificant or significant. If the combined impact of the variances is insignificant, unfavorable variances are closed as debits (increases) to Cost of Goods Sold (CGS); favorable variances are credits (decreases) to CGS. Thus, unfavorable variances decrease operating income because of the higher-than-expected costs. Favorable variances increase operating income because of the lower-than-expected costs. Even if the year's entire production has not been sold yet, this variance treatment is based on the immateriality of the amounts involved.

Significant Variances In contrast, large variances are prorated at year-end among ending inventories and Cost of Goods Sold so that the balances in those accounts approximate actual costs. Proration is based on the relative size of the account balances. Disposition of significant variances is similar to the disposition of large amounts of under- or overapplied overhead as shown in Chapter 6.

DEMO 10-5   LO10-5   Disposing of Standard Cost Variances

Part One: Disposing of a Significant Material Purchase Price Variance To illustrate the disposition of significant variances, assume that Nailz Company has a $20,000 unfavorable (debit) year-end Material Purchase Price Variance. The company considers this amount *significant*. Nailz makes one type of product, which requires a single raw material input. During the period, some of the raw material purchased by Nailz was placed into production. However, some purchased raw material remains in ending inventory at the end of the period. Of the material placed into production. Some was used in goods that were completed and were either sold or remain in ending FG inventory. Some of the raw material placed into production, though, remains in process with goods not yet completed. Thus, raw material may be in any of the three inventory accounts or in CGS. Prorating the material price variance requires allocating the favorable or unfavorable price to all of these accounts, using the following year-end account balances for Nailz Company.

Raw Material Inv	Work in Process Inv
49,126	28,072

Finished Goods Inv	CGS
70,180	554,422

Material Pur Price Var	
20,000	

Raw Material Inventory...............	$ 49,126
Work in Process Inventory...........	28,072
Finished Goods Inventory............	70,180
Cost of Goods Sold	554,422
Total of affected accounts..........	$701,800

The theoretically correct allocation of the material price variance would use actual material cost in each account at year-end. However, with regard to overhead, after the conversion process has begun, cost elements within account balances are commingled and tend to lose their identity. Thus, unless a significant misstatement would result, disposition of the variance can be based on the proportions of each account balance to the total.

◆ **What is the journal entry for Nailz Company to allocate the $20,000 unfavorable material purchase price variance to the affected account balances?**

The variance is allocated based upon the follow proportions.

Raw Material Inventory...............	7%	($ 49,126 ÷ $701,800)
Work in Process Inventory...........	4	($ 28,072 ÷ $701,800)
Finished Goods Inventory............	10	($ 70,180 ÷ $701,800)
Cost of Goods Sold	79	($554,422 ÷ $701,800)
Total............................	100%	

Applying these percentages to the $20,000 unfavorable material purchase price variance gives the amounts in the following journal entry to assign to the affected accounts.

Raw Material Inventory ($20,000 × 0.07)	1,400	
Work in Process Inventory ($20,000 × 0.04)	800	
Finished Goods Inventory ($20,000 × 0.10)	2,000	
Cost of Goods Sold ($20,000 × 0.79)	15,800	
Material Purchase Price Variance		20,000
To dispose of the material purchase price variance at year-end		

Part Two: Disposing of a Significant Labor Efficiency Variance All material and labor variances other than the material price variance occur as part of the conversion process. Because conversion includes only the raw material put into production (rather than raw material purchased), all remaining variances are prorated only to Work in Process Inventory, Finished Goods Inventory, and Cost of Goods Sold.

◆ **What is the journal entry for Nailz Company to allocate a $13,000 unfavorable labor efficiency variance to the affected account balances?**

Assume the company considers the variance to be *significant*. The variance is allocated based upon the following proportions.

Work in Process Inventory	$ 28,072	$ 28,072 ÷ $652,674 = 4%
Finished Goods Inventory	70,180	$ 70,180 ÷ $652,674 = 11%
Cost of Goods Sold	554,422	$554,422 ÷ $652,674 = 85%
Total of affected accounts	$652,674	

Note: Allocation percentages are rounded.

Thus, if Nailz had a $13,000 U labor efficiency variance, it would be allocated as a $520 increase to Work in Process Inventory, $1,430 increase to Finished Goods Inventory, and an $11,050 increase to Cost of Goods Sold.

Work in Process Inventory ($13,000 × 4%)	520	
Finished Goods Inventory ($13,000 × 11%)	1,430	
Cost of Goods Sold ($13,000 × 85%)	11,050	
Labor Efficiency Variance		13,000
To dispose of of labor efficiency variance at year-end		

Overhead variances are closed through the Overhead Control account and the ending over- or under-applied overhead balances are closed as discussed in Chapter 6.

Part Three: Disposing of Variances Considered Insignificant Assume instead that the $20,000 unfavorable material purchase price variance and the $13,000 unfavorable labor efficiency variance for Nailz Company are considered *insignificant*.

◆ **What is the journal entry for Nailz Company to dispose of the insignificant variances at year-end?**

The entry to dispose of the variances at year-end follows.

Cost of Goods Sold	33,000	
Material Purchase Price Variance		20,000
Labor Efficiency Variance		13,000
To dispose of variances		

Since the variances are considered insignificant, the entire balances are closed out to Cost of Goods Sold.

ADJUSTING STANDARDS

Standards should be set only after comprehensive investigation of prices and quantities for the various cost elements. Standards were traditionally retained for at least one year and, sometimes, for multiple years. However, the current operating environment (which includes suppliers, technology, competition, product design, and manufacturing methods) changes so rapidly that a standard may no longer be useful for management control purposes for an entire year.

Company management must decide if standards should be modified during a year when significant cost or quantity changes occur. Ignoring the changes is a simplistic approach that allows the same type of cost to be recorded at the same amount all year. Thus, for example, any material purchased during the year would be recorded at the same standard cost regardless of when it was purchased. Although making recordkeeping easy, this approach eliminates any opportunity to adequately control costs or evaluate performance. Additionally, such an approach could create large differentials between standard and actual costs, making standard costs unacceptable for external reporting.

Adjusting standards to reflect price or quantity changes would make some aspects of management control and performance evaluation more effective, and others more difficult. For instance, budgets prepared using the original standards would need to be adjusted before appropriate actual comparisons could be made against them. Changing standards also creates a problem for recordkeeping and inventory valuation. Accountants would have to decide whether products should be valued at the standard cost that was in effect when they were made or at the standard cost in effect when the financial statements were prepared. Although standards that were modified during the period would be more closely related to actual costs, the use of such standards might undermine many of the benefits discussed earlier in the chapter.

If possible, management should consider combining these two choices in the accounting system. The original standards can be considered "frozen" for budget purposes and a revised budget can be prepared using the new current standards. Differences between these two budgets would reflect variances related to operating environment cost changes. These variances could be designated as uncontrollable (such as those related to changes in the market price of raw material) or internally initiated (such as changes in standard labor time resulting from employee training or equipment rearrangement). Comparing the budget based on current standards with actual costs incurred would provide variances that more adequately reflect internally controllable causes, such as excess material and/or labor time usage caused by inferior material purchases. A combined "frozen" and revised budget system for variance analysis is depicted in **Exhibit 10.3**.

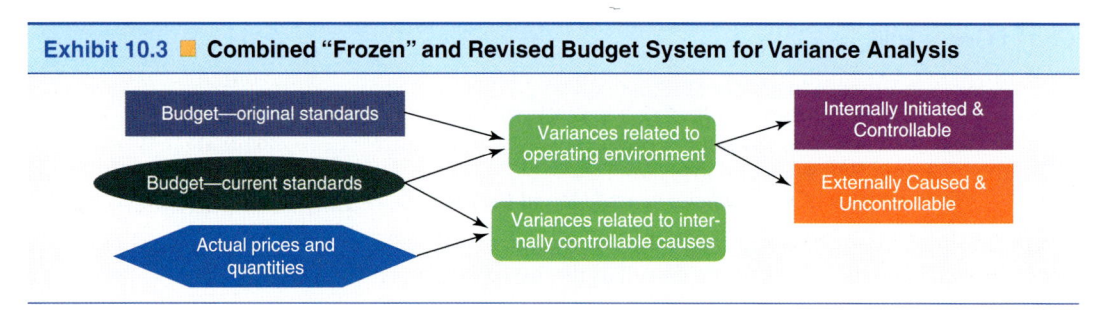

Exhibit 10.3 ■ Combined "Frozen" and Revised Budget System for Variance Analysis

REVIEW 10-5 — LO10-5 — Disposing of Standard Cost Variances

At year-end, the trial balance of Lane Corp. showed the following accounts and amounts.

	Debit	Credit
Raw material	$125,000	
Work in process	25,000	
Finished goods	75,000	
Cost of goods sold	400,000	
Material price variance		$5,000
Material quantity variance	10,000	
Labor rate variance		6,000
Labor efficiency variance	14,000	

a. Assume that, taken together, the variances are believed to be significant. Prepare the journal entries to close the variances at year-end.
b. Assume that, taken together, the variances are believed to be insignificant. Prepare the journal entry to close the variances at year-end.
c. **Critical Thinking:** What are the differences on the financial statements at year-end between parts *a* and *b*? What are the implications for standard setting in the future?

More practice: MC10-20, E10-57
Solution on p. 10-70.

MIX AND YIELD VARIANCES

Most companies combine *many materials and various classes of direct labor to produce goods.* In such settings, the material and labor variance computations presented in this chapter are insufficient.

When a product is made from multiple materials, a goal is to combine the materials in a way that produces the desired quality in the most cost-beneficial manner. Sometimes materials can be substituted for one another without affecting product quality. In other instances, only one specific material or type of material can be used. For example, a furniture manufacturer might use either oak or maple to build a couch frame and still have the same basic quality. However, a perfume manufacturer might have to use a very specific fragrance oil to achieve a desired scent.

Labor, like materials, can be combined in many different ways to make the same product. Some combinations are less expensive or more efficient than others. As with materials, some degree of interchangeability between labor categories is assumed. However, all potential combinations could not be viable. For example, unskilled workers could not be substituted for skilled craftspeople in making Baccarat crystal. The goal is to find the most effective and efficient selection of workers to perform specific tasks.

Each possible combination of materials or labor is called a **mix**. Experience, judgment, and experimentation are used to set the standards for the material mix and labor mix. Process **yield** is the output quantity that results from a specified input. Mix standards are used to calculate mix and yield variances for material and labor. An underlying assumption in product mix situations is that there can be substitution between the material and labor components. If this assumption is invalid, changing the mix cannot improve the yield and could even prove wasteful. In addition to mix and yield variances, price and rate variances are still computed for material and labor.

Material Price, Mix, and Yield Variances

A material price variance shows the dollar effect of paying prices that differ from the raw material standard. The **material mix variance** measures the effect of substituting a nonstandard mix of material during the production process. The **material yield variance** measures the difference between the actual total quantity of input and the standard total quantity allowed based on output; this difference reflects standard mix and standard prices. Summing the material mix and yield variances provides a material quantity variance similar to the one discussed in the chapter. The difference is that the sum of the mix and yield variances is attributable to multiple ingredients rather than to a single one. A company can have a mix variance without experiencing a yield variance. Computations for the price, mix, and yield variances are given in a format similar to that used in the chapter.

Actual Mix × Actual Quantity × Actual Price	Actual Mix × Actual Quantity × Standard Price	Standard Mix × Actual Quantity × Standard Price	Standard Mix × Standard Quantity × Standard Price
	Material Price Variance	Material Mix Variance	Material Yield Variance

Computing Material Price, Mix, and Yield Variances — LO10-6 DEMO 10-6A

Rizzo's Fish Market is used to illustrate the computation of price/rate, mix, and yield variances. The company recently began selling one-pound packages of seafood mix containing crab, shrimp, and oysters. Ingredients are mixed in 200-pound batches, and because seafood is purchased fully cleaned, there is no waste in processing. To some extent, one ingredient can be substituted for another. Standard and actual information for the company for December follows.

Standard Information for December		
Material standards for one batch (200 1-pound packages):		
Crab (30%).....................	60 pounds at $7.20 per pound...	$ 432
Shrimp (45%)...................	90 pounds at $4.50 per pound...	405
Oysters (25%)..................	50 pounds at $5.00 per pound...	250
Total.........................	200 pounds...................	$1,087

Actual Information for December

Actual production and cost data for December:
Production .... 40 batches

Material:
- Crab, purchased and used (28.5%*) .... 2,285.7 pounds at $7.50 per pound
- Shrimp, purchased and used (45.5%) ... 3,649.1 pounds at $4.40 per pound
- Oysters, purchased and used (26.0%)... 2,085.2 pounds at $4.95 per pound

Total .... 8,020.0 pounds

*2,285.7 ÷ 8,020.0 = 28.5%

♦ **Based on the information provided for Rizzo's Fish Market, what are the material price, mix, and yield variances for December?**

Computations necessary for the material variances are first detailed as follows.

Computations for Material Mix and Yield Variances

(1) Total actual data (mix, quantity, and prices):
- Crab—2,285.7 pounds × $7.50 .... $17,142.75
- Shrimp—3,649.1 pounds × $4.40 .... 16,056.04
- Oysters—2,085.2 pounds × $4.95 .... 10,321.74 $43,520.53

(2) Actual mix and quantity; standard prices:
- Crab—2,285.7 pounds × $7.20 .... $16,457.04
- Shrimp—3,649.1 pounds × $4.50 .... 16,420.95
- Oysters—2,085.2 pounds × $5.00 .... 10,426.00 $43,303.99

(3) Standard mix; actual quantity; standard prices:
- Crab—30% × 8,020 pounds × $7.20 .... $17,323.20
- Shrimp—45% × 8,020 pounds × $4.50 .... 16,240.50
- Oysters—25% × 8,020 pounds × $5.00 .... 10,025.00 $43,588.70

(4) Total standard data (mix, quantity, and prices):
- Crab—30% × 8,000 pounds × $7.20 .... $17,280.00
- Shrimp—45% × 8,000 pounds × $4.50 .... 16,200.00
- Oysters—25% × 8,000 pounds × $5.00 .... 10,000.00 $43,480.00

Using the amounts above, the material variances for Rizzo's Fish Market's seafood mix in December are calculated as shown below. Note that the material quantity variance is $176.01 F (a combination of the material mix variance of $284.71 F and the material yield variance of $108.70 U).

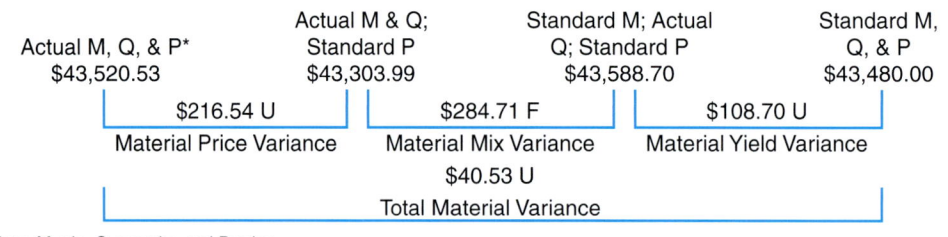

Actual M, Q, & P*	Actual M & Q; Standard P	Standard M; Actual Q; Standard P	Standard M, Q, & P
$43,520.53	$43,303.99	$43,588.70	$43,480.00

- $216.54 U — Material Price Variance
- $284.71 F — Material Mix Variance
- $108.70 U — Material Yield Variance
- $40.53 U — Total Material Variance

* Note: M mix, Q quantity, and P price.

These computations show a single price variance being calculated for all of the materials. To provide more useful information, separate price variances should be calculated for each ingredient.

```
Crab    = ($17,142.75 − $16,457.04) =   $685.71 U
Shrimp  = ($16,056.04 − $16,420.95) = − $364.91 F
Oysters = ($10,321.74 − $10,426.00) = − $104.26 F
```

The savings on shrimp and oysters did not offset the higher price for crab, so the total price variance was unfavorable. Also, less than the standard proportion of the most expensive ingredient (crab) was

Chapter 10 Flexible Budget, Standard Costing, and Variance Analysis

used, so it is reasonable that there would be a favorable mix variance. Rizzo's Fish Market also experienced an unfavorable yield because the 8,020 total actual pounds used was more than the 8,000 total pounds allowed for an output of 40 batches.

Labor Rate, Mix, and Yield Variances

When labor standards are prepared, the labor categories needed to perform various tasks and the amount of time each task is expected to take are established. During production, variances will occur if workers are not paid the standard rate, do not work in the standard mix on tasks, or do not perform those tasks in the standard time.

The labor rate variance is a measure of the cost of paying workers at other than standard rates. The **labor mix variance** is the financial effect associated with changing the relative hours of higher- or lower-paid workers in production. The **labor yield variance** reflects the monetary impact of using a higher or lower number of hours than the standard allowed. The sum of the labor mix and yield variances equals the labor efficiency variance. The diagram for computing labor rate, mix, and yield variances is as follows.

Actual Mix ×	Actual Mix ×	Standard Mix ×	Standard Mix ×
Actual Hours ×	Actual Hours ×	Actual Hours ×	Standard Hours ×
Actual Rate	Standard Rate	Standard Rate	Standard Rate

| Labor Rate Variance | Labor Mix Variance | Labor Yield Variance |

Standard rates are used for both the mix and yield computations.

Computing Labor Rate, Mix, and Yield Variances — LO10-6 DEMO 10-6B

Continuing with the Rizzo's Fish Market example, we assume two labor categories of helpers (A) and cooks (B) and a labor rate differential between these two categories. Standard and actual information for the company for December follow.

Standard Cost Information for December

Labor standards for one batch (200 1-pound packages):
Category A (75%).......	9 hours at $10.50 per hour	$94.50
Category B (25%).......	3 hours at $14.30 per hour	42.90
Total	12 hours..................	$137.40

Actual Cost Information for December

Labor :
Category A (90%*)........	450 hours at $10.50 per hour	
Category B (10%).........	50 hours at $14.40 per hour	
Total	500 hours	

*450 hours ÷ 500 hours = 90%

◆ **Based on the information provided for Rizzo's Fish Market, what are the labor rate, mix, and yield variances for December?**

Computations necessary for the labor variances are first detailed as follows.

Computations for Labor Mix and Yield Variances

(1) Total actual data (mix, hours, and rates):
 Category A—450 hours × $10.50............................... $4,725.00
 Category B—50 hours × $14.40................................ 720.00 $5,445.00

(2) Actual mix and hours; standard rates:
 Category A—450 hours × $10.50............................... $4,725.00
 Category B—50 hours × $14.30................................ 715.00 $5,440.00

continued

continued from previous page

Computations for Labor Mix and Yield Variances
(3) Standard mix; actual hours; standard rates:
Category A—75% × 500 × $10.50 . . . . $3,937.50
Category B—25% × 500 × $14.30 . . . . 1,787.50 $5,725.00
(4) Total standard data (mix, hours, and rates):
Category A—75% × 480* × $10.50 . . . . $3,780.00
Category B—25% × 480* × $14.30 . . . . 1,716.00 $5,496.00

* Because 12 hours is the standard for producing one batch of seafood mix, the standard number of hours allowed for production of 40 batches is 480 hours: 360 hours of A and 120 hours of B.

Using the amounts above and on the prior page, the labor variances for Rizzo's Fish Market's seafood mix in December are calculated as shown below. Note that the labor efficiency variance is $56 F (a combination of the labor mix variance of $285 F and the labor yield variance of $229 U).

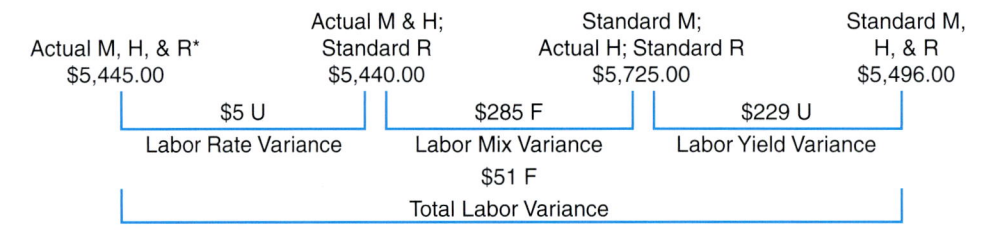

Actual M, H, & R*	Actual M & H; Standard R	Standard M; Actual H; Standard R	Standard M, H, & R
$5,445.00	$5,440.00	$5,725.00	$5,496.00
	$5 U	$285 F	$229 U
	Labor Rate Variance	Labor Mix Variance	Labor Yield Variance
		$51 F	
		Total Labor Variance	

*Note: M = mix, H = hours, and R = rate.

As with material price variances, separate rate variances should be calculated for each class of labor. Because category A does not have a labor rate variance, the total labor rate variance for December relates solely to category B.

Rizzo's Fish Market saved $285 by using the actual mix of labor rather than the standard. A higher proportion of the less expensive, unskilled class of labor (category A) than specified in the standard mix was used. One result of substituting a higher proportion of lower-paid workers seems to be that an unfavorable yield occurred because total actual hours were 20 hours higher than standard. However, the company saved a net of $51 by using the actual mix (even with the higher pay to category B workers) than the standard.

Because there are trade-offs in mix and yield when component qualities and quantities are changed, management should observe the integrated nature of price, mix, and yield. The effects of changes of one element on the other two need to be considered for managing cost efficiency and output quality. If mix and yield can be increased by substituting less expensive resources while maintaining quality, managers and product engineers should change the standards and the proportions of components. If costs are reduced but quality is maintained, selling prices could be reduced to gain a larger market share.

REVIEW 10-6 — LO10-6 — Mix and Yield Variances

Balanced Ltd. makes a protein powder. For a 50-pound batch, standard material and labor costs are as follows.

	Quantity	Unit Price
Plant-based blend.	30.00 pounds	$0.30 per pound
Soy	30.00 pounds	$0.20 per pound
Whey	15.00 pounds	$0.10 per pound
Skilled labor	1.12 hours	$15 per hour
Unskilled labor	0.28 hour	$10 per hour

During June, the following materials and labor were used in producing 700 batches of protein powder:

continued

	Quantity	Unit Price
Plant-based blend	25,200 pounds	$ 0.28 per pound
Soy	16,800 pounds	$ 0.25 per pound
Whey	17,000 pounds	$ 0.09 per pound
Skilled labor	560 hours	$17.5 per hour
Unskilled labor	364 hours	$11.5 per hour

a. Calculate the material price, mix, and yield variances.
b. Calculate the labor rate, mix, and yield variances.
c. **Critical Thinking:** Analyze the material and labor variances.

More practice: MC10-21, E10-58, E10-59, E10-60
Solution on p. 10-71.

Appendix 10A: Job Order Costing Using Standard Costs

Chapter 6 illustrated the use of actual historical cost data for direct material and direct labor in a *job order costing system*. However, using actual DM and DL costs may cause the costs of similar units to fluctuate from period to period or from job to job because of changes in component costs. Use of standard costs for DM and DL can minimize the effects of such cost fluctuations in the same way that predetermined rates do for overhead costs.

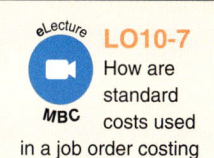

Standards can be used in a job order system only if a company typically works jobs that produce fairly similar products. One type of standard job order costing system uses standards only for input prices of material or only for labor rates. Such an approach is reasonable if all output relies on similar kinds of material or labor. If standards are used for price or rate amounts only, the debits to WIP Inventory become a *hybrid of actual and standard information*: actual quantities at standard prices or rates.

LO10-7 How are standard costs used in a job order costing system?

Computing Material Price and Labor Rate Variances for a Job LO10-7 DEMO 10-7A

Precise Painting, a house-painting company located in Denver, is used to illustrate the use of price and rate standards. Management has decided that, because of the climate, one specific brand of paint (costing $30 per gallon) is the best to use. Painters employed by the company are paid $18 per hour. These two amounts can be used as price and rate standards for Precise Painting. No standards can be set for the quantity of paint that will be used on a job or the amount of time that will be spent on the job. These items will vary based on the condition and texture of a structure's exterior as well as on the size of the structure being painted.

Assume that Precise Painting paints a house requiring 50 gallons of paint and 80 hours of labor time. The paint was purchased at a sale price of $27 per gallon (a total of $1,350). The actual labor rate paid to painters was $19 per hour.

◆ **How are the material price and the labor rate variances calculated for this job?**

Price and rate variances are calculated as follows.

Material price variance = (Actual price − Standard price) × Actual quantity

= ($27 − $30) × 50 gallons = −$150 or $150 F

Labor rate variance = (Actual price − Standard price) × Actual quantity

= ($19 − $18) × 80 hours = $80 U

The price variance is favorable because less was expended than what was expected. The rate variance is unfavorable because the amount spent is greater than what was expected.

Other job order companies produce output that is homogeneous enough to allow standards to be developed for *both* quantities and prices of material and labor. Such companies usually use distinct production runs for numerous similar products. In such circumstances, the output is homogeneous for each run, unlike the heterogeneous output of Precise Painting.

DEMO 10-7B LO10-7   Computing Material and Labor Variances for a Job

Green Manufacturing Inc. is a job order manufacturer that uses both price and quantity material and labor standards. Green uses recycled wood to produce flower boxes that are retailed through several chains of garden supply stores. Retailers contract for the boxes on a job order basis because of the changes in style, color, and size with each spring gardening season. Green produces the boxes in distinct production runs each month for each retail chain. Price and quantity standards for direct material and direct labor have been established and are used to compare the estimated and actual costs of monthly production runs for each type of box produced.

Material and labor standards set for the boxes sold to Mountain Gardens were the following.

> Material: 8 linear feet of 1" × 10" redwood plank at $0.60 per linear foot
> Labor: 1.4 direct labor hours at $15.00 per direct labor hour (DLH)

In June, 2,000 boxes were produced for Mountain Gardens. The actual quantities and costs for wood and labor related to this job follow.

> Material: 16,300 linear feet used; purchased at $0.58 per linear foot
> Labor: 2,700 actual hours worked at $15.10 per DLH

◆ **How are the material price and quantity variances and the labor rate and efficiency variances calculated for this job?**

Given this information, the following variances can be calculated.

Material Variances:

> **Material price variance = (Actual price − Standard price) × Actual quantity**
>
> = ($0.58 − $0.60) × 16,300 linear feet = −$326 or $326 F
>
> **Material quantity variance = Standard price × (Actual quantity − Standard quantity)**
>
> = $0.60 × (16,300 − (8 × 2,000)) = $180 U

Labor variance:

> **Labor rate variance = (Actual price − Standard price) × Actual quantity**
>
> = ($15.10 − $15.00) × 2,700 = $270 U
>
> **Labor efficiency variance = Standard price × (Actual quantity − Standard quantity)**
>
> = $15 × (2,700 − (1.4 × 2,000)) = −$1,500 or $1,500 F

A summary of variances follows:

Direct material price variance	$326 F
Direct material quantity variance	180 U
Direct labor rate variance	270 U
Direct labor efficiency variance	1,500 F
Net variance (cost less than expected)	$1,376 F

From a financial perspective, Green controlled its total material and labor costs well on the Mountain Gardens job.

Variances can be computed for actual-to-standard differences regardless of whether standards have been established for both quantities and prices or for prices or rates only. Standard costs for material and labor provide the same types of benefits as predetermined OH rates: more timely information and comparison benchmarks for actual amounts. In fact, a predetermined OH rate is simply a type of standard. It establishes a constant amount of overhead assignable as a component of product cost and eliminates any immediate need for actual overhead information in the calculation of product cost.

Standard cost job order systems are reasonable substitutes for actual or normal cost systems as long as the standards provide managers with useful information. Any cost accumulation system is acceptable in practice if it is effective and efficient in serving the company's unique production or performance needs, provides information desired by management, meets external reporting demands, and can be maintained at

Chapter 10 Flexible Budget, Standard Costing, and Variance Analysis

a cost that is reasonable when compared to the benefits received. These criteria apply equally well to both manufacturers and service companies.

> **Standard Costing**   LO10-7   REVIEW 10-7
>
> During July, Zap's Inc. worked on two production runs (Jobs #202 and #506) of the same product, a component of recreational equipment. Job #202 consisted of 1,000 units of the product, and Job #506 contained 900 units of the product. Because the component is routinely produced for one of Zap's long-term customers, standard costs have been developed for its production. The standard cost of material for each unit is $17; each unit contains six pounds of material at standard. The standard direct labor time per unit is 12 minutes for workers earning a standard rate of $20 per hour. The actual costs recorded for each job were as follows:
>
> | | Direct Material | Direct Labor |
> | --- | --- | --- |
> | Job #202....... | (3,650 pounds) $14,115 | (208 hours) $3,800 |
> | Job #506....... | (5,950 pounds) $18,720 | (300 hours) $5,900 |
>
> 1. Calculate the following variances for Job #202 and Job #506.
>   - a. Direct material price variance
>   - b. Direct material quantity variance
>   - c. Direct labor rate variance
>   - d. Direct labor efficiency variance
> 2. **Critical Thinking:** How can the variance results of Job #202 or Job #506 provide useful information to management about future jobs?
>
> More practice: E10-62, E10-63
> Solution on p. 10-72.

Appendix 10B: Conversion Cost as an Element in Standard Costing

As discussed in Chapter 2, conversion cost consists of direct labor and manufacturing overhead. The traditional view of separating product cost into three categories (direct material, direct labor, and overhead) is appropriate in labor-intensive production settings. However, in automated factories, direct labor cost often represents only a small part of total product cost. In such circumstances, one worker might oversee a large number of machines and deal more with troubleshooting machine malfunctions than with converting raw material into finished products. Within these new production operations, all production workers may be considered indirect labor, and therefore, their wages would be part of overhead.

Many automated companies have adapted their standard cost systems to provide for only two elements of product cost: direct material and conversion. In these situations, conversion cost is likely to be separated into variable and fixed components. Conversion cost can also be separated into direct and indirect categories based on the ability to trace such costs to a machine rather than to a product. Overhead can be applied under an activity-based costing methodology (see Chapter 8) using a variety of cost drivers such as number of machine hours, material cost, number of production runs, number of machine setups, or throughput time.

Variance analysis for conversion cost in automated plants normally focuses on the following:

- spending variances for overhead costs,
- efficiency variances for machinery and production costs rather than labor costs, and
- a volume variance for production.

These categories are similar to the traditional three-variance overhead approach. In an automated system, managers are better able to control not only the spending and efficiency variances but also the volume variance. Variance analysis under a conversion cost approach is illustrated in **Exhibit 10.4**. Regardless of how variances are computed, managers must analyze those variances and use them for cost control purposes to the extent that such control can be exercised.

LO10-8 How does the use of a single conversion element (rather than the traditional labor and overhead elements) affect standard costing?

Exhibit 10.4 ■ Variances Under Conversion Approach

$$\text{Conversion Rate per MH*} = \frac{\text{Budgeted Direct Labor Cost + Budgeted OH Cost}}{\text{Budgeted Machine Hours}}$$

(can be separated into variable and fixed costs)

*Other cost drivers could be more appropriate than MHs. If such drivers are used to determine the rate, they must also be used to determine the variances.

continued

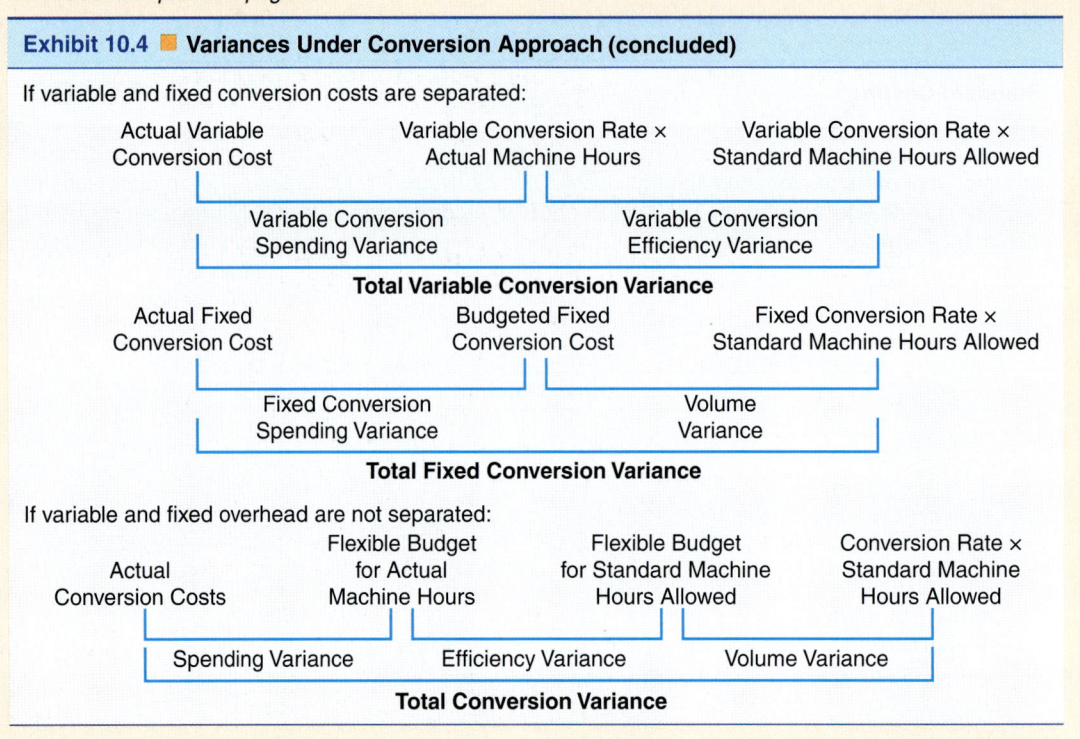

Exhibit 10.4 — Variances Under Conversion Approach (concluded)

If variable and fixed conversion costs are separated:

```
Actual Variable          Variable Conversion Rate ×      Variable Conversion Rate ×
Conversion Cost          Actual Machine Hours            Standard Machine Hours Allowed
         └──────────┬──────────┘         └──────────┬──────────┘
          Variable Conversion              Variable Conversion
           Spending Variance                Efficiency Variance
                        Total Variable Conversion Variance

Actual Fixed             Budgeted Fixed                  Fixed Conversion Rate ×
Conversion Cost          Conversion Cost                 Standard Machine Hours Allowed
         └──────────┬──────────┘         └──────────┬──────────┘
           Fixed Conversion                     Volume
           Spending Variance                   Variance
                        Total Fixed Conversion Variance
```

If variable and fixed overhead are not separated:

```
                    Flexible Budget         Flexible Budget         Conversion Rate ×
Actual              for Actual              for Standard Machine    Standard Machine
Conversion Costs    Machine Hours           Hours Allowed           Hours Allowed
      └──────┬──────┘      └──────┬──────┘      └──────┬──────┘
       Spending Variance   Efficiency Variance    Volume Variance
                        Total Conversion Variance
```

DEMO 10-8 LO10-8   Computing Conversion Cost Variances

Assume that Kalinda Corp. makes aluminum bike frames in a fully automated production facility; all labor required for this product is considered indirect. For simplicity, it is assumed that all overhead is applied on the basis of budgeted machine hours. Necessary annual production and cost information for bike frames is as follows.

Expected production.	48,000 units
Actual production	50,000 units
Actual machine time	37,100 MHs
Standard machine time allowed per unit	0.75 MH
Budgeted variable conversion cost	$144,000
Budgeted fixed conversion cost	$306,000
Actual variable conversion cost	$150,500
Actual fixed conversion cost	$304,600

Expected production time for the year = 48,000 × 0.75 = 36,000 MHs
Variable conversion rate: $144,000 ÷ 36,000 MHs = $4.00 per MH
Fixed conversion rate: $306,000 ÷ 36,000 MHs = $8.50 per MH
Standard machine hours allowed: 50,000 units × 0.75 MH per unit = 37,500 MHs

◆ **How is the variance for conversion costs calculated using a three-variance approach?**

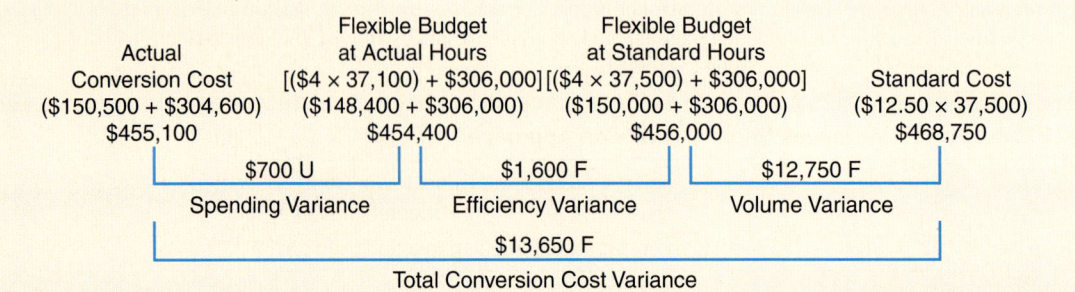

```
                        Flexible Budget              Flexible Budget
    Actual              at Actual Hours              at Standard Hours
Conversion Cost     [($4 × 37,100) + $306,000]  [($4 × 37,500) + $306,000]    Standard Cost
($150,500 + $304,600)   ($148,400 + $306,000)       ($150,000 + $306,000)    ($12.50 × 37,500)
     $455,100                $454,400                     $456,000                $468,750
          └────────┬────────┘       └────────┬────────┘       └────────┬────────┘
                 $700 U                   $1,600 F                  $12,750 F
            Spending Variance         Efficiency Variance          Volume Variance
                                      $13,650 F
                              Total Conversion Cost Variance
```

◆ **How can the spending variance calculated above be divided into its variable and fixed overhead components?**

The $700 U spending variance could be divided into a $2,100 U variable overhead spending variance and a $1,400 F fixed overhead spending variance as follows.

Variable conversion cost spending variance = Actual variable conversion cost − (Standard price × Actual quantity)

= $150,500 − ($4 × 37,100) = $150,500 − $148,400 = $2,100 U

Fixed Conversion cost spending variance = Actual fixed conversion cost − Budget fixed conversion cost

= $304,600 − $306,000 = $1,400 F

REVIEW 10-8 — Variances and Conversion Cost Category (LO10-8)

Liberty Inc. manufactures parts for commercial exercise equipment and has always applied overhead to production using direct labor hours. Recently, company facilities were upgraded resulting in significantly more automation. As a result, the accounting system was revised to show only two cost categories: direct material and conversion. Estimated variable and fixed conversion costs for the current month were $102,000 and $45,600, respectively. Expected output for the current month was 3,000 units, and the estimated number of machine hours was 6,000. During July, the firm actually used 5,400 machine hours to make 2,880 units while incurring $134,000 of conversion costs. Of this amount, $44,000 was fixed cost.

a. Using the four-variance approach, compute the variances for conversion costs.
b. **Critical Thinking:** If instead, the company continued to use the traditional cost system to measure direct material, direct labor, and overhead variances, are the results incorrect? Why or Why not?

More practice: E10-64, E10-65
Solution on p. 10-72.

Comprehensive Chapter Review

Key Terms

- bill of materials, p. 10-9
- budget variance, p. 10-22
- controllable variance, p. 10-22
- expected standards, p. 10-7
- fixed overhead spending variance, p. 10-19
- flexible budgets, p. 10-2
- four-variance approach, p. 10-17
- ideal standards, p. 10-8
- labor efficiency variance (LEV), p. 10-15
- labor mix variance, p. 10-29
- labor rate variance (LRV), p. 10-15
- labor yield variance, p. 10-29
- management-by-exception, p. 10-6
- material mix variance, p. 10-27
- material price variance (MPV), p. 10-12
- material quantity variance (MQV), p. 10-12
- material yield variance, p. 10-27
- methods-time measurement (MTM), p. 10-9
- mix, p. 10-27
- noncontrollable variance, p. 10-19
- one-variance approach, p. 10-21
- operations flow document, p. 10-9
- overhead efficiency variance, p. 10-23
- overhead spending variance, p. 10-23
- point-of-purchase model, p. 10-14
- point-of-usage model, p. 10-11
- practical standards, p. 10-7
- standard cost card, p. 10-9
- standard cost system, p. 10-5
- standard quantity allowed, p. 10-9
- standards, p. 10-5
- static budget, p. 10-2
- three-variance approach, p. 10-22
- total labor variance (TLV), p. 10-15
- total material variance (TMV), p. 10-13
- total overhead variance, p. 10-21
- two-variance approach, p. 10-22
- variable overhead efficiency variance, p. 10-18
- variable overhead spending variance, p. 10-17
- variance analysis, p. 10-5
- volume variance, p. 10-19
- yield, p. 10-27

Chapter Summary

LO10-1 **Flexible Budget (Page 10-2)**
- Flexible budgets can be used for planning
  - Budgets are prepared for activities within the relevant range.
  - The budget increment is equal to additional variable costs.
- Flexible budgets can be used to emphasize performance
  - Flexible budget can be prepared after the fact for control purposes.
  - Budget should be based on actual activity level
  - Variances are identified as the difference between actual and the flexible budget

LO10-2 **Setting Material, Labor, and Overhead Standards in a Standard Costing System (Page 10-5)**
- A standard cost system is used to
  - assist management in its planning, controlling, decision making, and evaluating performance functions.
  - motivate employees when the standards are
    - set at a level to encourage high-quality production and promote cost control.
    - seen as expected performance goals.
    - updated periodically so that they reflect actual economic conditions.
- Material standards require that management identify the
  - types of material inputs needed to make the product or perform the service.
  - quality of material inputs needed to make the product or perform the service.
  - quantity of material inputs needed to make the product or perform the service.
  - prices of the material inputs, given normal purchase quantities.
- A bill of materials contains all quantity and quality raw material specifications to make one unit (or batch) of output.
- Labor standards require that management identify the
  - types of labor tasks needed to make the product or perform the service.
  - amount of labor time needed to make the product or perform the service.
  - skill levels of personnel needed to make the product or perform the service.
  - wage rates or salary levels for the classes of labor skills needed.
- An operations flow document contains all labor operations necessary to make one unit (or batch) of output or perform a particular service.
- Overhead standards require that management identify the
  - variable and fixed overhead costs incurred in the organization.
  - estimated level of activity to be used in computing the predetermined overhead rate(s).
  - estimated variable and fixed overhead costs at the estimated level of activity.
  - predetermined overhead rate(s) used to apply overhead to production or service performance.
- A standard cost card summarizes the standard quantities and costs needed to complete one unit of product or perform a particular service.

LO10-3 **Calculating and Recording Material and Labor (Page 10-10)**
- Direct material variances are calculated as follows:
  - Material price variance = (Actual price × Actual quantity) − (Standard price × Actual quantity); generally calculated using quantity of material purchased
  - Material quantity variance = (Standard price × Actual quantity) − (Standard price × Standard quantity); calculated using quantity of material used
  - Total material variance = Material price variance + Material quantity variance; generally not calculated if the material price and quantity variances have been computed using different measures (purchased and used)
  - Compute material price variances based on usage rather than purchases.
- Direct labor variances are calculated as follows:
  - Labor rate variance = (Actual price × Actual quantity) − (Standard price × Actual quantity)
  - Labor efficiency variance = (Standard price × Actual quantity) − (Standard price × Standard quantity)
  - Total labor variance = Labor rate variance + Labor efficiency variance

LO10-4 **Calculating and Recording Overhead Variances (Page 10-16)**
- Variable overhead variances are calculated as follows:

Chapter 10 Flexible Budget, Standard Costing, and Variance Analysis

- VOH spending variance = Actual VOH − (Standard price × Actual quantity)
- VOH efficiency variance = (Standard price × Actual quantity of overhead application base) − Applied VOH
  - Note: Applied VOH = (Standard price × Standard quantity of overhead application base)
- Total VOH Variance = VOH spending variance + VOH efficiency variance
- Fixed overhead variances are calculated as follows:
  - FOH spending variance = Actual FOH − Budgeted FOH
    - Note: Budgeted FOH = Expected FOH amount for the period
  - Volume variance = Budgeted FOH − Applied FOH
    - Note: Applied FOH = (Standard price × Standard quantity of overhead application base)
  - Total FOH variance = FOH spending variance + Volume variance
- Recording standard costs and variances
  - Only standard costs are recorded in the inventory accounts.
  - Variances are recorded as either debit (unfavorable) or credit (favorable) differences between the standard cost and the actual cost incurred.

Disposition of Standard Cost Variances (Page 10-24) — LO10-5

- Variances are closed at the end of each accounting period.
  - Insignificant material and labor variances are closed to Cost of Goods Sold.
  - Significant material and labor variances are allocated among Cost of Goods Sold and the appropriate ending inventory accounts; the material price variance is the only one allocated to the Raw Material Inventory account.

Calculating Mix and Yield Variances (Page 10-27) — LO10-6

- Material mix variance measures the effect of substituting a nonstandard mix of materials during production.
- Material yield variance measures the difference between actual total quantity of input and standard total quantity allowed based on output.
- Labor mix variance is the financial effect associated with changing the relative hours of higher- or lower paid workers in production.
- The labor yield variance reflects the monetary impact of using a higher or lower number of hours than the standard allowed.

Job Order Costing Using Standard Costs (Page 10-31) — LO10-7

- Standards can be used in a job order system only if products in a job are fairly similar.
- Standard job order costing system can use standards
  - to establish input prices of material or for labor rates
  - to compute material quantity variance and/or labor efficiency variance

Standard Costing Using a Conversion Element (Page 10-33 — LO10-8

- If a conversion category is used rather than the traditional labor and overhead categories, overhead will commonly be separated into its variable and fixed categories.
  - overhead may be applied using activity-based costing.
  - the focus will be on
    - spending variances for variable and fixed overhead.
    - efficiency variances for machinery and production equipment rather than labor.
    - volume variance for production.

Solution Strategies

Variances in Formula Format — LO10-3

The following abbreviations are used:

AFOH	= actual fixed overhead		SM	= standard mix
AM	= actual mix		SP	= standard price
AP	= actual price or rate		SQ	= standard quantity
AQ	= actual quantity or hours		TAOH	= total actual overhead
AVOH	= actual variable overhead			
BFOH	= budgeted fixed overhead (remains at constant amount regardless of activity level as long as within the relevant range)			

© Cambridge Business Publishers

Materials and Labor Variances:

Material price variance = (AP − SP) × AQ
Material quantity variance = SP × (AQ − SQ)
Labor rate variance = (AP − SP) × AQ
Labor efficiency variance = SP × (AQ − SQ)

OH Four-Variance Approach:

Variable OH spending variance = AVOH − (VOH rate × AQ)
Variable OH efficiency variance = (VOH rate × AQ) − (VOH rate × SQ)
Fixed OH spending variance = AFOH − BFOH
Volume variance = BFOH − (FOH rate × SQ)

OH Three-Variance Approach:

Spending variance = TAOH − [(VOH rate × AQ) + BFOH]
Efficiency variance = [(VOH rate × AQ) + BFOH] − [(VOH rate × SQ) + BFOH]
Volume variance = [(VOH rate × SQ) + BFOH] − [(VOH rate × SQ) + (FOH rate × SQ)]
  (This is equal to the volume variance of the four-variance approach.)

OH Two-Variance Approach:

Budget variance = TAOH − [(VOH rate × SQ) + BFOH]
Volume variance = [(VOH rate × SQ) + BFOH] − [(VOH rate × SQ) + (FOH rate × SQ)]
  (This is equal to the volume variance of the four-variance approach.)

OH One-Variance Approach:

Total OH variance = TAOH − (Combined OH rate × SQ)

LO10-3 Variances in Diagram Format

Direct Material: Point-of-Usage

```
Actual Price ×           Standard Price ×          Standard Price ×
Actual Quantity Used     Actual Quantity Used      Standard Quantity
         └──── Material Price Variance ────┘└──── Material Quantity Variance ────┘
                         Total Material Variance
```

Direct Material: Point-of-Purchase

```
Actual Price ×              Standard Price ×
Actual Quantity Purchased   Actual Quantity Purchased
         └──── Material Price Variance ────┘

                  Standard Price ×          Standard Price ×
                  Actual Quantity Used      Standard Quantity
                           └──── Material Quantity Variance ────┘
```

Direct Labor

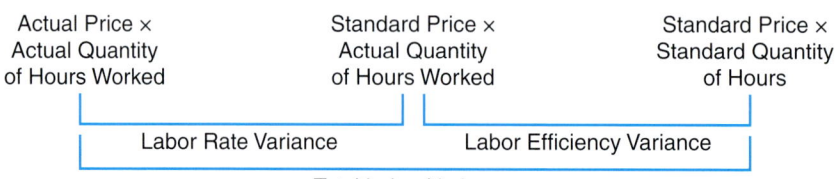

```
Actual Price ×        Standard Price ×         Standard Price ×
Actual Quantity       Actual Quantity          Standard Quantity
of Hours Worked       of Hours Worked          of Hours
      └──── Labor Rate Variance ────┘└──── Labor Efficiency Variance ────┘
                       Total Labor Variance
```

Overhead Four-Variance Approach

Variable Overhead

```
                    Budgeted VOH
                (based on actual hours)              Applied VOH
Actual VOH              SP × AQ                        SP × SQ
    |_____(a)_____|_____(b)_____|
         VOH Spending Variance      VOH Efficiency Variance
                        Total VOH Variance
```

Fixed Overhead

```
                                                  Applied FOH
                                          (for standard quantity allowed)
Actual FOH            Budgeted FOH                  SP × SQ
    |_____|_____|
      FOH Spending Variance          Volume Variance
                        Total FOH Variance
```

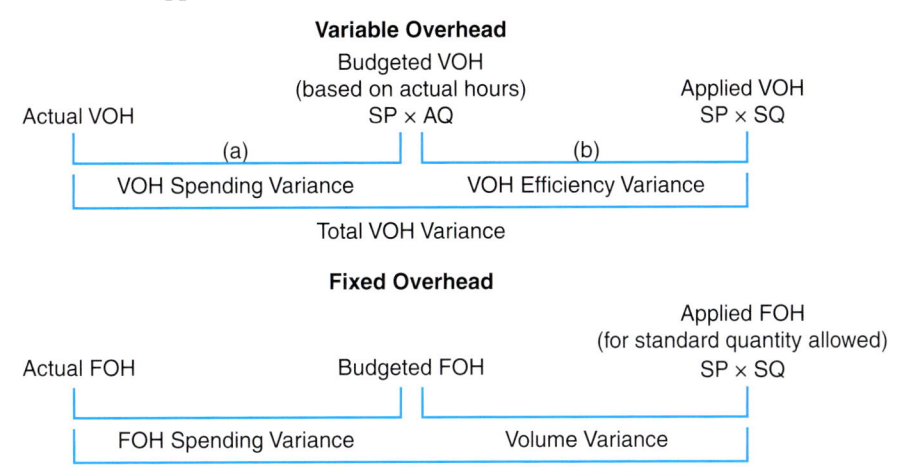

Overhead One-, Two-, and Three-Variance Approaches

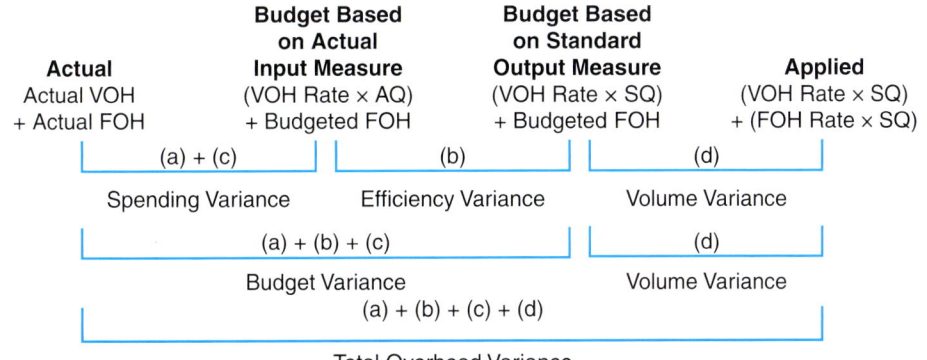

```
                    Budget Based        Budget Based
                     on Actual           on Standard
     Actual         Input Measure       Output Measure        Applied
   Actual VOH      (VOH Rate × AQ)      (VOH Rate × SQ)   (VOH Rate × SQ)
  + Actual FOH     + Budgeted FOH       + Budgeted FOH    + (FOH Rate × SQ)
      |____(a) + (c)____|_____(b)_____|_____(d)_____|
        Spending Variance   Efficiency Variance   Volume Variance
      |_____(a) + (b) + (c)_____|_____(d)_____|
              Budget Variance              Volume Variance
      |_____(a) + (b) + (c) + (d)_____|
                    Total Overhead Variance
              (Total Underapplied/Overapplied Overhead)
```

Chapter Demonstration Problem

LO10-3, 4

Filano Corp. has the following standards for one unit of product:

Direct material: 80 pounds × $6	$480
Direct labor: 3 hours × $16 per hour	48
Variable overhead: 1.5 hours of machine time × $50 per hour	75
Fixed overhead: 1.5 hours of machine time × $30 per hour	45

The predetermined OH rates were developed using a capacity of 6,000 units per year. Production is assumed to occur evenly throughout the year.

During May, the company produced 525 units. Actual data for May are as follows:

Direct material purchased: 45,000 pounds × $5.92 per pound
Direct material used: 43,020 pounds (all from May's purchases)
Total labor cost: $24,955 for 1,550 hours
Variable overhead incurred: $43,750 for 800 hours of machine time
Fixed overhead incurred: $22,800 for 800 hours of machine time

Required:
a. Calculate the following:
  1. Material price variance based on quantity purchased
  2. Material quantity variance
  3. Actual rate per direct labor hour

4. Labor rate variance
5. Labor efficiency variance
6. Variable overhead spending and efficiency variances
7. Budgeted annual and monthly fixed overhead
8. Fixed overhead spending and volume variances
9. Combined variable and fixed overhead rate
10. Overhead variances using a three-variance approach
11. Overhead variances using a two-variance approach
12. Overhead variance using a one-variance approach

b. Record the entries to recognize the variances.

Solution to Demonstration Problem

a. 1.

$AP \times AQ_p$ $SP \times AQ_p$
$5.92 \times 45,000$ $6.00 \times 45,000$
$266,400$ $270,000$

$3,600 F$
MPV

2. SQ = 525 × 80 pounds = 42,000 pounds

$SP \times AQ_u$ $SP \times SQ$
$6 \times 43,020$ $6 \times 42,000$
$258,120$ $252,000$

$6,120 U$
MQV

3. AR = $24,955 ÷ 1,550 hours = $16.10 per DLH

4. & 5. SQ = 525 × 3 hours = 1,575 DLHs

$AP \times AQ$ $SP \times AQ$ $SP \times SQ$
$16.10 \times 1,550$ $16 \times 1,550$ $16 \times 1,575$
$24,955$ $24,800$ $25,200$

$155 U$ $400 F$
LRV   LEV

6. SQ = 525 × 1.5 = 787.5 MHs

Actual VOH $SP \times AQ$ $SP \times SQ$
$43,750$ 50×800 50×787.5
     $40,000$ $39,375$

$3,750 U$ $625 U$
VOH Spending Variance   VOH Efficiency Variance

7. Annual BFOH = 6,000 × 1.5 hours × $30 = $270,000
Monthly BFOH = $270,000 ÷ 12 months = $22,500

8. SQ = 787.5 machine hours [from (5)]

Actual FOH   Budgeted FOH $SP \times SQ$
$22,800$ $22,500$ 30×787.50
          $23,625$

$300 U$ $1,125 F$
FOH Spending Variance   Volume Variance

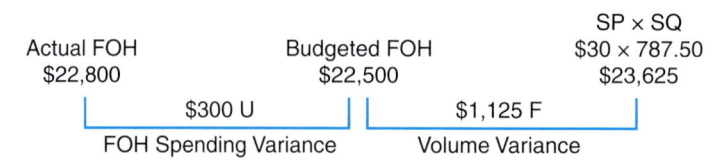

9. Combined OH = $50 + $30 = $80 per MH

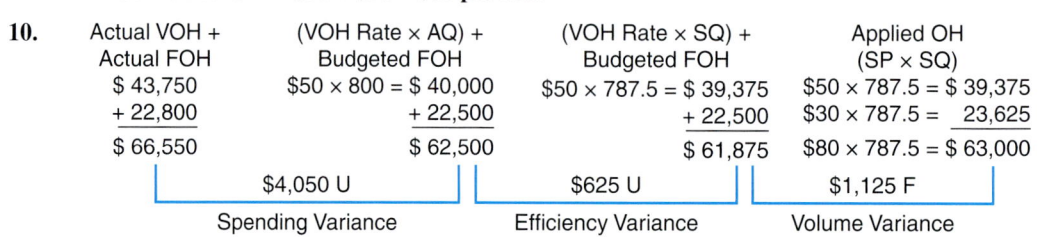

10.

Actual VOH + Actual FOH	(VOH Rate × AQ) + Budgeted FOH	(VOH Rate × SQ) + Budgeted FOH	Applied OH (SP × SQ)
$ 43,750	$50 × 800 = $ 40,000	$50 × 787.5 = $ 39,375	$50 × 787.5 = $ 39,375
+ 22,800	+ 22,500	+ 22,500	$30 × 787.5 = 23,625
$ 66,550	$ 62,500	$ 61,875	$80 × 787.5 = $ 63,000

$4,050 U$ $625 U$ $1,125 F$
Spending Variance   Efficiency Variance   Volume Variance

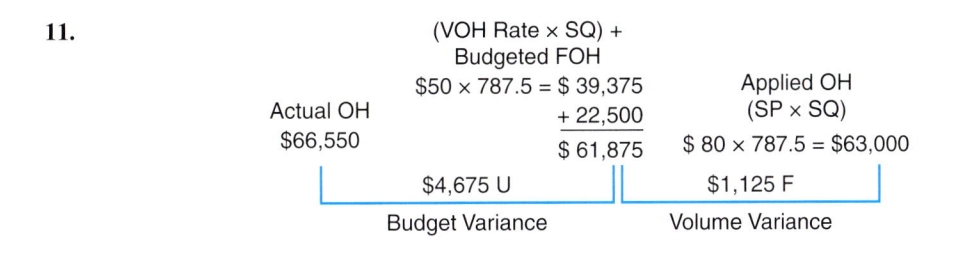

Chapter 10 Flexible Budget, Standard Costing, and Variance Analysis   10-41

11.

	(VOH Rate × SQ) + Budgeted FOH	
Actual OH	$50 × 787.5 = $ 39,375	Applied OH (SP × SQ)
$66,550	+ 22,500 $ 61,875	$ 80 × 787.5 = $63,000
$4,675 U		$1,125 F
Budget Variance		Volume Variance

12.

		Applied OH
Actual OH		SP × SQ
$66,550		$80 × 787.5 = $63,000
	$3,550 U	
	Total Overhead Variance (Total Underapplied Overhead)	

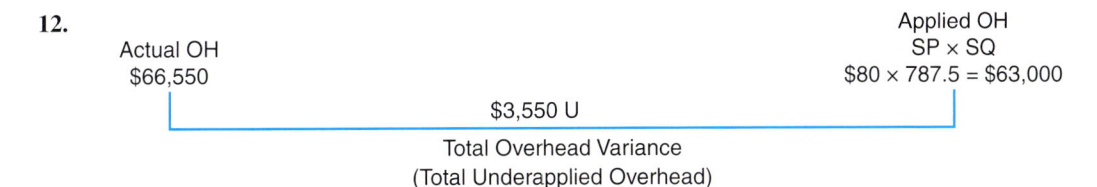

b. All amounts are taken from the computations shown in (a).

Raw Material Inventory.......................................	270,000	
Material Purchase Price Variance		3,600
Accounts Payable......................................		266,400
To record acquisition of material		
Work in Process Inventory..................................	252,000	
Material Quantity Variance................................	6,120	
Raw Material Inventory.....................................		258,120
To record issuance of material to production		
Work in Process Inventory	25,200	
Labor Rate Variance......................................	155	
Wages Payable...		24,955
Labor Efficiency Variance.................................		400
To record direct labor costs in all departments		
Work in Process Inventory	39,375	
Variable Overhead Efficiency Variance........................	3,750	
Variable Overhead Spending Variance........................	625	
Variable Manufacturing Overhead Control		43,750
To close variable OH		
Work in Process Inventory	23,625	
Fixed Overhead Spending Variance..........................	300	
Fixed Manufacturing Overhead Control		22,800
Volume Variance..		1,125
To close fixed OH		

Assignments with the ᴹᴮᶜ logo in the margin are available in *my*BusinessCourse.
Resources include demonstration videos, guided examples, and auto-graded homework.
See details in the Preface, and ask your professor how you can access the system.

Data Analytics

DA10-1. Using a flexible budget to illustrate best and worst case scenarios   LO10-1

Case Products manufactures two models of cell phone cases: regular and deluxe. Presented is standard cost information for each model, sold to retailers in packages of 6 units. During July, the company produced 8,000 regular and 3,500 deluxe packs of cell phone cases.

© Cambridge Business Publishers

Cost Components for a Pack	Regular		Deluxe	
Direct materials				
Plastic sheets	3 sheets × $12 =	$36.00	5 sheets × $12 =	$60.00
Assembly kit	=	5.00	=	5.00
Direct labor	0.5 hour × $20 =	10.00	0.75 hours × $20 =	15.00
Variable overhead	0.5 labor hr. × $5 =	2.50	0.75 labor hrs. × $5 =	3.75
Total		$53.50		$83.75

Required

a. Assume that budgeted selling prices for regular and deluxe packs are $60 and $90 respectively. The company expects to sell all of the products produced for the period. Management estimates that the best case scenario is that regular units increase by 10% and deluxe units increase by 20%. Management estimates that the worst case scenario is that regular units decrease by 10% and deluxe unit decrease by 15%. Create a schedule in Excel showing the contribution margin at budget, best, and worst case scenarios for regular and deluxe product.

b. Create a stacked column chart showing contribution margin of regular and deluxe products at budget, best case, and worst case. In what $10,000 range does the top of each bar fall under?

c. How could calculating a best and worst case scenario assist management in planning?

DA10-2. Budget variance analysis using Excel: management by exception

Preston Township's City Council will be evaluating costs incurred in the various city departments at its next meeting. In total, costs exceeded budgeted amounts in the prior year by $576,277. The Council president has asked for information about actual vs. budgeted costs by department and by expense type to help in the evaluation process. Transaction and budget information is included in the file available on the textbook's website. A video demonstrating Excel tools used to answer the questions in this problem is also available on the website.

Required

1. Create two PivotTables.
    a. One for actual costs by department and expense type.
    b. One for budgeted costs by department and expense type.
2. Create two Budget Variance reports (one for variances by department and one for variances by expense type).
    · Both reports should link actual and budget data from the PivotTables. *Hint:* Before copying the formula linking your report to the PivotTable down the column of your report, you must change the reference in your formula from the name in the cell to the cell address (A5, for example). *Hint:* When linking the data, you'll discover one referencing error due to a difference in account names. The referencing error can be resolved either by updating the account name in one of the data files or by using a hard reference to the desired data cell.
    · The reports should include columns for budgeted amounts, actual amounts, variance (in dollars), and variance (in percent). Show the unfavorable dollar variances as negative numbers, favorable variances as positive numbers. Show all percent variances as positive numbers. *Hint:* Use the ABS function in Excel in the formula to calculate percent variances.
3. Use the PivotTable and the variance reports to answer the following questions:
    a. Which department experienced the greatest variance between budgeted and actual cost (in dollars)? Which expense type in that department accounted for the largest share of the variance? *Hint:* Filter your PivotTables to update the variance reports.
    b. Which expense type had the highest unfavorable variance (in dollars)? Which department had the highest unfavorable variance in that expense type? Which expense type had the highest favorable variance (in dollars)? Which department had the highest favorable variance in that expense type?
    c. Which department had the highest percentage variance? Which type of expense was most over or under budget in that department? Which expense type had the highest percentage variance? Which department was most over or under budget in that expense type?
    d. Schools had the largest budget. Does it appear that the budget dollars were well managed? Explain your answer.
4. In general, should the council members be more concerned about the departments or expense types with the highest unfavorable dollar variances or the highest unfavorable percentage variances? Should the council members be concerned about departments or expense types with favorable variances? Explain your answers.

Data Visualization

Data Visualization Activities are available in myBusinessCourse. These assignments use Tableau Dashboards to expose students to visual depictions of data and introduce students to data analytics through data visualizations. These exercises are easily assignable and auto graded by MBC.

Potential Ethical Issues

1. Setting labor time standards extremely high so that variances on which performance is evaluated are consistently favorable
2. Evaluating each manager on the variances generated in his or her production area without regard for potential implications on other production areas
3. Estimating production at levels significantly higher than is necessary to meet current and anticipated sales, thereby lowering the predetermined fixed OH rate per unit and inventory cost, while increasing reported operating income
4. Producing unnecessary inventory to generate a high, favorable volume variance
5. Not adjusting standards for changed production conditions so that favorable variances will result
6. Using inappropriate material or labor mixes that create favorable price or rate variances but result in a lower-quality product

Questions

Q10-1. What are the three primary uses of a standard cost system? In a business that routinely manufactures the same products or performs the same services, why are standards helpful?

Q10-2. What is management by exception? Why is a standard cost system useful when managers control "by exception"?

Q10-3. What is a standard cost card? What information does it contain? How does it relate to a bill of materials and an operations flow document?

Q10-4. How is the material standard developed? Why are the quantities shown in the bill of materials not always the same quantities shown in the standard cost card?

Q10-5. A total variance can be calculated for each product cost component. Into what variances can this total be separated and to what does each relate?

Q10-6. What is meant by the term *standard hours*? Does the term refer to inputs or outputs?

Q10-7. When Domino's Pizza began operations in 1960, it had a "30 Minutes or It's Free" campaign. In making that promise, the company set a standard time to prepare and deliver a pizza. In a later year, Domino's completely removed that campaign. Discuss how setting such a standard might have been problematic for Domino's. Can you think of any other organizations in which guaranteeing specific labor time standards might create problems?

Q10-8. The overhead spending and overhead efficiency variances are said to be controllable, but the volume variance is said to be noncontrollable. Explain.

Q10-9. Discuss the following statement: Since standard costs are recorded in the inventory accounts in a standard cost system, actual costs are ignored.

Q10-10. How are insignificant variances closed at the end of an accounting period? How are significant variances closed at the end of an accounting period? Why is there a difference in treatment?

Q10-11. Why do managers care about capacity utilization? Are managers controlling costs when they control utilization?

Q10-12. Why should the use of ideal standards result in lower production costs?

Q10-13. When would adjusting standards within a period be reasonable?

Q10-14. What variances can be computed for direct material and direct labor when some materials or labor inputs are substitutes for others? What information does each of these variances provide?

Multiple Choice

LO10-1 MC10-15. A company reported the following cost information for the last fiscal year when it produced 100,000 units.

Direct labor	$200,000
Direct materials	100,000
Manufacturing overhead	200,000
Selling and administrative expenses	150,000

All costs are variable except for $100,000 of manufacturing overhead and $100,000 of selling and administrative expenses. Using flexible budgeting, what are the total costs associated with producing and selling 110,000 units?

a. $450,000.
b. $650,000.
c. $695,000.
d. $715,000.

LO10-2 MC10-16. All of the following statements concerning standard costs are correct except that
a. time and motion studies are often used to determine standard costs.
b. standard costs are usually set for one year.
c. standard costs can be used in costing inventory accounts.
d. standard costs are usually stated in total, while budgeted costs are usually stated on a per-unit basis.

LO10-3 MC10-17. Stevens Company manufactures electronic components used in automobile manufacturing. Each component uses two raw materials, Geo and Clio. Standard usage of the two materials required to produce one finished electronic component, as well as the current inventory, are shown below.

Material	Standard Per Unit	Price	Current Inventory
Geo	2.0 pounds	$15/lb.	5,000 pounds
Clio	1.5 pounds	$10/lb.	7,500 pounds

Stevens forecasts sales of 20,000 components for each of the next two production periods. Company policy dictates that 25% of the raw materials needed to produce the next period's projected sales be maintained in ending direct materials inventory.

Based on this information, the budgeted direct material purchases for the coming period would be

	Geo	Clio
a.	$450,000	$450,000
b.	$675,000	$300,000
c.	$675,000	$400,000
d.	$825,000	$450,000

LO10-3 MC10-18. MinnOil performs oil changes and other minor maintenance services (e.g., tire pressure checks) for cars. The company advertises that all services are completed within 15 minutes for each service. On a recent Saturday, 160 cars were serviced resulting in the following labor variances: rate, $19 unfavorable; efficiency, $14 favorable. If MinnOil's standard labor rate is $7 per hour, determine the actual wage rate per hour and the actual hours worked.

	Wage Rate	Hours Worked
a.	$6.55	42.00
b.	$6.67	42.71
c.	$7.45	42.00
d.	$7.50	38.00

LO10-4 MC10-19. Lee Manufacturing uses a standard cost system with overhead applied based on direct labor hours. The manufacturing budget for the production of 5,000 units for the month of June included 10,000 hours of direct labor at $15 per hour, $150,000. During June, 4,500 units were produced, using 9,600 direct labor hours, incurring $39,360 of variable overhead, and showing a variable overhead efficiency variance of $2,400 unfavorable. The standard variable overhead rate per direct labor hour was

Chapter 10 Flexible Budget, Standard Costing, and Variance Analysis

    a. $3.85.   *c.* $4.10.
    b. $4.00.   *d.* $6.00.

MC10-20. LaFlow Inc.'s account balances at year-end were as follows.   **LO10-5**

	Balances
Work in Process	$ 8,000
Finished Goods	16,000
Cost of Goods Sold	56,000
Total	$80,000

At year-end, the materials quantity variance is $4,000 U. How much of the variance would be allocated to Cost of Goods Sold if the variance is considered (1) significant or (2) insignificant?

    a. Significant: $4,000; Insignificant: $0.
    b. Significant: $3,200; Insignificant: $4,000.
    c. Significant: $4,000; Insignificant: $2,800.
    d. Significant: $2,800; Insignificant: $4,000.

MC10-21. Healthy Foods Inc. produces bags of organic dried mixed fruit of blueberries and mangos. Standard and actual information follow.   **LO10-6**

Standard quantities and cost per one pound bag	
Blueberries: 0.5 pound at $8 per pound	$4.00
Mangos: 0.5 pound at $6 per pound	$3.00

Actual quantities and cost for production of 7,200 bags
Blueberries: 4,000 pounds at $9 per pound
Mangos: 3,500 pounds at $5 per pound

What is the material yield variance?
    a. $2,600 F   *c.* $2,100 U
    b. $1,000 F   *d.* $1,050 U

MC10-22. Appendix; Which of the following statements regarding the use of a standard costing system in job order costing is not accurate?   **LO10-7**

    a. A standard costing system can only be used if jobs produce similar products.
    b. If a standard costing system is used, it must state all prices and quantities for material and labor at standard.
    c. Using standard costing means that unit costs of similar products will not fluctuate from job to job.
    d. Using a predetermined overhead rate is a type of standard.

MC10-23. Appendix; Assume the following amounts: **LO10-8**

Actual variable conversion cost	$294,000
Variable conversion rate × standard machine hours allowed	300,000
Variable conversion rate × actual machine hours	315,000

What is the variable conversion efficiency variance?
    a. $21,000 U   *c.* $15,000 F
    b. $21,000 F   *d.* $15,000 U

Exercises

E10-24. Flexible budget Tijuana Tile has gathered the following information on its utility cost for the past six months.   **LO10-1**

© Cambridge Business Publishers

Machine Hours	Utility Cost
1,300	$ 940
1,700	1,075
1,250	900
1,800	1,132
1,900	1,160
1,500	990

Prepare a flexible budget with separate variable and fixed categories for utility cost at 1,325, 1,500, and 1,675 machine hours.

LO10-1

E10-25. Flexible budget; variances; cost control The Sioux City Storage System's plant prepared the following flexible overhead budget for three levels of activity within the plant's relevant range.

	12,000 Units	16,000 Units	20,000 Units
Variable overhead	$48,000	$64,000	$ 80,000
Fixed overhead	32,000	32,000	32,000
Total overhead	$80,000	$96,000	$112,000

After discussion with the home office, the plant managers planned to produce 16,000 units of its single product during the year. However, demand for the product was exceptionally strong, and actual production for the year was 17,600 units. Actual variable and fixed overhead costs incurred in producing the 17,600 units were $69,000 and $32,800, respectively.

The production manager was upset because the company planned to incur $96,000 of costs and actual costs were $101,800. Prepare a memo to the production manager regarding the following questions.

a. Should the $101,800 actual total cost be compared to the $96,000 expected total cost for control purposes? Explain the rationale for your answer.

b. Analyze the costs and explain where the company did well or poorly in controlling its costs.

LO10-1

E10-26. Flexible budget Tom's Shoe Repair provides a variety of shoe repair services. Analysis of monthly costs revealed the following cost formulas when direct labor hours are used as the basis of cost determination:

Supplies	$y = \$0 + \$4.00X$
Production supervision and direct labor	$y = \$500 + \$7.00X$
Utilities	$y = \$350 + \$5.40X$
Rent	$y = \$450 + \$0.00X$
Advertising	$y = \$75 + \$0.00X$

a. Prepare a flexible budget at 250, 300, 350, and 400 direct labor hours.
b. Calculate a total cost per direct labor hour at each level of activity. Round amounts to two decimal places.

LO10-1

E10-27. Flexible budget

		Units		
	Rate per Unit	5,000	7,500	10,000
Direct material	a.	$20,000	b.	c.
Direct labor	d.	e.	11,250	f.
Variable overhead	$2	g.	h.	i.
Fixed overhead		j.	k.	l.
Total		m.	n.	$140,000

Required

Solve for items "a" through "n."

Chapter 10 Flexible Budget, Standard Costing, and Variance Analysis

E10-28. Terminology for a standard cost system Match each of the following terms *a* through *j* with the most appropriate description, 1 through 10. **LO10-1**

Terms
a. Appropriateness of a standard
b. Expected standard
c. Favorable variance
d. Ideal standard
e. Management-by-exception
f. Practical standard
g. Standard cost system
h. Standard
i. Unfavorable variance
j. Variance analysis

Description
1. ___ Standard costs or quantities were greater than actual
2. ___ Allows for a continual allocation of costs to products/services
3. ___ Investigation of variances outside of an acceptable limit
4. ___ Standard that is likely to reflect actual costs
5. ___ Classifies variances as favorable or unfavorable
6. ___ Standard that is unlikely to reflect actual costs
7. ___ Expected costs and quantities required to produce a product/service
8. ___ Reflects the relevance of factors used to determine the standard
9. ___ Standard that is likely to reflect actual costs, 60-70 percent of the time
10. ___ Standard costs or quantities were less than actual

E10-29. Cost control evaluation HardHead makes precast concrete steps for use with manufactured housing. The company had the following annual budget based on expected production of 6,400 units: **LO10-1**

	Standard Cost	Amount Budgeted
Direct material	$22.00	$140,800
Direct labor	12.00	76,800
Variable overhead		
Indirect material	4.20	26,880
Indirect labor	1.75	11,200
Utilities	1.00	6,400
Fixed overhead		
Supervisory salaries		80,000
Depreciation		30,000
Insurance		19,280
Total		$391,360

Cost per unit = $391,380 ÷ 6,400 = $61.15

Actual production was 7,000 units, and actual costs for the year were as follows:

Direct material used	$161,000
Direct labor	84,600
Variable overhead	
Indirect material	28,000
Indirect labor	13,300
Utilities	7,700
Fixed overhead	
Supervisory salaries	82,000
Depreciation	30,000
Insurance	17,600
Total	$424,200

Cost per unit = $424,200 ÷ 7,000 = $60.60

The plant manager, Tanzi Palate, whose annual bonus includes (among other factors) 20 percent of the net favorable cost variances, states that he saved the company $3,850 [($61.15 − $60.60) × 7,000]. He has instructed the plant cost accountant to prepare a detailed report to be sent to corporate headquarters comparing each component's actual per-unit cost with the per-unit amounts in the preceding annual budget to prove the $3,850 cost savings.

    a. Is the actual-to-budget comparison proposed by Palate appropriate? If his comparison is not appropriate, prepare a more appropriate comparison.
    b. How would you, as the plant cost accountant, react if Palate insisted on his comparison? Suggest what alternatives are available to you.

LO10-2 E10-30. **Behavioral implications of standard costing; research** Contact a local company that uses a standard cost system. Make an appointment with a manager at that company to interview her or him on the following issues.

- the characteristics that should be present in a standard cost system to encourage positive employee motivation
- how a standard cost system should be implemented to positively motivate employees
- the meaning of management by exception and how variance analysis often results in the use of this concept
- how employee behavior could be adversely affected when "actual to standard" comparisons are used as the basis for performance evaluation

Prepare a short report and an oral presentation based on your interview.

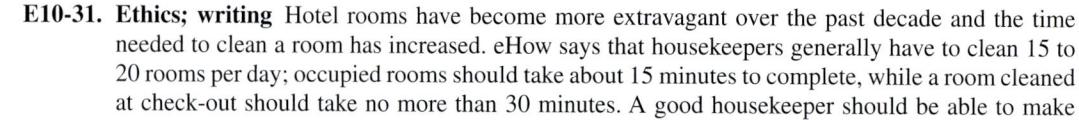

LO10-2 E10-31. **Ethics; writing** Hotel rooms have become more extravagant over the past decade and the time needed to clean a room has increased. eHow says that housekeepers generally have to clean 15 to 20 rooms per day; occupied rooms should take about 15 minutes to complete, while a room cleaned at check-out should take no more than 30 minutes. A good housekeeper should be able to make a bed in about one minute (http://www.ehow.com/about_4612024_hotel-housekeeping.html; last accessed 9/25/2023).

According to a study entitled "Creating Luxury, Enduring Pain" by Unite Here (the primary union representing hotel workers in the United States), housekeepers have the most dangerous jobs at hotels and have an injury rate of more than one in ten workers—almost twice that of other hotel employees. At one pricey hotel chain, it was estimated that a housekeeper who cleaned 15 rooms stripped approximately 500 pounds of soiled linens and replaced those with 500 pounds of clean linens . . . resulting in back and shoulder injuries, carpal tunnel syndrome, and bursitis.

Two articles relating to this situation are "New Study on Hotel Housekeeper Health and Safety," *Hotel News Resource* (April 25, 2006) (http://www.hotelnewsresource.com/article22006.html; last accessed 9/25/2023) and Frumin, Eric, et al. "Workload-Related Musculoskeletal Disorders among Hotel Housekeepers: Employer Records Reveal." (2006).

a. Why is it necessary for hotels to establish a standard for number of rooms to be cleaned by housekeepers?

b. The average annual wages of housekeepers is $31,920.[7] Assume that a large hotel chain is attempting to eliminate health-care benefits with a wage increase. Given the rate of job injuries, do you believe that the housekeepers are better off with the lower wage and health-care benefits or a higher wage and no health-care benefits? Explain.

c. In an eight-hour day (480 minutes), cleaning 15 rooms amounts to approximately 32 minutes per room. What makes it difficult for a housekeeper to strip and remake a bed, vacuum, lightly dust, and clean a bathroom in that period of time?

LO10-2 E10-32. **DL & OH; use of standard cost systems; ethics; writing** Many companies face the prospect of paying workers overtime wages; some of these payments are at time-and-a-half wages.

a. How does overtime pay affect direct labor cost? Variable overhead?

b. Obviously, paying overtime to already employed workers makes better financial business sense than does hiring additional workers. If workers would prefer not to work overtime but do so to maintain their jobs, how does overtime affect the ethical contract between employers and employees?

c. What effects might overtime have on job efficiency? On job effectiveness (such as quality of production)?

d. Would you be in favor of limiting allowable hours of overtime to have more individuals employed? Discuss this question from the standpoint of (1) the government, (2) the employer, (3) a currently employed worker, and (4) an unemployed individual.

LO10-2 E10-33. **Ethics; writing** Most hospitals are reimbursed according to diagnostic-related groups (DRGs). Each DRG has a specified standard "length of stay." If a patient leaves the hospital early, the hospital is financially impacted favorably, but a patient staying longer than the specified time costs the hospital money.

a. From the hospital administrator's point of view, would you want favorable length-of-stay variances? How might you try to obtain such variances?

---

[7] U.S Bureau of Labor Statistics, accessed 9/23/2023 at https://www.bls.gov/oes/current/oes372012.htm.

Chapter 10 Flexible Budget, Standard Costing, and Variance Analysis

    b. From a patient's point of view, would you want favorable length-of-stay variances? Answer this question from the point of view of (1) a patient who has had minor surgery and (2) a patient who has had major surgery.

    c. Would favorable length-of-stay variances necessarily equate to high-quality care?

E10-34. Standard setting; team project As a three-person team, choose an activity that is commonly performed every day, such as taking a shower/bath, preparing a meal, or doing homework. Have each team member time him- or herself performing that activity for two days and then develop a standard time for the team. Now have the team members time themselves performing the same activity for the next five days. **LO10-2**

    a. Using an assumed hourly wage rate of $16, calculate the labor efficiency variance for your team.

    b. Prepare a list of reasons for the variance.

    c. How could some of the variance have been avoided?

E10-35. Developing standard cost card One of Sure-Bet Sherbet's bestselling products is raspberry sherbet, which is manufactured in 10-gallon batches. Each batch requires six quarts of raspberries. The raspberries are sorted by hand before entering the production process, and because of imperfections, one quart of berries is discarded for every four quarts of acceptable berries. The standard direct labor sorting time to obtain one quart of acceptable raspberries is three minutes. After sorting, raspberries are blended with other ingredients; blending requires 12 minutes of direct labor time per batch. During the blending process, some sherbet is lost because it adheres to the blending vats. After blending, the sherbet is packaged in quart containers. The following cost information is relevant: **LO10-2**

- Raspberries are purchased for $0.80 per quart.
- All other ingredients cost a total of $0.45 per gallon.
- Direct labor is paid $9.00 per hour.
- The total cost of material and labor required to package the sherbet is $0.38 per quart of sherbet.

Develop the standard cost for the direct cost components of a 10-gallon batch of raspberry sherbet. The standard cost should identify standard quantity, standard price/rate, and standard cost per batch for each direct cost component.

E10-36. Standard cost card Cyclers Inc. manufactures vehicle bike racks and summarized the following information in order to develop standard costs for its bike rack. **LO10-2**

Direct Material Component	Quantity	Unit Cost
WF 05....................	1	$20.00
WR 05....................	1	25.00
B 05	2	10.00
HB 05	1	23.00
B 21	16	0.75
S 18	12	1.25
SP 05	1	17.00

Direct Labor Component	Hours	Rate
Painting..................	1.0	$15.00
Assembling...............	2.0	25.00
Testing	1.0	18.00
Packaging................	0.5	15.00

Variable overhead is applied at $22 per direct labor hour.
Fixed overhead is applied at $15 per direct labor hour.

    a. What is the standard cost of one bike rack?

    b. What is the standard quantity allowed for 500 bike racks for each of the following:
        1. Component B 05
        2. Component S 18
        3. Painting direct labor hours
        4. Assembling direct labor hours

    c. How can the standard cost estimated in part *a* be useful in operational decision making?

LO10-3 **E10-37. DM variances** In November, DayTime Publishing Company's costs and quantities of paper consumed in manufacturing its annual collegiate calendar were as follows:

Actual unit purchase price	$0.13 per page
Standard unit price	$0.14 per page
Standard quantity for good production	97,900 pages
Actual quantity purchased during November	115,000 pages
Actual quantity used in November	100,000 pages

    a. Calculate the total cost of purchases for November.
    b. Compute the material price variance (based on quantity purchased).
    c. Calculate the material quantity variance.

LO10-3 **E10-38. DM variances; journal entries** Skip Company produces a product called Lem. The standard direct material cost to produce one unit of Lem is four quarts of raw material at $2.50 per quart. During May, 4,200 quarts of raw material were purchased at a cost of $10,080. All the purchased material was used to produce 1,000 units of Lem.

    a. Compute the actual cost per quart and the material price variance for May.
    b. Assume the same facts except that Skip Company purchased 6,000 quarts of material at the previously calculated cost per quart, but used only 4,200 quarts. Compute the material price variance and material quantity variance for May, assuming that Skip identifies variances at the earliest possible time.
    c. Prepare the journal entries to record the material price and usage variances calculated in (b).
    d. Which managers at Skip Company would most likely assume responsibility for control of the variance computed in requirement (b)?

CPA ADAPTED

LO10-3 **E10-39. DM variances** Bell Inc. manufactures a product that requires five pounds of material. The purchasing agent has an opportunity to purchase the necessary material at a vendor's bankruptcy sale at $1.40 per pound rather than the standard cost of $2.10 per pound. The purchasing agent purchases 100,000 pounds of material on May 31. During the next four months, the company's production and material usage was as follows:

	Production	Quantity Used
June	3,000	16,400 lbs.
July	3,400	17,640 lbs.
August	2,900	14,950 lbs.
September	2,500	13,100 lbs.

    a. What is the material price variance for this purchase?
    b. What is the material quantity variance for each month for this material?
    c. What might be the cause of the unfavorable material quantity variances?

LO10-3 **E10-40. DM variances** McHenry Corp. makes wrought iron garden sculptures. During April, the purchasing agent bought 25,600 pounds of scrap iron at $0.64 per pound. During the month, 21,400 pounds of scrap iron were used to produce 600 sculptures. Although each sculpture is slightly different, McHenry uses a standard quantity per sculpture of 35 pounds of scrap iron at a standard cost of $0.70 per pound.

    a. For April, compute the direct material price variance (based on the quantity purchased) and the direct material quantity variance (based on quantity used).
    b. Identify the titles of individuals in the firm who would be responsible for each of the variances.
    c. Provide some possible explanations for the variances computed in (a).

LO10-3 **E10-41. Causes of DM and DL variances** Refer to the information in E10-35 to answer the following questions.

    a. Discuss the possible causes of unfavorable material price variances, and identify the individual(s) who should be held responsible for these variances.
    b. Discuss the possible causes of unfavorable labor efficiency variances, and identify the individual(s) who should be held responsible for these variances.

LO10-3 **E10-42. DL variances** Logen Construction builds standard prefabricated wooden frames for walls. Each frame requires five direct labor hours and the standard hourly direct labor rate is $18. During July, the company produced 670 frames and worked 3,310 direct labor hours. Payroll records indicate that workers earned $60,407.50.

Chapter 10 Flexible Budget, Standard Costing, and Variance Analysis

a. What were the standard hours for July production?
b. What was the actual hourly wage rate?
c. Calculate the direct labor variances.

E10-43. DL variances; journal entries Information on Hanley's direct labor costs for January is as follows:

Actual direct labor rate	$7.50
Standard direct labor hours allowed	9,000
Actual direct labor hours	10,000
Labor rate variance	$5,500 F

a. Compute the standard direct labor rate in January.
b. Compute the labor efficiency variance in January.
c. Prepare the journal entry to accrue direct labor cost and to record the labor variances for January.

CPA ADAPTED

E10-44. DL variances; journal entries Calista & Lane, CPAs, set the following standard for its inventory audit of Triumph Co.: 350 hours at an average hourly rate of $250. The firm actually worked 330 hours during the inventory audit process. The total labor variance for the audit was $3,500 unfavorable.

a. Compute the total actual payroll.
b. Compute the labor efficiency variance.
c. Compute the labor rate variance.
d. Prepare the entry to assign labor costs to inventory, record the labor variances, and accrue payroll costs.
e. Provide a brief explanation of these variances that is consistent with the labor rate and efficiency variances.

E10-45. Missing information for DL For each independent case, fill in the missing figures.

	Case A	Case B	Case C	Case D
Units produced	1,000	?	240	1,500
Standard hours per unit	3.5	0.9	?	?
Standard hours	?	900	600	?
Standard rate per hour	$ 7.25	?	$10.50	$ 7.00
Actual hours worked	3,400	975	?	4,900
Actual labor cost	?	?	$6,180	$31,850
Labor rate variance	$850 F	$975 F	$300 U	?
Labor efficiency variance	?	$765 U	?	$2,800 U

E10-46. DM & DL variances; journal entries In July, Zinger Corp. purchased 20,000 gallons of Numerol for $61,000 to use in the production of product #43MR7. During July, Zinger Corp. manufactured 3,900 units of product #43MR7. The following information is available about standard and actual quantities and costs:

	Standard for One Unit	Actual Usage for July
Direct material	4.8 gallons @ $3 per gallon	18,350 gallons
Direct labor	20 minutes @ $9 per DLH	1,290 DLHs @ $9.02 per DLH

a. Compute the material purchase price variance and the material quantity variance.
b. Compute the labor rate, labor efficiency, and total labor variance.
c. Prepare the journal entries for the material and labor variances.
d. Assume instead that the total labor variance for the period was zero. Does that mean that there were no labor variances?

E10-47. DM & DL variances; journal entries Madzinga's Draperies manufactures curtains. Curtain #4571 requires the following:

Direct material standard	10 square yards at $5 per yard
Direct labor standard	5 hours at $10 per hour

During the second quarter, the company purchased 17,000 square yards at a cost of $83,300 and used 16,500 square yards to produce 1,500 Curtain #4571s. Direct labor totaled 7,600 hours for $79,800.

a. Compute the material price and usage variances.
b. Prepare the journal entries for the purchase and use of direct material.
c. Compute labor rate and labor efficiency variances.
d. Prepare the journal entry to accrue direct labor cost and record the labor variances for the quarter.
e. Comment on the above variances. Identify possible causes and relationships among the variances that you computed.

CPA ADAPTED

LO10-3, 5

E10-48. DM & DL variances Green Tee produces 100 percent cotton t-shirts, with the following standard direct material and labor quantities and costs:

Direct material	2.0 yards × $3.00
Direct labor	0.7 hour × $7.50

Actual September production and costs for the company to produce 10,000 t-shirts were as follows:

	Quantity	Cost
Direct material		
Purchased	30,000 yards	$89,700
Requisitioned into production	20,120 yards	
Direct labor	7,940 hours	58,756

a. What is the standard quantity of material and the standard labor time for September's production?
b. Compute the direct material and direct labor variances.
c. How might the sales and production managers explain the direct material variances?
d. How might the production and human resources managers explain the direct labor variances?
e. Record the year-end adjusting entry to close the material and labor variances, assuming that they are insignificant.

LO10-3

E10-49. DM & DL variances In December, Sam Antari, president of Antari Inc., received the following information from Denise Sweet, the new controller, in regard to November production of travel bags:

November production	4,800 bags
Actual cost of material purchased and used	$14,550
Standard material allowed	0.5 square yard per bag
Material quantity variance	$600 U
Standard price per yard of material	$6
Actual hours worked	9,760 hours
Standard labor time per bag	2 hours
Labor rate variance	$1,464 F
Standard labor rate per hour	$17

Antari asked Sweet to provide the following information:

a. Standard quantity of material allowed for November production
b. Standard direct labor hours allowed for November production
c. Material price variance
d. Labor efficiency variance
e. Standard prime (direct material and direct labor) cost to produce one travel bag
f. Actual cost to produce one travel bag in November
g. An explanation for the difference between standard and actual cost; be sure that the explanation is consistent with the pattern of the variances

LO10-4

E10-50. OH variances Nelson Co. manufactures a product that requires 3.5 machine hours per unit. The variable and fixed overhead rates were computed using expected capacity of 144,000 units (produced evenly throughout the year) and expected variable and fixed overhead costs, respectively, of

$2,016,000 and $3,528,000. In October, Nelson manufactured 11,900 units using 41,800 machine hours. October variable overhead costs were $165,000; fixed overhead costs were $294,500.

a. What are the standard variable and fixed overhead rates?
b. Compute the variable overhead variances.
c. Compute the fixed overhead variances.
d. Explain the volume variance computed in (c).

E10-51. OH variances Sari Inc. has a fully automated production facility in which almost 97 percent of overhead costs are driven by machine hours. As the company's cost accountant, you have computed the following overhead variances for May:

Variable overhead spending variance............	$34,000 F
Variable overhead efficiency variance	41,200 F
Fixed overhead spending variance.............	28,000 U
Fixed overhead volume variance	20,000 U

The company's president is concerned about the variance amounts and has asked you to show her how the variances were computed and to answer several questions. Budgeted fixed overhead for the month is $1,000,000; the predetermined variable and fixed overhead rates are, respectively, $20 and $40 per machine hour. Budgeted capacity is 20,000 units.

a. Using the four-variance approach, prepare an overhead analysis in as much detail as possible.
b. What is the standard number of machine hours allowed for each unit of output?
c. How many actual hours were worked in May?
d. What is the total spending variance?
e. What additional information about the manufacturing overhead variances is gained by inserting detailed computations into the variable and fixed manufacturing overhead variance analysis?
f. How would the overhead variances be closed if the three-variance approach were used and the variances are considered insignificant?

E10-52. OH variances The manager of a vehicle warranty service provider has determined that it typically takes 30 minutes for the department's employees to register a new car for warranty coverage. The predetermined fixed overhead rate was computed on an estimated 10,000 direct labor hours per month and is $9 per direct labor hour, whereas the predetermined variable overhead rate is $3 per direct labor hour.

During July, 18,800 cars were registered and 9,500 direct labor hours were worked in registering those vehicles. For the month, variable overhead was $27,700 and fixed overhead was $90,800.

a. Compute overhead variances using a four-variance approach.
b. Compute overhead variances using a three-variance approach.
c. Compute overhead variances using a two-variance approach.

E10-53. Four OH variances; journal entries Kemp Manufacturing set 70,000 direct labor hours as the annual capacity measure for computing its predetermined variable overhead rate. At that level, budgeted variable overhead costs are $315,000. Kemp will apply budgeted fixed overhead of $140,400 on the basis of 3,900 budgeted machine hours for the year. Both machine hours and fixed overhead costs are expected to be incurred evenly each month.

During March, Kemp incurred 5,900 direct labor hours and 300 machine hours. Actual variable and fixed overhead were $26,325 and $11,400, respectively. The standard times allowed for March production were 5,980 direct labor hours and 290 machine hours.

a. Using the four-variance approach, determine the overhead variances for March.
b. Prepare all journal entries related to overhead for Kemp Manufacturing for March.

E10-54. Three OH variances Berlin Ltd. uses a combined overhead rate of $2.90 per machine hour to apply overhead to products. The rate was developed at an annual expected capacity of 264,000 machine hours; each unit of product requires two machine hours to produce. At 264,000 machine hours, expected fixed overhead for Munich Ltd. is $250,800.

During November, the company produced 11,960 units and used 24,700 machine hours. Actual variable overhead for the month was $47,100 and fixed overhead was $20,000.

Calculate the overhead spending, efficiency, and volume variances for November.

LO10-4 **E10-55. Missing data; three OH variances** Li Corporation's flexible budget formula for total overhead is $360,000 plus $8 per direct labor hour. The combined overhead rate is $20 per direct labor hour. The following data have been recorded for the year.

Actual total overhead	$580,000
Total overhead spending variance	16,000 F
Volume variance	24,000 U

Use a three-variance approach to determine the following:

a. Standard hours for actual production
b. Actual direct labor hours worked

LO10-4 **E10-56. OH variances** KrisKross Inc.'s total predetermined overhead rate is $50 per hour based on a monthly capacity of 59,400 machine hours. Overhead is 30 percent variable and 70 percent fixed.

During September, KrisKross produced 5,100 units of product and recorded 60,000 machine hours. September's actual overhead cost was $2,927,000. Each unit of product requires 12 machine hours.

a. What were standard hours for September?
b. What is total monthly budgeted fixed overhead cost?
c. What is the controllable overhead variance?
d. What is the noncontrollable overhead variance?

LO10-5 **E10-57. Variance journal entries** At year-end, the trial balance of Pennopscott Corp. showed the following accounts and amounts:

	Debit	Credit
Raw Material Inventory	$ 73,200	
Work in Process Inventory	87,840	
Finished Goods Inventory	131,760	
Cost of Goods Sold	1,171,200	
Material Price Variance	14,500	
Material Quantity Variance		$21,930
Labor Rate Variance		2,200
Labor Efficiency Variance	8,780	

Assume that, taken together, the variances are believed to be significant. Prepare the journal entries to close the variances at year-end. Round any necessary calculations to one decimal point.

LO10-6 **E10-58. Mix and yield variances** Hennessey Company produces 12-ounce cans of mixed pecans and cashews. Standard and actual information follows.

Standard Quantities and Costs (12-oz. can)	
Pecans: 6 ounces at $6.00 per pound	$2.25
Cashews: 6 ounces at $8.00 per pound	3.00

Actual Quantities and Costs for Production of 36,000 Cans
Pecans: 15,554 pounds at $5.80 per pound
Cashews: 12,726 pounds at $8.50 per pound

Determine the material price, mix, and yield variances.

LO10-6 **E10-59. Mix and yield variances** Coffen Corp. employs engineers and draftspeople. The average hourly rates are $60 for engineers and $30 for draftspeople. For one project, the standard was set at 400 hours of engineer time and 600 hours of draftsperson time. Actual hours worked on this project were:

Engineers—500 hours at $65 per hour
Draftspeople—500 hours at $32 per hour

Determine the labor rate, mix, and yield variances for this project.

Chapter 10 Flexible Budget, Standard Costing, and Variance Analysis

E10-60. Mix and yield variances Taglia Law Office has three labor classes: administrative assistants, paralegals, and attorneys. Standard wage rates are as follows: administrative assistants, $30 per hour; paralegals, $60 per hour; and attorneys, $125 per hour. For October, the numbers of actual direct labor hours worked and of standard hours for probate cases were as follows:

	Actual DLHs	Number of Standard Hours Allowed
Administrative assistant	900	1,008
Paralegal	2,520	2,772
Attorney	1,500	1,260

    a. Calculate October's direct labor efficiency variance as well as the direct labor mix variance and the direct labor yield variance.
    b. Discuss whether management used an efficient mix of labor.

E10-61. Appendix; Standard costing; writing Routine maintenance services are provided by Latamore Industries to oil and gas firms in their production facilities. Although many of the client services are relatively unique, some services are repetitive. The firm individually negotiates prices with each client. The CFO of Latamore Industries recently examined the profitability of a sample of the firm's service contracts and was surprised that contract profit amounts varied significantly. Additionally, production inputs (such as material and labor) often varied substantially from those budgeted at the time the service contracts were negotiated. The CFO has asked you, as a company intern, to write a memo describing how the adoption of standard costing could improve cost control and profit management for the firm's service contracts.

E10-62. Appendix; Standard costing Weingold Inc. engages in routine and customer print jobs for customers. In November, a client specified the use of one of the company's standard papers for a large job, but asked for a high level of customization relative to the print design. Thus, standard costs could be used for direct material but not for labor. The following DM costs were incurred for the client's job:

Actual unit purchase price	$0.032 per sheet
Standard unit price	$0.036 per sheet
Quantity purchased and used in November	980,000 sheets
Standard quantity allowed for good production	984,000 sheets

Calculate the material price variance and the material quantity variance for the client's job.

E10-63. Appendix; Standard costing Harvey Inc. uses a standard cost system for labor. Standard costs for material cannot be used because customers require unique materials and all jobs are different sizes. One of the company's jobs experienced the following results related to DL in December:

Actual hours worked	9,000
Standard hours for production	8,600
Actual direct labor rate	$9.65
Standard direct labor rate	$9.85

    a. Calculate the total actual payroll.
    b. Determine the labor rate variance.
    c. Determine the labor efficiency variance.
    d. What concerns do you have about the variances in (*b*) and (*c*)?

E10-64. Appendix; Variances and conversion cost category Auto Brakes Inc. manufactures brake rotors and has always applied overhead to production using direct labor hours. Recently, company facilities were automated, and the accounting system was revised to show only two cost categories: direct material and conversion. Estimated variable and fixed conversion costs for the current month were $170,000 and $76,000, respectively. Expected output for the current month was 5,000 rotors, and the estimated number of machine hours was 10,000. During July, the firm actually used 9,000 machine hours to make 4,800 rotors while incurring $228,000 of conversion costs. Of this amount, $150,000 was variable cost.

    a. Using the four-variance approach, compute the variances for conversion costs.
    b. Evaluate the effectiveness of the firm in controlling the current month's costs.

LO10-8 **E10-65. Appendix; Variances and conversion cost category** Svenson Technology considers direct labor cost too insignificant to separately account for and, therefore, uses a $22.50 per machine hour predetermined conversion cost rate (of which $16 is related to fixed overhead costs). The conversion rate was established based on expected capacity of 1,008,600 machine hours. One of Svenson Technology's products requires 4.1 machine hours to manufacture.

In September, the company manufactured 21,000 units of product and used 83,000 machine hours and 840 direct labor hours. Variable and fixed conversion costs incurred for September were $551,230 and $1,330,000, respectively.

a. What is the expected capacity per month in units and machine hours?
b. Prepare a four- and three-variance analysis of conversion costs for September.

Problems

LO10-1 **P10-66. Flexible budget** Flexible budgets; predetermined OH rates The Splash makes large fiberglass swimming pools and uses machine hours and direct labor hours to apply overhead in the Production and Installation departments, respectively. The monthly cost formula for overhead in Production is y = $7,950 + $4.05 MH; the overhead cost formula in Installation is y = $6,150 + $14.25 DLH. These formulas are valid for a relevant range of activity up to 6,000 machine hours in Production and 9,000 direct labor hours in Installation.

Each pool is estimated to require 25 machine hours in Production and 60 hours of direct labor in Installation. Expected capacity for the year is 120 pools.

a. Prepare a flexible budget for Production at possible annual capacities of 2,500, 3,000, and 3,500 machine hours. Prepare a flexible budget for Installation at possible annual capacities of 6,000, 7,000, and 8,000 machine hours.
b. Prepare a budget for next month's variable, fixed, and total overhead costs for each department assuming that expected production is eight pools.
c. Calculate the total overhead cost to be applied to each pool scheduled for production in the coming month if expected capacity is used to calculate the predetermined OH rates.

LO10-1 **P10-67. Flexible budget; multiple product performance report** Case Products manufactures two models of storage cases: regular and deluxe. Presented is standard cost information for each model:

Cost Components for a Pack	Regular			Deluxe		
Direct materials						
Acrylic sheets	3 sheets × $12	=	$36.00	5 sheets × $12	=	$60.00
Assembly kit		=	5.00		=	5.00
Direct labor	0.5 hour × $20	=	10.00	0.75 hour × $20	=	15.00
Variable overhead	0.5 labor hr. × $5	=	2.50	0.75 labor hr. × $5	=	3.75
Total			$53.50			$83.75

Budgeted fixed manufacturing overhead is $46,000 per month. During July, the company produced 8,000 regular and 3,500 deluxe storage cases while incurring the following manufacturing costs:

Direct materials	$561,300
Direct labor	130,800
Variable overhead	34,625
Fixed overhead	48,150
Total	$774,875

Required
Prepare a flexible budget performance report for the July manufacturing activities.

LO10-1 **P10-68. Flexible budget and performance evaluation** Kathy Vanderbosch, supervisor of housecleaning for Hotel Valhalla, was surprised by her summary performance report for March given below.

Chapter 10 Flexible Budget, Standard Costing, and Variance Analysis

	HOTEL VALHALLA Housekeeping Performance Report For the Month of March		
Actual	Budget	Variance	%Variance
$260,708	$252,000	$8,708 U	3.456% U

Kathy was disappointed. She thought she had done a good job controlling housekeeping labor and towel usage, but her performance report revealed an unfavorable variance of $8,708. She had been hoping for a bonus for her good work, but now expected a series of questions from her manager.

The cost budget for housekeeping is based on standard costs. At the beginning of a month, Kathy receives a report from Hotel Valhalla's Sales Department outlining the planned room activity for the month. Kathy then schedules labor and purchases using this information. The budget for the housekeeping was based on 8,000 room nights. Each room night is budgeted based on the following standards for various materials, labor, and overhead.

Shower supplies	4 bottles @ $0.50 each
Towels*	1 @ $4.00
Laundry	8 lbs. @ $0.25 a lb.
Labor	¾ hour @ $15.00 an hour
VOH	$3.00 per labor hour
FOH	$10 a room night (based on 8,000 room nights)

*Replacements for towels evaluated by housekeeping as inappropriate for cleaning and reuse.

With 8,600 room nights sold, actual costs and usage for housekeeping during April were

$14,620 for 36,550 bottles of shower supplies.
$32,121 for 7,740 towels.
$20,898 for 69,660 lbs. of laundry.
$91,504 for 6,020 labor hours.
$19,565 in total VOH.
$82,000 in FOH.

REQUIRED

a. Develop a complete budget column for the above performance report presented to Kathy. Break it down by expense category. The following format, with additional lines for expense categories, is suggested.

Account	Actual	Budget	Variance
Shower Supplies.	$ 14,620	?	?
⋮	⋮	⋮	⋮
Total	$260,708	$252,000	$8,708 U

b. Evaluate the usefulness of the cost center performance report presented to Kathy.
c. Prepare a more logical performance report where standard allowed is based on actual output. Also, split each variance into its price/rate/spending and quantity/efficiency components (except fixed of course). The following format, with additional lines for expense categories, is suggested.

Account	Actual	Flexible Budget	Total Variance	Price/Rate/Spending Variance	Quantity/Efficiency Variance
Shower Supplies.	$ 14,620	?	?	?	?
⋮	⋮	⋮	⋮		
Total	$260,708	?	?		

d. Explain to Kathy's boss what your report suggests about Kathy's department performance.
e. Identify additional nonfinancial performance measures management might consider when evaluating the performance of the housekeeping department and Kathy as a manager.

LO10-3 **P10-69. DM & DL variances; journal entries** Schmidt Co. has the following standard material and labor quantities and costs for one unit of Product SWK#468:

Material.......	1.85 pounds @ $3.50 per pound
Labor	0.04 hour @ $12 per hour

During July, the purchasing agent found a "good deal" on the raw material needed for Product SWK#468 and bought 100,000 pounds of material at $3.15 per pound. In July, the company produced 48,000 units of Product SWK#468 with the following material and labor usage:

Material.......	95,000 pounds
Labor	2,200 hours @ $12.10 (due to a renegotiated labor contract)

    a. What is the standard quantity of material and the standard labor time for July?
    b. Calculate the material and labor variances for July.
    c. Prepare the material and labor journal entries for July.
    d. Did the purchasing agent make a "good deal" on the raw material? Explain.

LO10-3 **P10-70. DM & DL variances; journal entries** Triscuit-Biscuit Corp. makes small plastic dog toys with the following material and labor standards:

	Standard Quantity	Standard Cost
Material.......	0.25 pound	$3.00 per pound
Labor	3 minutes	9.00 per hour

During October, 60,000 pounds of material were acquired on account at $3.08 per pound. During October, 24,800 pounds of that were used in production during the month to make 100,000 toys. Factory payroll for October showed 5,320 direct labor hours at a total cost of $46,816.

    a. Compute material and labor variances, basing the material price variance on the quantity of material purchased.
    b. Assuming a perpetual inventory system is used, prepare the relevant general journal entries for October.

LO10-3 **P10-71. DM & DL variances** Aquatica uses a standard cost system for materials and labor in producing small fishing boats. Production requires three materials: fiberglass, paint, and a purchased trim package. The standard costs and quantities for materials and labor are as follows:

Standards for One Fishing Boat	
2,000 pounds of fiberglass × $1.80 per pound............	$3,600
6 quarts gel coat paint × $15.00 per quart...............	90
1 trim package	200
40 hours of labor × $25.00 per hour...................	1,000
Standard cost for DM and DL.........................	$4,890

The following actual data related to the production of 600 boats was recorded for July:

Material Purchased on Account
Fiberglass—2,100,000 pounds × $1.83 per pound
Paint—1,000 gallons × $55.50 per gallon
Trim packages—640 × $205 per package

Material Used
Fiberglass—1,380,000 pounds
Paint—924 gallons
Trim packages—608

Direct Labor Used
23,850 hours × $23.50 per hour

Chapter 10 Flexible Budget, Standard Costing, and Variance Analysis

Calculate the material and labor variances for Aquatica for July. The material price variance should be computed for each type of material and on the quantity of material purchased.

P10-72. Incomplete data; variances; journal entries Surgical Products produces latex surgical gloves. Machines perform the majority of the processing for 1,000 pairs of gloves per hour. Each pair of gloves requires 0.85 square foot of latex, which has a standard price of $0.80 per square foot. Machine operators are considered direct labor and are paid $15 per hour.

LO10-3

During one week in May, Surgical Products produced 300,000 pairs of gloves and experienced a $1,440 unfavorable material quantity variance. The company had purchased 2,500 more square feet of material than had been used in production that week. The unfavorable material price variance for the week was $5,186. A $288 unfavorable total labor variance was generated based on 315 total actual labor hours to produce the gloves.

a. Determine the following amounts:
  (1) Standard quantity of material for production achieved
  (2) Actual quantity of material used
  (3) Actual quantity of material purchased
  (4) Actual price of material purchased
  (5) Standard hours for actual production
  (6) Labor efficiency variance
  (7) Labor rate variance
  (8) Actual labor rate
b. Prepare the journal entries for the above information.

P10-73. Incomplete data; variances Quinan Carpentry Co. makes wooden shelves. A small fire on October 1 partially destroyed the records relating to September's production. The charred remains of the standard cost card appear here.

LO10-3

	Standard Quantity	Standard Price
Direct material	3.1 board feet	
Direct labor		$9.80 per hour

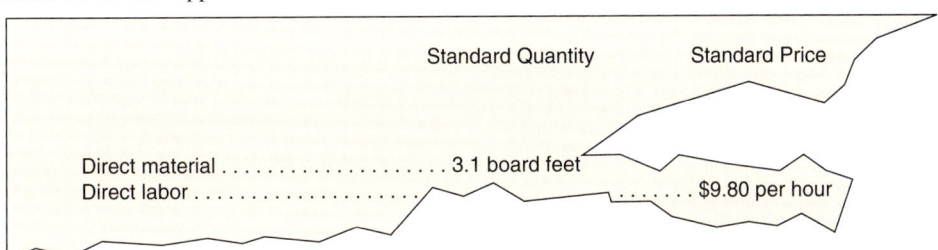

From other fragments of records and several discussions with employees, you learn the following:

- The purchasing agent's files showed that 50,000 board feet had been purchased on account in September at $1.05 per board foot. He was proud of the fact that this price was $0.05 below standard cost per foot.
- There was no beginning inventory of raw material on September 1, and since the raw material storage location is apart from the production facility, the fire caused no damage to the remaining raw material. Fourteen hundred board feet of raw material were on hand on October 1.
- The standard quantity of material allowed for September's production was 49,600 board feet.
- The September payroll for direct labor was $39,494 based on 4,030 actual hours worked.
- The production supervisor distinctly remembered being held accountable for 30 more hours of direct labor than should have been worked. She was upset because top management failed to consider that she saved hundreds of board feet of material by creative efforts that required extra time.

a. How many units were produced during September?
b. Calculate direct material variances for September.
c. What is the standard number of hours allowed for the production of each unit?
d. Calculate all direct labor variances for September.
e. Prepare general journal entries reflecting direct material and direct labor activity and variances for September, assuming a standard cost, perpetual inventory system.

P10-74. Adjusting standards ALOHA Corp., started in January 2007, manufactures Hawaiian muumuus. At that time, the following material and labor standards were developed:

LO10-3

Material	3.0 yards at $4 per yard
Labor	1.5 hours at $6 per hour

© Cambridge Business Publishers

In January, ALOHA Corp. hired a new cost accountant, Anulu Haoki. At the end of the month, Haoki was reviewing the production variances and was amazed to find that the company's material and labor standards had never been revised. Actual material and labor data for January, when 17,200 muumuus were produced, follow.

Material.	Purchased, 50,000 yards at $4.90
	Used 50,000 yards
Labor	17,800 hours at $9.05 per hour

Material prices have risen 4 percent each year beginning six years ago through the prior year), but the company can now buy at 95 percent of regular price due to increased purchase volume. Also, direct material waste has been reduced from 1/4 yard to 1/8 yard per muumuu; waste has always been included in the standard material quantity. Beginning six years ago, each annual labor contract has specified a 7 percent cost-of-living adjustment. Revision of the plant layout and acquisition of more efficient machinery has decreased the labor time per muumuu by one-third since the company began.

a. Determine the material and labor variances based on the company's original standards.
b. Determine the new standards against which Haoki should measure the January results. (Round adjustments annually to the nearest cent.)
c. Compute the variances for material and labor using the revised standards.

P10-75. OH variances Pier Corp. has an expected monthly capacity of 9,000 units but only 5,700 units were produced and 6,000 direct labor hours were used during August due to a flood in the manufacturing facility. Actual variable overhead for August was $48,165, and actual fixed overhead was $140,220.

Standard cost data follow:

	Standard Cost per Unit (One Unit Takes One Labor Hour)
Direct material	$ 9.00
Direct labor.	15.00
Variable overhead.	8.00
Fixed overhead.	16.00
Total	$48.00

a. Compute and compare the actual overhead cost per unit with the expected overhead cost per unit.
b. Calculate overhead variances using the four-variance method.
c. Explain why the volume variance is so large.

P10-76. OH variances; journal entries N Joy makes wooden picnic tables, swings, and benches. Standard hours for each product are as follows:

Picnic table	10 standard direct labor hours
Swing	3 standard direct labor hours
Bench	7 standard direct labor hours

The standard variable overhead rate is $4 per direct labor hour. The standard fixed overhead rate, computed using an expected annual capacity of 36,000 direct labor hours, is $2 per direct labor hour. The company estimates stable fixed overhead costs and direct labor hours each month of the annual period. March production was 100 picnic tables, 400 swings, and 60 benches; production required 2,780 actual direct labor hours. Actual variable and fixed overhead for March were $12,800 and $5,900, respectively.

a. Prepare a variance analysis using the four-variance approach. (Hint: Convert the production of each type of product into standard hours for all work accomplished for the month.)
b. Prepare journal entries to record actual overhead costs, application of overhead to production, and closing of the overhead variance accounts (assuming those variances are immaterial).
c. Evaluate the effectiveness of the managers in controlling costs.

Chapter 10 Flexible Budget, Standard Costing, and Variance Analysis

P10-77. OH variances with unknowns During December, Amin Corp. manufactured products requiring 8,000 standard labor hours. The following variance and actual information is available: LO10-4

Labor rate variance...................	$ 4,500 U
Labor efficiency variance	12,000 U
Actual variable overhead	162,000
Actual fixed overhead..................	84,000

Amin Corp.'s standard costs for labor and overhead were set at the beginning of the year and have remained constant through the year as follows:

Direct labor (4 hours × $12 per hour)................	$ 48
Factory overhead (10,000 DLHs expected capacity)	
Variable (4 hours × $16 per direct labor hour).........	64
Fixed (4 hours × $9 per direct labor hour)............	36
Total unit conversion cost...........................	$148

Calculate the following unknown amounts:

a. Number of units manufactured
b. Total applied factory overhead
c. Volume variance
d. Variable overhead spending variance
e. Variable overhead efficiency variance
f. Total actual overhead

P10-78. One-, two-, and three-variance approaches to OH variances Terkelsen Mfg. produces comforter sets with the following standard cost information: LO10-4

- Each comforter set requires 0.5 hours of machine time to produce.
- Variable overhead is applied at the rate of $9 per machine hour.
- Fixed overhead is applied at the rate of $6 per machine hour, based on an expected annual capacity of 30,000 machine hours.

Production Statistics for the year	
Number of comforter sets produced.............	62,000 units
Actual number of machine hours	33,300 hours
Variable overhead cost incurred.................	$265,400
Fixed overhead cost incurred...................	$177,250

a. Calculate variances using the one-variance approach.
b. Calculate variances using the two-variance approach.
c. Calculate variances using the three-variance approach.

P10-79. Comprehensive OH variances For the year, Riguilio Inc. set predetermined variable and fixed overhead rates, respectively, at $6.50 and $9.35 based on an expected monthly capacity of 4,000 machine hours. Each unit of product requires 1.25 machine hours.   LO10-4

During August, the company produced 3,360 units and incurred $27,000 of variable overhead costs and $41,400 of fixed overhead costs. The firm used 4,100 machine hours during August.

a. Using separate overhead rates, calculate overhead variances using the four-variance approach.
b. Using a combined overhead rate, calculate variances using the three-variance approach.
c. Using a combined overhead rate, calculate variances using the two-variance approach.
d. Using a combined overhead rate, calculate variances using the one-variance approach.

P10-80. Comprehensive Piedmont Manufacturing produces metal products with the following standard quantity and cost information: LO10-3, 4

Direct Material		
Aluminum	4 sheets @ $4	$ 16
Copper	3 sheets @ $8	24
Direct labor	7 hours @ $16	112
Variable overhead	5 machine hours @ $6	30
Fixed overhead	5 machine hours @ $4	20

Overhead rates were based on normal monthly capacity of 6,000 machine hours.

During November, the company produced only 850 units because of a labor strike, which occurred during union contract negotiations. After the dispute was settled, the company scheduled overtime to try to meet regular production levels. The following costs were incurred in November:

Material	
Aluminum	4,000 sheets purchased @ $3.80; used 3,500 sheets
Copper	3,000 sheets purchased @ $8.40; used 2,600 sheets

Direct Labor	
Regular time	5,200 hours @ $16 (pre-contract settlement)
Regular time	900 hours @ $17 (post-contract settlement)

Variable Overhead

$23,300 (based on 4,175 machine hours)

Fixed Overhead

$18,850 (based on 4,175 machine hours)

Determine the following and prepare the journal entries to record the standard costing information for November:

a. Total material price variance
b. Total material usage (quantity) variance
c. Labor rate variance
d. Labor efficiency variance
e. Variable overhead spending variance
f. Variable overhead efficiency variance
g. Fixed overhead spending variance
h. Volume variance
i. Budget variance

LO10-3, 4   **P10-81. Comprehensive; all variances; all methods** Hellier Contractors paints interiors of residences and commercial structures. The firm's management has established cost standards per 100 square feet of area to be painted.

Direct material ($18 per gallon of paint)	$1.50
Direct labor	2.00
Variable overhead	0.60
Fixed overhead (based on 600,000 square feet per month)	1.25

Management has determined that 400 square feet can be painted by the average worker each hour. During May, the company painted 600,000 square feet of space and incurred the following costs:

Direct material (450 gallons purchased and used)	$ 8,300.00
Direct labor (1,475 hours)	12,242.50
Variable overhead	3,480.00
Fixed overhead	7,720.00

a. Compute the direct material variances.
b. Compute the direct labor variances.

Chapter 10 Flexible Budget, Standard Costing, and Variance Analysis

c. Use a four-variance approach to compute overhead variances.
d. Use a three-variance approach to compute overhead variances.
e. Use a two-variance approach to compute overhead variances.
f. Reconcile your answers for (c) through (e).
g. Discuss other cost drivers that could be used as a basis for measuring activity and computing variances for this company.

P10-82. Variance disposition The following variances existed at year-end for Muckstadt Production Company: LO10-5

Material price variance	$23,400 U
Material quantity variance	24,900 F
Labor rate variance	5,250 F
Labor efficiency variance	36,900 U
Variance overhead spending variance	3,000 U
Variance overhead efficiency variance	1,800 F
Fixed overhead spending variance	6,600 F
Volume variance	16,800 U

In addition, the following inventory and Cost of Goods Sold account balances existed at year-end:

Raw Material Inventory	$ 320,600
Work in Process Inventory	916,000
Finished Goods Inventory	641,200
Cost of Goods Sold	2,702,200

a. Prepare the journal entry at December 31 to dispose of the variances, assuming that all are insignificant.
b. After posting your entry in (a), what is the balance in Cost of Goods Sold?
c. Prepare the journal entries at December 31 to dispose of the variances, assuming that all are significant. (Round to the nearest whole percentage.)
d. After posting your entries in (c), what are the balances in each inventory account and in Cost of Goods Sold?

P10-83. Variances and variance responsibility Namathe Industries manufactures children's footballs with the following standard costs per unit: LO10-3, 4

Material: one square foot of leather at $2.00	$ 2.00
Direct labor: 1.6 hours at $9.00	14.40
Variable overhead cost	3.00
Fixed overhead cost	3.00
Total cost per unit	$22.40

Per-unit overhead cost was calculated from the following annual overhead budget for 180,000 footballs.

Variable Overhead Cost

Indirect labor—90,000 hours @ $7.00	$630,000	
Supplies (oil)—180,000 gallons @ $0.50	90,000	
Allocated variable service department costs	90,000	
Total variable overhead cost		$ 810,000

Fixed Overhead Cost

Supervision	$ 81,000	
Depreciation	135,000	
Other fixed costs	45,000	
Total fixed overhead cost		261,000
Total budgeted overhead cost @ 180,000 units		$1,071,000

© Cambridge Business Publishers

Following are the charges to the manufacturing department for November when 15,000 units were produced:

Material (15,900 square feet @ $2.00)	$ 31,800
Direct labor (24,600 hours @ $9.10)	223,860
Indirect labor (7,200 hours @ $7.10)	51,120
Supplies (oil) (18,000 gallons @ $0.55)	9,900
Allocated service department variable OH costs	9,600
Supervision	7,425
Depreciation	11,250
Other fixed costs	3,750
Total	$348,705

Purchasing normally buys about the same quantity as is used in production during a month. In November, the company purchased 15,600 square feet of material at a price of $2.10 per foot.

a. Calculate the following variances from standard costs for the data given:
   1. Material purchase price
   2. Material quantity
   3. Direct labor rate
   4. Direct labor efficiency
   5. Overhead budget

b. The company has divided its responsibilities so that the Purchasing Department is responsible for the purchase price of materials and the Manufacturing Department is responsible for the quantity of materials used. Does this division of responsibilities solve the conflict between price and quantity variances? Explain your answer.

c. Prepare a report detailing the overhead budget variance. The report, which will be given to the Manufacturing Department manager, should only show that part of the variance that is her responsibility and should highlight the information in ways that would be useful to her in evaluating departmental performance and when considering corrective action.

d. Assume that the departmental manager performs the timekeeping function for this manufacturing department. From time to time, analyses of overhead and direct labor variances have shown that the manager has deliberately misclassified labor hours (i.e., listed direct labor hours as indirect labor hours and vice versa) so that only one of the two labor variances is unfavorable. It is not feasible economically to hire a separate timekeeper. What should the company do, if anything, to resolve this problem?

P10-84. Standards revision; writing Ripper Corp. uses a standard cost system for its aircraft component manufacturing operations. Recently, the company's direct material supplier went out of business, but Ripper's purchasing agent found a new source that produces a similar material. The price per pound from the original supplier was $7.00; the new source's price is $7.77. The new source's material reduces scrap, and thus, each unit requires only 1.00 pound rather than the previous standard of 1.25 pounds per unit. In addition, use of the new source's material reduces direct labor time from 24 to 22 minutes per unit because there is less machine setup time. At the same time, the recently signed labor contract increased the average direct labor wage rate from $12.60 to $14.40 per hour.

The company began using the new direct material on April 1, the same day that the new labor agreement went into effect. However, Ripper Corp. is still using the following standards that were set at the beginning of the calendar year:

Direct material	1.2 pounds @ $6.80 per pound	$ 8.16
Direct labor	20 minutes @ $12.30 per DLH	4.10
Standard DM and DL cost per unit		$12.26

Steve Wenskel, cost accounting supervisor, had been examining the following April 30 variance report.

Chapter 10 Flexible Budget, Standard Costing, and Variance Analysis

PERFORMANCE REPORT
STANDARD COST VARIANCE ANALYSIS FOR APRIL

	Standard	Price Variance	Quantity Variance	Actual
DM....	$ 8.16	($0.97 × 1.0) = $0.97 U	($6.80 × 0.2) = $1.36 F	$ 7.77
DL.....	4.10	[$2.10 × (22/60)] = 0.77 U	[$12.30 × (2/60)] = 0.41 U	5.28
	$12.26			$13.05

COMPARISON OF ACTUAL COSTS

	Average 1st Quarter Costs	April Costs	Percent Increase (Decrease)
DM.......	$ 8.75	$ 7.77	(11.2)
DL........	5.04	5.28	4.8
	$13.79	$13.05	(5.4)

When Cynthia Dirope, assistant controller, came into Wenskel's office, he said, "Cynthia, look at this performance report! Direct material price increased 11 percent, and the labor rate increased over 14 percent during April. I expected greater variances, yet prime costs decreased over 5 percent from the $13.79 we experienced during the first quarter of this year. The proper message just isn't coming through."

Dirope said, "This has been an unusual period. With all the unforeseen changes, perhaps we should revise our standards based on current conditions and start over."

Wenskel replied, "I think we can retain the current standards but expand the variance analysis. We could calculate variances for the specific changes that have occurred to direct material and direct labor before we calculate the normal price and quantity variances. What I really think would be useful to management right now is to determine the impact the changes in direct material and direct labor had in reducing our prime costs per unit from $13.79 in the first quarter to $13.05 in April—a reduction of $0.74."

a. Discuss the advantages of (1) immediately revising the standards and (2) retaining the current standards and expanding the analysis of variances.

b. Prepare an analysis that reflects the impact of the new direct material and new labor contract on reducing Ripper Corp.'s standard costs per unit from $13.79 to $13.05. The analysis should show the changes in direct material and direct labor costs per unit that are caused by (1) the use of the new direct material and (2) the labor rates of the new contract. This analysis should be in sufficient detail to identify the changes due to direct material price, direct labor rate, the effect of direct material quality on direct material usage, and the effect of direct material quality on direct labor usage.

P10-85. Mix and yield variances Polermo Inc. produces three-topping, 18-inch frozen pizzas and uses a standard cost system. The three pizza toppings (in addition to cheese) are onions, olives, and mushrooms. To some extent, discretion may be used to determine the actual mix of these toppings. The company has two classes of labor, and discretion also may be used to determine the mix of the labor inputs. The standard cost card for a pizza follows: **LO10-6**

Onions.................	3 ounces @ $0.10 per ounce
Olives..................	3 ounces @ $0.35 per ounce
Mushrooms..............	3 ounces @ $0.50 per ounce
Labor category 1	5 minutes @ $12 per hour
Labor category 2	6 minutes @ $8 per hour

During May, the company produced 48,000 pizzas and used the following inputs:

Onions.................	8,000 pounds
Olives..................	12,000 pounds
Mushrooms..............	8,000 pounds
Labor category 1	5,200 hours
Labor category 2	4,000 hours

During the month there were no deviations from standards on material prices or labor rates.

a. Determine the material quantity, mix, and yield variances.
b. Determine the labor efficiency, mix, and yield variances.
c. Prepare the journal entries to record the above mix and yield variances.

LO10-6 P10-86. Mix and yield variances Haddas Ltd. makes Healthy Life, a nutritional aid. For a 50-pound batch, standard material and labor costs are as follows:

	Quantity	Unit Price	Total
Wheat	25.0 pounds	$0.20 per pound	$5.00
Barley	25.0 pounds	0.10 per pound	2.50
Corn	10.0 pounds	0.05 per pound	0.50
Skilled labor	0.8 hour	12.00 per hour	9.60
Unskilled labor	0.2 hour	8.00 per hour	1.60

During June, the following materials and labor were used in producing 600 batches of Healthy Life:

Wheat	18,000 pounds @ $0.22 per pound
Barley	14,000 pounds @ $0.11 per pound
Corn	10,000 pounds @ $0.07 per pound
Skilled labor	400 hours @ $12.25 per hour
Unskilled labor	260 hours @ $9.00 per hour

a. Calculate the material quantity, mix, and yield variances.
b. Calculate the labor efficiency, mix, and yield variances.

LO10-7 P10-87. Appendix; Standard costing Modern Convenience specializes in making robotic conveyor systems to move materials within a factory. Model #89 accounts for approximately 60 percent of the company's annual sales. Because the company has produced and expects to continue to produce a significant quantity of this model, Modern Convenience uses the following standard costs to account for Model #89 production costs:

Direct material (28,000 pounds)	$ 56,000
Direct labor (1,720 hours at $20 per hour)	34,400
Overhead	76,000
Total standard cost	$166,400

For the 200 units of Model #89 produced during the year, the actual costs were

Direct material (6,000,000 pounds)	$11,600,000
Direct labor (178,400 hours)	6,957,600
Overhead	14,800,000
Total actual cost	$33,357,600

a. Compute a separate variance between actual and standard cost for direct material, direct labor, and manufacturing overhead for the Model #89 units produced during the year.
b. Is the direct material variance found in (a) driven primarily by the price per pound difference between standard and actual or the quantity difference between standard and actual? Explain.

LO10-7 P10-88. Appendix; Standard costing During July, Pull-Along worked on two production runs (Jobs #918 and #2002) of the same product, a trailer hitch component. Job #918 consisted of 1,200 units of the product, and Job #2002 contained 2,000 units. The hitch components are made from sheet metal. Because this component is routinely produced for one of Pull-Along's long-term customers, standard costs have been developed for its production. The standard cost of material for each unit is $18; each unit contains six pounds of material at standard. The standard direct labor time per unit is 12 minutes for workers earning a standard rate of $20 per hour. The actual costs recorded for each job were as follows:

Chapter 10 Flexible Budget, Standard Costing, and Variance Analysis

	Direct Material	Direct Labor
Job #918.......	(7,300 pounds) $23,525	(230 hours) $4,840
Job #2002......	(11,900 pounds) 37,440	(405 hours) 7,850

a. What is the standard direct cost of each trailer hitch component?
b. What was the total standard direct cost assigned to each of the jobs?
c. Compute the variances for direct material and for direct labor for each job.
d. Why should variances be computed separately for each job rather than for the aggregate annual trailer hitch component production?

P10-89. Appendix; Conversion cost variances The May budget for the Auberage Company shows $1,080,000 of variable conversion costs, $360,000 of fixed conversion costs, and 72,000 machine hours for the production of 24,000 units of product. During May, 76,000 machine hours were worked and 24,000 units were produced. Variance and fixed conversion costs for the month were $1,128,800 and $374,500, respectively.   LO10-8

a. Calculate the four conversion cost variances assuming that variable and fixed costs are separated.
b. Calculate the three conversion cost variances assuming that fixed and variable costs are combined.

P10-90. Appendix; Conversion cost variances Kieffer Company makes men's suit alterations for a major clothing store chain. No direct materials are used in the alterations process and overhead costs are primarily variable and relate very closely to direct labor charges. The company owner has decided to compute variances on a conversion cost basis. Standards for the year are as follows: LO10-8

Expected direct labor hours (DLHs; to be incurred evenly throughout the year)	60,000
Number of suits altered in October...	1,800
Standard DLHs per suit	3
Actual DLHs worked in October	5,490
Budgeted variable conversion cost per DLH	$ 18
Budgeted annual fixed conversion cost	$ 72,000
Actual variable conversion cost for October...............................	$103,100
Actual fixed conversion cost for October	$ 5,750

a. How many suits does Kieffer Company expect to alter during the year?
b. What is the predetermined fixed OH rate for Kieffer Company?
c. How many standard direct labor hours were allowed for October?
d. Calculate the four conversion cost variances assuming that variable and fixed costs are separated.
e. Calculate the three conversion cost variances assuming that fixed and variable costs are combined.

Review Solutions

Review 10-1

a.

	Direct Labor Hours			
	400	450	500	550
Variable costs:				
Supplies	$2,000	$2,250	$2,500	$ 2,750
Supervision and direct labor...........................	2,400	2,700	3,000	3,300
Utilities	1,600	1,800	2,000	2,200
Fixed costs:				
Supervision and direct labor...........................	850	850	850	850
Utilities	575	575	575	575
Rent	600	600	600	600
Advertising	85	85	85	85
Total cost	$8,110	$8,860	$9,610	$10,360

b.

	Direct Labor Hours			
	400	450	500	550
Cost per direct labor hour............................	$20.28	$19.69	$19.22	$18.84

c. The budget prepared in part *a* could be used for planning different scenarios before the period begins. The resources required at 400 direct labor hours are less than what is needed at 550 direct labor hours. Understanding the range of resources needed will help management make decisions on securing resources and for planning.

A flexible budget created based on actual hours incurred (after the fact) can be used for control purposes. Comparing actual activity to a budget at an equivalent volume level, provides a clearer picture of performance because it eliminates differences in costs due strictly to volume changes. For example, if the master budget was based on 400 hours but actual hours were 550, the variable costs will likely indicate costs are over budget, at least partially due to higher volumes.

Review 10-2

a.

Standard Cost Card		
Direct Materials		
Mixed berries (12* quarts × $1.25 per quart).........................	$15.00	
Other ingredients (15 gallons × $0.80).................................	12.00	$27.00
Direct Labor		
Sorting [(4 min. × 10 quarts) ÷ 60 min.) × $10.00].....................	6.67	
Blending [(15 min. ÷ 60) × $10.00].....................................	2.50	9.17
Packaging (128 ounces per gallon ÷ 16 ounces × 15 gallons) × $0.25..........		30.00
Overhead (0.50 × $20)...		10.00
Total cost per 15 gallon batch...		$76.17

*12 = 10 quarts × 6/5

b. 10 × 12 quarts = 120 quarts of mixed berries
10 × 15 gallons = 150 gallons of other ingredients
10 × 0.6667 hour = 6.67 hours
10 × 0.25 hour = 2.5 hours

c. If labor measurements are based on practical or ideal standards, standards would be more useful for evaluating performance than if expected standards are used. Providing a realistic target can encourage workers to stay efficient and even find small ways to improve efficiencies. If standards are not realistic, and with no support from management or formal programs in place to find new ways to reach the high standards, the standards would likely be ignored by workers.

Review 10-3

1. a. Material price variance:
   Stainless steel: $AQ_p \times (AP - SP) = 5{,}000 \times (\$6.20 - \$6.40) = \$1{,}000$ F
   Copper: $AQ_p \times (AP - SP) = 4{,}100 \times (\$8.20 - \$8.50) = \$1{,}230$ F
   Total: $2,230 F

   b. Material quantity variance:
   Stainless steel: $SP \times (AQu - SQ) = \$6.40 \times (5{,}500 - (5 \times 1{,}105)) = \$160$ F
   Copper: $SP \times (AQu - SQ) = \$8.50 \times (4{,}500 - (4 \times 1{,}105)) = \$680$ U
   Total: $520 U

   c. Labor rate variance: $AQ \times (AP - SP) = 7{,}700 \times (\$19 - \$20) = \$7{,}700$ F
   d. Labor efficiency variance: $SR \times (AH - SH) = \$20 \times (7{,}700 - (1{,}105 \times 7)) = \$700$ F

2.
Stainless Steel Material Inventory............................	32,000	
Stainless Material Price Variance.........................		1,000
Accounts Payable......................................		31,000
To record acquisition of material		

continued

continued from previous page

Copper Material Inventory	34,850	
Copper Material Price Variance		1,230
Accounts Payable.................................		33,620

To record acquisition of material

Work in Process Inventory	35,360	
Stainless Steel Material Quantity Variance.................		160
Stainless Steel Material Inventory		35,200

To record issuance of material to production

Work in Process Inventory	37,570	
Copper Material Quantity Variance............................	680	
Copper Material Inventory		38,250

To record issuance of material to production

Work in Process...	154,700	
Labor Rate Variance.................................		7,700
Labor Efficiency Variance.............................		700
Wages Payable.....................................		146,300

To record incurrence of direct labor

3. Both materials were purchased at a price less than standard causing favorable price variances. However, a higher quantity of product Copper was used than the standard allowed. The company could investigate whether the lower price paid for copper impacted the usage of copper. Regarding labor, both the rate and efficiency variances were favorable—a lower wage was paid than planned and hours incurred were less than standard hour allowed.

Review 10-4

1. a. VOH spending variance = Actual VOH − (Budgeted VOH at AHs) = $30,000 − (5,400 × $5) = $3,000 U
   b. VOH efficiency variance = (Budget at actual hours) − (Budget at SHs) = $27,000 − ($5 × 6 × 1,105) = $6,150 F
   c. FOH spending variance = Actual FOH − Budgeted FOH = $27,000 − (7,800 × $4) = $4,200 F
   d. Volume variance = Budgeted FOH − Applied FOH = (7,800 × $4) − ($4 × 6 × 1,105) = $4,680 U

2. a.

Variable Manufacturing Overhead Control	30,000	
Fixed Manufacturing Overhead Control	27,000	
Various accounts		57,000

To record actual overhead costs

b.

Work in Process Inventory	59,400	
Variable Manufacturing Overhead Control ($5 × 1,105 × 6).....		33,150
Fixed Manufacturing Overhead Control ($4 × 1,105 × 6)		26,250

To apply overhead to the month's production

c.

Variable Manufacturing Overhead Control	3,150	
Variable Overhead Spending Variance	3,000	
Variable Overhead Efficiency Variance.....................		6,150

To close the VOH Control account and recognize VOH variances

d.

Volume Variance...	4,680	
Fixed Overhead Spending Variance		4,200
Fixed Manufacturing Overhead Control		480

To close the FOH Control account and recognize FOH variances

3. The variable overhead spending variance was unfavorable (which could be caused by price or volume differences) while the variable overhead efficiency variance was favorable (which means less activity than planned). The fixed overhead volume variance was unfavorable (which means less product was produced than planned) while the fixed overhead spending variance was favorable (which means actual fixed OH spending was less than budget).

Review 10-5

a.

	Balance	% of Total	Allocation
Raw Material	$125,000	20%	$1,000
Work in Process	25,000	4%	200
Finished Goods	75,000	12%	600
Cost of Goods Sold	400,000	64%	3,200
Total	$625,000	100%	$5,000

Material Price Variance	5,000	
Raw Material Inventory		1,000
Work in Process Inventory		200
Finished Goods Inventory		600
Cost of Goods Sold		3,200

To dispose of the material price variances

All other variances: $ 18,000 U

	Balance	% of Total	Allocation
Work in Process	$ 25,000	5%	$ 900
Finished Goods	75,000	15%	2,700
Cost of Goods Sold	400,000	80%	14,400
Total	$500,000	100%	$18,000

Work in Process Inventory	900	
Finished Goods Inventory	2,700	
Cost of Goods Sold	14,400	
Labor Rate Variance	6,000	
Material Quantity Variance		10,000
Labor Efficiency Variance		14,000

To dispose of the remaining material and labor variances

b.

Cost of Goods Sold	13,000	
Material Price Variance	5,000	
Labor Rate Variance	6,000	
Material Quantity Variance		10,000
Labor Efficiency Variance		14,000

To dispose of variances

c. At year-end, treating variances as insignificant (as compared to the treatment in part *a*), causes an understatement of assets on the balance sheet and an overstatement of expenses on the income statement. The variance accounts are eliminated in either case. Overstating the unfavorable variances in the current period could impact how standards are budgeted for a future period. Because costs are overstated, the standard costs for the next period could be budgeted too high.

Chapter 10 Flexible Budget, Standard Costing, and Variance Analysis

Review 10-6

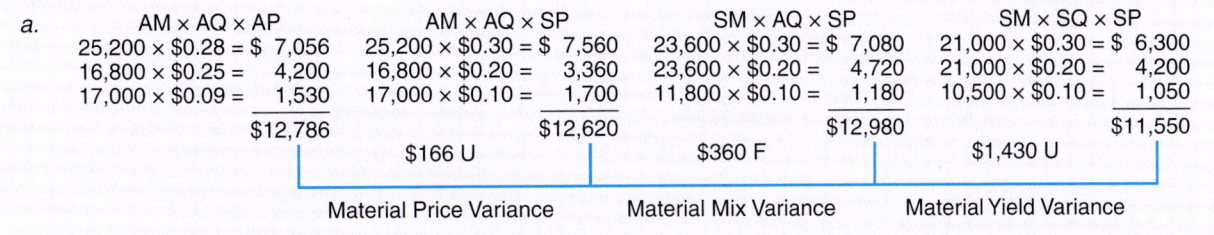

a.
```
        AM × AQ × AP              AM × AQ × SP              SM × AQ × SP              SM × SQ × SP
   25,200 × $0.28 = $ 7,056   25,200 × $0.30 = $ 7,560   23,600 × $0.30 = $ 7,080   21,000 × $0.30 = $ 6,300
   16,800 × $0.25 =   4,200   16,800 × $0.20 =   3,360   23,600 × $0.20 =   4,720   21,000 × $0.20 =   4,200
   17,000 × $0.09 =   1,530   17,000 × $0.10 =   1,700   11,800 × $0.10 =   1,180   10,500 × $0.10 =   1,050
                    $12,786                    $12,620                    $12,980                    $11,550
                           $166 U                     $360 F                     $1,430 U
                      Material Price Variance   Material Mix Variance   Material Yield Variance
```

Supporting calculations:
  Standard mix, actual quantity:
    Plant-based blend: 59,000 × (30 ÷ 75) = 23,600
    Soy: 59,000 × (30 ÷ 75) = 23,600
    Whey: 59,000 × (15 ÷ 75) = 11,800
  Standard mix, standard quantity:
    Plant-based blend: 700 × 30 = 21,000
    Soy: 700 × 30 = 21,000
    Whey: 700 × 15 = 10,500

Material quantity variance = $360 F + $1,430 U = $1,070 U

b.
```
        AM × AH × AR              AM × AH × SR              SM × AH × SR              SM × SH × SR
    560 × $17.50 = $ 9,800     560 × $15 = $ 8,400      739.20 × $15 = $11,088     784 × $15 = $11,760
    364 × $11.50 = $ 4,186     364 × $10 = $ 3,640      184.80 × $10 = $ 1,848     196 × $10 = $  1,960
                   $13,986                  $12,040                    $12,936                   $13,720
                         $1,946 U                   $896 F                     $784 F
                      Labor Rate Variance      Labor Mix Variance        Labor Yield Variance
```

Supporting calculations:
  Standard mix, actual quantity:
    Skilled: 924 × (1.12 ÷ 1.40) = 739.20
    Unskilled: 924 × (0.28 ÷ 1.40) = 184.80
  Standard mix, standard quantity:
    Skilled: 700 × 1.12 = 784
    Unskilled: 700 × 0.28 = 196

Labor efficiency variance = $896 F + $784 F = $1,680 F

c. While the material price variance was slightly unfavorable due to a combination of price differences, the material mix variance was favorable. A lower usage of the $0.20 part and a higher usage of the $0.10 part than budget was the largest contributing factor to the favorable mix variance. The material yield variance was unfavorable, because a higher quantity of all parts were used over the standard allowed.

For labor, the rate variance was unfavorable because both actual rates were above budget. The labor mix variance was favorable because a higher percentage of hours were incurred at the lower wage rate. The yield variance was positive because hours were below budget in both labor categories.

Review 10-7

1. Job #202
   a. Direct material price variance: 3,650 × [($14,115 ÷ 3,650) − $17/6)] = $3,773 unfavorable
   b. Direct material quantity variance: $17/6 × (3,650 − [6 × 1,000]) = $6,658 favorable
   c. Direct labor rate variance: 208 × ([$3,800 ÷ 208] − $20) = $360 favorable
   d. Direct labor efficiency variance: $20 × (208 − [12/60 × 1,000]) = $160 unfavorable

   Job #506
   a. Direct material price variance: 5,950 [($18,720 ÷ 5,950) − $17/6)] = $1,862 unfavorable
   b. Direct material quantity variance: $17/6 × (5,950 − [6 × 900]) = $1,558 unfavorable
   c. Direct labor rate variance: 300 × ([$5,900 ÷ 300] − $20) = $100 favorable
   d. Direct labor efficiency variance: $20 × (300 − [12/60 × 900]) = $2,400 unfavorable

2. Favorable or unfavorable variance results can help inform management on how to manage future jobs. For example, understanding why there are unfavorable material price variances could perhaps reverse the trend on future jobs. Is there another supplier that the company can use with better prices? Were there excess charges such as expedited shipping charges?

Review 10-8

a. Variable conversion spending variance: $90,000 − [(102,000 ÷ 6,000) × 5,400] = $1,800 F
Variable conversion efficiency variance: [(102,000 ÷ 6,000) × 5,400] − [(102,000 ÷ 6,000) × 5,760] = $6,120 F
Fixed conversion spending variance: $44,000 − $45,600 = $1,600 F
Volume variance: $45,600 − [($45,600 ÷ 6,000) × (2,880 × 6,000 ÷ 3,000)] = $1,824 U

b. The results would not be incorrect but tracking information for direct labor may not be cost beneficial. Because direct labor is not a significant product cost, the cost of tracking direct labor separately would likely be greater than the benefits received.

Data Visualization Solutions
(See page 10-4.)

a. At 1,000 units, the total costs are $350,300.

b. The flexible budget total cost amount appropriate for cost control depends upon the actual quantity of production. Each quantity within a relevant range has a specific budgeted cost. As quantity changes, variable costs change, which means that total costs change.

c. The master budget is based on 1,000 units at a total cost of $350,300. Compared to the master budget, the company is *under* budget. However, the relevant flexible budget shows total costs at $286,600. Compared to the flexible budget, the company's actual results are *over* budget.

d. The master budget is based on 1,000 units at a total cost of $350,300. Compared to the master budget, the company is *over* budget. However, the relevant flexible budget shows total costs at $382,150. Compared to the flexible budget, the company's actual results are *under* budget.

Chapter 11

Absorption/Variable Costing and Capacity Analysis

Road Map

LO	Learning Objective | Topics	Page	eLecture	Demo	Review	Assignments
11–1	**How do absorption and variable costing differ?** Absorption Costing :: Full Costing :: Functional Classification :: Variable Costing :: Direct Costing :: Cost Behavior :: Cost Accumulation :: Cost Presentation	11-2	e11-1	D11-1	Rev 11-1	MC11-11, MC11-12, MC11-14, MC11-16, E11-21, E11-23, E11-27, E11-29, E11-33, P11-40, P11-42, P11-43, P11-44, P11-47, P11-48
11–2	**How do changes in sales or production levels affect before-tax profit presented under absorption and variable costing?** Balance Sheet :: Absorption Costing Income Statement :: Variable Costing Income Statement :: Production Equals Sales :: Production Exceeds Sales :: Sales Exceeds Production :: Before-Tax Profit :: Phantom Profits :: Income Manipulation :: CVP Analysis	11-5	e11-2	D11-2	Rev 11-2	MC11-13, MC11-14, MC11-15, MC11-16, E11-22, E11-24, E11-25, E11-26, E11-27, E11-28, E11-30, E11-31, P11-39, P11-40, P11-43, P11-47, P11-48, DA11-1
11–3	**How does a volume variance impact the absorption and variable costing income statements?** Standard Cost System :: Absorption Costing Income Statement :: Variable Costing Income Statement :: Volume Variance	11-11	e11-3	D11-3	Rev 11-3	MC11-17, MC11-18, E11-32, E11-33, E11-34, E11-35, P11-41, P11-42, P11-44, P11-48, P11-50
11–4	**How does the measurement of capacity impact the results of absorption costing?** Theoretical Capacity :: Practical Capacity :: Normal Capacity :: Expected Capacity :: Budgeted FOH Rate :: Volume Variance :: Downward Demand Spiral	11-14	e11-4	D11-4	Rev 11-4	MC11-19, MC11-20, E11-36, E11-37, E11-38, P11-45, P11-46, P11-49, P11-50, DA11-2

© Cambridge Business Publishers

INTRODUCTION

In preparing financial reports, costs can be accumulated and presented in different ways. The choice of a cost accumulation method determines which costs are recorded as part of product costs and which are considered period costs. In contrast, the choice of a cost presentation method determines how costs are shown on external financial statements or internal management reports. Accumulation and presentation procedures are accomplished using one of two methods: absorption costing or variable costing. Either method can be used in job order or process costing (discussed in Chapters 6 and 7) and with actual, normal, or standard costs. We start with an overview of absorption and variable costing and demonstrate how the financial statements differ under the two methods. Next we discuss how the measurement of capacity impacts product costing under absorption costing. Capacity is a measurement of volume such as the number of seats available on a commercial airplane or the number of vehicles that can be produced in an automobile manufacturer's plant. How capacity is measured impacts the budgeted fixed overhead rate, which impacts the amount of fixed overhead applied to inventory. This discussion provides further analysis of the volume variance introduced in the last chapter.

OVERVIEW OF ABSORPTION AND VARIABLE COSTING

LO11-1 How do absorption and variable costing differ?

A debate exists over how to treat fixed manufacturing overhead costs in the valuation of inventory. The debate centers around whether fixed costs such as depreciation on manufacturing equipment should be considered an inventoriable product cost and treated as an asset cost until the inventory is sold, or as a period cost and recorded immediately as an operating expense. Absorption costing treats fixed manufacturing overhead as a product cost, whereas variable costing treats it as a period cost. Therefore, fixed manufacturing overhead is recorded initially as an asset (inventory) under absorption costing but as an operating expense under variable costing.

> **Fixed manufacturing costs**
> Absorption costing treats fixed manufacturing costs as product costs.
> Variable costing treats fixed manufacturing costs as period costs.

Since fixed product costs are eventually recorded as expenses under both variable and absorption costing by the time the inventory is sold, why does it matter whether fixed overhead is treated as a product cost or a period cost? It matters because the way it is treated affects the measurement of income for a *particular period* and the valuation assigned to inventory on the balance sheet at the end of the period. Because absorption costing presents fixed manufacturing overhead as a cost per unit rather than a total cost per period, management's perceptions of cost behavior and decisions based on perceptions of cost behavior, may also be affected.

Absorption Costing

Absorption costing treats the costs of all manufacturing components (direct material, direct labor, variable overhead, and fixed overhead) as inventoriable, or product, costs in accordance with GAAP. Absorption costing is also known as **full costing**, and this method fits the product cost definition given in Chapter 2. Under absorption costing, costs incurred in the nonmanufacturing areas of the organization are considered period costs and are expensed in the period that services are performed and revenue is generated. **Exhibit 11.1** depicts the absorption costing model. In addition, absorption costing presents expenses on an income statement according to their functional classifications. A **functional classification** is a group of costs that were incurred for the same principal purpose. Functional classifications generally include cost of goods sold (CGS), selling expense, and administrative expense.

Chapter 11 Absorption/Variable Costing and Capacity Analysis

Exhibit 11.1 ■ Absorption Costing Model

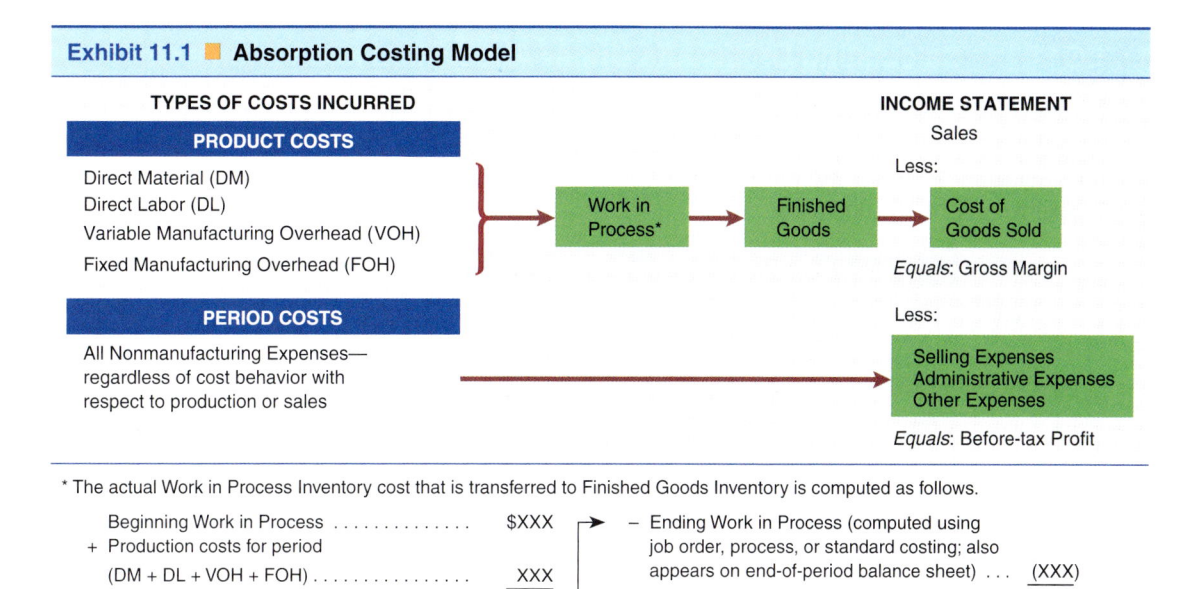

TYPES OF COSTS INCURRED

PRODUCT COSTS
- Direct Material (DM)
- Direct Labor (DL)
- Variable Manufacturing Overhead (VOH)
- Fixed Manufacturing Overhead (FOH)

→ Work in Process* → Finished Goods → Cost of Goods Sold

PERIOD COSTS
All Nonmanufacturing Expenses—regardless of cost behavior with respect to production or sales

INCOME STATEMENT
Sales
Less:
Cost of Goods Sold
Equals: Gross Margin
Less:
Selling Expenses
Administrative Expenses
Other Expenses
Equals: Before-tax Profit

* The actual Work in Process Inventory cost that is transferred to Finished Goods Inventory is computed as follows.

Beginning Work in Process	$XXX
+ Production costs for period (DM + DL + VOH + FOH)	XXX
= Total Work in Process to be accounted for . . .	$XXX
− Ending Work in Process (computed using job order, process, or standard costing; also appears on end-of-period balance sheet) . . .	(XXX)
= Cost of Goods Manufactured (CGM)	$ XXX

Variable Costing

In contrast, **variable costing** (also known as **direct costing**) is a cost accumulation method that includes only direct material, direct labor, and variable overhead as product costs. Unlike the absorption method, this method is *not* acceptable under GAAP, making it an option for a company's internal reporting only. This method treats fixed manufacturing overhead (FOH) as a period cost. Like absorption costing, variable costing treats costs incurred in the organization's selling and administrative areas as period costs. Variable costing income statements typically present expenses according to cost behavior (variable and fixed), although expenses can also be presented by functional classifications within the behavioral categories. See **Exhibit 11.2** for the variable costing model. The differences in the income statement presentation between variable and absorption costing are discussed in more detail in the next section.

Exhibit 11.2 ■ Variable Costing Model

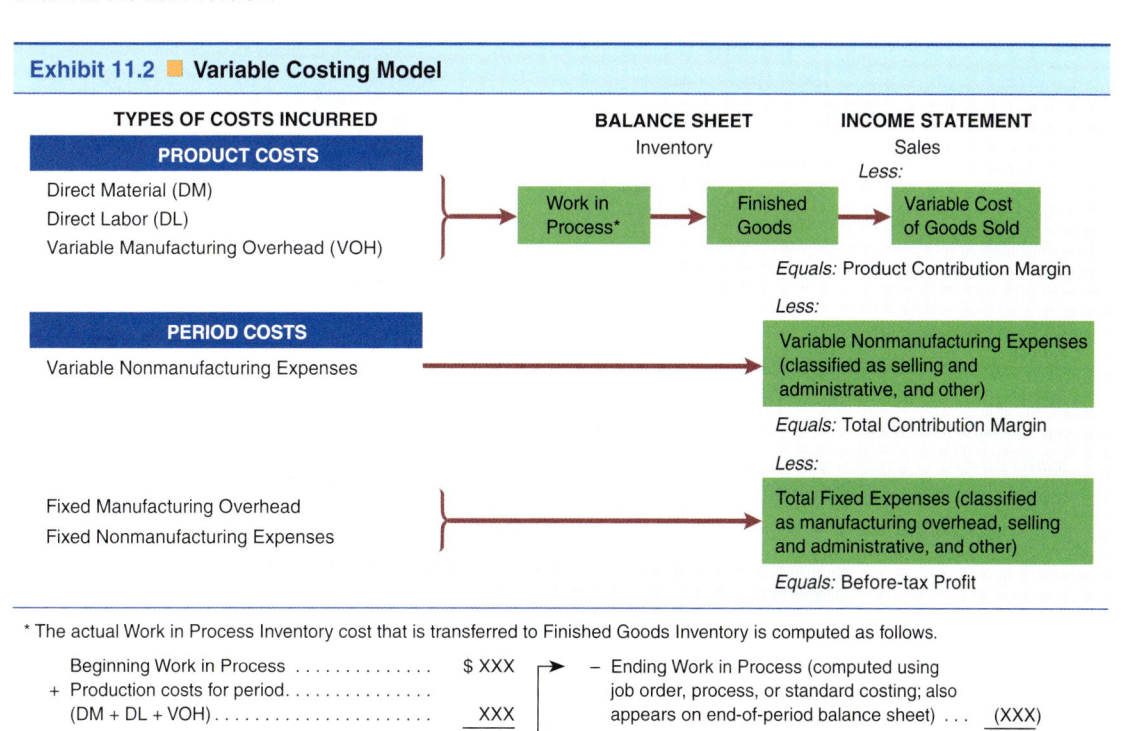

TYPES OF COSTS INCURRED

PRODUCT COSTS
- Direct Material (DM)
- Direct Labor (DL)
- Variable Manufacturing Overhead (VOH)

PERIOD COSTS
Variable Nonmanufacturing Expenses

Fixed Manufacturing Overhead
Fixed Nonmanufacturing Expenses

BALANCE SHEET
Inventory
→ Work in Process* → Finished Goods →

INCOME STATEMENT
Sales
Less:
Variable Cost of Goods Sold
Equals: Product Contribution Margin
Less:
Variable Nonmanufacturing Expenses (classified as selling and administrative, and other)
Equals: Total Contribution Margin
Less:
Total Fixed Expenses (classified as manufacturing overhead, selling and administrative, and other)
Equals: Before-tax Profit

* The actual Work in Process Inventory cost that is transferred to Finished Goods Inventory is computed as follows.

Beginning Work in Process	$ XXX
+ Production costs for period (DM + DL + VOH)	XXX
= Total Work in Process to be accounted for . . .	$ XXX
− Ending Work in Process (computed using job order, process, or standard costing; also appears on end-of-period balance sheet) . . .	(XXX)
= Cost of Goods Manufactured	$ XXX

© Cambridge Business Publishers

DEMO 11-1 LO11-1 Calculating Unit Costs Under Absorption and Variable Costing

Custom Covers began operations in Year 1 with a plan to make 300,000 car seat cushions. Product specifications are likely to be constant at least until model Year 4. To illustrate the difference in inventory valuations between absorption and variable costing, assume the following actual cost data at an annual volume of 300,000 units.

Production Costs	
Variable manufacturing cost per unit	
Direct material (DM)	$ 2.04
Direct labor (DL)	1.50
Variable manufacturing overhead (VOH)	0.18
Total variable manufacturing cost per unit	$ 3.72
Total fixed manufacturing overhead (FOH) costs for the year	$162,000
Nonproduction Expenses	
Variable selling expense per unit	$ 0.24
Total fixed selling and administrative expense for the year	$ 23,400

Assume that fixed overhead costs are applied based upon the budgeted number of units of production.

◆ **What is the total cost per unit of inventory under absorption costing versus variable costing?**

Under absorption costing, the total cost per unit of inventory is equal to total variable manufacturing cost per unit of $3.72 plus fixed overhead cost per unit of $0.54, calculated as follows.

FOH cost per unit = Budgeted annual FOH ÷ Budgeted annual units of production

= $162,000 ÷ 300,000 = $0.54

Total inventory cost per unit under absorption costing = $3.72 + $0.54 = $4.26.

Under variable costing, the total cost per unit of inventory is equal to total variable manufacturing cost per unit of $3.72.

The difference in the make-up of unit inventory costs is depicted in the following data visualizations.

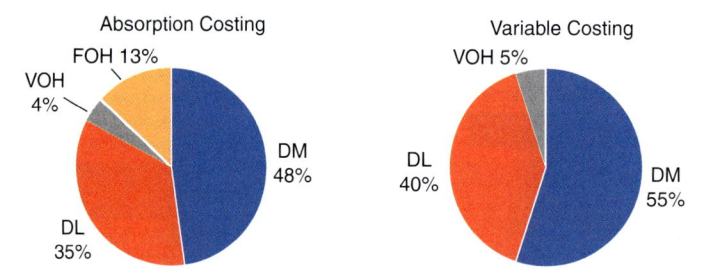

Absorption Costing: FOH 13%, VOH 4%, DL 35%, DM 48%

Variable Costing: VOH 5%, DL 40%, DM 55%

At an annual production volume of 300,000 units, Custom Cover's total component inventory cost per unit is $3.72 under variable costing and $4.26 under absorption costing. The $0.54 difference in total unit cost is attributed to the treatment of fixed overhead. The difference in the total component inventory valuation on the balance sheet between absorption and variable costing is the number of units in ending inventory times $0.54. (Note that the budgeted nonproduction expenses were *not* considered part of the inventory costs under either approach.)

For Custom Covers, assume the following activity for Year 1.

	Year 1
Actual units produced	300,000
Actual unit sales	270,000
Change in finished goods inventory, units	30,000
Beginning finished goods inventory, units	0
Ending finished goods inventory, units	30,000

Chapter 11 Absorption/Variable Costing and Capacity Analysis

Because Custom Covers began operations in Year 1, there is no beginning finished goods inventory. Because production exceeds sales, the company had 30,000 units of ending finished goods inventory. Custom Covers is assumed to complete all units started and, therefore, will have no Work-in-Process Inventory at the end of the period.

◆ **What is the total cost of ending finished goods inventory under absorption costing versus variable costing?**

Absorption costing ending inventory: **30,000 units × $4.26 = $127,800**

Variable costing ending inventory: **30,000 units × $3.72 = $111,600**

The $16,200 difference in the cost of ending inventory between the two methods is equal to fixed manufacturing overhead per unit of $0.54 × 30,000 units.

Calculating Costs Under Absorption vs. Variable Costing LO11-1 REVIEW 11-1

In the first year of business, Shalton Inc. produced 55,000 products. During its first year, the company sold 50,000 products. Costs incurred during the year were as follows:

Ingredients used	$280,000
Direct labor	120,000
Variable overhead	205,000
Fixed overhead	110,000
Variable selling expenses	25,000
Fixed selling and administrative expenses	1,000
Total actual costs	$741,000

a. What was the actual production cost per unit under variable costing?
b. What was the actual production cost per unit under absorption costing?
c. What was the value of ending inventory under variable costing?
d. What was the value of ending inventory under absorption costing?
e. **Critical Thinking:** Explain why there is a difference (if any) in your answers for parts c and d. What type of account will offset this difference (if any)? Why?

More practice:
MC11-12, E11-21, E11-23
Solution on p. 11-36.

INCOME UNDER ABSORPTION AND VARIABLE COSTING

One thing that is not different between absorption and variable costing methods is unit quantity: both methods track the same number of units in ending inventory and the same number of units sold. However, two differences exist between the two methods: one relates to cost accumulation and the other relates to cost presentation.

LO11-2 How do changes in sales or production levels affect before-tax profit presented under absorption and variable costing?

Cost Accumulation As described in the last section, absorption costing treats FOH as a product cost; variable costing treats it as a period cost. This treatment results in a difference in the accumulation of costs. Absorption costing advocates contend that products cannot be made without the production capacity provided by fixed manufacturing overhead costs, and, therefore, these costs "belong" to the product. Variable costing advocates contend that FOH costs would be incurred whether any products are manufactured; thus, such costs are not caused by production and cannot be product costs.

Cost Presentation When absorption costing is used, the income statement is usually formatted using the functional format. The functional income statement, used for financial reporting, subtracts manufacturing costs (represented by cost of goods sold) from revenues to calculate gross profit; selling and administrative costs are then subtracted from gross profit to calculate profit or income.

Under variable costing, cost of goods sold is more appropriately called variable cost of goods sold because it is comprised only of variable production costs. Sales minus variable cost of goods sold is called **product contribution margin** and indicates how much revenue is available to cover all period expenses and to provide net income.

Variable nonmanufacturing period expenses, such as sales commissions set at 10 percent of product selling price, are deducted from product contribution margin to determine the amount of total contribution margin. Total **contribution margin** is the difference between total revenues and total variable expenses. This amount measures the dollars available to "contribute" to cover all fixed expenses, both manufacturing and nonmanufacturing, and to provide net income. A variable costing income statement is also referred to as a contribution income statement. Note that this is similar to the *contribution income statement* introduced in Chapter 4, except now, VOH and FOH are explicitly stated. See **Exhibit 11.3** for a comparison of the cost relationships in absorption versus variable costing.

Major authoritative bodies of the accounting profession, such as the Financial Accounting Standards Board and the Securities and Exchange Commission, require the use of absorption costing to prepare external financial statements. Absorption costing is also required for filing tax returns with the Internal Revenue Service. The accounting profession has, in effect, disallowed the use of variable costing for external reporting purposes.

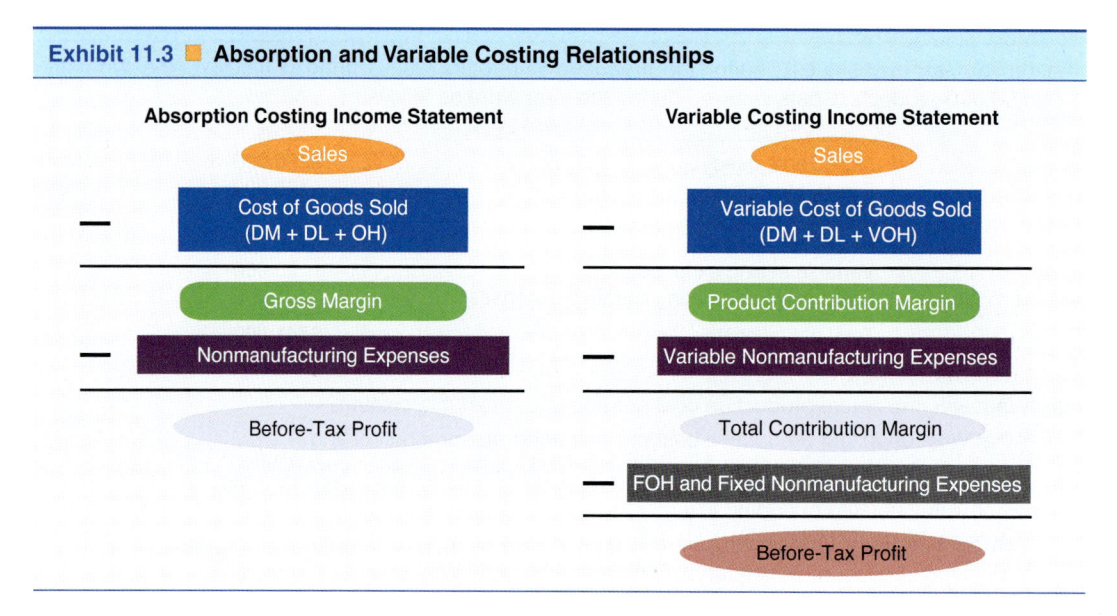

Exhibit 11.3 ■ Absorption and Variable Costing Relationships

Absorption Costing Income Statement
- Sales
- − Cost of Goods Sold (DM + DL + OH)
- = Gross Margin
- − Nonmanufacturing Expenses
- = Before-Tax Profit

Variable Costing Income Statement
- Sales
- − Variable Cost of Goods Sold (DM + DL + VOH)
- = Product Contribution Margin
- − Variable Nonmanufacturing Expenses
- = Total Contribution Margin
- − FOH and Fixed Nonmanufacturing Expenses
- = Before-Tax Profit

In the following demonstration, we illustrate how before-tax profit often differs under variable and absorption costing due to the treatment of fixed overhead described above.

DEMO 11-2   LO11-2   Comparing Absorption and Variable Costing Income Statement Results

We continue with the Custom Covers example, assuming that ending Year 1 inventory of 30,000 units is equal to Year 2 beginning inventory of 30,000 units. We also assume the same cost structure for both Year 1 and Year 2 (planned and actual results). The cost structures are considered constant over time to more clearly demonstrate the differences between absorption and variable costing and to reduce the complexity of the chapter explanations.

Planned and Actual Cost Data	
Variable manufacturing cost per unit	$ 3.72
Variable selling expense per unit	$ 0.24
Total fixed manufacturing costs	$162,000
Total fixed selling and administrative expenses	$ 23,400

With a consistent cost structure across years, we now focus on how a difference between production and sales volume affects before-tax profit under absorption and variable costing. For illustration purposes, we develop three scenarios for Year 2 with varying levels of sales, but with a uniform unit selling price of $6. Information regarding these three scenarios follows.

Chapter 11 Absorption/Variable Costing and Capacity Analysis

	Year 2 Scenario 1	Year 2 Scenario 2	Year 2 Scenario 3
Actual units produced.	300,000	300,000	300,000
Actual unit sales.	300,000	270,000	330,000
Change in finished goods inventory, units	0	30,000	(30,000)
Beginning finished goods inventory, units.	30,000	30,000	30,000
Ending finished goods inventory, units	30,000	60,000	0

◆ **In Year 2, how are absorption costing and variable costing income statements prepared under each of the three scenarios?**

Year Two, Scenario One: Production Volume Equals Sales Volume

Under absorption costing, cost of goods sold is determined by subtracting the full cost of ending inventory from the full cost of beginning inventory plus current manufacturing costs. Full cost includes fixed manufacturing costs. At a production level of 300,000 units, the full manufacturing cost per unit is $4.26, calculated as follows.

Variable manufacturing cost per unit	$3.72
Fixed manufacturing cost per unit ($162,000/300,000 units)	0.54
Total manufacturing cost per unit	$4.26

In Scenario 1, production units and sales units both total 300,000. With no change in inventory levels from the beginning to the end of the period, cost of goods sold under absorption costing is equal to the current manufacturing costs of the period of $1,278,000.

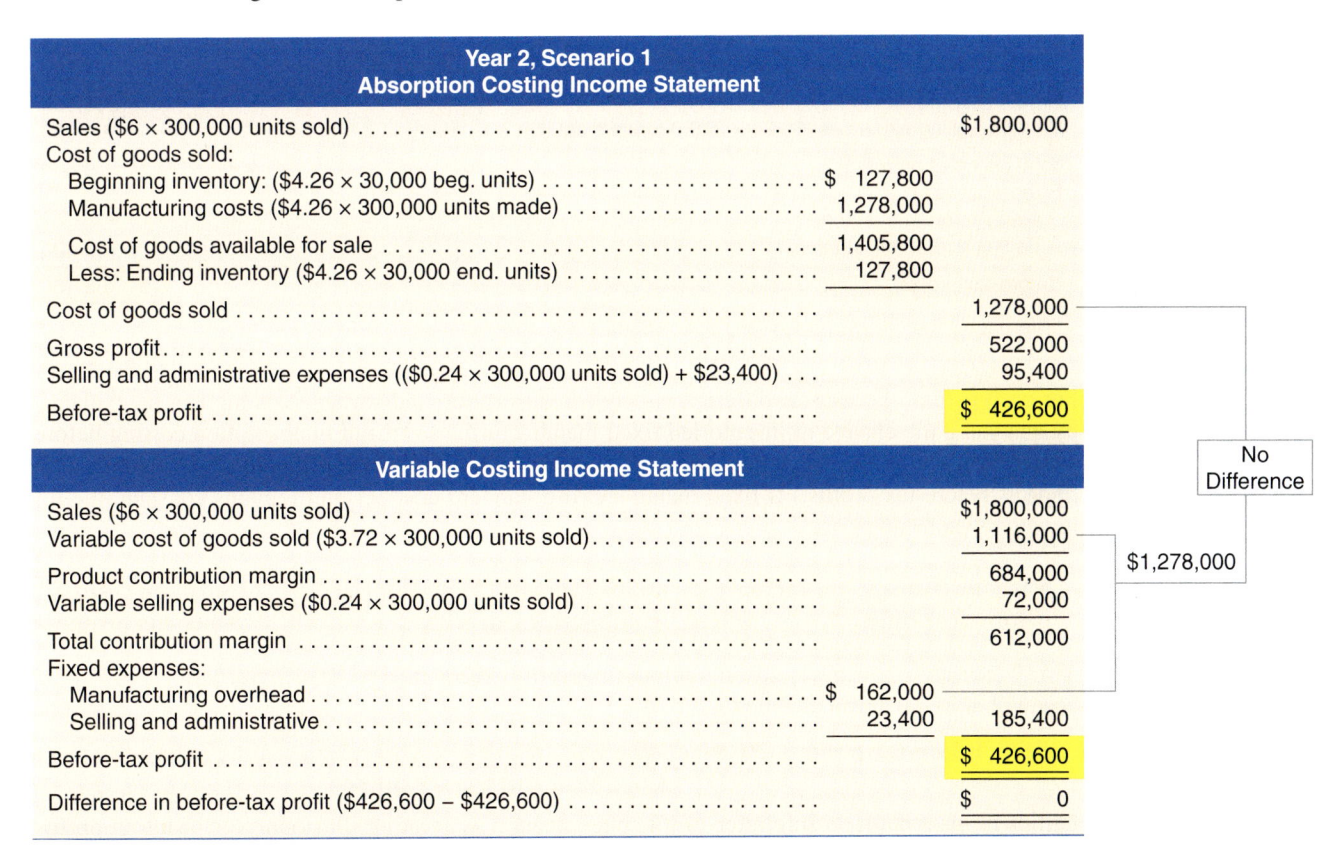

Year 2, Scenario 1
Absorption Costing Income Statement

Sales ($6 × 300,000 units sold)		$1,800,000
Cost of goods sold:		
Beginning inventory: ($4.26 × 30,000 beg. units)	$ 127,800	
Manufacturing costs ($4.26 × 300,000 units made)	1,278,000	
Cost of goods available for sale	1,405,800	
Less: Ending inventory ($4.26 × 30,000 end. units)	127,800	
Cost of goods sold		1,278,000
Gross profit		522,000
Selling and administrative expenses (($0.24 × 300,000 units sold) + $23,400)		95,400
Before-tax profit		$ 426,600

Variable Costing Income Statement

Sales ($6 × 300,000 units sold)		$1,800,000
Variable cost of goods sold ($3.72 × 300,000 units sold)		1,116,000
Product contribution margin		684,000
Variable selling expenses ($0.24 × 300,000 units sold)		72,000
Total contribution margin		612,000
Fixed expenses:		
Manufacturing overhead	$ 162,000	
Selling and administrative	23,400	185,400
Before-tax profit		$ 426,600
Difference in before-tax profit ($426,600 − $426,600)		$ 0

No Difference

$1,278,000

Because inventory levels did not change (again, assuming a consistent cost structure across years), the variable costing results mirror the absorption costing results. Under variable costing, current fixed manufacturing costs are always expensed in the current year. Thus, the variable cost of goods sold of

$1,116,000 plus fixed manufacturing overhead of $162,000 equals cost of goods sold under absorption costing of $1,278,000.

For any year in which there is no change in inventory from the beginning to the end of the year, both absorption and variable costing methods will result in the same before-tax profit, assuming similar cost structures. When the number of ending units does not change, no incremental costs are deferred of expensed.

Year Two, Scenario Two: Production Volume Exceeds Sales Volume

In Year 2, Scenario 2, *production exceeds sales* by 30,000 units. For any year in which inventory changes from the beginning to the end of the year, the absorption and variable costing methods will result in different values for before-tax profit.[1]

Year 2, Scenario 2
Absorption Costing Income Statement

Sales ($6 × 270,000 units sold)		$1,620,000
Cost of goods sold:		
Beginning inventory: ($4.26 × 30,000 beg. units)	$127,800	
Manufacturing costs ($4.26 × 300,000 units made)	1,278,000	
Cost of goods available for sale	1,405,800	
Less: Ending inventory ($4.26 × 60,000 end. units)	255,600	
Cost of goods sold		1,150,200
Gross profit		469,800
Selling and administrative expenses (($0.24 × 270,000 units sold) + $23,400)		88,200
Before-tax profit		$ 381,600

Variable Costing Income Statement

Sales ($6 × 270,000 units sold)		$1,620,000
Variable cost of goods sold ($3.72 × 270,000 units sold)		1,004,400
Product contribution margin		615,600
Variable selling expenses ($0.24 × 270,000 units sold)		64,800
Total contribution margin		550,800
Fixed expenses:		
Manufacturing overhead	$162,000	
Selling and administrative	23,400	185,400
Before-tax profit		$ 365,400
Difference in before-tax profit ($381,600 − $365,400)		$ 16,200

$16,200 Difference

$1,166,400

For each period, the income differences between absorption and variable costing can be explained by analyzing the change in inventoried fixed manufacturing overhead in absorption costing before-tax profit. (A difference in ending inventory causes a difference in cost of goods sold, which directly impacts before-tax profits.) If fixed manufacturing standard cost per unit remains constant, the following relationship exists.

> **Variable costing before-tax profit** + **Increase (or minus decrease) in inventoried fixed manufacturing overhead** = **Absorption costing before-tax profit**

Year 2, Scenario 2, variable costing before-tax profit is reconciled to Year 2, Scenario 2, absorption costing before-tax profit as follows.

Variable costing before-tax profit + (30,000 ending units × $0.54) = Absorption costing before-tax profit
$365,400 + $16,200 = $381,600

Critics of absorption costing refer to this phenomenon as creating illusionary or phantom profits. **Phantom profits** are temporary absorption costing profits caused by producing more inventory than is

---

[1] Although not shown, the Custom Covers income statement for Year 1 (Demo 11-1) would result in the same before-tax profit in both the absorption and variable costing income statements as Year 2, Scenario 2. The end results are the same because in both cases, costs structures across years are the same and ending inventory *increased* by 30,000 units.

Chapter 11 Absorption/Variable Costing and Capacity Analysis

sold. When previously produced inventory is sold, the phantom profits disappear. In contrast, variable costing expenses all FOH in the year it is incurred. In addition, no volume variance results when actual production volume is the same as planned production volume.

Year Two, Scenario Three: Sales Volume Exceeds Production Volume

In Year 2, Scenario 3, *sales exceeds production* by 30,000 units. Again, for any year in which inventory changes from the beginning to the end of the year, both absorption and variable costing methods will result in different values for before-tax profit.

Year 2, Scenario 3
Absorption Costing Income Statement

Sales ($6 × 330,000 units sold)		$1,980,000
Cost of goods sold		
Beginning inventory: ($4.26 × 30,000 beg. units)	$ 127,800	
Manufacturing costs ($4.26 × 300,000 units made)	1,278,000	
Cost of goods available for sale	1,405,800	
Less: Ending inventory ($4.26 × 0 end. units)	0	
Cost of goods sold		1,405,800
Gross profit		574,200
Selling and administrative expenses (($0.24 × 330,000 units sold) + $23,400)		102,600
Before-tax profit		**$ 471,600**

Variable Costing Income Statement

Sales ($6 × 330,000 units sold)		$1,980,000
Variable cost of goods sold ($3.72 × 330,000 units sold)		1,227,600
Product contribution margin		752,400
Variable selling expenses ($0.24 × 330,000 units sold)		79,200
Total contribution margin		673,200
Fixed expenses:		
Manufacturing overhead	$ 162,000	
Selling and administrative	23,400	185,400
Before-tax profit		**$ 487,800**
Difference in before-tax profit ($471,600 − $487,800)		$ (16,200)

$1,389,600
$16,200 Difference

Year 2, Scenario 3, variable costing before-tax profit is reconciled to Year 2, Scenario 3, absorption costing before-tax profit as follows.

Variable costing before-tax profit + (−30,000 units × $0.54) = Absorption costing before-tax profit
$$\$487,800 - \$16,200 = \$471,600$$

Summary of Effect on Before-Tax Profit of Absorption and Variable Costing

Whether absorption costing income is more or less than variable costing income depends on the relationship of production to sales. In all cases, to determine the effect on income, *it must be assumed that unit product costs are constant over time.* **Exhibit 11.4** summarizes the possible relationships between production and sales levels and the effects of these relationships on income. These relationships are as follows.

- If production equals sales, absorption costing income will equal variable costing income.
- If production is more than sales, absorption costing income is greater than variable costing income. This result occurs because some fixed manufacturing overhead cost is included in inventory cost on the balance sheet under absorption costing, whereas the total amount of fixed manufacturing overhead cost is expensed as a period cost under variable costing.
- If production is less than sales, income under absorption costing is less than income under variable costing. In this case, absorption costing expenses all of the current period fixed manufacturing overhead costs and releases some fixed manufacturing overhead cost from the beginning inventory where it had been deferred from a prior period.

Exhibit 11.4 ■ Production/Sales Relationships and Effects on Income

AC = Absorption Costing and VC = Variable Costing

	Absorption vs. Variable Income Statement: Before-Tax Profit
Units produced = Units sold	AC income = VC income
Units produced > Units sold	AC income > VC income
Units produced < Units sold	AC income < VC income

The effects of the relationships presented here are based on two qualifying assumptions:
(1) that unit costs are constant over time and
(2) that any under- or overapplied fixed overhead is written off when incurred rather than being prorated to inventory balances.

This process of deferring FOH costs into, and releasing FOH costs from inventory makes it possible to *manipulate income* under absorption costing by adjusting levels of production relative to sales to create phantom profits. Other times, sales in certain industries can vary by season, where inventory build-ups and sell-downs are a part of normal business cycles. For this reason, some believe that variable costing would be more useful for external reporting purposes than absorption costing. However, GAAP requires the use of absorption costing for financial statement presentation.

For internal reporting, variable costing information provides managers information about the behavior of the various product and period costs. To plan, control, and make decisions, managers must understand and be able to project how costs will change in reaction to changes in activity levels. Because absorption costing classifies expenses by functional category, cost behavior (relative to changes in activity) cannot be observed from an absorption costing income statement. Understanding cost behavior is extremely important for many managerial activities including budgeting, cost-volume-profit analysis, and relevant costing (See Chapters 4 and 5). For instance, the variable costing format provides information for determining the contribution margin ratio, a primary data item needed to determine the break-even point.

Data Visualization

Data Analytics

The following charts present two different cases of cost accumulation and presentation based on the *same* underlying economic situation.

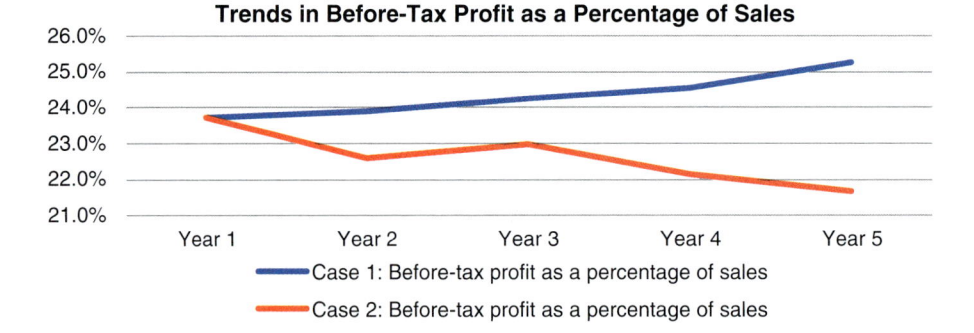

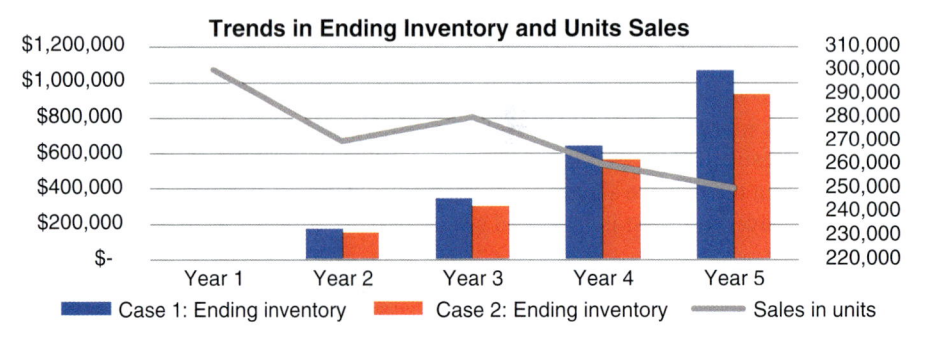

Trends in Before-Tax Profit as a Percentage of Sales

— Case 1: Before-tax profit as a percentage of sales
— Case 2: Before-tax profit as a percentage of sales

Trends in Ending Inventory and Units Sales

■ Case 1: Ending inventory ■ Case 2: Ending inventory — Sales in units

continued

Chapter 11 Absorption/Variable Costing and Capacity Analysis

continued from previous page

Refer to the data visualizations to answer the following questions.
a. In review of the first chart only, would you consider one case more economically favorable over the other? Why or why not?
b. Considering both charts, which presentation, Case 1 or Case 2, presents an absorption costing presentation, and which one presents a variable costing presentation? How do you know?
c. Considering both charts, comment on the financial position of the company.

Solution on p. 11-38.

Before-Tax Profit; Absorption vs. Variable Costing — LO11-2 — REVIEW 11-2

In the first year of business, Shalton Inc. produced 55,000 products. During its first year, the company sold 50,000 products. Costs incurred during the year were as follows.

Ingredients used	$280,000
Direct labor	120,000
Variable overhead	205,000
Fixed overhead	110,000
Variable selling expenses*	25,000
Fixed selling and administrative expenses	1,000
Total actual costs	$741,000

*Variable selling expenses change proportionately with sales units.

The products were sold for $20 per unit.

a. What was before-tax profit under variable costing?
b. What was before-tax profit under absorption costing?
c. What was before-tax profit under variable costing assuming instead that all 55,000 products were sold?
d. What was before-tax profit under absorption costing assuming instead that all 55,000 products were sold?
e. **Critical Thinking:** What causes the differences in the results (if any) between parts *a* and *b*, and parts *c* and *d*?

More practice: MC11-15, E11-22, E11-25, E11-26, E11-31
Solution on p. 3-36.

INCOME STATEMENT IMPACT OF A VOLUME VARIANCE

In this section, we demonstrate how a volume variance impacts the presentation of the absorption and variable costing income statements. Unlike the last section, we now assume that the company uses standard costs for material and labor and predetermined rates for variable and fixed overhead. In the demonstration that follows, volume variances result because actual production volume will now vary from the budgeted annual production of 300,000 units.

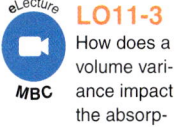

LO11-3 How does a volume variance impact the absorption and variable costing income statements?

Presenting Income Statements with a Volume Variance — LO11-3 — DEMO 11-3

We use the same initial cost data for Custom Covers, but now all actual costs are assumed to equal the standard and budgeted cost for the years presented. For simplicity, we assume that the cost structure remains constant over three years. Budgeted annual capacity for all three years is assumed to be 300,000 units. Thus, standard fixed manufacturing cost per unit is calculated by taking total standard fixed costs of $162,000 divided by budgeted annual production of 300,000 units, which equals $0.54 per unit.

Standard Cost Data		
Variable manufacturing cost per unit	$	3.72
Fixed manufacturing cost per unit ($162,000/300,000)		0.54
Total manufacturing cost per unit	$	4.26
Variable selling expense per unit	$	0.24
Total fixed manufacturing costs		$162,000
Total selling and administrative expenses		$ 23,400

© Cambridge Business Publishers

The following schedule is a comparison of actual unit production with actual unit sales to determine the change in inventory for each of the three years. (Note that different assumptions are made about units made and sold in the first two years compared to the earlier demonstrations.)

	Year 1	Year 2	Year 3	Total
Actual units made..........................	300,000	290,000	310,000	900,000
Actual unit sales.............................	300,000	270,000	330,000	900,000
Change in finished goods inventory, units........	0	20,000	(20,000)	0
Beginning finished goods inventory, units.........	0	0	20,000	0
Ending finished goods inventory, units............	0	20,000	0	0

Because the actual production volume shown above sometimes differs from the budgeted volume of 300,000 units, volume variances will result. We assume that any volume variances will be allocated to cost of goods sold and not to inventory.

There is no beginning finished goods inventory for the company's first year of operations. The next year, Year 2, also has no beginning inventory because all units produced in Year 1 were also sold in Year 1. In Year 2 and Year 3, production and sales quantities differ, which is a common situation because production frequently "leads" sales so that inventory can be stockpiled to satisfy future sales demand.

◆ **How does the company prepare absorption and variable costing income statements for Year 1, Year 2, and Year 3?**

Refer to the following schedule for Custom Covers' operating results for Year 1 through Year 3 using both absorption and variable costing.

Absorption Costing Income Statement	Year 1	Year 2	Year 3	Total
Sales ($6 per unit sold)......................	$1,800,000	$1,620,000	$1,980,000	$5,400,000
Cost of goods sold:				
Beginning inventory	0	0	85,200	0
Manufacturing costs ($4.26 × units made).......	1,278,000	1,235,400	1,320,600	3,834,000
Cost of goods available for sale	1,278,000	1,235,400	1,405,800	3,834,000
Less: Ending inventory ($4.26 × ending units).....	0	85,200	0	0
Cost of goods sold at standard.................	1,278,000	1,150,200	1,405,800	3,834,000
Volume variance............................	0	5,400	(5,400)	0
Cost of goods sold, adjusted	1,278,000	1,155,600	1,400,400	3,834,000
Gross margin	522,000	464,400	579,600	1,566,000
Selling and administrative expenses*...........	95,400	88,200	102,600	286,200
Before-tax profit	$ 426,600	$ 376,200	$ 477,000	$1,279,800

Variable Costing Income Statement	Year 1	Year 2	Year 3	Total
Sales ($6 per unit sold)......................	$1,800,000	$1,620,000	$1,980,000	$5,400,000
Variable CGS ($3.72 per unit sold).............	1,116,000	1,004,400	1,227,600	3,348,000
Product contribution margin	684,000	615,600	752,400	2,052,000
Variable selling expenses ($0.24 per unit sold)	72,000	64,800	79,200	216,000
Total contribution margin	612,000	550,800	673,200	1,836,000
Fixed expenses				
Manufacturing............................	162,000	162,000	162,000	486,000
Selling and administrative...................	23,400	23,400	23,400	70,200
Total fixed expenses	185,400	185,400	185,400	556,200
Before-tax profit	$ 426,600	$ 365,400	$ 487,800	$1,279,800
Differences in before-tax profit	$ 0	$ 10,800	$ (10,800)	$ 0

No Difference Over 3-Year Period

$3,834,000

*Year 1: (300,000 × $0.24) + $23,400 = $95,400; Year 2: (270,000 × $0.24) + $23,400 = $88,200; Year 3: (330,000 × $0.24) + $23,400 = $102,600

Year One: Actual Production Volume Equals Planned Production Volume

In Year 1, actual and planned production both total 300,000 units. No volume variance results when actual production volume is the same as planned production volume.

Year Two: Planned Production Volume Exceeds Actual Production Volume

Absorption Costing Actual production and operating costs have been assumed to equal the budgeted costs for Year 2. However, a difference in actual and budgeted capacity utilization occurred for Year 2, creating a volume variance for that year under absorption costing. As introduced in the last chapter, a volume variance reflects the monetary impact of a difference between the budgeted capacity used to determine the predetermined FOH rate and the actual capacity at which the company operated.

```
                                    Applied FOH
                             (for standard quantity allowed)
        Budgeted FOH                  SP × SQ
        |_____|
                      Volume Variance
```

For Year 2, the volume variance is calculated as follows.

Volume Variance = Budgeted FOH − Applied FOH

$$= \$162{,}000 - (\$0.54 \times 290{,}000 \text{ units})$$
$$= \$5{,}400 \text{ U}$$

The firm's standards are based on 300,000 units of production. In this case, the firm produced 10,000 *fewer* units than planned at $0.54 per unit, resulting in an unfavorable volume variance of $5,400. Because the company is not allocating variances to inventory, the entire unfavorable variance *increases* cost of goods sold at standard in Year 2.

Variable Costing No volume variance is shown under variable costing because fixed manufacturing overhead is not applied to products; the FOH is deducted in its entirety as a period expense.

Year Three: Actual Production Volume Exceeds Planned Production Volume

Absorption Costing In Year 3, just the opposite situation occurred compared to Year 2. Actual production volume exceeded planned production volume.

For Year 3, the volume variance is calculated as follows.

Volume Variance = Budgeted FOH − Applied FOH

$$= \$162{,}000 - (\$0.54 \times 310{,}000 \text{ units})$$
$$= \$5{,}400 \text{ F}$$

In Year 3, the firm produces 10,000 *more* units than planned at $0.54 per unit, resulting in a favorable volume variance of $5,400. Because the company is not allocating variances to inventory, the entire favorable variance *decreases* cost of goods sold at standard in Year 3.

Variable Costing No volume variance is shown under variable costing because fixed manufacturing overhead is not applied to products.

Reconciliation of Variable and Absorption Costing Before-Tax Profit

Over the three-year period, Custom Covers produced and sold 900,000 units (with an initial beginning inventory balance of zero). Thus, all the costs incurred (whether variable or fixed) are expensed in one year or another under either method which means that the total expenses for the three years is the same under both methods. The income difference in each year is caused *solely by the timing of the expensing of fixed manufacturing overhead.*

Year One Reconciliation In Year 1, production and sales both total 300,000 units. For any year in which there is no change in inventory from the beginning to the end of the year, both absorption and variable costing methods will result in the same before-tax profit, assuming consistent cost structures.

Year Two Reconciliation Units of production of 290,000 exceeded unit sales of 270,000 causing inventory to increase by 20,000 units. Year 2 variable costing before-tax profit is reconciled to Year 2 absorption costing before-tax profit as follows.

Variable costing before-tax profit + (20,000 ending units × $0.54) = Absorption costing before-tax profit

$365,400 + $10,800 = $376,200

Year Three Reconciliation In Year 3, inventory decreased by 20,000 units. This decrease, multiplied by the FOH rate of $0.54, explains the $10,800 by which Year 3 absorption costing income falls short of variable costing income.

Variable costing before-tax profit + (−20,000 ending units × $0.54) = Absorption costing before-tax profit

$487,800 − $10,800 = $477,000

Under absorption costing, not only is all Year 3 fixed manufacturing overhead expensed through Cost of Goods Sold, but also $10,800 of FOH that was retained in ending inventory of Year 2 is included in Cost of Goods Sold of Year 3. In contrast, only Year 3 fixed manufacturing overhead is shown on the Year 3 variable costing income statement.

Under these conditions, the data in the income statements demonstrate that, regardless of whether absorption or variable costing is used, the cumulative, three-year income before tax will be the same ($1,279,800). This is because there was zero Year 1 beginning inventory and zero Year 3 ending inventory, resulting in no net difference in inventory balances over the three-year period.

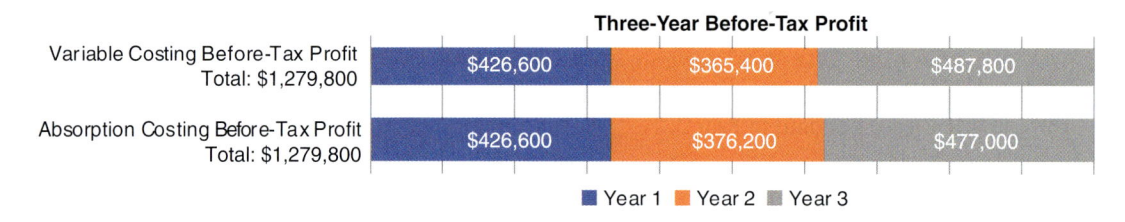

Three-Year Before-Tax Profit

	Year 1	Year 2	Year 3
Variable Costing Before-Tax Profit Total: $1,279,800	$426,600	$365,400	$487,800
Absorption Costing Before-Tax Profit Total: $1,279,800	$426,600	$376,200	$477,000

REVIEW 11-3 | **LO11-3** | Absorption and Variable Costing Income Statement with Volume Variance

In the first year of business, Shalton Inc. budgeted to produce 55,000 units of products. Budgeted costs for the year were as follows.

Budgeted Costs	
Variable manufacturing costs per unit made.............	$ 11.00
Variable selling expense per unit sold	$0.50
Total fixed manufacturing overhead	$110,000
Total fixed selling and administrative expenses	$ 1,000

During the year, the company produced 60,000 units of product and sold 50,000 units of products for $15 per unit. Assume that the actual costs in the table above were the same as budgeted costs for the year.

a. Prepare the company's absorption costing income statement for the year.
b. Prepare the company's variable costing income statement for the year.
c. Reconcile the difference in before-tax profit between the two statements.
d. **Critical Thinking:** Will the statement in part *a* or part *b* be used for cost-volume profit analysis? Why?

More practice: E11-32, E11-33, E11-35
Solution on p. 11-37.

IMPLICATIONS OF CAPACITY MEASUREMENTS

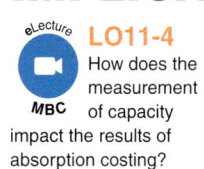

LO11-4
How does the measurement of capacity impact the results of absorption costing?

In this section, we discuss how capacity can be measured in different ways under different assumptions. We also explore how different measurements of capacity can impact the amount of fixed overhead that is applied and the timing of recognition of before-tax income.

Alternative Capacity Measures

The activity level used in setting the predetermined OH rate generally reflects a consideration of organizational capacity.

- **Theoretical capacity** is the estimated maximum potential activity for a specified time period. This measure assumes that all production factors are operating perfectly. Theoretical capacity disregards realities such as machinery breakdowns and reduced or stopped plant operations on holidays. Choosing this activity level for setting a predetermined OH rate nearly guarantees a significant amount of underapplied overhead cost. The amount by which overhead is underapplied reflects the difference between actual capacity and theoretical capacity.

- **Practical capacity** can be achieved during regular working hours. It is calculated by reducing theoretical capacity by ongoing, regular operating interruptions (such as holidays, downtime, and start-up time).

- **Normal capacity** considers historical and estimated future production levels and cyclical fluctuations. Normal capacity encompasses the firm's long-run (5–10 years) average activity and represents an attainable level of activity. Although it may generate substantial differences between actual and applied overhead in the short run, use of normal capacity has been required under GAAP.[2]

- **Expected capacity** is a short-run concept that represents the firm's anticipated activity level for the coming period based on *projected product demand*. Expected capacity level is determined during the budgeting process, which is discussed in Chapter 9. If actual results are close to budgeted results (in both dollars and volume), this measure should result in product costs that most closely reflect actual costs and, thus, generate an immaterial amount of underapplied or overapplied overhead.[3]

See **Exhibit 11.5** for a visual representation of capacity measures. Although expected capacity is shown in this diagram as much smaller than practical capacity, it is possible for expected and practical capacity to be more equal—especially in a highly automated plant.

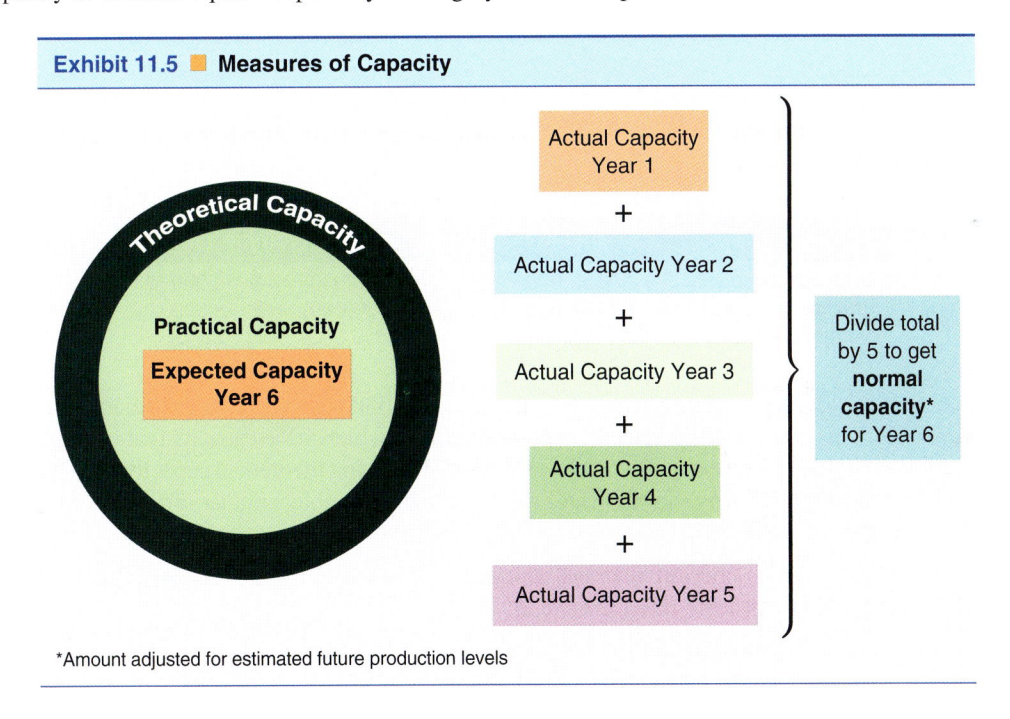

Exhibit 11.5 ■ Measures of Capacity

Theoretical Capacity
Practical Capacity
Expected Capacity Year 6

Actual Capacity Year 1
+
Actual Capacity Year 2
+
Actual Capacity Year 3
+
Actual Capacity Year 4
+
Actual Capacity Year 5

Divide total by 5 to get **normal capacity*** for Year 6

*Amount adjusted for estimated future production levels

---

[2] ASC 330-10-30 indicates that variations in production levels from period to period are expected and establish the normal capacity range. This capacity range will vary based on business- and industry-specific factors. The actual production level may be used if it approximates normal capacity. In periods of abnormally high production, the amount of fixed overhead allocated to each unit of production is decreased so that inventories are not measured above cost. The amount of fixed overhead allocated to each unit of production is not increased as a consequence of abnormally low production or an idle plant.

[3] Except where otherwise noted in the text, expected capacity has been chosen as the basis for calculating the predetermined fixed manufacturing overhead rate because it is believed to be the most prevalent practice. This choice, however, may not be the most effective for planning and control purposes as is discussed further in Chapter 10 with regard to standard cost variances.

Capacity Measurement Effect on Absorption Income

Recall from an earlier section that the budgeted fixed overhead rate is calculated as follows.

Predetermined FOH rate = Budgeted annual FOH ÷ Budgeted Annual Capacity in units

Based on this formula, the predetermined FOH rate varies inversely with the capacity measurement. As capacity increases (decreases), the FOH rate will decrease (increase). Therefore, the FOH rate will be lower if based on theoretical capacity as compared to a rate based on normal capacity. In a standard costing system, if actual production volume is closer to normal capacity than theoretical capacity, using normal capacity as the basis for the predetermined FOH rate will produce the lowest volume variance. This concept is illustrated in the following demonstration.

DEMO 11-4 LO11-4 Determining the Impact of Different Capacity Measures

Continuing with the Custom Covers example, let's assume that theoretical, practical, and normal capacity equal 450,000, 360,000 and 300,000 units, respectively.

♦ **With a total annual budgeted fixed overhead of $162,000, what is the budgeted FOH rate based upon theoretical, practical, and normal capacity?**

	Theoretical Capacity	Practical Capacity	Normal Capacity
Budgeted FOH	$162,000	$162,000	$162,000
Divided by capacity	÷ 450,000	÷ 360,000	÷ 300,000
Budgeted FOH rate	$ 0.36	$ 0.45	$ 0.54

As the capacity level decreases, the budgeted FOH rate increases.

♦ **What is the volume variance based upon theoretical, practical, and normal capacity, if actual volume manufactured is 330,000 units?**

	Budgeted FOH	Applied FOH	Volume Variance
Theoretical capacity	$162,000	− ($0.36 × 330,000)	= $ 43,200 U
Practical capacity	$162,000	− ($0.45 × 330,000)	= $ 13,500 U
Normal capacity	$162,000	− ($0.54 × 330,000)	= $(16,200) F

As capacity levels decrease relative to the actual volume of 330,000, the volume variance becomes more favorable. This is due to the decrease in **excess capacity**, which is the capacity that is not utilized. Intuitively, we would expect more unfavorable variances when using theoretical capacity because firms almost always have breakdowns and stoppages resulting in unfavorable variances from this somewhat unrealistic standard.

♦ **What is the impact on current year before-tax profit of using theoretical, practical, and normal capacity to allocate fixed overhead?**

Assume the same selling price per unit of $6, standard variable manufacturing costs per unit of $3.72 and standard fixed nonmanufacturing costs ($0.24 per unit plus $23,400) as shown in the prior demonstrations. Also assume beginning inventory of zero units and sales of 310,000 units. Thus, ending inventory is 20,000 units, equal to production of 330,000 units minus sales of 310,000 units.

	Theoretical Capacity	Practical Capacity	Normal Capacity
Sales ($6 × 310,000 units)	$1,860,000	$1,860,000	$1,860,000
Cost of goods sold:			
Beginning inventory	0	0	0
Manufacturing costs*	1,346,400	1,376,100	1,405,800
Cost of goods available for sale	1,346,400	1,376,100	1,405,800
Less: ending inventory**	81,600	83,400	85,200
Cost of goods sold (at standard)	1,264,800	1,292,700	1,320,600
Volume variance	43,200	13,500	(16,200)
Cost of goods sold	1,308,000	1,306,200	1,304,400
Gross margin	552,000	553,800	555,600
Selling and administrative expenses			
(($0.24 × 310,000 units) + $23,400)	97,800	97,800	97,800
Before-tax profit	$ 454,200	$ 456,000	$ 457,800

Totals $1,389,600 in Each Case (applies to Cost of goods available for sale and Volume variance rows)

*Manufacturing costs at standard:
($3.72 + $0.36) × 330,000 units = $1,346,400
($3.72 + $0.45) × 330,000 units = $1,376,100
($3.72 + $0.54) × 330,000 units = $1,405,800

**Inventory costs at standard:
($3.72 + $0.36) × 20,000 units = $81,600
($3.72 + $0.45) × 20,000 units = $83,400
($3.72 + $0.54) × 20,000 units = $85,200

In each instance, the total of cost of goods available for sale plus the volume variance is the same at $1,389,600. However, the difference in before-tax profit among the three scenarios is due to the amount of fixed overhead capitalized in the 20,000 units of finished goods inventory at period-end. For example, the difference between before-tax profit based on theoretical capacity and practical capacity is $1,800 (=$456,000 − $454,200). This difference is due to the difference in the amount of fixed overhead capitalized in ending inventory.

$$20,000 \text{ ending units} \times (\$0.45 - \$0.36) = \$1,800$$

Downward Demand Spiral

The amount of planned production of a product is largely based on expected customer demand for that product. If demand for a product suddenly drops causing a drop in planned production, fixed overhead will be allocated over fewer units of production, driving up the fixed cost per unit. For example, assume the following expected capacity levels over a three-year period.

    Year 1: $200,000 Fixed overhead ÷ 100,000 Expected capacity = $2.00 per unit

    Year 2: $200,000 Fixed overhead ÷ 80,000 Expected capacity = $2.50 per unit

    Year 3: $200,000 Fixed overhead ÷ 50,000 Expected capacity = $4.00 per unit

Assuming fixed costs remain constant, the fixed cost per unit increases sharply with each drop in expected capacity. To make matters worse, the increase in costs can prompt the company to increase prices. Increasing prices can result in even lower demand as shoppers search for other suppliers offering lower prices. This situation where fixed costs cannot be absorbed by a decreasing volume of product is known as a **downward demand spiral** (or a **death spiral**). A recent example of a death spiral is illustrated in the drop in customer demand for shopping in malls. The market value of U.S. regional malls has dropped dramatically due to changes in shopping patterns, competition, and the increase in virtual shopping.[4] The industry shows signs of a death spiral as demand continues to drop while the fixed costs related to mall physical structures do not. When malls lose stores, costs are allocated over fewer remaining stores leading to higher overhead costs per store. Malls often make up for these higher cost per store by raising the price of leases on the remaining stores. These increased prices often drive more stores to leave. The cycle continues until all stores leave because prices are too high.

---

[4] K. King, *Local Malls, Stuck in 'Death Spiral,' Plunge in Value*, Wall Street Journal, July 31, 2023.

REVIEW 11-4 — LO11-4: Predetermined OH Rates; Capacity Measures

Holley Inc. uses a standard cost system that applies overhead based on machine hours. The following budgeted data are available for the year.

- Fixed factory overhead at all levels between 20,000 and 118,000 machine hours is $531,000.
- Practical capacity is 118,000 machine hours; expected capacity is 75 percent of practical capacity.

a. What is the budgeted FOH rate using practical capacity?
b. What is the budgeted FOH rate using expected capacity?
c. During the year, the firm records 85,000 machine hours. What is the volume variance based upon (1) practical capacity and (2) expected capacity?
d. **Critical Thinking:** What do the results in part *c* indicate about excess capacity for the company and its impact on management decision making?

More practice: E11-37, E11-38
Solution on p. 11-37.

Comprehensive Chapter Review

Key Terms

absorption costing, p. 11-2
contribution margin, p. 11-6
death spiral, p. 11-17
direct costing, p. 11-3
downward demand spiral, p. 11-17
excess capacity, p. 11-16

expected capacity, p. 11-15
full costing, p. 11-2
functional classification, p. 11-2
normal capacity, p. 11-15
phantom profits, p. 11-8
practical capacity, p. 11-15

product contribution margin, p. 11-5
theoretical capacity, p. 11-15
variable costing, p. 11-3
volume variance, p. 11-13

Chapter Summary

LO11-1 Absorption and Variable Costing (Page 11-2)
- Absorption and variable costing differ in that
  - absorption costing
    - includes all manufacturing costs, both variable and fixed, as product costs.
    - presents nonmanufacturing costs on the income statement according to functional areas.
  - variable costing
    - includes only the variable costs of production (direct material, direct labor, and variable manufacturing overhead) as product costs.
    - presents both nonmanufacturing and manufacturing costs on the income statement according to cost behavior.

LO11-2 Changing Sales or Production Levels in Absorption and Variable Costing (Page 11-5)
- Differences between sales and production volume result in differences in income between absorption and variable costing because
  - absorption costing requires fixed costs to be expensed as a function of the number of units sold;
    - if production volume is higher than sales volume, some fixed costs will be deferred in inventory at year-end, making net income higher than under variable costing.
    - if sales volume is higher than production volume, the deferred fixed costs from previous periods will be expensed as part of Cost of Goods Sold, making net income lower than under variable costing.
  - variable costing requires all fixed costs to be expensed in the period incurred, regardless of when the related inventory is sold;
    - if production volume is higher than sales volume, all fixed manufacturing costs are expensed in the current period and are not deferred until the inventory is sold, making net income lower than under absorption costing.
    - if sales volume is higher than production volume, only current period fixed manufacturing costs are expensed in the current period, making net income higher than under absorption costing.

Chapter 11 Absorption/Variable Costing and Capacity Analysis

Volume Variance Impact on Absorption and Variable Costing Income Statements (Page 11-11) — LO11-3
- Absorption costing
  - Difference in actual and budgeted capacity utilization creates a volume variance
  - Volume variance equals budgeted FOH – Applied FOH
  - An unfavorable(favorable) volume variance increases(decreases) CGS (and possibly inventory levels)
- Variable costing
  - No volume variance is calculated because fixed manufacturing overhead is not applied to inventory, but is instead expensed as incurred

Predetermined Overhead Rates and Capacity (Page 11-14) — LO11-4
- Capacity measures affect the setting of predetermined OH rates because the use of
  - expected capacity (the budgeted capacity for the upcoming year) will result in a predetermined OH rate that would likely be most closely related to an actual OH rate.
  - practical capacity (the capacity that allows for normal operating interruptions) will generally result in a predetermined OH rate that is substantially lower than an actual OH rate would be.
  - normal capacity (the capacity that reflects a long-run average) can result in an OH rate that is higher or lower than an actual OH rate, depending on whether capacity has been over- or underutilized during the years under consideration.
  - theoretical capacity (the estimated maximum potential capacity) will result in a predetermined OH rate that is substantially lower than an actual OH rate; however, this rate reflects a company's utopian use of its capacity.

Solution Strategies

Absorption and Variable Costing — LO11-2, 3

Determine which method is being used (absorption or variable). The following abbreviations are used: VOH, variable manufacturing overhead; FOH, fixed manufacturing overhead; DM, direct material; DL, direct labor.
1. If absorption:
   - Determine the FOH application rate.
   - Determine the denominator capacity used in determining FOH.
   - Determine whether production was equal to the denominator capacity. If not, a FOH volume variance must be properly assigned to CGS and, possibly, inventories.
   - Determine the cost per unit of product, which consists of (DM + DL + VOH + FOH).
2. If variable:
   - Determine the cost per unit of product, which consists of (DM + DL + VOH).
   - Determine the total FOH and assign that amount to the income statement as a period expense.

Comparing Absorption to Variable Costing — LO11-2

1. Determine the relationship of production to sales.
   a. If production = sales, then absorption costing income = variable costing income.
   b. If production > sales, then absorption costing income > variable costing income.
   c. If production < sales, then absorption costing income < variable costing income.
2. The dollar difference between absorption costing income and variable costing income equals FOH rate × change in inventory units.

Chapter Demonstration Problem

LO11-1, 2, 3

White Plasto Company management uses predetermined VOH and FOH rates to apply overhead to its products. For Year 1, the company budgeted production at 27,000 units, which would require 54,000 direct labor hours (DLHs) and 27,000 machine hours (MHs). At that level of production, total variable and fixed manufacturing overhead costs were expected to be $13,500 and $105,300, respectively. Variable overhead is applied to production using direct labor hours, and fixed overhead is applied using machine hours. During Year 1, White Plasto Company produced 23,000 units and experienced the following operating volumes and costs: 46,000 direct labor hours; 23,000 machine hours; $11,980 actual variable manufacturing overhead; and $103,540 actual fixed manufacturing overhead. By the end of Year 1, all 23,000 units that were produced were sold; thus, the company began Year 2 with no beginning finished goods inventory.

© Cambridge Business Publishers

In Year 2 and Year 3, White Plasto Company management decided to apply manufacturing overhead to products using units of production (rather than direct labor hours and machine hours). The company produced 25,000 and 20,000 units, respectively, in Year 2 and Year 3. White Plasto's budgeted and actual fixed manufacturing overhead for both years was $100,000. Production in each year was projected at 25,000 units. Variable production cost (including variable manufacturing overhead) is $3 per unit. The following absorption costing income statements and supporting information are available:

	Year 2	Year 3
Net sales (20,000 units and 22,000 units)	$300,000	$330,000
Cost of goods sold (a)	(140,000)	(154,000)
Volume variance (0 and 5,000 units × $4)	0	(20,000)
Gross margin	$160,000	$156,000
Operating expenses (b)	(82,500)	(88,500)
Income before tax	$ 77,500	$ 67,500
(a) Cost of goods sold		
Beginning inventory	$ 0	$ 35,000
Cost of goods manufactured[a]	175,000	140,000
Goods available for sale	$175,000	$175,000
Ending inventory[b]	(35,000)	(21,000)
Cost of goods sold	$140,000	$154,000

[a] CGM
25,000 units × $7 (of which $3 are variable) = $175,000
20,000 units × $7 (of which $3 are variable) = $140,000

[b] EI
25,000 − 20,000 = 5,000 units; 5,000 × $7 = $35,000
5,000 + 20,000 − 22,000 = 3,000 units; 3,000 × $7 = $21,000

(b) Analysis of operating expenses		
Variable	$ 50,000	$ 55,000
Fixed	32,500	33,500
Total	$ 82,500	$ 88,500

Required
a. Determine the predetermined variable and fixed overhead rates for Year 1, and calculate how much underapplied or overapplied overhead existed at the end of that year.
b. Recast the Year 2 and Year 3 income statements on a variable costing basis.
c. Reconcile income for Year 2 and Year 3 between absorption and variable costing.

Solution to Demonstration Problem

a. VOH rate = $13,500 ÷ 54,000 DLHs = $0.25 per DLH
FOH rate = $105,300 ÷ 27,000 MHs = $3.90 per MH

Actual VOH	$ 11,980	Actual FOH	$103,540
Applied VOH (46,000 × $0.25)	(11,500)	Applied FOH (23,000 × $3.90)	(89,700)
Underapplied VOH	$ 480	Underapplied FOH	$ 13,840

Note that the large underapplication of FOH was caused mainly by a difference between the number of machine hours used to set the rate (27,000) and the number of machine hours that were actually worked (23,000): 4,000 × $3.90 = $15,600. The underapplication of FOH was constrained by the fact that the company incurred only $103,540 of FOH rather than the $105,300 the company expected to incur. The total underapplication is the combination of the negative machine hour effect and the positive total expenditure effect: $15,600 − ($105,300 − $103,540) = $13,840.

b.

	Year 2	Year 3
Net sales	$ 300,000	$ 330,000
Variable cost of goods sold	(60,000)	(66,000)
Product contribution margin	$ 240,000	$ 264,000
Variable operating expenses	(50,000)	(55,000)
Total contribution margin	$ 190,000	$ 209,000

continued

Chapter 11 Absorption/Variable Costing and Capacity Analysis

continued from previous page

(concluded)	Year 2	Year 3
Fixed costs		
Manufacturing	$ 100,000	$ 100,000
Operating	32,500	33,500
Total fixed costs	$(132,500)	$(133,500)
Income before tax	$ 57,500	$ 75,500

c. Reconciliation Year 2
    Absorption costing income before tax.................................. $77,500
    – FOH in ending inventory ($4.00 × 5,000) .... (20,000)
    Variable costing income before tax $57,500

    Reconciliation Year 3
    Absorption costing income before tax.................................. $67,500
    + FOH released from beginning inventory ($4.00 × 2,000) 8,000
    Variable costing income before tax $75,500

Assignments with the MBC logo in the margin are available in myBusinessCourse.
Resources include demonstration videos, guided examples, and auto-graded homework.
See details in the Preface, and ask your professor how you can access the system.

Data Analytics

DA11-1. Analyzing the effect of absorption or variable costing methods on before-tax profit LO11-2
Access the file included in MBC which includes forecasted data for Year 4 for Custom Covers, a manufacturer of car seat covers and complete the following requirements.

Required
a. Data is provided showing three different levels of budgeted production of units with an assumed sales budget. Prepare a clustered bar chart showing the forecasted Year 4, before-tax profit under the three production levels under absorption costing and under variable costing. *Hint*: Select data, click on Insert, and Clustered Bar chart.
b. Which bar charts show the most variability? Why?
c. How do the differences shown on the charts affect financial amounts in future periods?
d. How might the results shown in the bar chart affect management's actions in the current period assuming absorption costing is used?

DA11-2. Analyzing the impact of capacity on budgeted FOH rate LO11-4
A machine component part manufacturer has determined its annual budget for fixed manufacturing overhead for the upcoming year is $125,000. Capacity is measured in machine hours with a range of 30,000 hours at expected capacity to 100,000 hours at theoretical capacity.

Required
a. Create a line chart, showing the budgeted FOH rate per machine hour for the range from expected capacity to theoretical capacity, measured in machine hours in 10,000 hour increments.
b. Describe the shape of the line chart and indicate what is causing the shape.
c. Assuming actual machine hours for the year totaled 45,000, compute the resulting volume variances using the FOH rates per hour calculated in part *a* (expected to theoretical capacity). Next, create a line chart showing the volume variance at each measure of capacity used to calculate the budgeted fixed overhead rate.
d. What does the point where the line chart intercepts the X-axis represent?

Data Visualization

Data Visualization Activities are available in BusinessCourse. These assignments use Tableau Dashboards to expose students to visual depictions of data and introduce students to data analytics through data visualizations. These exercises are easily assignable and auto graded by MBC.

© Cambridge Business Publishers

Potential Ethical Issues

1. Using an inappropriately high capacity measurement to compute the predetermined OH rate, thereby reducing product cost and increasing operating income upon the sale of inventory—given that the closing of the underapplied manufacturing OH account would be deferred for multiple periods
2. Producing significantly more inventory than is necessary to meet current and anticipated sales, thereby lowering the predetermined FOH rate per unit under absorption costing, while increasing reported operating income
3. Manipulating sales around the end of an accounting period to shift revenues and expired product costs into the current period or into the following period
4. Choosing a financial statement presentation that better shows desired results in order to meet contractual agreements such as debt covenants.

Questions

Q11-1. How does absorption costing differ from variable costing in cost accumulation and income statement presentation?

Q11-2. Why is FOH treated differently in the absorption and variable costing methods?

Q11-3. What is meant by classifying costs (a) functionally and (b) behaviorally? Why would a company be concerned about functional and behavioral classifications?

Q11-4. Is variable or absorption costing generally required for external reporting? Why is this method preferred to the alternative?

Q11-5. Why does variable costing provide more useful information than absorption costing for making internal decisions?

Q11-6. What are the income relationships between absorption and variable costing when production volume differs from sales volume? What causes these relationships to occur?

Q11-7. Is an absorption and/or variable costing income statement useful for cost-volume-profit analysis?

Q11-8. How is the amount of cost of goods reported subject to manipulation under an absorption costing income statement but not under a variable costing income statement? What is the impact on before-tax profit of a cost of goods sold manipulation?

Q11-9. What are the differences between theoretical, practical, normal, and expected capacity? Which capacity measurements are geared more toward the potential for production and which are geared more toward product demand?

Q11-10. What is the impact on a company's ability to cover its fixed costs in the situation of a downward demand spiral?

Multiple Choice

MC11-11. Which of the following correctly shows the treatment of (1) factory insurance, (2) direct labor, and (3) finished goods shipping costs under absorption costing and variable costing?

	Absorption Costing		Variable Costing	
	Product Cost	Period Cost	Product Cost	Period Cost
a.	1, 2	3	2	1, 3
b.	2	1, 3	1, 2	3
c.	1, 2	3	1	2, 3
d.	1	2, 3	2, 3	1

MC11-12. Bethany Company has just completed the first month of producing a new product but has not yet shipped any of this product. The product incurred variable manufacturing costs of $5,000,000, fixed manufacturing costs of $2,000,000, variable marketing costs of $1,000,000, and fixed marketing costs of $3,000,000.

If Bethany uses the variable cost method to value inventory, the inventory value of the new product would be

Chapter 11 Absorption/Variable Costing and Capacity Analysis

  a. $5,000,000.
  b. $6,000,000.
  c. $8,000,000.
  d. $11,000,000.

MC11-13. Mill Corporation had the following unit costs for the recently concluded calendar year.

	Variable	Fixed
Manufacturing............	$8.00	$3.00
Nonmanufacturing	$2.00	$5.50

Inventory for Mill's sole product totaled 6,000 units on January 1 and 5,200 units on December 31. When compared to variable costing income, Mill's absorption costing income is
  a. $2,400 lower.
  b. $2,400 higher.
  c. $6,800 lower.
  d. $6,800 higher.

MC11-14. Dawn Company has significant fixed overhead costs in the manufacturing of its sole product, auto mufflers. For internal reporting purposes, in which one of the following situations would ending finished goods inventory be higher under direct (variable) costing rather than under absorption costing?
  a. If more units were produced than were sold during a given year.
  b. If more units were sold than were produced during a given year.
  c. In all cases when ending finished goods inventory exists.
  d. None of these situations.

MC11-15. A manufacturing company is contemplating switching from their current costing approach, variable costing, to absorption costing. Relevant data for the company in January of Year 2 is as follows.

Selling price	$ 30/unit
Units produced	40,000
Units sold	30,000
Inventory as of January 1, Year 2	None
Direct materials.........................	$ 6/unit
Direct labor..............................	$ 3/unit
Variable overhead.........................	$ 2/unit
Variable selling and administrative expense..........	$ 1/unit
Fixed selling and administrative expense............	$ 75,000
Fixed manufacturing overhead..................	$160,000

Based on the information above, the company's operating income using absorption costing is
  a. $415,000.
  b. $345,000.
  c. $335,000.
  d. $305,000.

MC11-16. Xylon Company uses direct (variable) costing for internal reporting and absorption costing for the external financial statements. A review of the firm's internal and external disclosures will likely find
  a. a difference in the treatment of fixed selling and administrative costs.
  b. a higher inventoriable unit cost reported to management than to the shareholders.
  c. a contribution margin rather than gross margin in the reports released to shareholders.
  d. internal income figures that vary closely with sales and external income figures that are influenced by both units sold and productive output.

MC11-17. An unfavorable volume variance considered insignificant for a period
  a. results in an increase to cost of goods sold under absorption costing only.
  b. results in a decrease to cost of goods sold under absorption costing only.
  c. results in an increase to cost of goods sold under variable costing only.
  d. results in an increase to cost of goods sold under both absorption and variable costing.

MC11-18. Fab Fixtures Inc., a producer of doorknobs, summarized the following information for its latest annual reporting period.

Budgeted annual capacity	160,000
Actual units produced for the year	145,000
Budgeted FOH	$ 40,000
Cost of goods sold, adjusted for volume variance	$303,750

What is the cost of goods sold at standard reported in the company's absorption costing income statement?

- a. $343,750
- b. $276,250
- c. $300,000
- d. $307,500

LO11-4 MC11-19. As capacity increases relative to actual volume, the volume variance
- a. becomes more favorable under absorption costing.
- b. becomes less favorable under absorption costing.
- c. becomes more favorable under variable costing.
- d. becomes less favorable under variable costing.

LO11-4 MC11-20. Landry Co. compiled the following information for the month of June from its production records.

Budgeted fixed factory overhead	$212,400
Actual fixed factory overhead	$180,000
Practical capacity (in machine hours)	47,200
Actual machine hours	34,000

Normal capacity is 80% of practical capacity. Applying FOH using a predetermined rate based on normal capacity, by how much is FOH -over or underapplied?

- a. $55,889 overapplied
- b. $32,500 underapplied
- c. $27,000 underapplied
- d. $11,250 overapplied

Exercises

LO11-1 E11-21. Absorption and variable costing comparisons: Production equals sales Assume that **Sweet and Spicy Inc.** manufactures and sells 45,000 cases of hot sauce each quarter. The following data are available for the third quarter of the year.

Total fixed manufacturing overhead	$ 675,000
Fixed selling and administrative expenses	1,225,000
Sales price per case	85
Direct materials per case	20
Direct labor per case	10
Variable manufacturing overhead per case	4

Compute the cost per case under both absorption costing and variable costing.

LO11-2 E11-22. Absorption and variable costing income statements: production equals sales Referring to the information in E11-21, answer the following questions.
- a. Compute net income under absorption costing.
- b. Compute net income under variable costing.
- c. Reconcile any differences in income. Explain.

LO11-1 E11-23. Absorption vs. variable costing Pete's Plant Stands manufactures wooden stands used by plant nurseries. In May, the company sold 16,560 stands. The cost per unit for the 18,000 stands produced in May was as follows:

Direct material	$ 9.00
Direct labor	6.00
Variable overhead	3.00
Fixed overhead	4.00
Total	$22.00

There were no beginning inventories for May and no work in process at the end of May.
- a. What is the cost of production per unit under absorption costing?
- b. What is the cost of production per unit under variable costing?
- c. What is the value of ending finished goods inventory using absorption costing?
- d. What is the value of ending finished goods inventory using variable costing?
- e. Which accounting method, variable or absorption, would have produced the higher net income for May?

Chapter 11 Absorption/Variable Costing and Capacity Analysis

E11-24. Absorption and variable costing income statements: production exceeds sales Century Company sells its product at a unit price of $20. Unit manufacturing costs are direct materials, $6.00; direct labor, $2.00; and variable manufacturing overhead, $1.00. Total fixed manufacturing costs are $255,000 per year. Selling and administrative expenses are $1.00 per unit variable and $185,000 per year fixed. Though 60,000 units were produced during the year, only 54,000 units were sold. There was no beginning inventory.

LO11-2

a. Prepare a functional income statement using absorption costing for the year.
b. Prepare a contribution income statement using variable costing for the year.

E11-25. Absorption and variable costing income statements: sales exceeds production Rad Development purchases, develops, and sells commercial building sites. As the sites are sold, they are cleared at an average cost of $8,000 per site. Storm drains and driveways are also installed at an average cost of $10,000 per site. Selling costs are 6% of sales price. Administrative costs are $600,000 per year. Two years ago, the company bought 2,000 acres of land for $7,500,000 and divided it into 200 sites of equal size. During that year, 95 sites were sold at an average price of $150,000. Last year, the company purchased and developed another 2,000 acres, divided into 200 sites. The purchase price was again $7,500,000. Sales totaled 250 sites last year at an average price of $150,000.

LO11-2

a. Prepare a functional income statement using absorption costing for the year.
b. Prepare a contribution income statement using variable costing for the year.

E11-26. Absorption vs. variable costing Reese's Tot Toy Boxes uses variable costing to manage its internal operations. The following data relate to the company's first year of operation, when 25,000 units were produced and 21,000 units were sold.

LO11-2

Variable costs per unit	
Direct material.............................	$50
Direct labor..................................	30
Variable overhead.........................	14
Variable selling costs....................	12
Fixed costs	
Selling and administrative.............	$750,000
Manufacturing...............................	500,000

How much higher (or lower) would the company's first-year net income have been if absorption costing had been used rather than variable costing? Show computations.

E11-27. Production cost; absorption vs. variable costing In its first year of business, Ollie's Olive Oil produced 104,000 quarts of olive oil. During its first year, the company sold 100,000 quarts of olive oil. Costs incurred during the year were as follows:

LO11-1, 2

Ingredients used.........................	$228,800
Direct labor.................................	104,000
Variable overhead.......................	197,600
Fixed overhead...........................	98,800
Variable selling expenses...........	50,000
Fixed selling and administrative expenses....	20,000
Total actual costs.......................	$699,200

a. What was the actual production cost per quart under variable costing? Under absorption costing?
b. What was variable cost of goods sold for the year under variable costing?
c. What was cost of goods sold for the year under absorption costing?
d. What was the value of ending inventory under variable costing? Under absorption costing?
e. How much fixed overhead was charged to expense for the year under variable costing? Under absorption costing?

E11-28. Net income; absorption vs. variable costing Tennessee Tack manufactures horse blankets. During the year, fixed overhead was applied to products at the rate of $8 per unit. Variable cost per unit remained constant throughout the year. In July, income under variable costing was $188,000. July's beginning and ending inventories were 20,000 and 10,400 units, respectively.

LO11-2

a. Calculate income under absorption costing assuming no variances.
b. Assume instead that the company's July beginning and ending inventories were 9,000 and 12,000 units, respectively. Calculate income under absorption costing.

LO11-1 **E11-29. Variable and absorption costing; writing** Because your professor is scheduled to address a national professional meeting at the time your class ordinarily meets, the class has been divided into teams to discuss selected issues. Your team's assignment is to prepare a report arguing whether fixed manufacturing overhead should be included as a component of product cost. You are also expected to draw your own conclusion about this issue and provide the rationale for your conclusion in your report.

LO11-2 **E11-30. Absorption costing income statement and income manipulation** In its first year of business, Troughton Company manufactures radio-controlled toy dogs. Summary budget financial data for Troughton for the current year are as follows:

Sales (5,000 units at $150 each)	$750,000
Variable manufacturing cost	400,000
Fixed manufacturing cost	100,000
Variable selling and administrative cost	80,000
Fixed selling and administrative cost	$150,000

Troughton uses an absorption costing system with overhead applied based on the number of units produced, with a denominator level of activity of 5,000 units. Underapplied or overapplied manufacturing overhead is considered insignificant and adjusts cost of goods sold. The $20,000 budgeted operating income from producing and selling 5,000 toy dogs planned for this year is of concern to Trudy George, Troughton's president. She believes she could increase operating income to $50,000 (her bonus threshold) if Troughton produces more units than it sells, thus building up the finished goods inventory.

a. How much of an increase in the number of units in the finished goods inventory would be needed to increase operating income from $20,000 to $50,000?
b. What are the ethical implications of this decision?

LO11-2 **E11-31. Absorption and variable costing income statements** A manufacturing company is contemplating switching from their current costing approach, variable costing, to absorption costing. Relevant data for the company in January 20X2 is as follows.

Selling price	$ 30/unit
Units produced	40,000
Units sold	30,000
Inventory as of 1/1/X2	None
Direct materials	$ 6/unit
Direct labor	$ 3/unit
Variable manufacturing overhead	$ 2/unit
Variable selling and administrative expense	$ 1/unit
Fixed selling and administrative expense	$ 75,000
Fixed manufacturing overhead	$160,000

a. Prepare a functional income statement for the year using absorption costing.
b. Prepare a contribution income statement for the year using variable costing.

LO11-3 **E11-32. Absorption costing; volume variance** Sports Drinks, Inc. began business in the current year selling bottles of a thirst-quenching drink. The budgeted fixed overhead rate for the year was applied based on the number of units produced budgeted to be 130,000 bottles. Planned fixed manufacturing overhead was $5,200 for the year. Production for the first year was 104,000 bottles, and sales were 98,000 bottles. Assume no beginning inventory balances. The selling price per bottle was $3.10.
Costs incurred during the year were as follows:

Ingredients used	$56,000
Direct labor	26,000
Variable manufacturing overhead	48,000
Fixed manufacturing overhead	5,200
Fixed selling and administrative expenses	55,000
Total actual costs	$190,200

a. What was the production cost per bottle under variable costing?
b. What was variable cost of goods sold?

c. Prepare a variable costing income statement.
d. What is the absorption production cost per unit?
e. Prepare an absorption costing income statement.
f. Reconcile the difference between parts c and e.

E11-33. Variable costing income statement, absorption income statement with volume variance Top Disc manufactures flying disks. The following information is available for the year, the company's first year in business when it produced 325,000 units. Revenue of $450,000 was generated by the sale of 180,000 flying disks. The predetermined fixed overhead rate was based on practical capacity of 375,000 units and planned fixed manufacturing overhead costs of $112,500 for the year.

LO11-1, 3

	Variable Cost	Fixed Cost
Production		
Direct material........	$150,000	
Direct labor..........	100,000	
Overhead...........	75,000	$112,500
Selling and administrative...	90,000	100,000

a. What is the variable production cost per unit?
b. Prepare a variable costing income statement.
c. What is the absorption production cost per unit?
d. Prepare an absorption costing income statement.
e. Reconcile the difference between part b and part d.

E11-34. Convert variable to absorption The April income statement for Fabio's Fashions has just been received by Diana Caffrey, Vice President of Marketing. The firm uses a variable costing system for internal reporting purposes.

LO11-3

Fabio's Fashions
Income Statement
For the Month Ended April 30

Sales..		$14,400,000
Variable cost of goods sold.......................		(7,200,000)
Product contribution margin......................		$ 7,200,000
Fixed expenses		
Manufacturing (budget and actual).............	$4,500,000	
Selling and administrative......................	2,400,000	(6,900,000)
Income before tax................................		$ 300,000

The following notes were attached to the statements:
- Unit sales price for April averaged $144.
- Unit manufacturing costs for the month were:

Variable cost......	$ 72
Fixed cost........	30
Total cost.......	$102

- The predetermined FOH rate was based on normal monthly production of 150,000 units.
- April production was 7,500 units in excess of sales.
- April ending inventory consisted of 12,000 units.

a. Caffrey is not familiar with variable costing.
  1. Recast the April income statement on an absorption costing basis.
  2. Reconcile and explain the difference between the variable costing and the absorption costing income figures.
b. Explain the features of variable costing that should appeal to Caffrey.

E11-35. Variable and absorption costing Porta Light manufactures a high-quality LED flashlight for home/office use. Data pertaining to the company's operations for the year are as follows:

LO11-3

Production for the year	45,000 units
Sales for the year (sales price per unit, $8)	48,750 units
Beginning inventory	8,750 units
Costs to produce one unit (This year and prior year):	
Direct material	$3.60
Direct labor	1.00
Variable overhead	0.60
Fixed overhead	0.40
Selling and administrative costs:	
Variable (per unit sold)	$0.40
Fixed (per year)	$150,000

The FOH rate is based on units of production based on an expected production capacity of 100,000 units per year.

a. What is budgeted annual fixed manufacturing overhead?
b. If budgeted fixed overhead equals actual fixed overhead, what is underapplied or overapplied fixed overhead for the year under absorption costing? Under variable costing?
c. What is the product cost per unit under absorption costing? Under variable costing?
d. How much total expense is charged against revenues for the year under absorption costing? Under variable costing?
e. Is income higher under absorption or variable costing? By what amount?

LO11-4

E11-36. Capacity measurements; before-tax profit The following predictions were made in the prior year for one of the plants of Windsor Inc.

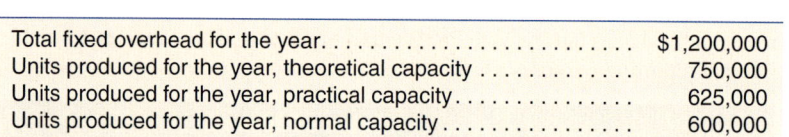

Total fixed overhead for the year	$1,200,000
Units produced for the year, theoretical capacity	750,000
Units produced for the year, practical capacity	625,000
Units produced for the year, normal capacity	600,000

Actual results for the month of January were as follows.

Units sold	51,000
Units produced	55,000

Assume a sales price per unit of $6 and fixed selling and administrative expenses of $55,000. Cost of goods sold at standard is $183,600, $199,920, and $204,000, at theoretical, practical, and normal capacity, respectively.

a. What is the budgeted FOH rate based upon theoretical, practical, and normal capacity?
b. What is the volume variance in January, if the budgeted FOH rate is based upon theoretical, practical, and normal capacity? Assume that budgeted FOH is assumed to be incurred evenly throughout the year.
c. Determine before-tax profit at theoretical, practical, and normal capacity.
d. Reconcile the differences between (1) before-tax profit at theoretical and practical capacity, and (2) before-tax profit at practical and normal capacity.

LO11-4

E11-37. Capacity measures For the year, Milltown Iron Manufacturing has estimated its annual production capacities as follows:

Theoretical capacity	400,000 units
Practical capacity	300,000 units
Normal capacity	260,000 units
Expected capacity	200,000 units

Milltown is trying to choose which capacity measure it should use to develop its predetermined OH rates for the year.

a. Why does the choice of capacity measure affect the amount of under- or overapplied overhead the firm will have at the end of the year?
b. Which capacity measure choice would likely result in the least amount of under- or overapplied overhead?
c. Which of the alternative capacity measures makes allowances for possible cycles in the industry?

Chapter 11 Absorption/Variable Costing and Capacity Analysis

E11-38. Predetermined OH rates; capacity measures Alberton Electronics makes inexpensive GPS navigation devices and uses a normal cost system that applies overhead based on machine hours. The following current year budgeted data are available:

LO11-4

Variable factory overhead at 100,000 machine hours	$1,250,000
Variable factory overhead at 150,000 machine hours	1,875,000
Fixed factory overhead at all levels between 10,000 and 180,000 machine hours	1,440,000

Practical capacity is 180,000 machine hours; expected capacity is two-thirds of practical.

a. What is Alberton Electronics' predetermined VOH rate?
b. What is the predetermined FOH rate using practical capacity?
c. What is the predetermined FOH rate using expected capacity?
d. During the year, the firm records 110,000 machine hours and $2,710,000 of overhead costs. How much variable overhead is applied? How much fixed overhead is applied using the rate found in (b)? How much fixed overhead is applied using the rate found in (c)? Calculate the total under- or overapplied overhead for the year using both fixed OH rates.

Problems

P11-39. Variable costing; ethics In its first year of operations, Utah Utility Trailers incurred the following costs:

LO11-2

Variable production cost	$2,800 per unit
Variable selling and administrative cost	$200 per unit
Fixed production cost	$200,000
Fixed selling and administrative cost	$80,000

For the year, the company reported the following results:

Sales ($5,000 per unit)	$ 500,000
Cost of goods sold	(400,000)
Gross margin	$ 100,000
Selling and administrative cost	(100,000)
Operating income	$ 0

a. Using the contribution margin ratio approach, compute the break-even point in sales dollars for this company. *Hint*: See Chapter 4.
b. How many units did the firm produce in its first year of operations?
c. Provide an explanation that reconciles your result in (a) to the income statement provided above.
d. Prepare a variable costing income statement for sales of 100 units.
e. Assume that Utah Utility Trailers is in need of a bank loan. Would it be unethical to use the income statement above, rather than the income statement compiled in (d), to present to the loan officer? Explain.

P11-40. Convert variable to absorption; ethics Georgia Shacks produces small outdoor buildings. The company began operations this year, producing 2,000 buildings and selling 1,500. A variable costing income statement for the year follows. During the year, variable production costs per unit were $800 for direct material, $300 for direct labor, and $200 for overhead.

LO11-1, 2

<table>
<tr><th colspan="3">Georgia Shacks
Income Statement (Variable Costing)
For the Year Ended December 31</th></tr>
<tr><td>Sales...</td><td></td><td>$3,750,000</td></tr>
<tr><td>Variable cost of goods sold</td><td></td><td></td></tr>
<tr><td> Beginning inventory ....</td><td>$ 0</td><td></td></tr>
<tr><td> Cost of goods manufactured ....</td><td>2,600,000</td><td></td></tr>
<tr><td> Cost of goods available for sale ....</td><td>$2,600,000</td><td></td></tr>
<tr><td> Less ending inventory..........................</td><td>(650,000)</td><td>(1,950,000)</td></tr>
<tr><td>Product contribution margin ....</td><td></td><td>$1,800,000</td></tr>
<tr><td>Less variable selling and administrative expenses.......</td><td></td><td>(270,000)</td></tr>
<tr><td>Total contribution margin ....</td><td></td><td>$1,530,000</td></tr>
<tr><td>Less fixed expenses</td><td></td><td></td></tr>
<tr><td> Fixed factory overhead ....</td><td>$1,500,000</td><td></td></tr>
<tr><td> Fixed selling and administrative expenses .....</td><td>190,000</td><td>(1,690,000)</td></tr>
<tr><td>Income before taxes..............................</td><td></td><td>$ (160,000)</td></tr>
</table>

The company president is upset about the net loss because he wanted to borrow funds to expand capacity.

a. Prepare a pre-tax absorption costing income statement.
b. Explain the source of the difference between the pre-tax income and loss figures under the two costing systems.
c. Would it be appropriate to present an absorption costing income statement to the local banker, considering the company president's knowledge of the net loss determined under variable costing? Explain.
d. Assume that during the second year of operations, Georgia Shacks produced 2,000 buildings, sold 2,200, and experienced the same total fixed costs as in the first year. For the second year:
   1. Prepare a variable costing pre-tax income statement.
   2. Prepare an absorption costing pre-tax income statement.
   3. Explain the difference between the incomes for the second year under the two systems.

LO11-3   P11-41. Absorption and variable costing Bird's Eye View manufactures satellite dishes used in residential and commercial installations for satellite-broadcasted television. For each unit, the following costs apply: $50 for direct material, $100 for direct labor, and $60 for variable overhead. The company's annual fixed overhead cost is $750,000; it uses expected capacity of 12,500 units produced as the basis for applying fixed overhead to products. A commission of 10 percent of the selling price is paid on each unit sold. Annual fixed selling and administrative expenses are $180,000. The following additional information is available:

	Year 1	Year 2
Selling price per unit........................	$ 500	$ 500
Number of units sold.........................	10,000	12,000
Number of units produced	12,500	11,000
Beginning inventory (units)..................	7,500	10,000
Ending inventory (units)	10,000	?

Prepare pre-tax income statements under absorption and variable costing for Year 1 and Year 2, with any volume variance being charged to Cost of Goods Sold. Reconcile the differences in income for the two methods.

LO11-1, 3   P11-42. Absorption costing vs. variable costing Since opening its business this year, Akron Aviation has built light aircraft engines and has gained a reputation for reliable and quality products. Factory overhead is applied to production using direct labor hours and any underapplied or overapplied overhead is closed at year-end to Cost of Goods Sold. The company's inventory balances for the past three years and income statements for the past two years follow.

Chapter 11 Absorption/Variable Costing and Capacity Analysis

Inventory Balances	Year 1	Year 2	Year 3
Direct Material	$22,000	$30,000	$10,000
Work in Process			
Costs	$40,000	$48,000	$64,000
Direct labor hours	1,335	1,600	2,100
Finished Goods			
Costs	$25,000	$18,000	$14,000
Direct labor hours	1,450	1,050	820

Comparative Income Statements

	Year 2	Year 3
Sales	$840,000	$1,015,000
Cost of goods sold		
Finished goods, Jan. 1	$ 25,000	$ 18,000
Cost of goods manufactured	556,000	673,600
Total available	$581,000	$691,600
Finished goods, Dec. 31	(18,000)	(14,000)
CGS before overhead adjustment	$563,000	$677,600
Underapplied factory overhead	17,400	19,300
Cost of goods sold	(580,400)	(696,900)
Gross margin	$259,600	$ 318,100
Selling expenses	$ 82,000	$ 95,000
Administrative expenses	70,000	75,000
Total operating expenses	(152,000)	(170,000)
Operating income	$107,600	$ 148,100

The same predetermined OH rate was used to apply overhead to production orders in Year 2 and Year 3. The rate was based on the following estimates:

Fixed factory overhead	$ 25,000
Variable factory overhead	$155,000
Direct labor cost	$150,000
Direct labor hours	25,000

In Year 2 and Year 3, actual direct labor hours expended were 20,000 and 23,000, respectively. Raw material costing $292,000 was issued to production in Year 2 and $370,000 in Year 3. Actual fixed overhead was $37,400 for Year 2 and $42,300 for Year 3, and the planned direct labor rate per hour was equal to the actual direct labor rate. Actual variable overhead was equal to applied variable overhead.

For both years, all of the reported administrative costs were fixed. The variable portion of the reported selling expenses results from a commission of 5 percent of sales revenue.

a. For the year ending December 31, Year 3, prepare a revised income statement using the variable costing method.
b. Describe both the advantages and disadvantages of using variable costing.

P11-43. Overhead application; absorption costing; ethics; writing Prior to the start of the fiscal year, managers of MultiTech hosted a web conference for its shareholders, financial analysts, and members of the financial press. During the conference, the CEO and CFO released the following financial projections for the current year to the attendees (amounts in millions):

LO11-1, 2

Sales	$40,000
Cost of goods sold	(32,000)
Gross margin	$ 8,000
Operating expenses	(4,000)
Operating income	$ 4,000

As had been their custom, the CEO and CFO projected confidence that the firm would achieve these goals, even though projections had been significantly more positive than the actual results from last year. Not surprisingly, the day following the web conference, MultiTech's stock rose 15 percent.

In early October, the CEO and CFO of MultiTech met and developed revised projections for the current fiscal year, based on actual results for the first three quarters of the year and projections for the final quarter. Their revised projections for the year follow:

Sales.	$ 38,000
Cost of goods sold	(30,500)
Gross margin	$ 7,500
Operating expenses	(4,000)
Operating income	$ 3,500

Upon reviewing these numbers, the CEO turned to the CFO and stated, "I think the market will be forgiving if we come in 5 percent light on the top line (sales), but if we miss operating income by 12.5 percent ($500 ÷ $4,000) our stock is going to get hammered when we announce fourth quarter and annual results."

The CFO mulled the situation over for a couple of days and started to develop a strategy to increase reported income by increasing production above planned levels. She believed this strategy could successfully move $500 million from Cost of Goods Sold to Finished Goods Inventory. If so, the firm could meet its early profit projections.

a. How does increasing production, relative to the planned level of production, decrease Cost of Goods Sold?
b. What other accounts are likely to be affected by a strategy of increasing production to increase income?
c. Is the CFO's plan ethical? Explain.
d. If you were a stockholder of MultiTech and carefully examined the current year financial statements, how might you detect the results of the CFO's strategy?

LO11-1, 3

P11-44. Absorption vs. variable costing Tomm's T's is a New York–based company that produces and sells t-shirts. The firm uses variable costing for internal purposes and absorption costing for external purposes. At year-end, financial information must be converted from variable costing to absorption costing to satisfy external requirements.

At the end of Year 1, management anticipated that Year 2 sales would be 20 percent above Year 1 levels. Thus, production for Year 2 was increased by 20 percent to meet the expected demand. However, economic conditions in Year 2 kept sales at the Year 1 unit level of 40,000. The following data pertain to Year 1 and Year 2:

	Year 1	Year 2
Selling price per unit.	$ 22	$ 22
Sales (units)	40,000	40,000
Beginning inventory (units)	4,000	4,000
Production (units)	40,000	48,000
Ending inventory (units)	4,000	?

Per-unit production costs (budgeted and actual) for Year 1 and Year 2 were:

Material.	$2.50
Labor	4.00
Overhead	1.75
Total.	$8.25

Annual fixed costs for Year 1 and Year 2 (budgeted and actual) were:

Production	$120,000
Selling and administrative	130,000
Total.	$250,000

Chapter 11 Absorption/Variable Costing and Capacity Analysis

The predetermined OH rate under absorption costing is based on an annual capacity of 60,000 units. Any volume variance is assigned to Cost of Goods Sold. Taxes are to be ignored.

a. Present the Year 2 income statement based on variable costing.
b. Present the Year 2 income statement based on absorption costing.
c. Explain the difference, if any, in the income figures. Assuming that there is no Work in Process Inventory, provide the entry necessary to adjust the book income amount to the financial statement income amount if an adjustment is necessary.
d. The company finds it worthwhile to develop its internal financial data on a variable costing basis. What advantages and disadvantages are attributed to variable costing for internal purposes?
e. Many accountants believe that variable costing is appropriate for external reporting; many others oppose its use for external reporting. List the arguments for and against the use of variable costing in external reporting.

P11-45. Overhead application Sunny Systems manufactures solar panels. The company has a theoretical capacity of 50,000 units annually. Practical capacity is 80 percent of theoretical capacity, and normal capacity is 80 percent of practical capacity. The firm is expecting to produce 30,000 units next year. The company president, Deacon Daniels, has budgeted the following factory overhead costs: **LO11-4**

Indirect material	$2.00 per unit
Indirect labor	$144,000 per year plus $2.50 per unit
Utilities for the plant	$6,000 per year plus $0.04 per unit
Repairs and maintenance for the plant	$20,000 per year plus $0.34 per unit
Material handling costs	$16,000 per year plus $0.12 per unit
Depreciation on plant assets	$210,000 per year
Rent on plant building	$50,000 per year
Insurance on plant building	$12,000 per year

a. Determine the cost formula for total factory overhead in the format of $y = a + bX$.
b. Determine the total predetermined OH rate for each possible overhead application base.
c. Assume that Sunny Systems produces 35,000 units during the year and that actual costs are exactly as budgeted. Calculate the overapplied or underapplied overhead for each possible overhead allocation base.

P11-46. Predetermined OH rates; flexible budget; capacity Battle Creek Storage Systems budgeted the following factory overhead costs for the upcoming year to help calculate variable and fixed predetermined overhead rates. **LO11-4**

Indirect material	$2.50 per unit produced
Indirect labor	$3.00 per unit produced
Factory utilities	$3,000 per year plus $0.02 per unit produced
Factory machine maintenance	$10,000 per year plus $0.50 per unit produced
Material handling	$8,000 per year plus $0.12 per unit produced
Machine depreciation	$0.03 per unit produced
Building rent	$12,000 per year
Supervisors' salaries	$72,000 per year
Factory insurance	$6,000 per year

The company produces only one type of product that has a theoretical capacity of 100,000 units of production during the year. Practical capacity is 80 percent of theoretical, and normal capacity is 90 percent of practical. The company's expected production for the upcoming year is 70,000 units.

a. Prepare a flexible budget for the company using each level of capacity.
b. Calculate the predetermined variable and fixed overhead rates for each capacity measure (round amounts to two decimal places when necessary).
c. The company decides to apply overhead to products using expected capacity as the budgeted level of activity. The firm actually produces 70,000 units during the year. All actual costs are as budgeted.
   1. Prepare journal entries to record the incurrence of actual overhead costs and to apply overhead to production. Assume cash is paid for costs when appropriate.
   2. What is the amount of underapplied or overapplied fixed overhead at year-end?
d. Which measure of capacity would be of most benefit to management, and why?

P11-47. Absorption and variable costing income statements Inman Inc. is a manufacturer of a single product and is starting to develop a budget for the coming year. Because cost of goods manufactured is the biggest item, Inman's senior management is reviewing how costs are calculated. In addition, senior management wants to develop a budgeting system that motivates managers and other workers to work toward the corporate goals. Inman has incurred the following costs to make 100,000 units during the month of September.

Materials	$400,000
Direct labor	100,000
Variable manufacturing overhead	20,000
Variable selling and administrative costs	80,000
Fixed manufacturing overhead	200,000
Fixed selling and administrative costs	300,000

Inman Inc.'s September 1 inventory consisted of 10,000 units valued at $72,000 using absorption costing. Total fixed costs and variable costs per unit have not changed during the past few months. In September, Inman sold 106,000 units at $12 per unit.

a. Using absorption costing, calculate Inman's September manufacturing cost per unit, Inman's September 30 inventory value, and Inman's September net income.

b. Using variable costing, calculate Inman's September manufacturing cost per unit, Inman's September 30 inventory value, and Inman's September net income

c. Identify and explain one reason why the income calculated in the previous two questions might differ.

d. Identify and discuss one advantage of using absorption costing and variable costing.

P11-48. Absorption and variable costing, analysis Barton Industries processes chemicals for the pharmaceutical industry. Wiley Richardson, company president, was eager to see the operating results for the just completed fiscal year as he believed that changes that were made during the year would result in increased profit on the expected sales volume of 1 million kg. At the beginning of the year, in response to a 10% increase in production costs, the sales price had been increased 12%, and the selling and administrative departments had been given strict instructions to hold expenses at the same level as the previous year. Therefore, Richardson was dismayed to learn that net income had dropped despite achieving the planned increase in sales volume. Shown below are comparative operating income statements for Barton Industries for the last two years along with budgeted operating and financial data. This year's cost of goods sold includes an adjustment of fixed overhead costs that were under-applied. Actual results were the same as budget, except for production volume. The company uses the first-in, first-out inventory valuation method, and has an ending inventory of 450,000 kg. this year.

Barton Industries
Comparative Operating Income Statements
($000 omitted)

	Previous Year	Current Year
Sales revenue	$9,000	$11,200
Cost of goods sold	6,600	8,815
Gross profit	$2,400	$2,385
Selling and administrative expense	1,500	1,500
Operating income	$900	$885

Barton Industries
Budgeted Operating and Financial Data

	Previous Year	Current Year
Sales price	$10.00/kg.	$11.20/kg.
Material cost	1.50/kg.	1.65/kg.
Direct labor cost	2.50/kg.	2.75/kg.
Variable overhead cost	1.00/kg.	1.10/kg.
Fixed overhead cost	3.00/kg.	3.30/kg.
Total fixed overhead costs	$3,000,000	$3,300,000
Selling and administrative expense	$1,500,000	$1,500,000
Sales volume	900,000 kg.	1,000,000 kg.
Beginning inventory	300,000 kg.	600,000 kg.

Chapter 11 Absorption/Variable Costing and Capacity Analysis

a. Explain why Barton Industries' operating income decreased in the current fiscal year despite the sales price and sales volume increases.
b. Prepare an operating income statement for the current fiscal year for Barton Industries using the variable (direct) costing method.
c. Prepare a reconciliation of the difference in Barton's operating income using the current method of absorption costing and using the variable (direct) costing method.
d. Identify two advantages and two disadvantages of using variable (direct) costing for internal reporting.

P11-49. Capacity Ecoclock manufactures four environmentally friendly consumer products, and the firm is organized as four operating centers, each responsible for a single product. The main mechanism of each product is the same and requires an identical initial processing step, although subsequent processing for each product is very different. Ecoclock's management has decided to centralize the initial processing function and purchase new equipment that has a 40,000 unit annual practical capacity. For budgeting and costing purposes, the initial processing function will be assigned to a new center, Center E. Shown below is the budgeted production for the product centers.

	Annual Production
Center A...	5,000
Center B...	7,500
Center C...	4,000
Center D...	6,000

A large part of the managers' compensation is derived from bonuses that they receive for meeting or exceeding cost targets. The mangers of centers A through D each agree that they should be charged with the variable costs per unit that are delivered by Center E. However, they disagree about the allocation of the fixed costs of Center E, primarily because they believe that the new equipment has a much larger capacity than is necessary and they do not want to be charged with the cost of the unused capacity. The fixed costs for Center E total $150,000, while the variable cost per unit is $6.

a. Assume fixed costs are allocated based on the proportion of units produced by each center. What is Center D's per unit cost?
b. What would be Center A's per unit cost if Center E's fixed costs are allocated based on practical capacity?
c. Although allocating Center E's fixed costs on a per-unit produced basis seems equitable, the manager of Center C is worried about Center B reducing the number of units produced to 5,000. Calculate Center C's per unit cost with no change in production.
d. If Center B reduces the number of units produced to 5,000, will Center C's cost increase or decrease and by how much?
e. The center managers are concerned that being charged for unused capacity will impact their bonus. Explain how company management could alleviate the concerns.
f. Identify three additional measures that could be used to evaluate manager performance.

P11-50. Service company; capacity, volume variance Fairbanks Express is a luxury passenger railway carrier in Alaska. All seats are first class, and the following data are available:

Number of passenger train cars used in a year	9,600
Number of seats per passenger train car.........	60
Percentage of seats filled at normal capacity......	75%
Average full passenger fare	$ 185
Average variable cost per passenger............	$ 60
Fixed operating cost per year..................	$28,800,000

Measured in the number of seats, the practical capacity under ideal conditions is 80% while the theoretical capacity is 91%. Costs for operating the railway carrier are allocated to passengers using a standard cost system.

Annual before-tax profits are estimated to be $25.2 million as shown.

Forecasted Annual Income Statement	
Sales.	$79,920,000
Variable costs	25,920,000
Fixed costs	28,800,000
Before-tax profits	$25,200,000

Actual percentage of seats filled for the four most recent years are shown below.

Actual information	Year 1	Year 2	Year 3	Year 4
Percentage of seats filled . . .	75%	78%	60%	65%

For simplicity, assume no differences in fixed operating costs or variable costs per passenger over the four-year period.

a. What is the budgeted fixed overhead rate considering theoretical capacity, practical capacity, and normal capacity?

b. What is the volume variance in each of the four years using the theoretical, practical and normal capacity to compute the FOH budgeted rates?

c. How do these calculations inform management on it unused capacity and/or the need to purchase additional capacity?

Review Solutions

Review 11-1

a. ($280,000 + $120,000 + $205,000) ÷ 55,000 = $11

b. ($280,000 + $120,000 + $205,000 + $110,000) ÷ 55,000 = $13

c. (55,000 − 50,000) × $11 = $55,000

d. (55,000 − 50,000) × $13 = $65,000

e. The ending inventory will be different between the two methods due to fixed overhead which is inventoriable under absorption costing, but not under variable costing. The offsetting account is cost of goods sold. Because no amount of fixed overhead is capitalized as inventory under variable costing, this amount is shown as an expense for the period. Thus, expenses will be higher under variable costing than under absorption costing with an increase in inventory.

Review 11-2

a. (50,000 × $20) − (50,000 × $11[1]) − ($25,000 + $110,000 + $1,000) = $314,000

b. (50,000 × $20) − (50,000 × $13[1]) − ($25,000 + $1,000) = $324,000

c. (55,000 × $20) − (55,000 × $11[1]) − ($27,500* + $110,000 + $1,000) = $356,500

d. (55,000 × $20) − (55,000 × $13[1]) − ($27,500 + $1,000) = $356,500

*$25,000/50,000 × 55,000

e. The difference in results between parts *a* and *b* relates to the amount of fixed overhead capitalized in inventory: $110,000/55,000 units produced = $2.00 FOH rate x 5,000 units of ending inventory (calculated as 55,000 − 50,000) = $10,000 The $10,000 is the difference between the before-tax profits of $324,000 and $314,000. There is no difference in the results between parts c and d because there is no inventory (units produced equal units sold). Thus, there is no FOH capitalized to inventory that would make the before-tax profit amounts differ.

[1]See rates calculated in Review 11-1.

Review 11-3

a.

Absorption Costing Income Statement
For the Year

Sales ($15 × 50,000)		$750,000
Cost of goods sold		
Beginning inventory		0
Manufacturing costs ($13 × 60,000)		780,000
Cost of goods available for sale		780,000
Less: Ending inventory ($13 × 10,000)		130,000
Cost of goods sold (at standard)		650,000
Volume variance*		(10,000)
Cost of goods sold		640,000
Gross margin		110,000
Selling and administrative expenses ($0.50 per units sold + $1,000)		26,000
Before-tax profit		$ 84,000

*$110,000 − ($2 × 60,000) = $(10,000) F

b.

Variable Costing Income Statement
For the Year

Sales revenue ($15 × 50,000)		$750,000
Less variable costs		
Cost of goods sold (50,000 × $11.00)	$550,000	
Selling and administrative	25,000	575,000
Contribution margin		175,000
Less fixed expenses		
Manufacturing overhead	$110,000	
Selling and administrative	1,000	111,000
Before-tax profit		$ 64,000

c. Difference: $2 (calculated as $110,000/55,000) × (60,000 − 50,000) = $20,000
($84,000 − $64,000 = $20,000)

d. The variable costing statement will be used for cost-volume-profit analysis because it indicates variable and fixed costs. The absorption statement is organized by function; thus, it does not provide the means to calculate contribution margin, which is the basis for cost-volume-profit calculations.

Review 11-4

a. $531,000 ÷ 118,000 = $4.50
b. $531,000 ÷ (118,000 × 75%) = $6.00
c. 1. Volume variance: $531,000 − ($4.50 × 85,000) = $148,500 U
   2. Volume variance: $531,000 − ($6.00 × 85,000) = $21,000 U

d. Based upon expected capacity, the company has an unfavorable volume variance which means that it is operating with excess capacity. When considering practical capacity, the company shows an even larger unfavorable variance. The volume variance is an indication of excess capacity. The company needs to determine how or whether to address the excess capacity. Are there other uses for the machine? Is there a demand for the product that could be satisfied with increased production? What are inventory storage costs?

Data Visualization Solutions

(See page 11-10.)

a. Considering only this chart, the first case appears to be more financially profitable because the before-tax profit percentage is going up, while in second case, the before-tax profit percentage is going down. However, since both charts represent the same underlying circumstances, the economic situation is not different. The differences are caused solely due to financial statement accumulation and presentation.

b. Case 1 presents an absorption costing scenario and Case 2 presents a variable costing scenario. Because both cases represent the same data set, the case where inventory is higher presents absorption costing because fixed costs are capitalized in ending inventory making the balance of ending inventory higher under absorption costing.

c. The financial position of the company is in a decline. It is evident that while sales are down, the company continues to build up more inventory. The result is that fixed costs are capitalized on the balance sheet under absorption costing, deferring the eventual expense to the income statement. Thus, the variable costing income statement is a better indicator of the financial troubles of the company.

Chapter 12

Allocation of Joint Costs and Accounting for By-Product/Scrap

Road Map

LO	Learning Objective | Topics	Page	eLecture	Demo	Review	Assignments
12-1	**What is the joint process and how is a decision to sell or process further made?** Joint Process :: Split-Off Point :: Joint Costs :: Joint Products :: Separate Costs :: Sell or Process Further :: Quantitative Considerations	12-2	e12-1	D12-1	Rev 12-1	MC12-11, MC12-12, E12-17, E12-18, E12-19, E12-20, E12-28, E12-30, E12-31, P12-48, P12-62
12-2	**How are the outputs of a joint process classified?** Outputs with a Sales Value :: Joint Products :: By-Products :: Scrap :: Output with No Sales Value :: Waste :: Management Judgment	12-7	e12-2	D12-2	Rev 12-2	MC12-10, E12-20, E12-21, E12-22, P12-49, P12-70
12-3	**How is the joint cost of production allocated to joint products?** Joint Cost Allocation :: Physical Measure Allocation :: Monetary Measure Allocation :: Sales Value at Split-Off :: NRV at Split-Off :: Net Realizable Value (NRV) :: Approximated NRV at Split-Off	12-9	e12-3	D12-3A D12-3B D12-3C D12-3D	Rev 12-3	MC12-13, MC12-14, E12-21, E12-23, E12-24, E12-25, E12-26, E12-28, E12-29, E12-30, E12-31, E12-32, P12-50, P12-51, P12-52, P12-53, P12-54, P12-55, P12-56, P12-57, P12-58, P12-59, P12-60, P12-61, P12-62, P12-70, DA12-1
12-4	**How are by-product and scrap accounted for?** Net Realizable Value Approach :: Offset Approach :: WIP Inventory Reduction Method :: CGS Reduction Method :: Realized Value Approach :: Other Income Approach :: Other Revenue Method :: Other Income Method :: Job Order Costing	12-16	e12-4	D12-4A D12-4B D12-4C	Rev 12-4	MC12-15, E12-30, E12-32, E12-33, E12-34, E12-35, E12-36, E12-37, E12-38, E12-39, E12-40, E12-41, E12-42, E12-43, P12-55, P12-56, P12-57, P12-58, P12-59, P12-60, P12-61, P12-62, P12-63, P12-64
12-5	**How should retail and not-for-profit organizations account for the cost of a joint activity?** Joint Costs :: Nonmanufacturing Businesses :: Retailer :: Not-For-Profit Organizations	12-22	e12-5	D12-5	Rev 12-5	MC12-16, E12-27, E12-37, E12-44, E12-45, E12-46, E12-47, P12-55, P12-65, P12-66, P12-67, P12-68, P12-69, P12-70

INTRODUCTION

Most companies produce and sell multiple products. Some companies engage in multiple production processes to manufacture a variety of products. Other companies have a single process that simultaneously generates different outputs. For example,

- a sugar cane processor generates cane sugar, molasses, and basasse (remaining fibrous substance of the sugar cane plant),
- crude oil refining can produce gasoline, motor oil, heating oil, and kerosene, and
- mining can produce copper, silver, and gold.

In a **joint process**, one product line cannot be manufactured without producing others. Such processes are common in the food, extractive, agricultural, and chemical industries. Additionally, the process of producing first-quality merchandise and factory seconds in a single operation can be viewed as a joint process. For example, if a manufacturing process is unstable in that it cannot "maintain output at a uniform quality level, [then] . . . the products that emerge from the [process] vary across one or more quality dimensions."[1]

This chapter discusses joint manufacturing processes, their related product outputs, and the accounting treatment of those processing costs. The total cost incurred for material, labor, and overhead during a joint process is called the *joint cost* of the production process. Joint cost is allocated only to the primary products of a joint process using either a physical or a monetary measure. Although joint cost allocations are necessary to determine financial statement valuations, such allocations should *not* be used in making internal decisions.[2] For example, in evaluating a specific joint product's profitability, the decision maker must understand that profitability is determined largely by the method used to allocate the joint cost to the product and that allocation process is an arbitrary one. In later production stages, additional *separate costs* may be incurred and these costs are assignable to the specific products to which those costs relate.

In addition, advertising and marketing expenditures can be joint costs. For example, a not-for-profit (NFP) organization could produce a brochure that serves the concurrent purposes of providing public service information and requesting donations. Joint costs for retail companies and NFPs are covered in the last section of the chapter.

THE JOINT PROCESS

LO12-1 What is the joint process and how is a decision to sell or process further made?

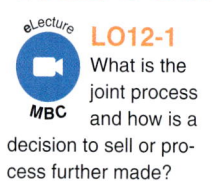

A company with a joint process typically uses a mass production process and a process costing accounting method. The point at which joint process outputs are first identifiable as individual products is called the **split-off point**. Possible outputs of a joint process at a split-off point include:

- Joint products: Key outputs of a joint process
- By-products: Salable product of a joint process, but not a key output
- Scrap: Salable product of a joint process, but with a lower selling price than a by-product
- Waste: Residual output of a joint process with no sales value

A joint process can have one or more split-off points, depending on the number and types of output produced. Output may be sold at the split-off point (if a market exists for products at that degree of completion) or may be processed further and then sold.

Joint cost includes all direct material, direct labor, and overhead costs incurred up to the split-off point. Financial reporting requires that all necessary and reasonable costs of production be attached to products. The following table indicates why a joint cost is allocated only to joint products rather than to all outputs of the joint process.

---

[1] James F. Gatti and D. Jacque Grinnell, "Joint Cost Allocations: Measuring and Promoting Productivity and Quality Improvements," *Cost Management* (July–August 2000), pp. 13–21.

[2] Sometimes correctly pricing a product depends on knowledge of the full cost of making the product, particularly when contractual agreements require cost-plus pricing. Joint cost allocation is also necessary to the costing of products for financial reporting.

Chapter 12 Allocation of Joint Costs and Accounting for By-Product/Scrap

Joint Cost	Rationale
Allocated only to joint products	• Necessary for financial statement valuations at split-off point • Underlying financial motivation for undertaking the production process • Not relevant for internal decision making because, at split-off, joint cost is a sunk cost
Not allocated to "other" output	• Not cost beneficial • Not significant to production process decision

If joint output is processed beyond the split-off point, additional **separate costs** will be incurred and must be assigned to the specific products for which those costs were incurred. **Exhibit 12.1** illustrates a joint process with multiple split-off points and the allocation of costs to products. For simplicity, the joint process shows no by-product production. Even if created in the joint process, other outputs (such as the scrap and waste produced from Joint Process 1) would not receive any joint cost allocation. Note that joint products B and C of Joint Process 1 become direct material for Joint Process 2. For accounting purposes, joint cost allocations will follow products B and C into Joint Process 2, but these allocated costs should not be used in making decisions about further processing in Departments 2, 3, or 4. Such decisions should be made only after considering whether the expected additional revenues from further processing are greater than the expected additional costs of further processing.

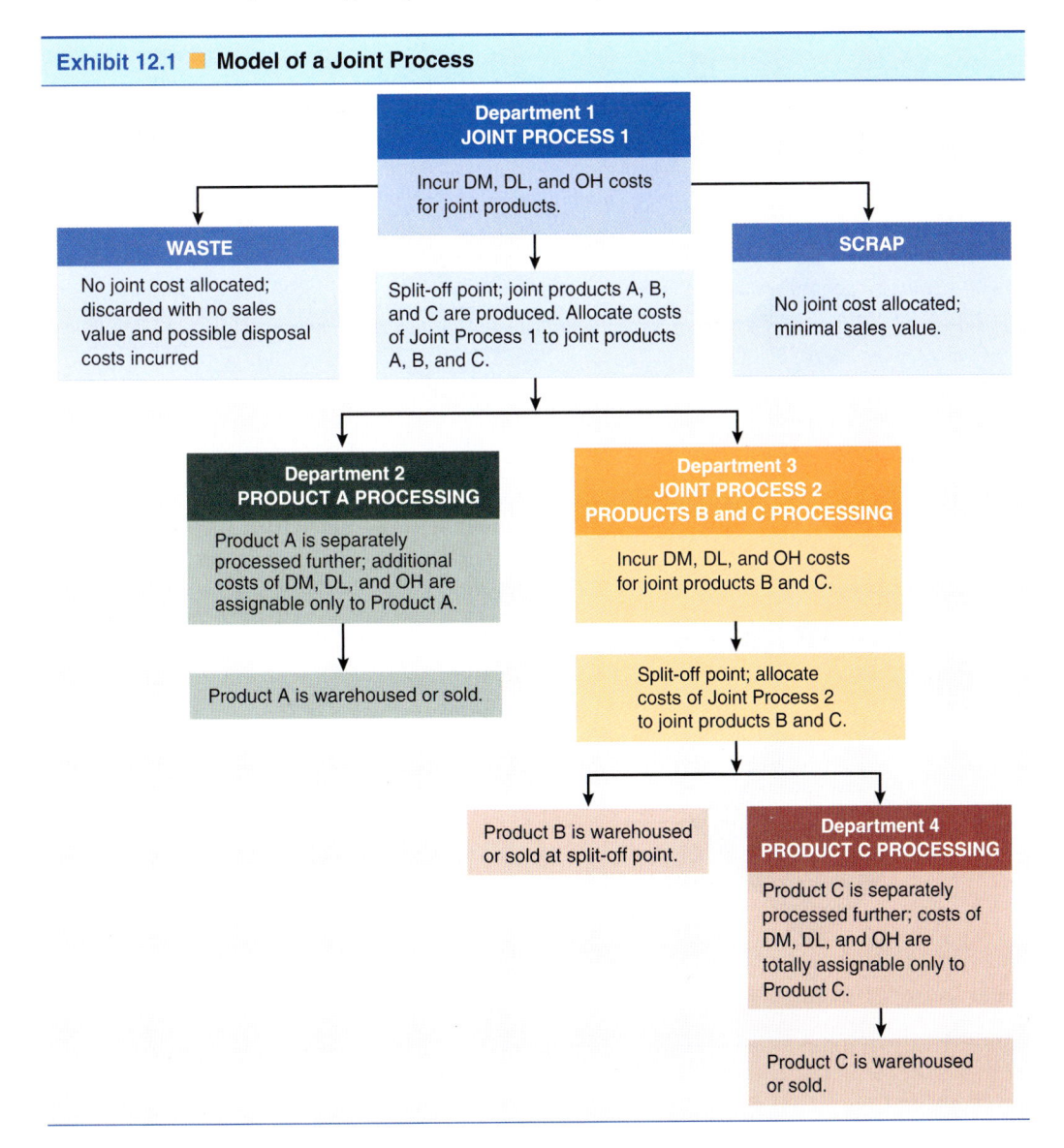

Exhibit 12.1 ■ Model of a Joint Process

Department 1 — JOINT PROCESS 1
Incur DM, DL, and OH costs for joint products.

WASTE
No joint cost allocated; discarded with no sales value and possible disposal costs incurred

Split-off point; joint products A, B, and C are produced. Allocate costs of Joint Process 1 to joint products A, B, and C.

SCRAP
No joint cost allocated; minimal sales value.

Department 2 — PRODUCT A PROCESSING
Product A is separately processed further; additional costs of DM, DL, and OH are assignable only to Product A.

Product A is warehoused or sold.

Department 3 — JOINT PROCESS 2 PRODUCTS B and C PROCESSING
Incur DM, DL, and OH costs for joint products B and C.

Split-off point; allocate costs of Joint Process 2 to joint products B and C.

Product B is warehoused or sold at split-off point.

Department 4 — PRODUCT C PROCESSING
Product C is separately processed further; costs of DM, DL, and OH are totally assignable only to Product C.

Product C is warehoused or sold.

Decisions in the Joint Process

Exhibit 12.2 indicates the four management decision points in a joint production process. The first two questions take place *before* the joint process begins.

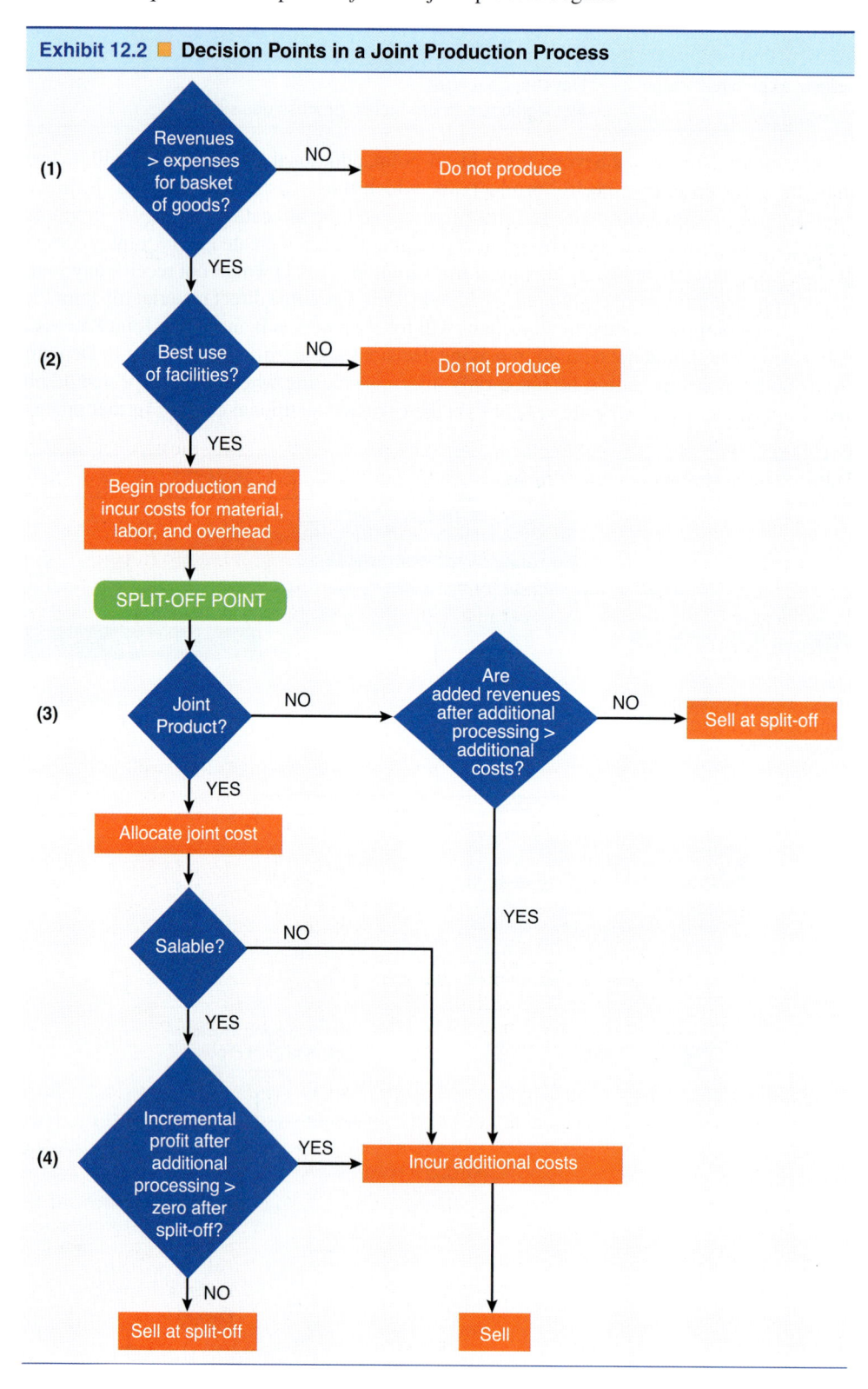

Exhibit 12.2 ■ Decision Points in a Joint Production Process

(1) Revenues > expenses for basket of goods? → NO → Do not produce
↓ YES

(2) Best use of facilities? → NO → Do not produce
↓ YES

Begin production and incur costs for material, labor, and overhead

SPLIT-OFF POINT

(3) Joint Product? → NO → Are added revenues after additional processing > additional costs? → NO → Sell at split-off
↓ YES   ↓ YES

Allocate joint cost

Salable? → NO ↓
↓ YES

(4) Incremental profit after additional processing > zero after split-off? → YES → Incur additional costs → Sell
↓ NO
Sell at split-off

Question #1: Will revenue from selling the joint output exceed costs? Before committing resources to a joint process, management's first decision is whether total expected revenue from selling the joint output "basket" of products is likely to exceed total expected processing cost, which includes

- joint cost,
- separate processing costs after split-off,
- selling expenses for the goods, and
- disposal costs for any waste materials.

Question #2: Is the joint process the best use of facilities? If total anticipated revenue exceeds total anticipated costs, managers should next decide whether this production process is the best use of the facilities. The income from this use of company resources would be compared to the income provided by the best alternative use. If the joint process income exceeds that of the best alternative, management would begin production.

The next two questions take place at a *split-off point*, only if the company decides to proceed with the joint process.

Question #3: Should joint output be sold or processed further? Management must decide whether to sell any or all joint output at split-off or to process it further. If joint products are salable at split-off, further processing should be undertaken only if the value added to the product, as reflected by the incremental revenue, exceeds the incremental cost.[3] This process is illustrated in Demo 12-1.

Question #4: How are joint process outputs classified and how are joint costs allocated? The fourth decision is to determine how to classify joint process outputs (refer to LO2). This classification decision is necessary because joint cost is assigned only to joint products (refer to LO3). Prior to allocation, however, the joint cost may be reduced by the sales value of any by-product or scrap (refer to LO4).

The Decision to Sell or Process Further

At split-off, management must decide whether to sell each joint product or process further. For example, does a cocoa bean processor make more profits from selling cocoa power at split-off or processing it further into a cake mix? The cocoa bean processor must decide whether further processing adds value to the product by comparing incremental revenues to incremental costs as illustrated in **Exhibit 12.3**.

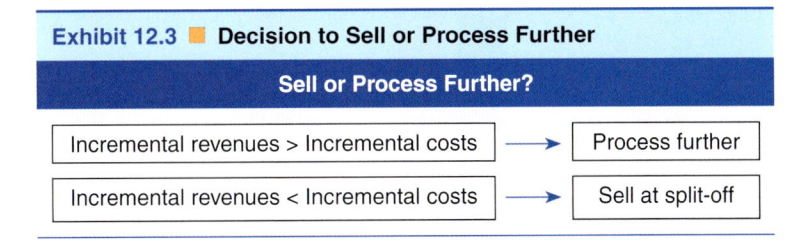

Exhibit 12.3 ■ Decision to Sell or Process Further

Sell or Process Further?	
Incremental revenues > Incremental costs	→ Process further
Incremental revenues < Incremental costs	→ Sell at split-off

If a primary product cannot be sold at split-off, additional costs must be incurred to make that product salable. For other output, management must also estimate whether the incremental revenue from additional processing will exceed the additional processing cost. By-product and scrap should also be processed further only if additional processing provides a net monetary benefit.

In making decisions at any potential sales point, managers must have a reasonable estimate of each joint output's selling price. Expected selling prices should be based on both cost and market factors. In the long run, the product selling prices and volumes must be sufficient to cover their total costs. However, current economic influences, such as competitors' prices and consumers' sensitivity to price changes, must be considered when estimating selling prices and forecasting revenues.

The following example illustrates a further processing decision.

---
[3] See Chapter 5 for a detailed discussion of incremental and relevant costs.

DEMO 12-1   LO12-1   Deciding Whether to Sell or Process Further

Assume that an organic cocoa bean processor can sell cocoa power for $8 per pound at split-off. The minimum selling price for cake mix after further processing is $8.50 per pound. The cost of additional processing is $0.40 per pound.

◆ **Should the company sell the cocoa power at split-off or process it further into cake mix?**

The company should compare incremental revenue to the incremental cost of processing further.

> **Incremental revenue = Revenue after additional processing − Revenue at split-off**

Incremental cost = $0.40 per pound
Incremental revenue = $8.50 − $8.00 = $0.50 per pound
$0.50 Incremental revenue − $0.40 Incremental cost = $0.10 per pound

Based on a quantitative analysis, the company should process the cocoa powder further because the incremental revenue exceeds the incremental costs.

Qualitative Considerations The quantitative result of a sell or process analysis suggests a course direction. However, it is important always to keep in mind that models do not make decisions—managers make decisions. The results of the model are an essential and necessary starting point in many decisions, but often there are other factors that weigh heavily on a decision that may cause the manager to go against the most economical alternative. There may be human resource, marketing, cultural, logistical, environmental, technological, or other factors that outweigh the analytics of a decision situation. It is in these situations where managers demonstrate leadership, problem-solving, and executive skill and potential, or the lack thereof.

Data Visualization

April Inc. produces three products (A, B, and C) and summarized the following information for each product.

Sell or Process Further Decision

Product	Sales Price at Split-Off	Final Sales Price	Allocated Joint Costs	Allocated Joint Costs Plus Separate Costs After Split-Off
Product A	$18	$20	$8	$10
Product B	$30	$35	$12	$15
Product C	$15	$18	$6	$10

Required

Solution on p. 12-47.   Which product (if any) should the company process further?

Chapter 12 Allocation of Joint Costs and Accounting for By-Product/Scrap   12-7

Deciding Whether to Sell or Process Further — LO12-1 — REVIEW 12-1

Clean Pools Inc. produces cleaning and sanitizing chemicals for residential pools. Assume the company processes raw material A into joint products B and C. Raw material A costs $8 per liter. It costs $150 to convert 100 liters of A into 60 liters of B and 40 liters of C. Product C can be sold immediately for $40 per liter or processed further into Product D at an additional cost of $12 per liter. Product D can then be sold for $56 per liter.

a. Determine whether Product C should be sold or processed further into Product D.
b. **Critical Thinking:** What qualitative factors might be considered in making the decision to sell or process further?

More practice: E12-17, E12-18, E12-19
Solution on p. 12-45.

OUTPUTS OF A JOINT PROCESS

In the prior section, we provided an overview of the joint process including the outputs of a joint process. In this section, we describe, in more detail, the classification of the outputs of a joint process. Output from a joint process can be classified as output with a sales value and output without a sales value.

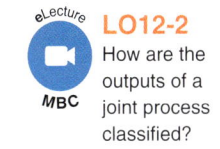

LO12-2 How are the outputs of a joint process classified?

Joint Process Outputs			
Output With a Sales Value			Output With No Sales Value
Joint Product	By-Product	Scrap	Waste

Output with a Sales Value

Joint products Key outputs of a joint process, or joint costs, have substantial revenue-generating ability and, as such, provide the financial motive for the company entering into the production process. Some joint products are dissimilar, while other joint products may be similar products that are finished in alternative ways or similar products of differing quality. For example, a poultry processor generates different grades of turkeys that, depending on certain characteristics defined by the U.S. Department of Agriculture, are graded as A, B, or C quality.

By-Products and Scrap In contrast, **by-product** and **scrap** are incidental outputs of a joint process. Both are salable (with by-products being the more valuable). However, *the sales values of these products alone would not be sufficient for management to undertake the joint process.* For example, **Ingredion Incorporated** would never undertake corn processing simply to generate the corn cob by-product that is ground and used in cosmetics and vitamins. **Krispy Kreme** would not manufacture doughnuts simply to generate the doughnut holes sold to customers. **Weyerhaeuser** would never process lumber merely to obtain the bark that is burned to produce power and steam.

Output with No Sales Value

Waste A final residual output from a joint process is **waste**, which has no sales value. In some cases, the expense incurred in disposing of waste may exceed its production cost. Many companies, though, have learned either to minimize their production waste by changing their processing techniques or to reclassify waste as by-product or scrap by finding a use that generates some minimal amount of revenue.

Reclassification of Outputs of a Joint Process

Over time, a product's classification may change because of technology advances, consumer demand, or ecological factors. New joint products may be developed from a production process, as illustrated in the ever-growing list for soybeans (**Exhibit 12.4**).

Instead of throwing away day-old bread or bagels, a bakery may decide to use them to make croutons, allowing what would have been waste to be reclassified as a by-product or scrap.

Exhibit 12.4 ■ Products from Soybeans

Soy Foods	Nonedible Products	
Animal feed	Adhesives	Lubricants and hydraulic fluids
Butter	Biodiesel fuel	Paints and coatings
Cereals	Building materials	Pesticides and herbicides
Chocolate coatings	Candles	Pharmaceuticals
Coffee	Cosmetics	Plastics
Flour	Crayons	Printing inks
Milk and creamers	Disinfectants	Road materials
Oil	Electrical insulation	Rubber
Salad dressing	Fiber (Yarn)	Shampoo and detergent
Sauce	Foam for furniture	Solvents
Sausage casings	Leather substitute	
Tofu		

Some products originally classified as by-products may be reclassified as joint products, and some joint products may be reduced to the by-product category. Even products originally viewed as scrap or waste can be upgraded to joint product or by-product status. For example, years ago, poultry processors considered unused chicken parts to be waste. These items are now recycled and processed further to produce valuable organic fertilizer and, therefore, may be classified as either by-product or scrap. Furthermore, chicken litter can, when gasified, be used to produce electricity.

Management Judgment Required in Classification

Joint process output is classified based on management's judgment about the relative sales values of outputs. Classifications are unique to each company.

DEMO 12-2 LO12-2 Classifying Joint Process Output

Assume that Company A and B both process soybeans. Company A regularly produces soy butter, milk, creamers, and oil. Company B only produces soy butter, milk, and creamers. Company B does not produce oil on a regular basis because of a lack of space in its processing facilities. Increasing production would require a capital investment that would not be cost beneficial.

◆ How might Company A and Company B classify their joint products?

Company A might classify soy butter, milk, creamers, and oil as joint products and Company B might classify soy butter, milk, and creamers as joint products and oil as a by-product. Unlike Company B, Company A likely has larger facilities that would allow processing of all joint products at costs substantially below the sales values of the multiple products.

REVIEW 12-2 LO12-2 Classification of Output from a Joint Process

Lathrop Co. makes a variety of products from a joint process. The joint cost per batch run is $55,000 and each batch produces the following products:

Product	# of Units	Sales Value per Unit at Split-Off
1	800	$10.00
2	14,000	2.00
3	5,000	.30
4	25	1.80
5	1,800	.80
6	300	3.50
7	1,000	5.00
8	10,000	4.00
9	650	2.20

a. How would you classify each product (joint, by-product, scrap, or waste)? Provide rationale for your answer.

b. **Critical Thinking:** What type of quantitative change might indicate that a joint product should be reclassified to another category?

ALLOCATION OF JOINT COST

Recall that joint costs include all manufacturing costs incurred up to the split-off point and that these costs are allocated only to joint products. In this section, we illustrate four methods of **joint cost allocation**.

Allocating Joint Costs			
Physical Measure Allocation	Sales Value at Split-Off	NRV at Split-Off	Approximated NRV at Split-Off

LO12-3 How is the joint cost of production allocated to joint products?

Apple Plus Inc. is used to demonstrate alternative methods of allocating joint costs. The company generates three primary (joint) products from the processing of harvested apples: Grade A, Grade B, and Grade C apples.[4] All remaining output is considered by-products of the joint process. Joint products can be either sold at split-off or processed further at an additional cost. Grade A apples can be processed further to produce candy apples; Grade B apples can be processed further into dried apples; and Grade C apples can be processed further into apple sauce. Certain marketing and disposal costs for advertising, commissions, and transportation are incurred regardless of when the products are sold.

Exhibit 12.5 provides assumed information on Apple Plus's processing operations and joint products for October. The company started processing 10,000 CWT (1 CWT equals 100 pounds) of apples during that month. Approximately 10 percent of the CWT started will become a by-product to be used in fertilizer pellets. Thus, the 10,000 CWT of input results in 9,000 CWT of joint product output and 1,000 CWT of by-product.

Exhibit 12.5 ■ Joint Cost Information for Apple Plus

Joint processing cost for period: $540,000

Joint Product	CWT Produced	Sales Price per CWT at Split-Off	Marketing Cost per CWT Regardless of When Sold	Separate Cost per CWT If Processed Further	Final Sales Price per CWT
Grade A	3,800	$280	$20	$10	$320
Grade B	2,400	180	10	10	210
Grade C	2,800	120	5	6	150

Diagram of problem assuming products are sold at split-off

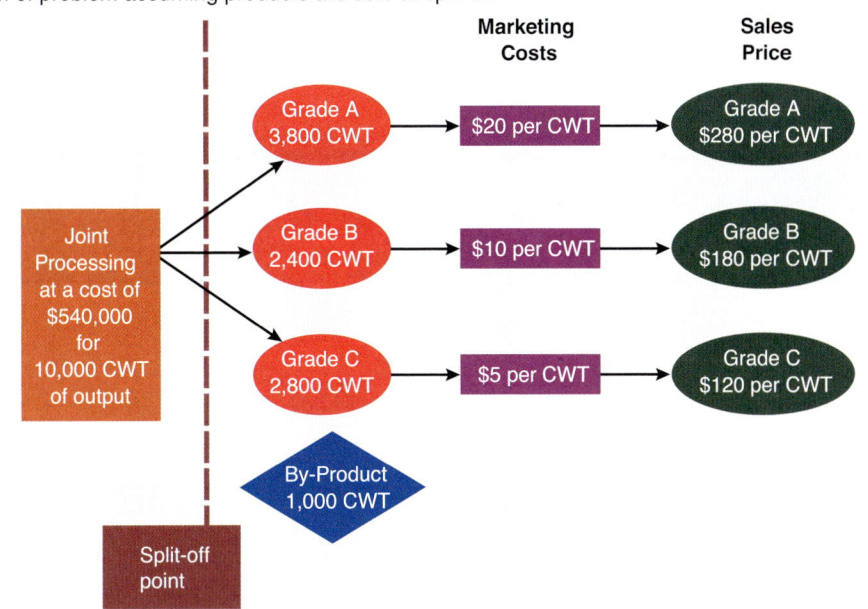

[Diagram: Joint Processing at a cost of $540,000 for 10,000 CWT of output splits at the Split-off point into Grade A (3,800 CWT) → $20 per CWT marketing → $280 per CWT sales price; Grade B (2,400 CWT) → $10 per CWT marketing → $180 per CWT sales price; Grade C (2,800 CWT) → $5 per CWT marketing → $120 per CWT sales price; and By-Product (1,000 CWT).]

---
[4] For simplification, we use Grade A, B, and C, which varies from the U.S. Standards of Extra Fancy, Fancy, and No. 1 for retail sale.

Physical Measure Allocation

An easy, objective way to prorate joint cost at the split-off point is to use **physical measure allocation** or proration using a common physical characteristic of the joint products such as:

- pounds of milk in the dairy industry,
- linear board feet in the lumber milling industry,
- barrels of oil in the petroleum refining industry, or
- number of computer chips in the semiconductor industry.

Physical measures provide an unchanging yardstick of output. Assuming that it is agreed that the word *ton* means "short ton" or 2,000 pounds (rather than a "long" or "metric ton"), a ton of output produced from a process 10 years ago is the same measurement as a ton produced from that process today. Physical measures are useful in allocating joint cost to products that have highly variable selling prices. These measures are also necessary in rate-regulated industries that use cost to determine selling prices. For example, assume that a rate-regulated company has the right to set the selling price of its product at 20 percent above cost. It would be circular logic to allocate joint cost using selling prices that were set based on production cost.

Allocating joint cost based on a physical measure, however, ignores the revenue-generating ability of individual joint products. Products that weigh the most or that are produced in the largest quantity will receive the highest proportion of joint cost allocation—regardless of their ability to bear that cost when they are sold.

DEMO 12-3A LO12-3 Applying the Physical Measure Allocation Method

◆ **Referring to the information provided in Exhibit 12.5 for Apple Plus, how are the joint costs of $540,000 allocated to joint products using the physical measure allocation method?**

The physical measure allocation process treats each weight unit of output as equally desirable and assigns each CWT the same per-unit cost. For Apple Plus, physical measure allocation assigns a cost of approximately $60 per CWT of apples, regardless of type.

Cost per physical measure = Total joint cost ÷ Total units of physical measurement

= $540,000 ÷ 9,000 CWT = $60 per CWT

The computations below show that, by allocating the same amount of joint cost to each CWT of joint product, Grade C apples generate the lowest gross profit per CWT of $60 (calculated as $120 − $60) of the three joint products.

Apple Plus's Joint Cost Allocation Based on Physical Measure					
Joint Product	CWT Produced	Sales Price per CWT at Split-Off	Total Sales Value at Split-Off	Allocated Joint Cost per CWT	Total Allocated Joint Cost
Grade A	3,800	$280	$1,064,000	$60	$228,000
Grade B	2,400	180	432,000	60	144,000
Grade C	2,800	120	336,000	60	168,000
Total	9,000		$1,832,000		$540,000

◆ **What are the journal entries to (1) incur the joint cost, (2) allocate the joint cost to the joint products, and (3) recognize the separate processing costs?**

The journal entries for incurring the joint cost, allocating it to the joint products, and recognizing the separate processing cost (assuming that all joint products are processed further) follow.

Chapter 12 Allocation of Joint Costs and Accounting for By-Product/Scrap

Work in Process Inventory—Apple Processing	540,000	
Various accounts		540,000
To record joint cost		
Work in Process Inventory—Grade A	228,000	
Work in Process Inventory—Grade B	144,000	
Work in Process Inventory—Grade C	168,000	
Work in Process Inventory—Apple Processing		540,000
To allocate joint cost		
Work in Process Inventory—Grade A (3,800 CWT × $10)	38,000	
Work in Process Inventory—Grade B (2,400 CWT × $10)	24,000	
Work in Process Inventory—Grade C (2,800 CWT × $6)	16,800	
Various accounts		78,800
To record separate processing costs (from Ex. 12.5)		

The marketing costs shown in **Exhibit 12.5** are not recorded until the products are sold.

Monetary Measure Allocation

The primary benefit of monetary over physical measure allocations is that the former recognizes the relative revenue generation of each product.[5] A problem with monetary measure allocations is that the allocation basis being used is a dynamic one. Because of fluctuations in general and specific price levels, a dollar of output today is different from a dollar of output from the same process five years ago. However, accountants customarily ignore price-level fluctuations when recording or processing data, so this particular flaw of monetary measures is manageable.

Process of Prorating All allocation methods employ a proration process. Because the physical measure allocation process is so simplistic, a detailed proration scheme is unnecessary. However, more complex monetary measure allocations use the following steps to prorate joint cost to joint products:

1. Choose a monetary allocation base.
2. List each joint product's base values.
3. Add the values in Step 2 to obtain total.
4. Divide each individual Step 2 value by the Step 3 total to obtain numerical proportions. These proportions should add to 100 percent.
5. Multiply the joint cost by each proportion to obtain the allocation for each product.
6. Divide each product's prorated joint cost by the number of product units[6] to obtain a cost per unit for valuation purposes.

Many different monetary measures can be used to allocate joint cost to primary output. The three presented in this text are sales value at split-off, net realizable value at split-off, and approximated net realizable value at split-off.

Sales Value at Split-Off The sales value at split-off allocation method assigns joint cost to joint products based on the relative split-off point sales values for the products. To use this method, all joint products must be salable at split-off.

Applying the Sales Value at Split-Off Allocation Method   LO12-3   DEMO 12-3B

◆ **Referring to the information provided in Exhibit 12.5 for Apple Plus, how are the joint costs of $540,000 allocated to the joint products using the sales value at split-off method?**

The table that follows presents the assignment of Apple Plus's joint cost to production using the sales value at split-off method. This allocation method uses a weighting technique based on both quantity produced and product selling price. The low selling price per CWT of Grade C apples compared to

---

[5] Monetary measures are more reflective of the primary reason a joint process is undertaken: profit. Physical measure allocations are sometimes of dubious value because they are based on the flawed assumption that all physical units are equally desirable.

[6] Given that joint products are generated in process costing environments, the units in this computation will actually be equivalent units of production as discussed in Chapter 7. The issue of EUP is ignored in this chapter.

the selling prices of other joint products results in a lower allocated cost ($34.71 per CWT) than was obtained using physical measure allocation ($60 per CWT). Account titles used in journal entries to record joint cost incurrence, allocate joint cost to joint products, and recognize separate processing cost are the same as those used in Demo 12-3A; however, the allocated cost amounts would be changed to those shown in the table below.

Apple Plus's Joint Cost Allocation Based on Sales Value at Split-Off

Joint Product	CWT Produced	Sales Price per CWT at Split-Off	Total Sales Value at Split-Off	% of Total Sales Value*	Joint Cost	Total Allocated Joint Cost	Total Allocated Joint Cost per CWT
Grade A	3,800	$280	$1,064,000	58%	$540,000	$313,200	$82.42
Grade B	2,400	180	432,000	24%	540,000	129,600	54.00
Grade C	2,800	120	336,000	18%	540,000	97,200	34.71
Total	9,000		$1,832,000	100%		$540,000	

* Proportions = Total sales value of joint product ÷ Total sales value
$1,064,000 ÷ $1,832,000 = 58% (rounded); $432,000 ÷ $1,832,000 = 24% (rounded); $336,000 ÷ $1,832,000 = 18% (rounded)

Net Realizable Value at Split-Off The **net realizable value at split-off allocation** method assigns joint cost based on an inventory valuation amount for the joint products at the split-off point. **Net realizable value (NRV)** is equal to sales value at split-off minus any expected completion and disposal costs.[7] This method requires that all joint products be salable at split-off and considers the costs that must be incurred at split-off to realize the estimated sales value. The marketing costs (shown in the fourth column of **Exhibit 12.5**) for Apple Plus's products are considered disposal costs and are incurred whether the product is sold at split-off or after further processing.

> NRV per CWT at split-off = Sales price at split-off − Marketing cost at point of sale

Grade A   NRV per CWT = $280 − $20 = $260
Grade B   NRV per CWT = $180 − $10 = $170
Grade C   NRV per CWT = $120 − $ 5 = $115

DEMO 12-3C   LO12-3   Applying the Net Realizable Value at Split-Off Allocation Method

◆ Referring to the information provided in Exhibit 12.5 for Apple Plus and the NRV amounts calculated above, how are the joint costs of $540,000 allocated to the joint products using the net realizable value at split-off method?

The table below provides the joint cost allocations based on each product's relative proportion of total NRV.

Apple Plus's Joint Cost Allocation Based on Net Realizable Value at Split-Off

Joint Product	CWT Produced	NRV per CWT at Split-Off	Total NRV at Split-Off	% of Total NRV*	Joint Cost	Total Allocated Joint Cost	Allocated Joint Cost per CWT
Grade A	3,800	$260	$ 988,000	57%	$540,000	$307,800	$81.00
Grade B	2,400	170	408,000	24%	540,000	129,600	54.00
Grade C	2,800	115	322,000	19%	540,000	102,600	36.64
Total	9,000		$1,718,000	100%		$540,000	

* Proportion = Total NRV of respective joint product ÷ Total NRV
$988,000 ÷ $1,718,000 = 0.57 (rounded down to sum to total); $408,000 ÷ $1,718,000 = 0.24 (rounded); $322,000 ÷ $1,718,000 = 0.19 (rounded)

---

[7] A complete discussion of net realizable value would also include the issues of "ceiling" and "floor" values under certain inventory valuation conditions. These issues are beyond the scope of this text and can be found in any intermediate accounting book.

Results in Demo 12-3B and Demo 12-3C are very similar because marketing costs incurred for each primary product are relatively low. When disposal costs are high, cost allocations based on sales values and on NRVs at split-off can differ substantially.

Approximated Net Realizable Value at Split-Off Often, some or all of the joint products are not salable at split-off. Thus, these products must be processed at an additional separate cost beyond the split-off point. This lack of marketability at split-off means that neither the sales value at split-off nor the NRV at split-off approach can be used. The **approximated net realizable value at split-off allocation** uses simulated NRVs for the joint products at split-off to calculate the joint cost allocation. For each product, this value is the final selling price minus all incremental processing, marketing, and disposal costs incurred between split-off and point of sale. For Apple Plus, the approximated NRV at split-off is calculated as follows.

Joint Product	Final Sales Price per CWT		Separate Cost per CWT after Split-Off		Approximated NRV at Split-Off
Grade A	$320	−	$30	=	$290
Grade B	210	−	20	=	190
Grade C	150	−	11	=	139

Allocating joint costs under the approximated NRV method requires two steps, (1) a sell or process further decision and (2) joint cost allocation, which are illustrated using the Apple Plus company.

Applying the Approximated Net Realizable Value at Split-Off Allocation Method — LO12-3 — DEMO 12-3D

◆ Referring to the information provided in Exhibit 12.5 for Apple Plus and the approximated NRV at split-off calculated above, how are the joint costs of $540,000 allocated to the joint products using the approximated net realizable value at split-off method?

Step One: Sell or Process Further Decision An underlying assumption of the approximated net realizable value at split-off method is that the incremental revenue from further processing is equal to or greater than the incremental costs of further processing and selling.

Joint Product	Sales Price per CWT at Split-Off	Final Sales Price per CWT	Marketing Cost per CWT at Split-Off	Further Processing Cost + Marketing Cost = Separate Cost per CWT after Split-Off
Grade A	$280	$320	$20	$10 + $20 = $30
Grade B	180	210	10	$10 + $10 = $20
Grade C	120	150	5	$ 6 + $ 5 = $11

Joint Product	Incremental Revenue	−	Incremental Cost	=	Incremental Profit
Grade A	$40		$10		$30
Grade B	30		10		20
Grade C	30		6		24

For all Apple Plus's products, incremental revenue exceeds increments costs as shown by the computations above. Thus, Apple Plus should process all joint products beyond the split-off point.

The same "process further" conclusion can be reached by comparing the approximated NRVs at split-off with the NRV at split-off.

Joint Product	(a) Approximated NRV per CWT at Split-Off	−	(b) NRV per CWT at Split-Off	=	Difference a − b
Grade A	$290		$260		$30
Grade B	190		170		20
Grade C	139		115		24

Step Two: Allocate Joint Costs Using the Approximated NRV Method Decisions made about further processing affect the values used to allocate joint cost with the approximated NRV method. If it is not economical to process one or more products beyond split-off, the base used for allocating joint cost will become a mixture of actual and approximated NRVs at split-off. Products that will not be processed further will be valued at their actual NRVs at split-off, whereas products that will be processed further are valued at approximated NRVs at split-off. Given that all products will be processed further, the joint cost allocation using the approximated NRV method is shown below.

Apple Plus's Joint Cost Allocation Based on Approximated Net Realizable Value at Split-Off

Joint Product	CWT Produced	Approximated NRV per CWT at Split-Off	Total Approximated NRV	% of Total NRV*	Joint Cost	Total Allocated Joint Cost	Allocated Joint Cost per CWT
Grade A	3,800	$290	$1,102,000	57%	$540,000	$307,800	$81.00
Grade B	2,400	190	456,000	23%	540,000	124,200	51.75
Grade C	2,800	139	389,200	20%	540,000	108,000	38.57
Total	9,000		$1,947,200	100%		$540,000	

*Proportion = Total approximated NRV of respective joint product ÷ Total approximated NRV
$1,102,000 ÷ $1,947,200 = 57% (rounded); $456,000 ÷ $1,947,200 = 23% (rounded); $389,200 ÷ $1,947,200 = 20% (rounded)

Recording Further Processing Using the Approximated NRV at Split-Off Method Apple Plus decides to further process its 1,000 CWT of Grade A apples into candy apples, 900 CWT of Grade B apples into dried apples, and 1,200 CWT of Grade C apples into apple sauce. (see **Exhibit 12.6**). For purposes of these calculations, the allocations are assumed to be the ones computed in Demo 12-3D. At the split-off point, the joint cost cannot be recouped and must be considered a "sunk" cost. Thus, the only relevant items in the decision to process further are the incremental revenue and incremental cost.

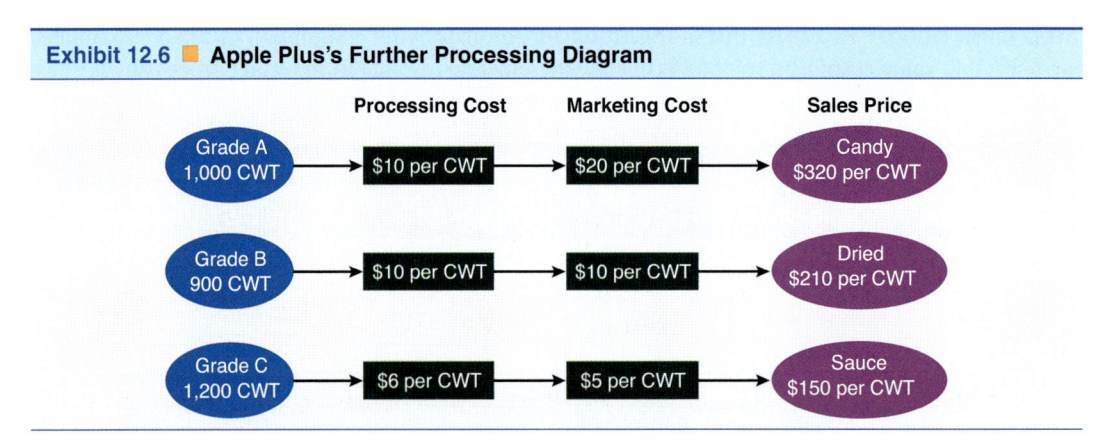

Exhibit 12.6 ■ Apple Plus's Further Processing Diagram

	Processing Cost	Marketing Cost	Sales Price
Grade A 1,000 CWT	$10 per CWT	$20 per CWT	Candy $320 per CWT
Grade B 900 CWT	$10 per CWT	$10 per CWT	Dried $210 per CWT
Grade C 1,200 CWT	$6 per CWT	$5 per CWT	Sauce $150 per CWT

The journal entries under the approximated NRV at split-off method to transfer allocated joint costs to new product inventories and to record separate processing costs are recorded below. Further processing does not change the joint cost allocations previously made. The new products are allocated some of the original joint cost and absorb their own separate processing cost. The marketing costs have not been recorded because the products have not yet been sold.

Work in Process Inventory—Candy (1,000 CWT × $81.00)	81,000	
Work in Process Inventory—Dried (900 CWT × $51.75)	46,575	
Work in Process Inventory—Sauce (1,200 CWT × $38.57)	46,284	
Work in Process Inventory—Grade A		81,000
Work in Process Inventory—Grade B		46,575
Work in Process Inventory—Grade C		46,284
To transfer allocated costs to new product inventories		

continued

continued from previous page

Work in Process Inventory—Candy (1,000 CWT × $10)	10,000	
Work in Process Inventory—Dried (900 CWT × $10)	9,000	
Work in Process Inventory—Sauce (1,200 CWT × $6)	7,200	
Various accounts		26,200
To record separate processing costs		

Comparison of Four Methods of Joint Cost Allocation

In summary, there are a number of ways that joint costs can be allocated to joint products. Based on the four methods described in this section, joint costs of $540,000 were allocated as follows.

Joint Product	Physical Measure (Demo 12-3A)	Sales Value at Split-Off (Demo 12-3B)	NRV at Split-Off (Demo 12-3C)	Approx. NRV at Split-Off (Demo 12-3D)
Grade A	$228,000	$313,200	$307,800	$307,800
Grade B	144,000	129,600	129,600	124,200
Grade C	168,000	97,200	102,600	108,000
Total	$540,000	$540,000	$540,000	$540,000

The results are also shown visually in the following data visualization.

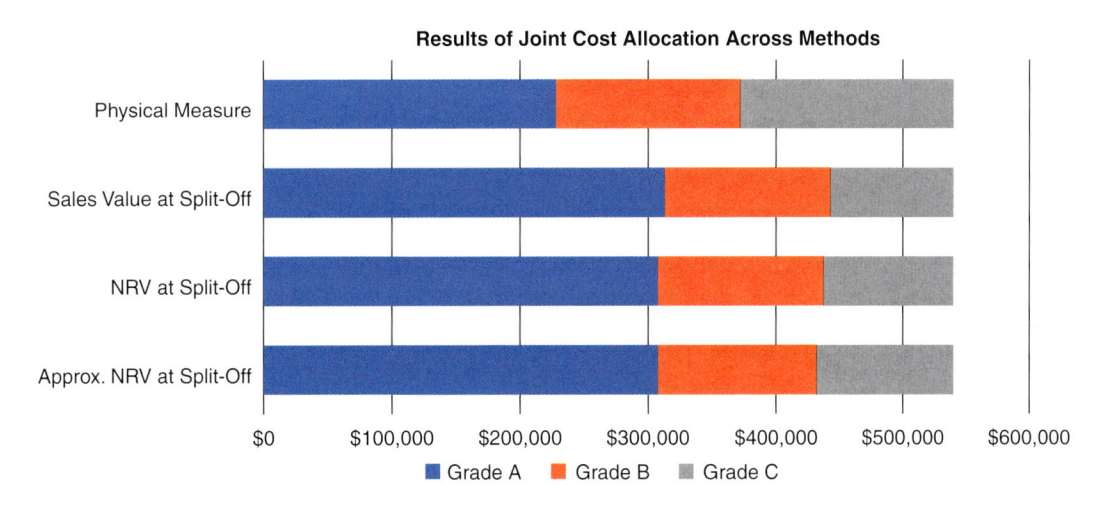

Results of Joint Cost Allocation Across Methods

Each allocation method assigns a different amount of joint cost to the joint products and results in a different per-unit cost for each product. Each method has advantages and disadvantages. For most companies, approximated NRV at split-off provides the *most logical* joint cost assignment because this method captures the

- intended level of separate processing,
- costs of separate processing,
- expected selling costs of each joint product, and
- expected selling price of each joint product.

Thus, approximated NRV measures the expected contribution of each product line to the coverage of joint cost. This method is, however, more complex than the others because estimations must be made about additional processing costs and potential future sales values.

REVIEW 12-3 — LO12-3: Allocation of Joint Costs and Decision on Processing Further

Oliver Inc. makes three types of olive oil that can be sold at split-off or processed further and then sold. The joint cost for October is $325,000.

Product	Units	Sales Price at Split-Off	Separate Cost After Split-Off	Final Sales Price
A	30,000	$5	$3	$12
B	45,000	4	1	10
C	20,000	8	2	15

The number of ounces in a bottle of each product is: Product A, twelve; Product B, sixteen; Product C, eighteen.

a. Allocate the joint cost based on (1) the number of units, (2) weight, (3) sales value at split-off, and (4) approximated net realizable. (Round proportions to the nearest whole percentage [without exceeding 100 percent] and dollar amounts to the nearest whole dollar.)

b. Prepare an analysis to determine whether each product should be processed further.

c. Assume that all products are processed further and completed. At the end of the period, the inventories are as follows: Product A, 800 units; Product B, 1,100 units; Product C, 1,900 units. Determine the values of the inventories based on answers obtained in (a). Round your final answer to the nearest whole dollar.

d. **Critical Thinking:** Analyze the differences (if any) in part *a* across the different methods. What causes methods to show different results? Will similar trends always be present when these methods are used?

More practice: MC12-13, MC12-14, E12-23, E12-24, E12-25, E12-26. Solution on p. 12-45.

ACCOUNTING FOR BY-PRODUCT AND SCRAP

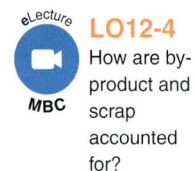

LO12-4 How are by-product and scrap accounted for?

The distinction between by-product and scrap is merely one of degree. Thus, in the following discussion, "scrap" can be substituted anywhere that "by-product" is used. Similar to the accounting for joint cost, a variety of methods exist in practice to account for a by-product. The choice of method should depend on the magnitude of the net realizable value of the by-product and the need for additional processing after split-off. As the sales value of the by-product increases, so does the need for inventory recognition. By-product sales value is generally recorded under either the NRV approach or realized value approach.[8]

- The net *realizable* value approach reflects the *expected* amount to be received from the by-product sale.
- The *realized* value approach reflects the *actual* amount that was received from by-product sale.

Thus, the NRV approach can be used in advance of revenue realization, whereas the realized value approach cannot be used until revenue is realized. Regardless of whether a company uses the NRV or the realized value approach, the specific method that will be used to account for by-product must be determined *before the joint cost is allocated to the joint products*. The following methods will be illustrated for each approach.

Net Realizable Value Approach		Realized Value Approach	
WIP Inventory Reduction Method	CGS Reduction Method	Other Revenue Method	Other Income Method

Net Realizable Value Approach

The **net realizable value approach** (or **offset approach**) reduces joint product cost for the NRV that will be created by the by-product's sale.

Alternative Presentations: Reduce WIP Inventory or CGS

When by-product is generated, the NRV is debited to inventory and credited to one of two accounts (Work in Process Inventory—Joint Products or Cost of Goods Sold for the joint products).

---

[8] Other alternative presentations include showing the realized value from the sale of by-product as (1) an addition to gross margin, (2) a reduction of the Cost of Goods Manufactured, or (3) a reduction of the Cost of Goods Sold. The major advantage of these simplistic approaches is clerical efficiency.

Using the Work in Process Inventory account allows the joint cost to be reduced immediately when the by-product is produced and *before the joint cost is allocated to the joint products.* However, recording the reduction in WIP Inventory or CGS immediately upon by-product production is less conservative than waiting until the by-product is actually sold. Additionally, the by-product could have sales potential beyond that currently known by management.

Using the NRV Approach to Account for By-Products — LO12-4 DEMO 12-4A

To illustrate the net realizable value approach, additional data is provided for Apple Plus, which produces fertilizer pellets as a by-product. The following table provides the October data.

October Data for By-Products of Apple Plus	
Total processing for month	10,000 CWT of apples
Total CWT of joint product output	9,000 CWT of joint products
By-products (fertilizer pellets) from joint product production	1,000 CWT (equivalent to 100,000 pounds)
Selling price per pound of fertilizer pellets	$0.30
Processing costs per pound of fertilizer pellets	$0.08 for labor and $0.02 for overhead
Net realizable value per pound of fertilizer pellets	$0.20
Sales for the month	$720,000
Operating expenses for the month	$160,000
Other income: Royalties for the month	$8,000
Also assume beginning and ending finished goods inventory of zero and 500 CWT, respectively.	

◆ **What are the journal entries to record Apple Plus's by-product production by initially reducing Work in Process Inventory—Joint Products, and the additional processing, completion, and sale of the by-product?**

Work in Process Inventory—Fertilizer Pellets (100,000 × $0.20)	20,000	
Work in Process Inventory—Joint Products		20,000
To record production of by-product; an alternative credit could have been made to Cost of Goods Sold from the sale of the joint products		
Work in Process Inventory—Fertilizer Pellets (100,000 × $0.10)	10,000	
Various accounts		10,000
To record additional separate processing costs for the by-product		
Finished Goods Inventory—Fertilizer Pellets (100,000 × $0.30)	30,000	
Work in Process Inventory—Fertilizer Pellets		30,000
To record completion of by-product		
Cash (or Accounts Receivable) (100,000 × $0.30)	30,000	
Finished Goods Inventory—Fertilizer Pellets		30,000
To record sale of by-product		

Financial Statement Effect of Reducing WIP vs. CGS

The choice of reducing WIP Inventory-Joint Products or Cost of Goods Sold creates alternative income statement presentations and balance sheet information.

◆ **How do the income statements differ under the net realizable value approach assuming the NRV of by-products reduces (a) WIP Inventory and (b) Cost of Goods Sold?** Assume that Apple Plus used a physical measure joint cost allocation.

WIP Inventory Reduction Method A reduction in WIP Inventory-Joint Products lowers the production cost per unit of the joint products. If by-product NRV were used to reduce WIP Inventory-Joint Products, the company's joint cost to allocate would have been $520,000 rather than $540,000: the difference is the 100,000 pounds of by-product multiplied by $0.20 NRV per pound.

$540,000 Joint costs − $20,000 NRV of by-product = $520,000 Joint cost to allocate

The reduction in WIP Inventory-Joint Products would create a corresponding reduction in cost of goods manufactured. Thus, the allocated joint cost per CWT would have been approximately $57.78 (or $520,000 ÷ 9,000) per CWT for any joint product rather than the $60 joint cost per CWT allocation shown in Demo 12-3A.

$$\$520,000 \text{ Joint cost} \div 9,000 \text{ CWT} = \$57.78 \text{ per CWT}$$

The reduced cost per CWT would affect not only the amount of CGS upon joint product sale but also the amount shown in the inventory account.

CGS Reduction Method Alternatively, reducing CGS by the NRV would not affect the $60 per CWT allocated cost of the joint products. The following statement shows the presentation of these two NRV approaches; the zero balance in beginning finished goods inventory highlights the differences in the CGS computation. Note that the $1,100 difference in pre-tax profits (= $76,000 − $74,890) is equal to

$$500 \text{ CWT} \times (\$60.00 - \$57.78) = \$1,110$$

NRV Approach to By-Products

	A	B	C
1	**(a) Net Realizable Value Approach: Reduce WIP—Joint Products**		
2	Sales		$ 720,000
3	Cost of goods sold		
4	Beginning finished goods (FG)	$ 0	
5	Cost of goods manufactured (CGM) ($540,000 − $20,000)	520,000	
6	Cost of goods available (CGA)	$ 520,000	
7	Ending FG (500 CWT @ $57.78 per CWT)	(28,890)	(491,110)
8	Gross margin		$ 228,890
9	Operating expenses		(160,000)
10	Income from principal operations		$ 68,890
11	Other income		
12	Royalties		8,000
13	Pre-tax profit		$ 76,890
14	**(b) Net Realizable Value Approach: Reduce Cost of Goods Sold**		
15	Sales		$ 720,000
16	Cost of goods sold		
17	Beginning FG	$ 0	
18	CGM	540,000	
19	CGA	$540,000	
20	Ending FG (500 CWT @ $60 per CWT)	(30,000)	
21	Unadjusted CGS	$510,000	
22	NRV of by-product	(20,000)	(490,000)
23	Gross margin		$ 230,000
24	Operating expenses		(160,000)
25	Income from principal operations		$ 70,000
26	Other income		
27	Royalties		8,000
28	Pre-tax profit		$ 78,000

Difference $1,110

Difference $1,110

Disadvantages of the NRV Method in Accounting for By-Products Although commonly used to account for such goods, the NRV method is not necessarily best for internal decision making or by-product management. This method does not indicate the revenues, expenses, or profits from the by-product and, thus, does not provide sufficient information to induce management to maximize the inflows from by-product sales.

Realized Value Approach

When management considers by-product to be a moderate source of income, the accounting and reporting methods used should help managers monitor by-product production and further processing as well as make effective decisions regarding this resource. The **realized value approach** (or **other income approach**) is the easiest approach to accounting for by-product because *no value is recognized for the by-product until it is sold*.

Alternative Presentations: Sale of By-Products in Other Revenues and in Other Income

Other Revenue Method This approach shows total sales of by-product under the Other Revenue caption. Costs of additional processing or disposal of the by-product are included as part of the cost of producing the joint products. This presentation provides little useful information to management because it does not match the costs of producing the by-product with its revenues.

Other Income Method This method requires that an inventory account be established for the by-product processing costs; the inventory account will be removed from the balance sheet upon sale of the by-product. By-product revenue, net of additional costs of processing and disposal, is then shown on the income statement. This presentation allows management to recognize the monetary benefit realized from managing the costs and revenues related to by-product.

Using the Realized Value Approach to Account for By-Products   LO12-4   DEMO 12-4B

To illustrate the realized value approach, we use the same data for Apple Plus from Demo 12-4A.

◆ **How are the incurrence of labor and overhead costs and the sale of by-products for Apple Plus recorded under the Other Income Method?**

The entries using the Other Income method for the incurrence of labor and overhead costs and sale of by-product for Apple Plus follow.

Work in Process Inventory—Fertilizer Pellets (100,000 pounds × $0.10) . . .	10,000	
Various accounts		10,000
To record the labor and overhead costs of by-product processing		
Cash (or Accounts Receivable) (100,000 pounds × $0.30)	30,000	
Work in Process Inventory—Fertilizer Pellets (see entry above)		10,000
Other Income ($30,000 – $10,000)		20,000
To record sale of by-product net of processing/disposal costs		

◆ **How do the income statements differ under the realized value approach using the (a) Other Revenue Method and the (b) Other Income Method?**

The statement that follows on the next page shows income statements using two different realized value presentations for accounting for by-product/scrap income for Apple Plus. The top section (a) of this statement assumes the use of physical measure joint cost allocation. Note that the cost per CWT for joint products has increased to approximately $61 (or $550,000 ÷ 9,000) per CWT from the $60 per CWT shown in Demo 12-3A because of the assignment of by-product costs to the joint products. In contrast, the bottom section (b) of this statement shows no effect on the allocated joint cost per joint product from the original computation because the processing costs for the by-product are netted from its sales value.

The Other Income method matches by-product revenue with related storage, further processing, transportation, and disposal costs. As such, this method

- presents detailed information on financial responsibility and accountability for disposition of these secondary outputs,
- provides better control opportunities than the realized value approach, and
- could improve performance because managers are more apt to look for new or expanded sales potential given that the net benefits of doing so are provided on the income statement.

By-product, scrap, and waste are created in all types of businesses, not just by manufacturers. Managers might not see the need to determine the cost of these secondary types of outputs. However, with the trend toward more emphasis on cost and quality control, companies are becoming more aware of the potential value of by-product, scrap, and waste and are devoting time and attention to developing those innovative revenue sources.

Realized Value Approaches to By-Products

	A	B	C
1	**(a) Net Realized Value Approach: Present as Other Revenue**		
2	Sales		$ 720,000
3	Other revenue		
4	By-product sales (100,000 × $0.30)		30,000
5	Total revenue		$ 750,000
6	Cost of goods sold		
7	Beginning finished goods (FG)	$ 0	
8	CGM (main products)	540,000	
9	CGM (by-product processing costs or 100,000 pounds × $0.10)	10,000	
10	Cost of goods available (CGA)	$550,000	
11	Ending FG (500 CWT × ($550,000/9,000) per CWT)	(30,556)	(519,444)
12	Gross margin		$ 230,556
13	Operating expenses		(160,000)
	Income from principal operations		$ 70,556
14	Other income		
15	Royalties		8,000
16	Pre-tax profit		$ 78,556
17	**(b) Net Realized Value Approach: Present as Other Income**		
18	Sales		$ 720,000
19	Cost of goods sold		
20	Beginning FG	$ 0	
21	CGM	540,000	
22	CGA	$540,000	
23	Ending FG (500 CWT × ($540,000/9,000) per CWT)	(30,000)	(510,000)
24	Gross margin		$ 210,000
25	Operating expenses		(160,000)
26	Income from principal operations		$ 50,000
27	Other income		
28	Royalties		$ 8,000
29	By-product sales ($30,000 − $10,000)		20,000
30	Pre-tax profit		$ 78,000

Difference $556

BY-PRODUCT AND SCRAP IN JOB ORDER COSTING

Although joint products are not normally associated with job order costing systems, accounting for by-product or scrap is common in these systems. Either the NRV or the realized value approach can be used to recognize the value of by-product/scrap.

In a job order system, the value of by-product/scrap is appropriately credited to either manufacturing overhead or the specific jobs in process. Overhead is credited if by-product/scrap is typically created by most jobs undertaken. This method reduces the amount of overhead that is applied to all products for the period. In contrast, if only a few or specific jobs generate substantial amounts of by-product/scrap, the individual jobs causing this output should be credited with its value. This method reduces the total costs assigned to those jobs.[9]

---

[9] Conceptually, the treatment of the profitability of by-product/scrap in a job order system is similar to the treatment of the costs of spoilage in a job order system, as discussed in Chapter 6.

Accounting for By-Products in Job Order Costing — LO12-4 DEMO 12-4C

To illustrate the realized value approach, we continue with the Apple Plus Company. Assume that Apple Plus occasionally prepares special runs of candied apples for large events. Every order generates scrap that is sold. Assume that Apple Plus received a special order in October resulting in the sale of $250 of scrap product.

◆ **What is the journal entry to record scrap using the realized value approach?**

Cash...	250	
Manufacturing Overhead		250
To record the sale of scrap		

Now assume instead that Apple Plus seldom has salable scrap on its special orders. However, during October, the company contracted with a client to process cherries for a special event, categorized as Job #101. Because Apple Plus does not normally process cherries, it must acquire specific raw material for the job and will charge the cost of all raw material directly to the client. Assume that the job generated $375 in sale of scrap. Because the raw material is directly related to the job, sale of scrap from that raw material also relates to that job.

◆ **What are the journal entries to record the production and sale of scrap using the net realizable value approach?**

Scrap Inventory—Cherries......................................	375	
Work in Process Inventory		375
To record the NRV of scrap produced by Job #101		
Cash...	375	
Scrap Inventory—Cherries		375
To record sale of the scrap		

In this case, the NRV approach is preferred because of the timing of recognition. The need to affect the specific job cost that caused an unusual incidence and quantity of scrap makes it essential to recognize the scrap at the point of production. Without prompt recognition, the job could be completed before the scrap could be sold, and thus, the reduction in the actual cost of the job would not be known.

Accounting for By-Products — LO12-4 REVIEW 12-4

Potato skins are generated as a by-product in making potato chips and frozen hash browns at Fit Food. The skins are sold to restaurants for use in appetizers. Processing and disposal costs associated with by-product sales are $0.08 per pound of potato skins. During October, Fit Food produced and sold 155,000 pounds of potato skins for $27,900. In addition, the joint cost for producing potato chips and hash browns was $90,000; separate costs of production were $55,000. In October, 85 percent of all joint production was sold for $335,000. Nonfactory operating expenses for October were $58,000.

a. Prepare an income statement for Fit Food assuming that the net realizable value of the by-product is subtracted from the joint cost of the main products under the Net Realizable Value Approach.
b. Prepare an income statement for Fit Food assuming that by-product sales are shown as Other Revenue and the processing and disposal costs for the by-product are shown as additional cost of goods sold of the joint products under the Realized Value Approach.
c. Prepare an income statement for Fit Food assuming that the net realizable value of the by-product is shown as Other Income under the Realized Value Approach.
d. **Critical Thinking:** Which presentation is preferable, part *b* or part *c*? Why?

More practice: MC12-15, E12-34, E12-35, E12-39, E12-40
Solution on p. 12-46.

JOINT COSTS IN NON-MANUFACTURING BUSINESSES AND NOT-FOR-PROFIT ORGANIZATIONS

LO12-5 How should retail and not-for-profit organizations account for the cost of a joint activity?

Allocation of joint costs is not unique to manufacturing organizations. Some costs incurred in non-manufacturing businesses, such as retail businesses and in not-for-profit organizations are considered joint costs in that such costs may need to be allocated among product lines, organizational locations, or types of organizational activities. For example, retail businesses and NFPs incur joint costs for advertising multiple programs, printing multipurpose documents, or holding multipurpose events. Additionally, NFPs often develop and distribute brochures providing information about the organization, its purposes, and its programs as well as appealing to readers for funds.

DEMO 12-5　LO12-5　Accounting for Joint Costs of a Retailer

A retail business can choose either a physical or a monetary allocation base to allocate joint costs.

◆ **For each joint cost in the two retail scenarios provided, how could the joint cost be allocated on a physical basis and on a monetary basis?**

	Physical Allocation	Monetary Allocation
a. A local bicycle and lawn mower repair company advertises a sale and lists all store locations in a single electronic ad.	Allocate ad cost equally to all locations.	Allocate ad cost based on sales volume for each location during the period of sale.
b. A grocery delivery service delivers multiple customer orders on the same trip.	Allocate cost of trip based on the number of bags or pounds delivered.	Allocate cost of trip based on the sales value of the orders delivered.

Allocating Joint Costs in an NFP

Although retail businesses may decide that allocating joint cost is not necessary, financial accounting requires that NFPs (and state and local government entities) meeting three tests allocate the costs of "joint activities" among fund raising, organizational program (program activities), and administrative functions (management and general activities).[10] If all three tests are not met, the entire cost associated with the "joint activity" must be charged to fund raising.[11] The tests relate to the following concepts.

Criterion	Meaning
Purpose	The activity includes accomplishing some program or management/general function.
Audience	The audience is suitable for accomplishing the activity's program or management/general functions.
Content	The content supports program or management/general functions.

The commonality among the criteria is that each creates some type of "call for action." Thus, a brochure that simply informs the audience about the NFP's purpose or a particular disease is not considered a call for action.

A critical element under the purpose criterion is the compensation test. If a majority of compensation or fees for anyone performing a part of the activity is tied to contributions raised, the activity automatically fails the purpose criterion and all costs of the activity must be charged to fund raising.[12] Thus, if professional fund raisers are used and paid a percentage of the amount raised, all costs of the activity must be charged to fund raising.

---

[10] ASC 958-720-45-29

[11] An exception to the rule is that costs for goods and services provided in exchange transactions (such as a meal provided at a function that failed to meet the three required criteria) that are part of joint activities should not be reported as fundraising costs; such costs should be reported as cost of sales for the activity (ASC 958-720-45-29).

[12] ASC 958-720-45-40

No specific allocation method is prescribed for the joint cost. ASC 958-720-45-54 merely states that the method must be

- rational and systematic,
- result in reasonable allocations, and
- applied in the same manner under similar situations.

A major purpose of this allocation process is to ensure that financial statement users are able to clearly determine amounts spent by the organization for various activities—especially fund raising. High fund raising costs may harm an NFP's credibility with donors who measure an organization's effectiveness by the percentage of funds that goes to programs furthering the entity's mission rather than the percentage going to raise more funds. High fund raising percentages may also jeopardize an NFP's standing with charity regulators.

REVIEW 12-5

Retail Organization Joint Cost — **LO12-5**

Recreation Inc. provides bicycle training classes for children and adults. During the year, the company had the following operating data:

	Children	Adults
Training hours taught	2,000	6,000
Hourly training fee	$50	$75

Direct instructional costs for the bicycle training classes for the year were $165,000; overhead costs for the two programs were $80,000. The store manager wants to know the cost of each program.

a. Determine each program's cost using a physical measure base.
b. Determine each program's cost using a physical measure for allocating direct instructional costs and revenues for allocating overhead.
c. **Critical Thinking:** If the total joint cost assigned is the same in parts *a* and *b*, why does the choice of methods make a difference in management decision making?

More practice: E12-27, E12-44, E12-45
Solution on p. 12-47.

Comprehensive Chapter Review

Key Terms

approximated net realizable value at split-off allocation, p. 12-13
by-product, p. 12-7
joint cost, p. 12-2
joint cost allocation, p. 12-9
joint process, p. 12-2
net realizable value approach, p. 12-16

net realizable value at split-off allocation, p. 12-12
net realizable value (NRV), p. 12-12
offset approach, p. 12-16
other income approach, p. 12-19
physical measure allocation, p. 12-10

realized value approach, p. 12-19
sales value at split-off allocation, p. 12-11
scrap, p. 12-7
separate costs, p. 12-3
split-off point, p. 12-2
waste, p. 12-7

Chapter Summary

Management Decisions about a Joint Process (Page 12-2) — **LO12-1**
- Two questions must be answered before the joint process is started:
  - Do total revenues exceed total (joint and separate) costs?
  - Is this process the best use of available facilities?
- Two questions must be answered at the split-off point:
  - Which products will be classified as joint products, by-product, scrap, or waste?
  - Which products will be sold at split-off, and which will be processed further?

LO12-2 **Classification of Joint Process Output (Page 12-7)**
- Joint products are the output with a relatively high sales value.
  - These products provide the primary incentive for undertaking production.
  - These products are identified at the split-off point.
  - These products are assigned the joint cost of the production process.
  - These products could have the related joint cost reduced by the net realizable value or realized value of by-product and scrap.
- By-products have a higher sales value than scrap but less than joint products.
- Scrap is output with the lowest sales value.
- Waste is the residual output with no sales value.

LO12-3 **Allocation of Joint Cost to Joint Products (Page 12-9)**
- There are two common methods of allocating joint cost to joint products.
  - Physical measures may be used. These measures
    - provide an unchanging yardstick of output over time and
    - treat each unit of product as equally desirable.
  - Monetary measures may be used. These measures consider different valuations of the individual joint products; these valuations can be based on
    - sales value at split-off,
    - net realizable value at split-off, or
    - approximated net realizable value at split-off.
- Allocated joint cost is a "sunk" cost and should not be used in decisions about further processing.
- Regardless of the method used to allocate joint cost to joint products, products should only be processed beyond split-off if the incremental revenue exceeds the incremental costs.

LO12-4 **Accounting for By-Product and Scrap (Page 12-16)**
- There are two common methods of accounting for by-product and scrap.
  - The net realizable value approach uses the expected NRV of the by-product to reduce either
    - Work in Process Inventory of the joint products when the by-product/scrap is produced or
    - Cost of Goods Sold of the joint products when the by-product/scrap is produced.
  - The realized value approach shows the actual value of the by-product/scrap on the income statement as either
    - other revenue when the by-product/scrap is sold or
    - other income when the by-product/scrap is sold.
- In a job order costing system, by-product and scrap may be accounted for using either the NRV or realized value approach.
  - The value of the by-product or scrap should be credited to manufacturing overhead if such items are created by most jobs.
  - The value of the by-product or scrap should be credited to individual jobs if by-product or scrap is not normally created; the net realized value approach is more appropriate because of timing of recognition.

LO12-5 **Accounting for the Cost of a Joint Activity in a Retail or Not-for-Profit Organization (Page 12-22)**
- Retail business may choose to allocate joint costs incurred for certain activities such as advertising; either a physical or monetary measure may be used.
- There are two alternatives for accounting for the cost of a joint activity by not-for-profit organizations:
  - The activity must meet three tests for its cost to be allocated:
    - purpose
    - audience
    - content
  - If all of the criteria are met, the cost is allocated among three categories:
    - fund raising,
    - program, and/or
    - management/general activities.
  - If all of the criteria are not met, the entire cost is allocated to fund raising.

Solution Strategies

Allocation of Joint Cost

LO12-3

Joint cost is allocated only to joint products; however, joint cost can be reduced by the value of by-product/scrap before the allocation process begins.

For physical measure allocation: Divide joint cost by the products' total physical measurements to obtain a cost per unit of physical measure.

For monetary measure allocation:
1. Choose an allocation base.
2. List the values that compose the allocation base for each joint process.
3. Sum the values in Step 2.
4. Calculate the percentage of the total base value associated with each joint product.
5. Multiply the joint cost by each percentage calculated in Step 4 to obtain the amount to be allocated to each joint product.
6. Divide the prorated joint cost for each product by the number of equivalent units of production (EUP) for each product to obtain a cost per EUP for valuation purposes.

Allocation bases, measured at the split-off point, by which joint cost is prorated to the joint products include the following:

Type of Measure	Allocation Base
Physical output	Physical measure of units of output (e.g., tons, feet, barrels, liters)
Monetary	Currency units of value
Sales value	Revenues of the several products
Net realizable value	Sales value minus incremental processing and disposal costs
	Final sales price minus incremental separate costs
	Approximated net realizable value

Chapter Demonstration Problem

LO12-3

Circle City Inc. produces two joint products—Primero and Segundo—from a single input. Further processing of product Primero results in a by-product designated Más. A summary of production and sales for the year follows.

- Circle City Inc. input 600,000 pounds of raw material into the Processing Department. Total joint processing cost was $520,000. During the joint processing, 90,000 pounds of material were lost.
- After joint processing, 60 percent of the joint process output was transferred to Division 1 to produce Primero, and 40 percent of the joint process output was transferred to Division 2 to produce Segundo.
- Further processing in Division 1 resulted in 70 percent of the input pounds becoming Primero and 30 percent of the input pounds becoming Más. The separate processing cost for Primero in Division 1 was $649,026.
- Total packaging costs for Primero were $122,094. After Division 1 processing and packaging, product Primero is salable at $8.00 per pound.
- Each pound of Más can be sold for $0.25 after incurring total selling cost of $5,000. The company accounts for Más using the net realizable value method and showing the NRV as a reduction in the cost of goods sold of the joint products.
- In Division 2, Segundo was further processed at a separate cost of $387,600. A completed pound of Segundo sells for $4.70.
- Selling (marketing) costs for Primero and Segundo are, respectively, $0.80 per pound and $0.15 per pound.

Required:
a. Prepare a process diagram similar to the one shown in **Exhibit 12.5** or **12.6**.
b. Record the journal entry to
   1. recognize incurrence of joint cost.
   2. allocate joint costs to the joint products using pounds as a physical measure and transfer the products into Divisions 1 and 2.
   3. record incurrence of separate processing costs for products Primero and Segundo in Divisions 1 and 2.

4. record incurrence of packaging cost for product Primero.
5. transfer completed products Primero and Segundo to finished goods.
c. Allocate the joint cost to products Primero and Segundo using approximated net realizable values at split-off. (Round proportions to nearest whole percentage.)
d. Circle City Inc. had no Work in Process or Finished Goods Inventory at the beginning of the year. Prepare an income statement through gross margin for Circle City Inc. assuming that
- 80 percent of the Primero and 90 percent of the Segundo produced for the year were sold.
- all the Más that was produced during the year was sold.
- joint cost was allocated using the physical measurement method in (b).

Solution to Demonstration Problem

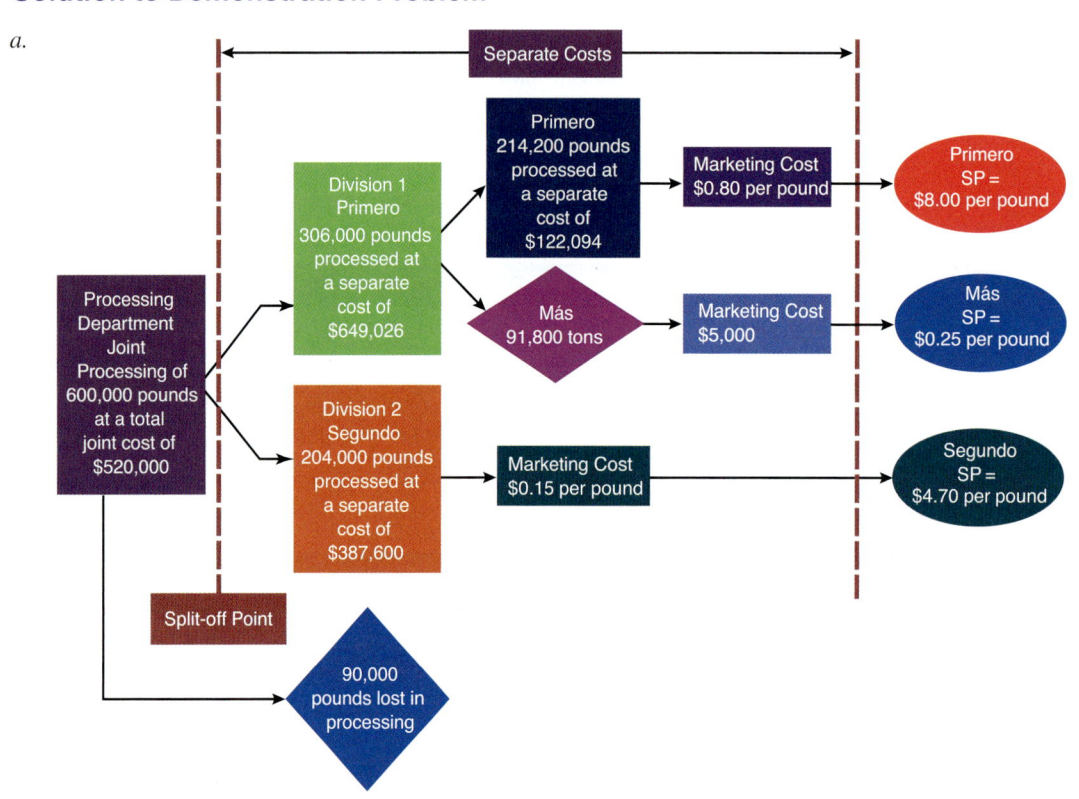

a.

```
                          ← Separate Costs →

                                    Primero
                                    214,200 pounds
                                    processed at       Marketing Cost         Primero
                     Division 1     a separate         $0.80 per pound        SP =
                     Primero        cost of                                   $8.00 per pound
                     306,000 pounds $122,094
                     processed at
                     a separate
   Processing        cost of                                                  Más
   Department        $649,026       Más                Marketing Cost         SP =
   Joint                             91,800 tons        $5,000                 $0.25 per pound
   Processing of
   600,000 pounds
   at a total
   joint cost of    Division 2
   $520,000         Segundo
                     204,000 pounds
                     processed at    Marketing Cost                           Segundo
                     a separate      $0.15 per pound                          SP =
                     cost of                                                  $4.70 per pound
                     $387,600

   Split-off Point

                     90,000
                     pounds lost in
                     processing
```

b.

1.	Work in Process Inventory—Processing		520,000	
	Various accounts			520,000
	To record annual joint processing costs			
2.	Work in Process Inventory—Division 1 (60%)		312,000	
	Work in Process Inventory—Division 2 (40%)		208,000	
	Work in Process Inventory—Processing			520,000
	To allocate joint cost to joint products			
3.	Work in Process—Division 1		649,026	
	Work in Process—Division 2		387,600	
	Various accounts			1,036,626
	To record separate processing costs			
4.	Work in Process Inventory—Division 1		122,094	
	Various accounts			122,094
	To record packaging costs for Primero			
5.	Finished Goods Inventory—Primero		1,083,120	
	Finished Goods Inventory—Segundo		595,600	
	Work in Process Inventory—Division 1			1,083,120
	Work in Process Inventory—Division 2			595,600
	To transfer completed production to finished goods			

c. **Approximated NRV Method**

Div. 1 = 0.6 × 510,000 lbs. = 306,000 lbs.; 306,000 × 0.7 = 214,200 lbs. Primero
Div. 2 = 0.4 × 510,000 lbs. = 204,000 lbs. Segundo
Ma´s = 306,000 × 0.3 = 91,800 lbs.

Product	Pounds Produced	NRV per Lb. at Split-Off*	Total NRV	Proportion	Joint Cost	Allocated Joint Cost
Primero......	214,200	$3.60	$ 771,120	59%	$520,000	$306,800
Segundo.....	204,000	2.65	540,600	41	520,000	213,200
			$1,311,720	100%		$520,000

*
	Primero	Segundo
Selling price per pound..................	$ 8.00	$ 4.70
Separate costs		
Division 1 ($649,026 ÷ 214,200)..........	(3.03)	
Packaging ($122,094 ÷ 214,200)	(0.57)	
Division 2 ($387,600 ÷ 204,000)..........		(1.90)
Selling...............................	(0.80)	(0.15)
Approximated net realizable value	$ 3.60	$ 2.65

d.

Circle City Inc.
Income Statement
For the Year Ended December 31

Sales			
Primero (214,200 × 0.80 × $8.00)		$1,370,880	
Segundo (204,000 × 0.90 × $4.70)		862,920	$ 2,233,800
Cost of Goods Sold			
Beginning finished goods inventories...................		$0	
Cost of goods manufactured [from (b5)]			
Primero..		1,083,120	
Segundo.......................................		595,600	
Available for sale		$1,678,720	
Ending finished goods inventories			
Primero ($1,083,120 × 0.20)......................		(216,624)	
Segundo ($595,600 × 0.10)		(59,560)	
Unadjusted cost of goods sold		$1,402,536	
NRV of Más [(91,800 × $0.25) – $5,000]		(17,950)	(1,384,586)
Gross margin			$ 849,214

Assignments with the MBC logo in the margin are available in *my*BusinessCourse.
Resources include demonstration videos, guided examples, and auto-graded homework.
See details in the Preface, and ask your professor how you can access the system.

Data Analytics

DA12-1. Comparing results of joint cost allocation methods LO12-3

Access the file included in MBC which includes joint cost allocation under four methods for an agricultural processor and complete the following requirements.

Required

a. Data is provided showing allocation of joint costs under the following methods: physical measure, sales value at split-off, NRV at split off, and approximated NRV at split-off . Prepare a stacked column chart showing how joint costs are allocated by method. Hint: Select data, click on Insert, and Clustered Bar chart. The methods should appear on the X-axis.

b. What are total joint costs? Do total joint costs vary across methods? Why or why not?

    c. Which column(s) shows a significantly different allocation and what could cause those results?
    d. How does your answer in part c impact the allocation method management chooses to use?

Data Visualization

Data Visualization Activities are available in myBusinessCourse. These assignments use Tableau Dashboards to expose students to visual depictions of data and introduce students to data analytics through data visualizations. These exercises are easily assignable and auto graded by MBC.

Potential Ethical Issues

1. Classifying a joint product as a by-product or scrap so that no joint cost will be allocated to that product and, thereby, increasing that product's appearance of profitability
2. Classifying a salable product as "waste" and then selling that product "off the books" for the personal benefit of a manager
3. Using the NRV approach for unsold by-products as a means to increase organizational income
4. Manipulating the assignment of joint costs such that joint products in inventory at period-end are assigned a disproportionately higher cost than joint products sold during the period so that higher income and higher inventory values are reported at period-end
5. Using the sales value of by-product/scrap generated by specific jobs to offset total manufacturing overhead and, thus, lowering the overhead allocation rate on all production rather than using that sales value to reduce the cost of the job specifically generating the by-product/scrap
6. Reducing or not incurring expenses by disposing of hazardous waste in a manner that causes harm to the environment or threatens humans and wildlife
7. Misallocating the cost of an activity to program and management/general activities solely to reduce the fund raising cost of a not-for-profit organization

Questions

Q12-1. How does management determine how to classify each type of output from a joint process? Is this decided before or after production?

Q12-2. In a company that engages in a joint production process, will all processing stop at the split-off point? Discuss the rationale for your answer.

Q12-3. By what criteria would management determine whether to proceed with processing at each decision point in a joint production process?

Q12-4. Why is cost allocation necessary in accounting? Why is it necessary in a joint process?

Q12-5. Compare the advantages and disadvantages of the two primary methods used to allocate joint cost to joint products.

Q12-6. Why are approximated, rather than actual, net realizable values at split-off sometimes used to allocate joint cost?

Q12-7. Which of the two common approaches used to account for by-product/scrap provides better information to management? Discuss the rationale for your answer.

Q12-8. When is by-product/scrap cost considered in setting the predetermined overhead rate in a job order costing system? When is such cost not considered?

Q12-9. Why must not-for-profit organizations determine when it is appropriate to allocate any cost for a joint activity among fund raising, program, and administrative activities?

Multiple Choice

MC12-10. In a production process where joint products are produced, the primary factor that will distinguish a joint product from a by-product is the
   a. relative total sales value of the products.
   b. relative total volume of the products.

c. relative ease of selling the products.
d. accounting method used to allocate joint costs.

MC12-11. A circuit board company conducts a joint manufacturing process to produce 10,000 units of Board A and 10,000 units of Board B. The total joint variable manufacturing cost to produce these two products is $2,000,000. The company can sell all 10,000 units of Board B at the split-off point for $300 per unit, or process Board B further and sell all 10,000 units at $375 per unit. The total additional cost to process Board B further would be $500,000, and all additional costs would be variable. If the company decides to process Board B further, what effect would the decision have on operating income?
a. $750,000 decrease in operating income.
b. $250,000 increase in operating income.
c. $2,250,000 increase in operating income.
d. $3,250,000 increase in operating income.

MC12-12. Jones Enterprises manufactures 3 products, A, B, and C. During the month of May Jones' production, costs, and sales data were as follows.

	Products			
	A	B	C	Totals
Units of production	30,000	20,000	70,000	120,000
Joint production costs to split-off point				$480,000
Further processing costs	$ 0	$60,000	$140,000	
Unit sales price				
At split-off	3.75	5.50	10.25	
After further processing	0	8.00	12.50	

Based on the above information, which one of the following alternatives should be recommended to Jones' management?
a. Sell both Product B and Product C at the split-off point.
b. Process Product B further but sell Product C at the split-off point.
c. Process Product C further but sell Product B at the split-off point.
d. Process both Products B and C further.

MC12-13. Tucariz Company processes Duo into two joint products, Big and Mini. Duo is purchased in 1,000 gallon drums for $2,000. Processing costs are $3,000 to process the 1,000 gallons of Duo into 800 gallons of Big and 200 gallons of Mini. The selling price is $9 per gallon for Big and $4 per gallon for Mini. Big can be processed further into 600 gallons of Giant if $1,000 of additional processing costs are incurred. Giant can be sold for $17 per gallon. If the net-realizable-value method were used to allocate costs to the joint products, the total cost of producing Giant would be
a. $5,600.   c. $5,520.
b. $5,564.   d. $4,600.

MC12-14. Fairchild Company processes raw material into two joint products, A and B. 8,000 gallons of A and 2,000 gallons of B were produced using $20,000 raw material and $30,000 processing costs were incurred. The per gallon selling price is $90 for A and $40 for B. If the sales value at split-off method is used to allocate joint costs to the final products, the per gallon cost (rounded to the nearest cent) of producing A is
a. $5.63 per gallon.   c. $4.50 per gallon.
b. $5.00 per gallon.   d. $3.38 per gallon.

MC12-15. A company produces products simultaneously through a refining process costing $186,000. The joint products, Alpha and Beta, have selling prices of $8 and $20 per pound, respectively, after additional processing costs of $4 per pound of each product are incurred after the split-off point. Omega, a by-product, is sold at the split-off point for $6 per pound. The number of pounds produced is shown below.

Alpha   10,000 pounds
Beta   5,000 pounds
Omega   1,000 pounds

Assuming the company inventories Omega, the joint cost allocated to Alpha using the net realizable value at split-off approach (WIP Inventory Reduction Method) is

a. $72,000.
b. $80,000.
c. $82,666.
d. $100,000.

LO12-5 MC12-16. Joint costs are allocated in
a. Manufacturing companies only.
b. Both manufacturing companies and retail companies only.
c. Manufacturing, retail, and not-for-profit companies.
d. None of the above.

Exercises

LO12-1 E12-17. Sell or process further Winn Mills processes cotton in a joint process that yields two joint products: fabric and yarn. May's joint cost is $120,000, and the sales values at split-off are $360,000 for fabric and $300,000 for yarn. If the products are processed beyond split-off, the final sales value will be $540,000 for fabric and $420,000 for yarn. Additional costs of processing are expected to be $120,000 for fabric and $102,000 for yarn.

a. Should the products be processed further? Show computations.
b. Were any revenues and/or costs irrelevant to the decision? If so, what were they and why were they irrelevant?

LO12-1 E12-18. Sell or process further Storey Corp. manufactures three products in a joint process. Each of the products can be sold at split-off or may be processed further. Using the following per unit information, determine which of the products should undergo further processing.

	JP#1	JP#2	JP#3
Sales value at split-off	$360	$290	$585
Sales value after further processing	410	330	650
Joint costs allocated at split-off	215	185	380
Costs of further processing	55	25	45

LO12-1 E12-19. Sell or process further Bright Red Cannery makes three products from a single joint process. For the year, the cannery processed all three products beyond split-off. The following data were generated for the year:

Joint Product	Incremental Separate Cost	Total Revenue
Candied apples	$26,000	$690,000
Apple jelly	32,000	775,000
Apple jam	15,000	271,000

Analysis of market data reveals that candied apples, apple jelly, and apple jam could have been sold at split-off for $670,000, $730,000, and $260,000, respectively.

a. Based on hindsight, evaluate management's production decisions.
b. How much additional profit could the company have generated if it had made optimal decisions at split-off?

LO12-1, 2 E12-20. Joint process analysis; research; writing Use the Internet to find five examples of businesses that have joint processes.

a. For each business, describe the various outputs from the processes; using logic, determine whether each output would be classified as a joint product, a by-product, scrap, or waste.
b. Recommend the most appropriate methods of allocating joint cost to the outputs you described in (a); express, in nontechnical terms, your justification for each of your recommendations.
c. For one of the businesses, diagram the flow of costs.

LO12-2, 3 E12-21. Joint process decision making; writing Bethany Lutrell's uncle has asked her to take over the family poultry processing plant. Provide Lutrell, who graduated in engineering, answers to the following issues:

a. What are the important questions to be answered about joint processes in a poultry processing plant? Also indicate the points in a joint process at which these questions should be answered.

b. How should joint costs be used in managerial decision making? When and why might a joint cost be used inappropriately in decision making?
c. How are joint process outputs similar and dissimilar?

E12-22. Classification of output from a joint process Organic Co. makes a variety of products from a joint process. The joint cost per batch run is $30,000 and each batch produces the following products:

Product	# of Units	Sales Value per Unit at Split-Off
Boco	1,200	$6.000
Loco	1,000	$1.750
Roco	5,000	$2.500
Soco	3,800	$4.200
Moco	4,100	$1.900
Coco	200	$0.250
Doco	300	$1.800
Joco	1,000	$0.020
Voco	6,000	$0.001

How would you classify each product (joint, by-product, scrap, or waste)? Provide rationale for your answer.

E12-23. Physical measure allocation and sell or process further Oregon Forests uses a joint process to manufacture two grades of wood: A and B. During October, the company incurred $16,200,000 of joint production cost in producing 27,000,000 board feet of Grade A and 9,000,000 board feet of Grade B lumber. The company allocates joint cost on the basis of board feet of lumber produced. The company can sell Grade A lumber at the split-off point for $0.70 per board foot and Grade B lumber at the split-off point for $0.50 per board foot. Alternatively, Grade A lumber can be further processed at a cost of $0.75 per board foot and then sold for $1.50 per board foot. No opportunity exists for processing Grade B lumber after split-off.

a. How much joint cost should be allocated to Grade A and to Grade B lumber using the physical units method?
b. If Grade A lumber is processed further and then sold, what is the incremental effect on Oregon Forests' net income? Should the additional processing be performed?

E12-24. Sales value and physical value allocation To-Go produces milk and sour cream from a joint process. During June, the company produced 240,000 quarts of milk and 190,000 pints of sour cream (there are two pints in a quart). Sales value at split-off point was $377,400 for the milk and $177,600 for the sour cream. The milk was assigned $125,800 of the joint cost. (Round proportions to the nearest whole percentage and dollar amounts to the nearest whole dollar.)

a. Using the sales value at split-off approach, determine the total joint cost for June.
b. Assume, instead, that the joint cost was allocated based on the number of quarts produced. What was the total joint cost incurred in June?

E12-25. Physical and sales value allocations FINS produces three products from its fish farm: fish, fish oil, and fish meal. During July, FINS produced the following average quantities of each product from each pound (16 ounces) of fish processed:

Product	Obtained from Each Pound of Fish
Fish	8 ounces
Fish oil	4
Fish meal	2
Total	14 ounces

Of each pound of fish processed, two ounces are waste. In July, FINS processed 37.5 tons of fish (1 ton equals 2,000 pounds). Joint cost amounted to $142,800. On average, each pound of product has the following selling prices: fish, $4.50; fish oil, $6.50; and fish meal, $2.

a. Allocate the joint cost using weight as the basis. (Round proportions to the nearest whole percentage and dollar amounts to the nearest whole dollar.)

b. Allocate the joint cost using sales value as the basis. (Round proportions to the nearest whole percentage and dollar amounts to the nearest whole dollar.)
c. Discuss the advantages and disadvantages of the answers to (a) and (b).

LO12-3

E12-26. Physical and sales value allocations and sell or process further Indianola Beef buys sides of beef to convert into three products: steaks, roasts, and ground beef. In April, Indianola bought multiple sides of beef for $20,000 that were converted into the following products at a cost of $6,400:

Product	# of Pounds	Sales Value at Split-Off
Steaks.	3,312	$4.25 per pound
Roasts	6,210	$3.80 per pound
Ground beef	4,278	$0.90 per pound

The remaining 1,200 pounds were lost as waste.

a. Allocate the joint cost to the three products using the physical units method. What problem do you find with this method?
b. Allocate the joint cost to the three products using the sales value at split-off method. (Round proportions to the nearest whole percentage.) Does this allocation eliminate the problem identified in (a)?
c. Assume that the ground beef could be processed into sausage that could be sold for $2.10 per pound to a distributor that wants a special label costing $0.15 per pound attached to the sausage. If Indianola Beef uses the sales value at split-off method to allocate joint cost, what is the maximum separate cost of processing that the company could incur to still appear to earn $0.40 per pound upon the sale? If this separate cost were incurred, would you consider the $0.40 per pound a "real" profit amount?

LO12-5

E12-27. Joint cost allocation; nonmanufacturing MediaForum has three operating groups: Games, News, and Documentaries. In May, the company incurred $24,000,000 of joint cost for facilities and administration. May revenues and separate costs of each group are as follows:

	Games	News	Documentaries
Revenue	$34,040,000	$30,720,000	$189,320,000
Separate costs	31,040,000	16,320,000	110,720,000

a. What amount of joint cost is allocated to each operating group using the profit before joint cost allocation as the basis for allocation? Compute the profit for each operating area after the allocation. (Round proportions to the nearest whole percentage and dollar amounts to the nearest whole dollar.)
b. What amount of joint cost is allocated to each operating group if the allocation is based on revenues? Compute the profit for each operating group after the allocation. (Round proportions to the nearest whole percentage and dollar amounts to the nearest whole dollar.)
c. Assume you are head of the Games Group. Would the difference in allocation bases create significant problems for you when you report to the top management of the company? Develop a short presentation for top management if the allocation base in (b) is used to determine each operating group's relative profitability. Be certain to discuss important differences in revenues and cost amounts for the Games and Documentaries groups.

LO12-1, 3

E12-28. Approximated net realizable value method and sell or process further Lauren Inc. makes three products that can be sold at split-off or processed further and then sold. The joint cost for April is $1,080,000.

Product	Bottles of Output	Sales Price at Split-Off	Separate Cost after Split-Off	Final Sales Price
Perfume	20,000	$7.00	$2.50	$16.50
Eau de toilette.	32,000	5.00	1.50	13.00
Body splash	28,000	5.00	2.00	12.00

The number of ounces in a bottle of each product is: perfume, one; eau de toilette, two; and body splash, three. Assume that all products are processed further after split-off.

Chapter 12 Allocation of Joint Costs and Accounting for By-Product/Scrap

a. Allocate the joint cost based on the number of bottles, weight, and approximated net realizable values at split-off. (Round proportions to the nearest whole percentage and dollar amounts to the nearest whole dollar.)

b. Assume that all products are processed further and completed. At the end of the period, the inventories are as follows: perfume, 600 bottles; eau de toilette, 1,600 bottles; and body splash, 1,680 bottles. Determine the values of the inventories based on answers obtained in (a). (Round your final answer to the nearest whole dollar.)

c. Do you see any problems with the allocation based on approximated net realizable value?

E12-29. Allocating joint cost Keiffer Production manufactures three joint products in a single process. The following information is available for August:

Product	Gallons	Sales Value at Split-Off per Gallon	Cost after Split-Off	Final Selling Price
JP-4539	4,500	$14	$4	$24
JP-4587	18,000	25	5	35
JP-4591	13,500	18	2	22

Allocate the joint cost of $558,000 to the production based on the

a. number of gallons.
b. sales value at split-off.
c. approximated net realizable values at split-off.

(Round proportions to the nearest whole percentage and dollar amounts to the nearest whole dollar.)

E12-30. Processing beyond split-off and cost allocations All-A-Buzz makes three products from a joint production process using honey. Joint cost for the process for the year is $123,200.

Product	Units of Output	Per Unit Selling Price at Split-Off	Incremental Processing Cost	Final Sales Price
Honey butter	10,000	4.00	$3.00	$ 6.00
Honey jam	20,000	6.40	4.00	14.00
Honey syrup	1,000	3.00	0.40	3.60

Each container of honey butter, jam, and syrup, respectively, contains 16 ounces, 8 ounces, and 3 ounces of product.

a. Determine which products should be processed beyond the split-off point.
b. Assume honey syrup should be treated as a by-product. Allocate the joint cost based on units produced, weight, and sales value at split-off. Use the net realizable value approach, assuming by-product revenues reduce joint production costs. (Round proportions to the nearest whole percentage and dollar amounts to the nearest whole dollar.)

E12-31. Joint cost allocation; sell or process further In a joint process, Wear Art produces precut fabrics for three products: dresses, jackets, and blouses. Joint cost is allocated on the basis of relative sales value at split-off. The company can choose to process each of the products further rather than sell the fabric at split-off. Information related to these products follows.

	Dresses	Jackets	Blouses	Total
Number of units produced	10,000	16,000	6,000	32,000
Joint cost allocated	?	$138,000	?	$360,000
Sales values at split-off point	?	$230,000	$ 80,000	$600,000
Additional costs of processing further	$ 26,000	$ 20,000	$ 78,000	$124,000
Sales values after all processing	$300,000	$268,000	$210,000	$778,000

a. What amount of joint cost should be allocated to dresses and blouses?
b. What is the sales value at the split-off point for dresses?
c. Should any of the products be processed beyond the split-off point? Show computations.
d. If 12,000 jackets are processed further and sold at the regular selling price, what is the gross profit on the sale?

LO12-3, 4

E12-32. Joint cost allocation; by-products Go-Go Co., which began operations in the current year, produces gasoline and a gasoline by-product. Go-Go accounts for the by-product at the time of production through a reduction in joint product cost of goods sold. The following information is available pertaining to annual sales and production:

Total production costs to split-off point	$240,000
Gasoline sales	540,000
By-product sales	60,000
Gasoline inventory, December 31	30,000
Additional by-product costs:	
Marketing	$ 20,000
Production	30,000

    a. Compute Go-Go's cost of sales for gasoline and for the by-product for the year.
    b. If Go-Go had used the by-product's NRV to reduce the joint cost of the gasoline, how (if at all) would the gross margin for the year change? No calculations are necessary.

CPA ADAPTED

LO12-4

E12-33. By-product/scrap; net realizable value vs. realized value Indicate whether each item that follows is associated with (1) the realized value approach or (2) the net realizable value approach.

    a. Is less conservative
    b. Has the advantage of better timing
    c. Uses an actual value for by-product sales
    d. Is easier to apply
    e. Presents proceeds from sale of the by-product as other revenue or other income
    f. Ignores value of by-product/scrap until it is sold
    g. Is used to reduce the cost of main products in the period the by-product is produced
    h. Should be used when the by-product's net realizable value is large
    i. Credits either cost of goods sold of main products or the joint cost when the by-product inventory is recorded
    j. Is appropriate if the by-product's net realizable value is small
    k. Has a greater likelihood for earnings management
    l. Is the most clerically efficient
    m. Uses an expected value for by-product sales

LO12-4

E12-34. By-product and cost allocation Georgia Co. raises peaches that, at harvest, are separated into three grades: premium, good, and fair. Joint cost is allocated to products based on bushels of output. The $337,500 joint cost for one harvest yielded the following output quantities.

Product	Output in Bushels
Premium	16,500
Good	43,560
Fair	5,940

The joint process also created a by-product that had a total net realizable value of $65,000. The company records the by-product inventory as a reduction to Work in Process Inventory—Joint Products. Allocate the joint cost to the joint products using bushels of output.

LO12-4

E12-35. By-product; net realizable value method Weinberg Canning produces fillet, smoked salmon, and salmon remnants in a single process. The same amount of disposal cost is incurred whether a product is sold at split-off or after further processing. In October, the joint cost of the production process was $142,000.

Product	Pounds Produced	Separate Cost	Final Selling Price
Fillet	18,000	$3.00	$16.00
Smoked	20,000	5.20	13.00
Remnants	2,000	0.30	1.50

    a. The remnants are considered a by-product of the process and are sold to cat food processors. Allocate the joint cost based on approximated net realizable value at split-off. Use the net realizable value method to account for the by-product, subtracting the by-product cost from the cost of Work in Process Inventory—Joint Products.

b. Determine the value of ending Finished Goods Inventory, assuming that 4,000 pounds of salmon fillets, 2,400 pounds of smoked salmon, and 350 pounds of salmon remnants were sold. (Round cost per pound to the nearest penny.)

E12-36. By-product accounting method selection; writing Your employer engages in numerous joint processes that produce significant quantities and types of by-product. You have been asked to give a report to management on the best way to account for by-product. Develop criteria for making such a choice and provide reasons for each criterion selected. On the basis of your criteria, along with any additional assumptions you wish to provide about the nature of the company you work for, recommend a particular method of accounting for by-product and explain why you consider it to be better than the alternatives.

LO12-4

E12-37. By-product and cost allocation Dover Studios shot hundreds of hours of footage that cost $20,000,000. From this footage, the company produced two movies: *Star World* and *Star World: The Sequel*. The sequel used better sound effects than the original, was significantly more expensive to produce, and was much better received at the box office.

LO12-4, 5

Dover Studios also generated revenue from admissions paid by numerous movie fans who wanted to tour the movie production set. The company accounted for this revenue as a by-product and used it to reduce joint cost before making allocations to the two feature-length movies.

The following information pertains to the two movies:

Products	Total Receipts	Separate Costs
Star World.................	$10,000,000	$ 6,800,000
Star World: The Sequel.............	58,000,000	41,200,000
Studio tours	800,000	480,000

a. If joint cost is allocated based on net realizable value, how much of the joint cost is allocated to each movie?
b. Based on your allocations in (a), how much profit was generated by each movie?

E12-38. Accounting for by-product Carvers Inc. manufactures wood statues, which yields sawdust as a by-product. Selling costs associated with the sawdust are $250 per ton sold. The company accounts for sawdust sales by deducting the sawdust's net realizable value from the major products' cost of goods sold. Sawdust sales for the year were 1,200 tons at $335 each. If the company changes its method of accounting for sawdust sales to show the net realizable value as Other Revenue (presented at the bottom of the income statement), how would its gross margin be affected?

LO12-4

E12-39. Accounting for by-product The Bishop's Falls Lumber Corporation harvests lumber and prepares it for sale to wholesalers of lumber and wood products. The main product is finished lumber, which is sold to wholesale construction suppliers. A by-product of the process is wood pellets, which are sold to wholesalers of wood pellet stoves. During December, the manufacturing process incurred $664,000 in total costs; 160,000 board feet of lumber were produced and sold along with 40,000 pounds of pellets. The finished lumber sold for $10 per board foot and the pellets sold for $4 per 100-pound bag. There were no beginning or ending inventories.

LO12-4

a. Compute the December gross margin for Bishop's Falls Lumber Corporation assuming that by-product revenues reduce joint production costs.
b. How would your answer change if by-products are accounted for as Other Revenue when sold?

E12-40. Accounting for by-product Potato skins are generated as a by-product in making potato chips and frozen hash browns at Zeena Foods. The skins are sold to restaurants for use in appetizers. Processing and disposal costs associated with by-product sales are $0.06 per pound of potato skins. During May, Zeena Foods produced and sold 135,000 pounds of potato skins for $20,250. In addition, the joint cost for producing potato chips and hash browns was $82,000; separate costs of production were $48,000. In May, 90 percent of all joint production was sold for $319,000. Non-factory operating expenses for May were $47,850.

LO12-4

a. Prepare an income statement for Zeena Foods assuming that by-product sales are shown as Other Revenue and the processing and disposal costs for the by-product are shown as additional cost of goods sold of the joint products.

b. Prepare an income statement for Zeena Foods assuming that the net realizable value of the by-product is shown as Other Income.
c. Prepare an income statement for Zeena Foods assuming that the net realizable value of the by-product is subtracted from the joint cost of the main products.
d. Would the presentation in (a), (b), or (c) be most helpful to managers? Why?

LO12-4 E12-41. Accounting for scrap Hammatt Inc. provides a variety of services for commercial clients. Hammatt destroys any paper client records after seven years and the shredded paper is sold to a recycling company. The net realizable value of the recycled paper is treated as a reduction to operating overhead. The following data pertain to operations for the year:

Budgeted operating overhead	$415,200
Actual operating overhead	$410,500
Budgeted net realizable value of recycled paper	$ 9,200
Actual net realizable value of recycled paper	$ 9,700
Budgeted billable hours	70,000
Actual billable hours	70,900

a. Assuming that number of billable hours is the allocation base, what was the company's predetermined overhead rate?
b. Record the journal entry for the sale of the recycled paper.
c. What was the company's underapplied or overapplied overhead for the year?

LO12-4 E12-42. Accounting for scrap Renaissance Creations restores antique stained glass windows. All jobs generate some breakage or improper cuts. This scrap can be sold to stained glass hobbyists. Renaissance Creations expects to incur approximately 45,000 direct labor hours during the year. The following estimates are made in setting the predetermined overhead rate for the year:

Overhead costs other than breakage		$297,200
Estimated cost of scrap	$25,200	
Estimated sales value of scrap	(7,400)	17,800
Total estimated overhead		$315,000

One job that Renaissance Creations completed during the year was a stained glass window of the Pierce family crest that took 125 hours, and direct labor is invoiced at $20 per hour. Total direct material cost for the job was $890. Scrap that was generated from this job was sold for $93.

a. What was the predetermined overhead rate (set on the basis of direct labor hours) for the year?
b. What was the cost of the Pierce stained glass window?
c. Prepare the journal entry to record the sales value of the scrap from the Pierce stained glass window.
d. Assume instead that only certain jobs generate scrap. What was the cost of the Pierce stained glass window?

LO12-4 E12-43. Accounting for scrap Mae-Doff Designs uses a job order costing system to account for the various architectural services offered to commercial clients. For each major job, architectural models of the completed structures are built for client presentations. At the completion of a job, models not wanted by clients are sold to an arts and crafts retailer. Mae-Doff Designs uses the realized value method of accounting for model sales. The sales value of each model is credited to the cost of the specific job for which the model was built. During the year, the model for the Hedge Fund Extraordinaire building was sold for $8,500.

a. Using the net realizable value approach, give the entry to record the sale.
b. Independent of your answer to (a), assume that a model's sales value is not credited to specific jobs. Give the entry to account for the sale of the Hedge Fund Extraordinaire model.
c. Which method would be preferable for Mae-Doff Designs to use, and why?

LO12-5 E12-44. Retail organization joint cost Wilke Realty separates its activities into two operating divisions: Rentals and Sales. In March, the firm spent $32,500 for general company promotions (as opposed to advertisements for specific properties). John, the corporate controller, has decided to allocate general promotion costs to the two operating divisions. He is considering whether to base his allocations on the (1) expected increase in divisional revenue from the promotions or (2) expected

Chapter 12 Allocation of Joint Costs and Accounting for By-Product/Scrap

increase in divisional profit from the promotions (before allocated promotion costs). General promotions had the following effects on the two divisions:

	Rentals	Sales
Increase in divisional revenue	$770,000	$105,000
Increase in profit (before allocated promotion costs)	104,500	85,500

a. Allocate the total promotion cost to the two divisions using change in revenue.
b. Allocate the total promotion cost to the two divisions using change in profit before joint cost allocation.
c. Which of the two approaches is more appropriate? Explain.

E12-45. Retail organization joint cost Abrula Archery provides archery training for children and adults. During the year, the camp had the following operating data:

	Children	Adults
Training hours taught	4,000	2,000
Hourly tuition	$35	$65

LO12-5

Direct instructional costs for the year were $120,000; overhead costs for the two programs were $55,500. Camp owners want to know the cost of each program.

a. Determine each program's cost using a physical measure base.
b. Determine each program's cost using the sales value at split-off method.
c. Make a case for the allocation method in (a) and (b).

E12-46. NFP program and support cost allocation Memphis Jazz Company is preparing a pamphlet that will provide information on the types of jazz, jazz terminology, and biographies of some of the better-known jazz musicians. In addition, the pamphlet will include a request for funding to support the jazz company. The company has tax-exempt status and operates on a not-for-profit basis.

LO12-5

The 10-page pamphlet cost $261,000 to design and print. Only 200,000 copies of the pamphlet were printed because the company director will be leaving and the pamphlet will soon be redesigned. One page of the pamphlet is devoted to fund solicitation; however, 98 percent of the design time was spent on developing and writing the jazz information.

a. If space is used as the allocation measure, how much of the pamphlet's cost should be assigned to program activities? To fund raising activities?
b. If design time is used as the allocation measure, how much of the pamphlet's cost should be assigned to program activities? To fund raising activities?

E12-47. NFP; research Look up three not-for-profit organization's Web sites and find a recent annual report or IRS filing. Many charities are also listed at http://www.charitynavigator.org.

LO12-5

a. How much did each of the organizations spend on program, administrative, and fundraising costs during the period?
b. What were the fundraising expenses percentages and fundraising efficiency amounts?
c. Go to the same organizations' home pages and find financial information. In what types of activities were the organizations engaged that might have generated joint costs needing to be allocated?

Problems

P12-48. Sell or process further Rose Hill, a soybean farm in northern Minnesota, has a herd of 25 dairy cows. The cows produce approximately 1,400 gallons of milk per week. The farm currently sells all its milk to a nearby processor for $1.25 per gallon, a significant drop from the $2.00 per gallon they were able to charge five years ago. It costs $1.60 per gallon to produce the milk.

LO12-1

The owners of Rose Hill are deciding whether to sell the dairy cows or expand into the artisan cheese market. Both owners have prior cheese-making experience and they already have all the needed equipment.

It takes 0.8 gallons of milk to make a pound of cheese. Costs to produce a pound of cheese are expected to total $7 per pound. Artisan cheeses are currently selling for $10 per pound at farmer's markets and upscale groceries.

a. How much incremental profit would Rose Hill recognize if half the milk each week was used to make cheese?
b. How much, in total, would Rose Hill earn each week if half the milk was used to make cheese and half was sold to the processor?
c. How much of the milk would need to be used to make cheese each week in order for Rose Hill to break even on its dairy operations assuming no cows were sold? (Note: Any milk not used to make cheese would still be sold to a processor.)
d. What other factors should the owners of Rose Hill consider when deciding whether to sell the dairy cows or expand into cheese-making?

LO12-2 P12-49. Joint product decision; ethics; research Production of ethanol, made from corn, is on the rise. Some states are even requiring that ethanol be blended in small amounts with gasoline to reduce pollution. The problem is that there is not enough corn being produced: the consumption of corn either as a food product (in all of its many forms) or as a fuel product will have to suffer. Research the issues regarding ethanol production from corn, and discuss what must be considered by farmers when determining whether corn output should be sold for consumption or for fuel.

LO12-3 P12-50. Joint costs; journal entries Natural Beauty Corp. uses a joint process to make two main products: Forever perfume and Fantasy lotion. Production is organized in two sequential departments: Combining and Heating. The products do not become separate until they have been through the heating process. After heating, the perfume is removed from the vats and bottled without further processing. The residue remaining in the vats is then blended with aloe and lanolin to become the lotion.

The following costs were incurred in the Combining Department during October: direct material, $42,000; direct labor, $11,340; and applied manufacturing overhead, $6,375. Prior to separation of the joint products, October costs in the Heating Department were direct material, $9,150; direct labor, $3,225; and applied manufacturing overhead, $4,860. After split-off, the Heating Department incurred separate costs for each product line as follows: bottles in which to package the Forever perfume, $3,180; and direct material, direct labor, and applied manufacturing overhead of $2,940, $4,680, and $6,195, respectively, for Fantasy lotion.

Neither department had beginning Work in Process Inventory balances, and all work that started in October was completed in that month. Joint costs are allocated to perfume and lotion using approximated net realizable values at split-off. For October, the approximated net realizable values at split-off were $238,365 for perfume and $79,455 for lotion.

a. Determine the joint cost allocated to, and the total cost of, Forever perfume and Fantasy lotion.
b. Prepare journal entries for the Combining and Heating Departments for October.
c. Post the entries to the accounts.

LO12-3 P12-51. Physical measure joint cost allocation Illinois Soybeans operates a processing plant in which soybeans are crushed to create soybean oil and soybean meal. The company purchases soybeans by the bushel (60 pounds). From each bushel, the normal yield is 11 pounds of soybean oil, 44 pounds of soybean meal, and 5 pounds of waste. For March, Illinois Soybeans purchased and processed 5,000,000 bushels of soybeans. The yield in March on the soybeans was equal to the normal yield. The following costs were incurred for the month:

Soybeans	$47,500,000
Conversion costs	2,300,000

At the end of March, there was no in-process or raw material in inventory. Also, there was no beginning Finished Goods Inventory. For the month, 60 percent of the soybean oil and 75 percent of the soybean meal was sold.

a. Allocate the joint cost to the joint products on the basis of pounds of product produced.
b. Calculate the cost of goods sold for March.
c. Calculate the cost of Finished Goods Inventory at the end of March.

LO12-3 P12-52. Physical measure joint cost allocation Powisett Farms Dairy began operations at the start of May. Powisett Farms operates a fleet of trucks to gather whole milk from local farmers. The whole milk is then separated into two joint products: skim milk and cream. Both products are sold at the split-off point to dairy wholesalers. For May, the firm incurred the following joint costs:

Whole milk purchase cost.	$400,000
Direct labor costs	180,000
Overhead costs	292,000
Total product cost	$872,000

During May, the firm processed 2,000,000 gallons of whole milk, producing 1,555,500 gallons of skim milk and 274,500 gallons of cream. The remaining gallons of the whole milk were lost during processing. There was no Raw Material or Work in Process Inventory at the end of May.

After the joint process, the skim milk and cream were separately processed at costs, respectively, of $67,660 and $83,310. Of the products produced, Powisett Farms Dairy sold 1,550,000 gallons of skim milk for $1,472,500 and 274,000 gallons of cream for $282,220 to wholesalers.

a. Powisett uses a physical measure (gallon) to allocate joint costs. Allocate the joint cost to production.
b. Calculate ending Finished Goods Inventory cost, Cost of Goods Sold, and gross margin for May.
c. A manager at Powisett Farms Dairy noted that the milk fat content of whole milk can vary greatly from farmer to farmer. Because milk fat content determines the relative yields of skim milk and cream from whole milk, the ratio of joint products can be partly determined based on the milk fat content of purchased whole milk. How could Powisett Farms Dairy use information about milk fat content in the whole milk it purchases to optimize the profit realized on its joint products?

P12-53. Monetary measure joint cost allocation Refer to the information in Problem P12-51. LO12-3

a. Assume the net realizable values of the joint products are as follows:

Soybean oil.	$0.50 per pound
Soybean meal.	$0.20 per pound

Allocate the joint cost incurred in March on the basis of net realizable value.
b. Calculate the cost of goods sold for March using the answer to (a).
c. Calculate the cost of Finished Goods Inventory at the end of March based on the answer to (a).
d. Compare the answers to (b) and (c) of Problem P12-51 to the answers to (b) and (c) of this problem. Explain why the answers differ.

P12-54. Monetary measure joint cost allocation Refer to the information in Problem P12-52. (Round to the nearest whole percentage and cent.) LO12-3

a. Calculate the sales price per gallon for skim milk and cream.
b. Using relative sales value, allocate the joint cost to the joint production.
c. Calculate ending Finished Goods Inventory cost, Cost of Goods Sold, and the gross margin for the month.

P12-55. Joint cost allocation; by-product; income determination Schneider Bank offers two primary financial services: commercial checking and credit cards. The bank also generates some revenue from selling identity fraud insurance as a by-product of its two main services. The monthly joint cost for conducting the two primary services is $800,000 and includes expenses for facilities, legal support, equipment, record keeping, and administration. The joint cost is allocated on the basis of total revenues generated from each primary service. LO12-3, 4, 5

The following table presents the results of operations and revenues for June:

Service	Number of Accounts	Total Revenues
Commercial checking	12,000	$1,914,000
Credit cards	28,000	1,386,000
Identity theft insurance	3,000	26,000

To account for revenues from the identity theft insurance, management reduces Cost of Services Rendered for primary services. The commissions are accounted for on a realized value basis as the policies are received.

For June, separate costs for commercial checking accounts and credit cards were $850,000 and 380,000, respectively.

a. Allocate the joint cost.
b. Determine the income for each primary service and the company's overall gross margin for June.
c. Assume instead that Schneider Bank uses the net realizable value approach for by-product revenue. How much joint cost would have been allocated to the commercial checking and the credit card products during June? Will the gross margin be the same as in (b)? Why or why not?

LO12-3, 4 **P12-56. Joint products; by-product** Fredericksburg Vegetable is a fruitpacking business. The firm buys peaches by the truckload in season and separates them into three categories: premium, good, and fair. Premium peaches can be sold as is to supermarket chains and to specialty gift stores. Good peaches are sliced and canned in light syrup and sold to supermarkets. Fair peaches are considered a by-product and are sold to Altas Company, which processes the peaches into jelly.

Fredericksburg Vegetable has two processing departments: (1) Cleaning and Sorting (joint cost) and (2) Cutting and Canning (separate costs). During the month, the company paid $15,000 for one truckload of fruit and $700 for labor to sort the fruit into categories. Fredericksburg Vegetable uses a predetermined overhead rate of 40 percent of direct labor cost. The following yield, costs, and final sales value resulted from the month's truckload of fruit.

	Premium	Good	Fair
Yield in pecks	1,500	2,000	500
Cutting and canning costs	$0	$2,000	$0
Total packaging and delivery costs	$1,500	$2,200	$500
Total final sales value	$30,000	$15,000	$4,500

a. Determine the joint cost.
b. Diagram Fredericksburg Vegetable's process in a manner similar to **Exhibits 12.5** and **12.6**.
c. Allocate joint cost using the approximated net realizable value at split-off method, assuming that the by-product is recorded when realized and is shown as Other Income on the income statement. (Round to the nearest whole percent.)
d. Using the allocations from (c), prepare the necessary entries assuming that the by-product is sold for $4,500 and that all costs were as shown.
e. Allocate joint cost using the approximated net realizable value at split-off method, assuming that the by-product is recorded using the net realizable value approach and that the joint cost is reduced by the net realizable value of the by-product. (Round to the nearest whole percent.)
f. Using the allocations from (d), prepare the necessary entries, assuming that the estimated realizable value of the by-product is $4,000.

LO12-3, 4 **P12-57. Process costing; joint cost allocation; by-product** GetAhead provides personal training services for, and sells apparel products to, its clients. GetAhead also generates some revenue from protein drink sales. The net realizable value from drink sales is accounted for as a reduction in the joint cost assigned to the Personal Training Services and Apparel Products. Protein drinks sell for $2.50 per bottle. The costs associated with making and packaging the drinks are $1.00 per bottle.

The following information is available for the year on apparel products, which are purchased by GetAhead:

Beginning inventory	$ 35,000
Ending inventory	21,500
Purchases	181,350

Joint cost is to be allocated to Personal Training Services and Apparel Products based on approximated net realizable values. For the year, total revenues were $753,000 from Personal Training Services and $289,000 from Apparel. The following joint costs were incurred:

Rent	$36,000
Insurance	43,750
Utilities	3,000

Separate costs were as follows:

	Personal Training	Apparel
Labor	$231,000	$33,250
Supplies	151,300	700
Equipment depreciation	165,000	1,200
Administration	103,000	3,700

For the year, 2,500 bottles of protein drinks were sold.

a. What is the total net realizable value of protein drinks used to reduce the joint cost assigned to Personal Training and Apparel?
b. What is the joint cost to be allocated to Personal Training and Apparel?
c. What is the approximated pre-tax realizable value of each main product or service for the year?
d. How much joint cost is allocated to each main product or service?
e. Determine the net income produced by each main product or service.

P12-58. Joint cost allocation; by-product Tangy Fresh produces orange juice and orange marmalade from a joint process. Second-stage processing of the marmalade creates an orange pulp by-product that can be sold for $0.05 per gallon. Expenses to distribute pulp total $90.

In May, 140,000 pounds of oranges costing $44,200 were processed in Department 1, with labor and overhead costs of $33,800 incurred. Department 1 processing resulted in 56,000 gallons of output, of which 40 percent was transferred to Department 2 to become orange juice and 60 percent was transferred to Department 3. Of the input going to Department 3, 20 percent resulted in pulp and 80 percent resulted in marmalade. Joint cost is allocated to orange juice and marmalade on the basis of approximated net realizable values at split-off.

The orange juice in Department 2 was processed at a total cost of $9,620; the marmalade in Department 3 was processed at a total cost of $6,450. The net realizable value of pulp is accounted for as a reduction in the separate processing costs in Department 3. Selling prices per gallon are $5.25 and $3.45 for orange juice and marmalade, respectively.

a. Diagram Tangy Fresh's process in a manner similar to **Exhibits 12.5** and **12.6**.
b. How many gallons leaving Department 1 were sent to Department 2 for further processing? To Department 3?
c. How many gallons left Department 3 as pulp? As marmalade?
d. What is the net realizable value of pulp?
e. What is the total approximated net realizable value of the orange juice? The marmalade?
f. What joint cost is assigned to each main product? (Round proportions to the nearest whole percentage and dollar amounts to the nearest whole dollar.)
g. If 85 percent of the final output of each main product was sold during May and Tangy Fresh had no beginning inventory of either product, what is the value of the ending inventory of orange juice and marmalade?

P12-59. By-product/joint product journal entries Arguillo Inc. is a 5,000-acre farm that produces two products: Zilla and Corma. Zilla sells for $3.50 per bushel (assume that a bushel weighs 60 pounds). Without further processing, Corma sells for $30 per ton (a ton equals 2,000 pounds). If the Corma is processed further, it can be sold for $45 per ton. Total joint cost up to the split-off point was $875,000. Arguillo produced 70 bushels of Zilla and 1 ton of Corma per acre. If all the Corma were processed further, separate costs would be $50,000.

Prepare the journal entries for Corma if it is:

a. transferred to storage at sales value as a by-product without further processing with a corresponding reduction of Zilla's production costs.
b. further processed as a by-product and transferred to storage at net realizable value with a corresponding reduction of the manufacturing costs of Zilla.
c. further processed and transferred to finished goods with joint cost allocated based on relative sales value at the split-off point. (Round proportions to the nearest whole percentage and dollar amounts to the nearest whole dollar.)

P12-60. Joint cost allocation; ending inventory valuation; by-product During March, the first month of operations, Pork Co. had the operating statistics shown in the following table.

Products	Weight in Pounds	Sales Value at Split-Off	Pounds Produced	Pounds Sold
Tenderloin.....	8,600	$132,000	6,440	5,440
Roast	13,400	86,000	16,740	14,140
Ham	10,800	22,400	8,640	7,640
Hooves	4,600	4,600	9,200	8,000

Costs of the joint process were direct material, $40,000; direct labor, $23,400; and overhead, $10,000. The company's main products are pork tenderloin, roast pork, and ham; pork hooves are a by-product of the process. The company recognizes the net realizable value of by-product inventory at split-off by reducing total joint cost. Neither the main products nor the by-product requires any additional processing or disposal costs, although management could consider additional processing.

   a. Calculate the ending inventory values of each joint product based on (1) relative sales value and (2) pounds. (Round proportions to the nearest whole percentage and dollar amounts to the nearest whole dollar.)
   b. Discuss the advantages and disadvantages of each allocation base for (1) financial statement purposes and (2) decisions about the desirability of processing the joint products beyond the split-off point.

LO12-3, 4 **P12-61. Joint cost allocation; scrap** DD's Linens produces terrycloth products for hotels. The company buys fabric in 60-inch-wide bolts. In the first process, the fabric is set up, cut, and separated into pieces. Setup can be for either robes and beach towels, or bath towels, hand towels, and washcloths.

During July, the company set up and cut 6,000 robes and 12,000 beach towels. Because of the irregular pattern of the robes, the process produces scrap that is sold to various prisons and hospitals for rags at $0.45 per pound. July production and cost data for DD's Linens are as follows:

Fabric used, 25,000 feet at $1.50 per foot	$37,500
Labor, joint process	$12,000
Overhead, joint process	$11,000
Pounds of scrap produced	3,600

DD's Linens assigns the joint processing cost to the robes and beach towels based on approximated net realizable value at split-off. Other data gathered include these:

	Per Robe	Per Beach Towel
Final selling prices	$20.00	$7.00
Costs after split-off	6.80	1.60

The selling price of the scrap is treated as a reduction of joint cost.
   a. Determine the joint cost to be allocated to the joint products for July.
   b. How much joint cost is allocated to the robes in July? To the beach towels? Prepare the journal entry necessary at the split-off point.
   c. What amount of cost for robes is transferred to Finished Goods Inventory for July? What amount of cost for beach towels is transferred to Finished Goods Inventory for July?

LO12-1, 3, 4 **P12-62. Joint cost allocation; by-products** Buchan's Junction Manufacturing Corporation uses a joint production process that produces three products at the split-off point. Joint production costs during March were $720,000. The company uses the sales-value method for allocating joint costs. March production information was as follows:

	Product		
	Alpha	Beta	Gamma
Units produced......................	2,500	5,000	7,500
Units sold	2,000	6,000	7,000
Sales prices:			
At the split-off point................	$100	$80	$20
After further processing	$150	$115	$30
Costs to process after split-off point.....	$150,000	$150,000	$100,000

Chapter 12 Allocation of Joint Costs and Accounting for By-Product/Scrap

a. Compute the amount of joint costs allocated to each product assuming that joint cost allocation is based on sales value at the split-off point. (Rounding is not needed.)
b. Assume that all three products are main products and that they can be sold at the split-off point or processed further, whichever is economically beneficial to the company. Compute the total cost of product Beta in March if joint cost allocation is based on sales value at split-off.
c. Assume that product Gamma is treated as a by-product and that the company accounts for the by-product at net realizable value as a reduction of joint cost. Products Beta and Gamma must be processed further before they can be sold. Compute the total cost of production of products Alpha and Beta in March if joint cost allocation is based on net realizable values. (Round proportions to the nearest whole percentage and dollar amounts to the nearest whole dollar.)

CIA ADAPTED
LO12-4

P12-63. Scrap; ethics; writing; research Some waste, scrap, and by-product materials have little value. In fact, for many meat and poultry producers, animal waste represents a significant liability because it is considered hazardous and requires significant disposal costs. Some companies, such as **Smithfield Foods Inc.** (the largest hog processor in the United States), gather the animal waste in "lagoons" and allow it to be used as "liquid fertilizer."

a. Review Willets and Tauss's article (October 31, 2018), "Smithfield Foods Says it Will Cover its Lagoons. Critics Say that's Just Lipstick on a Pig," accessed at https://indyweek.com/news/north carolina/smithfield-foods-cover-its-lagoons/ (accessed 10/17/2023) as well as the environmental policies at the company's website (https://www.smithfieldfoods.com (access 10/17/2023)). Discuss the ethical and legal implications of disposing of industrial waste in this manner.
b. What actions can people take to reduce this type of disposal?
c. Ethically, what obligation does the vendor/manufacturer of potentially toxic pollutants have to the consumer of the company's products?

LO12-4

P12-64. By-product; research Choose a fairly common product that you believe would generate multiple by-products.

a. Without doing any research, prepare a list of some items that you believe would be by-products from the common product you have chosen.
b. After you have completed your list, use the Web to find what by-products are actually associated with the product you have chosen.

LO12-5

P12-65. NFP joint cost Delores' Place is a not-for-profit that has a mission of helping parents prevent their children from abusing drugs. The NFP sends materials that discuss the dangers of drug abuse to parents of high school students. The materials encourage parents to discuss the dangers of drug use with children, explain how such abuse might be detected, and request contributions to continue the organization's mission. The materials sent to parents cost approximately $8,000 to produce. Similar materials are sent to other individuals without a contribution request. Discuss whether the $8,000 should be considered an allocable joint cost or if the entire cost should be considered fundraising.

AICPA ADAPTED
LO12-5

P12-66. NFP joint cost Get-Up-N-Go! is a not-for-profit organization with a mission of improving the quality of life for senior citizens; one objective within that mission is to increase seniors' physical activity. One four-page brochure distributed to over-65ers uses the first two pages to discuss a self-supervised exercise program and to encourage the undertaking of such a program. The remaining two pages of the brochure explain the Get-Up-N-Go! program and solicit contributions. Production of this brochure costs $10,000. A second four-page brochure provides specific information on exercise techniques for seniors; no contribution requests are made. Development and production of this brochure cost $14,000. The brochures are distributed to people over 65, regardless of their ability to contribute, and were developed by a public relations firm that was aware of the objectives of Get-Up-N-Go! through a letter requesting the help of the PR firm.

a. How much, if any, of the brochure costs should be considered allocable? Explain your reasoning.
b. If you have determined that any of the brochure costs should be allocated, should the allocation be to fund raising, program, or administrative functions? How would you allocate the joint cost?
c. How, if at all, would your answer change if Get-Up-N-Go! employs a fund raising consultant to develop the first brochure and pays that consultant 30 percent of the contributions received?

AICPA ADAPTED
LO12-5

P12-67. NFP joint cost WeeCare is a not-for-profit that provides food, clothing, and medical care to children in developing countries. U.S. television programs are sponsored by WeeCare to describe its programs, show the needy children, and ask for contributions. WeeCare's operating policies and internal management memos state that these programs are designed to educate the public about the needs of children in developing countries and to raise contributions. The employees producing the programs are familiar with WeeCare's programs; the executive producer is paid $25,000 plus will receive a $5,000 bonus if the aired program raises over $1,000,000 in contributions. Discuss whether the cost of the programs should be considered an allocable joint cost or if the entire cost should be considered fundraising.

AICPA ADAPTED

LO12-5 **P12-68. NFP joint cost** Debra's Diabetes Foundation was started by a family whose mother had died after suffering for many years with diabetes. A lecture that cost the foundation $360,000 was held on the fourth Tuesday in March, which is American Diabetes Alert Day. Advertisements were placed in social media, all local newspapers and were broadcast on local media channels. During the lecture, information was provided about the causes, symptoms, and treatment of diabetes, about help available for caregivers, and about the foundation and its mission. In addition to requesting contributions, members of the foundation asked attendees to take a quiz about diabetes, volunteer to distribute pamphlets about the disease to local businesses, write letters to their insurance companies about additional coverage availability, and participate in the Medicare Advocacy Program to gather information and identify problems encountered by beneficiaries and providers.

a. Did the lecture meet the audience criterion? Why or why not?
b. Did the lecture include a call for action? Explain.
c. Assume that 65 percent of the lecture time was related to the disease, 25 percent of the lecture was related to the foundation, and 10 percent was related to fundraising. Allocate the joint cost to the three activities.
d. Assume that the topics discussed at the lecture were not in specific order, and often, discussion was in response to questions that were asked by the attendees. How else might the joint cost be allocated among program, management, and fund raising activities?
e. Debra's Diabetes Foundation hired a consultant to help with the lecture. The consultant was paid $40,000 but has been informed that, if the lecture raised between $400,001 and $500,000, the fee would increase to $50,000; if the lecture raised over $500,000, the consultant would be paid $70,000. The consultant's fee was not included in the $360,000 joint cost. The Foundation was excited to find that the lecture raised $540,000. The time allocation given in (c) was representative of the time spent on topics during the lecture. How much of the $430,000 ($360,000 + $70,000) should be allocated to the three activities?

LO12-5 **P12-69. NFP joint cost; ethics; research; writing** Read Joseph McCafferty's article entitled "Misgivings" at *CFO.com* (January 2007); https://www.cfo.com/news/misgivings/675613/ (accessed 10/17/2023).

a. Discuss your thoughts about not-for-profits claiming to raise funds without incurring any costs.
b. What would you consider a "reasonable" cost of fund raising ratio, and why?
c. Why would some types of not-for-profits (such as educational institutions) have different types of fund raising ratios than others (such as museums or health-related organizations)?

LO12-2, 3, 5 **P12-70. NFP joint cost; joint revenues; decision making; writing** Throughout your college career, you have been employed on a part-time basis by the Center for Entrepreneurship of your business college. The Center for Entrepreneurship provides executive training and consulting for a fee to individuals and organizations located throughout the state. The condensed income statement that follows summarizes the operating results of the center for the year.

Fees	$ 2,625,000
Faculty and staff salaries	(1,050,000)
Facilities cost	(550,000)
Training materials	(375,000)
Marketing and promotions	(400,000)
Other costs of operations	(500,000)
Net operating loss	$ (250,000)

Given that the center operated at a loss for the year, the dean of the business college has asked the director to provide a justification for not closing the center. As the dean stated, "We're charged with a fundamental obligation of being good stewards of the state's resources. We cannot justify spending net resources to subsidize educational programs to corporations and other profit-oriented organizations."

The center director has made the dean's comments known to all employees and faculty of the center, and all are concerned about losing their employment should the center be closed.

Having just completed a chapter in your accounting course addressing joint products, you become curious as to whether the preceding income statement fairly reflects the value of all outputs of the center. Particularly, you believe that the center plays a crucial role in the generation of contributions made to the college by alumni and friends of the business college and university.

a. Discuss how the existence of joint products of the Center for Entrepreneurship would potentially modify the preceding income statement.
b. Discuss how you could use the concepts of joint products and joint cost allocation to demonstrate to the dean that the Center for Entrepreneurship is not consuming "net resources" of the state or college and that the center should continue its operations.

Review Solutions

Review 12-1

a. ($56 − $40) Incremental revenue − $12 Incremental costs = $4 Advantage of processing further
Based on the quantitative results, product C should be processed further into product D.

b. There are many qualitative considerations in a sell or process further decision. Do customers expect Product C to be available? What is the quality of Product C and D? Are there any capacity constraints in producing Product D? Are there any regulatory or environmental considerations of producing Product D?

Review 12-2

a.

# of Units	Sales per Unit	Total Sales	% of Total Sales		Product #
10,000	$ 4.00	$40,000	46.26%	Joint product	8
14,000	2.00	28,000	32.38	Joint product	2
800	10.00	8,000	9.25	By-product	1
1,000	5.00	5,000	5.78	By-product	7
5,000	0.30	1,500	1.73	Scrap	3
1,800	0.80	1,440	1.67	Scrap	5
650	2.20	1,430	1.65	Scrap	9
300	3.50	1,050	1.21	Scrap	6
25	1.80	45	0.05	Waste	4
Total sales.............		$86,465			

Note: All classifications are based on the respective proportional sales values. Other classifications may be justified with other factors. A further consideration would be any selling or disposal costs that would affect the net inflows to Lathrop Co.

b. An increase or decrease in the either the number of units produced or the sales price at split-off could indicate that a change in classification is required. This could be prompted by a change in process or inputs to a process that impact the outputs to the process.

Review 12-3

a. 1. Number of units
   Product A: $104,000 = 32% (30,000 ÷ 95,000) × $325,000
   Product B: $152,750 = 47% (45,000 ÷ 95,000) × $325,000
   Product C: $ 68,250 = 21% (20,000 ÷ 95,000) × $325,000

   2. Weight
   Product A: $ 81,250 = 25% (360,000 ÷ 1,440,000) × $325,000
   Product B: $162,500 = 50% (720,000 ÷ 1,440,000) × $325,000
   Product C: $ 81,250 = 25% (360,000 ÷ 1,440,000) × $325,000

   3. Sales value at split-off
   Product A: $ 97,500 = 30%* (150,000 ÷ 490,000) × $325,000
   Product B: $120,250 = 37 % (180,000 ÷ 490,000) × $325,000
   Product C: $107,250 = 33 % (160,000 ÷ 490,000) × $325,000
   *Percent rounded down in order for total not to exceed 100%.

4. Approximated NRV
   Product A: $ 94,250 = 29% (270,000 ÷ 935,000) × $325,000
   Product B: $139,750 = 43% (405,000 ÷ 935,000) × $325,000
   Product C: $ 91,000 = 28% (260,000 ÷ 935,000) × $325,000

b. Sell or process further
   Product A: Incremental revenue per unit ($7) – Incremental cost per unit ($3) = +$4; Process further
   Product B: Incremental revenue per unit ($6) – Incremental cost per unit ($1) = +$5; Process further
   Product C: Incremental revenue per unit ($7) – Incremental cost per unit ($2) = +$5; Process further

c. 1. Number of units
   Product A: $5,173   = ($104,000 ÷ 30,000 × 800) + ($3 × 800)
   Product B: $4,834   = ($152,750 ÷ 45,000 × 1,100) + ($1 × 1,100)
   Product C: $10,284 = ($68,250 ÷ 20,000 × 1,900) + ($2 × 1,900)

   2. Weight
   Product A: $4,567   = ($81,250 ÷ 30,000 × 800) + ($3 × 800)
   Product B: $5,072   = ($162,500 ÷ 45,000 × 1,100) + ($1 × 1,100)
   Product C: $11,519 = ($81,250 ÷ 20,000 × 1,900) + ($2 × 1,900)

   3. Sales value at split-off
   Product A: $5,000   = ($97,500 ÷ 30,000 × 800) + ($3 × 800)
   Product B: $4,039   = ($120,250 ÷ 45,000 × 1,100) + ($1 × 1,100)
   Product C: $13,989 = ($107,250 ÷ 20,000 × 1,900) + ($2 × 1,900)

   4. Approximated NRV
   Product A: $4,913   = ($94,250 ÷ 30,000 × 800) + ($3 × 800)
   Product B: $4,516   = ($139,750 ÷ 45,000 × 1,100) + ($1 × 1,100)
   Product C: $12,445 = ($91,000 ÷ 20,000 × 1,900) + ($2 × 1,900)

d. Product B is allocated the most joint costs across all methods. It has the highest relative number of total units, weight, sales value at split-off, and approximated NRV. This is not always the case that one product would be allocated the most costs under each method. There is no guarantee that the product with the most weight, for example, would have the highest sales price (i.e., some units could have a very low sales value per ounce).

Review 12-4

a.
Sales revenue (joint products)	$335,000
Cost of goods sold (85% × [($90,000 – $15,500*) + $55,000])	110,075
Gross profit	224,925
Non-factory expense	58,000
Income before taxes	$166,925

*($27,900 – ($0.08 × 155,000))

b.
Sales revenue (joint products)		$335,000
Other revenues (by-product sales)		27,900
Cost of goods sold:		
Joint cost (85% × $90,000)	$76,500	
Separate costs (85% × $55,000)	46,750	
By-products ($0.08 × 155,000)	12,400	135,650
Gross profit		227,250
Non-factory expense		58,000
Income before taxes		$169,250

Chapter 12 Allocation of Joint Costs and Accounting for By-Product/Scrap

c.
Sales revenue (joint products)	$335,000
Cost of goods sold ($76,500 + $46,750)	123,250
Gross profit	211,750
Non-factory expense	58,000
Income from operations	153,750
Other income (by-product sales, net)	15,500
Income before taxes	$169,250

d. The presentation of part *b* is preferable over the presentation of part *c* if the by-products are significant to the company's operations. (By-product revenue represents over 7% of total revenue and would likely be considered significant.) The presentation in part *b* shows both revenues and expenses related to by-products which offers more information to management for planning and control than the net number of $15,500 in part *c*. For one thing, the net profit of by-products gives management no indication of the magnitude of sales and expenses that comprise the net number reported.

Review 12-5

a.

	Children	Adult	Total
Direct costs	$41,250[1]	$123,750[2]	
Overhead cost	20,000[3]	60,000[4]	
Total cost assigned	$61,250	$183,750	$245,000

b.

	Children	Adult	Total
Direct costs	$41,250	$123,750	
Overhead cost	14,545[5]	65,455[6]	
Total cost assigned	$55,795	$189,205	$245,000

[1] $41,250 = (2,000/8,000) × $165,000
[2] $123,750 = (6,000/8,000) × $165,000
[3] $20,000 = (2,000/8,000) × $80,000
[4] $60,000 = (6,000/8,000) × $80,000
[5] $14,545 = (100,000/550,000) × $80,000
[6] $65,455 = (450,000/550,000) × $80,000

c. It is true that under different methods of allocating joint costs, the total amount allocated is the same. What differs is how much is allocated to each service (or product). Understanding the profitability of each service is important in order to determine which services are covering costs and which are not. In order to control costs, it is important to know the source of the costs.

Data Visualization Solutions

(See page 12-6.)

Product	Incremental Revenue	Incremental Cost	Incremental Profit (Loss)
Product A	$2	$2	$ 0
Product B	$5	$3	$ 2
Produce C	$3	$4	$ (1)

Based on an analysis of incremental revenue and incremental costs, only Product B should be processed further.

© Cambridge Business Publishers

Chapter 13

Responsibility Accounting, Support Department Cost Allocations, and Transfer Pricing

Road Map

LO	Learning Objective | Topics	Page	eLecture	Demo	Review	Assignments
13-1	**How is a management control system supported by a cost management system?** Management Information System (MIS) :: Management Control System (MCS) :: Detector :: Assessor: Effector :: Communications Network :: Cost Management System (CMS) :: Organizational Strategy :: Roles of a CMS	13-2	e13-1	D13-1	Rev 13-1	MC13-15, E13-23, E13-24, E13-25, E13-26, E13-27, P13-52, P13-53, P13-54, P13-55
13-2	**Which factors determine whether a firm should be decentralized or centralized?** Centralization :: Decentralization :: Continuum :: Shared Services :: Environmental Application	13-7	e13-2	D13-2	Rev 13-2	MC13-16, E13-28, E13-29, E13-30, E13-31, P13-56, P13-57
13-3	**How do responsibility reports help management conduct control activities?** Responsibility Accounting System :: Control Activities :: Multilevel Responsibility Report :: Variance Analysis :: Management-by-Exception Principle :: Goal Congruence	13-10	e13-3	D13-3	Rev 13-3	MC13-17, E13-32, E13-33, P13-58, P13-59, P13-60, P13-61
13-4	**What are the four primary types of responsibility centers, and what distinguishes them from each other?** Responsibility Center :: Cost Center :: Revenue Center :: Profit Center :: Investment Center :: Suboptimization	13-13	e13-4	D13-4	Rev 13-4	MC13-18, E13-34, E13-35, E13-36, E13-37, P13-61, P13-62, P13-63
13-5	**Why and how are support department costs allocated to operating departments?** Support Departments :: Service Department :: Administrative Department :: Allocation Bases :: Direct Method :: Step Method :: Benefits-Provided Ranking :: Algebraic Method :: Overhead Application Rates	13-15	e13-5	D13-5A D13-5B D13-5C	Rev 13-5	MC13-19, MC13-20, E13-38, E13-39, E13-40, E13-41, E13-42, E13-43, P13-64, P13-65, P13-66, P13-67, P13-68, P13-69, P13-70, P13-71, P13-78, DA13-1
13-6	**What types of transfer prices are used in organizations, and why are such prices used?** Transfer Pricing :: Pseudo-Profit Center :: Cost-Based Transfer Prices :: Market-Based Transfer Prices :: Negotiated Transfer Prices :: Dual Pricing :: Multinational Settings :: Arm's -Length Transaction	13-26	e13-6	D13-6	Rev 13-6	MC13-21, MC13-22, E13-31, E13-36, E13-44, E13-45, E13-46, E13-47, E13-48, E13-49, E13-50, E13-51, P13-72, P13-73, P13-74, P13-75, P13-76, P13-77, P13-78, P13-79, P13-80, P13-81, P13-82, P13-83

© Cambridge Business Publishers

13-1

INTRODUCTION

As an organization grows, its customer-base size and locations, product and service offerings, level of technology, distribution channels, and number of employees change. To cope with such changes, managers must recognize when and how the company's authority structure should be altered to support decision making, communication, and employee motivation. Global operations demand that managers in all regions effectively use corporate human and physical resources; product customization demands that managers be in close touch with customers; and coordination of larger and more diverse workforces demands that managers be more adept at employee training and development. Decisions often need to be made rapidly at a "grass-roots" level rather than at "the top" of the organizational hierarchy. Thus, one of the most common progressions made by high-growth companies is from highly centralized organizational structures to highly decentralized structures. When an organization has a centralized structure, top management retains the majority of decision-making authority. When top management delegates decision-making authority to subunit managers, decentralization exists. The cost management system utilized by the organization supports the needs of decision makers in a centralized or decentralized organizational structure. The first section of this chapter introduces management information and control systems, which offer a foundation and context for understanding the roles of the cost management system (CMS) first introduced in Chapter 2. This chapter also describes the accounting methods—responsibility accounting, support department cost allocations, and transfer pricing—that are appropriate in decentralized organizations.

MANAGEMENT INFORMATION AND CONTROL SYSTEMS

LO13-1 How is a management control system supported by a cost management system?

A fundamental concern of managers is identifying factors that affect organizational costs and benefits. This concern arises from the managerial focus on revenue growth and profit generation. To this end, a decision maker's access to accurate and relevant information is essential. **Exhibit 13.1** illustrates the types of information an organization needs to meet the requirements of internal parties performing managerial functions as well as requirements of external parties performing investment and credit-granting functions. A **management information system (MIS)** is a structure of interrelated elements used to collect, organize, and communicate data to managers so they can plan, control, make decisions, and evaluate performance. An MIS emphasizes satisfying *internal*, rather than external, demands for information.

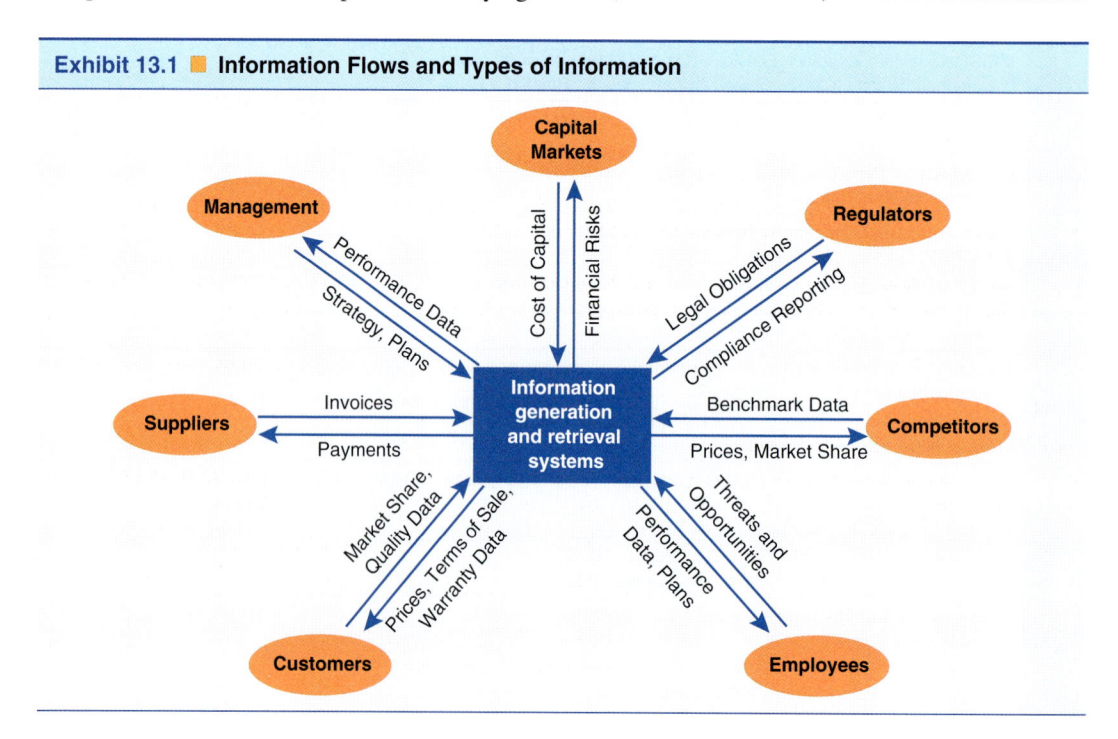

Exhibit 13.1 ■ Information Flows and Types of Information

The accounting function is charged with providing information about monetary receipts from, as well as purchases and payments to, interested internal parties (such as managers) and external parties (such as creditors and suppliers). In addition, government bodies such as the **Internal Revenue Service** and **Securities and Exchange Commission** receive mandatory reports from the accounting function. Because managers need external intelligence to govern their organizations, information to be included in the MIS is also gathered from various external parties, including competitors.

Components of a Management Control System

Because one managerial function requiring information is control, the MIS is part of the **management control system (MCS)**. As illustrated in **Exhibit 13.2**, a control system has the following four primary components:

1. A **detector** or **sensor**, which is a measuring device that identifies what is actually happening in the process being controlled.
2. An **assessor**, which is a device for determining the significance of what is happening. Usually, significance is assessed by comparing the information about what is actually happening with some standard or expectation of what should be happening.
3. An **effector**, which is a device that alters behavior if the assessor indicates the need for doing so. This device is often called feedback.
4. A **communications network**, which transmits information between the detector and the assessor and between the assessor and the effector.[1]

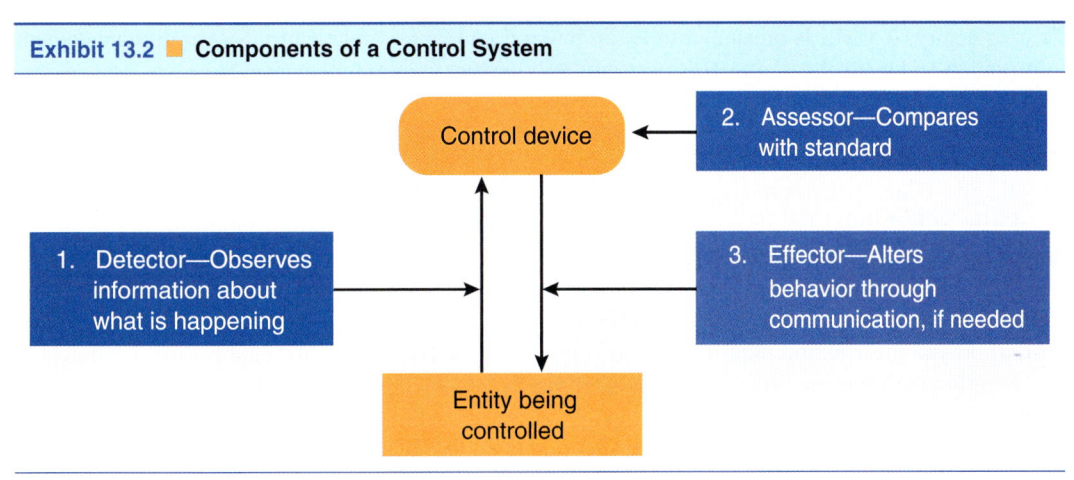

Exhibit 13.2 ■ Components of a Control System

- Control device
- 1. Detector—Observes information about what is happening
- 2. Assessor—Compares with standard
- 3. Effector—Alters behavior through communication, if needed
- Entity being controlled

Note: The arrows depict (4) the communication network.
Source: From Robert N. Anthony and Vijay Govindarajan, "Management Control Systems," 9th ed. (Burr Ridge, IL: Irwin/McGraw-Hill, 1998), p. 2. Copyright© 1998 The McGraw-Hill Companies, Inc.

Through these system components, information about organizational occurrences is gathered, comparisons are made against plans, changes are made when necessary, and communications take place among appropriate parties.

Identifying Components of a Management Control System   LO13-1   DEMO 13-1

Assume that a company's MIS automatically calculates differences between actual sales data and the sales budget. Sales analysts interpret and determine the causes of the detected variances. Management issues a variance report and encourages the sales staff to address detected unfavorable variances.

◆ For this example, what are the activities that are identified as detector, assessor, effector, and communications network?

---

[1] Robert N. Anthony and Vijay Govindarajan, *Management Control Systems*, 9th ed. (Burr Ridge, IL: Irwin/McGraw-Hill, 1998), pp. 1–2.

Control System Component	Activity
1. Detector	MIS automatically identifies variances.
2. Assessor	Sales analyst determines causes of variances.
3. Effector	Management issues report and encourages change to increase volume or prices.
4. Communications network	Sales analysts derive information from the MIS that is shared with management. Management communicates results to sales team and provides feedback.

Different managers can interpret and respond differently to the same information. In this respect, development of an MCS is not merely a mechanical process but requires expert judgment. Regardless of the specific actions taken, an MCS should serve to guide entities in designing and implementing strategies to achieve organizational goals and objectives.

Most businesses have a variety of control systems in place. For example, a control system could reflect a set of procedures for screening potential suppliers or employees, a set of criteria to evaluate potential and existing investments, or a statistical control process to monitor and evaluate product quality.

Defining a Cost Management System

A **cost management system (CMS)** consists of a set of formal methods developed for planning and controlling an organization's cost-generating activities relative to its short-term objectives and long-term strategies. A CMS is presumed to be an integral part of an organization's overall management information and control systems. Business entities face two major challenges:

- achieving profitability in the short run, and
- maintaining a competitive position in the long run.

An effective CMS provides managers the information needed to meet both challenges.

Refer to **Exhibit 13.3** for a summary of differences in the information requirements for organizational success in the short run relative to the long run. In the short run, organizational revenues must exceed costs and efficient use must be made of resources relative to revenues. Specific cost information is needed and must be delivered in a timely fashion to someone who can influence that cost. Short-run information requirements are often described as relating to organizational efficiency.

Meeting the long-run objective of survival depends on acquiring the right inputs from the right suppliers, selling the right product mix to the right customers, and using the right distribution channels. These decisions require only periodic information that is reasonably accurate.

Exhibit 13.3 ◾ Dual Focus of a Cost Management System

	Short Run	Long Run
Objective	Organizational efficiency	Survival
Focus	Specific costs: • manufacturing • service • marketing • administration	Cost categories: • customers • suppliers • products • distribution channels
Important characteristics of information	Timely Accurate Highly specific Short term	Periodic Reasonably accurate Broad focus Long term

Source: Adapted from Robin Cooper and Regine Slagmulder, "Operational Improvement and Strategic Costing," *Management Accounting* (September 1998), pp. 12–13. Copyright 1998 by Institute of Management Accountants. Reproduced with permission of Institute of Management Accountants in the format Textbook via Copyright Clearance Center.

The information generated from the CMS should benefit all an entity's functional areas. Thus, as shown in **Exhibit 13.4**, a CMS should integrate information from all areas of the organization and provide managers faster access to more cost information that is relevant, detailed, and appropriate for short- and long-term decision making.

Exhibit 13.4 ■ An Integrated Cost Management System

The Management Control System

Cost Management System

Surrounding elements: Employees, Manufacturing Processes and Capabilities, Competition, Investors and Creditors, Procurement, Inventory Management, Technology, Political Environment, Marketing and Distribution, Quality Assurance, Business Environment, Legal and Ethical Considerations, Product Pricing, Product Costing, Product Development, Customers, Environmental and Social Responsibility Issues

ORGANIZATIONAL STRATEGY

Roles of a Cost Management System

Crossing all functional areas, a CMS can be viewed as having six primary roles.

Develop Accurate Costs	Assess Performance	Improve Process Understanding	Control Costs	Measure Performance	Support Strategy

Develop accurate product/service costs Primarily, a CMS should provide the means of developing accurate product or service costs. Thus, the system must be designed to use cost driver information to trace costs to products and services. The system is not required to be the most accurate, but it should weigh the benefits of additional accuracy against costs of achieving such accuracy.

The product/service costs generated by the CMS are the inputs to managerial processes. These costs are used to

- plan,
- prepare financial statements,
- assess individual product/service profitability and periodic profitability,
- establish prices for cost-plus contracts, and
- create a basis for performance measurements.

If the costs generated by the CMS are not reasonably accurate, the execution of the preceding processes will be inappropriate for control and decision-making purposes.

Assess product/service life cycle performance Although product/service profitability may be calculated periodically (possibly as a requirement for external reporting), the financial accounting system does not provide profitability information over a product's entire life. The financial accounting system provides only a period-by-period look at product profitability. The CMS should provide information about a product's or service's life cycle performance. Without life cycle information, managers will not have a basis to relate costs incurred in one part of the life cycle to costs and profitability of other parts. For example, managers might not recognize that strong investment early in a product's life could provide significant returns later by reducing engineering change and quality-related costs. Further, if development/design cost is not traced to the related product or service, managers could be unable to recognize organizational investment "disasters."

Improve understanding of processes/activities A CMS should also help managers understand business processes and organizational activities. Only by understanding how an activity is accomplished and the reasons for cost incurrence can managers make cost-beneficial improvements in the production and processing systems. Managers desiring to implement new technology or production systems must be able to identify the costs and benefits that will arise from such actions. Such assessments can be made only if the managers understand how the processes and activities will differ after the change.

Control costs A cost accounting system's original purpose was to control costs and, given the current global competitive environment, this is still an important CMS function. A cost can be controlled only when the related activity is monitored, the cost driver is known, and information is available. For example, if units are spoiled during a process, the CMS should provide information on spoilage quantity and cost rather than "burying" that information in other cost categories. Additionally, the cost management system should allow managers to determine the underlying spoilage causes so that the cost of fixing the process can be compared with the benefits to be gained.

Measure performance Information generated from a CMS should also help managers measure and evaluate performance. The measurements can be used to evaluate human or equipment performance as well as future investment opportunities.

Support organizational strategy Finally, to maintain a competitive position, a firm must generate the information necessary to define and implement its organizational strategies. Strategy is the link among an organization's goals, objectives, and operational activities. In the current global market, firms must be certain that such a linkage exists. Information provided by a CMS enables managers to perform strategic analyses on issues such as determining core competencies and organizational constraints from a cost–benefit perspective and assessing the positive and negative financial and nonfinancial factors linked to strategic and operational plans. Thus, the CMS generates information for effective strategic resource management. For example, Walmart includes its mission statement on its website: "We save people money so they can live better."[2] Without a well-designed CMS, Walmart could not evaluate its progress toward accomplishing that mission. Thus, a CMS is instrumental in providing a foundation for companies with an organizational culture emphasizing cost savings and continuous improvement.

The world of business competition is dynamic and creative managers are constantly devising new business practices and innovative approaches to competition. Adapting to change requires that a CMS be flexible. A CMS system, for instance, must be able to support centralized or decentralized structures as discussed in the next section.

REVIEW 13-1 | **LO13-1** | **Cost Management System Roles in an Organization**

a. Match each of the following roles of a cost management system, 1 through 6, with the most appropriate example, *a* through *f*.

continued

---

[2] Wal-Mart Stores, Inc., "Frequently Asked Questions," https://stock.walmart.com/resources/investor-faqs/default.aspx (last accessed 10/25/2023).

continued from previous page

Cost Management System Role	Example
1. Develop accurate product/service costs	a. ___ Analyzing 5 years of warranty expense after an investment in a product update
2. Assess product/service life cycle performance	b. ___ Articulating how costs are accumulated in each particular job in a job costing system
3. Improve understanding of processes/activities	c. ___ Comparing quarterly revenue by major product to the prior year
4. Control costs	d. ___ Determining the financial and nonfinancial implications of a business purchase
5. Measure performance	e. ___ Determining total material variance and its quantity and usage components
6. Support organizational goals	f. ___ Using activity-based costing to determine the cost of providing a specific service

b. **Critical Thinking:** Does a company need to complete the types of tasks listed above in a cost management system with a high-level of accuracy to achieve its short-term and long-term goals? Why or why not?

More practice: E13-23, E13-25, E13-27
Solution on p. 13-58.

DECENTRALIZATION

The degree of centralization can be viewed as a *continuum*. With **centralization**, a single individual (usually the company owner or president) makes all major decisions and retains full authority and responsibility for that organization's activities. Alternatively, a purely decentralized organization would have virtually no central authority, and each subunit would act as a totally independent entity. **Decentralization** is a transfer of authority, responsibility, and decision-making rights from the top to the bottom of the organizational structure. Decentralization has both advantages and disadvantages, which are summarized in **Exhibit 13.5**.

LO13-2 Which factors determine whether a firm should be decentralized or centralized?

Exhibit 13.5 ■ Advantages and Disadvantages of Decentralization

Advantages
- Help top management recognize and develop managerial talent
- Allow managerial performance to be comparatively evaluated
- Can often lead to greater job satisfaction and provide job enrichment
- Make the accomplishment of organizational goals and objectives easier
- Reduce decision-making time
- Allow the use of management by exception

Disadvantages
- Can result in a lack of goal congruence or in suboptimization by subunit managers
- Require more effective communication abilities because decision making is removed from the home office
- Can create personnel difficulties upon introduction, especially if managers are unwilling or unable to delegate effectively
- Can be extremely expensive, including costs of training and of poor decision making

Either extreme of the centralization–decentralization continuum represents a clearly undesirable arrangement. In a totally centralized organization, a single individual would have neither the expertise nor sufficient and timely information to make effective decisions in all functional areas. In a totally decentralized organization, subunits could act in ways that are inconsistent with the whole entity's goals. An organization usually determines the appropriate degree of decentralization based on a combination of the

- managers' personal preferences,
- nature of decisions required for organizational growth, and
- types of activities in which the organization is engaged.

DEMO 13-2 LO13-2 Determining How Company Factors Impact Degree of Decentralization

◆ **How do each of the factors provided impact the degree of decentralization?**

Listed below are the characteristics of pure centralization and pure decentralization for each factor.

Degree of Decentralization in an Organizational Structure

FACTOR	Pure Centralization	→	Pure Decentralization
1. Age of organization	Young	→	Mature
2. Size of organization	Small	→	Large
3. Stage of product development	Stable	→	Growth
4. Growth rate of organization	Slow	→	Rapid
5. Expected impact on profits of incorrect decisions	High	→	Low
6. Top management's confidence in staff	Low	→	High
7. Historical degree of control in organization	Tight	→	Moderate or loose
8. Geographical diversity of operations	Local	→	Widespread
9. Cost of communications	Low	→	High
10. Ability to resolve conflicts	Easy	→	Difficult
11. Level of employee motivation	Low	→	Moderate to high
12. Level of organizational flexibility	Low	→	High
13. Time of response to changes	Slow	→	Rapid

Organizations tend to structure themselves according to the factors listed in Demo 13-2. Most businesses, however, are somewhere along the continuum.

Shared Services

Decentralization does not necessarily mean that a unit manager has the authority to make all decisions for that unit. Top management selectively determines the types of authority to delegate to, and withhold from, lower-level managers. Even highly decentralized companies often have certain organizational functions made centrally. The provision of a support function for various organizational units from a central location is often referred to as a **shared service**. Typical support functions are accounting/cash management, human resources, information technology, legal, and procurement. Whereas such services may be performed in-house at headquarters for decentralized units, organizations may also opt to outsource these functions to consultants or independent contractors.

Indication of a Need for Shared Services

Positive answers to the following questions may indicate that a particular organizational function should be centralized rather than being performed at multiple locations:

- Should the function be performed in a consistent manner throughout the organization?
- Are specialized skills/expertise, coordinated training, and/or a "best practices" model needed to perform the function effectively?
- Can the function be performed effectively without detailed interactions or coordination between the performers and the organizational units?
- Is there a high risk of negative impact to the organization if the function is performed incorrectly or improperly?
- Are there substantial monetary economies of scale if the function is performed centrally?
- Will the process be completed more rapidly if the function is performed centrally?
- Is there a distinct need (such as an ethical, sustainable, or a legal purpose) for organizational accountability for the function's performance?

Exhibit 13.6 provides some points for management to consider when deciding to centralize as a shared service or decentralize the responsibility for environmental issues, or more broadly, ESG considerations.

Exhibit 13.6 ■ Decentralization/Centralization Considerations for Environmental Issues

Decentralize Responsibility and Decision Making

- Local management is better informed and aware of local environmental problems, concerns, and requirements.
- Local management is more attuned to local laws related to environmental use.
- Decentralized responsibility will result in a higher motivation for management's more efficient and effective usage of natural resources.
- Decision making will be more reflective of local population input; local information is less likely to be "lost" in organizational aggregation of data.
- Decisions about problems can be made rapidly and without organizational bureaucracy.
- Greater opportunity may exist for governmental negotiation in the event of environmental failures because decision making was local rather than "external."
- Distrust of external influence may exist in the local population and/or political organizations.

Centralize Responsibility and Decision Making

- Decentralized units may make conflicting environmental decisions, especially if there is a difference in local laws.
- Decentralized units may lack environmental expertise, creating a need for additional communication and coordination.
- New regulations are enacted with broad implications on businesses, which could result in high costs for the organization if responses are insufficient.
- A greater level of transparency is likely because all environmental decisions will be made based on similar rules and policies.
- Fewer conflicts of interest relative to performance evaluation can exist among decentralized managers.
- More proactive decisions may be made if local influence differences are eliminated.
- Environmental protection is more likely to be seen as part of the organizational culture if established and monitored centrally.

A movement toward delegation of more authority to lower levels, increases the importance of an effective reporting system. An information system must provide relevant and timely information to the individuals who are making decisions that have cost control implications, and a MCS must be in place to evaluate the quality of those decisions. Top managers depend on the reporting system to keep all organizational subunits aligned with their subunit missions as well as with organizational goals and objectives. Reporting in a decentralized environment is discussed in the next section.

REVIEW 13-2

Centralization vs. Decentralization — LO13-2

a. Indicate whether each of the following descriptions is more characteristic of a centralized (C) or decentralized (D) company.

Description	Centralized	Decentralized
1. Hires highly motivated employees	_____	_____
2. Prioritizes training of employees at all levels	_____	_____
3. Has one owner, actively involved in operations	_____	_____
4. Is in the start-up stage	_____	_____
5. Has operations domestically and internationally	_____	_____
6. Is experiencing a rapid rate of growth	_____	_____
7. Delegates responsibilities	_____	_____
8. Establishes a uniform set of goals and objectives	_____	_____
9. Has total sales of $10,000	_____	_____
10. Has products in the growth stage of product development	_____	_____

b. **Critical Thinking:** During the pandemic, did companies generally move toward centralization or decentralization? Why?

More practice: MC13-16, E13-28, E13-29
Solution on p. 13-59.

RESPONSIBILITY ACCOUNTING SYSTEMS

LO13-3 How do responsibility reports help management conduct control activities?

A **responsibility accounting system** facilitates decentralization by providing information about the performance, efficiency, and effectiveness of organizational subunits and their managers. Responsibility accounting is the key management control tool in a decentralized organization.

Control Activities in a Responsibility Accounting System

A responsibility accounting system helps organizational unit managers to conduct the five basic control activities.

1. Prepare a plan (e.g., using budgets and standards) and use it to communicate output expectations and delegate authority.
2. Gather, record, summarize, and classify actual data for the unit in accordance with the organizational plan's specified activities and categories.
3. Compare and monitor the differences between planned and actual data at scheduled intervals. To assess performance, comparisons should be made using both flexible budgets at the actual activity level as well as the master budget.
4. Exert managerial influence in response to significant differences. Because of day-to-day contact with operations, unit managers should be aware of any significant variances before they are reported, identify the variance causes, and attempt to correct any problems. In contrast, top management might not know about operational variances until variance reports are received. By that time, subordinate managers should have corrected the problems causing the variances or have explanations as to why the problems were not or could not be resolved.
5. Continue comparing data and responding; at the appropriate time, the process will begin again. An important aspect of this control process is the preparation and analysis of a variance report, a type of responsibility report.

Responsibility Reports

A responsibility accounting system produces **responsibility reports** that assist each successively higher level of management in evaluating the performances of subordinate managers and their respective organizational units.

Monetary and Nonmonetary Information The reports should be tailored to fit the subordinate managers' planning, controlling, and decision-making needs and should include both monetary and nonmonetary information. **Exhibit 13.7** provides examples of information that is shown in responsibility reports. Depending on the type of responsibility unit for which the report is being generated, all types of information shown are not necessarily available.

Exhibit 13.7 ■ Information for Responsibility Reports

Monetary
- Budgeted and actual revenues
- Budgeted and actual costs (computed on a comparable basis)
- Variance computations for revenues and costs
- Asset investment base

Nonmonetary
- Capacity measures (theoretical and that used to compute predetermined overhead rates)
- Target rate of earnings on investment base
- Desired and actual market share
- Departmental or divisional throughput

continued

continued from previous page

Nonmonetary (continued)
- Number of defects (by product, product line, and supplier)
- Number of orders backlogged (by date, cost, and selling price)
- Number of customer complaints (by type and product); method of complaint resolution
- Percentage of orders delivered on time

- Manufacturing (or service) cycle efficiency
- Percentage of reduction of non-value-added time from previous reporting period (broken down by idle time, storage time, move time, and quality control time)
- Number and percentage of employee suggestions considered significant and practical
- Number and percentage of employee suggestions implemented
- Number of unplanned production interruptions or schedule changes
- Number and significance of environmental "instances"
- Number of engineering change orders; percentage change from previous period
- Number of safety violations; percentage change from previous period
- Number of days of employee absences; percentage change from previous period

Controllable and Noncontrollable Costs A manager's responsibility report should reflect the degree of the manager's influence and should include only the revenues and/or costs under that manager's control. Normally, some of an organizational unit's revenues or costs are noncontrollable (or only partially or indirectly controllable) by the unit manager. In such instances, the responsibility accounting report should separately classify all reported monetary information as controllable or noncontrollable by the manager. Alternatively, separate reports should be prepared for the organizational unit (showing all monetary amounts) and for the unit manager (showing only those monetary amounts under the manager's control).

Multilevel Reports Responsibility reports reflect the upward flow of information from operational units to company top management and illustrate the broadening scope of responsibility. Managers receive detailed information on the performance of their immediate control areas and summary information on all organizational units for which the managers are responsible. Summarizing results causes a pyramiding of information into a **multilevel responsibility report**. Reports at the lowest-level units are highly detailed, whereas more general information is reported to the top of the organization. Upper-level managers desiring more detail than is provided in summary reports can obtain it by reviewing subordinates' responsibility reports.

Variance Analysis Variances are itemized in performance reports at the lower levels so that the appropriate manager has the necessary details to take any required corrective action related to significant variances.[3] Under the **management-by-exception principle**, major deviations from expectations are highlighted under the subordinate manager's reporting section to assist upper-level managers in determining whether they need to become involved in subordinates' operations. In addition, such detailed variance analyses alert operating managers to items that require explanations for upper management.

Analyzing a Multilevel Responsibility Report with Variances — LO13-3 DEMO 13-3

The multilevel responsibility report on the following page shows the variance results for June for Kemp Company. Each area's budget is presented for comparative purposes. Production department data are aggregated or "rolled up" with data of the other departments under the production vice president's control. Similarly, the total costs of the production vice president's responsibility area are combined with other costs for which the company president is responsible.

---

[3] In practice, the variances presented in Demo 13-3 would be further separated into the portions representing price and quantity effects as shown in Chapter 10 on standard costing.

Kemp Company Responsibility Report (June)

President's Performance Report

	Budget	Actual	Variance Fav. (Unfav.)
Administrative office—president	$1,192,000	$1,196,800	$ (4,800)
Financial vice president	944,000	936,400	7,600
Production vice president	2,951,984	2,977,600	(25,616)
Sales vice president	1,100,000	1,105,600	(5,600)
Totals	$6,187,984	$6,216,400	$(28,416)

Production Vice President's Performance Report

	Budget	Actual	Variance Fav. (Unfav.)
Administrative office—vice president	$ 720,000	$ 728,800	$ (8,800)
Distribution and storage	498,800	504,000	(5,200)
Production department	1,733,184	1,744,800	(11,616)
Totals	$2,951,984	$2,977,600	$(25,616)

Distribution and Storage Manager's Performance Report

	Budget	Actual	Variance Fav. (Unfav.)
Direct material	$ 144,000	$ 141,600	$ 2,400
Direct labor	218,000	221,200	(3,200)
Supplies	18,800	21,200	(2,400)
Indirect labor	94,400	95,200	(800)
Repairs and maintenance	14,000	14,800	(800)
Other	9,600	10,000	(400)
Totals	$ 498,800	$ 504,000	$ (5,200)

Production Department Manager's Performance Report

	Budget	Actual	Variance Fav. (Unfav.)
Direct material	$ 477,200	$ 490,000	$(12,800)
Direct labor	763,520	752,108	11,412
Supplies	70,624	74,000	(3,376)
Indirect labor	185,152	188,080	(2,928)
Depreciation	154,612	154,612	0
Repairs and maintenance	49,628	51,600	(1,972)
Other	32,448	34,400	(1,952)
Totals	$1,733,184	$1,744,800	$(11,616)

◆ **Following the management-by-exception principle, which variance would each manager most likely be interested in analyzing, if variances over $10,000 are generally considered to be significant?**

- The production department manager would likely consider the unfavorable direct material variance of $12,800 and the favorable direct labor variance of $11,412 to be significant. These variance would likely require further explanation to the production vice president.
- The distribution and storage manager would not likely investigate the variances as they are under the general threshold for significance.
- The production vice president would be most concerned about the unfavorable production department variance which ties back to the production department manager's findings.
- The president would be most concerned about the unfavorable variance from the production vice president's report, of which, the production department variance is the most significant of the variances.

Challenges of Responsibility Accounting As Demo 13-3 illustrates, as each department is rolled up into another, the variances are aggregated. However, aggregation of information to each successively higher level allows potentially important details to be buried. If different units within the responsibility accounting system compete with each other for resources, managers could try to "promote their own agendas" by blaming problems on other organizational units. Alternatively, the competition could lead to a lack of goal congruence between or among organizational units. **Goal congruence** exists when the personal and organizational goals of decision makers throughout the firm are consistent and mutually supportive. Additionally, partitioning each responsibility unit as a separate part of the report might obscure interdependencies among units.

Responsibility accounting's focus is on the manager who has control over a particular cost object. In a decentralized company, the cost object is an organizational unit or *responsibility center*, such as a division, department, or geographical region.

Responsibility Report **LO13-3** **REVIEW 13-3**

The following costs were incurred for the month of June for the Process A23 Department.

	Budget	Actual
Sales in units	50,000	55,000
Variable manufacturing costs		
Direct material	$500,000	$522,500
Direct labor	225,000	236,500
Variable factory overhead	200,000	227,700
Fixed manufacturing costs		
Indirect labor	284,800	284,900
Depreciation	78,000	77,800
Property tax	25,000	25,000
Insurance	21,000	22,000
Other	18,000	18,000
Allocated corporate cost	35,000	35,000

a. Use this information to prepare a responsibility report for the month of June. (*Hint:* Convert the static budget to a flexible budget as described in Chapter 10.)

b. **Critical Thinking:** From part *a*, what is the most significant variance that management would need to investigate? Are small dollar variances always insignificant in that they do not require additional analysis?

More practice: E13-32, E13-33
Solution on p. 13-59.

TYPES OF RESPONSIBILITY CENTERS

Responsibility accounting systems identify, measure, and report on the performance of responsibility centers and their managers. **Responsibility centers** are generally classified according to their manager's scope of authority and type of financial responsibility: costs, revenues, profits, and/or asset base. The four primary types of responsibility centers are illustrated in **Exhibit 13.8** and discussed in the following sections.

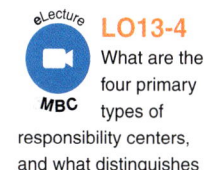

LO13-4
What are the four primary types of responsibility centers, and what distinguishes them from each other?

Exhibit 13.8 ■ Types of Responsibility Centers

Cost Center	Revenue Center	Profit Center	Investment Center
Manager is responsible for cost control	Manager is responsible for revenue generation	Manager is responsible for revenues, expenses, and net income	Manager is responsible for revenues, expenses, net income, and return on asset base

Cost Center

A **cost center** is an organizational unit whose manager has the authority only to incur costs and is specifically evaluated on the basis of how well costs are controlled. Such units (usually service and administrative departments) do not generate revenues or charge for services, but they do incur costs. The human resources, customer service, and accounting departments of most companies would likely be considered cost centers. In a traditional manufacturing environment, the production department is the largest cost center; individual assembly lines within the production department could also be viewed as separate cost centers. In a hospital, nursing, housekeeping, security, and medical records are typically designated as cost centers.

In some instances, a cost center can generate revenues, but the revenues are either not under the manager's control or not effectively measurable. The first situation exists in a community library that is provided a specific proration of property tax dollars but has no authority to levy or collect the related taxes. The second situation is reflected in research and development centers in which the outputs (revenues or benefits generated from the cost inputs) are not easily measured. In these two types of situations, revenues should *not* be included in the manager's responsibility accounting report.

Cost center managers often concentrate only on unfavorable standard cost variances and ignore the efficient performance indicated by favorable variances. However, significant favorable variances should not be disregarded if the management-by-exception principle is applied properly. Using this principle, top management should investigate all variances (both favorable and unfavorable) that fall outside the range of acceptable deviations.

Revenue Center

A **revenue center** is strictly defined as an organizational unit that is responsible for generating revenues and has no control over setting selling prices or budgeting costs. For instance, in many retail stores, each sales department is considered an independent unit, and managers are evaluated based on their departments' total revenues. Departmental managers, however, might have no authority to adjust selling prices to affect volume, and often they do not participate in the budgeting process. Additionally, the departmental managers might have no ability to affect costs. In a hospital, revenue centers might include the radiology, newborn intensive care, cancer care, and sleep disorders centers; a revenue center classification is likely if the hospital receives the majority of its funding from governmental sources that limit service payments to specific amounts based on the indicated DRG (diagnostic-related group) classification.

In most instances, pure revenue centers do not exist because managers are also responsible for managing some costs in their centers. A more appropriate term for such organizational units is a *revenue and limited cost center*.

Profit Center

A **profit center** is an organizational unit whose manager is responsible for generating revenues and managing expenses related to current activity. Thus, profit centers should be independent organizational units whose managers

- have the ability to obtain resources at the most economical prices,
- sell products at prices that will maximize revenue, and
- have a goal of maximizing the center's profit.

Costs not under a profit center manager's control are those related to long-term investments in plant assets; as such, separate evaluations should be made for the unit and its manager.

Investment Center

An **investment center** is an organizational unit whose manager is responsible for managing both revenues and expenses. In addition, the center's manager has the authority to acquire, use, and dispose of plant assets to earn the highest feasible rate of return on the center's asset base. Many investment centers are independent, freestanding divisions or corporate subsidiaries. This independence gives investment center managers the opportunity to make decisions about all matters affecting their organizational units and to be judged on the outcomes of those decisions. Because of their closeness to daily divisional activities, investment center managers should have more current and detailed knowledge than top management has about sales prices, costs, and other market information.

Regardless of the type of responsibility center overseen, managers will be evaluated on their performance. Thus, each manager may not always act harmoniously to accomplish the organization's goals and may instead act to optimize only his or her own isolated performance and that of his or her responsibility center. Losing sight of the organizational goals while working to achieve an independent responsibility center's conflicting goal results in **suboptimization**, which refers to the pursuit of goals and objectives that reflect personal, rather than organizational, best interests.

Chapter 13 Responsibility Accounting, Support Department Cost Allocations, and Transfer Pricing

A unique challenge for the design of responsibility centers arises from the instance in which one responsibility center supplies its outputs largely to other internal responsibility centers. In determining a unit's responsibility classification, top management often makes judgments about the nature and extent of the costs and revenues to include in those responsibility centers. Frequently, rather than attempting to make performance assessments about cost centers, management assigns costs incurred in cost centers to operating areas through a process of support department cost allocation. Alternatively, management can attempt to "create" revenues for the cost center by using an internal transfer pricing system for the center's tangible or intangible output that is used by other company units.

Identifying Responsibility Centers — LO13-4 — DEMO 13-4

◆ **Consider a retail store such as a Target store. What is an example of a cost center, revenue center, profit center, and investment center?**

Cost center An example of a cost center is the store's maintenance department. The department would control costs of maintaining the store, such as cleaning, repairs, and grounds upkeep, but it would not be responsible for the store revenue.

Revenue center An example of a revenue center is the electronics store sales team. If we assume the sales team is responsible for meeting store sales targets (and is not responsible for product costs), the sales team would be evaluated on the generation of revenue only.

Profit center An example of a profit center is the Furniture Department. If we assume the department is responsible for both ordering and selling furniture, the department could be evaluated on both revenue and costs of the department.

Investment center We can consider the entire store as an investment center. The store manager would be responsible for the profits as well as the return on the store's asset investments.

Responsibility Centers — LO13-4 — REVIEW 13-4

a. For each of the following organizational units, indicate whether the unit would most likely be classified as a cost center (C), a revenue center (R), a profit center (P), or an investment center (I).
   1. ___ A home cleaning service business
   2. ___ A specific Target store
   3. ___ Assembly department of a manufacturing company
   4. ___ Department of motor vehicles office
   5. ___ Battery division of Panasonic
   6. ___ Sales staff selling media ads
   7. ___ Information technology support department for a manufacturing company
   8. ___ Seasonal tax preparation center

b. **Critical Thinking:** How might an information technology support department's actions to successfully optimize its own departmental goals to reduce costs, negatively impact the organization?

More practice: MC13-18, E13-34
Solution on p. 13-59.

SUPPORT DEPARTMENT COST ALLOCATION

Organizations incur two types of overhead costs: those directly related to the operating (or primary revenue-generating) activities and those indirectly related to operating activities. Typically, as the number of product lines or service types increases, so does the need for additional indirectly related activities. **Support departments** include both service and administrative departments.

- **Service departments** (such as central purchasing, maintenance, engineering, security, or warehousing) perform specific functional tasks for other internal units.
- **Administrative departments** perform management activities that benefit the entire organization and include the human resources, accounting, legal, and insurance departments as well as organizational headquarters.

LO13-5 Why and how are support department costs allocated to operating departments?

All support department costs must be covered in the long run by sales of products and services. These costs may be allocated to operating departments to meet the objectives of full cost computation, managerial motivation, and managerial decision making. **Exhibit 13.9** identifies reasons for and against allocating support department costs in relationship to each allocation objective.

Exhibit 13.9 ■ Allocating Service Department Costs: Pros and Cons

Objective: To Compute Full Cost

Reasons *for*:
1. Provides for cost recovery.
2. Instills a consideration of support costs in production managers.
3. Reflects production's "fair share" of support costs.
4. Meets regulations in some pricing instances.

Reasons *against*:
1. Provides costs that are beyond production manager's control.
2. Provides arbitrary costs that are not useful in decision making.
3. Confuses the issues of pricing and costing. Prices should be set high enough so that product sales provide a profit margin large enough to cover all nonproduction costs.

Objective: To Motivate Managers

Reasons *for*:
1. Instills a consideration of support costs in production managers.
2. Relates individual production unit's profits to total company profits.
3. Reflects usage of services on a fair and equitable basis.
4. Encourages production managers to help support departments control costs.
5. Encourages the usage of certain services.

Reasons *against*:
1. Distorts production division's profit figures because allocations are subjective.
2. Includes costs that are beyond production manager's control.
3. Will not materially affect production division's profits.
4. Creates interdivisional ill will when there is lack of agreement about allocation base or method.
5. Is not cost beneficial.

Objective: To Compare Alternative Courses of Action

Reasons *for*:
1. Provides relevant information in determining corporate-wide profits generated by alternative actions.
2. Provides best available estimate of expected cost changes due to alternative actions.

Reasons *against*:
1. Is unnecessary if alternative actions will not change costs.
2. Presents distorted cash flows or profits from alternative actions because allocations are arbitrary.

Source: Adapted from Statements on *Management Accounting Number 4B: Allocation of Service and Administrative Costs* (June 13, 1985), pp. 9–10. Copyright by Institute of Management Accountants. Reproduced with permission of Institute of Management Accountants.

Allocation Bases

If support department costs are to be assigned to revenue-generating areas, a rational and systematic means by which to make the assignment must be developed. An improper cost allocation base will yield distorted cost allocations. A valid allocation base should

- measure the benefit the operating department receives from the support department;
- capture the causal relationship existing between factors in the operating department and costs incurred in the support department;
- reflect the fairness or equity of the allocations among operating departments; and
- measure the ability of operating departments to bear the allocated costs.

The first two criteria are used most often to select allocation bases because these criteria are reasonably objective and will produce rational allocations. Fairness is a valid theoretical basis for allocation, but its use can cause dissension because everyone does not agree on what is fair or equitable. The ability-to-bear criterion often results in unrealistic or profit-detrimental actions: managers might manipulate operating data related to the allocation base to minimize support department allocations. **Exhibit 13.10** indicates some appropriate bases for assigning various types of support department costs.

Exhibit 13.10 ■ Appropriate Service/Administrative Cost Allocation Bases to Divisions/Departments

Type of Cost	Acceptable Allocation Bases
Research and development	Estimated sales; assets employed; new products developed
Personnel functions	Number of employees; number of new hires
Accounting/treasury functions	Estimated time or usage; assets employed; payroll checks issued
Public relations and corporate promotion	Sales; number of advertisements developed; number of advertisements placed
Purchasing function	Dollar value of purchase orders; number of purchase orders; estimated time of usage; percentage of material purchases
Corporate executives' salaries	Sales; assets employed; pretax operating income
Legal, tax, or governmental affairs	Estimated time or usage; sales; assets employed
Property taxes	Square feet; real estate valuation
Data processing	Time of service; volume; storage capacity used; number of data mining searches run
Information technology	Number of service calls; number of computers or other IT devices; dollar value of technology employed
Custodial services	Square footage occupied; total labor hours

Methods of Allocating Support Department Costs

The idea underlying support department cost allocations is that the responsibility centers benefiting from the services provided by support units should bear the costs of such units. Therefore, all the allocation methods intend to accomplish the same result: assign the cost of support departments to their customers. The methods differ merely in their complexity and reliability of results.

Support Department Allocation Methods

Direct Method | Step Method | Algebraic Method

Direct Method The **direct method** assigns support department costs only to operating areas. For example, the human resources department costs can be assigned to production departments based on number of employees, and purchasing department costs can be assigned to production departments based on number of purchase orders generated for each department's manufacturing operations.

Under the direct method, costs associated with a cafeteria, which provides services for operating and other service departments, would be charged only to operating departments.

The direct method is the simplest allocation method, but it may result in distorted cost allocations if there is significant exchange of services between support departments or between support and operating departments.

Step Method In assigning costs, the **step method** allows a partial recognition of the effects of interactions among support departments. This method ranks the quantity of services provided by each support department to other support areas. A **benefits-provided ranking** begins with the support department providing the most service to all other support areas and ends with the support department providing the least service to all other support areas. Then, support department costs are sequentially allocated down the ranking until all costs have been assigned to the operating areas. For example, the human resources department might be the first department listed in the ranking because it provides assistance to all company areas. All other areas, including support areas, would receive an allocation of the human resources department's costs based on the proportion of human resources services used. Many approaches are used to implement the benefits-provided ranking. Two common methods are the dollar volume of services provided and the percentage of total assistance to other support areas.

Algebraic Method The **algebraic method** of allocating support department costs considers all departmental interrelationships and reflects these relationships in simultaneous equations. These equations provide for reciprocal allocation of total support costs among the support departments as well as to the operating departments. No benefits-provided ranking is needed. The algebraic method is the most complex of all the allocation techniques, but it is also the most theoretically correct and, if relationships are properly formulated, provides the most accurate and reliable allocations.

Data for McNally Supplements Co. (MNSC) illustrate the three methods of allocating budgeted support department costs.

- MNSC has two operating divisions: nutritionals and diet aids
- MNSC has three support departments: corporate administration, human resources, and maintenance.

Budgeted revenues for the year are $7,750,000 for nutritionals and $4,500,000 for diet aids. Budgeted costs of each support department are first allocated to each operating division using one of the three methods of support area cost allocation and are then added to the budgeted overhead costs of those divisions to determine an appropriate divisional overhead application rate. **Exhibit 13.11** provides an abbreviated annual budget of the direct and indirect costs for each support department (totals of which are highlighted in yellow) and operating division of MNSC.

Exhibit 13.11 ■ McNally Supplements Co. Budgeted Departmental and Divisional Costs

	Administration	Human Resources	Maintenance	Nutritionals	Diet Aids	Total
Direct departmental costs:						
Material	$ 0	$ 0	$ 0	$1,275,600	$ 669,600	$1,945,200
Labor	1,350,000	150,000	360,000	736,200	864,000	3,460,200
Total	$1,350,000	$150,000	$360,000	$2,011,800	$1,533,600	$5,405,400
Departmental overhead*	1,651,200	69,750	238,200	1,677,000	267,600	3,903,750
Total initial departmental costs	$3,001,200	$219,750	$598,200	$3,688,800	$1,801,200	$9,309,150

*Would be specified by type and cost behavior in actual budgeting process.

Exhibit 13.12 presents the bases selected for allocating MNSC's support department costs. These bases are proxies for the quantity of services consumed by each service area and operating division. The support departments are listed in a *benefits-provided ranking*. Management determined that administration provides the most assistance to all other support areas, human resources is second in the rank ordering, and maintenance supports only the operating areas (equipment used in other areas is under a lease maintenance arrangement and is not serviced by the company's maintenance department). All product research and development is conducted in a separate subsidiary company.

Exhibit 13.12 ■ Service Department Allocation Bases

Administration costs—allocated based on dollars of assets employed
Human resources costs—allocated based on number of employees
Maintenance costs—allocated based on machine hours used

	Dollars of Assets Employed	Number of Employees	Number of Machine Hours Used
Administration	$12,000,000	24	0
Human resources	3,600,000	6	0
Maintenance	6,000,000	18	0
Nutritionals	30,000,000	75	258,000
Diet aids	24,000,000	21	64,500

Direct Allocation Method   LO13-5   DEMO 13-5A

In the direct method of allocation, support department costs are assigned using the specified bases only to the operating areas.

◆ **How are support department costs allocated to nutritionals and diet aids using the direct allocation method?**

The direct method cost allocation for McNally Supplements Co. is shown in the following schedule.

Direct Allocation of Service Department Costs

	A	B	C	D	E	F
1		Base	Proportion of Total Base		Amount to Allocate	Amount Allocated
2	Administration costs (dollars of assets employed)					
3	Nutritionals	$30,000,000	30,000,000 ÷ 54,000,000 =	56%*	$3,001,200	**$1,680,672**
4	Diet aids	24,000,000	24,000,000 ÷ 54,000,000 =	44%*	3,001,200	1,320,528
5	Total	$54,000,000		100%		$3,001,200
6	Human resources costs (number of employees)					
7	Nutritionals	75	75 ÷ 96 =	78%*	$ 219,750	**$ 171,405**
8	Diet aids	21	21 ÷ 96 =	22%*	219,750	48,345
9	Total	96		100%		$ 219,750
10	Maintenance costs (number of machine hours used)					
11	Nutritionals	258,000	258,000 ÷ 322,500 =	80%	$ 598,200	**$ 478,560**
12	Diet aids	64,500	64,500 ÷ 322,500 =	20%	598,200	119,640
13	Total	322,500		100%		$ 598,200
14	*Rounded.					

Use of the direct method of support department allocation produces the total budgeted costs for nutritionals and diet aids, as shown in the following schedule. If budgeted revenues and costs equal actual revenues and costs, nutritionals would show a profit of $1,730,563, or 22.3 percent on revenues ($1,730,563 ÷ $7,750,000), and diet aids would show a profit of $1,210,287, or 26.9 percent on revenues ($1,210,287 ÷ $4,500,000).

Budgeted Before-Tax Profits Using the Direct Allocation Method

	A	B	C	D	E	F	G
1					**Nutritionals**	**Diet Aids**	**Total**
2	Total budgeted revenues (a)				$7,750,000	$4,500,000	$12,250,000
3	Direct costs (**Exhibit 13.11**)				2,011,800	1,533,600	3,545,400
4	Indirect costs						
5	Department overhead (**Exhibit 13.11**)				1,677,000	267,600	1,944,600
6	Allocated overhead (direct method)						
7	From administration				$1,680,672	$1,320,528	$3,001,200
8	From human resources				171,405	48,345	219,750
9	From maintenance				478,560	119,640	598,200
10	Subtotal				$2,330,637	$1,488,513	$3,819,150
11	Total overhead (for OH application rate determination)				4,007,637	1,756,113	5,763,750
12	Total budgeted costs (b)				6,019,437	3,289,713	9,309,150
13	Total budgeted before-tax profits (a – b)				$1,730,563	$1,210,287	**$2,940,850**
14			Verification of Allocation to				
15		**Administration**	**Human Resources**	**Maintenance**	**Nutritionals**	**Diet Aids**	**Total**
16	Initial costs	$3,001,200	$219,750	$598,200			$3,819,150
17	Costs from						
18	Administration	(3,001,200)			$1,680,672	$1,320,528	0
19	Human resources		(219,750)		171,405	48,345	0
20	Maintenance			(598,200)	478,560	119,640	0
21	Totals	$ 0	$ 0	$ 0	$2,330,637	$1,488,513	$3,819,150

DEMO 13-5B LO13-5 — Step Method Allocation

To apply the step method allocation, the benefits-provided ranking specified in **Exhibit 13.12** is used. (Administration first, human resources next, and maintenance last.) Costs are assigned using an appropriate, specified allocation base to the departments receiving support. After costs have been assigned from a department, no costs are charged back to that department. This means that the order in which the costs are applied makes a difference in the amount of service costs allocated to each operating department.

♦ **How are support department costs allocated to departments using the step allocation method?**

Step method allocation of MNSC support costs is shown in the schedule on the following page. First, the original administration cost of $3,001,200 is allocated to the two operating departments and to the remaining two service departments (human resources and maintenance). Next, total human resources cost of $399,822 is allocated to the two operating departments and to the remaining service department (maintenance).

$219,750 Original cost + $180,072 Allocated cost from administration = $399,822

Lastly, the total maintenance cost of $932,280 is allocated to the two operating departments.

$598,200 Original cost + $270,108 Allocated cost from administration
+ $63,972 Allocated cost from human resources = $932,280.

Chapter 13 Responsibility Accounting, Support Department Cost Allocations, and Transfer Pricing

Step Method Allocation to Revenue-Producing Areas

	A	B	C	D	E	F
1		Base	Proportion of Total Base		Amount to Allocate	Amount Allocated
2	Allocate first: Administration costs (dollars of assets employed)					
3	Human resources	$ 3,600,000	3,600,000 ÷ 63,600,000 =	6%*	$3,001,200	$ 180,072
4	Maintenance	6,000,000	6,000,000 ÷ 63,600,000 =	9%*	3,001,200	270,108
5	Nutritionals	30,000,000	30,000,000 ÷ 63,600,000 =	47%*	3,001,200	1,410,564
6	Diet aids	24,000,000	24,000,000 ÷ 63,600,000 =	38%*	3,001,200	1,140,456
7	Total	$63,600,000		100%		$3,001,200
8	Allocate second: Human resources costs (number of employees)					
9	Maintenance	18	18 ÷ 114 =	16%*	$ 399,822	$ 63,972
10	Nutritionals	75	75 ÷ 114 =	66%*	399,822	263,882
11	Diet aids	21	21 ÷ 114 =	18%*	399,822	71,968
12	Total	114		100%		$ 399,822
13	Allocate third: Maintenance costs (number of machine hours used)					
14	Nutritionals	258,000	258,000 ÷ 322,500 =	80%	$ 932,280	$ 745,824
15	Diet aids	64,500	64,500 ÷ 322,500 =	20%	932,280	186,456
16	Total	322,500		100%		$ 932,280
17	* Rounded.					

In this case, the amount of support department costs assigned to each operating area differs only slightly between the step and direct methods. However, in many situations, the difference can be substantial. If budgeted revenues and costs equal the actual revenues and costs for that year, the step method allocation process will cause nutritionals and diet aids to show the following profits.

Budgeted Before-Tax Profits Using Step Method Allocation

	A	B	C	D	E	F	G
1					Nutritionals	Diet Aids	Total
2	Total budgeted revenues (a)				$7,750,000	$4,500,000	$12,250,000
3	Direct costs (**Exhibit 13.11**)				2,011,800	1,533,600	3,545,400
4	Indirect costs						
5	Department overhead (**Exhibit 13.11**)				1,677,000	267,600	1,944,600
6	Allocated overhead (step method)						
7	From administration				$1,410,564	$1,140,456	$ 2,551,020
8	From human resources				263,882	71,968	335,850
9	From maintenance				745,824	186,456	932,280
10	Subtotal				$2,420,270	$1,398,880	$ 3,819,150
11	Total overhead (for OH application rate determination)				4,097,270	1,666,480	5,763,750
12	Total budgeted costs (b)				6,109,070	3,200,080	9,309,150
13	Total budgeted before-tax profits (a – b)				$1,640,930	$1,299,920	$ 2,940,850
14				Verification of Allocation to			
15		Administration	Human Resources	Maintenance	Nutritionals	Diet Aids	Total
16	Initial costs	$ 3,001,200	$ 219,750	$ 598,200			$3,819,150
17	Costs from						
18	Administration	(3,001,200)	180,072	270,108	$1,410,564	$1,140,456	0
19	Human resources		(399,822)	63,972	263,882	71,968	0
20	Maintenance			(932,280)	745,824	186,456	0
21	Totals	$ 0	$ 0	$ 0	$2,420,270	$1,398,880	$3,819,150

These profit figures reflect rates of return on revenues of 21.2 percent ($1,640,930 ÷ $7,750,000) and 28.9 percent ($1,299,920 ÷ $4,500,000), respectively.

The step method is a hybrid between the direct and the algebraic methods. This allocation approach is more realistic than the direct method in that the step method partially recognizes the exchange of services among support departments. Under this allocation process, a support department is "eliminated" once its costs have been assigned. Assistance provided by a support department further down the ranking sequence is not recognized as being given to departments higher in the benefits-provided ranking.

DEMO 13-5C LO13-5 — Algebraic Allocation Method

By recognizing all interrelationships among departments and making no decision about a rank ordering of support departments, the algebraic method of allocation eliminates the step method's two shortfalls. The algebraic method requires a set of equations be formulated to reflect reciprocal service among departments. Solving these equations simultaneously recognizes the fact that support departments both give and receive services.

◆ **How are support department costs allocated to nutritionals and diet aids using the algebraic allocation method?**

The algebraic method's starting point is choosing which base to use for measuring each department's consumption of services. A schedule is created to show each department's proportionate usage of the other departments' services. These proportions are then used to develop equations that, when solved simultaneously, give cost allocations that fully recognize the reciprocal services provided.

Using the bases shown in **Exhibit 13.12**, the allocation proportions for all departments of MNSC are shown below. The human resources department allocation is discussed to illustrate the derivation of these proportions. The allocation basis for human resources cost is number of employees. MNSC has 138 employees, excluding those in the human resources department. Human resources employees are ignored because costs are being removed from that department and assigned to other areas. Because maintenance has 18 employees, the proportionate amount of human resources services used by maintenance is 18 ÷ 138 or 13 percent (rounded).

	A	B	C	D	E	F	G
1	**Interdepartmental Proportional Relationships**	Administration (Dollars of Assets Employed)		Human Resources (Number of Employees)		Maintenance (Number of Machine Hours Used)	
2		Base	Percent*	Base	Percent*	Base	Percent*
3	Administration	N/A	N/A	24	18%	0	0%
4	Human resources	$ 3,600,000	6%	N/A	N/A	0	0
5	Maintenance	6,000,000	9	18	13	N/A	N/A
6	Nutritionals	30,000,000	47	75	54	258,000	80
7	Diet aids	24,000,000	38	21	15	64,500	20
8	Total	$63,600,000	100%	138	100%	322,500	100%
9	*Rounded.						

By using the calculated percentages, algebraic equations representing the interdepartmental usage of services can be formulated. The departments are labeled A (Administration), H (Human Resources), and M (Maintenance) in the equations. Initial costs of each support department are shown first in the formulas.

$$A = \$3{,}001{,}200 + 0.18H + 0.00M$$
$$H = \$219{,}750 + 0.06A + 0.00M$$
$$M = \$598{,}200 + 0.09A + 0.13H$$

These equations are solved simultaneously by substituting one equation into the others, gathering like terms, and reducing the unknowns until only one unknown exists. The value for this unknown is then computed and substituted into the remaining equations. This process is continued until all unknowns have been eliminated.

1. Substituting the equation for A into the equation for H gives the following.

$$H = \$219{,}750 + 0.06(\$3{,}001{,}200 + 0.18H) + 0.00M$$

Multiplying and combining terms produces the following results.

$$H = \$219{,}750 + \$180{,}072 + 0.01H$$
$$H = \$399{,}822 + 0.01H$$
$$H - 0.01H = \$399{,}822$$
$$0.99H = \$399{,}822$$
$$H = \$403{,}861$$

2. The value for H is substituted in the administration equation.

$$A = \$3{,}001{,}200 + 0.18(\$403{,}861) + 0.00M$$
$$A = \$3{,}001{,}200 + \$72{,}695$$
$$A = \$3{,}073{,}895$$

3. Substituting the values for A and H into the maintenance equation M gives the following.

$$M = \$598{,}200 + 0.09(\$3{,}073{,}895) + 0.13(\$403{,}861)$$
$$M = \$598{,}200 + \$276{,}651 + \$52{,}502$$
$$M = \$927{,}353$$

The amounts provided by these equations are then allocated among all the departments; costs are allocated both to and from the support areas. The resulting allocations are shown in the schedule that follows. Note that the net amount assigned to all support areas is $0.

Algebraic Solution of Service Department Costs

	A	B	C	D	E	F	G
1	Costs are allocated based on percentages computed in the prior schedule.						
2		Administration		Human Resources		Maintenance	
		Percent	Amount	Percent	Amount	Percent	Amount
3	Administration	N/A	N/A	18%	$ 72,695	0%	$ 0
4	Human resources	6%	$ 184,434	N/A	N/A	0	0
5	Maintenance	9	276,650	13	52,502	N/A	N/A
6	Nutritionals	47	1,444,731	54	218,085	80	741,882
7	Diet aids	38	1,168,080	15	60,579	20	185,471
8	Total	100%	$3,073,895	100%	$403,861	100%	$927,353
9	Note: Allocated amounts rounded to sum to totals.						

The $3,073,895 of administration costs calculated in the algebraic equations above is used to illustrate the computation of the amounts in the schedule above. Administration costs are assigned to the other areas based on dollars of assets employed. Human resources has 6 percent of MNSC's total asset dollars; thus, $184,434 (0.06 × $3,073,895) is assigned to that area. Maintenance has 9 percent of MNSC's total asset dollars; thus, $276,650 (0.09 × $3,073,895) is assigned to that area, and so on. A similar proration process is used for the other departments. Allocations from above are used in the table that follows to determine the reallocated costs and finalize the total budgeted overhead of nutritionals and diet aids.

Algebraic Method Allocation to Revenue-Producing Areas

	A	B	C	D	E	F	G
1		Total Service Department Costs (from equations)	Administration	Human Resources	Maintenance	Nutritionals	Diet Aids
2	Administration	$3,073,895	$ 0	$ 184,434	$ 276,650	**$1,444,731**	**$1,168,080**
3	Human resources	403,861	72,695	0	52,502	**218,085**	**60,579**
4	Maintenance	927,353	0	0	0	**741,882**	**185,471**
5	Total costs	$4,405,109	$ 72,695	$ 184,434	$ 329,152	$2,404,698	$1,414,130
6	Less reallocated costs	(586,281)	(72,695)	(184,434)	(329,152)		
7	Budgeted costs	$3,818,828	$ 0	$ 0	$ 0		

If budgeted revenues and costs equal the actual revenues and costs for that year, the algebraic method allocation process will cause nutritionals and diet aids to show the following profits.

Budgeted Before-Tax Profits

	A	B	C	D
1		Nutritionals	Diet Aids	Total
2	Total budgeted revenues (a)	$7,750,000	$4,500,000	$12,250,000
3	Direct costs (**Exhibit 13.11**)	2,011,800	1,533,600	3,545,400
4	Indirect costs			
5	Department overhead (**Exhibit 13.11**)	1,677,000	267,600	1,944,600
6	Allocated overhead (algebraic method)			
7	From administration	**$1,444,731**	**$1,168,080**	$ 2,612,811
8	From human resources	**218,085**	**60,579**	278,664
9	From maintenance	**741,882**	**185,471**	927,353
10	Subtotal	$2,404,698	$1,414,130	$ 3,818,828
11	Total overhead (for OH application rate determination)	4,081,698	1,681,730	5,763,428
12	Total budgeted costs (b)	6,093,498	3,215,330	9,308,828*
13	Total budgeted before-tax profits (a − b)	$1,656,502	$1,284,670	**$ 2,941,172***
14	*Amounts do not agree to total company costs and profits due to rounding difference of $322.			

Standalone Summary of Allocation Methods

Ignoring rounding differences, the total budgeted costs under all three methods is equal to $9,309,150 and, thus, the budgeted before-tax profit under all three methods is equal to $2,940,850 (see each income statement under the direct, step, and algebraic methods). However, the amounts of allocated service cost for the operating departments of nutritionals and diet aids, differ as shown in the following visuals.

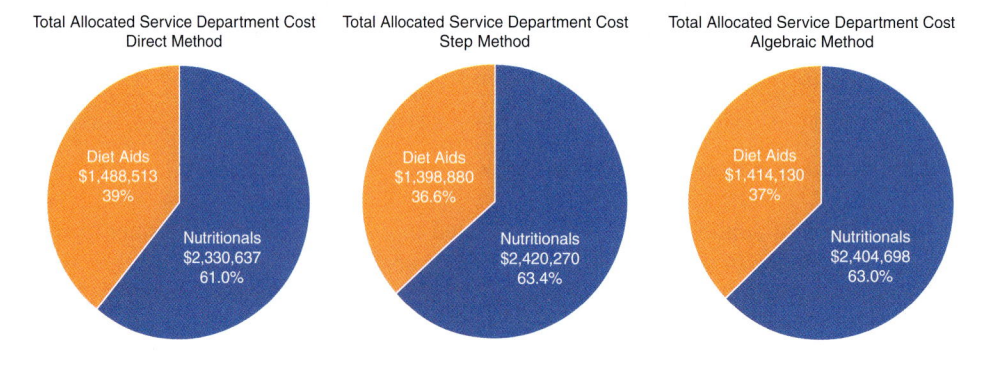

Total Allocated Service Department Cost — Direct Method
- Diet Aids $1,488,513 (39%)
- Nutritionals $2,330,637 (61.0%)

Total Allocated Service Department Cost — Step Method
- Diet Aids $1,398,880 (36.6%)
- Nutritionals $2,420,270 (63.4%)

Total Allocated Service Department Cost — Algebraic Method
- Diet Aids $1,414,130 (37%)
- Nutritionals $2,404,698 (63.0%)

Determining Overhead Application Rates

Regardless of the method used to allocate support department costs, the final step is to determine the overhead application rates for the operating areas. After support department costs have been assigned to production, they are included as part of production overhead and allocated to products or jobs through normal overhead assignment procedures.

As shown in the preceding schedule, the total allocated overhead costs of $4,081,698 and $1,681,730 for nutritionals and diet aids, respectively, will be divided by an appropriate overhead allocation base to assign both manufacturing and nonmanufacturing overhead to products. For example, assume that MNSC has chosen total ounces of diet aid products as the overhead allocation base for diet aids. The division expects to produce 2,250,000 ounces of diet aid products during the year. Thus, the support department overhead cost assigned to each ounce of diet aid product is $0.75 per ounce, calculated as follows.

$$\text{Allocated OH cost per ounce} = \text{Total support cost} \div \text{Total ounces of products}$$
$$= \$1,681,730 \div 2,250,000 \text{ ounces}$$
$$= \$0.75 \text{ per ounce (rounded)}$$

For simplicity, cost behavior in all departments has been ignored. A more appropriate allocation process would specify different bases in each department for the variable and fixed costs. Such differentiation would not change the allocation process but would change the results of the three methods (direct, step, or algebraic). Separation of variable and fixed costs would provide a more accurate allocation.

Before making any allocations, management should be certain that the allocation bases are reasonable. Allocations are often based on the easiest available measure, such as the number of people employed or number of documents processed. Use of such measures can distort the allocation process and result in inappropriate performance evaluations. However, regardless of the allocation method selected, the process of allocation does not change the organization's final profitability—but will change the "profitability" of individual divisions.

Allocating support department costs to operating divisions makes managers more aware of, and responsible for, controlling support service usage. However, if such allocations are made, evaluation of the operating division managers' performance should exclude these allocations. Operating division managers can control their usage of support services but not the actual incurrence of support department costs. The financial performance of an operating department manager should be evaluated using an incremental, rather than a full allocation, approach. For example, the diet aid manager's performance should be evaluated using a predetermined overhead rate based only on the incurrence of departmental overhead cost rather than total overhead cost. Thus, rather than being based on the $0.75 rate calculated earlier, the rate for the manager's performance evaluation would be $0.12 per ounce, calculated as follows.

$$\text{Diet aid departmental OH rate} = \$267,600 \div 2,250,000 \text{ ounces}$$
$$= \$0.12 \text{ per ounce (rounded)}$$

Comprehensive Support Department Allocations — LO13-5 — REVIEW 13-5

Management at Consulting Inc. has decided to allocate costs of the company's two support departments (administration and information technology) to the two revenue-generating consulting departments (financial consulting and operations consulting). Administration costs are to be allocated on the basis of dollars of assets employed; Information technology (IT) costs are to be allocated on the basis of number of employees. The following costs and allocation bases are available:

Department	Direct Costs	Number of Employees	Assets Employed
Administration............	$ 547,050	8	$ 270,970
Information technology....	344,890	6	204,190
Financial consulting......	870,565	20	968,050
Operations consulting.....	658,500	10	375,400
Totals................	$2,421,005	44	$1,818,610

a. Using the direct method, allocate the support department costs to the revenue-generating departments. (Round to the nearest whole percent and dollar.)

continued

continued from previous page

b. Using your answer to (a), what are the total costs of the revenue-generating departments after the allocations?

c. Assuming that the benefits-provided ranking is the order shown in the table, use the step method to allocate the support department costs to the revenue-generating departments.

d. Using your answer to (c), what are the total costs of the revenue-generating departments after the allocations?

e. Using the algebraic method, allocate the support department costs to the revenue-generating departments.

f. Using your answer to (c), what are the total costs of the revenue-generating departments after the allocations?

g. **Critical Thinking:** The total cost of support services is allocated to the operating departments according to the usage of the services as measured by the cost allocation bases. What are the overall implications of operations consulting incurring less of the cost allocation base than budgeted for the year?

More practice: E13-38, E13-40, E13-31, E13-43
Solution on p. 13-60.

TRANSFER PRICING

LO13-6 What types of transfer prices are used in organizations, and why are such prices used?

An alternative to using cost allocation is to "sell" support service to user departments using a **transfer price** or an internal charge for services (or goods) transferred between organizational units. The practice of using transfer prices for products is well established; using transfer prices for services is becoming more prevalent. Often transfer pricing systems are used when the selling unit offers services both inside and outside of the organization. Using transfer prices for services between organizational units has several advantages, as described in **Exhibit 13.13**. Top management must determine which method (allocation or transfer pricing) produces the most useful information.

Exhibit 13.13 ■ Advantages of Transfer Prices for Services

	Revenue Departments	Service Departments
User Involvement	Encourage ways to improve services to benefit internal users of the company	Promote development of services more beneficial to internal users of the company
Cost Consciousness	Relate to services used; restrict usage to those that are necessary and cost beneficial	Relate to cost of services provided; must justify transfer price established
Performance Evaluations	Include costs for making performance evaluations if control exists over amount of services used	Promote making a service department a profit center rather than a cost center and thus provide more performance evaluation measures

Transfer prices are established for a variety of reasons:

- help promote goal congruence;
- ensure optimal resource allocation;
- promote operating efficiency;
- make comparable performance evaluations among segments; and
- motivate managers to be more entrepreneurial.

In addition, transfer prices are used to "transform" a cost center into a **pseudo-profit center**.[4] Use of transfer prices allows a selling segment to create "artificial" revenue and a buying segment to create "artificial" costs.

---

[4] Pseudo-profit centers have been discussed for many years. One article by Ralph L. Benke, Jr., and James Don Edwards, "Should You Use Transfer Pricing to Create Pseudo-Profit Centers?" appeared in *Management Accounting* (now *Strategic Finance*) in February 1981. Such centers (termed microprofit centers) were also discussed at great length by Robin Cooper in *When Lean Enterprises Collide* (Boston, MA: Harvard Business School Press, 1995).

Although transfer prices can be used for services or products, for simplicity the following discussion will assume that a product is being transferred from a production department. Thus, all references to "products" or "goods" and "production" are equally applicable to "services" and "service performance." Transfer prices can be calculated in a number of ways, but the following general rules are appropriate.

- The *maximum* price should be no higher than the lowest market price at which the buying segment can acquire the goods or services externally.
- The *minimum* price should be no less than the sum of the selling segment's incremental costs associated with the goods or services plus the opportunity cost of the facilities used. An example of an opportunity cost is the contribution margin lost on product sold to external customers.

Determining Minimum and Maximum Transfer Prices — LO13-6   DEMO 13-6

Assume the West Division of a manufacturing company is currently producing 150,000 units of product per year for external customers, 50,000 units of product per year for the company's East Division, and it and has a total capacity of 200,000 units of product. The variable manufacturing cost of each unit is $30, and the annual fixed costs are $1,650,000. The lowest price that the product can be purchased for in the open market is $44 per unit.

◆ **What is the maximum and minimum transfer price per unit?**

Maximum transfer price is $44, the lowest external market price. Minimum transfer price is $30, the incremental cost per unit.

◆ **Assume the West Division could rent out its facilities for $50,000 if it decreased its production by 50,000 units for internal sales. How would that change the maximum and minimum transfer price?**

Maximum transfer price is still $44. However, the minimum transfer price is $31 ($30 + $50,000/50,000), the incremental cost per unit, plus the opportunity cost of the facilities used.

◆ **If the product is available in the open market for $28, where would the East Division purchase the product?**

The immediate short-run decision could be for the West Division to stop production and for the East Division to buy the product externally. This decision might be reasonable because, compared with the external suppliers, the West Division's activities do not appear to be cost efficient and elimination of the activity would release the facilities, people, and funds for other, more profitable purposes. A longer-run solution could be to have the West Division improve efficiency so that the internal cost of making the product is reduced. This solution could be implemented without stopping internal production, but some external purchases might be made until costs are reduced.

The difference between the upper and lower transfer price limits is the corporate "profit" (or savings) generated by producing internally rather than buying externally. Transfer prices act to "divide the corporate profit" between the buying and selling segments. Because they are internally set, transfer prices (and their "divided profits") are always eliminated for external reporting purposes, leaving only the actual cost of the items on balance sheets or income statements.[5]

In contrast, these "profits" can be extremely important for internal reporting. If performance is evaluated on a competitive basis, both buying and selling segment managers want to maximize their financial results in the responsibility accounting reports. The supplier-segment manager tries to obtain the highest transfer (selling) price, whereas the buying-segment manager tries to acquire the goods or services at the lowest transfer (purchase) price. Thus, the company's selling and buying segments should agree on the amount of a transfer price.

---

[5] Elimination of transfer prices within a company is similar to the elimination of any markup on the sale of inventory between a company and its subsidiaries (or among the subsidiaries of a single company) in preparing consolidated financial statements.

Data Visualization

Smith Manufacturing Inc. has a Parts Division that makes a machine part for sale to external customers and also supplies the part internally to the company's Small Equipment Division.

Assume that the data visualization depicts information helpful in determining a transfer price.

Transfer Price

A chart showing $ Amount per unit on the y-axis (ranging from $4 to $20) and Units on the x-axis (from 0 to 10,000). Two horizontal lines are shown: one at $16 labeled "Lowest external transfer price" and one at $10 labeled "Incremental cost to make."

Required

a. What is the company's overall cost savings (loss) if the Small Equipment Division purchases the part internally at a transfer price of $14?

b. How is the internal cost savings calculated in part *a* divided among the two divisions?

c. What is the company's overall cost savings (loss) if the Small Equipment Division purchases the part internally at a transfer price of $18?

d. How is the internal cost savings calculated in part *c* divided among the two divisions?

Solution on p. 13-62.

Types of Transfer Prices

There are three traditional types of transfer prices: cost-based, market-based, and negotiated; some companies may also use a dual pricing structure. Each type of transfer price is applicable to products or services.

Types of Transfer Prices			
Cost-Based	Market-Based	Negotiated	Dual Pricing

Exhibit 13.14 lists some questions that should be addressed for each type of transfer price. A discussion of each method and its advantages and disadvantages follows. Additional numerical examples of transfer price calculations are given in the Chapter Demonstration Problem at the end of the chapter.

Exhibit 13.14 — Types of Transfer Prices and Related Questions of Use

Cost-Based
1. What should be included in cost?
   - Variable production or performance costs
   - Total variable cost
   - Absorption production or performance costs
   - "Adjusted" absorption production or performance costs
2. Should cost be actual or standard?
3. Should a profit margin for the selling division be included?

Market-Based
1. What if there is no exact counterpart in the market?
2. What if internal sales create a cost savings (such as not having bad debts) that would not exist in external sales?
3. What if the market price is currently depressed?
4. Which market price should be used?

Negotiated
1. Do both parties have the ability to bargain with autonomy?
2. How will disputes be handled?
3. Are comparable product substitutes available externally?

Cost-Based Transfer Prices A cost-based transfer price would seem simple to implement until one realizes there are many definitions of the term *cost*, ranging from variable production cost to absorption cost plus additional amounts for selling and administrative costs (and, possibly, opportunity cost) of the selling division. If only variable costs are used to set a transfer price, the production division has little incentive to "sell" to another internal division because no contribution margin is generated on the transfer to help cover fixed costs. Transfer prices based on absorption cost at least provide a contribution toward covering the production division's fixed overhead. In the services area, cost-based transfer prices are commonly used for low-cost and low-volume services such as temporary maintenance and temporary office staff assistance.

Modifications can be made to reduce the problems of cost-based transfer prices. When variable cost is used as a base, an additional amount can be added to cover some fixed costs and provide a measure of profit to the production division. This adjustment is an example of a cost-plus arrangement. Some managers think cost-plus arrangements are acceptable substitutes for market-based transfer prices, especially when market prices for comparable substitute products are unavailable. Absorption cost can be modified by adding an amount for nonproduction costs associated with the product and/or an amount for profit to the production division. In contrast, a transfer price could be set at less than absorption cost if there were no other use for the capacity or if estimated savings (such as reduced packaging) in production costs were created by internal transfers.

Another consideration in a cost-based transfer price is whether actual or standard cost is used. Actual costs can vary according to the season, production volume, and other factors, whereas standard costs can be specified in advance and are stable measures of efficient production costs. Standard costs provide a superior basis for transfer pricing. Any variances from standard are borne by the selling division; if actual costs are used, the selling division's efficiencies or inefficiencies are passed on to the buying division.

Market-Based Transfer Prices To eliminate the problems of defining "cost," some companies use a market price approach to set transfer prices. Market price is believed to be an *objective, arm's-length measure* of value that simulates the selling price that would be offered and paid if the selling and buying divisions were independent companies. If operating efficiently relative to the competition, a selling division should be able to show a profit when transferring products or services at market prices. Similarly, an efficiently operating buying division would have to pay market price if the alternative of buying internally did not exist. Market-based transfer prices are effective for common high-cost and high-volume standardized services such as storage and transportation.

Several problems can exist, however, with the use of market prices for intracompany transfers.

- Transferred products may have no exact counterpart in the external market, which means there is no established market price.
- Internal sales reduce packaging, advertising, or delivery expenditures and eliminate bad debts; thus, market price is generally not entirely appropriate.
- In instances of a temporary downturn in market demand, the transfer price might be set at the artificially "depressed" price, which could cause inappropriate performance evaluations or decisions to be made.
- Different prices, discounts, and credit terms are allowed to different buyers, so there is a question of which is the "right" market price to use.

Negotiated Transfer Prices Because of the problems associated with both cost- and market-based prices, **negotiated transfer prices** are often set through a process of bargaining between the selling and buying unit managers. Such prices are typically below the normal market price paid by the buying unit but above the selling unit's combined incremental and opportunity costs. If internal sales would eliminate any variable selling costs, such costs are not considered. If external sales do not exist or a division cannot downsize its facilities, no opportunity cost is involved. To encourage cooperation between divisions, top management can consider joint divisional profits as one performance measurement for both the selling and the buying unit managers.

Negotiated transfer prices are often used for services because their value—as shown through expertise, reliability, convenience, or responsiveness—is often qualitative and can be assessed only judgmentally from the perspective of the parties involved. The transfer price should depend on the service's cost and volume level as well as whether comparable substitutes are available. Negotiated transfer prices are commonly used for customized high-cost and high-volume services such as risk management and specialized executive training.

Ability to negotiate a transfer price implies that segment managers have the autonomy to sell or buy products externally if internal negotiations fail. Because such extensive autonomy could lead to dysfunctional behavior and suboptimization, top management can provide a means of arbitrating a price in the event that the units cannot agree. Another way of reducing the difficulties in establishing a transfer price is simply to use a dual pricing approach.

Dual Pricing A **dual pricing arrangement** provides different transfer prices for the selling and buying segments by allowing the seller to record the transfer of goods at a market or negotiated market price and the purchaser to record the transfer at a cost-based amount. This arrangement provides a profit margin on the goods transferred from the selling division but a minimal cost to the buying division. Dual pricing eliminates the problem of having to artificially divide the profits between the selling and buying segments and allows managers to have the most relevant information for decision making and performance evaluation. However, an internal reconciliation (similar to that used in preparing consolidated statements when intercompany sales are made at an amount other than cost) is needed to adjust revenues and costs when company external financial statements are prepared.

Selecting a Transfer Pricing System

Setting a reasonable transfer price is not an easy task. Everyone involved in the process must be aware of both positive and negative aspects of each type of transfer price and be responsive to suggestions for change. The type of transfer pricing system selected should reflect the organizational units' characteristics as well as corporate goals. No single method of setting a transfer price is best in all instances, and all organizational units may not be able to use transfer pricing. For example, support departments that do not provide measurable benefits or cannot show a distinct cause-and-effect relationship between cost behavior and service use by other departments should not attempt to use transfer prices.

Transfer prices are not intended to be permanent; they are frequently revised in relation to changes in costs, supply, demand, competitive forces, and other factors. Flexibility by the selling segment to increase a transfer price when reduced productive capacity is present or to decrease a transfer price when excess productive capacity exists is a strong management lever. A company should evaluate the following potential negative and positive outcomes of transfer prices before instituting such a system.

Negative transfer pricing system outcomes:	Positive transfer pricing system outcomes:
• Disagreement between unit managers as to how the transfer price should be set	• An appropriate basis for calculating and evaluating segment performance
• Additional organizational costs and employee time	• Information to make rational acquisition decisions about transfers of goods and services between corporate divisions
• The potential for dysfunctional behavior among organizational units and for underutilization or overutilization of services	• The flexibility to respond to changes in demand or market conditions
• The need for year-end entries to eliminate the transfer prices	• A means of encouraging and rewarding goal congruence by managers in decentralized operations

Transfer Prices in Multinational Settings

A common use of transfer prices is to determine the tax effects created by moving products between organizational units located in different tax jurisdictions. Because of differences in tax systems, customs duties, freight and insurance costs, import/export regulations, and foreign-exchange controls, setting transfer prices for products and services becomes extremely difficult when a company has multinational operations.[6]

Although multinational enterprises (MNEs) can use different transfer prices for the same product being sent to, or received from, different countries, the company's transfer pricing policies should be

---

[6] Similar to international settings, multistate firms can employ transfer pricing strategies to move profits from state to state. The various states have different income tax rates—and some have no tax at all.

Chapter 13 Responsibility Accounting, Support Department Cost Allocations, and Transfer Pricing

followed consistently. For example, a parent company should not price services performed for foreign subsidiaries in a way that sends the greatest cost amount to the subsidiary in the country with the highest tax rate *unless* that method of pricing is reasonable and equitable to all subsidiaries. The general test of reasonableness is that a transfer price should reflect an **arm's-length transaction** or what the price would be on the open market.

As shown in **Exhibit 13.15**, the internal and external objectives of transfer pricing policies differ in multinational entities. In addition to MNE objectives, countries have specific goals in relation to transfer prices: to protect the country tax base and to encourage foreign direct investment and cross-border trade. Thus, tax authorities in both the home and host countries carefully scrutinize multinational transfer prices because such prices determine which country taxes the income from the transfer. The U.S. Congress is concerned about both U.S. multinationals operating in low-tax-rate countries and foreign companies operating in the United States. In either situation, Congress believes that companies could avoid paying U.S. corporate income taxes because of misleading or inaccurate transfer pricing. Thus, the Internal Revenue Service (IRS) can be quick to investigate U.S. subsidiaries that operate in low-tax areas and have unusually high profits.

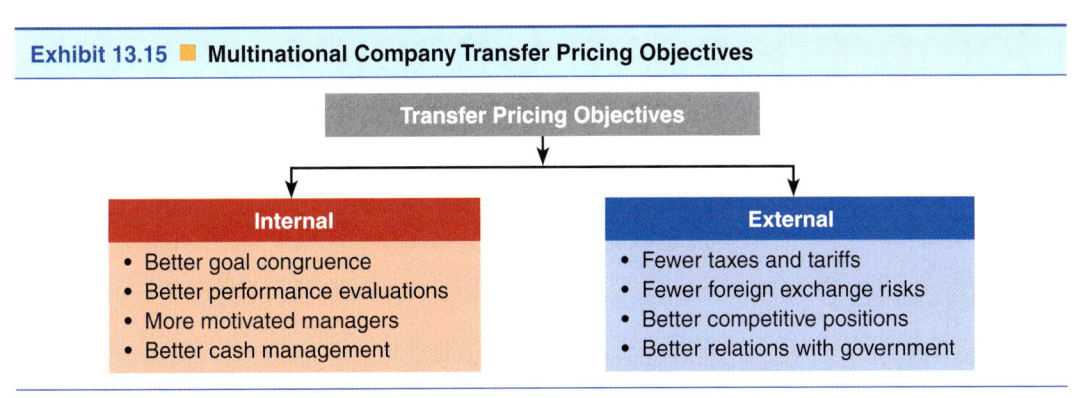

Exhibit 13.15 ■ Multinational Company Transfer Pricing Objectives

Transfer Pricing Objectives

Internal
- Better goal congruence
- Better performance evaluations
- More motivated managers
- Better cash management

External
- Fewer taxes and tariffs
- Fewer foreign exchange risks
- Better competitive positions
- Better relations with government

Source: Wagdy M. Abdallah, "Guidelines for CEOs in Transfer Pricing Policies," *Management Accounting* (September 1988), p. 61. Copyright 1988 by Institute of Management Accountants. Reproduced with permission of Institute of Management Accountants in the format Textbook via Copyright Clearance Center.

Additionally, current moves toward global tax reform in a highly complex regulatory environment is increasing the risk in transfer pricing policies and transactions. The vast majority (78 percent) of the respondents of a recent survey conducted by E&Y indicated that the most significant factor to affect change in transfer pricing models is tax risk management. The majority of the respondents also expect transfer price audits to increase over the next two years.[7] With the increase in regulatory pressure, potential for tax investigations with large reassessment and penalty implications, and pending tax law changes, companies are reevaluating transfer pricing policing in light of the increased risk level.

Transfer Pricing **LO13-6** **REVIEW 13-6**

Londen Inc., a division of Englend Enterprises, manufactures Product ABC to sell internally to other company divisions as well as externally. One unit of Product ABC sells externally for $90. Production and selling costs for a unit of Product ABC follow.

Direct material	$15.00
Direct labor	23.00
Variable overhead	8.50
Fixed overhead (based on production of 900,000 units)	12.00
Variable selling expense	5.00

continued

---

[7] Michalak, J., Fultz, T., "How Leaning into Transfer Pricing Transformation Helps Manage Tax Risk," (October 4, 2021), https://www.ey.com/en_us/tax/how-leaning-into-transfer-pricing-transformation-helps-manage-tax-risk (last accessed October 26, 2023).

> Canterbery Co., another division of Englend Enterprises, wants to purchase 75,000 units of Product ABC from Londen Inc. during the next year. No selling costs are incurred on internal sales.
>
> a. All the units of Product ABC that can be produced by Londen Inc. can be sold externally. Assume that Canterbery can purchase Product ABC from other suppliers at a price of $95 to $105. What should the minimum transfer price be?
> b. Assume that Londen Inc. is experiencing a slight slowdown in external demand and will be able to sell only 800,000 units of Product ABC externally next year at the $90 selling price. What should be the minimum selling price to Canterbery Co. under these conditions?
> c. Using the information in (a), compute a transfer price that divides the "profit" between the two divisions equally.
> d. **Critical Thinking:** If the company's policy is to allow for negotiated transfer prices, what factors could impact the negotiation process?

More practice:
MC13-21, E13-45, E13-46, E13-47, E13-48, E13-49
Solution on p. 13-61.

Comprehensive Chapter Review

Key Terms

administrative departments, p. 13-15
algebraic method, p. 13-18
arm's-length transaction, p. 13-31
assessor, p. 13-3
benefits-provided ranking, p. 13-17
centralization, p. 13-7
communications network, p. 13-3
cost center, p. 13-13
cost management system (CMS), p. 13-4
decentralization, p. 13-7
detector, p. 13-3

direct method, p. 13-17
dual pricing arrangement, p. 13-30
effector, p. 13-3
goal congruence, p. 13-12
investment center, p. 13-14
management-by-exception principle, p. 13-11
management control system (MCS), p. 13-3
management information system (MIS), p. 13-2
multilevel responsibility report, p. 13-11
negotiated transfer prices, p. 13-29

profit center, p. 13-14
pseudo-profit center, p. 13-27
responsibility accounting system, p. 13-10
responsibility centers, p. 13-13
responsibility reports, p. 13-10
revenue center, p. 13-14
sensor, p. 13-3
service departments, p. 13-15
shared service, p. 13-8
step method, p. 13-17
suboptimization, p. 13-14
support departments, p. 13-15
transfer price, p. 13-26

Chapter Summary

LO13-1 **Management Control Systems (Page 13-2)**
- Organizations have management control systems to
  - implement strategic and operating plans.
  - provide a means for comparison of actual to planned results for management control purposes.

Cost Management System (CMS)
- A CMS is a set of formal methods developed for planning and controlling an organization's cost-generating activities relative to its short-term objectives and long-term strategies.
- A CMS has a short-term goal of making efficient use of organizational resources.
- A CMS has a long-term goal of ensuring the organization's survival.
- Primary CMS components: detector, assessor, effector, communication network.

Roles of a Cost Management System
- Develop accurate product/service costs
- Assess product/service life cycle performance
- Improve understanding of processes/activities
- Control costs
- Measure performance
- Support organizational goals

Decentralization (Page 13-7)   LO13-2
- Decentralization is generally appropriate for companies that
  - are mature.
  - are large.
  - are in a growth stage of product development.
  - are growing rapidly.
  - can financially withstand incorrect decisions.
  - have high confidence in the employees' decision-making ability.
  - have widespread operations.
  - want to challenge, motivate, and mentor employees.
  - require rapid response to changing conditions or opportunities.

Relationship Between Decentralization and Responsibility Accounting (Page 13-10)   LO13-3
- Decentralization is made to work effectively through the use of responsibility accounting, which provides information about the
  - performance,
  - efficiency, and
  - effectiveness of organizational responsibility centers and their managers.
- Decentralization implies the acceptance of authority by subordinate managers, and the responsibility accounting system produces reports that indicate the "rolling up" of that authority back to upper management.
- Decentralization requires each responsibility center to report on the activities under its manager's immediate control.
- Decentralization uses the principle of management by exception, which is reflected in the successively aggregated responsibility reports.
- Decentralization seeks goal congruence and uses responsibility reports to highlight any suboptimal use of resources.

Types of Responsibility Centers (Page 13-13)   LO13-4
- Cost centers are organizational units in which managers are primarily responsible for controlling costs.
- Revenue centers are organizational units in which managers are primarily responsible for generating revenues, although in some instances, managers have control over revenues and some costs.
- Profit centers are organizational units in which managers are responsible for generating revenue, controlling costs, and maximizing their units' incomes.
- Investment centers are organizational units in which managers are responsible for generating revenue, controlling costs, and producing a satisfactory return on the asset base under their control.

Support Department Cost Allocations (Page 13-15)   LO13-5
- Support departments are service and administrative departments (i.e., non-revenue generating).
- Support department costs are allocated to producing departments to meet one or more objectives:
  - full cost computation,
  - managerial motivation, and/or
  - managerial decision making.
- Support department costs are allocated using the direct, step, or algebraic method:
  - The direct method assigns support department costs only to operating departments but does not consider assistance that can be provided from one support department to another.
  - The step method uses a benefits-provided ranking that lists support departments from the one providing the most assistance to other departments to the one providing assistance primarily to the operating areas. Costs are assigned from each department in order of the ranking.
  - The algebraic method recognizes the interrelationships among all departments through the use of simultaneous equations. This method provides the best allocation information and is readily adaptable to computer computations.

Transfer Prices (Page 13-26)   LO13-6
- Transfer prices are intracompany charges for goods or services bought and sold between segments of a decentralized company.
- Transfer prices may be cost based, market based, or negotiated; a dual pricing system can also be used to assign different transfer prices to the selling and buying units.
- Transfer prices are set between two boundaries:

- The upper price boundary is the lowest market price at which the product/service can be acquired externally.
- The lowest price boundary is the incremental cost of production or performance plus the opportunity cost of the facilities used.

■ Transfer prices are used in organizations to
  - enhance goal congruence.
  - make performance evaluations among segments more comparable.
  - change a cost center into a pseudo-profit center.
  - ensure optimal resource allocations.
  - promote responsibility center autonomy.
  - encourage motivation and communication among responsibility center managers.

■ Multinational companies must attempt to determine what transfer price would be considered "reasonable" as if generated in an arm's-length transaction.

■ Multinational companies face an increase in transfer pricing audits by tax authorities.

Solution Strategies

LO13-5 Service Department Cost Allocation

Direct Method
1. Determine rational and systematic allocation bases for each support department.
2. Assign costs from each support department directly to operating areas using specified allocation bases.
3. No costs are assigned to support areas.

Step Method
1. Determine rational and systematic allocation bases for each support department.
2. List support departments in a benefits-provided ranking from the one that provides the most assistance to all other areas (both operating and support) to the one that provides assistance only to operating areas.
3. Beginning with the first support department listed, allocate the costs from that department to all remaining departments; repeat the process until only operating departments remain.

Algebraic Method
1. Determine rational and systematic allocation bases for each department.
2. Develop equations that express the costs of, and service relationships among, support areas.
3. Solve the simultaneous equations for the support departments through an iterative process or by computer until all values are known.
4. Allocate costs using allocation bases developed in step 2. Eliminate "reallocated" costs from consideration.

LO13-6 Transfer Prices (Cost Based, Market Based, Negotiated, Dual)

Upper limit: Lowest price available from external suppliers

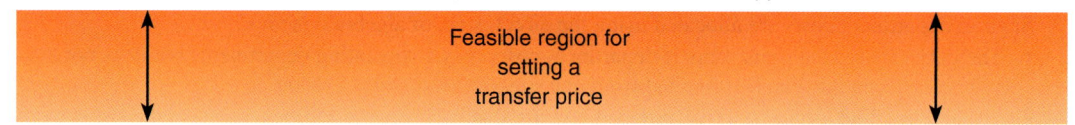

> Feasible region for setting a transfer price

Lower limit: Incremental costs of producing and selling the transferred goods or services plus the opportunity cost of the facilities used

Chapter Demonstration Problem

LO13-6 RaceFest Inc. has two operating divisions. The Ski Division makes water and snow skis, and the Binding Division makes rubber boots for water skis. The Binding Division estimates that 800,000 pairs of boots will be produced for the year; of those, 600,000 pairs will be sold to the Ski Division and 200,000 pairs will be sold externally. Managers of the two divisions are in the process of determining a transfer price for a pair of boots. The following information for the Binding Division is available:

Chapter 13 Responsibility Accounting, Support Department Cost Allocations, and Transfer Pricing

Direct material	$27
Direct labor	12
Variable overhead	7
Variable S&A (both for external and internal sales)	4
Total variable cost	$50
Fixed overhead (rate based on estimated annual production)	$10
Fixed selling and administrative (rate based on estimated annual sales)	5
Total fixed cost	15
Total cost per pair of boots	$65
Markup on total variable cost (40%)	20
List price to external customers	$85

Required:

a. Determine a transfer price based on variable production cost.
b. Determine a transfer price based on total variable cost plus normal markup.
c. Determine a transfer price based on full production cost.
d. Determine a transfer price based on total cost per pair of boots.
e. Prepare the journal entries for the Binding (selling) and Ski (buying) segments if the transfer is made at the external selling price for the selling division and the full production cost for the buying division.
   1. Seller's entries: The seller records the difference between the Intracompany Sales amount (equal to the seller's transfer price) and the Accounts Receivable amount (equal to the buyer's transfer price) as Intracompany Profits. The seller also records an entry to increase Intracompany CGS and reduce Finished Goods.
   2. Buyer's entry: The buying company records Inventory and Accounts Payable at its purchase price.
      Note: These intracompany transactions are eliminated at period end; however, these entries are beyond the scope of this text.
f. Assume that the Binding Division has no alternative use for the facilities that make the rubber boots for internal transfer. Also assume that the Ski Division can buy equivalent boots externally for $80. Calculate the upper and lower limits for which the transfer price should be set.
g. Using the information in (f), compute a transfer price that divides the "profit" between the two divisions equally.
h. Assume that a large portion of the facilities in which boots are produced can be rented for $600,000 if the Binding Division makes boots only for external sale. Determine the lower limit of the transfer price.

Solution to Demonstration Problem

a.
Direct material	$27
Direct labor	12
Variable overhead	7
Transfer price	$46

b.
Total variable cost	$50
Markup (40%)	20
Transfer price	$70

c.
Variable production cost	$46
Fixed production cost	10
Transfer price	$56

d.
Total variable cost	$50
Total fixed cost	15
Transfer price	$65

e. 1. Binding Division:

Accounts Receivable—Ski Division (600,000 × $56)	33,600,000	
Intracompany Profits (600,000 × $29)	17,400,000	
Intracompany Sales (600,000 × $85)		51,000,000
Intracompany Cost of Goods Sold (CGS) (600,000 × $56)	33,600,000	
Finished Goods (600,000 × $56)		33,600,000

2. Ski Division:

Inventory (600,000 × $56)	33,600,000	
Accounts Payable—Binding Division		33,600,000

f. Upper limit: Ski Division's external purchase price = $80
Lower limit: Total variable cost of Binding Division = $50

g. (Lower limit + Upper limit) ÷ 2 = ($50 + $80) ÷ 2 = $130 ÷ 2 = $65

h. $600,000 ÷ 600,000 pairs of boots = $1 opportunity cost per pair
Lower limit: Incremental variable cost of Binding Division + Opportunity cost = $50 + $1 = $51

Assignments with the MBC logo in the margin are available in myBusinessCourse.
Resources include demonstration videos, guided examples, and auto-graded homework.
See details in the Preface, and ask your professor how you can access the system.

Data Analytics

LO13-5

DA13-1. Comparing support cost allocation methods

Lean Mfg. has three support departments (human resources, administration, and maintenance) and three revenue-generating departments (Division 1, Division 2, and Division 3). The company calculated the allocation of support department costs under three methods: direct, step, and algebraic. Data is provided in MBC showing the total amount allocated to each of the three divisions using each of the three methods.

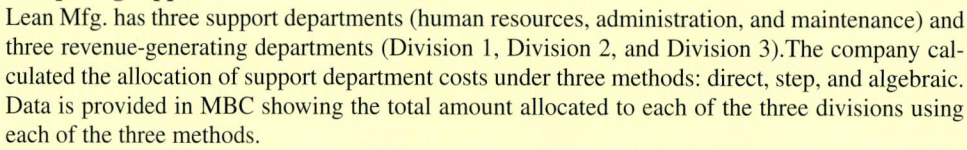

Required

a. Prepare a stacked bar chart showing how support costs are allocated by method. One bar should be displayed for each method showing the breakout of costs by division. Add labels showing dollar amounts for each cost segment. *Hint*: Select data, click on Insert, and Stacked Bar chart.

b. Describe the chart, both by division and in total. What likely causes the similarities or differences across the bar charts that you observe?

c. Which method would management of each of the divisions prefer, assuming a cost minimization strategy? Which method might the CEO of the company prefer, assuming an accurate cost allocation is the strategy? Will these preferences always be the case in future periods?

Data Visualization

Data Visualization Activities are available in myBusinessCourse. These assignments use Tableau Dashboards to expose students to visual depictions of data and introduce students to data analytics through data visualizations. These exercises are easily assignable and auto graded by MBC.

Potential Ethical Issues

1. Having managers engage in suboptimization acts that benefit themselves to the detriment of the overall firm
2. Creating responsibility reports that "bury" important details needed to accurately evaluate managerial performance in summary data
3. Allocating support department costs using an "ability-to-bear" criterion that results in profit-detrimental actions
4. Improperly estimating the benefits provided between departments to shift support department costs inappropriately
5. Establishing a transfer pricing system that does not allow managers who will be judged on profitability performance to buy or sell externally
6. Engaging in transfer pricing techniques that improperly shift costs to low- or no-tax locations
7. Using non-arm's-length transfer pricing techniques that create losses through aggressive tax planning

Questions

Q13-1. What is a control system? What purpose does a control system serve in an organization?

Q13-2. Wayne Litcomb is the president and chief operating officer of Litcomb Electronics. He founded the company and has led it to prominence in the electronics field. He has manufacturing plants or retail outlets in 40 states. Litcomb is finding, however, that he cannot "keep track" of things the way he did previously. Discuss the advantages and disadvantages of decentralizing the firm's decision-making activities among the various local and regional managers. Also discuss what functions Litcomb might want to be performed centrally and why he would choose these functions.

Q13-3. Why are responsibility reports prepared? Is it appropriate for a single responsibility report to be prepared for a division of a major company? Why or why not?

Q13-4. What is suboptimization, and what factors contribute to it in a decentralized firm?

Q13-5. Why are support department costs often allocated to operating departments? Is such an allocation process always useful from a decision-making standpoint? How might support department cost allocation create a feeling of cost responsibility among managers of operating departments?

Q13-6. "The four criteria for selecting an allocation base for support department costs should be applied equally." Discuss the merits of this statement.

Q13-7. Compare and contrast the direct, step, and algebraic methods of allocating support department costs. What are the advantages and disadvantages of each method?

Q13-8. When the algebraic method of allocating support department costs is used, total costs for each support department increase from what they were prior to the allocation. Why does this occur, and how are the additional costs treated?

Q13-9. What are transfer prices, and why do companies use them? How could the use of transfer prices improve or impair goal congruence?

Q13-10. What problems might be encountered when attempting to implement a cost-based transfer pricing system? A market-based transfer pricing system?

Q13-11. What type of transfer price would you recommend be used in each of the following selling and buying responsibility centers: cost, revenue, profit, and investment? How and why would such prices be set?

Q13-12. What is dual pricing? What is the intended effect of dual pricing on the performance of each division affected by the dual price?

Q13-13. How can support departments use transfer prices, and what advantages do transfer prices have over cost allocation methods?

Q13-14. Explain why the determination of transfer prices is more complex in a multinational, rather than in a domestic, setting.

Multiple Choice

LO13-1 MC13-15. What are the four primary components of a management control system?
a. Detector, assessor, effector, communications network
b. Controller, assessor, detector, effector
c. Sensor, effector, communications network, transmitter
d. Assessor, communications network, analytics, sensor

LO13-2 MC13-16. Which of the following is not an advantage of decentralization?
a. Reduces decision-making time
b. Allows for comparative evaluation
c. Develops managerial talent
d. Encourages goal congruence across segments

LO13-3 MC13-17. A company has the following financial information for its divisions.

	Alcohol	Soft Drink	Juice	Total
Sales..................	$700,000	$430,000	$270,000	$1,400,000
Variable costs...........	280,000	150,000	170,000	600,000
Fixed costs.............	300,000	100,000	120,000	520,000
Operating income (loss).....	$120,000	$180,000	$ (20,000)	$ 280,000

Which one of the following options reflects the current contribution margin ratio for each of the company's business segments?

	Alcohol	Soft Drink	Juice
a.	60%	65%	37%.
b.	60%	35%	63%.
c.	40%	65%	37%.
d.	40%	35%	63%

LO13-4 MC13-18. A company's production manager is accountable for controlling costs while manufacturing quality products. The manager also provides recommendations for equipment improvements and replacements. In this market, customers are very sensitive to the product's quality. What type of responsibility center is the production manager in charge of?
a. Cost center
b. Investment center
c. Profit center
d. Revenue center

LO13-5 MC13-19. Logo Inc. has two data services departments (the Systems Department and the Facilities Department) that provide support to the company's three production departments (Machining Department, Assembly Department, and Finishing Department). The overhead costs of the Systems Department are allocated to other departments on the basis of computer usage hours. The overhead costs of the Facilities Department are allocated based on square feet occupied (in thousands). Other information pertaining to Logo is as follows.

Department	Overhead	Computer Usage Hours	Square Feet Occupied
Systems............................	$200,000	300	1,000
Facilities...........................	100,000	900	600
Machining..........................	400,000	3,600	2,000
Assembly..........................	550,000	1,800	3,000
Finishing...........................	620,000	2,700	5,000
		9,300	11,600

If Logo employs the direct method of allocating service department costs, the overhead of the Systems Department would be allocated by dividing the overhead amount by
a. 1,200 hours.
b. 8,100 hours.
c. 9,000 hours.
d. 9,300 hours.

MC13-20. A company has the following financial information for its divisions.

	Support Departments		Operating Departments		
	Maintenance	Systems	Machining	Fabrication	Total
Budgeted overhead	$360,000	$95,000	$200,000	$300,000	$955,000
Support work finished					
From Maintenance ...		10%	50%	40%	100%
From Systems.......			50%	50%	100%

If Adam uses the step-down method, beginning with the Maintenance Department, to allocate support department costs to production departments, the total overhead (rounded to the nearest dollar) for the Machining Department to allocate to its products would be

a. $389,500.
b. $427,500.
c. $445,500.
d. $445,000.

MC13-21. Manhattan Corporation has several divisions that operate as decentralized profit centers. At the present time, the Fabrication Division has excess capacity of 5,000 units with respect to the UT-371 circuit board, a popular item in many digital applications. Information about the circuit board follows.

Market price	$48
Variable selling/distribution costs on external sales	5
Variable manufacturing cost	21
Fixed manufacturing cost	10

Manhattan's Electronic Assembly Division wants to purchase 4,500 circuit boards either internally, or else use a similar board in the marketplace that sells for $46. The Electronic Assembly Division's management feels that if the first alternative is pursued, a price concession is justified, given that both divisions are part of the same firm. To optimize the overall goals of Manhattan, the minimum price to be charged for the board from the Fabrication Division to the Electronic Assembly Division should be

a. $21.
b. $26.
c. $31.
d. $46.

MC13-22. Happy Time Industries uses segment reporting for all of its decentralized divisions. It has several products that are transferred from one division to other divisions. Happy Time wants to motivate the manager of the selling division to produce efficiently. Assuming the following methods are available, the optimal transfer pricing method should be a

a. cost-based transfer price that uses actual amounts.
b. cost-based transfer price that uses budgeted amounts.
c. variable cost-based transfer price that uses actual amounts.
d. market-based transfer price.

Exercises

E13-23. Management control system Match each of the following terms 1 through 4 with the most appropriate description, *a* through *d*. In addition, match each of the terms 1 through 4 with an example, *e* through *h*.

Term
1. Detector
2. Assessor
3. Effector
4. Communication network

Description
a. ___ Device altering behavior if required
b. ___ Device determining the significance of what is occurring
c. ___ Device measuring what is actually occurring
d. ___ Transmission of information

Example
   e. ___ Implementation of a procedure change in response to increased defects
   f. ___ Management reporting of trends of defects and any actions taken
   g. ___ Measuring product defects
   h. ___ Variance analysis (actual defects compared to prior period)

LO13-1 E13-24. Management control systems; writing A few years after graduation, Ibrahim and four of his friends from college organized an engineering consulting business called 5Q. All five individuals had earned degrees in engineering fields and were anxious to pool their expertise and work together in a successful business venture. Even though the business was very successful in attracting clients, the business failed within two years of its founding because the entrepreneurs were unable to control their costs. Discuss how the adoption of management controls could have improved the odds that the business would have been successful.

LO13-1 E13-25. Management control systems Following are activities that are components of a management control system in a production department. For each item listed, discuss whether it is a detector, assessor, effector, or communications network:
   a. Comparing actual costs to budgeted costs and calculating cost variances
   b. Reporting variances
   c. Implementing changes in production systems to correct the largest negative variances
   d. Measuring actual costs

LO13-1 E13-26. Cost management and strategy Following are descriptions of three businesses. For each, assume that you are the CEO. Identify the most critical information you would need to manage the strategic decisions of that business.
   a. Private hospital that competes on the basis of delivering high-quality services to an upscale clientele
   b. Small, high-technology firm that has just developed its first product, will begin sales in the coming quarter, and has five other products under development
   c. American Sugar Company, which is a large firm that competes in the commodity refined sugar industry.

LO13-1 E13-27. Cost management system roles in an organization Match each of the following roles of a cost management system, 1 through 6, with the most appropriate example, *a* through *f*.

Cost management system role	Example
1. Develop accurate product/service costs	a. ___ Reducing non-valued added costs in a process
2. Assess product/service life cycle performance	b. ___ Tracing research and development costs to a new product
3. Improve understanding of processes/activities	c. ___ Determining total cost per equivalent unit in a process costing system
4. Control costs	d. ___ Using data visualizations of activity over time for purposes of evaluation
5. Measure performance	e. ___ Assessing whether a company is meeting its goal of being a product differentiator
6. Support organizational goals	f. ___ Assessing the value of implementing AI production technology

LO13-2 E13-28. Centralization vs. decentralization Indicate whether a firm exhibiting each of the following characteristics would more likely be centralized (C) or decentralized (D).
   a. Few employees
   b. Wary of financial impacts of incorrect subordinate management decisions
   c. Subordinates highly trained and mentored in decision-making skills
   d. Slow growth rate
   e. Two years old
   f. Stable market environment
   g. Growth stage of product development
   h. High level of organizational flexibility
   i. Large number of employees who telecommute
   j. Tight management control
   k. Widely dispersed operating units
   l. High cost of gathering information
   m. Redundancy of functions is minimized
   n. Few interdependencies among organizational units

E13-29. Decentralization advantages and disadvantages Indicate whether each of the following is a potential advantage (A) or disadvantage (D) of decentralization. If an item is neither an advantage nor a disadvantage, use N.

    a. Promotion of goal congruence
    b. Use of management-by-exception principle by top management
    c. Development of leadership qualities
    d. Support of training in decision making
    e. Provision of increased job satisfaction
    f. Intricacies of communication process
    g. Cost of developing the planning and reporting system
    h. Speed of decisions
    i. Delegation of ultimate responsibility
    j. Placement of decision maker closer to time and place of problem

E13-30. Centralization vs. decentralization; research; writing Many companies are trying to determine the best organizational structure for information technology (IT) operations. Although IT operations had been decentralized in the past, there has been a growing trend to bring such operations back to a central location. Use the Internet to gather research to compare and contrast the advantages and disadvantages of centralized and decentralized IT operations. What other important information would you need to make a decision on such an organizational structure?

E13-31. Decentralization; transfer prices; research; writing Search the Internet to identify three highly decentralized companies. Based on the information you find on each, either determine directly or infer the types of responsibility centers used by these companies. Also, determine or speculate about whether the companies use transfer prices or allocation of costs for intracompany transfers of services. Prepare a report on your findings and inferences. In cases for which you had to infer, explain what information or reasoning led you to that inference. Why is decentralization appropriate for some companies but not for others?

E13-32. Performance evaluation Presented is the February performance report for the Production Department of Noel Manufacturing Inc.

Production Department Performance Report
For the Month of January

	Actual	Budget
Volume	52,000	48,000
Manufacturing costs		
Direct materials	$144,000	$132,000
Direct labor	110,000	108,000
Variable overhead	78,000	72,000
Fixed overhead	252,000	250,000
Total costs	$584,000	$562,000

    a. Evaluate the performance report.
    b. Prepare a more appropriate performance report.

E13-33. Performance analysis As a financial analyst, you have just been handed the annual financial report of Firm A, a large, global pharmaceutical company. Firm A competes in both traditional pharmaceutical products and in evolving biotechnology products. The following data (in billions) on Firm A and the pharmaceutical industry are available:

	Firm A	Industry Average
Sales	$2.00	$0.960
Net income	0.54	0.096
Advertising	0.04	0.160
Research and development	0.16	0.240
New investment in facilities	0.20	0.240

Given these data, evaluate the cost management performance of Firm A.

LO13-4 **E13-34. Responsibility centers** For each of the following organizational units, indicate whether the unit would most likely be classified as a cost center (C), a revenue center (R), a profit center (P), or an investment center (I):

   a. University-owned bookstore
   b. Local public television station's fund-raising telethon staffed by volunteers
   c. Corporate-owned local outlet of a fast-food restaurant
   d. Bloodmobile of a local hospital
   e. Beijing office of an international public accounting firm
   f. Wildlife management department in a national or state park
   g. Long-term parking lot at a regional airport
   h. City ticket office of an airline
   i. Cafeteria of a for-profit hospital
   j. Fine jewelry counter in a local department store
   k. Laundry of a large bed-and-breakfast
   l. Sales representative for a college textbook publisher
   m. Fraud investigation department of a major retailer

LO13-4 **E13-35. Responsibility centers; research** Go to your university's website and review the various organizational units within the university. Assuming no transfer pricing exists, make a list of the units that you believe would be classified as cost centers and profit centers.

LO13-4, 6 **E13-36. Responsibility centers** Nussbaum Inc. is a chemical company that is comprised of five independent divisions, located in three different countries. Divisional managers are evaluated based on divisional profitability. Home office functions include human resources, accounting, and environmental management (EM). Projects of the EM group are solicited and paid for by the contracting operating divisions. Nussbaum's transfer pricing policy requires EM to charge the operating divisions a market-based price for services.

   a. Is the EM group centralized or decentralized?
   b. What type of responsibility center is the EM group?
   c. What potential problems exist from having the EM group charge a market-based transfer price for its services?

LO13-4 **E13-37. Profit centers and allocations; research** Multiple-doctor medical practices are often structured with each doctor acting as a profit center.

   a. Discuss why such an organizational structure would be appropriate.
   b. Go to the web and find some software packages that could be used to account for such an organizational structure.
   c. List some costs of a medical practice that would be directly traceable to each physician.
   d. List some costs of a medical practice that might not be directly traceable to each physician. Provide possible allocation bases for such costs.

LO13-5 **E13-38. Direct method** Andreka Inc. uses the direct method to allocate support department costs to production departments (fabricating and finishing). Information for June follows.

	Human Resources	Administration
Service department costs	$630,000	$450,000
Services provided to other departments		
Human resources		10%
Administration	20%	
Fabricating	35%	50%
Finishing	45%	40%

   a. What amounts of human resources and administration costs should be assigned to Fabricating for June?
   b. What amounts of human resources and administration costs should be assigned to Finishing for June?

LO13-5 **E13-39. Direct method** Prosperous Bank has three support areas (administration, human resources, and accounting) and three revenue-generating areas (checking accounts, savings accounts, and loans). Monthly direct costs and the interdepartmental support structure are shown in the following benefits-provided ranking:

Chapter 13 Responsibility Accounting, Support Department Cost Allocations, and Transfer Pricing

Department	Direct Costs	Percentage of Service Used by					
		Admin.	Human Resources	Accounting	Checking	Savings	Loans
Administration......	$540,000		10	10	30	40	10
Human resources...	360,000	10		10	30	20	30
Accounting........	300,000	10	10		40	20	20
Checking..........	630,000						
Savings...........	337,500						
Loans............	675,000						

Compute the total cost for each revenue-generating area of the bank using the direct method.

E13-40. Step method Use the information in Exercise E13-39 to compute total cost for each revenue-generating area if Prosperous Bank uses the step method of cost allocation. **LO13-5**

E13-41. Step method Leander Mfg. has three support departments (human resources, administration, and maintenance) and two revenue-generating departments (assembly and finishing). The company uses the step method to allocate support department costs to operating departments. In October, human resources incurred $360,000 of costs, administration incurred $558,000, and maintenance incurred $170,000. Proportions of services provided to other departments for October follow. **LO13-5**

	Human Resources	Administration	Maintenance
Human resources......		10%	5%
Administration........	10%		15
Maintenance.........	15	10	
Assembly...........	40	50	45
Finishing............	35	30	35

a. Assuming that the departments are listed in a benefits-provided ranking, what amount of cost should be assigned from human resources to each of the other departments? From administration? From maintenance?
b. What total support department cost was assigned to assembly in October? To finishing?
c. Explain why the cost allocation is affected by the order in which costs are assigned.

E13-42. Algebraic method Use the information for Prosperous Bank in Exercise E13-39 to compute the total cost for each revenue-generating area using the algebraic method. **LO13-5**

E13-43. Algebraic method The following chart indicates the percentage of support department services used by other departments. Service departments are designated S1, S2, and S3; operating departments are designated RP1 and RP2. **LO13-5**

Department	Services Used				
	S1	S2	S3	RP1	RP2
S1...............	N/A	10%	20%	30%	40%
S2...............	40%	N/A	30	20	10
S3...............	20	30	N/A	40	10

Direct costs of the period were $170,000, $360,000, and $600,000 for S1, S2, and S3, respectively. Allocate the support department costs to the operating departments using the algebraic method.

E13-44. Transfer pricing in support departments Indicate whether each of the following statements constitutes a potential advantage (A), disadvantage (D), or neither (N) of using transfer prices for support department costs. **LO13-6**

a. Requires additional organizational data and employee time
b. Puts all support departments on an equal footing
c. Reduces goal congruence

d. Makes a support department into a profit center
   e. Increases resource waste
   f. Improves ability to evaluate performance
   g. Increases communication about which additional services are needed and which ones can be reduced or eliminated
   h. Increases disagreements among departments
   i. Causes certain services to be under- or overutilized
   j. Makes users and providers more cost conscious
   k. Measures benefits provided to operating departments
   l. Includes costs outside a manager's control

LO13-6 E13-45. Transfer pricing Mogi Corp. manufactures one primary product, which is processed through two divisions (P and R). Costs for each division are:

	P	R
Variable cost per gallon	$3	$15
Fixed cost per gallon (based on production of 25,000 and 40,000 gallons for P and R respectively)	2	12

P Division produces 25,000 gallons per month. R Division uses 40,000 gallons per month; of that, 25,000 gallons are purchased internally and 15,000 are purchased externally at $10 per gallon. After processing through R Division, a gallon of final product can be sold for $55.

   a. What would be P's transfer price to R Division if the price is set at 180 percent of variable cost?
   b. What would be P's transfer price to R Division if the price is set at 130 percent of full cost?
   c. What would be P's transfer price to R Division if the price is set at market value?
   d. What is Mogi Corp.'s operating profit if all 40,000 gallons of product produced are sold in the month?

LO13-6 E13-46. Transfer pricing Squish Corp. has two divisions: Production (which makes pillow foam) and Assembly (which makes pillows). Division managers can choose to purchase components internally or externally. For each pound of foam, the Production Division incurs $4 of variable cost and $1 of fixed cost with a production capacity of 30,000 pounds per month; the division recently increased its transfer price to Assembly to $5.50 to cover full production cost and provide a profit margin to the Production Division. Assembly's manager has decided to begin purchasing foam externally for $4.50 per pound.

   a. Assume that Production Division has no alternative uses for its manufacturing facilities. Fixed costs could not be avoided by external purchases. What is the monthly advantage (or disadvantage) to Squish Corp. if the foam is purchased internally?
   b. Assume that, rather than manufacturing foam, the Production Division manufacturing facilities can be rented for $25,000 per month. What is the monthly advantage (or disadvantage) to Squish Corp. if the foam is purchased internally?
   c. Assume that Squish decides to stop internal foam production and rent out the facilities for $25,000 per month. Thus, Assembly Division begins buying all of its production needs externally at $4.50 per pound. What short- or long-term effects would these transactions have on Squish Corp.?

LO13-6 E13-47. Transfer pricing Qvat Division, a subsidiary of Imogene Ltd., manufactures a silicon chip with the following costs:

Direct material	$15.00
Direct labor	26.25
Variable overhead	12.75
Fixed overhead	18.00
Total	$72.00

Some of the chips are sold externally for $162; others are transferred internally to the Kwak Division. Qvat Division's plant manager wants to establish a reasonable transfer price for chips transferred to Kwak. The purchasing manager of Kwak Division has informed the plant manager that comparable chips can be purchased externally in a price range from $112.50 to $172.50.

a. Determine the upper and lower limits for the transfer price between Qvat Division and Kwak Division.
b. If Qvat Division is presently selling all the chips it can produce to external buyers, what minimum price should be set for transfers to Kwak Division?

E13-48. Transfer pricing Elba Division of Haimes Industries manufactures product #54B89. Three-fourths of the production is transferred to the Crete Division of Haimes Industries; the remainder is sold externally for $67 per unit. The following information is available about product #54B89:

Total production annually	1,200,000 units
Variable production costs	$40
Variable selling costs (includes $4 per unit in advertising cost)	$16
Fixed overhead (allocated on the basis of units of production)	$1,800,000
Fixed selling costs	$2,400,000

a. Determine the transfer price under each of the following methods:
   (1) total variable cost
   (2) full production cost
   (3) total variable production cost plus allocated fixed selling costs
   (4) market price
b. What transfer price do you think Elba Division should use to "sell" the units to Crete Division?

E13-49. Transfer pricing Peyvandi Co., a profit center of California Enterprises, manufactures Product BP3751-9S to sell internally to other company divisions as well as externally. One unit of Product BP3751-9S sells for $72. Production and selling costs for a unit of Product BP3751-9S follow.

Direct material	$ 9.00
Direct labor	11.40
Variable overhead	4.80
Fixed overhead (based on production of 1,400,000 units)	16.50
Variable selling expense	3.00

Andersen Co., another division of California Enterprises, wants to purchase 50,000 units of Product BP3751-9S from Peyvandi Co. during the next year. No selling costs are incurred on internal sales.

a. All the units of Product BP3751-9S that can be produced by Peyvandi Enterprises can be sold externally. What should the minimum transfer price be? Explain.
b. Assume that Peyvandi Co. is experiencing a slight slowdown in external demand and will be able to sell only 1,200,000 units of Product BP3751-9S externally next year at the $72 selling price. What should be the minimum selling price to Andersen Co. under these conditions? Explain.
c. Assume that Joe Dhir, the manager of Andersen Co., offers to pay Peyvandi Co.'s production cost plus 25 percent for each unit of Product BP3751-9S. Dhir receives an invoice for $2,606,250 but was planning on only $1,575,000. How were these amounts determined? What created the confusion? Explain.

E13-50. Transfer pricing; management motivation; writing Great Taste Food Stores operates 20 large supermarkets in the East. Each store is evaluated as a profit center, and store managers have complete control over their purchases and inventory policy. Company policy is that transfers between stores will be made at cost if a store runs short of an item and another store has a sufficient supply.

During a recent period of rapid increases in food prices, company managers noticed that interstore transfers had decreased sharply. Store managers indicated that it was almost impossible to find another store with sufficient inventory to make a transfer when one store ran short of inventory. However, more in-depth checking revealed that many of the other stores did actually have the inventory items on hand.

a. Why would the store managers be reluctant to make the interstore transfers?
b. How could the transfer pricing policy be changed to avoid this type of situation?

LO13-6 **E13-51. Transfer pricing** Walsdorf Company's information technology department is developing a support department transfer price based on minutes of computer time. For the year, its expected capacity was 700,000 minutes, and theoretical capacity was 1,000,000 minutes. Annual costs of the IT department were expected to total $665,000.

  a. What is the IT transfer price based on expected capacity?
  b. What is the IT transfer price based on full capacity?
  c. Actual operating costs of the IT department for the year were $689,400, and actual capacity usage was 730,000 minutes. What were the total variances from budget if the IT department used a transfer price based on expected capacity? On full capacity? What are some possible causes of that variance?

Problems

LO13-1 **P13-52. Cost management and strategy; writing** You are the product manager at a silicon chip manufacturer. One of your products is a commodity chip widely used in cell phones, printers, and computers. As product manager, you have full profit responsibility for the commodity chip. The commodity chip is a "cash cow" for your company and enjoys an enviable market share in the industry. Because your company's chip has approximately the same features and functionality as chips available from competitors, market competition for this product is primarily based on price.

Because of your success in managing the commodity chip, you were recently promoted to product manager of ZX chip, your company's most innovative chip based on its data-processing speed, size, and functionality. The ZX chip has just completed final testing and will be ready to be presented to the market in two weeks.

You were successful in managing the commodity chip because you kept unit production cost low by achieving high volume and efficient production. Identify and discuss the key variables you will try to manage to make the ZX chip as successful as the commodity chip. Discuss whether your efforts to manage costs will be similar to or different from your efforts to manage costs of the commodity chip.

LO13-1 **P13-53. Cost management and customer service; writing** Companies sometimes experience difficult financial times—often so drastic that bankruptcy is declared. If a firm does not invest sufficient resources in its growth, then at some point it will experience diminishing revenues as its product revenues decline. Alternatively, if a firm invests too heavily in growth, costs can spiral out of control. Commonly, companies striving to maintain profitability vacillate between a focus on cost management or cost reduction and a focus on revenue growth. Often cost reduction is achieved by tactics such as across-the-board cost cutting. Seldom do companies maintain a balance of focus on cost management and revenue generation; however, one company, Alcoa, has taken a more strategic approach to both revenue growth and cost management. Even while in the middle of an effort to reduce costs by $1 billion per year, the company was focused on generating significant revenue growth. To achieve growth, the company breaks down its current revenue streams into five categories, including sales from existing customers and sales won from competitors' customers. By segmenting its revenue streams, the company can better evaluate the profitability of obtaining additional sales from different streams and focus on cost management and revenue growth simultaneously. The underlying idea is that growth in costs should occur only where there is a significant opportunity to increase profitability. Further, the company believes that cost management and revenue generation must be managed jointly so that managers understand how cost cutting affects customer value and revenue growth.[8]

  a. When are across-the-board spending cuts a rational approach to cost management?
  b. How can a cost management system help avoid adverse effects from cost cutting?
  c. Why is it necessary for managers to focus attention on both generating new revenue and managing costs to be successful?

LO13-1 **P13-54. Cost management; social responsibility; writing** Through its three sets of elements (motivational, informational, and reporting), a CMS focuses the attention of a given decision maker on the data and information that are crucial to that decision maker's responsibilities in the organization. However,

---

[8] Source: Joseph McCafferty, "Testing the Top Line: Analyzing a Company's Sources of Revenues Can Bring Insights into Growth," *CFO Magazine* (October 19, 2004), https://www.cfo.com/accounting-tax/2004/10/testing-the-top-line/ (last accessed 10/26/23).

the nature and scope of information generated by the CMS for that decision maker are often limited by traditions of financial reporting and the imaginations of CMS designers. A common omission from a CMS is information useful in meeting a firm's social responsibility. Consider the possibility that a CMS could be developed that would be informative relative to organizational performance from the following perspectives: local community, customers, employees, and the environment. Discuss how this information could be used to manage the following specific expenses:

   a. Product liability costs
   b. Local property taxes
   c. Pollution remediation
   d. Costs associated with employee turnover
   e. Warranty expense

P13-55. Information and cost management A product's or service's price is a function of its total production or performance costs. In turn, the total production or performance cost reflects the aggregate costs incurred throughout the supply chain.

Higher education is one industry that has been characterized by rapidly rising costs and prices. Study your college's or university's supply chain and prepare a table identifying specific ways in which improved communications with suppliers and customers could result in specific cost savings for the educational institution, its suppliers, or its customers (students). Organize your table in three columns as follows:

Specific Information to be Obtained	Information Source	Specific Cost to be Reduced

P13-56. Decentralization; ethics; writing A large U.S. corporation participates in a highly competitive industry. Company management has decided that decentralization will best allow the company to meet the competition and achieve profit goals. Each responsibility center manager is evaluated on the basis of profit contribution, market penetration, and return on investment. Failure to meet the objectives established by corporate management for these measures is not acceptable and usually results in demotion or dismissal of a center manager.

An anonymous survey of company managers showed that they felt extreme pressure to compromise their personal ethical standards to achieve corporate objectives. For example, managers at certain plants felt it necessary, for cost control purposes, to reduce quality control to such a level that it was uncertain whether all unsafe products were being rejected. Also, sales and human resources were encouraged to use questionable tactics to obtain orders, including offering gifts and other incentives to purchasing agents.

The chief executive officer is disturbed by the survey findings. In her opinion, the company cannot condone such behavior. She concludes that the company should do something about this problem.

   a. Discuss what might be the causes for the ethical problems described.
   b. Outline a program that could be instituted by the company to help reduce the pressures on managers to compromise personal ethical standards in their work.

P13-57. Decentralization; ethics; writing Although centralization and decentralization are commonly discussed in the context of business organizations and geographically distinct subunits, the concepts are also applicable within a single building. Consider that, in the last 25 years, most hospitals began shifting from centralized nursing stations to decentralized stations that were close to patients' rooms. This trend was thought to make it easier for nurses to attend to patients and to maintain their charts.

   a. Why did the shift from centralized stations to decentralized stations take place?
   b. What problems could be created by the decentralized nurse stations that did not exist when centralized stations were more common?

P13-58. Responsibility accounting reports Hippolito Inc. manufactures industrial tools and has annual sales of approximately $3.5 million with no evidence of cyclical demand. R&D is very important to Hippolito because its market share expands only in response to product innovation.

The company controller has designed and implemented a new annual budget system divided into 12 equal segments for use for monthly performance evaluations. The vice president of operations was upset upon receiving the following responsibility report for the Machining Department for October:

Machining Department
Responsibility Report
For the Month Ended October 31

	Budget	Actual	Variance
Volume in units	3,000	3,185	185 F
Variable manufacturing costs			
Direct material	$ 27,000	$ 28,028	$1,028 U
Direct labor	28,500	30,098	1,598 U
Variable factory overhead	33,300	35,035	1,735 U
Total	$ 88,800	$ 93,161	$4,361 U
Fixed manufacturing costs			
Indirect labor	$ 3,300	$ 3,334	$ 34 U
Depreciation	1,500	1,500	0
Property tax	300	300	0
Insurance	240	240	0
Other	930	1,027	97 U
Total	$ 6,270	$ 6,401	$ 131 U
Corporate costs			
Research and development	$ 2,400	$ 3,728	$1,328 U
Selling and administration	3,600	4,075	475 U
Total	$ 6,000	$ 7,803	$1,803 U
Total costs	$101,070	$107,365	$6,295 U

   a. Identify the weaknesses in the responsibility report for the Machining Department.
   b. Prepare a revised responsibility report for the Machining Department that reduces or eliminates the weaknesses indicated in (*a*).
   c. Deviations in excess of 5 percent of budget are considered material and worthy of investigation. Should any of the Machining Department's variances be investigated? Regardless of materiality, is there any area that the vice president of operations might wish to discuss with the manager of the Machining Department?

LO13-3 **P13-59. Responsibility reports** To respond to increased competition and a reduction in profitability, the nationwide law firm of O'Brien, New & Cave recently instituted a responsibility accounting system. One of the several responsibility centers established was the Civil Litigation Division. This division is treated as a cost center for control purposes. In the first year after the new system was established, the responsibility report for the Civil Litigation Division contained the following comparisons:

	Budget	Actual	Variance
Variable costs			
Professional labor	$3,000,000	$2,820,000	$180,000 F
Travel	150,000	120,000	30,000 F
Supplies	300,000	270,000	30,000 F
Fixed costs			
Professional labor	$1,200,000	$1,215,000	$ 15,000 U
Facilities	750,000	795,000	45,000 U
Insurance	240,000	234,000	6,000 F
Total	$5,640,000	$5,454,000	$186,000 F

For the year, the division projected it would handle 3,000 cases, but its actual case load was 2,970.
   a. What are the major weaknesses in the preceding responsibility report?
   b. Recast the responsibility report in a more meaningful format for cost control evaluation.
   c. If O'Brien, New & Cave uses a management-by-exception philosophy, which costs are likely to receive additional investigation? Explain.

Chapter 13 Responsibility Accounting, Support Department Cost Allocations, and Transfer Pricing

P13-60. Responsibility report; performance evaluation Swimmingly Corp. buys raw fish, cooks and processes it, and then cans it in single-portion containers. The canned fish is sold to several wholesalers, who specialize in providing food to school lunch programs in the northwest United States and western Canada. All processing is conducted in the firm's highly automated plant in Portland, Oregon. Amir Rigera, the production manager, is evaluated on the basis of a comparison of actual costs to standard costs. Only variable costs that Rigera controls are included in the comparison. Fish cost is noncontrollable. Standard costs per pound of fish follow.

LO13-3

Direct labor..............	$0.25
Repairs.................	0.05
Maintenance.............	0.30
Indirect labor............	0.05
Power..................	0.10

For the year, Swimmingly Corp. purchased 2.5 million pounds of fish and canned 1.5 million pounds. There were no beginning or ending inventories of raw, in-process, or canned fish for the year. Actual annual costs were:

Direct labor...........	$300,000
Repairs..............	80,000
Maintenance..........	325,000
Indirect labor.........	77,500
Power...............	157,500

a. Prepare a responsibility report for Rigera for the year.
b. As his supervisor, evaluate Rigera's performance based on the report in (a).
c. Rigera believes his performance is so good that he should be considered for immediate promotion to vice president of production operations. Do you agree? Discuss the rationale for your answer.
d. Do you believe that all of the costs shown on Rigera's responsibility report are truly under his control? Discuss the rationale for your answer.

P13-61. Profit center performance The accounting department at Kerrville College decided to offer a three-day ethics workshop for local CPAs in March. Rose Morris supervised the seminar's planning process and submitted the following budget to the departmental chairperson:

LO13-3, 4

Revenues ($900 per participant)		$ 90,000
Expenses		
Speakers ($2,500 each).............	$15,000	
Rent on facilities...................	3,600	
Advertising.......................	4,000	
Meals and lodging	33,390	
Departmental overhead allocation	23,560	(79,550)
Profit...........................		$ 10,450

The $3,600 facilities rent is a fixed rental, which is to be paid to a local hotel for the use of a meeting room. Advertising is also a fixed cost. Meal expense is budgeted at $10 per person per meal (a total of nine meals to be provided for each participant and each speaker); lodging is budgeted at the rate of $75 per participant and speaker per night. Departmental overhead includes a $10 charge per participant and speaker for supplies as well as a general allocation of 25 percent of revenues for use of departmental administrative and production resources. The budget was approved and Morris proceeded with the seminar.

a. Recast the budget in a segment margin income statement format.
b. The seminar's actual financial results were as follows:

Revenues (120 participants)............		$102,000
Expenses		
Speakers ($2,950 each).............	$17,700	
Rent on facilities...................	4,200	
Advertising.......................	4,900	
Meals and lodging	41,391	
Departmental overhead allocation	26,760	(94,951)
Profit...............................		$ 7,049

Because signups were below expectations, the seminar fee was reduced from $900 to $850, and advertising expense was increased. In budgeting for the speakers, Morris neglected to include airfare, which averaged $450 per speaker. With the increased attendance, a larger meeting room had to be rented from the local hotel. Actual lodging costs were as budgeted, but meals were 15 percent more expensive because of the gratuity. Recast the actual results in a segment margin income format.

   c. Identify and discuss the factors that are primarily responsible for the difference between the budgeted and the actual profit on the ethics seminar.

LO13-4

P13-62. Responsibility centers; research; writing Organizational spending on outsourced contact centers (previously referred to as call centers) continues to increase. Contact centers are critical to organizational success because these units often have primary responsibility for interactions with customers. In some companies, the contact centers are established primarily for customer support; in other companies (especially in the financial services sector), these centers not only provide customer support but also sell additional services to customers who call. Use library, web, or interview research to gather information on contact centers.

   a. Contact centers often have a large responsibility for customer relationship management (CRM). What is CRM, and why is it so important to companies?
   b. List five well-known companies that use such centers and indicate the primary purpose of those contact centers.
   c. How is artificial intelligence used to support the services provided in call centers?
   d. For each company identified in (b), do you think that its contact center would primarily be considered a cost or a profit center? Discuss the rationale for your answers.
   e. For each company in (b), list three possible methods of allocating the costs of contact centers to operating departments. Discuss the rationale for your answers.
   f. Although outsourced contact centers may create cost reductions, what other measurements might be useful in gauging contact center performance and customer satisfaction?

LO13-4

P13-63. Cost and profit centers; ethics; research; writing Many companies provide on-site child-care facilities for employees' children. In some situations, this service is provided free of charge; in other situations, employees are charged, usually on a sliding-scale basis relative to pay, for such services.

   a. If a company provides, but does not charge for, employee child care, the cost of such facilities would be considered a cost center. What potential ethical issues might arise when child-care facilities are viewed as a cost center?
   b. If a company charges for employee child care, do you think the company should establish a designated percentage of profitability that it wishes to earn on the facilities? Discuss the reason for your answer.
   c. Find information on two companies that have child-care facilities for employees' families and determine whether employees are charged for such facilities. What benefits are gained from the companies' perspectives from having such on-site facilities?

LO13-5

P13-64. Direct method Management of Shreveport Community Hospital has decided to allocate the budgeted costs of its three support departments (administration, public relations, and maintenance) to its three operating programs (surgery, in-patient care, and out-patient services). Budgeted information for the year follows.

Chapter 13 Responsibility Accounting, Support Department Cost Allocations, and Transfer Pricing

Budgeted costs	
Administration	$5,400,000
Public relations	1,100,000
Maintenance & janitorial	1,700,000
Allocation bases	
Administration	Dollars of assets employed
Public relations	Number of employees
Maintenance & janitorial	Hours of equipment operation

	Expected Utilizations		
	Assets Employed	Number of Employees	Hours of Equipment Operation
Administration	$1,480,180	8	2,040
Public relations	900,200	14	940
Maintenance & janitorial	1,651,360	10	3,060
Surgery	3,948,500	20	24,850
In-patient care	2,458,500	36	28,400
Out-patient services	1,043,000	44	17,750

Using the direct method, allocate the expected support department costs to the operating areas.

P13-65. Direct method Leyh Management Co. classifies its operations into three departments: commercial sales, residential sales, and property management. The owner, Ellen Leyh, wants to know the full cost of operating each department. Direct departmental costs and several allocation bases associated with each follow:

		Available Allocation Bases		
	Direct Costs	Number of Employees/ Salespersons	Assets Employed	Revenue
Administration	$ 1,500,000	20	$2,480,000	N/A
Accounting	990,000	15	1,364,000	N/A
Promotion	720,000	12	720,000	N/A
Commercial sales	10,490,000	45	900,000	$10,000,000
Residential sales	9,179,000	210	1,440,000	18,000,000
Property management	398,400	18	540,000	2,000,000

The support departments are shown in a benefits-provided ranking. Leyh has selected the following allocation bases for each department: number of employees/salespersons for administration, dollars of assets employed for accounting, and dollars of revenue for promotion.

a. Use the direct method to allocate the support department costs to the revenue-generating departments.
b. Determine the operating income for each division.

P13-66. Step method Use the information for Leyh Management Co. in Problem P13-65.

a. Allocate the support department costs to the revenue-generating departments using the step method.
b. Which department is apparently the most profitable?

P13-67. Direct and step methods Salado Inc. provides cleaning services through its Residential and Commercial divisions. Support services of the company are provided by Personnel and Administration areas. Costs of these two areas are allocated to the revenue producing departments. Personnel costs are allocated using number of employees; administration costs are allocated using direct department costs. The following annual budgeted information (presented in a benefits-provided ranking) is available:

	Personnel	Administration	Residential	Commercial
Direct costs	$140,000	$180,000	$480,000	$800,000
Number of employees	12	30	72	48
Direct labor hours			60,000	90,000
Square feet cleaned			450,000	570,000

a. Using the direct method, allocate the costs of Personnel and Administration to the Residential and Commercial divisions.

b. Using the step method, allocate the costs of Personnel and Administration to the Residential and Commercial divisions.

c. Salado prices jobs by the direct labor hour for Residential services and by the square foot cleaned for Commercial services. Compute the full cost of providing one direct labor hour of service for Residential and for one square foot cleaned for Commercial using (1) the direct method and (2) the step method. (Round cost per hour and cost per square foot to nearest cent.)

LO13-5

P13-68. Algebraic method Lombardi Printing has two support departments (administration and editorial) and two operating divisions (college texts and professional publications). Following are the direct costs and allocation bases for each of these areas:

	Allocation Bases		
Department	Direct Costs	Assets Employed	Number of Employees
Administration	$ 225,000	$310,000	5
Editorial	175,000	75,000	4
College texts	2,250,000	600,000	25
Professional publications	950,000	525,000	15

Company management has decided to allocate administration and editorial costs using dollars of assets employed and number of employees, respectively. Use the algebraic method to allocate the support department costs and determine the total operating costs of college textbooks and professional publications.

LO13-5

P13-69. Comprehensive support department allocations Management at C. Pier Press has decided to allocate costs of the paper's two support departments (administration and human resources) to the two revenue-generating departments (advertising and circulation). Administration costs are to be allocated on the basis of dollars of assets employed; human resources costs are to be allocated on the basis of number of employees. The following costs and allocation bases are available:

Department	Direct Costs	Number of Employees	Assets Employed
Administration	$ 390,750	5	$ 193,550
Human resources	246,350	4	145,850
Advertising	478,900	6	381,200
Circulation	676,300	13	935,150
Totals	$1,792,300	28	$1,655,750

a. Using the direct method, allocate the support department costs to the revenue-generating departments. (Round to the nearest whole percent and dollar.)

b. Using your answer to (a), what are the total costs of the revenue-generating departments after the allocations?

c. Assuming that the benefits-provided ranking is the order shown in the table, use the step method to allocate the support department costs to the revenue-generating departments.

d. Using your answer to (c), what are the total costs of the revenue-generating departments after the allocations?

e. Using the algebraic method, allocate the support department costs to the revenue-generating departments.

f. Using your answer to (e), what are the total costs of the revenue-generating departments after the allocations?

P13-70. Comprehensive support department allocations Wakowski Company's annual budget for its three support departments (administration, legal/accounting, and maintenance/engineering) and its two production departments (processing and finishing) is as follows:

LO13-5

	Annual Budget ($000 omitted)					
	Administration	Legal/ Accounting	Maintenance/ Engineering	Processing	Finishing	Total
Direct department costs:						
Direct labor	$1,400	$1,000	$1,800	$5,600	$4,000	$13,800
Direct material	140	400	180	800	2,400	3,920
Total direct department costs	$1,540	$1,400	$1,980	$6,400	$6,400	$17,720
Department overhead costs:						
Insurance	350	100	150	600	440	1,640
Depreciation	180	140	160	400	300	1,180
Miscellaneous	60	40	80	120	60	360
Total	$2,130	$1,680	$2,370	$7,520	$7,200	$20,900
Number of employees	80	40	60	400	300	880
Sq. ft. of floor space	800	600	400	1,600	2,000	5,400
Maint./Eng. hours	30	40	30	136	204	440

a. Prepare a cost distribution that allocates support department costs using the step method. Assume the benefits-provided ranking is the order in which the departments are listed. The allocation bases for the support department are (1) administration: number of employees; (2) legal/accounting: floor space; and (3) maintenance/ engineering: number of hours. Calculate the factory overhead (OH) rates used within the processing and finishing departments. For the cost allocation base, use both department overhead and allocated support costs. For the cost driver, use 400,000 direct labor hours in processing and 300,000 direct labor hours in finishing.

b. Allocate support department costs using the direct method. Next, calculate factory overhead rates for each department using department overhead plus allocated support costs in the cost allocation base and direct labor hours as the cost driver.

c. Allocate support department costs using the algebraic method. Next, calculate factory overhead rates for each department using department overhead plus allocated support costs in the cost allocation base and direct labor hours as the cost driver.

P13-71. Effect of support department allocations on reporting and evaluation; writing Kensington Corporation is a diversified manufacturing company with corporate headquarters in Easton, Massachusetts. The three operating divisions are Kennedy Division, Consumer Products Division, and Outerspace Products Division. Much of Kennedy Division's manufacturing activity is related to work performed for the government space program under negotiated contracts.

LO13-5

Kensington Corporation headquarters provides general administrative support and computer services to the three operating divisions. Computer services are provided through a computer time-sharing arrangement. The central processing unit (CPU) is located in Boston, and the divisions have remote terminals connected to the CPU by telephone lines. One standard from the Cost Accounting Standards Board provides that the cost of general administration may be allocated to negotiated defense contracts. Furthermore, the standards provide that, in situations in which computer services are provided by corporate headquarters, the actual costs (fixed and variable) of operating the computer department may be allocated to the Kennedy Division based on a reasonable measure of computer usage.

The general managers of the three divisions are evaluated on divisional before-tax performance. The November performance evaluation reports (in millions of dollars) for each division follow.

	Kennedy Division	Consumer Products Division	Outerspace Products Division
Sales	$46	$30	$110
Cost of goods sold	(26)	(14)	(76)
Gross profit	$20	$16	$34
Selling and administrative			
Division selling and administration costs	$10	$10	$16
Corporate general administration costs	2	0	0
Corporate computing	2	0	0
Total	$14	$10	$16
Profit before taxes	$6	$6	$18

Without a charge for computing services, the operating divisions might not make the most cost-effective use of the computer systems resources. Outline and discuss a method for charging the operating divisions for computer services usage that would promote cost consciousness by the operating divisions and operating efficiency by the computer systems services.

LO13-6 P13-72. Transfer prices In each of the following cases, the Speaker Division can sell all of its production of audio speakers externally or some internally to the Sound System Division and the remainder to outside customers. The Speaker Division's production capacity is 400,000 units annually. The data related to each independent case are as follows:

	Case 1	Case 2
Speaker Division		
Selling price to outside customers	$80	$65
Production costs per unit		
Direct material	32	22
Direct labor	12	10
Variable overhead	4	3
Fixed overhead (based on capacity)	1	1
Other variable selling and delivery costs per unit*	6	3
Sound System Division		
Number of speakers needed annually	40,000	40,000
Current unit price being paid to outside supplier	$70	$57

*In either case, $1 of the selling expenses will not be incurred on intracompany transfers.

a. For each case, determine the upper and lower limits for a transfer price for speakers.
b. For each case, determine a transfer price for the Speaker Division that will provide a $12 contribution margin per unit.
c. Using the information developed for (b), determine a dual transfer price for Case 1 assuming that Sound System will acquire the speakers from the Speaker Division at $12 below Sound System's purchase price from outside suppliers.

LO13-6 P13-73. Transfer price Ludmilla Corp. has two divisions: Engine and Mobile Systems. The Engine Division produces engines used by both the Mobile Systems Division and a variety of external industrial customers. External sales orders are generally produced in 50-unit lots. Using this typical lot size, the cost per engine is as follows:

Variable production cost	$4,200
Fixed manufacturing overhead	1,800
Variable selling expense	600
Fixed selling expense	840
Fixed administrative expense	1,280
Total unit cost	$8,720

An engine's external selling price is $10,464, providing the Engine Division with a normal profit margin of 20 percent. Because a significant number of sales are being made internally, Engine

Division managers have decided that the external selling price should be used to transfer all engines to Mobile Systems.

When the Mobile Systems Division manager learned of the new transfer price, she became very upset because it would have a major negative impact on her division's profit. Mobile Systems has asked for a lower transfer price from the Engine Division so that it earns a profit margin of only 15 percent. Mobile Systems' manager has asked corporate management whether the division can buy engines externally. Faye Ryan, Ludmilla's president, has gathered the following information on transfer prices to help the two divisional managers negotiate an equitable transfer price:

Current external sales price	$10,464
Total variable production cost plus a 20% profit margin ($4,200 × 1.2)	5,040
Total production cost plus a 20% profit margin ($6,000 × 1.2)	7,200
Bid price from external supplier (if motors are purchased in 50-unit lots)	9,280

a. Discuss advantages and disadvantages of each of these transfer prices to both the selling and buying divisions and to Ludmilla Corp.

b. If the Engine Division could sell all of its production externally at $10,464, what is the appropriate transfer price and why?

P13-74. Challenging: Transfer pricing journal entries Worldly Traveler's Roll-Em-On Division makes computer bags. The bags are sold to another internal division, SkyWheels, for inclusion in a luggage set and to external buyers. During the month just ended, SkyWheels acquired 4,000 bags from the Roll-Em-On Division, whose standard unit costs follow.   **LO13-6**

Direct material	$40
Direct labor	12
Variable factory overhead	16
Fixed factory overhead	24
Variable selling expense	8
Fixed selling and administrative expense	12

SkyWheels can acquire comparable bags externally for $160 each. Give the entries (*hint*: see the Chapter Demonstration Problem) for each division and for Roll-Em-On (assuming that no bags acquired by SkyWheels have been sold) for the past month if the transfer is to be recorded

a. at SkyWheels' external purchase price and no selling expenses were incurred on, or allocated to, internal transfers.

b. at a negotiated price of total variable cost plus 15 percent of full production cost.

c. by Roll-Em-On Division at SkyWheels' external price, and by SkyWheels at Roll-Em-On's variable production cost.

d. at Roll-Em-On's absorption cost.

P13-75. Transfer prices Cookie Delight Company has two divisions: Plain Cookies and Decorated Cookies. Lars Linden is the manager of Plain Cookies Division and Theresa Davis is the manager of Decorated Cookies Division. Company president Marie Strauss wants to develop a transfer pricing system that will instill goal congruence in the two division managers. Linden and Davis each get a bonus of 10 percent of the operating margins of his and her respective division. The following information is available: **LO13-6**

	Plain Cookies	Decorated Cookies
Sales (market price)	$2.00 per cookie	$4.00 per cookie
Variable costs (excluding direct costs)	$0.50 per cookie	$0.75 per cookie
Fixed costs	$300 per month	$500 per month
Units sold to outside market	3,000 per month	800 per month
Capacity (in units)	4,000 per month	850 per month

a. Create a contribution margin income statement for each division and for the company in total, assuming that the Decorated Cookie Division buys cookies from outside suppliers. Show both Linden's and Davis's bonuses separately.

b. Assuming there are no cost savings associated with the Plain Cookie Division selling directly to the Decorated Cookie Division, what is the lowest transfer price Linden should charge? What is the highest transfer price?
c. Prepare contribution income statements for each division and the company as a whole using the lowest and highest transfer prices computed in (b). What effect does each transfer price have on the two division managers?
d. How can Strauss encourage the division managers to agree to an arrangement that will be acceptable to them and also be the best price for the benefit of the company as a whole? Explain your answer.

P13-76. Transfer pricing; international Edge Products is a global supplier of medical products. They have one primary product which is manufactured in the United States, and two overseas subsidiaries which produce two key supplies for the primary product. Both subsidiaries also sell these supplies to other companies. The U.S. operation purchases the two supplies internally using transfer pricing. The supplies are of the same quality as any available from other suppliers and there would be no benefit to purchasing the supplies outside of the company. The market for the supplies is very competitive and prices are stable. For performance purposes, the U.S. operation is evaluated by department, such as marketing, IT, and sales, while the overseas operations are smaller and evaluated as a whole.

a. Define transfer pricing and identify the objectives of transfer pricing.
b. Explain the methods for determining transfer prices of (1) cost-based transfer prices, (2) market-based transfer prices, and (3) negotiated transfer prices.
c. Explain the advantages and disadvantages of each transfer pricing method described in part b.
d. Based on the scenario, which transfer pricing method should this company select? Explain your answer.
e. How could tariffs, customs duties, or taxes affect transfer pricing and related performance evaluation in this multinational company?

P13-77. Internal vs. external sale The president of Charlottetown Inc. has given the managers of the company's three decentralized divisions (O'Leary, Alberton, and Summerside) the authority to decide whether to sell externally or internally at a transfer price the division managers determine. Market conditions are such that internal or external sales will not affect market or transfer prices. Intermediate markets will always be available for the divisions to purchase their manufacturing needs or sell their product. Division managers attempt to maximize their contribution margin at the current level of operating assets for their divisions.

The Alberton Division manager is considering the following two alternative orders:

- Summerside Division needs 1,500 units of a motor that Alberton Division can supply. To manufacture these motors, Alberton would purchase components from O'Leary Division at a transfer price of $600 per unit; O'Leary's variable cost for these components is $300 per unit. Alberton Division would further process these components at a variable cost of $500 per unit.

  If Summerside cannot obtain the motors from Alberton, it will purchase the motors from Montague Company for $1,500 per unit. Montague Company would also purchase 1,500 components from O'Leary at a price of $400 for each motor; O'Leary's variable cost for these components is $200 per unit.

- New London Company wants to buy 1,750 similar motors from the Alberton Division for $1,250 per unit. Alberton would again purchase components from O'Leary Division, in this case at a transfer price of $500 per unit; O'Leary's variable cost for these components is $250 per unit. Alberton Division would further process these components at a variable cost of $400 per unit.

Alberton Division's plant capacity is limited, and therefore the company can accept either the New London contract or the Summerside order but not both. The president of Charlottetown Inc. and the manager of Alberton Division agree that it would not be beneficial in the short or long run to increase capacity.

a. If the Alberton Division manager wants to maximize the short-run contribution margin, determine whether Alberton Division should (1) sell motors to Summerside Division at the prevailing market price or (2) accept New London Company's contract. Support your answer with appropriate calculations.
b. Without prejudice to your answer to (a), assume that Alberton Division decides to accept the New London contract. Determine whether this decision is in the best interest of Charlottetown Inc. Support your answer with appropriate calculations.

Chapter 13 Responsibility Accounting, Support Department Cost Allocations, and Transfer Pricing   13-57

P13-78. Direct method; transfer price Tobias & Barfield LLC has three revenue departments: litigation (Lit.), family practice (FP), and legal consulting (LC). In addition, the company has two support departments, administration and EDP. Administration costs are allocated to the three revenue departments on the basis of number of employees. EDP's fixed costs are allocated to revenue departments on the basis of peak hours of monthly service expected to be used by each revenue department. EDP's variable costs are assigned to the revenue departments at a transfer price of $80 per hour of actual service. Following are the direct costs and the allocation bases associated with each of the departments:

LO13-5, 6

	Direct Costs (before transfer costs)	Allocation Bases: Number of Employees	Peak Hours	EDP Hours Used
Administration.........	$900,000	4	30	290
EDP—Fixed..........	600,000	2	N/A	N/A
EDP—Variable........	181,280	2	N/A	N/A
Lit..................	400,000	10	80	1,220
FP..................	510,000	5	240	650
LC..................	680,000	3	25	190

a. Was the variable EDP transfer price of $80 adequate? Explain.
b. Allocate all support department costs to the operating departments using the direct method.
c. What are the total costs of the operating departments after the allocation in (b)?

P13-79. Interdivisional transfers; deciding on alternatives Eekaydo Inc. is organized on a divisional basis with considerable vertical integration. Mary Sue Oehlke is the new controller of the CarryOn! Division of Eekaydo.

LO13-6

CarryOn! Division makes a variety of leather products, including a portfolio. Product sales have been steady, and the marketing department expects continued strong demand. Oehlke is looking for ways the CarryOn! Division can contain its costs and thus boost its earnings from future sales. She discovered that CarryOn! Division has always purchased its leather from HIDE, another part of Eekaydo. HIDE has been providing the three square feet of tanned leather needed for each portfolio for $9 per square foot.

Oehlke wondered whether it might be possible to purchase CarryOn!'s leather needs at comparable quality from an external supplier at a lower price. Top management at Eekaydo reluctantly agreed to allow the CarryOn! Division to consider purchasing outside the company.

CarryOn! Division management has issued an RFP (request for proposal) for the leather needed for 100,000 portfolios during the coming year. The two best supplier bids are $8 and $7 per square foot from Koenig and Thompson, respectively. Oehlke has been informed that another subsidiary of Eekaydo, Barrows Chemical, supplies Thompson the chemicals that are an essential ingredient of Thompson's tanning process. Barrows Chemical charges Thompson $2 for enough chemicals to prepare three square feet of leather. Barrows' profit margin is 30 percent.

HIDE Division wants to continue supplying CarryOn!'s leather needs at the same price per square foot as in the past. Tom Reed, HIDE's controller, believes the sales are necessary to maintain HIDE's healthy profit margin of 40 percent of sales.

As Eekaydo's finance vice president, you have called a meeting of the controllers of CarryOn! and HIDE. Oehlke is eager to accept Thompson's $7 bid. She points out that CarryOn!'s earnings will show a significant increase if the division can buy from Thompson.

Reed, however, wants Eekaydo to keep the business within the company and suggests that you require CarryOn! to purchase its needs from HIDE. He emphasizes that HIDE's profit margin should not be lost from the company.

From whom should the CarryOn! Division buy the leather? Consider both CarryOn!'s desire to minimize its costs and Eekaydo's corporate goal of maximizing profit on a companywide basis.

P13-80. Transfer prices; writing Rowling Inc. is a decentralized company, and each investment center has its own sales force and production facilities. Top management uses return on investment (income divided by assets) for performance evaluation. Potter Division has just been awarded a contract for a product that uses a component manufactured by Gondorf Division and by outside suppliers. Potter used a cost figure of $15.20 for the component when the bid was prepared for the new product. Gondorf supplied this cost figure in response to Potter's request for the average variable cost of the component.

LO13-6

© Cambridge Business Publishers

Gondorf has an active sales force that is continually soliciting new customers, and sales of the component are expected to increase. Gondorf's regular selling price is $26 for the component that Potter needs for the new product. Gondorf has the following costs associated with the component:

Standard variable manufacturing cost	$12.80
Standard variable selling and distribution cost	2.40
Standard fixed manufacturing cost	4.80
Total	$20.00

The two divisions have been unable to agree on a transfer price for the component. Corporate management has never established a transfer price because interdivisional transactions have never occurred. The following suggestions have been made for the transfer price:

- Regular selling price
- Regular selling price less variable selling and distribution expenses
- Standard manufacturing cost plus 15 percent
- Standard variable manufacturing cost plus 20 percent

a. Compute each suggested transfer price.
b. Discuss the effect that each of the transfer prices might have on the attitude of Gondorf Division management toward intracompany business.
c. Is the negotiation of a price between the Potter and Gondorf Divisions a satisfactory method for solving the transfer price problem? Explain your answer.
d. Should the corporate management of Rowling Inc. become involved in this transfer controversy? Explain your answer.

LO13-6 **P13-81. Transfer prices** Des Moines Industries consists of eight divisions that are evaluated as profit centers. All transfers between divisions are made at market price. Northeast, a division of Des Moines, sells approximately 20 percent of its output externally. The remaining 80 percent of Northeast's output is transferred to other divisions within Des Moines. No other Des Moines Industries division transfers internally more than 10 percent of its output.

With respect to any profit-based measure of performance, Northeast is the leading division within Des Moines Industries. Other divisional managers always find that their performance is compared to that of Northeast. These managers argue that the transfer pricing situation gives Northeast a competitive advantage.

a. What factors could contribute to any advantage that the Northeast Division might have over the other divisions?
b. What alternative transfer price or performance measure might be more appropriate in this situation?

LO13-6 **P13-82. International transfer prices; research** Go to the **Ernst & Young** website (https://www.ey.com/en_gl/tax-guides/worldwide-transfer-pricing-reference-guide-2020) to find information on the 2020–21 W*orldwide Transfer Pricing Global Reference Guide*. Choose five countries (other than the United States) and compare and contrast the transfer pricing penalties, penalty relief, documentation requirements, availability of APAs, and return disclosures/related party disclosures for those countries. Which of the countries you selected seems to be the (1) most stringent and (2) most lenient?

Ernst & Young

LO13-6 **P13-83. International transfer prices; writing** Why would intangible assets create significant difficulties in international transfer pricing?

Review Solutions

Review 13-1

a. *a.* 2 *b.* 3 *c.* 5 *d.* 6 *e.* 4 *f.* 1
b. Cost information needs to be reasonably accurate but will never be perfectly accurate as there is estimation necessary to quantify costs. Allocation of costs to products or services is an example of an estimation process. Achieving short run (organizational efficiency) and long run goals (survival) will more likely happen when the cost data used to make decisions is reasonably accurate.

Review 13-2

a.
1. Decentralized
2. Decentralized
3. Centralized
4. Centralized
5. Decentralized
6. Decentralized
7. Decentralized
8. Centralized
9. Centralized
10. Decentralized

b. The pandemic brought about abrupt change and much uncertainty. Companies generally needed to centralize decision making in order to make quick decisions in response to changing circumstances. For example, some Hollywood studios released movies directly to streaming platforms, bypassing the theaters. At times, high-stake decisions, impacting all facets of the company, were made in short order.

Review 13-3

a.

Process A23 Department
Responsibility Report
For the Month Ended June 30

	Budget	Actual	Variance
Sales in units	55,000	55,000	0
Controllable Costs			
Variable manufacturing costs			
Direct material	$ 550,000	$ 522,500	$27,500 F
Direct labor	247,500	236,500	11,000 F
Variable factory overhead	220,000	227,700	(7,700) U
Total controllable costs	1,017,500	986,700	30,800 F
Noncontrollable Costs			
Fixed manufacturing costs			
Indirect labor	284,800	284,900	(100) U
Depreciation	78,000	77,800	200 F
Property tax	25,000	25,000	0
Insurance	21,000	22,000	(1,000) U
Other	18,000	18,000	0
Total noncontrollable costs	426,800	427,700	(900) U
Total manufacturing costs	$1,444,300	$1,414,400	$29,900 F

b. The largest variance relates to the favorable direct material variance of $27,500, which would require investigation and analysis.

While a small dollar variance may fall below a dollar threshold established through the management-by-exception principle, it may still merit investigation. Sometimes, a small variance is a result of a netting of two large variances, which can have an impact on the company's current and future operations. For example, in Chapter 10, we dissected a material variance into the components of price and quantity variances. A large favorable price variance could offset a large unfavorable quantity variance. Understanding the individual variances could be useful information that would impact management decision making.

Review 13-4

a.
1. Profit
2. Investment
3. Cost
4. Cost*
5. Investment
6. Revenue
7. Cost
8. Profit

*Assumes that fees are regulated and not determined by the office personnel.

b. While the information technology department may reach its cost cutting goals, it could have a negative impact on the company which could include the following:

1. The quality of service to internal customers could be reduced affecting overall company productivity.
2. The technology department may be less inclined to invest in updated technology due to the costs which could make the company less competitive.
3. The technology department may have cut back on less visible yet important items such as security measures.

4. The technology department may have cut back on employees which could cause a delay in service and/or a drop in experience level, both of which could impact the quality of service provided.

Review 13-5

a. Direct method

Financial Consulting
Admin . . . . $393,876 = $547,050 × 72% (72% = $968,050 ÷ $1,343,450)
IT . . . . 231,076 = $344,890 × 67% (67% = 20 ÷ 30)
$624,952

Operations Consulting
Admin . . . . $153,174 = $547,050 × 28% (28% = $375,400 ÷ $1,343,450)
IT . . . . 113,814 = $344,890 × 33% (33% = 10 ÷ 30)
$266,988

b. Total costs

Financial	Operations	Total
$ 870,565	$658,500	$1,529,065
624,952	266,988	891,940
$1,495,517	$925,488	$2,421,005

c. Step-method

Administrative costs

Department	Base	Proportion of Base	Amount to Allocate	Amount Allocated
IT	$ 204,190	13%	$547,050	$ 71,117
Financial	968,050	63%	547,050	344,642
Operations	375,400	24%	547,050	131,292
	$1,547,640			$547,051*

*Difference due to rounding in departmental totals

IT Costs

Department	Base	Proportion of Base	Amount to Allocate	Amount Allocated
Financial	20	67%	$416,007	$278,724
Operations	10	33%	416,007	137,282
	30			$416,006*

*Difference due to rounding in departmental totals

d. Total costs

	Financial	Operations	Total
Direct costs......	$ 870,565	$658,500	$1,529,065
Allocated costs...	623,366*	268,574**	891,940
	$1,493,931	$927,074	$2,421,005

*$344,642 + $278,724 = $623,366
**$131,292 + $137,282 = $268,574

e. and f. Algebraic method

	Assets Employed	Proportion	# Employees	Proportion
Admin..........	N/A		8	21%
IT	$ 204,190	13%	N/A	
Financial........	968,050	63%	20	53%
Operations	375,400	24%	10	26%
	$1,547,640		38	

A = $547,050 + 0.21IT

IT = $344,890 + 0.13A

A = $547,050 + 0.21($344,890 + 0.13A)

A = $636,863

IT = $344,890 + 0.13 ($636,863)

IT = $427,682

	Admin	IT	Financial	Operations	Total
Direct costs.......	$547,050	$344,890	$ 870,565	$658,500	$2,421,005
Admin	(636,863)	82,792	401,224	152,847	0
IT	89,813	(427,682)	226,672*	111,197	0
	$ 0	$ 0	$1,498,461	$922,544	$2,421,005

*Amount adjusted due to rounding

g. If operations consulting uses less of an allocation base (such as a cut-back resulted in a few number of employees and/or assets employed), financial consulting would bear more of the service costs. This would happen even if financial consulting had the same number of employees and assets employed as budgeted.

Review 13-6

a. $85 = Incremental costs of $46.50 (calculated as $15 + 23 + $8.50) plus the opportunity cost of the contribution margin on lost sales of $38.50 (calculated as $90 − $15 − $23 − $8.50 − $5).

b. Because Londen Inc. has excess capacity, Londen Inc. has no opportunity cost so the minimum price should cover the incremental costs of $46.50 (calculated as $15 + 23 + $8.50).

c. The minimum price is $85 (see part a) and the maximum price is $95. The profit would be split evenly at $90 = ($85 + $95) ÷ 2.

d. Factors that could impact the negotiation process include:
   1. Capacity of production and external demand of product.
   2. Opportunity cost of the facility used in production such as downsizing of facilities or renting out facilities.
   3. Potential for internal selling costs that could be eliminated with the internal transfer.
   4. Quality of product compared to quality of comparable items in the market.
   5. Level of product customization, if any.
   6. Negotiating ability of management teams.
   7. Volatility of market place (i.e., prices constantly change).

Data Visualization Solutions

(See page 13-28.)

Note: All answers are shown as a cost per unit.

a. The overall cost savings is $6, calculated as $16 (purchase price in the market place) minus $10 (incremental cost to make).

b. The Parts Division records a $4 profit ($14 – 10) for the amount in excess of incremental costs. The Small Equipment Divisions realizes a $2 cost savings because it is $2 (= $16 – $14) cheaper to buy the part internally.

c. The overall cost savings is still the $16 (purchase price in the market place) minus $10 (incremental cost to make), which equals $6. Any internal profit or loss will be eliminated upon consolidation of the financial statements of Smith Manufacturing Inc.

d. The Parts Division records a $8 profit ($18 – 10) for the amount in excess of incremental costs. The Small Equipment Division realizes a $2 loss because it is $2 (= $18 – $16) more expensive to buy the part internally.

Chapter 14

Pricing, Sales Variances, and Customer Profitability

Road Map

LO	Learning Objective | Topics	Page	eLecture	Demo	Review	Assignments
14-1	**How are cost-based approaches applied to pricing?** Economic Pricing Approach :: Marginal Revenue :: Marginal Cost :: Cost-Based Pricing Approach :: Single-Product Companies :: Profit Equation :: Multiple-Product Companies :: Markup on Cost Base :: Markup on Variable Costs :: Markup on Total Manufacturing Costs :: Special Order Pricing :: Robinson-Patman Act :: Ad Hoc Discounts	14-2	e14-1	D14-1A D14-1B D14-1C	Rev 14-1	MC14-13, MC14-14, MC14-15, E14-22, E14-23, E14-24, E14-25, E14-26, E14-27, E14-28, E14-29, E14-30, E14-31, P14-50, P14-51, P14-52, P14-53, P14-54, P14-57, **DA14-1**
14-2	**What is target costing and its connection to the product life cycle?** Product Life Cycle:: Target Costing :: Value Engineering :: Design for Manufacture :: Chained Target Costing	14-8	e14-2	D14-2	Rev 14-2	MC14-16, MC14-17, E14-32, E14-33, E14-34, E14-35, E14-36, E14-37, E14-38, E14-39, P14-55, P14-56, P14-57, P14-58, P14-59, P14-60, P14-61
14-3	**What is the relation between target costing and continuous improvement costing?** Kaizen Costing :: Continuous Improvement :: Production Stage :: Cost Reduction Targets	14-13	e14-3	D14-3	Rev 14-3	MC14-18, E14-40, P14-62, P14-63
14-4	**How is the revenue variance decomposed and analyzed?** Revenue Variance :: Sales Price Variance :: Sales Volume Variance :: Price Elasticity	14-15	e14-4	D14-4	Rev 14-4	MC14-19, E14-41, E14-42, E14-43, E14-44, P14-64, P14-65, P14-66
14-5	**How is the contribution margin variance decomposed and analyzed?** Contribution Margin (CM) Variance :: Flexible Budget Variance :: Contribution Margin Volume Variance :: Sales Mix Variance :: Sales Quantity Variance	14-17	e14-5	D14-5A D14-5B D14-5C	Rev 14-5	MC14-20, E14-45, E14-46, P14-67
14-6	**How can a customer profitability analysis be useful in management decision making?** Customer Profitability Analysis :: Customer Profitability Profile :: Pareto Chart :: Activity-Based Costing :: Customer Profitability Ratio	14-23	e14-6	D14-6	Rev 14-6	MC14-21, E14-47, E14-48, E14-49, P14-68, **DA14-2**

INTRODUCTION

Cost-based pricing, target costing, and continuous improvement costing represent important concepts for product management professionals involved in the development, manufacture, and marketing of products and services. Virtually all such techniques are grounded in the notion of managing the value chain. This chapter examines pricing, the interrelation between price and cost, and the role of the product life cycle in target costing. We begin with an overview of the pricing model economists use to explain price equilibrium. Given the limitations of this long-run equilibrium model for determining price of a product or service, we consider the widely used cost-plus approach to identifying initial prices. We then examine how intense competition (such as that for the green car market) has inverted the cost-plus pricing model into one that starts with an acceptable market price and subtracts a desired profit to determine a target cost. We also consider how revenue and contribution variances are calculated and used to manage profitability. Lastly, we examine profitability at a more detailed level when we compute profitability of individual customers with customer profitability analysis.

COST-BASED APPROACHES TO PRICING

LO14-1 How are cost-based approaches applied to pricing?

Pricing products and services is one of the most important and complex decisions facing management. Pricing decisions directly affect the salability of individual products or services, as well as the profitability, and even the survival, of the organization. Many economists have spent their entire careers examining the foundations of pricing. To respond to the needs of pricing hundreds or thousands of individual items, managers may develop pricing guidelines *based on costs* which can then be compared to data obtained through consumer research.

Comparing Economic Pricing to Cost-Based Pricing

In economic models, the firm has a profit-maximizing goal and known cost and revenue functions. Typically, increases in sales quantity require reductions in selling prices, causing **marginal revenue** (the varying increment in total revenue derived from the sale of an additional unit) to decline as sales increase. Increases in production cause an increase in **marginal cost** (the varying increment in total cost required to produce and sell an additional unit of product). In economic models, profits are maximized at the sales volume at which marginal revenues equal marginal costs. Firms continue to produce as long as the marginal revenue derived from the sale of each additional unit exceeds the marginal cost of producing that unit.

Economic models provide a useful framework for considering pricing decisions. The ideal price is the one that will lead customers to purchase all units a firm can provide up to the point at which the last unit has a marginal cost exactly equal to its marginal revenue.

Despite their conceptual merit, economic models are seldom used for day-to-day pricing decisions. Perfect information and an indefinite time period are required to achieve equilibrium prices at which marginal revenues equal marginal costs. In the short run, most for-profit organizations attempt to achieve a target profit rather than a maximum profit. One reason for this is an inability to determine the single set of actions that will lead to profit maximization. Furthermore, managers are more apt to strive to satisfy a number of goals (such as profits for investors, job security for themselves and their employees, and being a "good" corporate citizen) than to strive for the maximization of a single profit goal. In any case, to maximize profits, a company's management would have to know the cost and revenue functions of every product the firm sells. For most firms, this information cannot be developed at a reasonable cost.

Cost-Based Pricing Approaches

Although cost is not the only consideration in pricing, it has traditionally been the most important for several reasons.

- *Cost data are available.* When hundreds or thousands of different prices must be set in a short time, cost could be the only feasible basis for product pricing.
- *Cost-based prices are defensible.* Managers threatened by legal action or public scrutiny feel secure using cost-based prices. They can argue that prices are set in a manner that provides a "fair" profit.

Chapter 14 Pricing, Sales Variances, and Customer Profitability   14-3

- *Revenues must exceed costs if the firm is to remain in business.* In the long run, the selling price must exceed the full cost of each unit.

Cost-based pricing is illustrated in **Exhibit 14.1**. The process begins with market research to determine customer wants. If the product requires components to be designed and produced by vendors, the process of obtaining prices can be time consuming. When some costs, such as those fixed costs at the facility level, are not assigned to specific products, a markup is added to cover these costs. An additional markup is added to achieve a desired profit. *The selling price is then set as the sum of the assigned costs, the markup to cover unassigned costs, and the markup to achieve the desired profit.*

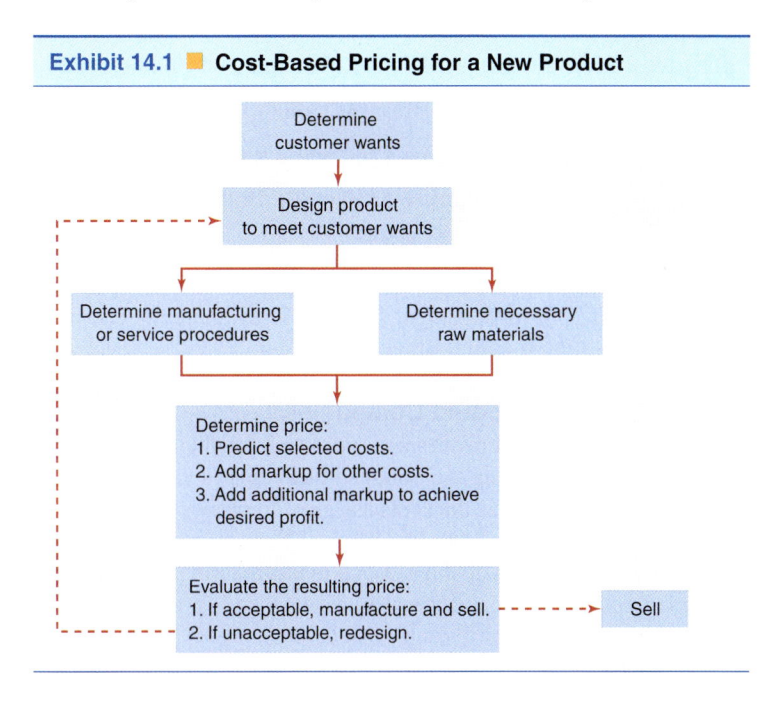

Exhibit 14.1 ■ Cost-Based Pricing for a New Product

```
Determine customer wants
        ↓
Design product to meet customer wants
        ↓
Determine manufacturing        Determine necessary
or service procedures          raw materials
        ↓
Determine price:
1. Predict selected costs.
2. Add markup for other costs.
3. Add additional markup to achieve
   desired profit.
        ↓
Evaluate the resulting price:
1. If acceptable, manufacture and sell.  ----→ Sell
2. If unacceptable, redesign.
```

The proposed selling price should be evaluated with regard to competitive information and what customers are willing to pay. If the price is acceptable, the product or service is produced. If the price is too high, the product might be redesigned, manufacturing procedures might be changed, and different types of materials might be considered until either an acceptable price is achieved or it is determined that the product cannot be produced at an acceptable price.

On the other hand, the selling price can sometimes be a major driver of a company's growth. Certain companies with differentiated products can reach budgeted sales targets by naming their own price. An example of this can be seen in the company **Tapestry** that owns the handbag brand, **Coach**. Despite signs of a slowdown in U.S. luxury purchases, the company increased the prices of Coach handbags based on its assessment of strong consumer demand for its products.[1] As a result, Tapestry's sales revenue forecast increased despite a general decline in consumer purchases. This is the exception, however, as most companies must set prices determined by the market.

Cost-Based Pricing in Single-Product Companies

Implementing cost-based pricing in a single-product company is straightforward if everything is known but the selling price. In this case, all known data are entered into the profit equation, which is then solved for the variable price.

Determining Cost-Based Price for a Single-Product Firm   LO14-1   DEMO 14-1A

Cleaner Rugs Inc. provides residential and commercial rug cleaning. Assume that one location's annual fixed facility-level costs are $200,000 and the unit cost of cleaning a rug is $10. Suppose management desires to achieve an annual profit of $30,000 at an annual volume of 10,000 rugs. To

---

[1] Sophia, D., "*Tapestry lifts forecast as Coach bags defy U.S. luxury gloom,*" Reuters, May 11, 2023, Accessed on October 30, 2023), https://www.reuters.com/business/retail-consumer/tapestry-raises-annual-profit-forecast-higher-prices-strong-demand-2023-05-11/.

© Cambridge Business Publishers

simplify the example, assume that management charges the same price regardless of the type, size, or shape of the rug.

◆ **What is the cost-based price of each rug using the profit equation?**

Using the profit equation, the cost-based price is determined to be $33.

$$\text{SP per unit } (X) - \text{VC per unit } (X) - \text{Total FC} = \text{Profit}$$

where SP = Selling price   VC = Variable cost
       X = Sales volume   FC = Fixed cost

$$(\text{SP per unit} \times 10{,}000 \text{ rugs}) - (\$10 \times 10{,}000 \text{ rugs}) - \$200{,}000 = \$30{,}000$$

Solving for the selling price:

$$(\text{SP per unit} \times 10{,}000) = \$300{,}000 + \$30{,}000$$
$$\text{SP per unit} = \$330{,}000 \div 10{,}000$$
$$= \$33$$

A selling price of $33 to clean a rug will allow ServiceMaster to achieve its desired profit. However, before setting the price at $33, management should also evaluate the competitive situation and consider what customers are willing to pay for this service.

Cost-Based Pricing in Multiple-Product Companies

In multiple-product companies, desired profits are estimated for the entire company, and standard procedures are established for determining the initial selling price of each product. These procedures typically specify the initial selling price as the costs assigned to products or services plus a markup to cover unassigned costs and provide for the desired profit. Depending on the sophistication of the organization's accounting system, possible cost bases in a manufacturing organization include markups based on a combination of cost behavior and function. The possible cost bases include the following.

- Direct materials costs
- Variable manufacturing costs
- Total variable costs (manufacturing, selling, and administrative)
- Full manufacturing costs

Regardless of the cost base, the general approach to developing a markup is to recognize that the markup must be large enough to provide for costs not included in the base (also referred to as the *unassigned* costs) plus the desired profit.

$$\text{Markup on cost base} = \frac{\text{Costs not included in the base} + \text{Desired profit}}{\text{Costs included in the base}}$$

DEMO 14-1B   LO14-1   Determining Cost-Based Price for a Multiple-Product Firm

First we illustrate a pricing decision with variable costs as the cost base; full manufacturing costs is the cost base in the second illustration.

Markup Based on Total Variable Costs When the markup is based on variable costs, it must be large enough to cover all fixed costs and the desired profit. Assume that the predicted annual variable and fixed costs for one of **Roku**'s divisions are as follows.

Variable		Fixed	
Manufacturing....................	$60,000	Manufacturing....................	$30,000
Selling and administrative..........	20,000	Selling and administrative..........	10,000
Total	$80,000	Total	$40,000

Chapter 14 Pricing, Sales Variances, and Customer Profitability

Furthermore, assume that Roku's division has total assets of $120,000.

◆ **If management believes that an annual return of 14 percent on total assets is appropriate in Roku's industry, what is the markup on variable cost?**

A 14 percent return translates into a desired annual profit of $16,800.

> Annual return on assets × Total assets = Desired annual profit
>
> 14% × $120,000 = $16,800

Assuming all cost predictions are correct, obtaining a profit of $16,800 requires a 71 percent markup on variable costs.

$$\text{Markup on variable cost} = \frac{\text{Fixed costs} + \text{Desired profit}}{\text{Variable costs}}$$

$$\text{Markup on variable cost} = \frac{\$40,000 + \$16,800}{\$80,000}$$

$$= 0.71$$

◆ **If the predicted variable cost for Product A1 is $12 per unit, what is the initial selling price for Product A1?**

> Variable cost per unit
> + (Variable cost per unit × Markup on variable cost)
> Initial selling price

$$= \$12 + (\$12 \times 0.71) = \$20.52$$

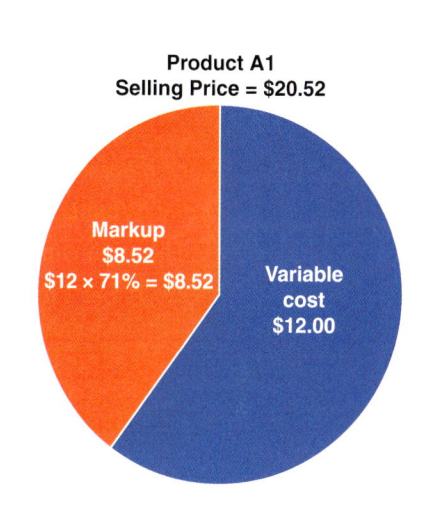

Product A1
Selling Price = $20.52
- Markup $8.52 ($12 × 71% = $8.52)
- Variable cost $12.00

Markup Based on Total Manufacturing Costs

When the markup is based on full manufacturing costs, it must be large enough to cover selling and administrative expenses and to provide for the desired profit. Again, it is necessary to determine the desired profit and predict all costs for the pricing period. The initial prices of individual products are then determined as their unit manufacturing costs plus the markup.

◆ **Assuming the same desired profit of $16,800 for Roku, what is the markup on manufacturing costs?**

$$\text{Markup on total manufacturing costs} = \frac{\text{Selling and administrative costs} + \text{Desired profit}}{\text{Total manufacturing costs}}$$

$$\text{Markup on total manufacturing costs} = \frac{(\$20,000 + \$10,000) + \$16,800}{(\$60,000 + \$30,000)}$$

$$= 0.52$$

◆ **If the predicted manufacturing cost for Product B1 is $10 per unit, what is the initial selling price for Product B1?**

> Manufacturing cost per unit
> + (Manufacturing cost per unit × Markup on manufacturing costs)
> Initial selling price

$$= \$10 + (\$10 \times 0.52) = \$15.20$$

Product B1
Selling Price = $15.20
- Markup $5.20 ($10 × 52% = $5.20)
- Total Manufacturing costs $10.00

Cost-Based Pricing for Special Orders

Many organizations use cost-based pricing to bid on unique projects called special orders. As explained in Chapter 5, the sales price quoted on a special order job should be high enough to at least cover the job's variable and incremental fixed cost. In addition, company management should consider any effects that the additional job will have on normal company activities. For example, without excess capacity, a company must give up a portion of regular sales. In this case, the associated contribution margin from the regular sales must be *subtracted* from the contribution margin gained from the special order. Also, a company should consider other opportunities for any unused capacity besides the special order.

In setting the bid price, management may specify a "reasonable" profit on the special order. If the project requires dedicated assets, the acquisition of new fixed assets, or an investment in employee training, the desired profit on the special order or project should allow for an adequate return on the dedicated assets or additional investment.

DEMO 14-1C   LO14-1   Determining a Price for a Special Order

Assume that Lee's Manufacturer's Inc. is considering the fulfillment of a special order of 100 units. Lee's unit variable production cost is $150 and fixed manufacturing costs for the period are $50,000. Lee has planned capacity of 5,000 units of production out of a total of 5,500 units of capacity. Lee has no other immediate opportunities for the excess capacity.

◆ **What is the minimum price per unit that Lee should charge for the special order?**

The minimum price per unit for the special order is $150, the incremental unit cost of the special order.

◆ **If Lee's management team believes that a normal profit margin of 11.4 percent on incremental unit cost for a special order is reasonable, what is the price Lee should charge for the special order?**

Selling price = Unit incremental cost + (Unit incremental cost × Markup on incremental cost)

=$150 + ($150 × 11.4%) = $167.10

Setting the special order bid price at $167.10 would cover the $150 variable production cost and provide the 11.4 percent profit margin ($17.10) on incremental unit cost. This computation illustrates a simplistic cost-plus approach to pricing but ignores both product demand and market competition. Landry's bid price should also reflect these considerations.

An additional consideration in making special pricing decisions in the United States is the **Robinson-Patman Act**, which, under certain circumstances, prohibits companies from pricing the same product at different levels when those amounts do not reflect related cost differences. Cost differences must result from actual variations in the cost to manufacture, sell, or distribute a product because of different methods of production or quantities sold.

Companies may, however, give **ad hoc discounts**, which are price concessions that relate to real (or imagined) competitive pressures rather than to where a buyer is located or the quantity of goods purchased. Such discounts are not usually subject to detailed justification because they are based on a competitive market environment. Although ad hoc discounts do not require intensive justification under the law, other types of discounts do because they could reflect some type of price discrimination. Prudent managers must understand the legalities of special pricing and the factors that allow for its implementation. For normally stocked merchandise, the only support for pricing differences is a difference in distribution or service costs.

Disadvantage of Cost-Based Pricing
Cost-based pricing has four major drawbacks.

1. Cost-based pricing requires accurate cost assignments. If costs are not accurately assigned, some products could be priced too high, losing market share to competitors. Other products could be priced too low, gaining market share but being less profitable than anticipated.
2. The higher the portion of unassigned costs, the greater is the likelihood of over- or underpricing individual products.

3. Cost-based pricing assumes that goods or services are relatively scarce and, generally, customers who want a product or service are willing to pay the price.
4. In a competitive environment, cost-based approaches increase the time and cost of bringing new products to market.

Cost-based pricing became the dominant approach to pricing during an era when products were relatively long-lived and there was relatively little competition. Also, these systems tend to focus on organizational units such as departments, plants, or divisions and not on activities or cost drivers. While easy to implement and justify, cost-based prices might not be competitive. Competition puts intense downward pressure on prices and removes slack from pricing formulas. There is little margin for error in pricing. In a highly competitive market, small variations in pricing make significant differences in success.

In contrast to the cost-based approach, users of a price-based approach start with a price that customers are willing to pay and then determine allowable costs as discussed in the next section.

REVIEW 14-1

Applying Cost-Based Approaches to Pricing LO14-1

Assume that **Prince**, a tennis equipment manufacturer, has the following current year contribution income statement.

PRINCE
Contribution Income Statement
For Year Ended December

Sales (100,000 units at $12 per unit)		$1,200,000
Less variable costs		
Manufacturing	$300,000	
Selling and administrative	150,000	(450,000)
Contribution margin		750,000
Less fixed costs		
Manufacturing	400,000	
Selling and administrative	200,000	(600,000)
Net income		$ 150,000

Assume Prince has total assets of $2,000,000 and management desires an annual return of 10 percent on total assets.

Required

a. Determine the dollar amount by which Prince exceeded or fell short of the desired annual rate of return for the year.

b. Given the current sales volume and cost structure, determine the selling price required to achieve an annual profit of $250,000.

c. Given your answer to requirement (b) and the current sales volume and cost structure, determine (1) the selling price as a percentage of variable manufacturing costs and (2) the markup as a percentage of variable manufacturing costs.

d. Restate your answer to requirement (c) for the markup as a percentage of variable manufacturing costs, dividing into two separate markup percentages:
  1. The markup on variable manufacturing costs required to cover unassigned costs.
  2. The additional markup on variable manufacturing costs required to achieve an annual profit of $250,000.

e. **Critical Thinking:** In part b, is the required selling price greater than or less than the current selling price? Does a change in selling price automatically mean that the company will achieve its profit goals?

More practice:
E14-23, E14-27,
E14-28, E14-29
Solution on p. 14-47.

LIFE CYCLE AND TARGET COSTING

LO14-2 What is target costing and its connection to the product life cycle?

Economists argue that cost-based prices are not realistic, because in the real world prices are determined by the confluence of supply and demand. However, when a new product is introduced into the market for which there is no previously existing supply or demand, there has to be a starting point. As discussed above, cost has often been the baseline for determining initial selling prices. All too often, however, companies introduce new products into the market based on what the designers and engineers "think" the market wants (or based on inadequate market research), only to find out later that either the market does not want the product, or it is not willing to buy the new product at a price sufficient to cover its cost plus an acceptable profit to the producer. This often leads to costly redesign, or in many cases, complete abandonment of the product, typically resulting in substantial financial losses.

As a result, companies must determine *before* a new product is introduced into the market, whether it can be produced at a cost that will make it profitable when sold at a price acceptable to customers. Understanding costs over a product's life cycle is critical because the company must cover all costs in order to be solvent and contribute toward profits. An awareness of the impact of today's actions on tomorrow's costs underlies the notion of **product life-cycle costs**, which include all costs associated with a product or service ranging from those incurred with the initial conception through development, introduction, growth, maturity, and decline.

Product Life Cycles

Product profit margins are typically judged on a period-by-period basis without consideration of the product life cycle. However, products, like people, have life cycles. The **product life-cycle** model depicts the stages through which a product class (not each product) passes from the time that an idea is conceived until production is discontinued. Those stages are development (which includes design), introduction, growth, maturity, and decline. **Exhibit 14.2** illustrates a conventional sales trend line as the product class passes through each life-cycle stage. Companies must be aware of where products are in their life cycles because, in addition to the sales effects, the life-cycle stage can have a tremendous impact on costs and profits.

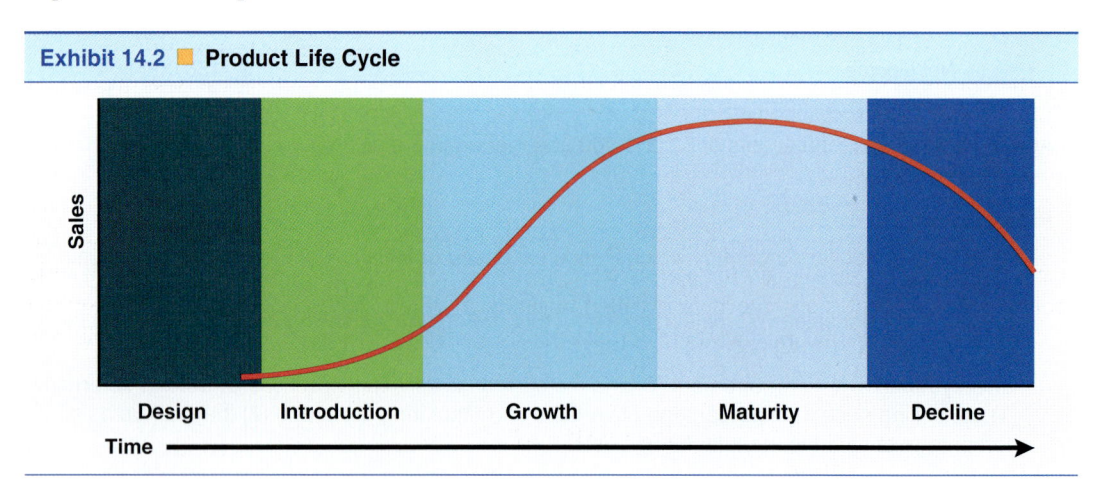

Exhibit 14.2 Product Life Cycle

[Chart showing Sales over Time across stages: Design, Introduction, Growth, Maturity, Decline]

- **Design stage** In the design stage, production methods, materials, and conversion operations are selected. Many of the product's quality, cost, and environmental impacts are set with the decisions made in this stage.
- **Introduction stage** During the product introduction stage, costs can be substantial and are typically related to engineering change orders, market research, and advertising/promotion. Sales are usually low and prices are often set in relation to the market prices of similar or substitute goods, if any are available.
- **Growth stage** The growth stage begins when the product has gained market acceptance and starts to show increased sales. Product quality also can improve during this life-cycle stage because of

learning curve effects (discussed in Chapter 3) or if competitors have made cost efficient improvements to the original production design. Prices are fairly stable during the growth stage because many substitutes exist or because consumers have become "attached" to the product and are willing to pay a premium price for it rather than buy a substitute.

- **Maturity stage** In the maturity stage, sales begin to stabilize or slowly decline, and firms often compete on selling price. Costs are often at their lowest level during this period because production techniques have become routine, so profits can be high. Some products remain at this stage for a long time; others pass through this stage quickly.
- **Decline stage** The decline stage reflects waning sales. Prices can be cut dramatically to stimulate business. Production cost per unit generally increases during this stage because fixed overhead is spread over a smaller production volume. The decrease in selling price and increase in fixed overhead cost per unit results in reduced profitability.

Target Costing

From a cost standpoint, product development is an extremely important stage that the traditional financial accounting model almost ignores. Financial accounting requires that development costs be expensed as incurred—even though most studies indicate that decisions made by the time the production design team has completed only 25–50 percent of its work actually determine approximately 80–90 percent of a product's total life-cycle costs.

Although technology and competition have tremendously shortened the time spent in the development stage, effective development efforts are critical to a product's life-cycle profitability. Decisions made during this stage can

- reduce production and life-cycle costs through material specifications,
- shorten manufacturing time through process design,
- increase quality by minimizing potential design defects, and
- add flexibility to product design or production processes.

After a product is designed, the producing firm has traditionally determined product cost and then set a selling price based, to some extent, on that cost. If the market will not bear the resulting selling price (possibly because competitors' prices are lower), the firm either earns less profit than desired or attempts to lower production costs. Because of intensified competition and surplus production capacity in many product markets, companies often have less discretion in setting prices now than in the past.

The Process of Target Costing

Today, most products are designed to be sold at a market price (the price point) that is associated with the preferences of a particular product market segment. To keep production costs in line with the price point, some companies use a technique called target costing. As expressed in the following formula, **target costing** develops an "allowable" product cost by using market research to estimate the price point for a product with specific characteristics.

$$TC = ESP - APM - S\&A$$

where   TC = target production cost
   ESP = estimated selling price
   APM = acceptable profit margin
   S&A = expected per-unit selling and administrative cost

Subtracting an acceptable profit margin and selling and administrative costs from the estimated selling price leaves an implied maximum per-unit target product cost, which is compared to an expected product cost. The target costing process is depicted in **Exhibit 14.3**.

Exhibit 14.3 ■ Target Costing Process

Step 1: Product/service characteristics desired
- New product marketing input →
- ← Customer input

Step 2: Target selling price
- Competitive market conditions →
- ← Customer input

Step 3: Target cost = Target price − Acceptable profit margin − Selling and administration costs
- Competitive market conditions →
- ← Management input/strategic plan

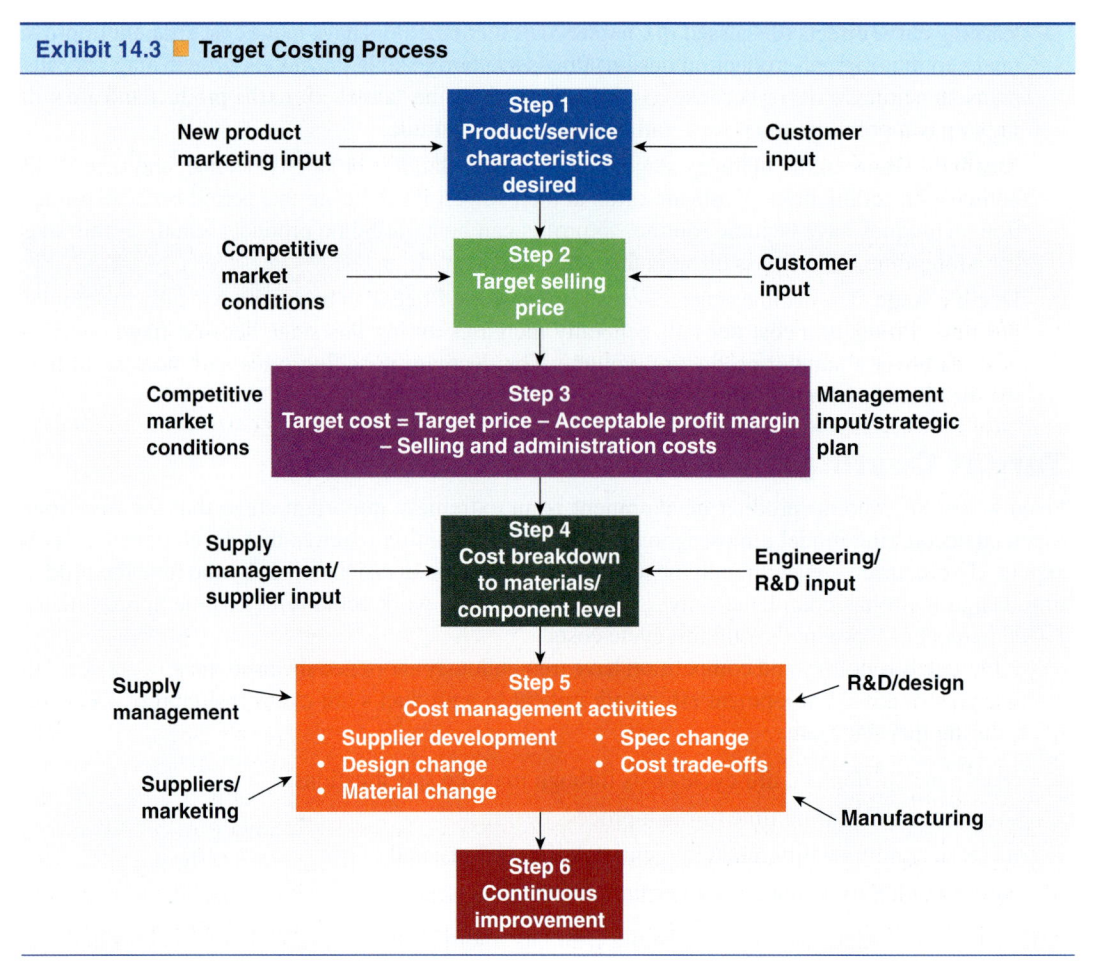

Step 4: Cost breakdown to materials/component level
- Supply management/supplier input →
- ← Engineering/R&D input

Step 5: Cost management activities
- Supplier development
- Design change
- Material change
- Spec change
- Cost trade-offs
- Supply management →
- Suppliers/marketing →
- ← R&D/design
- ← Manufacturing

Step 6: Continuous improvement

Source: From L.M. Ellram, "The Implementation of Target Costing in the United States: Theory versus Practice," *Journal of Supply Chain Management, 42*, no. 1, (Winter 2006), pp. 13ff. Copyright© 2006 Blackwell Publishing Ltd. Reproduced with permission of Blackwell Publishing Ltd.

If the expected product cost is higher than the target product cost, the company has several alternatives.

- First, cost databases can be used to help determine how the product design and/or production process can be adjusted to reduce costs. *Cost databases* provide information about the impact on product costs of using different input resources, manufacturing processes, and design specifications.
- Second, a less-than-desired profit margin can be accepted.
- Third, the company can decide not to enter this particular product market at the current time because the desired profit margin cannot be obtained.

If, for example, the target costing system used by **Canon** indicated that a product's life-cycle costs were too high to make an acceptable profit, the product would be abandoned unless it were strategically necessary to maintain a comprehensive product line or to create a "flagship" product.

Target costing requires a shift in the way managers think about the relations among cost, selling price, and profits. The traditional attitude has been that a product is developed, production cost is determined, a selling price is set (or a market price is met), and profits or losses result. Target costing takes a different perspective: a product is developed, a selling price and desired profit amount are determined, and maximum allowable costs are calculated. When allowable costs are constrained by selling price, all costs must be justified. Unnecessary costs should be eliminated without reducing quality.

An important step in successful product development is the process of **value engineering (VE)**, which involves a disciplined search for various feasible combinations of resources and methods that will increase product functionality and reduce costs. *Multidisciplinary teams* using various problem-solving tools such as brainstorming and Pareto analysis seek an improved product cost–performance ratio by considering such factors as reliability, conformity, and durability. Cost reduction, shortened production cycles, and increased quality are the major reasons to engage in VE. Additionally, companies are becoming more concerned about final disposal costs of products. As such, designing a product so that it can be recycled or will create a minimal environmental impact upon disposal has production cost and VE implications.

Target costing can be applied to services if they are sufficiently uniform to justify the modeling effort required.

Determining Target Cost   LO14-2   DEMO 14-2

Assume that a print shop wants to offer customers the opportunity to buy a variety of items personalized with photographs. A market survey indicates that the metropolitan area could sustain an annual 500-order volume and that customers believe $18 is a reasonable fee per service. The print shop manager desires a $6 profit for each customer order and estimates that marketing and administrative costs would be $3 per order.

◆ **What is the target cost of each order?**

$$TC = ESP - APM - S\&A$$

$$TC = \$18 - \$6 - \$3 = \$9$$

The allowable target cost is $9 per order: the manager will invest in the equipment necessary to provide the new service if the manager believes that the indicated volume suggested by market research is sufficient to support the costs of production and depreciation on the newly acquired equipment.

In designing a product to meet an allowable cost, engineers strive to eliminate all non-value-added activities from the production process. Such reductions in activities will, in turn, reduce costs. The production process and types of components to be used should be discussed among appropriate parties (including engineering, management, accounting, and marketing) in recognition of the product quality and cost desired. Suppliers also can participate in the design phase by making suggestions for modifications that would allow standard components to be used rather than more costly special order items.

Properly designed products should require only minimal engineering change orders (ECOs) after being released to production. Each time an ECO is issued, one or more of the following situations can occur and create additional costs: production documents must be reprinted; workers must relearn tasks; machine dies, jigs, or setups must be changed; and parts in stock or currently ordered can be made obsolete. If costs are to be affected significantly, any design changes must be made early in the process—preferably before production begins.

Target costing is more important for products with a relatively short market life cycle. Products with a long life cycle present many opportunities to continuously improve design and manufacturing procedures that are not available when a product has a short life cycle. Hence, extra care must go into the initial planning for short-lived products. This is especially true when short product life cycles are combined with increased worldwide competition. It is important to introduce a product first and at a price that ensures rapid market penetration. For example, for low-technology products with relatively long product lives, decisions committing the organization to spend money are made at approximately the same time the money is spent. However, for high-technology products with relatively short product lives, most of the critical decisions affecting cost, such as product design and the selection of manufacturing procedures, are made before production begins.

Advantages of Target Costing

Encourages Cost Management

Target costing takes a proactive approach to cost management, reflecting the belief that costs are best managed by decisions made during product development. This contrasts with the more passive cost-plus belief that costs result from design, procurement, and manufacture. Target costing helps orient employees toward the final customer and reinforces the notion that all departments within the organization and all organizations along the value chain must work together. Target costing also empowers employees who will be assigned the responsibility for carrying out activities necessary to deliver a product or service with the authority to determine what activities will be selected.

Encourages Design for Manufacture
In the absence of a target costing approach, design engineers are apt to focus on incorporating leading-edge technology and the maximum number of features in a product. Target costing keeps the customer's function, quality, and price requirements in the forefront at all times. If customers do not want leading-edge technology (which could be expensive and untested) and multiple product features, they will resist paying for them. Focusing on achieving a target cost keeps design engineers tuned into the requirements of the final customer.

Left on their own, design engineers might believe that their job ends when they design a product that meets the customer's functional requirements. The tendency is to simply pass on the design to manufacturing and let manufacturing determine how best to produce the product. Further down the line, if the product needs servicing, it becomes the service department's responsibility to determine how best to service the product. A target costing approach forces design engineers to explicitly consider the costs of manufacturing and servicing a product while it is being designed. This is known as **design for manufacture**.

Minor changes in design that do not affect the product's functioning can often produce dramatic savings in manufacturing and servicing costs. Examples of design for manufacture include the following:

- Using molded plastic parts to avoid assembling several small parts.
- Placing an access panel in the side of an appliance so service personnel can make repairs quickly.
- Using standard-size parts to reduce inventory requirements, to reduce the possibility of assembly personnel inserting the incorrect part, and to simplify the job of service personnel.
- Using manufacturing procedures that are common to other products.

Reduces Time to Introduce Products
By designing a product to meet a target cost (rather than evaluating the marketability of a product at a cost-plus price and having to recycle the design through several departments), target costing reduces the time required to introduce new products. Involving vendors in target costing design teams makes the vendors aware of the necessity of meeting a target cost. This facilitates the concurrent engineering of components to be produced outside the organization and reduces the time required to obtain components.

Disadvantages of Target Costing

Target Costing Requires Cost Information
Implementing target costing requires detailed information on the cost of alternative activities which require resources to obtain or develop. This information allows decision makers to select design and manufacturing alternatives that best meet function and price requirements. Tables that contain detailed databases of cost information for various manufacturing variables are occasionally used in designing products and selecting processes to meet target costs.

Target Costing Requires Extensive Coordination
Limitations of target costing are employee and supplier attitudes and the many meetings required to coordinate product design and to select manufacturing processes. All people involved must have a basic understanding of the overall processes required to bring a product to market and an appreciation of the cost consequences of alternative actions. They must also respect, cooperate, and communicate with other team members and be willing to engage in a negotiation process involving trade-offs. Finally, they must understand that reducing the total time required to bring a new product to market requires extensive upfront coordination.

This aspect of the process is even more difficult when suppliers must be brought in as part of the coordination process. This concept is frequently referred to as **chained target costing** because the supply chain's support is critical for the product to be both competitively priced and delivered to the final customer in a timely manner. When multiple suppliers are required, the organization must obtain everyone's support or the process will probably not be successful due to gaps in the reliability of delivery, quality, and cost control. Each organization and unit must understand that if the product is not brought to market within the defined constraints, all will lose. They must make firm commitments for the project undertaken and to have faith that each participant will carry out whatever part of the supply chain it has promised to fulfill. Coordination across the supply chain is vital in the overall process of continuous improvement as discussed later in this chapter.

Target Costing — LO14-2 — REVIEW 14-2

Unique Items Inc. has developed a new office product. The firm has conducted significant market research and estimated the following pattern for sales of the new product.

Year	Expected Volume	Expected Price per Unit
1	15,000	$15.00
2	32,000	18.00
3	58,000	20.00
4	62,000	20.00
5	20,000	10.00

The firm wants to net a minimum of $4.00 per unit in profit over the product's life, and selling and administrative expenses are expected to average $45,000 per year.

a. Calculate the life-cycle target cost per unit to produce the new product.
b. **Critical Thinking:** How can the target costing process address ESG considerations?

More practice: E14-36, E14-37
Solution on p. 14-48.

CONTINUOUS IMPROVEMENT COSTING

If a company decides to enter a market, the target cost computed at the beginning of the product life cycle does not remain the final focus. Over the product's life, the target cost is continuously reduced in an effort to spur a process of continuous improvement in actual production cost. **Kaizen costing** involves ongoing efforts for continuous improvement to reduce product costs, increase product quality, and/or improve the production process after manufacturing activities have begun. These cost reductions are designed to keep the profit margin relatively stable as the product price is reduced over the product life cycle.

LO14-3 What is the relation between target costing and continuous improvement costing.

Continuous improvement costing begins where target costing ends. Target costing takes a proactive approach to cost management during the conception, design, and preproduction stages of a product's life; continuous improvement costing takes a proactive approach to cost management during the *production stage* of a product's life.

```
                                Time
    ─────────────────────────────────────────────────────────▶
    Conception    Design    Preproduction  :  Production
    ─────────────────────────────────────── : ────────────────
              Target costing               :  Continuous improvement costing
```

Exhibit 14.4 compares target and kaizen costing.

Exhibit 14.4 ■ Comparison of Target and Kaizen Costing

	Target Costing	Kaizen Costing
What?	A procedural approach for determining a maximum allowable cost for an identifiable, proposed product, assuming a given target profit margin	A mandate to reduce costs, increase product quality, and/or improve production processes through continuous improvement efforts
Used for?	New products	Existing products
When?	Development stage (includes design)	Primary production stages (introduction and growth); possibly, but not probably, maturity

continued

continued from previous page

Exhibit 14.4	Comparison of Target and Kaizen Costing (concluded)
	Target Costing	**Kaizen Costing**
How?	Works best by aiming at a specified cost reduction objective; used to set original production standards	Works best by aiming at a specified cost reduction objective; reductions are integrated into original production standards to sustain improvements and provide new challenges
Why?	Extremely large potential for cost reduction because 80 to 90 percent of a product's lifelong costs are embedded in the product during the design and development stages	Limited potential for reducing cost of existing products, but may provide useful information for future target costing efforts
Focus?	All product inputs (material, labor, and overhead elements) as well as production processes and supplier components	Depends on where efforts will be most effective in reducing production costs; generally begins with the most costly component and (in more mature companies) ends with overhead components

Continuous improvement costing specifies a cost target to be achieved during a time period. First calculate the expected cost for the following period (due to growth, inflation, etc.). Next, calculate the target cost, based on the rate of desired cost reduction. Basically, the mathematics of the concept is quite simple, but its implementation is difficult.

DEMO 14-3 LO14-3 Determining Kaizen Cost Targets

To reduce the cost of merchandise handling in each of its stores, assume that **Walmart** sets a target cost reduction of 2 percent a year.

◆ **If a store had current annual merchandise handling costs of $100,000 and expected an increase the next year due to 10 percent expected growth, what would be the budget for the next year?**

The budget for the next year would be $107,800, calculated as follows.

$$\$100,000 \times 1.10 = \$110,000 \text{ Budget based on growth}$$
$$\$110,000 \times 0.98 = \$107,800 \text{ Budget based on target cost reduction}$$

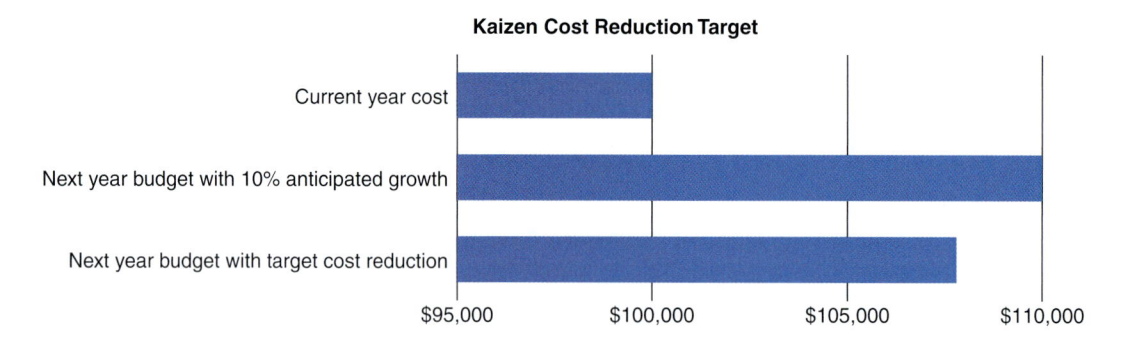

Kaizen Cost Reduction Target

Current year cost	$100,000
Next year budget with 10% anticipated growth	$110,000
Next year budget with target cost reduction	$107,800

Like target costing, Kaizen costing should be viewed as a serious attempt to make processes more efficient, while maintaining or improving quality, thereby making the company more competitive and profitable. In Kaizen costing, cost reductions can be achieved both internally and externally through continuous redesign and improved internal processes, and by working with vendors to improve their designs and processes. Kaizen initiatives often involve multifunctional teams that study specific production issues to lower costs or improve quality. Kaizen methods are also being used by companies to reduce energy consumption and the environmental impacts of operations.

Chapter 14 Pricing, Sales Variances, and Customer Profitability

The "Toyota Way" describes **Toyota's** method to set Kaizen cost reduction targets for each cost element, including purchased parts per car, direct materials per car, labor hours per car, and office utilities. Performance reports developed at the end of each month compare targeted and actual cost reductions. If actual cost reductions are more than the targeted cost reductions, the results are favorable. If the actual cost reductions are less than the targeted cost reductions, the results are unfavorable.

Because cost reduction targets are set before it is known how they will be achieved, continuous improvement costing can be stressful to employees. A critical element in motivating employee cooperation and teamwork in aggressive cost management techniques, such as target and continuous improvement costing, is to avoid using performance reports to place blame for failure. The proper response to an unfavorable performance report must be an offer of assistance to correct the failure.

REVIEW 14-3 — Analyzing the Impact of Continuous Improvement Initiatives (LO14-3)

Patel Company contracts manufacturing of compact security cameras. At its Pacific plant, cost control has become a concern of management. The actual costs per unit for the last two years were as follows.

	Year 1	Year 2
Direct materials		
Plastic case	$ 4.50	$ 4.40
Lens set	17.00	17.20
Electrical component set	6.60	5.70
Battery	11.00	10.00
Direct labor	32.00 (1.6 hours)	30.00 (1.5 hours)
Indirect manufacturing costs		
Variable	7.50	7.10
Fixed	3.00 (100,000 unit base)	2.85 (120,000 unit base)

The company manufactures all of the security camera components except the lens sets, which it purchases from several vendors. The company has used target costing in the past but has not been able to meet the very competitive global pricing. Beginning in Year 2, the company implemented a continuous improvement program that requires cost reduction targets.

Required

a. If continuous improvement (Kaizen) costing sets a target of a 5 percent reduction of the Year 1 variable costs per unit, what is the Year 2 cost variance by cost component? Assume that the company sets a target for fixed costs to remain constant in total.

b. **Critical Thinking:** How successful was the company in meeting its per unit cost reduction targets in Year 2? Analyze your results.

More practice: MC14-18, E14-40
Solution on p. 14-48.

REVENUE VARIANCE

The financial performance reports for revenue centers include a comparison of actual and budgeted revenues. In a revenue center, performance evaluations are limited because the manager has control over only one item: revenue.

If the organization is to meet its budgeted profit goal for a period, with its budgeted fixed and variable costs, the organization's revenue centers must meet their original revenue budgets. Consequently, the revenue variance is used to evaluate the financial performance of revenue centers.

Revenue Variance The **revenue variance** is the difference between the budgeted sales volume at the budgeted selling price (static budget) and the actual sales volume at the actual selling price (actual results). It can be presented as follows.

$$\text{Revenue variance} = (\text{Actual units} \times \text{Actual price}) - (\text{Budgeted units} \times \text{Budgeted price})$$

To compare budgeted and actual revenues, the price and volume components of revenue must be distinguished from one another. The separate impact of changing prices and volume on revenue is analyzed with the sales price and sales volume variances.

Sales Price Variance The **sales price variance** indicates the portion of the total revenue variance that is related to a change in selling price. It is computed as the change in selling price (SP) times the actual sales volume.

> **Sales price variance = (Actual selling price − Budgeted selling price) × Actual units**

Sales Volume Variance The **sales volume variance** indicates the impact of the change in sales volume on revenues, assuming there was no change in selling price. The sales volume variance is computed as the difference between the actual and the budgeted sales volumes times the budgeted selling price.

> **Sales volume variance = (Actual units − Budgeted units) × Budgeted selling price**

The net of the sales price and the sales volume variances is equal to the revenue variance.

```
                   Revenue Variance
                   _____|_____
                  |                 |
         Sales Price Variance   Sales Volume Variance
```

DEMO 14-4   LO14-4   Decomposing Revenue Variance into Sales Price and Sales Volume Variances

We assume that Spectator Inc. produces two stadium blankets: basic and deluxe. The following sales data was summarized for the current year.

	Basic	Deluxe
Actual units.	10,080	7,920
Budgeted units	10,010	8,190
Actual selling price per unit.	$40	$60
Budgeted selling price per unit.	$43	$58

◆ **How does the company calculate its revenue, sales price, and sales volume variances?**

The total revenue variance is decomposed into the sales price variance and sales volume variance as shown in the following calculations.

Decomposing Revenue Variance

	A	B	C	D	E	F	G
1				Basic			
2	Actual Units	10,080	Actual Units	10,080	Budgeted Units	10,010	
3	× Actual SP	$40	× Budgeted SP	$43	× Budgeted SP	$43	
4		$403,200		$433,440		$430,430	
5			$30,240 U		$3,010 F		
6			Sales Price Variance		Sales Volume Variance		
7				Deluxe			
8	Actual Units	7,920	Actual Units	7,920	Budgeted Units	8,190	
9	× Actual SP	$60	× Budgeted SP	$58	× Budgeted SP	$58	
10		$475,200		$459,360		$475,020	
11			$15,840 F		$15,660 U		
12			Sales Price Variance		Sales Volume Variance		
13							
14		$14,400 U	+	$12,650 U	=	$27,050 U	
15		Total Sales Price Variance		Total Sale Volume Variance		Total Revenue Variance	
16							

The following data visualization depicts the variances by product type.

Revenue Variance Analysis

[Bar chart showing Sales Price Variance, Sales Volume Variance, and Revenue Variance for Basic and Deluxe products, with values ranging from approximately -$30,000 to $20,000]

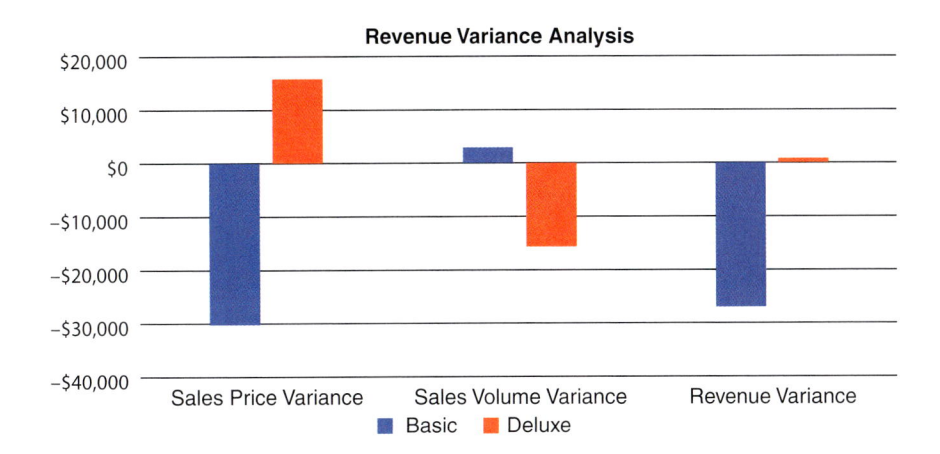

Analysis of Revenue Variance

Interpretation of revenue variances is subjective. In the case of the basic product, we could say that if the increase in sales volume had not been accompanied by a decline in selling price, revenues would have increased $3,010 instead of decreasing by $27,230 (=$30,240 U + $3,010 F). The $3.00 per unit decline in selling price cost the company $30,240 in revenues. Said in a different way, the $3 reduction in selling price was not offset by a large enough increase in sales volume. For the deluxe product, the $2 increase in the selling price over budget resulted in a favorable sales price variance. However, a corresponding decrease in volume nearly offset the favorable variance, with a resulting overall revenue variance of $180 F (=$15,840 F + $15,660 U). An economic analysis could explain the relationship as volume being sensitive to price (*price elasticity*).

Identifying Potential Problems and Opportunities Variances are merely signals that actual results are not proceeding according to plan. They help managers identify potential problems and opportunities. An investigation into their cause(s) could even indicate that a manager who received a favorable variance was doing a poor job, whereas a manager who received an unfavorable variance was doing an outstanding job. Consider Spectator's favorable sales volume variance for its basic product of $3,010. This occurred because actual sales exceeded budgeted sales slightly by 70 units (or less than 1 percent of budget), which on the surface meets expected performance. But what if the total market for the company's products exceeded the company's forecast by 10 percent? In this hypothetical case, Spectator's sales volume falls below its expected percentage share of the market. The favorable variance could occur (despite a poor marketing effort) because of strong customer demand that competitors could not fill. Volume variances are analyzed in further detail in the next section.

Decomposing the Revenue Variance — **LO14-4** — **REVIEW 14-4**

Presented is information pertaining to an item sold by Winding Creek General Store.

	Actual	Budget
Sales in units	150	125
Unit selling price	$26	$25

Required

a. Compute the revenue, sales price, and sales volume variances.
b. **Critical Thinking:** Analyze the variances in part *a*.

More practice: E14-41, E14-42, E14-43, E14-44
Solution on p. 14-49.

Contribution Margin Variance

While we have computed revenues variances, we now evaluate contribution margin (CM) variances by taking into account variable costs. Recall that contribution margin is calculated by subtracting variable costs from sales. Profit centers use variance analysis to compare actual contribution margin to budgeted contribution margin. In this section, we start with the CM variance, decomposing it into

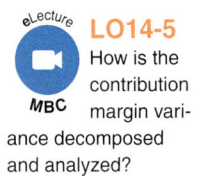

LO14-5 How is the contribution margin variance decomposed and analyzed?

the flexible budget and CM volume variance. To further analyze the CM volume variance, it is further decomposed as shown in the following diagram.

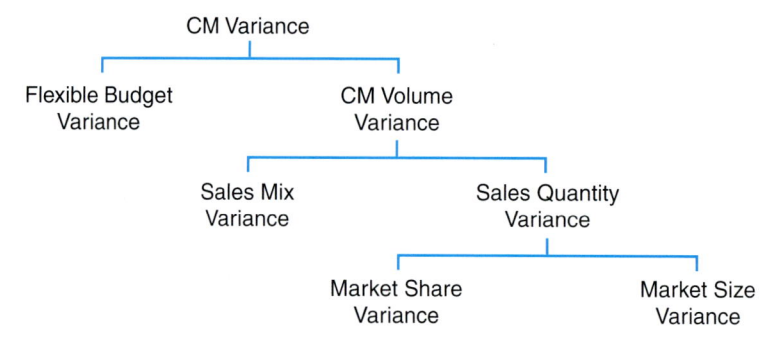

```
                        CM Variance
                            |
            ┌───────────────┴───────────────┐
      Flexible Budget                   CM Volume
         Variance                        Variance
                                            |
                              ┌─────────────┴─────────────┐
                          Sales Mix                   Sales Quantity
                          Variance                       Variance
                                                            |
                                               ┌────────────┴────────────┐
                                          Market Share              Market Size
                                            Variance                   Variance
```

Contribution Margin Variance The **contribution margin variance** is computed as the difference between the actual and budgeted contribution margin. It can be presented as follows.

> **Contribution margin variance = Actual contribution margin − Budgeted contribution margin**

The separate impact of changing prices and volume on the contribution margin variance is analyzed with the flexible budget and contribution margin volume variances.

Flexible Budget Variance The **flexible budget variance** indicates the portion of the total contribution margin variance that is related to a change in prices. A flexible budget is the difference between actual results and budgeted results adjusted to actual activity levels. It is computed as the change in contribution margin per unit times the actual units.

> **Flexible budget variance = (Actual CM per unit − Budgeted CM per unit) × Actual units**

Contribution Margin Volume Variance The **contribution margin volume variance** indicates the impact of the change in sales volume on total contribution margin, assuming there was no change in contribution margin per unit. The CM volume variance is computed as the difference between the actual and the budgeted sales volumes times the budgeted contribution margin per unit.

> **CM Volume variance = (Actual units − Budgeted units) × Budgeted CM per unit**

DEMO 14-5A   LO14-5 Decomposing CM Variance into Flexible Budget and CM Volume Variances

In addition to the data provided in Demo 14-4, additional data for Spectator Inc. is provided below.

	Budgeted Variable Cost per unit	Actual Variable Cost per unit
Basic.....	$23	$24
Deluxe ...	$34	$35

For both products, assume that the variable cost per unit increased over budget due to rising inflation.

◆ **How does the company calculate its flexible budget, CM volume, and CM variances?**

Given actual and budgeted selling price and variable cost per unit information, the actual and budgeted contribution margin per unit (selling price per unit − variable cost per unit) is calculated as follows for each product type.

	Budgeted CM per unit	Actual CM per unit
Basic.....	$20 ($43 − $23)	$16 ($40 − $24)
Deluxe ...	$24 ($58 − $34)	$25 ($60 − $35)

Using this and other previously provided information, the flexible budget and CM volume variances, and the total CM variance are calculated as follows.

Decomposing Contribution Margin Variance

	A	B	C	D	E	F	G	H	I
1				Basic					
2	Actual Units	10,080	Actual Units		10,080	Budgeted Units		10,010	
3	× Actual CM per unit	$16	× Budgeted CM per unit		$20	× Budgeted CM per unit		$20	
4		$161,280			$201,600			$200,200	
5				$40,320 U			$1,400 F		
6			Flexible Budget Variance			CM Volume Variance			
7				Deluxe					
8	Actual Units	7,920	Actual Units		7,920	Budgeted Units		8,190	
9	× Actual CM per unit	$25	× Budgeted CM per unit		$24	× Budgeted CM per unit		$24	
10		$198,000			$190,080			$196,560	
11				$7,920 F			$6,480 U		
12			Flexible Budget Variance			CM Volume Variance			
13									
14		$32,400 U	+		$5,080 U		=	$37,480 U	
15		Total Flexible Budget Variance			Total CM Volume Variance			Total CM Variance	
16									

The following data visualization depicts the variances by product type.

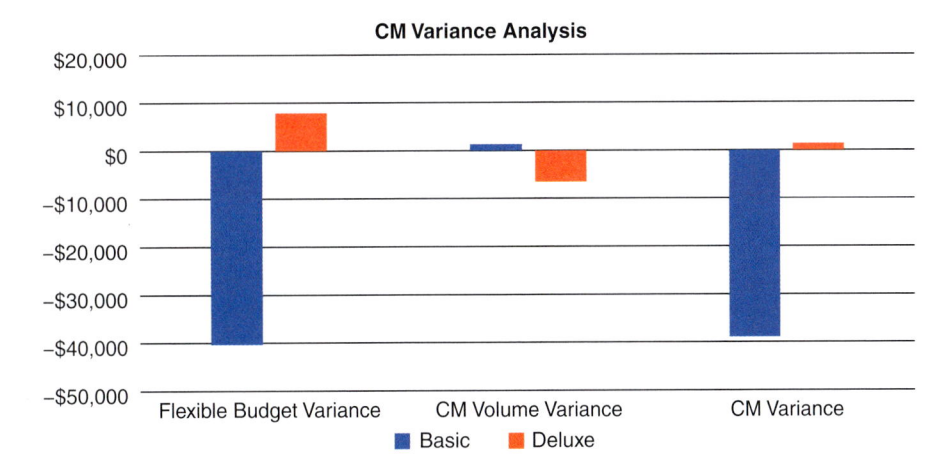

CM Variance Analysis The flexible budget variance is unfavorable because total actual contribution margin is less than total budgeted contribution margin. The basic product was the source of the overall unfavorable CM variance. Along with the sales price decrease, the variable cost per unit increased, both negatively impacting the flexible budget variance. The CM volume variance is unfavorable ($5,080 U) and is broken down into the sales mix variance and the sales quantity variance in the next section.

Contribution Margin Volume Variance

The separate impact of changing sales mix and sales quantity on the contribution margin volume variance is analyzed with the sales mix and sales quantity variances.

Sales Mix Variance The **sales mix variance** indicates the portion of the contribution margin volume variance that is related to the difference between planned and actual sales mix. Because different products can have different contribution margin percentages, a change in sales mix can result in more or less overall company contribution margin.

> **Sales mix variance =**
> **(Actual sales mix − Budgeted sales mix) × Total actual units × Budgeted CM per unit**

Sales Quantity Variance The **sales quantity variance** indicates the portion of the contribution margin volume variance that is related to the change in total units sold, assuming no change in sales mix.

> **Sales quantity variance =**
> **(Total actual units − Total budgeted units) × Budgeted sales mix × Budgeted CM per unit**

DEMO 14-5B LO14-5 Decomposing CM Volume Variance into Sales Mix and Sales Quantity Variances

In addition to the data provided in Demo 14-4 and Demo 14-5A, additional data for Spectator Inc. is provided below.

	Basic	Deluxe	Total
Actual units..................................	10,080	7,920	18,000
Actual sales mix (10,080/18,000; 7,920/18,000)	56%	44%	100%
Budgeted units...............................	10,010	8,190	18,200
Budgeted sales mix (10,010/18,200; 8,190/18,200).....	55%	45%	100%

Spectator Inc. sold more of its basic product compared to its deluxe product with a sales mix of 56 percent and 44 percent, respectively. Compared to the budget, the actual sales mix shifted slightly more toward the basic units and slightly less to the deluxe units.

◆ **What is the sales mix and sales quantity variances for the basic and deluxe products?**

The total CM volume variance is decomposed into the sales mix variance and sales quantity variance as shown in the following calculations.

Decomposing Contribution Margin Volume Variance

	A	B	C	D	E	F	G
1			Basic				
2	Total Actual Units	18,000	Total Actual Units	18,000	Total Budgeted Units	18,200	
3	× Actual Sales Mix	56%	× Budgeted Sales Mix	55%	× Budgeted Sales Mix	55%	
4	× Budgeted CM per unit	$20	× Budgeted CM per unit	$20	× Budgeted CM per unit	$20	
5		$201,600		$198,000		$200,200	
6			$3,600 F		$2,200 U		
7			Sales Mix Variance		Sales Quantity Variance		
8			Deluxe				
9	Total Actual Units	18,000	Total Actual Units	18,000	Total Budgeted Units	18,200	
10	× Actual Sales Mix	44%	× Budgeted Sales Mix	45%	× Budgeted Sales Mix	45%	
11	× Budgeted CM per unit	$24	× Budgeted CM per unit	$24	× Budgeted CM per unit	$24	
12		$190,080		$194,400		$196,560	
13			$4,320 U		$2,160 U		
14			Sales Mix Variance		Sales Quantity Variance		
15							
16		$720 U	+	$4,360 U	=	$5,080 U	
17		Total Sales Mix Variance		Total Sales Quantity Variance		Total CM Volume Variance	
18							

The following data visualization depicts the variances by product type.

CM Volume Variance Analysis

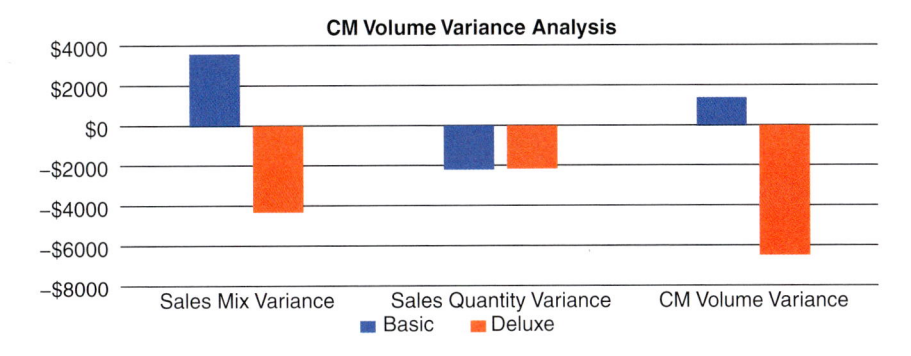

CM Volume Variance Analysis The sales mix variance was favorable for the basic product because a greater portion of the total units sold was reflected in sales than planned. The opposite was the case for the deluxe product resulting in a negative sales mix variance. Because total units sold were less than planned, the sale quantity variance was unfavorable. The sales quantity variance ($4,360 U) is broken down below into the market share variance and the market size variance in the next section.

Sales Quantity Variance

The separate impact of changing market share and market size on the sales quantity variance is analyzed with the market share and market size variances. The calculations use a budgeted weighted average CM per unit of a company's products, calculated as follows.

> Budgeted WA CM per unit = Total budgeted CM ÷ Total budgeted units

Market Share Variance The **market share variance** indicates the impact on the sales quantity variance of a difference between planned and actual market share.

> Market share variance =
> (Actual market share − Budgeted market share) × Actual total market units × Budgeted WA CM per unit

Market Size Variance The **market size variance** indicates the impact on the sales quantity variance of a change in total estimated units in the market, assuming no change in market share. The total number of estimated market units depends on what the customer demand is for Spectator's stadium blankets plus other similar blankets in the market.

> Market size variance =
> (Actual total market units − Budgeted total market units) × Budgeted market share × Budgeted WA CM per unit

Decomposing Sales Quantity Variance into Market Share and Size Variances LO14-5 DEMO 14-5C

In addition to the data provided in Demo 14-4, Demo 14-5A and Demo 14-5B, assume the following information about the market for the basic and deluxe products.

Actual total market units	75,000
Actual market share (18,000 units ÷ 75,000 units)	24%
Budgeted total market units	72,800
Budgeted market share (18,200 units ÷ 72,800 units) . . .	25%
Budgeted weighted average CM per unit	$21.80

The budgeted weighted average (WA) contribution margin per unit shown above was calculated as follows, using information from Demo 14-5A.

> Budgeted WA CM per unit = Total budgeted CM ÷ Total budgeted units

Budgeted WA CM per unit = ($196,560 + $200,200) ÷ (10,010 + 8,190) = $21.80

What is the market share and market size variance?

The total sales quantity variance is decomposed into the market share variance and market size variance as shown in the following calculations.

Decomposing Sales Quantity Variance

	A	B	C	D	E	F
1	Actual Total Market Units	75,000	Actual Total Market Units	75,000	Budgeted Total Market Units	72,800
2	× Actual Market Share	24%	× Budgeted Market Share	25%	× Budgeted Market Share	25%
3	× Budgeted WA CM per unit	$21.80	× Budgeted WA CM per unit	$21.80	× Budgeted WA CM per unit	$21.80
4		$392,400		$408,750		$396,760
5			$16,350 U		$11,990 F	
6			Market Share Variance		Market Size Variance	
7						
8		$16,350 U	+	$11,990 F	=	$4,360 U
9		Market Share Variance		Market Size Variance		Sales Quantity Variance

The following data visualization depicts the variances by type.

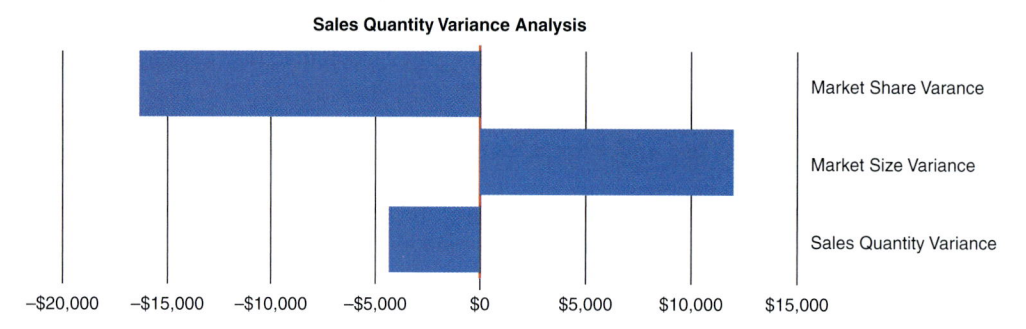

Sales Quantity Variance Analysis

Sales Quantity Variance Analysis The market share variance is unfavorable because the company obtained a smaller portion of the total market compared to budget. A lower share of the market equates to lost sales and lower profits. However, the market size variance was favorable because the actual total market demand was greater than anticipated. A total market or industry demand can fluctuate based on a number of reasons, including a change in economic conditions or in customer preferences. The two variances were offsetting resulting in an unfavorable sales quantity variance of $4,360.

REVIEW 14-5 **LO14-5** Decomposing the CM Volume Variances and the Sales Quantity Variances

A commercial small engine manufacturer summarized the following information for two products, Product X and Product Y, for the current year.

	Product X	Product Y	Total
Actual units.	5,544	7,056	12,600
Budgeted selling price per unit	$80	$120	
Budgeted variable cost per unit	$40	$ 72	
Budgeted units	4,800	4,800	9,600

Market Data

Actual total market In units	75,000
Budgeted total market in units	80,000

Required

More practice: E14-45, E14-46
Solution on p. 14-49.

a. Calculate the sales mix and sales quantity variances for Product X and Product Y.
b. Calculate the market share and market size variances.
c. **Critical Thinking:** Analyze the variances in parts a and b.

CUSTOMER PROFITABILITY ANALYSIS

In the prior sections, we examined tools to assess how sales and contribution margin of a company compare to budgetary information. However, there are considerable benefits in understanding which *particular customers contribute to profits as well*. Companies that have a large number of diverse customers also usually have widely varied profits from serving those customers. Many companies never attempt to calculate the profit earned from individual customers. They merely assume that if they are selling products above their costs, and that overall the company is earning a profit, then each of the customers must be profitable. Unfortunately, the cost incurred to sell goods and services to individual customers is not usually proportionate with the gross profit generated by those sales. Customers with high sales volume are not necessarily the most profitable. A **customer profitability analysis** assesses whether the gross profits from sales to individual customers exceed customer-specific costs of serving those customers. Some customers are simply more costly than others, and some may even be unprofitable, and the unprofitable customers can chip away at the total profits of the company. In an ideal world, only profitable customers would be retained, and unprofitable customers would be either converted to a profitable status or they would be dropped as customers.

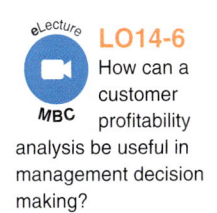

Customer Profitability Profile

If a company knows the amount of profits (or losses) generated by each of its customers, a **customer profitability profile** can be prepared similar to the one illustrated in the following exhibit. **Exhibit 14.5** depicts a **Pareto chart** where the cumulative total of customer profits is represented by the curved line. Each increment of profit added to the cumulative total comes from individual customers ranging from the most profitable to the least profitable.

Exhibit 14.5 ■ Customer Profitability Profile Graph

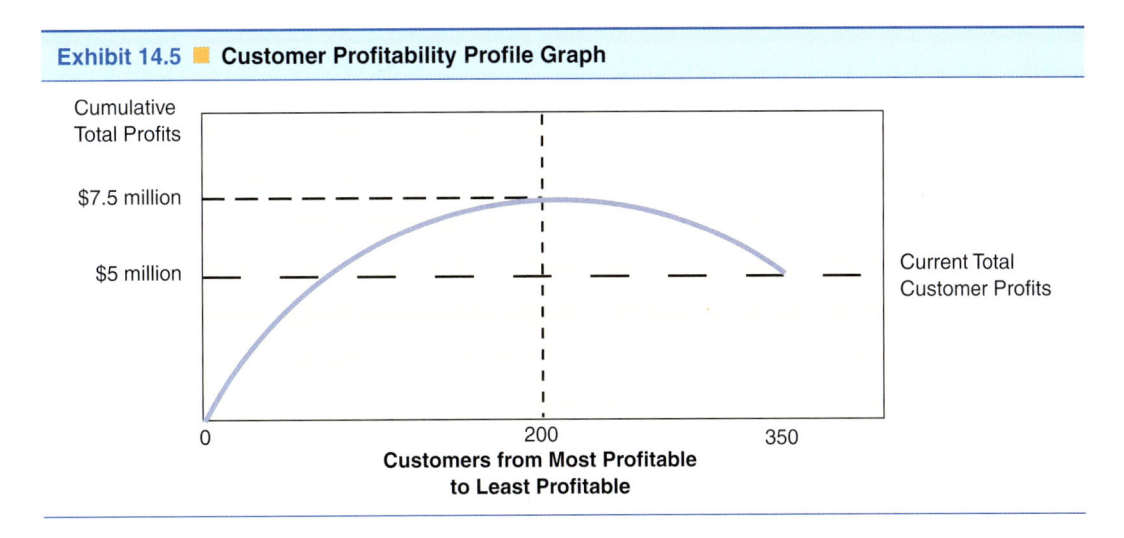

This hypothetical company has 350 customers and has current total profits of $5 million, but only 200 of its customers are profitable. Cumulative profits reach $7.5 million when the 200th customer is added to the graph, but the 201st through the 350th customers cause cumulative profits to decline to $5 million because they are unprofitable. Once a company has profitability data on each of its customers (or categories of customers), only then can it proceed to try to convert them to profitability, or seek to terminate the relationship with those customers.

Assessing a Customer Profitability Analysis — LO14-6 — DEMO 14-6

Pure Water Company is a "green" company located in the Midwest that manufactures and sells all-natural compounds for purifying water distributed through large public water systems. After five years in business, Pure Water has built a solid and growing customer base, but it has to invest significant time and expense servicing customers, especially those who have recently embraced its approach to water purification. Some customers require a lot of "hand-holding" with frequent visits and remote communication, and they tend to purchase frequently in small amounts, often requiring repackaging. Other customers require little attention and support, and many of them purchase in large amounts once a year.

Although the company is profitable, there is concern that profits could be higher if sales and other customer-related costs could be decreased. Pure Water's accountant has decided to conduct a *customer profitability analysis using activity-based costing*. As a first step, she determined that there were five primary activities related to serving customers: visits of customers by sales representatives, remote contacts, processing and shipping of customer orders, repackaging, and billing and collection. After numerous interviews and statistical analyses of activity and cost data, the accountant determined the following cost drivers and cost per unit of activity for the five customer-related activities.

Activity	Cost Driver	Cost per Unit of Driver Activity
Visits to customers	Visits	$800
Remote contacts	Number of contacts	75
Processing & shipping	Customer orders	450
Repackaging	Number of requests	250
Billing & collection	Invoices	90

After collecting activity driver data on each of these activities for its major customers, the accounting group prepared the customer activity cost and profitability analysis shown below for its five largest customers (in terms of sales dollars) in the order of greatest to least profit for the most recent year. Since Pure Water is selling only one product to all of its customers, and has the same pricing policy for all customers, there is a constant 40 percent gross profit ratio across all customers.

Customer Activity Cost and Profitability Analysis

	A	B	C	D	E	F	G
1		Clear Water District	Manhattan Water, Inc.	Great Lakes Utility	Gulf Coast Utilities	Open Water, Inc.	Total
2	**Customer Activity Cost Analysis**						
3	*Cost Driver Data*						
4	Visits to customers	3	5	4	1	1	
5	Remote contacts	5	7	8	2	3	
6	Processing & shipping	3	3	5	4	1	
7	Repackaging	0	2	3	0	0	
8	Billing & collection	3	3	5	4	1	
9	*Customer Activity Cost*						
10	Visits to customers	$ 2,400	$ 4,000	$ 3,200	$ 800	$ 800	
11	Remote contacts	375	525	600	150	225	
12	Processing & shipping	1,350	1,350	2,250	1,800	450	
13	Repackaging	0	500	750	0	0	
14	Billing & collection	270	270	450	360	90	
15	**Total Activity Cost**	$ 4,395	$ 6,645	$ 7,250	$ 3,110	$ 1,565	
16	**Customer Profitability Analysis**						
17	Customer sales	$17,500	$20,000	$12,000	$15,000	$16,250	$80,750
18	Less cost of goods sold	10,500	12,000	7,200	9,000	9,750	48,450
19	Gross profit on sales	7,000	8,000	4,800	6,000	6,500	32,300
20	Less activity costs	4,395	6,645	7,250	3,110	1,565	22,965
21	Customer profitability	$ 2,605	$ 1,355	$ (2,450)	$ 2,890	$ 4,935	$ 9,335
22	**Customer profitability ratio***	14.9%	6.8%	(20.4%)	19.3%	30.4%	11.6%
23	* Customer profitability ÷ Sales						
24	*Note:* As illustrated in Chapter 8, OH is allocated to customers (customer activity cost) by multiplying the allocation rates provided (cost per unit of driver activity) by the quantity of cost drivers (cost driver data) incurred for each customer. For example, the cost of visits to customers for the Clear Water District is equal to $800 × 3 = $2,400.						

◆ **What is the customer profitability ratio of all customers? Which two customers have the lowest customer profitability ratio?**

The combined net profitability of these customers is 11.6 percent of sales. However, all customers are not equally profitable. The high level of support required by Manhattan and Great Lakes resulted in a net customer loss from sales to Great Lakes and only a 6.8 percent customer profitability ratio for Manhattan.

◆ **What proactive steps could the company take to increase overall profitability?**

Informed by the data in the customer activity cost and profitability analysis, Pure Water can take proactive steps to increase its overall profitability ratio by decreasing activity costs incurred for less profitable customers.

Drop a Customer An obvious option would be to try to terminate its relationship with Great Lakes since the company is clearly losing money on that customer. If Great Lakes were terminated as a customer, and assuming that all of the activity costs associated with Great Lakes could be *avoided* by the termination, Pure Water's total sales would drop to $68,750, but its total profit would increase to $11,785, resulting in a profitability ratio on the remaining four customers of 17.1 percent.

Customer profitability ratio = Customer profitability ÷ Sales

Adjusted total sales ($80,750 − $12,000)	$68,750
Adjusted customer profitability [$9,335 − ($2,450)]	$11,785
Adjusted customer profitability ratio	17.1%

As discussed in a decision to drop a segment in Chapter 5, the analysis should differentiate fixed costs that will now have to be absorbed by other customers. If a customer is eliminated, any *unavoidable*

Data Visualization

Best Inc. Consulting prepared the following chart showing its cumulative total profits, ordered from the most profitable to the least profitable consulting client.

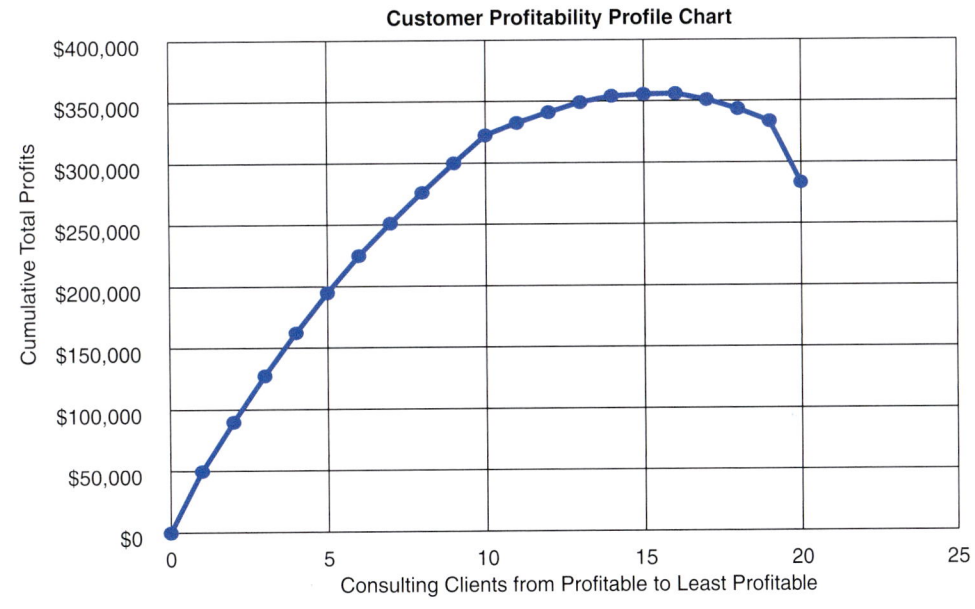

Customer Profitability Profile Chart

(Chart: x-axis "Consulting Clients from Profitable to Least Profitable" from 0 to 25; y-axis "Cumulative Total Profits" from $0 to $400,000. Cumulative profit rises steeply, peaks near $360,000 around client 15–17, then drops to about $290,000 by client 20.)

Using the data visualization, answer the following questions.
a. How many consulting clients does the company have?
b. What is the firm's total profits?
c. What is the profit(loss) from the firm's most profitable client and least profitable client?
d. How many customers are unprofitable?
e. How can this analysis be helpful to the firm?

Solution on p. 14-50.

expenses would merely shift to other customers. Thus, in a decision to drop a customer, only incremental revenue and incremental costs should be considered.

Lower Support Costs of Low-Profitability Customers A more proactive approach would be to work with Great Lakes and Manhattan that have high support requirements, such as repackaging, frequent visits, and remote contacts to try to lower the level of high-cost support activities without reducing sales to those customers. This could result in maintaining the current level of gross profit, but generating a significantly higher level of total net customer profitability.

Limitations to Customer Profitability Analysis

Two caveats should be considered when using activity cost data to manage customer profitability.

- First, there may be justifiable reasons (such as having a new customer that requires a high level of early-stage support, trying to penetrate a new geographic market, or existing relationships with other more profitable customers) for keeping customers that have lower profitability, or even customers that are not profitable. If so, these customers should be managed intensely to attempt to reduce the activities devoted to their support.

- Another caveat is that eliminating a customer may not immediately translate into an immediate reduction of activity costs. Some activity costs may not have a variable cost behavior pattern, and eliminating customers may merely create excess capacity in the short term. Of course, as stated previously, activity-based costing views virtually all costs as variable in the longer term. Despite these limitations, customer profitability analysis can provide valuable information to help keep an organization focused on its most profitable customers.

REVIEW 14-6 — LO14-6 — Analyzing Customer Profitability

Suppose SAP is a systems design and implementation firm that serves five different types of customers. Assume SAP's design and installation projects are fairly standardized and routine; hence, the pricing is also standardized for all customers. While the company is profitable overall, the CFO thinks the net margins should be higher. She is concerned that customer support costs are eating up some of the margin and has decided to do a customer profitability analysis based on the five different types of customers to see if some of the customer groups may actually be less profitable than others. The following data for the most recent period have been collected to support the analysis.

Support Activity	Driver	Cost per Driver Unit
A. Minor systems maintenance	Hours on jobs	$160
B. Visits to customer	Number of visits	$300
C. Communication	Number of calls	$ 50

Customer Group	Activity A	Activity B	Activity C	Profit Before Support Costs
1	69	25	128	$80,000
2	141	42	205	85,000
3	74	19	99	83,000
4	61	28	106	90,000
5	136	39	189	78,000

Required

a. Calculate the customer profitability for each customer group taking into account the support activity required for each customer group.

b. **Critical Thinking:** Comment on the usefulness of this type of analysis. What reasonable actions might the company take as a result of this analysis?

More practice: E14-47, E14-48
Solution on p. 14-50.

Chapter 14 Pricing, Sales Variances, and Customer Profitability

Comprehensive Chapter Review

Key Terms

ad hoc discounts, p.14-6
chained target costing, p.14-12
contribution margin variance, p.14-18
contribution margin volume variance, p.14-18
customer profitability analysis, p.14-23
customer profitability profile, p.14-23
design for manufacture, p.14-12
flexible budget variance, p.14-18
Kaizen costing, p.14-13
marginal cost, p.14-2
marginal revenue, p.14-2
market share variance, p.14-21
market size variance, p.14-21
Pareto chart, p.14-23
product life-cycle, p.14-8
product life-cycle costs, p.14-8
revenue variance, p.14-15
Robinson-Patman Act, p.14-6
sales mix variance, p.14-19
sales price variance, p.14-16
sales quantity variance, p.14-20
sales volume variance, p.14-16
target costing, p.14-9
value engineering (VE), p.14-10

Chapter Summary

Cost-Based Approach to Pricing (Page 14-2)   LO14-1
- In economic models, profits are maximized at the sales volume at which marginal revenues equal marginal costs.
- However, economic models are seldom used in pricing decisions because this information often cannot be developed at a reasonable cost.
- Cost-based pricing approaches are popular because cost data is available, cost-based prices are defensible, and in the long-run, selling prices must exceed costs.
- For single-product companies, the selling price is calculated using the profit equation and solving for selling price per unit.
- For multiple-product companies, the selling price is equal to costs plus markup to cover unassigned costs and provide for a profit.
- The general formula for a markup is (costs not included in the base + desired profit)/costs included in the bases.
- In a case of a special order, the bid price should be set to at least cover incremental costs plus any opportunity costs.
- Disadvantages of cost-based pricing include the following: cost-based pricing requires accurate cost assignments which is more difficult with a high proportion of unassigned costs, it assumes goods and services are scarce, and it increases the time and cost to bring a new product to market.

Product Life Cycle and Target Costing (Page 14-8)   LO14-2
- Product life cycles affect profitability because costs vary across the product life cycle, although most costs are determined in the development stage of the life cycle.
- Product life-cycle stages affect profitability because sales volume and selling prices vary across those stages.
- Target cost is calculated as expected selling price minus (acceptable profit margin + selling & administrative cost).
- Target costing is a tool to manage production costs
  - in the development stage of the product life cycle.
  - by developing an estimate of an "allowable" production cost (target cost) based on the estimated sales price of the product.
- Target costing forces managers to align the expected production cost with the target cost.
- Target costing utilizes value engineering through the use of multidisciplinary teams to increase product functionality and reduce costs.

Target Costing and Continuous Improvement Costing (Page 14-13)   LO14-3
- Kaizen costing involves ongoing efforts for continuous improvement to reduce product costs, increase product quality, and improve the production process.
- Continuous improvements takes place during the product's production stage.
- Under continuous improvement costing, the company works in multifunctional teams to achieve a target cost reduction.

© Cambridge Business Publishers

14-28   Chapter 14 Pricing, Sales Variances, and Customer Profitability

LO14-4   **Revenue Variances (Page 14-15)**
- Revenue centers calculate variances created by price or volume of units sold.
- The sales price variance indicates the portion of the total revenue variance that is related to a change in selling price.
- The sales volume indicates the impact of the change in sales volume on revenues, assuming there was no change in selling price.
- The total revenue variance is calculated as sales price variance + sales volume variance.

LO14-5   **Contribution Margin Variances (Page 14-17)**
- Contribution margin variance is calculated as the difference between the actual and budgeted contribution margin.
- Flexible budget variance indicates the portion of the total contribution margin variance that is related to a change in prices.
- CM volume variance indicates the impact of the change in sales volume on total contribution margin, assuming there was no change in contribution margin per unit.
- The sales mix variance indicates the portion of the contribution margin volume variance that is related to the difference between planned and actual sales mix.
- The sales quantity variance indicates the portion of the contribution margin volume variance that is related to the change in total units sold, assuming no change in sales mix.
- The market share variance indicates the impact on the sales quantity variance of a difference between planned and actual market share.
- The market size variance indicates the impact on the sales quantity variance of a change in total estimated units in the market, assuming no change in market share.

LO14-6   **Customer Profitability Analysis (Page 14-23)**
- A customer profitability analysis assesses whether the gross profits from sales to individual customers exceed customer-specific cost of serving those customers.
- A customer profitability profile shows cumulative total customer profits in increments of profit of individual customers, ordered from the most profitable to the least profitable customer.
- Customer profitability can be compared using the customer profitability ratio.

Solution Strategies

LO14-1 Cost-Based Pricing in Single-Product Companies

Selling price per unit(X) – Variable cost per unit(X) – Fixed costs = Profit
where X = Sales volume

$$\text{Markup on cost base} = \frac{\text{Costs not included in the base} + \text{Desired profit}}{\text{Costs included in the base}}$$

$$\text{Markup on variable cost} = \frac{\text{Fixed costs} + \text{Desired profit}}{\text{Variable costs}}$$

$$\text{Markup on total manufacturing costs} = \frac{\text{Selling and administrative costs} + \text{Desired profit}}{\text{Total manufacturing costs}}$$

LO14-2 Target Costing

Target cost = Expected long-range selling price – Acceptable profit – Selling & administrative costs

Compare predicted total life-cycle cost to target cost; if life-cycle cost is higher, determine ways to reduce it.

LO14-4 Revenue Variances

Revenue variance = (Actual units × Actual price) – (Budgeted units × Budgeted price)

Sales price variance = (Actual selling price – Budgeted selling price) × Actual units

Sales volume variance = (Actual units – Budgeted units) × Budgeted selling price

Sales price variance + Sales volume variance = Revenue variance

LO14-5 Contribution Margin Variances

Contribution margin variance = Actual contribution margin – Budgeted contribution margin

Flexible budget variance = (Actual CM per unit – Budgeted CM per unit) × Actual units

© Cambridge Business Publishers

Chapter 14 Pricing, Sales Variances, and Customer Profitability

CM Volume variance = (Actual units − Budgeted units) × Budgeted CM per unit

Flexible budget variance + CM volume variance = Contribution margin variance

Sales mix variance =
(Actual sales mix − Budgeted sales mix) × Total actual units × Budgeted CM per unit

Sales quantity variance =
(Total actual units − Total budgeted units) × Budgeted sales mix × Budgeted CM per unit

Sales mix variance + Sales quantity variance = CM Volume variance

Market share variance =
(Actual market share − Budgeted market share) × Actual total market units × Budgeted WA CM per unit

Market size variance =
(Actual total market units − Budgeted total market units) × Budgeted market share × Budgeted WA CM per unit

Market share variance + Market size variance = Sales quantity variance

Customer Profitability Ratio

LO14-6

Customer profitability ratio = Customer profitability ÷ Sales

Chapter Demonstration Problem

LO14-2

NewMaid has designed a new consumer product, a floor cleaner and wax, that is expected to have a five-year life cycle. Based on market research, NewMaid's management has determined that the product should be packaged in 32-ounce containers and should be sold at $6 per container in the first three years and $4 per container during the last two years. Unit sales are expected to be as follows:

Year 1	300,000
Year 2	400,000
Year 3	600,000
Year 4	400,000
Year 5	250,000
Total	1,950,000

Variable selling costs are expected to be $1 per container throughout the product's life. Annual fixed selling and administrative costs are estimated to be $500,000. NewMaid management desires a 25 percent profit margin on selling price.

Required:
a. Compute the life-cycle target cost to manufacture the product. (Round to the nearest cent.)
b. If NewMaid anticipates the new product will cost $3 per unit to manufacture in the first year, what is the maximum that manufacturing could cost in the last four years? (Round to the nearest cent.)
c. Suppose that NewMaid engineers determine that expected manufacturing cost per unit over the product life cycle is $2.25. What actions might the company take to reduce this cost?

Solution to Demonstration Problem

a. Step 1—Determine total product life-cycle revenue:

Year 1	300,000 × $6 =	$ 1,800,000
Year 2	400,000 × $6 =	2,400,000
Year 3	600,000 × $6 =	3,600,000
Year 4	400,000 × $4 =	1,600,000
Year 5	250,000 × $4 =	1,000,000
Total revenue		$10,400,000

© Cambridge Business Publishers

Step 2—Determine average unit revenue (AR) during product life:

$$AR = \text{Total revenue} \div \text{Total product life-cycle units}$$
$$= \$10,400,000 \div 1,950,000 \text{ units}$$
$$= \$5.33 \text{ (rounded)}$$

Step 3—Determine average unit fixed selling and administrative cost (AFS&A):

$$AFS\&A = (5 \text{ years} \times \$500,000) \div 1,950,000 \text{ units}$$
$$= \$2,500,000 \div 1,950,000$$
$$= \$1.28 \text{ (rounded)}$$

Step 4—Determine unit selling and administrative cost (US&AC):

$$US\&AC = AFS\&A + \text{Variable selling cost}$$
$$= \$1.28 + \$1.00$$
$$= \$2.28$$

Step 5—Calculate target cost (TC):

$$TC = AR - 0.25(AR) - US\&AC$$
$$= \$5.33 - (0.25 \times \$5.33) - \$2.28$$
$$= \$5.33 - \$1.33 - \$2.28$$
$$= \$1.72$$

b. Step 1—Determine total allowable cost over product life:

$$1,950,000 \text{ units} \times \$1.72 = \$3,354,000$$

Step 2—Determine expected total production cost in first year:

$$\$3 \times 300,000 \text{ units} = \$900,000$$

Step 3—Determine allowable unit cost in last four years:

$$(\$3,354,000 - \$900,000) \div 1,650,000 \text{ units} = \$1.49 \text{ (rounded)}$$

c. The following actions are potential options for the company:
- Product design and/or production processes can be changed to reduce costs. Cost tables can be used to provide information on the impact of using different input resources, processes, or design specifications.
- The 25 percent acceptable profit margin can be reduced.
- NewMaid can suspend consideration of the project at the present time.

Assignments with the MBC logo in the margin are available in BusinessCourse.
Resources include demonstration videos, guided examples, and auto-graded homework.
See details in the Preface, and ask your professor how you can access the system.

Data Analytics

LO14-1

United Parcel Service

DA14-1. Analyzing pricing trends

Access the data file for **UPS (United Parcel Service Inc.)** on the textbook's website with select information for the three quarters ended 2021 and 2022.

Required

a. Prepare line charts for each of the following.
  1. Average revenue per piece for the first three quarters of 2021
  2. Average revenue per piece for the first three quarters of 2022
  3. Average daily package volume for the first three quarters of 2021
  4. Average daily package volume for the first three quarters of 2022

b. Describe the trends in average revenue per piece over time and average daily package volume over time.

c. Sales for the nine months ended September 30, 2022, were up 4.2% from the same period in the prior year. What does this indicate about the company's pricing strategy in 2022?

DA14-2. Customer profitability profile chart

Access the file included in MBC which includes sales by customer for a small accounting firm, and complete the following requirements.

Required

a. Profits (losses) are provided for 25 customers. Sort the profits in the order from highest to lowest profits. *Hint:* Highlight data and right-click to quickly access the Sort function. Next, add a column to show cumulative profits. *Hint:* Start your cumulative column with a row for 0 customers at $0 profit. Create a line chart with your data points.

b. Review your chart and answer the following questions.
   1. What is the company's overall profit?
   2. At how many total customers is the company at its highest cumulative profit level? What is the profit at this level?
   3. Describe the line produced in the chart in part *a* and why it is shaped in this way.

Data Visualization

Data Visualization Activities are available in myBusinessCourse. These assignments use Tableau Dashboards to expose students to visual depictions of data and introduce students to data analytics through data visualizations. These exercises are easily assignable and auto graded by MBC.

Potential Ethical Issues

1. Using coercion to force suppliers to yield price concessions so that the cost of manufacturing a product is kept in line with the product's market price.
2. Allocating excess costs to a contracted manufacturing job when the contract is arranged to be paid at cost plus a designated profit.
3. Using a *predatory pricing policy* where products are sold below cost in order to eliminate competitors by forcing them to go out of business.
4. Charging different prices to different customers for the same product or service (perceived as discriminatory).
5. Setting prices unreasonably high when demand is greater than supply (such as during the pandemic).
6. Colluding with other companies to set prices at a particular level.

Questions

Q14-1. Why are economic models seldom used for day-to-day pricing decisions?

Q14-2. Identify three reasons that cost-based approaches to pricing have traditionally been important.

Q14-3. Identify four drawbacks to cost-based pricing.

Q14-4. How does target costing differ from cost-based pricing?

Q14-5. Distinguish between the marketing life cycles of products incorporating advanced technology (such as household electronic equipment) and those using more traditional technology (such as household paper products). Why would life-cycle costing be more important to a manufacturer of household electronic equipment than to a manufacturer of household paper products?

Q14-6. What is target costing, and how is it useful in assessing a product's total life cycle cost?

Q14-7. Why does the development stage have such a significant influence on a product's profitability over its life cycle?

Q14-8. What is kaizen costing, and how does it differ from target costing?

Q14-9. Should the actual performance of a revenue center be compared to the static budget or flexible budget? Why?

Q14-10. How does the contribution margin variance relate to the sales mix variance and the sales quantity variance?

Q14-11. What is the difference between the market share variance and the market size variance?

Q14-12. If a company shows an overall profitability, does this mean that all individual customers are profitable? Why or why not?

Multiple Choice

LO14-1

MC14-13. Companies that manufacture made-to-order industrial equipment typically use which one of the following?
  a. Cost-based pricing.
  b. Market-based pricing.
  c. Material-based pricing.
  d. Price discrimination.

LO14-1

MC14-14. Almelo Manpower Inc. provides contracted bookkeeping services. Almelo has annual fixed costs of $100,000 and variable costs of $6 per hour. This year the company budgeted 50,000 hours of bookkeeping services. Almelo prices its services at full cost and uses a cost-plus pricing approach. The company developed a billing price of $9 per hour. The company's mark-up level would be
  a. 12.5%.
  b. 33.3%.
  c. 50.0%.
  d. 66.6%.

LO14-1

MC14-15. Raymund Inc. currently sells its only product to Mall-Stores. Raymund has received a one-time-only order for 2,000 units from another buyer. Sale of the special order items will not require any additional selling effort. Raymund has a manufacturing capacity to produce 7,000 units. Raymund's Income Statement, before consideration of the one-time-only order, is as follows.

Sales (5,000 units at $20 per unit)		$100,000
Variable manufacturing costs	$50,000	
Variable selling costs	15,000	65,000
Contribution margin		35,000
Fixed manufacturing costs	16,000	
Fixed selling costs	4,000	20,000
Operating income		15,000

In negotiating a price for the special order, Raymund should set the minimum per unit selling price at
  a. $10.
  b. $13.
  c. $17.
  d. $18.

LO14-2

MC14-16. Which one of the following is not a characteristic of market-based costing?
  a. It has a customer-driven external focus.
  b. It is used by companies facing stiff competition.
  c. It is used by companies facing minimal competition.
  d. It starts with a target selling price and target profit.

LO14-2

MC14-17. Electronics Inc. is considering producing a new Bluetooth speaker that will offer several new features not widely available in the current market. After much market research, it has been determined that the appropriate target price for the new product is $90. To achieve its normal minimum profit margin of 20%, Electronics must be able to produce the product at a maximum total cost of
  a. $108.
  b. $70.
  c. $72.
  d. $18.

LO14-3

MC14-18. Orange Inc. produces electronic devices for personal use. It has recently introduced a health wearable band, but realizes that to compete effectively in the future, it must be able to lower the cost of production and the selling price. The current cost per unit for producing the band is $138, and Orange is estimating inflation on band components and supplies purchased externally to be 1.5% in the coming year. These components, expected to be impacted by inflation, amount to

Chapter 14 Pricing, Sales Variances, and Customer Profitability   14-33

$74 of the $138 total band cost. Despite these cost increases, Orange has adopted a Kaizen cost improvement model that targets a 5% cost decrease. Orange's Kaizen cost target (rounded to two decimal places) for the health band is

a. $131.11.
b. $132.15.
c. $133.07.
d. $130.05.

MC14-19. At the beginning of the year, a company budgeted to sell 600,000 units at a price of $12 per unit. It actually sold 585,000 units at a price of $12.50 per unit. The sales-volume variance is

a. $112,500 favorable.
b. $180,000 unfavorable.
c. $187,500 unfavorable.
d. $292,500 favorable.

LO14-4

MC14-20. Retailer Inc. sells two models of toaster ovens, premium and deluxe. Of the total units expected to be sold of 9,200, 50% are budgeted for premium toasters and 50% for deluxe toasters. Of the 10,000 actually sold, 4,200 are premium toasters and 5,800 are deluxe toasters.

If the budgeted contribution margin is $20 for premium toasters and $28 for deluxe toasters, what is the sales mix variance for premium and deluxe toasters?

a. Premium: $16,000 unfavorable; Deluxe: $22,400 favorable
b. Premium: $8,000 favorable; Deluxe: $11,200 favorable
c. Premium: $22,500 unfavorable; Deluxe: $11,200 favorable
d. Premium: $4,200 favorable; Deluxe: $5,800 unfavorable

LO14-5

MC14-21. To determine the profitability of individual customers of a manufacturer, from the sales to each individual customers, the following is subtracted

a. Cost of goods sold only.
b. Customer activity costs only.
c. Cost of goods sold and customer activity costs.
d. Cost of goods sold, customer activity costs, and common corporate costs.

LO14-6

Exercises

E14-22. Product pricing: single product Sue Bee Honey is one of the largest processors of its product for the retail market. Assume that one of its plants has annual fixed costs totaling $16,317,500, of which $5,250,500 is for administrative and selling efforts. Sales are anticipated to be 950,000 cases a year. Variable costs for processing are $35 per case, and variable selling expenses are 10% of selling price. There are no variable administrative expenses.

LO14-1

Required
If the company desires a pretax profit of $9,000,000, what is the selling price per case?

E14-23. Product pricing: single product Assume that you plan to open a Pinkberry franchise at a local shopping mall. Fixed operating costs for the year are projected to be $144,500. Variable costs per serving include the cost of the ice cream and cone, $1.50, and a franchise fee payable to Pinkberry, $0.20. A market analysis prepared by Pinkberry indicates that annual sales should total 130,000 servings.

LO14-1

Required
Determine the price you should charge for each serving to achieve a $125,000 pretax profit for the year.

E14-24. Product pricing A few years ago, Hotel Klingerhoffer, a large hotel chain, announced that because occupancy rates had declined during the previous quarter, it was raising room rates to cover the cost of its increase in vacant rooms. Although not referring to accounting or economics, several business journalists during the week following the announcement questioned the basis for the rate increases. One stated that "Hotel Klingerhoffer increases rates of vacant rooms."

LO14-1

Required
a. Did the journalist mean that vacant rooms would be more expensive? Explain.
b. Do you think Hotel Klingerhoffer's action to raise room rates was based on economics, accounting, or both?

E14-25. Flexible budget Tom's Shoe Repair provides a variety of shoe repair services. Analysis of monthly costs revealed the following cost formulas when direct labor hours are used as the basis of cost determination:

LO14-1

© Cambridge Business Publishers

Supplies	Y = $ 0 + $4.00X
Production supervision and direct labor	Y = $500 + $7.00X
Utilities	Y = $350 + $5.40X
Rent	Y = $450 + $0.00X
Advertising	Y = $ 75 + $0.00X

Tom's employees usually work 350 direct labor hours per month. The average shoe repair requires 1.25 labor hours to complete. Tom wants to earn a 40 percent margin on his cost. What should be the average charge per customer, rounded to the nearest dollar to achieve Tom's profit objective?

LO14-1

E14-26. Special order pricing Basic Computer Company (BCC) sells its laptop computers using bid pricing. It develops bids on a full cost basis. Full cost includes estimated material, labor, variable overheads, fixed manufacturing overheads, and reasonable incremental computer assembly administrative costs, plus a 10% return on full cost. BCC believes bids in excess of $925 per computer are not likely to be considered.

BCC's current cost structure, based on its normal production levels, is $500 for materials per computer and $20 per labor hour. Assembly and testing of each computer requires 12 labor hours. BCC's variable manufacturing overhead is $2 per labor hour, fixed manufacturing overhead is $3 per labor hour, and incremental administrative costs are $8 per computer assembled.

The company has received a request from the School Board for 500 computers. BCC's management expects heavy competition in bidding for this job. As this is a very large order for BCC, and could lead to other educational institution orders, management is extremely interested in submitting a bid which would win the job, but at a price high enough so that current net income will not be unfavorably impacted. Management believes this order can be absorbed within its current manufacturing facility.

What bid price should be recommended to BCC's management?

LO14-1

E14-27. Product pricing: Single product Presented is the current year contribution income statement of Grafton Products.

GRAFTON PRODUCTS
Contribution Income Statement
For Year Ended December

Sales (15,000 units)		$2,625,000
Less variable costs		
Cost of goods sold	$1,275,000	
Selling and administrative	150,000	(1,425,000)
Contribution margin		1,200,000
Less fixed costs		
Manufacturing overhead	685,000	
Selling and administrative	330,000	(1,015,000)
Net income		$ 185,000

Next year, Grafton expects an increase in variable manufacturing costs of $10 per unit and in fixed manufacturing costs of $30,000.

Required
a. If sales for next year remain at 15,000 units, what price should Grafton charge to obtain the same profit as last year?
b. Management believes that sales can be increased to 18,000 units if the selling price is lowered to $165. Is this action desirable? (Use the cost data from part *a*.)
c. After considering the expected increases in costs, what sales volume is needed to earn a pretax profit of $200,000 with a unit selling price of $165?

LO14-1

E14-28. Cost-based pricing and markups with variable costs Computer Consultants provides computerized inventory consulting. The office and computer expenses are $830,000 annually and are not assigned to specific jobs. The consulting hours available for the year total 18,000, and the average consulting hour has $40 of variable costs.

Required

a. If the company desires a profit of $250,000, what should it charge per hour?
b. What is the markup on variable costs if the desired profit is $322,000?
c. If the desired profit is $100,000, what is the markup on variable costs to cover (1) unassigned costs and (2) desired profit?

E14-29. Computing markups The predicted annual costs for Mighty Motors are as follows:

Manufacturing Costs		Selling and Administrative Costs	
Variable....................	$250,000	Variable....................	$250,000
Fixed.......................	350,000	Fixed.......................	550,000

Average total assets for the year are predicted to be $7,500,000.

Required

a. If management desires a 10% rate of return on total assets, what are the markup percentages based on total variable costs and based on total manufacturing costs?
b. If the company desires an 8% rate of return on total assets, what is the markup percentage on total manufacturing costs for (1) unassigned costs and (2) desired profit?

E14-30. Product pricing: Two products Assume **SnackPack Inc.** manufactures two snack products, almonds and organic chocolate covered almonds, both on the same assembly lines and packaged 5 pouches per pack. The predicted sales are 150,000 packs of almonds and 500,000 packs of chocolate covered almonds. The predicted costs for the year are as follows:

	Variable Costs	Fixed Costs
Materials...	$4,000,000	$1,560,000
Other...	2,000,000	2,052,500

Almonds use 25% of the materials costs and 10% of the other costs. Chocolate covered almonds use 75% of the materials costs and 90% of the other costs. The management of SnackPack desires an annual profit of $450,000.

Required

a. What price should the company charge for each pack if management believes the organic chocolate covered almonds sell for twice the price of the almonds?
b. What is the total profit per product using the selling prices determined in part *a*?

E14-31. Product pricing: two products Refer to the previous exercise, E14-30. Based on your calculations of the selling price and profit for almonds and organic chocolate covered almonds, how should the company evaluate the status of these two products? Should either almonds or organic chocolate covered almonds be discontinued? What additional information does the management of the company need in order to make an appropriate judgment on the future status of these two products?

E14-32. Setting prices during the product life cycle Match each of the following descriptions, *a* through *e*, with one of the following stages of a product life cycle: (1) development, (2) introduction, (3) growth, (4) maturity, or (5) decline.

a. ____ Even though sales are typically low in this stage, prices are set in line with prices of similar goods.
b. ____ Product quality is established based on decisions made in this stage
c. ____ Profits are typically lower in this stage due to lower sales volume and decreases in selling price.
d. ____ Stable prices are typical during this period with opportunities for cost savings realized through efficiencies.
e. ____ This stage is marked by low costs and stable or declining sales prices.

E14-33. Target costing Assume **Champion Power Equipment** wants to develop a new log-splitting machine for rural homeowners. Market research has determined that the company could sell 7,500 log-splitting machines per year at a retail price of $1,200 each. An independent catalog company would handle sales for an annual fee of $12,000 plus $75 per unit sold. The cost of the raw materials required to produce the log-splitting machines amounts to $200 per unit.

Required

If company management desires a return equal to 30% of the final selling price, what is the target conversion and administrative cost per unit? *Hint:* The target unit cost will only or should only include conversion costs and remaining or additional sales and administrative costs.

LO14-2 **E14-34. Product life cycle; writing** Recently you read an article regarding a new product introduced late last year by 5G Inc., a consumer products company. The article's author, although praising 5G Inc. for providing the marketplace with this innovative product, simultaneously criticized the company because the product had generated a $50 million loss for the year due to low unit sales. The author concluded the article by suggesting that company management had "missed the boat" with this product and should "dump it" as soon as possible. After reading this article you recall the concept of product life cycle and after contemplating how sales volume behaves over the product life cycle, you believe you can rebut the author of the 5G Inc. story. Write the rebuttal.

LO14-2 **E14-35. Product life cycle; writing** Joe Giles is a product engineer for a firm that makes various home and office electronic gadgets. Some of this company's products have long product life cycles and others have life cycles that are as short as nine months. Giles's company uses both target and kaizen costing to manage costs relative to the product life cycle of the firm's products. As an intern with the company, you recall a conversation in which Giles stated that kaizen cost management strategies were much more effective for products with longer life cycles than products with shorter life cycles, and that target costing techniques including value engineering were much more critical to products with short life cycles than to products with long life cycles. Do you agree with Giles? Why or why not?

LO14-2 **E14-36. Target costing** Utah Utensil has developed a new kitchen utensil. The firm has conducted significant market research and estimated the following pattern for sales of the new product:

Year	Expected Volume	Expected Price per Unit
1	48,000 units	$19
2	48,000 units	20
3	90,000 units	16
4	40,000 units	12

The firm wants to net a minimum of $3.50 per unit in profit over the product's life, and selling and administrative expenses are expected to average $50,000 per year. Calculate the life-cycle target cost per unit to produce the new utensil.

LO14-2 **E14-37. Target costing** The marketing department at Cleveland Furniture Mfg. has an idea for a new product that is expected to have a six-year life cycle. After conducting market research, the company found that the product could sell for $800 per unit in the first four years of life and for $650 per unit for the last two years. Unit sales are expected to be as follows:

Year 1	4,000
Year 2	3,600
Year 3	4,700
Year 4	5,000
Year 5	1,500
Year 6	1,000

Per-unit variable selling costs are estimated at $140 throughout the product's life; total fixed selling and administrative costs over the six years are expected to be $3,700,000. Cleveland Furniture Mfg. desires a profit margin of 15 percent of selling price per unit.

a. Compute the life-cycle target cost to manufacture the product. (Round to the nearest cent.)
b. If the company expects the product to cost $430 to manufacture in the first year, what is the upper bound for manufacturing cost in the following five years? (Round to the nearest cent.)
c. Refer to the original information. Assume that Cleveland Furniture Mfg. engineers indicate that the expected manufacturing cost per unit is $340. What actions might the company take to reduce this cost?

E14-38. Target costing; writing Mosquito MoJo is developing a propane-powered mosquito zapper for campers. Market research has indicated that potential purchasers would be willing to pay $145 per unit for this product. Company engineers have estimated that first-year production costs will amount to $120 per unit and selling and administrative expenses will be $20 per unit. On this type of product, Mosquito MoJo would normally expect to earn a $15 per unit profit. Using the concept of target costing, write a memo that (a) analyzes the prospects for this product and (b) discusses possible organizational strategies.

LO14-2

E14-39. Value engineering; research; writing Research the topic of value engineering on the Internet, and write a brief report on a company or an organization's experiences using this technique.

LO14-2

E14-40. Continuous improvement A paint manufacturer faced with a highly competitive market is adopting Kaizen costing. The company's manufacturing costs for the prior annual period based on production of 100,000 units are as follows.

LO14-3

Direct materials............	$300,000
Direct labor................	80,000
Overhead	240,000

All prices are expected to increase by 5% in the following year due to inflation. The cost reduction target per unit under Kaizen costing is 4%.

a. What is the target cost per unit for direct materials, direct labor, and overhead?
b. In what ways can the company try to reach its goal?

E14-41. Revenue variances Premiere Produce Inc. summarized the following results for its most recent fiscal year:

LO14-4

Budgeted revenue	$115,940
Actual revenue	122,575
Budgeted sales units	145,575
Actual units sold	168,750

Based on the sales information, compute the company's sales price variance and sales volume variance.

E14-42. Revenue variances For the year, Logitom planned to sell 460,000 units at a $39 selling price. The marketing manager was asked to explain why budgeted revenue had not been achieved for that year. Investigation revealed the following information:

LO14-4

| Actual sales volume .... | 473,000 units |
| Actual selling price .... | $38 per unit |

Analyze the information given and prepare the explanation that Logitom's marketing manager should present.

E14-43. Revenue variances You have asked your sales manager to explain why budgeted revenues for your division are below expectations. The budget indicated $472,500 of revenues based on a sales volume of 675,000 units. Sales records indicate that 682,000 product units were actually sold, but revenues were only $463,760. Analyze revenues and explain what occurred.

LO14-4

E14-44. Revenue variances Ha-Chin Yi delivers two-day statistical process control seminars for manufacturing workers. For each program, a $4,000 fee is normally paid. In Year 1, Yi presented 30 seminars, and he budgeted a 30 percent increase in seminars for Year 2. At the end of Year 2, Yi is disappointed that his actual revenue is only $154,350. He presented 42 seminars during the year.

LO14-4

a. What was Yi's expected revenue for Year 2?
b. What were Yi's sales price and sales volume variances?
c. Discuss why Yi did not achieve his budgeted revenue in Year 2.

E14-45. Contribution margin variances Zellow Inc. is analyzing its sales activity for its two main products in its commercial division for the past year. Zellow compiled the following information.

LO14-5

	Product W12	Product Y10
Actual units.	18,000	12,000
Budgeted units	14,000	14,000
Actual sales mix	60%	40%
Budgeted sales mix	50%	50%
Actual CM per unit	$80.00	$120.00
Budgeted CM per unit.	$88.00	$125.00

a. Based on the information provided, determine the sales mix and sales quantity variance for each product type and in total.
b. What is the total contribution volume variance?
c. What factors contributed to the variances calculated in part *a*?

LO14-5 E14-46. Market share and market size variances

Market Data	
Actual total market in units	100,000
Budgeted total market in units	112,000
Actual market share	30%
Budgeted market share	25%
Budgeted weighted average CM per unit	$106.50

Using the information from E14-45 for Zellow Inc., along with the additional market data provided above, answer the questions that follow.

a. Calculate the market share and market size variances.
b. What factors contributed to the variances calculated in part *a*?

LO14-6 E14-47. Customer profitability analysis Elite Services, Inc. provides residential painting services for three home building companies, Brookside, Edgewater, and Hillrose, and it uses a job costing system for determining the costs for completing each job. The job cost system does not capture any cost incurred by Elite for return touchups and refinishes after the homeowner occupies the home. Elite paints each house on a square footage contract price, which includes painting as well as all refinishes and touchups required after the homes are occupied. Each year, the company generates about one-third of its total revenues and gross profits from each of the three builders. The Elite owner has observed that the builders, however, require substantially different levels of support following the completion of jobs. The following data have been gathered:

Support Activity	Driver	Cost per Driver Unit
Major refinishes	Hours on jobs	$150
Touchups	Number of visits	$100
Communication.	Number of calls	$ 30

Builder	Major Refinishes	Touchups	Communication
Brookside	120	260	900
Edgewater	70	205	530
Hillrose	80	220	590

Assuming that each of the three customers produces gross profits of $150,000, calculate the profitability from each builder after taking into account the support activity required for each builder.

LO14-6 E14-48. Customer profitability analysis Leahy Inc. has 10 customers that account for all of its $1,472,000 of net income. Its activity-based costing system is able to assign all costs, except for $200,000 of general administrative costs, to key activities incurred in connection with serving its customers. A customer profitability analysis based on activity costing produced the following customer profits and losses:

Customer #1	$ 350,000
#2	262,000
#3	(75,000)
#4	240,000
#5	50,000
#6	375,000
#7	(100,000)
#8	325,000
#9	225,000
#10	(180,000)
Total	$ 1,472,000

Prepare a customer profitability profile similar to the one in **Exhibit 14.5**.

E14-49. Customer profitability analysis Refer to the previous exercise E14-48 for Leahy Inc.

    a. If Leahy were to notify customers 3, 7, and 10 that it will no longer be able to provide them services in the future, will that increase company profits by $355,000? Why or why not?

    b. What is the primary benefit of preparing a customer profitability analysis?

LO14-6

Problems

P14-50. Product pricing: two products **Macquarium Inc.** provides computer-related services to its clients. Its two primary services are Web page design (WPD) and Internet consulting services (ICS). Assume that Macquarium's management expects to earn a 35% annual return on the assets invested. Macquarium has invested $6 million since its opening. The annual costs for the coming year are expected to be as follows:

LO14-1

Macquarium Inc.

	Variable Costs	Fixed Costs
Consulting support	$250,000	$1,750,000
Sales and administration	150,000	850,000

The two services expend about equal costs per hour, and the predicted hours for the coming year are 15,000 for WPD and 25,000 for ICS.

Required

    a. If markup is based on variable costs, how much revenue must each service generate to provide the profit expected by corporate headquarters? What is the anticipated revenue per hour for each service? *Hint:* Start by determining the markup rate.

    b. If the markup is based on total costs, how much revenue must each service generate to provide the expected profit?

    c. Explain why answers in requirements (*a*) and (*b*) are either the same or different.

    d. Comment on the advantages and disadvantages of using a cost-based pricing model.

P14-51. Price setting: multiple products Tech Com's predicted variable and fixed costs for next year are as follows:

LO14-1

	Variable Costs	Fixed Costs
Manufacturing	$405,000	$ 424,200
Selling and administrative	102,000	594,000
Total	$507,000	$1,018,200

Tech Com is a small company producing a wide variety of electronic devices. Per-unit manufacturing cost information about one of these products, a fitness watch, is as follows:

Direct materials.	$8
Direct labor.	4
Manufacturing overhead	
Variable.	3
Fixed.	6
Total manufacturing costs.	$21

Variable selling and administrative costs for the watch are $4 per unit. Management has set a target profit for next year of $300,000 on the sale of the watches.

Required
- a. Determine the markup percentage on variable costs required to earn the desired profit.
- b. Use variable cost markup to determine a suggested selling price for the watch.
- c. For the watch, break the markup on variable costs into separate parts for fixed costs and profit. Explain the significance of each part.
- d. Determine the markup percentage on manufacturing costs required to earn the desired profit.
- e. Use the manufacturing costs markup to determine a suggested selling price for the watch.
- f. Evaluate the variable and the manufacturing cost approaches to determine the markup percentage.

P14-52. Price setting: multiple products Pipestem Golf produces a wide variety of golfing equipment. In the past, product managers set prices using their professional judgment. Samuel Snead, the new controller, believes this practice has led to the significant underpricing of some products (with lost profits) and the significant overpricing of other products (with lost sales volume). You have been asked to assist Snead in developing a corporate approach to pricing. The output of your work should be a cost-based formula that can be used to develop initial selling prices for each product. Although product managers are allowed to adjust these prices to meet competition and to take advantage of market opportunities, they must explain such deviations in writing. The following cost information from the current year accounting records is available:

	Manufacturing Costs	Selling and Administrative Costs
Variable.	$335,000	$ 55,000
Fixed.	245,000	365,000

During the year, Pipestem Golf reported earnings of $200,000. However, the controller believes that proper pricing should produce earnings of at least $250,000 on the same sales mix and unit volume. Accordingly, you are to use the preceding cost information and a target profit of $250,000 in developing a cost-based pricing formula. Selling and administrative expenses are not currently associated with individual products. However, you have obtained the following unit production cost information for the TW Irons:

Variable manufacturing costs	$145
Fixed manufacturing costs	105
Total.	$250

Required
- a. Determine the standard markup percentage for each of the following cost bases. Round answers to two decimal places.
    1. Full costs, including fixed and variable manufacturing costs, and fixed and variable selling and administrative costs.
    2. Manufacturing costs plus variable selling and administrative costs.
    3. Manufacturing costs.
    4. Variable costs.
    5. Variable manufacturing costs.
- b. Explain why the markup percentages become progressively larger from requirement (a), parts (1) through (5).

Chapter 14 Pricing, Sales Variances, and Customer Profitability

c. Determine the initial price of a set of TW Irons using the manufacturing cost markup and the variable manufacturing cost markup.
d. Do you believe the controller's approach to product pricing is reasonable? Why or why not?

P14-53. Special order Razor USA produces a variety of electric scooters. Assume that Razor has just received an order from a customer (Pulse Cycles) for 500 Power Core scooters. The following price, based on cost plus a 60% markup, has been developed for the order.

Manufacturing costs	
Direct materials.	$11,850
Direct labor	8,500
Factory overhead	15,800
Total	36,150
Markup (60%).	21,690
Selling price	$57,840

Pulse Cycles rejected this price and offered to purchase the 500 scooters at a price of $45,000. The following additional information is available.

- Razor has sufficient excess capacity to produce the scooters.
- Factory overhead is applied on the basis of direct labor dollars.
- Budgeted factory overhead is $8,000,000 for the current year. Of this amount, $6,000,000 is fixed. Of the $15,800 of factory overhead assigned to the Pulse Cycles order, only $3,950 is driven by the special order; $11,850 is a fixed cost.
- Selling and administrative expenses are budgeted as follows.

Fixed.	$3,000,000 per year
Variable.	$10 per unit manufactured and sold

Required
a. The president of Razor wants to know if he should allow Pulse Cycles to have the scooters for $45,000. Determine the effect on profits of accepting Pulse Cycles' offer.
b. Briefly explain why certain costs should be omitted from the analysis in requirement (a).
c. Assume Razor is operating at capacity and could sell the 500 scooters at its regular markup.
  1. Determine the opportunity cost of accepting Pulse Cycles' offer.
  2. Determine the effect on profits of accepting Pulse Cycles' offer.
d. What other factors should Razor consider before deciding to accept the special order?

P14-54. Special order pricing OneCo Inc. produces a single product. Cost per unit, based on the manufacture and sale of 10,000 units per month at full capacity, is shown below.

Direct materials.	$ 4.00
Direct labor.	1.30
Variable overhead.	2.50
Fixed overhead.	3.40
Sales commission.	0.90
Total.	$12.10

The $0.90 sales commission is paid for every unit sold through regular channels. Market demand is such that OneCo is operating at full capacity, and the firm has found it can sell all it can produce at the market price of $16.50.

Currently, OneCo is considering two separate proposals:

- Gatsby, Inc. has offered to buy 1,000 units at $14.35 each. Sales commission would be $0.35 on this special order.
- Zelda Productions, Inc. has offered to produce 1,000 units at a delivered cost to OneCo of $14.50 each.

a. What would be the effect on OneCo's operating income if it accepts of the proposal from Gatsby, but rejects the proposal from Zelda?

b. What would be the effect on OneCo's operating income if it accepts of the proposal from Zelda, but rejects the proposal from Gatsby?
c. What would be the effect on OneCo's operating income if it accepts both proposals?
d. Assume Gatsby has offered a second proposal to purchase 2,000 units at the market price of $16.50, but has requested product modifications that would increase direct materials cost by $0.30 per unit and increase direct labor and variable overhead by 15%. The sales commission would be $0.35 per unit. Should OneCo accept this order? Explain your recommendation.
e. Under the situation described above, would your recommendation be different if the company had excess capacity? Explain your answer.
f. Identify and describe at least two factors other than the effect on income that OneCo should consider before making a decision on the proposals.

LO14-2 P14-55. Target costing Assume Solar Inc. is a large global company providing large commercial solar panel installation. Assume that it is developing a new installation system for smaller, private companies. To attract small companies, Solar must keep the price low without giving up too many of the features of larger systems. A marketing research study conducted on the company's behalf found that the price range must be $50,000 to $75,000. Management has determined a target price to be $65,000. The company's minimum profit percentage of sales is normally 15%, but the company is willing to reduce it to 12% to get the new product on the market. The fixed costs for the first year are anticipated to be $8,000,000. If sales reach 400 installations, the company needs to know how much it can spend on variable costs, which are primarily related to installation.

Required
a. What is the amount of total cost allowed if the 12% profit target is allowed and the 400 installations sales target is met? Show the amount for fixed and for variable costs.
b. What is the amount of total costs allowed if the 15% normal profit target is desired at the 400 installations sales target? Show the amount for fixed and for variable costs.
c. Discuss the advantages of using a target costing model versus using cost-based pricing.

LO14-2 P14-56. Target costing The president of Houston Electronics was pleased with the company's latest electronic gadget. The proud president announced that this unique and innovative product would be an important factor in reestablishing the North American consumer electronics industry. Based on development costs and predictions of sales volume, manufacturing costs, and distribution costs, the cost-based price of the latest electronic gadget was determined to be $425. Following a market-skimming strategy, management set the initial selling price at $525. The marketing plan was to reduce the selling price by $50 during each of the first two years of the product's life to obtain the highest contribution possible from each market segment.

The initial sales of the gadget were strong, and Houston Electronics found itself adding second and third production shifts. Although these shifts were expensive, at a selling price of $525, the product had ample contribution margin to remain highly profitable. The president was talking with the company's major investors about the desirability of obtaining financing for a major plant expansion when the bad news arrived. A foreign company had announced that it would shortly introduce a similar product that would incorporate new design features and sell for only $350. The president was shocked. "Why," she remarked, "it costs us $375 to put a complete unit in the hands of customers."

Required
How could the foreign competitor profitably sell a similar product for less than the manufacturing costs to Houston Electronics? What advice do you have for the president concerning the gadget? What advice would you have to help the company avoid similar problems in the future?

LO14-1, 2 P14-57. Cost-based pricing, target costing Super Sonic Company manufactures audio speakers. The average costs for the production of speakers are summarized below.

	Per Unit	Per Year
Direct materials.	$10.00	
Direct labor.	20.50	
Variable manufacturing overhead.	1.50	
Variable selling and administrative expenses.	1.80	
Fixed manufacturing overhead.		$429,000
Fixed selling and administrative expenses		495,000

The pricing calculations are based on budgeted production and sales of 33,000 units per year. The company has invested $1,000,000 in this product and expects a return on investment of 12%. The markup rate on total manufacturing cost is 48%. A recent marketing research study reveals that due to increased competition the company must reduce the selling price to $45 in order to maintain the same level of sales volume.

a. Calculate the original target selling price of the product. Show your calculations.
b. Using the market-based pricing approach, calculate the target cost per unit given the competitive target price of $45. Show your calculations.
c. Identify and explain one advantage and one disadvantage of cost-based pricing and market-based pricing, respectively.
d. Define value engineering and explain how value engineering can help Super Sonic.
e. Identify and explain one reason why Super Sonic may want to set its selling price below $45.

P14-58. Product life cycles; writing Assume you are the CFO of an electronics manufacturer. Your firm is about to launch an extremely innovative new product. The product planning team has estimated life-cycle sales of the product to be as follows (in thousands):

Year	Units
Year 1	35,000
Year 2	75,000
Year 3	125,000
Year 4	90,000
Year 5	15,000

The life-cycle average sales price is projected by the product planning team to be $80. The team has recommended to top management and the marketing team that the introductory product price be set at $60.

a. As CFO, what is your reaction to the suggested introductory price of $60 relative to the expected life-cycle price of $80?
b. Most of the profit of consumer electronic products is realized early in the product life cycle. How would this fact influence your recommendation about where the price for this product should be set for Year 1?
c. As CFO, are you concerned that a significant portion of the forecasted life-cycle volume for this product is assigned to years 3 and 4? Explain.

P14-59. Product life cycles; writing **Sony Corp.** launched its PlayStation 4 in late 2013. It was introduced at a price point of $399. At the time of introduction, a technology firm performed a tear-down of the PlayStation and estimated its cost of production to be $381. Based on this cost estimate, the tech firm estimated Sony was making $18 per unit sold.

Source: IHS Electronics360 News Desk, "Exclusive Video Teardown: Sony Close to Breakeven on PS4," (November 19, 2013); Retrieved from https://electronics360.globalspec.com/article/3781/exclusive-video-teardown-sony-close-to-breakeven-on-ps4?cid=nl (last accessed 12-31-19).

a. Assume that Sony generates more profit on royalties from the games played on PlayStation than on the sales of PlayStation itself. In light of this explanation, is it rational for Sony to sell the PlayStation at a mere 4.5% gross profit rate? Explain.
b. How would setting the price of the PlayStation at $399, rather than a price reflecting a higher gross profit rate likely affect (1) early life-cycle sales and (2) total life-cycle sales of PlayStation 4?
c. Is Sony's pricing strategy (i.e., introductory price below production cost) more beneficial if the product's life cycle is long or short? Explain.

P14-60. Target costing Gourmet Grade has just completed its work on a new microwave entrée. After consumer research was conducted, the marketing group has estimated the following quantities of the product can be sold at the following prices over its life cycle:

Year	Quantity	Selling Price	Year	Quantity	Selling Price
1	100,000	$2.50	5	600,000	$2.00
2	250,000	2.40	6	450,000	2.00
3	350,000	2.30	7	200,000	1.90
4	500,000	2.10	8	130,000	1.90

Initial engineering estimates of direct material and direct labor costs are $1.70 and $0.40, respectively, per unit. Variable overhead per unit is expected to be $0.50, and fixed overhead is expected to be $200,000 per year. Gourmet Grade's management strives to earn a 25 percent gross margin on products of this type.

a. Estimate the target cost for the new entrée.
b. Compare the estimated production cost to the target cost. Discuss this comparison and how management might use the comparison to manage costs.
c. Based on your answer in (b), should Gourmet Grade begin production of the new entrée? Explain.

LO14-2 P14-61. **Target costing** StatPro has just been presented the following market and production estimates on Product X27, which has been under development in the company.

Projected market price of X27	$215	(based on 180,000 life-cycle unit sales over five-year life)
Projected gross margin per unit	35	
Estimated selling and administrative costs per unit	40	
Estimated production costs		
Direct material	$70	
Direct labor.	40	
Variable overhead.	15	
Fixed overhead.	$360,000 annually	

Use the concept of target costing to integrate the marketing and engineering information and interpret the results for StatPro.

LO14-3 P14-62. **Continuous improvement (Kaizen) costing** Samira Company does contract manufacturing of doorbell video cameras. At its Pacific plant, cost control has become a concern of management. The actual costs per unit for the previous two years were as follows:

	Year 1		Year 2	
Direct materials				
Plastic case.	$ 5.10		$ 4.75	
Lens set	12.00		10.90	
Electrical component set.	8.30		7.00	
Film track	10.50		10.05	
Direct labor.	48.00	(1.6 hours)	45.00	(1.5 hours)
Indirect manufacturing costs				
Variable.	5.60		5.00	
Fixed.	16.00	(100,000 unit base)	12.75	(120,000 unit base)

The company manufactures all of the camera components except the lens sets, which it purchases from several vendors. The company has used target costing in the past but has not been able to meet the very competitive global pricing. Beginning in Year 2, the company implemented a continuous improvement program that requires cost reduction targets.

Required
a. If continuous improvement (Kaizen) costing sets a target of a 10% reduction of the first year cost base, how successful was the company in meeting the per unit cost reduction targets in the second year? Support your answer with appropriate computations.
b. Evaluate and discuss Samira's use of Kaizen costing.

LO14-3 P14-63. **Continuous improvement (Kaizen) costing** Assume that GE Capital, a division of **General Electric**, has been displeased with the costs of servicing its consumer loans. Assume that it has decided to implement a Kaizen-based cost improvement program. For the current year, GE Capital incurred the following costs ($ millions):

General Electric

Loan processing.	$12,500
Customer relations	2,800
Printing, mailing, and postage	550

For the next two years, GE Capital expects an increase in consumer loans of 8% annually with related increases in costs.

Required

a. If the company has a continuous improvement goal of 4% each year, develop a budget for the next two years for the consumer loan department.
b. Identify some possible ways that GE Capital can achieve the Kaizen costing goal.
c. Discuss the potential benefits and limitations of GE's Kaizen costing model.

P14-64. Revenue variances Cardiff Sports sells footballs and shoulder pads. For the year, company management budgeted the following:

	Footballs	Shoulder Pads
Sales revenue.	$1,200,000	$1,800,000
Unit sales price.	$60	$45

At the end of the year, management was told that actual sales of footballs were 21,000 units and the sales price variance was $63,000 unfavorable. Sales of shoulder pads generated $1,680,000 of revenue, with an unfavorable sales volume variance of $360,000.

a. Compute the budgeted sales volume for each product.
b. Compute the sales volume variance for footballs.
c. Compute the sales price variance for shoulder pads.
d. What conditions might have contributed to the revenue variances?

P14-65. Revenue variances Kessla Taub manages the marketing department at Electronic Village. Company management has been concerned about the sales of three products and has informed Taub that, regardless of other sales, her performance for the year will be evaluated on whether she has met the sales budget for the following items:

	Sales Price per Unit	Budgeted Unit Sales
Wireless backup camera	$120	1,600
Heated seat cushion.	68	2,100
Wireless car phone charger	60	1,050

Actual sales for these three products, generated for the year, were as follows:

	Sales Price per Unit	Sales Revenue
Wireless backup camera	$115	$195,500
Heated seat cushion.	70	141,400
Wireless car phone charger	55	228,250

a. Compute the sales price variances by product.
b. Compute the sales volume variances by product.
c. Assuming that the variances computed in (a) and (b) are controllable by Taub, discuss what actions she may have taken to cause actual results to deviate from budgeted results.
d. What problems might be caused by the manner in which Taub was evaluated?

P14-66. Revenue variances Folsom Fashions sells a line of dresses. Folsom's performance report for November is shown below. The company uses a flexible budget to analyze its performance and measure the effect on operating income of the various factors affecting the difference between budgeted and actual operating results.

	Actual	Budget
Dresses sold.	5,000	6,000
Sales.	$ 235,000	$ 300,000
Variable costs	(145,000)	(180,000)
Contribution margin	$ 90,000	$ 120,000
Fixed costs	(84,000)	(80,000)
Operating income	$ 6,000	$ 40,000

a. Compute the sales price variance and the sales volume variance for November.
b. Determine the impact of the sales volume variance on Folsom's contribution margin for the month of November.
c. What additional information is needed for Folsom to calculate the dollar impact of a change in the market share on operating income for November? What would be the overall benefit to Folsom's sales managers of having such information?
d. Explain why performance evaluation at Folsom Fashions is limited if the company's evaluation of management is based solely on sales price and volume variances.

LO14-5 P14-67. Contribution margin variances Keller Inc. manufactures and sells two types of water bottles: plastic and stainless steel. The company summarized the following actual and budgeted information for the past year.

	Plastic	Stainless Steel
Actual units.	55,250	29,750
Budgeted units	44,800	35,200
Actual selling price per unit.	$25	$60
Budgeted selling price per unit.	$25	$55
Actual variable cost per unit	$10	$25
Budgeted variable cost per unit	$9	$26

In addition, the company's marketing manager estimated the industry market for water bottles to be 1,000,000 for the past year. However, due to an economic downturn, actual results were much less at an estimated 850,000 water bottles.

a. Calculate the components of the revenue variance: sales price and sales volume variances.
b. Calculate the components of the contribution margin variance: flexible budget and contribution margin volume variances.
c. Calculate the components of the contribution margin volume variance: sales mix and sales quantity variances.
d. Calculate the components of the sales quantity variance: market share and market size variances.
e. Analyze your results.

LO14-6 P14-68. Customer profitability analysis Remington Aeronautics LTD is a British aeronautics subcontract company that designs and manufactures electronic control systems for commercial airlines. The vast majority of all commercial aircraft are manufactured by **Boeing** in the U.S. and **Airbus** in Europe; however, there is a relatively small group of companies that manufacture narrow-body commercial jets. Assume for this exercise that Remington does contract work for the two major manufacturers plus three companies in the second tier.

Because competition is intense in the industry, Remington has always operated on a fairly thin 20% gross profit margin; hence, it is crucial that it manage nonmanufacturing overhead costs effectively in order to achieve an acceptable net profit margin. With declining profit margins in recent years, Remington Aeronautics' CEO, John Remington, has become concerned that the cost of obtaining contracts and maintaining relations with its five major customers may be getting out of hand. You have been hired to conduct a customer profitability analysis.

Remington Aeronautics' nonmanufacturing overhead consists of $2 million of general and administrative (G&A) expense (including, among other expenses, the CEO's salary and bonus and the cost of operating the company's corporate jet) and selling and customer support expenses of $3.15 million (including 5% sales commissions and $750,000 of additional costs).

The accounting staff determined that the $750,000 of additional selling and customer support expenses related to the following four activity cost pools:

Activity	Cost Driver	Cost per Unit of Activity
1. Sales visits	Number of visit days	$1,000
2. Product adjustments	Number of adjustments	1,600
3. Phone and email contacts	Number of calls/contacts	100
4. Promotion and entertainment events	Number of events	3,000

Financial and activity data on the five customers follow (Sales and Gross Profit data in millions):

Customer	Sales	Gross Profit	Activity 1	Activity 2	Activity 3	Activity 4
A	$19	$3.8	90	10	160	21
B	14	2.8	105	20	200	20
C	5	1.0	95	18	100	17
D	6	1.2	30	8	35	12
E	4	0.8	30	4	25	14
	$48	$9.6	350	60	520	84

Quantity of Sales and Support Activity

In addition to the above, the sales staff used the corporate jet at a cost of $1,000 per hour for trips to customers as follows:

Customer A	16 hours
Customer B	32 hours
Customer C	8 hours
Customer D	0 hours
Customer E	5 hours

The total cost of operating the airplane is included in general and administrative expense; none is included in selling and customer support costs.

Required

a. Prepare a customer profitability analysis for Remington Aeronautics that shows the gross profits less all expenses that can reasonably be assigned to the five customers.
b. Now assuming that the remaining general and administrative costs are assigned to the five customers based on relative sales dollars, calculate net profit for each customer.
c. Discuss the merits of the analysis in part *a* versus part *b*.

Review Solutions

Review 14-1

a.

Desired annual profit ($2,000,000 × 0.10)	$200,000
Actual profit	(150,000)
Amount actual profit fell short of achieving the desired return	$ 50,000

b.

Predicted costs		
Variable	$450,000	
Fixed	600,000	$1,050,000
Desired profit		250,000
Required revenue		$1,300,000
Unit sales		÷ 100,000
Required unit selling price		$ 13

c.

Variable manufacturing costs per unit ($300,000/100,000 units)	= $3
Selling price as a percent of variable manufacturing costs	= $13/3
	= 433⅓%
Markup as a percent of variable manufacturing costs ($10/$3)	= 333⅓%

d. Detail of markup on variable manufacturing costs:

1.
Unassigned costs		
Variable selling and administrative	$150,000	
Fixed costs	600,000	$750,000
Variable manufacturing costs		÷ 300,000
Markup on variable manufacturing costs to cover unassigned costs		250%

2.
Desired profit	$250,000
Variable manufacturing costs	÷ 300,000
Additional markup on variable manufacturing costs to achieve desired profit ($250,000)	83 1/3 %

e. In order to achieve the desired profits, the company would have to increase its selling price from $12 a unit to $13 a unit. If sales quantity did not change, the company would increase profits. However, if sales quantity goes down due to the increase in price, the company would not achieve its profit goals.

Review 14-2

a. $3,401,000 = ($15 × 15,000) + ($18 × 32,000) + ($20 × 58,000) + ($20 × 62,000) + ($10 × 20,000)
$2,428,000 = $3,401,000 − $748,000* − $225,000**
$12.98 = $2,428,000 ÷ 187,000

*$748,000 = $4 × (15,000 + 32,000 + 58,000 + 62,000 + 20,000)
**$225,000 = $45,000 × 5

b. ESG concerns can be addressed in a number of ways during the target costing process. For example, the product can be designed to include less packaging. The manufacturing process can be planned to minimize resources used as well as scrap materials produced. The design team can consider how the product can be effectively recycled at the end of its useful life.

Review 14-3

a.
Item	Year 1	× Target %	Year 2 Target	Year 2 Actual	Variance
Direct materials (per unit):					
Plastic case	$ 4.50	0.95	$ 4.275	$ 4.40	$ 0.125 U
Lens set	17.00	0.95	16.15	17.20	1.05 U
Electrical set	6.60	0.95	6.27	5.70	0.57 F
Battery	11.00	0.95	10.45	10.00	0.45 F
Direct labor (per unit)	32.00	0.95	30.40	30.00	0.40 F
Indirect mfg (per unit)					
Variable costs	7.50	0.95	7.125	7.10	0.025 F
Indirect mfg (in total)					
Fixed costs	$300,000	1.00	$300,000	$342,000	$42,000 U

b. The company made progress during Year 2 with favorable variances for all components except cases and lens sets. The variances related to the lens sets may require more consideration since the lens sets are vendor purchased. Maybe new vendors can be found, or current vendor contracts may be renegotiated.

The fixed manufacturing costs also need attention. The total fixed costs increased from $300,000 (100,000 × $3) to $342,000 (120,000 × $2.85). If they are fixed, why did they increase? Did increased production or other factors cause the increase? If it was volume driven, maybe some of the costs are not fixed.

Chapter 14 Pricing, Sales Variances, and Customer Profitability

Review 14-4

a.

Actual Units	150	Actual Units	150	Budgeted Units	125		
× Actual SP	$26	× Budgeted SP	$25	× Budgeted SP	$25		
	$3,900		$3,750		$3,125		

$150 F		$625 F
Sales Price Variance		Sales Volume Variance

$150 F	+	$625 F	=	$775 F
Sales Price Variance		Sale Volume Variance		Revenue Variance

b. The sales price variance was favorable due to the $1 increase in the actual selling price over the budgeted selling price. The sales volume variance also produced favorable results due to the increase in actual units sold of 150 over budgeted units sold of 125. The net of the two variances is a positive revenue variance of $775.

Review 14-5

a.

Product X

Total Actual Units	12,600	Total Actual Units	12,600	Total Budgeted Units	9,600		
× Actual Sales Mix[1]	44.0%	× Budgeted Sales Mix	50.0%	× Budgeted Sales Mix	50.0%		
× Budgeted CM per unit[2]	$ 40	× Budgeted CM per unit	$ 40	× Budgeted CM per unit	$ 40		
	$221,760		$252,000		$192,000		

$30,240 U	$60,000 F
Sales Mix Variance	Sales Quantity Variance

Product Y

Total Actual Units	12,600	Total Actual Units	12,600	Total Budgeted Units	9,600		
× Actual Sales Mix[3]	56.0%	× Budgeted Sales Mix	50.0%	× Budgeted Sales Mix	50.0%		
× Budgeted CM per unit[4]	$ 48	× Budgeted CM per unit	$ 48	× Budgeted CM per unit	$ 48		
	$338,688		$302,400		$230,400		

$36,288 F	$72,000 F
Sales Mix Variance	Sales Quantity Variance

b.

Actual Total Market Units	75,000	Actual Total Market Units	75,000	Budgeted Total Market Units	80,000		
× Actual Market Share[5]	16.8%	× Budgeted Market Share	12.0%	× Budgeted Market Share	12.0%		
× Budgeted WA CM per unit[6]	$44	× Budgeted WA CM per unit	$44	× Budgeted WA CM per unit	$44		
	$554,400		$396,000		$422,400		

$158,400 F	$26,400 U
Market Share Variance	Market Size Variance

[1] 5,544/12,600 = 44%; 4,800/9,600 = 50%
[2] $80 − $40 = $40
[3] 7,056/12,600 = 56%; 4,800/9,600 = 50%
[4] $120 − $72 = $48
[5] 12,600/75,000 = 16.8%; 9,600/80,000 = 12.0%
[6] (($80 − $40) × 50%) + (($120 − $72) × 50%) = $44

c. The company's sales mix shifted more toward Product Y than budgeted (56% actual sales mix versus 50% budgeted sales mix). This resulted in an overall favorable sales mix of $6,048 (=$36,288 F + $30,240 U) because Product Y has a higher budgeted CM per unit. The favorable sales quantity variance for both Product X and Product Y is due to the overall increase in company sales units of 12,600 over budgeted units of 9,600.

The market share variance is favorable because the company had a 16.8% share of the market over the budgeted market share of 12%. This favorable variance was partially offset because the market shrunk from 80,000 units to 75,000 resulting in an unfavorable market size variance. Thus, the company benefited from a larger market share but of a smaller market size.

Review 14-6

a. Activity A—Minor systems maintenance
    Activity B—Visits to customers
    Activity C—Communication

Activity	1	2	3	4	5
A (@ $160)	$11,040	$22,560	$11,840	$9,760	$21,760
B (@ $300)	7,500	12,600	5,700	8,400	11,700
C (@ $50)	6,400	10,250	4,950	5,300	9,450
Total support costs	$24,940	$45,410	$22,490	$23,460	$42,910
Profit before support costs	80,000	85,000	83,000	90,000	78,000
Customer profits	$55,060	$39,590	$60,510	$66,540	$35,090
Ratio of support costs to profit before support costs	31%	53%	27%	26%	55%

b. This analysis is beneficial to SAP because it shows that Groups 2 and 5 are outliers among the five customer groups in terms of support services required. Groups 2 and 5 are significantly larger consumers of activities for all three of the support activities. Note also that Group 4 customers are relatively light users of minor systems maintenance, and Group 3 are relatively light users of communication. Calculating the ratio of total support costs to profit before support costs provides additional insight into the relative profitability of the customer groups. All five customer groups are profitable; however, this analysis provides useful information for improving profits by working with Groups 2 and 5 to control support activities and related costs and attempt to bring their support costs in line with the other customer groups.

Data Visualization Solutions

(See page 14-25.)

a. 20 clients
b. Approximately $280,000
c. Most profitable client is approximately +$50,000 and the least profitable client is approximately −$50,000.
d. Four customers as the last four customers show a downward trajectory in the chart.
e. This analysis can be helpful for the firm to recognize the effect of its unprofitable clients on its overall profitability. The company can take measures to improve profitability of those clients or perhaps drop these clients, unless the company has a strategy that requires keeping these clients.

Chapter 15

Performance Measurement, Balanced Scorecards, and Performance Rewards

Road Map

LO	Learning Objective | Topics	Page	eLecture	Demo	Review	Assignments
15-1	**How are performance measures designed?** Mission Statement :: Values Statement :: Performance Measures :: Internal Performance Measures :: External Performance Measures :: Design Criteria :: Financial Performance Goals :: Nonfinancial Performance Goals (NFPMs)	15-2	e15-1	D15-1	Rev 15-1	MC15-17, E15-26, E15-27, E15-28, E15-29, E15-30, P15-60, P15-68, P15-74, P15-78, P15-81, P15-82
15-2	**How do companies use segment reports and the statement of cash flows to measure financial performance?** Financial Performance Measures :: Segment Reports :: Contribution Income Statement Format :: Segment Contribution Margin :: Segment Margin :: Contribution Margin Ratio :: Segment Profit Margin Ratio :: Statement of Cash Flows	15-7	e15-2	D15-2	Rev 15-2	MC15-18, MC15-19, MC15-20, E15-28, E15-31, E15-32, E15-34, P15-58, P15-59, P15-60, P15-64, P15-74, DA15-1, DA15-2, DA15-3
15-3	**How are the financial measures of return on investment, residual income, and economic value added calculated and used?** Financial Performance Measures :: Return on Investment (ROI) :: Du Pont Model :: Profit Margin :: Asset Turnover :: Residual Income (RI) :: Economic Value Added (EVA)	15-12	e15-3	D15-3A D15-3B D15-3C D15-3D	Rev 15-3	MC15-21, MC15-22, E15-33, E15-34, E15-35, E15-36, E15-37, E15-38, E15-39, E15-40, E15-41, E15-42, E15-43, E15-44, P15-61, P15-62, P15-63, P15-64, P15-65, P15-66, P15-74, P15-82
15-4	**What are types of nonfinancial, quantitative measures and how are they selected?** Nonfinancial Performance Measures :: Throughput :: Manufacturing Cycle Efficiency :: Process Productivity :: Process Quality Yield :: Quality Measures :: Lead Time :: Environment-Related Metrics :: Greenhouse Gas (GHG) Emissions	15-18	e15-4	D15-4	Rev 15-4	MC15-22, MC15-23, E15-45, E15-46, E15-47, E15-48, P15-67, P15-69, P15-74, DA15-4
15-5	**How can a balanced scorecard be used to measure performance?** Balanced Scorecard (BSC) Approach :: Lagging Indicators :: Leading Indicators :: Financial :: Internal Business :: Customer :: Learning and Growth :: Sustainability :: Strategy Map :: Dashboard :: Multinational Settings	15-24	e15-5	D15-5	Rev 15-5	MC15-24, E15-49, E15-50, E15-51, E15-52, E15-53, E15-54, P15-69, P15-70, P15-71, P15-72, P15-73, P15-74, P15-75, P15-76, P15-77, P15-79
15-6	**What is compensation strategy, and what factors must be considered in designing the compensation strategy?** Compensation Strategy :: Pay-for-Performance Plans :: Build Mission :: Harvest Mission :: Pay Versus Performance :: Profit Sharing :: Employee Stock Ownership Plans (ESOP) :: Tax Implications :: Ethical Considerations	15-32	e15-6	D15-6	Rev 15-6	MC15-25, E15-55, E15-56, E15-57, P15-63, P15-78, P15-79, P15-80, P15-81, P15-82

© Cambridge Business Publishers

INTRODUCTION

An organization's performance evaluation and reward systems are key tools for aligning the efforts and goals of workers, managers, and owners.[1] The manager's primary function is to maximize shareholder value. When employees help control costs and profits increase, stockholders benefit through higher dividends and/or stock market prices. One of the most important ways of motivating employees to maximize shareholder value is through the design and implementation of effective employee performance metrics and remuneration structures.

Performance assessments are chosen to be consistent with organizational goals and objectives and to motivate or "drive" managers toward designated achievements. These assessments can be

- quantitative or nonquantitative,
- financial or nonfinancial, and
- short term or long term.

For example, if a subunit is expected to generate a specified annual profit amount, the performance measure has been set to be quantitative, financial, and short term. A longer-term performance measure might be an average increase in profit or change in stock price over a five- to ten-year period. Performance measures and rewards should be designed to

- support organizational missions and competitive strategies,
- motivate employees and managers to act in the best interest of the organization and its subunits, and
- help recruit and retain qualified employees.

Once defined, the criteria used to measure performance should be linked to the organizational incentive system because "you get what you measure." This linkage sends the message to managers that they will be rewarded based on the quality of their organizational and subunit decisions and, thereby, their contributions to achieving the organizational mission.

DESIGNING PERFORMANCE MEASUREMENT SYSTEMS

LO15-1 How are performance measures designed?

Before performance measurements can be created and assessed, the company needs to have a clear understanding of its mission. A performance measurement system should assess the company's progress toward its mission.

Organization Mission Statements

Every organization has a reason or mission for existing. The **mission statement** expresses an organization's purpose and should identify how the organization will meet targeted customers' needs through its products or services. For example, **Intel**'s mission statement is "We create world-changing technology that improves the life of every person on the planet."[2] Mission statements must be communicated not only externally to customers but internally to employees. Internal communication can be made in numerous ways, including conference room posters and tag lines that can be added to company logos or electronic signatures.

In addition to a mission statement, many companies have developed a **values statement** that reflects the organization's culture by identifying fundamental beliefs about what is important to the organization. These values may be objective (such as increased profitability and market share) or subjective (such as ethical behavior and respect for individuals). Intel's values communicated through its website are as follows.

- Customer first
- Fearless innovation
- Results driven
- One Intel
- Inclusion
- Quality
- Integrity

Mission and values statements are two of the underlying bases for setting organizational goals (abstract targets to be achieved) and objectives (quantified targets with expected completion dates). Goals and

---

[1] The authors use the term *employees* to refer to all personnel of an organization. The terms *workers* and *managers* are used to identify mutually exclusive groups of employees.

[2] Intel, General Company Information; http://www.intel.com/intel/company/corp1.htm (accessed November 5, 2023).

objectives can be short term or long term, but they are inexorably linked. Without achieving at least some short-run success, there will never be long-run success. Without engaging in long-run planning, short-run success will rapidly fade.

Critical Elements for Performance Measurement

In fulfilling organizational missions, managers design and implement strategies that apply organizational resources to activities. The organizational structure reflects the manner in which a firm assigns and coordinates its people to deploy strategies. Subunits can be created and charged with making specific contributions to the business strategy. The extent to which each subunit succeeds in its mission can be assessed using carefully designed **performance measures** that capture the subunit's important performance dimensions.

Management talent and time are dedicated to planning, controlling, decision making, and evaluating performance. For an organization to be successful, managers must devise appropriate information systems to track and gauge the effective and efficient use of organizational resources. An *effective* use of organizational resources produces the intended results. An *efficient* use of organizational resources produces results at maximum productivity with minimal waste. Two conditions must exist to make such determinations:

1. the terms effective and efficient must be defined for the specific circumstances, and
2. performance measures consistent with those definitions must be formulated.

Definitions of effective and efficient may relate to historical organizational performance, competitive benchmarks, or stakeholder expectations. Once defined, effectiveness and efficiency can be assessed by comparing actual performance with defined and targeted performance goals.

As indicated in **Exhibit 15.1**, performance measures should exist for *all elements that are critical to an organization's success in a competitive market*. Thus, not setting performance measures for any of an organization's critical elements is tantamount to stating that the ignored element is unimportant. All elements are linked because high performance in one element should lead to high performance in the others.

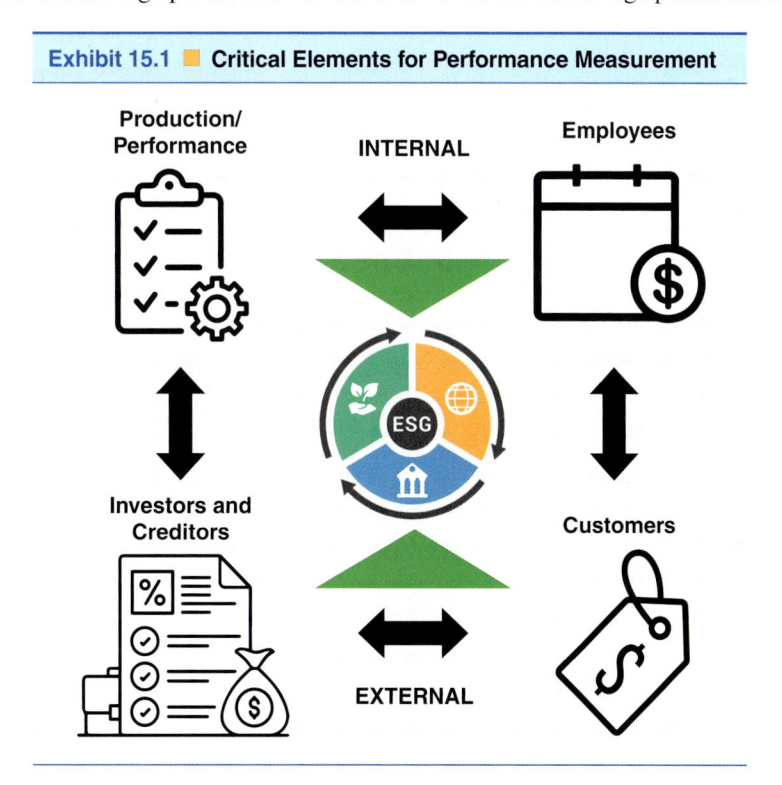

Exhibit 15.1 ■ Critical Elements for Performance Measurement

Internal Performance Measures

Production/Performance Management must develop internal measures that provide a focus on the efficiency and effectiveness of production and service processes. Inadequate processes make it more difficult for a company to manufacture a product or perform a service that will engender both employee pride and customer satisfaction. Internal process measures should reflect concern for streamlined production, high quality, minimization of product complexity, and reduction/ elimination of negative environmental impacts. Products and services compete with others on the dimensions of price, quality, and product features (including aspects of sustainability). Superior performance in any of these three areas can provide the competitive advantage needed for success. Developing performance measures for each competitive dimension can help to identify alternative ways to leverage a firm's competencies.

Employees Employee performance is also a critical element of organizational success. Each successive management level establishes target measures for subordinates. These measures communicate organizational mission, goals, and strategies and motivate staff to accomplish the stated targets. Measures, such as comparing actual to budgeted results in responsibility reports, are also used for implementing organizational control over activities. Employee performance comparisons are used for promotion and retention decisions. A firm searching for new ways to provide customers with more value at lower cost must develop an organizational culture that promotes employee learning, job satisfaction, and production efficiency.

Sustainability Sustainability concerns may relate to product production or service performance. Company management must be aware of the organization's impact on the environment from the organization's building design, to resource (especially recycled ones) usage, to product packaging, to employee training, and to research and development activities related to sustainability processes and strategies.

External Performance Measures
Externally, performance measures must signal an organization's ability to satisfy its customers, investors/creditors, and other stakeholders.

Customers The quality and quantity of firms competing in the global market have placed consumers at the center of attention. Although profit may be the ultimate measure of success in serving customers, other measures that indicate relative accomplishment in specific areas of market performance can be developed. For example, performance measures must reflect characteristics, such as product/service reliability, value, quality, and on-time delivery, that customers highly value. Such performance measures should result in a high level of customer loyalty, as measured by customer retention. Meeting or exceeding the performance targets set for customers should result in the increased likelihood of meeting or exceeding the performance targets set for investors and creditors.

Investors and Creditors The most common organizational performance metric is profit, which can be measured as operating income or net income, and can be expressed on a gross or per-share basis. Generally accepted accounting principles are formulated to provide information that is comparable across firms. This comparability facilitates investor/creditor judgments about which firms are worthy of capital investments and which firms can provide appropriate returns relative to the investment risks borne. Financial performance measures typically determine whether top management is retained or dismissed. Meeting or exceeding the market's performance expectations should create capital inflows that fund improving processes, hiring more qualified employees, and creating more satisfied customers. Management must be careful to realize, after recent accounting scandals in the business community, that "good" financial performance should not be sought by improper accounting methods—whether in regard to "managing" revenues or expenses.

Sustainability Sustainability must be measured from an external as well as internal perspective. In addition to the stakeholders already mentioned, an organization must be concerned with its local and more global communities. As such, an extremely common performance metric is level of (or reduction in level of) pollutant emissions into the air, water, and soil. But additional measures may also be important: proportion of suppliers that are "green," number of or fines from environmental "incidents," increase/decrease in percentage of local jobs from the organization, paid hours for community volunteer work, and dollars of investments in disaster relief projects. External sustainability metrics should reflect strategic organizational priorities.

Identifying Performance Measurements   LO15-1   DEMO 15-1

◆ What are possible performance measurements for each of the following critical elements of performance measurement: Production/performance, employees, sustainability, customers, and investors and creditors?

Critical Element	Performance Measurement
1. Production/Performance	Level of quality Number of defects Inventory turnover
2. Employees	Number of days of training Employee satisfaction surveys Number of employees participating in wellness program
3. Sustainability	Rate of emissions Quantity of packaging per product Quantity of water used in production
4. Customers	Market share variance Rate of on-time shipments Number of customer referrals
5. Investors and Creditors	Operating cash flows Operating profit Dividend payouts

Performance Measurement System Criteria

In creating any performance measurement system, it is important to remember that people focus on the items that are measured by supervisors. Thus, an essential question to address when implementing a performance measurement system is, "What behavior will this metric encourage?" The performance measurement system should be designed to encourage behaviors that will result in outcomes that generate organizational success.

Regardless of the results that are being measured, the employee level at which the measurement is occurring, or the type (monetary or nonmonetary) of measure that is being used, five general criteria should be considered in designing a performance measurement system as outlined in **Exhibit 15.2**.

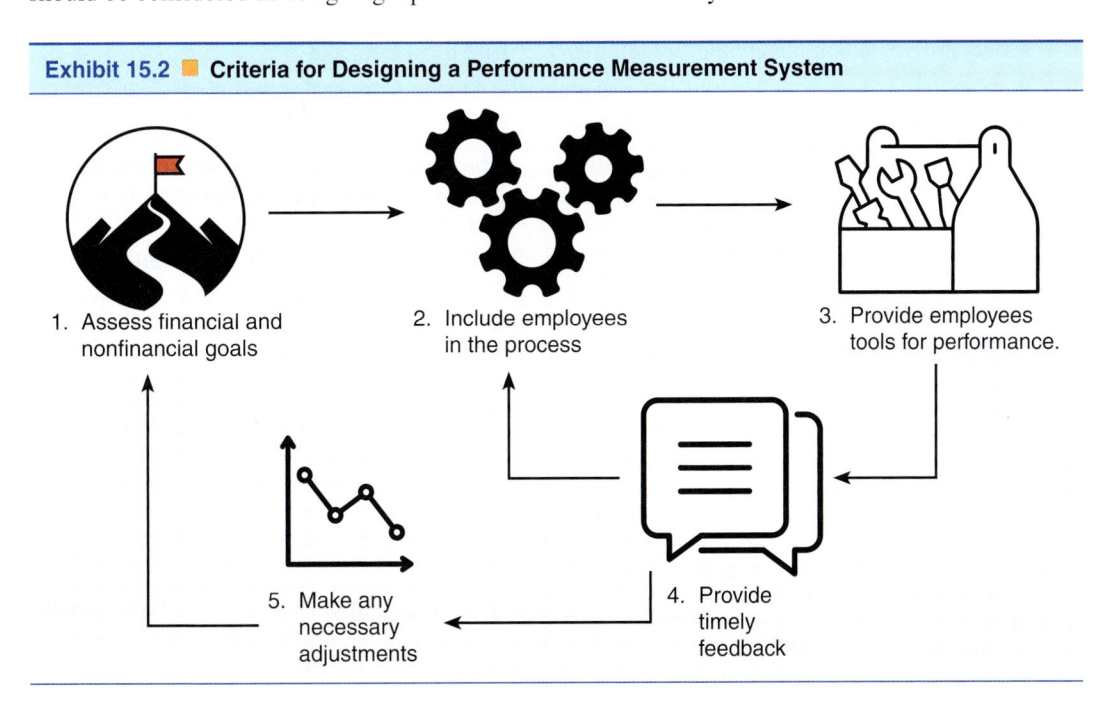

Exhibit 15.2 ■ Criteria for Designing a Performance Measurement System

1. Assess financial and nonfinancial goals
2. Include employees in the process
3. Provide employees tools for performance.
4. Provide timely feedback
5. Make any necessary adjustments

Assess Financial and Nonfinancial Goals

Organizations have a variety of objectives, including the need to be financially viable. Therefore, financial performance measures must be relevant for the type of organization or subunit being evaluated and must reflect an understanding of accounting information and its potential for manipulation. In addition to financial success, many companies are now establishing operational targets of total customer satisfaction, zero defects, lead time to market, and environmental and social responsibility. These goals generally cannot be measured directly using traditional, short-term financial methods. Alternative methods are needed to capture the nonfinancial performance dimensions. **Nonfinancial performance measures (NFPMs)** that indicate progress—or lack thereof—toward the achievement of a world-class company's critical success factors can be developed.

Include Employees in the Process

Regardless of the number or types of measures chosen, top management must set high performance standards and communicate them to others. The measures should promote harmonious operations rather than suboptimization among organizational units. Because people are expected to act in accordance with the way they are measured, they must be aware of and understand the performance measures being used. Withholding measurement information does not allow people to perform at their highest level, which frustrates them and does not foster feelings of mutual respect and cooperation.

If standards or budget comparisons are used to assess performance, people should be involved in setting those standards or the budget. Participation results in a "social contract" between participants and evaluators by generating an understanding, and acceptance of, the standards or budget. Also, people who have participated in setting targets generally attempt to achieve the results to affirm that the plans were well founded.

Provide Employees Tools for Performance

For performance measures to be fair, people must first possess or obtain the appropriate skills for their jobs. Given job competence, people must then be provided the necessary tools (equipment, resources, information, and authority) to perform their jobs in a manner consistent with the measurement process. If the appropriate support is unavailable, managers cannot presume that employees will be able to reach their objectives.

In decentralized firms, there may be little opportunity to directly observe subordinates' actions and managers must make evaluations based on the outcomes that are captured by performance measures. Thus, the performance measures selected should

- highly correlate with the subunit mission,
- reflect fairly and completely the subunit manager's performance, and
- measure performance dimensions that are under the subunit manager's control.

To evaluate performance, benchmarks are established as reference points for performance measures. Benchmarks can be monetary (such as standard costs or budget appropriation amounts) or nonmonetary (such as zero defects or another organization's market share).

Provide Timely Feedback and Make Any Necessary Adjustments

Performance should be monitored, and feedback (both positive and negative) should be provided to the appropriate individuals on a continuing basis. Waiting to give feedback on performance until a known evaluation point is reached does not allow employees an opportunity for early adjustment. Thus, if employee performance reviews and evaluations are performed at a certain date annually, feedback on performance should be provided periodically during the year so that employees are aware of how they are doing and have ample opportunities to maximize positive results and correct negative results, so those employees are not "blindsided" during performance reviews.

The ultimate feedback is that organizational stakeholders exhibit belief in the firm's viability. The primary determinant of this belief is typically provided by short-run financial performance measures.

Managers should provide feedback on employee performance often so that employees are rewarded for successful results while having an opportunity to continually improve or correct poor results.

Classifying Performance Measures — LO15-1 — REVIEW 15-1

1. For each of the following performance measures, indicate whether the measure is an internal performance measure or an external performance measure and whether the measure primarily relates to the element of production/performance, employees, sustainability, investors and creditors, or customers.
   a. Amount of machine downtime
   b. Rate of on-time deliveries
   c. Retention rate of managers within the company
   d. Percentage of recyclable packaging in products
   e. Amount of revenue reported each annual reporting period
   f. Hours of community service performed by employees during company sponsored functions
2. **Critical Thinking:** Which of the measures above would normally be assessed during the process of preparing financial statements? What does your answer indicate about the importance of carefully choosing performance measures that align with the company's mission?

More practice: E15-26
Solution on p. 15-65.

FINANCIAL PERFORMANCE MEASURES

We discuss financial performance measures, followed by nonfinancial performance measures. For financial measures, we focus on segment reports and the statement of cash flows in LO15-2 and ratio analysis in LO15-3. Types of quantitative, nonfinancial measures are examined in LO15-4.

eLecture LO15-2 How do companies use segment reports and the statement of cash flows to measure financial performance?

Segment Margin

As discussed in Chapter 13 relative to responsibility centers and responsibility accounting, each manager in a firm is expected to make specific organizational contributions. *Measurements selected to gauge managerial performance must be appropriate for the types of responsibility assigned and behavior desired.* Traditionally, managerial performance was judged primarily on monetary measures such as profits, achievement of and variations from budget objectives, and cash flow.

The ability to use monetary measures is, however, affected by the type of responsibility center being evaluated because managers should be evaluated only with metrics that reflect authority and responsibility.

- In a *cost center*, the primary financial performance measurements are variances from budgeted or standard costs, discussed in Chapter 10.
- In a *pure revenue center*, performance can be judged primarily by comparing budgeted with actual revenues and through sales variances, as discussed in the last chapter.
- *Profit center* managers are responsible for revenues and expenses; thus, profit (or cash flow) is an appropriate performance measure.
- *Investment center* managers are responsible for revenues, expenses, and return on investment; thus, a variety of measures are appropriate.

Segment reports are income statements for portions or segments of a business that are profit or investment centers. Segment reporting is used primarily for internal purposes, although generally accepted accounting principles also require some disclosure of segment information for public corporations.

Although segment reports are normally produced to coincide with managerial lines of responsibility, some companies also produce segment reports for smaller slices of the business that do not represent separate responsibility centers. These parts of the business are not significant enough to be identified as "strategic" business units as defined, but management could want information about them on a continuing basis.

Preparing a Segment Report

Even though there are many different types of segment reports, at least three steps are basic to the preparation of all segment reports.

- Identification of the segments
- Assignment of direct costs to segments
- Allocation of indirect costs to segments

The format of segment income statements varies depending on the approach adopted by a company for reporting income statements internally. The contribution income statement format, introduced in Chapter 4, can be used for segment reporting, or the traditional income statement format can be used. Data availability can, however, dictate the format used. Regardless of the format adopted, it is essential that costs be separable into those directly traceable to the segments and those not directly traceable to segments. See **Exhibit 15.3**, below, for how the three steps above can be incorporated in the development of segment income using the *contribution income statement format*.

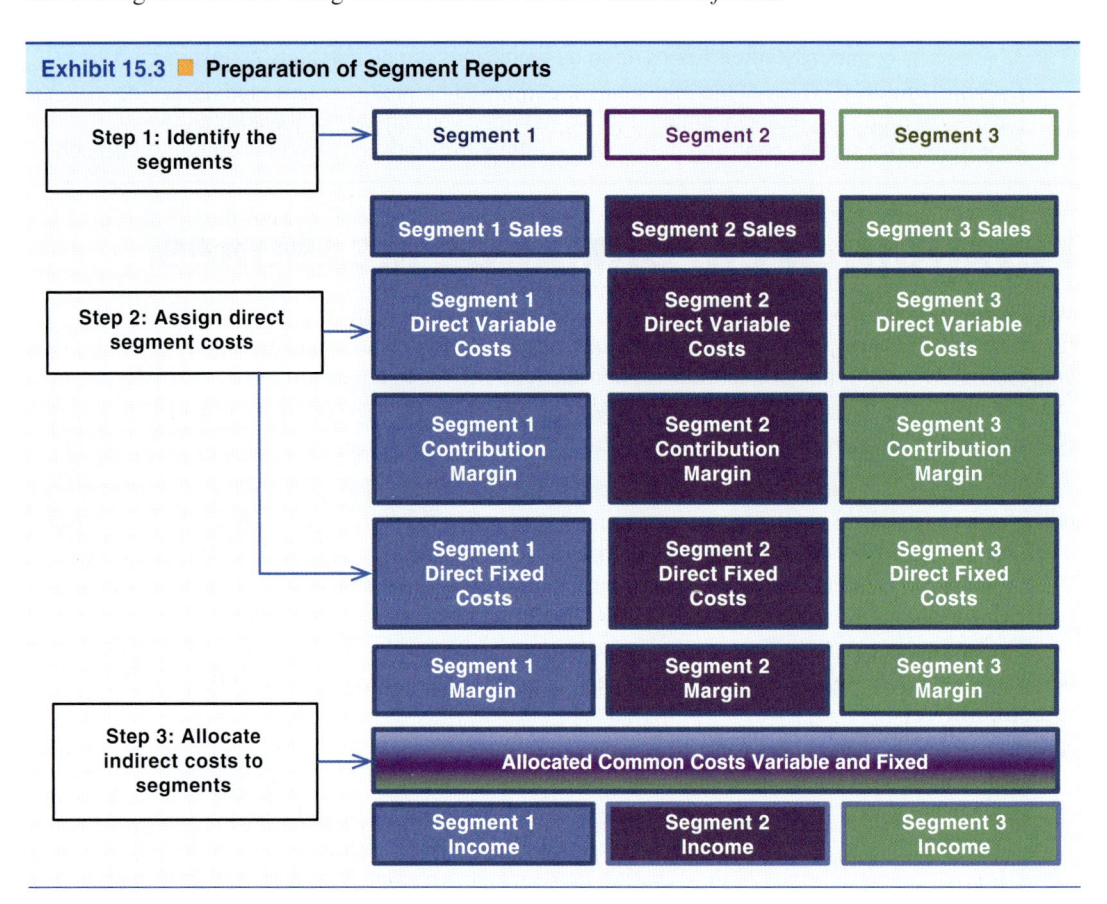

Exhibit 15.3 ■ Preparation of Segment Reports

	Segment 1	Segment 2	Segment 3
Step 1: Identify the segments			
	Segment 1 Sales	Segment 2 Sales	Segment 3 Sales
Step 2: Assign direct segment costs	Segment 1 Direct Variable Costs	Segment 2 Direct Variable Costs	Segment 3 Direct Variable Costs
	Segment 1 Contribution Margin	Segment 2 Contribution Margin	Segment 3 Contribution Margin
	Segment 1 Direct Fixed Costs	Segment 2 Direct Fixed Costs	Segment 3 Direct Fixed Costs
	Segment 1 Margin	Segment 2 Margin	Segment 3 Margin
Step 3: Allocate indirect costs to segments	Allocated Common Costs Variable and Fixed		
	Segment 1 Income	Segment 2 Income	Segment 3 Income

The subtotals depicted in **Exhibit 15.3** are described in further detail.

- **Direct segment variable costs** vary in proportion to the level of segment sales and are subtracted from segment sales in calculating *segment contribution margin*.
- **Direct segment fixed costs** are nonvariable costs directly traceable to the segments, incurred for the specific benefit of the respective segments.
- **Segment margin** equals the segment contribution margin minus the direct segment fixed costs. Segment margin represents the amount that a segment contributes directly to the company's profitability in the short run.
- **Allocated common segment costs** are costs incurred for the common benefit of all related segments that can be reasonably allocated to segments, even though they cannot be directly traced to the various segments based on benefits received.
- **Segment income** represents all revenues of the segment minus all costs directly or indirectly charged to it.

Unallocated common segment costs are common costs that cannot reasonably be allocated to the segments. Although not shown as part of the segment report in **Exhibit 15-3**, unallocated common segment costs are subtracted from total segment income to arrive at net income for the company. For example, if the cost of a national ad campaign could not be reasonably allocated to regional divisions, the cost would not be charged to the regions. However, to calculate net income of all segments combined, the amount would be subtracted from total segment income.

Segment Margin as Performance Measure

The **segment margin** of a profit or investment center is frequently used to measure segment performance.[3] Segment margin is an appealing financial metric because it does not include allocated costs, which managers of the segment do not control. Actual and budgeted segment margins are compared, and variances are computed to determine the point at which targets were exceeded or not achieved. The segment margin can also be compared to prior year results or available industry data.

Additionally, companies measure the performance of a segment through the use of ratios. Ratios are useful in comparing the performance of two segments or divisions because they allow for the comparability of segments with different sales volumes.

Segment Contribution margin ratio. The segment contribution margin ratio measures the portion of each segment sales dollar that can be used to cover segment direct fixed and allocated costs, and provide segment income and is calculated as follows.

> **Segment contribution margin ratio = Segment contribution margin/Segment sales**

Segment profit margin ratio The segment profit margin ratio measures the portion of each segment sales dollar that can be used to cover allocated costs and provide segment income and is calculated as follows.

> **Segment profit margin ratio = Segment margin/Segment sales**

Potential Issues with Segment Reporting

One problem with using segment margin to measure performance is that (as with many other accounting measures) individual components are subject to manipulations, such as the following.

- If a cost flow method other than first-in, first-out is used, inventory purchases can be accelerated or deferred at the end of the period to manage the period's Cost of Goods Sold for retailing and wholesaling firms. Managers in manufacturing firms can increase or decrease production to manage earnings. For example, production can be increased so that fixed cost per unit declines and earnings rise.
- Replacement of workers who have resigned or been dismissed can be deferred to minimize salary expense for the period.
- Routine maintenance can be delayed or eliminated to reduce perceived expenses in the short run.
- Sales recognition can be delayed or accelerated.
- Advertising expenses or other discretionary costs can be delayed or accelerated.
- Depreciation methods can be changed to affect depreciation expense.

These tactics can be used to "cause" reported segment margin to conform to budget expectations, but such manipulations are normally not in the center's long-run best interest and could even be improper accounting.

Preparing a Segment Report   LO15-2   DEMO 15-2

Randal Supplies Inc. summarized the following information for the current year.

---

[3] However, because segment reporting ignores the amount of assets invested in the segment, additional performance measures would be required for an investment center as described in later sections.

Sales revenue—Division 1	$3,000,000
Sales revenue—Division 2	5,000,000
Direct variable costs—Division 1	1,200,000
Direct variable costs—Division 2	2,250,000
Direct fixed costs—Division 1	400,000
Direct fixed costs—Division 2	550,000
Allocated fixed costs—Division 1	250,000
Allocated fixed costs—Division 2	350,000
Unallocated common fixed costs	150,000

◆ **How would the company prepare a segment report using the contribution income statement, incorporating a companywide total column?**

The following segment report shows segment income of $1,150,000 and $1,850,000 for Division 1 and Division 2, respectively.

	Division 1	Division 2	Company Total
Segment sales revenue	$3,000,000	$5,000,000	$8,000,000
Segment direct variable costs	1,200,000	2,250,000	3,450,000
Segment contribution margin	1,800,000	2,750,000	4,550,000
Segment direct fixed costs	400,000	550,000	950,000
Segment margin	1,400,000	2,200,000	3,600,000
Allocated fixed costs	250,000	350,000	600,000
Segment income	$1,150,000	$1,850,000	3,000,000
Unallocated common fixed costs			150,000
Total income			$2,850,000

◆ **How would the company evaluate the segment performance of Division 1 and Division 2?**

Segment margin could be used to evaluate the performance of Division 1 and Division 2.

Segment Margin

- Division 1: $1,400,000
- Division 2: $2,200,000

Because the division managers would not have direct control over the allocated fixed costs, it is unlikely that the division managers would be responsible for those costs. Based on total segment margin, Division 2 had a stronger performance relative to Division 1.

The company could also use the performance measures of segment contribution margin ratio and segment profit margin ratio to compare the two divisions.

	Division 1	Division 2
Segment contribution margin	$1,800,000	$2,750,000
Segment sales	$3,000,000	$5,000,000
Segment contribution margin ratio	60%	55%
Segment margin	$1,400,000	$2,200,000
Segment sales	$3,000,000	$5,000,000
Segment profit margin ratio	47%	44%

Ratio Summary

- Segment profit margin ratio: Division 1 — 47%; Division 2 — 44%
- Segment contribution margin ratio: Division 1 — 60%; Division 2 — 55%

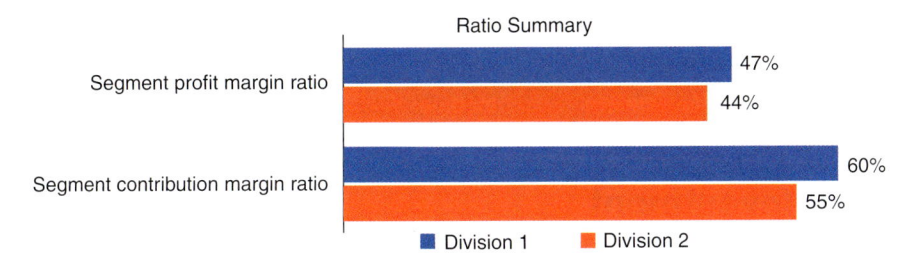

Division 2 is a larger segment relative to Division 1 with sales 167 percent of Division 1 sales. Thus, it is expected that its segment margin would be larger than that of Division 1. However, relative to the amount of sales, Division 1 had a stronger performance over Division 2. For each dollar of sales, Division 1 more effectively and efficiently produced both segment contribution margin and segment margin. For a more complete understanding of the segment performance, these results should be compared to budget, prior year results, and industry data.

Statement of Cash Flows

To succeed, an entity or an investment center must meet two requirements:

- long-run profitability and
- continuous liquidity.

The statement of cash flows (SCF) provides information about the sources and uses of cash from operating, investing, and financing activities.

- **Operating cash flows:** Net cash flows generally related to activities that generate net income.
- **Investing cash flows:** Net cash flows generally related to purchasing (selling) long-term assets
- **Financing cash flows:** Net cash flows generally related to debt and company stock transactions.

Such information is useful when managing cash outflow commitments, adapting to adverse changes in business conditions, and assessing new cash commitments. Furthermore, because this statement identifies the relationships between segment margin (or net income) and net cash flow from operations, the SCF assists managers in judging the reliability of the entity's earnings. Analysis of the SCF in conjunction with budgets and other financial reports provides information on cost reductions, collection policies, impact of capital projects on total cash flows, and liquidity position.

Statement of Cash Flows

Net cash flows from operating activities	
Net income	$#
Adjust for net reconciling items	#
Total	#
Net cash flows from investing activities	
Purchase (sale) of plant and equipment	#
Sale (purchase of investments)	#
Other investing cash flows	#
Total	#
Net cash flows from financing activities	
Issuance (payment) of notes payable	#
Payment of dividends	#
Total	#
Net change in cash	$#

REVIEW 15-2 — Calculating Segment Margin and Ratios (LO15-2)

The following annual information is available for Lakewood Industries, an investment center.

Sales	$453,000
Direct variable operating expenses	225,000
Direct fixed costs	160,000
Allocated fixed costs	17,000

a. Prepare a segment income statement using the contribution income statement format.
b. Calculate the segment contribution margin ratio.
c. Calculate the segment profit margin ratio.
d. **Critical Thinking:** How would your answers change to parts a, b, and c if Lakewood Industries was a profit center instead of an investment center?

More practice:
MC 15-19, MC15-20,
E15-31, E15-32
Solution on p. 15-65.

LO15-3 How are the financial measures of return on investment, residual income, and economic value added calculated and used?

In this section, we examine three ratios used to measure financial performance.

| Return on Investment | Residual Income | Economic Value Added |

Return on Investment

Return on investment (ROI) is a ratio relating income generated by an investment center or organization to the resources (or asset base) used to produce that income. The return on investment formula is

$$\text{ROI} = \text{Income} \div \text{Assets invested}$$

Defining Terms in the ROI Formula

To use ROI, both terms in the formula must be specifically defined. Alternative definitions and preferred definitions are provided in **Exhibit 15.4**. With internal performance measures, no specific guidelines are required which means that the measure can be adapted to the company's needs. Once definitions have been assigned to the terms, ROI can be used to evaluate individual entities and to make intracompany, intercompany, and multinational comparisons. However, managers making these comparisons must consider differences in the entities' characteristics and accounting methods.

Exhibit 15.4 ROI Definitional Questions and Answers

Question	Preferable Answer
Is income defined as segment margin or segment income?	Segment margin The manager does not have short-run control over unavoidable fixed expenses and allocated corporate costs.
Is income on a before-tax or after-tax basis?	Before-tax Investment centers might pay higher or lower tax rates than the overall organization.
Should assets be defined as • total assets utilized; • total assets available for use; or • net assets (equity)?	Total assets available for use If duplicate or unused assets were eliminated from the formula, there would be no encouragement for managers to dispose of those assets and gain additional cash flow that could be used for more profitable projects. Alternatively, if the objective is to measure how well the segment is performing, given the funds provided for that segment, then net assets should be used to measure return on equity.
Should plant assets be included at • original cost; • depreciated book value; or • current value?	Current value As assets age and net book value declines, an investment center earning the same income each year would show a continuously increasing ROI. Although more difficult to obtain and possibly more subjective, current values measure the opportunity cost of using the assets.
Should beginning, ending, or average assets be used?	Average assets The numerator income amount is for a period of time, the denominator base should reflect for the same time frame.

Data for Nationwide Services (**Exhibit 15.5**) are used to illustrate return on investment computations. The company has investment centers in Denver, San Diego, and Raleigh. All three divisions operate in the same industry, offer the same types of services to customers, and are charged with similar missions. Similarity in business lines and missions allows for comparisons among the three centers.

Exhibit 15.5 ■ Data for Nationwide Services

Financial Data for Denver, San Diego, and Raleight

	A	B	C	D	E
1			Investment Centers		
2	(in $000s)	Denver	San Diego	Raleigh	Total
3	Revenues	$ 3,200,000	$ 675,000	$ 430,000	$ 4,305,000
4	Direct costs				
5	Variable	(1,120,000)	(310,000)	(172,000)	(1,602,000)
6	Fixed (avoidable)	(550,000)	(118,000)	(60,000)	(728,000)
7	Segment margin	$ 1,530,000	$ 247,000	$ 198,000	$ 1,975,000
8	Allocated common fixed costs	(372,000)	(78,000)	(50,000)	(500,000)
9	Segment income	$ 1,158,000	$ 169,000	$ 148,000	$ 1,475,000
10	Taxes (34%)	(393,720)	(57,460)	(50,320)	(501,500)
11	Net income	$ 764,280	$ 111,540	$ 97,680	$ 973,500
12	Current assets	$ 48,500	$ 33,120	$ 20,000	
13	Fixed assets	6,179,000	4,610,000	900,000	
14	Total asset cost	$ 6,227,500	$ 4,643,120	$ 920,000	
15	Accumulated depreciation	(1,232,500)	(1,270,000)	(62,500)	
16	Total asset book value	$ 4,995,000	$ 3,373,120	$ 857,500	
17	Liabilities	(2,130,000)	(600,000)	(162,500)	
18	Net assets	$ 2,865,000	$ 2,773,120	$ 695,000	
19	Proportion of total assets utilized	100%	93%	85%	
20	Current value of total assets	$ 5,500,000	$ 2,400,000	$ 780,000	
21	Fair value of invested capital (for EVA)	$18,250,000	$ 2,400,000	$ 500,000	
22	*Note:* A summarized corporate balance sheet would not balance with the investment center balance sheets because of the existence of general corporate assets and liabilities.				

The following schedule provides the return on investment rates (using a variety of bases) for Nationwide Services' investment centers. The rates vary because different numerator and denominator definitions are used in each case, and this does not even include all possible variations! These variations demonstrate why the income and assets involved must be defined before making computations or comparisons.

	Denver	San Diego	Raleigh			Denver	San Diego	Raleigh
Segment income / Asset utilization	$1,158,000 / $4,995,000	$169,000 / $3,137,002	$148,000 / $728,875		Segment margin / Asset book value	$1,530,000 / $4,995,000	$247,000 / $3,373,120	$198,000 / $857,500
ROI	23.2%	5.4%	20.3%		ROI	30.6%	7.3%	23.1%
Segment income / Asset current value	$1,158,000 / $5,500,000	$169,000 / $2,400,000	$148,000 / $780,000		Segment margin / Asset current value	$1,530,000 / $5,500,000	$247,000 / $2,400,000	$198,000 / $780,000
ROI	21.1%	7.0%	19.0%		ROI	27.8%	10.3%	25.4%
Segment margin / Total asset cost	$1,530,000 / $6,227,500	$247,000 / $4,643,120	$198,000 / $920,000		Segment margin / Net assets	$1,530,000 / $2,865,000	$247,000 / $2,773,120	$198,000 / $695,000
ROI	24.6%	5.3%	21.5%		ROI	53.4%	8.9%	28.5%

ROI Using the Du Pont Model

The ROI formula can be restated to provide useful information about two individual factors that compose the rate of return: profit margin and asset turnover. This restatement, called the **Du Pont model**, is

$$\text{ROI} = \text{Profit margin} \times \text{Asset turnover}$$
$$= (\text{Income} \div \text{Sales}) \times (\text{Sales} \div \text{Assets})$$

■ **Profit margin** is the ratio of income to sales and indicates what proportion of each sales dollar is not used for expenses (and, thus, becomes profit). Profit margin can be used to judge management's efficiency with regard to the relationship between sales and expenses.

- **Asset turnover** measures asset productivity and shows the number of sales dollars generated by each dollar of assets. This metric can be used to judge management's effective utilization of assets relative to revenue production.

DEMO 15-3A   LO15-3   Computing ROI Using the Du Pont Model

For this demo, we define the terms used in the formula of ROI to be *segment margin* as the income value, and *total asset cost* as the asset value.

◆ **How is ROI calculated and analyzed for each of Nationwide Services' investment centers using the Du Pont Model?**

ROI for each center using the Du Pont Model is calculated as follows.

Denver

$$\text{ROI} = (\text{Income} \div \text{Sales}) \times (\text{Sales} \div \text{Assets})$$
$$= (\$1{,}530{,}000 \div \$3{,}200{,}000) \times (\$3{,}200{,}000 \div \$6{,}227{,}500)$$
$$= 0.478 \times 0.514 = 24.6\%$$

San Diego

$$\text{ROI} = (\text{Income} \div \text{Sales}) \times (\text{Sales} \div \text{Assets})$$
$$= (\$247{,}000 \div \$675{,}000) \times (\$675{,}000 \div \$4{,}643{,}120)$$
$$= 0.366 \times 0.145 = 5.3\%$$

Raleigh

$$\text{ROI} = (\text{Income} \div \text{Sales}) \times (\text{Sales} \div \text{Assets})$$
$$= (\$198{,}000 \div \$430{,}000) \times (\$430{,}000 \div \$920{,}000)$$
$$= 0.460 \times 0.467 = 21.5\%$$

ROI

Center	ROI
Denver	24.6%
San Diego	5.3%
Raleigh	21.5%

Denver Center The Denver investment center has both the highest profit margin and highest turnover. This center may be benefiting from scale economies relative to the other divisions, which could partially account for its superior performance. Additionally, Denver is better at leveraging its assets; as shown in **Exhibit 15.5**, the center's assets are 100 percent utilized.

San Diego Center The San Diego center is performing very poorly compared to the other two investment centers. Based on the relationship between the accumulated depreciation and fixed asset cost amounts shown in **Exhibit 15.5**, the San Diego center appears to be the oldest, which could be a factor driving its poor operating performance. San Diego's manager should consider purchasing more modern facilities to generate more sales and greater profits. Such an investment could, however, *cause ROI to decline because the asset base would increase*. Rate of return computations can encourage managers to retain and use old plant assets (especially when accumulated depreciation is deducted from the asset base) to keep ROIs high as long as those assets can keep revenues up and expenses down.

Raleigh Center The Raleigh investment center is the newest of the three based on the low proportion of accumulated depreciation to fixed asset cost based on the information in **Exhibit 15.5**. With increased asset utilization, the Raleigh investment center should generate a higher asset turnover and raise its ROI.

Improving ROI

Sales prices, volume and mix of products sold, expenses, and capital asset acquisitions and dispositions affect ROI. Return on investment can be increased through various management actions including

- raising sales prices if demand will not be impaired;
- decreasing expenses; and

- decreasing investment in assets, especially nonproductive ones.

Actions should be taken only after considering relationships among the factors that determine ROI. For instance, a sales price increase could reduce sales volume if demand is elastic with respect to price.

Profit margin, asset turnover, and ROI can be assessed as favorable or unfavorable only if each component is compared with a valid benchmark. Comparison bases include expected results, prior results, or results of other similar entities.

Residual Income

An investment center's **residual income (RI)** is the profit earned that exceeds an amount "charged" for funds committed to the center. The "charged" amount is equal to a specified target rate of return multiplied by the asset base and is comparable to an imputed rate of interest on the divisional assets used.[4] The rate can be changed to compensate for market rate fluctuations or for risk. The RI computation follows.

> Residual income = Income − (Target rate × Asset base)

An application of residual income is noted in **Berkshire Hathaway Inc.**'s 2021 annual report: one of its manufacturing divisions analyzes loan applicants using guidelines that incorporate residual income.

Residual income yields a dollar figure rather than a percentage. Expansion (or additional investments in assets) should occur in an investment center if *positive* RI (dollars of return) is expected on the dollars of additional investment.

Calculating Residual Income LO15-3 DEMO 15-3B

We continue with the Nationwide Services example but now assume that the company has established a 15 percent target return on total assets and has defined income as *segment margin* and asset base as *total asset cost*.

◆ **What is the company's residual income of each of its investment centers?**

Residual income calculations follow.

Denver	RI = $1,530,000 − (0.15 × $6,227,500) = $1,530,000 − $934,125 = $595,875
San Diego	RI = $247,000 − (0.15 × $4,643,120) = $247,000 − $696,468 = $(449,468)
Raleigh	RI = $198,000 − (0.15 × $920,000) = $198,000 − $138,000 = $60,000

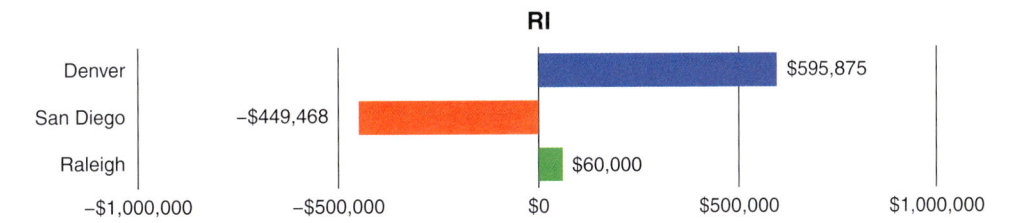

RI

- Denver: $595,875
- San Diego: −$449,468
- Raleigh: $60,000

Denver and Raleigh show positive RIs, but San Diego's negative RI indicates that income is significantly low relative to asset investment.

Economic Value Added

A measure that has been developed to more directly align managerial interests with common stockholders' interests is **economic value added (EVA®)**.[5] Conceptually similar to RI, EVA measures the profit produced above the cost of capital (assumed to be the after-tax, weighted average cost of the various sources (debt and equity) of funds that compose a firm's financial structure). However, EVA

---

[4] This target rate is similar to the discount rate used in capital budgeting (discussed in Chapter 19). For management to invest in a capital project, that project must earn at least a minimum specified rate of return. In the same manner, the ROI of an investment center must be equal to or higher than the target rate used to compute residual income.

[5] EVA is a registered trademark of Stern Stewart & Co. It was first discussed by Alfred Marshall, an English economist, in about 1890. More information about EVA can be found at https://sternvaluemanagement.com/eva (last accessed November 7, 2023).

applies the target rate of return to the fair value of the capital invested rather than the asset book values that are used to calculate RI. Furthermore, EVA is calculated on net income, or the after-tax income available to stockholders. The EVA calculation is as follows.

> **EVA = After-tax income − (Cost of capital % × Fair value of invested capital)**

As an example of its relevance, both **Dell Corporation** and **Ford Motor Company** list economic value added as a possible performance criteria used to measure performance goals in recent Proxy reports filed with the **Securities and Exchange Commission**.

DEMO 15-3C LO15-3   Calculating Economic Value Added

◆ Using information on net income and fair values given in Exhibit 15.5, what is the EVA for each Nationwide Services investment center?

The cost of capital is assumed to be 13 percent. EVA calculations follow.

Denver	EVA = $764,280 − (0.13 × $18,250,000) = $764,280 − $2,372,500 = $(1,608,220)
San Diego	EVA = $111,540 − (0.13 × $2,400,000) = $111,540 − $312,000 = $(200,460)
Raleigh	EVA = $97,680 − (0.13 × $500,000) = $97,680 − $65,000 = $32,680

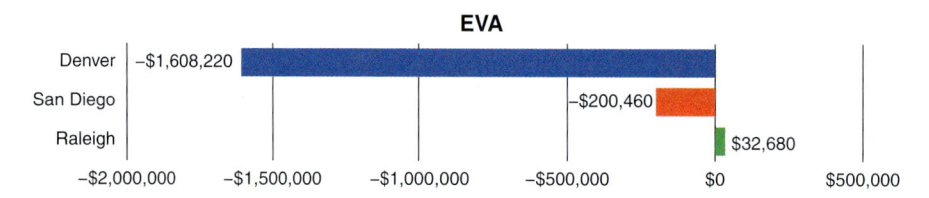

EVA

- Denver: −$1,608,220
- San Diego: −$200,460
- Raleigh: $32,680

As the difference between the fair value of invested capital (total equity and interest-bearing debt) and the book value of assets increases, so do the relative benefits of using EVA rather than RI as a performance measure. The results show a different portrayal of performance than those given by ROI and RI. EVA shows the Raleigh center to be the stellar performer. By failing to capture the large difference between the market and cost values of the Denver investment center, ROI and RI significantly overstate Denver's performance. San Diego still appears to be performing poorly, although better than Denver.

Despite its popularity, EVA cannot measure all dimensions of performance and is short-term focused. Accordingly, the EVA measure can discourage investment in long-term projects because such investments cause *an immediate increase in the amount of invested capital, but only later in time do they increase after-tax profits*. For greatest benefit, EVA should be supplemented with longer-term financial and nonfinancial performance measures.

Limitations of Return on Investment, Residual Income, and Economic Value Added

Each financial measure of performance discussed has certain limitations. For example, the limitations of divisional profit and cash flow are, respectively, their potential for income and cash flow manipulation. ROI, RI, and EVA have three primary limitations.

Use of Accounting Income The first limitation reflects the use of accounting income. Income can be manipulated or managed in the short run, depending on the accounting methods selected to account for items such as inventory or depreciation. For valid comparisons to be made, all investment centers must use the same accounting methods. Because neither cash flows nor the time value of money are considered, income may not always provide the best basis for evaluating performance.

Measurement of the Asset Base The second limitation of ROI, RI, and EVA relates to the asset investment base used. Asset investment can be difficult to properly measure and assign to center managers. Some investments (such as research and development costs) have value beyond the accounting period but are not capitalized and, thus, create an understated asset base. Previous managers could have acquired assets and, if those managers are no longer heading the center, current managers can potentially be judged on investment decisions over which the current managers had no control. If fixed assets and inventory are not restated for price-level increases, net income could be overstated (or understated, in the event of price-level decreases), and the investment base could be understated (or overstated). Managers who keep and use older assets can report much higher ROIs than managers using new assets. For EVA, this situation exists for the income measure, but not for the asset measure, because EVA focuses on the fair value of capital employed.

Conflicts with Companywide Goals The third limitation of these measures is a single, potentially critical problem: the measures direct attention to how well an investment center performed in isolation rather than relative to companywide objectives. Such a focus can result in resource suboptimization so that the firm is not maximizing its operational effectiveness and efficiency.

Suboptimizing Returns with ROI Focused-Decisions | LO15-3 DEMO 15-3D

Assume that the Raleigh investment center, shown to have an ROI of 21.5 percent in Demo 15-3A, has an opportunity to increase income by $40,000 by installing a new $200,000 service kiosk.

◆ **What is the ROI for the investment and how would the investment impact the overall ROI for the Raleigh investment center?**

This specific investment has an ROI of 20 percent.

$$\text{ROI of Investment} = \$40{,}000 \div \$200{,}000 = 20\%$$

However, as shown in the following calculation, installing the kiosk would cause Raleigh's overall ROI to decline slightly from its current rate of 21.5 percent.

$$\text{New Raleigh ROI} = (\$198{,}000 + \$40{,}000) \div (\$920{,}000 + \$200{,}000)$$
$$= \$238{,}000 \div \$1{,}120{,}000$$
$$= 21.25\%$$

21.50%   21.25%

If investment center managers are evaluated only on the basis of ROI, the Raleigh center manager will not accept this investment opportunity. However, if Nationwide Services has a 15 percent target rate of return on investment, the Raleigh manager's decision to reject the new opportunity suboptimizes companywide returns. This venture should be accepted because it provides a return higher than the *firm's target rate*. Top management should be informed of such opportunities, made aware of the effects that acceptance might have on divisional performance measurements, and be willing to reward such acceptance based on the impact on company performance. Aligning goals of the company with performance measures is discussed further in LO15-6.

Multi-Year Financial Performance Measures

The examples shown in this section are calculated over a single year. However, as mentioned previously, a substantial investment can cause an immediate increase in the amount of invested capital, but profits could follow in subsequent periods. Thus, large projects could be rejected because of the immediate impact on measures such as ROI, RI, and EVA. One advantage of evaluating segments using a *multi-year financial performance measure* is that it allows the performance measure to capture the future benefits directly related to the initial investment. An example of a multi-year performance measure is described in the 2023 Proxy Statement of **Lowe's Companies, Inc.** The company considers a 3-year average return on invested capital (ROIC) one of its most important performance measures. ROIC, a non-GAAP measure defined by Lowe's, incorporates operating profit and balance sheet performance.[6] Lowe's considers this performance measure to be aligned with its shareholders in creating long-term value.

---

[6] Lowe's ROIC is calculated by "dividing the Company's lease adjusted net operating profit after taxes for the year by the average of the Company's invested capital as of the beginning and end of the fiscal year. "Invested capital" for these purposes means the average of current year and prior year ending debt and shareholders' (deficit)/equity." See Lowe's 2023 Notice of Annual Meeting of Shareholders & Proxy Statement found at https://www.sec.gov/Archives/edgar/data/60667/000119312523099980/d392221ddef14a.htm).

Data Visualization

The following data visualizations relate to two divisions operating in the same industry, offering the same types of services to customers, and are charged with similar missions. Each division has the same target rate of return of 15 percent.

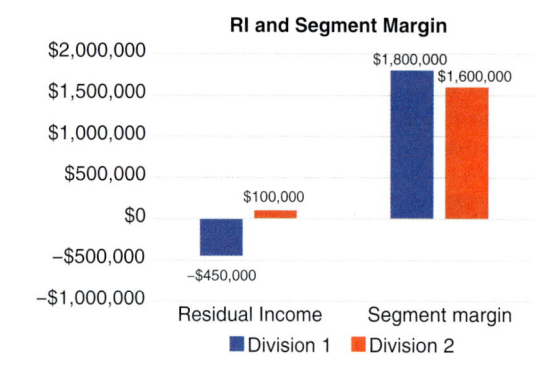

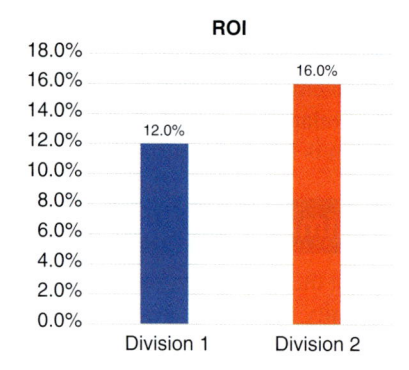

RI and Segment Margin

	Division 1	Division 2
Residual Income	−$450,000	$100,000
Segment margin	$1,800,000	$1,600,000

ROI

Division 1	Division 2
12.0%	16.0%

Referring to the data visualizations above, answer the following questions.

a. Which division had more favorable results?
b. Which of the two divisions had a higher sales volume?
c. What are total assets for Division 1? Division 2?

Solution on p. 15-67.

REVIEW 15-3 — LO15-3 — Calculating ROI, RI, and EVA

The following annual information is available for Lakewood Industries, an investment center.

Total assets, beginning of year	$190,000	Variable operating expenses	$225,000
Total assets, end of year	180,000	Direct fixed costs	160,000
Average fair value of invested capital for the year	238,000	Allocated fixed costs	17,000
Sales	453,000		

Cost of capital:	8%
Target rate of return for RI:	12%
Tax rate:	21%

a. Calculate ROI (return on investment). Base your calculations on segment margin and average assets. (Round percentage to one decimal point.)
b. Calculate segment profit margin ratio. (Round percentage to one decimal point.)
c. Calculate asset turnover. Base your calculations on average assets. (Round amount to two decimal points.)
d. Using (b) and (c), prove your answer to (a) using the Du Pont Model. (Round percentage to one decimal point.)
e. Compute the annual RI (residual income). Base your calculations on segment margin and average assets.
f. Calculate the EVA (economic value added). Base your calculations on after tax-segment margin.
g. **Critical Thinking:** Analyze the results of your calculations. What additional information could be useful in analyzing the results?

More practice: E15-33 to E15-40
Solution on p. 15-66.

NONFINANCIAL, QUANTITATIVE PERFORMANCE MEASURES

LO15-4 What are types of nonfinancial, quantitative measures and how are they selected?

Performance can be evaluated qualitatively and quantitatively. Qualitative measures are often subjective. For example, a manager could be evaluated using low-to-high rankings on job skills such as technical knowledge, quality of work, and need for supervision. Rankings can be given for an individual on a stand-alone basis, in relationship to other managers, or on a group or team basis. Although such measures provide useful information, at some point and in some way, performance should also be compared to a quantitative—but not necessarily financial—standard. People are generally more comfortable with, and respond better to, quantitative rather than qualitative measures of performance because quantitative measures provide a defined target at which to aim. Quantitative performance measures are of two types: financial (previously discussed) and nonfinancial.

Selection of Nonfinancial Quantitative Measures

Nonfinancial performance measures use information contained in the cost management, rather than the financial accounting, system. Thus, NFPMs are based on nonmonetary details, such as *time* (such as, manufacturing cycle time or setup time), *quantities* (such as, number of patents generated or pounds of material moved), and *ratios* (such as, percentage of good units to total units produced or percentage change in pollutant emissions from prior period). Appropriate nonfinancial metrics are those that

- can be clearly articulated and defined,
- are relevant to the objective,
- can trace responsibility,
- rely on valid data,
- have target objectives, and
- have established internal and/or external benchmarks.

As indicated in **Exhibit 15.6**, NFPMs have many distinct advantages over financial performance measures.

Exhibit 15.6 ■ Advantages of Nonfinancial over Financial Performance Measures

Compared to financial measures, nonfinancial performance measures are more
- **relevant** to nonmanagement employees who are generally more familiar with nonfinancial items (such as times and quantities) than financial items (such as costs or profits).
- **timely** than historical financial data and, thus, more apt to identify problems or benefits.
- **reflective** of the leading indicators of activities, such as manufacturing and delivering quality goods and services and providing customer service, that create shareholder wealth.
- **causal** of goal-congruent behavior (rather than suboptimization) because they promote long-term success rather than the short-term success promoted by financial measures.
- **integrated** with organizational effectiveness because they can be designed to focus on processes rather than simply outputs.
- **indicative** of productive activity and the direction of future cash flows.
- **appropriate** for gauging teamwork because they can focus on outputs that result from organizational effort (such as quality) rather than inputs (such as costs).
- **cross-functional** than financial measures, which are generally related to one function.
- **comparable** for benchmarking externally than financial measures (which can be dramatically affected by differences in accounting methods).
- **aligned** with the reward system because they are more likely to be under the control of lower-level employees than are financial measures.

Selecting Essential Short-Run and Long-Run Success Measures Using a very large number of NFPMs is counterproductive and wasteful. Additionally, there may be considerable dependence among some measures. For example, increased product quality should increase customer satisfaction, and additional worker training should decrease poor service performance. An organization must determine which factors are essential to long-term success and develop short- and long-run metrics for such factors to steer the company toward success. A **short-run success measure** for quality is the number of customer complaints in the current period; a **long-run success measure** for quality is the number of patents obtained for quality improvements of company products. Choosing appropriate performance measures can also help a company focus on the activities that cause costs to be incurred and, thus, control costs and improve processes. As discussed in Chapter 8 on activity-based management (ABM), if an activity is controlled, the cost resulting from that activity is controlled.

Types of Nonfinancial Performance Measures

The following discussion addresses four important nonfinancial performance measures.

Throughput	Quality Measures	Lead Time	Environment-Related Metric

Throughput One significant NFPM is **throughput**, which reflects the movement of inputs through a process to become outputs. Throughput provides a measure of productive activity for firms. For example, **Kinder Morgan Energy Partners'** completion of a terminal facility project in Houston, Texas, will provide a throughput capacity of ten million tons of coal per year.[7] Top performing **Chipotle Mexican Grill** locations can serve 300 customers per hour: "that rate of service—'throughput'—is a Chipotle obsession."[8]

For a manufacturer, throughput could reflect the number of units that are produced during a period. For a service business, throughput could reflect the number of customers served during a period. However, two additional factors should be considered in the actual determination of throughput.

- First, organizations should not count units, services, or work performed as truly being throughput unless they would be deemed acceptable for purchase by customers.
- Second, because a firm's primary goal is to earn income, only goods or services that are actually sold should be considered throughput. *Therefore, goods or services that are either unacceptable or produced only to be stored in inventory should not be viewed as throughput.*

Throughput can be analyzed as a set of component elements (similar to the manner in which the Du Pont model includes components of ROI). Components of throughput include manufacturing cycle efficiency, process productivity, and process quality yield.[9] Throughput can be calculated as follows.

$$\text{Manufacturing cycle efficiency} \times \text{Process productivity} \times \text{Process quality yield} = \text{Throughput}$$

$$\frac{\text{Value-added processing time}}{\text{Total processing time}} \times \frac{\text{Total units}}{\text{Value-added processing time}} \times \frac{\text{Good units}}{\text{Total units}} = \text{Throughput}$$

- **Manufacturing cycle efficiency** The proportion of value-added (VA) processing time to total processing time is manufacturing cycle efficiency. VA processing time reflects activities that increase the product's worth to the customer, such as assembly, customizing, and packaging. In contrast, non-value-added activities that do not increase the product's worth to the customer include items such as transporting materials, moving work in process inventory, and reworking product.
- **Process productivity** Total units produced during the period divided by the VA processing time determines process productivity. Production activities can produce both good and defective units.
- **Process quality yield** The proportion of good units resulting from activities is the process quality yield.

If we cancel out value-added processing time and total units from the numerators and denominators, throughput can simply be stated as good units divided by total processing time.

$$\frac{\cancel{\text{Value-added processing time}}}{\text{Total processing time}} \times \frac{\cancel{\text{Total units}}}{\cancel{\text{Value-added processing time}}} \times \frac{\text{Good units}}{\cancel{\text{Total units}}} = \frac{\text{Good units}}{\text{Total processing time}} = \text{Throughput}$$

---

[7] Business Wire, "Kinder Morgan and Arch Coal Sign Throughput Agreement to Further Expand Coal Terminal Network," Mining.com (January 25, 2012); http://www.mining.com/2012/01/25/kinder-morgan-and-arch-coal-sign-throughput-agreementto-further-expand-coal-terminal-network/ (last accessed 1/28/12).

[8] D. A. Kaplan, "Chipotle's Growth Machine," *Fortune* (September 26, 2011), p. 138.

[9] These terms and formulas are based on the following article: Carole Cheatham, "Measuring and Improving Throughput," *Journal of Accountancy* (March 1990), pp. 89–91. One assumption that must be made with regard to this model is that the quantity labeled "throughput" is sold. Another assumption is that the units started are always completed before the end of the measurement period.

Calculating Throughput

LO15-4 DEMO 15-4

Assume the following data for a manufacturing process.
- Total processing time . . . . 80,000 hours
- Total value-added processing time . . . . 20,000 hours
- Total quantity of product manufactured . . . . 100,000 tons
- Total quantity of good production manufactured and sold . . . . 88,000 tons

◆ What is the manufacturing cycle efficiency, process productivity, process quality yield, and throughput?

Manufacturing cycle efficiency (MCE) = VA processing time ÷ Total processing time

$$= 20{,}000 \div 80{,}000 = 25\%$$

This measure indicates 75 percent of processing time is non-value-added.

Process productivity (PP) = Total units ÷ VA processing time

$$= 100{,}000 \div 20{,}000 = 5 \text{ tons per hour}$$

This measure indicates 5 tons can be produced per hour.

Process quality yield (PQY) = Good units ÷ Total units

$$= 88{,}000 \div 100{,}000 = 88\%$$

This measure means that 88 percent of the tons were acceptable, or 12 percent were defective.

Throughput = MCE × PP × PQY

$$= 0.25 \times 5 \times 0.88 = 1.1$$

This measure means that 1.1 good tons are produced per hour of total processing time, compared with the 5 tons actually produced per value-added hour.

Alternatively, throughput can be calculated as follows.

Throughput = Good units ÷ Total time

$$= 88{,}000 \div 80{,}000 = 1.1$$

Ways to Increase Throughput Management should strive to increase throughput by engaging in one or several of the following methods:

- decreasing non-value-added (NVA) activities,
- increasing total unit production and sales,
- decreasing the per-unit processing time, and/or
- increasing process quality yield.

Some companies have increased throughput significantly by the use of flexible manufacturing systems and, in some cases, by reorganizing production operations. Computer technologies such as sophisticated production scheduling technology have also enhanced throughput at many firms. Improved throughput means a greater ability to respond to customer needs and demands, reduce production costs, and reduce inventory levels, and therefore, the NVA costs of moving and storing goods.

Quality Measures Companies operating in the global environment are also generally concerned with high product and service quality and the need to develop measurements of quality such as those presented in **Exhibit 15.7**. For example, if a performance measurement is the cost of defective units produced during a period, the expectation is that defects will occur and management will accept some amount of defect cost. If, instead, the performance measurement is zero defects, the expectation is that no defects will occur and such a standard would create an atmosphere more conducive to eliminating defects than would the first. As quality improves, management's threshold of "acceptable" performance becomes more demanding and performance is evaluated against progressively more rigorous benchmarks.

A detailed discussion of calculating the cost of quality is included in Chapter 17.

Exhibit 15.7 ■ Nonfinancial Quality Measurements

Element	Measure	Element	Measure
Prevention	Design review (number of hours) Preventive maintenance (number of hours) Employee training (number of hours) Quality circles (number of hours) Quality engineering (number of hours)	Internal failure	Scrap (number of units) Rework (number of units) Spoilage (number of units) Quality-related downtime (number of hours) Inspection of rework (number of units)
Appraisal	Material inspection (number of inspections) Work in Process inspection (number of inspections) Finished Goods inspection (number of inspections) Sample preparation (number of samples) Product simulation (number of simulations)	External failure	Warranty claims (number of claims) Complaint processing (number of complaints) Loss of goodwill (percentage of nonreturning customers*) Liability suits (number of suits) Product recalls (number of recalls)

*Not as originally listed in article.

Source: Ronald C. Kettering, "Accounting for Quality with Nonfinancial Measures: A Simple No-Cost Program for the Small Company," *Management Accounting Quarterly* (Spring 2001), p. 17. Copyright 2001 by Institute of Management Accountants. Reproduced with permission of Institute of Management Accountants in the format Textbook via Copyright Clearance Center.

Lead Time A NFPM related to customer service is **lead time**, which reflects how quickly customers receive their goods after placing their orders. Measuring lead time should result in products becoming more rapidly available for customers. In addition, using fewer parts, interchangeable parts, and product designs that require few or no engineering changes after the start of production shortens lead time. Lead time incentives could also drive changes in facility layout to speed work flow, increase workforce productivity, and reduce defects and rework. Last, lead time incentives should cause managers to observe and correct any NVA activities or constraints that are creating production, performance, or processing delays. Some companies are implementing activity-based management techniques to remove any implied acceptance of NVA activities. Activity-based management can provide information on the overhead impact created by reengineered processes meant to streamline activities and minimize nonquality work.

Environment-Related Metrics The environmental dimension of sustainability concerns an organization's impacts on the earth's ecosystems.

Climate-Related Metrics To assess such impacts, one NFPM is the organization's carbon footprint, which reflects the total of all **greenhouse gas (GHG) emissions** created by that organization's activities during a specified time. The GHG Protocol, created in coordination between the World Resources Institute and the World Business Council for Sustainable Development, is a widely accepted accounting standard. The protocol provides a consistent framework for companies to both measure and report specific greenhouse gasses such as carbon dioxide and methane. The GHG Protocol classifies emissions into three levels called Scope 1, and Scope 2, and Scope 3.

- **Scope 1 Emissions** Direct GHG emissions occur from company owned or controlled sources such as from company vehicles, equipment, or buildings.
- **Scope 2 Emissions** The primary source of Scope 2 emissions is the generation of purchased energy, namely, electricity purchased by a company from a power provider.
- **Scope 3 Emissions** Emissions that result from company activities but are not generated by the company from sources it owns or controls. It includes for example, emissions associated with employee business travel or the disposal of a company's product after customer use.[10]

---

[10] Securities and Exchange Commission: The Enhancement and Standardization of Climate-Related Disclosures for Investors; Release Nos. 33-11042; 34-94478; File No. S7-10-22; March 21, 2022; https://www.sec.gov/files/rules/proposed/2022/33-11042.pdf (accessed on November 7, 2023).

As of the writing of this text, the **Securities and Exchange Commission** is finalizing disclosure requirements related to emissions for public companies. The goal is to provide investors and creditors information about the climate-related risk of companies by requiring certain **climate-related metrics** such as greenhouse gas emissions.

Other Environmental Metrics Many companies, especially public companies, summarize their sustainability goals in annual sustainability reports. These reports include goals (such as the year in which the company will achieve a net-zero greenhouse gas emission), metrics (such as the rate of GHG emissions), and actual results (such as the amount of emissions in the recent year). A selection of goals related to environmental metrics found in sustainability reports follows.

- Reduce or eliminate water usage in manufacturing processes
- Reduce or eliminate landfill waste from manufacturing processes
- Increase the use of electric vehicles
- Increase the use of carbon-free electricity to power operations
- Increase the use of recycled or renewable materials in production
- Increase the use of agricultural ingredients that are sustainably resourced
- Increase the amount of packaging that is recyclable

While formal standards are being developed which will provide for consistent disclosure across companies, many companies have voluntarily established goals, performance measurements, and in many cases, reward management for reaching these goals through compensation, as discussed in a later section.

Establishment of Comparison Bases

Once the NFPMs are selected, benchmark performance levels should be established against which actual data are compared. These levels can be developed internally (such as from a world-class division) or determined from external sources (such as competitors, companies in other industries, or database reporting initiatives). In addition, a system of monitoring and reporting comparative performance levels should be established at appropriate intervals. Typically, lower-level results are monitored more frequently (continuously, daily, or weekly) than upper-level results (monthly, quarterly, and annually). Measures used by middle management are intermediate links between the lower- and upper-level performance measures and require monitoring at intermediate points (weekly, monthly, and annually). Annual measurements can be plotted to reveal long-run trends and progress toward long-run objectives.

A general model for measuring an activity's relative success compares a numerator representing number of successes with a logical and valid denominator representing total outcome volume. For example, delivery success could be measured for a period based on success or failure information. Assume that Nationwide Services made 1,000 deliveries during a period; of those, 922 were on time and 78 were late. The company's measurement of delivery success and failure is as follows.

922 On-time deliveries ÷ 1,000 Total deliveries = 92.2% Delivery success

or

78 Late deliveries ÷ 1,000 Total deliveries = 7.8% Delivery failure

Determination of how well or poorly the company performed for the period would require comparison with

- previous periods,
- a target rate of success (such as 100 percent on-time deliveries), or
- a benchmark with a world-class competitor.

Analysis of the types and causes of the 78 late deliveries should allow management to determine what actions would eliminate these causes in the process of continuous long-term improvement.

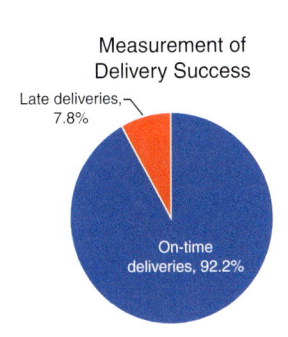

> **REVIEW 15-4** **LO15-4** — Calculating Throughput
>
> Lopez Corp. wants to compute its throughput for March. The following production data are available.
>
> | | |
> |---|---|
> | Good units produced and sold | 150,650 |
> | Total units produced | 188,475 |
> | Total processing time (in hours) | 54,230 |
> | Value-added time (in hours) | 22,900 |
>
> a. Determine the manufacturing cycle efficiency. (Round percentage to one decimal point.)
> b. Determine the process productivity. (Round amount to one decimal point.)
> c. Determine the process quality yield. (Round percentage to one decimal point.)
> d. Determine the throughput using only good units and total time. (Round amount to one decimal point.)
> e. **Critical Thinking:** How could the company improve its process quality yield?
>
> More practice: E15-45, E15-46
> Solution on p. 15-66.

USING A BALANCED SCORECARD FOR MEASURING PERFORMANCE

LO15-5 How can a balanced scorecard be used to measure performance?

In recognition of the multiple facets of performance, some companies use a **balanced scorecard (BSC)** approach to performance measurement. A balance scorecard approach encompasses both internal and external performance measures and leading and lagging indicators.

Leading and Lagging Indicators

Accounting information helps managers to measure dimensions of performance that are important in accomplishing strategic goals. In the past, management spent significant time analyzing historical financial data to assess whether organizational strategy was effective. Today, firms use a variety of information to determine not only how the organization has performed but also how it is likely to perform in the future. Financial measures such as historical financial data reflect **lag indicators** or outcomes that resulted from past actions. For example, an increase in operating profits (lag indicator) could occur after a new production process is installed. Unfortunately, lag indicators are often recognized and assessed too late to significantly improve current or near-future actions.

In contrast, **lead indicators** project future outcomes and thereby help assess strategic progress and guide decision making before lag indicators are known. For example, a lead indicator is the number of employees trained on a new accounting information system. The expectation is that the more employees who are trained to use the new system, the more rapidly orders will be processed, the more satisfied customers will be with turnaround time after placing an order, and the more quickly profits will be realized. If training (lead indicator) was provided to fewer employees than planned, future profits (lag indicator) will decrease (or not increase as expected) because some customers will be unhappy with sales order turnaround time. Measurements for improving performance should involve tracking leading indicators or data about the actionable steps that will create the results desired.

Managing for the long run has commonly been viewed as managing a series of short runs. Theoretically, if a firm performs well in each successive short period, its future is secure. Although appealing, this approach fails when the firm does not keep pace with long-range technical and competitive trends. Thinking only of short-run performance and ignoring the time required to make long-term improvements can doom a firm in the globally competitive environment.

Short-run objectives focus on the effective and efficient management of current operating, investing, and financing activities. A firm's long-term objectives involve resource investments and proactive efforts, such as customer satisfaction, quality, delivery, price, service, and sustainability to enhance competitive position. Because competitive position results from the interaction of various factors, a firm must identify the most important drivers (not just predictors) for achieving a particular long-run objective. For example, predictors of increased market share might include increased spending on employee training, research and development, or capital improvements. The true drivers of a firm's increased market share, however, are likely to be product and service quality, speed of delivery, and reputation relative to the competitors. Measurements of success in these areas would be *leading indicators* of increased market share and profitability.

Need for Multiple Performance Measures

A performance measurement system should encompass a variety of measures, especially those that track factors considered necessary for mission achievement and long-run success. Although internal measures of performance are useful, only a company's customers can truly assess organizational performance. Good performance is typically defined as providing a product or service that equals or exceeds a customer's quality, price, and delivery expectations. This definition is totally unrelated to internal measurements such as standard cost variances or capacity utilization. Companies that cannot meet customer expectations will find themselves at some point without customers and without any need for financial performance measures.

Knowing that performance is to be judged using external criteria should cause companies to implement concepts such as just-in-time inventory (Chapter 18), total quality management (Chapter 17), and continuous improvement (Chapter 14). Two common themes of these concepts are to make the organization, its products, and its processes (production as well as customer responsiveness) more effective and efficient and to generate higher value through lower costs.

Exhibit 15.8 provides ideas for judging managerial performance in five areas. Some of these measures should be monitored for both short-run and long-run implications. For example, a short-run measure of market improvement is the growth rate of sales. A long-run measure is change in market share. Brainstorming about both short-run and long-run measures can be an effective approach to identifying measurements. Because measures should reflect the organization's mission and culture as well as management's expectations and philosophies, changes in any of these factors should also create changes in performance measures.

Exhibit 15.8 ■ Examples of Performance Measurements

	Qualitative	Quantitative Nonfinancial	Quantitative Financial
Human Resources	• Acceptance of additional responsibility • Increased job skills • Need for supervision • Interaction with upper- and lower-level employees	• Proportion of direct to indirect labor (low or high depending on degree of automation) • Diversity of ethnic background in hiring and promotion • Scores on standardized examinations	• Comparability of personnel pay levels with those of competitors • Savings from using part-time personnel
Market	• Addition of new product features • Increased product durability • Improved efficiency (and/or effectiveness) of product	• Number of sales transactions • Percentage repeat customers • Number of new ideas generated • Number of customer complaints • Delivery time	• Increase in revenue from previous period • Percent of total market revenue • Revenue generated per advertising dollar (by product or product line)
Costs	• Better traceability of costs • Increased cost consciousness • Better employee suggestions for cost reductions • Increased usage of automated equipment for routine tasks	• Time to design new products • Number of engineering change orders issued • Length of process time • Proportion of products with defects • Number of different product parts • Number of days of inventory • Proportion of material generated as scrap/waste • Reduction in setup time since prior period	• Reduction in production cost (DM, DL, & OH and in total) since prior period • Reduction in distribution and scrap/waste cost since prior period • Variances from standard • Cost of engineering changes
Benefits (Profitability)	• Customer satisfaction • Product brand loyalty	• Proportion of on-time deliveries • Degree of accuracy in sales forecasts of demand	• Change in market price per share • Return on investment • Change in net income
Environmental Sustainability	• Natural habitats that have been protected or restored • Energy reduction initiatives • Environmental protection training for employees • Environmental management system certification status	• Greenhouse gas emissions • Proportion of inputs from recycled sources • Number of sanctions for environmental noncompliance • Number of environmental audits	• Environmental protection expenditures by type • Amount of environmental fines • Savings from environmental initiatives (such as packaging reduction)

Balanced Scorecard Approach

The balanced scorecard (BSC) is a framework that translates an organization's strategy into clear and objective performance measures (both leading and lagging) that focus on customers, internal business processes, employees, and shareholders. Thus, the BSC provides a means by which actual business outcomes can be evaluated against performance targets. Examples of companies that use a balance scorecard for performance measurement include **Ford Motor Company**, **Hilton Hotels Corp.**, **IBM**, **Indiana University**, and **Wells Fargo Bank**.[11]

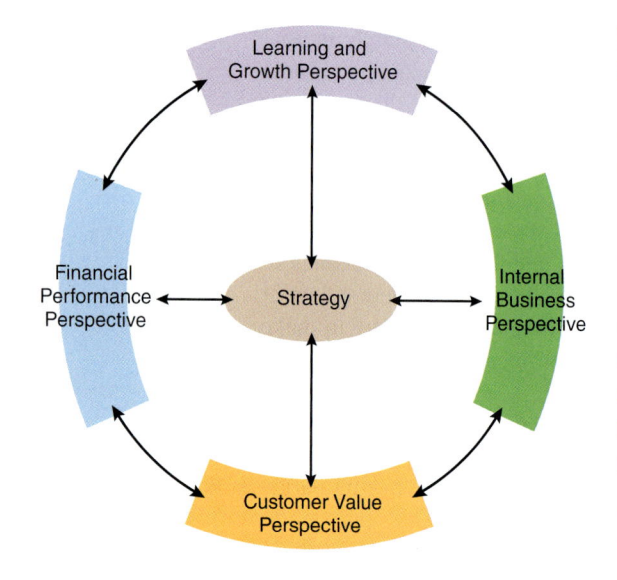

The BSC includes short- and long-term, internal and external, and financial and nonfinancial measures to balance management's view and execution of strategy.

The BSC provides a set of measurements that "complements financial measures of past performance with measures of the drivers of future performance."[12] The scorecard should reflect an organization's mission and strategy and typically includes performance measures from four perspectives:

- financial,
- internal business,
- customer, and
- learning and growth.

Managers choosing to apply the BSC demonstrate a belief that traditional financial performance measures alone are insufficient to assess how the firm is doing and how it is likely to do in the future.

Companies adapt the balanced scorecard to fit their own structures and environments.

- **Financial measures** of the BSC should reflect stakeholder-relevant issues of profitability, organizational growth, and market price of stock. Such measures are lagging indicators of the other perspectives.
- **Customer measures** lead financial perspective measures and should indicate how the organization is faring relative to customer issues of speed (delivery time), quality, service, and price (both at and after purchase).
- **Internal process** measures should focus on organizational actions designed to meet customer needs and expectations. Measures in this area are usually quantitative.
- **Learning and growth** measures lead customer perspective measures and should focus on using the organization's intellectual capital to adapt to changing customer needs or influence new customer needs and expectations through product or service innovations. Learning and growth measures tend to be quantitative, long-term targets. Learning and growth measures can help an organization ascertain its ability to learn, grow, improve, and survive.

DEMO 15-5 LO15-5   Identifying Balanced Scorecard Performance Measures

◆ What are potential performance measures in each section of the balanced scorecard?

Financial:	Subunit operating income, net income, cash flow, change in market share, and return on assets.
Customer:	Rate of on-time deliveries, product (service) satisfaction scores and customer retention rates.

continued

---

[11] Balanced Scorecard Institute, accessed on November 8, 2023 at https://balancedscorecard.org/bsc-basics/about-the-balanced-scorecard/balanced-scorecard-adopters/

[12] Robert S. Kaplan and David P. Norton, *The Balanced Scorecard* (Boston: Harvard Business School Press, 1996), p. 8.

continued from previous

Internal process:	Process quality yields, manufacturing or service cycle efficiency, time to market on new products, and cost variances.
Learning and growth:	Number of patents or copyrights applied for, percentage of research and development projects resulting in patentable products, average time of R&D project from conception to commercialization, and percentage of capital invested in "high-tech" projects.

Exhibit 15.9 illustrates a balanced scorecard and provides some performance measures for the various goals.

Exhibit 15.9 ■ Balanced Scorecard and Perspectives

Learning and Growth Perspective

Goals	Measures	TARGET
Technology leadership	Time to develop next generation	
Manufacturing learning	Process time to maturity	
Product focus	Percent of products that equals 80% of sales	
Time to market	New product introduction versus competition	

Internal Business Perspective

Goals	Measures	TARGET
Technology capability	Manufacturing ability versus competition's	
Manufacturing excellence	Cycle time	
	Unit cost	
	Yield	
Design productivity	Engineering efficiency	
New product introduction	Actual production schedule versus plan	

Customer Value Perspective

Goals	Measures	TARGET
New products	Percent of sales from new products	
	Percent of sales from proprietary products	
Responsive supply	On-time delivery (defined by customer)	
Preferred supplier	Share of key accounts' purchases	
Customer partnership	Number of cooperative engineering efforts	

Financial Performance Perspective

Goals	Measures	TARGET
Survive	Cash flow	
Succeed	Quarterly sales growth and operating income by division	
Prosper	Increased market share and return on equity (or investment)	

Source: Robert S. Kaplan and David P. Norton, "The Balanced Scorecard—Measures That Drive Performance," *Harvard Business Review* (January–February 1992), pp. 72–76. Copyright © 1992 by The Harvard Business School Publishing Corporation. All rights reserved.

Strategy Map

One concern about the traditional four-box BSC diagram was that companies might select objectives for each perspective "without making sure they are linked or aligned… [which] could lead to silo activities" and noncohesive and nonintegrated strategies.[13] Many of the present BSCs are depicted as "strategy maps" rather than as the traditional four-box template. The **strategy map** indicates the linkages between and among the scorecard performance measurements and perspectives. **Exhibit 15.10** provides such a strategy map presentation using the BSC from Crown Castle International, which owns and manages wireless infrastructures including towers for the communications industry.

---

[13] B. Marr, What Is a Modern Balanced Scorecard?, *Management Case Study*, The Advanced Performance Institute (2010), p. 4; http://www.ap-institute.com/media/3967/what_is_a_modern_balanced_scorecard.pdf (accessed 1/28/2012).

Exhibit 15.10 ■ Strategy Map

FINANCIAL PERSPECTIVE

Maximize Shareholder Value

Grow Organic Revenue | Expand Recurring Revenue Margins | Allocate Capital | Extend Revenue (Adjacencies)

- Increase BBEs
- Increase Pipeline
- Increase Recurring Revenue
- Reduce Operating Costs
- Increase Installation Margin
- Reduce A/R, Unbilled, and WIP
- Expand Revenue Around Assets

CUSTOMER PERSPECTIVE

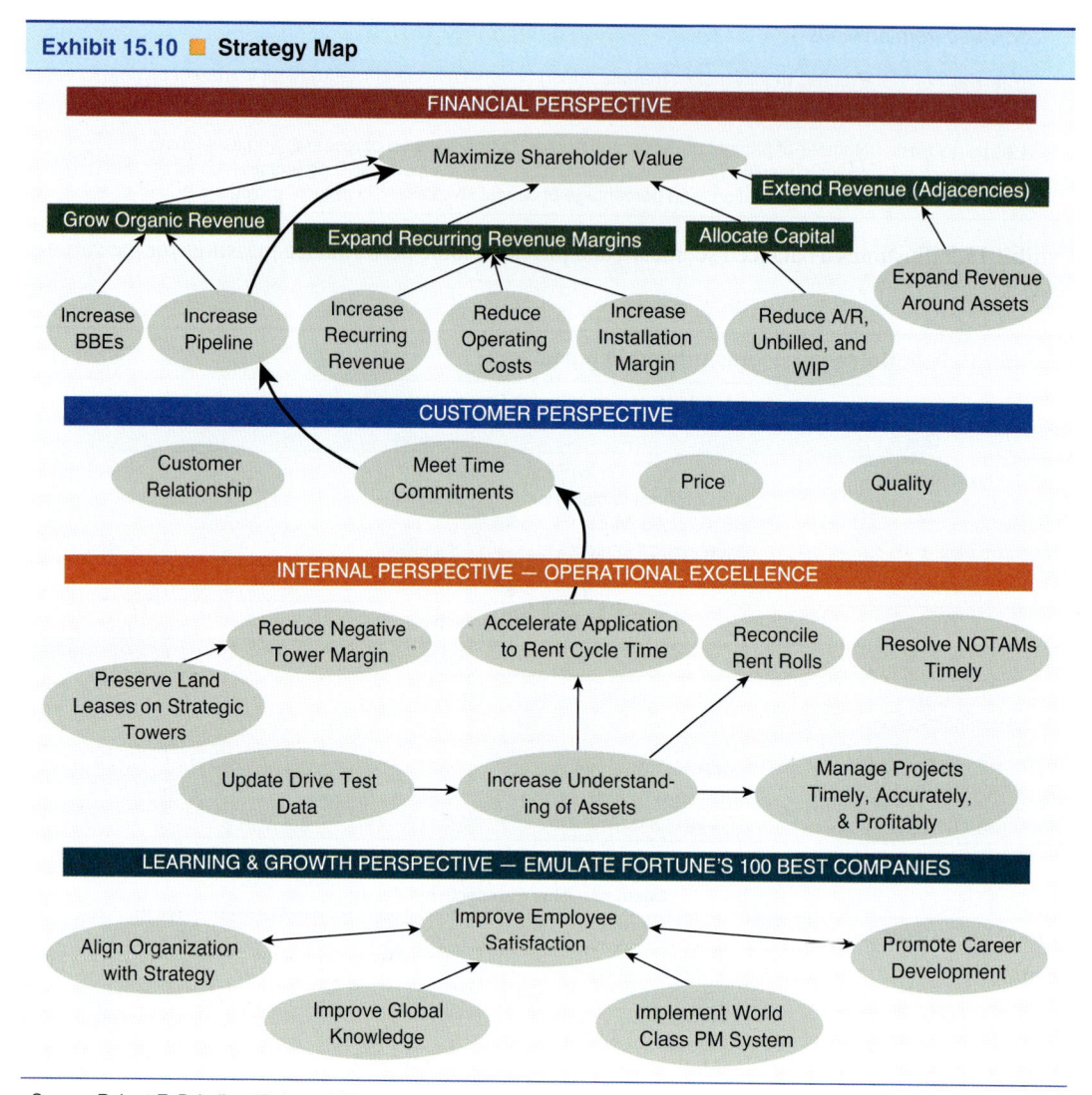

- Customer Relationship
- Meet Time Commitments
- Price
- Quality

INTERNAL PERSPECTIVE — OPERATIONAL EXCELLENCE

- Preserve Land Leases on Strategic Towers
- Reduce Negative Tower Margin
- Accelerate Application to Rent Cycle Time
- Reconcile Rent Rolls
- Resolve NOTAMs Timely
- Update Drive Test Data
- Increase Understanding of Assets
- Manage Projects Timely, Accurately, & Profitably

LEARNING & GROWTH PERSPECTIVE — EMULATE FORTUNE'S 100 BEST COMPANIES

- Align Organization with Strategy
- Improve Employee Satisfaction
- Promote Career Development
- Improve Global Knowledge
- Implement World Class PM System

Source: Robert E. Paladino, "Balanced Forecasts Drive Value," *Strategic Finance* (January 2005) p. 36. Copyright 2005 by Institute of Management Accountants. Reproduced with permission of Institute of Management Accountants in the format Textbook via Copyright Clearance Center.

BSCs may be used in organizations at multiple levels: top management, subunit, and even individual employees. When a BSC is implemented at lower levels of the organization, care should be taken to make certain that the measurements used can "roll up" into higher-level measurements that will ultimately provide the organizational results desired. Regardless of the managerial level at which the scorecard is used or the type of organization using the scorecard, this technique allows measurement data to be compiled in a way that reflects the organizational mission. "Taken together, the measures provide a holistic view of what is happening both inside and outside the organization or level, thus allowing all constituents of the organization to see how their activities contribute to attainment of the organization's overall mission."[14]

Inclusion of Sustainability Metrics

Because a clear trend in performance measurement is accounting for environmental impact and sustainability of operations, many firms are beginning to include sustainability metrics in BSCs. Three possible approaches to including such metrics are to

---

[14] Chee W. Chow, Denise Ganulin, Kamal Haddad, and Jim Williamson, "The Balanced Scorecard: A Potent Tool for Energizing and Focusing Healthcare Organization Management," *Journal of Healthcare Management* (May–June 1998), pp. 263–280.

- incorporate them as a fifth dimension in a traditional BSC,
- develop a separate sustainability scorecard, or
- integrate them across the four existing BSC categories.[15]

Exhibit 15.11 illustrates a framework that not only incorporates "green" information technology (IT) initiatives into the original four BSC perspectives but also includes a separate environmental and social sustainability perspective.

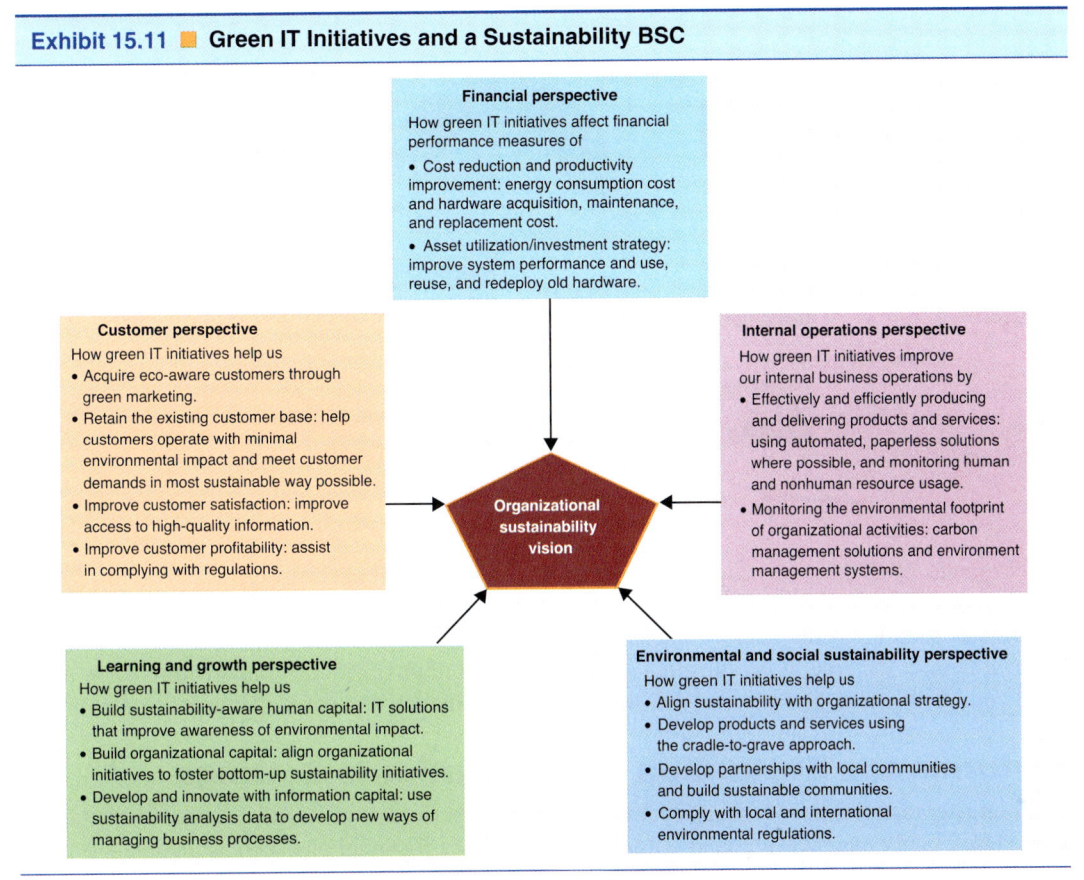

Exhibit 15.11 ■ Green IT Initiatives and a Sustainability BSC

Financial perspective
How green IT initiatives affect financial performance measures of
- Cost reduction and productivity improvement: energy consumption cost and hardware acquisition, maintenance, and replacement cost.
- Asset utilization/investment strategy: improve system performance and use, reuse, and redeploy old hardware.

Customer perspective
How green IT initiatives help us
- Acquire eco-aware customers through green marketing.
- Retain the existing customer base: help customers operate with minimal environmental impact and meet customer demands in most sustainable way possible.
- Improve customer satisfaction: improve access to high-quality information.
- Improve customer profitability: assist in complying with regulations.

Internal operations perspective
How green IT initiatives improve our internal business operations by
- Effectively and efficiently producing and delivering products and services: using automated, paperless solutions where possible, and monitoring human and nonhuman resource usage.
- Monitoring the environmental footprint of organizational activities: carbon management solutions and environment management systems.

Organizational sustainability vision

Learning and growth perspective
How green IT initiatives help us
- Build sustainability-aware human capital: IT solutions that improve awareness of environmental impact.
- Build organizational capital: align organizational initiatives to foster bottom-up sustainability initiatives.
- Develop and innovate with information capital: use sustainability analysis data to develop new ways of managing business processes.

Environmental and social sustainability perspective
How green IT initiatives help us
- Align sustainability with organizational strategy.
- Develop products and services using the cradle-to-grave approach.
- Develop partnerships with local communities and build sustainable communities.
- Comply with local and international environmental regulations.

Source: Adapted from R. P. Jain, R. Benbunan-Fich, and K. Mohan, "Assessing Green IT Initiatives Using the Balanced Scorecard," *IT Pro* (January/February 2011), p. 27.

Monitoring Balanced Scorecard Metrics

A company can use a balanced scorecard to develop performance metrics for managers from the top of the company to the lowest-level department. The scorecard becomes a vehicle for communicating the factors that are key to the success of managers, factors that upper management will monitor in evaluating the success of lower managers in carrying out the corporate strategy. To make balanced scorecards more user friendly, several companies use performance monitoring **dashboards**, which present scorecard results using graphics, some of which mimic the instrument displays on an automobile dashboard. A sample of a dashboard with key indicators is included below. This allows management a way to easily track areas of concern and make necessary adjustments before period end. For purposes of this example, sustainability metrics are integrated within the four existing BSC perspectives.

---

[15] J. B. Butler, S. C. Henderson, and C. Raiborn, "Sustainability and the Balanced Scorecard: Integrating 'Green' Measures into Business Reporting," *Management Accounting Quarterly* (Winter 2011), pp. 1–10.

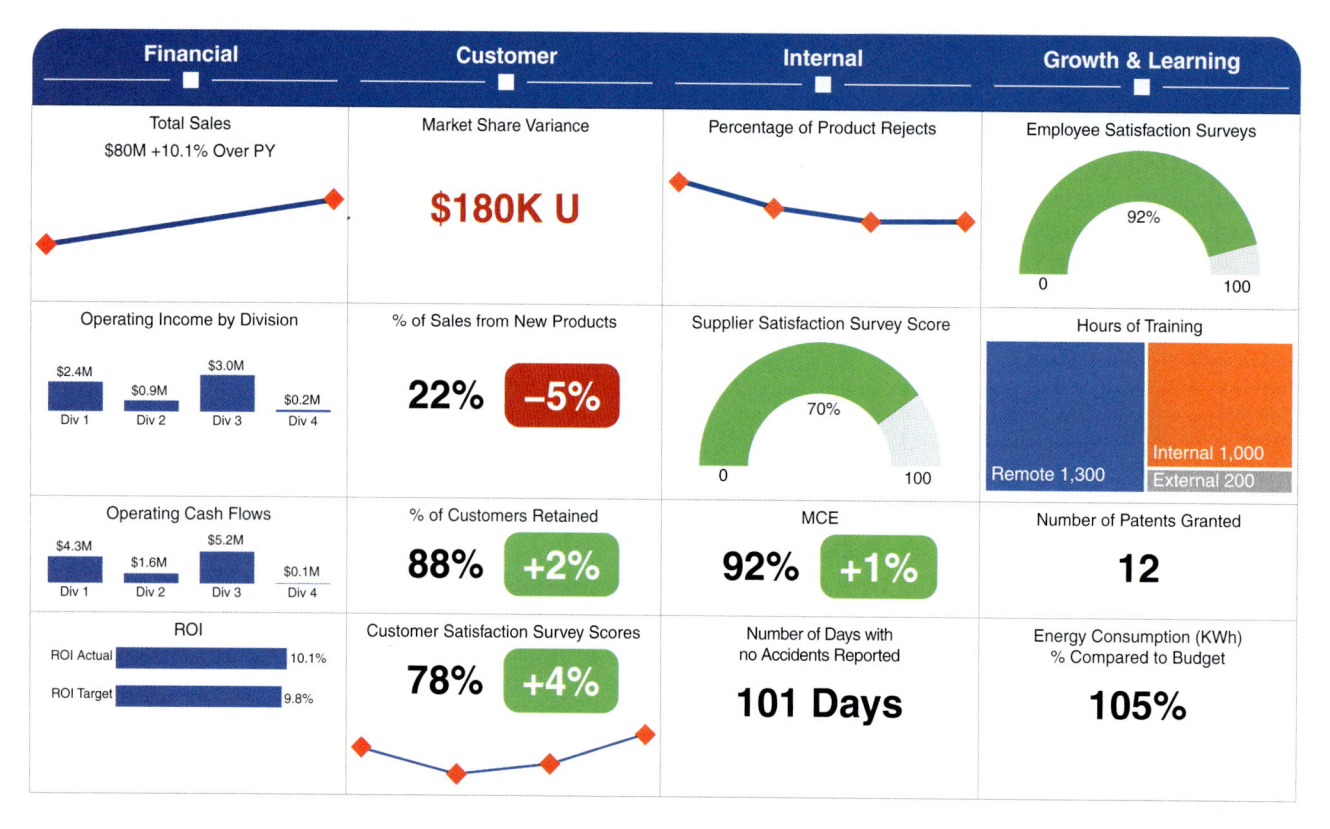

Financial	Customer	Internal	Growth & Learning
Total Sales $80M +10.1% Over PY	**Market Share Variance** $180K U	**Percentage of Product Rejects**	**Employee Satisfaction Surveys** 92%
Operating Income by Division Div 1 $2.4M, Div 2 $0.9M, Div 3 $3.0M, Div 4 $0.2M	**% of Sales from New Products** 22% −5%	**Supplier Satisfaction Survey Score** 70%	**Hours of Training** Remote 1,300; Internal 1,000; External 200
Operating Cash Flows Div 1 $4.3M, Div 2 $1.6M, Div 3 $5.2M, Div 4 $0.1M	**% of Customers Retained** 88% +2%	**MCE** 92% +1%	**Number of Patents Granted** 12
ROI ROI Actual 10.1%; ROI Target 9.8%	**Customer Satisfaction Survey Scores** 78% +4%	**Number of Days with no Accidents Reported** 101 Days	**Energy Consumption (KWh) % Compared to Budget** 105%

No single BSC, measurement system, or set of performance measurements is appropriate for all organizations or, possibly, even all responsibility centers within the same company. Although some performance measurements, such as financial viability, zero defects, and customer service, are important regardless of the type of organization or its location, foreign operations may require some additional considerations in performance measurement and evaluation compared to domestic operations.

Performance Evaluation in Multinational Settings

Many large companies have foreign operations in which performance must be measured and evaluated. Use of only one measurement criterion—especially a financial one such as income—is even less appropriate for multinational segments than it is for domestic responsibility centers.

The investment cost necessary to create the same type of organizational unit in different countries can differ substantially. For example, because of exchange rates and legal costs, it is significantly more expensive for a U.S. company to open a Japanese subsidiary than an Indonesian one. If performance were measured using residual income calculated with the same target rate of return, the Japanese unit would be placed at a distinct disadvantage because of its larger investment base. However, the company could believe that the possibility of future Japanese joint ventures or market inroads justifies the larger investment. One method of handling such a discrepancy in investment bases is to assign a lower target rate when computing residual income for the Japanese subsidiary than for the Indonesian one. This type of differential might also be appropriate because of the lower political, financial, and economic risks.

Income comparisons between multinational units could be invalid because of differences in trade tariffs, income tax rates, currency fluctuations, political risks, and the possibility of restrictions on the transfer of goods or currencies among countries. Income earned by a multinational unit can also be affected by conditions totally outside its control, such as protectionism of local companies, government aid, or varying wage rates caused by differing standards of living, levels of industrial development, and/or the amount of social services. If the multinational subunit adopts the local country's accounting practices, differences in international standards can make income comparisons among units difficult and inconvenient even after the statements are translated to a single currency basis.

Firms with multinational profit or investment centers (or subsidiaries) need to establish flexible systems of measuring performance. Such systems should recognize that differences in sales volumes, accounting standards, economic conditions, and risk might be outside the control of an international subunit's manager. Qualitative performance measures such as market share increases, quality improvements (defect reductions), inventory management improvements with the related reduction in working capital, and new product development could become significantly more useful.

Regardless of location, performance measures reflect on accomplishments of employees. By linking performance measures to an organization's mission and reward structure, employees are motivated to improve performance that will result in long-run organizational viability.

Balanced Scorecard — LO15-5 — REVIEW 15-5

a. Match each of the objectives listed, 1 through 15, with its most appropriate perspective: financial, internal business, customer, or learning and growth. In addition, for each objective listed, identify the most appropriate performance measure listed as *a* through *o*.

Objective	Perspective	Performance Measure
1. Decrease use of water for manufacturing process	___	___
2. Improve customer perception of product quality	___	___
3. Improve responsible sourcing of raw materials	___	___
4. Improve satisfaction of customer	___	___
5. Increase employee efficiency with technology	___	___
6. Increase income generated from assets	___	___
7. Increase involvement of employees	___	___
8. Increase market share	___	___
9. Increase number of new products released	___	___
10. Increase production process quality	___	___
11. Increase revenue of specified products	___	___
12. Increase satisfaction of employees	___	___
13. Increase throughput	___	___
14. Reduce non-recyclable packaging	___	___
15. Reduce selling variable cost per unit	___	___

Perspective
1. Financial
2. Internal business
3. Customer
4. Learning and growth
5. Environmental and social sustainability

Performance Measures
a. Customer survey ratings
b. Employee satisfaction surveys
c. Gallons of water used for manufacturing process
d. Hours of employee IT training
e. Manufacturing cycle efficiency
f. Number of implemented improvement suggestions submitted by employees
g. Number of new products released per quarter
h. Number of products with 100 percent recyclable packaging
i. Number of reworked products divided by total units produced
j. Percentage of products supplied from sustainable sources
k. Product returns as a percentage of sales
l. Return on investment
m. Revenue for specified products
n. Sales as a percentage of total market sales
o. Variable unit cost

b. **Critical Thinking:** Why must balanced scorecards be customized to each company or even segment?

More practice: E15-53
Solution on p. 15-66.

COMPENSATION STRATEGY

LO15-6 What is compensation strategy, and what factors must be considered in designing the compensation strategy?

The many organizational changes (technological advances, globalization, customer focus, product/service quality, and sustainability issues) that have occurred in the recent past have created opportunities and challenges in establishing responsibility and rewarding individuals for their performance. Each organization should determine a **compensation strategy** that addresses the role that pay should play in the firm. The foundation for the actual compensation plan should tie organizational goals, mission, and strategies to performance measurements and employee rewards. The relationships among the activities underlying an integrated planning, performance, and reward structure are shown in **Exhibit 15.12**.

The traditional U.S. compensation strategy differentiates among three employee groups: executives, middle management, and workers.

- **Executives** are generally granted compensation packages that include a salary element and contingent pay tied to incentives for meeting or exceeding targeted objectives such as companywide net income or earnings per share.
- **Middle managers** are typically given salaries with the opportunity for future raises (and possibly bonuses) based on some performance measure such as segment income or divisional return on investment.
- **Workers** are paid wages (usually specified by union contract, established by skill level or seniority, or tied to the minimum-wage law) for the number of hours worked or production level achieved. Current or year-end bonuses may be paid if performance exceeds some specified quantitative measure.

The motivational elements link all managerial performance to stockholder welfare through compensation contracting that cascades down from executives through the organizational hierarchy. These motivational elements create the incentive for managers to outperform the budget, increase earnings, and raise stock price.

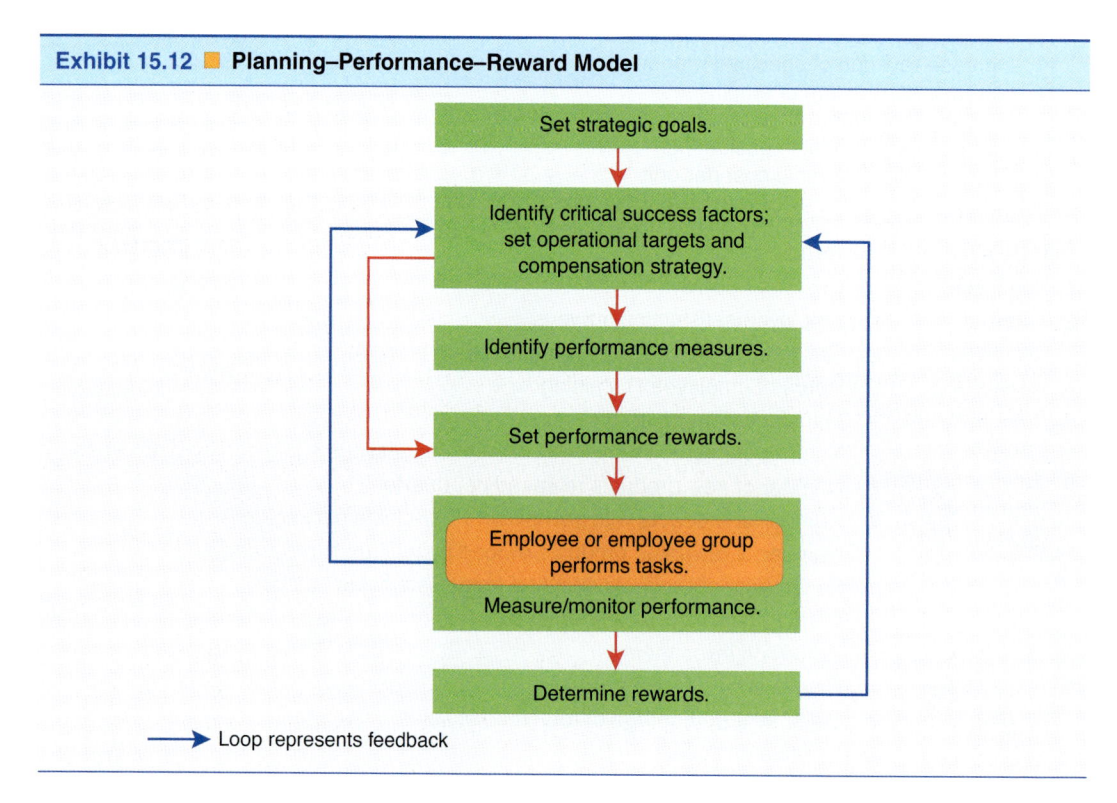

Exhibit 15.12 Planning–Performance–Reward Model

Set strategic goals.
↓
Identify critical success factors; set operational targets and compensation strategy.
↓
Identify performance measures.
↓
Set performance rewards.
↓
Employee or employee group performs tasks.
Measure/monitor performance.
↓
Determine rewards.

→ Loop represents feedback

Pay-for-Performance Plans

Compensation plans should encourage higher levels of employee performance and loyalty, while lowering overall costs and raising profits. The plans must encourage behavior essential to achieving organizational goals and maximizing shareholder value. More than any other goal or objective, maximization of shareholder wealth (a long-term goal) drives the design of reward systems.

Link Performance Measures to Corporate Goals Approximately 83 percent of respondents of a survey of large S&P 500 firms indicated that they use some type of annual incentive pay, with profits and revenues as the most common metrics.[16] In a pay-for-performance plan, the defined performance measures must be highly correlated with the organization's operational targets. For example, because Intel has established sustainability as a corporate goal, a portion of employee compensation is linked to corporate responsibility factors.[17] If such correlations do not exist, suboptimization can occur, and workers can earn incentive pay even though the organization's broader objectives are not achieved.

Analyzing Effect of Compensation on Goal Congruence — LO15-6 — DEMO 15-6

The board of directors of an organic food manufacturer supports a *build* mission for the company. The board establishes a target ROI of 20 percent. The company's West division is considering a new investment to expand its product line. Operating income and total assets are provided below before considering the investment and the expected results from the investment.

	Current Division Results (Before Investment)	Expected Results From Investment
Operating income	$268,800	$ 92,400
Total assets	$960,000	$385,000

◆ **If executive bonuses for West division are based upon ROI, would the executives be motivated to make the investment?**

The calculations for ROI for the division before and after the investment follow.

	Current Division Results (Before Investment)	Expected Results (After Investment)
Operating income	$268,800	$ 361,200
Total assets	÷ $960,000	÷ $1,345,000
ROI	28.0%	26.9%

Based on the performance measurement of ROI, the executives would not be incentivized to make the investment because ROI would decrease. This is the case even though the investment exceeds the company's target ROI of 20 percent.

$$\text{Investment ROI} = \$92,400 \div \$385,000 = 24\%$$

◆ **If executive bonuses for West division are based upon RI, would the executives be motivated to make the investment, assuming a target rate of 15%?**

	Current Division Results (Before Investment)	Expected Division Results (After Investment)
RI	$268,800 − (15% × $960,000) = $124,800	$361,200 − (15% × $1,345,000) = $159,450

In this case, the executives would be more likely to make the investment based upon the measure used to evaluate performance. To achieve goal congruence between the mission of the company (in this case a build mission) and management, the performance measures that determine compensation must also reward a build mission.

---

[16] Groysberg, et.al., "Compensation Packages that Actually Drive Performance," *Harvard Business Review*, January-February 2021, https://hbr.org/2021/01/compensation-packages-that-actually-drive-performance (accessed on November 9, 2023).

[17] Intel, *Corporate Responsibility Report*, (2022-23), https://www.intel.com/content/www/us/en/corporate-responsibility/csr-report-builder.html (accessed November 9, 2023)

© Cambridge Business Publishers

Include Short-Run and Long-Run Measures A second consideration when designing a performance-based reward system is that the measures should not focus solely on the short run. The most common short-run measure on which to base pay-for-performance is a financial one, such as income. However, nonfinancial measures such as safety, quality, customer retention, or workforce diversity focus employees on the impact of decisions that create longer-term value. In order to be effective, the nonfinancial measures must be linked to the company's strategy and key goals.[18] In other words, short-run measures are not necessarily viable proxies for the long-run wealth maximization that is the primary objective of U.S. businesses.

Pay-for-performance criteria should encourage workers to adopt a long-range perspective. Many financial incentives now involve shares of corporate common stock or stock options. Employees (regardless of level) who become stockholders in their employing company tend to develop, to some degree, the same perspective as other stockholders: long-run wealth maximization.

To illustrate, cash is the most obvious reward for short-term performance. All managers receive some compensation in cash to provide for living expenses. However, once a manager receives a cash reward, its value does not depend on the firm's future performance. In contrast, a stock option that is not exercisable until a future time provides a manager with an incentive to be more concerned about long-term performance. A stock option's ultimate value is determined when the option is exercised rather than when it is received. Thus, the option's value is related more to long-term than to short-term organizational performance. For example, assume that a stock option received by an executive represents the right to purchase a specified number of shares of stock at a future date for $25 per share (the current market price). The employee has an incentive to help improve the value of the company such that a share of the company's stock is worth more than $25 in the future.

Link Subunit Employee Rewards to Subunit's Mission Because each organizational subunit has a unique mission and possesses unique competencies, the performance measurement system and reward structure for subunit employees should be crafted with the subunit's mission in mind. What is measured and rewarded affects the focus of employees, and that focus should be directed toward factors that determine the success of the whole organization as well as its subunits. Managers of subunits charged with a **build mission** should receive long-term incentives and be evaluated based on longer-term performance measures. These managers need to be concerned about long-term success and be willing to make short-term sacrifices for long-term gains. In contrast, managers of subunits charged with a **harvest mission** must be more oriented to the short term. These subunits are expected to generate as much cash and profit as possible from their operations. Accordingly, incentives should be in place to encourage these managers to have a short-term focus in decision making. **Exhibit 15.13** indicates how the form of reward is influenced by the subunit mission.

Exhibit 15.13 ■ Different Strategic Missions: Compensation Implications

	← MISSION CONTINUUM →		
	Build	**Hold**	**Harvest**
Base salary.	Low	⟶	High
Incentives tied to sales growth	High	⟶	Low
Incentives tied to profitability	Low	⟶	High
Incentives tied to cost control.	Low	⟶	High
Incentives tied to nonfinancial performance measures	High	⟶	Low
Incentive compensation formula criteria.	Subjective	⟶	Objective
Incentive compensation time horizon.	Long term	⟶	Short term

Consider Employee Job Commitment Job commitment of employees can also be an important factor in designing employee incentive plans. It is possible that younger employees have a longer-term perspective than older employees, especially those who will retire from the firm within a few years. In designing employee incentives, any difference in time-frame perspectives among employees should

---

[18] Korn Ferry, "Non-Financial Performance Metrics: Strategic Use in LTI Plans," *The Executive Edition* (April 2017); http://static.kornferry.com/media/sidebar_downloads KFHG_Executive_Edition_April_2017.pdf (accessed 12/17/19).

be considered. Soon-to-leave employees could suboptimize to see short-run, rather than long-run, benefits of investment projects.

Pay Versus Performance

The last section detailed how to link pay to performance that is in line with a company's goals. Taking this one additional step, a recent pay versus performance rule[19] enacted by the **Securities and Exchange Commission** (SEC) requires companies to illustrate how actual compensation paid aligned with the actual performance of the company. **Pay versus performance** is a term that refers to the relationship between executive compensation and the financial results of the company. Among the rules, registrants of the SEC are required to complete the following.

- Provide a table showing specified executive compensation and financial performance measures. These financial measures include (1) total shareholder return[20], (2) total shareholder return for the company's peer group, (3) net income, and (4) the most important financial measure used by the company to link compensation to performance.
- Describe the relationship between financial performance measures in the table described above, and paid compensation. Along with this comparison, the company is required to describe the relationship between the company's total shareholder return and its peer group's total shareholder return.
- List three to seven of the company's "most important performance measures." This list can include financial and nonfinancial measures.

The required disclosures are often included in the company's *proxy statement* (SEC Schedule 14A), which is an SEC required filing that provides information about matters that will be addressed at an annual shareholder meeting.

The following chart shows the disclosures for a selection of SEC registrants of their most important performance measurements.

Company	Most Important Performance Measurements				
Meta Platforms, Inc.	Revenue				
Intel Corporation	Revenue	Gross margin percentage	Cash flow from operations		
Workday, Inc.	Subscription revenue	Annual customer satisfaction score	Workday Class A common stock price		
Ralph Lauren Corp.	Adjusted operating profit margin	Total company revenue	Relative total shareholder revenue	Environmental, social, and governance scorecard	
Lowe's Companies, Inc.	Sales	Operating income (as adjusted)	Inventory turnover	Pro Sales Growth	3-year average ROIC	3-year relative TSR vs. the median of S&P 500 companies

Note: The source of the information for each company is the applicable 2023 Proxy statement filed with the SEC.

From this selection of performance measures, a form of sales or revenue, as defined, is included for all companies. Nonfinancial items were identified in some companies as important including inventory turnover and environmental, social, and governance scorecard (a form of the balanced scorecard

---

[19] As required by the Dodd-Frank Act, the Securities and Exchange Commission (SEC) issued rules on pay versus performance disclosure requirements (see Item 402(v) of Regulation S-K).

[20] The sum of the Ending Stock Price minus the Beginning Stock Price, plus the amount of any dividends and distributions paid on a per share basis (as define) cumulatively over the performance period, divided by the Beginning Stock Price. See sec.gov for further information on this performance measure.

discussed in the last section). Also, a multi-year example, a long-term measure, was listed for Lowe's Companies, Inc.

LINKS BETWEEN PERFORMANCE MEASURES AND REWARDS

When the compensation strategy and target objectives are known, performance measures for individual employees or employee groups can be determined based on their required contributions to the operational plan. Performance measures should, directly or indirectly, link individual actions to basic business strategies. Rewards in a performance-based compensation plan should use monetary and nonmonetary as well as short-term and long-term measures. If an organization makes numerous measurements but only rewards financial outcomes, employees will quickly realize what is truly important in the work environment and what is being measured simply for the sake of measurement.

Degree of Control over Performance Output

Actual performance is a function of employee effort, employee skill, and random effects. Random effects include performance measurement error, problems or inefficiencies created by co-workers or adjacent workstations, illness, and weather-related production problems. After the actual performance is measured, determining the contributions of the controllable and noncontrollable factors to the achieved performance is impossible in many instances. Using performance-based pay systems causes employees to bear more risk than does the use of less comprehensive input–output measurements to determine compensation. For example, consider the following three compensation packages.

Option 1: Fixed compensation per month for 12 months

Option 2: Variable compensation based on segment profits

Option 3: Partial fixed compensation and partial variable compensation, based on segment profits

In Option 1, the employee bears little risk because the salary is the same each month and is not dependent upon performance. However, while a fixed salary provides an incentive to do the necessary work to maintain the job, the pay structure does not provide incentives for the employee to improve segment profit which could provide additional efforts.

In Option 2, the employee bears risk because the employee will only receive pay if the segment performs well. Even if there are circumstances outside of the customer's control such as an economic recession, the employee's compensation will be impacted.

In Option 3, the employee shares the risk with the company because there is some security with the salary portion of compensation, but there is also incentives to take risks to improve segment profits. It partially protects the employee from circumstances that affect profit, but are outside the employee's control.

At the worker level, performance measures should be specific and typically have a short-run focus—usually on cost and/or quality control. Each higher level in the organizational hierarchy should include increasingly more elements related to the critical success factors under an individual's control and responsibility. As the level of responsibility increases, performance measures should, by necessity, become less specific, focus on a longer time horizon, and be more concerned with organizational longevity than with short-run cost control or income. When the compensation strategy, operational targets, and performance measurements have been determined, appropriate target rewards can be specified. Rewards should motivate employees to contribute in a manner congruent with the operational objectives, and employees must be able to relate their performance to the reward structure.

Incentives Relative to Organizational Level

Individuals at different organizational levels typically view monetary rewards differently because of the relationship of pay to standard of living. Relative pay scales are essential to recognizing the value of monetary rewards to different employees. At lower employee levels, most incentives should be monetary and short term (to enhance current lifestyles), but some nonmonetary and long-term incentives should also be included so these individuals will take a long-run organizational ownership view. At higher levels, most incentives should be nonmonetary and long term (such as stock and stock options), so that top management will be more concerned about the organization's continuing well-being rather than their own short-term personal gains.

Performance Plans and Feedback

As employees perform their required tasks, performance related to the measurement standards is monitored. The two feedback loops in the model shown in **Exhibit 15.12** exist so that problems identified in one period can be corrected in future periods. The first feedback loop relates to monitoring and measuring performance, which must be considered in setting targets for the following periods. The second feedback loop relates to the rewards given and the compensation strategy's effectiveness. Both loops are essential in the managerial planning process.

Worker Pay and Performance Links

The competitive environment in many industries has evolved to use more automation and less labor-intensive technology. Also, management philosophies now emphasize the need for workers to perform in teams and groups. An interesting paradox has been created by these changes. Workers are more detached from the production function and more involved with higher-technology tasks. Thus, the trend is to rely more on performance-based evaluation and less on direct supervision to control worker behavior. This trend is consistent with the movement to empower workers and decrease levels of supervision and layers of management. Research has indicated that pay-for-performance is increasing in large organizations for four primary reasons:

- to better align activities with business strategies;
- to create better linkages between corporate and individual performance;
- to improve organizational or team performance; and
- to ensure market competitiveness.[21]

Promoting Overall Success

Many performance-based plans have the express goal of causing employees to act in the best interest of shareholders. One popular arrangement is **profit sharing**, which refers to compensation that is contingent on the level of organizational profit generated. These current and/or deferred incentive payments are contingent on organizational performance and can be in the form of cash or stock. Allocation of the total profit-sharing payment among individual employees is made on the basis of personal performance, seniority, team performance, managerial judgment, and/or specified formulas. One popular profit-sharing compensation program is the **employee stock ownership plan (ESOP)**, in which investments are made in the employer's securities.

An ESOP conforming to the Internal Revenue Code rules offers both tax and incentive advantages. Under an ESOP, the employer makes tax-deductible payments of cash or stock to a trust fund. If cash is contributed, it is used by the trust to purchase shares of the employing company's stock. Trust beneficiaries are the employees, and their wealth grows with both the employer contributions and advances in the stock price. Of course, employees are at risk of losing some or all of these benefits if the employing company goes bankrupt.

Nonfinancial Incentives

Besides various forms of monetary compensation, workers can also be motivated by nonfinancial factors. Although all employees value and require cash to satisfy basic human needs, other human needs cannot necessarily be fulfilled with monetary wealth. Employees are typically more productive when they think their efforts are appreciated. The results of a survey of HR professionals showed that 80 percent of the respondents used some form of noncash incentive. The survey also indicated that when incentives were tied to organizational values, the outcome was a positive impact on

- employee engagement (90 percent);
- employee happiness (86 percent);
- added humanity to the workplace (85 percent);
- improved employee relationships (84 percent); and
- reinforcement of corporate values (88 percent).[22]

---

[21] WorldatWork, "Employers Increasing Proportion of Variable Pay in Employee Pay Programs," WorldatWork.org (July 8, 2010); http://www.worldatwork.org/waw/adimComment?id=39253 (accessed 1/29/12).

[22] SHRM Online Staff, "SHRM Survey Findings: Employee Recognition Programs—2015" *SHRM.org* (June 22, 2015); https://www.shrm.org/hr-today/trends-and-forecasting/research-and-surveys/Documents/SHRM-Globoforce-Employee-Recognition-2015.pdf (accessed 12/17/19).

Supervisors can formally recognize contributions of subordinates through simple gestures such as compliments and small awards. For example, because sustainability is a corporate goal, Intel employees can earn nonfinancial awards for community volunteering and engaging in environmental, energy-conservation, and pollution prevention programs.[23] Nonfinancial incentives contribute to making employment socially fulfilling and let employees know that superiors are attentive to, and appreciative of, their contributions.

Tax Implications of Compensation Elements

Differences in tax treatments of compensation components are important because taxes affect the take-home pay received by employees and the actual employer cost of the pay plan. There are three different tax treatments for employee compensation:

- full and immediate taxation,
- deferral of taxation, and
- exemption from taxation.

Tax deferral indicates that taxation occurs in the future rather than currently. *Tax exemption* is the most desirable form of tax treatment because the income is never subject to income taxation.

When analyzing the compensation plan, employers and employees must consider the entire package—not simply one element of the package. For employers, compensation beyond wages and salaries creates additional costs; for employees, such compensation creates additional benefits. Fringe benefits can include employee health insurance, child care, physical fitness facilities, and pension plans. However, different types of fringe benefits have different tax consequences. Certain employee fringe benefits are tax exempt to the employee but are fully deductible by the employer.[24]

Global Compensation

As more companies engage in multinational operations, compensation systems should be developed that reward all employees and managers on a fair and equitable basis. A very important issue related to global compensation is the manner in which expatriates are compensated. **Expatriates** (expats) are parent-company and third-country nationals assigned to a foreign subsidiary or foreign nationals assigned to the parent company. Relocating individuals to foreign countries requires consideration of compensation. A fair and reasonable compensation package in one locale might not be fair and reasonable in another.

The compensation package paid to expats must reflect labor market factors, cost-of-living considerations, and currency fluctuations as well as recognize tax consequences. Typically, an expat's base salary and fringe benefits should reflect what he or she would have been paid domestically—adjusted for reasonable cost-of-living factors. These factors could be quite apparent (such as providing for housing, education, and security needs similar to those that would have been available in the home country or compensating for a spouse's loss of employment), or they could be less obvious (such as a need to hire someone in the home country to care for an elderly relative or to handle real estate investments).

Expats can be paid in the currency of the country in which they reside, in their home currency, or in a combination of both. Frequently, price-level adjustment clauses are built into the compensation system to counteract any local currency inflation or deflation. Regardless of the national currency that comprises the pay package, fringe benefits related to retirement must be related to the home country and should be paid in that currency.

Tying compensation to performance is essential because all workers recognize that what gets measured and rewarded determines what gets accomplished. Organizations must focus their reward structures to motivate employees to succeed at all activities that will create shareholder, stakeholder, and personal value. In this highly competitive age, the new paradigm of success is to provide quality products and services at a reasonable price while generating a reasonable profit margin. Top management compensation has traditionally been tied to financial measures of performance; more and more organizations

---

[23] Chorn, *ibid.*,p.3.

[24] Information about fringe benefits and taxes can be found in IRS Publication 15-B; http://www.irs.gov/publications/p15b/ ar02.html#en_US_2012_publink1000193627 (accessed November 9, 2023).

are beginning to tie the compensation of all levels of workers to one or more nonfinancial performance measures.

Ethical Considerations of Compensation

A major issue of discussion and contention involves perceptions of disparity between the pay of ordinary workers and top managers. Plato argued that no one should earn more than five times the income earned by the lowest-paid worker. In the early 1900s, however, **J. P. Morgan** stated that the differential should be no more than 20 times. Today, numerous CEOs earn untold multiples of the pay of the average worker.[25]

As a result of the Dodd-Frank Act, the Securities Exchange Commission requires its registrants to provide a **Pay Ratio Disclosure**. The ratio is calculated as the proportion of the company's principal executive officer compensation to the median employee's compensation. The SEC indicated that the ratio should provide shareholders additional information on the individual company's compensation practices rather than a means of comparison to other companies.[26]

Compensation and Goal Congruence **LO15-6** **REVIEW 15-6**

Compensation and a Company's Mission

1. An organization with a mission to *build* is in rapid expansion and growth. An organization with a mission to *harvest* is in a mature market. Assuming compensation is based on each of the factors listed in *a* through *e*, determine whether the mission of the related company is more aligned with a mission to *build* or with a mission to *harvest*.

    a. Base salary of $50,000 — Build or harvest?
    b. Based on 1 percent of gross profit — Build or harvest?
    c. Based on 5 percent of sales — Build or harvest?
    d. Based on a five-year sales incentive target — Build or harvest?
    e. Based on a reduction of administrative expenses/sales — Build or harvest?

2. **Critical Thinking:** How can disclosures on *pay versus performance* help shareholders determine whether there is a link between executive compensation and either a build or harvest mission?

More practice: E15-56
Solution on p. 15-67.

Comprehensive Chapter Review

Key Terms

asset turnover, p. 15-14
balanced scorecard (BSC), p. 15-24
build mission, p. 15-34
climate-related metrics, p. 15-23
compensation strategy, p. 15-32
dashboards, p. 15-29
Du Pont model, p. 15-13
economic value added (EVA®), p. 15-15
employee stock ownership plan (ESOP), p. 15-37
expatriates, p. 15-38

greenhouse gas (GHG) emissions, p. 15-22
harvest mission, p. 15-34
lag indicators, p. 15-24
lead indicators, p. 15-24
lead time, p. 15-22
long-run success measure, p. 15-19
mission statement, p. 15-2
nonfinancial performance measures (NFPMs), p. 15-6
pay ratio disclosure, p. 15-39
pay versus performance, p. 15-35

performance measures, p. 15-3
profit margin, p. 15-13
profit sharing, p. 15-37
residual income (RI), p. 15-15
segment margin, p. 15-9
segment reports, p. 15-7
short-run success measure, p. 15-19
strategy map, p. 15-27
throughput, p. 15-20
values statement, p. 15-2

---

[25] In April of each year, *The Wall Street Journal* provides a special report on executive pay.

[26] SEC; Commission Guidance on Pay Ratio Disclosure; 17 CFR Part 229 and 249; https://www.sec.gov/files/rules/final/2015/33-9877.pdf (accessed November 7, 2023).

Chapter Summary

LO15-1 **Mission Statement (Page 15-2)**
- A mission statement is important to an organization because it
  - expresses the organization's purpose.
  - identifies how the organization intends to meet its customers' needs through its products/services.
  - communicates organizational purposes and goals to employees.
  - acts as a foundation for setting organizational strategy.

Performance Measures
- Performance measures in organizations serve to
  - assess organizational performance.
  - relate organizational goals and missions to managerial performance.
  - foster growth of subordinate managers.
  - motivate managers.
  - enhance organizational communication.
  - evaluate comparative managerial performance.
  - implement organizational control.
- The design of performance measures should be guided by
  - assessing progress toward organizational mission, goals, and objectives.
  - allowing the people being evaluated to participate in the development of the measures.
  - hiring people who have the appropriate skills and talents (or training people to have such) and providing those people with the necessary equipment, resources, information, and authority to be successful.
  - providing feedback to people in a timely and useful manner.
  - establishing a set of measures that will provide a variety of information about performance.

LO15-2 **Segment Reports and Statement of Cash Flows (Page 15-7)**
- Common short-term financial performance measures include
  - segment margin, which is
    - calculated as segment sales minus (direct variable expenses and direct fixed expenses).
    - used to assess whether segmental profitability goals were achieved.
  - Segments can be compared through the
    - segment contribution margin ratio and the
    - segment profit margin
  - cash flow (by segment or responsibility unit), which is
    - calculated as cash provided (used) from operating activities, investing activities, and (if appropriate) financing activities.
    - used to assess the profitability of the responsibility unit, liquidity to pay debts as they arise, adaptability to adverse conditions, and ability to undertake new commitments.

LO15-3 **Return on Investment, Residual Income, Economic Value Added (Page 15-12)**
- Return on investment is
  - calculated as profit margin multiplied by asset turnover.
  - used to assess the generation of income relative to the resources used to produce that income.
- Residual income is
  - calculated as income earned above a target rate on the unit's asset base.
  - used to assess the generation of income relative to the resources used to produce that income.
- Economic value added is
  - calculated as after-tax income less the product of the fair value of invested capital multiplied by the cost of capital percentage.
  - used to assess the generation of income relative to the fair value of the resources used to produce that income.
- Company management should focus on long-term performance because such a perspective reflects
  - leading indicators of future performance.
  - technical and competitive trends.
  - a more intensive investigation of resource allocations.
  - proactive efforts to enhance competitive position.

Nonfinancial Performance Measures (Page 15-19)   LO15-4
- When selecting nonfinancial performance measures, managers should consider that
  - people are more comfortable with quantitative rather than qualitative measures.
  - the measures must be clearly defined and communicated to those who will be evaluated by the measures.
  - the measures must be relevant to the objective, trace responsibility, and be evaluated against internal or external benchmarks.
  - the measures must use valid data that can be obtained in a cost-beneficial manner.
  - too many measures are counterproductive.

Balanced Scorecard (Page 15-24)   LO15-5
- A balanced scorecard
  - indicates critical goals and targets needed to operationalize strategy.
  - measures success factors for learning and growth, internal business, customer satisfaction, and financial value.
  - includes financial and nonfinancial, internal and external, long- and short-term, and lead and lag indicators.
- Multiple measures of performance should be used because an organization's success depends on a variety of factors, each of which should be reviewed for contribution toward the organization's mission, goals, and objectives.
- A balanced scorecard can be used to measure performance by providing a set of measurements that reflect the organization's mission and strategy from a(n)
  - financial perspective.
  - customer perspective.
  - internal process perspective.
  - learning and growth perspective.
- Some companies are including a sustainability perspective in their BSCs.

Compensation Strategy (Page 15-32)   LO15-6
- The role compensation should play in an organization must be addressed.
- The underlying structure for the compensation plan includes consideration of
  - employees' control over performance output.
  - employees' positions in the organization.
  - employees' opportunities to gain feedback and adapt performance.
  - the alignment of organizational mission, goals, and objectives with the performance measurements and employee rewards.
  - tax and ethical implications of compensation.
- Measuring performance for multinational firms often creates difficulties because of differing
  - labor and tax laws.
  - employee work ethics.
  - market and political stability.
  - inflation, exchange, and labor rates.
  - consumer wealth and purchasing power.
  - financing costs.
  - accounting practices.

Solution Strategies

Performance Measures for Responsibility Centers   LO15-2
- **Cost Center**

      Budgeted costs
    – Actual costs
    ―――――――――――――
      Variances (consider materiality)

- **Revenue Center**

Budgeted revenues
− Actual revenues
Variances (consider materiality)

- **Profit Center**

Budgeted profits		Cash inflows
− Actual profits		− Cash outflows
Variances (consider materiality)		Net cash flow (adequate for operations?)

- **Investment Center**

Budgeted profits		Cash inflows
− Actual profits		− Cash outflows
Variances (consider materiality)		Net cash flow (adequate for operations?)

LO15-3 Note: For the following ratios, income (and assets) must be defined. As noted in LO2, the preferred definition for income is segment margin.

Return on investment	= Income ÷ Assets invested (high enough rate?)
Du Pont model ROI	= Profit margin × Asset turnover
	= (Income ÷ Sales) × (Sales ÷ Assets) (high enough rate?)
Residual income	= Income − (Target rate × Asset base) (positive or negative? amount?)
Economic value added	= After-tax income − (Cost of capital % × Fair value of invested capital) (positive or negative? amount?)

LO15-4 Throughput

$$\text{Manufacturing cycle efficiency} \times \text{Process productivity} \times \text{Process quality yield} = \text{Throughput}$$

$$\frac{\text{Value-added processing time}}{\text{Total processing time}} \times \frac{\text{Total units}}{\text{Value-added processing time}} \times \frac{\text{Good units}}{\text{Total units}} = \text{Throughput}$$

LO15-6 Reward System

The design of an effective reward structure depends heavily on each organization's unique characteristics. It is impossible to design a generic incentive model that would be effective in all firms. However, affirmative answers to the following questions provide guidance as to the applicability of a proposed incentive and reward plan for a particular organization.

1. Are the organizational objectives more likely to be achieved if the proposed compensation structure is implemented?
2. Is the proposed structure consistent with organizational design and culture as well as management philosophy?
3. Are there reasonable and objective performance measures that are good surrogates for the organizational objectives and subunit missions?
4. Are factors beyond employee/group control minimized under the performance measures of the proposed compensation structure?
5. Is the ability of employees to manipulate the performance measurements limited?
6. In light of the interests of managers, workers, and stockholders, is the proposed reward structure fair and does it encourage and promote ethical behavior?
7. Is the proposed reward structure arranged to take advantage of potential employee/employer tax benefits?
8. Does the proposed reward structure promote harmony among employee groups?
9. Is there an adequate balance between group and individual incentives?
10. Can the reward system be adapted to accommodate international constraints and considerations?

Chapter Demonstration Problem 1

Household Products is a division of Delaware Electronics. The division had the following performance targets for the year: **LO15-3**

Asset turnover	3.1
Profit margin	6%
Target rate of return on investments for RI	15%
Cost of capital	9%
Income tax rate	35%

At the end of the year, the following actual information concerning the company's performance is available:

Total assets at beginning of year	$24,800,000
Total assets at end of year	29,600,000
Average fair value of invested capital for year	36,000,000
Sales	68,000,000
Variable operating costs	34,800,000
Direct fixed costs	27,440,000
Allocated fixed costs	2,700,000

Required:

a. Compute the segment margin and average assets for Household Products.
b. Based on segment margin and average assets, compute the profit margin, asset turnover, and ROI.
c. Evaluate the ROI performance of Household Products.
d. Using your answers from (b), compute the residual income for Household Products.
e. Compute the EVA for Household Products using after-tax segment margin. What causes EVA and RI to differ?
f. Based on the data given in the problem, discuss why ROI, EVA, and RI could be inappropriate measures of performance for Household Products.

Solution to Demonstration Problem 1

a.
Sales	$ 68,000,000
Variable operating costs	(34,800,000)
Direct fixed costs	(27,440,000)
Segment margin	$ 5,760,000

Average assets = ($24,800,000 + $29,600,000) ÷ 2 = $27,200,000

b. Profit margin = $5,760,000 ÷ $68,000,000 = 8.47%

Asset turnover = $68,000,000 ÷ $27,200,000 = 2.50

ROI = 8.47% × 2.5 = 21.18%

c. The target ROI for the division was 18.6 percent (6% × 3.1). The division generated an ROI of 21.18 percent. The division exceeded its target profit margin but fell short of its target asset turnover. Because the profit margin effect dominated the asset turnover effect, the achieved ROI was above the target ROI by more than 2.5 percent.

d. RI = $5,760,000 − (0.15 × $27,200,000)
= $5,760,000 − $4,080,000
= $1,680,000

© Cambridge Business Publishers

e. After-tax income = Pre-tax segment income − Taxes
= $5,760,000 − ($5,760,000 × 0.35)
= $5,760,000 − $2,016,000
= $3,744,000

EVA = $3,744,000 − ($36,000,000 × 0.09)
= $3,744,000 − $3,240,000
= $504,000

EVA and RI differ for three reasons. First, RI is based on pre-tax, rather than after-tax, income; RI is based on the book value of investment whereas EVA is based on the fair value of investment; and the target rates of return differ between the methods.

f. ROI, RI, and EVA are all measures of short-term performance. These measures may be particularly inappropriate for divisions that have long-term missions (such as high growth). In this case, the relatively large growth (19.35 percent) in assets of Household Products from the beginning to the end of the period could indicate that this division is oriented toward growth. If so, the ROI, RI, and EVA measures will provide an incentive contrary to the growth mission.

Chapter Demonstration Problem 2

LO15-4 Birmingham Hardwood Frames makes picture frames. During November, managers compiled the following data:

Total frames manufactured	1,850,000
Good frames produced and sold	1,731,000
Total processing time (minutes)	21,120
Value-added processing time (minutes)	6,920

Required:
a. Calculate the manufacturing cycle efficiency (MCE).
b. Calculate the process productivity (PP).
c. Calculate the process quality yield (PQY).
d. Calculate throughput using one ratio.
e. Confirm your answer to (d) using the results of (a), (b), and (c).

Solution to Demonstration Problem 2

a. MCE = Value-added processing time ÷ Total processing time
= 6,920 ÷ 21,120 = 32.77%

b. PP = Total frames manufactured ÷ Value-added processing time
= 1,850,000 ÷ 6,920 = 267.34 frames per minute of VA time

c. PQY = Good frames manufactured ÷ Total frames manufactured
= 1,731,000 ÷ 1,850,000 = 93.57%

d. Throughput = Good frames manufactured ÷ Total processing time
= 1,731,000 ÷ 21,120 = 82 frames per minute

e. Throughput = MCE × PP × PQY
= 0.3277 × 267.34 × 0.9357 = 82 frames per minute

Chapter 15 Performance Measurement, Balanced Scorecards, and Performance Rewards   15-45

Assignments with the MBC logo in the margin are available in myBusinessCourse.
Resources include demonstration videos, guided examples, and auto-graded homework.
See details in the Preface, and ask your professor how you can access the system.

Data Analytics

DA15-1. Segment profitability reports using Excel

LO15-2

Southern Comforts Inc. is a department store chain with stores in North Carolina, Tennessee, Kentucky, and West Virginia. Its corporate headquarters are located in Charlotte, North Carolina. In the past, the store owners only received financial reports for the company operations overall. They have recently asked for reports of costs and profitability by segment (location and department). Southern Comforts' locations include the four stores (Charlotte, Nashville, Virginia Beach, and Louisville) and the corporate office (Charlotte HQ). Departments include the product lines (Men's, Women's, Kids, Shoes, and Home) and the overhead expense types (Facilities, Labor, and Other). Provided is an Excel file that includes Southern Comfort transactions for the year. The first step is to make sure the data is in the form needed by separating revenue transactions from expense transactions (all transactions are currently in the Transactions column). After the data is in a useful format, we will then use the data to analyze profitability by store.

Part 1 Preparing the data
1. Download Excel file found in myBusinessCourse.
2. Add two new column headers, Revenues and Expenses.
3. Convert the schedule to a table. *Hint:* Click on any cell in the data; click on Insert, Table. Check the My table has headers box.
4. Use the IF function to add data to the Revenues column and Expenses column. *Hint:* In F2, enter =IF(E2>0,E2," "). The formula will be copied down to all cells in the Revenues column. Enter the formula to identify expenses in G2.
5. Add a new column after Month and call it Month Name.
6. Use the TEXT function to convert the date format to a text format. *Hint:* =TEXT(cell reference,"mmmm")—returns a full month name, as January–December.

Part 2 Creating PivotTables
1. Create PivotTable 1 on a new worksheet showing revenues, expenses, and net income per store. *Hint:* To change from Count of to Sum of, open the dropdown menu next to the fields in Values. Select Value Field Settings and click Sum in the Summarize value field by box. Drag Store to Rows and Revenue and Expenses to Values (change to "sum of"). Create a calculated field for net income by clicking on PivotTable Analyze, Fields, Items & Sets, and Calculated fields. The formula for net income will be Revenues + Expenses because expenses are negative numbers.
2. Indicate which store was the most profitable (in dollars)? What was the store's net income?
3. Indicate which store had the most revenue? What was the store's revenue?
4. Create PivotTable 2 showing revenues by store by month. *Hint:* Drag Store to Columns and Month Name to Rows, and Revenues to Values (change to "sum of").
5. Indicate which month had the highest revenue. What was the amount?
6. Duplicate PivotTable 2 (called PivotTable 2A) on the same worksheet and display each amount in a column as a percentage of the total of that column in this new table. *Hint:* Click on Sum of Revenues in Values and select Value Field Settings. Open the Show Values As tab and select % of Column Total.
7. Identify what percentage of total sales occurred during the month indicated in part 5. Round percentage to two decimal places.
8. Create PivotTable 3 showing net income by month.
9. Indicate which month was the least profitable (in dollars). What was the net profit that month?
10. Create PivotTable 4 showing gross profit by month and by store. *Hint:* Create a PivotTable showing net income by store. Drag Month Name to Columns, Store to Rows, Net income to Values. Click anywhere inside the PivotTable and open the PivotTable Analyze tab. Click Insert Slicer and select Department. Use the slicer to include the retail departments only (Mens, Womens, Kids, Shoes, and Home). After the overhead expense categories are removed, the "net income" amount will equal gross margin (sales minus the direct costs for each retail department).
11. List the total gross margin (in dollars) for 2020. Which store had the highest gross margin (in dollars)? List the amount of gross margin in dollars.

© Cambridge Business Publishers

15-46   Chapter 15 Performance Measurement, Balanced Scorecards, and Performance Rewards

12. Create PivotTable 5 showing department cost categories by store. *Hint:* Drag Department to Columns, Store to Rows, Expenses (sum of) to Values.
13. Indicate which store had the highest labor costs and which store had the highest facilities cost. List the dollar amounts.

Part 3   Summarizing results
1. For the two stores with the largest sales, compute the gross profit percentage (gross profit/sales), labor as a percentage of total sales, facilities as a percentage of total sales, and other as a percentage of total sales. *Hint:* Use data from the various PivotTables to calculate the expense percentages.
2. Indicate which of the two stores in Question 1 had the (a) lowest gross profit, (b) highest percentage of labor over sales, (c) highest percentage of facilities over sales, and (d) the highest percentage of other items over sales.

LO15-2

DA15-2. Segment profitability reports using Tableau
Available in MBC, this problem uses Tableau to analyze the profitability of segments.

LO15-2

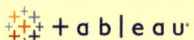

DA15-3. Segment analysis
Refer to the data available in MBC to answer the following questions.

Required
a. Prepare a column chart using information in part *a*, showing sales and income for each of the 3 product segments.
b. Prepare a column chart using information in part *b*, showing sales and income for each of the 3 territories.
c. Prepare a column chart using information in part *c*, showing sales and income for the Americas territory for the 3 product segments.
d. Calculate the profit margin percentage (margin/sales) for each segment in each of the 3 charts.
e. Using the 3 charts created above, answer the following questions.
   1. In reviewing the first chart, what conclusions do you draw on sales per product segment and profitability per product segment?
   2. In reviewing the second chart, what conclusions do you draw about profitability across territories?
   3. Comparing the third chart to the first chart, what conclusions do you draw that make the trends shown in the Americas product segments different from overall company product segment trends?
   4. Pick one product segment or territory segment from Chart 1 or 2 and make a case for why the company would want to invest resources in that segment.

LO15-4

DA15-4. Analysis of Scope 3 emissions reporting
Apple Inc. reports greenhouse gas emissions for Scope 1, Scope 2, and Scope 3. Data on emissions from Apple's 2022 Environment Progress Report are included in an Excel file in MBC.

Required
a. Prepare a stacked area chart showing the totals only of Scope 1, Scope 2, and Scope 3 greenhouse gas emissions (with the earliest time period on the left). Comment on the relative size of Scope 1, Scope 2, and Scope 3 emissions.
b. Prepare a stacked area chart showing the components of Scope 3 emissions only. Comment on the relative size of the Scope 3 components.
c. Generally speaking, what is the source of the largest component of Scope 3 emissions?
d. What is the general trend in Scope 3 emissions for Apple? What are some significant factors to consider when analyzing the trend in Scope 3 emissions over time?

Data Visualization

Data Visualization Activities are available in myBusinessCourse. These assignments use Tableau Dashboards to expose students to visual depictions of data and introduce students to data analytics through data visualizations. These exercises are easily assignable and auto graded by MBC.

© Cambridge Business Publishers

Potential Ethical Issues

1. Creating an unbalanced performance measurement system that places excessive emphasis on short-term performance
2. Putting excessive emphasis on accounting earnings such that managers experience extreme pressure to manipulate financial reports
3. Reporting fraudulent or manipulated accounting numbers so that a higher bonus will be paid or the adverse effects of the actual performance on compensation will be avoided
4. Evaluating mid- and lower-level managers using performance criteria that are beyond the influence of such managers
5. Not informing or explaining fully all performance criteria by which employees and managers will be evaluated
6. Not providing timely feedback to employees and managers during the period so that corrective action can be taken on a timely basis
7. Rewarding only financial performance and ignoring other important performance criteria such as innovation and organizational learning
8. Engaging in suboptimization practices that are personally beneficial but detrimental to the organization as a whole
9. Compensating expats or employees in foreign operations in a manner that would be considered "inappropriate" from an external perspective because of the wage rate/salary being paid, work hours being demanded, or work conditions being provided

Questions

Q15-1. What are the benefits of organizational mission and values statements? How are organizational missions and strategies related to performance measures?

Q15-2. Why is performance measurement important to the success of businesses? Should performance measures be qualitative, quantitative, or both? Justify your answer. For performance measurements to be meaningful, why is it necessary to establish benchmarks?

Q15-3. What benefits can be gained by allowing a manager to participate in developing the performance measures that will be used to assess that manager's performance?

Q15-4. On what basis should the performance of a responsibility center be measured? What are the traditional financial performance measures for each type of responsibility center? Why can the same quantitative measures of performance not be used for all types of responsibility centers?

Q15-5. How can cash flow be used as a performance measure? In what ways is cash flow a relatively stronger or weaker performance measure than accrual measures such as segment income?

Q15-6. At Lockhart Inc., divisional managers are evaluated on the basis of a variety of net income measures. The controller informs the president that such measures could be misleading. What are the major concerns in defining the "income" measures? Are internal or external measures more susceptible to manipulation? Explain.

Q15-7. What is residual income, and how is it used to measure divisional performance? How is it similar to, and different from, the return on investment measure? How is residual income similar to, and different from, economic value added? How is economic value added superior to residual income as a performance measure?

Q15-8. In designing a performance measurement system, why should managerial rewards be linked to performance measures? Why would an effective compensation strategy treat top managers, middle managers, and other workers differently?

Q15-9. What is the balanced scorecard? What perspectives are considered in selecting performance measures for the balanced scorecard, and why is each of these perspectives important?

Q15-10. Why would a company want to include sustainability as a perspective in a balanced scorecard?

Q15-11. If worker performance measures used in a pay-for-performance plan are not highly correlated with corporate goals, what is the likely result for the organization? For the workers?

Q15-12. How does the time perspective of a performance-based plan affect the selection of performance measures?

Q15-13. Why should different missions for two subunits result in different performance reward structures for the managers of those subunits? How does the mission of an organizational subunit affect the mix of financial and nonfinancial, and short-term and long-term, rewards?

Q15-14. How can feedback, both positive and negative, be used to improve managerial performance? How is feedback used in a performance-based reward system?

Q15-15. Many pay structures involve compensation combining both cash and stock. Why do firms want employees to be holders of the firm's common stock? What additional performance measurement and reward issues are created when managers are not shareholders in their firms?

Q15-16. What are some of the important equity issues in designing reward structures? Why is the achievement of equity in the reward structure important?

Multiple Choice

LO15-1 **MC15-17.** Which of the following is not a key criterion in designing a performance measurement system?
 a. Proving timely feedback.
 b. Including customers in the design process.
 c. Providing tools necessary for employee success.
 d. Assessing both financial and nonfinancial goals.
 e. Making adjustments to the process as required.

LO15-2 **MC15-18.** A company has the following financial information for its divisions.

	Alcohol	Soft Drink	Juice	Total
Sales.	$700,000	$430,000	$270,000	$1,400,000
Variable costs	280,000	150,000	170,000	600,000
Fixed costs	300,000	100,000	120,000	520,000
Operating income (loss)	$120,000	$180,000	$ (20,000)	$ 280,000

Which one of the following options reflects the current contribution margin ratio for each of the company's business segments?

	Alcohol	Soft Drink	Juice
a.	60%	65%	37%
b.	60%	35%	63%
c.	40%	65%	37%
d.	40%	35%	63%

LO15-2 **MC15-19.** Next Generation Inc. has two divisions (Individual and Business) and has the following information available for the current year:

Sales revenue—Individual	$1,200,000
Sales revenue—Business.	2,000,000
Variable cost—Individual	480,000
Variable cost—Business.	900,000
Direct fixed cost—Individual	160,000
Direct fixed cost—Business	220,000
Allocated fixed cost—Individual	100,000
Allocated fixed cost—Business	140,000
Unallocated common fixed cost	60,000

Next Generation Inc.'s Business segment income is
 a. $960,000   c. $880,000
 b. $740,000   d. $706,100

LO15-2 **MC15-20.** Refer to the previous question. What is the segment margin for Next Generation Inc.'s Individual segment margin?
 a. $620,000   c. $460,000
 b. $720,000   d. $560,000

MC15-21. A company has recently implemented responsibility accounting in all seven segments of the company. The following information is available for Segment W for the last quarter.

Net working capital...................	$1,200,000
Property, plant and equipment, net......	3,175,000
Revenues..........................	8,000,000
Cost of sales........................	6,350,000
General and administrative expenses ...	180,000

Based on the information provided, if the company treats Segment W as an investment center, what is the return on investment for the last quarter?
- a. 33.6%
- b. 37.7%
- c. 46.3%
- d. 74.4%

MC15-22. To ensure that a divisional vice president places appropriate focus on both the short-term and the long-term objectives of the division, the best approach would be to evaluate the vice president's performance by using
- a. return on investment (ROI) which permits easy and quick comparisons to other similar divisions.
- b. residual income since it will eliminate the rejection of capital investments that have a return less than ROI but greater than the cost of capital.
- c. division segment margin or profit margin.
- d. financial and nonfinancial measures, including the evaluation of quality, customer satisfaction, and market performance.

MC15-23. For a manufacturing process, if throughput is 1.28, process productivity is 4.0, and manufacturing cycle efficiency is 0.40, what is process quality yield?
- a. 3.12
- b. 0.51
- c. 0.80
- d. Insufficient information provided

MC15-24. Which one of the following statements about a balanced scorecard is incorrect?
- a. It seeks to address the problems associated with traditional financial measures used to assess performance.
- b. The notion of value chain analysis plays a major role in the drawing up of a balanced scorecard.
- c. It relies on the perception of the users with regard to service provided.
- d. It is directly derived from the scientific management theories.

MC15-25. A company currently sells 46,000 units of its product annually at a sales price of $38 per unit. Variable costs per unit total $21 and the total fixed costs each year are $749,000. Fixed costs include the annual salary of three sales staff, which is $55,000 each. Management is considering changing the sales staff's compensation. Under this proposal, sales staff salaries would decrease to $25,000, but sales staff would also receive a commission of $2 per unit for each unit sold. Management estimates this option will increase sales 10 percent. Should management change to the commission-based plan, and why?
- a. Yes, because it will increase operating income by $67,000.
- b. Yes, because it will increase net income by $67,000.
- c. No, because it will decrease net income by $23,000.
- d. No, because it will decrease operating income by $23,000.

Exercises

E15-26. Classifying performance measures For each of the following performance measures, indicate (a) whether the measure is an internal performance measure or an external performance measure and (b) whether the measure primarily relates to the element of production/performance, employees, sustainability, investors and creditors, or customers.
1. Product quality rating on a five-star scale
2. Hours of volunteer work of employees
3. Number of parts per product
4. Employee turnover
5. Operating profit
6. Supplier lead time
7. Greenhouse gas emissions
8. Market share
9. Level of employee absenteeism
10. Return on investment
11. Environmental building certifications

LO15-1

E15-27. Selecting performance measures; writing Theta Property Management provides management services for commercial real estate development projects. The firm recently started a new division to market video conferencing equipment to existing clients. The new division will purchase and maintain the video conferencing equipment placed in client buildings. Clients will be paid 25 percent of gross video conferencing equipment revenues.

Theta has hired you to report on recommended performance measures to be used in monitoring and evaluating the success of the new division and its manager. Begin your report with a discussion of your perception of the new division's strategic mission.

LO15-1, 2

E15-28. Selecting performance measures; research; writing Choose a company that has either gone out of business or is currently in poor financial condition. Use the Internet to research that company's history. Prepare a report on your findings, concentrating on indicators that might have provided a perspective of failure. Describe these indicators either as short-term or long-term and as leading or lagging.

LO15-1

E15-29. Performance measurement; writing Recall the various ways in which your academic performance has been measured and rewarded. Have the ways that your class grades were determined always provided the best indications of performance? Provide at least two positive and two negative examples. What would you have done to change the measurement system in the negative examples?

LO15-1

E15-30. Measuring long-run performance; writing The company president has asked you, as the new controller, to comment on any deficiencies of the firm. After saying you believe that the firm needs long-run performance measurements, the president says that the long run is really just a series of short runs. He says that if you do a good job of evaluating the short-run performance, the long run will take care of itself. He sees that you are unconvinced and agrees to keep an open mind if you can make a good case for measuring and evaluating long-run performance. Prepare a report supporting your case.

LO15-2

E15-31. Segment reporting Blue Mountain operates retail stores throughout the United States. Blue Mountain has three divisions, where each operates their own independent retail stores: Apparel, Shoes, and Sports Equipment. The manager of each division is responsible for the revenues and costs of the division. All investment decisions are made by the corporate headquarters. Blue Mountain had a history of financial success until last year when it incurred a net loss of $250,000. President Bob Johnson does not understand why the company incurred a loss and has assigned accountant Hillary Ryan with the job of analyzing the results.

Last Year's Operating Results	
Sales.............	$ 7,500,000
Variable expenses ...	4,000,000
Fixed expenses......	3,750,000
Net loss...........	$($250,000)

A breakout of operating data by division is shown below.

	Apparel	Shoes	Sports Equipment
Revenues..........	$3,750,000	$1,500,000	$2,250,000
Variable expenses ...	1,500,000	500,000	2,000,000

Ryan analyzed fixed expenses and found that $1,000,000 is traceable to Apparel, $750,000 is traceable to Shoes, and $1,500,000 is traceable to Sports Equipment. The remaining fixed expenses relate to the corporate headquarters.

a. Prepare a segment report using the contribution income statement approach.
b. What is the segment contribution margin ratio for each segment?
c. Which division of Blue Mountain is least profitable and how can Blue Mountain improve this division's profitability?

LO15-2

E15-32. Segment reporting Health Care Consulting Firm provides three types of client services in three health-care-related industries. The sales, contribution margin ratio, and direct and allocated fixed expenses for each of the three types of services are as follows:

	Hospitals	Physicians	Nursing Care
Sales.................................	$272,000	$164,000	$220,000
Contribution margin ratio	25%	35%	30%
Direct fixed expenses and services	$29,200	$6,800	$15,000
Allocated common fixed services expense.....	$6,800	$2,000	$3,200

a. Prepare a segment report using the contribution income statement format, including a column for the entire firm in the statement. Assume total fixed costs for the company are $124,000.
b. What is the segment profit margin ratio for each segment?
c. Analyze the relative profitability of the segments.

E15-33. ROI Data for the three autonomous divisions of Dakota Mining, Inc. for the year follow.

	Division 1	Division 2	Division 3
Segment income.	$ 320,000	$ 450,000	$ 4,850,000
Asset investment	2,700,000	2,000,000	30,200,000

Compute the return on investment for each division. (Round to one decimal point.)

E15-34. ROI For the most recent fiscal year, the Southern Division of Fargo Corporation generated an asset turnover ratio of 5 and a segment profit margin ratio of 6 percent on sales of $3,950,000.
a. Compute the average assets employed.
b. Compute the segment margin.
c. Compute the ROI.

E15-35. ROI; Du Pont Model; RI The following information for the year is available for Leffingwell Industries: average assets invested, $8,200,000; sales, $31,400,000; and expenses, $27,600,000.
a. Calculate return on investment. (Round to one decimal point.)
b. Calculate profit margin. (Round to one decimal point.)
c. Calculate asset turnover. (Round to one decimal point.)
d. Using the Du Pont Model and parts b and c, prove your answer to part a. (Round to one decimal point.)
e. Assuming Leffingwell's cost of capital is 14 percent, compute residual income.

E15-36. RI Ribocon Corp. has established a 12 percent target ROI for its Lynchfield Division. The following data have been gathered for the division's operations for the year: average total assets, $14,200,000; revenues, $28,000,000; and expenses, $26,500,000. What is the division's residual income? Did the division successfully meet the target ROI?

E15-37. RI Carrington Co. operates its two divisions as investment centers. Information about these divisions follows.

	Division 1	Division 2
Sales.	$5,200,000	$1,850,000
Total variable costs	2,630,000	330,000
Total fixed costs	490,000	840,000
Average assets invested.	7,180,000	875,000

a. What is the residual income of each division if the "charge" on invested assets is 13 percent? Which division is doing a better job?
b. If the only change expected for next year is a sales increase of 20 percent, what will be the residual income of each division? Which division will be doing a better job financially?
c. Why were the percentage changes in residual income determined in (b) so different for Divisions 1 and 2?

E15-38. ROI; Du Pont Model; RI; change in definition of denominator Schulz GmbH, a German company, set an 18 percent target rate of return for its U.S. division for the year. The U.S. division generated $39,000,000 of annual revenue on average assets of $25,000,000. The division's variable costs were 45 percent of sales, and fixed costs were $6,750,000. Compute the following items for the U.S. division:
a. ROI
b. Residual income
c. Profit margin (Round to one decimal point.)
d. Asset turnover (Round to one decimal point.)
e. Using the Du Pont Model and parts c and d, prove your answer to a.
f. How does your answer to part a change if instead, assets are defined as assets at fair value? Assume assets at fair value are equal to $36,000,000.

LO15-3 **E15-39. EVA** Mountain Mist Inc.'s cost of capital is 11 percent. For the year, one of the firm's divisions generated an EVA of $1,130,000. The fair value of the capital investment in that division was $29,500,000. How much after-tax income was generated by the division?

LO15-3 **E15-40. EVA** EVA is used by top management at College Learning Technologies to measure and evaluate the performance of segment managers. The company's cost of capital is 11 percent. For the year, its Audio/Visual subsidiary generated after-tax income of $2,260,000, with $8,900,000 fair value of invested capital.
 a. Compute the subsidiary's EVA.
 b. As the controller of College Learning Technologies, how would you determine the fair value of capital investment for a particular division?

LO15-3 **E15-41. Performance measurement changes** Following is a list of transactions that affected one division within a multiple-division company. Indicate, for the current fiscal year, whether each transaction would increase (I), decrease (D), have no effect (N), or have an indeterminate (?) effect on each of the following: asset turnover, profit margin, ROI, and RI. Analyze each transaction separately.
 a. In September, the division fired its R&D manager; the position will not be filled during the current fiscal year.
 b. At mid-year, the division manager increased scheduled annual production by 5,000 units. This decision has no effect on scheduled sales.
 c. Equipment with an original cost of $680,000 was sold for $139,000. At the time of sale, the book value of the equipment was $170,000. The equipment sale had no effect on production or sales activities.
 d. The division wrote down obsolete finished goods by debiting Cost of Goods Sold and crediting Finished Goods Inventory for $96,000.
 e. The division manager automated a previously labor-intensive operation. The action had no effect on sales, but total annual operating expenses declined by 17 percent.
 f. Because of significant changes in its cost of capital, the company lowered the division's target rate of return from 12 to 10 percent.
 g. A special overseas order was accepted at a selling price significantly less than that for domestic business. The selling price, however, was sufficient to cover all traceable costs of the order.
 h. During the year, the division manager spent an additional $165,800 on advertising, which sparked an immediate increase in sales.

LO15-3 **E15-42. ROI; changing definition of ROI denominator** College Spirit Inc. owns a number of screen print shops, which specialize in the printing of t-shirts for college events. Its Madison print shop is considering the purchase of new screen printing equipment for $100,000 in order to increase sales volume. The Madison print shop estimates that the purchase would result in an increase in income for the first year of $20,000. Before the consideration of the investment, the Madison shop summarized the following financial data.

	Division 1
Sales.	$380,000
Variable costs	247,000
Contribution margin	133,000
Direct fixed costs	18,000
Segment margin	115,000
Indirect fixed and allocated costs . . .	24,000
Segment income.	91,000
Taxes (30%)	27,300
Net income	$ 63,700
Average asset book value. $500,000	
Fair value of total assets. $600,000	

 a. What is the shop's current ROI? Base your calculations on segment margin and average asset book value.
 b. What is the ROI for the purchase of the equipment?
 c. What is the ROI of the shop, assuming the purchase of the equipment?
 d. If the shop is measured based upon ROI, would the shop make the investment, considering only the ROI implications?

e. How do your answers to parts a to d change, now basing your ROI calculations on segment margin and fair value of total assets?

E15-43. ROI; RI; impact of a new investment The Eastern Division of Tooling Inc. had an operating income of $750,000 and net assets of $3,500,000. Tooling Inc. has a target rate of return of 18 percent.

a. Compute the return on investment.
b. Compute the residual income.
c. The Eastern Division has an opportunity to increase operating income by $165,000 with an $800,000 investment in assets.
   1. Compute the Eastern Division's return on investment if the project is undertaken. (Round your answer to three decimal places.)
   2. Compute the Eastern Division's residual income if the project is undertaken.

E15-44. ROI, RI, EVA; changing definition of ROI denominator Exceptional Inc. has a target return on capital of 10 percent. In evaluating operations, management looks at book values (GAAP compliant) and current values. Current values reflect management's estimates of asset values. The following financial information is available for March ($ thousands):

	Software Division (Value Base)		Consulting Division (Value Base)		Tax Division (Value Base)	
	Book	Current	Book	Current	Book	Current
Sales.............	$200,000	$200,000	$450,000	$450,000	$625,000	$625,000
Pretax income......	35,000	37,200	37,000	38,500	63,000	43,200
Operating assets ...	250,000	310,000	185,000	175,000	700,000	720,000
Current liabilities....	30,000	30,000	20,000	20,000	65,000	65,000

a. Compute the return on investment using both book and current values for each division. (Round answers to three decimal places.) For ROI calculations, Exceptional Inc. uses operating assets as the investment base.
b. Compute the residual income for both book and current values for each division.
c. Compute the economic value-added income for both book and current values for each division if the tax rate is 20 percent and the weighted average cost of capital is 8 percent.
d. Does book value or current value provide a better basis for performance evaluation? Which division do you consider the most successful?

E15-45. Throughput Completely Nuts, a macadamia nut cannery, is analyzing its throughput for September. The following statistics are obtained for the month:

Cans packed and sold	700,000
Total cans packed..................	742,040
Value-added processing time	650 hours
Total processing time	2,750 hours

a. Calculate the manufacturing cycle efficiency. (Round to one decimal point.)
b. Calculate the process productivity. (Round to one decimal point.)
c. Calculate the process quality yield. (Round to one decimal point.)
d. Calculate the throughput using only good units and total time. (Round to one decimal point.)
e. Verify your answer to (d) by using your answers to (a), (b), and (c).

E15-46. Throughput Hernandez Corp. wants to compute its throughput for August. The following production data are available:

Good units produced and sold	2,923,200
Total units produced	3,460,000
Total processing time	144,000 hours
Value-added time	50,300 hours

a. Determine the manufacturing cycle efficiency. (Round to one decimal point.)
b. Determine the process productivity. (Round to one decimal point.)
c. Determine the process quality yield. (Round to one decimal point.)
d. Determine the throughput using only good units and total time.
e. What can company management do to raise hourly throughput?

LO15-4 E15-47. Throughput Management at Lantana Inc. has decided to begin using throughput as a divisional performance measure. The Carolina Division is a job shop that carefully crafts furniture to customer specifications. The following first quarter information is available for the division:

Good units started, completed, and sold	98,400
Total units completed	104,500
Total value-added hours of processing time	15,160
Total hours of divisional time	25,000

a. What is the division's manufacturing cycle efficiency? (Round to one decimal point.)
b. What is the division's process productivity? (Round to one decimal point.)
c. What is the division's process quality yield? (Round to one decimal point.)
d. What is the total hourly throughput? (Round to one decimal point.)
e. Discuss whether throughput is as useful a performance measurement in a job shop as in an automated plant. Why would you expect process quality yield to be high in a job shop? Why might a job shop such as Carolina Division have a low manufacturing cycle efficiency?

LO15-4 E15-48. Manufacturing cycle efficiency; value-added activities Randolph Inc. runs one 8-hour shift per day. Three different machines are used in the production of skateboards, Randolph's sole product. The operations manager at Randolph is looking at ways to be more efficient and has gathered the following information:

Manufacturing Time per Batch of 50 Skateboards	
Function	Time
Actual processing time per batch of skateboards	2.5 hours
Time spent moving a batch of skateboards between work stations	1.25 hours
Time spent on control testing, per batch	45 minutes
Time spend on machine setup, per batch	30 minutes

a. What is the value-added processing time?
b. What is the total processing time?
c. What is the manufacturing cycle efficiency?
d. What are some practical steps that the company can take to improve its efficiency?

LO15-5 E15-49. Balanced scorecard Management at Krazy Klothing wants to implement a balanced scorecard. The company has a single location in Seattle, Washington, and 15 employees. The primary customers are college students between 18 and 25. Clothing prices range from $10 to $150; most clothes are all-natural fibers, and all are made in the western part of the United States. The company is owned by Pam and Meg Pash. What objectives and measurements for those objectives at Krazy Klothing do you think should be included for the financial perspective of the BSC?

LO15-5 E15-50. Balanced scorecard Use the information from Exercise E15-49. What objectives and measurements for those objectives at Krazy Klothing do you think should be included for the customer perspective of the BSC?

LO15-5 E15-51. Balanced scorecard Use the information from Exercise E15-49. What objectives and measurements for those objectives at Krazy Klothing do you think should be included for the internal perspective of the BSC?

LO15-5 E15-52. Balanced scorecard Use the information from Exercise E14-49. What objectives and measurements for those objectives at Krazy Klothing do you think should be included for the sustainability perspective of the BSC?

LO15-5 E15-53. Balanced scorecard Match each of the following measures, *a* through *h*, with the most appropriate section of the balanced scorecard: (1) Learning and growth perspective, (2) Internal business perspective, (3) Customer value perspective (4) Financial performance perspective.
a. ___ Level of sales by product line
b. ___ Number of new customers
c. ___ Employee job satisfaction measured on a 5-point scale
d. ___ Number of defective products discovered in quality testing
e. ___ Average customer rating on a 5-point scale based on product satisfaction
f. ___ Administrative expenses as a percentage of sales
g. ___ Turnover of production floor employees
h. ___ Number of new product introductions

E15-54. Balanced scorecard; writing You attended a conference on the balanced scorecard last week and your manager has asked you to prepare a short report to answer the following questions.
    a. Why is a balanced scorecard used in a business?
    b. What are some benefits of a balanced scorecard approach to measuring organizational performance?
    c. What are some disadvantages of using a balanced scorecard approach?

LO15-5

E15-55. Pay plan and suboptimization Thomas Owan is a division manager of Weatfarl Inc. He is in the process of evaluating a $4,000,000 investment. The following net annual increases, before depreciation, in divisional income are expected during the investment's five-year life:

Year 1	$ 300,000
Year 2	500,000
Year 3	760,000
Year 4	3,200,000
Year 5	2,900,000

All company assets are depreciated using the straight-line method. Owan receives an annual salary of $300,000 plus a bonus of 2 percent of any divisional pre-tax profit. Before consideration of the potential investment project, he anticipates that his division will generate $4,000,000 annually in pre-tax profit.
    a. Compute the effect of the new investment on the level of divisional pre-tax profits for years 1 through 5.
    b. Determine the effect of the new project on Owan's compensation for each of the five years.
    c. Based on your computations in (b), will Owan want to invest in the new project? Explain.
    d. Would upper management likely view the new investment favorably? Explain.

LO15-6

E15-56. Compensation; goal congruence Assuming compensation is based on each of the factors listed in *a* through *e*, determine whether the mission of the related company is more aligned with a mission to build or with a mission to harvest.
    a. Compensation is distributed in restricted stock units where the employee will receive shares of the company stock after a 3-year restricted period ends.
    b. Compensation is based on variances between actual manufacturing costs and costs at standard.
    c. Compensation is based on overall company net income.
    d. Compensation is based on an average ROI over a two-year period.
    e. Compensation is fixed at $8,000 per month.

LO15-6

E15-57. Variable pay and incentives In recent years, salaries for chief financial officers (CFOs) of large U.S. corporations averaged only about 20 percent of the total CFO compensation package; the other 80 percent was performance-based, variable compensation that included mostly stock options and short-term and long-term incentive bonuses. Among major corporate officers, typically, only CEOs had a higher percentage of pay that was variable.
    a. What does the high portion of variable CFO pay indicate about the importance of CFOs to their organizations?
    b. What does the high portion of variable CFO pay indicate about the risk level tolerance of CFOs?
    c. Discuss any concerns investors should have about such a high percentage of CFO pay being variable.
    d. Discuss any concerns CFOs should have about the high percentage of pay being variable.

LO15-6

Problems

P15-58. Divisional profit The Mergers & Acquisitions Division (M&A) of Global Financial Services is evaluated by corporate management based on a comparison of budgeted and actual pre-tax profit. For the year, M&A's budgeted income statement was as follows:

Sales	$ 36,000,000
Variable costs	(25,200,000)
Contribution margin	$ 10,800,000
Fixed costs	(7,200,000)
Pre-tax profit	$ 3,600,000

LO15-2

At the end of the year, M&A's actual results were as follows:

Sales	$ 39,000,000
Variable costs	(29,230,000)
Contribution margin	$ 9,770,000
Fixed costs	(7,230,000)
Pre-tax profit	$ 2,540,000

a. Based on the preceding information, evaluate M&A's performance. What was the principal reason for the poor profit performance? How can the contribution margin ratio be used to assess the performance?

b. Why do complete income statements provide a more comprehensive basis for evaluating the profit performance of a manager than mere comparisons of the bottom lines of the budgeted and actual income statements?

LO15-2   P15-59. Statement of cash flows San Francisco Sea Salt's controller prepared the following statements of cash flow (in thousands of dollars) for the past two years, the current year (Year 3), and the upcoming year (Year 4):

	Year 1	Year 2	Year 3	Year 4 Budget
Net cash flows from operating activities				
Net income	$ 41,700	$ 39,200	$ 43,700	$ 45,100
Add net reconciling items	2,200	4,300	3,000	4,000
Total	$ 43,900	$ 43,500	$ 46,700	$ 49,100
Net cash flows from investing activities				
Purchase of plant and equipment	$(18,700)		$(12,200)	$ (4,600)
Sale (purchase) of investments	8,700	$ (3,600)	(12,600)	(15,800)
Other investing inflows	1,200	800	600	2,400
Total	$ (8,800)	$ (2,800)	$(24,200)	$(18,000)
Net cash flows from financing activities				
Payment of notes payable	$(12,000)	$(24,000)	$(15,000)	$ (7,000)
Payment of dividends	(20,000)	(7,000)	(13,300)	(20,000)
Total	$(32,000)	$(31,000)	$(28,300)	$(27,000)
Net change in cash	$ 3,100	$ 9,700	$ (5,800)	$ 4,100

After preparation of the budgeted statement of cash flows for Year 4, Lana Kaslowski, the company president, asked you to recompile it based on a separate set of facts. She is evaluating a proposal to purchase an artificial intelligence software system for the company at a total cost of $50,000. The proposal has been deemed to provide a satisfactory rate of return. However, she does not want to issue additional stock and would prefer not to borrow any more money to finance the project.

Projecting the fair value of the accumulated investments for Year 2 and Year 3 ($3,600 and $12,600) reveals an estimate that these investments could be liquidated for $18,400. Kaslowski said the investments scheduled for Year 4 could be delayed indefinitely and that dividends could be reduced to 40 percent of the budgeted amount. These are the only changes that can be made to the original forecast.

a. Evaluate the cash trends for the company during the Year 1–Year 4 period.
b. Giving effect to the preceding changes, prepare a revised Year 4 budgeted statement of cash flows and present the original and revised versions in a comparative format.
c. Based on the revised budgeted statement of cash flows, can the system be purchased if Kaslowski desires an increase in cash of at least $1,000?
d. Comment on the usefulness of the report prepared in (b) to Kaslowski.

LO15-1, 2   P15-60. Cash flow; ethics Wayne Coyle, the controller of PEI Potato Co., is disillusioned with the company's system of evaluating the performance of divisional profit centers and their managers. The present system focuses on a comparison of budgeted to actual income from operations. Coyle's major concern with the current system is the ease with which profit center managers can manipulate the measure "Income from operations." Most corporate sales are made on credit, and most purchases

Chapter 15 Performance Measurement, Balanced Scorecards, and Performance Rewards 15-57

are made on account. The profit centers are organized according to product line. Following is the second quarter income statement for one of the company's profit centers:

Sales.	$ 31,500,000
Cost of goods sold	(25,500,000)
Gross profit.	$ 6,000,000
Selling and administrative expenses	(4,500,000)
Income from operations	$ 1,500,000

Coyle has suggested that company management replace the accrual-based income from operations evaluation measure with a cash flow from operations measure. He believes this measure will be less susceptible to manipulation by profit center managers. To defend his position, he compiles a statement of cash flows for the same profit center:

Cash receipts from customers	$ 26,400,000
Cash payments for production labor, materials, and overhead.	(21,600,000)
Cash payments for selling and administrative activities	(4,200,000)
Cash flow from operations	$ 600,000

a. If Coyle is correct that profit center managers are manipulating the income measure, where are manipulations likely taking place?
b. Explain whether the proposed cash flow measure would be less subject to manipulation than the income measure.
c. Explain whether manipulation would be reduced if both the cash flow and income measures were utilized.
d. Do the cash and income measures reveal different information about profit center performance? Explain.
e. How could the existing income statement be used more effectively in evaluating performance?

P15-61. ROI; Du Pont Model; industry targets Evergreen Industries operates a chain of lumber stores. Corporate management examined industry-level data and determined the following performance targets for lumber retail stores:

LO15-3

Asset turnover	1.9
Profit margin	7.0%

The actual annual results for the company's lumber retail stores are as follows:

Total assets at beginning of year	$10,200,000
Total assets at end of year	12,300,000
Sales.	28,250,000
Operating expenses	25,885,000

a. For the year, how did the lumber retail stores perform relative to their industry norms? (Round percentages to one decimal point.)
b. Which, as indicated by the performance measures, are the most likely areas to improve performance in the retail lumber stores?
c. What are the advantages and disadvantages of setting a performance target at the start of the year compared with one that is determined at the end of the year based on actual industry performance?

P15-62. ROI; Du Pont Model RI Fashion Fabrics sells sewing and craft materials to specialty retail and department stores. For the year, the company's New York Division had the following performance targets:

LO15-3

Asset turnover	3.0
Profit margin	5.5%

Actual information concerning the performance of the New York Division for the year follows.

© Cambridge Business Publishers

Total assets at beginning of year	$ 8,400,000
Total assets at end of year	9,900,000
Sales	25,000,000
Operating expenses	23,160,000

a. For the year, did the New York Division achieve its target objectives for ROI, asset turnover, and profit margin? (Round computations to one decimal point.)

b. Which, as indicated by the performance measures, are the most likely areas to improve performance?

c. If the company has an overall target return of 13 percent, what was the New York Division's residual income for the year?

LO15-3, 6

P15-63. Adjusting income for ROI purposes; RI: ethics Imelda Sanchez, manager of the Arias Division of Poncé Chemical, is evaluated based on the division's return on investment and residual income. Near the end of November, she was reviewing the division's financial information as well as some activities projected for the remainder of the year. The information she was reviewing follows.

1. Annual sales were projected at 100,000 units, each with a selling price of $30. Sanchez has received a purchase order from a new customer for 5,000 units. The purchase order states that the units should be shipped on January 3 of next year, for arrival on January 5.
2. The division's beginning inventory was 500 units, each with a cost of $11. Purchases of 99,500 units have been made steadily throughout the year, and the per-unit cost has been constant at $10. Sanchez intends to make a purchase of 5,200 units before year-end, providing a 200-unit balance in inventory after making the shipment to the new customer. Carrying costs for the units are quite high, but ordering costs are extremely low. The division uses a last-in, first-out (LIFO) cost flow assumption for inventory.
3. Shipping expenses are $0.50 per unit sold.
4. Sanchez has just received a notice from her primary supplier that he is going out of business and is selling his remaining stock of 15,000 units for $9 each. She makes a note to herself to place her final order for the year from this supplier.
5. Division advertising is $5,000 per month for newspaper inserts and television spots. No advertising has yet been purchased for December, but Sanchez intends to have her sales manager call the paper and TV station early next week.
6. Salaries through the end of the year are projected at $700,000. This amount assumes that the position to be vacated by the division's personnel manager will be filled on December 1. The personnel manager's job pays $66,000 per year. Sanchez has an interview on Monday with an individual who appears to be a good candidate for the position.
7. Other general and administrative costs for the full year are estimated to total $590,000.
8. As Sanchez was reviewing the divisional information, she received a phone call from the division's maintenance supervisor. He informed her that $10,000 of electrical repairs to the office heating system are necessary. When asked if the repairs were essential, the supervisor replied, "No, the office won't burn down if you don't make them, but they are advisable for energy efficiency and long-term operation of the system." Sanchez tells the supervisor to see her on Monday at 8:00 A.M.

Using her information, Sanchez prepared a budgeted income statement and was fairly pleased with the division's results. Although providing the 13 percent rate of return on investment desired by corporate management, the results did not reach the 16 percent rate needed for Sanchez to receive a bonus for the year.

a. Prepare a budgeted income statement for the Arias Division for the year. Determine the division's residual income, assuming that the division has an asset investment base of $4,500,000.

b. Sanchez's less-than-scrupulous friend, John Greer, walked into the office at this time. When he heard that she was not going to receive a bonus, Greer said, "Here, let me take care of this for you." He proceeded to recompute the budgeted income statement and showed Sanchez that, based on his computation of $723,000 in income, she would receive her bonus. Prepare Greer's budgeted income statement.

c. What future difficulties might arise if Sanchez acts in a manner that will make Greer's pro forma income statement figures a reality?

LO15-2, 3

P15-64. Segment margin; ROI; RI Morton Industrial produces stamping machinery for manufacturers. Four years prior, the company expanded vertically by acquiring a supplier, Lancaster Company. Lancaster is now operated as a divisional investment center.

Morton monitors its divisions on the basis of both unit contribution and return on investment (ROI), with investment defined as average operating assets employed. Management bonuses are determined based on ROI. All investments in operating assets are expected to earn a minimum return of 10 percent before income taxes.

Lancaster's cost of goods sold is entirely variable, whereas the division's administrative expenses are totally fixed. Selling expenses are a mixed cost with 40 percent attributed to sales volume. Last year, Lancaster's ROI was 13.6 percent. During this fiscal year ended November 30, Lancaster contemplated a capital acquisition with an estimated ROI of 11.5 percent; however, division management decided that the investment would decrease Lancaster's overall ROI.

The division's operating assets employed were $15,750,000 at November 30, a 5 percent increase over the prior year-end balance. The division's income statement follows.

Lancaster Division
Income Statement
For the Fiscal Year Ended November 30
($000 omitted)

Sales revenue		$ 25,000
Less expenses		
Cost of goods sold	$16,500	
Administrative expenses	3,955	
Selling expenses	2,700	(23,155)
Income from operations before income taxes		$ 1,845

a. Calculate the segment margin for the Lancaster Division, assuming that 1,484,000 units were produced and sold during the year ended November 30.
b. Calculate the following performance measures for the year for the Lancaster Division:
  1. pre-tax ROI and
  2. residual income calculated on the basis of average operating assets employed.
c. Explain why the management of the Lancaster Division would have been more likely to accept the contemplated capital acquisition if residual income rather than ROI were used as a performance measure.
d. Identify several items that Lancaster should control if it is to be evaluated fairly by either the ROI or residual income performance measures.

P15-65. Decisions based on ROI and RI Miami Marine uses ROI to evaluate the performance of both its Powerboat and Sailboat Division managers. The following estimates of relevant measures have been made for the upcoming year:

	Powerboats	Sailboats	Total Company
Sales	$18,000,000	$48,000,000	$66,000,000
Expenses	16,200,000	42,000,000	58,200,000
Divisional assets	15,000,000	30,000,000	45,000,000

Both division managers have the autonomy to make decisions regarding new investments. The Powerboats manager is considering investing in a new asset that would generate a 14 percent ROI; the Sailboats manager is considering an investment that would generate an 18 percent ROI.

a. Compute the projected ROI for each division, disregarding the contemplated new investments.
b. Based on your answer in (a), which manager is likely to actually invest in the additional assets under consideration?
c. Are the outcomes of the investment decisions in (b) likely to be consistent with overall corporate goals? Explain.
d. If the company evaluated the division managers' performances using a residual income measure with a target return of 15 percent, would the outcomes of the investment decisions be different from those described in (b)? Explain.

P15-66. EVA As one of the division managers for Premier Inc., your performance is evaluated primarily on a single measure: after-tax divisional segment income less the cost of capital invested in divisional assets. The fair value of invested capital in your division is $20,000,000, the required return on capital is 10 percent, and the tax rate is 40 percent. Income projections for the year follow.

Sales	$ 30,000,000
Expenses	(26,250,000)
Segment income	$ 3,750,000
Taxes	(1,500,000)
After-tax segment income	$ 2,250,000

You are considering an investment in a new product line that would, according to projections, increase pre-tax segment income by $600,000. The investment cost is not yet determinable because negotiations about several factors are still under way.

   a. Ignoring the new investment, what is your projected EVA for the year?
   b. In light of your answer in (a), what is the maximum amount that you would be willing to invest in the new product line?
   c. Assuming that the new product line would require an investment of $3,100,000, what would be the revised projected EVA for your division if the investment were made?

LO15-4 **P15-67. Throughput** Justin Fawber is a divisional manager within GPS Guidance Systems. Fawber is concerned about the amount of the division's production. The following production data are available for April:

Total units completed	1,023,000
Total good units completed and sold	838,860
Total value-added hours of processing time	18,600
Total hours of processing time	62,000

Determine each of the following for this division for April.

   a. What is the manufacturing cycle efficiency?
   b. What is the process productivity?
   c. What is the process quality yield?
   d. What is the total throughput per hour? (Round to one decimal point.)
   e. If only 660,000 of the units produced in April had been sold, would your answers to any of the preceding questions differ? If so, how? If not, why not? (Round to one decimal point.)
   f. If Fawber can eliminate 20 percent of the NVA (non-value added) time, how would throughput per hour for these data differ? (Round to one decimal point.)
   g. If Fawber can increase quality output to a yield of 90 percent and eliminate 20 percent of the NVA time, how would throughput per hour for these data differ? (Round to one decimal point.)
   h. How would Fawber determine how the NVA time was being spent in the division? What suggestions do you have for decreasing NVA time and increasing yield?

LO15-1 **P15-68. Providing feedback on performance; writing** Terry Travers is the manufacturing supervisor of the Aurora Manufacturing Company, which produces a variety of plastic products. Some of these products are standard items that are listed in the company's catalog, whereas others are made to customer specifications. Each month, Travers receives a performance report displaying the budget for the month, the actual activity for the period, and the variance between budget and actual. Part of Travers's annual performance evaluation is based on his department's performance against budget. Aurora's purchasing manager, Bob Christensen, also receives monthly performance reports and is evaluated in part on the basis of these reports.

The most recent monthly reports were just distributed when Travers met Christensen in the hallway outside their offices. Travers began the conversation, "I see we have another set of monthly performance reports indicating that our performance is down again."

Christensen: "Yes, and I'll have to spend a lot of time reviewing the report and preparing explanations. The worst part is that the information is almost a month old, and we spend all this time on history."

Travers: "My biggest problem is that our production activity varies a lot from month to month, but we're given an annual budget that's written in stone. Last month, we were shut down for three

Chapter 15 Performance Measurement, Balanced Scorecards, and Performance Rewards

days when a strike delayed delivery of the basic material used in our plastic formulation, and we had already exhausted our inventory. When we got what we needed from an alternate supplier on a rush basis, we had to pay more than we normally do."

Christensen: "I expect problems like that to pop up from time to time—that's part of my job—but now we'll both have to take a careful look at the report to see where charges are reflected for that rush order. Every month, I spend more time making sure I should be charged for each item reported than I do making plans for my department's daily work. It's really frustrating to see charges for things I have no control over."

Travers: "The way we get information doesn't help, either. I don't get copies of the reports you get, yet a lot of what I do is affected by your department, and by most of the other departments we have."

Christensen: "I seem to get more reports than I need, and I am never asked to comment until top management calls me about my department's shortcomings. Do you ever hear comments when your department shines?"

Travers: "I guess they don't have time to review the good news. One of my problems is that all the reports are in dollars and cents. I work with people, machines, and materials. I need information to help me solve this month's problems—not another report of the dollars expended last month or the month before."

a. Based on the conversation between Travers and Christensen, describe the likely motivation and behavior of these two employees resulting from Aurora Manufacturing Company's performance reporting system.
b. 1. When performance reporting systems have been properly implemented, both employees and companies should benefit from them. Describe the benefits that can be realized from using a performance reporting system.
2. Based on the situation presented here, recommend ways for Aurora Manufacturing Company to improve its performance system to increase employee motivation.

P15-69. Performance measurement; BSC For each of the following items, indicate two performance measurements that could be obtained from a cost management system. Classify each item into one of the four balanced scorecard perspectives.   LO15-4, 5

a. Quality
b. Cost
c. Production line flexibility
d. People productivity and development
e. Inventory management
f. Lead time
g. Responsive after-sales service
h. Customer satisfaction and retention
i. Product and process design
j. Manufacturing planning process
k. Procurement process
l. Manufacturing process
m. Management accomplishments
n. Marketing/sales and customer service
o. Delivery performance
p. Financial accounting services

P15-70. Balanced scorecard Assume that management at Subway has decided to implement a balanced scorecard for the organization. Visit the company's site map at http://www.subway.com/subway root/sitemap.aspx. Using the information there as well as other information you can obtain from the Internet, prepare a balanced scorecard for the organization.   LO15-5

P15-71. Balanced scorecard; writing You have been elected president of your university's newly chartered accounting honor society. The society is a chapter of a national organization that has the following mission: "To promote the profession of accountancy as a career and to imbue members with high ethical standards."   LO15-5

a. Determine the balanced scorecard categories that you believe would be appropriate for the honor society.
b. Under each category, determine between four and six important performance measures.
c. How would you choose benchmarks against which to compare your chapter to others of the national organization?

P15-72. Balanced scorecard; research; writing One of the fundamental performance measurements in an organization's balanced scorecard learning and growth perspective is the number of patents obtained. The following schedule shows the total U.S. patents issued for 2022.   LO15-5

Company	Total Patents
1. Samsung	6,248
2. IBM	4,398
3. Taiwan Semiconductor	3,024
4. Huawei	2,836
5. Canon	2,694
6. LG	2,641
7. Qualcomm	2,625
8. Intel	2,418
9. Apple	2,285
10. Toyota	2,214

Source: J. Koetsler, "Samsung Beats IBM, Apple, Intel, Google For 2022 Patent Crown; 56% Of U.S. Patents Go To Foreign Firms," Forbes (January 14, 2023); https://www.forbes.com/sites/johnkoetsier/2023/01/14/samsung-beats-ibm-apple-intel-google-for-2022-patent-crown-56-of-us-patents-go-to-foreign-firms/?sh=270bcece1891.

In a team of three or four people, research these companies on the web and prepare a written report on their financial performance, customers' perceptions of their service and product quality, and manufacturing operations (such as level of automation in plants).

P15-73. Balanced scorecard; government As part of the mayor's advisory team, you are to develop a balanced scorecard for Hogwart City, which has a population of 65,000. The city's strategic themes are planning and community development, sustainability, resource management, and community safety. The city has decided that the perspectives it desires in its BSC are financial, customer, and internal processes. Prepare a BSC for Hogwart City that includes at least three goals and measurements in each category.

P15-74. Balanced scorecard; EVA; writing Chesterville Manufacturing makes a variety of glass products having both commercial and household applications. One of its newest divisions, ColOptics, manufactures fiber optic cable and other high-tech products. Recent annual operating results (in millions) for ColOptics and two older divisions follow.

	ColOptics	Industrial Glass	Kitchenware
Sales	$500	$1,800	$1,500
Segment income	50	184	170

Chesterville Manufacturing uses economic value added (EVA) as its only segment performance measure. Clare Cole, CEO of Chesterville, posed some serious questions in a memo to the controller, Doug Larsen, after studying the operating results.

> *Doug:*
> *I'm concerned about ColOptics. Its key competitor's sales and market share are growing at about twice the pace of ColOptics. I'm not comforted by the fact that ColOptics is generating substantially more profits than the competitor. The mission we have established for ColOptics is high growth. Do you think we should use EVA to measure the division's performance and as a basis to compensate ColOptics' divisional management? Do we need to change our performance criteria?*

After pondering the memo and studying the operating results, Larsen passed the memo and operating results to you, his newest employee in the controller's office, and asked you to respond to the following questions:

a. Why would the use of EVA discourage a high-growth strategy?
b. Could the concept of the balanced scorecard be used to encourage a higher rate of growth in ColOptics? Explain.

P15-75. Balanced scorecard; research; writing As the cost of health care continues to increase, hospital and clinic managers need to be able to evaluate the performance of their organizations. Numerous articles have been written on performance measurements for health-care organizations. Obtain some of these articles and prepare a report on what you believe to be the best set of balanced scorecard measures for such organizations.

P15-76. Balanced scorecard The Coca-Cola Company has taken sustainability to heart by specifying seven core areas in which to set goals and measure progress. Review the company's 2022 Business and Sustainability Report at https://www.coca-colacompany.com/content/dam/company/us/en/reports/coca-cola-business-sustainability-report-2022.pdf

 a. Which three of the six 2022 sustainability goal topics do you think are most important to the company's long-term success? Why did you choose these three?
 b. At the time the report was issued, Coca-Cola operated in more than 200 countries and territories. Do you think the sustainability goals and measures might be more difficult to attain in some countries than in others? Explain your answer.

P15-77. Balanced scorecard; sustainability Go to http://www.carbonfootprint.com/calculator.aspx to compute your approximate carbon footprint. What goals and measurements would you put on a balanced scorecard to reduce the size of that footprint?

P15-78. Performance evaluation; ethics; writing In September, Lyon Precision Corporation (LPC) decided to launch an expansion plan for some product lines. To finance this expansion, the firm has decided to issue $400,000,000 of new common stock in November.

Historically, the firm's innovative smartphone was a significant contributor to corporate profits. However, a competitor has recently introduced its new generation of smartphones that has rendered LPC's smartphone obsolete. The controller has informed LPC's president that the inventory value of the smartphones needs to be reduced to its net realizable value. Because LPC has a large inventory of the smartphones in stock, the write-down will have a detrimental effect on both the balance sheet and income statement.

The president, whose compensation is determined in part by corporate profits and in part by stock price, has suggested that the write-downs be deferred until January of the following year. He argues that, by deferring the write-down, existing shareholders will realize more value from the shares to be sold in November because the stock market will not be informed of the pending write-downs.

 a. What effects are the performance evaluation measures of the president likely to have on his decision to defer the write-down of the obsolete inventory?
 b. Is the president's decision to defer the write-down of the inventory an ethical treatment of existing shareholders? Of potential new shareholders?
 c. If you were the controller of Lyon Precision Corporation, how would you respond to the president's decision to defer the write-down until after issuance of the new stock?

P15-79. Pay plans and goal congruence The lead story in your college newspaper reports the details of the hiring of the current football coach. The previous football coach was fired for failing to win games and attract fans. In his last season, his record was 1 win and 11 losses. The news story states that the new coach's contract provides for a base salary of $600,000 per year plus an annual bonus computed as follows:

Win less than five games	$ 0
Win five to seven games	75,000
Win eight games or more	150,000
Win eight games and conference championship	250,000
Win eight games, win conference, and get a bowl bid	350,000

The coach's contract has essentially no other features or clauses.

The first year after the new coach is hired, the football team wins three games and loses eight. In the second year, the team wins six games and loses five. In the third year, the team wins nine games, wins the conference championship, and is invited to a prestigious bowl. Shortly after the bowl game, articles appear on the front page of several national sports publications announcing that your college's football program has been cited by the National Collegiate Athletic Association (NCAA) for nine major rule violations including cash payoffs to players, playing academically ineligible players, illegal recruiting tactics, illegal involvement of alumni in recruiting, and so on. The national news publications agree that the NCAA will disband your college's football program. One article also mentions that during the past three years, only 13 percent of senior football players managed to graduate on time. Additional speculation suggests that the responsible parties, including the coaching staff, athletic director, and college president, will be dismissed by the board of trustees.

 a. Compute the amount of compensation paid to the new coach in each of his first three years.
 b. Did the performance measures in the coach's contract foster goal congruence? Explain.

c. Would the coach's actions have been different if other performance measures had been added to the compensation contract? Explain.
d. What performance measures should be considered for the next coach's contract, assuming the football program is allowed to continue?

LO15-6 **P15-80. Compensation; ethics; research; writing** American firms increasingly adopt stock compensation plans to compensate mid- to high-level managers. Companies are motivated to use stock options and restricted stock units as a large portion of the compensation mix because boards of directors view stock options and restricted stock units as aligning manager and stockholder interests better than most other forms of compensation. Research the linkage between reported accounting abuses (e.g., manipulating reported earnings) and the increased use of stock options and restricted stock units for managerial compensation. Discuss your findings.

LO15-1, 6 **P15-81. Performance evaluation; compensation; ethics; writing** A survey of U.S. chief financial officers provided compelling evidence that managers are willing to take extraordinary measures to achieve financial earnings targets. For example, the survey found 26 percent were willing to sacrifice some long-term value of the firm to achieve short-term earnings goals. Further, 55 percent were willing to delay the start of new projects to achieve higher earnings, and 80 percent indicated they would reduce spending on research and development to achieve short-term earnings targets.

Source: J. R. Graham, C. R. Harvey, and S. Rajgopal, "The Economic Implications of Corporate Financial Reporting," *Journal of Accounting and Economics* 40 (2005), pp. 3–73.

a. Discuss the ethics of managers forfeiting long-term value of their firms to achieve short-term earnings goals and earn higher short-term compensation.
b. How can boards of directors create incentives and performance measures that will discourage top managers from optimizing reported short-run performance at the expense of long-term performance?

LO15-1, 3, 6 **P15-82. Performance and compensation** Family Fun Vehicle Co. (FFV), a subsidiary of Drummondville Automotive, manufactures go-carts and other recreational vehicles. Family recreational centers that feature go-cart tracks, miniature golf, batting cages, paint ball wars, and arcade games have increased in popularity. As a result, FFV has been receiving some pressure from Drummondville Automotive top management to diversify into some of these other recreational areas. Great Games Inc. (GGI), one of the largest firms that leases arcade games to family recreation centers, is looking for a friendly buyer. Drummondville Automotive management believes that GGI's assets could be acquired for an investment of $6.4 million and has strongly urged Sam Peach, division manager of FFV, to consider acquiring GGI.

Peach has reviewed GGI's financial statements with his controller, Molly Howe, and they believe that the acquisition may not be in FFV's best interests. "If we decide not to do this, the Drummondville Automotive people are not going to be happy," said Peach. "If we could convince them to base our bonuses on something other than return on investment, maybe this acquisition would look more attractive. How would we do if the bonuses were based on residual income using the company's 15 percent cost of capital?"

Drummondville Automotive has traditionally evaluated all of its divisions on the basis of return on investment, which is defined as the ratio of operating income to total assets; the desired rate of return for each division is 20 percent. The management team of any division reporting an annual increase in the return on investment is automatically eligible for a bonus. The management of divisions reporting a decline in the return on investment must provide convincing explanations for the decline to be eligible for a bonus, and this bonus is limited to 50 percent of the bonus paid to divisions reporting an increase. Presented below are condensed financial statements for both FFV and GGI for the fiscal year ended May 31.

	FFV	GGI
Sales revenue	$ 21,000,000	
Leasing revenue		$ 5,600,000
Variable expenses	(14,000,000)	(2,000,000)
Fixed expenses	(3,000,000)	(2,400,000)
Operating income	$ 4,000,000	$ 1,200,000
Current assets	$ 4,600,000	$ 3,800,000
Long-term assets	11,400,000	2,600,000
Total assets	$ 16,000,000	$ 6,400,000
Current liabilities	$ 2,800,000	$ 1,900,000
Long-term liabilities	7,600,000	2,600,000
Shareholders' equity	5,600,000	1,900,000
Total liabilities and shareholders' equity	$ 16,000,000	$ 6,400,000

a. Under the present bonus system, how would the acquisition of GGI affect Peach's bonus expectations? (Round percentages to one decimal.)
b. If Peach's suggestion to use residual income as the evaluation criterion is accepted, how would acquisition of GGI affect Peach's bonus expectations?
c. Given the present bonus arrangement, is it fair for Drummondville Automotive management to expect Peach to acquire GGI?
d. Is the present bonus system consistent with Drummondville Automotive's goal of expansion of FFV into new recreational products?

Review Solutions

Review 15-1

1. a. Internal; production/performance
   b. External; customers
   c. Internal; employees
   d. Internal; sustainability
   e. External; Investors and creditors
   f. External; sustainability

2. The only performance measure that would be included as part of the financial statement preparation process is part e, tracking the amount of revenue each period. This means that specific tracking mechanisms and related controls must be implemented for any of the other measures used. Thus, given a company's limited resources, it is important that the measures chosen truly indicate whether or not the company is advancing its mission. For instance, if a company's mission is high quality service, measuring the rate of on-time deliveries is likely an indicator that the company is advancing that mission.

Review 15-2

a.
Sales	$453,000
Direct variable operating expenses	225,000
Contribution margin	228,000
Direct fixed costs	160,000
Segment margin	68,000
Allocated fixed costs	17,000
Segment income	$ 51,000

b.
Contribution margin	$228,000
Sales	÷ $453,000
Contribution margin ratio	50% (rounded)

c.

Segment margin．．．．．．．．．．．．．．．．．．．．．．．．．．．．．	$ 68,000
Sales．．	÷ $453,000
Segment profit margin ratio．．．．．．．．．．．．．．．．．．	15% (rounded)

d. The answers to parts *a*, *b*, and *c* would not change if the segment were a profit center instead of an investment center. However, because it is an investment center, calculating additional ratios (as explained in the next section), will be necessary as the segment report above does not take into account the underlying asset investment.

Review 15-3

a. 36.8% = ($453,000 − $225,000 − $160,000) ÷ $185,000*
   *$185,000 = ($190,000 + $180,000)/2
b. 15.0% = ($453,000 − $225,000 − $160,000) ÷ $453,000
c. 2.45 = $453,000 ÷ $185,000
d. 36.8% = 15.0% × 2.45
e. $45,800 = ($453,000 − $225,000 − $160,000) − (12% × $185,000)
f. $34,680 = [($453,000 − $225,000 − $160,000) × (1 − 0.21)] − (8% × $238,000)
g. The investment center has an ROI of 36.8 percent. However, if assets were instead defined as average fair value of invested capital, the ROI would be lower at 28.6% (=$68,000 ÷ $238,000). This illustrates how an investment center is more apt to keep older assets if its performance is measured on ROI, calculated using the book value of assets.

   The company also has a positive RI and EVA at $45,800 and $34,680 respectively. Both measures indicate that the operations segment is favorable.

   Additional data that would be helpful are the budgeted levels, prior year results, and industry averages of each of the following: ROI, profit margin, asset turnover, RI, and EVA. Also, the asset utilization percentage could be helpful in analyzing the asset turnover ratio.

Review 15-4

a. 42.2% = 22,900 ÷ 54,230
b. 8.2 units per hour = 188,475 ÷ 22,900
c. 79.9% = 150,650 ÷ 188,475
d. 2.8 units per hour = 150,650 ÷ 54,230
e. The process quality yield can be improved by moving toward a goal of zero defects. The failure rate appears high at 20.1 percent, which implies that 2 out of every 10 units are defective.

Review 15-5

a.

Objective	Perspective	Performance Measurements
Decrease use of water for manufacturing process	Sustainability	Gallons of water used for manufacturing process
Improve customer perception of product quality	Customer	Product returns as a percentage of sales
Improve responsible sourcing of raw materials	Sustainability	Percentage of products supplied from sustainable sources
Improve satisfaction of customer	Customer	Customer survey ratings
Increase employee efficiency with technology	Learning and Growth	Hours of employee IT training
Increase income generated from assets	Financial	Return on investment
Increase participation by employees	Learning and Growth	Number of implemented suggestions submitted by employees
Increase market share	Customer	Sales as a percentage of total market sales
Increase number of new products released	Learning and Growth	Number of new products released per quarter
Increase production process quality	Internal business	Number of reworked products divided by total units produced
Increase revenue of specified products	Financial	Revenue for specified products
Increase satisfaction of employees	Learning and Growth	Employee satisfaction surveys
Increase throughput	Internal business	Manufacturing cycle efficiency
Reduce nonrecyclable packaging	Sustainability	Number of products with 100% recyclable packaging
Reduce selling variable cost per unit	Financial	Variable unit cost

b. A key feature of the balanced scorecard is that it includes performance measurements that map to the company's mission. Thus, a balanced scorecard is adapted to the individual company's mission. In addition, industries and markets are unique, as well as the product or service that a company provides. Performance measurements are tailored for the unique set of circumstances. For example, a balanced scorecard for a manufacturer will include different measures than that of a service provider. Or, a company competing in a competitive market place will be focused on different metrics than that of a company with a differentiated product/service without heavy competition.

Review 15-6
1. *a.* harvest   *b.* harvest   *c.* build   *d.* build   *e.* harvest
2. The trend of executive compensation paid should match trends in a company's progress toward achieving its goals/mission. If a company's strategy is to build, increasing trends in executive compensation should correlate with increasing trends in sales and profits due to expansionary activity such as new product lines, business acquisitions, capital acquisitions, etc. However, if the company's strategy is to harvest, increasing trends in executive compensation should correlate with cost reductions due to manufacturing efficiencies, continuous improvement activity, design improvements of current products, etc.

Data Visualization Solutions

(See page 15-18.)

a. Division 2 had more favorable results. Even though it had a lower segment margin, it was more efficient and effective in using its assets, evidenced by a positive residual income and a higher ROI.

b. The segment margin does not indicate the sales value. For example, a higher segment margin does not necessarily mean the company had higher sales--it could have had lower sales, but less relative expenses. Therefore, there is not enough information to discern which company had the higher sales.

c. Division 1: RI = Segment Income − (Target rate × Assets)
   $450,000 = $1,800,000 − (15% × Assets)
   Assets = $15,000,000

   Division 2: RI = Segment Income − (Target rate × Assets)
   $100,000 = $1,600,000 − (15% × Assets)
   Assets = $10,000,000

Chapter 16

Approaches to Cost Control and Managing Uncertainty

Road Map

LO	Learning Objective | Topics	Page	eLecture	Demo	Review	Assignments
16–1	**What are the functions of a cost control system?** Cost Control System :: Preventive :: Corrective :: Diagnostic :: Planning Phase :: Time to Market :: Strategic Alliances with Suppliers :: Control Phase	16-2	e16–1	D16-1	Rev 16-1	MC16-13, E16-22, E16-23, E16-24, E16-25, E16-26, P16-56, P16-57, P16-58, P16-59
16–2	**What factors cause costs to change from period to period or to deviate from expectations?** Cost Consciousness :: Cost Understanding :: Volume Changes :: Flexible Budget :: Inflation/Deflation :: General Price-Level Changes :: Consumer Price Index :: Supply/Supplier Cost Adjustments :: Price Elasticity :: Quantity Purchased	16-5	e16–2	D16-2	Rev 16-2	MC16-14, MC16-15, E16-27, E16-28, E16-30, E16-31, E16-32, P16-59, P16-60
16–3	**What are the generic approaches to cost control?** Cost Containment :: Cost Avoidance :: Cost Reduction :: Benchmarking :: Outsourcing :: Implementing a Cost Control System :: Spend Analysis	16-9	e16–3	D16-3	Rev 16-3	MC16-16, E16-23, E16-29, E16-36, E16-37, P16-56, P16-59, P16-60, P16-67
16–4	**What are the two primary types of fixed costs, and what are the characteristics of each?** Committed Fixed Costs :: Discretionary Fixed Costs	16-13	e16–4	D16-4	Rev 16-4	MC16-17, E16-38, E16-39, P16-67
16–5	**What are the typical approaches to controlling discretionary fixed costs?** Planning :: Discretionary Cost Appropriation :: Budgeting :: Measuring Benefits :: Controlling :: Efficiency and Effectiveness Measures :: Engineered Cost Variances :: Flexible Budget Variance Analysis	16-15	e16–5	D16-5A D16-5B D16-5C	Rev 16-5	MC16-18, E16-22, E16-40, E16-41, E16-42, E16-43, E16-44, P16-61, P16-62, P16-63, P16-67
16–6	**What are the objectives managers strive to accomplish in managing cash?** Optimal Cash Level :: Sources of Cash :: Working Capital :: Cash Conversion Cycle :: Days Sales in Inventory :: Days Sales in Receivables :: Days Payable :: e-Procurement Systems :: Cost of Carrying Cash :: Banking Relationships	16-23	e16–6	D16-6	Rev 16-6	MC16-19, MC16-20, E16-45, E16-46, E16-47, E16-48, E16-49, E16-50, P16-64, P16-65, P16-66, P16-68
16–7	**What are the four generic approaches to managing uncertainty?** Uncertainty :: Regression Analysis :: Coefficient of Determination :: Sensitivity Analysis :: Degree of Operating Leverage :: Options and Forward Contract :: Hedging :: Insurance	16-29	e16–7	D16-7	Rev 16-7	MC16-21, E16-51, E16-52, E16-53, E16-54, E16-55, P16-69, P16-70, P16-71, **DA16-1**

© Cambridge Business Publishers

16-1

INTRODUCTION

This chapter presents a variety of topics that explain some of the key contributions of accounting and finance specialists to business organizations. The discussion begins with a description of cost control systems and general cost management strategies. While companies should always strive for cost efficiencies, companies tend to become more focused on cost controls when faced with uncertain economic times, such as high inflationary conditions or pending economic downturns. The discussion then turns to the responsibilities and tools of the treasury function including cash management and the importance of monitoring cash budgets and liquidity ratios. The chapter concludes with a presentation of methods and tools for dealing with uncertainty in budgeting and cost management.

FUNCTIONS OF A COST CONTROL SYSTEM

LO16-1 What are the functions of a cost control system?

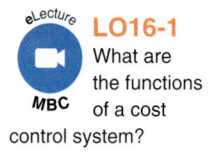

An integral part of the overall organizational decision support system is the **cost control system**, which is the set of formal and informal tools and methods designed to manage organizational costs. This system focuses on intraorganizational information and contains the detector, assessor, effector, and network components discussed in Chapter 13. Relative to the cost management system, the cost control system provides information for planning and control from the point activities are being planned until after they are performed, as indicated in **Exhibit 16.1**. **Preventive** functions include budgeting and standard setting before an event. **Corrective** functions include monitoring and correction during an event. **Diagnostic** functions include analysis and the providing of feedback after an event.

Exhibit 16.1 Functions of an Effective Cost Control System

Control Point	Reason	Cost Control Method
Before an event	Preventive • Reflects planning	Budgeting and standard setting methods
During an event	Corrective • Ensures that the event is being pursued according to plans • Allows management to correct problems as they occur	Monitoring and correcting methods
After an event	Diagnostic • Guides future actions	Analysis and feedback methods

DEMO 16-1 LO16-1 Identifying Functions of a Cost Control System

◆ Are the following cost control methods classified as preventive, corrective, or diagnostic?

a.	Establishing budgets	**Preventive**
b.	Providing feedback after variance analysis is complete	**Diagnostic**
c.	Continual comparison of activities and costs against budgets	**Corrective**
d.	Periodic monitoring of ongoing activities	**Corrective**
e.	Setting policies for the approval for deviations from standard costs	**Preventive**
f.	Establishing ethical guidelines	**Preventive**
g.	Discussing responsibility report with segment manager	**Diagnostic**
h.	Avoidance of excessive expenditures	**Corrective**
i.	Expressing qualitative objectives	**Preventive**
j.	Establishing standard costs	**Preventive**

The general planning and control model in **Exhibit 16.2** illustrates that control is part of a management cycle that begins with planning. Without first preparing organizational plans (such as the budgets discussed in Chapter 9), control cannot be achieved because no operational targets and objectives have been established. The planning phase establishes performance targets that become the inputs to the control phase. Cost control however, starts in the product/service design stage, even before budgets are established.

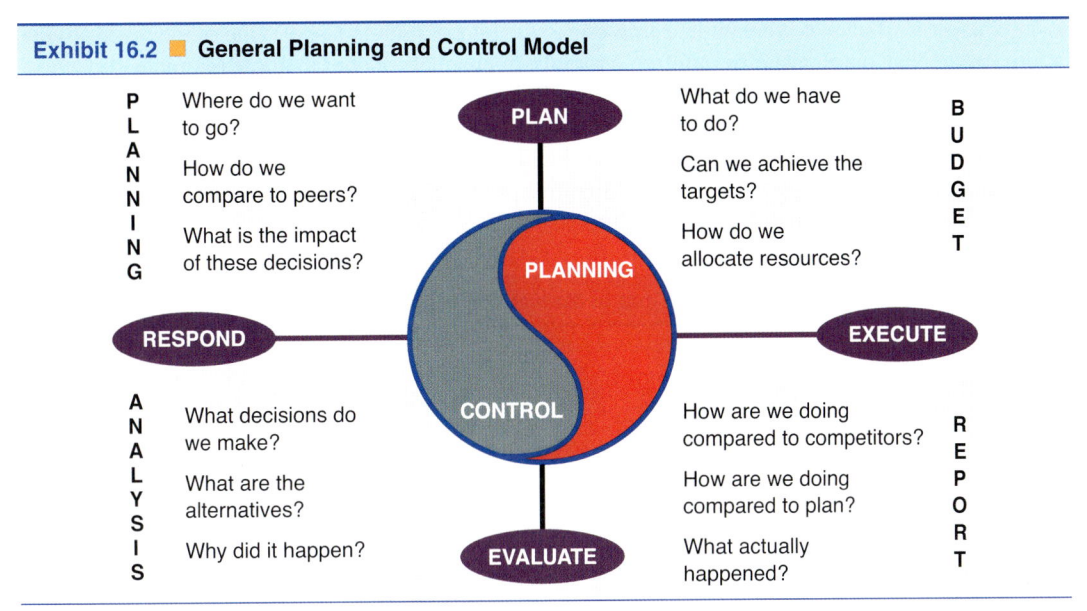

Exhibit 16.2 ■ General Planning and Control Model

PLANNING
- Where do we want to go?
- How do we compare to peers?
- What is the impact of these decisions?

PLAN
- What do we have to do?
- Can we achieve the targets?
- How do we allocate resources?

BUDGET

RESPOND

EXECUTE

ANALYSIS
- What decisions do we make?
- What are the alternatives?
- Why did it happen?

EVALUATE
- How are we doing compared to competitors?
- How are we doing compared to plan?
- What actually happened?

REPORT

Source: Kathryn Jehle, "Budgeting as a Competitive Advantage," *Strategic Finance* (October 1999), p. 57. Copyright 1999 by Institute of Management Accountants. Reproduced with permission of Institute of Management Accountants in the format Textbook via Copyright Clearance Center.

Cost Control Implications in the Planning Phase

Manufacturing and service firms have aggressively adopted advanced technology, which creates substantial costs associated with the plant, equipment, and infrastructure investments that provide the capacity to produce goods and services. These costs are higher in industries that depend on technology for competing on the basis of quality and price.

Reducing Time to Market

In pursuing either a differentiation or cost leadership strategy, the management of high technology costs requires beating competitors to the market with new products. Being first to market can enable a company to set a price that leads to a larger market share and, in turn, an industry position of cost leader. Alternatively, the leading-edge company can set a product price that provides a substantial per-unit profit for all sales generated before competitors are able to offer alternative products. For example, when first introduced, Apple's iPhone had no direct competing product. Only years later did the iPhone have competing offerings. Time to market is critical in the high-tech industry because profitability depends on selling an adequate number of units at an acceptable price. Because per-unit prices in the technology sector have been falling steadily for years, getting a new product to the market late can be disastrous.

Monitoring the external environment is a key activity to manage revenues and costs over the longer term. For instance, the evolution of social media has created new channels for product distribution, advertising, customer outreach, and market intelligence. Failure to stay abreast of market and technology trends may lead to business model stagnation and lost opportunities to improve cost management and generate new revenues.

"Faster time to market and shorter product life cycles are pushing companies into more frequent product transitions, requiring managers to confront the potential rewards and challenges associated with product introductions and phaseouts."[1] Missing the "right" time to provide a product to customers may also mean missing the "best" price at which that product can be sold.

Getting products to market quickly and profitably requires a compromise between product innovation and superior product design. Rapid time to market could mean that a firm incurs costs (such as engineering changes) associated with design flaws that could have been avoided if more time had been

---
[1] Feryal Erhun, Paulo Gonçalves, and Jay Hopman, "The Art of Managing New Product Transitions," *MIT Sloan Management Review* (Spring 2007), p. 73.

allowed for the product's development. This situation was evident when the **Samsung** Galaxy Note 7 was released in August of 2016, only to have production permanently halted two months later. The issue was due to a battery malfunction which caused the phone to generate excessive heat and to combust. As a result all phones were under recall due to the phone's safety issues. One of the results of the failure was to push out Samsung's timeframe for introducing new phones to allow for quality updates.[2]

When a flawed product is marketed, costs will likely be incurred for returns, warranty work, or customer "bad will" regarding the firm's reputation for product quality. Time to market is important because of the competitive advantages it offers and because of compressed product life cycles. The faster a product gets to market, the fewer competitive products will exist; consequently, a greater market share can be captured (see **Exhibit 16.3**).

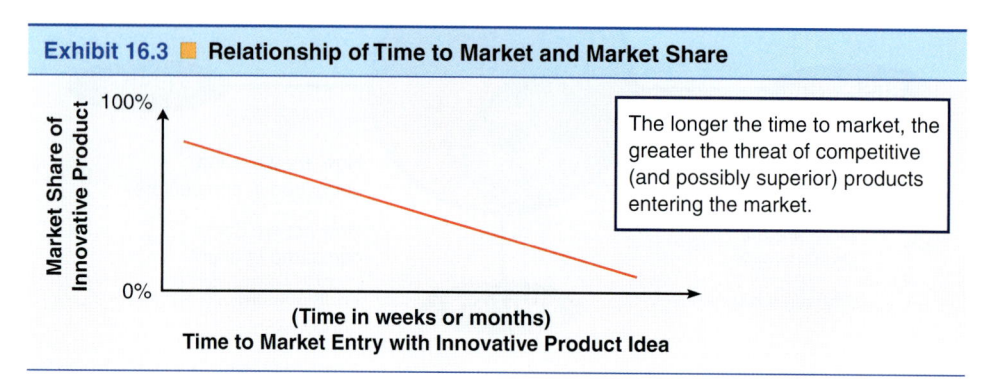

Exhibit 16.3 ■ Relationship of Time to Market and Market Share

The longer the time to market, the greater the threat of competitive (and possibly superior) products entering the market.

Other Preventive Actions

Reducing time to market is one way a company can cut costs; other preventive techniques are indicated in **Exhibit 16.4**. Most actions to reduce product cost are associated with the *early product life cycle stages*. Thus, product profitability is largely determined by an effective design and development process.

Exhibit 16.4 ■ Preventive Actions to Substantially Reduce Product Costs

- Use target costing to reduce non-value-added activities
- Standardize product parts and processes
- Reduce variability of processes
- Increase product and process quality
- Manufacture products to order
- Design products to limit engineering change orders
- Implement new technologies
- Outsource non-core competencies
- Train employees to obtain learning curve effects
- Develop long-term and sole-source supplier relationships
- Stress the importance of a quality culture

Supplier Strategic Alliances

Supplier relationships constitute another aspect of an organization's operating environment that impacts cost controls. Many companies that have formed strategic alliances with suppliers have found such relationships to be effective cost control mechanisms. For example, by involving suppliers early in the design and development stages of new products, a company should achieve a better design for manufacturability and improve the likelihood of meeting cost targets.

The traditional supply chain structure had clear distinctions between supplier and customer firms—there were no "fuzzy boundaries" that created an inability to determine where one firm ended its contribution to the supply chain and another began its contribution. Now, however, companies often have incentives to develop interorganizational agreements that go beyond normal supplier/customer arrangements. Generically, these agreements are called **strategic alliances**, which reflect agreements involving two or more firms with complementary core competencies to jointly contribute to the supply chain.

---

[2] M. Lopez, "Samsung Explains Note 7 Battery Explosions, And Turns Crisis Into Opportunity," *Forbes*, January 22, 2017, https://www.forbes.com/sites/maribellopez/2017/01/22/samsung-reveals-cause-of-note-7-issue-turns-crisis-into-opportunity/?sh=466c30c124f1. Accessed November 10, 2023.

Strategic alliances can take many forms including joint ventures, equity investments, licensing, joint R&D arrangements, technology swaps, and exclusive buyer/seller agreements. A strategic alliance differs from the usual interactions between (or among) independent firms in that the output produced reflects a joint effort between (or among) the firms and the rewards of that effort are split between (or among) the allied firms. For example, GlaxoSmithKline collaborated with Propeller Health (a technology startup company) to track the use of inhalers using sensor technology, in order to reduce health care cost and increase market share.[3]

The strategic alliance is typical of many other business arrangements. A strategic alliance

- involves the exploitation of partner knowledge,
- includes partners with access to different markets, and
- allows sharing of risks and rewards.

Strategic alliances allow companies to collaborate and attract new customers, often resulting in the creation of a new entity.

A typical strategic alliance involves the creation of a new entity. In structuring the new entity, the contributions required of the parent organizations must be determined. Beyond simply contributing cash, many new ventures will require inputs of human capital, technology, access to distribution channels, patents, and supply contracts. Furthermore, a governing board or set of directors must be established for the entity, and agreement must be reached as to how many directors can be appointed by each parent. Composition of the governing board determines which of the "parents" is more influential in managing the new entity. Simultaneous agreements must be executed to express the parent organizations' rights in sharing gains and to specify obligations for bearing losses. Such agreements will have significant implications for the risks borne by the parent companies.

As discussed in this section and in prior chapters, product/service costs are heavily influenced by actions that take place in the planning phase. Going forward in this chapter, we focus primarily on cost controls that take place during the control phase, which follows the planning phase.

Identifying Functions in a Cost Control System **LO16-1** **REVIEW 16-1**

1. Indicate whether each of the cost control methods listed in *a* through *f* is (1) preventive, (2) corrective, or (3) diagnostic.
   a. ____ Preparation of an annual production budget of variable and fixed costs.
   b. ____ Analysis of cost variances in excess of 10 percent over the prior quarter.
   c. ____ Performing a market study on innovative ways to reduce the amount of packaging materials.
   d. ____ Comparison of actual production costs to budgeted production costs during the period.
   e. ____ Asking for competitive bids on materials from a new supplier pool due to an unexpected price increase in product from a current supplier.
   f. ____ Using year-to-date information to update standard costs effective for the next fiscal year.
2. **Critical Thinking:** In what function can management have the most impact in cost control, preventive, corrective, or diagnostic? Why?

More practice: MC16-13, E16-24
Solution on p. 16-54.

COST CONSCIOUSNESS ATTITUDE

A good control system encompasses not only the managerial functions shown in **Exhibit 16.2** but also the ideas about cost consciousness shown in **Exhibit 16.5**. Cost consciousness refers to a companywide employee attitude toward the topics of understanding cost changes, cost containment, cost avoidance, and cost reduction. Each of these topics is important for a particular stage of cost control. Cost understanding takes place before the event occurs and is discussed further in this section. Cost containment and cost avoidance take place during the event as a way to reduce costs *before* they occur.

LO16-2 What factors cause costs to change from period to period or to deviate from expectations?

---

[3] W. Engelbrecht, et. al., "Strategic Alliances Drive Competitive Advantage," *The Wall Street Journal*, December 10, 2019, https://deloitte.wsj.com/cmo/strategic-alliances-drive-competitive-advantage-01576011366. Accessed on November 10, 2023.

Based on feedback indicating excess costs, cost reduction techniques can reduce *future* costs. Cost containment, avoidance, and reduction are discussed in LO16-3.

Managers alone cannot control costs. An organization is composed of many individuals whose attitudes and efforts affect how an organization's costs are controlled. Cost control is a continual process that requires the support and involvement of all employees at all times.

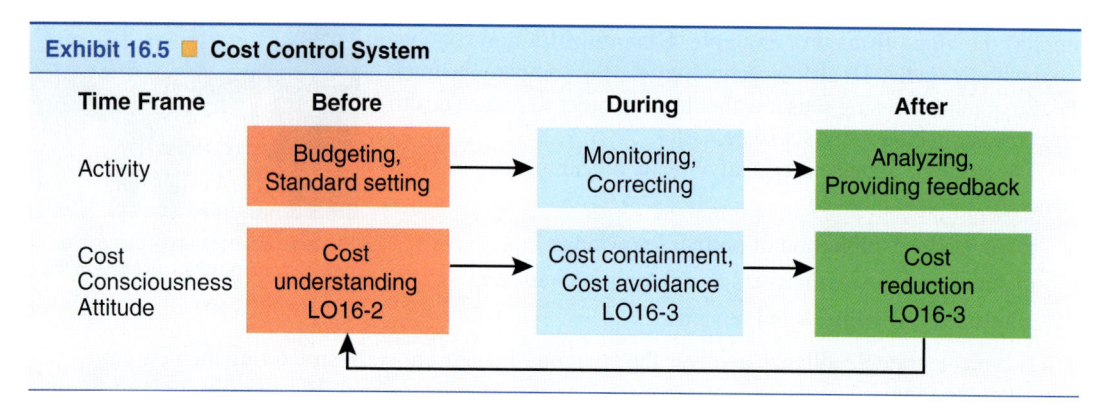

Exhibit 16.5 Cost Control System

Time Frame	Before	During	After
Activity	Budgeting, Standard setting	Monitoring, Correcting	Analyzing, Providing feedback
Cost Consciousness Attitude	Cost understanding LO16-2	Cost containment, Cost avoidance LO16-3	Cost reduction LO16-3

Understanding Cost Changes

Control requires that a set of expectations exists. Thus, cost control begins when the budget is prepared. However, budgets cannot be prepared without understanding why costs change from period-to-period, and cost control cannot be achieved without understanding why costs may differ between periods or from the budgeted amounts. Common causes of cost changes include the following.

Volume Changes	Inflation/Deflation	Supply/Supplier Cost Adjustments	Quantity Purchased

In considering these factors, remember that an external price becomes an internal cost when a good or service is acquired.

Volume Changes

Some costs change because of their underlying behavior. Total variable or mixed costs increase or decrease with, respectively, increases or decreases in activity. If the current period's actual activity differs from that of a prior period or from the budgeted activity level, total actual variable or mixed costs will differ from that of the prior period or from the budget. A *flexible budget* can compensate for such differences by providing expected costs at any activity level, as shown in Chapter 10. By using a flexible budget, managers can make valid budget-to-actual cost comparisons to determine whether costs were properly controlled. For costs to be controlled most effectively relative to their cost behaviors, it is important that the driver of the cost (as discussed in Chapter 8) be determined as accurately as possible.

Inflation/Deflation

Fluctuations in the value of money, called **general price-level changes**, cause the prices of goods and services to change. If all other factors are constant, general price-level changes affect prices approximately equally and in the same direction. In the United States, the **Consumer Price Index** (CPI) is the most often cited measure of general price-level changes. The CPI measures the average change in prices over time, paid by urban consumers for a representative basket of goods and services. For example, the CPI in September of 2023 shows a +0.4 percent increase in prices over the prior month.[4] Inflation and deflation indexes by industry or commodity can be examined to obtain more accurate information about inflation/deflation effects on prices of particular inputs, such as energy resources. Inflationary periods can be especially challenging for management to navigate. In response to high inflation, a survey of CFOs indicated that approximately 80 percent of the respondents passed on the cost increases through higher prices. If this wasn't possible, the respondents reported using other

---

[4] U.S. Bureau of Labor Statistics, https://www.bls.gov/cpi/#news, accessed on November 11, 2023.

Chapter 16 Approaches to Cost Control and Managing Uncertainty

approaches in addition to absorbing or reducing margins, such as reducing costs in other areas, substituting product offerings, adding contingency clauses into contracts, and turning away business.[5]

In some instances, other factors can cause a product/service to drop in price, despite general inflationary trends. Among electrical energy sources, solar power is becoming more competitive relative to the alternatives because industry capacity to produce solar photovoltaics (the active material used in many solar panels) has increased dramatically, causing prices to drop.[6] Thus there may be deflation in the cost of solar energy versus inflation in alternative electrical energy sources.

Inflationary Effect Inflation, or deflation, can distort the comparisons of financial information between periods because the statements are based on historical dollars, not on dollars of the same value. Allowances must be made for these effects, or the analysis is distorted. To illustrate, assume that Etson Company has Year 1 sales of $100,000 and cost of sales totaling $40,000. During Year 2, when inflation is 5 percent, the company's selling prices increase by 5 percent, while its costs have a net increase of only 3 percent due to beginning inventory available at Year 1 prices. In Year 3, when inflation is 5 percent, both selling prices and costs go up by 5 percent. Therefore, the company has an increase in Year 2 gross profit due *primarily* to inflation of $3,800 and an increase in Year 3 gross profit of $3,190 due *solely* to inflation (ignoring any offsetting factors which had no net effect).

	Year 1	Year 2	Year 3
Sales.	$100,000	$105,000	$110,250
Cost of sales.	40,000	41,200	43,260
Gross profit.	$ 60,000	$ 63,800	$ 66,990
Dollar increase in gross profit over prior period		$ 3,800	$ 3,190
Percentage increase in gross profit over prior period.		6.3%	5.0%

A manager must be careful to avoid stating that the company has increased operating *efficiency when all it did was keep pace with inflation*. As a general rule, ignoring inflation produces favorable results when other things remain equal. Inflation can even produce favorable results when actual, constant dollar results are unfavorable. We must remember that external financial statements are presented in historical dollars that have not been adjusted for inflation.

Some companies include price-escalation clauses in sales contracts to cover the inflation occurring from order to delivery. Such escalators are especially prevalent in industries with production activities that require substantial lead time. Some government benefits and penalties are also inflation adjusted. For example, Congress passed the Debt Collection Improvement Act of 1996, which contained a provision to periodically adjust the Environmental Protection Agency's fines in the event of inflation. The law allows the EPA's penalties to keep pace with inflation and thereby maintain the deterrent effect that Congress intended when penalties were originally specified.[7]

Supply/Supplier Cost Adjustments

Availability of goods/services The relationship between the availability of a good or service and the demand for that item affects its selling price. If supply is reduced but demand remains high, the selling price of the item increases. The higher price often stimulates greater production, which, in turn, increases supply. In contrast, if demand falls but supply remains constant, the price falls. This reduced price should motivate lower production, which lowers supply. Therefore, the relationship of supply and demand consistently and circularly influences price. Price changes resulting from independent causes are specific price-level changes, which can move in the same or opposite direction as a general

---

[5] "CFOs Reporting Rising Costs that Could Last Through 2022," *Duke University and the Federal Reserve Banks of Richmond and Atlanta*, December 2, 2021, https://www.richmondfed.org/research/national_economy/cfo_survey/data_and_results/2021/20211202_data_and_results. Accessed on November 13, 2023.

[6] Human Development Report 2021-22, (September 8, 2022), https://hdr.undp.org/content/human-development-report-2021-22, accessed on November 11, 2023.

[7] 61 FR 69360, Civil Monetary Penalty Inflation Adjustment Rule; https://www.govinfo.gov/app/details/FR-1996-12-31/96-32972 (last accessed November 11, 2023).

price-level change. The relationship between price changes and supply and demand changes varies across products. **Price elasticity** is a numerical measure of the relationship of supply or demand to price changes. Price elasticities can be calculated for specific products using historical data by relating price changes to supply and demand changes. If price elasticity is low, then a large change in price will lead to only a small change in supply or demand; alternatively, if price elasticity is high, a large change in price leads to a large change in supply or demand.

Specific price-level changes Specific price-level changes are also caused by advances in technology. As a general rule, as suppliers advance the technology of producing a good or performing a service, the cost of that product or service to producing/performing firms declines. Assuming competitive market conditions, such cost declines are often passed along to consumers of that product or service in the form of *lower prices*.

Alternatively, additional production or performance costs are typically passed on by suppliers to their customers in the form of *higher* prices. Such costs can be within or outside the supplier's control. For example, the increase in demand for corn to develop ethanol fuel caused corn prices to rise. As a result, the cost of many food products using inputs derived from corn (such as corn syrup) have increased.

Number of suppliers The number of suppliers of a product or service can also affect selling prices. As the number of suppliers increases in a competitive environment, price tends to fall. Likewise, a reduction in the number of suppliers will, all else remaining equal, cause prices to increase. A change in the number of suppliers is not the same as a change in the quantity of supply. If the supply of an item is large, one normally expects a low price. However, if there is only one supplier, the price can remain high because the market is controlled by the supplier. For example, when drugs are first introduced under patent, the supply can be readily available, but the selling price is high because the prescription drug comes from only a single source. As patents expire and generic drugs become available, selling prices decline because more suppliers compete to produce and market the medication.

Regulatory requirements Sometimes, cost increases are caused by higher taxes or additional regulatory requirements. For example, airlines continually face more stringent noise abatement and safety legislation. Complying with these regulations increases airline costs. The companies can

- pass along the costs to customers as price increases to maintain the same income level,
- decrease other costs to maintain the same income level, or
- experience a decline in net income.

Quantity Purchased
Suppliers normally give customers quantity discounts, up to some maximum level, when bulk purchases are made. Therefore, a cost per unit can change because quantities are purchased in lot sizes differing from those of previous periods or from the lot sizes projected. Involvement in group purchasing arrangements can make quantity discounts easier to obtain.

DEMO 16-2 LO16-2   Understanding How Factors Cause Cost Changes

◆ **In general, do the following factors likely indicate an increase or decrease in total cost?**

a. The static budget for the production of electric vehicles is based on 100,000 units and actual units produced were 110,000.
   Answer: *Variable and mixed costs will increase over budget when actual units exceed the static budget.*

b. The Consumer Price Index decreased 0.2 percent in December.
   Answer: *A decrease in the CPI indicates generally, that prices decreased over the prior month; thus, costs in general, decreased.*

c. Supply of construction materials is high, while the rate of new residential construction decreased.
   Answer: *If supply is high for a low demand product, prices generally will drop.*

d. An organic food manufacturer purchases ingredients in bulk.
   Answer: *Generally, the cost of ingredients should drop due to quantity discounts offered by the supplier.*

Chapter 16 Approaches to Cost Control and Managing Uncertainty

The preceding discussion indicates why costs change. Next, the discussion addresses actions firms can take to contain (control) costs.

Factors Causing Cost Changes — **LO16-2** — **REVIEW 16-2**

1. For each description of a cost change in items *a* through *h*, indicate whether the cause is due to (1) underlying cost behavior, (2) inflation or deflation, (3) supply or supplier cost adjustments, or (4) changes in quantities purchased.
   a. ___ A large manufacturer exceeded its variable overhead budget by 20 percent due to an unexpected spike in sales volume that required additional production runs.
   b. ___ An office furniture retailer chartered alternative ships, specially designed for cost effectiveness, to transport overseas merchandise at a 20 percent cost reduction.
   c. ___ An organic food retailer canceled advertising contracts with marketing consultants, and instead hired an in-house expert at a significant cost reduction.
   d. ___ A consulting firm upgraded its cellular phone contracts and received substantially more data, faster speed, and higher bandwidth for a lower price.
   e. ___ A decrease in the domestic sales budget of a mid-sized manufacturer resulted in production running at less than capacity, which increased fixed costs per unit.
   f. ___ A restaurant chain experienced an increase in raw materials costs, when an E. coli breakout was attributed to contaminated romaine lettuce from its main supplier, causing the company to find higher priced, temporary supply solutions.
   g. ___ A large supplier of a retailer opened up a new distribution center, which allowed the retailer to order goods as needed, increasing efficiencies and reducing storage and handling costs by 10 percent.
   h. ___ Costs of parts for a boat manufacturer are expected to increase over the prior year due to inflation.
2. **Critical Thinking:** How can data analytics be used by management to predict cost changes and to determine any impact on selling prices?

More practice: E16-27, E16-28, E16-29
Solution on p. 16-54.

Cost Containment

To the extent possible, period-by-period increases in per-unit variable and total fixed costs should be minimized through a process of **cost containment**. Cost containment is not possible for inflation effects, tax and regulatory changes, and supply and demand adjustments because these forces occur outside the organization.

Costs that rise because of reduced supplier competition, seasonality, and quantities purchased are, however, subject to cost containment activities. A company should look for ways to *cap upward changes in these costs*. For example, in response to an increase in supplier costs, the company could conduct workshops and offer training on the topics of supply chain management for its supply chain partner in order to achieve overall cost reductions. Alternatively, a cost containment activity is to find alternative suppliers with lower costs who can provide product at equivalent quality.

Alternative supply sources Purchasing agents should be aware of alternative suppliers for goods and services and determine which, if any, of those suppliers can reliably provide items in the quantity, quality, and time desired. Comparing costs and finding new sources of supply can increase buying power and reduce costs.

Supplier negotiation If bids are used to select suppliers, the purchasing agent should remember that a bid is merely the first step in the negotiation process. Although a low bid may eliminate some competition from consideration, additional negotiations between the purchasing agent and the remaining suppliers could result in a purchase price even lower than the bid amount or other relevant concessions (such as faster and more reliable delivery) may be gained. Purchasing agents must also remember that the supplier offering the lowest bid is not necessarily the best supplier to choose because factors such as quality, service, and reliability are important.

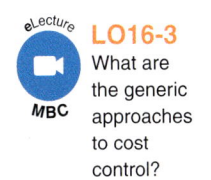

LO16-3 What are the generic approaches to cost control?

Seasonality considerations A company can circumvent seasonal cost changes by postponing or advancing purchases of goods and services. However, such purchasing changes should not mean buying irresponsibly or incurring excessive carrying costs. Economic order quantities, safety stock levels, and materials requirements planning as well as the just-in-time philosophy should be considered when making purchases.[8]

As to services, seasonality is often important in cost control. It is often possible for employees to repair rather than to replace items that have seasonal cost changes. For example, maintenance workers might find that a broken heat pump can be repaired and used during spring and replaced in summer when the cost of servicing is lower.

Product redesign Another cost containment option is to redesign the product while still maintaining the features and quality that customers require. For example, the use of more cost effective materials or packaging could offset increases in supplier costs. Or a company could even pivot to a product substitute with lower costs, which would not require price increases for its customers.[9]

Cost Avoidance and Cost Reduction

Cost containment can prove very effective if it can be implemented. However, when cost containment is not possible, cost avoidance strategies may be applied instead. **Cost avoidance** involves finding acceptable alternatives to high-cost items and/or not spending money for unnecessary goods and services. Avoiding one cost may require incurring an alternative, lower cost. For example, **United Parcel Service, Inc. (UPS)** has contracted with **Arrival** to make 10,000 electric vehicles. UPS is replacing fossil fuel vehicles with electric vehicles that cost the same or less than the fossil fuel vehicles and have lower operating costs than fossil fuel vehicles.[10]

Closely related to cost avoidance, the intent of **cost reduction** is to lower costs. *Benchmarking* is especially important in this area so that companies can become aware of excessively high costs. Benchmarking is the formal comparing of one organization's operations to those of another company and is discussed further in the next chapter. Companies can reduce costs by *outsourcing functions* such as data processing, legal, and distribution rather than maintaining internal departments. Even the function of marketing may be outsourced given the expertise required including social media marketing, data analytic, and website design skills.

Sometimes money must be spent to generate cost savings. For example, some of the large accounting firms (such as **PricewaterhouseCoopers**) have their own in-house studios and staffs and provide customized web-based training to new employees. Although the cost of producing an online presentation is high, the firms believe the cost is justified because the presentation can be used multiple times at very low cost.

Technology can play an important role in company's efforts to cut costs. Consider **IKEA**, which sells affordable furniture, packaged in flatpacks, allowing for easy transport. Experience shows that one out of every 20 items purchased in IKEA's U.S. locations is returned. To make the return process more cost effective, the company uses an AI system with machine learning algorithms. Based on the type of item and its condition, the system suggests the most profitable way to manage the returned inventory. The AI system uses historical data and real-time data showing how well certain items are selling in different channels to make a recommendation. For instance, the system could suggest whether the item should be returned to inventory, be shipped immediately to a store, or be sold to an outlet.[11] Technology allows companies to employ cost cutting methods more effectively through the prescriptive data analytics (data analysis that suggests action).

---

[8] These concepts are discussed in Chapter 18.

[9] "Five Ways to ADAPT Pricing to Inflation," *McKinsey & Company*, February 25, 2022, https://www.mckinsey.com/capabilities/growth-marketing-and-sales/our-insights/five-ways-to-adapt-pricing-to-inflation. Accessed on November 13, 2023.

[10] "UPS invests in Arrival, accelerates fleet electrification with a commitment to purchase up to 10,000 electric vehicles," *UPS*, January 29, 2020, https://about.ups.com/us/en/newsroom/press-releases/sustainable-services/ups-invests-in-arrival-accelerates-fleet-electrification-with-order-of-10-000-electric-delivery-vehicles.html#:~:text=Along%20with%20the%20investment%20in,%2DAssistance%20Systems%20(ADAS). Accessed on November 11, 2023.

[11] J. Council, "IKEA Seeks to Cut Costs, Waste in the U.S. With Smarter Approach to Customer Returns," March 2, 2020, https://www.wsj.com/articles/ikea-seeks-to-cut-costs-waste-with-smarter-approach-to-customer-returns-11583145000. Accessed on November 13, 2023.

Chapter 16 Approaches to Cost Control and Managing Uncertainty

Some companies are also beginning to look outside for information about how and where to cut costs. Consulting firms, such as Dallas-based **Ryan, LLC**, review files for overpayment of state and local taxes. This firm often works on a contingent fee basis and gets paid only if tax overpayments are found.

Identifying Generic Approaches to Cost Control LO16-3 DEMO 16-3

◆ **Does the action listed primarily represent initiatives for cost containment, cost avoidance, or cost reduction?**

a. After taking into account differences in shipping costs, some of the suppliers with lower invoice costs had higher shipping costs making them a more expensive option.
  Answer: Cost reduction *(choosing the lowest cost provider, considering all costing including shipping).*

b. An accounting firm used optical character recognition to recognize text in client contracts, which saved multiple hours of staff time.
  Answer: Cost avoidance *(avoided labor costs of manual process)/cost reduction (reduces labor costs).*

c. A data analysis of supplier costs of a manufacturing company with multiple plants across the U.S. indicated that bulk discounts could be achieved by combining certain purchases.
  Answer: Cost reduction *(reduce supplier costs through quantity discounts).*

d. A health care provider determined that outsourcing its payroll processing would be more cost effective and efficient.
  Answer: Cost reduction *(reduce costs through outsourcing).*

e. A contract with a supplier was renegotiated at a lower rate per unit, secured over a 9-month period.
  Answer: Cost containment *(cost with supplier contained over a set period of time).*

f. A retailer reduced the space leased at its retail locations as a result of its rise in online sales and decline of in-store sales.
  Answer: Cost reduction *(lease costs are reduced).*

Implementing a Cost Accounting System

Managers can adopt the five-step method of implementing a cost control system shown in **Exhibit 16.6**:

- **Step 1:** Understand the type of costs incurred by an organization. Are the costs under consideration fixed or variable, product or period? What are the drivers of those costs? From whom were purchases made? When were purchases made? The generation of answers to these types of questions is generically referred to as **spend analysis**.
- **Step 2:** Communicate the need for cost consciousness to all employees. Employees must be aware of which costs need to be better controlled and why cost control is important individually and organizationally.
- **Step 3:** Educate employees in cost control techniques, encourage suggestions on ways to control costs, and motivate employees to take the concepts to heart. Incentives can range from simple verbal recognition to monetary rewards to time off with pay. Managers must also be flexible enough to allow for changes from the current method of operation.
- **Step 4:** Generate reports that indicate actual results, compare budget to actual, and calculate variances. Management must evaluate these costs to determine why costs were or were not controlled in the past. Such analysis can provide insight about cost drivers so that activities driving costs can be better controlled in the future.
- **Step 5:** Develop a view that the cost control system is a long-run process, not a short-run solution. Organizations need "to examine new kinds of questions, learn to experience time differently (long-term solutions versus quick fixes), [and] notice how systems work."[12] Proposed cost controls should be assessed using realistic circumstances rather than improbable assumptions.

---

[12] Sid Gardner and Alan Brown, "Cost Savings and Achievement Potential of Prevention Programs: Smart Cuts, Dumb Cuts, and a Process to Tell the Difference," *PM. Public Management* (March 2009), pp. 20–23.

© Cambridge Business Publishers

Exhibit 16.6 — Implementing a Cost Control System

1. Identify and understand the types of costs incurred by the organization.
2. Communicate the need for cost consciousness to all employees.
3. Motivate employees through education and incentives.
4. Compare actual results to budgets and analyze for future methods of improvement.
5. View cost control as a long-run process, not a short-term solution.

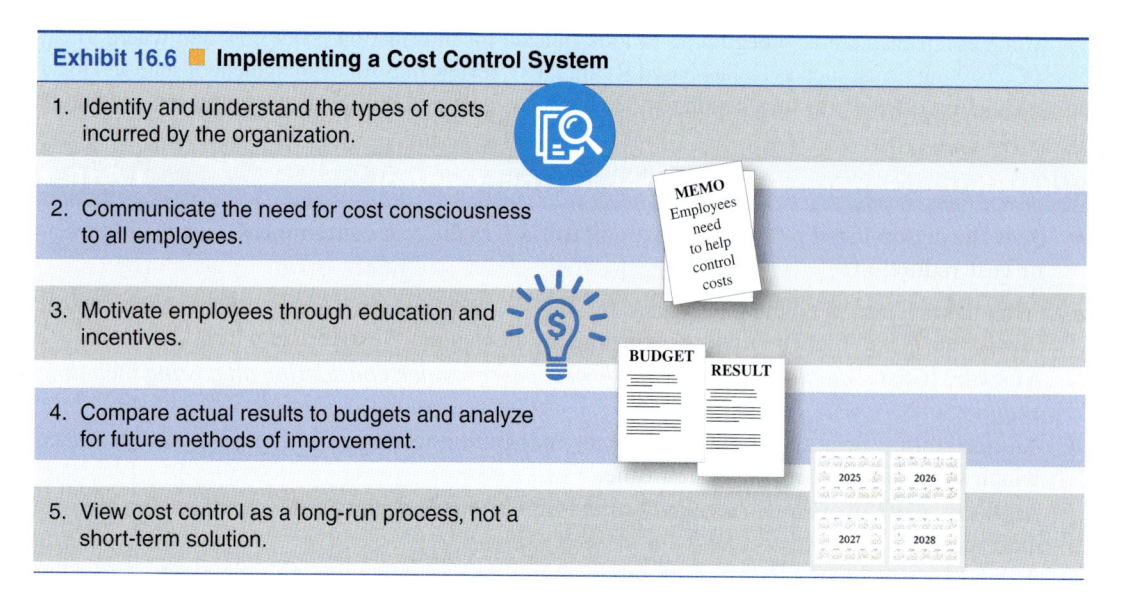

Following these five steps will provide an atmosphere conducive to controlling costs as effectively as possible and to deriving the most benefit from costs incurrence. A cost–benefit analysis should be performed before a commitment is made to incur a cost. Costs should also be incorporated into the budgeting system because costs cannot be controlled after they have been incurred. Future costs, on the other hand, can be controlled based on information learned about past costs.

Data Visualization

The following data visualization depicts travel costs per employee in each business segment over the preceding year.

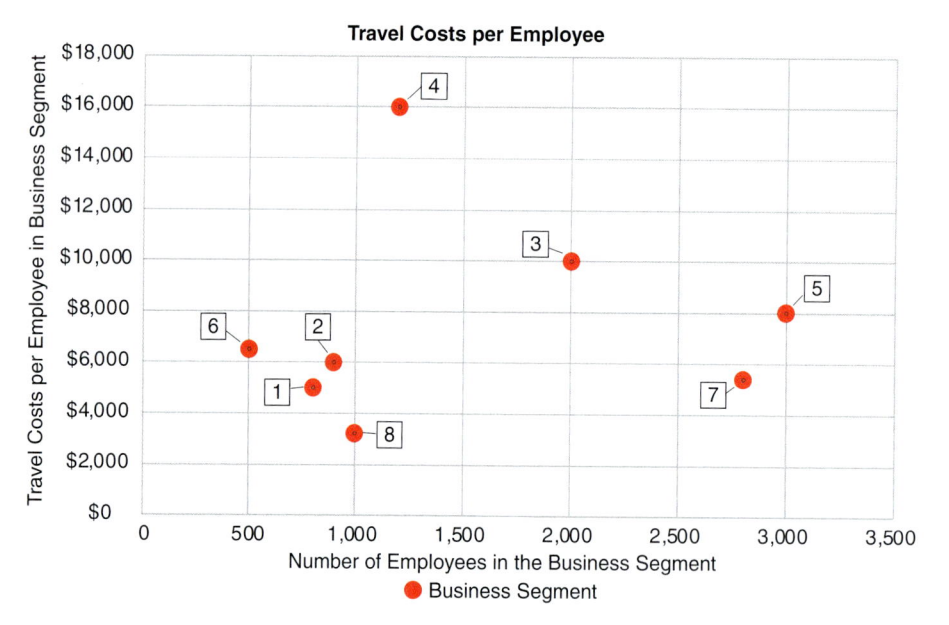

Travel Costs per Employee (scatter plot of Travel Costs per Employee in Business Segment vs. Number of Employees in the Business Segment):
- 1: ~800 employees, ~$5,000
- 2: ~900 employees, ~$6,000
- 3: ~2,000 employees, ~$9,800
- 4: ~1,200 employees, ~$16,000
- 5: ~3,000 employees, ~$7,800
- 6: ~600 employees, ~$6,500
- 7: ~2,800 employees, ~$5,300
- 8: ~1,000 employees, ~$3,200

Using the data visualization, answer the following questions.

a. How is benchmarking applied in this visualization?
b. How many employees were in the business segment with the highest travel cost per employee?
c. How many employees were in the business segment with the lowest travel cost per employee?
d. For which business segment(s) might the Sales VP of the company have questions regarding travel expenses per employee?
e. What other information would be useful in analyzing travel costs per employee?

Chapter 16 Approaches to Cost Control and Managing Uncertainty 16-13

REVIEW 16-3

Approaches to Cost Control — LO16-3

1. Indicate whether the actions listed *a* through *h*, primarily represent initiatives for cost containment (CC), cost avoidance (CA), or cost reduction (CR). Indicate what costs were contained, avoided, or reduced as support for your answer.
   a. _____ A small manufacturer outsourced its payroll processing function resulting in an overall drop in costs due to efficiencies gained by not using internal resources.
   b. _____ The sales staff of a large insurance company are provided a daily per diem amount for travel expenditures.
   c. _____ A mid-sized manufacturer of auto supplies reduces price volatility by negotiating six-month price contracts with its suppliers.
   d. _____ A small retailer instituted a new policy allowing employees to voluntarily take unpaid time-off during non-peak times, which resulted in lower salaries costs and increased employee morale.
   e. _____ An online retailer renegotiated its contract with a supplier, which now requires the supplier to insure the goods in transit (formerly paid for by the retailer).
   f. _____ In order to maintain its current medical insurance costs, a service provider increased each employee's deductible on each medical service by 25 percent.
   g. _____ A health care provider invested in web conference software and video screens in order to eliminate travel costs for off-site training.
   h. _____ A retailer relocated its corporate office rental space to a location with lower rent and easier accessibility to the airport for travel purposes.
2. **Critical Thinking:** How can benchmarking be useful in management decision making related to cost control?

More practice: MC16-16, E16-35
Solution on p. 16-54.

CLASSIFYING FIXED COSTS

Cost control should not cease at the end of a fiscal period or because costs were reduced or controlled during the current period. Managers are charged with planning and controlling the types and amounts of costs necessary to conduct business activities. Many activities required to achieve business objectives involve fixed costs. All fixed costs (and the activities that create them) can be categorized as either committed or discretionary. The difference between the two categories is primarily the time period for which management obligates itself to the activity and its cost.

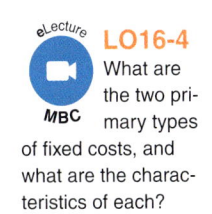

LO16-4 What are the two primary types of fixed costs, and what are the characteristics of each?

Committed Fixed Costs

Costs associated with plant assets and human resources are known as **committed fixed costs**. The amount of committed costs is normally dictated by long-run management decisions involving the desired scale and scope of operations. Committed costs cannot be reduced easily even during temporarily diminished activity.

A committed cost is most logically controlled prior to the expenditure being made.

Controlling Committed Costs

One method of controlling committed costs is to compare expected benefits of plant assets (or human resources) with expected costs of such investments. Managers must identify activities necessary to attain company objectives and what (and how many) assets are needed to support those activities. Once assets are acquired, managers are committed to both the activities and their related costs for the long run. But managers must understand how committed fixed costs could affect income in the event of changes in operations.

A second method of controlling committed costs is to compare actual and expected results from plant asset investments. During this process, managers are able to see and evaluate the accuracy of their cost and revenue predictions relative to the investment. This comparison is called a postinvestment audit and is discussed in Chapter 19.

An organization cannot operate without some basic plant and human assets. Considerable control can be exercised over the process of determining how management chooses fundamental assets and designs the human resources structure. The most logical point in time to control committed fixed costs is *prior* to making the investment in plant assets or hiring human resources. The benefits from committed costs generally can be predicted and commonly are compared with actual results in the future.

Discretionary Fixed Costs

In contrast to a committed cost, a **discretionary fixed cost** is one "that a decision maker must periodically review to determine if it continues to be in accord with ongoing policies."[13] Discretionary costs relate to company activities that are important, but the level of funding is subject to judgment. Discretionary cost activities are usually *service-oriented*.

There is no "correct" amount at which to set funding for discretionary costs because the relationship between the amount of cost incurred and the amount of benefit created can be determined only *subjectively*. Further, there are no specific activities for which all organizations consider the costs to be discretionary. A discretionary fixed cost reflects a management decision to fund a particular activity at a specified amount for a specified period of time. In the event of cash flow shortages or forecasted operating losses, discretionary fixed costs can be more easily reduced than committed fixed costs.

Though costs associated with university recruitment are discretionary costs, they can have a direct impact on admissions and ultimately, the number of graduates.

Discretionary costs, then, are generated by activities that vary in type and magnitude from day to day and whose benefits are often not measurable in monetary terms. Just as discretionary cost activities vary, performance quality can also vary according to the tasks involved and skill levels of the persons performing them. These two factors—varying activities and varying quality levels—usually cause discretionary costs not to be susceptible to the precise measures available to plan and control variable production costs or the cost–benefit evaluation techniques available to control committed fixed costs. We further discuss the planning and controlling of discretionary costs in the next section.

DEMO 16-4   LO16-4   Classifying Discretionary and Committed Fixed Costs

◆ How are the following fixed costs commonly classified as either committed or discretionary?

Employee travel	**Discretionary**	Advertising	**Discretionary**
Repairs and maintenance	**Discretionary**	Property taxes	**Committed**
Depreciation on building	**Committed**	Research and development	**Discretionary**
Lease payments	**Committed**	Employee training and development	**Discretionary**
Charitable contributions	**Discretionary**	Staff salaries	**Committed**

REVIEW 16-4   LO16-4   Identifying Committed and Discretionary Fixed Costs

1. Choose letter C (for committed fixed cost) or D (for discretionary fixed cost) to indicate the common classification of each of the following described costs.
   - a. ___ Professional meeting attendance fees
   - b. ___ Depreciation on office equipment
   - c. ___ Property insurance premiums
   - d. ___ Equipment maintenance
   - e. ___ Sales salaries
   - f. ___ Travel costs for continuing education
   - g. ___ Catered business meetings
   - h. ___ Health insurance premiums
   - i. ___ Research and development costs
   - j. ___ Social media advertising costs
   - k. ___ Internet provider fees

More practice: MC16-17, E16-38, E16-39
Solution on p. 16-54.

2. **Critical Thinking:** How does a company's classification of fixed costs as committed or discretionary affect management decision making in times of economic downturns?

---

[13] Institute of Management Accountants (formerly National Association of Accountants), *Statements on Management Accounting Number 2: Management Accounting Terminology* (Montvale, NJ, June 1, 1983), p. 35.

PLANNING AND CONTROLLING DISCRETIONARY FIXED COSTS

During periods of financial well-being, organizations can make large expenditures on discretionary cost items. However, because the benefits of discretionary cost activities cannot be assessed definitively, these activities are often among the first to be cut when profits are lagging. Thus, proper planning for discretionary activities and costs can be more important than subsequent control measures. Control after the planning stage is often restricted to monitoring expenditures to ensure conformity with budget classifications and preventing managers from overspending budgets.

Planning for Discretionary Costs

Described in Chapter 9 as both planning and controlling devices, budgets serve to officially communicate a manager's authority to spend up to a predetermined amount (**appropriation**) or rate for each budget item. Budget appropriations serve as a baseline for comparison with actual costs. Accumulated expenditures in each budgetary category are periodically compared with appropriated amounts to determine whether funds have been under- or overexpended.

Budgeting Discretionary Costs Before addressing *control* of discretionary costs, top management must translate company goals into specific objectives and policies that will contribute to organizational success. Cash flow and income expectations for a coming period need to be reviewed and discretionary cost activities must be prioritized before funding levels can be set. Management must then budget the types and quantities of discretionary activities to accomplish those objectives. Management tends to be more generous about making discretionary cost appropriations when the economic outlook for the organization is strong rather than weak.

Discretionary costs are generally budgeted on the basis of three factors:

- the related activity's perceived significance to achieving goals and objectives;
- the next period's expected level of operations; and
- the ability of managers to effectively negotiate during the budgetary process

For some discretionary costs, managers are expected to spend the full amount of their appropriations within the specified time frame. For other discretionary cost activities, the "less-is-better" adage is appropriate.

Spending Appropriation is Desirable As an example of "less is *not* better," consider the cost of preventive maintenance. This cost can be viewed as discretionary, but reducing it could result in diminished quality, production breakdowns, or machine inefficiency. Although the benefits of maintenance expenditures cannot be precisely quantified, most managers believe that incurring less maintenance cost than budgeted is not effective cost control. In fact, spending (with supervisory approval) more than originally appropriated could be necessary or even commendable—assuming that positive results (such as a decline in quality defects or an extension of equipment life) are obtained. Such a perspective illustrates the perception mentioned earlier that cost control should be a long-run process rather than a short-run concern.

Spending Less than Appropriation is Desirable Alternatively, spending less than the amount budgeted on travel and entertainment (while achieving the desired results) would probably be considered positive performance, whereas spending on travel and entertainment in excess of budget appropriations might be considered irresponsible—especially in difficult economic times.

If revenues, profits, or cash flows are lower than expected, funding for discretionary expenditures should be evaluated, not simply in reference to reduced operations but also relative to activity priorities. Eliminating the funding for one or more discretionary activities altogether could be possible if other funding levels are maintained at the previously determined amounts. For example, faced with a downturn in product demand, a company often reduces its discretionary advertising budget—a potentially illogical reaction. Instead, increasing the advertising budget and reducing the corporate executives' travel budget might be more appropriate.

The difference in managerial attitude between committed and discretionary costs has to do with the ability to measure the benefits provided by those costs. Although benefits of committed fixed costs can be measured on a "before" and "after" basis (through the capital budgeting and postinvestment audit processes), the benefits from discretionary fixed costs are often not distinctly measurable in monetary terms, or the benefits may not even be identifiable.

Measuring Benefits from Discretionary Costs Because benefits from some activities traditionally classified as discretionary cannot be adequately measured, companies often assume that the benefits—and, thus, the related activities—are unimportant. However, many activities previously described as discretionary (repairs, maintenance, R&D, and employee training) are *critical to survival* in a world-class environment. In the long run, these activities create quality products and services; therefore, before reducing or eliminating expenditures in these areas, managers should attempt to more appropriately recognize and measure the benefits of these activities.

Funds are spent on discretionary activities to provide some desired output, but the value of discretionary costs must often be judged using nonmonetary, surrogate measures. Devising such measures sometimes requires substantial time and creativity. **Exhibit 16.7** presents some useful surrogate measures for determining the effectiveness of various types of discretionary costs. Some of these measures are verifiable and can be gathered quickly and easily; others are abstract and require a longer time horizon before they can be obtained.

Exhibit 16.7 ■ Examples of Nonmonetary Measures of Output from Discretionary Costs

Discretionary Cost Activity	Surrogate Measure of Results
Preventive maintenance	• Reduction in equipment failures • Reduction in unplanned downtime • Reduction in production interruptions caused by preventive maintenance activities
Advertising	• Increase in unit sales in the two weeks after an advertising effort relative to the sales two weeks prior to the effort • Number of customers referring to the ad • Number of website clicks
University admissions recruiting trip	• Percentage of students met who requested an application • Number of students from area visited who requested to have ACT/SAT scores sent to the university • Number of admissions that year from that area
Prevention and appraisal quality activities	• Reduction in number of customer complaints • Reduction in number of warranty claims • Reduction in number of product defects discovered by customers
Staffing law school indigent clinic	• Number of clients served • Percentage of cases effectively resolved • Percentage of cases won
Executive retreat	• Proportion of participants providing positive feedback • Number of useful suggestions made • Values tabulated from an exit survey

Controlling Discretionary Activities

After the planning stage, discretionary costs are controlled to ensure that costs are expended as planned and are producing the desired results. Three methods to control discretionary activities are discussed in this section.

| Efficiency and Effectiveness Measures | Engineered Cost Variances | Flexible Budget Variance Analysis |

Efficiency and Effectiveness Measures

Comparing input costs and output results can help determine whether there is a reasonable cost–benefit relationship. Managers can judge this cost–benefit relationship by how *efficiently* inputs (costs) were used and how *effectively* incurrence of the costs achieved the intended results. These relationships can be seen in the following model.

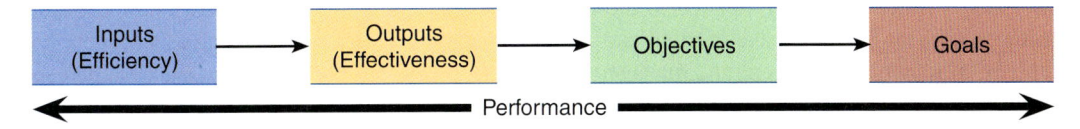

Inputs (Efficiency) → Outputs (Effectiveness) → Objectives → Goals
← Performance →

The degree to which a satisfactory relationship occurs when comparing outputs to inputs reflects the activity's efficiency. **Efficiency** is a yield concept and is usually measured by a ratio of output to input. For instance, one measure of automobile efficiency is miles driven (output) per gallon of fuel consumed (input). The higher the miles per gallon, the greater is the car's fuel efficiency.

Comparing actual output results to desired results indicates the **effectiveness** of an activity or how well the activity's objectives were achieved. When a valid output measure is available, efficiency and effectiveness can be determined as follows.

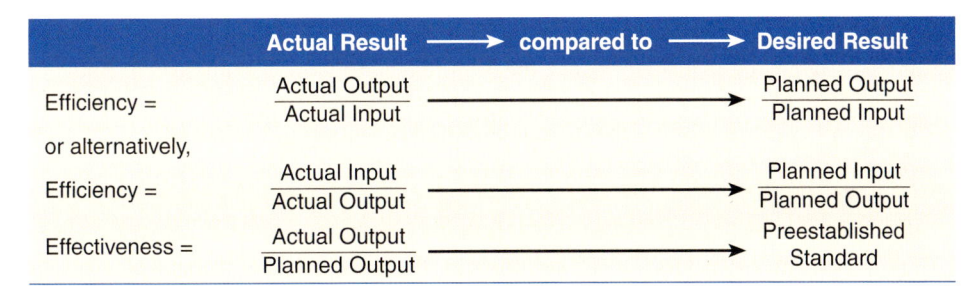

	Actual Result → compared to →	Desired Result
Efficiency =	Actual Output / Actual Input	Planned Output / Planned Input
or alternatively,		
Efficiency =	Actual Input / Actual Output	Planned Input / Planned Output
Effectiveness =	Actual Output / Planned Output	Preestablished Standard

Efficiency A reasonable measure of efficiency can exist only when inputs and outputs can be matched in the same period and when a credible causal relationship exists between them. These two requirements make measuring the efficiency of discretionary costs *very difficult*.

- First, several years could pass before output occurs from some discretionary cost expenditures. Consider, for example, the length of time between expenditures made for research and development or a drug rehabilitation program and the time at which results of these expenditures are visible.
- Second, frequently a dubious cause-and-effect relationship exists between discretionary inputs and resulting outputs.

Effectiveness In contrast to the measurement of efficiency, measurement of effectiveness does not require the consideration of inputs. Effectiveness is determined for a particular period by comparing results achieved with results desired. Determination of an activity's effectiveness is unaffected by whether the designated output measure is stated in monetary or nonmonetary terms. Management can only subjectively attribute some or all of the effectiveness of the cost incurred to the results. Subjectivity is required because comparison of actual to planned output *does not indicate a perfect causal relationship between activities and output results*.

Measuring Effectiveness of Performance — LO16-5 DEMO 16-5A

Assume that last month Precision Industrial increased its customer service training expenditures and, during this month, customer satisfaction ratings improved by 12 percent. The planned increase in customer satisfaction was 15 percent.

◆ **What is the company's rate of effectiveness?**

The rate of effectiveness is calculated is follows.

Effectiveness = Actual output ÷ Planned output

= 12% Actual increase in customer satisfaction ratings ÷ 15% Planned increase in customer satisfaction ratings
= 80% effectiveness

♦ **Is the customer service training the cause of the change in effectiveness?**

Although management was 80 percent effective in achieving its goal of increased customer satisfaction, that result was not necessarily related to the customer service training expenditures. The increase in customer satisfaction could have resulted partially or entirely from other causes such as a reduction in complex customer orders. Therefore, management does not know for certain whether the customer service training program was the most effective way in which to increase customer satisfaction.

The relationship between discretionary costs and desired results is inconclusive at best, and the effectiveness of such costs can be inferred only from the relationship of actual to desired output. Because many discretionary costs result in benefits that must be measured on a nondefinitive and nonmonetary basis, exercising control of these costs is difficult.

Engineered Cost Variances

Some discretionary activities are repetitive enough to allow the development of standards similar to those for manufacturing costs. Such activities result in **engineered costs**, which are costs that have been found to bear observable and known relationships to a quantifiable activity base. Such costs can be treated as either variable or fixed. Discretionary cost activities that fit into the engineered cost category are usually geared to a performance measure related to work accomplished. Budget appropriations for engineered costs are based on the static master budget. However, control can be exerted through the use of flexible budgets if the expected level of activity is not achieved.

DEMO 16-5B LO16-5   Measuring the Efficiency of Engineered Costs

To illustrate the use of engineered costs, assume that Precision Industrial has found that routine machine inspections of machining lathes can be treated as an engineered cost. Because Precision Industrial uses only one type of lathe, inspections are similar enough to allow management to develop a standard inspection time. Precision Industrial managers summarized the following estimates, based on the observation of inspections.

Inspection time per lathe	20 minutes
Number of inspections per hour	3

From this information, the company can obtain a fairly valid estimate of what inspection costs should be based on the inspection activity level and can compare actual cost against the standard cost each period. The activity base of this engineered cost is the number of inspections performed.

In May, Precision Industrial management makes the following predictions.

Budgeted number of inspections	10,500
÷ Number of budgeted inspections per hour	3
Budgeted inspection time in hours	3,500

If the standard average hourly pay rate for inspectors is $50, the May budget for this activity is calculated as follows.

$$\$50 \text{ per hour} \times 3{,}500 \text{ hours} = \$175{,}000 \text{ budgeted inspections costs}$$

Actual information for May is summarized as follows.

	May
Actual number of inspections	10,770
Actual number of hours of inspections	3,600
Actual cost of inspections	$176,400
Actual cost per hour of inspections ($176,400/3,600)	$ 49

♦ **Using the generalized cost analysis model for variance analysis presented in Chapter 10, how are the price and efficiency variances calculated for inspection costs?**

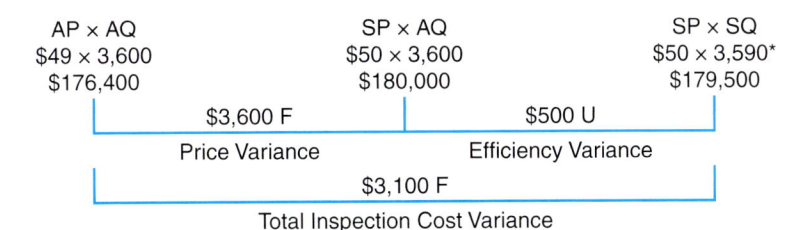

```
     AP × AQ              SP × AQ              SP × SQ
   $49 × 3,600          $50 × 3,600          $50 × 3,590*
    $176,400             $180,000             $179,500
          └─────$3,600 F─────┘└─────$500 U─────┘
             Price Variance      Efficiency Variance
          └──────────────$3,100 F──────────────┘
                  Total Inspection Cost Variance
```

*10,770 Actual inspections ÷ 3 Budgeted inspections per hour = 3,590 standard inspection hours allowed

The inspection cost variances are visually depicted as follows.

Inspection Cost Variance

Price Variance	$3,600
Efficiency Variance	$(500)

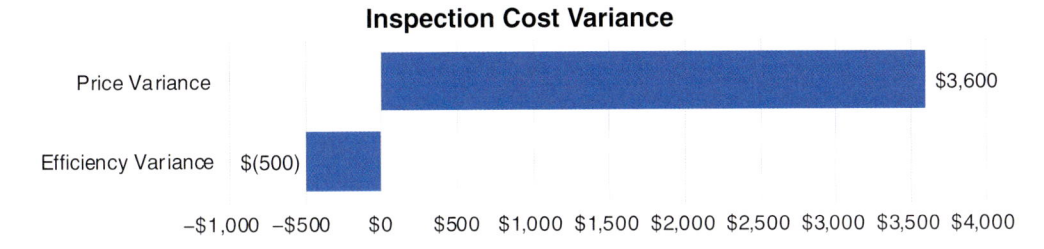

The price variance shows that, on average, Precision Industrial paid $1 less per hour for inspectors during May than was planned.

$49 Actual inspection cost per hour − $50 Budgeted inspection cost per hour = $(1)

The unfavorable efficiency variance results from using 10 hours more than standard for May.

3,600 Actual inspection hours − 3,590 Standard inspection hours allowed = 10 hours

The preceding analysis is predicated on the company's willingness and ability to hire the exact number of inspection hours needed and a continual availability of lathes to inspect. If Precision Industrial can employ only full-time employees on a salary basis, analyzing inspection costs in the preceding manner is not very useful. In this instance, quality inspection cost becomes a discretionary fixed cost, and Precision Industrial might prefer the following type of fixed overhead variance analysis.

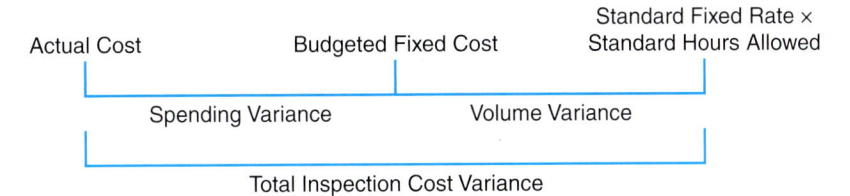

```
                                           Standard Fixed Rate ×
   Actual Cost       Budgeted Fixed Cost    Standard Hours Allowed
        └─────Spending Variance─────┘└─────Volume Variance─────┘
                  Total Inspection Cost Variance
```

The method of variance analysis and, thus, cost control must be appropriate to the cost category and management information needs. Regardless of the variance levels or the explanations provided, managers should always consider whether the activity itself and, therefore, its cost incurrence were sufficiently justified. Postincurrence audits of discretionary costs are often important in determining an expenditure's value.

Flexible Budget Variance Analysis

After discretionary cost budget appropriations have been made, monetary control is provided through the use of flexible budget-to-actual comparisons in the same manner as for other budgeted costs. Actual results are compared to expected results, and explanations should be provided for variances. Such explanations often can be found by recognizing cost consciousness attitudes. The following illustration involving two discretionary cost activities provides a flexible budget-to-actual comparison that demonstrates employee cost consciousness.

DEMO 16-5C LO16-5 — Preparing a Flexible Budget Analysis

Assume that Precision Industrial is one of many companies that outsource payroll processing activities to Payroll Financial Services (PFS). PFS has prepared the condensed budget for the first quarter of the year. Allison James, the controller for PFS, estimates 1,200,000 electronic paychecks will be processed during that period. The company charges clients $0.75 per electronic check processed.

Payroll Financial Services Budget—First Quarter

	A	B	C
1			Total
2	Revenues		
3	Processing fees (1,200,000 × $0.75)		$ 900,000
4	Expenses		
5	Employee training (fixed)	$ 80,000	
6	Maintenance ($1.20 × (1,200,000/50))	28,800	
7	Office ($100 × 600 budgeted office hours)	60,000	
8	Wages and fringe benefits (600 budgeted office hours × 10 employees × $30 per hour)	180,000	
9	Salaries and fringe benefits (fixed)	120,000	
10	Depreciation (fixed)	75,000	(543,800)
11	Operating income before tax		$ 356,200

In pursuing a strategy of total quality management and continuous improvement, PFS's management has chosen to fund employee training to improve employee and customer satisfaction. The company also considers maintenance a discretionary cost, and the budget allows a $1.20 processing fee per 50 checks processed. Office costs include utilities, phone service, supplies, and delivery. These costs are variable and are budgeted at $100 per office hour. PFS expects to operate at 600 office hours in the budget quarter. Wages are for ten employees, who are paid an average wage of $30 per hour. Salaries and fringe benefits are for management level personnel and, like depreciation, are fixed costs.

James collected the revenue and expense data shown below during the first quarter of the year for the processing of 1,300,000 electronic checks. Because of computer downtime during the quarter, PFS worked five extra hours on four different workdays, for a total of 620 hours (= 600 hours + (5 hours × 4 days)). Additional contracts were responsible for the majority of the increase in checks processed.

Payroll Financial Services Actual Results—First Quarter

	A	B	C
1			Total
2	Revenues		
3	Processing fees (1,300,000 × $0.75)		$ 975,000
4	Expenses		
5	Employee training	$ 70,000	
6	Maintenance	26,300	
7	Office	63,860	
8	Wages and fringe benefits	192,200	
9	Salaries and fringe benefits	116,450	
10	Depreciation	85,000	(553,810)
11	Operating income before tax		$ 421,190

◆ **What are the variances between actual results for the first quarter and the flexible budget for the first quarter?**

The original static budget is adjusted for actual activity to produce the flexible budget. Variances are calculated as the differences between the flexible budget and the actual results.

Payroll Financial Services Budget-to-Actual Comparison for First Quarter

	A	B	C	D	E	F	G	H
1		Budget Item No.	Original Budget	Budget for Actual Results		Actual	Variances	
2	Revenues							
3	Processing fees		$900,000	$975,000		$975,000	$ 0	
4	Expenses							
5	Training	(1)	$ 80,000	$ 80,000		$ 70,000	$ 10,000	F
6	Maintenance	(2)	28,800	31,200	a	26,300	4,900	F
7	Office	(3)	60,000	62,000	b	63,860	1,860	U
8	Wages and fringe benefits	(4)	180,000	186,000	c	192,200	6,200	U
9	Salaries and fringe benefits	(5)	120,000	120,000		116,450	3,550	F
10	Depreciation	(6)	75,000	75,000		85,000	10,000	U
11	Total expenses		$543,800	$554,200		$553,810	$ 390	F
12	Operating income before tax		$356,200	$420,800		$421,190	$ 390	F

a $1.20 × (1,300,000/50) = $31,200   b $100 × 620 hours = $62,000   c 10 employees × 620 hours × $30 per hour = $186,000

The flexible budget variances are visually depicted as follows.

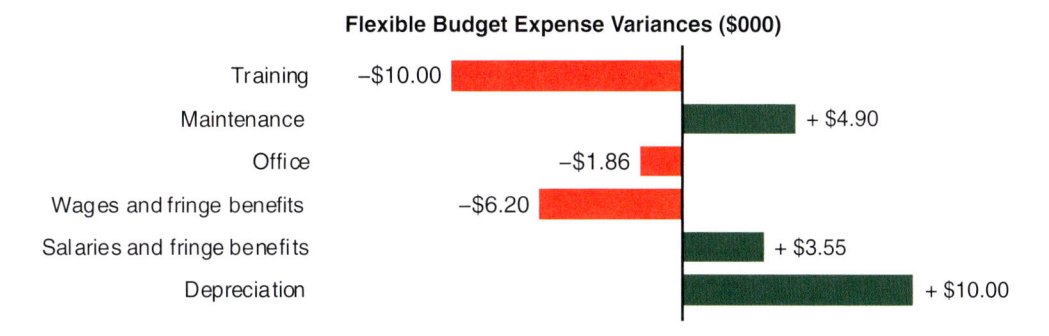

Flexible Budget Expense Variances ($000)

Training	−$10.00
Maintenance	+ $4.90
Office	−$1.86
Wages and fringe benefits	−$6.20
Salaries and fringe benefits	+ $3.55
Depreciation	+ $10.00

Variance Explanations Because actual costs exceeded the original budget, the board questioned whether costs had been effectively controlled. Assume that PFS's board of directors requested explanations for the cost variances. James provided the following explanations for the variances utilizing a flexible budget variance approach. Each explanation is preceded by the related budget item number.

1. **Training** The discretionary cost for employee training decreased because the vendor providing training services announced a new, higher price for its services. PFS chose to decrease training services while researching the pricing structure of other training service vendors. *Comment: This explanation reflects a cost containment approach to short-term management of training costs. In the long term, the company must provide at least the original level of training to avoid an eventual decline in quality and customer service. If a lower cost source of training services cannot be identified, the company may need to consider raising prices to maintain profitability.*

2. **Maintenance** Managers obtained a favorable price on maintenance supplies obtained from a new vendor which caused maintenance costs to decrease. *Comment: This explanation reflects an understanding of how to reduce costs without adversely affecting quality. The company has found a way to reduce costs while maintaining high client service quality. Costs have been reduced by obtaining the maintenance inputs at a lower unit cost.*

3. **Office** Office expenses were influenced by two factors: the additional 20 hours of operation and an increase in local utility rates, which caused PFS's costs to rise $3 per operating hour.

620 hours × $103 = $63,860 Actual office expenses

Comment: The first part of the explanation reflects an understanding of the nature of variable costs—working additional hours caused additional costs to be incurred. The second part of the explanation reflects an understanding of the nature of specific price-level adjustments. The increase in utility rates was caused by an increase in fuel prices paid by the utility company and passed along to customers through a higher rate.

4. **Wages and fringe benefits** The increase in wages was caused by two factors: 20 additional operating hours and a $1 increase in the hourly cost of fringe benefits because of an increase in health insurance premiums.

10 employees × 620 hours × $30 per hour................	$186,000
Increase in fringe benefit costs (10 × 620 × $1)...........	6,200
Total wages cost....................................	$192,200

Comment: These cost changes reflect the nature of variable costs and an unavoidable increase caused by a vendor cost adjustment.

5. **Salaries and fringe benefits** A new purchasing agent, hired at the beginning of the quarter, is being paid $14,200 (or $3,500 per quarter = $14,200/4) less per year than the previous agent.
Comment: Salaries are usually higher for more experienced managers. The new manager is less experienced than the previous manager and, therefore, is being paid a lower salary.

6. **Depreciation** The depreciation increase was related to the purchase and installation of a new electronic data interchange (EDI) system. The purchase was made with board approval when a competitor went bankrupt during the quarter and had a distress liquidation sale. Purchase of this technology had been included in the capital budget for the fourth, not the first, quarter.
Comment: Acquiring the EDI technology is a good example of the cost containment concept. PFS wanted to buy the software and equipment and had an opportunity to buy it at a substantial savings, but earlier than anticipated. This purchase created an unfavorable cost variance for depreciation in the first quarter, but it shows an instance of planning, foresight, and flexibility. The long-run benefits of this purchase are twofold. First, the capital budget will show a favorable variance when this equipment's actual and expected costs are compared. Second, in future periods, the budgeted committed cost for depreciation will be less than it would have been had the purchase not been made at this time.

Note that the variance computations compare a revised budget using actual electronic checks processed as the cost driver to actual revenues and costs. When comparing budgeted and actual expenditures, managers must be careful to analyze variances using an equitable basis of measurement. These variance computations illustrate the use of flexible budgeting. Comparisons between the original budget and actual results for the variable cost items would not have been useful for control purposes because variable costs automatically change with changes in cost driver volume levels.

In addition to effective cost control, management also must develop tools that are effective in managing a critical organizational resource: cash (discussed in the next section).

REVIEW 16-5 | **LO16-5** | **Controlling Discretionary Costs**

Part One: Measuring Efficiency and Effectiveness of Discretionary Cost

My Fitness Inc., an athletic club, hires athletic trainers at its facilities primarily to offer individualized training sessions for its club members. However, trainers are involved in other general activities including some administrative functions. The company believes it can treat the cost of the training as an engineered cost. The following data is summarized related to the training sessions.

continued

> | | |
> |---|---|
> | Planned number of one-hour training sessions | 385 |
> | Budgeted trainer hours | 480 |
> | Actual number of one-hour training sessions | 340 |
> | Actual trainer hours | 455 |
>
> a. Calculate the degree of effectiveness of the training program relative to the number of one-hour training sessions.
> b. Calculate planned efficiency of the trainers.
> c. Calculate the actual efficiency of the trainers.
> d. **Critical thinking:** Did the company exceed effectiveness and efficiency expectations?
>
> **Part Two: Engineered Cost Variance Analysis**
>
> Management at Premiere Manufacturers Inc. has estimated that each quality control inspector should be able to make an average of 40 inspections per hour. The standard rate is $30 per hour. During the first month, 145,800 inspections were made, and the total pay to the inspectors was $122,300 for 4,200 hours of work.
>
> a. Perform a variance analysis for management on the quality control labor cost.
> b. **Critical thinking:** Analyze your results.
>
> More practice: E16-41, E16-42, E16-43
> Solution on p. 16-55.

CASH MANAGEMENT

Of all organizational resources, cash is one of the most important and challenging to manage. Cash is the organizational resource that is the medium of exchange in most business transactions. Two key cash management tools were introduced in Chapter 9.

- Cash budget
- Budgeted (pro forma) cash flow statement

This section provides an overview of cash management objectives and tools.

An organization's liquidity depends on having sufficient cash available to retire debts and other obligations as they come due. However, holding too much cash reduces a firm's profitability because the return on idle cash is below both the return that can be earned on other productive assets and the cost of capital.

Firms hold cash to liquidate transactions, to cover unexpected events, and for speculation. Objectives of managing cash are similar to objectives of managing inventories. Cash levels should be sufficient to cover all needs but low enough to constrain opportunity costs associated with alternative uses of the cash. Models useful in managing inventory (discussed in Chapter 18) are also useful for managing cash levels. Optimal cash management requires answers to the three questions posed in the following sections.

LO16-6 What are the objectives managers strive to accomplish in managing cash?

What Variables Influence the Optimal Level of Cash?

The cash budget and pro forma statement of cash flows provide managers information about the amounts and timing of cash flows. These data are the primary inputs to determining the "inventory" of cash that should be available at a specific point in the budget year. However, the actual level of cash maintained can differ from that necessary to meet the cash flow requirements in the cash budget.

The level of confidence that managers have in the cash budget is a nonquantitative factor that influences the desired cash balance. For example, the less certain managers are of either the amount or timing of cash inflows or outflows, the higher is the amount of cash that managers will hold. If actual cash flows fail to match budgetary amounts, more cash could be required to satisfy transactions. Similarly, the greater the variability in cash requirements throughout the year, the more conservative managers must be in managing cash. To avoid liquidity problems, managers of firms with high variability in the operating cycle must hold a greater amount of cash than managers of firms with very stable, predictable operating cycles. Firms that would have difficulty arranging for short-term credit to cover unexpected cash shortages are forced to hold higher amounts of cash to cover contingencies.

Also, securities ratings (particularly bond ratings) can induce firms to hold larger cash balances than is justified based on all other considerations. A favorable bond rating is contingent on the organization paying interest and principal when these amounts are due. Security rating agencies encourage organizations to demonstrate conservative practices in managing cash. Related to bond ratings, firms with debt may be obligated by loan covenants to maintain minimum levels of cash.

What Are the Sources of Cash?

There are three usual sources of cash:

- sales of goods or services (the primary source);
- sale of equity or debt securities and other shorter-term instruments; and
- sale of assets that are no longer necessary or productive.

The capital budget is the key control tool for the last two sources of cash (refer to Chapter 19).

Management of cash consumed by and derived from the operating cycle is integral to the management of working capital. **Working capital** is a measure of liquidity and is calculated as follows.

$$\text{Working capital} = \text{Current assets} - \text{Current liabilities}$$

Current assets represent cash and other assets that will be converted into cash (either directly or indirectly) through operations within a reasonably short period of time. Under normal operating conditions, cash is generated by sales of inventory and collection of accounts receivable. **Current liabilities** are financial obligations that will become due within a relatively short period of time and will be paid from cash currently available and from the pool of cash generated from current assets.

In the operating cycle of a manufacturer, cash is first invested in material and conversion costs, then in finished goods inventory, followed by (or concurrently with) marketing and administrative activities, and finally in accounts receivable. The cycle is completed when the accounts receivable are collected. **Exhibit 16.8** illustrates the cash conversion cycle.

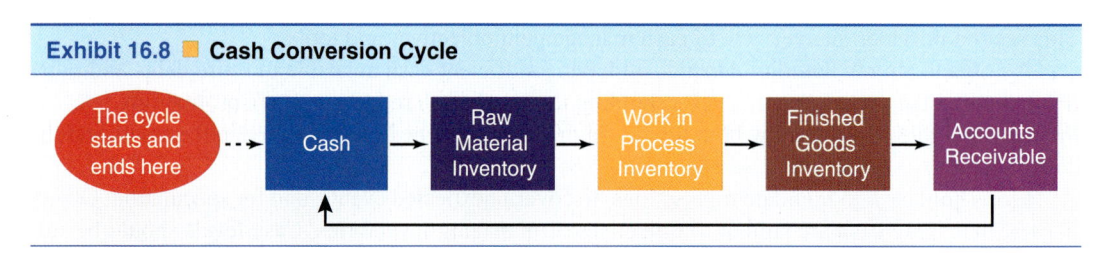

Exhibit 16.8 ■ Cash Conversion Cycle

The cycle starts and ends here → Cash → Raw Material Inventory → Work in Process Inventory → Finished Goods Inventory → Accounts Receivable

Cash Conversion Cycle

The **cash conversion cycle** is calculated as follows.

$$\text{Cash conversion cycle} = \text{Days sales in inventory} + \text{Days sales in receivables} - \text{Days payable}$$

The cash conversion measures the time it takes for a company to convert its inventory into cash receipts from operations. To calculate the cash conversion cycle, three ratios must first be calculated.

Cash Conversion Cycle

Days Sales in Inventory   Days Sales in Receivables   Days Payable

Days sales in inventory An indication of how many days of sales, on average, the inventory balance could supply is **days sales in inventory**, calculated as follows.

$$\text{Days sales in inventory} = \frac{\text{Average Inventory}}{\text{Average daily cost of goods sold}}$$

The average daily cost of goods sold is calculated by dividing cost of goods sold by the number of days in a year (365 days). Days sales in inventory is often regarded as both a measure of liquidity and a measure of performance. As a liquidity measure, days sales in inventory reveals the number of days, on average, inventory is in production or held before being sold. The goal is to decrease this ratio. As a performance measure, days sales in inventory reveals how well the firm is managing investments in inventory. *Inventory turnover*, calculated as cost of goods sold divided by average inventory, can also be used to measure a company's success in reducing inventory (see Chapter 18).

Days Sales in Receivables Next to cash and marketable securities, receivables are the most liquid assets. They are converted directly into cash in the normal course of business. **Days sales in receivables** measures the average number of days it takes to generate the value of uncollected credit sales at a point in time and is calculated as follows.

$$\text{Days sales in receivables} = \frac{\text{Average accounts receivable}}{\text{Average daily credit sales}}$$

The average daily credit sales is calculated by dividing credit sales by the number of days in a year (365 days). Days sales in receivables is a measure of both liquidity and performance. As a measure of liquidity, it reveals how many days on average it takes to convert accounts receivable into cash. As a performance measure, days sales in receivables reveals how well the firm is managing the credit extended to customers. The longer the collection period, the less cash is available for daily operations; thus, a larger ratio is less desirable.

Days Payable The measurement of the amount of time, on average, that a company pays off its short-term debts is called **days payable**, and is calculated as follows.

$$\text{Days payable} = \frac{\text{Average accounts payable}}{\text{Average daily cost of goods sold}}$$

A longer days payable means that the company holds on to cash for a relatively longer period of time which could then be invested, providing an additional source of income. This means that a larger ratio is desirable.

Calculating the Cash Conversion Cycle — LO16-6 DEMO 16-6

Assume the following selected information for Breckenridge Company.

	Current Year	Prior Year
Selected balance sheet data		
Cash and cash equivalents	$ 60,075	$ 53,640
Accounts receivable	75,510	55,440
Inventories	76,636	57,560
Accounts payable	70,380	49,120
Total current assets	236,070	180,880
Total current liabilities	101,160	69,680
Selected income statement data		
Sales	$438,000	$321,120
Cost of goods sold	273,750	193,720

◆ Measured at the end of the current year, what is (1) working capital, (2) days sales in inventory, (3) days sales in receivables, (4) days payable, and (5) cash conversion cycle?

1. Working capital

$$\text{Working capital} = \text{Current assets} - \text{Current liabilities}$$

$$\text{Working capital} = \$236,070 - \$101,160 = \$134,910$$

This means that Breckenridge Company has $134,910 that it can use as operating funds in the near future.

2. Days sales in inventory

$$\frac{\text{Average inventory}}{\text{Average daily cost of goods sold}}$$

$$\frac{(\$76{,}636 + \$57{,}560)/2}{(\$273{,}750/365 \text{ days})} = \frac{\$67{,}098}{\$750} = 89.5 \text{ days}$$

During the year, the average inventory available was sufficient to meet the average sales needs for 89.5 days. Since ending inventory is somewhat higher than the average inventory for the year, inventory at year-end is sufficient to supply somewhat more than 89.5 days' average sales.

3. Days sales in receivables

$$\frac{\text{Average accounts receivable}}{\text{Average daily credit sales}}$$

$$\frac{(\$75{,}510 + \$55{,}440)/2}{(\$438{,}000/365 \text{ days})} = \frac{\$65{,}475}{\$1{,}200} = 54.6 \text{ days}$$

At the end of the current year, Breckenridge Company had receivables equal to the average sales for 54.6 days.

4. Days payable

$$\frac{\text{Average accounts payable}}{\text{Average daily cost of goods sold}}$$

$$\frac{(\$70{,}380 + \$49{,}120)/2}{(\$273{,}750/365 \text{ days})} = \frac{\$59{,}750}{\$750} = 79.7 \text{ days}$$

Breckenridge takes on average, 79.7 days to pay its accounts payable balance.

5. Cash conversion cycle

Cash conversion cycle = Days sales in inventory + Days sales in receivables − Days payable

Cash conversion cycle = 89.5 days + 54.6 days − 79.7 days = 64.4 days

The cash conversion cycle for Breckenridge indicates that on average, the company converts its inventory into cash from sales in 64.4 days.

Effective management of the cash conversion cycle can both reduce the demand for cash and increase its supply. For example, if cash invested (such as in inventories and receivables) during the operating cycle can be reduced by accelerating the cycle, the cash balance will increase. In the utopian case, raw material would be instantly obtained when a customer placed an order but paid for at a later date. That material would then be instantly converted into a finished product that would instantly be transferred to the customer who would instantly pay in cash. Even without achieving the utopian ideal, any reduction in the length of the operating cycle will reduce inventory and accounts receivable balances and increase the cash and accounts payable balances.

Decreasing Days Sales in Inventory Managers can take explicit measures to decrease days sales in inventory by accelerating inventory turnover. For example, inventory levels can be reduced if products can be manufactured more quickly after customer orders are received. Inventory levels can also be reduced through the sharing of information and managing costs in supply-chain interactions. **Exhibit 16.9** depicts three significant supply-chain interactions and dependencies. The most obvious interaction is the downstream flow of goods and services. However, many supply-chain costs are associated with the other two arrows: the upstream flow of information and the upstream flow of payments.

Exhibit 16.9 ■ Supply-Chain Relationships

Suppliers → Firms and Their Internal Processes → Final Customers

Flow of Goods and Services →

← Flow of Information

← Flow of Payments

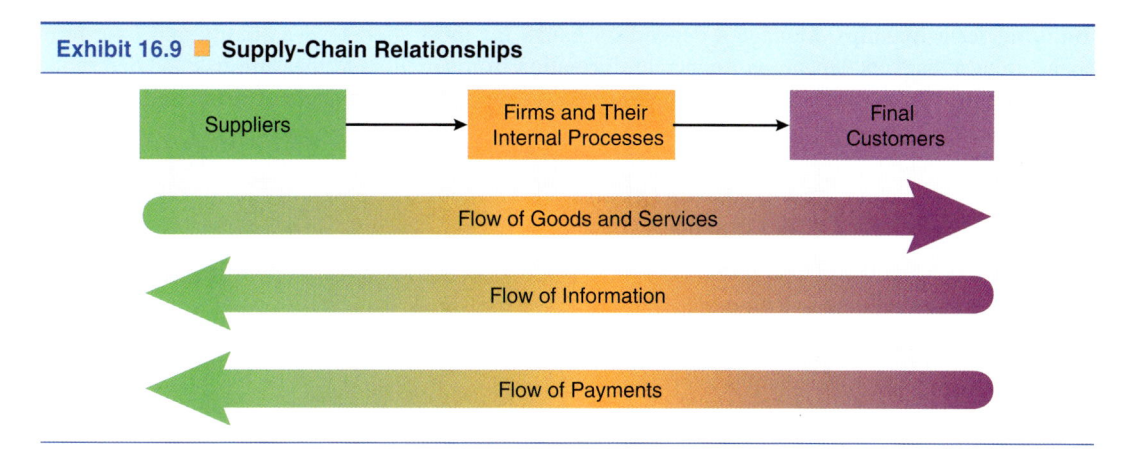

In the past, a significant amount of time and other resources was spent ordering parts and materials from suppliers and issuing payments for those inputs. The downstream firm typically prepared a material requisition form, purchase order, and receiving report. The upstream firm issued documents to control the production, shipping, and billing of the ordered goods. Collectively, these control processes and documents created significant supply-chain costs.

Today, firms increasingly use **e-procurement systems** to virtually purchase goods and services, exchange information and payments, and reduce purchasing transaction costs. Such systems are electronic B2B (business-to-business) applications that control the requisitioning, ordering, and payment functions for inputs.

Decreasing Days Sales in Receivables In addition to reducing inventory, cash collections can be accelerated to increase cash levels. Accounts receivable turnover can be directly influenced by terms given on credit sales, policies governing credit approval, discounts given for early payment, and use of the services of financial intermediaries that specialize in purchasing (or "factoring") accounts receivable. Other practices can be implemented to accelerate customer payments including using

- electronic invoicing,
- electronic funds transfers or online deposits,
- customer credit card payments, and
- lock boxes.

Centralizing cash collection functions at organizational headquarters may also allow accounts receivable to be converted to cash more quickly.

Increasing Days Payable Alternatively, the cash balance can be increased by slowing down payments for inputs. Managers can search among alternative vendors for the most desirable credit terms and policies. Credit rather than cash can be used to purchase inputs. Rather than paying factory employees weekly, a bimonthly or monthly pay plan can be instituted. Also, decentralizing cash disbursement functions can increase the interval from when a check is issued until it clears the financial banking system.

What Variables Influence the Cost of Carrying Cash?

The cost of carrying cash varies over time, and there are two classes of costs to manage: the cost of borrowing and the cost of issuing equity capital. For example, short-term borrowing costs will rise and fall with changes in inflation rates, creditworthiness of the borrower, and availability of funds for lending. The higher the short-term borrowing costs, the greater the incentive to minimize idle cash balances.

Second, there is an opportunity cost of holding cash. Excess cash can be invested in productive projects or returned to investors. Firms with multiple investment opportunities have a greater incentive to convert idle cash to other assets. Even if few investment opportunities are available, managers can always return cash to investors by reducing debt or repurchasing stock. The higher a firm's cost of capital, the greater the opportunity cost of holding idle cash.

Banking Relationships Managers depend on banks for most short-term liquidity and long-term loans. In turn, bankers depend on financial information from creditors to measure risk and determine loan eligibility. Accounting and cash flow information are key determinants of loan eligibility, loan limits, and credit terms.

From the bank's perspective, credit risk is a primary concern in determining whether, and how much, a bank will lend to an entity. Credit risk also is a key input in determining the borrower's interest rate. To assess credit risk, banks examine

- the borrower's credit history,
- the borrower's ability to generate cash flow,
- quality of collateral offered by the borrower,
- character of senior officers of the borrower, and
- the borrower's operational plans and strategies.

A loan agreement includes covenants or restrictions that prescribe minimal financial thresholds that the borrower must maintain over the loan term. For instance, covenants can stipulate minimum acceptable ratios for debt to assets, current assets to current liabilities, and interest coverage.

Accountants must monitor the firm's compliance with loan agreement covenants. By projecting revenues, expenses, and cash flows, accountants can identify potential problems before they are encountered and help develop plans to avoid covenant violations. If a covenant violation is inevitable, accountants can work with the bank to negotiate a solution to the situation. Furthermore, accountants should understand the bank's standard lending policies, such as margin requirements for short-term assets, and manage the firm's compliance with those policies.

Trust is an important element of a good relationship between a bank and a borrower. Development of trust depends on accountants providing the bank with accurate, conservative financial data as well as timely information about operating results. Accountants have the responsibility of preparing the reports provided to the bank and providing interpretations of the data to help bank personnel understand the financial and operating results.

Bankers abhor surprises. If a firm is facing bad news, such as the potential for missed loan payments or bankruptcy, the bank should be kept informed about the circumstances and efforts being made to overcome the challenge. By maintaining a trusting relationship with a bank and its officers, a firm will have a valuable partner in weathering financial storms.

In addition to building relationships with banks and other lenders, the trend is to build stronger ties to suppliers and providers of other necessary inputs as well.

REVIEW 16-6 LO16-6 Cash Conversion Cycle

A merchandiser summarized the following financial statement information for the current and prior year.

	Current Year	Prior Year
Selected balance sheet data		
Accounts receivable	$122,100	$138,200
Inventories	96,200	105,300
Current assets	397,800	519,400
Accounts payable	78,600	84,800
Current liabilities	153,300	222,500
Selected income statement data		
Sales	$706,800	$963,600
Cost of goods sold	426,180	603,600

a. Calculate the company's days sales in inventory, days sales in receivables, and days payable.
b. What is the company's cash conversion cycle?
c. **Critical Thinking:** Analyze your results.

More practice: E16-48, E16-49
Solution on p. 16-55.

COPING WITH UNCERTAINTY

The world of the management and cost accountant is split into two spheres separated by time. The first sphere is the historical, in which the accountant is concerned with accounting accurately and fairly for events and activities that have already occurred; examples include determining the production cost for the period, determining the cost of equipment that has been purchased, and ascertaining a department's or division's operating costs. The focus of financial accounting is accurately reporting historical accounting data.

The second sphere is future oriented, in which accountants deal with events and activities yet to unfold; examples include budgeting future production costs for organizational products, estimating the cost of equipment to be purchased, and projecting the impact of future events on departmental or divisional costs and revenues. Effectiveness of accountants in this second realm is determined in part by their abilities to cope with and manage uncertainty. **Uncertainty** reflects the doubt or imprecision in specifying future outcomes. Uncertainty arises from lack of complete knowledge about future events and is the reason accountants are less accurate in assigning costs to future events and activities than to historical events and activities. Much of management accountants' activity deals with uncertainty.

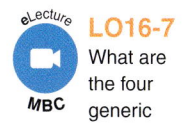

The Nature and Causes of Uncertainty

Before discussing specific strategies for dealing with effects of uncertainty in cost management, it is first necessary to understand the nature of uncertainty and its causes. Uncertainty in cost management has two main sources.

Understanding Uncertainty Causes and Effects First, uncertainty arises from a lack of identification or understanding of cost drivers. To estimate and budget future costs, accountants assess the relationship between a cost and its cost driver. In a simple and perfect world, each organizational cost would have a single driver that would perfectly explain every fluctuation in the related cost. However, in the real world, some costs may be predicted with accuracy based on the cost driver-to-cost relationship, but rarely is a cost predicted perfectly because cost is not entirely related to a single cost driver. In the context of cost prediction and cost understanding, **random** refers to the fact that some portion of a cost cannot be predicted from a specified cost driver or that a cost is stochastically, rather than deterministically, related to the cost driver.

For example, a cost accountant may use machine hours as the basis for predicting factory utility costs. Although changes in machine hour volume may account for nearly all of the change in factory utility cost, other factors, such as weather and number of employees, may account for some part of the cost. If machine hours alone are used as the basis for predicting utility costs, the prediction might be close to the actual cost, but the prediction will contain some error. This error is evidence that part of the utility cost is only randomly related to the machine-hour cost driver. Furthermore, logic suggests that whereas machine hours may explain with relative accuracy the quantity of kilowatt-hours of electricity consumed, machine hours may have no relationship to the price the utility company charges for each kilowatt-hour consumed.

Occurrence of Unforeseen Events A second source of uncertainty is unforeseen events. For example, the events of the pandemic dealt a severe economic blow to most industries in the United States, but for the airline industry, the impact was especially severe due to the immediate slow-down of travel. This industry is characterized by high fixed operating costs, and events that shock demand are a source of significant risk for any business, including the airlines. Without significant aid from the U.S. government, airlines may not have survived the direct impact the restrictions and behavioral responses had on travel. Very few firms anticipated the severity of the downturn and how extensively the global economy would be affected.

When firms plan for unforeseen events, it is impossible to know the magnitude of all potential contingencies. Accordingly, no reasonable plan to deal with unforeseen events will provide solutions for all possible occurrences. Even so, managers must develop strategies for reducing the level of uncertainty to which firms are exposed.

Four Strategies for Dealing with Uncertainty

There are four generic strategies applicable to cost management in the face of uncertainty:

| Use Regression and Sensitivity Analysis | Adjust Cost Structure | Use Options and Forward Contracts | Insure for Specific Events |

Regression and Sensitivity Analysis Typically, the historical relationship between a cost and its cost driver is used to assess the extent to which the cost and its cost driver are related. Statistical tools are often used in this type of analysis. In Chapter 3, least squares regression was introduced as a statistical tool to predict costs by estimating values for a and b in the following prediction equation, in which Y is the cost or other item to be predicted (dependent variable); a and b are, respectively, the intercept and slope in the prediction equation; and X is the predictor variable (independent variable).

$$Y = a + bX$$

When alternative independent variables exist, least squares regression can help select the independent variable that is the best predictor of the dependent variable. For example, managers can use least squares to decide whether machine hours, ambient temperature, factory production hours, or another variable best explains and predicts changes in factory utility expense. Recall that a coefficient of determination value of 0 means the predictor variable is not useful in predicting the dependent variable, and a value of 1 means the predictor variable is ideal. **Exhibit 16.10** illustrates a hypothetical relationship between factory utility costs and two possible predictor variables: machine hours and plant production hours. The exhibit features the relationships between dependent and independent variables based on six months of recent data. Ordinary least squares was used to estimate the exhibit's regression lines. The calculated coefficient of determination reflects the proximity of the data points to the fitted regression line. If the coefficient of determination is 1, all data points will fall on the ordinary least squares regression line. Given the relationships, neither of the candidate predictor variables provide a coefficient of determination of 1. However, the machine hour data points are much closer to the line than are the plant production hour data points. Thus, it follows that the coefficient of determination is higher for the machine hours regression (0.91) than for the plant production hours regression (0.59).

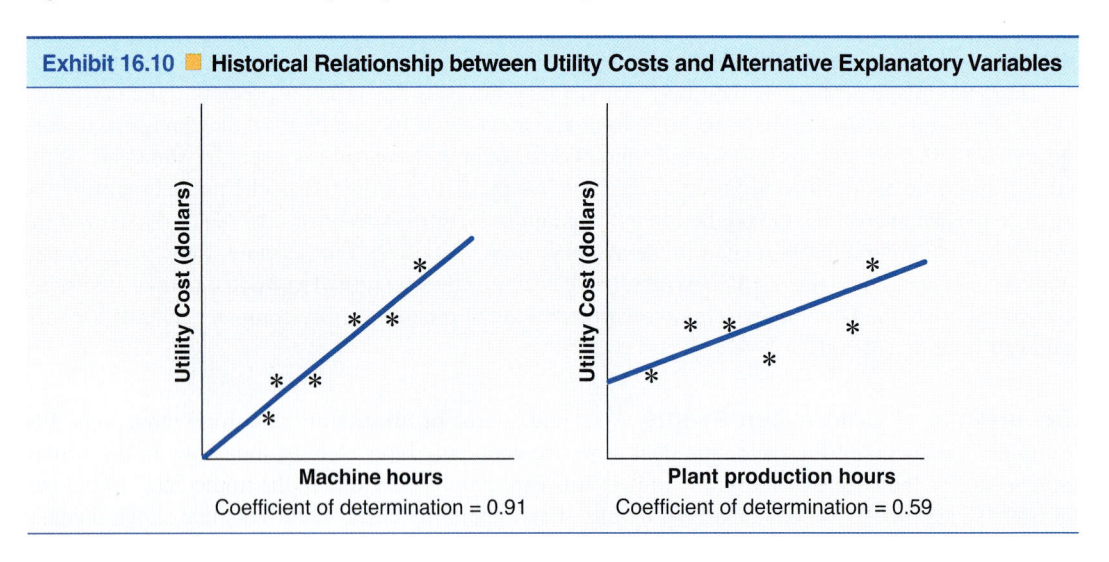

Exhibit 16.10 ■ **Historical Relationship between Utility Costs and Alternative Explanatory Variables**

Machine hours
Coefficient of determination = 0.91

Plant production hours
Coefficient of determination = 0.59

Using the coefficient of determination as a tool to select the best among candidate predictor variables will reduce the uncertainty regarding estimated costs or revenues. *All other things being equal, the higher the coefficient of determination, the lower is the uncertainty regarding the resulting prediction or forecast.* Other statistical techniques such as computer simulations and more multiple regression analysis as well as nonlinear relationships between independent and dependent variables, can also be used to select predictor variables. Use of these more advance techniques reduces the prediction error and the effects of uncertainty on prediction accuracy.

The alternative approach to explicitly considering the effects of uncertainty in cost estimates is to examine the sensitivity of costs and/or revenues to estimation errors. Because tools such as ordinary least squares regression provide predictions of a single value, it is useful to examine effects of errors in estimates. Sensitivity analysis is a tool commonly used for this purpose.

Performing a Sensitivity Analysis — LO16-7   DEMO 16-7

To illustrate, assume that Precision Industrial predicts its factory maintenance costs (Y) as a function of machine hours (X). Following is the prediction equation.

$$\text{Annual factory maintenance cost function: } Y = \$60{,}000{,}000 + \$50X$$

Precision Industrial expects to work 2,000,000 machine hours in the coming year. However, the possible range of activity is between 1,900,000 to 2,100,000 machine hours. The lower level reflects the most pessimistic level of customer demand, while the higher level reflects the most optimistic level of customer demand. As customer demand increases, more machine hours will have to be incurred to produce the demanded units.

◆ **What are estimated costs at the expected level of activity, the most pessimistic level, and the most optimistic level?**

Inserting the expected, minimum, and maximum values into the cost equation yields the following cost estimates.

$$\text{Maintenance cost at expected demand} = \$60{,}000{,}000 + \$50(2{,}000{,}000)$$
$$= \$160{,}000{,}000$$
$$\text{Maintenance cost at most pessimistic demand} = \$60{,}000{,}000 + \$50(1{,}900{,}000)$$
$$= \$155{,}000{,}000$$
$$\text{Maintenance cost at most optimistic demand} = \$60{,}000{,}000 + \$50(2{,}100{,}000)$$
$$= \$165{,}000{,}000$$

The predicted range of maintenance costs is depicted below.

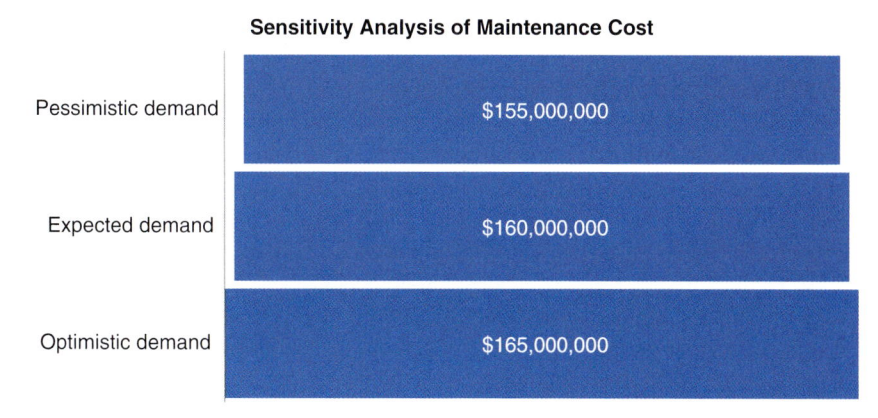

Sensitivity Analysis of Maintenance Cost

Pessimistic demand	$155,000,000
Expected demand	$160,000,000
Optimistic demand	$165,000,000

This approach yields very useful information in instances where there is uncertainty about volume of operations, perhaps because of uncertain customer demand. If Precision Industrial's managers are confident of the relationship between machine hours and factory maintenance costs as well as estimates of customer demand, the managers can be relatively confident that factory maintenance cost will fall between $155,000,000 and $165,000,000 for the coming year.

Structuring Costs to Adjust to Uncertain Outcomes As discussed earlier, the events of the pandemic were financially disastrous for the airline industry. The airline industry is characterized by very high levels of fixed costs, and in the short run, the level of costs is very insensitive to the level of customer demand. Consequently, if demand spikes, profits soar, and if demand falters, profits plummet and losses are quickly experienced. The greater the uncertainty about demand, the greater is the risk of allowing fixed costs to comprise a high proportion of total costs.

Consider the cost and revenue graphs that are shown in **Exhibit 16.11** for Companies A and B. Company A has a cost structure that is entirely variable, and Company B has a cost structure that is entirely fixed (has a higher degree of operating leverage). The space between the revenue and total cost lines in the graphs represents profits or losses. Note how the amount of profit varies greatly with small changes in volume for Company B. Alternatively, Company A's profits change slowly as volume changes. Accordingly, Company A's profits are less exposed to the effects of uncertainty. The degree of operating leverage is discussed in detail in Chapter 4 with regard to cost-volume-profit analysis.

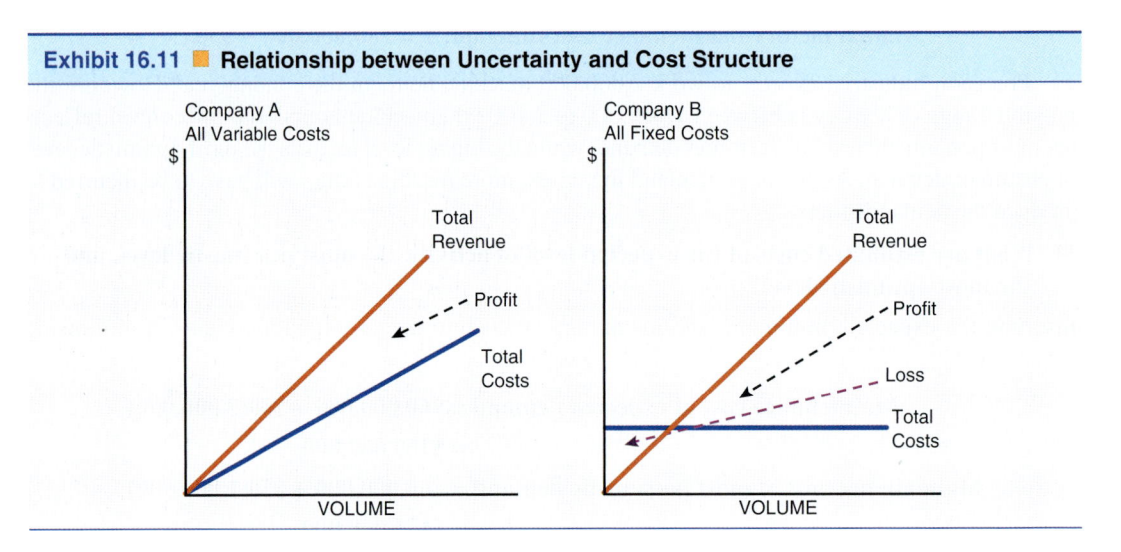

Exhibit 16.11 Relationship between Uncertainty and Cost Structure

Although fixed and variable costs are not completely substitutable, most companies have substantial opportunities to change their cost structures. For example, in the airline industry, managers could choose to lease rather than to purchase airplanes. The shorter the term of the lease, the more the cost of airplanes can approximate a variable cost. Thus, as demand changes, airplane leases can be added or canceled.

Options and Forward Contracts Uncertainty about input costs arises from two sources: the quantity and cost of inputs consumed. Although input quantity is typically highly correlated with customer demand and production volume, input price can be influenced by many other factors. Accordingly, even though machine hours may, on a long-term basis, prove to be highly correlated with utility cost, machine hours are more highly correlated with the quantity, rather than the price, component of cost. Thus, although the uncertainty surrounding quantity of input usage may be best resolved by an improved understanding of volume drivers, other strategies will be necessary to deal with price uncertainty.

Some companies operate in industries that are intensely competitive, and if input costs unexpectedly increase, companies may be unable to increase prices sufficiently to cover the cost increases. Such companies in particular need effective strategies for dealing with input cost uncertainty. Two tools used in such strategies are options and forward contracts.

Options and **forward contracts** are agreements that give the holder the right to purchase a given quantity of a specific input at a specific price at a specific time. Generically, the use of options and forward contracts to manage risk is known as **hedging**. To illustrate, companies such as food and soft drink manufacturers are heavily exposed to risks of price changes for corn. These companies can use options and forward contracts to protect against such price increases. Consider also airlines that hedge against fluctuations in fuel prices. For example, **Southwest Airlines** has a multi-year fuel hedging program that significantly offset market price increases in jet fuel in 2022. In fact, the value of the fuel hedges in 2022 was approximately $1 billion.[14]

---

[14] Reed, T. "Southwest Airlines holds $1 Billion in Fuel Hedges," *Forbes*, July 28, 2022, https://www.forbes.com/sites/tedreed/2022/07/28/southwest-airlines-reports-record-quarter-with-gains-from-fuel-hedging/?sh=5b9521525bf4 (accessed on November 15, 2023).

Forward contracts or options can be executed between a company and a specific vendor, or options can be purchased on organized exchanges such as the Chicago Mercantile Exchange, Chicago Board of Trade, and New York Mercantile Exchange. **Exhibit 16.12** lists items commonly traded on the organized exchanges. Just as the consumer of a commodity such as diesel fuel can use a forward contract or option to hedge against cost uncertainty, a producer of diesel fuel can use a forward contract or option to hedge against revenue uncertainty.

Exhibit 16.12 ■ Examples of Items Commonly Hedged

Energy	Metals	Interest Rates
heating oil	gold	short term
crude oil	silver	long term
gasoline	copper	
natural gas	aluminum	**Agriculture**
electricity	platinum	livestock
coal		meats
propane	**Currencies**	grains
		cotton

Insuring against Occurrences of Specific Events The final strategy for coping with uncertainty involves use of insurance contracts, in which one party (an insurer) in exchange for a payment (premium) agrees to reimburse a second party (an insured) for the costs of certain occurrences. Whereas other strategies for dealing with uncertainty largely address uncertainty about costs deriving from quantity and price variability, insurance is purchased to cope with uncertainty about occurrences of specific events. The types of events are limited only by the imagination of the contracting parties, but are typically those that, in the absence of insurance, would dramatically increase costs (e.g., to rebuild a factory following a fire) or decrease revenues (e.g., business is interrupted by a labor strike in a company's only factory). Common types of occurrences for which insurance protection are sought include events often described as "acts of nature" such as tornados, hailstorms, floods, and earthquakes. Other types of common events covered by insurance include fire, theft, vandalism, accidental death of a key employee, and product failure. Companies can also obtain D&O (directors' and officers') insurance that can protect the board members and corporate officers from being personally liable while they are acting on the company's behalf. However, D&O insurance does not typically protect directors and officers who engage in dishonest, fraudulent, or illegal actions.

Uncertainty in Estimating Costs — LO16-7 — REVIEW 16-7

Skyway Inc. identified a cost pool related to material handling costs for its manufacturing process. Using historical data and ordinary least squares regression, Skyway summarized two different equations to estimate the cost of material handling. The first equation uses pounds of materials as the cost driver and the second equation uses number of units produced as the cost driver.

Variable	Coefficient of Determination	Estimation Equation
Pounds of materials handled . . .	0.73	$Y = \$2{,}500 + \$60x$
Number of units produced	0.33	$Y = \$7{,}480 + \$53x$

The range of activities for the year is estimated to be 225 to 275 pounds of material or 200 to 300 units of production.

a. Which is the preferred cost driver for estimating material handling costs?
b. What is the best estimate for the range of costs related to materials handling costs?
c. **Critical Thinking:** How is a range of cost estimates useful in management decision making?

More practice:
MC16-21, E16-51
Solution on p. 16-55.

Comprehensive Chapter Review

Key Terms

appropriation, p. 16-15	current liabilities, p. 16-24	general price-level changes, p. 16-6
cash conversion cycle, p. 16-24	days payable, p. 16-25	hedging, p. 16-32
committed fixed costs, p. 16-13	days sales in inventory, p. 16-24	options, p. 16-32
Consumer Price Index, p. 16-6	days sales in receivables, p. 16-25	preventive, p. 16-2
corrective, p. 16-2	diagnostic, p. 16-2	price elasticity, p. 16-8
cost avoidance, p. 16-10	discretionary fixed cost, p. 16-14	random, p. 16-29
cost consciousness, p. 16-5	effectiveness, p. 16-17	spend analysis, p. 16-11
cost containment, p. 16-9	efficiency, p. 16-17	strategic alliances, p. 16-4
cost control system, p. 16-2	engineered costs, p. 16-18	uncertainty, p. 16-29
cost reduction, p. 16-10	e-procurement systems, p. 16-27	working capital, p. 16-24
current assets, p. 16-24	forward contracts, p. 16-32	

Chapter Summary

LO16-1 Cost Control Systems (Page 16-2)
- An effective cost control system helps manage costs
  - prior to an event through
    - establishment of budgets and standards, or
    - other stated expectations of performance outcomes;
  - during an event by
    - identifying deviations from plans or budgets, or
    - monitoring other aspects of operations relative to expectations; and
  - following an event by providing feedback on performance.

LO16-2 Cost Changes and Deviations (Page 16-5)
- Costs can change from one period to the next, or deviate from expectations, as a result of
  - variable costs moving with changes in volume.
  - inflation or deflation of prices.
  - supplier-changed prices
    - in response to changes in demand or
    - due to changes in cost of production.
  - purchase volume changes, which affect purchase discounts related to volume.

LO16-3 Generic Approaches to Cost Control (Page 16-9)
- Three generic approaches to cost control include
  - cost containment, which is an approach to minimize cost increases;
  - cost avoidance, which means finding ways to avoid high-cost inputs by substituting lower-cost inputs; and
  - cost reduction, which involves finding ways to alter operations to lower costs.

LO16-4 Fixed Costs (Page 16-13)
- Two primary types of fixed cost are
  - committed fixed costs, which are associated with an organization's basic infrastructure and are determined by long-run strategy (examples include depreciation, lease payments, and property taxes); and
  - discretionary fixed costs, which are incurred for activities for which the level and nature are determined by management judgment (examples include research and development, advertising, and employee training).

LO16-5 Controlling Discretionary Fixed Costs (Page 16-15)
- Control of discretionary fixed costs can apply
  - before an event by the use of budgets or by treating those costs as engineered costs if they are associated with repetitive activities;

Chapter 16 Approaches to Cost Control and Managing Uncertainty

- during an event by comparing budgets to actual expenditures; and
- after an event by calculating variances for engineered costs.

Managing Cash (Page 16-23)   *LO16-6*

- The objectives in managing cash are to
  - maintain an organization's liquidity by making certain there is enough cash to cover cash expenses and to retire debt; and
  - invest any idle cash so that a return is generated on cash balances exceeding liquidity needs.
  - Cash can be managed through the monitoring of the cash conversion cycle.

Uncertainty (Page 16-29)   *LO16-7*

- Uncertainty is greater for future events than for past events because
  - cause-and-effect relationships are incompletely understood.
  - events that are unforeseen can alter outcomes.
- Four generic strategies for dealing with uncertainty are to
  - explicitly consider uncertainty when estimates are generated by
    - using best predictor variables in generating estimates and
    - analyzing effects of estimation errors on estimates using sensitivity analysis;
  - structure costs to adjust to uncertain outcomes;
  - use options and forward contracts to manage price risks; and
  - use insurance to indemnify against occurrences of specific events such as
    - acts of nature or
    - fire, theft, and liability risks.

Solution Strategies

Measuring Benefit of Discretionary Costs   *LO16-5*

Effectiveness: Relationship of actual output and desired output
Efficiency: Relationship of input and output

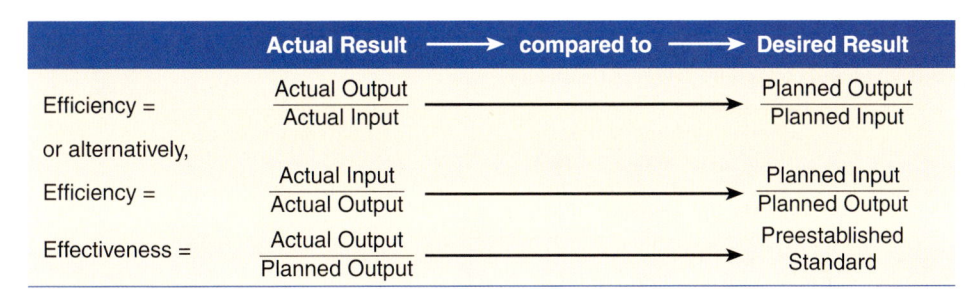

	Actual Result ⟶ compared to ⟶ Desired Result
Efficiency =	$\dfrac{\text{Actual Output}}{\text{Actual Input}}$ ⟶ $\dfrac{\text{Planned Output}}{\text{Planned Input}}$
or alternatively,	
Efficiency =	$\dfrac{\text{Actual Input}}{\text{Actual Output}}$ ⟶ $\dfrac{\text{Planned Input}}{\text{Planned Output}}$
Effectiveness =	$\dfrac{\text{Actual Output}}{\text{Planned Output}}$ ⟶ Preestablished Standard

Cost Variances   *LO16-5*

Comparison of actual costs with budgeted costs: allows management to compare discrepancies from the original plan

Comparison of actual costs with budgeted costs at actual activity level: allows management to determine how well costs were controlled; this approach requires a flexible budget

Variance analysis using standards for discretionary costs: allows management to compute variances for routine, structured discretionary costs

For discretionary costs susceptible to engineered cost treatment:

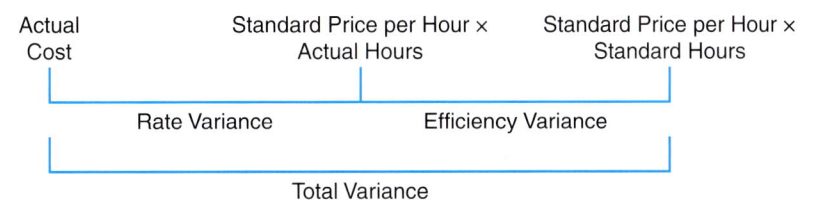

```
    Actual          Standard Price per Hour ×     Standard Price per Hour ×
     Cost                 Actual Hours                  Standard Hours
      └──────────────────────┴─────────────────────────────────┘
           Rate Variance              Efficiency Variance
      └────────────────────────────────────────────────────┘
                           Total Variance
```

© Cambridge Business Publishers

For discretionary costs that are managed as lump-sum fixed costs:

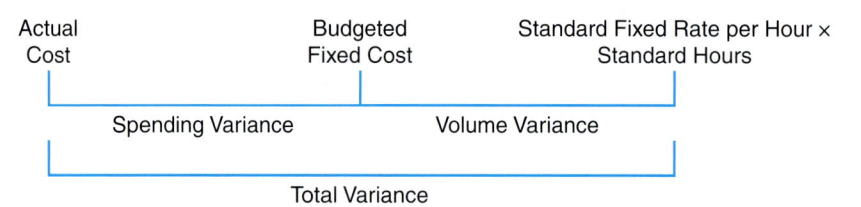

```
Actual              Budgeted              Standard Fixed Rate per Hour ×
Cost                Fixed Cost            Standard Hours
  |_____|_____|
        Spending Variance        Volume Variance
  |_____|
                     Total Variance
```

For discretionary costs involving both fixed and variable elements:

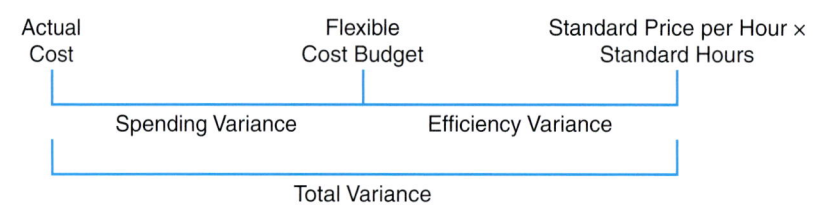

```
Actual              Flexible              Standard Price per Hour ×
Cost                Cost Budget           Standard Hours
  |_____|_____|
        Spending Variance        Efficiency Variance
  |_____|
                     Total Variance
```

LO16-6 Liquidity Ratios

Working capital = Current assets − Current liabilities

Cash conversion cycle = Days sales in inventory + Days sales in receivables − Days payable

Days sales in inventory = Average inventory ÷ Average daily cost of goods sold

Days sales in receivables = Average accounts receivable ÷ Average daily credit sales

Days payable = Average accounts payable ÷ Average daily cost of goods sold

Chapter Demonstration Problem

LO16-5 BigBiz, Inc., a firm with global operations, has developed a training program for compliance with company policy and international laws regarding hiring practices. The company believes it can treat the cost of this training as an engineered cost. The following data were extracted from documents addressing the training plan and from records regarding actual performance:

Planned volume of training	21,600 employees
Total budgeted trainer days	120
Actual volume of training	24,800 employees
Actual trainer days	130

Required:
a. Calculate the degree of effectiveness of the training program relative to number of employees trained.
b. Calculate planned efficiency for the trainers.
c. Calculate the actual efficiency of the trainers.
d. Comment on the performance of the trainers.

Solution to Demonstration Problem

a. Degree of effectiveness = Actual employees trained ÷ Budgeted employees trained
   = 24,800 ÷ 21,600
   = 1.148, or 115 percent (rounded)

b. Planned efficiency = Planned output ÷ Planned input
   = 21,600 employees ÷ 120 trainer days
   = 180 employees per trainer day

c. Actual efficiency = Actual output ÷ Actual input
   = 24,800 employees ÷ 130 trainer days
   = 191 employees per trainer day (rounded)

d. The performance of the trainers exceeded both effectiveness and efficiency expectations.

Data Analytics

DA16-1. Predicting maintenance costs using regression and scenario analysis

LO16-7

A large machine parts manufacturer with several plant locations would like to predict its machine maintenance costs for the next 12 months. Access the file included in MBC which includes data on maintenance hours, machine hours, and total maintenance costs for the last 18 months and complete the following requirements.

Required

a. Use regression analysis in Excel to develop a cost-estimating equation for total maintenance costs using total maintenance hours as the predictor. *Hint*: Under the Data tab, click on Data analysis, Regression, and select the cells for the Y Range and X Range.
   1. List the estimating equation and the R^2.
   2. Determine total maintenance costs for the year using 150,000 maintenance hours as expected annual hours.
b. Use regression analysis in Excel to develop a cost-estimating equation for total maintenance costs using total machine hours as the predictor.
   1. List the estimating equation and the R^2.
   2. Determine total maintenance costs for the year using 1,480,000 machine hours as expected annual hours.
c. Is total maintenance hours or total machine hours a better predictor of total maintenance costs?
d. Using the predictor identified in part *c*, perform a scenario analysis by developing expected, low, and high volume scenarios. The low volume scenario should reflect a decrease in hours of 10% from expected hours and a high volume scenario should reflect an increase in volume of 10% over expected hours. How could this information be useful to management in managing uncertainty?

Data Visualization

Data Visualization Activities are available in myBusinessCourse. These assignments use Tableau Dashboards to expose students to visual depictions of data and introduce students to data analytics through data visualizations. These exercises are easily assignable and auto graded by MBC.

Potential Ethical Issues

1. Including price escalation clauses in sales contracts but refusing to grant sales price decreases in the event of substantial cost reductions
2. Artificially reducing the supply of a product or service to force an increase in price (or maintain an artificially high price) to customers
3. Acquiring raw material inputs in excessively high quantities to obtain a low price merely to generate a favorable variance for an individual manager or responsibility center (especially if that manager is primarily evaluated on the basis of price variances) while simultaneously ignoring the related non-value-added carrying costs related to the purchase
4. Engaging in cost avoidance by acquiring counterfeit goods at a lower price than their name-brand counterparts
5. Outsourcing production or procurement activities to companies that violate acceptable (as perceived from the firm's domicile country) labor or environmental laws
6. Delaying payments to suppliers simply to generate larger investment returns on cash balances, especially when those suppliers do a high, or the highest, percentage of their business with the company
7. Manipulating or falsifying financial statements to obtain additional credit or lower interest rates on borrowings

Questions

Q16-1. How does the cost control system interact with the overall cost management system?

Q16-2. Why does the general control model begin with planning activities?

Q16-3. At what points in time is cost control for any specific organizational activity exercised? Why are these points of cost control important?

Q16-4. What factors can cause costs to change? Which of these factors are subject to cost containment and which are not? What creates the difference in controllability?

Q16-5. Differentiate between committed and discretionary fixed costs. Could a cost be considered discretionary by one firm and committed by another? If so, discuss and give an example. If not, discuss why not.

Q16-6. Why is it often difficult to measure the output of activities funded by discretionary costs?

Q16-7. Define the terms *efficiency* and *effectiveness*, and distinguish one from the other. Why is measuring the efficiency of discretionary costs often difficult? Explain how the effectiveness of discretionary cost activities can be measured.

Q16-8. What types of discretionary costs are subject to control as engineered costs? Provide several examples.

Q16-9. Why do firms hold cash balances? Why do some firms hold larger cash balances than other firms?

Q16-10. How is technology affecting supply-chain purchasing practices and transaction costs?

Q16-11. What are the four generic approaches to reducing uncertainty? Describe the context in which each approach is typically used.

Q16-12. What factors create uncertainty when estimating future costs and revenues?

Multiple Choice

LO16-1 MC16-13. Monitoring operations in a manufacturing facility in order to determine whether throughput is at the level planned is part of which cost control function?
  a. Preventive
  b. Diagnostic
  c. Cost consciousness
  d. Corrective

LO16-2 MC16-14. If the supply of hearing aid disposable batteries remains at a consistent level, but the overall demand for hearing aids with non-rechargeable batteries suddenly *drops*, what would likely happen to the cost of hearing aid disposable batteries in the short-term?
  a. Stay the same
  b. Increase
  c. Decrease
  d. Increase or decrease

LO16-2 MC16-15. Due to unfavorable economic conditions, Zelda Inc. is reporting profits under budget in its high-end clothing line. Which of the following conditions does the company have the most control over in the current year?
  a. Increase in general price levels due to inflation.
  b. Drop in the overall industry demand of high-end clothing.
  c. A reduction in the number of suppliers due to bankruptcies and consolidations which resulted in supplier price increases.
  d. Decrease in quantity of goods purchased due to an unexpected drop in Zelda's sales budget.

LO16-3 MC16-16. A decision by a charitable organization to outsource cyber security services to be more cost efficient is an example of
  a. Cost containment
  b. Cost avoidance
  c. Cost reduction
  d. Cost understanding

LO16-4 MC16-17. A type of cost that is often the result of structural decisions about the size and nature of a firm is called a (an)
  a. Committed fixed cost
  b. Controllable fixed cost
  c. Discretionary fixed cost
  d. Objective fixed cost

Chapter 16 Approaches to Cost Control and Managing Uncertainty

MC16-18. If the total inspection cost variance is $2,500 U, the actual inspection costs were $1,000,000, the price variance is $50,000 U, and the standard inspection hours allowed are 10,500 hours, what is the standard price per labor hour for inspections?
  a. $90.00
  b. $100.00
  c. $95.00
  d. $95.50

MC16-19. Cornwall Corporation's net accounts receivable balances were $68,000 and $47,000 at the beginning and end of the year, respectively. Cornwall's condensed Income Statement is shown below.

Sales	$900,000
Cost of goods sold	527,000
Operating expenses	175,000
Operating income	198,000
Income tax	79,000
Net income	$119,000

Cornwall's average number of days' sales in accounts receivable (using a 360-day year) is
  a. 8 days
  b. 13 days
  c. 19 days
  d. 23 days

MC16-20. The following financial information is given for Anjuli Corporation (in millions of dollars).

	Prior Year	Current Year
Sales	$10	$11
Cost of goods sold	6	7
Current assets		
Cash	2	3
Accounts receivable	3	4
Inventory	4	5

Between the prior year and the current year, did the days sales in inventory and days sales in receivables for Anjuli increase or decrease? Assume a 365-day year and use year-end inventory balances in your calculations.

	Days Sales in Inventory	Days Sales in Receivables
a.	Increased	Increased
b.	Increased	Decreased
c.	Decreased	Increased
d.	Decreased	Decreased

MC16-21. A simple regression equation has an R^2 of 0.85. This means that
  a. 85% of the variation of the dependent variable is explained by the regression line.
  b. 85% of the variation of the independent variable is explained by the regression line.
  c. the dependent and independent variables have a correlation coefficient of 0.85.
  d. the dependent variable does not have a strong correlation with the independent variable.

Exercises

E16-22. Cost control systems; writing Lois Jilg, the CEO of Minnesota Consulting, was concerned about the amount the firm had spent on travel and entertainment in the previous quarter. Jilg called Alice Briggs, the CFO, and expressed her concern, "Alice, according to our latest quarterly report, we spent $50,000 on travel and entertainment costs. Isn't that way too much?"

As an intern working for Briggs, how would you proceed to answer this query about control of quarterly travel and entertainment costs at Minnesota Consulting?

E16-23. Cost control; financial records; writing Idaho Industrial is a medium-size manufacturing corporation in a capital-intensive industry. Currently, actual profits are not meeting expectations. As a result, new investment funds are limited, and hiring is restricted. These consequences of the corporation's problems have placed a strain on the plant's repair and maintenance program. The result has been a reduction in work efficiency and cost control effectiveness in the repair and maintenance area.

The assistant controller proposes installing a maintenance work order system to overcome these problems. This system would require a work order to be initiated for each repair request from the department requesting service, and automatically for each regular maintenance activity. The maintenance superintendent would enter in the system the estimated time to complete a job, which would be visible in the system to the department in which the work would be performed. The work order would also serve as a job cost sheet. Actual cost of parts and supplies used on the job as well as actual labor costs incurred in completing the job would be entered in the system for the work order. The completed work order would be the basis for the charge to the department in which the repair or maintenance activity occurred.

The maintenance superintendent opposes the new system because of the additional time it will take to enter the information in the system. Plus, the superintendent believes that the department is currently understaffed.

a. Discuss how such a maintenance work order system would aid in cost control.
b. Explain how a maintenance work order system might assist the maintenance superintendent in getting authorization to hire more staff.

LO16-1

E16-24. Functions in a cost control system Indicate whether each of the cost control methods listed in *a* through *g* is (1) preventive, (2) corrective, or (3) diagnostic.

a. Increasing time to market to avoid costly product recalls.
b. Comparing inventory turnover at period-end to the industry average.
c. Continually applying a *management by exception* approach by identifying significant differences between actual and budgeted labor costs.
d. Establishing metrics and goals for sustainability measures related to carbon emissions.
e. Collaborating with a key supplier during a product's design stage in order to meet a target cost.
f. Identifying the primary reason for a cost overrun and taking steps to fix the problem so that it will not recur next period.
g. Monitoring a dashboard of critical performance measures during the period in order to identify potential problems that require immediate action.

LO16-1

E16-25. Strategic alliances; research In their annual reports, companies provide brief descriptions of their most important contracts, including strategic alliances. Select a large publicly traded company and obtain a copy of its most recent annual report (On the EDGAR portion of the SEC's Web site at https://www.sec.gov/edgar/search/#, enter the key word "strategic alliances"). Review the portions of the annual report that discuss strategic alliances. Based on your review, prepare a written report in which you discuss the following points:

a. Motivations for establishing strategic alliances.
b. Extent to which strategic alliances are used to conduct business.
c. Relative financial success of the strategic alliances.

LO16-1

E16-26. Strategic alliances; research; writing Assume you are employed by a technology company that is considering entering into a strategic alliance with a communications company to provide certain innovative services delivered via the Internet. As a financial professional, how could you contribute to the organization and management of the strategic alliance?

LO16-2

E16-27. Causes of cost changes; writing Identify in the following scenarios whether the cost change is attributable to effects of cost behavior (CB), inflation/deflation (I/D), supplier cost adjustment (CA), or quantity purchased (QP). Defend your answer.

a. Allison Mfg. experienced an increase in fuel costs following an increase in crude oil prices by members of OPEC.
b. Foremost Plastics experienced an increase in the cost of plastic resins when its main supplier merged with one of its competitors.
c. The amount Kimball Co. spent on raw materials declined when its sales volume dropped by 20 percent because of diminished overseas demand for its products.
d. Minerva Industrial reduced the price it paid for fasteners when it consolidated the purchases made from five vendors to just one vendor.
e. The price of corn syrup purchased by California Confectionary increased when the demand for corn-based ethanol jumped dramatically.
f. The amount Madison Beef Processing expended for direct labor jumped 25 percent when demand for the company's products jumped following the EU's removal of its U.S. beef import restrictions.

g. The price Villanova Steel paid for its metal products increased when it adopted JIT manufacturing practices and began purchasing steel in small lot sizes.
h. The cost of executive travel at Hudson Financial Services dropped by 20 percent when two new airlines began providing services at the airport nearest the firm's headquarters.

E16-28. Factors affecting cost changes Indicate if the following factors will generally cause an increase or decrease in cost levels.

a. Artificial intelligence is used by a biotechnology company to more quickly and comprehensively analyze patient data. The objective is to develop viable new drugs more efficiently.
b. A video game developer filed a patent for a new video game which quickly gained popularity.
c. A federal regulation affects an auto service shop. The rule requires that any person working on a motor vehicle air conditioner must have prerequisite training.
d. A furniture manufacturer reduces its production plan compared to budget due to an unexpected 20% decrease in the sales static budget.
e. The primary supplier of a machine manufacturer fell behind on production due to operational issues. As a result, the machine manufacturer must order needed component parts from a number of new suppliers in smaller quantities.
f. CPI index indicates a 3.7% increase over the prior year.
g. A pharmaceutical commonly prescribed for diabetes was discovered to be helpful for anxiety disorders. The unexpected increase in demand suddenly depleted the pharmaceutical inventory levels.

E16-29. Approaches to cost control Indicate whether the actions listed *a* through *g*, primarily represent initiatives for cost containment (CC), cost avoidance (CA), or cost reduction (CR). Indicate what costs were contained, avoided, or reduced as support for your answer. More than one answer may apply.

a. A retailer implemented a new distribution system that makes deliveries more efficient by changing and/or combining routes.
b. A retailer decided not to add a new product line because of the additional costs required for capabilities that were not available in-house.
c. A manufacturer reduces its energy costs and water usage in line with its sustainability goals by implementing operational efficiencies.
d. A cost variance system is implemented in a manufacturing setting to identify favorable and unfavorable variances in real time which helps control costs.
e. In order to save money on health care costs, a medium-sized manufacturer determined that self-insuring for medical costs falling under catastrophic levels is more cost beneficial that using a fully insured plan.
f. The president of a consulting firm indicated that the current year departmental budgets for selling costs need to be 10% less than the prior year actual amounts. As a result, a number of administrative positions were consolidated, resulting in a net reduction of staff.
g. A fast food retailer added self-service kiosks for customer food ordering to replace staff in response to increasing labor costs due to new regulations.

E16-30. Understanding costs; flexible budget Suppose you receive the following performance report from the accounting department for your first month as plant manager for a new company. Your supervisor, the vice president of manufacturing, has concerns that the report does not provide an accurate picture of your performance in the area of cost control.

	Actual	Budgeted	Variance
Units	10,000	12,000	2,000 U
Costs			
Direct materials	$ 299,000	$ 360,000	$ 61,000 F
Direct labor	345,500	432,000	86,500 F
Variable factory overhead	180,000	216,000	36,000 F
Fixed factory overhead	375,000	360,000	15,000 U
Total costs	$1,199,500	$1,368,000	$168,500 F

Prepare a revised budget that better reflects your performance.

LO16-2

E16-31. Understanding costs; assessing inflationary effects The president of Office Products Inc. is pleased with the progress her company has made in recent years, but she cannot understand why the company is always having to borrow funds when sales continually increase. Her office staff is small, and the largest cost outside of merchandise inventory is sales commissions, which are 10% of sales. As the cost of merchandise changes, she continually changes retail prices. Thus, she believes the profit margin should remain near the same percentage level for each period. However, even with her best efforts, the company continues to experience cash shortages. After gathering financial data, you prepare the following set of information for the past four years.

	Year 1	Year 2	Year 3	Year 4
Sales.............	$220,000	$228,800	$238,638	$246,500
Cost of goods sold ...	$121,000	$127,000	$133,500	$140,000
Current ratio........	1.60	1.55	1.43	1.35
Inventory turnover....	6.20	6.21	6.19	6.22
Inflation rate........	5.0%	5.0%	5.0%	5.0%

What conclusions can be drawn about the operating condition of Office Products Inc.? Explain. *Hint*: Consider analyzing trends.

LO16-2

E16-32. Understanding costs; assessing inflationary effects The Innovation Products Company wants to launch a new product to replace a current product that is technologically inferior. First-year sales for the replacement product are expected to be 50,000 units at a unit selling price of $12. The initial cost of the product is $9 per unit variable and $125,000 fixed. The expected sales growth is 1,000 units per year, and the expected inflation rate is in a range of 3% to 4% for both sales and variable costs.

a. Determine the anticipated profit margin for the new product for the first four years assuming
 1. No inflation
 2. Inflation at 4%
b. Compute the profit margin difference between no inflation and 4% inflation. Would this information make a difference in your evaluation of the new product? Explain.

LO16-3

E16-33. Cost control activities Rogal and Associates Legal Services hires full- and part-time professional employees. Full-time experienced staff can be hired for a salary of $60,000 per year; fringe benefit costs for each full-time employee amount to 20 percent of base salary. Rogal and Associates pays part-time professional employees $50 per hour but does not provide any fringe benefits. If a part-time employee has worked for the firm for more than 1,500 hours by year-end, he or she receives a $4,500 bonus.

a. Does the firm's policy of hiring part-time professional staff represent an example of cost containment, cost avoidance, or cost reduction? Explain.
b. For a given professional position, at what level of annual hours worked should the firm consider hiring full-time rather than part-time professional staff?

LO16-3

E16-34. Cost consciousness; research; team activity; writing All organizations seek to be aware of and control costs. In a three- or four-person team, choose one of the following industries and do web research to identify methods that have been used to control costs:

- Internet retailers
- Automobile manufacturers
- Hospitals
- Software companies
- Government entities

Discuss the various methods of cost control, dollars of costs saved (if available), and your perceptions of the positive and negative implications of each cost control methodology. You may choose a particular company within the industry should you so desire.

LO16-2, 3

E16-35. Cost control activities; writing Brenda Barnes has just been appointed the new director of Youth Hot-Line, a not-for-profit organization that operates a hot line for teenage individuals experiencing emotional difficulties. The phones are staffed by qualified social workers and psychologists who are paid on an hourly basis. Barnes took the following actions in the first week on her new job. Indicate whether the actions represent cost understanding (CU), cost containment (CC), cost avoidance (CA), or cost reduction (CR). Some actions may have more than one control technique; if they do, indicate the reason.

Chapter 16 Approaches to Cost Control and Managing Uncertainty

  a. Increased the advertising budget appropriation for the hotline.
  b. Exchanged the land line system (which is more costly to maintain and to expand) with cellular phones.
  c. Eliminated the call-forwarding answering service because Youth Hot-Line will now be staffed 24 hours a day.
  d. Eliminated two paid administrative positions and replaced these individuals with volunteers.
  e. Ordered blank notepads for the counselors to keep by their phones; the old notepads (stock now depleted) had the Youth Hot-Line logo and address printed on them.
  f. Negotiated a new contract with the telecommunications company which allows unlimited minutes with up to 20 cellular phones for a flat fee. Under the previous plan, charges were accrued per line. With the increased staff, Barnes needs five additional cellular phones.

E16-36. Outsourcing decision Suppose a technology firm, DataTech, offers Uber a one-year contract to manage all of Uber's data storage service at a cost of $15,000 per month. Assume monthly miles driven average 300,000 miles. Uber is now faced with the decision to continue to supply the data storage service internally or outsource the technology to DataTech. An analysis of the decision reveals that if Uber accepts the offer, it will be able to reduce the following:

- Variable platform and data storage costs by $0.20 per 10 miles.
- Fixed platform and data storage costs by $5,000.

Should Uber supply storage service internally or outsource it? *Hint*: Refer to Chapter 5.

E16-37. Outsourcing research A PricewaterhouseCoopers' (PwC) Global Operations Survey offers a narrower view of the role of outsourcing in operations. Rather than recommending outsourcing as a way to change the firm's cost structure, PwC views outsourcing as a way to focus on operations that truly differentiate the firm. The PwC study divides a company's capabilities into four groups:

  1. Differentiating capabilities
  2. Competitive necessities
  3. Basic capabilities
  4. Other activities

Access the PricewaterhouseCoopers report at https://www.pwc.com/gx/en/operations/reimagining-operations.pdf and answer the following questions.

  a. Describe each of the four groups of capabilities.
  b. Which group does PwC recommend focusing the most resources on in order to achieve the greatest returns?
  c. Which group does PwC recommend to outsource where possible?
  d. Which group does PwC recommend where the focus should be on efficiency and reducing costs?
  e. Which group does PwC indicate may be comprised of at least some non-valued-added services?

E16-38. Committed vs. discretionary costs; writing A list of committed and discretionary costs follows.

Annual audit fees	Internal audit salaries
Annual report preparation and printing	Marketing research
Building flood insurance	Preventive maintenance
Charitable contributions	Property taxes
Corporate advertising	Quality control inspection
Employee continuing education	Research and development salaries
Equipment depreciation	Research and development supplies
Interest on bonds payable	Administrative salaries

  a. Classify each of these costs as normally being either committed (C) or discretionary (D).
  b. Which of these costs can be either committed or discretionary based on management philosophy?
  c. For the expenses marked discretionary in (a), provide a monetary or nonmonetary surrogate output measure. For each output measure, briefly discuss any objections that could be raised to it.

E16-39. Committed vs. discretionary costs Choose letter C (for committed cost) or D (for discretionary cost) to indicate the type of each of the following described costs. Explain the rationale for your choice.

  a. Control is first provided during the capital budgeting process.
  b. Typical examples include advertising, research and development, and employee training.
  c. This type of cost cannot be easily reduced even during temporary slowdowns in activity.
  d. There is usually no "correct" amount at which to set funding levels.

© Cambridge Business Publishers

e. Typical examples include depreciation, lease rentals, and property taxes.
f. This type of cost often provides benefits that are not monetarily measurable.
g. Temporary reductions can usually be made without impairing the firm's long-range capacity or profitability.
h. This cost is primarily affected by long-run decisions regarding desired capacity levels.
i. It often is difficult to ascribe outcomes as being closely correlated with this type of cost.
j. This cost usually relates to service-type activities.

LO16-5 E16-40. Effectiveness measures Houston Health Clinic has used funds during the year for the following purposes:

a. Sent two cost accounting staff members to seminars on activity-based costing.
b. Purchased a kidney dialysis machine.
c. Built an attached parking garage for the clinic.
d. Redecorated the main lobby.
e. Placed an advertisement on four local discount-priced web sites.
f. Acquired new software to track patient charges and prepare itemized billings.

Provide nonmonetary, surrogate measures that would help evaluate the effectiveness of the monies spent.

LO16-5 E16-41. Effectiveness and efficiency measures Allridge University formed a new department to recruit top out-of-state students. The department's funding for the year was $1,600,000, and the department was given the goal of recruiting 600 new nonresident students. By year-end, the department was credited with recruiting 660 new students. The department actually consumed $1,873,200 in its recruiting efforts.

a. How effective was the newly formed department? Show calculations.
b. How efficient was the department? Show calculations.

LO16-5 E16-42. Engineered cost variances Fred's Freight employs three drivers who are paid $20 per hour for regular time and $30 for overtime. A single pickup and delivery requires, on average, one hour of driver time. Drivers are paid for a 40-hour week because they must be on call all day. One driver stands by for after-hour deliveries. Analyze the labor cost variances for one week in which the company made 105 daytime deliveries and 12 after-hour deliveries. The payroll for drivers for that week was $2,780. The employees worked 120 hours of regular time and 15 hours of overtime.

LO16-5 E16-43. Engineered cost variances Management at Robo Weld Inc. has estimated that each quality control inspector should be able to make an average of 24 inspections per hour. Retired factory supervisors are excellent quality control inspectors because of their familiarity with the products and processes in the plant. Robo Weld management has decided to staff the quality control program with these individuals and has set $20 as the standard hourly rate. During the first month of the new program, 50,040 inspections were made, and the total pay to the inspectors was $38,950 for 2,050 hours of work.

a. Perform a variance analysis for management on the quality control labor cost.
b. Assume that management could hire eight full-time inspectors for a monthly salary of $4,500 each and hire part-timers for the overflow. Each full-time inspector would work 170 hours per month. How would the total cost of this alternative compare to the cost of a 2,050-hour month at the standard rate of $20 per hour?

LO16-5 E16-44. Variance analysis; ethics; writing Cost control in the human resources office of Eastern Wholesale is evaluated based on engineered cost concepts. The office incurs both variable and fixed costs. The variable costs are largely driven by the amount of employee turnover. For the year, budgeted costs in the human resources office were:

Fixed.........	$400,000
Variable.......	800,000 (based on projected turnover of 2,000 employees)

For the year, actual costs in the human resources office were:

Fixed.........	$440,000
Variable.......	900,000 (actual turnover of 2,100 employees)

Chapter 16 Approaches to Cost Control and Managing Uncertainty

Using traditional variance analysis, evaluate the control of fixed and variable costs in the office. Does this method of evaluation encourage the human resources office managers to hire low-quality workers? Explain.

E16-45. Cash management; writing New England Automotive manufactures aftermarket automobile parts that are sold in a variety of outlets including auto parts stores and discount retailers. The following account data (in millions) have been taken from a recent balance sheet:

Current Assets	
Cash	$ 20
Accounts Receivable	280
Finished Goods Inventory	50
Work in Process Inventory	340
Raw Material Inventory	180
Current Liabilities	
Accounts Payable	$44
Other Liabilities	14

LO16-6

Discuss recommendations that New England Automotive managers could use to improve its cash position. Focus your discussion on the operating cycle rather than on other means of raising cash.

E16-46. e-Procurement; writing You are employed by a firm engaging in heavy manufacturing. Its direct materials are sourced globally, but its nonoperating inputs are sourced from a variety of U.S. vendors. You have been charged with making a presentation to the CFO about the benefits of e-procurement for nonoperating inputs. Outline the benefits your firm could expect to realize if it replaced its internet purchases with a state-of-the-art e-procurement system.

LO16-6

E16-47. Cash management Assume that a manufacturing company is determining the optimal minimum level of cash to maintain in a financial institution to cover short-term needs. *Separately* consider each of the following scenarios, *a* through *g*, and determine whether each item would be more likely to cause the optimal minimum level of cash to increase or decrease.

LO16-6

a. The company opened a new short-term line of credit.
b. Management is uncertain about the timing of cash inflows and outflows related to a new product launch.
c. The company signed a loan with a debt covenant requiring compliance with a minimum current ratio level.
d. The company is intent on maintaining its favorable bond rating on bonds outstanding.
e. The company's cost of capital increased.
f. Timing between when supplies are purchased for production and when cash is ultimately received from the sale of the final product is expected to vary month to month due to a change in market conditions.
g. Short-term borrowing costs increased.

E16-48. Cash conversion cycle Stellar Inc. summarized the following ratios for the current and prior years.

LO16-6

	Current Year	Prior Year
Days sales in receivables	45.2	48.1
Days sales in inventory	40.1	42.1
Days payable	43.8	42.5

a. What is the cash conversion cycle for the current year and the prior year?
b. Did the company's liquidity improve or worsen over the prior year?

E16-49. Cash conversion cycle Unique Products Inc. reported annual sales of $828,000. Average balances for the year for inventory, accounts receivable, and accounts payable were $115,000, $75,000, and $78,000, respectively.

LO16-6

a. If cost of goods sold reported for the year was $580,000, what is the company's cash conversion cycle?
b. Analyze your results.

LO16-6 **E16-50. Working capital** Indicate whether each of the following combined transactions would increase, decrease, or have no effect on net working capital.
1. A $1 million decrease in cash, and a $1 million increase in inventory.
2. A $1 million decrease in cash, and a $1 million decrease in accounts payable.
3. A $1 million decrease in cash, and a $1 million increase in fixed assets.
4. A $1 million increase in cash, and a $1 million increase in long-term debt.

LO16-7 **E16-51. Scenario analysis** Amund Inc. estimated the following information related to its annual shipping costs.

Fixed costs..............	$40,000
Variable costs per unit......	$ 5.45

Amund Inc. expects to ship 80,000 units. Shipping costs are dependent upon demand which could vary from a predicted low of 70,000 units to a predicted high of 94,000 units.

a. What is the cost equation for the company's shipping costs?
b. Determine estimated shipping costs at the expected level of activity, at the low level of activity, and at the high level of activity.
c. Calculate the cost per unit for each level described in part b.
d. How is the information in parts b and c useful to management for decision making?

LO16-7 **E16-52. Regression; coefficient** The following two cost equations were derived through regression analysis using two different predictors.
1. Cost equation using number of shipments as the predictor of shipping costs.
   $Y = 6.65X + \$287,801$
   $R^2 = 0.6045$
2. Cost equation using weight shipped as the predictor of shipping costs.
   $Y = 818.98X + \$109,934$
   $R^2 = 0.8591$

a. What is the dependent and independent variable in each equation?
b. Which equation has the lower uncertainty regarding the resulting prediction of shipping costs?

LO16-7 **E16-53. Coping with uncertainty; writing** You have been assigned the task of projecting the cost of annual employee fringe benefits for your firm and have identified number of employees, total labor hours, and total labor cost as candidate independent variables for use in the estimation equation. Using historical data and ordinary least squares regression, you calculate the coefficient of determination for each of the candidate variables. You get the following results:

Variable	Coefficient of Determination
Number of employees.........	0.87
Total labor hours.............	0.95
Total labor cost..............	0.81

a. Discuss how you would use the coefficient of determination to select the best predictor variable.
b. What are the highest and lowest possible values for the coefficient of determination? Explain.

LO16-7 **E16-54. Coping with uncertainty; writing** Omaha Metal Products manufactures a variety of industrial products from stock metal components. The firm is engaged in its annual process of budgeting costs and revenues for the coming year. The cost of metal consumes approximately 50 percent of total revenues. Discuss which strategies for dealing with uncertainty would be appropriate for Omaha Metal Products to use in estimating and managing its metal costs for the coming year.

LO16-7 **E16-55. Coping with uncertainty; writing** Johnson Consumer Electronics operates in an industry in which the demand for products is cyclical and often unpredictable. Discuss a strategy for dealing with uncertainty associated with the cycles that would be appropriate for Johnson Consumer Electronics to employ to maintain its profitability throughout the cycles.

Problems

P16-56. Cost control; writing Slydell Industries produces a variety of consumer goods including lamps, home office desks, and storage cabinets. Many products sold by the company are purchased disassembled and then assembled by the customer. To assist the customer with assembly, Slydell provides a free hotline staffed 24 hours daily and provides an assembly manual with each item sold. The firm produces the assembly manuals in-house and maintains very tight control over the production costs of the manuals. For the latest year, the company spent $9,000,000 writing, publishing, and packaging assembly manuals for its products. The manager tasked with managing the production of assembly manuals was speaking with the CEO and noted that "our actual production cost of $9,000,000 for assembly manuals was $700,000 under budget. I am very proud of my employees and their efforts to control costs for the company."

The CEO pondered the statement for a moment and then responded, "According to survey results that reached my desk only this morning, 65 percent of our customers use the hotline for assistance with product assembly; only 7 percent ever open their manual."

a. In light of the survey results, did the company effectively control costs of assembly manuals? Explain.
b. In the long term, why must cost control efforts be viewed through the eyes of the customer rather than through the accounting system only?

LO16-1, 3

P16-57. Cost control; writing Temporary or part-time employees may be used rather than full-time employees in each of the following situations:

a. To teach undergraduate accounting courses at a university.
b. To serve as security guards.
c. To staff a health clinic in a rural area.
d. To write articles for a monthly technical help website.
e. To clean the office when the custodial staff is ill.
f. To answer questions on a tax help-line during tax season.
g. To work in department stores during the seasonal peak.
h. To do legal research in a law firm.
i. To perform quality control work in a car manufacturing plant.
j. To do seamstress work in a custom dress shop.
k. To work as a clerk/cashier in a small retail store. The store has a single owner, and the clerk is the only employee in the store when the clerk/cashier works.

Indicate the potential advantages and disadvantages of the use of temporaries in each of these situations. These advantages and disadvantages can be viewed from the standpoint of the employer or the user of the employer's products or services.

LO16-1

P16-58. Strategic alliances; writing Strategic alliances and joint ventures are being used with increasing frequency to exploit market opportunities. Virtually all larger firms are involved in several to many strategic alliances.

a. From the perspective of controlling the quality of production, discuss how a strategic alliance is significantly different from a typical vendor/customer relationship.
b. How can the accounting function contribute to the management of quality for strategic alliances?

LO16-1

P16-59. Cost control; ethics; writing Primary care clinics often use nurse practitioners (NPs) instead of medical doctors (MDs) as a cost effective way to address the shortage of MDs. Research referenced on the AANP.org (American Association of Nurse Practitioners) website indicates that NPs provide safe and effective care that is comparable in quality to that of MDs.

a. Discuss the use of nurse practitioners from the perspective of controlling costs.
b. How could the use of nurse practitioners impair the quality of work performed by the medical clinics?
c. Is it ethical for the medical clinics to bill the time of NPs at the same rate as MDs? Discuss.
d. How could the use of NPs affect the effectiveness and efficiency of work performed in the medical clinics?

LO16-1, 2, 3

P16-60. Cost consciousness The Hansens are preparing their household financial budget for December. They have started with their November budget and are adjusting it to reflect the difference between November and December in planned activities. The Hansens are expecting out-of-town guests

LO16-2, 3

for two weeks over the holiday season. The following list describes the budgetary changes from November to December that are contemplated by the Hansen family:

a. Increase the grocery budget by $165.
b. Decrease the commuter transportation budget by $70 to reflect the days off from work.
c. Change food budget to reflect serving pizza rather than steak and lobster each weekend.
d. Budget an extra $80 for utilities.
e. Reduce household maintenance budget by $90 to reflect the fact that outside housekeeping services will not be used over the holiday period.
f. Buy generic breakfast cereal rather than name brand due to the quantity the guests will consume.
g. Use paper plates to avoid using the dishwasher as often.
h. Buy the institutional-size packages of paper plates rather than smaller-size packages.
i. Budget the shipping charges at $40 less because there will be no need to mail packages to the relatives who will be visiting from England.
j. Budget movie costs at $9 for the month for a streaming service rather than $12 per person to go to the movies.
k. Postpone purchasing of needed work clothes until the January sales.
l. Budget funds for plans to repair car, rather than take the car to a garage in January.

Indicate whether each of these items indicates cost understanding (CU), cost containment (CC), cost avoidance (CA), or cost reduction (CR). Some items may have more than one answer.

LO16-5 P16-61. Efficiency standards Lucy Liu has been asked to monitor the efficiency and effectiveness of a newly installed machine as part of the company's sustainability initiatives. The machine has been guaranteed by the manufacturer to produce 2,000 engine gaskets per kilowatt hour (kWh). The rate of defects on production is estimated at 2 percent. The machine is equipped with a device to measure the number of kWhs used. During the first month of use, the machine manufactured 350,000 gaskets, of which 5,000 packages were flawed, and used 180 kWhs.

a. What is the efficiency standard for flawless output?
b. Calculate the achieved efficiency for the first month and briefly comment on it.
c. Determine the achieved effectiveness and briefly comment on it.
d. Assume that the company was charged $4.50 per kWh during the first month this machine was in service. Estimate the company's savings or loss in power costs because of the machine's efficiency level in the first month of operations.
e. If you were a customer buying this company's gaskets for use in automobile production, what level of quality control would you want the company to have, and why?

LO16-5 P16-62. Effectiveness/efficiency; ethics; writing Top management of Capital Services observed that the budget for the EDP department had been growing far beyond what was anticipated for the past several years. Each year, the EDP manager would demonstrate that increased usage by the company's non-EDP departments would justify a larger appropriation. The administrative vice president commented that she was not surprised because user departments were not charged for the EDP department services, and EDP department personnel were creative and eager to continue expanding services. A review of the current year's statistics of the EDP department revealed the following:

Budgetary appropriation............	$2,000,000, based on 4,000 hours of run time; $1,600,000 of this appropriation is related to fixed costs
Actual department expenses	Variable, $370,500 (incurred for 3,900 hours of run time) Fixed, $1,630,000

a. Did the EDP manager stay within his appropriation? Show calculations.
b. Was the EDP department effective? Show calculations. Comment.
c. Was the EDP department efficient? Show calculations. (Hint: Treat variable and fixed expenses separately.)
d. Using the formulas for analyzing variable and fixed costs, calculate the variances incurred by the EDP department.
e. Propose a rate per hour to charge user departments for EDP services. Do you think charging users will affect the demand for services by user departments? Why or why not?
f. Discuss whether it would be ethical to evaluate the EDP department manager based only on comparing budgeted versus actual costs and ignoring differences between budgeted and actual volume.

Chapter 16 Approaches to Cost Control and Managing Uncertainty

P16-63. Budget-to-actual comparison Birmingham Chemical evaluates performance in part through the use of flexible budgets. The selling expense budgets at three activity levels within the relevant range follow.

LO16-5

Activity Measures			
Unit sales volume	15,000	17,500	20,000
Dollar sales volume	$15,000,000	$17,500,000	$20,000,000
Number of orders processed	1,500	1,750	2,000
Number of salespersons	100	100	100
Monthly Selling and Administrative Expenses			
Advertising and promotion	$ 1,600,000	$ 1,600,000	$ 1,600,000
Administrative salaries	80,000	80,000	80,000
Sales salaries	100,000	100,000	100,000
Sales commissions	600,000	700,000	800,000
Salesperson travel	200,000	225,000	250,000
Sales office expense	445,000	452,500	460,000
Shipping expense	650,000	675,000	700,000
Total	$ 3,675,000	$ 3,832,500	$ 3,999,000

The following assumptions were used to develop the selling expense flexible budgets:

- The average size of the company's sales force during the year was planned to be 100 people.
- Salespersons are paid a monthly salary plus commission on gross dollar sales.
- The travel costs have both a fixed and a variable element. The fixed portion is related to the number of salespersons, and the variable portion tends to fluctuate with gross dollars of sales.
- Sales office expense is a mixed cost, with the variable portion related to the number of orders processed.
- Shipping expense is a mixed cost, with the variable portion related to the number of units sold. (An order consists of 10 units.)

A salesforce of 90 persons generated a total of 1,600 orders, resulting in a sales volume of 16,000 units during November. The gross dollar sales amounted to $14.9 million. The selling expenses incurred for November were as follows:

Advertising and promotion	$1,550,000
Administrative salaries	80,000
Sales salaries	101,000
Sales commissions	609,000
Salesperson travel	185,000
Sales office expense	500,000
Shipping expense	640,000
Total	$3,665,000

    a. Explain why the selling expense flexible budget would not be appropriate for evaluating the company's November selling expense, and indicate how the flexible budget would have to be revised.

    b. Determine the budgeted variable cost per salesperson and variable cost per sales order for the company.

    c. Prepare a selling expense report for November that the company can use to evaluate its control over selling expenses. The report should have a line for each selling expense item showing the appropriate budgeted amount, the actual selling expense, and the monthly dollar variation.

    d. Determine the actual variable cost per salesperson and variable cost per sales order processed for the company.

    e. Comment on the effectiveness and efficiency of the salespersons during November.

P16-64. Working capital, cash conversion cycle A retailer summarized the following financial statement information for Year 1, Year 2, and Year 3 (the most recent year).

LO16-6

	Year 3	Year 2	Year 1
Accounts receivable	$ 149,700	$ 159,100	$ 145,200
Cost of goods sold	1,072,875	914,595	1,056,000
Current assets	495,000	396,000	445,500
Accounts payable	134,200	138,000	130,000
Current liabilities	300,000	247,500	341,000
Inventory	246,000	183,150	214,500
Sales	1,761,125	1,633,375	1,320,000

a. Calculate the company's working capital for Year 3 and Year 2.
b. Calculate the company's days sales in inventory, days sales in receivables, and days payable for Year 3 and Year 2.
c. What is the company's cash conversion cycle for Year 3 and Year 2?
d. Analyze your results.

LO16-6

P16-65. Cash management; research Prior to the Tax Cuts and Jobs Act of 2018 (TCJA), multinational firms domiciled in the United States did not have to pay U.S. income taxes on foreign earnings, unless those earnings were returned (repatriated) to the United States. Accordingly, the U.S. income tax system acted as a deterrent to firms to bring cash earned abroad back to the United States. In 2018, the U.S. Congress passed the Tax Cuts and Jobs Act which resulted in a shift to a territorial system where only income earned in the United States is subject to corporate income tax. Research the TCJA and answer the following questions:

a. What was the incentive included in the Act to induce firms to bring cash earned abroad under the old system back to the United States?
b. What is the goal of repatriation of cash?
c. Approximately how much cash was repatriated during 2018?

LO16-6

P16-66. Cash management; writing José Martin founded a firm that manufactures innovative toys. Since its founding, the firm has experienced steady growth. However, in the past six months, the firm's products were featured on two popular online toy review sites. As a result of that exposure, the demand for the firm's products jumped dramatically. To meet demand, the firm ramped up production by adding a second shift of workers. With the added production capacity, the firm has been producing at 80 percent above levels of the prior year. One of the surprising side effects of this growth has been a severe cash crunch. Just this morning, Martin obtained the following balance sheet information from his CFO:

Current assets		Current liabilities	
Cash	$ 200,000	Accounts payable	$2,900,000
Accounts receivable	950,000	Wages payable	900,000
Inventory	3,900,000	Taxes payable	300,000

a. Discuss how the high rate of growth has created the cash crunch Martin's firm is currently experiencing.
b. What strategies would you propose to Martin to deal with the cash shortage?

LO16-3, 4, 5

P16-67. Comprehensive; analyzing cost control The financial results for the Business Education Department of Omega Educational Services Corporation for November are presented in the schedule at the end of this problem. Caroline Roper, president of Omega Educational Services, is pleased with the final results but has observed that the revenue and most of the costs and expenses of this department exceeded the budgeted amounts. Bret Shulman, vice president of the Business Education Department, has been requested to provide an explanation for any amount that exceeded the budget by 5 percent or more.

Shulman has accumulated the following facts to assist in his analysis of the November results:

- The budget for the calendar year was finalized in December of the preceding year, and at that time, a full program of business education courses was scheduled to be held in St. Louis during the first week of November. The schedule allowed eight courses to be run on each of the five days during the week. The budget assumed that there would be 425 participants in the program and 1,000 participant days for the week.
- Omega Educational Services charges a flat fee of $150 per day of course instruction, so the fee for a three-day course is $450. Omega grants a 10 percent discount to persons who subscribe to its publications. The 10 percent discount is also granted to second and subsequent registrants for the same course from the same organization. However, only one discount per registration is allowed.

Chapter 16 Approaches to Cost Control and Managing Uncertainty

Historically, 70 percent of the participant day registrations are at the full fee of $150 per day, and 30 percent of the participant day registrations receive the discounted fee of $135 per day. These percentages were used in developing the November budgeted revenue.
- The following estimates were used to develop the budgeted figures for course-related expenses:

Food charges per participant day (lunch/coffee breaks)	$ 27
Course materials per participant	8
Instructor fee per day	1,000

- A total of 530 individuals participated in the St. Louis courses in November, accounting for 1,280 participant days. This number included 20 persons who took a new, two-day course on pension accounting that was not on the original schedule; thus, on two of the days, nine courses were offered, and an additional instructor was hired to cover the new course. The breakdown of the course registrations follows.

Full fee registrations	704
Discounted fees	
Current periodical subscribers	128
New periodical subscribers	128
Second registration from the same organization	320
Total participant day registrations	1,280

A combined promotional mailing was used to advertise the St. Louis program and a program in Boston that was scheduled for December. The incremental costs of the combined promotion were $5,000, but none of the promotional expenses ($20,000) budgeted for the Boston program in December will have to be incurred. This earlier-than-normal promotion for the Boston program has resulted in early registration fees collected in November as follows (in terms of participant days):

Full fee registrations	140
Discounted registrations	60
Total participant day registrations	200

- Omega Educational Services includes $2,000 in each monthly budget for the purpose of updating courses or adding new ones. The additional amount spent on course development during November was for an unscheduled course that will be offered in February for the first time.

Shulman has prepared the following quantitative analysis of the November variances:

Omega Educational Services Corporation
Statement of Operations Business Education Department
For the Month Ended November 30

	Budget	Actual	Favorable (Unfavorable) Dollars	Favorable (Unfavorable) Percent
Revenue: Course fees	$145,500	$212,460	$ 66,960	46.0
Expenses				
Food charges	$ 27,000	$ 32,000	$ (5,000)	(18.5)
Course materials	3,400	4,770	(1,370)	(40.3)
Instructor fees	40,000	42,000	(2,000)	(5.0)
Instructor travel	9,600	9,885	(285)	(3.0)
Staff salaries and benefits	12,000	12,250	(250)	(2.1)
Staff travel	2,500	2,400	100	4.0
Promotion	20,000	25,000	(5,000)	(25.0)
Course development	2,000	5,000	(3,000)	(150.0)
Total expenses	$116,500	$133,305	$(16,805)	(14.4)
Revenue over expenses	$ 29,000	$ 79,155	$ 50,155	172.9

continued

continued from previous page

Omega Educational Services Corporation Analysis of November Variances		
Budgeted revenue		$145,500
Variances		
Quantity variance [(1,280 − 1,000) × $145.50]...............	$40,740 F	
Mix variance [($143.25 − $145.50) × 1,280].................	2,880 U	
Timing difference ($145.50 × 200)........................	29,100 F	66,960 F
Actual revenue		$212,460
Budgeted expenses		$116,500
Quantity variances		
Food charges [(1,000 − 1,280) × $27].....................	$ 7,560 U	
Course materials [(425 − 530) × $8]......................	840 U	
Instructor fees (2 × $1,000)	2,000 U	10,400 U
Price variances		
Food charges [($27 − $25) × 1,280].......................	$ 2,560 F	
Course materials [($8 − $9) × 530]	530 U	2,030 F
Timing differences		
Promotion..	$ 5,000 U	
Course development	3,000 U	8,000 U
Variances not analyzed (5% or less)		
Instructor travel.....................................	$ 285 U	
Staff salaries and benefits	250 U	
Staff travel	100 F	435 U
Actual expenses...		$133,305

After reviewing Shulman's quantitative analysis of the November variances, prepare an email to Roper explaining the following:

a. The cause of the revenue mix variance.
b. The implication of the revenue mix variance.
c. The cause of the revenue timing difference.
d. The significance of the revenue timing difference.
e. The primary cause of the unfavorable total expense variance.
f. How the favorable food price variance was determined.
g. The impact of the promotion timing difference on future revenues and expenses.
h. Whether the course development variance has an unfavorable impact on the company.

LO16-6 P16-68. Supply-chain management; writing Your employer, Lawson Brake Systems, implemented an e-procurement system last year for purchasing nonoperating inputs. The installation has been such a success that the firm is now considering using the same system to acquire operating inputs (such as, direct material and product components).

However, some executives in the firm are reluctant to implement such a system for operating inputs because it does not support the rich collaboration that is necessary for effective supply-chain cost management. Current systems support exchange of only basic transactional information: price, product availability, shipping terms and dates, and routine transaction processing including electronic ordering and electronic payments.

a. Assume that you are the firm's controller. Would you support the use of the e-procurement system for purchasing operating inputs? Why or why not?
b. Assume that you are vice president of product development. Would you support installation of the e-procurement system? Why or why not?

LO16-7 P16-69. Coping with uncertainty As an accounting intern working for your local police department, you learn that the department is considering starting a citizen's police academy. In recent years, there have been several events that have created friction between the police department and the citizens. The police academy is intended to create goodwill within the community and increase communication between the department and the community. You have been invited to advise the departmental management about managing the financial risk associated with the academy. You have learned that there is a federal program that provides grants to fund citizen police academies and that the program provides a reimbursement of costs up to $600 per participant. Following are estimated costs of the academy as determined by the departmental sponsors of the academy:

Variable costs	
Supplies........................	$200
Meals..........................	$80
Equipment.....................	$150
Fixed cost	
Rental for training facilities........	$25,000

Although the chief of police is very supportive of the police academy proposal, he is adamant that there is no slack in the department's budget to cover unreimbursed costs; thus, he has asked for assurance that the costs of the police academy will be covered by the federal grant program.

a. How many citizens must participate in the program to reach the breakeven point?
b. Is there financial risk in the proposed police academy for the police department? Explain.
c. What advice would you offer the proponents of the police academy to minimize losses the department could incur in offering the police academy?

P16-70. Coping with uncertainty; writing After reviewing financial results for the year, Chicago Cannery's president sent the following e-mail to his CFO and controller, Willie Logan.

> Dear Willie:
> I'm disappointed in the financial results for the year just completed. As you know, profits were $2 million below budget. In comparing the actual results to the budget, I note that the cost of natural gas exceeded budget by almost $1.3 million, and that cost alone accounts for 65 percent of the profit deficiency. This is the second year in a row that energy costs have dramatically reduced profits. I am calling a meeting on Tuesday to review our financial results, and I would like you to offer a presentation on the following topics:
> 1. Why our estimates of energy costs have been dramatically below actual costs.
> 2. What actions you intend to take to improve our ability to estimate these costs.
> 3. What actions the company could take to better manage these costs.

As the most recent hire in the Financial Department of Chicago Cannery, Logan has asked you for help.

a. What suggestions will you give Logan to improve the estimates of energy costs for future budgeting cycles?
b. What suggestions will you give Logan to improve the management of energy costs in the future?

P16-71. Coping with uncertainty; writing Wilson Ceramics manufactures holiday ornaments in its sole plant located in Wisconsin. Because the demand for the company's products is very seasonal, the company builds inventory throughout the first nine months of the year and draws down inventory the last three months of the year as demand in those months greatly exceeds production capacity. The company recently designated a member of management to be Chief Risk Officer (CRO). This individual has been charged with developing strategies to manage the effects of uncertainty on the business. The CRO has identified the following major sources of uncertainty:

1. Financing costs of inventory.
2. The cost of resin, which is the main material used in production.
3. "Acts of nature" that could harm or destroy the production facility.
4. The price to be realized for products.
5. The level of demand for the company's products.

As a risk consultant, you have been retained by the CRO to develop strategies to deal with each of these major sources of uncertainty. Identify the sources of risk for each of the five sources of uncertainty and provide recommendations on how to manage that uncertainty.

Review Solutions

Review 16-1

1. a. Preventive   c. Preventive   e. Corrective
   b. Diagnostic   d. Corrective   f. Diagnostic

2. Management can likely be *most* effective in cost control by implementing preventive methods. Because product profitability is largely determined by an effective design and development process, the most impact can be made *before* costs are incurred. For example, in target costing, supplier alliances can be formed to achieve a more effective design for manufacture.

Review 16-2

1. a. 1: Variable costs increase with an increase in production.
   b. 3: Change in transportation provider resulted in a decrease in costs.
   c. 3: Change in the provider of advertising services resulted in a decrease in costs.
   d. 3: Savings from supplier technology advances passed on to customer.
   e. 1: Drop in quantity will cause an increase in fixed costs per unit.
   f. 3: Changing suppliers caused prices to go up.
   g. 4: While the ordering process moved to a just-in-time model, handling and storage costs decreased.
   h. 2: The result of inflation is increasing prices.

2. Management can use data analytics to monitor trends in supplier quoted prices in real-time, along with other similar publicly available cost data on product substitutes. Data analytics can also be used by management to monitor final prices of products (including competitors' products) in relation to customer demand. Analysis of the data will help management determine whether there are any unexpected cost trends and gauge how customers are reacting to any pricing changes in the market place.

   For example, an analysis of past and real-time data can produce different cost scenarios to predict how passing along the price increases to customers would impact sales.

Review 16-3

1. a. Cost reduction (reduce costs of internal inefficiencies)
   b. Cost containment (keep sales costs in check)
   c. Cost containment (keep supplier costs in check)
   d. Cost reduction (reduce labor costs)
   e. Cost avoidance (avoid transportation insurance costs)
   f. Cost containment (control medical costs)
   g. Cost avoidance (avoid travel costs of training)
   h. Cost reduction (reduce costs of rent and travel)

2. Benchmarking can be used to help management identify cost inefficiencies. Benchmarking can provide the basis for setting cost reduction goals and provide ideas for cost reduction initiatives. Benchmarking can help management make decisions on ways to become more cost effective. For example, comparing cost of services with industry benchmarks could help management determine where to expend efforts in supplier cost negotiations. Or, benchmarking can indicate where the company's costs (or costs as a percentage of sales) are higher than the industry average. This could help management determine where to expend efforts on cost avoidance and reduction initiatives.

Review 16-4

1. a. Discretionary   d. Discretionary   g. Discretionary   j. Discretionary
   b. Committed   e. Committed   h. Committed   k. Committed (Likely considered
   c. Committed   f. Discretionary   i. Discretionary   committed for most companies)

2. During economic downturns, management will be more focused on cost reduction and avoidance measures in order to stay viable. Thus, more attention will be turned toward cutting discretionary costs, which could be the easiest to cut in the near term. For example, a company could place a temporary freeze on employee training and travel or delay projects or cut employee bonus plans. Cutting committed fixed costs could also be a focus, but often requires restructuring or renegotiations to effect change. For example, down-sizing an operation would take time for planning and implementation.

Chapter 16 Approaches to Cost Control and Managing Uncertainty

Review 16-5
Part One
a. 88.3% = Actual one-hour sessions (340) ÷ budgeted one-hour sessions (385)
b. 80.2% = Planned number of sessions (385) ÷ Planned trainer hours (480)
c. 74.7% = Actual number of sessions (340) ÷ Actual trainer hours (455)
d. The company was less effective (88% of target) and less efficient (74.7% vs. 80.2% target).

Part Two
a. Rate variance = $3,700 favorable = $122,300 − (4,200 × $30)
   Quantity variance = $16,650 unfavorable = $126,000 − [($145,800 ÷ 40) × $30]
b. The favorable rate variance resulted from the inspectors being paid less per hour ($122,300/4,200 = $29.12 rounded) than budgeted per hour ($30). The quantity variance was unfavorable because the actual hours of 4,200 exceeded the standard hours allowed of 3,645 ($145,800/40).

Review 16-6
a. Days sales in inventory

$$\frac{\text{Average inventory}}{\text{Average daily cost of goods sold}}$$

$$\frac{(\$96,200 + \$105,300)/2}{(\$426,180/365 \text{ days})} = \frac{\$100,750}{\$1,168} = 86.3 \text{ days}$$

Days sales in receivables

$$\frac{\text{Average accounts receivable}}{\text{Average daily credit sales}}$$

$$\frac{(\$122,100 + \$138,200)/2}{(\$706,800/365 \text{ days})} = \frac{\$130,150}{\$1,936} = 67.2 \text{ days}$$

Days payable

$$\frac{\text{Average accounts payable}}{\text{Average daily cost of goods sold}}$$

$$\frac{(\$78,600 + \$84,800)/2}{(\$426,180/365 \text{ days})} = \frac{\$81,700}{\$1,168} = 70.0 \text{ days}$$

b. Cash conversion cycle = Days sales in inventory + Days sales in receivables − Days payable
   Cash conversion cycle = 86.3 days + 67.2 days − 70.0 days = 83.5 days

On average, inventory was sold and replenished in approximately 86 days. The company had a receivable balance equal to approximately 67 days of sales. The company takes on average, 70 days to pay off its accounts payable balance. This means that the estimated cash conversion cycle is 83.5 days, or the time it takes to convert its resources into cash. This measure can be compared to the company's prior year ratio, its budgeted or target ratio, and to the industry average.

Review 16-7
a. Pounds of materials handled (higher coefficient of determination)
b. Low-end estimate: $2,500 + ($60 × 225) = $16,000
   High-end estimate: $2,500 + ($60 × 275) = $19,000
c. A range of cost estimates is useful for decision making because it helps to account for uncertainty. The level of activity is an estimate; thus, if a range of activity is used in the estimate, if provides management information on how volatility impacts the cost. Knowing the range helps management to plan for high activity fluctuations and low activity fluctuations.

Data Visualization Solutions

(See page 16-12.)
a. The travel costs per employee of other business segments within the company are used as the benchmark for a particular business segment's performance.
b. Approximately 1,200 employees

c. Approximately 1,000 employees
d. Business segment No. 4, and even No. 3, seem to have higher travel expenditures per employee than the other segments. The VP may also be interested in Business segment No. 8. with a low value of travel cost per employee. Are the employees traveling enough to make the contacts needed to meet sales targets and maintain customer relationships?
e. Other data that would be useful is travel costs as a percentage of sales. Did higher travel costs per employee produce more sales for the business segments?

Chapter 17

Implementing Quality Concepts

Road Map

LO	Learning Objective | Topics	Page	eLecture	Demo	Review	Assignments
17–1	**What is quality, and from whose viewpoint should it be evaluated?** Quality :: Production View of Quality :: Quality Control (QC) :: Statistical Process Control (SPC) :: Common Cause Variation :: Special Cause Variation :: Control Charts :: Mean :: Standard Deviation :: Upper Control Limit :: Lower Control Limit	17-2	e17–1	D17-1	Rev 17-1	MC17-11, MC17-12, E17-20, E17-21, E17-22, E17-23, E17-24, E17-25, E17-26, E17-27, P17-53, P17-54, P17-55, DA17-1, DA17-2
17–2	**What is benchmarking, and why do companies engage in it?** Internal benchmarking :: Results Benchmarking :: Reverse Engineering :: Process Benchmarking :: Strategic Benchmarking :: Steps in Benchmarking	17-8	e17–2	D17-2	Rev 17-2	MC17-13, MC17-14, E17-23, E17-28, E17-29, E17-30, E17-31, 17-32, 17-33, P17-53
17–3	**What constitutes the total quality management philosophy?** Total Quality Management (TQM) :: Continuous Improvement :: Zero Defects :: Employee Participation :: Product/Service Improvement :: Customer Profitability Analysis :: Supplier Partnerships :: Organizational Culture	17-12	e17–3	D17-3	Rev 17-3	MC17-15, E17-34, E17-35, E17-36, E17-37, E17-38, E17-39, P17-66
17–4	**What are the types of quality costs, and how are those types related?** Quality Costs :: Prevention Costs :: Appraisal Costs :: Internal Failure Costs :: External Failure Costs :: TQM's Cycle of Benefit :: Cost of Compliance :: Cost of Noncompliance	17-16	e17–4	D17-4	Rev 17-4	MC17-16, MC17-17, MC17-18, E17-23, E17-30, E17-40, E17-41, E17-42, E17-43, E17-44, E17-45, E17-46, E17-47, P17-53, P17-58, P17-59
17–5	**How is cost of quality reported and measured?** Identifying Quality Costs :: New Quality Accounts :: Coding Quality Transactions :: Cost of Quality Reports :: Pareto Analysis :: Cost of Quality Formula :: Balanced Scorecard	17-19	e17–5	D17-5	Rev 17-5	MC17-19, E17-23, E17-44, E17-48, E17-49, E17-50, E17-51, E17-52, P17-56, P17-57, P17-60, P17-61, P17-62, P17-63, P17-64, P17-65, DA 17-3, DA17-4, DA17-5

INTRODUCTION

Managers recognize that pursuit of high quality is a fundamental organizational strategy for competing in a global economy. Businesses, both domestic and foreign, compete to attract customers by offering more choices to satisfy customer needs and wants. Competition elicits the best in companies, and international competition has generated continuously higher-quality products and services.

Although consumers desire a wide variety of product and service choices, companies have resource constraints and must make trade-offs among price, quality, service, and promptness of delivery—thereby providing customers with a limited set of purchase options. Customers' ready access to multinational vendors motivates producers to improve quality and customer service. Vendors are continuously adopting more dynamic approaches to improve products, processes, and customer service.

This chapter discusses the issues of quality, benchmarking, total quality management, and quality costs and their measurement as well as how a cost management system and balanced scorecard are used to support quality initiatives. Many managers realize that current expenditures on quality improvements can be more than recouped through future material, labor, and overhead cost reductions and sales volume increases. Thus, regardless of the treatment for financial accounting purposes, quality improvement costs should be viewed not as expenses or losses but as recoverable investments with the potential for profit generation. Because of the potential financial consequences, accountants must understand the short- and long-run implications of the choice between higher and lower product/service quality.

WHAT IS QUALITY?

LO17-1 What is quality, and from whose viewpoint should it be evaluated?

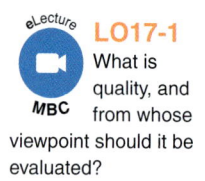

Before an organization can improve its product or service quality, the term *quality* must be defined. The **American Society for Quality (ASQ)** defines quality in a technical usage as having two meanings:

1. The characteristics of a product/service that bear on its ability to satisfy stated or implied customer needs
2. A product/service free of defects or shortfalls.[1]

The late Joseph Juran, noted quality expert, defined quality as "fitness for use." Other quality authorities define quality in different ways, but a fairly inclusive definition of **quality** is the summation of all characteristics of a product or service that influence its ability to meet the stated or implied needs of the person acquiring that product or service.

Quality should be viewed as a production/performance, profitability, and longevity issue. All organizational processes (such as production, procurement, distribution, finance, and promotion) are involved in quality improvement efforts. Thus, two quality perspectives are relevant.

> Production View of Quality   Consumer View of Quality

Production View of Quality

Productivity is measured by the quantity of good output generated from a specific amount of input during a time period. Any factor that either slows (or stops) a production process or causes unnecessary work reduces productivity. Activity analysis can be used to highlight such factors.

Reduction of Non-Value-Added Activities

As discussed in Chapter 8, the actions performed in making a product or providing a service can be classified into value-added (VA) and non-value-added (NVA) categories. VA activities increase the product's or service's worth to the customer. NVA activities consume time and generate costs but add no customer value. If impediments to good production are reduced or eliminated, managers can expect to realize productivity increases and production of higher-quality goods as indicated in **Exhibit 17.1**.

---

[1] *Quality Glossary*, American Society for Quality, https://asq.org/quality-resources/quality-glossary/q, accessed on November 15, 2023.

Chapter 17 Implementing Quality Concepts

Exhibit 17.1 ■ Reducing NVA Activities

NVA Activities	Reduce NVA Activities By	Reductions Create Positive Benefits Of
• Reworking spoiled or defective units • Replacing spoiled or defective units • Repairing spoiled or defective units • Producing and storing products with little demand • Moving materials unnecessarily • Experiencing unscheduled production interruptions	• Implementing better product design • Using conforming materials • Instituting value-added production processes • Using advanced production technology • Fitting machinery for mistake-proof operations • Hiring more skilled workers • Increasing worker training • Having suppliers pre-inspect raw materials for conformity to specifications • Rearranging production areas for better work flow • Instituting a just-in-time inventory system	• Decreased product failure rates • Decreased scrap and rework costs • Decreased product breakage rates • Increased product life • Increased manufacturing productivity • Increased competitiveness • Decreased time-to-market • Increased recyclability of products or product components

Elimination of Special-Cause Variation

All attempts to reduce variability and product defects reflect the implementation of **quality control (QC)**. QC places the primary responsibility for product or service quality at the source: with the maker or provider. In implementing QC, many companies use **statistical process control (SPC)** techniques to analyze where variations (or fluctuations) occur in the process. SPC is based on the theory that a process has common cause variation and special-cause variation.

- **Common cause variation** is due to many random causes that are inherent to any process. Manufacturing processes, for example, are not precise, and some variability within the process is expected. Random causes are not predictable and to reduce or remove them often requires a redesign of the process. For example, reducing random causes in a manufacturing process may require the purchase of higher quality equipment, standardized training programs, or a consistent purchasing of higher quality materials.

- **Special-cause variation** is abnormal variability due to a special or assignable cause that disrupts the process. This generally means that something changed that has affected the process. Special causes are few in number and can be identified, analyzed, and resolved or eliminated. For example, a particular batch of raw material may be defective. If discovered early enough, production can stop using the defective material and any affected product can be reworked.

To analyze process variations, control charts are developed to record the occurrence of specified performance measures at preselected points in a process. **Control charts**, such as the one in **Exhibit 17.2**, graph actual process results and indicate upper and lower control limits. A process is considered either "in" or "out of" control depending on whether

- results are within established limits (i.e., the upper and lower control limits) and
- patterns reflect only random variation (e.g., there is not a run of eight observations on one side of the mean line).

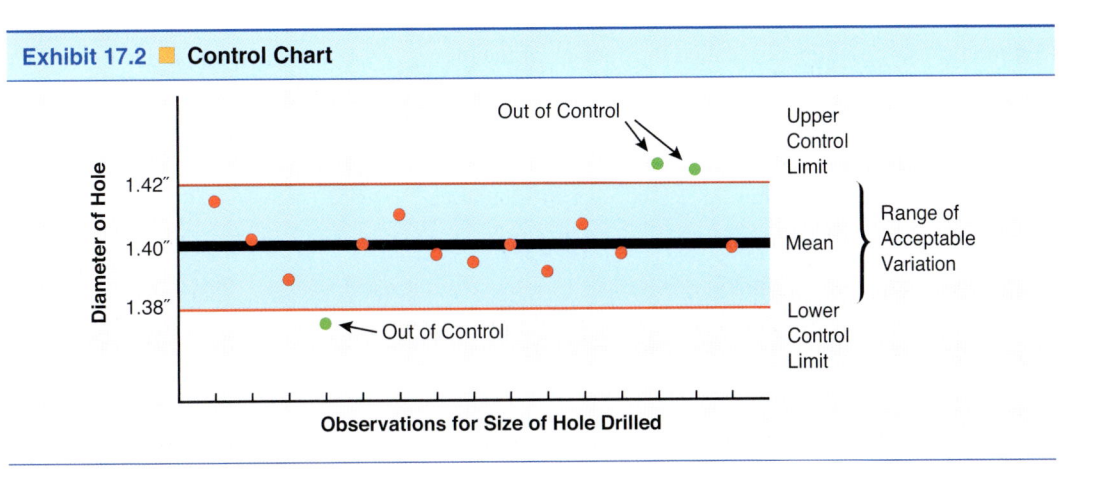

Exhibit 17.2 ■ Control Chart

In a control chart, the center straight line is the mean or average of the observations. The upper line shows the upper control limit, and the lower line shows the lower control limit. One practice is to set the upper control limit as the mean plus three standard deviations and the lower control limit as the mean minus three standard deviations. The **standard deviation** is a statistical calculation of the variation around the average line (the derivation of which can be found in statistics textbooks). The standard deviation for a sample of a population can be calculated in Excel using the function STDEV.S(number1, number2, . . .). In practice, managers estimate the mean and the control limits through the use of sample data from a process.

In effect, control charts use the management-by-exception principle and indicate the need for workers to respond to occurrences that are outside a predetermined limit or that form nonrandom, telltale patterns. This means that generally only observations due to special-cause or nonrandom variation are investigated. Control charts help a process communicate to workers what is occurring in that process, and whether the process is in control or out of control. If workers understand and react to that communication, potential product defects and process malfunctions can be prevented.

Control charts must be prepared consistently and accurately for a useful analysis of conditions to be made. Accountants are often directly involved in selecting appropriate performance measures and interpreting the charts. Often the measures selected to prepare control charts are nonfinancial, such as number of defective parts, quantity of waste created, and time consumed for task completion.[2]

DEMO 17-1 LO17-1   Statistical Process Control

Use **Exhibit 17.2**, which graphs dimension observations of holes drilled in wood in a construction site, to answer the following questions.

◆ **What is the average diameter of the measurements observed?**

The average diameter (or the mean) is shown as the center line at 1.4 inches.

◆ **Assuming that the company sets its control limits using two standard deviations, what is the value of one standard deviation?**

The distance between the mean and the upper control limit (as well as the distance to the lower control limit) is 0.02 inches. Since limits were established using two standard deviations, one standard deviation is equal to 0.02 inches/2 = 0.01 inches.

◆ **How many points are caused by special-cause variation and what are three possible special-causes for this scenario?**

Three points are shown outside of the control limits. Examples of special causes include the following.

- Drill malfunction that caused a new drill to be replaced.
- Defect in the wood that was used in the project.
- Temporary worker filled in for the job and was not properly trained.

◆ **What are possible causes of random variation in the process?**

Common cause variation, also called the "noise" of the process, is expected variation due to random causes. Examples of random-causes for this scenario include the following.

- Minor tool wear based upon the manufacturing specifications and quality level of the drills used.
- Typical environmental factors such as humidity and the amount of lighting that may impact the drilling process.
- Expected differences due to human variability in techniques used or performance levels.

---

[2] Selection of performance measures to assess quality is discussed in Chapter 15.

Data Visualization

Assume the following charts all pertain to a particular process, but represent different time periods of that process.

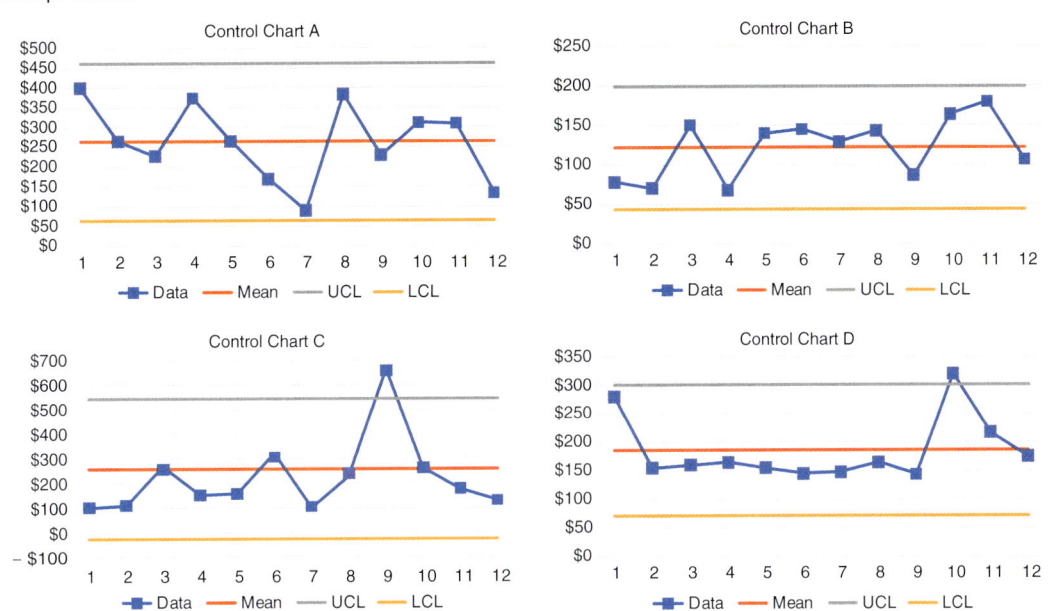

Control Chart A — data ranges roughly $50–$400, Mean ≈ $250, UCL ≈ $450, LCL ≈ $50.

Control Chart B — data ranges roughly $70–$180, Mean ≈ $120, UCL ≈ $200, LCL ≈ $50.

Control Chart C — data mostly $100–$300 with one point near $650 exceeding UCL ≈ $550; Mean ≈ $280, LCL ≈ $0.

Control Chart D — data mostly $150–$180 with one point near $320 exceeding UCL ≈ $300; Mean ≈ $190, LCL ≈ $75.

Indicate which visualization is best described by each of the following explanations. More than one chart may apply.

1. Special-cause variance is present in the process.
2. Only common cause variance is present in the process.
3. Only common cause variance is present, and it shows the least amount of common cause variance.
4. Improvement to the system could be made using short-term measures.
5. Improvements to the system can be made through long-term strategies.

Solution on p. 17-48.

Consumer View of Quality

Every consumer who acquires a product or service obtains a set of product/service characteristics and a set of organizational characteristics.

Product/Service Characteristics	Organizational Characteristics
Features and aesthetics	Convenience of access
Warranty and serviceability	Timeliness of delivery and service
Packaging	Reputation
Price (purchase and after-purchase)	Credit availability
Durability	Responsiveness to customer
Ease of disposal and/or recyclability	
Performance	

The consumer's view of quality reflects more than whether the product or service delivers what was intended or the probability of purchasing a defective unit. The customer perceives quality as a product's or service's ability to meet and satisfy all specified needs at a reasonable cost. In other words, from a consumer's perspective, quality relates to both performance and value. This quality perspective derives from

- increased competition,
- public interest in product safety, and
- litigation relative to products and product safety.

When high-quality producers dominate a market, successful entering companies must understand both their own customers' quality expectations and their competitors' quality standards.

Customers' Characteristics of Quality

Exhibit 17.3 lists eight characteristics that are commonly included in a customer's definition of product quality. An important difference between the first six and last two characteristics is level of objectivity. Characteristics A through F can be reasonably evaluated through objective methods, whereas G and H are strictly subjective. Thus, *the first six are much more susceptible to organizational control than are the other two*. Most, if not all, of the quality characteristics in **Exhibit 17.3** apply equally to companies making tangible products and those providing services. For example, a hotel might consider the provision of in-room high-speed internet access and luxury spas as "features" and low noise levels in guest rooms as high "performance." In the exhibit, illustrative examples are given for **The Ritz-Carlton**, an upscale hotel chain dedicated to service quality.

Service quality reflects the manner in which an output is delivered to a customer. Some firms use outside "secret shoppers" to assess the level of service provided. For example, an undercover hotel "guest" at an exclusive hotel could put a nonperforming light bulb in a room lamp to determine whether housekeeping detects the outage and replaces that bulb. Other companies simply reward customers for observations about service conditions: one large discount club pays customers $1 if the cashier does not address them by the name shown on their membership cards.

Exhibit 17.3 ■ Characteristics of Quality

Objective Measurement:

A. **Performance** refers to the operating features and relative importance of multiple characteristics such as ease of use and speed. Performance at The Ritz-Carlton might include comfortable beds, universal electronic charging stations for smart phones and laptops, and high-speed in-room Internet connections.

B. **Features** are the extras needed to customize a product. The Ritz-Carlton might include flowers in a customer's room at check-in, provide guests with spacious hotel rooms and fully equipped health club facilities, or offer electric vehicle charging stations in the hotel front drive.

C. **Reliability** refers to the likelihood that a product/service will perform on time as expected without a glitch. Ritz-Carlton customers expect on-time room cleanup and evening turn-down service with quality chocolates on the pillows.

D. **Conformance** is the extent to which products comply with prespecified standards. Ritz-Carlton guests may expect granite countertops on vanities and bathtubs with spa jets.

E. **Durability** refers to expected product life before deterioration and the need for replacement. Ritz-Carlton guests might expect hotel rooms to be refurbished every five years or a fresh fruit basket to be placed in the room every third day of a stay.

F. **Serviceability and Responsiveness** reflect the convenience, ease, and speed with which courteous and competent service staff complete work. Ritz-Carlton customers expect prompt responses to room service and maintenance requests.

Subjective Measurement:

G. **Aesthetics** refers to the environmental ambiance required by the discerning customer. The Ritz-Carlton might provide designer towels in the bathrooms and robes and slippers for in-room use.

H. **Perceived Value** is a customer's opinion of the product based on perceptions formed from advertising or product/service reputation. When customers stay at The RitzCarlton, they generally expect "royal" treatment.

Source: Adapted from David Garvin, "Competing on the Eight Dimensions of Quality." https://hbr.org/1987/11/competing-on-the-eight-dimensions-of-quality (last accessed 12/22/2019); and David Garvin, "What Does 'Product Quality' Really Mean?" *Sloan Management Review* (Fall 1984), pp. 25–43.

In addition to the quality characteristics in **Exhibit 17.3** that apply to all organizations, the following additional quality characteristics apply to service organizations:

- **assurance** (customers expect employees to be knowledgeable, courteous, and trustworthy);
- **tangibles** (customers expect high-quality physical facilities, equipment, and appearance of personnel); and
- **empathy** (customers expect employees to express an appropriate level of caring and attention).

Maximizing Value

Not all customers can afford the same grade of product or service. **Grade** is the quality level that a product or service has relative to the inclusion or exclusion of characteristics (especially price) to satisfy customer needs. Customers try to maximize their satisfaction within the context of their willingness and ability to pay. They view a product or service as a **value** when it meets the highest number of their needs at the lowest possible total cost (which includes an item's purchase price plus its operating, maintenance, and disposal costs). Thus, although customers may have a collective vision of what constitutes "high quality," some choose to accept a lower grade of product or service because it satisfies their functional needs at a lower cost. Note that "high quality" is a more encompassing concept than "high grade." Someone with 20 minutes left for lunch can find more value in a fast-food hamburger than a sit-down restaurant's sirloin steak.

To illustrate the difference between quality and grade, assume that Ron Reeves is in the market for a new car for traveling to and from work, running errands, and going on vacation. He has determined that reliability, gas mileage, safety, and comfort are the most important features to him. He may believe the Lexus is the highest-quality car available, but his additional needs are that the car's price is within his budget and that repair and maintenance services are readily available at a reasonable cost. Thus, he will search for the *highest-quality product that maximizes his set of quality-characteristic preferences within the grade of car he can afford.*

Quality Comparisons Across Industries Customers often make quality assessments by comparing a product or service to an ideal rather than to an actual product or service of the same type or in the same industry. For example, on business trips, Melanie Stringfellow frequently stays at The Ritz-Carlton hotels; the company has received all major awards from the hospitality industry and leading consumer groups. On a recent trip, Stringfellow called a rental car company to arrange for a car. She could compare the service quality she received from the rental company with the high-quality service she receives from The Ritz-Carlton rather than how well this company compared to other rental car companies. Stringfellow is unconcerned that car company employees may not have received the same customer satisfaction training as Ritz-Carlton employees or that The Ritz-Carlton corporate culture is dedicated to high quality whereas the rental company may not have yet made such a quality commitment. Formally comparing one organization's quality levels to those of another company is called competitive benchmarking.

Statistical Process Control Chart **LO17-1** **REVIEW 17-1**

A parts manufacturer is aiming to decrease water wasted in its production process. As a result, the company tracked its water waste in gallons for the last 6 months.

	Water Gallons (000)
Month 1.	10.3
Month 2.	4.9
Month 3.	8.9
Month 4.	11.7
Month 5.	6.3
Month 6.	7.7
Standard deviation	2.5

The following visualization tracks the 6-month data, and sets upper and lower control limits at three standard deviations.

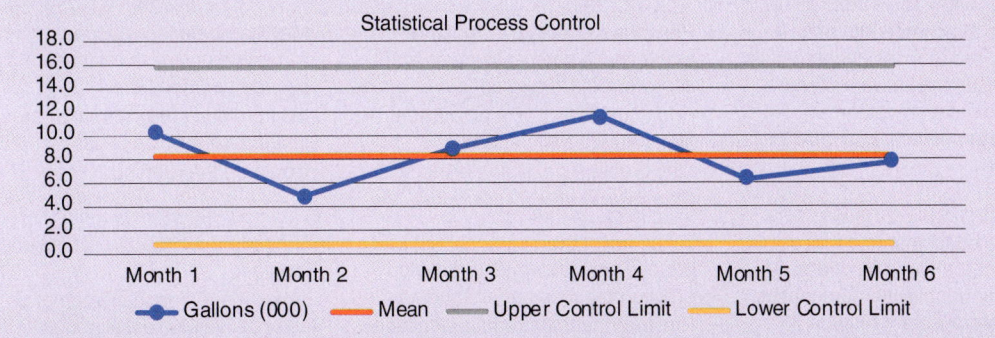

a. At what value (in gallons) is the mean line set? Show your calculations.
b. At what values (in gallons) are the upper and lower control limits set? Show your calculations.
c. What point(s) represent special-cause variation?
d. **Critical Thinking:** What does the control chart indicate about the effectiveness of the manufacturer's efforts to decrease water waste?

More practice:
MC17-11, E17-21, E17-27
Solution on p. 17-47.

BENCHMARKING

LO17-2 What is benchmarking, and why do companies engage in it?

Because each company has its own unique philosophy, products, and people, "copying" such elements is neither appropriate nor feasible. Therefore, a company should attempt to imitate those ideas that are readily transferable but, more importantly, to upgrade its own effectiveness and efficiency by improving on methods used by others.[3] **Benchmarking** involves investigating, comparing, and evaluating a company's products, processes, and/or services against those of either competitors or companies believed to be the "best in class." Companies may be motivated by a variety of reasons (see **Exhibit 17.4**) to perform benchmarking, but the end result is that an understanding of another company's production and performance methods is gained that allows the comparing company to identify its own strengths and weaknesses.

Exhibit 17.4 ■ Reasons to Benchmark

1. To increase awareness of the competition
2. To understand competitors' production and performance methods as well as cost structures
3. To identify areas of competitors' internal strengths and weaknesses
4. To identify external and internal threats and opportunities
5. To justify and accelerate a plan for continuous process improvement and change
6. To create a framework for program and process assessment and evaluation
7. To establish a focus for mission, goals, and objectives
8. To establish performance improvement targets
9. To understand customers' needs and expectations
10. To encourage creative thinking
11. To identify state-of-the-art business practices and new technologies

Types of Benchmarking

As indicated in **Exhibit 17.5**, there are four primary types of benchmarking.

Exhibit 17.5 ■ Types of Benchmarking

Type	Description	Advantages	Disadvantages
Internal	An approach to benchmarking that allows organizations to learn from "sister" companies, divisions, or operating units. Performance improvement may be 10 percent.	• Provides highest degree of process detail and simplified access to process information • Provides rapid and easy-to-adopt improvements • Is low cost • Provides a deeper understanding of in-house process	• Gives an internal focus that tends to be operational rather than strategic and bound by the organization's cultural norms • Creates an internal bias • Does not provide a significant stretch • May not find best-in-class practices
Results	An approach to benchmarking that targets specific product designs, process capabilities, or administrative methods used by one's direct competitors. Performance improvement may be 20 percent or better.	• Provides a strategic insight into marketplace competitiveness and can provide a "wake-up" call to action • Prioritizes areas of improvement according to competition • May create a possible partnership • Can show similar regulatory issues	• May generate legal issues regarding business relations between competitors • May provide study data that are insufficient for diagnosis • Could be threatening
Process	An approach to benchmarking that seeks information from the same functional area within a particular application or industry. Performance improvement may be 35 percent or better.	• Takes advantage of functional and professional networks to develop detailed process understanding • Provides industry trend information • Provides quantitative comparisons • Can review common business functions	• Tends to best support operational studies • Takes more time than internal or competitive studies, although it uses an external perspective • May be difficult to find common functions

continued

---

[3] The American Productivity and Quality Center has established a code of conduct for benchmarking activities. The code addresses issues such as equal exchange of information, confidentiality, avoidance of antitrust issues and illegalities, and inter-organizational courtesy; the code can be found at https://www.apqc.org/resource-library/resource-listing/benchmarking-code-conduct-0 (accessed 11/15/2023).

Chapter 17 Implementing Quality Concepts

continued from previous page

Exhibit 17.5 ■ Types of Benchmarking (concluded)

Type	Description	Advantages	Disadvantages
Strategic	An approach to benchmarking that seeks process performance information from outside one's own industry. Enablers are translated from one organization to another through the interpretation of their analogous relationship. Performance improvement may be 35 percent or better.	• Provides the greatest opportunity for process breakthroughs • Generates reliable, detailed data because noncompeting organizations are used • Is innovative • Has high potential for discovery	• Is difficult to develop an analogy between dissimilar businesses • Is hard to determine which companies to benchmark • Has a high cost • Takes a long time to plan

Source: Adapted from U.S. Patent and Trademark Office, Office of Quality Management, *Benchmarking Workbook* (September 2000), p. 15.

Internal Benchmarking

Internal benchmarking addresses how and why one organizational unit is performing better than another. The techniques of the higher-performing unit are then implemented, to the extent possible, in the lower-performing units. For example, the gross profit margin of one business segment of a company is compared to the gross profit margin of its other segments. Strategies to increase sales and decrease costs used by the higher performing segments are shared with the lower performing segments. The primary difficulty with internal benchmarking is that *none of the organizational units may be performing on a quality level attained by external parties*.

Results Benchmarking

Results benchmarking uses a specific product/service feature or capability of a *competitor(s)* as the target. In some cases, an end product or software program is examined using a process called **reverse engineering**. For a product, reverse engineering refers to disassembling the product to determine how it was designed and how it operates—generally so as to duplicate or enhance the product. In other cases, competitor products are tested in labs to determine strengths, weaknesses, and quality levels. The focus is on product/service specifications and performance results. Results benchmarking helps companies determine which other companies are "best in class" in a particular category. If, however, results benchmarking leads to making an exact replica of another's product (especially for software), serious ethical and legal considerations exist.

A wide variety of metrics can serve as benchmarks including cost per unit, time to market, time of service, and customer retention rates. Website benchmarks are another way a company can compare its performance to that of its competitors. Knowing how a company's website is trending compared to others in its industry is a useful benchmarking exercise. **Google Analytics** produce benchmarking reports that track items such as website sessions and new users. A company can compare their data to that of the market to assess its performance.[4]

Process Benchmarking

Although benchmarking against direct competitors is necessary, it can also create the risk of becoming stagnant. For example, General Motors, Chrysler, and Ford historically competitively benchmarked among themselves and, over time, their processes became similar. When foreign competitors entered the U.S. market with totally different, and better, processes, the U.S. automotive companies were forced to change and improve their quality systems.

Because of potential stagnation, comparisons should also be made against companies that are the best in a specific characteristic rather than just the best in a specific industry. Focusing on how best-in-class companies achieve their results is called **process benchmarking**. For example, **Kellogg Co.** determined that they needed to expand beyond internal benchmarking to understand their business operations. As a result, they partnered with **American Productivity & Quality Center (APC)** to gain access to standardized business process measures such as the cost of processing a purchase order. Currently, Kellogg Co.

---

[4] Zaric, S., "Google Analytics Benchmarking Reports: Use, Examples & Best Practices," *Databox*, https://databox.com/google-analytics-benchmarking-reports. Accessed on November 18, 2023.

© Cambridge Business Publishers

uses over a hundred benchmarks at least annually.[5] Looking at noncompetitors is extremely valuable in process benchmarking.

Many companies and organizations are now benchmarking environmental management and sustainability programs among peers and noncompetitors with an eye toward continuous improvement of operations, lowered emissions and resource conservation, green energy usage, and waste conservation.

Strategic Benchmarking

Strategic benchmarking is also non–industry specific but focuses on strategy and how companies compete. This type of benchmarking is most important at many Japanese companies because their managers focus more on long-run performance than on the short-run benefits that can be gained from process and results benchmarking. In the United States, some network carrier airlines have tried to do strategic benchmarking against Southwest Airlines: the network carriers had some success in their benchmarking efforts relative to hedging activities against jet fuel costs but had some failures in starting up low-cost subsidiaries.[6]

DEMO 17-2 LO17-2   Performing Benchmark Analysis

For billing purposes, assume Phoenix Family Medical Clinic classifies its services into one of four major procedures, X1 through X4. The actual rates charged for the procedures are included in the chart below and are generally based on markups from cost. Rates for the Tucson Family Medical Clinic (part of the same health care system), a competing clinic, and the industry are also provided.

Phoenix Clinic Cost Data

	A	B	C	D	E
1		Phoenix Rate per Procedure	Tucson Rate per Procedure	Competitor Rate per Procedure	Industry Average Rate per Procedure
2	X1	$100	$110	$125	$150
3	X2	200	205	195	200
4	X3	60	62	80	90
5	X4	300	250	240	245

◆ **How can the Phoenix clinic complete a variance analysis using internal benchmarking, results benchmarking, and process benchmarking?**

The rate for each procedure can be compared to each benchmark and the difference in dollars can be calculated.

Phoenix Clinic Benchmark Analysis

	A	B	C	D
1		Internal Benchmarking $ Variance	Results Benchmarking $ Variance	Process Benchmarking $ Variance
2	X1	$(10)	$(25)	$(50)
3	X2	(5)	5	0
4	X3	(2)	(20)	(30)
5	X4	50	60	55

Based on this analysis, management may want to further investigate the rates for three of the procedures.

X1: The Phoenix clinic appears to be undercharging for services. The company should complete a detailed pricing analysis of the X1 service and ensure the cost system is capturing all costs.

X2: The price of the service shows little variation across clinics.

---

[5] Maurer, M., "How Kellogg Uses Standardized Benchmarks to Boost Cost Savings," *The Wall Street Journal*, January 6, 2023, https://www.wsj.com/articles/how-kellogg-uses-standardized-benchmarks-to-boost-cost-savings-11672953730. Accessed on November 18, 2023.

[6] Paul Muddle and Parvez Sopariwala, "Cost Restructuring and Revenue Building: A Strategic Benchmarking Analysis," *Cost Management* (January/February 2008), pp. 36ff.

Chapter 17 Implementing Quality Concepts   17-11

X3: The internal benchmarking shows a slight variation, but the rates seem low compared to the competitor's rate and that of the industry. Further analysis should be done on the rate and associated costs.

X4: Phoenix's rate seems high compared to the various benchmarks. Analysis is required on the rate charged, the cost support for the charge, and/or any cost efficiencies that could be gained.

Benchmarking Steps

Benchmarking steps are detailed in **Exhibit 17.6**. Some companies have more steps than others but all have a structured approach. After the negative gap analysis (Step 6) is completed, everyone in the firm is expected to work toward both closing that gap and becoming a best-in-class organization. Through benchmarking, companies are working to improve their abilities to deliver high-quality products from the perspectives of how products are made and how customers perceive those products. Integrating these two perspectives requires involvement of all organizational members in the implementation of a total quality management system.

Exhibit 17.6 ■ Steps in Benchmarking

1. Determine the specific area in which improvements are desired and/or needed.
2. Select the characteristic that will be used to measure quality performance.  
3. Identify the best-in-class companies based on quality characteristics. Remember that these companies do not have to be industry, product, or service specific. 
4. Ask for cooperation from the best-in-class companies. This may be handled directly or through a consulting firm. Be prepared to share information and respect requests for confidentiality.
5. Have the people who are associated with the specific area being analyzed collect the needed information. 
6. Analyze the "negative gap" between the company's product, process, or service and that of the best-in-class firm. 
7. Act on the negative gap analysis and make improvements. 
8. Do not become complacent. Strive for continuous improvement. 

Benchmarking   LO17-2   REVIEW 17-2

Based on a recent time study over a three-week period, a Cincinnati fast-food restaurant estimates its average service time per food order to be 4.0 minutes. The company currently does not use self-service kiosk ordering. The company would like to use benchmarking to assess its performance in this competitive industry. The following additional information is available.

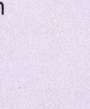

- The company performed a similar time study six months prior and the average service time per food order was 4.5 minutes.
- The average service time per food order for another fast-food restaurant within the company's franchise is 4.2 minutes. The restaurant is also located in Cincinnati.
- Based on a small sample of visits to a competing fast-food restaurant, the average service time per food order is 3.9 minutes. The competing restaurant is also located in Cincinnati.
- An industry benchmark for similar fast-food restaurants is 3.5 minutes.
- For a large, highly rated online merchandiser, the average time it takes for a customer to complete an online purchase after the item is in a shopping cart is 2.30 minutes.

continued

continued from previous page

> a. Using historical information, compare the company's performance to the prior period by computing the difference between actual service time and the prior period service time.
> b. Use internal benchmarking by computing the difference between actual service time and the service time of another restaurant in the franchise.
> c. Use results benchmarking by computing the difference between actual service time and the service time of a competing restaurant.
> d. Use process benchmarking by computing the difference between actual service time and the industry benchmark.
> e. Use strategy benchmarking by computing the difference between actual service time and the average time for a large online merchandiser to complete an online order.
> f. **Critical Thinking:** Analyze your results.

More practice: E17-28, E17-29, E17-31, E17-32
Solution on p. 17-47.

TOTAL QUALITY MANAGEMENT

LO17-3 What constitutes the total quality management philosophy?

Total quality management (TQM) is a "management approach of an organization, centered on quality, based on the participation of all its members and aiming at long-term success through customer satisfaction, and benefits to all members of the organization and to society."[7]

Tenets of TQM

TQM is based on four important tenets.

| Continuous Improvement | Employee Participation | Product/Service Improvement | Supplier Partnerships |

Continuous Improvement

Effective quality management requires the implementation of a system that provides information about process quality so managers can plan, control, evaluate performance, and make decisions for continuous improvement. Traditionally, consideration of quality has not been part of the planning process. Most often, it has involved an after-the-fact measurement of errors because a certain level of defects was tolerated as part of the "natural" business process. Action was not triggered until a predetermined error threshold was exceeded. In contrast, a total quality system should be designed to reorient thinking to emphasize a goal of *zero defects* through continuous improvement.

Old Way →	New Emphasis →	End Results
Ignored prior to occurrence	Planned for in every process and product	Ability to set goals and methods for quality improvements
Inspection	Prevention	System for measuring quality (or lack thereof) and providing feedback on quality enhancements
Tolerance of defects	Zero defects and continuous improvement	Encouragement of teamwork
		Move organizational attitude from product inspection and defect correction to proactive quality assurance

✓ **Zero Defects**

Employee Participation

TQM recognizes that all organizational levels share responsibility for product/service quality. Workers should be viewed as effectors of success, not creators of problems. Training workers to handle multiple job functions helps improve efficiency and quality. Upper-level management must

- be involved in the quality process,
- develop an atmosphere that is conducive to quality improvements,

---
[7] ISO 8402, *Total Quality Management* (Geneva: ISO, 1994), definition 3.7.

- set an example of commitment to TQM,
- provide constructive feedback about opportunities for improvement, and
- provide positive feedback when improvements are made.

Encouraging employee suggestions can produce substantial annual or, more commonly, enduring cost savings and increase productivity in all types and sizes of organizations. For example, employees at **Audi** saved the company $133 million in 2017 at the company's plants in Ingolstadt and Neckarsulm. In one case, two maintenance workers noticed the ventilation system in their buildings was operating around the clock. Two employees suggested running the system during the week from 6 a.m. until 10 p.m. Reducing the fans' speed when employees weren't present saved approximately $122,000 a year.[8]

Product/Service Improvement

Total quality management focuses attention on the relationship between the internal production/service process and the external customer whose satisfaction is the ultimate evidence of success. Therefore, TQM requires that companies first know who their customers are.

Identifying Value-Adding Customers In analyzing their customers, companies must recognize that they may need to stop serving some groups of customers based on the results of cost–benefit analyses, activity-based costing, and data-mining techniques. Some customers simply cost more than they add in revenues and/or other benefits as illustrated earlier in LO 14-6. Each revenue dollar does not contribute equally to organizational profitability because the cost to serve customers varies. The concept that shedding one or more sets of customers would be good for business is difficult to believe at first, but most organizations have some clients who drain, rather than improve, those organizations' ability to provide quality products and service. Managers should be attuned to customers that are not cost-beneficial and first attempt to find a way to make them profitable. If no solution is found, "nonperforming" customers should be sent to do business elsewhere so that the company can focus its attention on its current profitable customers and attract new, profitable customers. Organizations must recognize that customer loyalty and customer profitability are not the same thing.

Instituting customer service programs often produces valuable information. For example, many chains use loyalty app reward programs to develop databases of customer information. These systems typically contain information on purchases made, amounts spent, and customer likes/dislikes. A hotel chain may accumulate the same types of information as well as personal and family interests, preferred credit cards, and any previous difficulties encountered by a customer at a hotel. Such data can be used to sort customers and to decide whether a customer relationship merits additional investment. However, customer service programs should not be taken to the extreme: some customers, such as those that demand exorbitant service but are not willing to pay the related price, are not profitable to an organization.

Identifying Preferences of Value-Adding Customers After identifying its value-adding customers, a company must then understand what those customers want. The primary characteristics currently desired by customers are

- quality,
- value, and
- good service.

"Good" service is an intangible and means different things to different people. But most customers would agree that "good" service reflects the interaction between themselves and organizational employees—including response time in the event of problems or questions. Frequently, only service quality separates one product from its competition. The need for customer satisfaction information is essential to organizations embracing TQM because poor service can be disastrous. A study conducted in 2018 revealed that poor customer service experiences are costing companies more than $75 billion annually. In fact, 67 percent of customers are willing to switch brands because of a poor customer experience.[9]

---

[8] A. Alaniz, "Even the Smallest Idea Can Save Millions," (Jan. 20, 2018); https://www.motor1.com/news/227974/audi-employees-save-133-million/ (Accessed on November 18, 2023).

[9] S. Hyken, "Businesses Lose $75 Billion Due To Poor Customer Service" *Forbes* (5/17/18); https://www.forbes.com/sites/shephyken/2018/05/17/businesses-lose-75-billion-due-to-poor-customer-service/?sh=414b9c1716f9. Accessed November 20, 2023.

Supplier Partnerships

Adopting TQM encourages companies to review their supply chain and establish long-term relationships with preferred suppliers. The TQM philosophy sees suppliers as a distinct part of a company's ability to either satisfy customers or create extreme dissatisfaction. For example, **General Motors** made a binding agreement with LG Chem to supply Cathode Active Material (CAM) over eight years. CAM is used in GM's electric vehicle production and represents about 40 percent of the cost of a battery cell. General Motors emphasized both the importance of the high-quality product and their commitment to strong supplier relationships.[10]

To ensure compliance with expectations of their suppliers, some companies perform supplier quality audits. Such audits identify nonconformances in production, shipping, engineering changes, invoicing, and quality processes. After problems are identified, the parties agree on and implement effective changes; sometimes, cost recoveries are requested from suppliers. However, some companies that have adopted TQM and developed long-term supplier relationships have chosen to stop performing quality audits because they are viewed as non-value-added activities.

Given the extent to which outsourcing is currently used and the economic difficulties currently faced by many organizations, companies must be certain that they are "linking up" with suppliers that enhance product quality and customer satisfaction. Failure costs caused by defective materials or parts cannot be tolerated when companies are struggling to survive. Suppliers can indirectly enhance customer satisfaction, by finding more direct ways to accommodate customers. For example, hotels can recommend high-quality restaurants to guests and arrange for seamless transportation to desired destinations.

Some TQM critics have called it nothing more than a management fad that does not work when practical attempts are made to implement its concepts. One rebuttal to such criticisms follows: "Poor management, not poor ideas, may be responsible for the inconsistency of TQM or other managerial interventions."[11] Companies using TQM have cited many positive outcomes and benefits, such as those included in **Exhibit 17.7**.

As electric vehicles technology advances and production volume increases, it will be critical for vehicle manufacturers to partner with key suppliers to ensure that quality standards keep pace with the rapid changes.

Exhibit 17.7 ■ Benefits of TQM

Internal
- Improved response time to change
- Increased ability to compete profitably in the marketplace
- Decreased cost through reduction/elimination of non-value-added activities and waste
- Increased profitability through reduced costs
- Improved products, services, and customer relations
- Increased employee morale, motivation, and retention
- Improved internal communications and organizational focus
- Enhanced employee decision-making abilities and teamwork
- Increased innovation and acceptance of new ideas
- Reduced number of errors
- Increased benchmarks for evaluating employee performance

External
- Increased customer trust and loyalty
- Enhanced customer satisfaction
- Improved response time to customer requests
- Decreased prices resulting from reduced internal costs

---

[10] "LG Chem and General Motors Reach Agreement for Long-Term Supply of Cathode Active Material to Support EV Growth," *General Motors* (July 26, 2022), https://investor.gm.com/news-releases/news-release-details/lg-chem-and-general-motors-reach-agreement-long-term-supply, accessed on November 20, 2023.

[11] David Lemak, Neal Mero, and Richard Reed, "When Quality Works: A Premature Post-Mortem on TQM," *Journal of Business and Management* (Fall 2002), pp. 391ff.

Chapter 17 Implementing Quality Concepts

Understanding Total Quality Management Tenets — LO17-3   DEMO 17-3

◆ For each of the following items, which tenet of TQM applies: (1) continuous improvement, (2) employee participation, (3) product/service improvement, or (4) supplier partnerships?

1. Measuring and responding to customer satisfaction surveys on quality. . . . . Product/service improvement
2. Incorporating quality in the planning process with a goal of zero defects . . . . Continuous improvement
3. Building out long-term purchase schedules with key suppliers . . . . Supplier partnerships
4. Management communicating regularly with employees on cost quality initiatives . . . Employee participation

Quality as an Organizational Culture

Quality, propelled by changing customer needs and better competition, must be viewed as a moving target; thus, TQM is inseparable from the concept of continuous improvement. To provide the sense of working toward a common goal, continually higher performance standards must be set for everyone in the organization (not just for people in the production or service area). The TQM philosophy provides a new focus. In the future, it will not be the company with the "best" products or the "lowest" costs that will be successful; it will be the company that is the best at learning to do things better.[12]

The behavior of organizational personnel comprises the basis for TQM. Consistent and committed top management leadership is the catalyst for moving the company toward a culture in which all individuals, regardless of rank or position, are focused on exceeding customer expectations. Such an attitude should permeate all areas of the company, from R&D to product design, production, marketing, and distribution, to customer and supplier relations to accounting and information processing. Management can effectively change its organizational culture by providing an environment in which employees know that the company cares about them, is responsive to their needs, and will appreciate and reward excellent results. This knowledge goes a long way in motivating employees to increase cooperation and making them feel trusted, respected, and comfortable. Such employees are more likely to treat customers in a similar manner.

The firm must empower employees to participate fully in the quest for excellence by providing the means by which employees gain pride, satisfaction, and substantive involvement. The new corporate work environment involves the effective and appropriate use of teams, and employees should be recognized and rewarded for being involved in

- team problem solving,
- contributing ideas for improvement,
- monitoring work processes,
- developing new skills, and
- sharing their knowledge and enthusiastic attitudes with their colleagues.

With its focus on process and customers, TQM is founded on one very obvious and simple principle:

Do the right things right the first time, all the time, on time, and continuously improve.

The heart of this principle is zero defects now and in the future. For example, a non-TQM production policy statement might read: "Defective production cannot be greater than one percent of total production." In contrast, TQM would state: "Zero-defect production will be achieved." Such a statement necessitates that management provide employees with the proper

- training,
- equipment,
- materials quality,
- encouragement,
- empowerment opportunities, and
- work environment to achieve the goal.

---

[12] Tom Richman, "What Does Business Really Want from Government?" *The State of Small Business* (1995), p. 96.

"High quality" is not a static concept; when one problem has been solved, another one is always waiting for a solution. The TQM philosophy cannot be integrated into an organization quickly. According to Dr. W. Edwards Deming, organizational changes take at least seven years. Therefore, in the time it takes for the changes necessitated by TQM implementation to be effected, today's organizations are bombarded with numerous technological innovations that require a reassessment of how customers view quality and how competitors are addressing quality issues. Achieving world-class status does not mark an ending point; it is only a resting point until the competition catches up and tries to race ahead.

REVIEW 17-3 — **LO17-3** — **Total Quality Management**

1. Total quality management (TQM) is based on four tenets of (1) continuous improvement, (2) employee participation, (3) product/service improvement, and (4) supplier partnerships. Review each of the following items, *a* through *e*, and determine which tenet of TQM applies.
   a. _____ Employees of a warehouse are cross-trained by rotating through the functions of receiving orders, picking orders, and packing orders for shipment.
   b. _____ A study conducted by a large CPA firm of its clients resulted in the firm dismissing clients that posed the largest risks for audit failures.
   c. _____ Equipment was redesigned in order to avoid a machining process that resulted in occasional product defects.
   d. _____ A fast food service provider offers a customer loyalty program where the customer is rewarded with free menu items after a short survey is completed within five days of the last visit.
   e. _____ An equipment parts manufacturer teams up with its international suppliers to review labor practices.

More practice: E17-34
Solution on p. 17-47.

2. **Critical Thinking:** What circumstances make a condition of high quality today *not* a condition of high quality in a year or even a month from now?

TYPES OF QUALITY COSTS

LO17-4 What are the types of quality costs, and how are those types related?

Instituting TQM in an organization creates a new focus on costs and their incurrence. This focus results in the tracking of costs of compliance and noncompliance.

The **cost of compliance** (or costs of controlling quality) include prevention and appraisal costs.

> Cost of compliance = Prevention costs + Appraisal costs

- **Prevention costs** are incurred to improve quality by precluding product defects and improper processing from occurring. Amounts spent to implement training programs, research customer needs, and acquire improved production equipment are prevention costs.
- **Appraisal costs** are incurred to inspect, monitor and compensate for mistakes not eliminated through prevention activities.

Compliance costs are incurred to reduce or eliminate the present and future costs of failure; thus, expenditures for compliance are proactive. Furthermore, effective investments in prevention activities can even minimize the costs of appraisal.

The **cost of noncompliance** (or failure costs) results from production imperfections. Cost of noncompliance includes internal and external failure costs.

> Cost of noncompliance = Internal failure costs + External failure costs

Chapter 17 Implementing Quality Concepts 17-17

- **Internal failure costs** are expenditures, such as scrap or rework, incurred to remedy defective units before they are shipped to customers.
- **External failure costs** are expenditures for items, such as warranty work, customer complaints, litigation, and defective product recalls, that are incurred after a faulty unit of product has been shipped to (or an improper service has been performed for) the customer.

Although both types of failure costs can be expensive, an organization would prefer to incur internal, rather than external, failure costs.

Quality costs, like other costs, can have variable, fixed, mixed, or step behaviors. Some quality costs are variable in relation to the quantity of defective output, some are step fixed with increases at specific levels of defective output, and some are fixed for a specific time. For example, rework cost could vary directly with the total quantity of production and, therefore, be a variable cost. In contrast, training expenditures are fixed costs if set by management because they will not vary regardless of the quantity of output produced in a given period.

The total quality management process will result in a cycle of benefit shown in **Exhibit 17.9**. This cycle will continue and produce a company that is profitable and secure in its market share—two primary goals of any organization.

Exhibit 17.9 ■ TQM's Cycle of Benefit

- Increase amounts spent for prevention
- Reduce or eliminate NVA activities
- Install technologically advanced equipment

→

- Decrease appraisal and failure costs
- Increase productivity and quality

→

- Decrease selling price or increase value

↓

- Increase in sales and profitability

←

- Increase R&D investments
- Increase worker training

←

- Generate new product ideas
- Raise customer service levels

↑

Thus, the TQM philosophy indicates that total costs decline, rather than increase, as an organization makes quality improvements. It seems that it is the *lack* of high quality, rather than the *pursuit* of high quality, that is expensive. Understanding the types and causes of quality costs helps managers prioritize improvement projects and provide feedback that supports and justifies improvement efforts.

Determining Types of Prevention, Appraisal, Internal Failure, and External Failure Costs LO17-4 DEMO 17-4

◆ **What are examples of prevention, appraisal, internal failure, and external failure costs?**

The following table provides specifics of each type of quality cost.

© Cambridge Business Publishers

COSTS OF COMPLIANCE		COSTS OF NONCOMPLIANCE	
Prevention Costs	**Appraisal Costs**	**Internal Failure Costs**	**External Failure Costs**
Employees: • Hiring for quality • Providing training and awareness • Establishing participation programs Customers: • Surveying needs • Researching needs • Conducting field trials Machinery: • Designing to detect defects • Arranging for efficient flow • Arranging for monitoring • Incurring preventive maintenance • Testing and adjusting equipment • Fitting machinery for mistake-proof operations Suppliers: • Assessing for quality • Educating suppliers • Involving suppliers Product Design: • Developing specifications • Engineering and modeling • Testing and adjusting for conformity, effective and efficient performance, durability, ease of use, safety, comfort, appeal, and cost	Before Production: • Inspecting at receipt Production Process: • Monitoring and inspecting • Keeping the process consistent, stable, and reliable • Using procedure verification • Automating During and After Production: • Conducting quality audits Information Process: • Recording and reporting defects • Measuring performance Organization: • Administering quality control department	Product: • Reworking • Creating waste • Storing and disposing of waste • Reinspecting rework Production Process: • Reprocessing • Creating unscheduled interruptions • Experiencing unplanned downtime • Retesting Organization: • Making inappropriate decisions because of lost or missing information • Incurring non-value-added activities • Losing revenue from selling items as "seconds"	Organization: • Staffing complaint departments • Staffing warranty claims departments Customer: • Losing future sales to current or potential customers • Losing reputation • Losing goodwill Product: • Repairing • Replacing • Reimbursing • Recalling • Litigating Service: • Providing unplanned service • Expediting • Serving after purchase

Time-Phased Model for Quality Costs The points in the production–sales cycle at which quality costs are usually incurred are shown in **Exhibit 17-10**. An information feedback loop should be in effect to link the types and causes of failure costs to future prevention costs. Alert managers and employees continuously monitor failures to discover their causes and adjust prevention activities to close the gaps that allowed the failures to occur. These continuous rounds of action, reaction, and action are essential to continuous improvement initiatives for products currently in production and related products in the design stage.

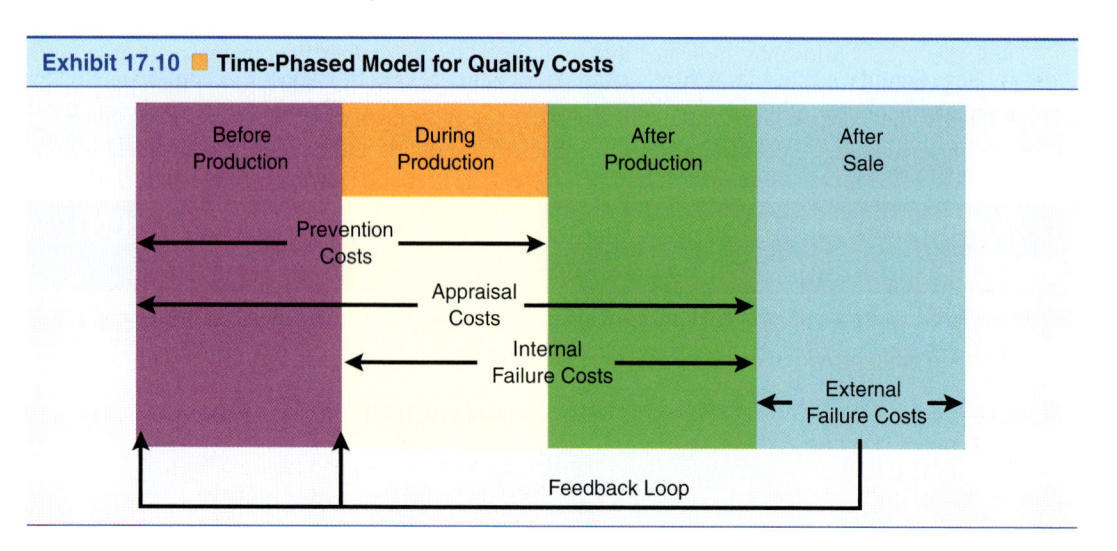

Exhibit 17.10 ■ Time-Phased Model for Quality Costs

REVIEW 17-4

Identifying Quality Costs   LO17-4

1. Identify each of the costs listed as *a* through *h* as one of the following: (1) prevention cost, (2) appraisal cost, (3) internal failure cost, or (4) external failure cost.
   a. _____ Reworking a product due to a problem discovered during inspection.
   b. _____ Cost of inspecting a product at two points during production.
   c. _____ Approving a new supplier based on preestablished criteria.
   d. _____ Cost due to a recall of a product due to the possibility of injury.
   e. _____ Costs to adjust equipment in order to avoid material waste.
   f. _____ Loss of customer loyalty on future purchases due to unsatisfactory service.
   g. _____ Replacing a labor-intensive process with an automated process to reduce human error.
   h. _____ Holding a customer focus group in order to get feedback on a product prototype's functionality.
2. **Critical Thinking:** How are prevention and appraisal costs a result of proactive management decisions, while failure costs require a reactionary management response?

More practice: MC17-16, MC17-17, MC17-18, E17-40, E17-41
Solution on p. 17-48.

MEASURING THE COST OF QUALITY

A company that wants to use TQM and continuous improvement should record and report its quality costs separately so that managers can plan, control, evaluate, and make decisions about the activities that cause those costs. However, merely generating quality cost information does not enhance quality. Managers and workers must consistently and aggressively use the information as a basis for creatively and intelligently advancing quality.

LO17-5 How is cost of quality measured and reported?

Because accounting records are commonly kept primarily to serve financial accounting requirements, the quality cost behaviors relative to activity changes as well as the appropriate drivers for these costs must be separately developed or estimated, and tracked for quality management purposes. A system in which quality costs are readily available or easily determined provides useful information to managers trying to make spending decisions by pinpointing areas having the highest cost–benefit relationships. Additionally, quality cost information will indicate how a shift in one or more costs will affect the others. When quality costs are not reflected specifically in the accounting records, managers have no idea how large or pervasive these costs are and, therefore, have little incentive to reduce them.

Identifying and Tracking Quality Costs

The first step in making quality information readily available is to first identify the costs. A company can identify its quality costs in its accounting system by either adding new quality general ledger accounts or by coding quality transactions.

Adding New Quality Accounts A firm's chart of accounts can be expanded to accommodate either tracing separately or allocating quality costs to new accounts. **Exhibit 17.11** indicates some suggested accounts that will help management focus on quality costs. *Opportunity costs*, including lost future sales and a measure of the firm's loss of reputation, are also associated with poor quality. Although opportunity costs are real and may be estimated, they are not recorded in the accounting system because they do not result from specific transactions.

Exhibit 17.11 ■ New Quality Accounts

Prevention Cost Accounts	Often "Buried" In
Quality training	Manufacturing overhead (salaries/wages expense)
Quality market research	Marketing expense; Advertising expense
Quality technology	Assets; Factory overhead (depreciation)
Quality product design	Engineering salaries/Wages expense
Preventive maintenance	WIP inventory; FG inventory; Factory overhead

continued

continued from previous page

Exhibit 17.11 ■ New Quality Accounts

Appraisal Cost Accounts	Often "Buried" In
Quality inspections	Manufacturing overhead (salaries/wages expense)
Procedure verifications	Manufacturing overhead (salaries/wages expense)
Measurement equipment	Assets; Manufacturing overhead (depreciation)

Internal Failure Cost Accounts	Often "Buried" In
Reworking products	WIP inventory; FG inventory; Manufacturing overhead
Scrap and waste	WIP inventory; FG inventory
Storing and disposing of waste	Manufacturing overhead; loss
Reprocessing	WIP inventory; FG inventory
Rescheduling and setup	Manufacturing overhead

External Failure Cost Accounts	Often "Buried" In
Complaint handling	Salaries/Wages expense
Warranty handling	Warranty expense
Repairing or replacing returns	Warranty expense
Customer reimbursements after failure	Accounts Receivable credit
Expediting replacements	Shipping expense
Product recalls	Marketing expense; Advertising expense
Image improvements after failure	Marketing expense; Advertising expense

Coding Quality Transactions If a firm has a database management system, transactions can be coded so that reports can be generated without expanding the chart of accounts. Coding permits quality transaction types and amounts to be accessible and the generation of a cost of quality report such as the one shown in the schedule that follows (which uses assumed numbers).

Preparing a Cost of Quality Report

Two important assumptions underlie this report: stable production and a monthly reporting system. If wide fluctuations in production or service levels occur, period-to-period comparisons of absolute amounts may not be appropriate. Amounts might need to be converted to percentages to have valid meaning. Additionally, in some settings (such as the just-in-time environment discussed in Chapter 18), a weekly reporting system is more appropriate because of the need for continuous monitoring.

Cost of Quality Report

	A	B	C	D	E	F
1		Cost of Current Period	Cost of Prior Period	Percent Change from Prior Period	Current Period Budget	Percent Change from Budget
2	*Prevention Costs*					
3	Quality training	$ 5,800	$ 5,600	+4	$ 6,000	−3
4	Quality participation	8,200	8,400	−2	8,000	+3
5	Quality market research	9,900	7,700	+29	11,000	−10
6	Quality technology	9,600	10,800	−11	15,000	−36
7	Quality product design	16,600	12,200	+36	16,500	+1
8	Total	$50,100	$44,700	+12	$56,500	−11
9	*Appraisal Costs*					
10	Quality inspections	$ 3,300	$ 3,500	−6	$ 3,000	+10
11	Procedure verifications	1,200	1,400	−14	1,500	−20
12	Measurement equipment	2,700	3,000	−10	3,200	−16
13	Test equipment	1,500	1,200	+25	1,500	0
14	Total	$ 8,700	$ 9,100	−4	$ 9,200	−5

continued

continued from previous page

Cost of Quality Report

	A	B	C	D	E	F
15		Cost of Current Period	Cost of Prior Period	Percent Change from Prior Period	Current Period Budget	Percent Change from Budget
16	*Internal Failure Costs*					
17	Reworking products	$ 8,500	$ 8,300	+2	N/A*	
18	Scrap and waste	2,200	2,400	−8	N/A*	
19	Storing and disposing of waste	4,400	5,700	−23	N/A*	
20	Reprocessing	1,800	1,600	+13	N/A*	
21	Rescheduling and setup	900	1,200	−25	N/A*	
22	Total	$ 17,800	$ 19,200	−7		
23	*External Failure Costs*					
24	Complaint handling	$ 5,800	$ 6,200	−6	N/A*	
25	Warranty handling	10,700	9,300	+15	N/A*	
26	Repairing or replacing returns	27,000	29,200	−8	N/A*	
27	Customer reimbursements	12,000	10,700	+12	N/A*	
28	Expediting	1,100	1,300	−15	N/A*	
29	Total	$ 56,600	$ 56,700	0		
30	Total quality costs	$133,200	$129,700	+3	$65,700	+103

*TQM advocates planning for zero defects; therefore, zero failure costs would be included in the budget.

Theoretically, if prevention and appraisal costs were prudently incurred, failure costs would become $0. However, because prevention and appraisal costs must still be incurred to identify and reduce failures, total quality costs can never actually be zero. But quality guru Philip Crosby proposes that, if the organizational benefits from increased sales and greater efficiency exceed the sum of compliance and noncompliance costs, then quality is essentially free.[13] The following example indicates that quality may not only be "free" but even *profit enhancing* if the cost of eliminated failure costs (e.g., less warranty work and customer returns) can be estimated.

Expenditures on prevention	$ (450,000)
Expenditures on appraisal	(250,000)
Total quality compliance costs	$ (700,000)
Total failure costs eliminated	1,000,000
Addition to profit	$ 300,000

Management should analyze the quality cost relationships and spend money for quality in ways that balance costs and benefits. Such an analysis requires measuring the cost of quality to the extent possible and practical and estimating the benefits of quality costs.

Determining the Causes of Variances

Pareto analysis is a statistical technique based on the Pareto principle that can be used to separate the "vital few" from the "trivial many." Such an analysis reviews the causes of a problem so as to determine which ones occur most often. Data analysis has repeatedly shown that approximately 20–30 percent of the population (regardless of whether that population is inventory items, number of donors resulting from participants at a charity event, or sources of defects) accounts for 70–80 percent of the cost or values. Thus, a disproportionate benefit can be achieved by addressing a limited number of "problems." Pareto analysis can be used by management to decide where to concentrate the quality prevention budget. This technique classifies the causes of process problems according to impact on an objective. For example, a laptop manufacturer might classify its warranty claim costs for the past year according to defects in screens, CPUs, ports, keyboards, and other. The following table lists the

---
[13] Philip Crosby, *Quality Is Free* (New York: Signet, 1979).

defects in order from the highest warranty costs to the lowest warranty costs in dollars, as a percentage of total dollars, and as a cumulative percentage of total dollars.

Phoenix Clinic Cost Data

	A	B	C	D
1		Warranty Cost	% of Total	Cumulative
2	Screen	$ 50,880	44%	44%
3	CPU	36,360	32%	76%
4	Ports	12,000	10%	86%
5	Keyboard	9,000	8%	94%
6	Other (10 claim types)	6,760	6%	100%
7	Total	$115,000	100%	

Warranty costs and the cumulative percentage of warranty costs are shown in the following Pareto chart.

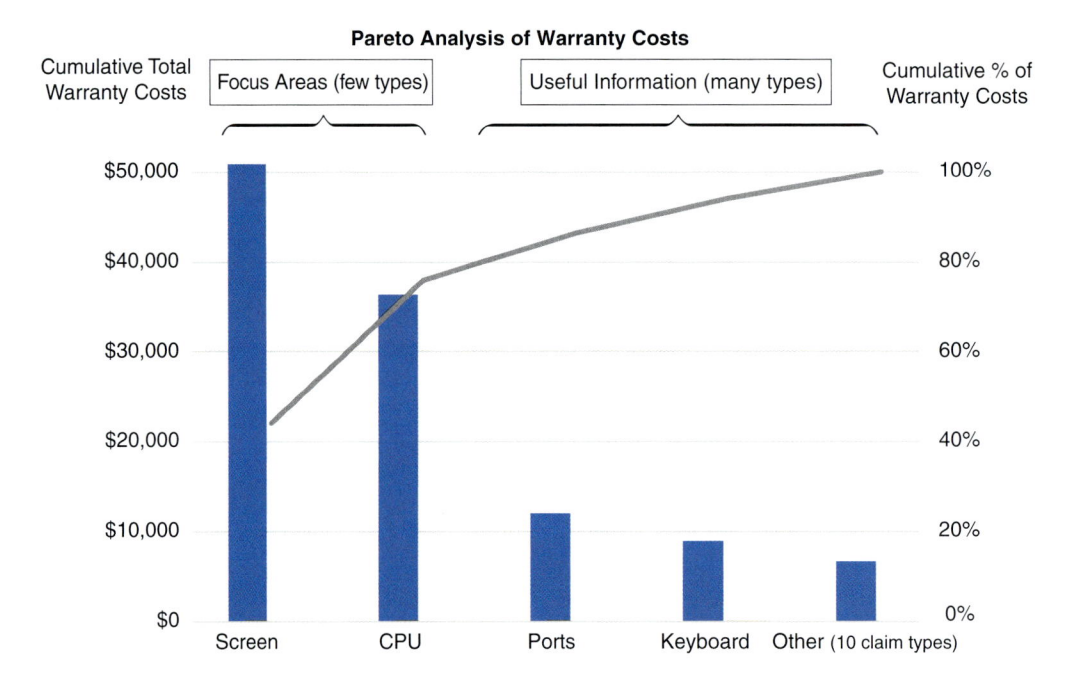

Pareto Analysis of Warranty Costs

Screen	CPU	Ports	Keyboard	Other (10 claim types)
$50,880	$36,360	$12,000	$9,000	$6,760

Focus Areas (few types): Screen, CPU
Useful Information (many types): Ports, Keyboard, Other

Listing the total failure costs of all models in descending order of magnitude indicates that screen and CPU failures account for 76 percent (44% + 32%) of total warranty costs. Therefore, management should focus efforts on identifying the causes of screen and CPU problems for all laptops, rather than investigating all of the different warranty issues. This type of information allows management to devote the appropriate portion of its prevention efforts to minimizing or eliminating specific problems. In this way, the company prioritizes its efforts, using its limited resources in a cost beneficial way. This analysis should be conducted sufficiently often to detect trends quickly and make adjustments rapidly. As another example, a large restaurant chain could use Pareto analysis to prioritize service problems and thus determine where to devote the majority of its training efforts.

Calculating the Total Cost of Quality

Exhibit 17.12 provides formulas for calculating an organization's total quality cost, using the prevention, appraisal, and failure categories. Some amounts used in these computations are, by necessity, estimates. It is more appropriate for businesses to use reasonable estimates of quality costs than to ignore such costs because of a lack of verifiable or precise amounts.

Chapter 17 Implementing Quality Concepts

Exhibit 17.12 ■ Formulas for Calculating Total Quality Cost

Calculating Lost Profits
Profit lost by selling units as defects = (Total defective units − Number of units reworked) × (Profit for good unit − Profit for defective unit)

$$Z = (D - Y)(P_1 - P_2)$$

Calculating Total Internal Costs of Failure
Rework cost = Number of units reworked × Cost to rework defective unit

$$R = (Y)(r)$$

Calculating Total External Costs of Failure
Cost of processing customer returns = Number of units returned × Cost of a return

$$W = (D_r)(w)$$

Total failure cost = Profit lost by selling units as defects + Rework cost + Cost of processing customer returns + Cost of warranty work + Cost of product recalls + Cost of litigation related to products + Opportunity cost of lost customers

$$F = Z + R + W + PR + L + O$$

Calculating the Total Quality Cost
Total quality cost = Total compliance cost + Total failure cost
T = (Prevention cost + Appraisal cost) + Total failure cost

$$T = K + A + F$$

Prevention and appraisal costs are total estimated amounts; no formulas are appropriate. As the cost of prevention rises, the number of defective units should decline. Additionally, as the cost of prevention rises, the cost of appraisal should decline; however, appraisal cost should never become zero.

Source: Adapted from James T. Godfrey and William R. Pasewark, "Controlling Quality Costs," *Management Accounting* (March 1988), p. 50. Copyright 1988 by Institute of Management Accountants. Reproduced with permission of Institute of Management Accountants in the format Textbook via Copyright Clearance Center.

Calculating the Total Cost of Quality — LO17-5 DEMO 17-5

Consider the following April operating information for O'Reilly Company.

Defective units (D)	5,000	Units reworked (Y)	2,400
Profit for good unit (P_1)	$50	Profit for defective unit (P_2)	$30
Cost to rework defective unit (r)	$10	Units returned (Dr)	800
Cost of return (w)	$15	Prevention cost (K)	$80,000
Appraisal cost (A)	$14,400		

Note: Assume no PR, L, or O.

◆ **What is the amount of lost profit, internal failure cost, external failure cost, total failure cost, and total cost of quality?**

Substituting these values into the cost of quality formulas provided in **Exhibit 17.13** gives the following results.

$Z = (D - Y)(P_1 - P_2)$ = (5,000 − 2,400)($50 − $30) = 2,600 × $20 = $52,000 Lost profit

$R = (Y)(r)$ = (2,400)($10) = $24,000 Internal failure cost

$W = (D_r)(w)$ = (800)($15) = $12,000 External failure cost

$$F = Z + R + W = \$52{,}000 + \$24{,}000 + \$12{,}000 = \underline{\$88{,}000} \text{ Total failure cost}$$

$$T = K + A + F = \$80{,}000 + \$14{,}400 + \$88{,}000 = \underline{\$182{,}400} \text{ Total quality cost}$$

Of the $182,400 total quality cost, O'Reilly's managers need to identify the causes of the $88,000 failure costs and work to eliminate those causes. If sales for the same period were $4,500,000, the total quality cost as a percentage of sales is 4 percent.

$$\$182{,}400 \text{ total quality cost} \div \$4{,}500{,}000 \text{ Sales} = 4.0\%$$

Decreasing failure costs by increasing future spending on prevention and appraisal efforts should result in lower quality cost as a percentage of sales.

Incorporating Quality into a Balanced Scorecard

Today's business strategy of focusing on customers and quality requires a firm to manage costs so that a reasonable value-to-price relationship can be achieved. Although prices are commonly set in reference to the competitive market rather than to costs, companies lacking appropriate cost management skills cannot expect to succeed in the long run. Thus, organizations need to engage in cost management.

Cost management can be viewed as the use of management accounting information for the purpose(s) of

- setting and communicating organizational strategies;
- establishing, implementing, and monitoring the success of methods to accomplish the strategies; and
- assessing the level of success in meeting the promulgated strategies.

An organization's cost management system (CMS) should accumulate and report information related to organizational success in meeting or exceeding customer needs and expectations as well as quality-related goals and objectives. Managers can analyze and interpret such information to plan and control current activities and to make decisions about current and future courses of action.

In designing a CMS, consideration must be given to cost accumulation and process measurement activities. Cost accumulation for financial accounting purposes can be inadequate for strategy-based decisions. For instance, financial accounting requires that research and development (R&D) costs be expensed as incurred, but a product's cost is largely determined during the design stage. Design has implications for perceived product value, necessary production technology, ease of product manufacturability, product durability, and likelihood of product failure. Consequently, a CMS should accumulate design costs as part of product cost. This cost need not appear on the financial accounting statements, but it must exist for decision-making purposes in the cost management system.

In contrast to its treatment of R&D costs, financial accounting requires all production costs to be inventoried and does not distinguish whether they add customer value. A useful CMS differentiates between costs that add value and those that do not so that managers and employees can work to reduce the NVA costs and enhance continuous improvement.

Another CMS function relates to the production process. Financial accounting is monetarily based and, therefore, does not directly measure nonfinancial organizational activities. For example, the percent of automated production, percent of reworked units, number of customer complaints, and percent of repeat customers are not recorded in financial accounting. Additionally, many activities critical to success in a quality-oriented, global marketplace are related to time—a nonmonetary characteristic. A truly useful CMS ensures the availability of information related to nonmonetary occurrences (such as late deliveries or defect rates) and incorporates that information into a balanced scorecard (BSC) so that management can achieve TQM and profitability goals. Goals and measurements for the BSC perspectives are shown in **Exhibit 17.13**.[14]

---

[14] Chapter 15 provides more discussion of the BSC.

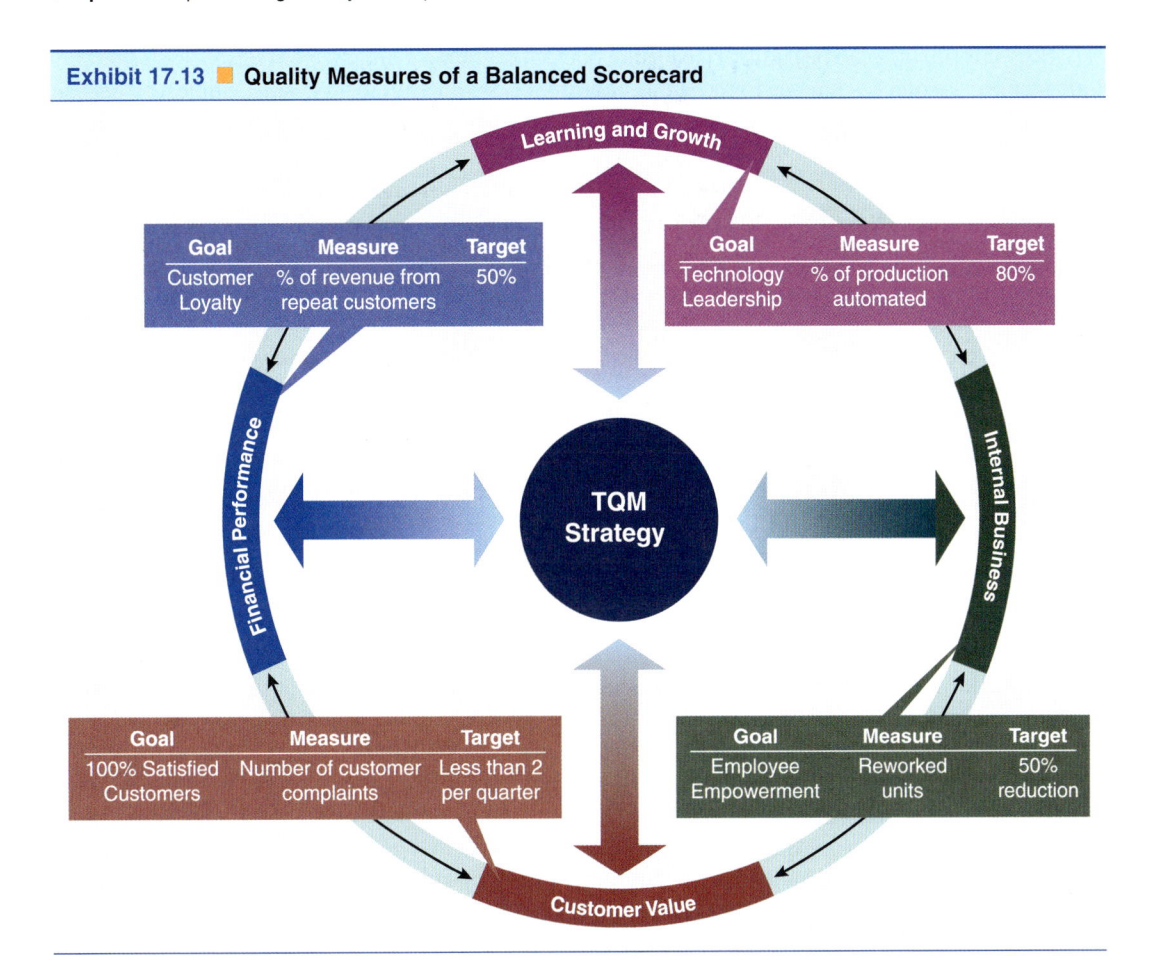

Exhibit 17.13 ■ Quality Measures of a Balanced Scorecard

Learning and Growth
- Goal: Customer Loyalty | Measure: % of revenue from repeat customers | Target: 50%
- Goal: Technology Leadership | Measure: % of production automated | Target: 80%

Customer Value
- Goal: 100% Satisfied Customers | Measure: Number of customer complaints | Target: Less than 2 per quarter
- Goal: Employee Empowerment | Measure: Reworked units | Target: 50% reduction

Center: TQM Strategy

Perspectives around the circle: Learning and Growth, Internal Business, Customer Value, Financial Performance

---

The BSC can be used to provide information on quality and help frame management decision processes. Assume that a company wants to fully automate its fiber-optic production line by year-end to reduce the number of product defects. The following processes organized in the BSC will help to ensure a focus on quality through the automation process.

Perspective	Process
Learning and Growth	Train employees to use new technologies and evaluate those employees on their success. Focus performance measurements on employee satisfaction, retention, and productivity.
Internal Business	Empower employees to troubleshoot production problems and manage quality. Monitor stoppages and compare NVA wait times and product defects before and after employee empowerment.
Customer Value	Ensure that all employees are focused on important customer criteria, such as speed (lead time), quality, service, and price (both original and after-purchase amounts). Empower sales staff to satisfy customers by offering discounts and allowances when production time is longer than expected or by servicing a product for a short time after the warranty period ends. Survey customers on satisfaction levels and compare with prior performance. Compare customer retention rates before and after new technologies were implemented.
Financial Performance	Analyze changes in revenues, sales returns, and cost of goods sold from prior periods. Compare market share before and after new technologies were implemented.

BSC information can be summarized using computer graphics organized in *dashboards* that provide managers a quick reference to the status of current BSC measurements. An example of a generic dashboard of a balanced scorecard used by management to monitor progress is shown here.

Financial	Customer		Internal		Growth & Learning	
Variance from Prior Period	Current	Variance from Budget	Current	Variance from Budget	Current	Variance from Budget
Change in Gross Profit % Over Prior Period	Rate of customers retained		Percentage of Product Defects		Employee Satisfaction Surveys	
0.8%	88%	−2%	0.06%	+0.01%	90%	+4%
Change in Sales Return Rate Over Prior Period	Customer Satisfaction Survey Scores		Percentage of Time in Work Stoppage		Employee Retention	
−2.8%	82%	+8%	8.4%	−1.1%	80%	−2%

Long-term Focus Continuous improvement is a long-term, rather than a short-term, organizational goal. Unfortunately, financial accounting reflects a short-term perspective of operating activity. Gathering monetary information and forcing it into a specific 12-month period does not clearly indicate to managers how today's decisions will affect the organization's long-run financial success. For instance, not investing in R&D would cause a company's short-run profitability to improve but could be disastrous in the long run.

Thus, a CMS should report more of the costs and benefits of organizational activities than do financial accounting reports. Having strategy-based information included in a BSC allows managers to make informed assessments of the company's performance in the value chain, its position of competitive advantage (or disadvantage), and its progress toward achieving the organization's mission.

REVIEW 17-5 | **LO17-5** | **Measuring Cost of Quality**

1. The following production information about quality costs has been gathered for September.

Total defective units	1,660
Number of units reworked	1,100
Number of units returned	195
Total prevention cost	$63,480
Total appraisal cost	$19,550
Per-unit profit for defective units	$45
Per-unit profit for good units	$110
Cost to rework defective units	$40
Cost to handle returned units	$32
Litigation costs related to product failure	$92,000

    Using these data, calculate the following.
    a. Total cost to rework
    b. Profit lost from not reworking all defective units
    c. Cost of processing customer returns
    d. Total failure costs
    e. Total quality cost

2. If sales for September were $6 million, what is the cost of compliance as a percentage of sales and cost of noncompliance as a percentage of sales?

3. **Critical Thinking:** How can the company reduce the total cost of quality as a percentage of sales?

More practice: E17-50, E17-51
Solution on p. 17-48.

Chapter 17 Implementing Quality Concepts

Comprehensive Chapter Review

Key Terms

appraisal costs, p. 17-16
benchmarking, p. 17-8
common cause variation, p. 17-3
control charts, p. 17-3
cost of compliance, p. 17-16
cost of noncompliance, p. 17-16
external failure costs, p. 17-17
grade, p. 17-6

internal benchmarking, p. 17-9
internal failure costs, p. 17-17
Pareto analysis, p. 17-21
prevention costs, p. 17-16
process benchmarking, p. 17-9
quality, p. 17-2
quality control (QC), p. 17-3
results benchmarking, p. 17-9

reverse engineering, p. 17-9
special-cause variation, p. 17-3
standard deviation, p. 17-4
statistical process control (SPC), p. 17-3
strategic benchmarking, p. 17-10
total quality management (TQM), p. 17-12
value, p. 17-6

Chapter Summary

Quality Definition and Perspective (Page 17-2) — LO17-1
- Quality is the sum of all characteristics of a product or service that influence its ability to meet the needs of the person acquiring that product or service.
- Quality, from a production viewpoint, is defined as conformity with requirements and, from this viewpoint, can be improved by
  - increasing the good output generated from a specific amount of input during a period.
  - reducing variability, often by adding automation in the process.
  - reducing the product's or service's failure rate.
- Determination of conformity to standards is often made using statistical process control techniques, including control charts.
- Many companies focus on a Six Sigma production view of quality, which means that a process produces no more than 3.4 defects per million "opportunities."
- Quality, from a consumer viewpoint, is defined as the ability to meet and satisfy all specified needs at a reasonable cost.
- Characteristics of product quality from a consumer viewpoint include
  - performance,
  - features,
  - reliability,
  - conformance,
  - durability,
  - serviceability and responsiveness,
  - aesthetics, and
  - perceived value.
- A consumer viewpoint is typically seen as the better perspective and should encompass
  - making certain that the product or service delivers what was intended.
  - ascertaining that the product or service fulfills consumer needs relative to a grade versus value perspective.

Benchmarking Definition, Rationale, and Types (Page 17-8) — LO17-2
- Benchmarking refers to investigating, comparing, and evaluating a company's products, processes, and/or services against those of competitors or companies believed to be "best in class."
- A company benchmarks to obtain an understanding of another's production and performance methods so that the company can identify its strengths and weaknesses.
- Benchmarking may be one of four types:
  - internal benchmarking, in which organizational units are compared to each other, with the lower performers "learning" from the higher performers;
  - results benchmarking, in which an end product or service is examined using reverse engineering to focus on product/service specifications and performance results; this type of benchmarking is performed on competitors' products or services;
  - process benchmarking, in which a specific process is examined to determine how a "best-in-class" company achieves its results; this type of benchmarking is often performed on noncompetitors although competitors may also be used; and
  - strategic benchmarking, in which the focus is on understanding how successful companies compete.

© Cambridge Business Publishers

LO17-3 Total Quality Management (TQM) (Page 17-12)
- TQM involves all organizational employees and places the customer at the center of focus.
- TQM is defined as seeking continuous improvement in processes so as to meet or exceed customer expectations.
- TQM requires the following conditions to yield full benefits:
  - sharing planning and decision making among personnel;
  - eliminating non-value-added activities;
  - enhancing technology in hardware, production processes, and management systems that increase productivity;
  - increasing consumer awareness of the numerous types and grades of products available; and
  - using competitive benchmarking to close any performance gaps.

Quality as Part of Organizational Culture
- Quality can be instilled as part of an organization's culture by
  - having committed and consistent top management leadership.
  - developing an esprit de corps among all employees so that they are eager to meet and exceed customer expectations.
  - making certain that a work environment is provided in which employees know that the company cares about and will reward efforts to achieve high quality.
  - empowering employees.
  - providing job and quality training.
  - encouraging the pursuit of quality awards.

LO17-4 Types and Relationships of Quality Costs (Page 17-16)
- Quality costs include costs of compliance (or assurance), which are expenditures incurred to reduce or eliminate the current costs of quality failure and to continuously improve in the future. Compliance costs include
  - prevention costs that are incurred to minimize or eliminate the production of nonconforming products and services. The incurrence of prevention costs tends to reduce the costs of appraisal and failure.
  - appraisal costs that are incurred to identify units of output that do not conform to product specifications. The incurrence of appraisal costs tends to reduce the costs of external failure and increase the costs of internal failure.
- Quality costs include the costs of noncompliance (or quality failure), which include
  - internal failure costs that are incurred to remediate a nonconforming product that is detected through appraisal activities before that product is shipped to a customer. Incurrence of internal failure costs tends to reduce external failure costs.
  - external failure costs that are incurred to remediate a nonconforming product that is not detected until after being shipped to the customer.
- Compliance and noncompliance costs are inversely related. As compliance costs increase, noncompliance costs will fall.

LO17-5 Measurement and Reporting of the Cost of Quality (Page 17-9)
- The total cost of quality is equal to prevention cost plus appraisal cost plus failure cost.
- The cost of failure includes the following costs:
  - profits lost by selling defective units,
  - rework of defective goods,
  - processing customer returns,
  - warranty work,
  - product recalls,
  - litigation related to products, and
  - opportunity cost of lost customers.
- The CMS can be used to compute the
  - quality costs incurred for production/service activities,
  - costs of non-value-added activities,
  - product/service life cycle costs, and/or
  - rework costs.
- A CMS can be used to excerpt quality information that is typically "buried" in traditional financial accounting cost categories.
- The BSC can be used to develop measurements to compute
  - manufacturing cycle efficiency,
  - time to market for new products,
  - customer satisfaction levels,
  - on-time deliveries,

Chapter 17 Implementing Quality Concepts

- defect rates, and/or
- success rates of research and development activities.

Solution Strategies

Cost of Quality Components
LO17-4

Total Cost of Quality = Cost of Compliance + Cost of Noncompliance

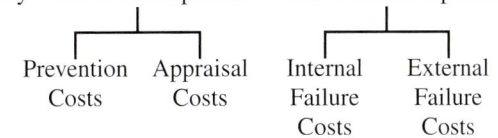

Cost of Compliance: Prevention Costs, Appraisal Costs
Cost of Noncompliance: Internal Failure Costs, External Failure Costs

Costs of noncompliance are inversely related to the costs of compliance and are a direct result of the number of defects.

Dimensions of product quality include
- conformity to specifications,
- effective and efficient performance,
- durability,
- ease of use,
- safety,
- comfort of use, and
- appeal.

Cost of Quality Formulas
LO17-5

Profit lost by selling units as defects = (Total defective units − Number of units reworked) × (Profit for good unit − Profit for defective unit)

$$Z = (D - Y)(P_1 - P_2)$$

Rework cost = Number of units reworked × Cost to rework defective unit

$$R = (Y)(r)$$

Cost of processing customer returns = Number of units returned × Cost of a return

$$W = (D_r)(w)$$

Total failure cost = Profit lost by selling units as defects + Rework cost + Cost of processing customer returns + Cost of warranty work + Cost of product recalls + Cost of litigation related to products + Opportunity cost of lost customers

$$F = Z + R + W + PR + L + O$$

Total quality cost = Total compliance cost + Total failure cost
T = Prevention cost + Appraisal cost + Total failure cost

$$T = K + A + F$$

Chapter Demonstration Problem

Burrow Corp.'s quality report for October showed the following information:
LO17-5

Profit for a good unit	$76
Profit for a defective unit	$44
Cost to rework a defective unit	$14
Cost to process a returned unit	$20
Total prevention cost	$54,000
Total appraisal cost	$32,000
Litigation related to product failure	$140,000
Opportunity cost of lost customers while litigation is being settled	$100,000
Total defective units	4,000
Number of units reworked	2,800
Number of customer units returned	1,300

© Cambridge Business Publishers

Required:

Compute the following:

a. Profit lost by selling unreworked defects
b. Total rework cost
c. Cost of processing customer returns
d. Total failure cost
e. Total quality cost

Solution to Demonstration Problem

a. $Z = (D - Y)(P_1 - P_2)$ $= (4,000 - 2,800)(\$76 - \$44) = 1,200(\$32) = \underline{\underline{\$38,400}}$

b. $R = (Y)(r)$ $= (2,800)(\$14) = \underline{\underline{\$39,200}}$

c. $W = (D_r)(w)$ $= (1,300)(\$20) = \underline{\underline{\$26,000}}$

d. $F = Z + R + W + L + O$ $= \$38,400 + \$39,200 + \$26,000 + \$140,000 + \$100,000 = \underline{\underline{\$343,600}}$

e. $T = K + A + F$ $= \$54,000 + \$32,000 + \$343,600 = \underline{\underline{\$429,600}}$

Assignments with the MBC logo in the margin are available in *myBusinessCourse*.
Resources include demonstration videos, guided examples, and auto-graded homework.
See details in the Preface, and ask your professor how you can access the system.

Data Analytics

LO17-1

DA17-1. Statistical process control with adjustments to standard deviation

A food processor is evaluating its production process for a cheese dip that requires 16 ounces of cheese. A variation in the results of the final product indicates that there may be variation in the amount of cheese that is used in the process. Data for 5 items in 20 batches is included the Excel file that can be found in MBC and will be used to answer the following questions.

a. What is the mean of the 20 batches. *Hint*: First calculate the mean of each batch and then calculate the mean of the 20 batches using the Average function in Excel. Round your final answer to one decimal place.
b. Estimate the standard deviation using the 100 data points. *Hint*: Use the STDEV.S function in Excel. Round your answer to one decimal place.
c. What is the upper and lower control limit assuming three standard deviations?
d. Create a statistical process control chart using three standard deviations. *Hint*: In a table, create four columns: original data points, the mean, upper control limit, and lower control limit. The last three columns will have the same amount repeated next to each data point. Highlight your data and create a line chart.
e. Which point(s) are due to special-cause variation? *Hint*: Use conditional formatting in your tables to identify the outliers.
f. Repeat parts c, d and e, but now use two standard deviations to set your control limits. What causes your answers to change?
g. What is the risk of considering random variation to be special-cause variation?

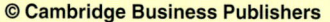

LO17-1

DA17-2. Statistical process control

Johnny Cantalore, owner of Ba-Da-Bing Pizza, has a policy to put 36 slices of pepperoni on a large pizza. Cantalore recently hired two college students to work part-time making pizzas and decided to observe them at their jobs for a few days. Cantalore gathered data on number of pepperoni slices being used on the pizzas and is included in an Excel file in MBC.

a. What is the mean of the two observation dates. *Hint*: First calculate the mean of each day and then calculate the mean of the two days using the Average function in Excel. Round your final answer to one unit.
b. Estimate the standard deviation using all of the data points. *Hint*: Use the STDEV.S function in Excel. Round your answer to one unit.
c. What is the upper and lower control limit assuming three standard deviations?
d. Create a statistical process control chart using three standard deviations. *Hint*: In a table, create four columns: original data points, the mean, upper control limit, and lower control limit. The last three columns will have the same amount repeated next to each data point. Highlight your data and create a line chart.

Chapter 17 Implementing Quality Concepts   17-31

  e. Which point(s) are due to special-cause variation?
  f. What information does the chart provide to Cantalore?

DA17-3. Quality analysis using pareto chart LO17-5
 Refer to the information in E17-48 and access the related Excel file in MBC to answer the following questions.
  a. Create a table in Excel including the number of complaints, the percentage of total complaints, and the cumulative percentage of total complaints.
  b. Create a Pareto chart using the data from part a. *Hint*: Highlight the data and select Pareto chart from the histogram chart options. What do the bars represent? What does the line represent?
  c. How does the combination of the line and the bars provide information to support the 80/20 rule?

DA17-4. Quality analysis using pareto chart with decision making LO17-5
 Refer to the information in E17-49 and access the related Excel file in MBC to answer the following questions.
  a. Create a table in Excel including the number of complaints, the percentage of total complaints, and the cumulative percentage of total complaints.
  b. Create a Pareto chart using the data from part *a*. *Hint*: Highlight the data and select Pareto chart from the histogram chart options. What do the bars represent? What does the line represent?
  c. How does the combination of the line and the bars provide information to support the 80/20 rule?
  d. How should management use the analysis in decision making?

DA17-5. Correlation vs. causation LO17-5
 Assume that you are a cost accountant working with a plant that manufacturers machinery components. You have noticed that quality costs (including inspection costs and costs of reworking rejected parts) have increased over the last year. Overhead costs for the plant are allocated using a single overhead cost pool and a single cost driver. In order to better understand the increase in quality costs, you first identified a pool of quality costs over the past year ranging from approximately $17,200 to $24,600. You prepared a data visualization showing the relationship between units of products produced and quality costs (see MBC).
  a. Explain whether or not quality costs correlate with units produced.
  b. Explain the factors you would consider in determining whether or not units produced cause quality costs.
  c. After discussions with production workers on the factory floor, you determine that the number of line setups may impact the number of rejected parts (the more setups, the more rejects). How might this information affect (1) additional data visualizations that you develop and (2) your understanding of correlation and causation of quality costs?

Data Visualization

Data Visualization Activities are available in myBusinessCourse. These assignments use Tableau Dashboards to expose students to visual depictions of data and introduce students to data analytics through data visualizations. These exercises are easily assignable and auto graded by MBC.

Potential Ethical Issues

1. Ignoring the actual range of acceptable variation on control charts to accept a higher level of defects than allowed and, thus, creating a higher possibility of external failure costs
2. Using lower-grade raw material and components than specified for production activities to reduce costs while continuing to promote the company's high-quality products
3. Using the benchmarking process as an opportunity to illegally gain information or product designs from competitors
4. Creating a set of preferred supplier characteristics that fosters discrimination against other suppliers
5. Consciously choosing to discount internal information about product defects and failures that could result in significant consumer or environmental harm
6. Minimizing estimates of internal and external failure costs to justify retaining current practices rather than engaging in expenditures that would, in the long run, be cost beneficial

© Cambridge Business Publishers

Questions

Q17-1. What is meant by the term *quality*? In defining quality, from what two perspectives can a definition be formulated? Why are both important?

Q17-2. What does it mean for a process to be "in control" or "out of control?"

Q17-3. In conducting activity analyses, the presence of certain activities indicates low production process quality. List five examples of these activities.

Q17-4. Compare and contrast the eight characteristics that constitute overall quality from the customer's perspective with the three additional characteristics that constitute service quality from the customer's perspective.

Q17-5. Locate a well-described product on the Internet. Discuss how that product exemplifies the eight overall quality characteristics. Prepare a balanced scorecard for this product assuming that its manufacturer has a total quality management strategy.

Q17-6. Describe four types of benchmarking.

Q17-7. What is TQM? What are the four important tenets of TQM, and why are they important?

Q17-8. In the production–sales cycle, what are the four points at which quality costs are incurred? How are these costs interrelated through these points?

Q17-9. How can Pareto analysis help focus managerial efforts on reducing the costs of quality-related problems?

Q17-10. How can a firm track quality costs within the accounting system to allow systematic report generation of quality costs?

Multiple Choice

LO17-1

MC17-11. Assume that a **McDonald's** restaurant is analyzing the time it takes to process a customer order. Using a sample size of 100, the restaurant estimates the mean processing time to be 3.4 minutes with a standard deviation of 0.5 minutes. The highest individual observation was 5.1 minutes and the lowest individual observation was 1.2 minutes. If the restaurant decides to establish control limits based on three standard deviations, what are the upper and lower control limits of the time it takes to process orders?

a. Upper control limit is 3.9 minutes and the lower control limit is 2.9 minutes.
b. Upper control limit is 4.6 minutes and the lower control limit is 1.7 minutes.
c. Upper control limit is 4.9 minutes and the lower control limit is 1.9 minutes.
d. Upper control limit is 5.1 minutes and the lower control limit is 1.2 minutes.

LO17-1

MC17-12. Indicate whether the customer perspective quality metrics of *reliability* and *perceived value* are typically evaluated objectively or subjectively.

	Reliability	Perceived Value
a.	Objectively	Objectively
b.	Objectively	Subjectively
c.	Subjectively	Subjectively
d.	Subjectively	Objectively

LO17-2

MC17-13. Retail Partners Inc., which operates eight discount store chains, is seeking to reduce the costs of its purchasing activities through reengineering and a heavier use of electronic data interchange (EDI). Which of the following benchmarking techniques would be appropriate in this situation?

I. A comparison of the purchasing costs and practices of each of Retail Partners' store chains to identify their internal "best in class."

Chapter 17 Implementing Quality Concepts

II. A comparison of the practices of Retail Partners to those of Discount City, another retailer, whose practices are often considered "best in class."
III. A comparison of the practices of Retail Partners to those of Capital Airways, an international airline, whose practices are often considered "best in class."
IV. An in-depth review of a retail trade association publication on successful electronic data interchange applications.

 a. II and IV only
 b. I and II only
 c. I and IV only
 d. I, II, III, and IV

MC17-14. All of the following are examples of benchmarking standards except
 a. the performance of the unit during the previous year.
 b. the best performance of the unit in comparable past periods.
 c. a comparison with a similar unit within the same company.
 d. the best performance of a competitor with a similar operation.

MC17-15. Which of the following is not a benefit of total quality management?
 a. Improved internal communication
 b. Elimination of non-value-added activities
 c. Improved response time to change
 d. Increase in employee turnover

MC17-16. When measuring the cost of quality, the cost of inspecting incoming raw materials is a(n)
 a. prevention cost.
 b. appraisal cost.
 c. internal failure cost.
 d. external failure cost.

MC17-17. When evaluating the cost of quality in an organization, which one of the following would be considered an internal failure cost?
 a. The cost to rework defective units
 b. The cost to inspect units produced
 c. The warranty repair costs
 d. Product testing

MC17-18. A company is currently performing a cost of quality analysis of one of its facilities. The following are costs compiled by the facility accountant.

Inspection	$1,500
Warranty repair	2,800
Testing of new materials	400
Product testing	950
Spoilage	645
Scrap	150
Preventive equipment maintenance	590
Liability claims	1,870
Rework	1,285

Total internal failure cost is
 a. $2,080
 b. $2,785
 c. $4,945
 d. $5,955

MC17-19. Lancelot Manufacturing Inc. incurred the following costs of quality over the last six months.

Product design	$26,000
Warranty resolution	$30,000
Reworking of products	$28,000
Quality inspections	$10,000

If sales are $400,000 for the six-month period, what is the quality compliance costs as a percentage of sales and total failure costs as a percentage of sales?

	Quality Compliance Costs As a Percentage of Sales	Total Failure Costs As a Percentage of Sales
a.	7.0%	14.5%
b.	6.5%	17.0%
c.	9.0%	14.5%
d.	14.0%	9.5%

© Cambridge Business Publishers

Exercises

LO17-1 E17-20. Production view of quality; consumer view of quality Review each of the following items, *a* through *f*, and determine whether the item supports a (1) production view of quality or a (2) consumer view of quality.
- a. _____ Applying management-by-exception through the use of control charts.
- b. _____ Distinguishing between value-added and non-value added activities.
- c. _____ Evaluating the number of features which customize a product.
- d. _____ Hiring a secret shopper to assess the responsiveness of a service provider.
- e. _____ Measuring durability or the expected product's life.
- f. _____ Using statistical process control to analyze variances.

LO17-1 E17-21. Statistical process control Diamond Inc. summarized the following data for inspection costs for the last ten months, along with the estimated standard deviation.

	Inspection Costs
Month 1.	$15,100
Month 2.	14,200
Month 3.	15,200
Month 4.	14,500
Month 5.	14,900
Month 6.	15,500
Month 7.	12,900
Month 8.	14,500
Month 9.	15,400
Month 10.	14,200
Standard deviation	722

Based on this information, and setting its upper and lower control limits based on two standard deviations, the company prepared the following chart.

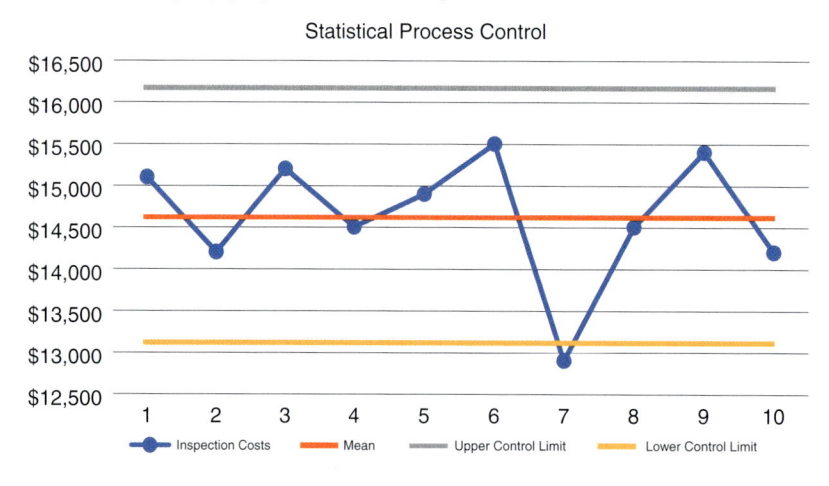

- a. At what value is the main line set? Show your calculations.
- b. At what values are the upper and lower control limits set? Show your calculations.
- c. What point(s) represent special-cause variation?
- d. Why is some variation expected in a system which is still in control?
- e. What is your recommendation based upon this analysis?

LO17-1 E17-22. Quality definition; research; writing Use the Internet to find four definitions of quality.
- a. Compare and contrast each of the four definitions with specific emphasis on whether the definition includes conformity or customer orientation.
- b. Assume that you are the manager of (1) a print and shipping services store and (2) a kitchen blender manufacturer. Prepare definitions of quality to distribute to your employees and discuss how you would measure service/product adherence to those definitions.

Chapter 17 Implementing Quality Concepts

E17-23. True/False Mark each of the following statements as true or false and explain why the false statements are incorrect. *LO17-1, 2, 4, 5*
  a. Appraisal cost is used to monitor and correct mistakes.
  b. Total quality management focuses on production processes rather than on customer satisfaction.
  c. Results benchmarking relies only on comparisons to firms within the same industry.
  d. Pareto analysis is used to help managers identify areas in which to focus quality-improvement efforts.
  e. SPC control charts are used to plot the costs of quality over time.
  f. Higher quality yields lower profits but higher productivity.
  g. Traditional accounting systems have separate accounts to capture quality costs.
  h. As the number of defective products manufactured rises, internal failure costs also rise but external failure costs are expected to decline.
  i. Quality is free.
  j. The total quality cost is the sum of prevention cost plus failure cost.

E17-24. Statistical process control; writing Statistical process control (SPC) can be used in any process with identified errors, defects, or problems. Assume that you are in charge of analyzing defect at a software manufacturing facility. *LO17-1*
  a. What is the primary goal of SPC?
  b. How would you define a defect in your organization?
  c. What defect information would you want to record in such an organization?
  d. Why would you want to record the types of defects?
  e. How do severity and priority of the defect affect your actions?

E17-25. Quality characteristics; writing Choose one product and one service with which you are well acquainted. Indicate how the product and service each meet (or do not meet) the eight overall quality characteristics. For the service, indicate how it meets (or does not meet) the three additional characteristics for service quality. *LO17-1*

E17-26. Definition of quality; quality characteristics; writing In a three-person team, role-play the following individuals who are visiting a local car dealership: (1) a 19-year-old college student, (2) one-half of a young married couple with two children, and (3) a retired person. Each individual is interested in purchasing a new automobile. *LO17-1*
  a. How does each customer define quality in an automobile? Explain the reasons for the differences.
  b. What vehicle characteristics are important to each type of buyer? Which vehicle characteristics are unique to each buyer?

E17-27. Statistical process control Via Inc. produces a product that requires the purchase of direct materials for which it has established a standard cost per unit. Using its material price variances for the last 30 weeks, the company produced the following process control chart, setting control limits based on three standard deviations. *LO17-1*

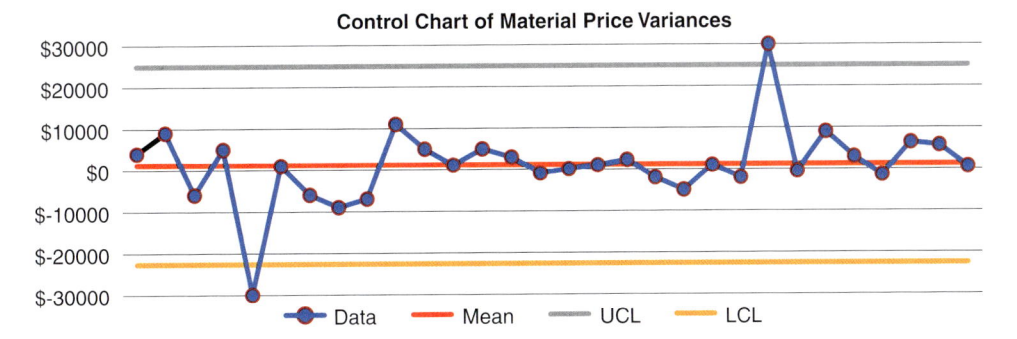

Control Chart of Material Price Variances

  a. Is the process in control in terms of the control chart? How do you know?
  b. How would the control chart change if there was less special cause variation?
  c. Can common cause variation be eliminated from the process?
  d. How would the control chart change if there was less common cause variation?
  e. What do you recommend for management to further investigate based on this analysis of its material price variances?

LO17-2 **E17-28. Benchmarking** The call center of Wobegon Electric Company handles 1.2 million calls per year. The average call requires six minutes of operator time, and 40 percent of the calls require a supervisor to be involved for at least half of the call time. Operators are paid $18 per hour, and supervisors are paid $24 per hour. After Wobegon Electric engaged in process benchmarking, which resulted in the purchase of AI software to add a chatbot to pre-screen questions, call times were reduced by one minute, and the number of supervisor-involved calls were reduced by 15 percent. The benchmarking study and related technology purchases cost Wobegon Electric Company $850,000.

   a. What was Wobegon Electric's total labor cost and the average labor cost per call at the call center prior to benchmarking?
   b. What was Wobegon Electric's total labor cost and the average labor cost per call at the call center after benchmarking? (Round up to the nearest penny.)
   c. If the new results are expected to continue for three years, was engaging in the benchmarking study profitable to Wobegon Electric Company? Show calculations.

LO17-2 **E17-29. Benchmarks** Fuel economy vehicle leaders ranked by fueleconomy.gov[15] for all vehicles and excluding plug-ins include the following:

> **All 2024 Vehicles:**
> 2024 Hyundai Ioniq 6 Long range RWD (18 inch Wheels) at 140 MPGe*
> **All 2024 Vehicles Excluding Plug-ins:**
> 2024 Toyota Prius at 57 MPG
> *Miles per gallon of gasoline equivalent.

The fuel ranking report includes the following additional information on other all-electric and hybrid vehicles:

All-electric 2024 vehicles	
2024 Kia EV6 Standard range RWD	117 MPGe
2024 Polestar 2 Single Motor (19 inch wheels)	115 MPGe
2024 Hyundai Ioniq 5 Long range RWD	114 MPGe
2024 Lucid Air Pure RWD with 20 inch wheels	130 MPGe
2024 BMW i4 eDrive35 Gran Coupe (18 inch Wheels)	120 MPGe

Hybrid 2024 vehicles	
2024 Kia Niro	49 MPG
2024 Hyundai Eliantra Hybrid	50 MPG
2024 Honda Accord Hybrid	48 MPG
2024 Toyota Corrala Hybrid	47 MPG
2024 Lexus ES 300h	44 MPG

   a. How do each of the all-electric vehicles and the hybrid vehicles compare to the top vehicle in each class according to the report? Consider the leader in the "all 2024 vehicles" to be the benchmark for all-electric vehicles and the leader in the "all 2024 vehicles excluding plug-ins" to be the leader for hybrid vehicles. Prepare a variance report with MPG/MPGe differences compared to the benchmark in each class and as a percentage of the benchmark.
   b. Which vehicles (other than the leaders) performed the best according to the benchmarks and the worst according to the benchmarks?
   c. Consider the all-gasoline model of the 2024 Toyota Camry with a 32 MPG (www.toyota.com). How does it measure up to the hybrid benchmark standard?
   d. What other factors may be relevant in comparing vehicles besides the benchmark of MPG/MPGe?

LO17-2, 4 **E17-30. Benchmarks; quality costs** For a benchmark, assume that the average firm incurs quality costs in the following proportions:

---

[15] Source: U.S. Department of Energy, "Fueleconomy.gov Top Ten," *EPA*, https://www.fueleconomy.gov/feg/topten.jsp?year=2024&action=All. Accessed on November 18, 2023.

Chapter 17 Implementing Quality Concepts

Prevention.	30%
Appraisal.	25%
Internal failure.	15%
External failure	30%
Total costs.	100%

1. When are each of the costs of quality incurred during the product life cycle: before production, during production, after production, and/or after sale?
2. Would each of the following industries be inclined to have a spending pattern on quality costs that differs from the benchmark? Why or why not?
   a. Pharmaceutical company
   b. Discount merchandiser
   c. Computer manufacturer competing on the basis of quality.
   d. Used-car retailer with focus on maintaining a high reputation for service.
   e. Local lawn service company with high priority on employee safety.

E17-31. Benchmarks; variance The Memphis manufacturing plant of Odyssey Inc. has a total of $2,362,500 in production overhead costs. Assume that the Memphis plant uses the following activity centers, costs, and cost drivers to apply overhead to products.

Cost Pool	Amount	Cost Driver	Amount
Utilities	$ 750,000	No. of machine hours	75,000
Setup	193,500	No, of setups	1,290
Material handling	1,419,000	No. of pounds of material . . .	330,000

   a. Determine the following cost pools rates for the Memphis plant: utilities cost per machine hour, setup cost per number of setups, and material handling cost per number of pounds of material.
   b. Based on an internal benchmarking initiative, Odyssey Inc. reviewed cost pool rates across all of its plant locations across the U.S. that produce similar products. Odyssey established the following benchmarks based on its analysis: $6 utilities cost per machine hour, $140 setup cost per number of setups, and $5.00 material handling cost per number of pounds of material.

   For the Memphis plant, determine the variances between its actual cost pool rates and the benchmark rates in dollars and as a percentage.
   c. What are examples where internal benchmarking may provide an incentive for a change in Odyssey's Memphis manufacturing plant? In what instances may the internal benchmarks not be practical for Memphis?

E17-32. Benchmarks; variance In a report filed with the Securities and Exchange Commission[16], a significant investment group of Bed Bath & Beyond (BBBY) shared a strategic plan detailing modern retail strategies to improve earnings per share. The report included the following data of inventory turns of BBBY compared to its peers.

	Inventory Turnover		Inventory Turnover
Target Corporation	5.6	Tractor Supply Company	3.3
Bed Bath & Beyond	5.6	Williams-Sonoma, Inc.	2.8
The Home Depot, Inc..	5.5	Tuesday Morning Corporation . . .	2.7
Ross Stores, Inc.	5.3	DICK'S Sporting Goods, Inc. . . .	2.7
TJX Companies Inc..	5.3	Macy's Inc.	2.7
Kirkland's Inc..	3.9	The Michaels Group	2.2
Lowe's Companies inc..	3.9	Pier 1 Imports, Inc..	2.2
The Container Store Group, Inc.. . .	3.7	At Home Group, Inc..	1.8
Kohl's Corporation	3.3		

---

[16] 1DFAN14A (Proxy soliciting materials) filed by Bed Bath & Beyond Inc. on 04-26-2019 with the SEC found at https://www.sec.gov/Archives/edgar/data/886158/000092189519001180/ex1dfan14a09050028_04262019.pdf.

a. What is BBBY's benchmark for inventory turnover using its peer average inventory turnover ratio?
b. If BBBY's inventory turnover over ratio is 2.9, what is BBBY's inventory turnover ratio as a percentage of the peer average?
c. What are the advantages BBBY's management identified for improving its inventory to be more in line with the peer average?
d. How can executive management impact inventory turns on a store level?

LO17-2

E17-33. Benchmarks; variance Better Health Inc. is a health care provider which has clinics across the U.S. Indicate whether each of the following examples of benchmarking for Better Health is considered (1) internal benchmarking, (2) results benchmarking, (3) process benchmarking, or (4) strategic benchmarking.

a. _____ At Better Health, customers may set up an appointment in advance or through a walk-in sign-up process. Better Health is comparing its processes to the appointment processes of a retail technology store that services computers, cellular phones, and other high-tech products.
b. _____ The results of a customer satisfaction survey from a new clinic in Minneapolis are compared to the results of customer satisfaction surveys from five well-performing Better Health clinics in the Midwest.
c. _____ Better Health Inc. identified the survey results from current patients who had recently transferred from a competing clinic in the area as a way to identify how their services compared to its competitor.
d. _____ The process of scheduling an appointment at a new clinic in Minneapolis is compared to a well-documented industry study that analyzed data from the processes of health care clinics across the U.S.

LO17-3

E17-34. Total quality management tenets Total quality management (TQM) is based on four tenets of (1) continuous improvement, (2) employee participation, (3) product/service improvement, and (4) supplier partnerships. Review each of the following items, *a* through *e*, and determine which tenet of TQM applies.

a. Performing a customer profitability analysis in order to determine which customers to prioritize and which customers to possibly drop.
b. Instituting long-term measures in order to reduce common cause variation in the system's processes.
c. Hosting brainstorming sessions where employees are encouraged to submit new ideas for process improvement.
d. Creating a dashboard shared with key suppliers that reports performance metrics such as inspection failure rates of incoming materials, on-time delivery rates, overall defect rates, etc.

LO17-3

E17-35. TQM; writing Different sources indicate differing key elements of total quality management, but integrity, training, leadership, and communication are four items that seem to be essential. Discuss why you think that these four elements are critical to an effective TQM program and why disregard of each could invalidate such a program.

LO17-3

E17-36. Cost and benefit of TQM; writing Colleges and universities have a variety of internal and external customers. Use a team of three or four individuals to answer the following:

a. Who are three internal and two external customers of a college or university?
b. How would each of the customers from (a) define product or service quality at a college or university? Do any of these views conflict and, if so, how?
c. Are a college or university's internal customers as important as external customers? Explain the rationale for your answer.

LO17-3

E17-37. TQM; sustainability; writing Discuss how corporate sustainability programs are similar in direction and implementation to total quality management programs.

LO17-3

E17-38. Research; supplier partnerships; writing Find a company's website that provides information on the characteristics that are desired for that company when establishing long-term/preferred supplier relationships.

a. What characteristics are listed? Why do you think each of these is important?
b. Did the characteristics within the list or elsewhere on the website address supplier diversity? Do you believe that supplier diversity is necessary? Why or why not?

Chapter 17 Implementing Quality Concepts

E17-39. Supplier quality; writing Honda Motor Company has paid for full-page advertisements in *The Wall Street Journal* that did not discuss any Honda products, refer to year-end earnings, or announce a new stock issuance. Instead, the ads informed readers that "buying quality parts is important to this company." The ads named Honda suppliers and identified their locations. Prepare a brief essay to answer the following questions:

a. Why would Honda want newspaper readers to know what suppliers it uses?
b. Do you think these advertisements would have any benefit for Honda itself? Discuss the rationale for your answer.

E17-40. Costs of quality Leese Inc. has the following quality financial data for its most recent fiscal year.

Rework costs	$110,000
Warranty repair costs	280,000
Product line inspection	95,000
Design engineering	300,000
Supplier evaluation	240,000
Labor training	150,000
Product testing	65,000
Breakdown maintenance	70,000
Product scrap	195,000
Cost of returned goods	180,000
Customer complaint support	35,000
Product liability claims	80,000

What are the total prevention, appraisal, internal failure, and external failure costs for the year?

E17-41. Quality costs; ESG Classify each of the following costs related to environmental activities as prevention, appraisal, internal failure, or external failure costs.

1. Costs of environmental audits to assess the environmental impact of a company's manufacturing operations.
2. Legal costs to defend lawsuits related to environmental damage caused by the company's product
3. Costs of employee training on compliance with environmental regulations.
4. Clean-up and remediation costs of contaminated ground water due to an operational environmental spill.
5. Research and development costs to develop environmentally-friendly products.
6. Costs to measure carbon emissions of a company's manufacturing operations.
7. Costs to dispose of waste materials that were mishandled within the manufacturing facility.
8. Fines and penalties related to environmental violations.

E17-42. Quality costs Hartigay Manufacturing is evaluating its quality control costs for the current year and preparing the budget for next year. Quality costs incurred at the company for this year are as follows:

Prevention costs	$ 450,000
Appraisal costs	150,000
Internal failure costs	525,000
External failure costs	150,000
Total	$1,275,000

a. Which categories of quality costs would be affected by the decision to spend $2,250,000 on new equipment that would replace older equipment? Why?
b. If projected external failure costs for next year can be reduced 60 percent (relative to the current year's levels) by spending either $75,000 more on appraisal or $120,000 more on prevention, why might the firm opt to spend the $120,000 on prevention rather than the $75,000 on appraisal?

E17-43. Quality costs Seymour Inc. has prepared the following summary quality cost report for the year:

Prevention costs	$1,560,000
Appraisal costs	1,800,000
Internal failure costs	2,280,000
External failure costs	1,680,000
Total quality costs	$7,320,000

The company is actively striving to reduce total quality costs. Its current strategy is to increase spending in one or more quality cost categories in the hope of achieving greater spending cuts in other quality cost categories. Prepare a presentation that answers the following questions.

a. What are total quality compliance costs as a percentage of total cost of quality? What are total failure costs as a percentage of total cost of quality?
b. Which spending categories are most susceptible to control by managers? Why?
c. Why is it more logical for the company to increase spending in the prevention cost and appraisal cost categories than in the failure cost categories?
d. Which cost category is the most likely target for an increase in spending? Explain.
e. How would the adoption of a TQM philosophy affect the focus in reducing quality costs?

LO17-4, 5

E17-44. Quality costs The accounting system for Dolment Co. reflected the following quality costs for Year 1 and Year 2:

	Year 1	Year 2
Customer refunds for poor product quality	$37,000	$29,000
Fitting machines for mistake-proof operations	9,400	11,800
Supply chain management activities	9,000	10,000
Waste disposal	44,000	36,000
Quality training	26,000	30,000
Litigation claims for product defects	81,000	64,000

a. Which of these are costs of compliance, and which are costs of noncompliance?
b. Calculate the percentage change in each cost and for each category. (Round to the nearest whole percentage.)
c. Discuss the pattern of the changes in the two categories.

LO17-4

E17-45. Quality costs Harmon's Hardware has gathered the following data on its quality costs for Year 1 and Year 2:

Defect Prevention Costs	Year 1	Year 2
Quality training	$4,500	$6,250
Quality technology	4,750	5,200
Quality production design	2,000	4,700

External Failure Costs	Year 1	Year 2
Warranty handling	$7,500	$4,600
Customer reimbursements	5,500	3,900
Customer returns handling	3,500	1,900

a. Compute the percentage change in the two quality cost categories from Year 1 to Year 2.
b. Describe the pattern of change in the two categories.

LO17-4

E17-46. Quality costs; writing Sometimes a company, in its efforts to reduce costs, might also reduce quality.

a. What kinds of costs could an organization reduce that would almost automatically lower product/service quality?
b. If quality improvements create cost reductions, why would cost reductions not create quality improvements?
c. Are there instances in which cost reductions would create quality improvements? Explain.

LO17-4

E17-47. Quality costs; ethics; writing By building quality into a process rather than having quality inspections at the end of the process, certain job functions (such as that of quality control inspector) can be eliminated. Additionally, the installation of automated equipment to monitor product processing could eliminate some line worker jobs.

Chapter 17 Implementing Quality Concepts

In a company facing bankruptcy, would attempts to implement quality improvements that resulted in employee terminations be appreciated or condemned? Discuss your answer from the standpoint of a variety of concerned constituencies, including the consumers who purchase the company's products.

E17-48. Cost of quality Management at Goliath Corp. (located in Birmingham, Alabama) wants to determine what issues to address relative to customer service at its call center. A survey was taken of customers and the following information was gathered about customer complaints.

Type of Complaint	Number of Complaints
Long wait times	405
Limited hours	63
Unfriendly agents	49
Hard to navigate automated system	30
Inadequate agent communication skills	124
Agents didn't understand problem	110
Other (comprised of 10 different causes)	18

a. Determine the percentage of complaints in each category and the cumulative percentage beginning with the largest complaint category.
b. Referring to part *a*, how many different types of complaints make up 80% of the complaints? How should this analysis impact management decision making?
c. What actions would you suggest to Goliath's management to help resolve customer complaint issues?

E17-49. Cost of quality Customer returns were getting out of control at The Electronic Toy Shack. Approximately 65 percent of the toys carried by the company are made in China or Taiwan. Customers were queried by sales personnel when goods were returned about the reason for the return. After six months of gathering information from customers who provided responses, Toy Shack management had the following data.

Type of Complaint	Number of Complaints
Did not perform as expected	28
Found item cheaper elsewhere	125
Instructions too complicated	59
Instruction wording unclear	85
Missing parts/manual	14
Changed mind	17
Used too many batteries too quickly	31
Wasn't fun	19
Other (comprised of 9 different complaints)	12

a. Determine the percentage of complaints in each category and the cumulative percentage beginning with the largest complaint category.
b. What actions would you suggest to Toy Shack's management to help resolve customer complaint issues?

E17-50. Cost of quality Managers at Wellington LTD want to determine the company's cost of quality. For the month of August, the company reported sales of $1.8 million and gathered the following additional information.

Defective units	6,000
Units reworked	1,200
Defective units returned	400
Appraisal costs	$17,500
Cost per unit for rework	$18
Prevention costs	$85,000
Profit per good unit produced and sold	$85
Profit per defective unit sold	$43
Cost per unit for customer returns	$14
Cost of warranty work	$9,000

Compute the following:

a. Lost profits from selling defective work
b. Total costs of failure
c. Total quality costs
d. Calculate as a percentage of total sales: prevention costs, appraisal costs, and failures costs.

LO17-5 **E17-51. Cost of quality** The following production information about quality costs has been gathered for June:

Total defective units	720
Number of units reworked	595
Number of units returned	85
Total prevention cost	$27,600
Total appraisal cost	$8,500
Per-unit profit for defective units	$20
Per-unit profit for good units	$55
Cost to rework defective units	$18
Cost to handle returned units	$14

Using these data, calculate the following:

a. Total cost to rework
b. Profit lost from not reworking all defective units
c. Cost of processing customer returns
d. Total failure costs
e. Total quality cost

LO17-5 **E17-52. Quality information system; team activity; writing** Your company is interested in developing information about quality but has a traditional accounting system that does not provide such information directly. In a three- or four-person team, prepare a set of recommendations about how to improve the company's information system to eliminate or reduce this deficiency. In your recommendations, also explain in what areas management would have the most difficulty satisfying its desire for more information about quality and why these areas were chosen.

Problems

LO17-1, 2, 4 **P17-53. Quality problems; benchmarking; cost of quality** In 2022, pharmaceutical company **Sage Therapeutics** approved drug Zuranolone for postpartum depression, but not for major depressive disorder (MDD). The denial by the FDA for the drug's use for MDD was a sizable setback for Sage Therapeutics and for **Biogen**, a company that jointly developed the drug. In the Sage Therapeutic's third quarter, 2023 report filed with the SEC, the company reported the following.

> We cannot guarantee that future financing will be available in sufficient amounts or on terms acceptable to us, if at all. Any time we encounter a major setback in our development or regulatory activities, as is the case with the CRL issued by the FDA to our NDA for zuranolone for the treatment of MDD, or in our commercialization efforts, or receive negative data from a key clinical program, our stock price is likely to decline which would make a future financing more difficult and potentially more dilutive to our existing stockholders. For example, in August 2023, after the announcement of the CRL issued by the FDA to our NDA for zuranolone for the treatment of MDD, our stock price declined significantly.

Stock prices at month ends of June through October 2023 are shown here.

Stock prices:

June 30, 2023	$47.02	August 31, 2023	$19.72	October 31, 2023	$18.73
July 31, 2023	$34.68	September 30, 2023	$20.58		

Chapter 17 Implementing Quality Concepts

a. How did the stock prices change from June 30, 2023 to October 31, 2023? What contributed to the change?
b. Obtain the net income for the first three quarters of 2023 for Sage Therapeutics (SAGE) and the following companies with these ticker symbols: APLS, KRTX, PRTA, BPMC, and ACAD. *Hint:* Quarterly income can be looked up easily for each company at finance.yahoo.com or in quarterly 10-Q reports. How does Sage's net income compare to its peer group?
c. Discuss why a total quality management system would be more important in pharmaceutical companies than in most other companies.

P17-54. Quality and strategy; writing Three possible goals for a business are to (1) maximize profits, (2) maximize shareholder wealth, and (3) satisfy customer wants and needs. If goal (1) or (2) is chosen, the primary measurements of "success" are organizational profitability or stock price.   LO17-1

a. Do you believe that one of these three goals can be chosen to the exclusion of the others? Discuss the rationale for your answer.
b. How can total quality management help an organization meet all of these goals?
c. How might the selection of goal (1) or (2) lead to quality problems in an organization? Would the selection of goal (3) be likely to lead to quality problems? Explain.

P17-55. Statistical process control chart; special-cause variation Certain rules can help identify special-value variation in a statistical control chart besides a depiction of one point outside of the control limits.   LO17-1

a. What are common rules that indicate the system is out of control? See the website of the **American Society for Quality** at https://asq.org/quality-resources/control-chart.
b. Match each of the rules to the most relevant problem described below.
   1. Indicates a large shift from the average.
   2. Indicates a small shift from the average.
   3. Indicates a prolonged shift from the average.
   4. One observation is out of control.

P17-56. Quality costs; Pareto analysis Pierre-Paul Appliances identified the following failure costs during the year: LO17-5

Product	Cost of Failure by Type				
	Motor	Wiring	Housing	All Other	Total Dollars
Blender........	$28,000	$24,000	$ 56,000	$22,560	$130,560
Mixer..........	32,000	28,000	20,480	12,000	92,480
Breadmaker	4,000	3,920	32,000	9,040	48,960
Total.........	$64,000	$55,920	$108,480	$43,600	$272,000

a. Rearrange the rows in descending order of magnitude based on the Total Dollars column, and prepare a table using Pareto analysis with the following headings:

Product	Dollars	% of Total	Cumulative % of Total

b. Which products account for almost 80 percent of all failure costs?
c. Focusing on the products identified in (b), prepare a table using Pareto analysis to identify the types of failure causing the majority of failure costs. (*Hint:* Rearrange the cost of failure types in descending order of magnitude.) Use the following headings for your table:

Failure Type	Dollars	% of Total	Cumulative % of Total

d. Describe the problem areas for which to use preventive measures first. How, if at all, does this answer reflect the concept of leveraging expenditures?

P17-57. Quality costs; Pareto analysis Altazar Electronics has identified the following warranty costs for one of the company products. The information has been categorized according to the type of product failure.   LO17-5

Model	Electrical	Motor	Structural	Mechanical	Total Dollars
Chic	$45,360	$50,000	$26,760	$11,200	$133,320
Elegant	57,640	64,000	52,200	12,000	185,840
Others	17,660	33,180	12,360	21,640	84,840
Total	$120,660	$147,180	$91,320	$44,840	$404,000

a. Rearrange the rows in descending order of magnitude based on the Total Dollars column, and prepare a table using Pareto analysis with the following headings:

Model	Dollars	% of Total	Cumulative % of Total

b. Which model(s) account for the vast proportion of all failure costs? Discuss.
c. Devise a plan for Altazar Electronics to address the prioritization of preventive measures based on the findings in the Pareto analysis.

LO17-4

P17-58. Quality costs; research; writing New automobiles are often equipped with artificial intelligence capabilities that support the driver up to the point of allowing fully autonomous operations. The inspection process of these vehicles is evolving. Vehicles could be tested on a test track, simulator, or even in certain cities.

What implications does the manufacturing of fully autonomous vehicles have on the four types of quality costs within the manufacturing process? Outside the manufacturing process?

LO17-4

P17-59. External failure cost; research; writing Many companies' products have had flaws; some of these companies have been more forthcoming than others in publicly acknowledging such flaws.

a. Do you think admitting that a product is defective hurts or helps a company's reputation? Explain the rationale for your answer.
b. Discuss the costs and benefits of halting sales when product flaws are discovered.
c. Use the Internet to find an example of a company that has continued to sell its product in spite of complaints and other negative feedback about quality. What have been the results?

LO17-5

P17-60. Cost of quality Elijah Electronics makes wireless headphone sets. The firm produced 45,000 wireless headphone sets during its first year of operation. At year-end, it had no inventory of finished goods. Elijah sold 42,300 units through regular market channels, but 450 of the units produced were so defective that they had to be sold as scrap. The remaining units were reworked and sold as seconds. For the year, the firm spent $240,000 on prevention costs and $120,000 on quality appraisal. There were no customer returns. An income statement for the year follows.

Sales		
Regular channel	$8,460,000	
Seconds	213,750	
Scrap	15,750	$ 8,689,500
Cost of goods sold		
Original production costs	$2,876,400	
Rework costs	63,000	
Quality prevention and appraisal	360,000	(3,299,400)
Gross margin		$ 5,390,100
Selling and administrative expenses (all fixed)		(1,470,000)
Profit before income taxes		$ 3,920,100

a. Compute the total pre-tax profit lost by the company in its first year of operations by selling defective units as seconds or as scrap rather than selling the units through regular channels.
b. Compute the total failure cost for the company in its first year.
c. Compute total quality cost incurred by the company in its first year.
d. What evidence indicates that the firm is dedicated to manufacturing and selling high-quality products?

LO17-5

P17-61. Cost of quality During its first year of operations, Ridenour Company produced 39,800 electronic tablets. Of total production, 1,000 were found defective by quality appraisers. Six hundred of the defective units were reworked and sold through regular channels at the original price; the rest were sold as seconds without rework. (The uncorrected defect did not pose a hazard to customers.) The electronic tablets are sold with a two-year warranty; seconds have a six-month warranty.

Ridenour Company spent $450,000 for prevention measures and $196,000 on appraisal. Following is the firm's income statement, which appropriately does not reflect any income taxes:

Ridenour Company
Income Statement
For Year Ended December 31

Regular sales (39,400 units)	$10,244,000	
Sales of seconds (400 units)	56,000	$10,300,000
Cost of goods sold		
Original production costs	$ 3,200,000	
Rework costs (600 units)	21,000	
Prevention and appraisal costs	646,000	(3,867,000)
Gross margin		$ 6,433,000
Selling and administrative expenses (all fixed)		(2,400,000)
Net income		$ 4,033,000

a. Compute the total profit lost by Ridenour Company in its first year of operation by selling defective units as seconds rather than reworking them and selling them at the regular price.
b. Compute the company's total failure cost for the year.
c. Compute the company's total quality cost for the year.
d. Assume that selling and administrative expenses include $300,000 to operate a customer complaint center. How should this cost be categorized relative to quality costs?
e. Are the costs included in the income statement completely reflective of Ridenour's quality costs?

P17-62. Cost of quality Golf courses are demanding in their quest for high-quality carts because of the critical need for lawn maintenance. Antaris Co. manufactures golf carts and is a recognized leader in the industry for quality products. In recent months, company managers have become more interested in trying to quantify the company's cost of quality. As an initial effort, the company identified the following annual costs by categories that are associated with quality:

LO17-5

Prevention Costs	
Quality training	$ 30,000
Quality technology	100,000
Quality circles	64,000

Appraisal Costs	
Quality inspections	$36,000
Test equipment	28,000
Procedure verifications	18,000

Internal Failure Costs	
Scrap and waste	$13,000
Waste disposal	4,200

External Failure Costs	
Warranty handling	$19,000
Customer reimbursements/returns	15,200

Managers were also aware that 500 of the 16,000 carts produced had to be sold as seconds. These 500 carts were sold for $160 less profit per unit than "good" carts. Also, the company incurred rework costs amounting to $12,000 to sell 400 other carts through regular market channels.

a. Using these data, calculate Antaris Co.'s expense for the following:
 1. Lost profit from the 500 units
 2. Total failure cost
 3. Total quality cost

b. Assume that the company is considering expanding its existing five-year warranty to a seven-year warranty. How would such a change be reflected in quality costs?

LO17-5 **P17-63. Cost of quality** BreatheWell is very aware that its scuba diving tanks must be of the highest quality to maintain its reputation of excellence and safety. The company has retained you as a consultant, and you have suggested that quantifying the costs would be important to the understanding and management of quality. Your experience as a cost accountant helped you determine annual costs of quality from the company's accounting records as follows:

Prevention Costs	
Foolproofing machinery	$20,000
Quality training	60,000
Educating suppliers	44,000
Appraisal Costs	
Quality inspections	$24,000
Recording defects	18,000
Procedure verifications	12,000
Internal Failure Costs	
Waste disposal	$9,000
Unplanned downtime	2,800
External Failure Costs	
Warranty handling	$12,800
Customer reimbursements/returns	10,200

You also determined that 2,400 of the 200,000 tanks made during the year had to be sold "for swimming pool use only" for $70 less profit per tank than regular tanks. BreatheWell also incurred $8,000 of rework costs that had been buried in overhead (in addition to the failure costs listed) in producing the tanks sold at the regular price.

  a. BreatheWell's management has asked you to determine the "costs" of the following:
     1. Lost profit from the sale of the 2,400 units limited to use in swimming pools
     2. Total failure cost
     3. Total quality cost
  b. Assume that the company is considering expanding its existing full two-year warranty to a full three-year warranty. How would such a change be reflected in quality costs?

LO17-5 **P17-64. Balanced scorecard; writing; ethics** Assume that you are in charge of Physicians Social Service Agency, which provides counseling services to low-income families. The agency's costs have been increasing with no corresponding increase in funding. In an effort to implement some cost reductions, you took the following actions:

- Empowered counselors to make their own decisions about the legitimacy of all low-income claims.
- Told counselors not to review processed claims a second time to emphasize the concept of "do it right the first time."
- Set an upper and lower control limit of 5 minutes on a standard 15-minute time for consultations to discourage "out-of-control" conditions.

  a. Discuss the ethics as well as the positive and negative effects of each of the ideas listed.
  b. Develop a balanced scorecard for Physicians Social Service Agency that incorporates the three changes listed.

LO17-5 **P17-65. Balanced scorecard; writing** Assume that you are in the market for a new car. Since your promotion at work, price is no object. You are considering purchasing a **Porsche**, but your spouse has suggested the purchase of a **Kia**.

  a. What do you perceive to be Porsche's strategy relative to value and grade of its automobiles?
  b. How might Porsche modify its strategy to compete better against Kia vehicles? Do you think such a change in strategy would be profitable for Porsche? Explain.
  c. If Porsche were to change its strategy, develop a balanced scorecard that would provide measurements of the new strategy.

Chapter 17 Implementing Quality Concepts

P17-66. Quality culture; research; writing Choose an organization with which you have a solid familiarity. You have been placed in charge of initiating a quality culture in that organization. Access at least four websites that refer to this subject; these sites may contain general information about creating a quality culture or specific information about how a quality culture was created (or enhanced) in a particular organization. Write a short paper to present to your organization's leaders with your suggestions on how such a culture should be established (or enhanced) in your organization.

LO17-3

Review Solutions

Review 17-1

Answers are in (000) gallons
a. The mean is equal to 8.3 gallons (=(10.3 + 4.9 + 8.9 + 11.7 + 6.3 + 7.7) ÷ 6).
b. Upper control limit: 8.3 + (3 × 2.5) = 15.8 gallons
   Lower control limit: 8.3 − (3 × 2.5) = 0.8 gallons
c. No points appear outside of the upper and lower control limits with no unusual patterns indicating that the points are all in control and the variation is due to random causes in the process and not to special causes.
d. The control chart indicates that the company has not made substantive or lasting progress toward a waste water reduction as the data is operating within the control limits. It could be that the initiatives that have taken place take time to be established and there is a delay in results.

Review 17-2

		Actual Current Average (minutes)	Historical Average (minutes)	Difference (minutes)
a.	Historical Comparison	4.0	4.5	−0.5

		Actual Current Average (minutes)	Benchmark (minutes)	Difference (minutes)
b.	Internal benchmarking	4.0	4.2	−0.2
c.	Results benchmarking	4.0	3.9	0.1
d.	Process benchmarking	4.0	3.5	0.5
e.	Strategy benchmarking	4.0	2.3	1.7

f. The fast-food restaurant reduced its average service time over the prior year and is performing better than another restaurant within the franchise. However, the fast-food restaurant is underperforming related to its direct competitor and industry averages. The company may want to determine whether it could reduce service time with self-service ordering. The company could use insights gained from efficient online ordering to implement a self-service system.

Review 17-3

1. a. 2   b. 3   c. 1   d. 3   e. 4
2. What is defined as a condition of high quality from a customer perspective today, can change in the future due to a number of reasons such as:
   a. Customer preferences, expectations, or needs can change. Consider how homeowners might describe a high quality dining room table now versus ten years ago (likely more formal in prior years).
   b. Quality standards can change quickly with advances in technology and new innovations due to increased competition. Consider how quickly, for example, the capabilities of cell phones change as each major supplier turns out its latest update.

Review 17-4

1. a. 3   b. 2   c. 1   d. 4   e. 1   f. 4   g. 1   h. 1
2. Management must take actions to implement prevention and appraisal controls that require proactive steps. The steps are taken proactively, in an attempt to avoid failure in the future. If failure happens, either internal or external, the company must take action in a reactionary way, to address the failure that already occurred.

Review 17-5

1. a. Total cost to rework: $44,000 = $40 × 1,100
   b. Profit lost from not reworking all defective units: $36,400 = (1,660 − 1,100) × ($110 − $45)
   c. Cost of processing customer returns: $6,240 = $32 × 195
   d. Total failure costs: $178,640 = $44,000 + $36,400 + $6,240 + $92,000
   e. Total quality cost: $261,670 = $63,480 + $19,550 + $178,640
2. Cost of compliance: $ 83,030 ÷ $6,000,000 = 1.4%
   Cost of noncompliance: $178,640 ÷ $6,000,000 = 3.0%
3. In order to reduce total cost of quality as a percentage of sales, the company will likely need to increase prevention and appraisal costs in order to prevent the more costly noncompliance costs. Also, using the dollars on prevention and appraisal costs effectively should also be a consideration.

Data Visualization Solutions

(See page 17-5.)

1. Charts C and D: In Chart C, one observation is outside of the control limits. In Chart D, 8 points are on one side of the mean, and one point is outside of the upper control limit.
2. Charts A and B: No special-cause variation appears on the chart.
3. Chart B: While both charts A and B show only common cause variation, the range around the mean is much tighter in Chart B.
4. Charts C and D: Special-cause variation can be investigated and addressed more readily than common cause variation.
5. Charts A, B, C, and D: All systems have common cause variation, which can be reduced through long-term strategies.

Chapter 18
Inventory and Production Management

Road Map

LO	Learning Objective | Topics	Page	eLecture	Demo	Review	Assignments
18–1	**What costs are associated with buying, producing, and carrying inventory?** Gross Profit Ratio :: Inventory Costs :: Purchasing Cost :: Production Cost :: Ordering Cost :: Setup Cost :: Carrying Cost :: Opportunity Cost :: Stockout Cost	18-2	e18–1	D18-1	Rev 18-1	MC18-11, MC18-12, E18-20, E18-21, E18-22, E18-23, E18-24, E18-25, E18-26, E18-42, E18-43, P18-49, P18-50, P18-51, P18-53, **DA18-1**
18–2	**How is economic order quantity used in a push system of production?** Push System :: Pull System :: Economic Order Quantity (EOQ) :: Economic Production Run (EPR) :: Order Point :: Usage :: Lead Time :: Safety Stock :: Pareto Inventory Analysis	18-4	e18–2	D18-2A D18-2B D18-2C D18-2D	Rev 18-2	MC18-13, MC18-14, E18-22, E18-27, E18-28, E18-29, E18-30, E18-31, E18-32, E18-33, E18-34, E18-35, E18-36, P18-50, P18-52, P18-53, P18-54, P18-55
18–3	**How is the just-in-time philosophy used in a pull system and how is performance measured?** Just-in-Time :: Kanban :: Supplier Relationships :: Product Design :: Engineering Change Orders (ECOs) :: Product Processing :: Plant Layout :: Inventory Turnover :: Gross Margin Return on Inventory Investment (GMROI) :: JIT ECO Variances :: Flexible Manufacturing Systems (FMS) :: Lean Manufacturing	18-10	e18–3	D18-3	Rev 18-3	MC18-15, E18-29, E18-37, E18-38, E18-39, E18-40, E18-41, E18-42, E18-43, P18-56, P18-58, **DA18-2**, **DA18-3**
18–4	**How is backflush costing used to account for just-in-time inventory systems?** Backflush Costing :: Raw and In-Process (RIP) Inventory :: Alternative Entries	18-17	e18–4	D18-4	Rev 18-4	MC18-16, MC18-17, E18-44, E18-45, P18-57, P18-58
18–5	**How can the theory of constraints help in determining production flow?** Theory of Constraints :: Constraint :: Bottlenecks	18-20	e18–5	D18-5	Rev 18-5	MC18-18, MC18-19, E18-46, E18-47, E18-48

INTRODUCTION

Manufacturing and retail firms face two significant challenges in managing inventory. First, these firms must have the inventory available to match the demand from their customers. To meet this challenge, firms must produce or order the right products at the right price and have them available when customers want those products. Second, to avoid excessive costs and remain competitive, firms must avoid producing or ordering inventory that is not demanded by their customers. Less often do firms hold inventory until a customer decides to make a purchase; they ardently strive to avoid investing cash in inventory until customers actually place orders.

Other than plant assets and human resource development, inventory is often the largest investment a company makes—although this investment yields no return until the inventory is sold. We begin with a discussion on categories of inventory costs, followed by the application of the economic order quantity concept. While this concept is based on the cost effectiveness of inventory ordering, the remainder of the chapter addresses ways companies minimize their monetary commitments to inventory while still satisfying customer demands.

BUYING/PRODUCING AND CARRYING INVENTORY

LO18-1 What costs are associated with buying, producing, and carrying inventory?

Before we examine the components of inventory costs, we first review how the cost of inventory is recognized in the financial statements.

Financial Statement Presentation of Inventory Costs

As discussed in Chapter 2, the inventory classification on the balance sheet depends on the type of organization. The following table includes excerpts from recent annual reports of Target Corporation (a merchandiser) and General Motors Company (a manufacturer).

($ millions)	Merchandiser: Target 2022	Manufacturer: General Motors 2022
Merchandise Inventory	$ 13,499	n/a
Total productive material, supplies and work in process	n/a	$ 8,014
Finished product, including service parts	n/a	7,353
Total inventory cost	13,499	15,366
Total assets	53,335	264,037
Sales	107,588	143,975
Cost of goods sold	82,229	126,892
Gross profit	$ 25,359	$ 17,083

Note: Financial report amounts are rounded, and thus, they may not exactly sum to totals and subtotals.

On the balance sheet, Target carries merchandise inventory making up approximately 25 percent of its total assets and General Motors carries material, supplies, work in process, and finished goods inventory making up close to 6 percent of its total assets.

On the income statement, gross profit, (sales minus cost of goods sold), is $25.4 billion for Target and $17.1 billion for General Motors. Recall that cost of goods sold is made up of the cost of the inventory which has been sold to customers. These costs were previously shown on the balance sheet as inventory. The gross profit ratio is calculated as follows.

Gross profit ratio = Gross profit ÷ Sales

Target's gross profit ratio = $25,359 ÷ $107,588 = 23.6%

General Motor's gross profit ratio = $17,083 ÷ $143,975 = 11.9%

Managing inventory costs is a critical aspect of cost control because inventory is a substantive asset on the balance sheet and the cost of inventory sold directly impacts the gross profit on the income statement. Investors and creditors of a company pay careful attention to the trends in these measures.

In manufacturing organizations, production begins with the acquisition of raw material. Although not always the largest production cost, raw material purchases cause a continuous cash outflow. Work in process is partially completed inventory, while finished goods is the inventory stored and available for immediate sale. Similarly, retailers make significant investments in merchandise purchased for sale to customers.

Profit margins in both types of organizations can benefit from reducing or minimizing inventory investments, assuming that product demand can still be met. The term *inventory* is used in this chapter to refer to direct material, work in process, finished goods, indirect material (supplies), and retail merchandise. Efficient inventory management largely relies on cost-minimization strategies.

Primary Inventory Costs

The primary costs associated with inventory include the following.

Inventory Costs		
Purchasing or Producing	Ordering or Setup	Carrying or Stockout

Purchasing Cost Inventory **purchasing cost** is the quoted purchase price minus any discounts allowed, plus shipping charges. Discounts come from purchasing inventory in bulk or from paying suppliers within the period of time established to quality for a purchase discount.

Production Cost For a manufacturer, **production cost** refers to the costs associated with purchasing direct material, paying for direct labor, and absorbing variable and fixed overhead. Of these production costs, fixed manufacturing overhead is the least susceptible to short-run cost minimization. An exception is that management is able to somewhat control the fixed component of unit product cost by managing production capacity utilization relative to short-run demand. Most efforts to minimize fixed manufacturing overhead costs involve long-run measures.

Ordering Cost An **ordering cost** is the cost of an activity performed for each purchase order such as the cost for purchase approvals, issuing purchase orders, receiving and inspecting purchases, and paying for the purchase.

Setup Cost Costs to prepare equipment to produce a specific product, or to change from producing one product to another product are **setup costs**.

Carrying Cost The total variable cost of carrying one unit of inventory in stock for one year is the **carrying cost** of inventory. Carrying costs include warehousing, logistics, insurance, financing, and the risk of loss due to theft, damage, or technological or customer preference changes. Carrying cost also includes the opportunity cost of capital invested in inventory, measured as follows.

$$\text{Opportunity Cost} = \text{Inventory cost} \times \text{Rate of return}$$

For example, if a company's expected rate of return is 16 percent and the company carries, on average, $50,000 of inventory, the opportunity cost of holding the inventory is $8,000.

$$\text{Opportunity cost} = \$50,000 \times 16\% = \$8,000$$

In other words, the company could earn $8,000 if it invested the cash tied up in inventory in another investment assumed to be of similar risk.

Stockout Cost A stockout is the condition of not having inventory available upon need or request. A company may incur a **stockout cost** to schedule a special production run or to expedite a shipping order from a supplier. If the sale is lost, however, the opportunity cost includes lost contribution margin and customer goodwill.

DEMO 18-1 LO18-1 Classifying Inventory Costs

◆ Are the following costs classified as purchasing, production, ordering, setup, carrying, or stockout?

		Inventory Cost Type
a.	Quoted price of merchandise inventory less any applicable purchase discounts.	Purchasing
b.	Shipping charges of purchased merchandise inventory.	Purchasing
c.	Direct materials, direct labor, overhead costs.	Production
d.	Costs to prepare purchase order, inspect goods, and to make payments.	Ordering
e.	Labor cost to set up machine plus cost of any machine downtime.	Setup
f.	Cost of storing, handling, insuring, and taxing finished goods inventory.	Carrying
g.	Losses from obsolescence, damage, and theft.	Carrying
h.	Opportunity cost of invested capital in inventory.	Carrying
i.	Expedited shipping charges to fill an order because inventory was not readily available to sell.	Stockout
j.	Setup cost to reschedule a production run to fill inventory shortfall.	Stockout
k.	Lost customer goodwill and contribution because inventory was not readily available to sell.	Stockout

REVIEW 18-1 LO18-1 Calculating Inventory Costs

Lakeside Inc., a merchandiser of water recreational equipment, summarized the following for a unit of inventory of its primary product.

Cost to approve, place, and pay for order.	$ 15 per unit
Cost to receive and inspect the product.	$ 10 per unit
Invoice cost.	$375 per unit
Shipping costs—in bound.	$ 50 per unit
Handling costs.	$ 50 per unit
Insurance on inventory held.	$ 5 per unit
Warehousing costs.	$100 per unit

a. What are the total purchasing costs per unit?
b. What are the total ordering costs per unit?
c. What are the total carrying costs per unit if the company's expected rate of return is 18%?
d. **Critical Thinking:** Are opportunity costs recorded in a company's accounting system? Why or why not?

More practice: MC18-12, E18-24, E18-26
Solution on p. 18-39.

ECONOMIC ORDER QUANTITY IN A PUSH SYSTEM

LO18-2 How is economic order quantity used in a push system of production?

The two theoretical approaches to producing inventory are push systems and pull systems.

Push System Versus a Pull System

In the traditional **push system** approach (illustrated in **Exhibit 18.1**), production occurs in anticipation of customer orders and work centers buy or produce inventory according to lead time, economic order size, or production quantity requirements. Current sales demand and current production may be poorly correlated. Excess inventory is stored until it is needed by other work centers.

Exhibit 18.1 ■ Push System of Production Control

Purchases and production are constantly *pushed* down into storage locations until need arises.

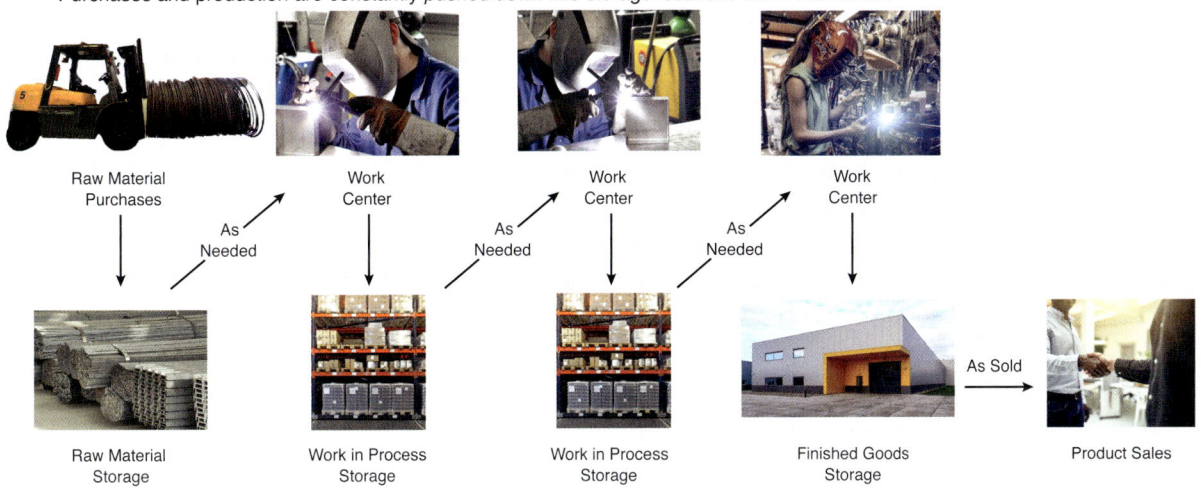

To reduce the cost of carrying inventory until needed at some point in the future, many firms have implemented **pull systems** of production control (depicted in **Exhibit 18.2**). In these systems, inventory is delivered or produced only as it is needed by the next work center in the value chain. Although necessity dictates that companies carry some minimal amount of inventory, work centers do not produce to compensate for lead times or to meet some economic production run model. The pull system approach to inventory management is more consistent with environmentally sustainable business models because there is a focus on both cost minimization and quality maximization.

Exhibit 18.2 ■ Pull System of Production Control

Product sales dictate total production. Purchases and production are *pulled* through the system on an as-needed basis.

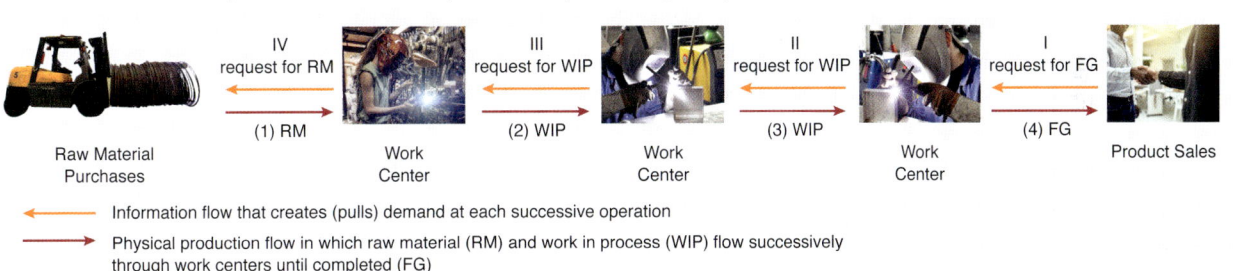

← Information flow that creates (pulls) demand at each successive operation

→ Physical production flow in which raw material (RM) and work in process (WIP) flow successively through work centers until completed (FG)

Economic order quantity is a tool that is used in conjunction with traditional "push" production and inventory management systems and is covered next. Because economic order quantity implies acquiring and holding inventory before it is needed, it is *incompatible* with "pull" systems such as JIT, which is covered in LO3.

Economic Order Quantity

Companies making purchasing (rather than production) decisions often compute the **economic order quantity (EOQ)**, which represents the least costly number of units to order. Thus, the focus is not on minimizing inventory, but instead, cost effectiveness in ordering inventory. EOQ indicates the optimal balance between ordering and carrying costs by mathematically equating total ordering costs to total carrying costs. At this point, the issue of stockouts is ignored. Annual ordering and carrying costs are calculated as follows.

Total annual ordering costs = Number of orders per year × O

Total annual carrying costs = Average inventory in units × C

where Average inventory in units = (Quantity of an order [new inventory received]
+ 0 [inventory level depleted to zero])/2

O = estimated cost of placing one order

C = estimated cost to carry one unit in stock for one year

Purchasing managers should first determine which supplier can offer the appropriate quality of goods at the best price in the most reliable manner. After the supplier is selected, the most economical inventory quantity to order—at a single time—is determined using calculus. The EOQ formula is as follows.

$$EOQ = \sqrt{\frac{(2QO)}{C}}$$

where EOQ = economic order quantity in units

Q = estimated annual quantity used in units (can be found in the annual purchases budget)

O = estimated cost of placing one order

C = estimated cost to carry one unit in stock for one year

Note that unit purchase cost is not included in the EOQ formula. Purchase cost relates to the question of from whom to buy, which is considered separately from the question of how many to buy at a single time. Except to the extent that opportunity cost is calculated on the basis of investment, inventory unit purchase cost does not affect the other costs in the EOQ formula.

All inventory-related costs must be evaluated when purchasing or production decisions are made. The costs of ordering and carrying inventory oppose each other when estimating the economic order quantity: as units are purchased more often, fewer units must be kept in inventory.

DEMO 18-2A LO18-2   Computing Economic Order Quantity

Marshall Industrial uses 64,000 pounds of one material in producing ceramic products. The cost associated with placing each order is $40. The carrying cost of one pound of the material is $2 per year.

◆ **What is Marshall's EOQ?**

Marshall's EOQ for this material is calculated as follows.

$$EOQ = \sqrt{\frac{(2 \times 64{,}000 \times \$40)}{\$2}} = 1{,}600 \text{ pounds}$$

The EOC can also be calculated in Excel: =SQRT(number)
=SQRT((2*64000*40)/2)
= 1,600 pounds

◆ **At the EOQ, what are annual ordering costs and annual carrying costs?**

Total annual ordering costs at EOQ = Number of orders per year[†] × O

= 64,000/1,600 × $40 = $1,600

Total annual carrying costs at EOQ = Average inventory in units × C

= [(1,600 + 0)/2] × $2 = $1,600

[†] Units required for a year ÷ number of units in an order or 64,000/1,600 EOQ = 40 orders.

The EOQ selects the inventory quantity (1,600 pounds) that makes the ordering costs ($1,600) equal to the carrying costs ($1,600). Total ordering and carrying costs are $3,200 (=$1,600 + $1,600).

◆ **Assuming instead that Marshall ordered its materials in orders of 1,000 pounds, what would be the total annual ordering costs and total annual carrying costs?**

Chapter 18 Inventory and Production Management

Total annual ordering costs at 1,000 per order = Number of orders per year × O

= 64,000/1,000 × $40 = $2,560

Total annual carrying costs at 1,000 per order = Average inventory in units × C

= [(1,000 + 0)/2] × $2 = $1,000

Total ordering and carrying costs are $3,560 (=$2,560 + $1,000), which exceeds the total costs at the EOQ of $3,200.

Economic Production Run

In a manufacturing company, managers are concerned not only with how many units of raw material to buy, but with how many finished units to produce in a batch. The EOQ formula can be modified to calculate the appropriate number of units to manufacture in an **economic production run (EPR)**. This estimate reflects the production quantity that minimizes the total costs of setting up a production run and of carrying one unit in stock for one year. The only change in the EOQ formula is that the equation's terms are redefined as manufacturing rather than as purchasing costs.

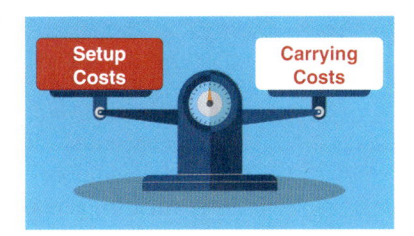

$$EPR = \sqrt{\frac{(2QS)}{C}}$$

where EPR = economic production run in units

Q = estimated annual quantity to be produced in units (can be found in the annual production budget)

S = estimated cost of setting up a production run

C = estimated cost to carry one unit in stock for one year

Computing Economic Production Run — LO18-2 DEMO 18-2B

Marshall manufactures 183,750 ceramic sinks per year. Setup cost for a ceramic sink run is $240, and the annual carrying cost for each sink is $5.

◆ **What is Marshall's EPR?**

The economic production run quantity is determined as follows.

$$EPR = \sqrt{\frac{(2 \times 183,750 \times \$240)}{\$5}} = 4,200 \text{ sinks}$$

The EPR can also be calculated in Excel: =SQRT((2*183750*240)/5)
= 4,200 sinks

◆ **At the EPR, what are annual setup costs and annual carrying costs?**

Total annual setup costs at EPR = Number of setups per year × O

= 183,750/4,200 × $240 = $10,500

Total annual carrying costs at EPR = Average inventory in units × C

= [(4,200 + 0)/2] × $5 = $10,500

Similar to the EPR, we see that the EOQ selects the quantity (4,200 sinks) that make the setup costs of ($10,500) equal to the carrying costs ($10,500).

Cost differences among various run sizes around the EPR might not be significant. If such costs are insignificant, management would have a range of acceptable, economical production run quantities.

Disadvantages The critical step in using either an EOQ or an EPR model is to properly identify costs, especially carrying costs. This process is often difficult, and some costs (such as those for facilities, operations, administration, and accounting) that were traditionally viewed as irrelevant fixed costs could, in actuality, be long-term relevant variable costs. Also, the EOQ or EPR model does not provide any direction for managers attempting to control all of the separate costs that collectively compose ordering and carrying costs. By considering only the trade-off between ordering (or producing) and carrying costs, these models do not lead managers to consider inventory management alternatives that can simultaneously reduce both categories of costs.

Additionally, as companies significantly reduce the necessary setup time (and thus cost) for operations and move toward a "stockless" inventory policy, a more comprehensive cost perspective will indicate a substantially smaller cost per setup and a substantially larger annual carrying cost. These changes will reduce the EOQ and EPR.

Order Point and Safety Stock

The EOQ or EPR model indicates how many units to order or produce, respectively. Managers are also concerned with the **order point**, which reflects the inventory level that triggers placement of an order for additional units. If the EPR model was being used, the concern would be about the inventory level that triggers production. Determination of order or production point is based on three factors: daily usage, lead time, and safety stock.

- **Daily usage** refers to the quantity of inventory used or sold each day.
- **Lead time** of an order reflects the days between issuing an order (externally or internally) to obtaining or producing the necessary goods. Companies can often project a constant, average figure for both usage and lead time.
- **Safety stock** is the inventory quantity kept by a company in the event of fluctuating usage or unusual delays in lead time.

Assuming No Safety Stock If usage is entirely constant and lead time is known with certainty, the order point equals daily usage multiplied by lead time.

$$\text{Order point} = \text{Daily usage} \times \text{Lead time}$$

DEMO 18-2C LO18-2 Computing Order Point with No Safety Stock

Marshall uses 5,000 pounds of silica sand per day and the supplier can have the material to Marshall in two days.

♦ How many units should Marshall have on hand when a new order is placed?

$$\text{Order point} = \text{Daily usage} \times \text{Lead time}$$

$$= 5{,}000 \text{ pounds} \times 2 \text{ days} = 10{,}000 \text{ pounds}$$

When the stock of silica sand reaches 10,000 pounds, Marshall should place an order for additional silica sand.

Accounting for Safety Stock The order point formula minimizes a company's inventory investment. Orders would arrive at precisely the time the inventory reached zero. This formula, however, does not take into consideration unusual events such as variations in production schedules, defective products being provided by suppliers, erratic shipping schedules of the supplier, or late arrival of units shipped. To provide for such events, managers carry a "buffer" safety stock of inventory to protect the company from being out of stock. When a safety stock is maintained, the order point formula becomes the following.

$$\text{Order point} = (\text{Daily usage} \times \text{Lead time}) + \text{Safety stock}$$

Safety stock size should be determined based on how crucial the item is to production or to retail sales, the item's purchase cost, and the amount of uncertainty related to both usage and lead time. For example, a hospital's supply of medicines used in emergency situations would be crucial to have in stock at all times.

One way to estimate safety stock quantity is to allow one factor to vary from the norm. For example, either excess usage during normal lead time or normal usage with excess lead time can be considered in the safety stock calculation.

Computing Order Point with Safety Stock — LO18-2 DEMO 18-2D

Assume that Marshall never uses more than 8,000 pounds of silica sand in one day. Given this information, the estimate of the necessary safety stock is 6,000 pounds, computed as follows.

Maximum daily usage............	8,000	pounds
Normal daily usage.............	(5,000)	pounds
Excess usage.................	3,000	pounds
Lead time....................	× 2	days
Safety stock	6,000	pounds

◆ Using this estimate of safety stock, at what level of inventory should a new order be placed?

Order point = (Daily usage × Lead time) + Safety stock

= (5,000 pounds × 2 days) + 6,000 = 16,000 pounds

Accounting for safety stock, Marshall should order silica sand when 16,000 pounds are on hand.

Pareto Inventory Analysis

Unit cost commonly affects the degree of control that should be maintained over an inventory item. As unit cost increases, internal controls (such as inventory access) are typically tightened and a perpetual inventory system is more often used. Recognition of cost–benefit relationships can result in a **Pareto inventory analysis**, which separates inventory into three groups based on annual cost-to-volume usage.

Items having the highest value are referred to as A items; C items represent the lowest dollar volume of usage. All other inventory items are designated as B items. **Exhibit 18.3** illustrates the results of a typical Pareto inventory analysis: 20 percent of the inventory items (A items) account for 80 percent of the cost; an additional 30 percent of the items (B items), taken together with the first 20 percent (the A items), account for 90 percent of the cost; and the remaining 50 percent of the items (C items) account for the remaining 10 percent of the cost.

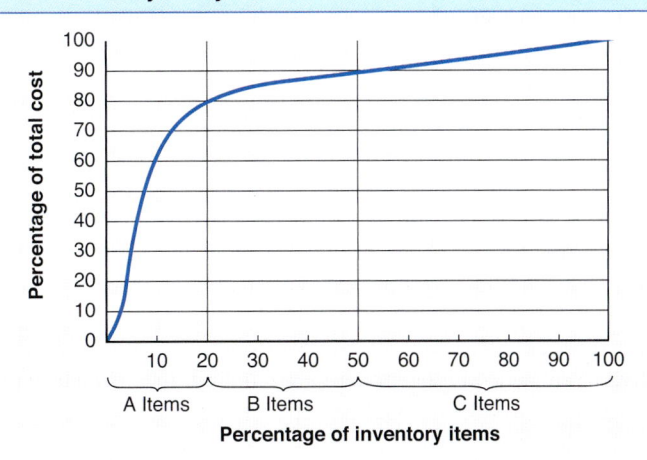

Exhibit 18.3 ■ Pareto Inventory Analysis

Once inventory is categorized as A, B, or C, management can determine the best inventory control method for items in each category. A-type inventory should require a perpetual inventory system and would be a likely candidate for JIT purchasing techniques (discussed in the next section) to minimize the funds tied up in inventory investment. The highest control procedures would be assigned to these items. Such a treatment reflects the financial accounting concept of materiality.

The control placed on C items is probably minimal because inventory cost is immaterial. The type of inventory system (perpetual or periodic) and the level of internal control associated with items in the B category will depend on management's judgment. Influencing characteristics include the item's significance to the production process, suppliers' response time, and estimates of benefits to be gained by increased accounting or access controls.

REVIEW 18-2 | **LO18-2** | Economic Order Quantity and Economic Production Run

Part One: Economic Order Quantity

Compute the economic order quantity for oats based upon the following information related to a manufacturer of granola; round to the nearest whole unit. Assume that the company operates 260 days out of the year.

Annual usage of oats	5,000 pounds
Average number of days delay between initiating and receiving an order	5
Estimated cost per order	$30
Estimated annual cost of carrying a pound of oats	$0.75

Part Two: Economic Production Run

Lazer Inc. custom manufactures medical device replacement parts. The following data relate to production of Product #101.

Annual quantity produced in units	10,080
Cost of setting up a production run	$840
Cost of carrying one unit in stock for a year	$6

a. Compute the economic production run for Product #101; round to the nearest whole unit.

b. **Critical Thinking:** EPR is not an ideal tool for companies striving for minimal inventory levels. In what types of situations would companies benefit the most from using EPR?

More practice: E18-31, E18-33, E18-34
Solution on p. 18-39.

JUST-IN-TIME IN A PULL SYSTEM

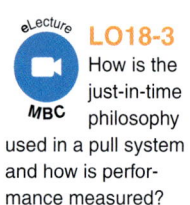

LO18-3
How is the just-in-time philosophy used in a pull system and how is performance measured?

Just-in-time (JIT) is a philosophy about when to do something. The "when" is as needed and the "something" is a production, purchasing, or delivery activity. The JIT philosophy is applicable in all departments of all types of organizations. JIT's three primary goals are

- eliminating any production process or operation that does not add value to the product/service,
- continuously improving production/performance efficiency, and
- reducing the total cost of production/performance while increasing quality.

These goals are totally consistent with, and supportive of, the total quality management (TQM) program discussed in Chapter 17. Elements of the JIT philosophy are outlined in **Exhibit 18.4**. A logical starting point for discussing JIT is in regard to manufacturing or production activities. JIT manufacturing originated in Japan where a card, or **kanban** (pronounced "kahn-bahn"), was used to communicate between work centers to control the flow of in-process products. A **just-in-time manufacturing system** attempts to acquire components and produce inventory units only as they are needed (i.e., a pull system), minimize product defects, and reduce cycle/setup times for acquisition and production.

Chapter 18 Inventory and Production Management

Exhibit 18.4 ■ Elements of a JIT Philosophy

- Quality is essential at all times; work to eliminate defects and scrap.
- Employees often have the best knowledge of ways to improve operations; listen to them.
- Employees generally have more talents than are being used; train them to be multiskilled and increase their productivity.
- Ways to improve operations are always available; constantly look for them, being certain to make fundamental changes rather than superficial ones.
- Creative thinking doesn't cost anything; use it to find ways to reduce costs before making expenditures for additional resources.
- Suppliers are essential to operations; establish and cultivate good relationships with suppliers and, if possible, use long-term contracts.
- Inventory is an asset that generates no revenue while it is held in stock, so it can be viewed as a "liability"; eliminate it to the extent possible.
- Storage space is directly related to inventories; eliminate it in response to the elimination of inventories.
- Long cycle times cause inventory buildup; keep cycle times as short as possible by using frequent deliveries.

Production has traditionally been dictated by the need to smooth operating activities over time. Although allowing a company to maintain a steady workforce and continuous machine utilization, smooth production often creates products that must be stored until they are sold. Additionally, maintaining high levels of raw material and work in process inventories can compensate for inefficiencies in acquisition and/or production. Solving issues due to quality, poor scheduling, or vendor problems can be avoided because there is extra inventory to fill in the gaps. Alternatively, JIT exposes the issues because only goods that are needed are produced, forcing the company to eliminate the issues.

Changes Needed to Implement JIT Manufacturing

Implementation of a just-in-time system requires a long-term commitment. JIT depends on the ability of employees and suppliers to compress the time, distance, resources, and activities and to enhance interactions needed to produce a company's products and services. Consider that **Toyota** invested more than 20 years to develop the JIT system and realize significant benefits from it. However, any company—not simply a large manufacturer—can now put a system in place and recognize benefits fairly rapidly. In a world in which managers work diligently to produce improvements of a percentage point or two, some numbers simply do not look realistic even though they are.

For just-in-time production to be effective, certain modifications must be made to each of the following.

| Value Chain Partnerships | Product Design | Product Processing | Plant Layout |

Value Chain Partnerships A **value chain approach** to inventory management requires that managers consider their suppliers' and customers' strategies, goals, and objectives, if they hope to compete successfully in a global marketplace.

Supplier → Production Plant → Finished Goods → Distribution Center → Customers

By improving cooperation, communication, and integration, entities within a value chain can treat each other as extensions of themselves and, thereby, increase quality, throughput, and cost efficiency. Entities can share expertise and engage in problem solving to reduce or eliminate non-value-added activities and enhance value-added activities. Firms can provide products and services faster and with fewer defects as well as perform activities more effectively and reliably with fewer errors and less redundancy. Consider the following areas in which opportunities for improvement between entities exist:

- communicating product/component requirements, specifications, and needs;
- clarifying requests for products or services;
- providing feedback about unsatisfactory products or services;
- planning, controlling, and problem solving; and
- sharing managerial and technical expertise, supervision, and training.

Selecting suppliers Factors commonly considered in choosing suppliers include a vendor's reliability and responsiveness, delivery performance, ability to provide service, human resources qualifications, research and development strength, production capacity, and environmental policies. The optimal JIT situation is to contract with only one vendor for any given item. Such an ideal, however, creates the risk of not having alternative sources (especially for critical inputs) in the event of vendor business failure, production strikes, unfair pricing, or shipment delays. Thus, it is often more realistic to limit the number of suppliers to a select few that are recognized by the company for quality and reliability.

Consider the impact on the supply chain due to the pandemic when companies could not obtain needed product from key suppliers due to factory shut-downs. These circumstances have caused some companies to reconsider their reliance on a single supplier or suppliers from a single country. For instance, **Apple Inc.**'s iPhone manufacturer, **Foxconn**, expanded its manufacturing operations (focused primarily in China) into India in 2023 in order to diversify its operations.[1] The following excerpt from a recent SEC report of **WidePoint Corporation**, explains how the company needed to pivot from the use of just-in-time to respond to market changes that caused supply chain issues.

> We continue to experience ongoing supply chain issues and have changed from just-in-time inventory for accessory items to keeping sufficient stock on hand and having to locate alternative sources if traditional suppliers cannot fulfill in a timely manner. In addition, we continue to experience supply price increases that we seek to mitigate by seeking volume discounts. Overall, the customers are understanding that these supply chain issues are [indications of a global problem] and not just impacting orders they place with us and have been willing to work with us to find alternative solutions or delay the purchases until the requested products are available. It is difficult to forecast when and if the supply chain will normalize.[2]

Forming partnerships with fewer vendors on a long-term basis provides the opportunity to continuously improve quality and substantially reduce costs. For example, such partnerships permit members of the supply chain to eliminate redundancies in warehousing, packaging, labeling, transportation, and inventories. Partnerships also allow for long-term purchasing arrangements which provide pricing stability. However, companies need to carefully select their supply partners and consider if any supplier diversification strategies are necessary to limit risk of any future market disruptions.

Product Design Products should be designed to use the fewest number of dissimilar parts and to minimize production steps and risks. Assume for example, a company found that 29 different types of screws were being used to manufacture a single product. Changing to one type of screw can significantly reduce production time. Parts standardization does not necessarily result in identical finished products. Many companies find they can produce a larger number of variations in finished products from just a few basic models.

Products should be designed for the quality desired and should require no, or a minimal number of, **engineering change orders** (ECOs) after the design is released for production. An effective arrangement for a vendor–purchaser partnership is to have the vendor's engineers participate in the design phase of the purchasing company's product. Another option is to provide product specifications and allow the vendor company to draft the design for approval.

Good product design should address all the intended users' concerns, including product recyclability. For instance, an automobile plant can be equipped to receive and take apart old models, remanufacture various parts, and send the cars back into the marketplace. Thus, companies are considering remanufacturing as part of their design and processing capabilities. The environmental effects

---

[1] Paul Page, "Here's How Supply Chains Are Being Reshaped for a New Era of Global Trade," *The Wall Street Journal* (2023).
[2] Source: June 30, 2023 10Q SEC filing for WidePoint Corporation, p. 23

of products can be dramatically altered if products are designed to be remanufactured or recycled at the end of their useful lives.

Product Processing In the product processing stage, one primary JIT consideration is the reduction of machine setup time so that processing can shift between products more often and at a lower cost. Costs of reducing setup time are more than recovered by the savings derived from reducing downtime, in-process inventory, and material handling as well as by increasing safety, process flexibility, and ease of operation.

Another essential part of product processing is the institution of high-quality standards because JIT has the goal of zero defects. Under JIT systems, quality is determined continuously rather than at quality control checkpoints. First, the quality of vendors' products is ensured at purchase. Then, workers and machines (such as optical scanners) monitor production quality. Controlling quality on an ongoing basis significantly reduces the assessment cost of obtaining high quality. The JIT philosophy recognizes that it is less costly not to make mistakes than to correct them after they have been made.

Plant Layout Traditionally, manufacturing plants were designed to conform with functional areas; similar machines and workers with similar specialized skills were placed together. For JIT to work effectively, the physical plant must be conducive to the flow of goods and the location of workers as well as to increasing the value added per square foot of plant space. Manufacturing plants should be designed to minimize material handling time, lead time, and movement of goods from raw material input to completion of the finished product. This goal often requires that machines or workers be arranged in S- or U-shaped production groupings, commonly referred to as **manufacturing cells** (see **Exhibit 18.5**), to generate the most efficient and effective production process for a particular product type. This streamlined design allows for more visual controls to be instituted for problems such as excess inventory, production defects, equipment malfunctions, and out-of-place tools. The design also allows for greater teamwork and quicker exchange of vital information.

The informational arrows in **Exhibit 18.5** indicate how production is "pulled" through the system as successive downstream work centers issue kanbans to acquire needed goods or services from upstream suppliers so that the goods or services demanded by downstream customers can be produced.

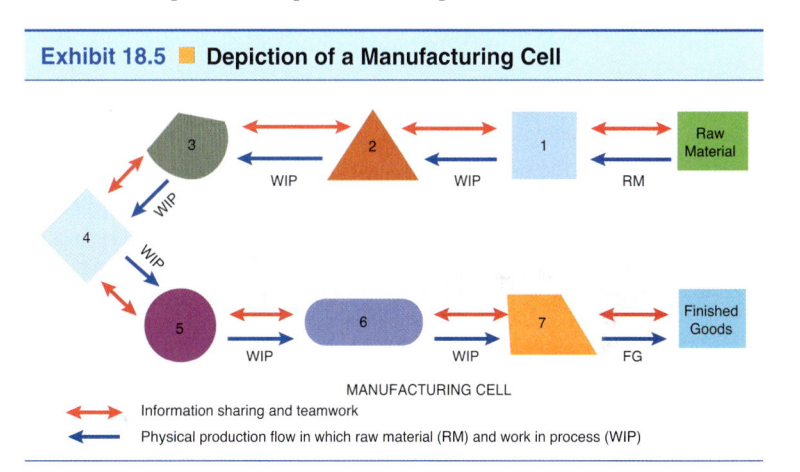

Exhibit 18.5 ■ Depiction of a Manufacturing Cell

Information sharing and teamwork
Physical production flow in which raw material (RM) and work in process (WIP)

Performance Measures Under JIT

In accordance with the goal of eliminating inventory and reducing cycle time to processing time, JIT supportive performance measures emphasize inventory turnover, cycle time, and **manufacturing cycle efficiency** (the ratio of value-added to non-value-added manufacturing activities discussed in Chapter 15).

Inventory Turnover (units) When applied to a specific item of raw materials or finished goods, **inventory turnover** is computed as the annual demand in units divided by the average inventory in units.

$$\text{Inventory turnover (in units)} = \frac{\text{Annual demand in units}}{\text{Average inventory in units}}$$

Progress toward the goal of reducing inventory is measured by comparing successive inventory turnover ratios. Generally, the higher the inventory turnover, the better.

Inventory Turnover (dollars) When measured with inventory dollars instead of inventory units, inventory turnover can be used as a measure of the organization's overall success in reducing inventory, or in increasing sales in relation to inventories. This financial measure can be derived directly from a firm's financial statements.

$$\text{Inventory turnover (in dollars)} = \frac{\text{Cost of goods sold}}{\text{Average inventory (in dollars)}}$$

Gross Margin Return on Inventory Investment Another ratio often used to monitor the effectiveness of inventory levels in retail organizations, such as **Whole Foods** or **Macy's**, is gross margin return on inventory investment (GMROI), calculated as follows.

$$\text{GMROI} = \frac{\text{Gross margin (in dollars)}}{\text{Average inventory (in dollars)}}$$

The GMROI indicates the gross margin earned for each dollar of inventory.

JIT Material Quantity and JIT ECO Variances In JIT systems, traditional variance reporting and analysis essentially disappear because such information is untimely. Variances first appear physically (rather than financially). Thus, JIT mandates immediate recognition of variances so that causes can be ascertained and, if possible, promptly remedied if unfavorable or exploited if favorable. Therefore, the number and monetary significance of end-of-period variances being reported for managerial control should be extremely rare. For example, long-term price agreements have been made with vendors, so material price variances should be minimal. Also, because better control of raw material quality is expected, few (if any) material quantity variances should be caused by substandard material.

One type of quantity variance is *not* caused by errors but by engineering changes made to the product specifications. A JIT system typically has two comparison standards: an annual standard and a current standard. Design modifications would change the current standard but not the annual one. The annual standard provides a basis for preparing and executing the company's master budget, and the annual standards are ordinarily kept intact because the annual financial plans and arrangements are predicated on the standards and plans used to prepare the master budget. Using two standards allows comparisons to be made that indicate the cost effects of ECOs implemented after a product has begun to be manufactured.

DEMO 18-3   LO18-3   Computing JIT Material Quantity and JIT ECO Variances

The following information is provided for Material M and Material N: actual, current standard, and annual standard information.

Production during month	9,000 units
Actual material cost	
Material M (64,800 feet × $3.05)	$ 197,640
Material N (52,200 feet × $3.35)	174,870
Total cost of material used	$ 372,510
Current standard	
Material M (7 feet × $3.05)	$21.35
Material N (6 feet × $3.35)	20.10
	$41.45
Annual standard	
Material M (8 feet × $3.05)	$24.40
Material N (5 feet × $3.35)	16.75
	$41.15

◆ What is the JIT material quantity variance and the JIT ECO variance for Material M, Material N, and in total?

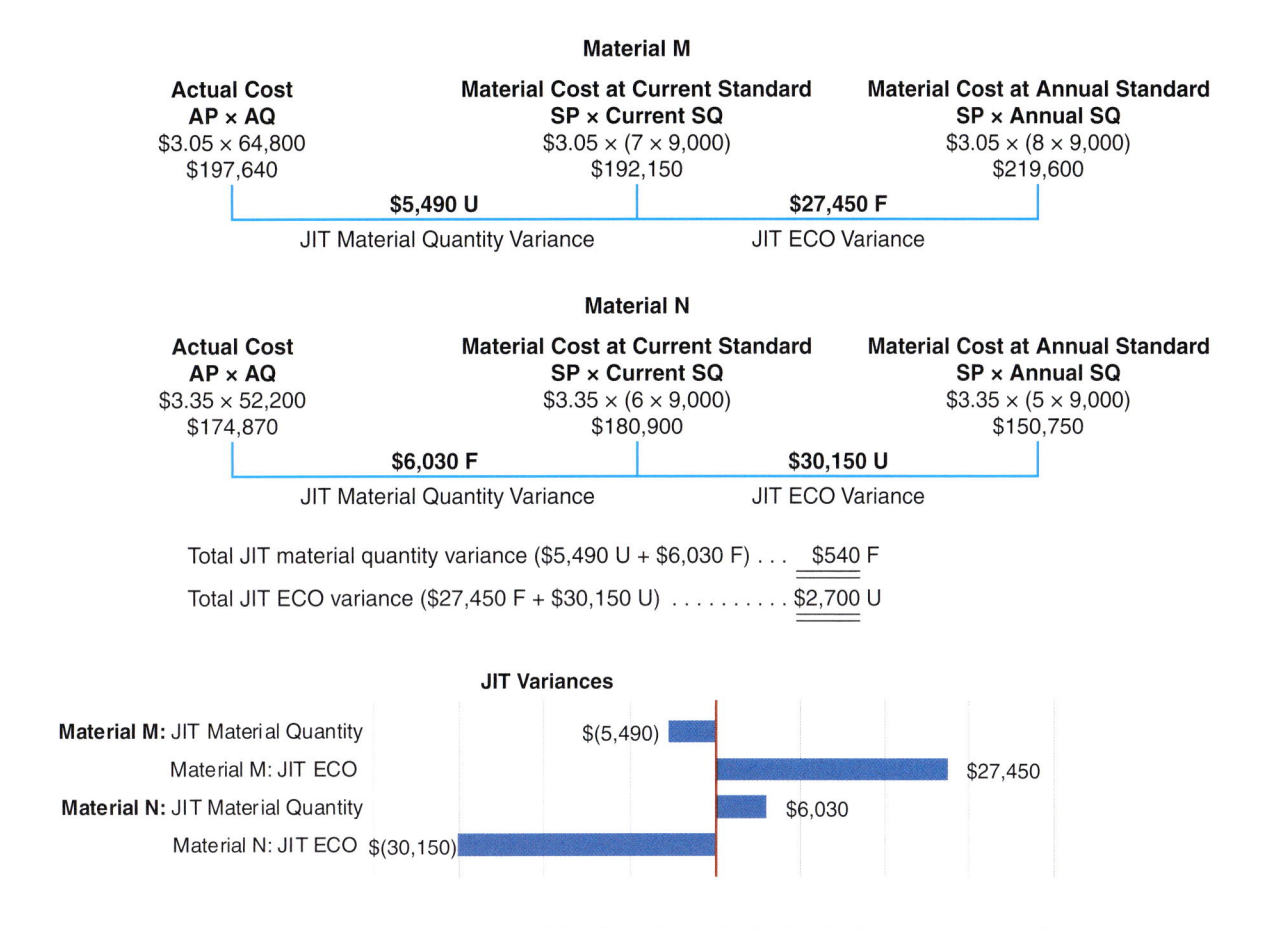

Material M

Actual Cost AP × AQ $3.05 × 64,800 $197,640	Material Cost at Current Standard SP × Current SQ $3.05 × (7 × 9,000) $192,150	Material Cost at Annual Standard SP × Annual SQ $3.05 × (8 × 9,000) $219,600
	$5,490 U JIT Material Quantity Variance	$27,450 F JIT ECO Variance

Material N

Actual Cost AP × AQ $3.35 × 52,200 $174,870	Material Cost at Current Standard SP × Current SQ $3.35 × (6 × 9,000) $180,900	Material Cost at Annual Standard SP × Annual SQ $3.35 × (5 × 9,000) $150,750
	$6,030 F JIT Material Quantity Variance	$30,150 U JIT ECO Variance

Total JIT material quantity variance ($5,490 U + $6,030 F) . . . $540 F

Total JIT ECO variance ($27,450 F + $30,150 U) . . . . $2,700 U

JIT Variances

- Material M: JIT Material Quantity $(5,490)
- Material M: JIT ECO $27,450
- Material N: JIT Material Quantity $6,030
- Material N: JIT ECO $(30,150)

The portion of the total quantity variance caused by the ECO ($2,700 U) is shown separately from that caused by efficiency ($540 F). While the total ECO variance is only $2,700 U, the data visualization depicts how the favorable ECO variance of Material M offset a majority of the unfavorable ECO variance of Material N.

Labor, overhead, and/or conversion can also have ECO variances. However, labor variances in an automated just-in-time system should be minimal if standard rates and times have been set appropriately.

Flexible and Lean Manufacturing Systems

In adopting a JIT philosophy, a number of manufacturers have adopted either a flexible manufacturing system, a lean manufacturing system, or a combination of both.

Flexible Manufacturing Systems Traditionally, most manufacturing firms employed long production runs to make thousands of identical products; this process was encouraged by the idea of economies of scale. After each run, the machines would be stopped and a slow and expensive setup would be made to prepare for the next massive production run. Instead, many companies use a **flexible manufacturing system (FMS)**. An FMS involves a network of robots and material conveyance devices monitored and controlled by computers that allows for rapid production and responsiveness to changes in production needs. **Exhibit 18.6** contrasts a traditional manufacturing system with an FMS.

Modular factories commonly employ FMSs and output can be customized upon request by customers because such systems can introduce new products quickly, produce in small lot sizes, make rapid machine and tool setups, and communicate and process large amounts of information. Information is transferred through an electronic network to computers that control the robots performing most of the production activities. Companies are able to operate at high speeds and can quickly and inexpensively stop producing one item and start producing another, making it possible to minimize product costs while building a large assortment of high-quality products to offer customers.

Exhibit 18.6 Comparison of Traditional Manufacturing and Flexible Manufacturing System

Factor	Traditional Manufacturing	Flexible Manufacturing System
Product variety	Limited	Extensive
Response time to market needs	Slow	Rapid
Worker tasks	Specialized	Diverse
Production runs	Long	Short
Lot sizes	Massive	Small
Performance rewards basis	Individual	Team
Setups	Slow and expensive	Fast and inexpensive
Product life cycle expectations	Long	Short
Work area control	Centralized	Decentralized
Production activity	Labor intensive	Technology intensive
Information requirements	Batch based	Online, real-time
Worker knowledge of technology	Low to medium	High

Lean Enterprises **Lean manufacturing** refers to the process of making only those items demanded by customers and making those items without waste. Lean enterprises use many of the management tools, such as cellular manufacturing and JIT discussed earlier in this section. A major theme in lean enterprises is the same as that of JIT: inventory should be eliminated to the extent possible because it hides production problems and wastes resources. Five principles of lean processes provide the framework for a lean enterprise.

- Value from a customer standpoint is defined.
- Value stream is mapped including all steps to turn materials into the final product.
- System flow is maximized in a pull-production system.
- Employees are empowered to measure and control the process.
- The ultimate goal is perfection of the process.[3]

Lean enterprises, such as **Toyota** and **Rockwell Automation**, put pressure on the entire value chain to minimize waste, maximize quality, eliminate NVA activities, and shorten the lead time for delivering products and services. Two concepts are central to a lean enterprise's success and that of its value chain: *leveraging technology and training employees*. Technology allows for short cycle times, high-quality products, and quick changeovers of production lines. Well-trained employees manage the technology, identify ways to become more efficient, and focus on satisfying customer needs. With the ability to quickly develop and sell high-quality products having minimal defects, lean enterprises have raised the competitive bar in many industries. For some industries, these competitive pressures have led to reduced product life cycles and dramatically reduced new product time to market.

REVIEW 18-3 | **LO18-3** | **JIT Variances**

New Products Inc. uses a JIT system. The following standards are related to materials A and B, which are used to make one unit of the company's final product:

Annual Material Standards
2 pounds of Material A @ $5.80 per pound
3 pounds of Material B @ $6.40 per pound

Current Material Standards
3 pounds of Material A @ $5.80 per pound
2 pounds of Material B @ $6.40 per pound

continued

---

[3] Frances A. Kennedy, and B. Maskell. "Lean Enterprise Fundamentals," *Statements on Management Accounting, Institute of Management Accountants IMA* (2006): 1–32.

Chapter 18 Inventory and Production Management

continued from previous page

Actual Usage During August	
Units produced..........................	9,000 units
Material A used	17,000 pounds
Material B used	24,000 pounds

Current material standards differ from the original because of an engineering change made near the end of July. Assume all material is acquired at the standard cost per pound.

a. Calculate the material quantity variance.
b. Calculate the ECO material variance.
c. **Critical Thinking:** Analyze the variances.

More practice: E18-37, E18-38
Solution on p. 18-39.

BACKFLUSH COSTING USED IN JUST-IN-TIME SYSTEMS

Under the JIT philosophy, a pull system ensures that inventory is manufactured to sell, leaving minimal to no inventory balances. Thus, a JIT system can have a major impact on inventory accounting. In addition to minimizing and adjusting the variance calculations, companies no longer require a separate raw material inventory classification because material is acquired only when needed for production. JIT companies can use a combined **Raw and In-Process (RIP) Inventory account** in a system called backflush costing.

Backflush costing is a streamlined cost accounting method that speeds up, simplifies, and minimizes accounting effort in an environment that minimizes inventory balances, requires few allocations, uses standard costs, and has few variances from standard. During the period, this costing method records purchases of raw material and accumulates actual conversion costs. Then, at a predetermined trigger point, such as (1) at completion of production or (2) upon the sale of goods, an entry is made to allocate the total costs incurred to Cost of Goods Sold or to Finished Goods Inventory using standard production costs.

LO18-4 How is backflushing used to account for just-in-time inventory systems?

Accounting for Inventory Using Backflushing — LO18-4   DEMO 18-4

Information for Marshall Industrial, a ceramics producer, is used to illustrate JIT system backflush entries. During July, Marshall produced 20,000 units and sold 19,800 units at $110 per unit. Marshall Industrial's standard production cost per unit is as follows.

Direct material	$19.25
Conversion	46.00
Total cost........................	$65.25

No beginning inventories exist. The following events took place in July.

- Purchased $392,500 of direct materials at a long-term contract price of $19.25 per unit.
- Incurred $921,750 of conversion costs.
- Applied conversion costs to Raw and In-Process Inventory based on a rate of $46 per unit.

To establish a foundational set of transactions from which to illustrate subsequent alternative recordings in a backflush costing system, entries for one of Marshall's products are presented on the next page.

◆ **Using information from the six entries that follow, how would Randall record journal entries in July under four backflush costing alternatives including (a) journal raw material purchases when production is complete (b) combine entries to complete and sell inventory (c) journal upon product sale and (d) charge cost of goods sold upon product sale with subsequent backflush?**

(1) Purchased $392,500 of direct material in July:
Raw and In-Process (RIP) Inventory 392,500
    Accounts Payable.. 392,500
To record material purchased at standard cost under a long-term agreement with supplier*

(2) Incurred $921,750 of conversion costs in July:
Conversion Cost Control..................................... 921,750
    Various accounts 921,750
To record conversion costs; various accounts include Wages Payable for direct and indirect labor, Accumulated Depreciation, Supplies, etc.

(3) Applied conversion costs to RIP for 20,000 units completed:
Raw and In-Process Inventory (20,000 × $46.00) 920,000
    Conversion Cost Control................................. 920,000
To apply labor and overhead to units completed

(4) Transferred 20,000 units of production in July:
Finished Goods Inventory (20,000 × $65.25)..................... 1,305,000
    Raw and In-Process Inventory 1,305,000
To transfer completed goods from RIP

(5) Sold 19,800 units on account in July for $110 each:
Accounts Receivable (19,800 × $110) 2,178,000
    Sales.. 2,178,000
To record goods sold on account

Cost of Goods Sold (19,800 × $65.25)........................... 1,291,950
    Finished Goods Inventory................................ 1,291,950
To record cost of goods sold

(6) In addition, there are underapplied conversion costs of $1,750, considered immaterial, (calculated as $921,750 − $920,000) which would be eliminated through the following entry:
Cost of Goods Sold 1,750
    Conversion Cost Control................................. 1,750
To close underapplied overhead

Ending inventories:
Raw and In-Process Inventory ($1,312,500 − $1,305,000) .... $ 7,500
Finished Goods Inventory ($1,305,000 − $1,291,950).................. $13,050

*A long-term contract with Marshall's direct material supplier indicates a cost of $19.25 per unit, so no material price variance occurs at purchase.

The following selected T-accounts summarize the activity presented above.

Raw and In-Process Inventory				Conversion Cost Control			
(1)	392,500	(4)	1,305,000	(2)	921,750	(3)	920,000
(3)	920,000						
Bal.	7,500			Bal.	1,750		

Finished Goods Inventory				Cost of Goods Sold			
(4)	1,305,000	(5)	1,291,950	(5)	1,291,950		
Bal.	13,050						

Accounts Receivable				Sales			
(5)	2,178,000					(5)	2,178,000

Alternative Entries in Backflush Costing

Four alternatives to the entries presented above follow.

a. **Journal Raw Material Purchases When Production Is Complete** First, if production time were extremely short, Marshall might not journalize raw material purchases until production is complete. In this case, and in addition to recording entries (2), (5), and (6), the entry to replace entries (1), (3), and (4) follows. Completion of the finished goods is the trigger point for this entry.

Raw and In-Process Inventory	7,500	
Finished Goods Inventory (20,000 × $65.25)	1,305,000	
Accounts Payable		392,500
Conversion Cost Control (20,000 × $46.00)		920,000
To record completed production and accounts payable, and adjust RIP inventory account valuation		

b. **Combine Entries to Complete and Sell Inventory** Second, if completed goods were shipped immediately to customers, Marshall could use another alternative in which the entries to complete and sell products would be combined. Doing so would replace entries (3), (4), and the second part of (5). Entries (1), (2), the first part of (5), and (6), would still be needed. Sale of the products is the trigger point for this entry.

Finished Goods Inventory (200 × $65.25)	13,050	
Cost of Goods Sold (19,800 × $65.25)	1,291,950	
Raw and In-Process Inventory (20,000 × $19.25)		385,000
Conversion Cost Control (20,000 × $46.00)		920,000
To record sale of products and adjust RIP and FG inventory account valuations		

c. **Journal upon Product Sale** The third alternative reflects the ultimate JIT system: other than entry (2) and (6), the only entry made is to record product sales. All account adjustments would be made through this entry. For Marshall, the entry would be as follows.

Raw and In-Process Inventory (minimal overpurchases)	7,500	
Finished Goods Inventory (minimal overproduction)	13,050	
Cost of Goods Sold	1,291,950	
Accounts Payable		392,500
Conversion Cost Control		920,000
To adjust inventory account valuations and record accounts payable		

d. **Charge Cost of Goods Sold upon Product Sale with Subsequent Backflush** A fourth alternative charges all costs to the Cost of Goods Sold account, with a subsequent backflush of costs to the Raw and In-Process Inventory and the Finished Goods Inventory accounts at the end of the period. The following entries replace entries (1), (3), (4), the second part of (5), and (6). Entry (2) and the first part of (5) would still be made at the product sale trigger point.

Cost of Goods Sold	1,312,500	
Accounts Payable		392,500
Conversion Cost Control		920,000
To charge all material, labor, and overhead costs to CGS		
Raw and In-Process Inventory	7,500	
Finished Goods Inventory	13,050	
Cost of Goods Sold		20,550
To adjust inventory account valuations		

Importantly, the accounts will have the same balances at period-end, no matter which alternative is followed.

Implementing JIT can create significant cost reductions and productivity improvements. Management should consider the costs of, and benefits provided by, the inventory control alternatives before

REVIEW 18-4 — LO18-4 — Backflush Costing

During June, Urban Fit Inc. produced 45,000 units and sold 40,000 units. The standard cost for each item follows.

Direct material	$ 4
Conversion costs	8
Total cost	$12

The company had no inventory on June 1. The following events took place in June:

- Purchased $192,000 of direct material and incurred $354,000 of conversion costs
- Applied $360,000 of conversion costs to Raw and In-Process Inventory
- Finished 45,000 units and sold 40,000 units for $20 each

a. Prepare journal entries including the entry to close underapplied or overapplied overhead (assumed to be immaterial) to cost of goods sold. Use the following inventory account names: Raw and In-Process Inventory and Finished Goods Inventory.

b. What are the ending balances in the following accounts: Raw and In-Process Inventory, Finished Goods, and Cost of Goods Sold?

c. Instead assume that backflush costing is used where the trigger point is the product sale. Record the entry to adjust inventory and cost of goods sold upon sale.

d. **Critical Thinking:** Why are detailed variance entries not required for management decision-making purposes under JIT costing systems?

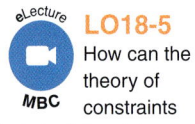

More practice: MC18-16, MC18-17, E18-44
Solution on p. 18-39.

THEORY OF CONSTRAINTS

LO18-5 How can the theory of constraints help in determining production flow?

The **theory of constraints (TOC)** can help management reduce cycle time. This theory indicates that the flow of goods through a production process cannot be at a rate faster than the slowest constraint in the process.[4] A **constraint** is anything that confines or limits the ability of a person or machine to perform a project or function.

Production limitations in a manufacturing environment are caused by human, material, and machine constraints. Some constraints relate to process speed, whereas others relate to absolute production limits such as availability of material or machine time. Still other constraints relate to people and any limitations those people have on their ability to understand, react, or perform at some particular rate of speed. Because the labor content contained in products is declining rapidly as automation increases, constraints caused by machines are often of more concern than human constraints in reducing cycle time.

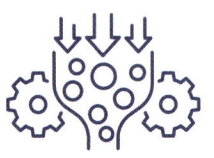

Constraints, also called **bottlenecks**, are points at which the processing levels are sufficiently slow as to cause the other processing mechanisms in the network to experience idle time. Bottlenecks cause an activity's processing to be impeded. Even a totally automated process will have some constraints because all machines do not operate at the same speed or handle the same capacity. Therefore, the constraints must be identified and corrected to the extent possible.

DEMO 18-5 — LO18-5 — Analyzing Bottlenecks

Consider the following simplistic illustration of a production process constraint.

---

[4] The theory of constraints was introduced to business environments by Eliyahu Goldratt and Jeff Cox in the book *The Goal* (New Haven, CT: North River Press, Inc./Spectrum Publishing Company, 1986).

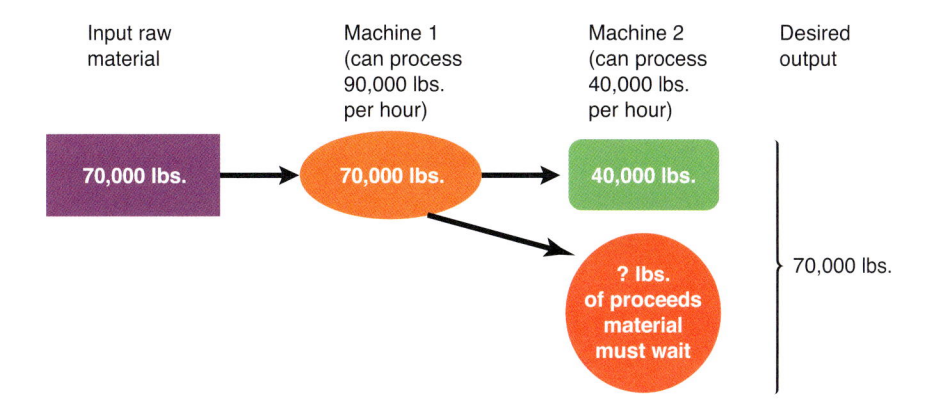

Chapter 18 Inventory and Production Management

[Diagram: Input raw material 70,000 lbs. → Machine 1 (can process 90,000 lbs. per hour) 70,000 lbs. → Machine 2 (can process 40,000 lbs. per hour) 40,000 lbs. and ? lbs. of proceeds material must wait → Desired output 70,000 lbs.]

♦ **If Machine 1 passes 70,000 pounds to Machine 2, how many pounds of material will be waiting at Machine 2 to be processed after one hour of Machine 2 processing time?**

Assume that each unit moves directly from Machine 1 to Machine 2 with no lag time. Although Machine 1 can process 90,000 pounds of raw material in an hour, Machine 2 can handle only 40,000 pounds. Of the 70,000 pounds of input, 30,000 pounds of processed material will be waiting at the constraining machine (Machine 2) after an hour of processing. The constraint's effect on production is obvious, but the implications are not quite as clear. Managers have a tendency to want to see machines working, not sitting idle.

♦ **How many pounds of material will be waiting at Machine 2 to be processed if Machine 1 processing is maximized and produces 450,000 total pounds over 5 hours?**

If Machine 1 were kept in continual use, all 450,000 pounds would be processed through Machine 1 in five hours. However, a backlog of 250,000 pounds of processed material would now be waiting at Machine 2.

$$(5 \text{ hours} \times 90{,}000 \text{ pounds}) - (5 \text{ hours} \times 40{,}000 \text{ pounds}) = 250{,}000 \text{ pounds}$$

All of this material would require storage space and create additional NVA costs.

Machine constraints also impact quality control. Managers normally choose quality control points to follow completion of a particular process. When constraint points are known, quality control points should always be placed before a constrained process. "If you scrap a part before it reaches the bottleneck, all you have lost is a scrapped part. But if you scrap the part after it's passed through the bottleneck, you have lost time that cannot be recovered."[5]

As soon as constraints are known, managers should determine what is the best use of constrained process time or productive capacity and then limit the constraints' impacts on performance. Options such as adding more machines to perform the constrained activity or processing material through other machines that would reduce limitations should be investigated. Managing constraints is a process of continuous improvement.

Data Visualization

A manufactured product requires time in three processes using Machine 1, Machine 2, and Machine 3. Data visualizations regarding machine processing follow.

Maximum Units per Hour

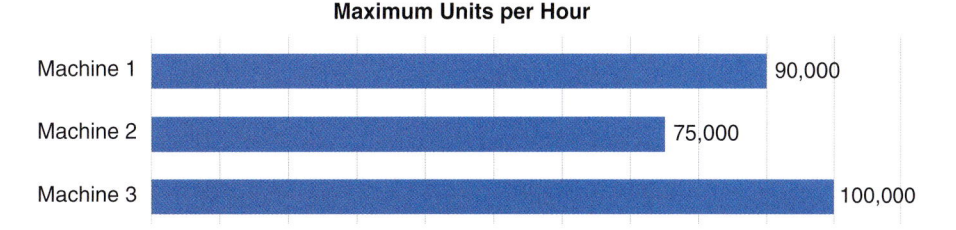

Machine	Units
Machine 1	90,000
Machine 2	75,000
Machine 3	100,000

continued

---
[5] Ibid., p. 156.

continued from previous page

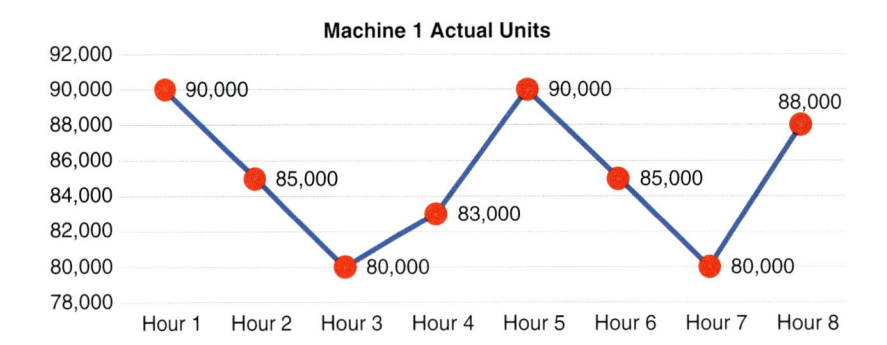

Machine 1 Actual Units

Hour	Units
Hour 1	90,000
Hour 2	85,000
Hour 3	80,000
Hour 4	83,000
Hour 5	90,000
Hour 6	85,000
Hour 7	80,000
Hour 8	88,000

Based on the data visualizations above, answer the following questions.
a. Which machine(s) is the bottleneck in the process? Assume that each unit moves directly from Machine 1 to Machine 2 to Machine 3 with no lag time.
b. What is the maximum that can be processed each hour by Machine 2? Machine 3?
c. After 8 hours, how many units will be unfinished at Machine 2? Machine 3?

Solution on p. 18-40.

REVIEW 18-5 — LO18-5 — Theory of Constraints

Better Buy Inc. produces equipment in a three-department operation: Department 1 is labor intensive and Department 2 and 3 are highly automated. The average output of Department 1 is 56 units per hour. Units from Department 1 are transferred to Department 2 (which manufactures a maximum of 48 units per hour) and then to Department 3 (which manufactures a maximum of 55 units per hour).

Department One produced the following units: first hour: 48 units, second hour: 60 units, third hour: 55 units, and fourth hour: 49 units.

a. Which department is the bottleneck in the manufacturing process?
b. How much inventory is on hand in the bottleneck operation at the end of four hours? Assume that beginning inventory in all three departments is zero and inventory is passed to the next department at *the end of an hour of production*.
c. **Critical Thinking:** How can the company better manage the production limitations due to the constraint?

More practice: MC18-18, E18-46, E18-48
Solution on p. 18-40.

Comprehensive Chapter Review

Key Terms

backflush costing, p. 18-17
bottlenecks, p. 18-20
carrying cost, p. 18-3
constraint, p. 18-20
economic order quantity (EOQ), p. 18-5
economic production run (EPR), p. 18-7
engineering change orders, p. 18-12
flexible manufacturing system (FMS), p. 18-15
inventory turnover, p. 18-13

just-in-time (JIT), p. 18-10
just-in-time manufacturing system, p. 18-10
kanban, p. 18-10
lead time, p. 18-8
lean manufacturing, p. 18-16
manufacturing cells, p. 18-13
manufacturing cycle efficiency, p. 18-13
ordering cost, p. 18-3
order point, p. 18-8
Pareto inventory analysis, p. 18-9
production cost, p. 18-3

pull systems, p. 18-5
purchasing cost, p. 18-3
push system, p. 18-4
raw and in-process (RIP) inventory account, p. 18-17
safety stock, p. 18-8
setup costs, p. 18-3
stockout cost, p. 18-3
theory of constraints (TOC), p. 18-20
usage, p. 18-8
value chain approach, p. 18-11

Chapter Summary

Costs Associated with Inventory — LO18-1
- The primary cost associated with inventory is either the cost of purchasing or producing the goods.
  - Purchasing cost for inventory is the quoted purchase price minus any discounts allowed, plus shipping charges.
  - Production cost for inventory is the summation of costs associated with purchasing direct material, paying for direct labor, and absorbing variable and fixed overhead.
- Ordering costs include amounts for invoice preparation, receiving, inspection, and payment.
- Setup costs include labor costs and machine downtime costs.
- Carrying costs of inventory include storage, handling, insurance, property taxes, obsolescence losses, and the opportunity cost of invested capital.
- Stockout costs include loss of customer goodwill, special ordering expenses, and setup costs for rescheduled production.
- Managing inventory costs is important to the firm because inventory
  - produces no value for the firm until it is sold.
  - can hide inefficiencies in production activities.
  - is a significant investment.

Economic Order Quantity Concepts — LO18-2
- Economic order quantity: Calculation of the least number of units to order that optimizes the balance between ordering and carrying costs.
- Economic production run: Reflects the production quantity that minimizes the total costs of setting up a production run and of carrying one unit in stock for one year.
- Order point: Reflects the inventory level that triggers placement of an order for additional units.
- Order point can be adjusted for safety stock.
- Pareto inventory analysis: separates inventory into three groups based on annual cost-to-volume usage.

Push and Pull Inventory Systems — LO18-3
- Push systems produce goods to satisfy a production schedule based on economic production run concepts.
- Pull systems produce goods only in response to current customer demand.

Just-in-Time (JIT) Inventory System
- JIT is a philosophy that states production should not occur until a customer demands the product.
- Successful implementation of JIT requires
  - elimination of non-value-added activities.
  - a focus on continuous improvement.
  - persistent efforts to reduce inventory.
  - a focus on improving quality of processes.
  - high-quality inputs from vendors.
- JIT can require modifications to the accounting system to recognize
  - variances immediately upon occurrence rather than at period end.
  - that inventories be sufficiently small to no longer justify separate accounting for raw, in-process, and finished goods.

Manufacturing Systems
- A flexible manufacturing system
  - integrates computer systems with automated production equipment.
  - is often used in plants organized for cellular manufacturing.
  - minimizes the time required to set up for production.
  - is ideal for low-volume, high-quality products.
- Lean manufacturing refers to making only those items in demand by customers and making those items without waste.
- Lean enterprises put pressure on their entire value chains to minimize waste, maximize quality, eliminate activities that add product cost but not value, and shorten delivery lead time for products and services.
- Lean enterprises emphasize an organization's ability to leverage technology and train employees.
- Lean enterprises have raised the competitive bar in many industries by quickly developing and selling high-quality products that have few defects.

LO18-4 **Backflush Costing Used in JIT Systems**
- Streamlined cost accounting method that speeds up, simplifies, and minimizes accounting effort.
- Backflush accounting is possible because inventory balances are minimal, few allocations are required, standard costs are used, and there are typically few variances from standard.
- JIT companies can use a Raw and In-Process (RIP) Inventory account.
- Entries are recorded at a predetermined trigger point such as when production is complete or upon sale.

LO18-5 **Theory of Constraints (TOC)**
- TOC is a tool for reducing cycle time by
  - maximizing the flow of products through production bottlenecks.
  - overcoming constraints in the flow of goods through a production system.

Solution Strategies

LO18-1 **Gross Profit Analysis**

$$\text{Gross profit ratio} = \text{Gross profit} \div \text{Sales}$$

LO18-2 **Economic Order Quantity Concepts**

$$\text{Total annual ordering costs} = \text{Number of orders per year} \times O$$
$$\text{Total annual carrying costs} = \text{Average inventory in units}^* \times C$$

*(Quantity of an order [new inventory received] + 0 [inventory completely depleted])/2
O = estimated cost of placing one order
C = estimated cost to carry one unit in stock for one year

$$EOQ = \sqrt{\frac{(2QO)}{C}}$$

where EOQ = economic order quantity in units
Q = estimated annual quantity used in units (can be found in the annual purchases budget)
O = estimated cost of placing one order
C = estimated cost to carry one unit in stock for one year

$$EPR = \sqrt{\frac{(2QS)}{C}}$$

where EPR = economic production run in units
Q = estimated annual quantity to be produced in units (can be found in annual production budget)
S = estimated cost of setting up a production run
C = estimated cost to carry one unit in stock for one year

$$\text{Order point} = (\text{Daily usage} \times \text{Lead time}) + \text{Safety stock}$$

LO18-3 **Inventory Ratios**

$$\text{Inventory turnover (in units)} = \frac{\text{Annual demand in units}}{\text{Average inventory in units}}$$

$$\text{Inventory turnover (in dollars)} = \frac{\text{Cost of goods sold}}{\text{Average inventory (in dollars)}}$$

$$\text{GMROI} = \frac{\text{Gross margin (in dollars)}}{\text{Average inventory (in dollars)}}$$

LO18-3 **Material and Labor Variances under JIT**

Two standards can exist:
1. an annual standard (set and held constant for the year), and
2. a current standard (based on design modifications or engineering change orders).

Generally, firms have minimal, if any, material price variances because prices are set by long-term contracts. A labor rate variance can occur and is calculated in the traditional manner.

Chapter 18 Inventory and Production Management

JIT Material Quantity Variance

Actual material cost
− Material cost at current standard
Material quantity variance

JIT Labor Efficiency Variance

(Actual labor hours × Current standard rate)
− (Standard labor hours × Current standard rate)
Labor efficiency variance

JIT Engineering Change Order Variance for Material

Material cost at current standard
− Material cost at annual standard
ECO variance

JIT Engineering Change Order Variance for Labor

(Standard labor hours × Current standard rate)
− (Standard labor hours × Annual standard rate)
ECO variance

(Exists only if a change occurs in the mix of labor used to manufacture the product or through the automation of processes.)

Chapter Demonstration Problem

CAN-DO Inc. manufactures home-improvement products in a JIT environment. The annual and current material standards for one of the company's products follow.

LO18-3

Annual Material Standards

Material 1: 4 pounds × $3.75	$15.00
Material 2: 12 pounds × $2.25	27.00
	$42.00

Current Material Standards

Material 1: 8 pounds × $3.75	$30.00
Material 2: 8 pounds × $2.25	18.00
	$48.00

The current material standards differ from the original because an engineering change order was made near the end of August. During September, the company manufactured 1,000 units of product and used 7,500 pounds of Material 1 and 8,200 pounds of Material 2. All material is acquired at the standard cost per pound.

Required:
a. Calculate the material variance and the ECO material variance.
b. Explain the effect of the ECO on product cost.

Solution to Demonstration Problem

a.

Actual Material Usage

Material 1: 7,500 × $3.75	$28,125
Material 2: 8,200 × $2.25	18,450
Total material cost	$46,575

Material Cost at Current Standard

Material 1: 1,000 × 8 × $3.75	$30,000
Material 2: 1,000 × 8 × $2.25	18,000
Total material cost	$48,000

Material Cost at Annual Standard

Material 1: 1,000 × 4 × $3.75	$15,000
Material 2: 1,000 × 12 × $2.25	27,000
Total material cost	$42,000

continued

continued from previous page

Variances	
Material cost at current standard	$48,000
Actual material cost	(46,575)
Material quantity variance	$ 1,425 F
Material cost at annual standard	$42,000
Material cost at current standard	(48,000)
ECO variance	$ (6,000) U

b. The effect of the ECO was to substitute the higher-priced Material 1 for the lower-priced Material 2. The financial effect of this change was to increase expected production cost for August by $6,000. However, the cost increase could have been offset by an increase in price, assuming the change in mix of materials increased product quality.

Assignments with the MBC logo in the margin are available in myBusinessCourse.
Resources include demonstration videos, guided examples, and auto-graded homework.
See details in the Preface, and ask your professor how you can access the system.

Data Analytics

LO18-1 **DA18-1. Analyzing trends in gross profit margin and unit costs**

Access the file included in MBC which includes sales, cost of goods sold, and units shipped for the first three quarters of the year and annually for five years for **Harley-Davidson, Inc.** and complete the following requirements.

Required
a. Calculate the gross profit ratio and the cost per unit sold for each period presented.
b. Create a combo chart in Excel showing the gross profit margin as a Clustered column chart and the Cost per unit shipped as a Line chart (secondary axis). *Hint*: Choose the "Clustered Column – Line on Secondary Axis Chart" after arranging the data in two columns.
c. What was the impact of the pandemic on the trends?
d. What are the general trends in cost per unit shipped over the five-year time period?
e. In general, how do current gross profit trends compare to trends prior to the pandemic?

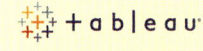

LO18-3 **DA18-2. Using Tableau to analyze inventory**

Coca-Cola Company
NYSE :: KO

You recently joined the **Coca-Cola Company** (in the consumer staples segment) as a cost accountant. You have learned of the importance of a company being able to sell its products in a timely fashion, and that the ratio of days sales in inventory provides this useful information. You decide a dashboard would be helpful in seeing if this ratio is improving or declining in the consumer discretionary and the consumer staples segments between 2017 and 2018. You will later compare your company results to this industry data. You build two sheets that are included in the dashboard. The first sheet shows the level of the ratio for each segment for the two years in question. The second sheet shows the change in the ratio between the two years. (Data is included in MBC.)

Required
Has the ratio days sales in inventory improved or declined in the consumer discretionary and the consumer staples segments between 2017 and 2018. By how much?

LO18-3 **DA18-3. Analyzing inventory turnover ratio**

Applying data visualization techniques for existing data sets is a proficiency included in the CGMA Competency Framework. Creating data visualizations under best practices is essential in communicating an accurate message to your audience.

Review the following data visualizations for Company A and Company B over the last three years. Assume that both companies adopted lean manufacturing techniques that resulted in an increase in inventory turnover over a three-year period.

Company A: Inventory Turnover

Year	Turnover
Year 1	~19.6
Year 2	~19.8
Year 3	~20.1

(Scale: 19.3 19.4 19.5 19.6 19.7 19.8 19.9 20.0 20.1 20.2)

Company B: Inventory Turnover

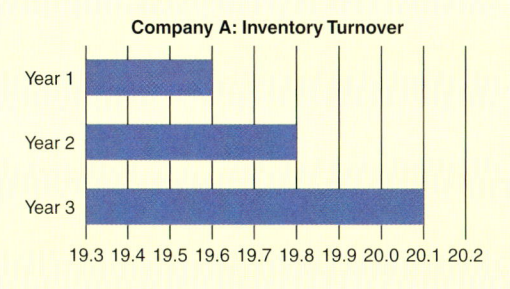

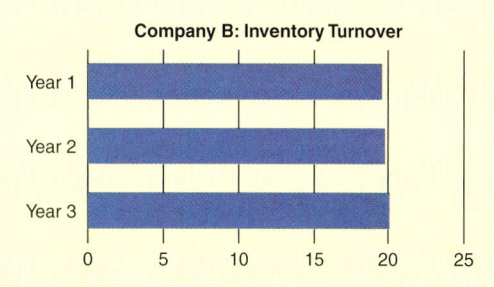

Year	Turnover
Year 1	~20
Year 2	~20
Year 3	~20

(Scale: 0 5 10 15 20 25)

Required

Which company showed a more favorable impact on inventory turnover over the three-year period when lean manufacturing methods were adopted? Explain your answer. *Hint:* Review the *Data Visualization* report issued by the **IMA** found at https://www.imanet.org/research-publications/statements-on-management-accounting/data-visualization

Data Visualization

Data Visualization Activities are available in *BusinessCourse*. These assignments use Tableau Dashboards to expose students to visual depictions of data and introduce students to data analytics through data visualizations. These exercises are easily assignable and auto graded by MBC.

Potential Ethical Issues

1. Producing inventory that is not needed relative to current sales demand to increase reported operating profits
2. Avoiding the adoption of innovative production and inventory management methods because of short-run negative effects on profits
3. Blaming suppliers for inventory problems that are, in actuality, artifacts of in-house inventory management mistakes
4. Failing to write-down obsolete or spoiled inventory as soon as information regarding these conditions becomes known
5. Using the adoption of evolving production and inventory management methods as a justification to dismiss workers

Questions

Q18-1. What are the three costs associated with inventory? Explain each and give examples.
Q18-2. Differentiate between the push and pull systems of production. Is JIT a push or a pull system?
Q18-3. How are ordering costs and carrying costs related?
Q18-4. What is Pareto inventory analysis? Why do A items and C items warrant different inventory control methods? What are some methods that can be employed to control C items?
Q18-5. What are the primary goals of the JIT philosophy, and how does JIT attempt to achieve these goals?
Q18-6. What changes must occur in a production environment to effectively implement JIT? Why are these changes necessary?
Q18-7. How would switching from a traditional manufacturing system to a flexible manufacturing system affect a firm's inventory and production control systems?
Q18-8. What are the key principles of lean processes?
Q18-9. Why is a raw materials account not typically used in JIT systems? What alternative account would typically be used?
Q18-10. What is the theory of constraints? How is this concept appropriate for manufacturing and service companies?

Multiple Choice

LO18-1 **MC18-11.** All of the following are carrying costs of inventory except
- *a.* storage costs.
- *b.* insurance.
- *c.* shipping costs.
- *d.* opportunity costs.

LO18-1 **MC18-12.** A review of the inventories of Cedar Grove Company shows the following cost data for entertainment centers.

Invoice price	$400.00 per unit
Freight and insurance on shipment	20.00 per unit
Insurance on inventory	15.00 per unit
Unloading	140.00 per order
Cost of placing orders.	10.00 per order
Cost of capital, 25%	

What are the total carrying costs of inventory for an entertainment center?
- *a.* $105.
- *b.* $115.
- *c.* $120.
- *d.* $420.

LO18-2 **MC18-13.** Moss Products uses the Economic Order Quantity (EOQ) model as part of its inventory management process. A decrease in which one of the following variables would increase the EOQ?
- *a.* Annual sales.
- *b.* Cost per order.
- *c.* Safety stock level.
- *d.* Carrying costs.

LO18-2 **MC18-14.** James Smith is the new manager of inventory at American Electronics, a major retailer. He is developing an inventory control system, and knows he should consider establishing a safety stock level. The safety stock can protect against all of the following risks, except for the possibility that
- *a.* customers cannot find the merchandise they want, and they will go to the competition.
- *b.* shipments of merchandise from the manufacturers is delayed by as much as one week.
- *c.* the distribution of daily sales will have a large variance, due to holidays, weather, advertising, and weekly shopping habits.
- *d.* new competition may open in the company's market area.

LO18-3 **MC18-15.** Presario Inc. recently installed just-in-time production and purchasing systems. If Presario's experience is similar to that of other companies, Presario will likely
- *a.* reduce the number of suppliers with which it does business.
- *b.* increase the size of individual orders of raw materials.
- *c.* increase the dollar investment in finished goods inventory.
- *d.* be less reliant on sales orders as a "trigger" mechanism for production runs.

LO18-4 **MC18-16.** Reality Inc. follows a JIT system with standard direct material cost of $15 per unit and conversion cost of $18 per unit. Assume that the company produced 1,000 units and sold 900 units with no price or usage variances for the period. The entry to transfer completed goods from Raw and In-Process Inventory to Finished Goods Inventory will include the following:
- *a.* Debit to Raw and In-Process Inventory for 33,000.
- *b.* Debit to Finished Goods Inventory for $33,000.
- *c.* Debit to Finished Goods Inventory for $29,700.
- *d.* Credit to Raw and In-Process Inventory for $29,700.

LO18-4 **MC18-17.** Larken Manufacturing uses backflush costing to assign costs to inventory at month-end. Assume that the company had zero inventory on January 1, and after one month of production, the company had zero inventory in work in process and materials inventory. Additional information for January is as follows.

	January
Units produced	500
Units sold	400
Manufacturing cost per unit	$20.00

Chapter 18 Inventory and Production Management   18-29

The journal entry to assign costs to finished goods at month-end includes the following:
- a. Debit to Cost of Goods Sold for $2,000.
- b. Credit to Finished Goods Inventory for $8,000.
- c. Credit to Cost of Goods Sold for $2,000.
- d. Debit to Finished Goods Inventory for $1,000.

MC18-18. A manufacturing process consists of two processes: Process 1 and Process 2. In Process 1, 1,050 units were completed in the first hour and 1,100 were completed in the second hour. Process 2 started with zero inventory. Inventory passes from Process 1 to Process 2 at the end of an hour of production. If the number of unfinished units remaining in Process 2 after three hours is 150 units, what is the maximum hourly production of Process 2?   LO18-5
- a. 2,000 units
- b. 1,000 units
- c. 1,150 units
- d. 1,300 units

MC18-19. According to the theory of constraints, all of the following activities help to relieve the problem of a bottleneck in operations except   LO18-5
- a. eliminating idle time at the bottleneck operation.
- b. reducing setup time at the bottleneck operation.
- c. shifting products that do not have to be made on bottleneck machines to non-bottleneck machines.
- d. increasing the efficiency of operations at non-bottleneck machines.

Exercises

E18-20. Inventory cost management; research Included in MBC are data from recent annual reports from five merchandisers and five manufacturers.   LO18-1
- a. Calculate total merchandise inventory to total assets for the five merchandisers, along with the average ratio of the five merchandisers.
- b. Calculate the following ratios for each of the manufacturers, along with the average of the five manufacturers.
  - Raw Material Inventory to total assets
  - Work in Process Inventory to total assets
  - Finished Goods Inventory to total assets
  - Total inventory to total assets
- c. On average, which inventory component comprises the largest percentage of total inventory for the manufacturers?
- d. Do your answers to parts *a*, *b*, and *c* suggest that effective inventory management is crucial to the success of these ten firms? Discuss.
- e. Calculate the gross profit ratio for the merchandisers and manufacturers, along with the average of each firm type. How do the ratios differ by firm type?
- f. How does the reduction of inventory cost per unit impact the gross profit, assuming no change in selling price per unit?

E18-21. Inventory cost management Indicate whether each of the following costs would be considered an ordering cost (O), a carrying cost (C), or a stockout cost (S). For any costs that do not fit these categories, indicate N/A for "not applicable."   LO18-1
- a. Travel costs to inspect items at a supplier's site
- b. Cost of labor to inspect incoming shipments of materials
- c. Purchasing agent's salary
- d. Purchase price of product
- e. Customer goodwill lost due to unavailability of product
- f. Wage cost to update purchase order
- g. Freight-in cost on product
- h. Insurance for products in inventory
- i. Wages of receiving clerks
- j. Preparing and issuing electronic payment to suppliers
- k. Contribution margin lost due to unavailability of product
- l. Storage costs for products on hand

© Cambridge Business Publishers

m. Quantity discounts on products ordered
n. Opportunity cost of funds invested in inventory
o. Property taxes on warehouses
p. Handling costs for products on hand
q. Excess ordering and shipping charges for rush orders of standard product lines
r. Spoilage of products awaiting use

E18-22. Inventory cost management; EOQ; writing A plant manager and her controller were discussing the plant's inventory control policies. The controller suggested to the plant manager that the ordering policies should be reviewed because new technology had been implemented in the plant, including installation of (1) computerized inventory tracking, (2) electronic data interchange capabilities with the plant's major suppliers, and (3) in-house facilities for electronic fund transfers.

   a. As technology changes, why should managers update ordering policies for inventory?
   b. Write a memo to the plant manager describing the likely impact of the changes made in this plant on the economic order quantity of material input.

E18-23. Inventory cost management Indicate whether each of the following costs related to inventory, *a* through *l*, would be considered (1) a purchasing cost, (2) an ordering cost, (3) a carrying cost, or (4) a stockout cost.

   a. _____ Approving and preparing electronic payment to supplier for merchandise ordered.
   b. _____ Cost of renting storage space for finished goods inventory.
   c. _____ Freight-in on merchandise purchased.
   d. _____ Inspection of goods received.
   e. _____ Overnight shipping charges to move inventory from supplier to customer for goods not on hand.
   f. _____ Insurance cost for finished goods warehouse.
   g. _____ Insurance cost on in-transit inventory purchased from a supplier.
   h. _____ Lost contribution margin on inventory purchased from a competitor due to a stockout.
   i. _____ Labor to process returns of defective goods received.
   j. _____ Losses from inventory damaged when moved within finished goods warehouse.
   k. _____ Supplier quantity discount lost by not purchasing merchandise inventory in bulk to hold until sale.
   l. _____ Opportunity cost of cash tied up in inventory.

E18-24. Calculating inventory cost In June, Milestone Inc. received an invoice with a per unit cost of $175 from a vendor for its latest inventory purchase. Milestone plans to pay the invoice within 10 days to take advantage of a 2% discount. Shipping cost for the purchase amounts to $5 per unit. Other costs incurred for the inventory item include the following.

Staff costs to prepare purchase order and obtain required approvals . . .	$ 2.00 per unit
Costs to inspect item upon receipt	$ 1.50 per unit
Storage and insurance costs	$ 8.00 per unit
Shipping costs to customer	$10.00 per unit

   a. What are the total purchasing costs per unit?
   b. What are the total ordering costs per unit?
   c. What are the total carrying costs per unit if the company's expected rate of return is 16%?

E18-25. Inventory cost management; writing The supply management director at Texas Oil Field Services has contracted to purchase $4 million of spare parts that are currently unneeded at a 50% discount. His rationale for the contract was that the parts were currently available at a significantly reduced price from the standard price. The company just hired a new president who, on learning about the contracts, stated that the purchase contract should be canceled because the parts would not be needed for at least a year. The supply management director informed the president that the penalties of $2,100,000 for canceling the contracts would cost more than letting the orders go through. Determine the best course of action if warehousing and insurance costs for the year are estimated to be 10% of the purchase price, personnel costs to receive and inspect the inventory are expected to be $10,000, and the opportunity cost of capital is 16%.

E18-26. Carrying costs Determine the carrying costs for an item costing $6.80, given the following per-unit cost information:

Storage cost	$0.24
Handling cost	0.28
Production labor cost	1.70
Insurance cost	0.44
Opportunity cost	8% of investment

E18-27. Push vs. pull systems Consider the following circumstances and discuss whether you would recommend a push system or a pull system in each particular case.   LO18-2

    a. _____ Gluten-free bread manufacturer, supplying local specialty stores.
    b. _____ High-volume manufacturer of seasonal outdoor patio furniture.
    c. _____ High-end customized furniture manufacturer.
    d. _____ Large battery manufacturer that supplies large retailers with predictable sales orders.
    e. _____ Furniture manufacturer that changes out its production lines for different types of products.
    f. _____ Start-up manufacturer of leather handbags.

E18-28. Push vs. pull systems; writing Tonight you are going to dine at the restaurant of your choice. To choose the restaurant, you are going to consider the fact that some manage their food production on a push basis and others manage their food production on a pull basis.   LO18-2

    a. Discuss the difference between managing food production in a restaurant on a push versus a pull basis.
    b. Are there any circumstances in which you would prefer to dine at a restaurant that uses a push model of food production? Discuss.
    c. Are there any circumstances in which you would prefer to dine at a restaurant that uses a pull model of food production? Discuss.

E18-29. Push vs. pull systems; writing Everyone in your company seems excited about the suggestion that the firm implement a JIT system. Being a cautious person, however, your company president has asked you to write a report describing situations in which JIT will not work. Prepare such a report.   LO18-2, 3

E18-30. Carrying costs Farm Fresh manufactures a variety of animal food products from alfalfa "pellets." The firm has determined that its EOQ is 80,000 pounds of pellets. Based on the EOQ, the firm's annual ordering cost for pellets is $16,700. Given this information, what is the firm's annual carrying cost of pellets? Explain.   LO18-2

E18-31. Multiproduct EOQs A retail cosmetics chain carries three types of skin products: face cream, lotion, and powder. Determine the economic order quantity for each, given the following information: LO18-2

Product	Order Cost	Carrying Cost	Demand
Face cream.	$12	$2.00	2,000 units
Lotion	40	1.45	1,000 units
Powder	15	1.25	900 units

Round each answer to the nearest whole unit.

E18-32. Product demand The annual estimated demand for a product is 3,200 units, carrying cost is $0.35 per unit, and ordering cost is $140.00 per order.   LO18-2

    a. Compute the economic order quantity.
    b. Assume that a company enters into a partnership with one of its suppliers which cuts the ordering cost in half per order. What is the new EOQ? How does it compare to the prior EOQ?

E18-33. EPR UpTown Mfg. custom manufactures machine parts used by other companies. The following data relate to production of Part #33:   LO18-2

Annual quantity produced in units	3,600
Cost of setting up a production run.	$600
Cost of carrying one unit in stock for a year	$ 2

    a. Calculate the economic production run for Part #33; round to the nearest whole unit.
    b. At the EPR, what are annual setup costs and annual carrying costs?
    c. If the company is currently manufacturing 2,000 parts in a production run, what are the total setup and carrying costs? How does this amount compare to the EPR?

LO18-2 **E18-34. EPR** Rachelle Razer has taken a job as production superintendent in a plant that makes, among other products, jewelry cases. She is trying to determine how many cases to produce on each production run (EPR). Discussions reveal that last year the plant made 15,000 such cases, and this level of demand is expected for the coming year. The setup cost of each run is $400, and the cost of carrying a case in inventory for a year is estimated at $2.50.

 a. Calculate the EPR for jewelry cases and the total cost associated with it. Round the EPR to the nearest whole unit.
 b. Recalculate the EPR and total cost if the annual cost of carrying a case in inventory is $10 and the setup cost is $100. Round the EPR to the nearest whole unit.

LO18-2 **E18-35. Calculating total order and carrying costs; discounts lost** Valley Inc. uses 400 lbs. of a rare isotope per year. The isotope costs $500 per lb., but the supplier is offering a quantity discount of 2% for order sizes between 30 and 79 lbs., and a 6% discount for order sizes of 80 lbs. or more. The ordering costs are $200. Carrying costs are $100 per lb. of material and are not affected by the discounts. If the purchasing manager places eight orders of 50 lbs. each, what is the total cost of ordering and carrying inventory, including discounts lost?

LO18-2 **E18-36. Safety stock; order point** Lander Inc. uses 16,000 pounds of materials on average in its manufacturing process each day. Lander uses no more than 20,000 pounds of materials on a particular day. Due to a supplier issue, the current supplier is taking 7 days to ship the order.

 a. Compute the safety stock in pounds.　　b. Compute the order point.

LO18-3 **E18-37. JIT variances** Oklahoma Pneumatic uses a JIT system. The following standards are related to materials A and B, which are used to make one unit of the company's final product:

Annual Material Standards	
3 pounds of Material A × $2.50 ...	$ 7.50
4 pounds of Material B × $3.40 ...	13.60
	$21.10

Current Material Standards	
2 pounds of Material A × $2.50 ...	$ 5.00
5 pounds of Material B × $3.40 ...	17.00
	$22.00

Current material standards differ from the original because of an engineering change made near the end of June. During July, the company produced 3,000 units of its final product and used 11,000 pounds of Material A and 10,000 pounds of Material B. All material is acquired at the standard cost per pound.

 a. Calculate the material quantity variance and the engineering change order (ECO) material variance.
 b. Explain the effect of the ECO on product cost.

LO18-3 **E18-38. JIT variances** Natural Gardens makes recyclable pots for plants and uses JIT to manage inventories and production. The following are standards for a typical one-gallon pot:

Annual Material Standards	
32 ounces of Component X × $0.02 ...	$0.64
2 ounces of Component Y × $0.05 ...	0.10
	$0.74

Current Material Standards	
27 ounces of Component X × $0.02 ...	$0.54
4 ounces of Component Y × $0.05 ...	0.20
	$0.74

In-house experiments indicated that changing the material standard would make the pots stronger, so the company issued an engineering change order for the product in February; this ECO established the current material standards. March production was 8,000 pots. Usage of raw material (all purchased at standard price) in March was 220,000 ounces of Component X and 31,000 ounces of Component Y.

 a. Calculate the material quantity variance.
 b. Calculate the ECO variance.
 c. Summarize the company's effectiveness in managing March production costs.
 d. Comment on the circumstances in which a company would institute an ECO that results in the expected product cost being unchanged.

LO18-3 **E18-39. JIT implementation; writing** Duggan Mfg. began implementing a just-in-time inventory system several months ago. The production and purchasing managers, however, have not seen any dramatic improvements in throughput. The managers have decided that the problems are related to company suppliers. The company's three suppliers seem to send the wrong materials at the wrong

Chapter 18 Inventory and Production Management

times. Prepare a discussion of the problems that might exist in this situation. Be certain to address the following items: internal and external communications; possible engineering changes and their impacts; number, quality, and location of suppliers; and length of system implementation.

E18-40. Flexible manufacturing systems; research; writing On the Internet, research the topic of manufacturing cells and write a brief report on company experiences using those cells.

LO18-3

E18-41. Flexible manufacturing systems; writing Installation of a flexible manufacturing system (FMS) allows firms to make a variety of products in small batches. Assume Johnson Steel, a metal fabricating company, is considering switching from a traditional assembly line production process to an FMS. Provide answers to the following questions.

LO18-3

    a. How would the adoption of an FMS likely affect the inventory levels?
    b. How would the adoption of an FMS likely affect the quantity of production employees needed?
    c. Would the adoption of an FMS require employees to be retrained? Explain.

E18-42. Inventory management metrics Below are data for four scenarios, a base scenario (Scenario 1) followed by three modifications (2, 3, and 4) to the base scenario.

LO18-1, 3

	Scenario 1	Scenario 2	Scenario 3	Scenario 4
Sales.............	$120,000	$140,000	$120,000	$120,000
Cost of goods sold....	84,000	84,000	72,000	84,000
Gross profit.........	$ 36,000	$ 56,000	$ 48,000	$ 36,000
Average inventory.....	$ 14,400	$ 14,400	$ 14,400	$ 9,600

    a. For each scenario calculate the gross profit ratio, the inventory turnover (in dollars), and the gross margin return on inventory investment (GMROI).
    b. For Scenarios 2 through 4, explain what change occurred relative to Scenario 1 to cause GMROI to change. For example, was the change in GMROI caused by a change in inventory turns, a change in gross margin percent, or by reducing inventory levels?
    c. What general conclusions can be made from the calculations and observations regarding the factors that influence GMROI?

E18-43. JIT, inventory turnover, GMROI, gross profit ratio The following information was included or calculated from recent annual reports of Hasbro Inc. (and is also included in an Excel file in MBC).

LO18-1, 3

($ millions)	2022	2021	2020	2019	2018	2017
Sales.............	$5,856.7	$6,420.4	$ 5,465.4	$4,720.2	$4,579.6	$5,209.8
Cost of goods sold.......	1,911.8	1,927.5	1,718.9	1,807.8	1,850.7	2,033.7
Gross profit............	$3,944.9	$ 4,492.9	$ 3,746.5	$2,912.4	$2,728.9	$3,176.1
Merchandising inventory...	$ 676.8	$ 552.1	$ 395.6	$ 446.1	$ 443.4	$ 433.3
Average inventory........	614.5	473.9	420.9	444.8	438.4	410.5
Total assets.............	9,295.9	10,037.8	10,818.4	8,855.6	5,263.0	5,290.0

    a. Calculate inventory as a percentage of total assets and inventory turnover for each year presented.
    b. Calculate GMROI and the gross profit ratio for each of the years presented.
    c. What caused the change in the inventory turnover ratio in 2022 and how did it relate to a change in just-in-time trends? *Hint*: See the "Working Capital Requirements: Seasonality" section in Item 1 of the Hasbro Inc. December 25, 2022 10K, which can be found at https://investor.hasbro.com.

E18-44. Backflush costing Consider the following data pertaining to March for a firm that has adopted JIT.

LO18-4

Production	8,000 units
Sales ($20 per unit)	7,900 units
Standard production costs	
Direct material	$4
Conversion costs	8

Assume that there were no cost or usage variances for March, and the quantity of material used equaled the quantity purchased. All material is purchased on account, and all units started were completed.

a. Assuming that the company uses a traditional costing system, record the journal entries to recognize the following:
   1. purchase of material
   2. incurrence of conversion costs
   3. completion of the month's production
   4. sale of the month's production
b. Assuming that the company initially charges all costs to Cost of Goods Sold and then uses backflush costing to assign costs to inventories at the end of the period, record the journal entries to recognize the following:
   1. incurrence of conversion costs
   2. completion of production
   3. backflushing of costs to inventories

LO18-4

E18-45. Backflush costing Durham Denim uses backflush costing to account for production costs of its one-size-fits-all ponchos. During August, the firm produced 150,000 ponchos and sold 149,000. The standard cost for each poncho is:

Direct material	$2
Conversion costs	4
Total cost	$6

The firm had no inventory on August 1. The following events took place in August:

- Purchased $302,000 of direct material
- Incurred $608,000 of conversion costs
- Applied $600,000 of conversion costs to Raw and In-Process Inventory
- Finished 150,000 ponchos
- Sold 149,000 ponchos for $10 each

a. Prepare journal entries using backflush costing using the method shown in Demo 18-4. Include the entry to close underapplied or overapplied overhead (assumed to be immaterial) to cost of goods sold.
b. Post the amounts in *a* to T-accounts.
c. Calculate any inventory account balances at month-end.

LO18-5

E18-46. Theory of constraints Best Furniture Inc. produces chairs in a three-department operation: Cutting, Assembly, and Finishing. Units from Department 1 (which completes a maximum of 850 items in a day) are transferred to Department 2 (which completes a maximum of 780 items in a day) and then to Department 3 (which completes a maximum of 900 items per day). For simplicity, assume a continual flow of production from one department to the next with no lag time (i.e., in one day of production, all of Department 1's production can pass through all three departments if capacity allows it to).

Department 1 produced the following units: first day: 790 units, second day: 840 units, third day: 850 units, fourth day: 800 units, and fifth day: 825 units.

a. Which department is the bottleneck in the manufacturing process?
b. How much inventory is on hand in the bottleneck operation at the end of five days?
c. How many units were finished after five days?
d. How does your answer change to parts *b* and *c* if Department 2 maximum production increases to 800 items per day?

LO18-5

E18-47. Production constraints Xcaliber manufactures high-end flatware. One of the crucial processes in flatware production is polishing. The company normally operates three polishing machines to maintain pace with the upstream and downstream production operations. However, one of the polishing machines broke yesterday, and management has been informed that the machine will not be back in operation until repairs are completed in three weeks. Two machines cannot keep pace with the volume of product flowing to the polishing operation. You have been hired as a consultant to improve the throughput of the polishing operation. Discuss the tactics you would recommend Xcaliber to employ for handling the capacity limitation.

Chapter 18 Inventory and Production Management   18-35

E18-48. **Production constraints** Promotional Products produces commercial banner flags in a two-department operation: Department 1 is labor intensive and Department 2 is automated. The average output of Department 1 is 45 units per hour. Units from Department 1 are transferred to Department 2 to be completed by a robot. The robot can finish a maximum of 45 units per hour. The company needs to complete 180 units this afternoon for an order that has been backlogged for four months. The production manager has informed the people in Department 1 that they are to work on nothing else except this order from 1:00 P.M. until 5:00 P.M. The supervisor in Department 2 has scheduled the same times for the robot to work on the order. Department 1's activity for each hour of the afternoon is as follows:

LO18-5

Time	1:00–2:00 P.M.	2:00–3:00 P.M.	3:00–4:00 P.M.	4:00–4:58 P.M.
Production	40 units	44 units	50 units	46 units

Each unit moves directly from Department 1 to Department 2 with no lag time. Did Promotional Products complete the 180 units by 5:00 P.M.? If not, explain and provide detailed computations.

Problems

P18-49. **Inventory cost management; ethics** Restaurant Brands International (RBI), which includes the fast food chain Burger King, included a goal in its 2022 sustainability report of 100% cage-free eggs globally.

LO18-1

  a. Discuss how the implementation of RBI's goal at its supplier locations might affect the prices Burger King pays for its products.
  b. Evaluate the ethics of the supplier policy from the point of view of a Burger King patron, assuming that the new supplier policy will likely increase prices charged for food products.
  c. Evaluate the ethics of the policy from the point of view of a supplier who will now face higher costs in providing Burger King with products.

P18-50. **Inventory cost management; writing** IMeg manufactures various electronic assemblies that are sold primarily to computer manufacturers. IMeg's reputation has been built on quality, timely delivery, and products that are consistently on the cutting edge of technology. IMeg's typical product has a short life; products are in development for about a year and in the growth stage, with sometimes spectacular growth, for about a year. Each product then experiences a rapid decline in sales as new products become available.

LO18-1, 2

IMeg's competitive strategy requires a reliable stream of new products to be developed each year, which is the only way that the company can overcome the threat of product obsolescence. IMeg's products go through the first half of the product life cycle similar to products in other industries; however, differences occur in the second half of the products' life cycles. IMeg's products never reach the mature product or declining product stage. Near the end of the growth stage, products just "die" as new ones are introduced.

  a. In the competitive market facing IMeg, what would be key considerations in production and inventory control?
  b. How would the threat of immediate product obsolescence affect IMeg's practices in purchasing product components and materials?
  c. How would the threat of product obsolescence affect the inventory carrying costs for a typical product produced by IMeg?

P18-51. **Identification of inventory costs** Tyler Tubing's management has been evaluating company policies with respect to control of costs of corrugated metal, one of the firm's major component materials. The firm's controller has gathered the following financial data, which may be pertinent to controlling costs associated with the metal tubing:

LO18-1

Ordering Costs	
Annual salary of purchasing department manager.	$61,500.00
Depreciation of equipment in purchasing department	$42,300.00
Cost per order for purchasing department supplies	$0.90
Typical communication expense per order placed	$6.06
Monthly expense for heat and light in purchasing department	$700.00

© Cambridge Business Publishers

Carrying Costs	
Annual depreciation on materials storage building........................	$30,000.00
Annual inventory insurance premium (per dollar of inventory value)...........	$0.15
Annual property tax on materials storage building.......................	$7,500.00
Obsolescence cost per dollar of average annual inventory..................	$0.16
Annual salary of security officer assigned to the materials storage building......	$38,000.00

    a. Which of the ordering costs should Tyler Tubing's controller consider in performing short-run decision analysis? Explain.

    b. Which of the carrying costs should Tyler Tubing's controller consider in performing short-run decision analysis? Explain.

LO18-2

P18-52. Push vs. pull systems Assume that you are a management consultant who advises manufacturing firms regarding production technologies. One of the hot issues you often discuss with management is whether a pull system or a push system is superior in a particular situation. Consider the following circumstances and discuss whether you would recommend a push system or a pull system in each particular case:

    a. The firm manufactures two consumer products; 75 percent of annual sales are made during the year-end holiday sales cycle.

    b. The firm manufactures a variety of goods for the petroleum industry; most products are sold in low volumes and have a high unit cost.

    c. The firm manufactures products subject to rapid obsolescence and that have relatively short product life cycles.

    d. The firm manufactures products that have a limited shelf life.

    e. The firm manufactures a limited line of products for which there is predictable, but seasonal, demand and the products have long life cycles.

LO18-1, 2

P18-53. Push vs. pull systems; writing **Electronics Inc.** makes high-quality speakers for a variety of applications. Electronics Inc. is a St. Louis-based company but has significant manufacturing operations in China. When manufacturing operations were moved to China, the company's president was a strong proponent of just-in-time inventory management. Although the company maintained significant orders of component parts, finished goods were produced only to satisfy customer orders. Accordingly, work in process and finished goods inventories were small. However, moving production offshore significantly increased the complexity of the firm's logistics. Unexpected changes in product mix and product demand caused the firm's backlog of orders to rise significantly. In response, the company discontinued the use of JIT inventory management and instead, increased the stock of inventory on hand.

    Why does globalization of a firm's production operations increase the challenges in controlling inventories using the JIT philosophy (pull system)?

LO18-2

P18-54. EOQ Diane Delbert operates a health food bakery that uses a special type of ground flour in one of its high-margin products. The bakery operates 365 days a year. Delbert finds that she seems to order either too much or too little special flour and asks for your help. After some discussion, you find that she has no idea of when or how much to order. An examination of her records and answers to further questions reveals the following information:

Annual usage of special flour..	7,000 pounds
Average number of days delay between initiating and receiving an order......	12
Estimated cost per order..	$32.00
Estimated annual cost of carrying a pound of special flour in inventory........	$0.50

    a. Calculate the economic order quantity for flour. (Round to the nearest whole pound.)

    b. Assume that Delbert desires a safety stock cushion of seven days' usage. Calculate the appropriate order point. (Round the order point to the nearest whole pound.)

LO18-2

P18-55. EPR Gale's Garden grows and sells a variety of indoor and outdoor plants and garden vegetables. One of the firm's more popular vegetables is a red onion, which has an annual sales quantity of approximately 30,000 pounds. Two of the major inputs in the growing of onions are seeds and fertilizer. Due to the poor germination rate, two seeds must be purchased for each onion plant grown (a mature onion plant provides 0.5 pound of onion). Also, 0.25 pound of fertilizer is required for each pound of onion produced. The following information summarizes costs for onions, seeds, and fertilizer. Carrying costs for onions are expressed per pound of onion; carrying costs for seeds are

Chapter 18 Inventory and Production Management

expressed per seed; and for fertilizer, carrying costs are expressed per pound of fertilizer. To plant onions, the company incurs a cost of $50 to set up the planter and the fertilizing equipment.

	Onions	Seeds	Fertilizer
Carrying cost	$ 0.25	$0.01	$0.05
Ordering cost	—	$4.25	$8.80
Setup cost	$50.00	—	—

a. What is the economic production run for onions? (Round to the nearest whole pound.)
b. How many production runs will Gale's Garden make for onions annually? (Round to the nearest whole production run.)
c. What are the economic order quantities for seeds and fertilizer? (Round to the nearest whole seed or whole pound.)
d. How many orders will be placed for seeds? For fertilizer? (Round to the nearest whole order.)
e. What is the total annual cost of ordering, carrying, and setting up for onion production?
f. How is the planting of onions similar to and different from a typical factory production run?
g. Are there any inconsistencies in your answers to a–c that need to be addressed? Explain.

P18-56. JIT features Indicate by letter which of the three categories apply to the following features of just-in-time systems. Use as many letters as appropriate.

LO18-3

D = desired immediate result of using JIT
U = ultimate goal of JIT
T = technique associated with JIT

a. Reducing setup time
b. Reducing total cost of producing and carrying inventory
c. Using focused factory arrangements
d. Designing products to minimize design changes after production starts
e. Monitoring quality on a continuous basis
f. Using manufacturing cells
g. Minimizing inventory stored
h. Measuring variances caused by an engineering change order
i. Using automation processes
j. Pulling purchases and production through the system based on sales demand

P18-57. JIT journal entries Cosmo Industries recorded the following transactions for its first month of operations:

LO18-4

(1) Direct Material Inventory.................................... 24,000
    Accounts Payable....................................... 24,000
    To record purchase of direct material

(2) Work in Process Inventory................................... 24,000
    Direct Material Inventory................................ 24,000
    To record distribution of material to production

(3) Conversion Cost Control..................................... 40,000
    Various accounts....................................... 40,000
    To record incurrence of conversion costs

(4) Work in Process Inventory................................... 40,000
    Conversion Cost Control................................ 40,000
    To assign conversion cost to WIP

(5) Finished Goods Inventory.................................... 64,000
    Work in Process Inventory.............................. 64,000
    To record completion of products

(6) Accounts Receivable... 116,000
    Sales... 116,000
    To record sale of products

    Cost of Goods Sold... 62,000
    Finished Goods Inventory.............................. 62,000
    To record cost of goods sold

Because Cosmo employs JIT, the company's CEO has asked how the accounting system could be simplified.

a. Prepare the journal entries, assuming that no transactions are recognized until goods are completed.
b. Prepare the journal entries, assuming that goods are shipped to customers as soon as they are completed and that no journal entries are recorded until goods are completed.
c. Prepare the journal entries, assuming that sale of product is the trigger point for journal entries.
d. Prepare the journal entries, assuming that sale of product is the trigger point for journal entries and that the firm uses backflush costing.

LO18-3, 4 **P18-58. JIT journal entries; advanced** Wisconsin Wire (WW) has implemented a just-in-time inventory system for the production of its insulated wire. Inventories of raw material and work in process are so small that WW uses a Raw and In-Process account. In addition, almost all labor operations are automated, and WW has chosen to cost products using standards for direct material and conversion costs. The following production standards are applicable at the beginning of the year for one roll of insulated wire:

Direct material (100 yards × $2).............	$200
Conversion (4 machine hours × $35).........	140
Total cost............................	$340

The conversion cost of $35 per machine hour was estimated on the basis of 500,000 machine hours for the year and $17,500,000 of conversion costs. The following activities took place during the year:

1. Raw material purchased and placed into production totaled 12,452,000 yards. All except 8,000 yards were purchased at the standard price of $2.00 per yard. The other 8,000 yards were purchased at a cost of $2.06 per yard; the higher price was due to the placement of a rush order. The order was approved in advance by management. All purchases are on account.
2. From January 1 to February 28, WW manufactured 20,800 rolls of insulated wire. Conversion costs incurred to date totaled $3,000,000. Of this amount, $600,000 was for depreciation, $2,200,000 was paid in cash, and $200,000 was on account.
3. Conversion costs are applied to the Raw and In-Process account from January 1 to February 28 on the basis of the annual standard.
4. The Engineering Department issued a change order (ECO) to the operations flow document effective March 1. The change decreased the machine time to manufacture one roll of wire by five minutes per roll. However, the standard raised the amount of direct material to 100.4 yards per roll. The Accounting Department requires that the annual standard be continued for costing the Raw and In-Process Inventory for the remainder of the year. The effects of ECOs should be shown in two accounts: Material Quantity ECO Variance and Machine Hours ECO Variance.
5. Total production for the remainder of the year was 103,200 rolls of wire. Total conversion costs for the remaining 10 months of the year were $14,442,000. Of this amount, $4,000,000 was depreciation, $9,325,000 was paid in cash, and $1,117,000 was on account.
6. The standard amount of conversion cost is applied to the Raw and In-Process Inventory for the remainder of the year.

Note: Some of the journal entries for the following items are not explicitly covered in the chapter. This problem challenges students regarding the accounting effects of the implementation of a JIT system.

a. Prepare entries for items 1, 2, 3, 5, and 6.
b. Determine the increase in material cost due to the ECO related to direct material.
c. Prepare a journal entry to adjust the Raw and In-Process Inventory account for the ECO cost found in b.
d. Determine the reduction in conversion cost due to the ECO related to machine time.
e. Prepare a journal entry to reclassify the actual conversion costs by the savings found in d.
f. Making the entry in e raises conversion costs to what they would have been if the ECO related to machine time had not been made. Are conversion costs under- or overapplied and by what amount?
g. Assume that the reduction in machine time could not have been made without the corresponding increase in material usage. Is the net effect of these ECOs cost beneficial? Why?

Review Solutions

Review 18-1

a. $375 + $50 = $ 425
b. $15 + $10 = $25
c. ($425 × 0.18) + $50 + $5 + $100 = $ 231.50
d. Opportunity costs are not tracked in the accounting system for reporting because they do not represent actual cost outlays. An opportunity cost is the trade-off of not investing in inventory. Even though this is an important aspect of controlling and managing inventory, it is not practical or even feasible for the costs to be included in the accounting system.

Review 18-2

Part 1:
EOQ = 632 pounds = $\sqrt{\dfrac{(2 \times 5{,}000 \times \$30)}{\$0.75}}$

Part 2:
a. EPR = 1,680 units = $\sqrt{\dfrac{(2 \times 10{,}080 \times \$840)}{\$6}}$

b. Using EPR would be beneficial in a number of situations such as the following: demand is erratic and unpredictable, suppliers are unreliable and partnerships are not feasible, production lead times are lengthy (e.g., shipped on barges internationally); or there is a risk of a supply chain disruption (e.g., pandemic).

Review 18-3

a. [($5.80 × 17,000) + ($6.40 × 24,000)] − [($5.80 × 3 × 9,000) + ($6.40 × 2 × 9,000)] = $19,600 F
b. [($5.80 × 3 × 9,000) + ($6.40 × 2 × 9,000)] − [($5.80 × 2 × 9,000) + ($6.40 × 3 × 9,000)] = $5,400 F
c. Computing the material quantity variance based on the original standard, the variance was favorable ($19,600). However, the engineering change order resulted in an incremental favorable variance of $5,400. This resulted because less of the more expensive Material B was used and replaced with Material A as a result of the engineering change order.

Review 18-4

a.

	Debit	Credit
Raw and In-Process Inventory	192,000	
Accounts Payable		192,000
Conversion Cost Control	354,000	
Various accounts		354,000
Raw and In-Process Inventory	360,000	
Conversion Cost Control		360,000
Finished Goods Inventory	540,000	
Raw and In-Process Inventory		540,000
Accounts Receivable	800,000	
Sales		800,000
Cost of Goods Sold	480,000	
Finished Goods Inventory		480,000
Conversion Cost Control	6,000	
Cost of Goods Sold		6,000

b. Raw and In-Process Inventory balance: $12,000 = $192,000 + $360,000 − $540,000
Finished Goods Inventory balance: $60,000 = $540,000 − $480,000
Cost of Goods Sold balance: $474,000 = $480,000 − $6,000

c.
Raw and In-Process Inventory	12,000	
Finished Goods	60,000	
Costs of Goods Sold	480,000	
Accounts Payable		192,000
Conversion Cost Control		360,000

d. Under JIT costing systems, detailed variance entries are not required for management decision-making purposes because they should be irrelevant if the system is working properly. Variances report historical information, but under JIT, variance information is tracked in real time, such as through constantly monitored statistical control charts. Thus, problems are recognized immediately and course correction is immediate. Thus, only minimal variances should result from the process.

Review 18-5

a. Department 2 is the bottleneck in the system as this department cannot process as quickly as Department 1, causing unfinished inventory to be held in Department 2.

b. 19 units are on hand in Department 2 after four hours (see table below).

	Maximum Hourly Production	First Hour	Second Hour	Third Hour	Fourth Hour
Dept. 1 production		48	60	55	49
Dept. 2 production	48	0	48	48	48
Dept. 2 unfinished units		0	0	12	19
Dept. 3 production	55	0	0	48	48
Dept. 3 unfinished units		0	0	0	0

c. Management can focus on Department 2, which is the source of the bottleneck. Because Department 2 is fully automated, it seems that the company could benefit by making updates to the machine to increase its throughput, re-purposing a different machine to be used in Department 2, or purchasing a new machine with more capacity. The company may also consider outsourcing the work in Department 2 if it is cost effective to do so.

Data Visualization Solutions

(See page 18-21.)

a. Machine 2 is a bottleneck because capacity is at 75,000 but Machine 1 has a capacity of 90,000. However, Machine 1 is a bottleneck for Machine 3 because it can't produce enough units to fully utilize Machine 3.

b. Machine 2 and Machine 3 will process at the maximum, 75,000 units an hour with Machine 2 processing its maximum, which flows into Machine 3.

c. After 8 hours, 81,000 units will be unfinished at Machine 2, but no units will be unfinished at Machine 3 (see table).

	Maximum Hourly Production (units)	1 Hour	2 Hour	3 Hour	4 Hour	5 Hour	6 Hour	7 Hour	8 Hour
Machine 1 production		90,000	85,000	80,000	83,000	90,000	85,000	80,000	88,000
Machine 2 production	75,000	75,000	75,000	75,000	75,000	75,000	75,000	75,000	75,000
Machine 2 unfinished units		15,000	25,000	30,000	38,000	53,000	63,000	68,000	81,000
Machine 3 production	90,000	75,000	75,000	75,000	75,000	75,000	75,000	75,000	75,000
Machine 3 unfinished units		0	0	0	0	0	0	0	0

Chapter 19
Capital Budgeting

Road Map

LO	Learning Objective | Topics	Page	eLecture	Demo	Review	Assignments
19–1	**How is payback period computed, and what does it measure?** Capital Assets :: Capital Budgeting :: Cash Flows :: Financing Decision :: Investment Decision :: Time Line :: Payback Period :: Unequal Cash Flows :: Equal Cash Flows :: Annuity	19-2	e19–1	D19-1A D19-1B D19-1C	Rev 19-1	MC19-17, MC19-18, E19-27, E19-28, E19-29, E19-30, E19-31, E19-32, E19-33, E19-48, E19-54, E19-55, P19-56, P19-57, P19-58, P19-59, P19-61, P19-62, P19-64, P19-70, P19-71
19–2	**How are the net present value, profitability index, and internal rate of return of a project computed, and what do they measure?** Time Value of Money :: Discounting :: Discount Rate :: Cost of Capital (COC) :: Net Present Value (NPV) :: Profitability Index (PI) :: Internal Rate of Return (IRR) :: Hurdle Rate :: Qualitative Considerations	19-5	e19–2	D19-2A D19-2B D19-2C	Rev 19-2	MC19-19, MC19-20, E19-33, E19-34, E19-35, E19-36, E19-37, E19-38, E19-39, E19-40, E19-41, E19-47, E19-49, P19-58, P19-59, P19-60, P19-61, P19-62, P19-64, P19-69, P19-70, P19-71
19–3	**How do taxation and depreciation affect project cash flows?** Depreciation :: Tax Shield :: Tax Benefit :: After-Tax Net Present Value	19-12	e19–3	D19-3	Rev 19-3	MC19-21, E19-42, E19-44, P19-63, P19-64, P19-65, P19-66, P19-67
19–4	**How do managers evaluate and rank investment projects, considering the assumptions and limitations of the different evaluation methods?** Cost-Benefit Analysis :: Screening Decision :: Preference Decision :: Mutually Exclusive Projects :: Independent Projects :: Mutually Inclusive Projects :: Reinvestment Assumptions	19-15	e19–4	D19-4	Rev 19-4	MC19-22, E19-43, E19-45, E19-46, E19-47, P19-65, P19-66
19–5	**How is risk considered in capital budgeting analyses?** Risk :: Judgmental Method :: Risk-Adjusted Discount Rate Method :: Sensitivity Analysis :: Discount Rate :: Annual Net Cash Flows :: Project Life	19-20	e19–5	D19-5A D19-5B D19-5C D19-5D	Rev 19-5	MC19-23, E19-38, E19-48, E19-49, P19-60, P19-63, 19-65, DA19-1, DA19-2
19–6	**How and why should management conduct a postinvestment audit of a capital project?** Postinvestment Audit :: Postinvestment Net Present Value	19-24	e19–6	D19-6	Rev 19-6	MC19-24, E19-50, P19-68, P19-69
19–7	**(Appendix 19A) How are present values calculated?** Future Value :: Simple Interest :: Compound Interest :: Compounding Period :: Present Value of a Single Cash Flow :: Present Value of an Annuity :: Ordinary Annuity :: Annuity Due	19-26	e19–7	D19-7A D19-7B	Rev 19-7	MC19-25, E19-51, E19-52, E19-53
19–8	**(Appendix 19B) What are the advantages and disadvantages of the accounting rate of return method?** Accounting Rate of Return :: Accrual Accounting	19-28	e19–8	D19-8	Rev 19-8	MC19-26, E19-45, E19-46, E19-54, E19-55, P19-70, P19-71

INTRODUCTION

Choosing the assets in which an organization will invest is one of the most important business decisions a manager will make. Organizations invest in working capital assets, such as merchandise inventory, supplies, and raw material. Organizations must also invest in **capital assets**, which are long-term assets used to generate future revenues or cost savings or to provide distribution, service, or production capacity. A capital asset can be a tangible fixed asset (such as a piece of machinery or a building), a partial or complete acquisition of another firm, or an intangible asset (such as a finance lease or drug patent).

Financial managers, assisted by cost accountants, are responsible for analyzing alternative investment opportunities through the process of capital budgeting. **Capital budgeting** involves evaluating and ranking alternative future investments to effectively and efficiently allocate limited capital. The process includes planning for and preparing the capital budget as well as reviewing past investments to assess the success of past decisions and to enhance future decisions. Planned annual expenditures for capital projects for the near term (five years or less) and summary information for the long term (six to ten years) are shown in the capital budget, which is a key instrument in implementing organizational strategies.

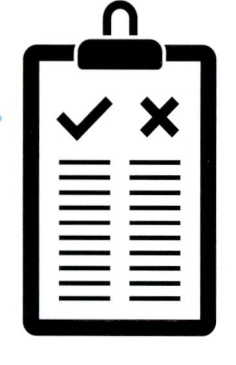

Capital budgeting involves comparing and evaluating alternative projects. Managers and accountants apply quantitative and qualitative criteria to evaluate the feasibility of alternative projects. Although financial criteria are used to judge virtually all projects, firms now also use nonfinancial criteria to critically assess activities that have benefits that are difficult to quantify. For example, high-technology and R&D investments as well as sustainability projects are often difficult to evaluate using only financial criteria.

Providing information about the estimated financial returns of potential capital projects is an important task of cost accountants. This chapter discusses techniques used in evaluating the expected financial costs and benefits of proposed capital projects. Several of these techniques are based on an analysis of the amounts and timing of investment cash flows.

PAYBACK PERIOD

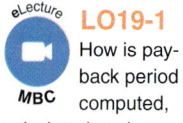

LO19-1 How is payback period computed, and what does it measure?

All investments undertaken by organizations are expected to earn some type of return. For example, investments in bonds are expected to earn interest, and investments in other companies are expected to earn dividends. In general, such interest and dividends are cash returns. Similarly, investments in capital assets are evaluated from a financial perspective based on their cash costs and cash benefits. Accordingly, aside from the effects on cash tax flows, accounting accruals are typically not considered in capital budget analysis. Accrual accounting recognizes revenues when performance obligations are satisfied rather than when cash is received and recognizes expenses when they are incurred rather than when cash is paid. *Using cash flow information puts all investment returns on an equivalent basis.*

Identifying Cash Flows

Capital budgeting investment decisions can be based on a variety of quantitative techniques, including the following.

Payback Period	Net Present Value	Profitability Index	Internal Rate of Return
LO1	LO2	LO2	LO2

All of these methods[1] focus on **cash flows** (cash receipts or disbursements).

Cash Receipts from	Cash Disbursements for
• Project revenues, earned and collected	• Asset acquisition
• Savings in operating costs	• Cash invested in working capital
• Sale of asset at end of useful life	• Costs related to project

---

[1] One method that focuses on accrual accounting instead of cash flows is the annual rate of return, covered in LO8.

Chapter 19 Capital Budgeting

In evaluating capital projects, a distinction is made between operating cash flows and financing cash flows. Interest expense is a cash outflow associated with debt financing and is not part of the project selection process. Project funding is a financing, not an investment, decision.

- A **financing decision** involves choices regarding the method of raising capital to fund an investment. Financing is based on an entity's ability to issue and service debt and equity securities.
- On the other hand, an **investment decision** is a judgment about which assets to acquire to accomplish an entity's mission.

Cash flows generated by the two types of decisions should not be combined. Company management must justify an asset's acquisition and use prior to justifying the method of financing that asset.

Including financing receipts and disbursements with other project cash flows confuses the evaluation of a project's profitability because financing costs relate to all of an entity's projects rather than to a specific project. Assignment of financing costs to a specific project is often arbitrary, which causes problems in comparing projects that are acquired with different financing sources. In addition, including financing effects in an investment decision creates a problem in assigning responsibility. Divisional managers, or top managers with input from divisional managers, make investment decisions. An organization's treasurer in conjunction with top management typically makes financing decisions.

Cash flows from a capital project are received and paid at different points in time over the project's life. Some cash flows occur at the beginning of a period, some during the period, and others at the end. To simplify capital budgeting analysis, most analysts assume that all cash flows occur at a specific, single point in time—typically, either at the beginning or end of the time period in which they actually occur. A **time line** visually illustrates the points in time when projected cash flows are received or paid, making it a helpful tool for analyzing cash flows of a capital investment proposal. On a time line, cash inflows are shown as positive amounts and cash outflows are shown as negative amounts.

Creating a Cash Flow Time Line — LO19-1 DEMO 19-1A

Assume that various capital projects are being considered by Family One Stop, a retail chain selling consumer goods in 55 locations throughout the Midwest. One investment being considered by the firm is the acquisition of photovoltaic power technology to light all parking lots owned by the chain. In addition to long-term cost savings, this investment would reduce the company's carbon footprint.

The expected cost to purchase and install the technology as well as the operating cost savings over the investment's seven-year useful life appear in **Exhibit 19.1**.

Exhibit 19.1 ■ Family One Stop's Photovoltaic Technology Decision Information

Cash Outflows	
Year 0	$13,500,000
Year 1	500,000
Year 2	300,000

Cash Inflows	
Electricity cost savings:	
Year 1	$2,700,000
Year 2	2,900,000
Year 3	3,200,000
Year 4	3,900,000
Year 5	4,200,000
Year 6	2,100,000
Year 7	1,000,000

◆ Using the information in Exhibit 19.1, how does a time line illustrate net cash flows over the seven-year period?

The following time line represents the cash flows associated with Family One Stop's potential photovoltaic technology investment (in thousands).

End of period	0	1	2	3	4	5	6	7
Inflows	$ 0	$2,700	$2,900	$3,200	$3,900	$4,200	$2,100	$1,000
Outflows	(13,500)	(500)	(300)	(0)	(0)	(0)	(0)	(0)
Net cash flow	$(13,500)	$2,200	$2,600	$3,200	$3,900	$4,200	$2,100	$1,000

Considering the initial investment, the project generates a net negative cash flow in the first year and net positive cash flows thereafter. On a time line, the date of initial investment represents time point 0, which marks the start of the cash flows pertaining to the project. Each year after the initial investment is represented as a full time period; periods serve only to separate the timing of cash flows. Nothing is presumed to happen *during* a period. Thus, for example, cash inflows each year from product sales are shown as occurring at the end of, rather than during, the time period. A less conservative assumption would show the cash flows occurring at the beginning of, or middle of, the period.

Calculating the Payback Period

Information on the timing of net cash flows is an input to a simple and often-used capital budgeting technique called **payback period**. This method measures the time required for a project's cash inflows to equal the original investment. A project's payback is complete when the organization has recouped its investment.

In one sense, payback period measures a dimension of project risk by focusing on the timing of cash flows. The assumption is that the longer it takes to recover the initial investment, the greater is the project's risk, because cash flows in the more distant future are more uncertain than relatively near-term cash flows. Another reason for concern about long payback periods relates to capital reinvestment. The faster that capital is returned from an investment, the more rapidly the capital can be invested in other projects.

Unequal Cash Flows Payback period for a project having unequal cash inflows is determined by accumulating cash flows until the original investment is recovered.

Equal Cash Flows When equal periodic cash flows are generated from a project (an **annuity**), the payback period is determined as follows.

$$\text{Payback period} = \text{Investment} \div \text{Annuity amount}$$

DEMO 19-1B LO19-1 Calculating Payback Period with Unequal Cash Flows

◆ Using the information shown in Exhibit 19.1 and the time line presented in Demo 19-1A, what is the photovoltaic technology investment payback period calculated using a yearly cumulative total of inflows?

Year	Annual Net Cash Flow	Cumulative Total
0	$(13,500)	$(13,500)
1	2,200	(11,300)
2	2,600	(8,700)
3	3,200	(5,500)
4	3,900	(1,600)
5	4,200	2,600
6	2,100	4,700
7	1,000	5,700

Payback is complete between Year 4 and Year 5

Note: Amounts in thousands

At the end of the fourth year, all but $1,600,000 of the initial $13,500,000 investment has been recovered. The $4,200,000 inflow in the fifth year is assumed to occur evenly throughout the year.

Full years (Year 1 – Year 4)	= 4.00 years
Partial Year 5 ($1,600,000/$4,200,000)	= 0.38 years
Total payback period	4.38 years

Chapter 19 Capital Budgeting

Therefore, the payback period for this project is 4.38 years (equivalent to 4 years and 4.6 months).

Calculating Payback Period with Equal Cash Flows — LO19-1 DEMO 19-1C

Assume that another technology investment being considered by Family One Stop requires an initial investment of $200,000 and is expected to generate equal annual cash flows of $32,000 in each of the next ten years.

◆ **What is the payback on the investment?**

The payback period would equal 6.25 years (equivalent to 6 years and 3 months).

$$\text{Payback period} = \$200{,}000 \div \$32{,}000 = 6.25 \text{ years}$$

Family One Stop's management typically sets a maximum acceptable payback period as one of the financial evaluation criteria. If the company has set five years as the longest acceptable payback period, the photovoltaic technology investment would be considered acceptable, but the second technology investment project would be considered unacceptable.

Disadvantages of Payback Period Most companies use payback period in conjunction with other quantitative criteria. After being found acceptable in terms of payback period, a project is then evaluated using other capital budgeting criteria. A second evaluation criterion is usually necessary because the payback period method ignores three things:

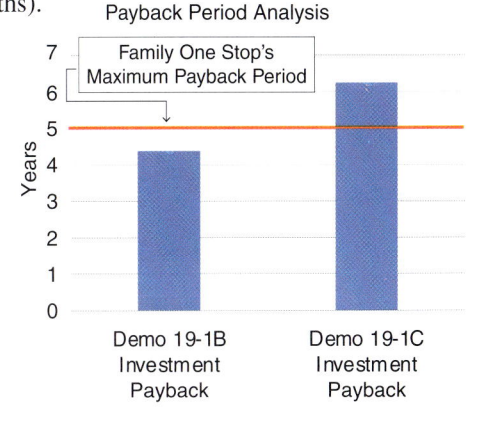

- cash inflows occurring after the payback period has been reached,
- the company's desired rate of return, and
- the time value of money.

These issues are considered in the decision process using discounted cash flow techniques in the next section.

Payback Period Analysis (chart showing Family One Stop's Maximum Payback Period at 5 years; Demo 19-1B Investment Payback approximately 4.4 years; Demo 19-1C Investment Payback approximately 6.25 years)

Payback Period — LO19-1 REVIEW 19-1

Keenlen Inc. is considering the purchase of new manufacturing equipment requiring an initial $580,000 investment and having an expected eight-year useful life. At the end of its life, the equipment would have no salvage value. By installing the new equipment, the firm's annual labor and quality costs would decline by $130,000.

a. Compute the payback period for this equipment.

b. Assume instead that the annual cost savings would vary according to the following schedule:

Years	Annual Cost Savings	Years	Annual Cost Savings
1.....	$100,000	5.....	160,000
2.....	130,000	6.....	120,000
3.....	150,000	7.....	120,000
4.....	160,000	8.....	100,000

Compute the payback period under the revised circumstances.

c. **Critical Thinking:** How can management use the information in parts *a* and *b* in decision making?

More practice: MC19-18, E19-31, E19-32
Solution on p. 19-49.

DISCOUNTED CASH FLOW METHODS

LO19-2 How are the net present value, profitability index, and the internal rate of return of a project computed, and what do they measure?

A time value is associated with money because interest is paid or received on money.[2] For example, $1 received today has more value than $1 received one year from today because money received today can be invested to generate a return that will cause it to accumulate to more than $1 over time.

---

[2] The time value of money and present value computations are covered in Appendix 19A of this chapter. These concepts are essential to understanding the rest of this chapter; be certain they are clear before continuing.

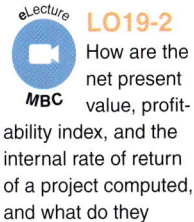

This effect is referred to as the **time value of money**. Discounted cash flow techniques are used in most capital budgeting situations to account for the effect of the time value of money.

Discounting means reducing future cash flows by removing the portion of the future values representing interest. This "imputed" amount of interest is based on two considerations:

- the length of time until the cash flow is received or paid, and
- the rate of interest assumed.

After discounting, all future values associated with a project are stated in a common base of current dollars, known as **present values (PVs)**. Cash receipts and disbursements occurring at the beginning (time 0) of a project are already stated in their present values and are not discounted.

Capital project evaluations require estimates of related cash flows. It is extremely important, therefore, to have the best possible estimates of all potential cash inflows and outflows, and the rate of return on capital required by the company. This rate of return, called the **discount rate**, is used to determine the imputed interest portion of future cash flows. The discount rate should equal or exceed the company's **cost of capital (COC)**, which is the weighted average cost of the various sources (debt and equity) of funds that compose a firm's financial structure.[3] For example, if a company has a COC of 10 percent, then each year an amount equal to 10 percent of investment capital is required to finance the company. To determine whether a capital project is a worthwhile investment, this company should generally use a minimum rate of 10 percent to discount its projects' future cash flows.

A distinction must be made between cash flows representing a return *of* capital and those representing a return *on* capital. A **return *of* capital** is the recovery of the original investment (or the return of principal), whereas a **return *on* capital** is income and equals the discount rate multiplied by the investment amount. For example, $1.00 invested in a project that yields a 10 percent rate of return will grow to a sum of $1.10 in one year. Of the $1.10, $1.00 represents the return *of* capital and $0.10 represents the return *on* capital. The return *on* capital is computed for each period of the investment life. For a company to benefit from making an investment, a project must produce cash inflows that exceed the investment made and the cost of capital. To determine whether a project meets a company's desired rate of return, one of several discounted cash flow methods can be used.

Discounted Cash Flow Methods		
Net Present Value	Profitability Index	Internal Rate of Return

Each of these methods is defined and illustrated in the following sections.

Net Present Value Method

The **net present value method** determines whether a project's rate of return is equal to, higher than, or lower than the desired rate of return. All cash flows from a project are discounted to their present values using the company's desired rate of return. Subtracting the total present value of all an investment project's cash outflows from the total present value of all cash inflows yields the project's **net present value (NPV)**.

DEMO 19-2A LO19-2   Calculating Net Present Value

◆ Referring to the cash flow data in Exhibit 19.1, what is the net present value of the investment assuming a 7 percent discount rate?

The net present value calculation is shown in **Exhibit 19.2**.

---

[3] All examples in this chapter use an assumed discount rate or cost of capital. The computations required to estimate a company's cost of capital are discussed in any basic finance text.

Exhibit 19.2 ■ NPV Calculation for Photovoltaic Technology

Discount Rate = 7%

Cash Flow	Time	a Amount	×	b Discount Factor	=	c Present Value
Initial investment	t_0	$(13,500,000)		1.0000		$(13,500,000)
Year 1 net cash flow	t_1	2,200,000		0.9346		2,056,120
Year 2 net cash flow	t_2	2,600,000		0.8734		2,271,840
Year 3 net cash flow	t_3	3,200,000		0.8163		2,612,160
Year 4 net cash flow	t_4	3,900,000		0.7629		2,975,310
Year 5 net cash flow	t_5	4,200,000		0.7130		2,994,600
Year 6 net cash flow	t_6	2,100,000		0.6663		1,399,230
Year 7 net cash flow	t_7	1,000,000		0.6228		622,800
Net present value						$ 1,432,060

Excel Function	Solution
=PV(RATE,NPER,PMT,FV)	PV
=PV(0.07,1,0,−2200000)	$ 2,056,075
=PV(0.07,2,0,−2600000)	2,270,941
=PV(0.07,3,0,−3200000)	2,612,153
=PV(0.07,4,0,−3900000)	2,975,291
=PV(0.07,5,0,−4200000)	2,994,542
=PV(0.07,6,0,−2100000)	1,399,319
=PV(0.07,7,0,−1000000)	622,750
Initial investment	(13,500,000)
NPV calculated in Excel	$ 1,431,071*

*Difference due to rounding of factors in Appendix A

The factors used to compute NPV are obtained from the present value tables provided in Appendix A on the book's website, rounded to four decimal places. Each period's cash flow is multiplied by a factor obtained from Table 1 (PV of $1) for 7 percent and the appropriate time period designated for the cash flow.

Similar results can be obtained using Excel, with differences due to rounding errors from use of rounded factors in present value tables. The formula to solve for the present value is preset in the present value function in Excel. The inputs to the function are called arguments (commonly referred to as variables) and are defined as follows. Each variable can also be solved for as a function.

Excel Argument	Description
RATE	Discount rate for each compounding period.
NPER	Number of compounding periods.
FV	Future value or the value at a future date that assumes an investment increased by interest accumulation.
PV	Present value or the value today of a future amount that is discounted to the present with interest discounting.
PMT	Fixed payment per period.

After entering values in Excel for each variable, the PV function will return the present value amount. Note that in Excel, if a negative amount is entered (representing a cash outflow), a positive amount will be returned (representing a cash inflow). The opposite is also true.

The net present value represents the net cash benefit (or, if negative, the net cash cost) of acquiring and using the proposed asset.

- If the NPV is zero, the project's actual rate of return is equal to the required rate of return.
- If the NPV is positive, the actual rate of return is more than the required rate of return.
- If the NPV is negative, the actual rate of return is less than the required rate of return.

Note that the exact rate of return is not indicated under the NPV method, but its relationship to the desired rate can be determined. If all estimates about the investment are correct, the photovoltaic technology being considered by Family One Stop has an NPV of $1,432,060 and will provide a rate of return of more than 7 percent.

If Family One Stop's management chose any rate other than 7 percent and used that rate in conjunction with the same facts, a different net present value would have resulted. For example, if the company set 9 percent as the discount rate, an NPV of $469,310 would have resulted for the project (see **Exhibit 19.3**, which gives the project's net present values at other selected discount rates). The computations for these values are made in a manner similar to those at 7 and 9 percent. (To confirm your understanding of the NPV method, you may want to prove these computations.)

Exhibit 19.3 ■ Alternative NPV Calculation for Photovoltaic Technology

Discount Rate = 9%

Cash Flow	Time	a Amount	×	b Discount Factor	=	c Present Value
Initial investment......	t_0	$(13,500,000)		1.0000		$(13,500,000)
Year 1 net cash flow ...	t_1	2,200,000		0.9174		2,018,280
Year 2 net cash flow ...	t_2	2,600,000		0.8417		2,188,420
Year 3 net cash flow ...	t_3	3,200,000		0.7722		2,471,040
Year 4 net cash flow ...	t_4	3,900,000		0.7084		2,762,760
Year 5 net cash flow ...	t_5	4,200,000		0.6499		2,729,580
Year 6 net cash flow ...	t_6	2,100,000		0.5963		1,252,230
Year 7 net cash flow ...	t_7	1,000,000		0.5470		547,000
Net present value ...						$ 469,310

Net present value with a 5 percent discount rate: $2,494,590
Net present value with an 8 percent discount rate: $938,060
Net present value with a 10 percent discount rate: $23,210

Excel Function	Solution
=PV(RATE,NPER,PMT,FV)	PV
=PV(0.09,1,0,−2200000)	$ 2,018,349
=PV(0.09,2,0,−2600000)	2,188,368
=PV(0.09,3,0,−3200000)	2,470,987
=PV(0.09,4,0,−3900000)	2,762,858
=PV(0.09,5,0,−4200000)	2,729,712
=PV(0.09,6,0,−2100000)	1,252,161
=PV(0.09,7,0,−1000000)	547,034
Initial investment.........	(13,500,000)
NPV calculated in Excel...	$ 469,469*

*Difference due to rounding of factors in Appendix A

Demo 19-2A illustrates that the NPV is not a single, unique amount but is a function of two factors.

- **Discount rate** Changing the discount rate while holding the amounts and timing of cash flows constant affects the NPV. Increasing the discount rate causes NPV to decrease; decreasing the discount rate causes NPV to increase.

    Discount rate ↑ NPV ↓

    Discount rate ↓ NPV ↑

- **Cash flows** Changing the estimated amounts or timing of cash inflows and outflows affects a project's NPV. Effects of cash flow changes on NPV depend on the changes themselves. For example, decreasing the estimate of cash outflows causes NPV to increase; reducing the stream of cash inflows causes NPV to decrease. When amounts and timing of cash flows change, the effects of the changes on NPV can be determined only by calculation.

    Cash outflows ↓ NPV ↑

    Cash inflows ↓ NPV ↓

The information provided by the NPV allows managers to eliminate from consideration any project producing a negative NPV because such a project would have an unacceptable rate of return.

Profitability Index

Comparisons of projects requiring different levels of investment are made using a variation of the NPV method known as the profitability index. The **profitability index (PI)** is a ratio of a project's net cash inflows to the project's net investment.

PI = Present value of net cash inflows ÷ Net investment

The present value (PV) of net cash inflows equals the PV of future cash inflows minus the PV of future cash outflows. The PV of net cash inflows represents an output measure of the project's worth, whereas the net investment represents an input measure of the project's cost. By relating these two measures, the PI gauges the efficiency of the firm's use of capital. *The higher the index, the more efficient is the capital investment.*

Chapter 19 Capital Budgeting

Calculating Profitability Index   LO19-2 DEMO 19-2B

Family One Stop is considering two investments: a distribution warehouse costing $3,440,000 and distribution equipment costing $1,700,000 for an existing storage facility. Corporate managers have computed the present values of the investments by discounting all future expected cash flows at a rate of 12 percent. Present values of the expected net cash inflows are $4,200,000 for the distribution warehouse and $2,360,000 for the distribution equipment.

◆ **What is the profitability index and net present value of the warehouse and the distribution equipment?**

Dividing the PV of the net cash inflows by net investment gives the PI for each investment. Subtracting asset cost from the present value of the net cash inflows provides the NPV. Results follow.

	PV of Inflows	Cost	PI	NPV
Warehouse...............	$4,200,000	$3,440,000	1.22	$760,000
Distribution equipment	2,360,000	1,700,000	1.39	660,000

Although the warehouse's NPV is higher, the profitability index indicates that the distribution equipment is a more efficient use of corporate capital. The higher PI reflects a higher rate of return per investment dollar on the distribution equipment than on the warehouse. The higher a project's PI, the more profitable that project is per investment dollar. However, two conditions must exist for the PI to provide better information than the NPV method.

- First, the decision to accept one project must require the other project to be rejected.
- Second, the availability of funds for capital acquisitions must be limited.

If a capital investment is to provide a return on capital, the PI should be equal to or greater than 1.00. This criterion is the equivalent of an NPV equal to or greater than zero. Like the NPV method, the PI does not indicate the project's expected rate of return. However, another discounted cash flow method, the internal rate of return, provides the expected rate of return to be earned on an investment.

Internal Rate of Return

A project's **internal rate of return (IRR)** is the discount rate that causes the present value of the net cash inflows to equal the present value of the net cash outflows. The IRR is the project's expected rate of return. If the IRR is used as the discount rate to determine a project's NPV, the NPV will be zero. Data in **Exhibit 19.3** indicate that Family One Stop's photovoltaic technology investment would generate an IRR slightly above 10 percent because a discount rate of 10 percent produced an NPV of $23,210, which is relatively close to $0 relative to the initial investment cost of $13,500,000.

Computing IRR Using Present Value Tables

The IRR is most easily computed for projects having equal annual net cash inflows. When an annuity exists, the NPV formula can be restated as follows.

$$\text{NPV} = -\text{Net investment} + \text{PV of annuity amount}$$
$$= -\text{Net investment} + (\text{Cash flow annuity amount} \times \text{PV factor})$$

The investment and annual cash flow amounts are known from the expected data, and the NPV is known to be zero at the IRR. The IRR and its present value factor are unknown. To determine the internal rate of return, substitute known amounts into the formula, rearrange terms, and solve for the unknown (the PV factor).

$$\text{NPV} = -\text{Net investment} + (\text{Annuity} \times \text{PV factor})$$
$$\$0 = -\text{Net investment} + (\text{Annuity} \times \text{PV factor})$$
$$\text{Net investment} = (\text{Annuity} \times \text{PV factor})$$

PV factor = Net Investment ÷ Annuity

The solution yields a present value factor for the number of annuity periods corresponding to the project's life at an interest rate equal to the IRR. Finding this PV factor in an annuity table and reading the interest rate at the top of the column in which the factor is found provides the internal rate of return.

Manually finding the IRR of a project that has unequal annual cash flows is more complex and requires an iterative trial-and-error process. An initial estimate is made of a rate believed to be close to the IRR, and the NPV is computed. If the resulting NPV is negative, a lower rate is estimated (because of the inverse relationship mentioned earlier), and the NPV is computed again. If the NPV is positive, a higher rate is selected, and the NPV is calculated. This process is continued until the NPV equals zero, at which time the IRR has been found.

Computing IRR Using Excel

Alternatively, IRR may be calculated through the RATE function in Excel when there are *equal annual net cash flows* related to the project.

$$=RATE(NPER,PMT,PV,FV)$$

When solving for RATE, enter the cash outflow as a negative amount and the cash inflow as a positive amount. Entering both values as either negative or positive will result in an error in Excel. Alternatively, the IRR function can be used in Excel. Simply include the initial outflow (with a negative sign) in a column, followed by each annual cash flow. Identify the data as the values in the IRR function: =IRR(values).

DEMO 19-2C **LO19-2** **Calculating Internal Rate of Return**

Assume that Family One Stop is considering the purchase of a warehouse distribution management system. The system would cost $1,500,000, be installed immediately, and generate cost savings of $300,000 per year over its seven-year life. The system has no expected salvage value.

◆ **What is the IRR, estimated using the applicable present value table?**

First, solve for the present value factor.

> PV factor = Net Investment ÷ Annuity
> = $1,500,000 ÷ $300,000
> = 5.0000

Next, the PV of an ordinary annuity table (Appendix A, Table 2) is examined to find the IRR. In the table, find the row representing the project's life (in this case, seven periods) and find the PV factor resulting from the equation solution. In row 7, a factor of 5.03295 appears under the column headed 9 percent. Thus, the internal rate of return for this investment is very near 9 percent.

◆ **How is the IRR calculated using Excel instead?**

By using Excel, IRR of the warehouse distribution management system is calculated as 9.2 percent.

Excel Function	Solution
=RATE(NPER,PMT,PV,FV)	RATE
=RATE(7,300000,−1500000,0)	9.2%

Analyzing the IRR The project's IRR is then compared with management's required **hurdle rate**, which is the rate of return specified as the lowest acceptable return on investment. Like the discount rate mentioned earlier, this rate should generally be at least equal to the cost of capital. In fact, the hurdle rate is commonly the discount rate used in computing NPV amounts. *If a project's IRR is equal to or greater than the hurdle rate, the project is considered viable from a financial perspective.*

The higher the IRR, the more financially attractive is the investment proposal. In choosing among alternative investments, however, managers cannot look solely at internal rates of return, because they do not reflect the dollars involved. An investor would normally rather have a 20 percent return on $1,000 than a 100 percent return on $5!

Chapter 19 Capital Budgeting

Using the IRR for capital project evaluation has three drawbacks.

- When uneven cash flows exist, the iterative process is inconvenient and time consuming if using PV tables.
- Unless PV tables provide factors for fractional interest rates, finding a project's precise IRR is difficult.
- Some projects can have several rates of return that will make the NPV of the cash flows equal zero. This phenomenon usually occurs when, at other than time 0, there are net cash inflows in some years and net cash outflows in other years of the investment project's life.

Note that the first two problems are eliminated when using Excel.

Multiple Evaluation Criteria Quantitative and qualitative criteria used by the forest products industry to evaluate capital projects are provided by **Exhibit 19.4**. These criteria were obtained from a survey of industry practices and are not presented in rank order in the exhibit; similar criteria are generally used by firms in other industries. Most firms evaluate projects using multiple criteria and include *quantitative and qualitative considerations* in their analyses. By evaluating potential capital projects using a portfolio of criteria, managers can be confident that they have carefully considered all project costs and contributions. Additionally, using multiple criteria allows for a balanced evaluation of short- and long-term benefits as well as the effects of capital spending on all significant organizational stakeholders.

Exhibit 19.4 ■ Project Evaluation Criteria

Quantitative Criteria	Qualitative Criteria
1. Accounting rate of return	1. Employee morale
2. Payback period	2. Employee safety
3. Discounted payback period	3. Employee responsibility
4. Net present value	4. Corporate image
5. Internal rate of return	5. Social responsibility
6. Profitability index	6. Market share
	7. Growth
	8. Strategic planning
	9. Sustainability

Source: Liliya S. Hogaboam and Steven R. Shook, "Capital Budgeting Practices in the U.S. Forest Products Industry: A Reappraisal," *Forest Products Journal* (December 2004), p. 149.

In performing discounted cash flow analyses, accrual-based accounting information generally must be converted to cash flow data. One accrual detailed in the next section is depreciation. Although not a cash flow, depreciation has cash flow implications because it affects income tax payments—which *are* cash flows.

Data Visualization

The following data visualization uses the cash flows from **Exhibit 19.1**, but changes the interest rate and the resulting net present value amounts.

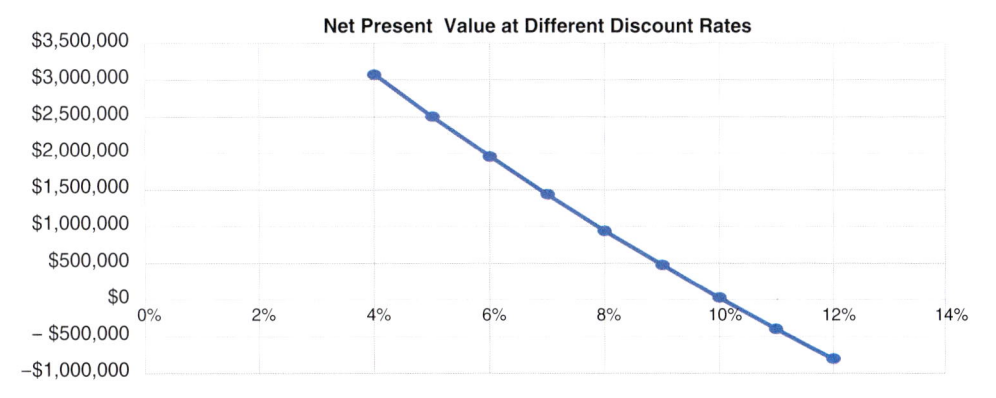

Net Present Value at Different Discount Rates

continued

continued from previous page

Using the data visualization, answer the following questions.

a. What is the relationship between the discount rate and the net present value, assuming no change to cash flows?

b. If the company's discount rate is 8 percent, would the company make the investment? Would the company make the investment at a discount rate of 14 percent?

c. What is the approximate internal rate of return of the project?

Solution on p. 19-53.

REVIEW 19-2 — LO19-2 — Net Present Value, Profitability Index, Internal Rate of Return

C. Gomez, corporate engineer of Allied Products Ltd. is proposing the replacement of existing equipment with more efficient equipment. According to information received by Gomez, the proposed equipment's cost is $1,300,000 and has an expected life of ten years. Data relating to the existing and replacement equipment follow.

Existing Equipment	
Original cost	$117,600
Carrying value	$ 67,200
Annual cash operating costs	$279,000
Fair value	$ 10,000
Salvage value	$ 0
Remaining useful life	10

Replacement Equipment	
Cost	$1,300,000
Annual cash operating costs	$ 60,000
Salvage value	$ 0
Useful life	10

a. Assume that the company's cost of capital is 8 percent, which is to be used in discounted cash flow analysis. Compute the net present value of investing in the new equipment. (Ignore tax and round to the nearest whole dollar.)

b. Compute the profitability index (PI) of investing in the new equipment. (Ignore taxes and round PI to two decimal points.)

c. Rounding to the nearest whole percentage, compute the internal rate of return for the equipment investment.

d. **Critical Thinking:** Should the company purchase the equipment?

More practice: MC19-19, E19-34, E19-35, E19-36, E19-37, E19-39, E19-41
Solution on p. 19-49.

RELEVANT AFTER-TAX CASH FLOWS

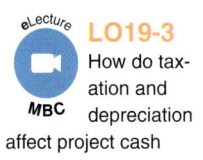

LO19-3 How do taxation and depreciation affect project cash flows?

Income taxes represent a significant cash expense for businesses and, therefore, are the subject of managerial planning and decision-making processes. Large organizations often have an individual designated "Director of Taxation" to oversee tax planning and tax compliance. This person typically has expertise in federal, state, and international tax laws. Tax considerations have a large impact on overall business profitability and managers typically make decisions only after examining how those decisions will affect company taxes. In evaluating capital projects, managers should use after-tax cash flows to determine project acceptability.

Depreciation expense is *not* a cash flow item: no funds are paid or received for it. However, depreciation on capital assets, like interest on debt, affects cash flows by reducing a company's income tax expense. Thus, depreciation provides a **tax shield** against the payment of taxes. The tax shield produces a **tax benefit** equal to the amount of taxes saved.

$$\text{Tax benefit} = \text{Depreciation expense} \times \text{Tax rate}$$

The concepts of tax shield and tax benefit are shown on the following income statements. The tax rate is assumed to be 40 percent.

Chapter 19 Capital Budgeting

No Depreciation Deduction Income Statement		Depreciation Deduction Income Statement	
Sales.	$ 500,000	Sales.	$ 500,000
Cost of goods sold	(350,000)	Cost of goods sold	(350,000)
Gross margin	$ 150,000	Gross margin	$ 150,000
Expenses other than depreciation . . .	(75,000)	Expenses other than depreciation . . .	(75,000)
Depreciation expense.	0	Depreciation expense.	(75,000)
Income before taxes.	$ 75,000	Income before taxes.	$ 0
Tax expense (40%).	(30,000)	Tax expense (40%).	0
Net income	$ 45,000	Net income	$ 0

In this example, the

- tax shield is the $75,000 depreciation expense, and the
- tax benefit is $30,000 (the difference between $30,000 of tax expense on the first income statement and $0 of tax expense on the second income statement).

The tax benefit is also calculated as follows.

> **Tax benefit = Depreciation expense × Tax rate**
>
> = $75,000 × 40% = $30,000

Because taxes are reduced by $30,000 because of the depreciation, the pattern of cash flows is improved.

It is the depreciation taken for *income tax purposes* rather than the depreciation taken for financial accounting purposes that is relevant in discounted cash flow analysis. Income tax laws regarding depreciation deductions are subject to frequent revision. For example, Congress allows very rapid depreciation (even immediate expensing in some cases) of certain assets to stimulate economic growth in the United States. In analyzing capital investments, managers should use the most current tax regulations for depreciation. Different depreciation methods can have significant impacts on after-tax cash flows. For a continuously profitable business, an accelerated method of depreciation, such as the modified accelerated cost recovery system (MACRS) allowed for U.S. tax computations, will produce higher tax benefits in the early years of an asset's life than will the straight-line method. These higher tax benefits will translate into a higher NPV for the investment's cash flows if the tax rate is constant across years.

Risk of Tax Law Changes Alternative depreciation methods and asset depreciable lives for tax purposes could dramatically affect projected after-tax cash flows, net present value, profitability index, and internal rate of return expected from a capital investment. Because capital projects are analyzed and evaluated before investments are made, managers should be aware of the inherent risk of tax law changes. Original assumptions made about the depreciation method or asset life could be invalid by the time an investment is actually made and an asset is placed into service. However, an asset can generally be depreciated using the method and tax life allowed when the asset was purchased and placed into service regardless of the tax law changes occurring after that time.

Calculating After-Tax Net Present Value LO19-3 DEMO 19-3

To illustrate changes that would affect a project's cash flows, assume that Family One Stop is considering a $6 million investment in new point-of-sale store equipment.

Initial investment.	$6,000,000
Expected annual before-tax cash flows . . .	850,000
Straight-line tax depreciation (10 years). . .	600,000
Expected economic life.	10 years
Discount rate	5%

For simplification, we assume corporate assets are depreciated on a straight-line basis for tax purposes.

Prior to making the point-of-sale equipment investment, Family One Stop's cost accountant, Sarah Brown, calculated the project's NPV. Because Brown was concerned about proposed changes in the U.S. tax rate, she also analyzed the project assuming that tax rates changed.

- Situation A: At the time of the analysis, the company's tax rate is 30 percent.
- Situation B: To model a potential tax decrease, Situation B assumes a 25 percent tax rate.
- Situation C: To model a potential tax increase, Situation C assumes a 40 percent tax rate.

♦ **What is the net present value of the investment purchase under the three different tax situations?**

	Situation		
Years 1–10	A	B	C
Cash flow before tax	$ 850,000	$ 850,000	$ 850,000
Tax	(255,000)	(212,500)	(340,000)
Depreciation tax benefit	180,000[1]	150,000[2]	240,000[3]
Cash flow after tax	$ 775,000	$ 787,500	$ 750,000

[1] $600,000 × 30% [2] $600,000 × 25% [3] $600,000 × 40%

Situation A—Tax Rate 30%

Cash Flow	Time	Amount	Discount Factor	Present Value
Investment	t_0	$(6,000,000)	1.0000	$(6,000,000)
Annual inflows	t_1–t_{10}	775,000	7.7217	5,984,318
Net present value				$ (15,682)

Excel Function	Solution
=PV(RATE,NPER,PMT)	PV
=PV(0.05,10,−775000)	$5,984,345
Initial investment	(6,000,000)
NPV calculated in Excel	$ (15,655)

Situation B—Tax Rate 25%

Cash Flow	Time	Amount	Discount Factor	Present Value
Investment	t_0	$(6,000,000)	1.0000	$(6,000,000)
Annual inflows	t_1–t_{10}	787,500	7.7217	6,080,839
Net present value				$ 80,839

Excel Function	Solution
=PV(RATE,NPER,PMT)	PV
=PV(0.05,10,−787500)	$6,080,866
Initial investment	(6,000,000)
NPV calculated in Excel	$ 80,866

Situation C—Tax Rate 40%

Cash Flow	Time	Amount	Discount Factor	Present Value
Investment	t_0	$(6,000,000)	1.0000	$(6,000,000)
Annual inflows	t_1–t_{10}	750,000	7.7217	5,791,275
Net present value				$ (208,725)

Excel Function	Solution
=PV(RATE,NPER,PMT)	PV
=PV(0.05,10,−750000)	$5,791,301
Initial investment	(6,000,000)
NPV calculated in Excel	$ (208,699)

Note that the tax benefit from the depreciation tax shield is added to cash flows after taxes to obtain the amount of after-tax cash flow. The PV amounts are obtained by multiplying the after-tax cash flows by the appropriate PV of an annuity factor from Table 2 in Appendix A on the book's website, rounded to four decimal places. The NPV evaluation technique indicates the acceptability of the capital investment. Even though the depreciation tax benefit increases (decreases) as taxes increase (decrease), the overall cash flow after tax goes down (up) with an increase (decrease) in the tax rate. This means that the net present value amount goes down with an increase in taxes. If tax policy is in a state of uncertainty, management will be more likely to defer non-urgent investment decisions because a change in the tax rate can impact an accept/reject decision.

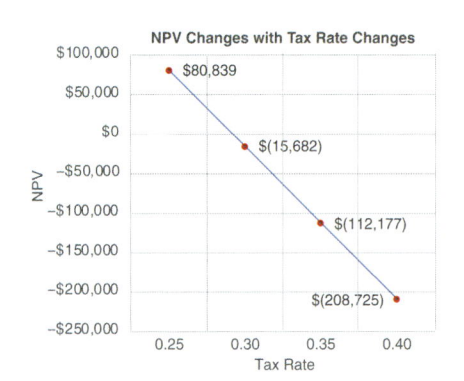

Using NPV as an investment criterion, a decrease in the tax rate makes the point-of-sale equipment a more acceptable investment; an increase has the opposite effect. Since multinational firms operate in countries having federal tax rates from 0 to greater than 50 percent, the tax jurisdiction in which a new asset is located can dramatically influence that asset's NPV.

Understanding how depreciation and taxes affect the various capital budgeting techniques allows managers to make the most informed decisions about capital investments. If the substantial resource commitment required can be justified, managers are more likely to have confidence in the company's capital investments. Justification is partially achieved by determining whether a capital project fits into an organization's strategic plans. To be confident of their conclusions, managers must also comprehend the assumptions and limitations of each capital budgeting method.

After-Tax Net Present Value — **LO19-3** — **REVIEW 19-3**

SavingsPlus Inc. is considering an investment in computer technology. The project would require an initial investment of $240,000 and have an expected life of six years with no salvage value. The pre-tax increase in income is expected to be $55,000 in each of the first four years and $50,000 in each of the next two years. The company's discount rate is 6 percent, its tax rate is 21 percent, and the investment would be depreciated for tax purposes using the straight-line method with no consideration of salvage value over a five-year period and for accounting purposes over a six-year period with no salvage value.

a. Calculate the after-tax NPV on the project.

b. **Critical Thinking:** How does an increase and a decrease in the tax rate impact the NPV? If federal tax policy is likely to change in the near future but the change is unpredictable, how are management investment decisions impacted?

More practice: MC19-21, E19-42, E19-44
Solution on p. 19-50.

EVALUATING AND RANKING PROJECTS USING DIFFERENT METHODS

The capital budgeting methods described in the prior sections are used to analyze potential capital projects as part of an approval process. However, first, the company must determine whether the investment is in line with the company's goals and objectives.

LO19-4 How do managers evaluate and rank investment projects, considering the assumptions and limitations of the different evaluation methods?

Investment Decision

Management must identify the best asset(s) to acquire for fulfilling the company's goals and objectives; to do so requires answers to the questions appearing in the following four subsections.

Is the Activity Worthy of an Investment?

A company acquires assets when they have value in relation to specific current or desired organizational activities. For example, **Pioneer Hi-Bred International** invests heavily in product development because that activity is that firm's primary path to new revenues. Before making asset acquisition decisions, company management must be certain that the activity for which the assets are needed justifies an investment.

An activity's worth is measured by *cost–benefit analysis*. For most capital budgeting decisions, costs and benefits are measured in monetary terms. If the monetary benefits exceed the monetary costs, the activity is potentially worthwhile. In some cases, though, the benefits provided by capital projects are difficult to quantify. Difficulty in quantification is no reason to exclude such benefits from capital budgeting analyses. Often surrogate quantifiable measures can be obtained for qualitative benefits. For example, benefits from investments in daycare centers for employees' children could be estimated through the reduction in employee time-off and turnover. At a minimum, managers should attempt to subjectively include qualitative benefits in the analytical process.

Many companies today invest in implementing green workplace programs to reduce environmental impact, even though the costs may exceed the financial benefits of doing so.

In other circumstances, management could know in advance that the monetary benefits of the capital project will not exceed the costs but that the project is essential for other reasons. For instance, a company could consider renovating the employee workplace with new carpet, furniture, paint, and artwork. The renovation would not make the employees' work any easier, faster, or safer but would make the workplace more comfortable. Such a project could be deemed "worthy" regardless of the results of a cost–benefit analysis. Companies could also invest in unprofitable products to maintain market share of a product group and, therefore, protect the market position of profitable products. Further, a company may invest in technology that reduces energy consumption and pollution even though the investment is not wholly justified on financial grounds alone.

Which Assets Can Be Used for the Activity?
Identifying appropriate assets to use for the proposed activity is closely related to an evaluation of the activity's worth. Management must determine how much the assets will cost to decide whether the activity should be pursued. Management should gather, for each asset being considered, the specific monetary and nonmonetary information shown in **Exhibit 19.5** to make this determination.

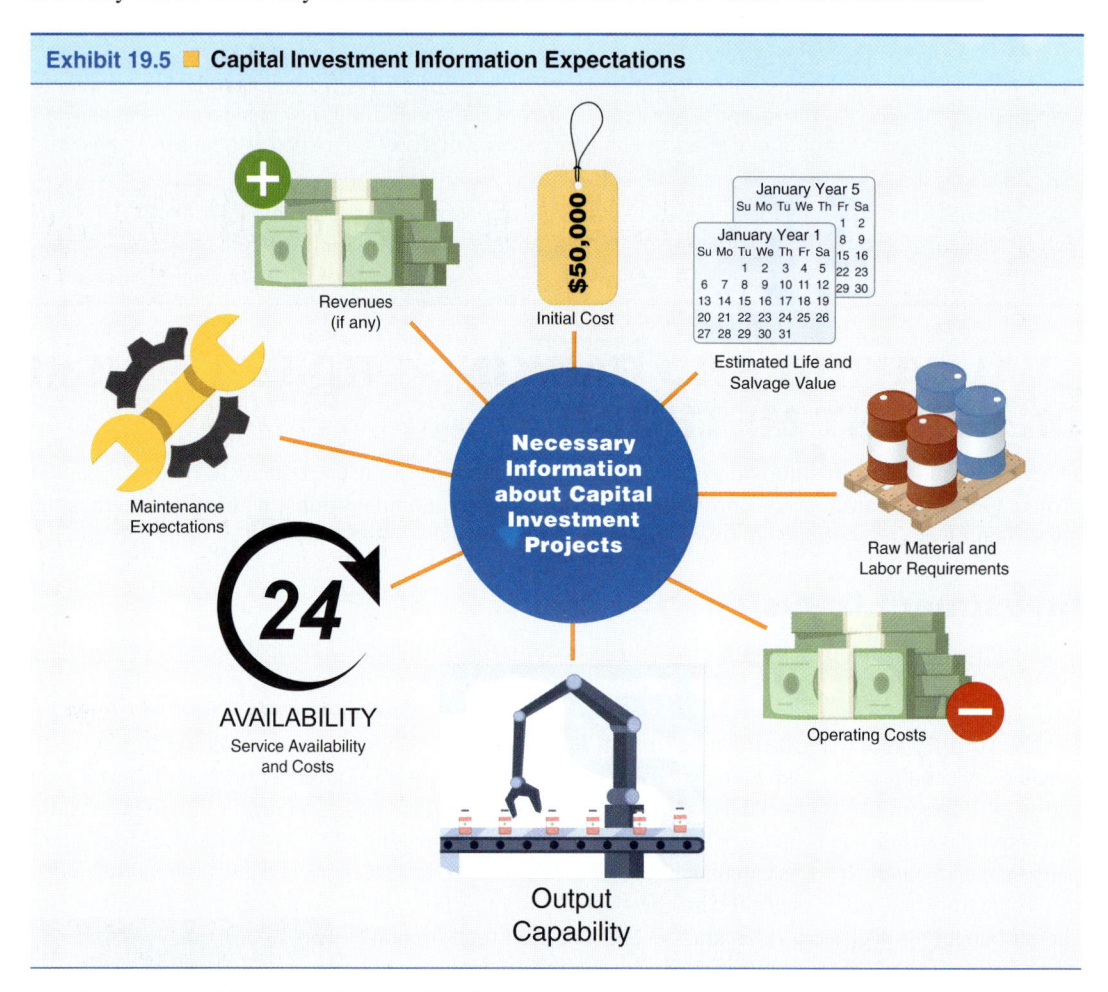

Exhibit 19.5 Capital Investment Information Expectations

Necessary Information about Capital Investment Projects:
- Revenues (if any)
- Initial Cost ($50,000)
- Estimated Life and Salvage Value
- Raw Material and Labor Requirements
- Operating Costs
- Output Capability
- Availability: Service Availability and Costs
- Maintenance Expectations

As mentioned in the previous section, information used in a capital project analysis may include surrogate, indirect measures. Management must have both quantitative and qualitative information about each asset and recognize that some projects are simply more crucial to the firm's future than others.

Of the Available Assets for Each Activity, Which Is the Best Investment?
Using all available information, management should select the best asset from the candidates and end consideration of all others. In most instances, companies have committees that discuss, evaluate, and approve capital projects. In judging capital project acceptability, a committee should recognize that two types of capital budgeting decisions must be made.

- A **screening decision** determines whether a capital project is desirable based on some previously established minimum criterion or criteria (such as NPV = 0). A project that does not meet the minimum standard(s) is excluded from further consideration.

- A **preference decision** ranks projects according to their impact on the achievement of company objectives.

Chapter 19 Capital Budgeting

Deciding which asset is the best investment requires the use of one or more of the evaluation techniques discussed previously. Some techniques are used to screen project acceptability; other techniques are used to rank projects. Although different companies use different techniques for screening and ranking purposes, *payback period is commonly used only for screening decisions* because payback focuses on only the short run and does not consider the time value of money. The other techniques previously discussed can be used to screen or rank capital projects.

The assumptions and limitations of each method discussed are summarized in **Exhibit 19.6**. To maximize benefits of the capital budgeting process, managers should understand the similarities and differences of the various methods and use multiple methods to evaluate projects.

Exhibit 19.6 ■ Assumptions and Limitations of Capital Budgeting Methods

Assumptions	Limitations
Payback Method	
• Speed of investment recovery is the key consideration. • Timing and magnitude of cash flows are accurately predicted. • Risk (uncertainty) is lower for a shorter payback project.	• Cash flows after payback are ignored. • Cash flows and project life are treated as deterministic without explicit consideration of probabilities. • Time value of money is ignored. • Cash flow pattern preferences are not explicitly recognized.
Net Present Value	
• Discount rate used is valid. • Timing and size of cash flows are accurately predicted. • Project life is accurately predicted. • If the shorter lived of two projects is selected, the proceeds of that project will continue to earn the discount rate of return through the theoretical completion of the longer-lived project.	• Cash flows and project life are treated as deterministic without explicit consideration of probabilities. • Alternative project rates of return are not known. • Cash flow pattern preferences are not explicitly recognized. • IRR on project is not reflected.
Profitability Index	
• Assumptions are the same as NPV. • Size of PV of net future cash inflows relative to size of present value of investment measures efficient use of capital.	• Limitations are the same as NPV. • A relative answer is given but dollars of NPV are not reflected.
Internal Rate of Return	
• Hurdle rate used is valid. • Timing and size of cash flows are accurately predicted. • Project life is accurately predicted. • If the shorter lived of two projects is selected, the proceeds of that project will continue to earn the IRR through the theoretical completion of the longer-lived project.	• The IRR, rather than dollar size, is used to rank projects for funding. • Dollars of NPV are not reflected. • Cash flows and project life are treated as deterministic without explicit consideration of probabilities. • Cash flow pattern preferences are not explicitly recognized. • Multiple rates of return can be calculated on the same project.
Accounting Rate of Return (presented in Appendix 19B of this chapter)	
• Effect on accounting earnings relative to average investment is key consideration. • Timing and size of increase in earnings, investment cost, project life, and salvage value can be accurately predicted.	• Cash flows are not considered. • Time value of money is not considered. • Earnings, investment, and project life are treated as deterministic without explicit consideration of probabilities.

All methods in **Exhibit 19.6** have two similar limitations.

- Except to the extent that payback indicates promptness of investment recovery, none of the methods provides a mechanism to include management preferences with regard to the timing of cash flows. This limitation can be partially overcome by discounting cash flows occurring further in the future at higher rates than those in earlier years, assuming that earlier cash flows are preferred.
- All methods use single, deterministic measures of cash flows rather than probabilities. This limitation can be minimized through the use of probability estimates of cash flows. Such estimates can be input into a computer program to determine a distribution of answers for each method under various conditions of uncertainty.

Of the "Best Investments" for All Worthwhile Activities, in Which Ones Should the Company Invest?

Although many worthwhile investment activities exist, each company has limited resources available and must allocate them in the most profitable manner. Therefore, after choosing the best asset for each activity, management must decide which activities and assets to fund. Investment projects are classified as mutually exclusive, independent, or mutually inclusive.

- **Mutually exclusive projects** compete to fill the same function. One project will be chosen from such a group, excluding all others from further consideration. A proposal under consideration could be to replace a current asset with one that provides the same functionality. If the company keeps the old asset, the new one will not be purchased. If the new asset is purchased, the old asset will be sold. Thus, the two assets are mutually exclusive. For example, if a small bakery decides to buy a new delivery truck, it would no longer need the existing truck and would sell it to help finance the new truck.

- **Independent projects** have no specific bearing on one another. For example, acquiring an office computer system is not related to purchasing a factory lathe. These project decisions are analyzed and accepted or rejected independently of one another. Although limited resources may preclude the acquisition of all acceptable projects, the projects themselves are not mutually exclusive.

- **Mutually inclusive projects** have multiple investments linked to a primary project. In such a situation, if the primary project is chosen, all related projects are also selected. Alternatively, rejection of the primary project dictates rejection of the others. For example, when a firm chooses to invest in new technology, investing in an employee training program for the new technology would also be necessary.

Exhibit 19.7 illustrates a typical investment decision process in which a company is determining the best way to provide transportation for its sales force. Answers to the four questions asked in the subheadings to this section are provided for the transportation decision.

Exhibit 19.7 ■ **Typical Investment Decision Process**

Activity—Provide transportation for a sales force of 10 people.

1. Is the activity worthy of an investment?
   Yes; this decision is based on an analysis of the cost of providing transportation in relation to the dollars of gross margin to be generated by the sales force.

2. Which assets can be used for the activity?
   Available: Bus passes, bicycles, motorcycles, automobiles (purchased), automobiles (leased), automobiles (currently owned), small airplanes.
   Infeasible: Bus passes, bicycles, and motorcycles are rejected because of inconvenience and inability to carry a reasonable quantity of merchandise; airplanes are rejected because of inconvenience and lack of landing sites near customers.
   Feasible: Various types of automobiles to be purchased (assume asset options A through G); various types of leasing arrangements (assume availability of leases 1 through 5); current fleet.
   Gather all relevant quantitative and qualitative information on all feasible assets (purchased assets; leased assets; current fleet).

3. Of the available assets for each activity, which is the best investment? Compare all relevant information and choose the best asset candidate from the purchase group (assume Asset D) and the lease group (assume Lease 2).

4. Of the "best investments" for all worthwhile activities, in which ones should the company invest? Comparing the best asset candidate from the purchase group (Asset D) and the lease group (Lease 2) represents a mutually exclusive, multiple-candidate project decision. The best candidate is found to be Type D assets. Comparing the Type D assets to the current fleet is a mutually exclusive project. The best investment is deemed to be the purchase of a new fleet of 10 Type D automobiles concurrently with the sale of the old fleet.

To ensure that capital funds are invested in the best projects available, managers must carefully evaluate all projects and decide which represent the most effective and efficient use of resources—a difficult determination. The evaluation process should consider activity priorities, cash flows, and project risk. Projects should then be ranked in order of acceptability. Ranking could be required for both independent and mutually exclusive projects. Ranking independent projects is required to efficiently allocate scarce capital to competing uses. Ranking mutually exclusive projects is required when selecting the best project from a set of alternatives.

Ranking Multiple Capital Projects

Accept/Reject Decision for Single Asset When managers must make an accept/reject decision for a single asset, all time value of money evaluation techniques normally point to the same decision alternative. A project is acceptable under the NPV method if its net present value is not negative. Acceptability of a capital investment is also indicated by a profitability index of 1.00 or more. Because the PI is an adaptation of the NPV method, these two evaluation techniques always provide the same screening result. To be acceptable using the IRR model, a project must have an internal rate of return equal to or greater than the specified hurdle rate. The IRR method gives the same accept/reject decision as the NPV and PI methods if the hurdle rate is used as the discount rate.

Ranking Multiple Mutually Exclusive Projects More often, however, managers must choose among multiple, mutually exclusive projects. Multiple project evaluation decisions require that a ranking be made, generally using net present value, profitability index, and/or internal rate of return. Payback period also can be used to rank multiple projects. However, the payback method does not provide as much useful information as do NPV, PI, and IRR because the payback method ignores both cash flows beyond the payback period and the time value of money.

Managers can use results from the evaluation techniques to rank projects in descending order of acceptability.

- For the NPV and PI methods, rankings are based on the magnitude of the NPV and PI index, respectively. Although based on the same figures, the NPV and PI methods do not always provide the same rank order because the former is a dollar measure and the latter is a percentage measure.
- When the IRR is used, rankings of multiple projects are based on expected rates of return. Rankings provided by the IRR method are not necessarily the same as those given by the NPV or PI methods.

Reinvestment Assumptions Conflicting results arise, in part, among the three methods because of differing underlying **reinvestment assumptions**. The reinvestment assumption focuses on how the cash flows received during a project's life are assumed to be reinvested until the end of that project's life.

- The NPV and PI techniques assume that cash inflows are reinvested at the discount rate, which is typically the weighted average cost of capital.
- The IRR method assumes that cash inflows are reinvested at the expected internal rate of return, which is higher than the COC for projects with positive NPVs.

In such a case, the IRR method could provide a misleading indication of project success because additional projects having the same high return might not be found.

In addition to ranking projects based on financial criteria, managers must evaluate whether there are differences in risks across potential projects.

Ranking Investments   LO19-4   DEMO 19-4

Grocer Warehouse Inc. is considering three unrelated capital investments. Each investment has an initial cost of $81,000, but each has different cash flows over a three-year period. The payback, net present value, and profitability index are provided for each investment.

	Proposal A	Proposal B	Proposal C
Payback	2 years	2 years	1 year
Net present value	$22,321	$19,718	$(7,364)
Profitability index	1.28	1.24	0.91

◆ Which project should management choose if only one project can be selected?

Based on the payback method, Proposal C is preferable because it has the shortest payback. However, considering the net present value and the profitability index, Proposal A is preferable. Because the payback considers only the time required to recover the investment and not profitability or timing of cash flows, the stronger case is for Proposal A.

REVIEW 19-4 **LO19-4** **Ranking Capital Projects**

Management of Last Call Inc. is considering the following capital projects

Project	Cost	Annual After-Tax Cash Flow	Number of Years
A	$2,000,000	$400,000	15
B	3,000,000	560,000	9
C	4,000,000	560,000	14
D	3,500,000	500,000	20
E	2,400,000	425,000	15
F	800,000	220,000	8

Assume that all projects have no salvage value and that the company uses a discount rate of 10 percent. Management has decided that no more than $6,000,000 can be spent in the current year for capital projects.

a. Determine the net present value, profitability index, and internal rate of return for each of the six projects.
b. Rank the six projects according to each method used in *a*.
c. **Critical Thinking:** Indicate how you would suggest to the management of the company that the funds be spent.

More practice:
MC19-22, E19-47
Solution on p. 15-50.

COMPENSATING FOR RISK IN CAPITAL PROJECT EVALUATION

LO19-5
How is risk considered in capital budgeting analyses?

When choosing among multiple projects, managers must consider the risk or uncertainty associated with each project. In accounting, **risk** reflects uncertainty about differences between the expected and actual future returns from an investment. For example, the purchase of a $100,000, 2 percent Treasury note would provide a virtually risk-free return of $2,000 annually because such notes are backed by the full faith and credit of the U.S. government. If the same $100,000 were used to purchase stock, the returns could range from −100 percent (losing the entire investment) to an abnormally high return. The potential for extreme variability makes the stock a much riskier investment than the Treasury note.

Managers considering a capital investment should understand and compensate for the degree of risk involved in that investment. There are three approaches to compensate for risk.

Approaches to Compensate for Risk		
Judgmental Method	Risk-Adjusted Discount Rate Method	Sensitivity Analysis

These methods do not *eliminate* risk, but they do help managers understand and *evaluate* risk in the decision-making process.

Judgmental Method

The **judgmental method** of risk adjustment allows decision makers to use logic and reasoning when deciding whether a project provides an acceptable rate of return in relation to its risk. The decision maker is presented all available information for each project, including the payback period, NPV, PI, and IRR. After reviewing the information, the decision maker chooses from among acceptable projects based on personal judgment of the risk-to-return relationship. The judgmental approach provides no formal process for adjusting data for the risk element. Although such a method sounds unorthodox, experienced business managers are generally able to use this method with a high level of reliability.

Chapter 19 Capital Budgeting

Risk-Adjusted Discount Rate Method

A more formal method of considering risk requires making adjustments to the discount (or hurdle) rate. Under the **risk-adjusted discount rate method**, the decision maker increases the rate used for discounting future cash inflows and decreases the rate used for discounting future cash outflows to compensate for increased risk. As the discount rate is increased (or decreased), the PVs of future cash flows are reduced (or increased). Therefore, larger cash inflows are required to "cover" the investment and provide an acceptable rate of return. Changes in the discount rate should reflect the degree of risk, other investment opportunities, and corporate objectives. If the internal rate of return were used for higher-risk project evaluation, the risk-adjusted discount rate method would increase the hurdle rate to which the IRR is compared.

Compensating for Risk by Using a Higher Discount Rate — LO19-5 DEMO 19-5A

Assume that Family One Stop's management is considering the purchase of an automated product-ordering system. The $1,500,000 system would be used for ten years and then would be sold for $50,000.

Initial installation cost	$1,500,000
After-tax net cash flows	
Years 1–5	260,000
Years 6–10	220,000
Year 10 (sale)	50,000

Family One Stop's management generally uses its 10 percent cost of capital as the discount rate in evaluating capital projects using the NPV method. However, Soloman Klatz, a capital projects committee member, believes that this project has substantially above-normal risk.

- First, the cost savings realized from the system could be significantly less than planned.
- Second, the system's salvage value in ten years could vary substantially from the $50,000 estimate.

Klatz wants to compensate for these risk factors by using a 14 percent discount rate rather than the 10 percent rate. Determining the adjustment of the discount rate (from 10 to 14 percent, for example) is most commonly an arbitrary one. Thus, even though a formal process is used to compensate for risk, the process still involves a degree of judgment on the part of the project evaluators.

◆ **Ignoring taxes, what is the net present value of the investment using a 10 percent discount rate and using a 14 percent discount rate?**

The following tables show the NPV computations using both discount rates, with factors rounded to four decimal places.

NPV Using 10% Discount Rate

Cash Flow	Time	Amount	Discount Factor	Present Value
Value Investment	t_0	$(1,500,000)	1.0000	$(1,500,000)
Annual inflows	t_1–t_5	260,000	3.7908	985,608
Annual inflows	t_6–t_{10}	220,000	2.3538[a]	517,836
Final inflow	t_{10}	50,000	0.3855	19,275
Net present value				$ 22,719

Excel Function	PV at t_5	Solution
=PV(0.10,5,−260000)		$ 985,605
=PV(0.10,5,−220000)	$833,973	
=PV(0.10,5,0,−833973)		517,832
=PV(0.10,10,0,−50000)		19,277
Initial investment		(1,500,000)
NPV calculated in Excel		$ 22,714

NPV Using 14% Discount Rate

Cash Flow	Time	Amount	Discount Factor	Present Value
Value Investment	t_0	$(1,500,000)	1.0000	$(1,500,000)
Annual inflows	t_1–t_5	260,000	3.4331	892,606
Annual inflows	t_6–t_{10}	220,000	1.7830[b]	392,260
Final inflow	t_{10}	50,000	0.2697	13,485
Net present value				$ (201,649)

Excel Function	PV at t_5	Solution
=PV(0.14,5,−260000)		$ 892,601
=PV(0.14,5,−220000)	$755,278	
=PV(0.14,5,0,−755278)		392,268
=PV(0.14,10,0,−50000)		13,487
Initial investment		(1,500,000)
NPV calculated in Excel		$ (201,644)

[a] Factor for 10 periods at 10% − Factor for 5 periods at 10% = Factor for periods 6–10 at 10% = 6.1446 − 3.7908 = 2.3538
[b] Factor for 10 periods at 14% − Factor for 5 periods at 14% = Factor for periods 6–10 at 14% = 5.2161 − 3.4331 = 1.7830

© Cambridge Business Publishers

When the discount rate is raised to 14 percent, the project's NPV is reduced and shows the project to be unacceptable. Thus, using a higher hurdle rate adjusted for risk, the project would likely be rejected.

Applying Risk Adjustment to Payback and ARR The same type of risk adjustment can be used for payback period or accounting rate of return (ARR, which is discussed in Appendix 19B of this chapter). If the payback method is used, managers can choose to shorten the maximum allowable payback period to compensate for increased risk. This adjustment assumes that cash flows occurring in the more distant periods are riskier than cash flows occurring sooner. If the ARR method is used, managers can increase the hurdle rate against which the ARR is compared to compensate for risk. Another way in which risk can be included in the decision process is through the use of sensitivity analysis.

Sensitivity Analysis

Sensitivity analysis is a process of determining the amount of change that must occur in a variable before a different decision would be made. Sensitivity analysis examines what happens if a variable were different from that originally expected. In a capital budgeting situation, sensitivity analysis can be conducted for the

- discount rate,
- annual net cash flows, or
- project life.

Except for the initial purchase price, all information used in capital budgeting is estimated. Use of estimates creates the possibility of introducing errors, and sensitivity analysis identifies an "error range" for the various estimated values over which the project will still be acceptable. The following sections consider how sensitivity analysis relates to the discount rate, cash flows, and asset life.

Range of the Discount Rate A capital project providing a rate of return equal to or greater than the discount or hurdle rate is considered an acceptable investment. A project's NPV will change, however, if the discount rate changes. Because the minimal discount and hurdle rates should be set at the organization's cost of capital, an increase in the COC would cause an increase in the discount rate—and a corresponding decrease in the project's NPV. The COC, for instance, can increase because of increases in interest rates on new issues of debt.

Sensitivity analysis allows a company to determine how much the estimated COC (and, therefore, the related discount rate) could increase before a project becomes unacceptable. The upper limit of increase in the discount rate (COC) is the project's internal rate of return. At the IRR, a project's NPV is zero; therefore, the PV of the cash inflows equals the PV of cash outflows. As long as the IRR for a project is equal to or greater than the COC, or alternative discount rate, the project is acceptable.

DEMO 19-5B   LO19-5   Compensating for Risk Through a Range of Discount Rates

To illustrate the use of sensitivity analysis, assume that Family One Stop has an opportunity to invest $340,000 in new delivery equipment that has a ten-year life and will generate cost savings of $75,000 per year.

◆ **Using a 10 percent COC rate for Family One Stop, what is the equipment's NPV?**

Excel Function	Solution
=PV(RATE,NPER,PMT)	PV
=PV(0.10,10,−75000)	$460,843
Initial investment	(340,000)
NPV calculated in Excel	$120,843

After-tax cash flows for 10 years discounted at 10% ($75,000 × 6.1446) ... $ 460,845
Initial investment.. (340,000)
Net present value.. $ 120,845

The equipment provides a positive NPV and is considered an acceptable investment candidate.

Family One Stop's management wants to know how high the discount rate can rise before the investment would become unacceptable.

◆ **What is the discount rate that equates the initial investment to the present value of the cash flows?**

To find the upper limit of the discount rate, the PV factor for an annuity of 10 periods at the unknown interest rate is computed as follows.

PV factor = Net Investment ÷ Annuity

= $340,000 ÷ $75,000
= 4.5333

Excel Function	Solution
=RATE(NPER,PMT,PV,FV)	RATE
=RATE(10,75000,–340000,0)	17.8%

Assume that the factors in a present value of an ordinary annuity table are 4.659 and 4.494 at 17% and 18%, respectively, for 10 periods. As long as Family One Stop's COC is less than or equal to approximately 17.5 percent, this investment is acceptable. (Through Excel, we can calculate the actual rate of 17.8 percent.) As the discount rate increases and approaches the IRR, the investment becomes less desirable. These calculations assume that the cash flows and equipment life have been properly estimated. This means that the COC could fall in the range of 10.0 percent to 17.8 percent and the project would still be considered an acceptable investment candidate, assuming all other assumptions are valid.

Range of the Discount Rate

- Upper End COC: NPV = $0 — 17.80%
- Estimated COC: NPV = $120,845 — 10%

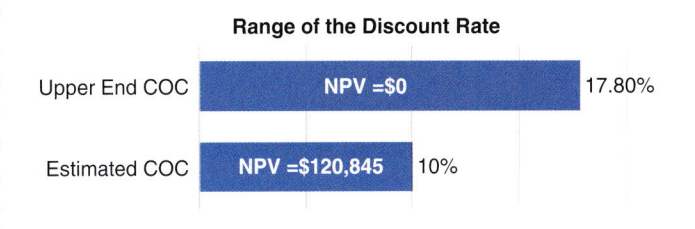

Range of the Cash Flows Another factor sensitive to changes in estimation is the investment's projected cash flows.

Compensating for Risk Using a Range of Cash Flows   LO19-5   DEMO 19-5C

Family One Stop's data for the $340,000 delivery equipment investment are used to illustrate how to determine the range of acceptable cash flows over the ten-year useful life.

♦ **How small can the net annual cash inflow be and still have the investment remain desirable?**

This determination requires that the present value of the cash flows for 10 periods, discounted at 10 percent, be equal to or greater than the investment cost of $340,000. The PV factor for 10 periods at 10 percent is 6.1446 (rounded). The equation from the preceding section can be used to find the lowest acceptable annuity.

Cash flow × PV factor = Investment

Cash flow × 6.1446 = $340,000
Cash flow = $340,000 ÷ 6.1446
Cash flow = $55,333

Excel Function	Solution
=PMT(RATE,NPER,PV)	PMT
=PMT(0.10,10,–340000)	$55,333

As long as the net annual after-tax cash flow equals or exceeds $55,333, the delivery equipment will be financially acceptable. Alternatively, solve for PMT in Excel to arrive at the payment amount of $55,333. This means that the annual cash flow could fall in the range of $55,333 to $75,000 and the project would still be considered an acceptable investment candidate, assuming all other assumptions are valid.

Range of Annual Cash Flow

- Lower end cash flow: NPV = $0 — $55,333
- Estimated cash flow: NPV = $120,845 — $75,000

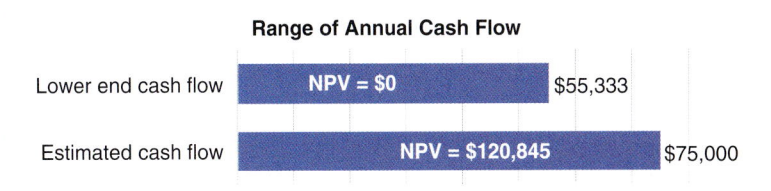

Range of the Life of the Asset Asset life is related to many factors, some of which (such as the amount and timing of maintenance and equipment) are controllable. Other factors, such as technological advances and actions of competitors, are noncontrollable. Misestimating the project's life will change the number of periods from which cash inflows are to be derived. This change could affect the accept/reject decision for a project.

DEMO 19-5D LO19-5 Compensating for Risk Using a Range of Number of Periods

The Family One Stop's delivery equipment example is used to determine the acceptable range of the life of the asset.

◆ **What is the minimum length of time the cash flows must be received for the investment to be acceptable?**

The solution requires setting the present value of the cash flows of $75,000 discounted at 10 percent equal to the investment of $340,000. This computation yields the PV factor for an unknown number of periods.

Excel Function	Solution
=NPER(RATE,PMT,PV)	NPER
=NPER(0.10,75000,−340000)	6.34

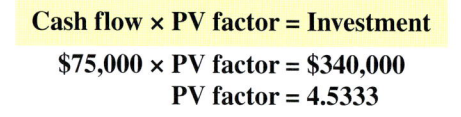

Cash flow × PV factor = Investment

$75,000 × PV factor = $340,000
PV factor = 4.5333

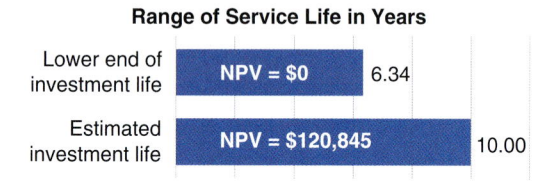

Range of Service Life in Years

- Lower end of investment life: NPV = $0 — 6.34
- Estimated investment life: NPV = $120,845 — 10.00

Review the present value of an annuity table in Appendix A under the 10 percent interest column to find the 4.5333 factor. The investment life is between six and seven years. If the cash inflows were to stop at any point before approximately 6.5 years, the investment would be unacceptable. Through Excel, we can calculate the actual period of 6.34 years by solving for NPER. This means that the investment life could fall in the range of 6.34 years to 10 years and the project would still be considered an acceptable investment candidate, assuming all other assumptions are valid.

Sensitivity analysis does not reduce the uncertainty about each variable. Such analysis does, however, provide management a sense of the tolerance for estimation errors by providing upper and lower ranges for selected variables. The preceding presentation simplistically focuses on single changes in each of the variables. If all factors change simultaneously, this type of sensitivity analysis is useless. More advanced treatments of sensitivity analysis, which allow for simultaneous ranging of all variables, can be found under the topic of simulation in an advanced mathematical modeling text.

REVIEW 19-5 LO19-5 Sensitivity Analysis

Star Co. is considering the installation of new equipment for its warehouse. The equipment has an initial cost of $600,000, expected annual operational cash savings of $100,000, and an expected useful life of ten years. It is assumed that the equipment will lower production costs by increasing operational efficiencies.

a. If the company estimates its cost of capital to be 8 percent, what is the annual operational cash savings necessary to minimally justify the investment?

b. Assume instead that the company is fairly small; thus the CEO is uncertain about the company's actual cost of capital. To the nearest whole percent, what is the maximum the company's cost of capital could be for this project to be acceptable if estimated annual cash savings were projected to be $100,000?

c. **Critical Thinking:** What is the range of operational cash savings for the investment to be acceptable? What is the percentage difference between the low end of the range and the estimated amount? What is the range of cost of capital for the investment to be acceptable? What is the percentage difference between the estimated amount and the high end of the range? How is this information useful for management decision-making purposes?

More practice:
MC19-23, E19-48, E19-49
Solution on p. 15-51.

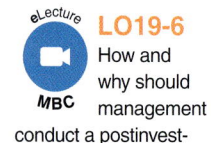

POSTINVESTMENT AUDIT

LO19-6 How and why should management conduct a postinvestment audit of a capital project?

In a **postinvestment audit** of a capital project, information on actual project results is gathered and compared to expected results. This process provides a feedback or control feature to both the persons who submitted the original project information and those who approved it. Comparisons should be made using the same technique or techniques used originally to determine project acceptance. Actual data should be extrapolated to future periods in which such information would be appropriate. For cases in which significant learning or training is necessary, start-up costs of the first year may not be representative of future costs. Such projects should be given a chance to stabilize before conducting the project audit.

As the size of the capital expenditure increases, a postinvestment audit becomes more crucial. Although an audit cannot change a past investment decision, it can pinpoint project areas that are out of line with expectations so that problems can possibly be corrected before they get out of hand.

An audit can also provide feedback on the accuracy of the original project cash flow estimates. Sometimes project sponsors are biased in favor of their own projects and provide overly optimistic forecasts of future revenues or cost savings. Project sponsors should be required to explain all major variances. Knowing that postinvestment audits will be made could cause project sponsors to provide more realistic cash flow forecasts in their capital requests.

Performing a postinvestment audit is not an easy task. The actual information might be in a different form from the original estimates, and some project benefits can be difficult to quantify. Project returns fluctuate considerably over time, so results gathered at a single point might not be representative of the complete project results. Regardless of the difficulties involved, however, postinvestment audits provide information that can help managers make better capital investment decisions in the future.

Preparing a Postinvestment Audit — LO19-6 DEMO 19-6

The following table provides information pertinent to a postinvestment audit of the photovoltaic technology investment presented in **Exhibit 19.2**. This postinvestment audit is occurring after all actual cash flows associated with the investment are known; i.e., after period t_7. Thus, none of the actual amounts are projected or estimated.

Postinvestment Audit of Photovoltaic Technology Investment
Discount Rate = 7%

Cash Flow	Time	Planned Amount (Exhibit 19.2)	Actual Amount
Initial investment	t_0	$(13,500,000)	$(14,250,000)
Year 1 net cash flow	t_1	2,200,000	2,250,000
Year 2 net cash flow	t_2	2,600,000	2,650,000
Year 3 net cash flow	t_3	3,200,000	3,340,000
Year 4 net cash flow	t_4	3,900,000	4,200,000
Year 5 net cash flow	t_5	4,200,000	4,125,000
Year 6 net cash flow	t_6	2,100,000	1,000,000
Year 7 net cash flow	t_7	1,000,000	550,000

As shown in **Exhibit 19.2**, the projected NPV of the investment was $1,432,060.

◆ **What is the NPV of the investment using a discount rate of 7 percent and the actual amounts of net cash flows based on the postinvestment audit?**

The following table provides the NPV calculation on the actual data using the 7 percent discount rate.

NPV Calculation for Postinvestment Audit of Photovoltaic Technology Investment
Discount Rate = 7%

Cash Flow	Time	a Amount	×	b Discount Factor	=	c Present Value
Initial investment	t_0	$(14,250,000)		1.0000		$(14,250,000)
Year 1 net cash flow	t_1	2,250,000		0.9346		2,102,850
Year 2 net cash flow	t_2	2,650,000		0.8734		2,314,510
Year 3 net cash flow	t_3	3,340,000		0.8163		2,726,442
Year 4 net cash flow	t_4	4,200,000		0.7629		3,204,180
Year 5 net cash flow	t_5	4,125,000		0.7130		2,941,125
Year 6 net cash flow	t_6	1,000,000		0.6663		666,300
Year 7 net cash flow	t_7	550,000		0.6228		342,540
Net present value						$ 47,947

=PV(RATE,NPER,PMT,FV)	PV
=PV(0.07,1,0,−2250000)	$ 2,102,804
=PV(0.07,2,0,−2650000)	2,314,613
=PV(0.07,3,0,−3340000)	2,726,435
=PV(0.07,4,0,−4200000)	3,204,160
=PV(0.07,5,0,−4125000)	2,941,068
=PV(0.07,6,0,−1000000)	666,342
=PV(0.07,7,0,−550000)	342,512
Initial investment	(14,250,000)
NPV calculated in Excel	$ 47,934

Projected Versus Actual NPV

- Actual NPV: $47,947
- Projected NPV: $1,432,060

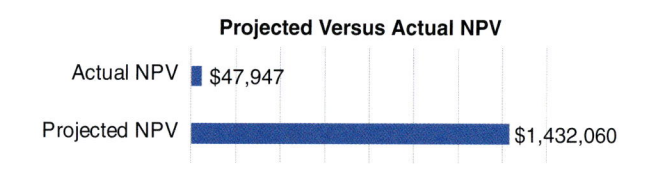

As shown to the left, the investment's actual NPV was $47,947. Whereas the NPV is positive and the project generated a return in excess of 7 percent, the realized NPV was far less than the projected NPV of $1,432,060. This analysis reveals the difference between the planned and actual NPV is attributable to three primary factors.

1. The initial acquisition cost of $14,250,000 exceeded the expected investment cost of $13,500,000. This accounts for $750,000 of the difference between the planned and actual NPVs.
2. The actual cash inflows in years one through four exceeded the planned cash inflows. Further investigation revealed actual energy prices were higher than were anticipated in the project proposal. Hence, the energy savings were greater than originally estimated.
3. The actual cash inflows in years six and seven were far less than planned levels. The investigation revealed that actual repair and maintenance costs were much higher than planned. Simply put, extending the investment's actual life to the seven-year planned life required extraordinary maintenance and repair activities. Accordingly, the cash inflows late in the investment's life were far below expectations.

REVIEW 19-6 — LO19-6 — Postinvestment Audit

Four years ago, based on a pre-tax NPV analysis, Harper Inc. decided to add new equipment with a cost of $85,000, allowing the company to expand its product offerings. The data used in the analysis were as follows:

Discount rate	6%
Useful life	4 years
Contribution margin expected increase:	
Year 1	$46,000
Year 2	46,000
Year 3	50,000
Year 4	55,000
Annual incremental fixed costs	20,000
Salvage value of equipment	5,000

The management team decided to conduct a postinvestment audit to assess the accuracy of the planning process. The team is expecting the net present value to be better than expected because they were able to decrease fixed costs to $16,000 based upon renegotiated contracts. Actual contribution margin for years 1, 2, 3, and 4 were $40,000, $42,000, $48,000 and $48,000, respectively. Due to the unexpected market changes, the equipment does not have a salvage value.

a. Determine the original projected NPV on the product line investment.
b. Determine the actual NPV of the project based on the postinvestment audit.
c. **Critical Thinking:** Identify factors that are responsible for the differences between the projected NPV and the actual postinvestment audit NPV.

More practice: MC19-24, E19-50
Solution on p. 15-52.

Appendix 19A: Time Value of Money

LO19-7 How are present values calculated?

The time value of money can be discussed in relation to either its future or its present value. **Future value (FV)** refers to a cash flow occurring in the future. Alternatively, present value is the amount that future cash flows are worth currently given a specified rate of interest.[4] Thus, FVs and PVs depend on three things:

- amount of the cash flow,
- rate of interest, and
- timing of the cash flow.

---

[4] Interest can be earned or owed, received or paid. To simplify the discussion, the topic of interest is viewed only from the inflow standpoint.

Chapter 19 Capital Budgeting

Future and present values are related: a PV is an FV discounted to time 0. The rate of return used in PV computations is called the discount rate.

In computing FVs and PVs, simple or compound interest is used. **Simple interest** means that interest is earned only on the original investment or principal amount. **Compound interest** means that interest earned in prior periods is added to the original investment, so interest is earned in each successive period on both principal and previously accrued interest. The time between each interest computation is called the **compounding period**. The more often interest is compounded, the higher the actual interest rate being received relative to the stated rate. The following discussion is based on the use of compound interest because most analyses use this method. Additionally, only PVs are discussed because they are more relevant to the types of management decisions discussed in this text.

Interest rates are typically stated in annual terms, and compounding is assumed to occur annually. To compensate for more frequent compounding periods, the number of years is multiplied by the number of compounding periods per year, and the annual interest rate is divided by the number of compounding periods per year.

Present Value of a Single Cash Flow

The present value of s single cash flow is the current worth of a single, specified amount of money to be received at some future date at some interest rate.

Calculating Present Value of a Single Cash Flow   LO19-7   DEMO 19-7A

Assume that Stevie Wild's investment account has an expected return of 10 percent per year, compounded annually.

◆ **What amount should Stevie invest now to achieve the goal of accumulated $100,000 in five years?**

The following diagram presents the situation.

Time period	t_0	t_1	t_2	t_3	t_4	t_5
Future value						$100,000
Present value	?					

The formula to solve for the present value is as follows.

$$PV = FV \div (1 + i)^n$$

where PV = present value of a future amount,
 FV = future value of a current investment,
  i = interest rate per compounding period, and
  n = number of compounding periods.

Substituting known values into the formula gives the following.

$$PV = \$100{,}000 \div (1 + 0.10)^5$$
$$PV = \$100{,}000 \div 1.61051$$
$$PV = \$62{,}092$$

In capital budgeting analyses, many future value amounts must be converted to present values. Rather than using formulas to find PVs, a table of factors for the PV of $1 (Table 1) for various interest rates and time periods is provided in Appendix A on the book's website for ease of computation. The discount factors for single period cash flows are obtained from the formula $[1 \div (1 + i)^n]$. Such factors are also built into Excel and can be solved as follows.

=PV(RATE,NPER,PMT,FV)	PV
=PV(0.10,5,0,−100000)	$62,092

Present Value of an Annuity

An annuity is a cash flow (either positive or negative) that is repeated over consecutive periods. In an **ordinary annuity**, cash flows occur at the end of each period. In contrast, cash flows for an **annuity due** occur at the beginning of each period.

© Cambridge Business Publishers

DEMO 19-7B LO19-7 — Calculating Present Value of an Annuity

To illustrate the computation of the PV of an annuity, consider the following situation. Joe and Jenny Clack are planning for their daughter's college education. Their daughter, Carleigh, will need $25,000 per year for the next four years.

◆ **How much should the Clacks invest currently at 8 percent so that Carleigh can withdraw $25,000 per year?**

The following diagram presents the situation.

Time period	t_0	t_1	t_2	t_3	t_4
Future value		$25,000	$25,000	$25,000	$25,000
Present value	?				

The present value of each single cash flow can be found using 8 percent factors in Table 1 of Appendix A (rounded to four decimal places) as follows.

Excel Function	Solution
=PV(RATE,NPER,PMT)	PV
=PV(0.08,4,–25000)	$82,803*

*Difference due to rounding of factors in Appendix A

PV of first receipt: $25,000 × 0.9259 .... $23,148
PV of second receipt: $25,000 × 0.8573 21,433
PV of third receipt: $25,000 × 0.7938 19,845
PV of fourth receipt: $25,000 × 0.7350 18,375
Total present value of future cash flows $82,801

The PV factor for an ordinary annuity can also be determined by adding the PV factors for all periods having a future cash flow. Table 2 in Appendix A provides PV of ordinary annuity factors for various interest rates and time periods. From this table, the factor of 3.31213 can be obtained and multiplied by $25,000 to yield $82,803, or approximately the same result as just calculated. (The difference is caused by decimal-fraction rounding.)

REVIEW 19-7 LO19-7 — Present Value Computations

a. What amount of investment earning 4 percent should you make today to have $20,000 in 20 years?

b. Would you rather have $20,000 today or receive $5,000 at the end of each year over the next 6 years, earning 5 percent interest?

c. How much money did you invest 15 years ago, to now have $50,000? Assume your investment earned 8 percent annually.

d. What is the present value of the following expected payments over the next 5 years: Year 1, $8,000; Year 2, $10,000; Year 3, $15,000; Year 4, $20,000; Year 5, $25,000. Assume that the money is invested to earn 7 percent compounded annually.

e. You have just won the lottery, which will pay you $500,000 at the end of each year for the next five years. Assuming a tax rate of 40 percent, and that you plan to invest the net payments to earn 5 percent compounded annually, what is the present value of your award? (For simplicity, assume that the interest earned is not taxable.)

f. **Critical Thinking:** Referring to part e, how would your answer change if the annual payment was instead made in quarterly installments and compounded quarterly? Why does your answer change?

More practice: MC19-25, E19-53
Solution on p. 15-52.

Appendix 19B: Accounting Rate of Return

LO19-8 What are the advantages and disadvantages of the accounting rate of return method?

The **accounting rate of return (ARR)** measures the rate of earnings obtained on the average capital investment over a project's life. This evaluation method is consistent with the accounting model and uses profits from accrual-basis accounting. It is the one evaluation technique that is not based on cash flows. The formula for computing the accounting rate of return follows.

Chapter 19 Capital Budgeting

> **ARR = Average annual profits from project ÷ Average investment in project**

Investment in project refers to project cost as well as working capital items (such as inventory) to support the project. Investment in project, salvage value, and working capital released at the end of the project's life are summed and divided by 2 to obtain the average investment over the life of the project.[5] The cost and working capital needed represent the initial investment, and the salvage value and working capital released represent the ending investment.

Calculating the Accounting Rate of Return — LO19-8 DEMO 19-8

The following information pertains to a new product line being considered by Family One Stop. The information is used to illustrate after-tax calculation of the ARR.

Beginning investment	
Initial cost of equipment and software	$4,000,000
Additional working capital needed for the product line	2,000,000
Return over life of project	
Average increase in profits after taxes	500,000
Return at end of project	
Salvage value of investment in 10 years (end of life of product line)	1,000,000
Working capital released at the end of 10 years	2,000,000

◆ **What is the accounting rate of return of this project?**

$$\text{ARR} = \$500{,}000 \div [(\$6{,}000{,}000 + \$3{,}000{,}000) \div 2]$$
$$= \$500{,}000 \div \$4{,}500{,}000$$
$$= 11.1\% \text{ (rounded)}$$

The 11.1 percent ARR on this investment can be compared with a hurdle rate set in advance by management. This hurdle rate need not be the same as the desired discount rate because the data used in calculating the ARR are not strictly cash flows. The ARR hurdle rate can be set higher than the discount rate because the discount rate automatically compensates for the time value of money. In addition, the 11.1 percent ARR for this project should be compared with ARRs on other projects under investment consideration by Family One Stop to see which projects have the higher accounting rates of return.

Accounting Rate of Return — LO19-8 REVIEW 19-8

Westend Inc is evaluating the purchase of equipment that costs $385,000, has a ten-year life, and has no salvage value at the end of its life. The company's controller estimates that the system will annually generate $182,000 of cash receipts and create $77,000 of cash operating costs. The company's tax rate is expected to be 25 percent during the life of the asset, and the company uses straight-line depreciation.

a. Compute the accounting rate of return for this equipment. (Round percentage to one decimal place.)
b. **Critical Thinking:** How does the company use the accounting rate of return to evaluate the investment?

More practice: MC19-26, E19-54, E19-55
Solution on p. 19-52.

---

[5] Sometimes ARR is computed using initial cost rather than average investment as the denominator. Such a computation ignores the return of funds at the end of the project's life and is less appropriate than the computation shown.

© Cambridge Business Publishers

Comprehensive Chapter Review

Key Terms

accounting rate of return (ARR), p. 19-28
annuity, p. 19-5
annuity due, p. 19-27
capital assets, p. 19-2
capital budgeting, p. 19-2
cash flows, p. 19-2
compounding period, p. 19-27
compound interest, p. 19-27
cost of capital (COC), p. 19-6
discounting, p. 19-6
discount rate, p. 19-6
financing decision, p. 19-3
future value (FV), p. 19-26
hurdle rate, p. 19-10
independent projects, p. 19-18
internal rate of return (IRR), p. 19-9
investment decision, p. 19-3
judgmental method, p. 19-20
mutually exclusive projects, p. 19-18
mutually inclusive projects, p. 19-18
net present value method, p. 19-6
net present value (NPV), p. 19-6
ordinary annuity, p. 19-27
payback period, p. 19-4
postinvestment audit, p. 19-24
preference decision, p. 19-16
present values (PVs), p. 19-6
profitability index (PI), p. 19-8
reinvestment assumptions, p. 19-19
return of capital, p. 19-6
return on capital, p. 19-6
risk, p. 19-20
risk-adjusted discount rate method, p. 19-21
screening decision, p. 19-16
sensitivity analysis, p. 19-22
simple interest, p. 19-27
tax benefit, p. 19-12
tax shield, p. 19-12
time line, p. 19-3
time value of money, p. 19-6

Chapter Summary

LO19-1 Payback Period (Page 19-2)
- The payback period
  - is computed by summing the annual net cash inflows until they total the original investment.
  - is the length of time required for cash inflows to recoup the initial cost of a capital project.

LO19-2 Net Present Value, Profitability Index, and Internal Rate of Return (Page 19-5)
- Net present value (NPV) and profitability index (PI) use discounted cash flows to measure the expected returns on potential capital projects.
  - NPV is the present value (PV) of cash inflows minus the PV of cash outflows.
    - To be acceptable, a project must generate an NPV of $0 or more.
  - PI is the PV of cash inflows divided by the PV of cash outflows.
    - To be acceptable, a project must generate a PI of at least 1.
- The internal rate of return (IRR) of a project is the discount rate that causes the NPV to equal zero.
  - IRR can be calculated by trial and error. Using the NPV framework, a discount rate can be arbitrarily selected and an NPV calculated.
    - If the resulting NPV is positive, select a higher discount rate and again calculate the NPV.
    - If the resulting NPV is negative, select a lower discount rate and again calculate the NPV.
    - Repeat the process until the discount rate selected causes the NPV to equal zero.
  - IRR can be calculated by many handheld calculators and computers.
  - If the only cash inflow is an annuity, the IRR can be found by using the PV of an ordinary annuity table.

LO19-3 Taxation and Depreciation (Page 19-12)
- Taxation and depreciation impact a project's cash flows because
  - operating profit is subject to income tax, which reduces the cash inflows from capital projects.
  - depreciation reduces the amount of taxes paid because depreciation is deducted in determining taxable income from projects.

LO19-4 Evaluation Method Assumptions and Limitations (Page 19-15)
- Each capital project evaluation method has certain underlying assumptions and limitations.
  - Payback method
    - Assumptions
      - The speed of investment recovery is the most important investment criterion.

- The timing and amounts of cash flows can be accurately predicted.
- The risk is lower for projects with shorter paybacks.
  - Limitations
    - Cash flows occurring after payback are ignored.
    - All cash flows are treated as deterministic.
    - The time value of money is ignored.
    - Any managerial preferences in the pattern of cash flows are ignored.
    - This method should be used in conjunction with another method because it ignores both the cash flows after the payback period is reached and the time value of money.
- NPV method
  - Assumptions
    - The discount rate used is valid for that project.
    - The timing and amounts of cash flows can be accurately predicted.
    - Cash flows received from projects can be reinvested at the discount rate for the life of the project. When comparing projects with unequal lives, the NPV method assumes that the cash inflows from the shorter project can be reinvested at the discount rate for the life of the longer project.
  - Limitations
    - All cash flows are treated as deterministic.
    - The actual rate of return for projects is not revealed.
    - Any managerial preferences in the pattern of cash flows are ignored.
- PI method
  - Assumptions
    - The discount rate used is valid for that project.
    - The timing and amounts of cash flows can be accurately predicted.
    - Cash flows received from projects can be reinvested at the discount rate for the life of the project. When comparing projects with unequal lives, the NPV method assumes that the cash inflows from the shorter project can be reinvested at the discount rate for the life of the longer project.
    - The present value of cash inflows relative to the present value of the investment measures the efficiency of capital projects.
  - Limitations
    - All cash flows are treated as deterministic.
    - The actual rate of return for projects is not revealed.
    - Any managerial preferences in the pattern of cash flows are ignored.
    - Actual dollars of net present value are ignored.
- IRR method
  - Assumptions
    - The hurdle rate used is a valid return benchmark.
    - The timing and amounts of cash flows can be accurately predicted.
    - The life of projects can be accurately predicted.
    - Cash flows received from projects can be reinvested at the internal rate of return for the life of the projects. When comparing projects with unequal lives, the IRR method assumes that the cash inflows from the shorter project can be reinvested at the internal rate of return for the life of the longer project.
  - Limitations
    - All cash flows are treated as deterministic.
    - The actual rates of return for projects are not revealed.
    - Any managerial preferences in the pattern of cash flows are ignored.
    - The dollar magnitude of return on projects is ignored.
    - Multiple IRRs can be generated on the same project.

Ranking Investment Projects
- Managers can rank capital projects using the following guidelines:
  - Shorter payback period is preferred to longer payback period.
  - Higher NPV is preferred to lower NPV.
  - Higher PI is preferred to lower PI.
  - Higher IRR is preferred to lower IRR.

LO19-5 Risk (Page 19-20)
- Capital budgeting analysis considers risk by
  - requiring a shorter payback period for riskier projects.
  - applying a higher discount rate for riskier projects when the NPV or PI method is used.
  - applying a higher discount rate for riskier cash flows when the NPV or PI method is used.
  - requiring a higher IRR for riskier projects.
  - applying sensitivity analysis to the original project assumptions and estimates.

LO19-6 Postinvestment Audits (Page 19-24)
- Postinvestment audits of projects should be
  - conducted after the project has stabilized rather than shortly after start-up.
  - to compare actual project performance against expected performance to
    - evaluate the accuracy of original projections.
    - diagnose problems with implementation.
    - assess credibility of project sponsors' information.
  - in greater depth for high-value investment projects.
  - using the same technique or techniques originally used to determine project acceptance.

Solution Strategies

LO19-1 Payback Period

1. For projects with an equal annual cash flow:

    Payback period = Investment ÷ Annuity

2. For projects with unequal annual cash flows:

    Find the length of time required for the sum of the annual cash inflows to equal the initial investment cost. If the payback period is equal to or less than a preestablished maximum number of years, the project is acceptable.

LO19-2 Net Present Value

```
− Investment made currently (no discounting required)
+ PV of future cash inflows or cost savings
− PV of future cash outflows
= NPV
```

If NPV is equal to or greater than zero, the project is expected to return a rate equal to or greater than the discount rate, and it is acceptable.

Profitability Index

```
+ PV of future cash inflows or cost savings
− PV of future cash outflows
= PV of net cash flows
```

PI = PV of net cash flows ÷ Net investment

If PI is 1.00 or higher, the project is expected to return a rate equal to or greater than the discount rate, and the project is acceptable.

Internal Rate of Return

1. For projects with equal annual cash flows:

    PV factor = Net investment ÷ Annuity

    Find the PV factor (or the one closest to it) in the annuity table on the row for the number of periods of the cash flows. The percentage at the top of the column where this factor is found will approximate the IRR. (*Note:* For projects with equal annual cash flows, this factor also equals the payback period.)

Chapter 19 Capital Budgeting

- The timing and amounts of cash flows can be accurately predicted.
- The risk is lower for projects with shorter paybacks.
- Limitations
  - Cash flows occurring after payback are ignored.
  - All cash flows are treated as deterministic.
  - The time value of money is ignored.
  - Any managerial preferences in the pattern of cash flows are ignored.
  - This method should be used in conjunction with another method because it ignores both the cash flows after the payback period is reached and the time value of money.
- NPV method
  - Assumptions
    - The discount rate used is valid for that project.
    - The timing and amounts of cash flows can be accurately predicted.
    - Cash flows received from projects can be reinvested at the discount rate for the life of the project. When comparing projects with unequal lives, the NPV method assumes that the cash inflows from the shorter project can be reinvested at the discount rate for the life of the longer project.
  - Limitations
    - All cash flows are treated as deterministic.
    - The actual rate of return for projects is not revealed.
    - Any managerial preferences in the pattern of cash flows are ignored.
- PI method
  - Assumptions
    - The discount rate used is valid for that project.
    - The timing and amounts of cash flows can be accurately predicted.
    - Cash flows received from projects can be reinvested at the discount rate for the life of the project. When comparing projects with unequal lives, the NPV method assumes that the cash inflows from the shorter project can be reinvested at the discount rate for the life of the longer project.
    - The present value of cash inflows relative to the present value of the investment measures the efficiency of capital projects.
  - Limitations
    - All cash flows are treated as deterministic.
    - The actual rate of return for projects is not revealed.
    - Any managerial preferences in the pattern of cash flows are ignored.
    - Actual dollars of net present value are ignored.
- IRR method
  - Assumptions
    - The hurdle rate used is a valid return benchmark.
    - The timing and amounts of cash flows can be accurately predicted.
    - The life of projects can be accurately predicted.
    - Cash flows received from projects can be reinvested at the internal rate of return for the life of the projects. When comparing projects with unequal lives, the IRR method assumes that the cash inflows from the shorter project can be reinvested at the internal rate of return for the life of the longer project.
  - Limitations
    - All cash flows are treated as deterministic.
    - The actual rates of return for projects are not revealed.
    - Any managerial preferences in the pattern of cash flows are ignored.
    - The dollar magnitude of return on projects is ignored.
    - Multiple IRRs can be generated on the same project.

Ranking Investment Projects
- Managers can rank capital projects using the following guidelines:
  - Shorter payback period is preferred to longer payback period.
  - Higher NPV is preferred to lower NPV.
  - Higher PI is preferred to lower PI.
  - Higher IRR is preferred to lower IRR.

LO19-5 Risk (Page 19-20)

- Capital budgeting analysis considers risk by
  - requiring a shorter payback period for riskier projects.
  - applying a higher discount rate for riskier projects when the NPV or PI method is used.
  - applying a higher discount rate for riskier cash flows when the NPV or PI method is used.
  - requiring a higher IRR for riskier projects.
  - applying sensitivity analysis to the original project assumptions and estimates.

LO19-6 Postinvestment Audits (Page 19-24)

- Postinvestment audits of projects should be
  - conducted after the project has stabilized rather than shortly after start-up.
  - to compare actual project performance against expected performance to
    - evaluate the accuracy of original projections.
    - diagnose problems with implementation.
    - assess credibility of project sponsors' information.
  - in greater depth for high-value investment projects.
  - using the same technique or techniques originally used to determine project acceptance.

Solution Strategies

LO19-1 Payback Period

1. For projects with an equal annual cash flow:

$$\text{Payback period} = \text{Investment} \div \text{Annuity}$$

2. For projects with unequal annual cash flows:

   Find the length of time required for the sum of the annual cash inflows to equal the initial investment cost. If the payback period is equal to or less than a preestablished maximum number of years, the project is acceptable.

LO19-2 Net Present Value

```
− Investment made currently (no discounting required)
+ PV of future cash inflows or cost savings
− PV of future cash outflows
= NPV
```

If NPV is equal to or greater than zero, the project is expected to return a rate equal to or greater than the discount rate, and it is acceptable.

Profitability Index

```
+ PV of future cash inflows or cost savings
− PV of future cash outflows
= PV of net cash flows
```

$$PI = \text{PV of net cash flows} \div \text{Net investment}$$

If PI is 1.00 or higher, the project is expected to return a rate equal to or greater than the discount rate, and the project is acceptable.

Internal Rate of Return

1. For projects with equal annual cash flows:

$$\text{PV factor} = \text{Net investment} \div \text{Annuity}$$

Find the PV factor (or the one closest to it) in the annuity table on the row for the number of periods of the cash flows. The percentage at the top of the column where this factor is found will approximate the IRR. (*Note:* For projects with equal annual cash flows, this factor also equals the payback period.)

Chapter 19 Capital Budgeting

2. For projects with unequal annual cash flows:

   Make an estimate of the rate provided by the project; compute NPV. If NPV is positive (negative), try a higher (lower) rate until the NPV is zero. Compare IRR to the required hurdle rate. If the IRR is equal to or greater than the hurdle rate, the project is acceptable.

Tax Benefit of Depreciation   LO19-3

$$\text{Tax benefit} = \text{Depreciation amount} \times \text{Tax rate}$$

Accounting Rate of Return   LO19-8

$$\text{ARR} = \text{Average annual profits from project} \div \text{Average investment in project}$$

$$\text{Average investment} = (\text{Beginning investment in project} + \text{Recovery of investment at end of project life}) \div 2$$

Compare calculated ARR to hurdle ARR. If the calculated ARR is equal to or greater than the hurdle ARR, the project is acceptable.

Basic Concepts of Capital Budgeting Techniques   LO19-4, 8

	Payback	NPV	PI	IRR	ARR
Uses time value of money?	No	Yes	Yes	Yes	No
Indicates a specific rate of return?	No	No	No	Yes	Yes
Uses cash flow?	Yes	Yes	Yes	Yes	No
Considers returns during life of project?	No	Yes	Yes	Yes	Yes
Uses discount rate in calculation?	No	Yes	Yes	No*	No*

*Discount rate is not used in the calculation, but it can be used as the hurdle rate.

Chapter Demonstration Problem

Elton Credit Co. is considering an investment in a web-based store front. The project would require an initial investment of $400,000 and have an expected life of six years with no salvage value. At the end of the fourth year, the firm anticipates spending $70,000 to update some hardware and software. This amount would be fully deductible for tax purposes in the year incurred.   LO19-1, 2

Management requires that investments of this type be recouped in five years or less. Management also requires this project to generate an accounting rate of return of at least 8 percent. The pre-tax increase in income is expected to be $95,000 in each of the first four years and $80,000 in each of the next two years. The company's discount rate is 8 percent, its tax rate is 30 percent, and the investment would be depreciated for tax purposes using the straight-line method with no consideration of salvage value over a five-year period and for accounting purposes over a six-year period with no salvage value.

Required:
a. Prepare a time line for displaying cash flows. Be certain to consider the effects of taxes.
b. Calculate the after-tax payback period.
c. Calculate the after-tax NPV on the project.
d. Calculate the profitability index of the project.
e. Discuss whether this is an acceptable investment.

Solution to Demonstration Problem

a.

End of period	0	1	2	3	4	5	6
Investment	$(400,000)						
Operating inflows[a]		$66,500	$66,500	$66,500	$66,500	$56,000	$56,000
Depreciation tax benefit[b]		24,000	24,000	24,000	24,000	24,000	
Operating outflows[c]					(49,000)		
Total cash flows	$(400,000)	$90,500	$90,500	$90,500	$41,500	$80,000	$56,000

[a] $95,000 × (1 − 0.30) = $66,500
$80,000 × (1 − 0.30) = $56,000
[b] ($400,000 ÷ 5) × 0.30 = $24,000
[c] $70,000 × (1 − 0.30) = $49,000

b.

Year	Annual Flow	Cumulative Flow
0	$(400,000)	$(400,000)
1	90,500	(309,500)
2	90,500	(219,000)
3	90,500	(128,500)
4	41,500	(87,000)
5	80,000	(7,000)
6	56,000	49,000

The payback is complete in 5.125 years or in the middle of February in the sixth year. The portion of the sixth year (0.125) required to complete the payback equals $7,000 ÷ $56,000.

Excel Function	Solution
=PV(RATE,NPER,PMT,FV)	PV
=PV(0.08,3,−90500,0)	$233,227
=PV(0.08,4,0,−41500)	30,504
=PV(0.08,5,0,−80000)	54,447
=PV(0.08,6,0,−56000)	35,289
Initial investment	(400,000)
NPV calculated in Excel	$ (46,533)

c.

Cash Flow	Time	Amount	Discount Factor*	Present Value
Investment	t_0	$(400,000)	1.0000	$(400,000)
Annual flow	t_1–t_3	90,500	2.5771	233,228
Annual flow	t_4	41,500	0.7350	30,503
Annual flow	t_5	80,000	0.6806	54,448
Annual flow	t_6	56,000	0.6302	35,291
Net present value				$ (46,530)

*Rounded to four decimal places.

d. The profitability index = Present value of net cash inflows ÷ Net investment
= ($400,000 − $46,530) ÷ $400,000 = 0.88

e. The project is unacceptable based on the payback period. The project also fails to qualify based on all the discounted cash flow criteria. Accordingly, from strictly a financial perspective, the project is not acceptable. However, nonquantitative factors, such as effects on competitive position and ability to adopt future technological advances, must be considered.

Assignments with the MBC logo in the margin are available in BusinessCourse.
Resources include demonstration videos, guided examples, and auto-graded homework.
See details in the Preface, and ask your professor how you can access the system.

Data Analytics

LO19-5 **DA19-1. Use a sensitivity analysis to adjust discount rate in NPV**
Refer to the data provided in MBC for three separate cases to answer the following questions.

Required

a. Prepare a table in Excel to compute the net present value for each proposal, A, B and C. In your formulas, reference the discount rate used for all of your calculations to a single cell. *Hint*: By referencing all of your calculations to a single cell, you can easily develop a sensitivity analysis by changing the discount rate in that cell and the output (net present value) will update automatically.

b. Prepare a new table listing the discount rate from 5 percent to 20 percent along with the net present value for each proposal, A, B, and C. *Hint*: Using the table from part *a*, enter each percentage. Take the results and copy and paste values into the new table.

c. Prepare a line chart showing the net present value of proposals A, B, and C with discount rates ranging from 5 percent to 20 percent.

d. Using the chart in part *c*, answer the following questions.
1. Which project has the highest net present value for each interest rate in your chart?
2. Which project has the lowest net present value for each interest rate in your chart?
3. Using only the chart and no additional calculations, what is the approximate internal rate of return for each project?
4. Does the net present value increase or decrease as the interest rate changes? Why?
5. How does this sensitivity analysis take into account the risk of the investment? Should each project be discounted at the same interest rate?
6. What's the highest discount rate that generates a net present value for all proposals that's not a negative amount?

Chapter 19 Capital Budgeting   19-35

7. Based on the net present value, which proposal would you recommend, assuming that you must choose one?

DA19-2. Use a sensitivity analysis to adjust cash flows in NPV   LO19-5
Refer to the data provided in MBC for three separate cases to answer the following questions.

Required
a. Prepare a table in Excel to compute the net present value for Proposal A and consider this the *likely* scenario. Next, prepare an optimistic and pessimistic scenario. For the *optimistic* scenario, increase each cash inflow by 10 percent and for the *pessimistic* scenario, decrease each net cash inflow by 10 percent.
b. Prepare a bar chart showing the net present value for the likely, optimistic, and pessimistic scenarios.
c. Using the chart in part *b*, answer the following questions.
   1. Indicate whether any of the three scenarios meet the screening test based on net present value.
   2. Would you recommend that the company move forward with proposal A?

Data Visualization

Data Visualization Activities are available in *BusinessCourse*. These assignments use Tableau Dashboards to expose students to visual depictions of data and introduce students to data analytics through data visualizations. These exercises are easily assignable and auto graded by MBC.

Potential Ethical Issues

1. Using only financial criteria to evaluate projects that enhance employee safety or reduce detrimental environmental impact
2. Changing assumptions or estimates for projects solely so that they will meet required criteria for investment approval
3. Using an inappropriately low discount rate relative to the risk of a project so that the project will generate a positive NPV and be acceptable
4. Failing to conduct postinvestment audits to hold project sponsors accountable for differences between the investment proposal and actual results achieved by projects
5. Choosing projects based only on their impact on accounting earnings and not on discounted cash flow analyses

Questions

Q19-1. What is a capital asset? How is it distinguished from other assets?
Q19-2. Why do capital budgeting evaluation methods use cash flows rather than accounting income?
Q19-3. How are time lines helpful in evaluating capital projects?
Q19-4. What does the payback method measure? What are its major weaknesses?
Q19-5. What is the distinction between a return *of* capital and a return *on* capital?
Q19-6. What is measured by the net present value (NPV) of a potential project? If the NPV of a project is $0, is it an acceptable project? Explain.
Q19-7. Will the NPV amount determined in the capital budgeting process be the same amount as that which actually occurs after a project is undertaken? Why or why not?
Q19-8. How is the profitability index (PI) related to the NPV method? What does the PI measure?
Q19-9. What is measured by the internal rate of return? When is a project considered acceptable using this method?
Q19-10. Because depreciation is not a cash flow, why is it important in capital budgeting evaluation techniques that use discounted cash flows?
Q19-11. What four questions should managers ask when choosing the investment proposals to fund?

© Cambridge Business Publishers

Q19-12. How is risk defined in capital budgeting analysis? List several aspects of a project in which risk is involved and how risk can affect a project's net present value.

Q19-13. How is sensitivity analysis used in capital budgeting?

Q19-14. Why are postinvestment audits performed? When should they be performed?

Q19-15. (*Appendix 1*) What is meant by the term *time value of money*? Why is a present value always less than the future value to which it relates?

Q19-16. (*Appendix 2*) How is the accounting rate of return computed? How does this rate differ from the discount rate and the internal rate of return?

Multiple Choice

LO19-1

MC19-17. Which one of the following is not a shortcoming of the payback method?
- a. It offers no consideration of cash flows beyond the expiration of the payback period.
- b. It ignores the time value of money.
- c. It offers no indication of a project's liquidity.
- d. It encourages establishing a short payback period.

LO19-1

MC19-18. A company is considering the purchase of five construction cranes for its recently awarded construction project. The cranes cost $20,000 each. These cranes are projected to provide a total cash savings of $190,000 over the next eight years. The projected cash savings by year are shown below.

Year	Cash Savings	Year	Cash Savings
0	$ 0	5	$24,000
1	35,000	6	20,000
2	32,000	7	15,000
3	28,000	8	10,000
4	26,000		

The payback period is closest to
- a. 4.0 years.
- b. 3.2 years.
- c. 3.4 years.
- d. 3.0 years.

LO19-2

MC19-19. Jenson Copying Company is planning to buy a coping machine costing $25,310. The net present values (NPV) of this investment, at various discount rates, are as follows.

Discount Rate	NPV
4%	$2,440
6%	$1,420
8%	$ 460
10%	$ (440)

Jenson's approximate internal rate of return on this investment is
- a. 6 percent.
- b. 8 percent.
- c. 9 percent.
- d. 10 percent.

LO19-2

MC19-20. A company is interested in a capital project that has a net present value of $0. The company should
- a. accept the project because the company's required rate of return has been met.
- b. accept the project because the company's value will increase.
- c. reject the project because its cash inflows equal the project's cash outflows.
- d. reject the project because its internal rate of return is 0 percent.

LO19-3

MC19-21. For each of the next six years Atlantic Motors anticipates net income of $10,000, straight-line tax depreciation of $20,000, a 40 percent tax rate, a discount rate of 10 percent, and cash sales of $100,000. The depreciable assets are all being acquired at the beginning of year 1 and will have a salvage value of zero at the end of six years. The present value of the total depreciation tax savings would be
- a. $8,000.
- b. $27,072.
- c. $34,842.
- d. $87,100.

Chapter 19 Capital Budgeting

MC19-22. Molar Inc. is evaluating three independent projects for the expansion of different product lines. The Finance Department has performed an extensive analysis of each project and the chief financial officer has indicated that there is no capital rationing in effect. Which of the following statements are correct?
  I. Reject any project with a payback period which is shorter than the company standard.
  II. The project with the highest internal rate of return (IRR) exceeding the hurdle rate should be selected and the others rejected.
  III. All projects with positive net present values should be selected.
  IV. Molar should reject any projects with negative IRRs.
  a. I, II, and IV only.
  b. I, II, III, and IV.
  c. II and III only.
  d. III and IV only.

MC19-23. The Cuisine Shop is evaluating a capital expenditure proposal with the following predicted cash flows:

Initial investment....................	$(85,000)
Operations, each year for four years ...	30,000
Salvage........................	8,000
Discount rate, 14%	

Using sensitivity analysis, how far can the discount rate rise before the investment would become unacceptable? Compute your answer using Excel.
  a. 17.9 percent
  b. 15.4 percent
  c. 20.5 percent
  d. 16.1 percent

MC19-24. Refer to the information in MC19-23 but now assume that a postinvestment audit revealed that cash inflows were $28,000 over the four years and salvage value was only $2,000. Using Excel, what is the net present value based on the original estimated data and the net present value using actual cash flows?
  a. NPV using estimates: $25,721; NPV using actual amounts: $2,411
  b. NPV using estimates: $(2,325); NPV using actual amounts: $(4,600)
  c. NPV using estimates: $7,148; NPV using actual amounts: $(2,232)
  d. NPV using estimates: $2,411; NPV using actual amounts: $(3,416)

MC19-25. Appendix; An initial investment of $66,200 is to be returned in six equal annual payments. Determine the amount of each payment if the interest rate is 10 percent.
  a. $11,033
  b. $13,818
  c. $14,800
  d. $15,200

MC19-26. Appendix; Referring to MC 19-23, the accounting rate of return on the investment is
  a. 0.706
  b. 0.645
  c. 0.353
  d. 0.176

Exercises

E19-27. Cash flows, accounting accruals Snappel Inc. is considering the purchase of new equipment for a purchase price of $105,000. The equipment has an estimated useful life of 5 years and an estimated cash salvage value of $8,000. Incremental annual fixed costs for operating the equipment over its 5-year useful life are as follows: Year 1, $18,000; Year 2, $20,000; Year 3, $20,000; Year 4, $25,000; and Year 5, $22,000. Incremental contribution margin generated from additional sales are estimated as follows: Year 1, $35,000; Year 2, $50,000; Year 3, $55,000; Year 4, $55,000; and Year 5, $60,000. The company uses the straight-line method for depreciation purposes.

  a. Prepare a time line for this purchase that shows cash flows over the life of the proposed equipment purchase. Ignore taxes.
  b. Prepare a time line for this purchase that shows the earnings effects for the equipment's five-year life on an accrual basis. Ignore taxes.
  c. What is the net amount of cash flows from part *a* over the 5-year period?
  d. What is the net amount of accounting earnings from part *b* over the 5-year period?

LO19-1 **E19-28. Cash flows vs. accounting accruals; writing** In discussing your cost accounting class with friends, you explained that you were currently studying methods of evaluating capital investments. You mentioned that most of these methods rely upon cash flow analysis. One particularly sophisticated friend was surprised to hear that these analyses used cash flows rather than accounting earnings. He said, "It seems to me that investors are only interested in accounting earnings and don't pay much attention to cash flows. In fact, you never hear market commentators talk about cash flow; they always talk about a firm's income and whether earnings will match investor and analyst expectations."

Provide a written explanation to your friend that provides the rationale for capital budgeting techniques focusing on cash flows rather than accounting earnings.

LO19-1 **E19-29. Cash flows vs. accounting accruals** Lundholm Corp. is considering the purchase of a robotic machine that would replace a manual labor production task. The purchase and installation of this machine would require an upfront cash commitment of $3,000,000. The machine would have a five-year expected life (and zero salvage value) and generate annual labor cost savings of $900,000. The machine will be depreciated over its expected life. Prepare a time line (including a total column) for this purchase that shows both the cash flow and accounting earnings effects for the machine's five-year life. Ignore taxes.

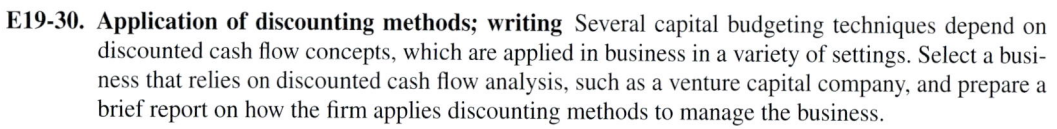

LO19-1 **E19-30. Application of discounting methods; writing** Several capital budgeting techniques depend on discounted cash flow concepts, which are applied in business in a variety of settings. Select a business that relies on discounted cash flow analysis, such as a venture capital company, and prepare a brief report on how the firm applies discounting methods to manage the business.

LO19-1 **E19-31. Payback period** Laredo Laminates is considering the purchase of new production technology equipment requiring an initial $3,000,000 investment and having an expected ten-year life. At the end of its life, the equipment would have no salvage value. By installing the new equipment, the firm's annual labor and quality costs would decline by $600,000.

a. Compute the payback period for this equipment.
b. Assume instead that the annual cost savings would vary according to the following schedule:

Years	Annual Cost Savings
1–5	$300,000
6–10	400,000

Compute the payback period under the revised circumstances.

LO19-1 **E19-32. Payback period** Houston Fashions is considering a new product line that would require an investment of $140,000 in fixtures and displays and $180,000 in working capital. Store managers expect the following pattern of net cash inflows from the new product line over the life of the investment.

Year	Amount
1	$70,000
2	78,000
3	72,000
4	56,000
5	50,000
6	48,000
7	44,000

a. Compute the payback period for the proposed new product line. Houston Fashions requires a four-year pre-tax payback period on its investments. (Round to one decimal point.) Should the company make this investment? Explain.
b. Should Houston Fashions use any other capital project evaluation method(s) before making an investment decision? Explain.

LO19-1, 2 **E19-33. Comparing capital budgeting methods** Match each of the following descriptions, *a* through *h*, with a capital budgeting method: (1) payback method, (2) net present value, (3) profitability index, or (4) internal rate of return. More than one method may apply.

a. _____ Requires the use of a hurdle rate to interpret results.
b. _____ May not recognize all relevant project cash flows.
c. _____ Provides the relation of an output measure to an input measure.
d. _____ The calculation relies on the use of a valid discount rate.

Chapter 19 Capital Budgeting

  e. ____ Does not consider the time value of money.
  f. ____ Used to rank projects based on each project's cash inflows relative to initial investment.
  g. ____ Assumes that the life of a project is accurately estimated.
  h. ____ Of primary consideration is a rapid recovery of the initial investment.

E19-34. NPV Commodity Copper is considering the installation of a $1,800,000 production conveyor system that would generate the following labor cost savings over its 10-year life:

Years	Annual Labor Cost Savings
1–2	$280,000
3–5	340,000
6–8	288,800
9–10	260,000

The system will have no salvage at the end of its 10-year life, and the company uses a discount rate of 12 percent. What is the pre-tax net present value of this potential investment?

E19-35. NPV Birmingham Bolt, Inc., has been approached by one of its customers about producing 800,000 special-purpose parts for a new home product. The customer wants 100,000 parts per year for eight years. To provide these parts, Birmingham would need to acquire a $500,000 new production machine. The new machine would have no salvage value at the end of its eight-year life.

The customer has offered to pay Birmingham $7.50 per unit for the parts. Birmingham's managers have estimated that, in addition to the new machine, the company would incur the following costs to produce each part:

Direct labor	$2.00
Direct material	2.50
Variable overhead	2.00
Total	$6.50

In addition, annual fixed out-of-pocket costs related to the production of these parts would be $20,000.

  a. Compute the net present value of the machine investment, assuming that the company uses a discount rate of 9 percent to evaluate capital projects.
  b. Based on the NPV computed in *a*, is the machine a worthwhile investment? Explain.
  c. In addition to the NPV, what other factors should Birmingham's managers consider when making the investment decision?

E19-36. PI A manager at Shannon's Custom Cabinets is interested in purchasing a computer, software, and peripheral equipment costing $240,000 that would allow company salespeople to demonstrate to customers how a finished carpet installation would appear. Using this cost, the manager has determined that the investment's net present value is $18,000. Compute the investment's profitability index. (Round to two decimal points.)

E19-37. PI Cedar City Public Transportation is considering adding a new bus route. To do so, the entity would be required to purchase a new $600,000 bus, which would have a 10-year life and no salvage value. If the new bus is purchased, Cedar City Public Transportation's managers expect net cash inflows from bus ridership would rise by $91,000 per year for the life of the bus. Cedar City Public Transportation uses a 9 percent required rate of return for evaluating capital projects.

  a. Compute the profitability index of the bus investment. (Round to two decimal points.)
  b. Should Cedar City Public Transportation buy the new bus?
  c. What is the minimum acceptable value for the profitability index for an investment to be acceptable? Explain.

E19-38. IRR; sensitivity analysis White Sands Resort is considering adding a new dock to accommodate large yachts. The dock would cost $700,000 and would generate $144,000 annually in new cash inflows. Its expected life would be eight years, with no salvage value. The resort's cost of capital and discount rate are 7 percent.

  a. Calculate the internal rate of return for the proposed dock addition (round to the nearest whole percent).
  b. Based on your answer to *a*, should the resort add the new dock?
  c. How much annual cash inflow would be required for the project to be minimally acceptable?

LO19-2 **E19-39. IRR** Latin Cuisine is considering the purchase of new food processing technology, which would cost $1,800,000 and would generate $300,000 in annual cost savings. No salvage is expected on the technology at the end of its 10-year life. The firm's cost of capital and discount rate are both 10 percent.

a. Calculate the internal rate of return for the project. (Round to the closest one-half percent.) Does the IRR indicate the project is acceptable?
b. What qualitative factors should the company consider in evaluating the investment?

LO19-2 **E19-40. NPV; IRR** Jenna Smith recently purchased an annuity contract that will pay her $375,000 per year for the next seven years. According to Smith's calculations, the estimated internal rate of return on this investment is 12 percent. If Smith's cost of capital is 10 percent, what is the estimated NPV of the annuity investment?

LO19-2 **E19-41. NPV, PI, IRR** Good Products Inc. is evaluating a capital expenditure proposal that has the following predicted cash flows:

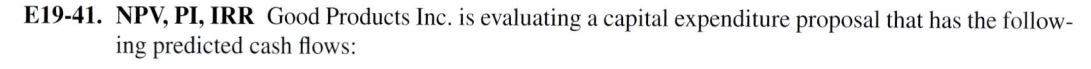

Initial investment.	$100,000
Operational cost savings per year over 3 years	$ 45,000

a. Determine the payback period.
b. Using a discount rate of 12 percent, determine the net present value of the investment proposal, assuming the salvage value is $0.
c. Determine the project's profitability index.
d. Determine the project's internal rate of return using Excel.
e. Would you recommend that the project be accepted?

LO19-3 **E19-42. Depreciation; PV** Yankee Freight provides truck freight services throughout the northeast United States. The firm is considering an investment in improved logistics management requiring a mainframe computer and communications software, which would cost $1,000,000 and have an expected life of eight years. For tax purposes, the investment will be depreciated using the straight-line method, with no salvage value. The company's cost of capital and tax rates are 8 and 30 percent, respectively.

a. Compute the present value of the depreciation tax benefit.
b. Assume instead that Yankee Freight uses the double-declining-balance method of depreciation for tax purposes with a five-year life. Compute the present value of the depreciation tax benefit.
c. Why is the depreciation tax benefit computed in *b* larger than that computed in *a*?

LO19-4 **E19-43. Alternative depreciation methods; NPV** Kansas Salt Co. is considering an investment in computer-based production technology as part of a business reengineering process. The necessary equipment will cost $18,000,000, have a life of eight years, and generate annual net before-tax cash flows of $3,100,000 from operations. Cost of installation and training is considered nominal. The equipment will have no salvage value at the end of its eight-year estimated life.

The company's tax rate and cost of capital are, respectively, 30 percent and 5 percent.

a. If Kansas Salt Co. uses straight-line depreciation for tax purposes, is the project acceptable using the net present value method?
b. Assume that the tax law allows the company to take accelerated annual depreciation on this asset in the following manner:

Years 1–2	23% of cost
Years 3–8	9% of cost

What is the net present value of the equipment? Is it acceptable?
c. Recompute *a* and *b* assuming the tax rate is increased to 40 percent.

LO19-3 **E19-44. Tax effects of asset sale** Three years ago, Girston Gravel Pit purchased a material conveyor system. The company has decided to sell the system and acquire more advanced technology. Data relating to the existing system follow.

Current fair value	$37,000
Original cost	99,000
Current book value for tax purposes	18,000
Current book value for financial accounting purposes	35,000
Corporate tax rate	30%

Chapter 19 Capital Budgeting

a. How much depreciation has been taken on the conveyor system for (1) tax and (2) financial accounting purposes?
b. What will be the after-tax cash flow from the sale of this asset?
c. What will be the after-tax cash flow from the sale of the asset if its fair value is $9,000 rather than $37,000?

E19-45. Assumptions of capital budgeting methods For each of the following assumptions that underlie the capital project evaluation methods, indicate to which method, or methods, the assumption applies. Consider all of the following methods: payback, NPV, PI, IRR, and ARR (from Appendix 19B). — LO19-4, 8

a. Speed of investment recovery is a key investment criterion.
b. Cash inflows can be reinvested at the hurdle rate.
c. Cash inflows can be reinvested at the IRR.
d. Timing and size of cash flows can be accurately predicted.
e. Life of project can be accurately predicted.
f. Risk is higher for cash flows in the more distant future.
g. Key consideration in evaluating projects is their effects on accounting earnings.

E19-46. Limitations of capital budgeting methods For each of the following limitations of the capital project evaluation methods, indicate to which method, or methods, the limitation applies. Consider all of the following methods: payback, NPV, PI, IRR, and ARR (from Appendix 19B). — LO19-4, 8

a. Treats cash flows as deterministic.
b. Ignores some cash flows.
c. Ignores cash flows.
d. Ignores the time value of money.
e. Ignores effects on accounting earnings.
f. Does not specifically consider cash flow preferences.
g. Can provide multiple rates of return for the same project.
h. Ignores dollar value of project benefits.

E19-47. Capital rationing Management of Frisco Films is considering the following capital projects: — LO19-2, 4

Project	Cost	Annual After-Tax Cash Flows	Number of Years
New film studios	$20,000,000	$3,100,000	15
Cameras and equipment	3,200,000	800,000	8
Land improvement	5,000,000	1,180,000	10
Motion picture #1	17,800,000	4,970,000	5
Motion picture #2	11,400,000	3,920,000	4
Motion picture #3	8,000,000	2,300,000	7
Corporate aircraft	2,400,000	770,000	5

Assume that all projects have no salvage value and that the firm uses a discount rate of 10 percent. Management has decided that only $25,000,000 can be spent in the current year for capital projects.

a. Determine the net present value, profitability index, and internal rate of return for each of the seven projects.
b. Rank the seven projects according to each method used in a.
c. Indicate how you would suggest to the management of Frisco Films that the money be spent. What would be the total net present value of your selected investments?

E19-48. Uncertain annual cash flow Sepchek Oil Field Services is considering the installation of a new electronic surveillance system for its warehouse. The system has an initial cost of $160,000 and an expected life of five years. For its life, the system will save the company labor costs for security guards. — LO19-1, 5

a. If the company's cost of capital is 10 percent, how much annual increase in cash flows is necessary to minimally justify the investment?
b. Based on your answer to a, what would be the payback period for this investment?

E19-49. NPV; uncertain cost of capital Brenda's Bees is considering the purchase of new honey processing equipment. The equipment would cost $100,000, have an expected life of seven years, and save $28,000 annually in maintenance, operating, and cleanup costs. The firm's cost of capital is estimated to be 10 percent. — LO19-2, 5

a. Calculate the NPV of the proposed project.

b. Because the company is fairly small, the CEO is uncertain about her firm's actual cost of capital. To the nearest whole percent, what is the maximum the firm's cost of capital could be for this project to be acceptable? Compute your answer using Excel.

LO19-6

E19-50. Postinvestment audit Bayside Inc. is performing a postinvestment audit on a purchase of industrial equipment made six years ago. Predicted and actual initial cash outflow amounts and annual net cash inflow amounts from operations are as follows.

	Estimate	Actual
Initial outlay......	$(350,000)	$(385,000)
Year 1..........	137,500	0
Year 2..........	137,500	165,000
Year 3..........	137,500	137,500
Year 4..........	66,000	66,000
Year 5..........	66,000	66,000
Year 6..........	66,000	66,000

a. What was the estimated net present value of the project?
b. What was the actual net present value of the project?
c. What accounted for the difference between part *a* and part *b*?

LO19-7

E19-51. Appendix; FV You just invested $80,000 in a mutual fund account that guarantees to pay you 6 percent interest, compounded annually. At the end of five years, how much money will have accumulated in your investment account? (Ignore taxes.)

LO19-7

E19-52. Appendix; PV You have just purchased a new car, making a down payment of $8,000 and financing the balance of the purchase cost on an installment credit plan. According to the credit agreement, you will pay $800 per month for a period of 48 months. If the credit agreement is based on a monthly interest rate of 1 percent, what is the cost of the car? Compute your answer using Excel.

LO19-7

E19-53. Appendix; PV Use the tables in Appendix A from the book's website to determine the answers to the following questions. Ignore taxes in all circumstances.

a. Titus wishes to have $50,000 in six years. He can make an investment today that will earn 8 percent each year, compounded annually. What amount of investment should he make today to achieve his goal?
b. Jacob is going to receive $400,000 on his 50th birthday, 20 years from today. He has the opportunity to invest money today in a government-backed security paying 5 percent compounded annually. How much would he be willing to receive today instead of the $400,000 in 20 years?
c. Jason has $60,000 today that he intends to use as a down payment on a house. How much money did Jason invest 20 years ago to have $60,000 now if his investment earned 8 percent compounded annually?
d. Lonnie is the host of a television game show that gives away thousands of dollars each day. One prize on the show is an annuity, paid to the winner, in equal installments of $200,000 at the end of each year for the next five years. If a winner has an investment opportunity to earn 8 percent, annually, what present amount would he or she take in exchange for the annuity?
e. Keri is going to be paid modeling fees for the next ten years as follows: Year 1, $50,000; Year 2, $55,000; Year 3, $60,000; Years 4–8, $100,000; Year 9, $70,000; and Year 10, $45,000. She can invest her money at 7 percent compounded annually. What is the present value of her future modeling fees?
f. Dave has just won the lottery, which will pay him $200,000 per year for the next five years. If this is the only asset Dave owns, will he be a millionaire (one who has a net worth of $1,000,000 or more)? Explain.

LO19-1, 8

E19-54. Appendix; Payback; ARR Portsmouth Port Services creates and maintains shipping channels at various ports around the world. The company is considering the purchase of a $72,000,000 ocean-going dredge that has a five-year life and no salvage value. The company depreciates assets on a straight-line basis. This equipment's expected annual cash flow on a before-tax basis is $20,000,000. Portsmouth requires that an investment be recouped in less than five years and have a pre-tax accounting rate of return of at least 18 percent.

a. Compute the payback period and accounting rate of return for this equipment. (Round to one decimal point.)

Chapter 19 Capital Budgeting

   b. Is the equipment an acceptable investment for Portsmouth? Explain.

E19-55. Appendix; Payback; ARR Kurt's Office Services is evaluating the purchase of a state-of-the-art desktop publishing system that costs $40,000, has a six-year life, and has no salvage value at the end of its life. The company's controller estimates that the system will annually generate $15,000 of cash receipts and create $3,000 of cash operating costs. The company's tax rate is expected to be 30 percent during the life of the asset, and the company uses straight-line depreciation.
LO19-1, 8

   a. Determine the annual after-tax cash flows from the project.
   b. Determine the after-tax payback period for the project. (Round to one decimal point.)
   c. Determine the after-tax accounting rate of return for the project. (Assume tax and financial accounting depreciation are equal.) (Round to one decimal point.)

Problems

P19-56. Financing decision; ethics; writing Although they should be considered independently, investing and financing decisions are often considered together. Consider the case of a consumer acquiring a new car. The consumer can purchase a car by either paying cash or borrowing money through the car dealer or a bank. Alternatively, the consumer can acquire the car through a lease arrangement. When the consumer compares the options of financing or leasing the car, the better option may not be obvious. Indeed, the consumer may not have sufficient information, or skill, to identify the better alternative, and the car dealer and/or manufacturer may exploit that circumstance.
LO19-1

Complex lease contracts combined with hidden costs complicate the decision to lease or buy. However, key lease terms such as the cost of the car are disclosed to consumers. Laws in some states, as well as Federal Reserve Board Regulation M and leasing data available on the Internet, are prompting dealers to make increased disclosures. Unfortunately, some fees, including the interest rate the dealer uses to calculate the lease payment (known in the industry as the money factor), still remain unknown to the consumer.

   a. Why might some consumers find leasing a car to be more appealing than purchasing one?
   b. Is the practice of not disclosing lease information ethical for car dealers and manufacturers even if such disclosure is not required by law? Discuss.
   c. As an accountant, how could you aid a client in a car-buying situation?

P19-57. Ethics; qualitative information; writing Joey Hernandez was reprimanded by the home office for recommending a pollution abatement project because the project did not meet the standard financial criterion of an 8 percent rate of return. However, Hernandez had concluded that the $950,000 piece of equipment was necessary to prevent small amounts of arsenic from seeping into the city's water system. No EPA warnings have been issued to the company.
LO19-1

   a. Discuss the company requirement of an 8 percent rate of return on all projects.
   b. What might be the ultimate consequence to Hernandez's employer if it fails to prevent future arsenic seepage into the water system?
   c. How should Hernandez justify the purchase of the equipment to the home office?

P19-58. Time line; payback; NPV Holly's Fashions is considering expanding its building so it can stock additional merchandise for travelers and tourists. Store manager Jill Eliason anticipates that building expansion costs would be $190,000. The firm's suppliers are willing to provide inventory on a consignment basis so there would be no additional working capital needed upon expansion. Annual incremental fixed cash costs for the store expansion are expected to be as follows:
LO19-1, 2

Year	Amount	Year	Amount
1	$20,000	5	$30,000
2	27,000	6	30,000
3	27,000	7	30,000
4	27,000	8	33,000

Eliason estimates that annual cash inflows could be increased by $60,000 of contribution margin generated from the additional merchandise sales. Because of uncertainty about the future, Eliason does not want to consider any cash flows after eight years. The firm uses an 8 percent discount rate.

   a. Construct a time line for the investment.

b. Determine the payback period. (Ignore taxes.)
c. Calculate the net present value of the project. (Ignore taxes.)

LO19-1, 2

P19-59. Time line; payback; NPV Austin Audio Systems is considering the purchase of a new delivery truck to replace an existing unit. The truck would cost $45,000 and would have a life of seven years with no salvage value. The existing truck could be sold currently for $4,000, but if it is kept, it will have a remaining life of seven years with no salvage value. By purchasing the truck, Austin Audio Systems' managers would anticipate operating cost savings as follows:

Year	Amount	Year	Amount
1	$5,900	5	$8,000
2	8,100	6	8,300
3	8,300	7	9,200
4	8,000		

Austin Audio Systems' cost of capital and capital project evaluation rate is 8 percent.

a. Construct a time line for the purchase of the truck.
b. Determine the payback period. (Ignore taxes.) (Round time to one decimal point.)
c. Calculate the net present value of the truck. (Ignore taxes.)

LO19-2, 5

P19-60. NPV; PI; sensitivity analysis Westside Warehouse is considering reengineering some production operations with automated equipment. The new equipment would have an initial cost of $5,000,000 including installation. The vendor has indicated that the equipment has an expected life of seven years with an estimated salvage value of $400,000. Estimates of annual labor savings and incremental costs associated with operating the new equipment follow.

Annual labor cost savings (14 workers)	$950,000
Annual maintenance costs	40,000
Annual property taxes	28,000
Annual insurance costs	44,000

a. Assuming the company's cost of capital is 6 percent, compute the NPV of the automated equipment. (Ignore taxes.)
b. Based on the NPV, should the company invest in the new equipment?
c. Compute the profitability index for this potential investment. (Ignore taxes.) (Round to two decimal points.)
d. Assume Westside's managers are least confident of the estimates of labor cost savings. Calculate the minimum annual labor savings that must be realized for the project to be financially acceptable.
e. What other qualitative factors should the company consider in evaluating this investment?

LO19-1, 2

P19-61. Payback; IRR Shelly's Tax Services prepares tax returns for individuals and small businesses. The firm employs four tax professionals. Currently, all tax returns are prepared on a manual basis. The firm's owner, Shelly Foster, is considering purchasing a computer system that would allow the firm to serve all its existing clients with only three employees. To evaluate the feasibility of the computerized system, Foster has gathered the following information:

Initial cost of the hardware and software	$140,000
Expected salvage value in four years	$0
Annual depreciation	$30,000
Incremental annual operating costs	$8,500
Incremental annual labor savings	$47,500
Expected life of the computer system	4 years

Foster has determined that she will invest in the computer system if its pre-tax payback period is less than 3.5 years and its pre-tax IRR exceeds 12 percent.

a. Compute the payback period for this investment. (Round time to one decimal point.) Does the payback meet Foster's criterion? Explain.
b. Compute the IRR for this project to the nearest percentage. Based on the computed IRR, is this project acceptable to Foster? Explain.
c. What qualitative factors should Foster consider in evaluating the project?

Chapter 19 Capital Budgeting

P19-62. NPV; PI; payback; IRR Pete's Paving provides custom paving of sidewalks and driveways. One of the most labor-intensive aspects of the paving operation is preparing and mixing materials. Sharon Guillon, corporate engineer, has found new computerized equipment to mix (and monitor the mixing of) materials. According to information received by Guillon, the equipment's cost is $580,000 and has an expected life of eight years. If purchased, the new equipment would replace manually operated equipment. Data relating to the existing and replacement mixing equipment follow.

LO19-1, 2

	Existing Equipment
Original cost	$56,000
Present book value	$32,000
Annual cash operating costs	$150,000
Fair value	$12,000
Fair value in eight years	$0
Remaining useful life	8 years

	Replacement Equipment
Cost	$580,000
Annual cash operating costs	$30,000
Fair value in eight years	$0
Useful life	8 years

    a. Assume that the company's cost of capital is 10 percent, which is to be used in discounted cash flow analysis. Compute the net present value and profitability index of investing in the new equipment. Should Pete's Paving purchase the machine? Why or why not? (Ignore taxes and round PI to one decimal point.)
    b. Compute the payback period for the investment in the new equipment. (Ignore taxes and round time to one decimal point.)
    c. Rounding to the nearest whole percentage, compute the internal rate of return for the equipment investment.

P19-63. NPV; taxes; sensitivity analysis The owner of Midwest Grocer's Warehouse is considering a $195,000 installation of a new refrigerated storage room. The storage room has an expected life of 20 years with no salvage value. The storage room is expected to generate net annual cash revenues (before tax, labor, utility, and maintenance costs) of $46,000 and would increase annual labor, utility, and maintenance costs by $21,000. The firm's cost of capital is 9 percent, and its tax rate is 30 percent.

LO19-3, 5

    a. Using straight-line depreciation, calculate the after-tax net present value of the storage room.
    b. Based on your answer to *a*, is this investment financially acceptable? Explain.
    c. What is the minimum amount by which net annual cash revenues must increase to make this an acceptable investment?

P19-64. After-tax cash flows; payback; NPV; PI; IRR Forester Fashions is considering the purchase of computerized design software. The software is expected to cost $320,000, have a useful life of five years, and have no salvage value at the end of its useful life. Assume that tax regulations permit the following depreciation pattern for this software:

LO19-1, 2, 3

Year	Percent Deductible
1	20
2	32
3	19
4	15
5	14

The company's tax rate is 35 percent, and its cost of capital is 8 percent. The software is expected to generate the following cash savings and cash expenses:

Year	Cash Savings	Cash Expenses
1	$122,000	$18,000
2	134,000	16,000
3	144,000	26,000
4	120,000	18,000
5	96,000	10,000

    a. Prepare a time line presenting the after-tax operating cash flows.
    b. Determine the following on an after-tax basis: payback period, net present value, profitability index, and internal rate of return (using Excel). (Round time and PI to one decimal point.)

LO19-3, 4, 5   **P19-65. NPV; project ranking; risk** West Coast Real Estate Management is expanding operations, and the firm's president, Mike Mayberry, is trying to make a decision about new office space. The following are the firm's options:

Maple Commercial Plaza . . .	5,000 square feet; cost, $800,000; investment period, 10 years; salvage value in 10 years, $400,000
High Tower	20,000 square feet; cost, $3,400,000; investment period, 10 years; salvage value in 10 years, $1,500,000

If Maple Commercial Plaza is purchased, West Coast Real Estate Management will occupy all of the space. If High Tower is purchased, West Coast Real Estate Management will rent the extra space for $620,000 per year. Both buildings will be depreciated on a straight-line basis for tax purposes using a 25-year life with no salvage value. Purchasing either building will save the company $210,000 annually in rental payments. All other costs of the two options (such as land cost) are expected to be the same. The firm's tax rate is 40 percent. Either building would be sold after 10 years.

    a. Determine the before-tax net cash flows from each project for each year.
    b. Determine the after-tax cash flows from each project for each year.
    c. Determine the net present value for each project if West Coast Real Estate Management's cost of capital is 11 percent. Which purchase is the better investment based on the NPV method?
    d. Mayberry questions whether the excess space in High Tower can be rented for the entire 10-year period. To compute the NPV for that portion of the project's cash flows, he has decided to use a discount rate of 20 percent to compensate for risk. Compute the NPV using Excel, and determine which investment is more acceptable.

LO19-3, 4   **P19-66. NPV; taxes; sensitivity analysis** Georgia Properties is considering purchasing a 50-room motel outside of Atlanta as an investment. The current owners state that the motel's occupancy rate averages 80 percent each of the 300 days per year the motel is open. Each room rents for $70 per day, and variable cash operating costs are $20 per occupancy day. Fixed annual cash operating costs are $250,000.

Savannah Roe, Georgia Properties' owner, is considering paying $1,500,000 for the motel. Georgia Properties would keep the motel for 14 years and then dispose of it. Because the market for motels is difficult to predict, Roe estimates a zero salvage value at the time of disposal. Depreciation (rounded to the nearest dollar) will be taken on a straight-line basis for tax purposes. Roe's tax rate is estimated at 25 percent for all years.

    a. Determine the after-tax net present value of the motel to Georgia Properties, assuming a cost of capital rate of 10 percent.
    b. What is the highest discount rate that will allow this project to be considered acceptable to Georgia Properties?
    c. What is the minimum amount the net after-tax cash flows must be to allow the project to be considered acceptable by Georgia Properties, assuming a cost of capital rate of 10 percent?
    d. What is the fewest number of years for which the net after-tax cash flows can be received and the project still be considered acceptable?

LO19-3   **P19-67. NPV; taxes** Dave's Drilling is considering the acquisition of new manufacturing equipment that has the same capacity as the current equipment. The new equipment will provide $150,000 of annual operating efficiencies in direct and indirect labor, direct material usage, indirect supplies, and power during its estimated four-year life.

The new equipment costs $300,000 and would be purchased at the beginning of the year. Given the time of installation and training, the equipment will not be fully operational until the

Chapter 19 Capital Budgeting

second quarter of the year in which it is purchased. Thus, only 60 percent of the estimated annual savings can be obtained in the year of purchase. Dave's Drilling will incur a one-time expense of $80,000 to transfer the production activities from the old equipment to the new. No loss of sales will occur, however, because the plant is large enough to install the new equipment without disrupting operations of the current equipment.

Although the current equipment is fully depreciated and carried at zero book value, its condition is such that it could be used an additional four years. A salvage dealer will remove the old equipment and pay Dave's Drilling $5,000 for it.

The company currently leases its manufacturing plant for $60,000 per year. The lease, which will have four years remaining when the equipment installation would begin, is not renewable. The company must remove any equipment in the plant at the end of the lease term. Cost of equipment removal is expected to equal the salvage value of either the old or the new equipment at the time of removal.

Dave's Drilling uses the sum-of-the-years'-digits depreciation method for tax purposes. A full year's depreciation is taken in the first year an asset is put into use. The company is subject to a 40 percent income tax rate and requires an after-tax return of at least 11 percent on new investment.

a. Calculate the annual incremental after-tax cash flows for the company's proposal to acquire the new manufacturing equipment.
b. Calculate the net present value of the new manufacturing equipment using the cash flows calculated in a and indicate what action Dave's management should take. Assume all recurring cash flows occur at the end of the year.

P19-68. Postinvestment audit CXI has formal policies and procedures to screen and approve capital projects. Proposed capital projects are classified as one of the following types:

1. expansion requiring new plant and equipment,
2. expansion by replacement of present equipment with more productive equipment, or
3. replacement of old equipment with new equipment of similar quality.

All expansion and replacement projects that will cost more than $50,000 must be submitted to the top management capital investment committee for approval. The investment committee evaluates proposed projects considering the costs and benefits outlined in the supporting proposal and the long-range effects on the company.

Projected revenue and/or expense effects of projects, once they are operational, are included in the proposal. After a project is accepted, the committee approves an expenditure budget from the project's inception until the project becomes operational. Annual required expenditures for expansions or replacements are also incorporated into CXI's annual budget procedure. Budgeted revenue and/or cost effects of the projects for the periods in which they become operational are incorporated into the five-year forecast.

CXI does not have a procedure for evaluating projects once they have been implemented and become operational. The vice president of finance has recommended that CXI establish a postinvestment audit program to evaluate its capital expenditure projects.

a. Discuss the benefits a company could derive from a postinvestment audit program for capital expenditure projects.
b. Discuss the practical difficulties in collecting and accumulating information that would be used to evaluate a capital project once it becomes operational.

P19-69. Postinvestment audit Ten years ago, based on a pre-tax NPV analysis, Sante's Sporting Goods decided to add a new product line. The data used in the analysis were as follows:

Discount rate	10%
Life of product line	10 years
Annual sales increase	
Years 1–4	$115,000
Years 5–8	$175,000
Years 9–10	$100,000
Annual fixed cash costs	$20,000
Contribution margin ratio	40%
Cost of production equipment	$130,000
Investment in working capital	$10,000
Salvage value	$0

Because the product line was discontinued this year, corporate managers decided to conduct a postinvestment audit to assess the accuracy of their planning process. Actual cash flows generated from the product line were found to be as follows:

Actual Investment	
Production equipment.	$110,000
Working capital.	17,500
Total	$127,500

Actual Revenues	
Years 1–4	$120,000
Years 5–8	200,000
Years 9–10	103,000

Actual Fixed Cash Costs	
Years 1–4	$15,000
Years 5–8	17,500
Years 9–10	25,000
Actual contribution margin ratio	35%
Actual salvage value.	$ 6,000
Actual cost of capital.	10%

    a.   Determine the original projected NPV on the product line investment.
    b.   Determine the actual NPV of the project based on the postinvestment audit.
    c.   Identify the factors that are most responsible for the differences between the projected NPV and the actual postinvestment audit NPV.

LO19-1, 2, 8   **P19-70. Appendix; Payback; NPV; ARR** New England Metals is considering adding a new product line that has an expected life of eight years. Setup costs for the new product line would total $6,400,000. All product line revenues will be collected as earned. Variable costs will average 35 percent of revenues. All expenses, except for the amount of straight-line depreciation, will be paid in cash when incurred. Following is a schedule of annual revenues and fixed cash operating expenses (excluding $800,000 of annual depreciation on the investment) associated with the new product line.

Year	Revenues	Fixed Expenses
1	$3,000,000	$1,480,000
2	3,200,000	1,280,000
3	3,720,000	1,280,000
4	5,120,000	1,440,000
5	6,400,000	1,280,000
6	6,400,000	1,280,000
7	4,480,000	1,280,000
8	2,720,000	1,120,000

The company's cost of capital is 8 percent. Management uses this rate in discounting cash flows for evaluating capital projects.

    a.   Calculate the payback period. (Ignore taxes and round time to one decimal point.)
    b.   Calculate the net present value. (Ignore taxes.)
    c.   Calculate the accounting rate of return. (Ignore taxes and round to one decimal point.)
    d.   Should New England Metals invest in this product line? Discuss the rationale, including any qualitative factors, for your answer.

LO19-1, 2, 8   **P19-71. Appendix; Comprehensive** Pittsburgh Pipe management is evaluating a proposal to buy a new turning lathe to replace a less efficient piece of similar equipment that would then be sold. The new lathe's cost, including delivery and installation, is $1,420,000. If the lathe is purchased, Pittsburgh Pipe will incur $40,000 to remove the current lathe and revamp service facilities. The current lathe

Chapter 19 Capital Budgeting

has a book value of $800,000 and a remaining useful life of 9 years. Technical advancements have made this lathe outdated, so its current resale value is only $340,000. The following comparative manufacturing cost tabulation is available:

	Current Lathe	New Lathe
Annual production in units	780,000	1,000,000
Cash revenue from each unit	$1.20	$1.20
Annual costs		
Labor	$160,000	$100,000
Depreciation (10% of asset book value or cost)	$80,000	$142,000
Other cash operating costs	$192,000	$80,000

Management believes that if it does not replace the lathe now, the company will have to wait seven years before the replacement is justified. The company uses a 10 percent discount rate in evaluating capital projects and expects all capital project investments to recoup their costs within five years.

Both lathes are expected to have a negligible salvage value at the end of 9 years.

a. Determine the net present value of the new lathe. (Ignore taxes.)
b. Determine the internal rate of return on the new lathe. (Ignore taxes.)
c. Determine the payback period for the new lathe. (Ignore taxes and round time to one decimal point.)
d. Determine the accounting rate of return for the new lathe. (Ignore taxes and round to one decimal point.)
e. Determine whether the company should keep the present lathe or purchase the new lathe. Provide discussion of your conclusion.

Review Solutions

Review 19-1

a. $580,000 ÷ $130,000 = 4.46 years
b. Four years = $100,000 + $130,000 + $150,000 + $160,000 = $540,000
   0.25 year = ($580,000 − $540,000) ÷ 160,000
   Total payback period = 4.25 years
c. The payback period is often used as a screening tool for management. If the project pays back the initial investment within an acceptable time period, the project would be subject to further analysis. If the project does not meet the desired payback period, it would be rejected.

Review 19-2

a. Net cash flows = $219,000 = $279,000 − $60,000
   PV of cash inflows = $1,469,508 = PV(0.08,10,−219000)
   NPV = $179,508 = $1,469,508 − ($1,300,000 − $10,000)
   Or
   PV of cash flows = $1,469,512 = $219,000 × 6.7101
   NPV = $179,512 = $1,469,512 − ($1,300,000 − $10,000)
b. 1.14 = $1,469,508 ÷ $1,290,000
   Or
   1.14 = $1,469,512 ÷ $1,290,000
c. 11% = RATE(10,219000,−1290000)
   Or
   FACTOR = $1,290,000 ÷ $219,000 = 5.890
   11% return at 10 periods with a factor of 5.890.
d. Yes; NPV is positive and the IRR of 11 percent exceeds the company's 8 percent cost of capital. However, the company should also consider any qualitative factors such as safety features of the new equipment or the environmental impact of using the new equipment.

Review 19-3

a.

	1	2	3	4	5	6	Total
Cash flow—after tax*	$43,450	$43,450	$43,450	$43,450	$39,500	$39,500	
Tax shield**	10,080	10,080	10,080	10,080	10,080	—	
Total cash flows	53,530	53,530	53,530	53,530	49,580	39,500	
Present value***	$50,500	$47,642	$44,945	$42,401	$37,049	$27,846	$250,383
OR							
Total cash flows	$53,530	$53,530	$53,530	$53,530	$49,580	$39,500	
Factor	0.9434	0.8900	0.8396	0.7921	0.7473	0.7050	
Present value	$50,500	$47,642	$44,944	$42,401	$37,051	$27,848	$250,386

*$43,450 = $55,000 × (1 − 0.21); $39,500 = $50,000 × (1 − 0.21)
**$10,080 = ($240,000 ÷ 5) × 0.21
***$50,500 = PV(0.06,1,0,−53530); $47,642 = PV(0.06,2,0,−53530); $44,945 = PV(0.06,3,0,−53530);
42,401 = PV(0.06,4,0,−53530); $37,049 = PV(0.06,5,0,−49580); $27,846 = PV(0.06,6,0,−39500)

b. Even though the depreciation tax benefit increases (decreases) as taxes increase (decrease), the overall cash flow after tax goes down (up) with an increase (decrease) in the tax rate. This means that the net present value amount goes down with an increase in taxes. If tax policy is in a state of uncertainty, management will be more likely to defer non-urgent investment decisions because a change in the tax rate can impact an accept/reject decision.

Review 19-4
Solutions in Excel

a.

Project	NPV	PI	IRR
A	$1,042,432	1.52	18.42%
B	225,053	1.08	11.86%
C	125,345	1.03	10.57%
D	756,782	1.22	13.06%
E	832,584	1.35	15.73%
F	373,684	1.47	21.84%

Project A: NPV = (PV(0.10,15,−400000)) − $2,000,000
PI = (PV(0.10,15,−400000)) ÷ $2,000,000
IRR = RATE(15,400000,−2000000)

Project B: NPV = (PV(0.10,9,−560000)) − $3,000,000
PI = (PV(0.10,9,−560000)) ÷ $3,000,000
IRR = RATE(9,560000,−3000000)

Project C: NPV = (PV(0.10,14,−560000)) − $4,000,000
PI = (PV(0.10,14,−560000)) ÷ $4,000,000
IRR = RATE(14,560000,−4000000)

Project D: NPV = (PV(0.10,20,−500000)) − $3,500,000
PI = (PV(0.10,20,−500000)) ÷ $3,500,000
IRR = RATE(20,500000,−3500000)

Project E: NPV = (PV(0.10,15,−425000)) − $2,400,000
PI = (PV(0.10,15,−425000)) ÷ $2,400,000
IRR = RATE(15,425000,−2400000)

Project F: NPV = (PV(0.10,8,−220000)) − $800,000
PI = (PV(0.10,8,−220000)) ÷ $800,000
IRR = RATE(8,220000,−800000)

b.

Net Present Value		Profitability Index		Internal Rate of Return	
A...	$1,042,432	A...	1.52	F...	21.84%
E...	832,584	F...	1.47	A...	18.42%
D...	756,782	E...	1.35	E...	15.73%
F...	373,684	D...	1.22	D...	13.06%
B...	225,053	B...	1.08	B...	11.86%
C...	125,345	C...	1.03	C...	10.57%

c. Project A..... $2,000,000
    Project E..... 2,400,000
    Project F.....   800,000
    Total $5,200,000

The profitability index is a useful measure in comparing different projects at different investment levels. Projects A, E and F have the highest profitability indexes. These three projects also have the highest IRRs.

Solutions with Present Value Tables

a.

Project	NPV	PI	IRR
A.......	$1,042,440	1.52	18.0%
B.......	225,040	1.08	12.0%
C.......	125,352	1.03	10.5%
D.......	756,800	1.22	13.0%
E.......	832,593	1.35	15.5%
F.......	373,678	1.47	20.0%

Project A: NPV = (7.6061 × $400,000) − $2,000,000
PI = (7.6061 × $400,000) ÷ $2,000,000
Estimated factor = $2,000,000 ÷ $400,000 = 5.0000

Project B: NPV = (5.7590 × $560,000) − $3,000,000
PI = (5.7590 × $560,000) ÷ $3,000,000
Estimated factor = $3,000,000 ÷ $560,000 = 5.3571

Project C: NPV = (7.3667 × $560,000) − $4,000,000
PI = (7.3667 × $560,000) ÷ $4,000,000
Estimated factor = $4,000,000 ÷ $560,000 = 7.1429

Project D: NPV = (8.5136 × $500,000) − $3,500,000
PI = (8.5136 × $500,000) ÷ $3,500,000
Estimated factor = $3,500,000 ÷ $500,000 = 7.000

Project E: NPV = (7.6061 × $425,000) − $2,400,000
PI = (7.6061 × $425,000) ÷ $2,400,000
Estimated factor = $2,400,000 ÷ $425,000 = 5.6471

Project F: NPV = (5.3349 × $220,000) − $800,000
PI = (5.3349 × $220,000) ÷ $800,000
Estimated factor = $800,000 ÷ $220,000 = 3.6364

b. and c. No change in rankings or in recommendations from the results shown for Excel.

Review 19-5

a. $89,418 = PMT(0.08,10,−600000)
   Or
   $89,417 = $600,000 ÷ 6.7101

b. 10.56% = RATE(10,100000,−600000)
   Or
   Estimated factor = $600,000 ÷ $100,000 = 6.000
   10.5% (from table)

c. The range of the operational cash savings is from $89,418 (low end) to $100,000 (estimated). As a percentage, it is an 11.8 percent difference (=$10,582/$89,418). The range of the cost of capital is from 8 percent (estimated) to 10.5 percent (high end). As a percentage, it is a 31.3 percent difference (=2.5%/8.0%). This information is useful for management decision making because the company understands how far off the estimated targets can be from the actual amounts, and still result in the same accept/reject decision. This information, combined with the company's risk tolerance, will help management make a more informed investment decision.

Review 19-6

a.

Year	Cash Flow	Excel Formula	Net Present Value	Formula by Table	Net Present Value
0	$(85,000)	n/a	$(85,000)	n/a	$(85,000)
1	26,000	PV(0.06,1,0,−26000)	24,528	$26,000 × 0.9434	24,528
2	26,000	PV(0.06,2,0,−26000)	23,140	$26,000 × 0.8900	23,140
3	30,000	PV(0.06,3,0,−30000)	25,189	$30,000 × 0.8396	25,188
4	40,000	PV(0.06,4,0,−40000)	31,684	$40,000 × 0.7921	31,684
			$19,541		$19,540

b.

Year	Cash Flow	Excel Formula	Net Present Value	Formula by Table	Net Present Value
0	$(85,000)	n/a	$(85,000)	n/a	$(85,000)
1	24,000	PV(0.06,1,0,−24000)	22,642	$24,000 × 0.9434	22,642
2	26,000	PV(0.06,2,0,−26000)	23,140	$26,000 × 0.8900	23,140
3	32,000	PV(0.06,3,0,−32000)	26,868	$32,000 × 0.8396	26,867
4	32,000	PV(0.06,4,0,−32000)	25,347	$32,000 × 0.7921	25,347
			$12,997		$12,996

c. Decrease in NPV of $6,544 over projection ($12,996 − $19,540).

Decrease is due to the decrease in contribution margin which was not fully offset by the decrease in fixed costs. In addition, the company overestimated the salvage value.

Review 19-7

	Excel Formula	Answer	Rate Formula	Answer
a.	PV(0.04,20,0,−20000)	$ 9,127.74	0.4564 × $20,000	$ 9,128.00
b.*	PV(0.05,6,−5000)	$ 25,378.46	5.0757 × $5,000	$ 25,378.50
c.	PV(0.08,15,0,−50000)	$ 15,762.09	0.3152 × $50,000	$ 15,760.00
d.	PV(0.07,1,0,−8000)	$ 7,476.64	0.9346 × $8,000	$ 7,476.80
	PV(0.07,2,0,−10000)	8,734.39	0.8734 × $10,000	8,734.00
	PV(0.07,3,0,−15000)	12,244.47	0.8163 × $15,000	12,244.50
	PV(0.07,4,0,−20000)	15,257.90	0.7629 × $20,000	15,258.00
	PV(0.07,5,0,−25000)	17,824.65	0.7130 × $25,000	17,825.00
e.	PV(0.05,5,−300000)	$1,298,843.00	4.3295 × $300,000	$1,298,850.00

*Choose the annuity payment with a present value of $25,378.

f. PV(0.05/4,5*4,−300000/4) = $1,319,949

The NPV increased because of the change in the compounding of interest from annually to quarterly. Because interest is earned on each quarter, interest is earned on the interest in the earlier quarters of a year versus under annual compounding, where interest is earned once at the end of the year.

Review 19-8

a. 25.9% = [($182,000 − $77,000 − $38,500) × (1 − 25%)] ÷ ($385,000/2)

b. The ARR of 25.9 percent would need to be compared to the company's established hurdle rate and to the ARR of other projects under consideration. Also, managers can increase the hurdle rate against which the ARR is compared to compensate for any perceived risk of the project.

Data Visualization Solutions

(See page 19-11.)

a. As the interest rate goes up, the net present value goes down. Higher rates yield lower present values because, at the higher rates, more of the future cash inflows is imputed interest.

b. Yes at 8 percent because the net present value is positive, but no at 14 percent, because the net present value is negative.

c. The actual return of the project is slightly above 10 percent where the net present value is zero.

Appendix A
Compound Interest Tables

TABLE 1 — Present Value of Single Amount

$p = 1/(1 + i)^t$

Interest Rate

Period	0.01	0.02	0.03	0.04	0.05	0.06	0.07	0.08	0.09	0.10	0.11	0.12
1	0.99010	0.98039	0.97087	0.96154	0.95238	0.94340	0.93458	0.92593	0.91743	0.90909	0.90090	0.89286
2	0.98030	0.96117	0.94260	0.92456	0.90703	0.89000	0.87344	0.85734	0.84168	0.82645	0.81162	0.79719
3	0.97059	0.94232	0.91514	0.88900	0.86384	0.83962	0.81630	0.79383	0.77218	0.75131	0.73119	0.71178
4	0.96098	0.92385	0.88849	0.85480	0.82270	0.79209	0.76290	0.73503	0.70843	0.68301	0.65873	0.63552
5	0.95147	0.90573	0.86261	0.82193	0.78353	0.74726	0.71299	0.68058	0.64993	0.62092	0.59345	0.56743
6	0.94205	0.88797	0.83748	0.79031	0.74622	0.70496	0.66634	0.63017	0.59627	0.56447	0.53464	0.50663
7	0.93272	0.87056	0.81309	0.75992	0.71068	0.66506	0.62275	0.58349	0.54703	0.51316	0.48166	0.45235
8	0.92348	0.85349	0.78941	0.73069	0.67684	0.62741	0.58201	0.54027	0.50187	0.46651	0.43393	0.40388
9	0.91434	0.83676	0.76642	0.70259	0.64461	0.59190	0.54393	0.50025	0.46043	0.42410	0.39092	0.36061
10	0.90529	0.82035	0.74409	0.67556	0.61391	0.55839	0.50835	0.46319	0.42241	0.38554	0.35218	0.32197
11	0.89632	0.80426	0.72242	0.64958	0.58468	0.52679	0.47509	0.42888	0.38753	0.35049	0.31728	0.28748
12	0.88745	0.78849	0.70138	0.62460	0.55684	0.49697	0.44401	0.39711	0.35553	0.31863	0.28584	0.25668
13	0.87866	0.77303	0.68095	0.60057	0.53032	0.46884	0.41496	0.36770	0.32618	0.28966	0.25751	0.22917
14	0.86996	0.75788	0.66112	0.57748	0.50507	0.44230	0.38782	0.34046	0.29925	0.26333	0.23199	0.20462
15	0.86135	0.74301	0.64186	0.55526	0.48102	0.41727	0.36245	0.31524	0.27454	0.23939	0.20900	0.18270
16	0.85282	0.72845	0.62317	0.53391	0.45811	0.39365	0.33873	0.29189	0.25187	0.21763	0.18829	0.16312
17	0.84438	0.71416	0.60502	0.51337	0.43630	0.37136	0.31657	0.27027	0.23107	0.19784	0.16963	0.14564
18	0.83602	0.70016	0.58739	0.49363	0.41552	0.35034	0.29586	0.25025	0.21199	0.17986	0.15282	0.13004
19	0.82774	0.68643	0.57029	0.47464	0.39573	0.33051	0.27651	0.23171	0.19449	0.16351	0.13768	0.11611
20	0.81954	0.67297	0.55368	0.45639	0.37689	0.31180	0.25842	0.21455	0.17843	0.14864	0.12403	0.10367
21	0.81143	0.65978	0.53755	0.43883	0.35894	0.29416	0.24151	0.19866	0.16370	0.13513	0.11174	0.09256
22	0.80340	0.64684	0.52189	0.42196	0.34185	0.27751	0.22571	0.18394	0.15018	0.12285	0.10067	0.08264
23	0.79544	0.63416	0.50669	0.40573	0.32557	0.26180	0.21095	0.17032	0.13778	0.11168	0.09069	0.07379
24	0.78757	0.62172	0.49193	0.39012	0.31007	0.24698	0.19715	0.15770	0.12640	0.10153	0.08170	0.06588
25	0.77977	0.60953	0.47761	0.37512	0.29530	0.23300	0.18425	0.14602	0.11597	0.09230	0.07361	0.05882
30	0.74192	0.55207	0.41199	0.30832	0.23138	0.17411	0.13137	0.09938	0.07537	0.05731	0.04368	0.03338
35	0.70591	0.50003	0.35538	0.25342	0.18129	0.13011	0.09366	0.06763	0.04899	0.03558	0.02592	0.01894
40	0.67165	0.45289	0.30656	0.20829	0.14205	0.09722	0.06678	0.04603	0.03184	0.02209	0.01538	0.01075

TABLE 2 — Present Value of Ordinary Annuity

$p = \{1 - [1/(1 + i)^t]\}/i$

Interest Rate

Period	0.01	0.02	0.03	0.04	0.05	0.06	0.07	0.08	0.09	0.10	0.11	0.12
1	0.99010	0.98039	0.97087	0.96154	0.95238	0.94340	0.93458	0.92593	0.91743	0.90909	0.90090	0.89286
2	1.97040	1.94156	1.91347	1.88609	1.85941	1.83339	1.80802	1.78326	1.75911	1.73554	1.71252	1.69005
3	2.94099	2.88388	2.82861	2.77509	2.72325	2.67301	2.62432	2.57710	2.53129	2.48685	2.44371	2.40183
4	3.90197	3.80773	3.71710	3.62990	3.54595	3.46511	3.38721	3.31213	3.23972	3.16987	3.10245	3.03735
5	4.85343	4.71346	4.57971	4.45182	4.32948	4.21236	4.10020	3.99271	3.88965	3.79079	3.69590	3.60478
6	5.79548	5.60143	5.41719	5.24214	5.07569	4.91732	4.76654	4.62288	4.48592	4.35526	4.23054	4.11141
7	6.72819	6.47199	6.23028	6.00205	5.78637	5.58238	5.38929	5.20637	5.03295	4.86842	4.71220	4.56376
8	7.65168	7.32548	7.01969	6.73274	6.46321	6.20979	5.97130	5.74664	5.53482	5.33493	5.14612	4.96764
9	8.56602	8.16224	7.78611	7.43533	7.10782	6.80169	6.51523	6.24689	5.99525	5.75902	5.53705	5.32825
10	9.47130	8.98259	8.53020	8.11090	7.72173	7.36009	7.02358	6.71008	6.41766	6.14457	5.88923	5.65022
11	10.36763	9.78685	9.25262	8.76048	8.30641	7.88687	7.49867	7.13896	6.80519	6.49506	6.20652	5.93770
12	11.25508	10.57534	9.95400	9.38507	8.86325	8.38384	7.94269	7.53608	7.16073	6.81369	6.49236	6.19437
13	12.13374	11.34837	10.63496	9.98565	9.39357	8.85268	8.35765	7.90378	7.48690	7.10336	6.74987	6.42355
14	13.00370	12.10625	11.29607	10.56312	9.89864	9.29498	8.74547	8.24424	7.78615	7.36669	6.98187	6.62817
15	13.86505	12.84926	11.93794	11.11839	10.37966	9.71225	9.10791	8.55948	8.06069	7.60608	7.19087	6.81086
16	14.71787	13.57771	12.56110	11.65230	10.83777	10.10590	9.44665	8.85137	8.31256	7.82371	7.37916	6.97399
17	15.56225	14.29187	13.16612	12.16567	11.27407	10.47726	9.76322	9.12164	8.54363	8.02155	7.54879	7.11963
18	16.39827	14.99203	13.75351	12.65930	11.68959	10.82760	10.05909	9.37189	8.75563	8.20141	7.70162	7.24967
19	17.22601	15.67846	14.32380	13.13394	12.08532	11.15812	10.33560	9.60360	8.95011	8.36492	7.83929	7.36578
20	18.04555	16.35143	14.87747	13.59033	12.46221	11.46992	10.59401	9.81815	9.12855	8.51356	7.96333	7.46944
21	18.85698	17.01121	15.41502	14.02916	12.82115	11.76408	10.83553	10.01680	9.29224	8.64869	8.07507	7.56200
22	19.66038	17.65805	15.93692	14.45112	13.16300	12.04158	11.06124	10.20074	9.44243	8.77154	8.17574	7.64465
23	20.45582	18.29220	16.44361	14.85684	13.48857	12.30338	11.27219	10.37106	9.58021	8.88322	8.26643	7.71843
24	21.24339	18.91393	16.93554	15.24696	13.79864	12.55036	11.46933	10.52876	9.70661	8.98474	8.34814	7.78432
25	22.02316	19.52346	17.41315	15.62208	14.09394	12.78336	11.65358	10.67478	9.82258	9.07704	8.42174	7.84314
30	25.80771	22.39646	19.60044	17.29203	15.37245	13.76483	12.40904	11.25778	10.27365	9.42691	8.69379	8.05518
35	29.40858	24.99862	21.48722	18.66461	16.37419	14.49825	12.94767	11.65457	10.56682	9.64416	8.85524	8.17550
40	32.83469	27.35548	23.11477	19.79277	17.15909	15.04630	13.33171	11.92461	10.75736	9.77905	8.95105	8.24378

TABLE 3 — Future Value of Single Amount

$f = (1 + i)^t$

Interest Rate

Period	0.01	0.02	0.03	0.04	0.05	0.06	0.07	0.08	0.09	0.10	0.11	0.12
1	1.01000	1.02000	1.03000	1.04000	1.05000	1.06000	1.07000	1.08000	1.09000	1.10000	1.11000	1.12000
2	1.02010	1.04040	1.06090	1.08160	1.10250	1.12360	1.14490	1.16640	1.18810	1.21000	1.23210	1.25440
3	1.03030	1.06121	1.09273	1.12486	1.15763	1.19102	1.22504	1.25971	1.29503	1.33100	1.36763	1.40493
4	1.04060	1.08243	1.12551	1.16986	1.21551	1.26248	1.31080	1.36049	1.41158	1.46410	1.51807	1.57352
5	1.05101	1.10408	1.15927	1.21665	1.27628	1.33823	1.40255	1.46933	1.53862	1.61051	1.68506	1.76234
6	1.06152	1.12616	1.19405	1.26532	1.34010	1.41852	1.50073	1.58687	1.67710	1.77156	1.87041	1.97382
7	1.07214	1.14869	1.22987	1.31593	1.40710	1.50363	1.60578	1.71382	1.82804	1.94872	2.07616	2.21068
8	1.08286	1.17166	1.26677	1.36857	1.47746	1.59385	1.71819	1.85093	1.99256	2.14359	2.30454	2.47596
9	1.09369	1.19509	1.30477	1.42331	1.55133	1.68948	1.83846	1.99900	2.17189	2.35795	2.55804	2.77308
10	1.10462	1.21899	1.34392	1.48024	1.62889	1.79085	1.96715	2.15892	2.36736	2.59374	2.83942	3.10585
11	1.11567	1.24337	1.38423	1.53945	1.71034	1.89830	2.10485	2.33164	2.58043	2.85312	3.15176	3.47855
12	1.12683	1.26824	1.42576	1.60103	1.79586	2.01220	2.25219	2.51817	2.81266	3.13843	3.49845	3.89598
13	1.13809	1.29361	1.46853	1.66507	1.88565	2.13293	2.40985	2.71962	3.06580	3.45227	3.88328	4.36349
14	1.14947	1.31948	1.51259	1.73168	1.97993	2.26090	2.57853	2.93719	3.34173	3.79750	4.31044	4.88711
15	1.16097	1.34587	1.55797	1.80094	2.07893	2.39656	2.75903	3.17217	3.64248	4.17725	4.78459	5.47357
16	1.17258	1.37279	1.60471	1.87298	2.18287	2.54035	2.95216	3.42594	3.97031	4.59497	5.31089	6.13039
17	1.18430	1.40024	1.65285	1.94790	2.29202	2.69277	3.15882	3.70002	4.32763	5.05447	5.89509	6.86604
18	1.19615	1.42825	1.70243	2.02582	2.40662	2.85434	3.37993	3.99602	4.71712	5.55992	6.54355	7.68997
19	1.20811	1.45681	1.75351	2.10685	2.52695	3.02560	3.61653	4.31570	5.14166	6.11591	7.26334	8.61276
20	1.22019	1.48595	1.80611	2.19112	2.65330	3.20714	3.86968	4.66096	5.60441	6.72750	8.06231	9.64629
21	1.23239	1.51567	1.86029	2.27877	2.78596	3.39956	4.14056	5.03383	6.10881	7.40025	8.94917	10.80385
22	1.24472	1.54598	1.91610	2.36992	2.92526	3.60354	4.43040	5.43654	6.65860	8.14027	9.93357	12.10031
23	1.25716	1.57690	1.97359	2.46472	3.07152	3.81975	4.74053	5.87146	7.25787	8.95430	11.02627	13.55235
24	1.26973	1.60844	2.03279	2.56330	3.22510	4.04893	5.07237	6.34118	7.91108	9.84973	12.23916	15.17863
25	1.28243	1.64061	2.09378	2.66584	3.38635	4.29187	5.42743	6.84848	8.62308	10.83471	13.58546	17.00006
30	1.34785	1.81136	2.42726	3.24340	4.32194	5.74349	7.61226	10.06266	13.26768	17.44940	22.89230	29.95992
35	1.41660	1.99989	2.81386	3.94609	5.51602	7.68609	10.67658	14.78534	20.41397	28.10244	38.57485	52.79962
40	1.48886	2.20804	3.26204	4.80102	7.03999	10.28572	14.97446	21.72452	31.40942	45.25926	65.00087	93.05097

TABLE 4 — Future Value of an Ordinary Annuity

$f = [(1 + i)^t - 1]/i$

Interest Rate

Period	0.01	0.02	0.03	0.04	0.05	0.06	0.07	0.08	0.09	0.10	0.11	0.12
1	1.00000	1.00000	1.00000	1.00000	1.00000	1.00000	1.00000	1.00000	1.00000	1.00000	1.00000	1.00000
2	2.01000	2.02000	2.03000	2.04000	2.05000	2.06000	2.07000	2.08000	2.09000	2.10000	2.11000	2.12000
3	3.03010	3.06040	3.09090	3.12160	3.15250	3.18360	3.21490	3.24640	3.27810	3.31000	3.34210	3.37440
4	4.06040	4.12161	4.18363	4.24646	4.31013	4.37462	4.43994	4.50611	4.57313	4.64100	4.70973	4.77933
5	5.10101	5.20404	5.30914	5.41632	5.52563	5.63709	5.75074	5.86660	5.98471	6.10510	6.22780	6.35285
6	6.15202	6.30812	6.46841	6.63298	6.80191	6.97532	7.15329	7.33593	7.52333	7.71561	7.91286	8.11519
7	7.21354	7.43428	7.66246	7.89829	8.14201	8.39384	8.65402	8.92280	9.20043	9.48717	9.78327	10.08901
8	8.28567	8.58297	8.89234	9.21423	9.54911	9.89747	10.25980	10.63663	11.02847	11.43589	11.85943	12.29969
9	9.36853	9.75463	10.15911	10.58280	11.02656	11.49132	11.97799	12.48756	13.02104	13.57948	14.16397	14.77566
10	10.46221	10.94972	11.46388	12.00611	12.57789	13.18079	13.81645	14.48656	15.19293	15.93742	16.72201	17.54874
11	11.56683	12.16872	12.80780	13.48635	14.20679	14.97164	15.78360	16.64549	17.56029	18.53117	19.56143	20.65458
12	12.68250	13.41209	14.19203	15.02581	15.91713	16.86994	17.88845	18.97713	20.14072	21.38428	22.71319	24.13313
13	13.80933	14.68033	15.61779	16.62684	17.71298	18.88214	20.14064	21.49530	22.95338	24.52271	26.21164	28.02911
14	14.94742	15.97394	17.08632	18.29191	19.59863	21.01507	22.55049	24.21492	26.01919	27.97498	30.09492	32.39260
15	16.09690	17.29342	18.59891	20.02359	21.57856	23.27597	25.12902	27.15211	29.36092	31.77248	34.40536	37.27971
16	17.25786	18.63929	20.15688	21.82453	23.65749	25.67253	27.88805	30.32428	33.00340	35.94973	39.18995	42.75328
17	18.43044	20.01207	21.76159	23.69751	25.84037	28.21288	30.84022	33.75023	36.97370	40.54470	44.50084	48.88367
18	19.61475	21.41231	23.41444	25.64541	28.13238	30.90565	33.99903	37.45024	41.30134	45.59917	50.39594	55.74971
19	20.81090	22.84056	25.11687	27.67123	30.53900	33.75999	37.37896	41.44626	46.01846	51.15909	56.93949	63.43968
20	22.01900	24.29737	26.87037	29.77808	33.06595	36.78559	40.99549	45.76196	51.16012	57.27500	64.20283	72.05244
21	23.23919	25.78332	28.67649	31.96920	35.71925	39.99273	44.86518	50.42292	56.76453	64.00250	72.26514	81.69874
22	24.47159	27.29898	30.53678	34.24797	38.50521	43.39229	49.00574	55.45676	62.87334	71.40275	81.21431	92.50258
23	25.71630	28.84496	32.45288	36.61789	41.43048	46.99583	53.43614	60.89330	69.53194	79.54302	91.14788	104.60289
24	26.97346	30.42186	34.42647	39.08260	44.50200	50.81558	58.17667	66.76476	76.78981	88.49733	102.17415	118.15524
25	28.24320	32.03030	36.45926	41.64591	47.72710	54.86451	63.24904	73.10594	84.70090	98.34706	114.41331	133.33387
30	34.78489	40.56808	47.57542	56.08494	66.43885	79.05819	94.46079	113.28321	136.30754	164.49402	199.02088	241.33268
35	41.66028	49.99448	60.46208	73.65222	90.32031	111.43478	138.23688	172.31680	215.71075	271.02437	341.58955	431.66350
40	48.88637	60.40198	75.40126	95.02552	120.79977	154.76197	199.63511	259.05652	337.88245	442.59256	581.82607	767.09142

Index

A

Abnormal loss, 6-24
Absorption costing, 11-2
   before-tax profit, reconciliation of, 11-13–11-14
   calculating unit costs under, 11-4–11-5
   cost relationships in, 11-6e
   income statement
      results, comparing, 11-6–11-7
      with volume variance, 11-11–11-14
   income under, 11-5–11-11
   model of, 11-3e
   production/sales relationships and effects on income, 11-10e
Accounting rate of return (ARR), 19-28–19-29
Activity analysis, 8-3–8-5
Activity-based approach, 9-5–9-6
Activity-based costing (ABC), 8-2, 8-8, 8-14–8-18
   activity center, 8-14
   activity driver, 8-14
   criticisms of, 8-22–28-23
      environmental barriers, 8-22
      individual barriers, 8-22
      organizational barriers, 8-22
   process complexity, 8-16
   product complexity, 8-16
   product variety, 8-16
   two-stage allocation method, 8-14–8-18
   usefulness, determining, 8-18–8-22
      business environment, changes in, 8-21–8-22
      high product/process complexity, 8-19–8-20
      irrationality of current cost allocations, 8-21
      lack of commonality in overhead costs, 8-20–8-21
      large product/service variety, 8-19
Activity-based management (ABM), 8-2–8-7
   business-value-added (BVA) activity, 8-3
   non-value-added (NVA) activity, 8-3
   value-added (VA) activity, 8-3
Activity center, 8-14
Activity driver, 8-14
Actual cost systems, 6-4
Ad hoc discounts, 14-6
Adjusting standards, 10-25–10-26
Administrative departments, 13-15
After-tax cash flows, 19-12–19-15
Allocation
   bases, 13-16–13-17, 13-19e
   of joint cost, 12-9–12-16

American Institute of CPAs (AICPA), 1-20
Annuity, 19-4
Annuity due, 19-27
Applied overhead, 6-6
Appraisal costs, 17-16
Appropriateness, 10-7
Approximated NRV at split-off, 12-13
Artificial intelligence (AI), 1-13–1-16
Asset turnover, 15-14
Attainability, 10-7
Augmented intelligence, 1-14
Authority, 1-8
Autonomous intelligence, 1-14

B

Backflush costing
   just-in-time, 18-17–18-20
Balanced scorecard
   approach of, 15-26–15-30
   leading and lagging indicators, 15-24–15-25
   metrics, monitoring, 15-29–15-30
   multinational settings, performance evaluation in, 15-30–15-31
   multiple performance measures, 15-25
   for performance measurement, 15-24–15-31
   performance measures, identifying, 15-26–15-27
   and perspectives, 15-27e
   quality measures of, 17-24–17-26, 17-25e
   strategy map, 15-27–15-28, 15-28e
   sustainability metrics, inclusion of, 15-28–15-29
Batch-level activity, 3-19
Batch-level costs, 8-9–8-10
Benchmarking
   analysis, performing, 17-10–17-11
   internal, 17-9
   process, 17-9–17-10
   reasons to, 17-8e
   results, 17-9
   steps in, 17-11, 17-11e
   strategic, 17-10
   types of, 17-8–17-10, 17-8–17-9e
Benefits-provided ranking, 13-17–13-18
Big data, 1-13
Bill of materials, 10-9
Blockchain, 1-16–11-17
Blocks, 1-16
Board of directors, 1-8
Bottlenecks, 18-20
Break-even chart, 4-7
Break-even point (BEP), 4-4–4-9
   contribution income statement proof, 4-8–4-9

formula approach to, 4-5
graphing approach to, 4-6
identifying, 4-5–4-8
profit-volume (PV) graph, 4-7–4-8
in sales dollars, solving for, 4-6
in sales units, solving for, 4-5
traditional break-even graph, 4-6–4-7
Budget manual, 9-35
Budget padding, 9-33
Budget slack, 9-33
Budget variance, 10-22
Budgeted financial statements, 9-23–29-27
Budgeting process, 9-2–9-35. *See also* Master budget
   general approaches to, 9-5–9-7
      activity-based approach, 9-5–9-6
      incremental approach, 9-6
      minimum level approach, 9-6–9-7
      output/input approach, 9-5
   impact of environmental considerations on, 9-27–9-29
   long-term strategic planning, 9-2
   short-term tactical planning, 9-3–9-5
Business-value-added (BVA) activity, 8-3
By-product
   accounting for, 12-16–12-20
   in job order costing, 12-20–12-21

C

Capacity, 8-23
Capacity measures, 11-15, 11-15e
   absorption income, effect on, 11-16–11-17
   expected capacity, 11-15
   impact of, determining, 11-16–11-17
   normal capacity, 11-15
   practical capacity, 11-15
   theoretical capacity, 11-15
Capital assets, 19-2
Capital budgeting, 19-2–19-29
   after-tax cash flows, 19-12–19-15
   discounted cash flow methods, 19-5–19-12
   investment decision, 19-15–19-19
   payback period, 19-2–19-5
   postinvestment audit, 19-24–19-27
   present value of annuity, 19-27–19-29
   present value of single cash flow, 19-27
   ranking multiple capital projects, 19-19–19-20
   risk in, compensation for, 19-20–19-24
Carbon offsets, 9-28
Carrying cost, 18-3
Cash budget, 9-17–9-23
Cash conversion cycle, 16-24

Note: The letter "e" refers to an exhibit on the stated page, and the letter "n" indicates that the information is included in a footnote on the given page. For example, 11-3n1 means footnote 1 on page 11-3.

Index

Cash flows, 19-2–19-4
Cash management, 16-23–16-28
    cost of carrying cash, 16-27–16-28
    optimal level of cash, 16-23–16-24
    sources of cash, 16-24–16-27
Centralization, 13-7
    for environmental issues, 13-9
Certified Management Accountant (CMA), 1-2
Certified Public Accountant (CPA), 1-2
Chained target costing, 14-12
Chartered Global Management Accountant (CGMA), 1-2
Chartered Institute of Management Accountants (CIMA), 1-20
Chief executive officers (CEOs), 1-8, 1-19
Chief financial officers (CFOs), 1-8, 1-19
Classification categories of cost, 2-2–2-3
    association with cost object, 2-2–2-3
    conversion cost, 2-10
    cost driver, 2-7
    distribution cost, 2-10
    financial statements, 2-9, 2-11
    fixed cost, 2-4–2-5
    inventoriable costs, 2-10
    mixed cost, 2-6–2-7
    period costs, 2-10
    predictor, 2-7
    prime cost, 2-10
    product cost, 2-10
    reaction to changes in activity, 2-4–2-8
    relevant range, 2-4
    step cost, 2-7
Coefficient of determination, 3-12
Coefficients, 3-11
Committed fixed costs, 16-13–16-14
Common cause variation, 17-3
Compensation strategy
    ethical considerations of, 15-39
    global compensation, 15-38–15-39
    pay-for-performance plans, 15-32–15-35
    pay versus performance, 15-35–15-36
    planning-performance-reward model, 15-32e
    tax implications of, 15-38
Competence, 1-20, 1-21
Competitive bidding, 6-13
Compound interest, 19-27
Compounding period, 19-27
Confidentiality, 1-20–1-21
Constraint, 18-20
Consumer Price Index (CPI), 16-6
Continuous budget, 9-32
Continuous improvement costing, 14-13–14-15
Continuous loss, 7-21
Contribution income statements, 4-2, 4-8–4-9
Contribution margin (CM), 4-2–4-4, 5-11, 11-6
Contribution margin per unit (CM per unit), 4-3
Contribution margin ratio (CM%), 4-4
Contribution margin variance, 14-17–14-19
Contribution margin volume variance, 14-19–14-21
Control charts, 17-3, 17-3e
Controllable variance, 10-22
Controllers, 1-8
Conversion cost (CC), 2-10, 7-5
Conversion process, 2-14–12-18

    degrees of, 2-14e
    retailers *versus* manufacturers/service companies, 2-15–12-18
Core competency, 1-6–1-7
Corrective functions, 16-2
Cost, 2-2
Cost accountants, 2-11
Cost accounting, 1-2, 1-4–1-5
    Cost Accounting Standards Board (CASB), 1-5
    financial accounting, 1-2
    guidelines, 1-5
    intersection, 1-4
    management accounting, 1-2–1-4
    product cost, 1-4
    relationship of, 1-4
    service cost, 1-4
    standards, 1-5
Cost Accounting Standards Board (CASB), 1-5
Cost accumulation systems, 6-2–6-3
    job order costing system, 6-3
    process costing systems, 6-3
Cost allocation, 2-18
Cost avoidance, 16-10–16-12
Cost-based pricing
    for single-product companies, 14-3–14-4
    for multiple-product companies, 14-4–14-6
    for special orders, 14-6–14-7
    disadvantages of, 14-6–14-7
    approaches to, 14-2–14-7, 14-3e
    and economic pricing, 14-2
Cost-based transfer price, 13-28e, 13-29
Cost behavior analysis
    factors affecting cost behavior patterns, 3-4–3-5
    linear total cost estimating equation, 3-3–3-4
Cost behavior analysis, 3-2–3-5
    factors affecting cost behavior patterns
        cost type, 3-4–3-5
        time period, 3-4
    variable costs, 3-2–3-3
    patterns, 3-2e
    fixed costs, 3-3
    mixed costs, 3-3
    step costs, 3-3
Cost-benefit analysis, 1-2
Cost center, 13-13–13-14
Cost changes
    inflation/deflation, 16-6–16-7
    quantity purchased, 16-8–16-9
    supply/supplier cost adjustments, 16-7–16-8
    volume changes, 16-6
Cost consciousness, 16-5–16-9
Cost containment
    quantity purchased, 16-9–16-10
Cost control system, 16-2–16-5
    functions of, 16-2–16-5
    implications in planning phase, 16-3–16-5
Cost cross-subsidization, 6-9, 8-17–8-18
Cost driver, 2-7, 8-8–8-13
    levels at which costs are incurred, 8-9–8-11
    product profitability analysis, 8-11–8-13
Cost driver, classification
    customer cost hierarchy, 3-20–23-21
        customer-level activity, 3-20

        market-segment-level activity, 3-20
        project-level activity, 3-21
        order-level activity, 3-20
        organizational/facility-level activity, 3-20
        unit-level activity, 3-20
    manufacturing cost hierarchy, 3-19–3-20
        batch-level activity, 3-19
        organizational/facility-level activity, 3-19
        product/process-level activity, 3-19
        unit-level activity, 3-19
Cost estimation, 3-5–3-13
    changes in technology/prices, 3-16–13-17
    high-low cost estimation, 3-8–3-9
    identifying relevant cost drivers, 3-17
    least squares regression, 3-9–3-13
    matching activity and costs, 3-17
    reliability of data, 3-17–13-18
    scatter diagrams, 3-5–3-7
Cost leadership, 1-7
    strategy, 1-7
Cost management system (CMS), 2-2
    definition of, 13-4, 13-5e
    dual focus of, 13-4e
    information flows, 13-2e
    information types, 13-2e
    roles of, 13-5–13-6
Cost object, 2-2
    association with cost object, 2-2–2-3
    direct costs, 2-3
    indirect costs, 2-3
Cost of capital (CC), 19-6
Cost of compliance, 17-16
Cost of goods manufactured (CGM), 2-20–2-22
Cost of goods sold (CGS), 2-20–2-22, 10-24
Cost of noncompliance, 17-16
Cost of production report, 7-11
Cost of quality
    balanced scorecard, quality measures of, 17-24–17-26, 17-25e
    measuring, 17-19–17-26
    new quality accounts, 17-19, 17-19–17-20e
    Pareto analysis, 17-21–17-22
    report, preparing, 17-20–17-21
    total cost of quality, calculating, 17-22–17-24, 17-23e
Cost of Services Provided, 6-19
Cost-plus contract, 6-13
Cost prediction, 3-9
Cost reduction, 16-10–16-12
Cost system, 2-18–2-21
    actual cost system, 2-20
    perpetual inventory accounting system, 2-19
Cost-volume-profit (CVP) analysis, 4-2, 4-9–4-10
    fixed amount of profit, 4-10–4-11
    fixed amount of profit
        after-tax profit, 4-11
        before-tax profit, 4-10–4-11
    managing risks of, 4-19–4-22
        margin of safety, 4-19–4-20
        operating leverage, 4-20–4-22

Note: The letter "e" refers to an exhibit on the stated page, and the letter "n" indicates that the information is included in a footnote on the given page. For example, 11-3n1 means footnote 1 on page 11-3.

© Cambridge Business Publishers

Cost-volume-profit (CVP) analysis, *(continued)*
   in multiproduct environment, 4-16–4-19
      break-even in multiple product mix, 4-17–4-18
      change in sales mix, 4-18–4-19
   profit per unit, specific amount of, 4-11–4-14
   profit per unit, specific amount of
      after-tax profit per unit, 4-12–4-13
      before-tax profit per unit, 4-11–4-12
      contribution income statement proof, 4-13
   underlying assumptions of, 4-22–4-23
Credibility, 1-20–1-21
Cumulative average time learning curve, 3-15
Current assets, 16-24
Current liabilities, 16-24
Customer-level activity, 3-20
Customer profitability analysis
   assessing, 14-23–14-26
   customer profitability profile, 14-23, 14-23e
   limitations to, 14-26
Customer profitability profile, 14-23, 14-23e

D

Data analytics, 1-12–1-13
   accountants, 1-13
   types of, 1-12–1-13
Days payable, 16-25–16-27
Days sales in inventory, 16-24–16-25
Days sales in receivables, 16-25
Death spiral. *See* Downward demand spiral
Decentralization, 13-7–13-9
   advantages of, 13-7e
   disadvantages of, 13-7e
   for environmental issues, 13-9
   shared services, 13-8–13-9
Decision making, 5-2–5-24. *See also under* Relevant costs
   bearing on the future, 5-3–5-5
   decision maker, importance to, 5-3
   relevant information for, 5-2–5-24
Degree of conversion, 2-14
Degree of operating leverage (DOL), 4-20
Department overhead allocation method, 6-8
Descriptive analytics, 1-12
Design for manufacture, 14-12
Diagnostic functions, 16-2
Diagnostic analytics, 1-12
Differential cost, 5-2
Differential revenue, 5-2
Direct costing. *See* Variable costing
Direct costs, 2-3
Direct labor (DL), 2-10, 6-4, 12-12–12-13
Direct labor budget, 9-14
Direct material (DM), 2-10, 2-11, 6-4
Discount rate, 19-6
Discounting, 19-6
Discrete loss, 7-21
Discretionary costs
   planning for, 16-15–16-16
Discretionary fixed costs, 16-14
   controlling discretionary activities, 16-16–16-22
   planning for, 16-15–16-16
Distribution cost, 2-11

Downstream costs, 1-3
Downward demand spiral, 11-17
Dual pricing arrangement, 13-30

E

E-procurement systems, 16-27
Earnings management, 1-19
Economic order quantity (EOQ), 18-4–18-10
Economic pricing vs. cost-based pricing, 14-2
Economic production run (EPR), 18-7–18-8
Economic value added
   calculating, 15-16
   limitations of, 15-16–15-17
Effectiveness, 16-17
Efficiency, 16-17
Employee stock ownership plan (ESOP), 15-37
Engineered cost variances, 16-18–16-19
Engineered costs, 16-18
Engineering change orders (ECOs), 18-12
Enterprise resource planning (ERP) system, 1-13
Environmental constraint, 1-9
Environmental, social, and governance (ESG), 1-9
Equivalent units of production (EUP), 7-4
Excess capacity, 11-16
Expatriates, 15-38
Expected capacity, 11-15
Expected standards, 10-7
External failure costs, 17-17

F

False Claims Act (FCA), 1-21
Financial accounting, 1-2
Financial Accounting Standards Board (FASB), 1-2
Financial budget, 9-7
Financial vs. management accounting, 1-3
Financial, management, and cost accounting, comparison, 1-2–1-5
Financial performance measures
   economic value added, 15-15–15-16
   multi-year, 15-17–15-18
   residual income, 15-15
   return on investment, 15-12–15-15
   segment margin, 15-7–15-11
   statement of cash flows, 15-11–15-12
Financial reporting, classification on, 2-9–2-10
Financing decision, 19-3
Finished goods (FG), 2-15
First-in, first-out (FIFO), 7-2, 7-6, 7-13–17-18
Fixed cost, 2-4–2-5, 3-3, 16-13–16-14
Fixed overhead, 2-13, 10-18–10-21
Fixed overhead spending variance, 10-19
Flexible budget variance, 14-18, 16-19–16-22
Flexible budgets, 10-2–10-5
   for performance measurement, 10-3–10-4
   for planning, 10-2–10-3
Flexible manufacturing system (FMS), 18-15–18-16
Foreign Corrupt Practices Act (FCPA), 1-22
Forward contracts, 16-32
Four-variance approach, 10-17, 10-18–10-21
Full costing. *See* Absorption costing
Functional classification, 11-2
Future value (FV), 19-26

G

General Motors (GM), 1-10
General price-level changes, 16-6
Generally accepted accounting principles (GAAP), 1-2, 2-11
Goal congruence, 13-12–13-13
Greenhouse gas (GHG) emissions, 15-22
Gross margin return on inventory investment (GMROI), 18-14

H

Hedging, 16-32
High-low cost estimation, 3-8–3-9
High-low method of cost estimation, 3-8
Hybrid costing system, 7-20–27-21

I

Ideal standards, 10-8
IMA's Statement of Ethical Professional Practice, 1-20
Imposed budgets, 9-33
Incremental analysis, 4-14
   for short-run changes, 4-14–14-16
Incremental approach, 9-6
Incremental cost, 5-2
Incremental loss, 5-3
Incremental profit, 5-3
Incremental revenue, 5-2
Incremental unit time learning curve, 3-14–3-15
Independent projects, 19-18
Indirect costs, 2-3
Indirect labor costs, 2-12
Indirect material cost, 2-11
Insignificant variance, 10-24
Institute of Management Accountants (IMA), 1-3, 1-5
Integrity, 1-20–1-21
Intellectual capital, 1-9
Internal benchmarking, 17-9
Internal failure costs, 17-17
Internal rate of return (IRR), 19-9–19-12
Inventoriable costs, 2-10
Inventory and production management, 18-2–18-22
Inventory costs
   financial statement presentation of, 18-2–18-3
Inventory turnover, 18-13–18-14
Investment center, 13-14–13-15
Investment decision, 19-3, 19-15–19-19

J

Job order costing system, 6-2–6-26
   to assist managers, 6-22–6-24
   by-product in, 12-20–12-21
   illustration, 6-13–6-18
   product and material losses in, 6-24–6-26
      abnormal loss, 6-24
      defects, 6-24
      normal loss, 6-24
      rework cost, 6-24
      spoilage, 6-24
   scrap in, 12-20–12-21

Note: The letter "e" refers to an exhibit on the stated page, and the letter "n" indicates that the information is included in a footnote on the given page. For example, 11-3n1 means footnote 1 on page 11-3.

Index

Job order costing system, *(continued)*
    in service organizations, 6-18–6-21
    sheet, 6-13, 6-17
    specifically identified with a particular job, 6-25
    weighted average costing method, 7-6–7-13
Joint costs, 12-2
Joint process, 12-1–12-23. *See also* Realized value approach
    allocation of, 12-9–12-16
        approximated net realizable value, 12-13
        monetary measure allocation, 12-11–12-15
        NRV at split-off, 12-12
        physical measure allocation, 12-10–12-11
        sales value at split-off, 12-11–12-12
    outputs of, 12-7–12-8
    decisions in, 12-4–12-7, 12-4e
    model of, 12-3e
    in non-manufacturing businesses, 12-22–12-23
    in not-for-profit organizations, 12-22–12-23
Judgemental method, 19-20
Just-in-time (JIT), 8-7
    backflush costing, 18-17–18-20
    manufacturing system, 18-10
    pull system, 18-10–18-16

K

Kaizen costing, 14-13
    Kaizen cost targets, determining, 14-14–14-15
    vs. target costing, 14-13–14-14e
KPMG, 1-2

L

Labor efficiency variance (LEV), 10-15
Labor mix variance, 10-29
Labor rate variance (LRV), 10-15
Labor standards, 10-9
Labor variances, 10-10–10-16
Labor yield variance, 10-29
Lag indicators, 15-25
Lead indicators, 15-24
Lead time, 15-22
Lean manufacturing, 18-16
Least squares regression, 3-9–3-13
Line personnel, 1-8
Linear programming (LP), 5-13
Long-run success measure, 15-19

M

Machine learning, 1-14
Make-or-buy decision, 5-6
Management accounting, 1-2–1-4
    career opportunities, in, 1-3–1-4
    job duties of, 1-4
    not-for-profit organization, 1-2–1-3
    strategic and problem-solving skills, 1-4
Management-by-exception principle, 10-6, 13-11
Management control system (MCS), 13-3
    components of, 13-3–13-4, 13-3e
Management information system (MIS), 13-2–13-3

Management style, 1-9
Manufacturer, 2-15–12-18
Manufacturing cells, 18-13
Manufacturing cycle efficiency (MCE), 8-6–8-7, 18-13
Margin of safety (MS), 4-19–4-20
Marginal cost, 14-2
Marginal revenue, 14-2
Market-based transfer price, 13-28e, 13-29
Market-segment-level activity, 3-20
Market share variance, 14-21
Market size variance, 14-21
Mass customization, 8-19
Master budget, 9-7–9-11. *See also* Budgeting process
    budgeted financial statements, 9-23–9-27
    capital budget, 9-17
    cash budget, 9-17–9-23
    direct labor budget, 9-14
    financial budget, 9-7
    operating budget, 9-7
    overhead budget, 9-14–19-15
    overview of, 9-9e
    production budget, 9-12–19-13
    purchases budget, 9-13–19-14
    quality of, 9-31–9-35
    sales budget, 9-9–9-12
    selling and administrative expense budget, 9-15–9-16
    for service provider, 9-29–9-31
Material mix variance, 10-27
Material price variance (MPV), 10-12
Material quantity variance (MQV), 10-12–10-13
Material requisition document, 6-14
Material standards, 10-8–10-9
Material variances, 10-10–10-16
    journal entries for, 10-13
    material price variance (MPV), 10-12
    material quantity variance (MQV), 10-12–10-13
    point-of-purchase model, 10-14
    point-of-usage model, 10-11–10-13
    total material variance (TMV), 10-13
Material yield variance, 10-27
Materiality, 6-10
Mayo Clinic hospital, 1-2
Merchandiser, 2-13
Method of neglect, 7-21
Methods-time measurement (MTM), 10-9
Minimum level approach, 9-6–9-7
Mission statement, 1-6, 15-2
Mixed cost, 2-6–2-7, 3-3
Monetary measure allocation, 12-11–12-15
Multilevel responsibility report, 13-11–13-12
Multinational corporations, ethics in, 1-22–1-23
Multiple capital projects, ranking, 19-19–19-20
Multiple regression, 3-13
Mutually exclusive projects, 19-18
Mutually inclusive projects, 19-18

N

Natural language processing (NLP), 1-14
Negotiated transfer price, 13-28e, 13-29–13-30
Net present value method, 19-6–19-8

Net realizable value (NRV), 12-16–12-18
    at split-off, 12-12
Nodes, 1-16
Non-manufacturing businesses, 12-22–12-23
Non-value-added (NVA) activities, 8-3, 8-5–8-6, 17-2, 17-3e
Noncontrollable variance, 10-19
Nonfinancial performance measures (NFPMs)
    advantages over financial performance measures, 15-19e
    comparison bases, establishment of, 15-23
    environment-related metrics, 15-22
    lead time, 15-22
    quality measures, 15-21–15-22, 15-22e
    selection of, 15-19
    throughput, 15-20–15-21
    types of, 15-20–15-23
Normal capacity, 11-15
Normal cost systems, 6-4, 6-6–6-9
    applying overhead to production, 6-6–6-9
    predetermined OH rate, 6-6
Normal loss, 6-24
Not-for-profit organization (NFP), 1-2, 1-3, 9-31, 12-22–12-23

O

One-variance approach, 10-21–10-22
Operating budget, 9-7
Operating leverage, 4-20–4-22
Operations flow document, 10-9
Opportunity cost, 5-3
Options contracts, 16-32
Order-level activity, 3-20
Order point, 18-8–18-9
Ordering cost, 18-3
Ordinary annuity, 19-27
Organisation of Economic Co-operation and Development (OECD), 1-22
Organization chart, 1-8
Organizational constraints, 1-9
Organizational strategy, 1-6–1-9
    core competency, 1-6–1-7
    environmental constraints, 1-9
    factors influencing, 1-6
    management style, 1-9
    organizational constraints, 1-9
    organizational structure, 1-8, 1-9
Organizational structure, 1-8–1-9
Organizational/facility-level activity, 3-19–3-20
Organizational/facility-level costs, 8-11
Other income approach. *See* Realized value approach
Outliers, 3-5
Output/input approach, 9-5
Outsourcing, 5-6
Outsourcing decisions, 5-6–5-11
    benefits of, 5-6
    factors, 5-7
    with opportunity cost, 5-9–5-10
    qualitative decision factors, 5-10
    risk, 5-7–5-9
    in service organizations, 5-11
    short-run vs. long-run decision making, 5-10–15-11

Note: The letter "e" refers to an exhibit on the stated page, and the letter "n" indicates that the information is included in a footnote on the given page. For example, 11-3n1 means footnote 1 on page 11-3.

© Cambridge Business Publishers

Overapplied overhead
   causes of, 6-10
   disposition to, 6-10–6-12
Overhead (OH), 2-10, 2-13, 6-4, 8-2
Overhead budget, 9-14–9-15
Overhead efficiency variance, 10-23
Overhead spending variance, 10-23
Overhead standards, 10-9
Overhead variance, 10-16–10-23
   alternative approaches, 10-21–10-23

P

Pareto analysis, 17-21–17-22
Pareto chart, 14-23e
Pareto inventory analysis, 18-9–18-10
Pareto principle, 8-19
Participatory budget, 9-33
Pay-for-performance plans, 15-32–15-35
Pay vs. performance, 15-35–15-36
Pay ratio disclosure, 15-39
Payback period, 19-2–19-5
Performance measurement. *See also* Financial performance measures; Nonfinancial performance measures
   balanced scorecard for, using, 15-24–15-31
      approach of, 15-26–15-30
      leading and lagging indicators, 15-24–15-25
      multinational settings, performance evaluation in, 15-30–15-31
      multiple performance measures, need for, 15-25
   compensation strategy, 15-32–15-36
      pay-for-performance plans, 15-32–15-35
      pay vs. performance, 15-35–15-36
   designing, 15-2–15-7
      organization mission statements, 15-2–15-3
      criteria for, 15-5–15-6
      critical elements for, 15-3–15-4, 15-3e
      identifying, 15-5
   external performance measures, 15-4
   financial performance measures, 15-7–15-18
      economic value added, 15-15–15-16
      multi-year, 15-17–15-18
      residual income, 15-15
      return on investment, 15-12–15-15
      segment margin, 15-7–15-11
      statement of cash flows, 15-11–15-12
   internal performance measures, 15-3–15-4
   nonfinancial, quantitative performance measures, 15-18–15-24
      comparison bases, establishment of, 15-23
      selection of, 15-19
      types of, 15-20–15-23
   and rewards, links between, 15-36–15-39
      compensation elements, tax implications of, 15-38
      compensation, ethical considerations of, 15-39
      global compensation, 15-38–15-39
Period costs, 2-10
Phantom profits, 11-8–11-9
Physical measure allocation, 12-10–12-11

Planning-performance-reward model, 15-32e
Plant layout, 18-13
Plantwide overhead allocation method, 6-8
Point-of-purchase model, 10-14
Point-of-usage model, 10-11–10-13
Postinvestment audit, 19-24–19-29
Practical capacity, 11-15
Practical standards, 10-7–10-8
Predetermined OH rate, 6-4
Predictive analytics, 1-12
Predictor, 2-7
Preference decision, 19-16
Prescriptive analytics, 1-12
Present values (PVs), 19-6
Prevention costs, 17-16
Preventive functions, 16-2
Price elasticity, 16-8
Primary inventory costs, 18-3–18-4
Prime cost, 2-10
Process benchmarking, 17-9–17-10
Process complexity, 8-16
Process costing, 6-3, 7-2–7-29
   equivalent units of production: the denominator, 7-4–7-6
   in multidepartment setting, 7-18–7-20
   production costs: the numerator, 7-3
   unit cost calculation in, 7-2–7-6
Product complexity, 8-16
Product contribution margin, 11-5
Product cost, 1-4, 2-10–12-14
   cost accumulation systems, 6-2–6-3
   in cost system, 2-18–2-21
   direct labor, 2-12–2-13
   direct material, 2-11
   overhead, 2-13
   valuation methods, 6-4–6-5
Product design, 18-12–18-13
Product differentiation, 1-7
Product life cycle
   model, 14-8–14-9, 14-8e
   costs, 14-8
Product line, 5-22–5-24
Product processing, 18-13
Product profitability analysis, 8-11–8-13
Product variety, 8-16
Production budget, 9-12–9-13
Production cost, 18-3
Product/process-level activity, 3-19
Product/process-level costs, 8-10–8-11
Professional ethics, 1-19–1-23
   earnings management, 1-19
   ethical standards in accounting, 1-19–1-21
   IMA statement of ethical professional practice, 1-20
   multinational corporations, ethics in, 1-22–1-23
   unethical practices, 1-19
Profit center, 13-14
Profit margin, 15-13
Profit sharing, 15-37
Profit-volume (PV) graph, 4-7–4-8
Profitability index (PI), 19-8–19-9
Project-level activity, 3-21
Pseudo-profit center, 13-26, 13-26n4
Public Company Accounting Oversight Board (PCAOB), 1-2

Pull system, 18-5
   just-in-time (JIT), 18-10–18-16
Purchases budget, 9-13–9-14
Purchasing cost, 18-3
Push system
   economic order quantity in, 18-4–18-10

Q

Qualitative factors, 5-6
Quality. *See also* Benchmarking
   characteristics of, 17-6e
   concepts, implementing, 17-1–17-26
   consumer view of, 17-5–17-7
   definition of, 17-2
   as organizational culture, 17-15–17-16
   production view of, 17-2–17-5
Quality control (QC), 17-3
Quality costs. *See also* Cost of quality
   appraisal costs, 17-16
   external failure costs, 17-17
   identifying and tracking, 17-19–17-20
   internal failure costs, 17-17
   prevention costs, 17-16
   time-phased model for, 17-18, 17-18e
   types of, 17-16–17-18
Quantitative factors, 5-6

R

Ranking investments, 19-19–19-20
Raw and In-Process (RIP) Inventory account, 18-17
Raw material (RM), 2-15
Realized value approach, 12-19–12-20
Regression line, 3-9
Reinvestment assumptions, 19-19
Relevant costs
   outsourcing decisions, 5-6–5-11
   product line, 5-22–5-24
   sales mix decisions, 5-14–5-19
   scarce resource decisions, 5-11–5-14
   segment decisions, 5-22–5-24
   special order decisions, 5-19–5-21
   for specific decisions, 5-5–5-24
Relevant range, 2-4
Residual income
   calculating, 15-15
   limitations of, 15-16–15-17
Responsibility, 1-8
Responsibility accounting system
   challenges of, 13-12–13-13
   control activities in, 13-10
   cost center, 13-13–13-14
   investment center, 13-14–13-15
   profit center, 13-14
   responsibility centers, types of, 13-13–13-15
   responsibility reports, 13-10–13-13, 13-10–13-11e
   revenue center, 13-14
Responsibility centers, 13-13–13-15
Results benchmarking, 17-9
Retailer, 2-13, 2-15
Retailers vs. manufacturers/service companies, 2-15–2-18
   business input-output relationships, 2-16e
   finished goods, 2-15

Note: The letter "e" refers to an exhibit on the stated page, and the letter "n" indicates that the information is included in a footnote on the given page. For example, 11-3n1 means footnote 1 on page 11-3.

Index

Retailers vs. manufacturers/service companies, (*continued*)
    manufacturers *versus* service companies, 2-17–2-18
    production, stages and costs of, 2-16–2-17e
    raw material, 2-15
    work in process, 2-15
Return of capital, 19-6
Return on investment
    formula, defining terms in, 15-12–15-13
    improving, 15-14–15-15
    limitations of, 15-16–15-17
    using Du Pont model, computing, 15-13–15-14
Revenue center, 13-14
Revenue variance, 14-15
    analysis of, 14-17
    contribution margin variance, 14-17–14-19
    contribution margin volume variance, 14-19–14-21
    sales quantity variance, 14-21–14-22
Reverse engineering, 17-9
Rework cost, 6-24
Risk-adjusted discount rate method, 19-21–19-22
Robinson-Patman Act, 14-6
Rolling budget, 9-32

S

Safety stock, 18-8–18-9
Sales budget, 9-9–9-12
Sales mix decisions, 5-14–5-19
    advertising budget changes, 5-18–5-19
    sales compensation changes, 5-17–5-18
    sales price changes, 5-15–5-17
Sales mix variance, 14-19
Sales price variance, 14-16
Sales quantity variance, 14-20–14-22
Sales value at split-off, 12-11–12-12
Sales volume variance, 14-16
Sarbanes-Oxley Act of 2002 (SOX), 1-2, 1-19
Scarce resource decisions, 5-11–15-14
Scatter diagrams, 3-5–3-7
Scatter plot, 3-5
Scrap
    accounting for, 12-16–12-20
    in job order costing, 12-20–12-21
Screening decision, 19-16
Segment decisions, 5-22–5-24
Segment margin, 5-23
    as performance measures, 15-9
    segment reporting, potential issues with, 15-9
    segment reports, preparing, 15-7–15-9, 15-8e, 15-9–15-11
Selling and administrative (S&A) expense budget, 9-15–9-16
Semivariable costs, 3-3
Sensitivity analysis, 19-22–19-24
Separate costs, 12-3
Service company, 2-15
Service cost, 1-4–1-5, 6-18
Service cycle efficiency (SCE), 8-7
Service departments, 13-15
Service differentiation, 1-7
Service provider, 2-13

Setup costs, 18-3
Shared services, 13-8–13-9
Short-run success measure, 15-19
Significant variance, 10-24
Simple interest, 19-27
Simple regression, 3-9
Special-cause variation, 17-3
Special order decisions, 5-19–5-21
Speed analysis, 16-11
Split-off
    approximated NRV at, 12-13
    sales value at, 12-11–12-12
    split-off point, 12-2
Spoilage, 6-24, 7-21–7-24
Staff personnel, 1-8
Standard, 10-5
    establishing, considerations in
        appropriateness, 10-7
        attainability, 10-7
        expected standards, 10-7
        ideal standards, 10-8
        labor standards, 10-9
        material standards, 10-8–10-9
        overhead standards, 10-9
        practical standards, 10-7–10-8
        standard cost card, 10-9–10-10
Standard cost card, 10-9–10-10
Standard cost system, 10-5–10-10
    adjusting standards, 10-25–10-26
    benefits of, 10-5–10-7
        controlling, 10-5–10-6
        decision making, 10-7
        motivation, 10-5
        performance evaluation, 10-7
        planning, 10-5
    disposition of, 10-24–10-25
    establishing, considerations in, 10-7–10-10
    general variance analysis model, 10-11
    labor rate, mix and yield variances, 10-29–10-31
    material price, mix and yield variances, 10-27–10-29
Standard cost system, 6-5
Standard quantity allowed, 10-9
Starbucks, 1-2
Statement of cash flows (SCF), 15-11–15-12
Statements on Management Accounting (SMAs), 1-5
Static budgets, 10-2
Statistical process control (SPC), 17-4
Step costs, 2-7, 3-3
Step fixed cost, 2-7
Step variable costs, 2-7
Stockout cost, 18-3–18-4
Straight-line formula, 3-3
Strategic alliances, 16-4–16-5
Strategic benchmarking, 17-10
Strategy map, 15-27–15-28, 15-28e
Suboptimization, 13-14
Sunk costs, 5-3–5-5
Support department cost allocations
    algebraic allocation method, 13-22–13-24
    allocation bases, 13-16–13-17, 13-19e
    direct allocation method, 13-19–13-20
    methods of, 13-17–13-18

    overhead application rates, determining, 13-24–13-25
    pros and cons, 13-16e
    step method allocation, 13-20–13-22
Sustainability, 1-9

T

Target costing
    advantages of, 14-11–14-12
    determining, 14-11
    disadvantages of, 14-12–14-13
    and Kaizen costing, 14-13–14-14e
    process of, 14-9–14-11, 14-10e
Tax benefit, 19-12
Tax shield, 19-12
Theoretical capacity, 11-15
Theory of constraints (TOC), 18-20–18-22
Three-variance approach, 10-22–10-23
Throughput, 5-9, 15-20–15-21
Time-driven activity-based costing (TDABC), 8-23–8-25
    capacity, 8-23
    unused capacity, 8-23
Time line, 19-3
Time-phased model, for quality costs, 17-18, 17-18e
Time value of money, 19-6
Total cost accounted for, 7-8
Total cost to account for, 2-21, 7-8
Total labor variance (TLV), 10-15
Total material variance (TMV), 10-13
Total overhead variance, 10-21
Total physical units accounted for, 7-9
Total physical units to account for, 7-9
Total quality management (TQM)
    benefits of, 17-14e
    continuous improvement, 17-12
    cycle of benefit, 17-17e
    employee participation, 17-12–17-13
    product/service improvement, 17-13
    quality as organizational culture, 17-15–17-16
    supplier partnerships, 17-14
    tenets of, 17-12–17-15
Traditional income statement, 4-2
Transfer pricing, 13-26–13-31
    advantages of, 13-26e
    cost-based, 13-28e, 13-29
    dual pricing, 13-30
    market-based, 13-28e, 13-29
    minimum and maximum, determining, 13-27–13-28
    in multinational settings, 13-30–13-31, 13-31e
    negotiated, 13-28e, 13-29–13-30
    selecting, 13-30
    types, 13-28–13-30
Transferred-in cost, 7-18
Treasurers, 1-8
Two-variance approach, 10-22

U

Uncertainty, coping with, 16-29–16-33
    insuring, 16-33
    nature and causes of, 16-29
    options and forward contracts, 16-32–16-33

Note: The letter "e" refers to an exhibit on the stated page, and the letter "n" indicates that the information is included in a footnote on the given page. For example, 11-3n1 means footnote 1 on page 11-3.

© Cambridge Business Publishers

Uncertainity, coping with, *(continued)*
   regression and sensitivity analysis, 16-30–16-31
   structuring costs to adjust to, 16-31–16-32
Underapplied overhead
   causes of, 6-10
   disposition to, 6-10–6-12
Unit-level activity, 3-19,–3-20
Unit-level costs, 8-9
Units started and completed, 7-10
Unused capacity, 8-23
Upstream costs, 1-3

V

Valuation methods, 6-4–6-5
   direct labor (DL), 6-4
   direct material (DM), 6-4
   overhead (OH), 6-4
   work in process (WIP) inventory, 6-4
Value-added (VA) activity, 8-3
Value chain, 1-10–1-18, 18-11
   artificial intelligence, 1-13–1-16
   blockchain technology, 1-16–1-17
   components of, 1-11
   data analytics, 1-12–1-13
Value engineering (VE), 14-10
Values statement, 15-2
Variable cost ratio (VC%), 4-7
Variable costing, 2-4, 3-2–3-3, 11-3
   before-tax profit, reconciliation of, 11-13–11-14
   calculating unit costs under, 11-4–11-5
   cost relationships in, 11-6e
   income statement results, comparing, 11-6–11-7
   income statement with volume variance, 11-11–11-14
   income under, 11-5–11-11
   model of, 11-3e
   production/sales relationships and effects on income, 11-10e
Variable overhead, 2-13, 10-17–10-18
Variable overhead efficiency variance, 10-18
Variable overhead spending variance, 10-17–10-18
Variance analysis, 10-5
Volume variance, 10-19, 11-13

W

Weighted average (WA), 7-2, 7-6
Work in process (WIP), 2-15, 6-4, 7-2
Working capital, 16-24

Z

Zero-based budgeting, 9-6

Note: The letter "e" refers to an exhibit on the stated page, and the letter "n" indicates that the information is included in a footnote on the given page. For example, 11-3n1 means footnote 1 on page 11-3.

© Cambridge Business Publishers